DAY BY DAY: THE SIXTIES

Volume II
1965–Index

by **Thomas Parker**
and
Douglas Nelson

Facts On File®

AN INFOBASE HOLDINGS COMPANY

DAY BY DAY: THE SIXTIES

Library of Congress Cataloging in Publication Data

Parker, Thomas
  Day by day, the sixties.

  Includes index.
  1. History, Modern—1945-   —Chronology. I. Title.
D848.L4   1985   909.82′02′02   80-22432
ISBN 0-87196-384-1 Vol. 1
ISBN 0-87196-046-X Vol. 2
ISBN 0-87196-648-4 Vol. Set

Photographs courtesy of Wide World Photos

Printed in the United States of America

KP LOG 10 9 8 7 6 5 4

1965

Two armed Klansmen guard a meeting of the Ku Klux Klan in Pine Bluff, Ark.

Pope Paul VI enters St. Patrick's Cathedral on Oct. 4 during his visit to New York City.

Merrymakers dance around a bonfire in Harlem during the Nov. 9 blackout affecting much of the Northeast.

Soviet leaders wave from atop the Lenin Mausoleum during the May Day parade in Moscow's Red Square. They are, from left to right, Leonid Brezhnev, First secretary of the Communist Party, Alexei Kosygin, Premier, Nikolai Podgorny, Presidium member and Mikhail Suslov, chief party theoretician.

Civil rights marchers walk from Selma to Montgomery, Alabama, on March 23 demonstrating against voting restrictions in the state.

Ferdinand Marcos, is elected President of the Philippines on Nov. 11.

National Guard soldiers patrol the streets of Watts after riots in that city.

Gary Player gets set to toss his hat into the air after sinking a putt giving him a three-stroke margin and a victory in the World Series of Golf.

CBS correspondent Edward R. Murrow, who died April 27.

Maj. Edward White takes a walk in space during the flight of Gemini 4 on June 8.

	World Affairs	Europe	Africa & the Middle East	The Americas	Asia & the Pacific
Jan.	Indonesia withdraws from the U.N.	Sir Winston Churchill dies in London at 90.	Reports indicate that the traditional land-holding elite of Iran is resisting the Shah's land reform program.	Panama begins talks with the U.S. on a new Canal Treaty.	Military leaders of South Vietnam oust the civilian government of Premier Tran Van Huong.
Feb.	Britain offers to make a permanent committment of logistical support for a U.N. force.	Turkish Premier Ismet Inonu resigns after losing a vote of confidence in parliament.	Congolese guerrillas attack government troops in various parts of the country.	Cuba accuses the U.S. of trying to infiltrate Cuban exiles into Cuba.	U.S. planes attack North Vietnam for the first time since Aug. 1964. . . .South Vietnamese military council dismisses army chief Nguyen Khanh.
March	At the U.N. Turkey accuses Cypriote officials of abusing the island's Turkish minority.	Britain says that it will make big cuts in defense spending.	Former French Congolese government officials report that Communist China is the most influential country in the newly independent state.	An Argentine poll indicates that the Peronists are still a strong force.	U.S. planes begin to make regular raids against North Vietnam.
April	At the U.N. Western delegates call for greater birth control efforts in the developing world.	Communists delay traffic to Berlin in reprisal for a scheduled meeting of the West German parliament in West Berlin.	Reports indicate that Belgian officials are back in the Congo as administrators.	Dominican government collapses as army factions battle for power.	India and Pakistan accuse each other of major border incursions.
May	U.N. calls for a cease-fire in the Dominican Republic.	A Soviet political rally hails Stalin for the first time since 1956.	Rhodesian P.M. Ian Smith wins a decisive victory in parliamentary elections.	A de facto cease-fire begins in the Dominican Republic.	U.S. resumes the bombing of North Vietnam after a six-day lull brings no response.
June	OAS says that it will publish a plan for an interim government in the Dominican Republic.	West European nations react favorably to the less radical government in Algeria.	Algerian army ousts Pres. Ahmed Ben Bella.	Continued fighting leaves more than 100 dead in the Dominican Republic.	Air Vice Marshall Nguyen Cao Ky becomes South Vietnamese premier.
July	Pres. Johnson names Associate Supreme Court Justice Arthur Goldberg to the US Amb.-to-UN.	France begins a boycott of Common Market meetings.	Col. Houari Boumedienne assumes the leadership of the Algerian government.	Guatemala lifts the state of seige as guerrilla activity declines.	Observers report that North Vietnam is increasing preparations for a major war.
Aug.	At the U.N. India and Pakistan accuse each other of border incursions.	Greek deputies topple the government as left-wing demonstrations spread throughout Greece.	Egyptian Pres. Nasser and Saudi King Faisal agree to a compromise solution to the Yemeni situation.	Dominican junta resigns in favor of an interim government.	Fighting breaks out between India and Pakistan in Kashmir. . .Singapore declares its independence from Malaysia.
Sept.	U.N. observers monitor a shaky truce in Kashmir.	Soviet Union backs India in the Indian-Pakistani war.	Congo (Leopoldvill) accuses the former Frence Congo (Brazzaville) of border intrusions.	U.S. troops begin to leave the Dominican Republic after Hector Garcia-Godoy becomes the interim president.	India and Pakistan agree to a truce after several weeks of intensive fighting.
Oct.	United Nations Children's Fund wins the Nobel Peace Prize.	British PM Harold Wilson leaves London for independence talks in Rhodesia.	Observers say that Egypt is pulling many of its troops out of Yemen.	Brazilian Pres. Humberto Castelo Branco assumes additional powers and abolishes political parties.	Indonesian army arrests thousands of Communists after a Communist coup attempt fails to topple Pres. Sukarno.
Nov.	U.N. calls on Britain to use force against Rhodesia.	Britain declares economic sanctions against Rhodesia.	Rhodesia declares its independence from British rule. . . .Congolese Gen. Joseph Mobutu deposes Pres. Joseph Kasavubu in a bloodless coup.	Leftist students attack Sen. Robert Kennedy at the University of Conception in Chile.	Philippine Senator Ferdinand Marcos wins presidential elections.
Dec.	U.N. African delegates walk out during an address by British P.M. Harold Wilson.	French Pres. de Gaulle wins presidential elections with 54.7% of the vote.	Rhodesia rations gas in the face of economic sanctions.	Sporadic fighting flares up in Santo Domingo as U.S. troops continue to leave.	U.S. planes refrain from bombing North Vietnam during a week as a peace signal.

A	B	C	D	E
Includes developments that affect more than one world region, international organizations and important meetings of major world leaders.	Includes all domestic and regional developments in Europe, including the Soviet Union, Turkey, Cyprus and Malta.	Includes all domestic and regional developments in Africa and the Middle East, including Iraq and Iran and excluding Cyprus, Turkey and Afghanistan.	Includes all domestic and regional developments in Latin America, the Caribbean and Canada.	Includes all domestic and regional developments in Asia and Pacific nations, extending from Afghanistan through all the Pacific Islands, except Hawaii.

U.S. Politics & Social Issues	U.S. Foreign Policy & Defense	U.S. Economy & Environment	Science, Technology & Nature	Culture, Leisure & Life Style
Pres. Johnson sends Congress a budget containing the biggest expansion of domestic welfare programs since the New Deal.	An AP survey of 83 U.S. Senators shows a sharp division over future American policy in South Vietnam in the U.S. Senate.	Pres. Johnson is reportedly trying to cut gold backing for the dollar.	U.S. officials foresee 125,000 deaths from cigarette smoking in 1965.	T(homas) S(tearns) Eliot, the American-born British poet, dies at 76 in London.
Alabama state troopers attack black protestors with night sticks and electric cattle prods in Selma, Ala.	U.S. is reportedly planning a limited air war as a lever against North Vietnam.	House backs Pres. Johnson's partial repeal of the gold backing of the U.S. dollar.	U.S. and Britain agree to coordinate research on a fast-breeder reactor.	Anglican and Eastern Orthodox church leaders agree to discuss their doctrinal differences.
Pres. Johnson calls for civil rights progress and pledges "We Shall Overcome" before a joint session of Congress.	Most Senators and Representatives voice support for the increased bombing of North Vietnam.	Organized labor states its opposition to trade with communist countries.	Soviet astronaut Aleksei Leonev floats in space for 10 minutes.	Pope Paul celebrates a mass in Italian for the first time.
House approves a Medicare bill by 313-115.	U.S. sends 2,500 airborne troops into the Dominican Republic in wake of rioting.	U.S. officials say that the 4.7% jobless rate is the lowest since 1957.	U.S. scientists fear that the introduction of commercial supersonic air travel may bring about substantial climate changes.	Edward R. Murrow, former CBS news correspondent and chief of the U.S. Information Agency, dies of cancer.
Senate approves a major voting rights bill by 77-19.	U.S. dispatches a total of 14,000 troops to the Dominican Republic.	U.S. economists agree that the economic outlook is excellent.	A U.S. scientist stops a charging bull with electronic impulses sent by wires to its brain.	British authorities recover a stolen portrait of the Duke of Wellington by Goya.
Observers report that many Southern schools are pressing for integration in order not to lose federal aid.	U.S. officials acknowledge that U.S. troops are engaged in an active combat role in South Vietnam.	Pres. Johnson says that the federal budget deficit will be $3.8 billion.	Scientists say that the finding of blue galaxies lacks the "big bang" theory in astronomy.	Observers report that social issues are splitting the Roman Catholic Church in Latin America.
Pres. Johnson signs the Medicare bill for the elderly.	Pres. Johnson orders 50,000 more men to Vietnam and doubles the draft; Congress expresses its approval.	U.S. cash receipts rise by $4 billion despite the tax cut.	Mariner 4 photos of Mars depict a desolate planet.	U.S. Amb.-to-UN Adlai Stevenson dies in London at 65.
Large-scale rioting leaves 33 dead in the black neighborhoods of Los Angeles.	Former Pres. Eisenhower and former V.P. Nixon back Pres. Johnson's escalation of the Vietnam War.	U.S. officials warn N.Y.C. that it could run out of water during 1966.	U.S. officials report that the U.S. birth rate continued to decline during 1965.	Swiss architect Le Corbusier dies at Cap Martin in France at 77.
U.S. officials say that school integration is up 50% in the South.	U.S. cuts off arms aid to Pakistan and India.	Steelworkers Union ratifies a new pact covering three years.	U.S. scientists discover their second comet within a week.	Vatican bishops debate the utility of Sigmund Freud's writings.
Abe Fortas becomes a member of the Supreme Court.	U.S. says it may airlift supplies to Zambia if Rhodesia blocks it access to the sea.	General Motors earnings break all profit records.	U.S. officials say that they are ahead of the Soviet Union in space.	Cezanne's *Maisons a l'Estaque* sets the world's auction record for impressionist paintings.
U.S. officials say school integration in the South is proceeding with relatively few violent incidents.	Defense Secy. Robert McNamara says that the Vietnam War will be long and costly.	U.S. officials foresee a $7 billion federal deficit.	A power failure snarls the Northeast for more than six hours.	Pope Paul VI reaffirms the Church's birth control prohibitions.
Martin Luther King Jr. says that the civil rights movement must begin operating in the North.	Observers say that U.S. labor unions are solidly behind U.S. Vietnam policy.	Federal Reserve Board defies Pres. Johnson and raises the discount rate to 4.5%.	Five independent international scientific teams claim to have identified indications of the primordial flash that occurred when the universe was thought to have been created.	Roman Catholic and Eastern Orthodox Churches agree to nullify the Anathema of 1054 which communicated the leaders of each church.

F	G	H	I	J
Includes elections, federal-state relations, civil rights and liberties, crime, the judiciary, education, health care, poverty, urban affairs and population.	*Includes formation and debate of U.S. foreign and defense policies, veterans' affairs and defense spending. (Relations with specific foreign countries are usually found under the region concerned.)*	*Includes business, labor, agriculture, taxation, transportation, consumer affairs, monetary and fiscal policy, natural resources, and pollution.*	*Includes worldwide scientific, medical and technological developments, natural phenomena, U.S. weather, natural disasters, and accidents.*	*Includes the arts, religion, scholarship, communications media, sports, entertainment, fashions, fads and social life.*

	World Affairs	Europe	Africa & the Middle East	The Americas	Asia & the Pacific
Jan. 1	Indonesia threatens to leave the U.N. if Malaysia is given a Security Council seat.	Intermetall, an international steel trust comprised of the Soviet Union and five East European countries, begins its operations in Budapest.	Nigerian Pres. Nuamdi Azikiwe refuses to resign in the face of a newly elected hostile parliament.		
Jan. 2	Indonesia's Ambassador-to-U.N., L.N. Palar, declares: "This is a confrontation between Indonesia and British neo-colonialism."	Congolese government (Leopoldville) postpones legislative elections.			South Vietnamese forces suffer a major defeat at Binh Gia.
Jan. 3				The ruling military Bolivian junta announces that the army has smashed a federal police plot to overthrow the government of Pres. Rene Barrientos.	The chief spokesman of South Vietnam's Buddhists, Thich Tham Cham, urges the ouster of the South Vietnamese government on the grounds that it lacks popular support and is hostile to Buddhists.
Jan. 4	Britain sends an additional 1,000 soldiers to strengthen its 10,000-man garrison in Malaysia and orders an aircraft carrier to leave Mombassa, Kenya for Singapore.	Rumania, which had refused to join Intermetall, is reported to have signed a contract with the Firestone Co. of Akron, Ohio.			South Vietnamese troops remain in possession of Binh Gia after the longest and one of the most costly battles of the war.
Jan. 5	The Soviet ambassador to Indonesia expresses Moscow's opposition to Indonesia's threat to leave the U.N.		Maj. General Hamoud al-Jaifa resigns as premier of North Yemen to protest the continued presence of Egyptian troops in his country.	A five-year Cuban-Communist Chinese trade agreement is announced in Havana and Peking.	At least thirty-three persons are killed and hundreds injured in clashes between supporters of the recently elected President of Pakistan, Ayub Khan, and his opponent Fatima Jinnah.
Jan. 6	Communist Chinese Ambassador-to-Indonesia is reported to have expressed Peking's strong endorsement of Indonesia's position.	The Albanian CP's newspaper charges in an editorial that the new Soviet leaders are "Khrushchevian revisionists."	President Nahum Goldman of the World Zionist Organization tells the 26th World Zionist Congress in Jerusalem that he is convinced that West Germany will extend the twenty-year statute of limitations for the prosecution of Nazi war criminals.		The U.S. military mission in Saigon reports that 136 Americans were killed and 1,022 were wounded in the fighting in South Vietnam during 1964.
Jan. 7		West Germany is reportedly seeking talks with East Germany under the auspices of the Big Four.	Kuwait says it wants a blending of capitalism and socialism for its economy.		Communist China is reportedly advising Indonesia to build up its armed forces.
Jan. 8			Israeli agents are reportedly trying to kill a German rocket expert working for Egypt.	Panamanian Pres. Marco Aurelio Robles appeals for calm as the anniversary of the 1964 anti-US riots approaches.	Indonesia lands 14 guerrillas in Southern Malaysia.
Jan. 9	Indonesia announces it is closing its U.N. mission.		Congolese troops have reportedly executed more than 500 rebel troops in Katanga province.		Australia is reportedly increasing its military strength in response to the Vietnam War.
Jan. 10		NATO is reportedly considering an atom mine field to block any Soviet invasion.			Communist China hails Indonesia's plans to withdraw from the U.N.
Jan. 11		France is reportedly widening its ties to East European countries.			Buddhist protest strikes disrupt life in three central Vietnamese cities.
Jan. 12		Britain agrees to reduce its military presence in Libya.	Arab countries criticize West Germany's recent arms sales to Israel.	Tear gas halts Panamanian protesters as they advance towards the Canal Zone.	South Vietnamese Buddhists insist on the ouster of the government as protests continue.
	A	B	C	D	E
	Includes developments that affect more than one world region, international organizations and important meetings of major world leaders.	Includes all domestic and regional developments in Europe, including the Soviet Union, Turkey, Cyprus and Malta.	Includes all domestic and regional developments in Africa and the Middle East, including Iraq and Iran and excluding Cyprus, Turkey and Afghanistan.	Includes all domestic and regional developments in Latin America, the Caribbean and Canada.	Includes all domestic and regional developments in Asia and Pacific nations, extending from Afghanistan through all the Pacific Islands, except Hawaii.

U.S. Politics & Social Issues	U.S. Foreign Policy & Defense	U.S. Economy & Environment	Science, Technology & Nature	Culture, Leisure & Life Style	
		Pres. Johnson orders a study of recent steel price hikes.		Former U.S. Bar Association head Allen Klots dies in Laurel Hollow, N.Y. at 75.	Jan. 1
Martin Luther King, Jr. tells a Negro rally in Selma, Ala., that a new voter registration drive will be launched throughout Ala.	Senate Minority Leader Everett Dirksen proposes that Pres. Johnson call an immediate conference to decide whether the U.S. should continue to fight in South Vietnam.				Jan. 2
	State Secy. Dean Rusk says that the U.S. should neither withdraw from South Vietnam nor expand the war.	The Commerce Department forecasts record production and sales in all major industries during 1965.		Milton Clark Avery, the American abstract painter, dies at 71 in New York.	Jan. 3
In the annual State of the Union Message, President Lyndon Johnson speaks about plans for a great society and invites Soviet leaders to participate in an exchange of T.V. broadcasts to the U.S. and Soviet peoples.		The AFL-CIO's Civil Rights Dept. opens a special office in Atlanta, Ga. whose goal is to fight job discrimination.		T(homas) S(tearns) Eliot, the American-born British poet, dies at 76 in London.	Jan. 4
A discussion about racial problems scheduled for Bogalusa, La. is cancelled because of threats of violence by the Ku Klux Klan.	Senator Wayne Morse (D, Ore.) calls the U.S. presence in South Vietnam an "open violation" of the U.N. Charter.				Jan. 5
	An AP survey of 83 U.S. senators shows sharp divisions over future American policy in South Vietnam.				Jan. 6
Liberal Democrats are reportedly making gains in key congressional posts.	Former US Amb-to-UN Henry Cabot Lodge says the U.S. must not leave South Vietnam.	Pres. Johnson is reportedly trying to cut gold backing for the dollar.			Jan. 7
Pres. Johnson calls for an end to all barriers for voting in the South.		U.S. Treasury says French purchases of U.S. gold will not deter the U.S. from selling gold at $35 an ounce.		U.S. lawyer Fowler Harper, challenger of birth control laws, dies in New Haven, Conn. at 67.	Jan. 8
U.S. officials report that the nation's crime rate is still climbing.				U.S. says it plans to restore Independence Hall, Philadelphia to its original 1776 style.	Jan. 9
FBI agents are reportedly making progress in the investigation of the 1965 slaying of three civil rights workers near Philadelphia, Miss.			A heavy snow snarls traffic in N.Y.C.	Austrian conductor Karl Boehm conducts a performance at the New York Metropolitan Opera.	Jan. 10
Columbia Univ. officials call for improved relations with the local community.	U.S. officials acknowledge that the U.S. foreign aid program will decline.		U.S. officials foresee 125,000 deaths from cigarettes in 1965.	First Lord of the British Admiralty, Earl Alexander, dies in London at 79.	Jan. 11
Pres. Johnson proposes a major increase in spending for education.				U.S. author Lorraine Hansberry dies in N.Y.C. at 34 of cancer.	Jan. 12

F	G	H	I	J
Includes elections, federal-state relations, civil rights and liberties, crime, the judiciary, education, health care, poverty, urban affairs and population.	Includes formation and debate of U.S. foreign and defense policies, veterans' affairs and defense spending. (Relations with specific foreign countries are usually found under the region concerned.)	Includes business, labor, agriculture, taxation, transportation, consumer affairs, monetary and fiscal policy, natural resources, and pollution.	Includes worldwide scientific, medical and technological developments, natural phenomena, U.S. weather, natural disasters, and accidents.	Includes the arts, religion, scholarship, communications media, sports, entertainment, fashions, fads and social life.

	World Affairs	Europe	Africa & the Middle East	The Americas	Asia & the Pacific
Jan. 13		Soviet Union announces plans to convert 400 industrial plants to a system based on demand economics.	Islam is reportedly gaining converts in black Africa.		Communist gunners shoot down two U.S. planes over central Laos.
Jan. 14	At the U.N. U.S. criticizes the Soviet Union for refusing to pay dues because of displeasure about the U.N.'s operations in the Congo.	Two Irish prime ministers meet for the first time since Ireland was partitioned more than 40 years ago.			U.S. planes knock out a key Laotian bridge along the Ho Chi Minh trail.
Jan. 15		West German Socialists propose border talks with Poland.	Tanzania expels two U.S. diplomats for alleged subversive activities.	Canada and the U.S. agree to end all manufacturer's tariffs on automobiles.	
Jan. 16		Former British P.M. Winston Churchill suffers a serious stroke in London.	Black guerrilla activity is reportedly growing in Rhodesia.		Communist China is reportedly building up air defense systems in Laos and North Vietnam.
Jan. 17	U.N. reconvenes in the midst of serious financial problems.			Cuban exiles claim to have set fire to sugar cane fields in Western Cuba.	Government troops kill four anti-government protestors in central South Vietnamese cities of Hue and Dalat.
Jan. 18		Former British P.M. Winston Churchill continues to grow weaker.	Several hundred European mercenaries are reportedly fighting for Congolese Premier Moise Tshombe.	Dominican Republic ousts the head of the country's national police force.	Indonesia is reportedly seeking closer ties with Communist China.
Jan. 19	At the U.N. Britain appeals to the Soviet Union to pay its back dues.				South Vietnamese and Communist forces clash outside of Saigon.
Jan. 20		Reports indicate that the relations between French Pres. de Gaulle and West German Chancellor Ludwig Erhard are somewhat strained.	Israel makes additional arms purchases from West Germany.		Communist China urges the Soviet Union to return the Kuriles Islands to Japan.
Jan. 21	Indonesia formally withdraws from the U.N.	Soviet Union calls for a compromise on the Cyprus problem.	Lebanon is reportedly debating whether to invite in an Arab peace-keeping force.		South Vietnamese troops crush a Viet Cong force in the Mekong Delta.
Jan. 22	Reports indicate that U.N. officials are making progress solving the organization's fiscal crisis.	Former British P.M. Winston Churchill's condition continues to deteriorate.	Kenya accuses Communist China of trading with South Africa.	Latin American governments are reportedly embarrassed by a U.S. request for material support for South Vietnam.	Saigon Buddhists stone the U.S. library.
Jan. 23	At the U.N. African delegates criticize Western investment in South Africa.	Sir Winston Churchill dies in London at 90.	Several hundred Congolese guerrillas seize a village 200 miles from Leopoldville.	Anti-government student protesters demonstrate at the University of Buenos Aires in Argentina.	Buddhist demonstrators sack the U.S. Information Service library in Hue.
Jan. 24	At the U.N. Arab delegates accuse Israel of trying to provoke a war.	French Pres. de Gaulle calls Winston Churchill the greatest man of his era.	Lebanon warns Israel not to divert the tributaries of the Jordan River.		Communist China calls for a completely new kind of U.N.
Jan. 25		Soviet Union denies that its recent nuclear explosion violated the nuclear test-ban treaty.	Congolese Premier Moise Tshombe bans the country's opposition newspaper.	Canada sells Communist China $54 million in wheat.	South Vietnam declares martial law in Hue.
Jan. 26		Turkey bars a visit of a U.S. nuclear merchant ship.	Syria sentences eight government opponents to death.		Military leaders of South Vietnam oust the civilian government of Premier Tran Van Huong.

A	B	C	D	E
Includes developments that affect more than one world region, international organizations and important meetings of major world leaders.	Includes all domestic and regional developments in Europe, including the Soviet Union, Turkey, Cyprus and Malta.	Includes all domestic and regional developments in Africa and the Middle East, including Iraq and Iran and excluding Cyprus, Turkey and Afghanistan.	Includes all domestic and regional developments in Latin America, the Caribbean and Canada.	Includes all domestic and regional developments in Asia and Pacific nations, extending from Afghanistan through all the Pacific Islands, except Hawaii.

U.S. Politics & Social Issues	U.S. Foreign Policy & Defense	U.S. Economy & Environment	Science, Technology & Nature	Culture, Leisure & Life Style	
	Pres. Johnson is reportedly displeased with Japanese Premier Eisaku Sato's recent overtures to Communist China.			U.S. publisher Robert Kelly dies in N.Y.C. at 58.	Jan. 13
	Pres. Johnson makes the lowest foreign aid request in the program's history.				Jan. 14
U.S. sues Alabama, charging that its new voter registration test is too difficult.	U.S. is reportedly giving South Vietnam new military aid.		Sweden says it has detected an underground Soviet nuclear test.		Jan. 15
U.S. officials arrest 18 men in connection with the 1964 slaying of three civil rights workers in Philadelphia, Miss.	Pres. Johnson says he still favors a mixed-manned nuclear surface fleet within NATO.				Jan. 16
Pres. Johnson announces 88 new anti-poverty projects.				U.S. banker William Keith dies in Newark at 53.	Jan. 17
A segregationist punches Martin Luther King Jr. as he registers at a formerly segregated hotel in Selma, Ala.	U.S. says its recent air raid in Laos is justified because of Communist violations of the 1962 Geneva accord.				Jan. 18
Civil rights leader Martin Luther King Jr. seeks an injunction against Sheriff James Clark of Selma, Ala.	U.S. says that a recent Soviet underground nuclear test may have broken the test-ban treaty because of radioactive debris.		U.S. launches an unmanned Gemini spacecraft down the Atlantic Test Range.	World Council of Churches authorizes a regular exchange of meetings with Roman Catholic officials.	Jan. 19
	Pres. Johnson calls for advances in the desegregation movement as he takes the oath as President.	U.S. West Coast businessmen urge trade with Communist China.		Disk jockey Alan Freed dies in Palm Springs, Calif. at 43.	Jan. 20
	Defense Secy. Robert McNamara says he will remain at his post.		U.S. officials say they are expanding the government's birth control program.		Jan. 21
			U.S. launches Tiros 9, a weather satellite.		Jan. 22
					Jan. 23
				Reports indicate that European designers are turning increasingly to plastics in the creation of esthetic household goods.	Jan. 24
Pres. Johnson sends Congress a budget containing the biggest expansion of domestic welfare programs since the New Deal.				Pope Paul designates 27 new Cardinals.	Jan. 25
	The U.S. House of Representatives bars food aid to Egypt.	GSA calls for 17 new car safety features.		French artist Jean Despujols dies in Shreveport, La. at 78.	Jan. 26

F	G	H	I	J
Includes elections, federal-state relations, civil rights and liberties, crime, the judiciary, education, health care, poverty, urban affairs and population.	Includes formation and debate of U.S. foreign and defense policies, veterans' affairs and defense spending. (Relations with specific foreign countries are usually found under the region concerned.)	Includes business, labor, agriculture, taxation, transportation, consumer affairs, monetary and fiscal policy, natural resources, and pollution.	Includes worldwide scientific, medical and technological developments, natural phenomena, U.S. weather, natural disasters, and accidents.	Includes the arts, religion, scholarship, communications media, sports, entertainment, fashions, fads and social life.

	World Affairs	Europe	Africa & the Middle East	The Americas	Asia & the Pacific
Jan. 27		Thousands pass former British P.M. Winston Churchill's bier in London.		Cuba accuses the Dominican Republic of aiding Cuban exiles.	Buddhist demonstrators temporarily halt protests in South Vietnam.
Jan. 28		Portuguese government accuses the country's CP of trying to infiltrate the army.			Communist China condemns the concept of peaceful co-existence.
Jan. 29	At the U.N. Israel accuses Egypt of inciting guerrilla action from the Gaza Strip.		Reports indicate that the traditional land-holding elite of Iran is resisting the Shah's land reform program.		South Vietnamese and Viet Cong forces clash near Saigon.
Jan. 30		Body of Sir Winston Churchill is buried amidst sorrow and regal pageantry in England.	Reports indicate that Iran's ties with the U.S. are slackening in the wake of improved U.S.-USSR relations.	Panama begins talks with the U.S. on a new Canal Treaty.	South Vietnamese and Viet Cong troops clash in the Mekong Delta.
Jan. 31		Soviet Union is reportedly trying to strengthen its ties with Mongolia.	Egypt orders the Congo to close its embassy in Cairo.	Campaign to elect half of Argentina's deputies begins.	British troops stationed in Malaysia clash with a small group of Indonesian infiltrators.
Feb. 1	U.N. recesses to avoid a showdown between the U.S. and the Soviet Union about unpaid dues.		Britain's Queen Elizabeth begins a visit to Ethiopia.		Laos puts down an attempted coup by army officers.
Feb. 2	U.N. Secy. Gen. U Thant says that the U.N. must reduce its expenses.	British P.M. Harold Wilson says the British economy must become more competitive.	Royalist forces in Yemen report that Egyptian forces are preparing a new offensive.		
Feb. 3	U.S. and Britain agree to a plan to improve the U.N.'s finances.	Soviet Premier Aleksei Kosygin leaves on a trip to Asia.		Cuba accuses Cuban exiles of shelling an oil tank installation near Havana.	Rival army troops battle in Vientiane, Laos.
Feb. 4		France calls for a return to the gold standard.			A Laotian rightist rebellion is reportedly crushed.
Feb. 5	At the U.N. African delegates criticize South Africa's apartheid policy.				Presidential assistant McGeorge Bundy tells feuding South Vietnamese leaders they must unite to prosecute the war more effectively.
Feb. 6	U.N. is expected to recess within a week in order to avoid a financial crisis.		Congolese Premier Moise Tshombe is reported to have won major financial concessions from Belgium.	Cuba reports the capture of two armed infiltrators.	Viet Cong kill seven U.S. soldiers in the central highlands.
Feb. 7			Egypt says it will cut its ties with West Germany if it continues its arms sales to Israel.	Argentine officials meet with U.S. officials about a possible financial loan.	U.S. planes attack North Vietnam for the first time since August 1964.
Feb. 8	U.N. Secy. Gen. U Thant offers a plan for volunteer U.N. payments.	Soviet Union pledges air defense aid to North Vietnam in the wake of U.S. air attacks.	Ghana sentences five anti-government conspirators to death.		South Vietnamese planes bomb a communication center in North Vietnam.
Feb. 9	At the U.N. Arab delegates criticize American support of Israel.		Congolese guerrillas attack government troops in various parts of the country.		
	A	B	C	D	E
	Includes developments that affect more than one world region, international organizations and important meetings of major world leaders.	Includes all domestic and regional developments in Europe, including the Soviet Union, Turkey, Cyprus and Malta.	Includes all domestic and regional developments in Africa and the Middle East, including Iraq and Iran and excluding Cyprus, Turkey and Afghanistan.	Includes all domestic and regional developments in Latin America, the Caribbean and Canada.	Includes all domestic and regional developments in Asia and Pacific nations, extending from Afghanistan through all the Pacific Islands, except Hawaii.

U.S. Politics & Social Issues	U.S. Foreign Policy & Defense	U.S. Economy & Environment	Science, Technology & Nature	Culture, Leisure & Life Style	
Atlanta, Ga. city officials praise Martin Luther King's civil rights work in the South.	U.S. is reportedly resigned to having the South Vietnamese military rule the country.			U.S. painter Abraham Walkowitz dies in N.Y.C. at 84.	Jan. 27
Pres. Johnson appoints Nicholas B. Katzenbach as Attorney General.		Pres. Johnson predicts that 1965 will be a very prosperous year in America.		French W.W. II Gen. Maxime Weygand dies in Paris at 98.	Jan. 28
American Bar Association says that recent Supreme Court decisions have tipped the scales of justice too far in favor of criminals at the expense of the public's safety.				Opera singer Franco Corelli makes his seasonal debut at New York's Metropolitan Opera.	Jan. 29
	U.S. agrees to widen cultural ties with the Soviet Union.				Jan. 30
Senate votes for poverty funds for Appalachia.				U.S. magazine editor Yelta Arenstein dies in N.Y.C. at 53.	Jan. 31
Alabama officials arrest 700 Negroes as they demonstrate against the state's voter registration requirements in Selma, Ala.	White House announces it is sending national security adviser McGeorge Bundy to South Vietnam.	House backs President Johnson's partial repeal of the gold backing of the U.S. dollar.			Feb. 1
Alabama officials arrest 500 more Negroes protesting the state's voter registration laws in Selma, Ala.	Administration is reportedly becoming increasingly pessimistic about the situation in Vietnam.				Feb. 2
Alabama officials arrest 1,000 Negroes as voter registration protests continue.	Pres. Johnson says that he hopes to meet with Soviet leaders during 1965.				Feb. 3
An Alabama federal judge issues an order making it easier for Negroes to vote in Selma, Ala.	Pres. Johnson asks the House to give him a free hand for dealing with the issue of food aid to Egypt.			Ghanaian independence leader Joseph Dangnah dies in Accra while in detention.	Feb. 4
Martin Luther King Jr. calls for new legislation guaranteeing Negroes the right to vote.	U.S. vows to back the Laotian neutralists and not the rightist dissidents.			A theater group plans to stage plays in the Waterford, Conn. home of Eugene O'Neill.	Feb. 5
White House says that Pres. Johnson will ask for new legislation to eliminate voting barriers for Negroes in the South.		Pres. Johnson opposes any increase in interest rates for the time-being.			Feb. 6
			American Medical Association begins to organize its supporters to defeat the administration's Medicare bill.	Former Uruguayan Pres. Luis Giannattasio dies in Montevideo at 70.	Feb. 7
	House agrees to allow Pres. Johnson to grant Egypt food aid if he believes it is in the national interest.	Pres. Johnson asks for increased federal power to curb pollution.			Feb. 8
Officials report that major crime is up 9% in N.Y.C. over the previous year.	U.S. agrees to sell $1 billion in arms to Britain and Australia.				Feb. 9
F	G	H	I	J	
Includes elections, federal-state relations, civil rights and liberties, crime, the judiciary, education, health care, poverty, urban affairs and population.	Includes formation and debate of U.S. foreign and defense policies, veterans' affairs and defense spending. (Relations with specific foreign countries are usually found under the region concerned.)	Includes business, labor, agriculture, taxation, transportation, consumer affairs, monetary and fiscal policy, natural resources, and pollution.	Includes worldwide scientific, medical and technological developments, natural phenomena, U.S. weather, natural disasters, and accidents.	Includes the arts, religion, scholarship, communications media, sports, entertainment, fashions, fads and social life.	

	World Affairs	Europe	Africa & the Middle East	The Americas	Asia & the Pacific
Feb. 10		West Germany orders a temporary halt in arms sales to Israel in the face of Arab pressure.	Congolese planes strafe rebel forces in the Northern Congo.		South Vietnamese planes attack supply dumps in North Vietnam.
Feb. 11		Poland announces significant industrial gains over the last several years.			One hundred sixty U.S. and South Vietnamese planes attack military bases in North Vietnam.
Feb. 12	U.N. Secy. Gen. U Thant calls for restraint in Vietnam.	Turkey is reportedly loosening its ties with the U.S. as a result of the 1964 Cyprus crisis.			Twenty-one protesters die in language riots in southern India.
Feb. 13		Turkish Premier Ismet Inonu resigns after losing a vote of no-confidence in Parliament.			Communist China attacks U.S. bombardment of North Vietnam.
Feb. 14		West Germany is reportedly reconsidering the Hallstein doctrine.	Tanzania recalls its envoy from the U.S. to protest alleged U.S. subversion.		
Feb. 15		West Germany threatens to end its aid to Egypt if Pres. Nasser sees East German Pres. Walter Ulbricht.		Cuban Premier Castro dismisses several orthodox Communists from party posts.	Communist China calls for reprisals against the U.S. in the wake of the bombing of North Vietnam.
Feb. 16		France calls for a negotiated settlement of the Vietnam War.	A Ugandan mob shreds a U.S. flag to protest U.S. support of Congolese Premier Moise Tshombe.		North Vietnam is reportedly receiving anti-aircraft missiles from the Soviet Union.
Feb. 17	At the U.N. Arab delegates accuse Israel of wanting to expand to the Nile River and the Euphrates River.	Soviet Union asserts that its submarine fleet now equals America's.			South Vietnamese and Viet Cong forces clash in the Mekong Delta.
Feb. 18	U.S. decides not to force a showdown with the Soviet Union about its back dues at the U.N.	British P.M. Harold Wilson will reportedly visit French Pres. de Gaulle on April 1-3.	Gambia becomes an independent nation.		South Vietnamese military overthrows Lieut. Gen. Nguyen Khanh.
Feb. 19	U.N. Secy. Gen. U Thant says that the U.N. must find additional funds for the current year.		Congolese Premier Moise Tshombe accuses Uganda of making border incursions.	Police and student protesters clash briefly at the Univ. of Santiago in Chile.	Lieut. Gen. Nguyen Khanh regains control in Saigon and calls on dissident officers to surrender.
Feb. 20	U.N. will try to help India lower its birth rate.	France is reportedly seeking closer ties with the Arab world.			South Vietnamese military is reportedly applying pressure on Gen. Nguyen Khanh to resign as army staff chief.
Feb. 21			Congo is seeking the return of ousted European teachers.		South Vietnamese military council dismisses army chief Nguyen Khanh.
Feb. 22	At the U.N. African delegates call for majority rule in South Africa.	Several hundred people in London demonstrate against the Vietnam War.		Cuba accuses the U.S. of trying to infiltrate Cuban exiles into Cuba.	
Feb. 23	Britain offers to make a permanent commitment of logistical support for a U.N. peace-keeping force.	Soviet Union criticizes the recent U.S. bombing of North Vietnam.	Syria hangs Farhan Attassi, a naturalized U.S. citizen, for alleged spy activities.		Indonesian Pres. Sukarno rules out the possibility of improved relations with the U.S.
Feb. 24	U.N. Secy. Gen. U Thant calls for Vietnam talks leading to a U.S. pull-out.	West Germany cuts off its aid to Egypt.	Egyptian Pres. Nasser receives East German Pres. Walter Ulbricht in Cairo.		U.S. planes, manned entirely by Americans, attack Viet Cong positions for the first time in South Vietnam.
	A	B	C	D	E
	Includes developments that affect more than one world region, international organizations and important meetings of major world leaders.	Includes all domestic and regional developments in Europe, including the Soviet Union, Turkey, Cyprus and Malta.	Includes all domestic and regional developments in Africa and the Middle East, including Iraq and Iran and excluding Cyprus, Turkey and Afghanistan.	Includes all domestic and regional developments in Latin America, the Caribbean and Canada.	Includes all domestic and regional developments in Asia and Pacific nations, extending from Afghanistan through all the Pacific Islands, except Hawai'i.

U.S. Politics & Social Issues	U.S. Foreign Policy & Defense	U.S. Economy & Environment	Science, Technology & Nature	Culture, Leisure & Life Style	
Alabama officials attack Negro protesters with night sticks and electric cattle prods in Selma, Ala.	U.S. warns the Soviet Union to curb protesters attacking the U.S. embassy in Moscow.	Pres. Johnson urges restraint in U.S. investing abroad to cut its payments deficit.			Feb. 10
	U.S. officials stress that they do not want an expanded war in South Vietnam.		U.S. launches a Titan 3-A rocket.	Pope Paul indirectly calls for a negotiated Vietnam settlement.	Feb. 11
	Administration is reportedly undecided about continuing aerial attacks against North Vietnam.		U.S. and Britain agree to coordinate research on a fast-breeder reactor.	U.S. historian Arthur Schlesinger Jr. is reportedly writing a book on the Kennedy administration.	Feb. 12
Former V.P. Richard Nixon is reportedly stepping into a leadership vacuum in the Republican Party.	U.S. is reportedly considering troop increases to South Vietnam.		Soviet Union conducts an underground nuclear test.		Feb. 13
A fire-bomb damages the home of black nationalist leader Malcolm X but causes no personal injuries.	Johnson administration is reportedly deeply worried about the ability of South Vietnam to defend itself.			Two delegates from the Eastern Orthodox church meet with Pope Paul in Rome.	Feb. 14
Martin Luther King Jr. leads 2,800 Negroes in three Ala. voter rights marches.	Pres. Johnson confers with State Secy. Dean Rusk about Vietnam.				Feb. 15
	U.S. says that Communist China is reportedly preparing a second atomic test.	Pres. Johnson calls for public support of his Medicare proposal for the elderly.	U.S. launches a giant winged satellite into orbit.		Feb. 16
Four hundred Negro high school students throw bricks at store windows in Brooklyn, N.Y.	Pres. Johnson asserts that the U.S. will persist in its Vietnam policy.		U.S. says that the Soviet Union is stalling on agreed exchange of weather information.		Feb. 17
Three hundred Negro high school students riot for a second day in Brooklyn, N.Y.		Pres. Johnson again urges U.S. business to cut its spending abroad.			Feb. 18
U.S. authorities begin an investigation into the recent attacks by state troopers on Negro demonstrators in Selma, Ala.			U.S. astronaut John Glenn says a race to the moon with the Soviet Union would be foolish.		Feb. 19
		AFL-CIO says it will seek a $2 minimum wage.	U.S. Ranger Eight spacecraft hits its target on the moon.	Pope Paul discloses that he has sought direct contact with the parties to the Vietnam conflict.	Feb. 20
A Negro assassin kills black nationalist Malcolm X.	Former presidential candidate Barry Goldwater calls for more air strikes against North Vietnam.		The moon's surface is still in doubt despite Ranger Eight's photos.		Feb. 21
A fire destroys a Black Muslim building in Harlem.			Soviet Union launches a weather satellite.	Former Supreme Court Justice Felix Frankfurter dies in Washington D.C. at 82.	Feb. 22
N.Y.C. police fear a vendetta is growing out of the recent assassination of Malcolm X.					Feb. 23
Abolition of the death penalty is reportedly gaining supporters in the N.Y. Legislature.	U.S. officials admit that U.S. advisers are taking a more active role in conducting the Vietnam War.				Feb. 24

F	G	H	I	J
Includes elections, federal-state relations, civil rights and liberties, crime, the judiciary, education, health care, poverty, urban affairs and population.	Includes formation and debate of U.S. foreign and defense policies, veterans' affairs and defense spending. (Relations with specific foreign countries are usually found under the region concerned.)	Includes business, labor, agriculture, taxation, transportation, consumer affairs, monetary and fiscal policy, natural resources, and pollution.	Includes worldwide scientific, medical and technological developments, natural phenomena, U.S. weather, natural disasters, and accidents.	Includes the arts, religion, scholarship, communications media, sports, entertainment, fashions, fads and social life.

	World Affairs	Europe	Africa & the Middle East	The Americas	Asia & the Pacific
Feb. 25		About 2,000 Univ. of Madrid students vote to stage a sit-in strike.		Tensions are reportedly growing between the French and English communities in Canada.	U.S. jets pound Viet Cong positions in South Vietnam.
Feb. 26		Turkey is reportedly trying to improve its relations with the Soviet Union.	Egyptian Pres. Nasser, in an apparent gesture to the West, restates his differences with communism.		Indonesia seizes rubber estates belonging to U.S. concerns.
Feb. 27		Soviet Premier Aleksei Kosygin visits East Germany.	Algeria denounces Western aid as being 'imperialist.'		Japanese citizens are reportedly beginning to make private trips to Communist China.
Feb. 28		Soviet Union calls for a pull-out of U.S. troops from South Vietnam.	Egypt has reportedly called up several thousand army reservists during the last six weeks.		South Vietnamese and Viet Cong troops clash in the Mekong Delta.
March 1		A conference of 19 pro-Soviet Communist parties opens in Moscow.	Congolese rebels are reportedly exploiting gold mines in the northern Congo.		
March 2	U.S. announces that it will donate $60 million to a U.N. technical assistance fund.	Threat of a doctors' strike eases as Britain grants a pay increase.	Egypt threatens not to pay its financial debts to West Germany.		More than 100 U.S. planes bomb a North Vietnamese munitions depot.
March 3		Britain says that it will make big cuts in defense spending.	Congo accuses Uganda of conducting border raids.		U.S. planes bomb the Ho Chi Minh trail.
March 4	U.N. Secy. Gen. U Thant voices hope for a fund for the U.N.'s Mideast force.	Soviet police rout 2,000 Asian students demonstrating at the U.S. embassy in Moscow.	Syria nationalizes nine oil concerns.		U.S. says it will close its information libraries in Indonesia.
March 5		Soviet Union apologizes for attacks on the U.S. embassy in Moscow.	Communist China is reportedly the most influential country in the former French Congo.		Viet Cong batter three South Vietnamese battalions near Danang.
March 6	At the U.N. Israel denounces Arab guerrilla attacks on its territory.				Students in Peking protest outside of the Soviet embassy.
March 7		West Germany indicates it wants diplomatic relations with Israel.	Iraqi Kurds say they expect a government offensive in the spring.		U.S. marines land near Danang and guard a large airbase.
March 8	U.N. Secy. Gen. U Thant calls for negotiations in Vietnam.		Yemeni royalists may get U.S. food.	Anti-government students demonstrate at the Univ. of Mexico.	India receives Soviet MiG fighters.
March 9	U.N. delegates criticize arrests of apartheid opponents in South Africa.	Spanish students vote to suspend mass protest meetings in Madrid.	Arab states push their drive to punish West Germany's overtures toward Israel.		
March 10		British government announces that P.M. Harold Wilson will visit the U.S. in April 1965.	Egypt warns West Germany not to recognize Israel.		Indonesian naval officers go on strike.
March 11	At the U.N. African delegates criticize minority rule in Rhodesia.	Soviet Union denies Communist Chinese charges of Soviet police brutality in quelling Chinese demonstrators at the U.S. embassy in Moscow.	Israel has reportedly asked West Germany for a guarantee of her frontiers as the price for formal diplomatic relations.		Laotian Communist troops blow up a supply bridge.
	A	B	C	D	E
	Includes developments that affect more than one world region, international organizations and important meetings of major world leaders.	Includes all domestic and regional developments in Europe, including the Soviet Union, Turkey, Cyprus and Malta.	Includes all domestic and regional developments in Africa and the Middle East, including Iraq and Iran and excluding Cyprus, Turkey and Afghanistan.	Includes all domestic and regional developments in Latin America, the Caribbean and Canada.	Includes all domestic and regional developments in Asia and Pacific nations, extending from Afghanistan through all the Pacific Islands, except Hawaii.

U.S. Politics & Social Issues	U.S. Foreign Policy & Defense	U.S. Economy & Environment	Science, Technology & Nature	Culture, Leisure & Life Style	
	State Secy. Dean Rusk says that North Vietnam must end its aggression in South Vietnam before talks can begin.		U.S. officials say that the Mariner Four spacecraft heading towards Mars is functioning smoothly.	Anglican and Orthodox Church leaders agree to discuss their doctrinal differences.	Feb. 25
Police charge a Black Muslim, Norman 3X Butler, with the murder of Malcolm X.	A U.S. white paper brands North Vietnam as an "aggressor" and hints at increased attacks.	U.S. officials report that the consumer price index rose one-tenth of one percent during January.			Feb. 26
Harlem crowds watch the funeral rites of Malcolm X in silence.	Pres. Johnson is reportedly undecided about selling arms to Saudi Arabia.				Feb. 27
House takes up a proposed $1.25 billion school aid bill.	U.S. is reportedly planning a limited air war as a lever against North Vietnam.			Pope Paul reportedly wants the Church's internal debate on birth control to end.	Feb. 28
Supreme Court rules that de facto segregation does not violate the Constitution.		Organized labor states its opposition to trade with communist countries.		Russian film The Overcoat opens in N.Y.C.	March 1
Pres. Johnson asks for rent subsidies to spur housing construction.			U.S. launches a weather satellite.		March 2
Senate unit suggests that Congress should consider a bill to legalize wiretapping.	U.S. is reportedly considering selling arms to Israel.				March 3
		Pres. Johnson says that unemployment is still too high.		Vatican has reportedly told U.S. bishops not to participate in joint worship services with Protestants.	March 4
Fire destroys a civil rights Freedom School in Indianola, Miss.	U.S. protests attacks on its embassy in Moscow.			National Chinese official Chen Cheng dies in Taipei at 67.	March 5
Seventy white Alabamians stage a march to support Negroes in Selma, Ala.	U.S. sends 3,500 more marines to Vietnam.		Soviet Union launches a weather satellite.		March 6
Police use gas and clubs to rout protesting Negroes in Selma, Ala.	U.S. officials say that they are trying to exploit the Sino-Soviet split.			Pope Paul celebrates a mass in Italian for the first time.	March 7
Martin Luther King Jr. leads a civil rights demonstration in Selma, Ala.	U.S. is considering sending naval craft to protect the South Vietnamese coast from infiltrators.				March 8
Martin Luther King Jr. leads 1,500 Negroes and whites on a second attempted protest march in Selma, Ala.	U.S. denies that its food aid to Yemeni royalists means that it no longer recognizes the republican government.				March 9
U.S. sues to void a state ban on marches in Alabama.	Pres. Johnson confers with his top aides on Vietnam.			Pres. Johnson submits a $10 million plan to promote the arts.	March 10
U.S. officials say they will prosecute Alabama police for tear gas attacks on protesting Negroes.	Pentagon hints that more U.S. troops may be going to Vietnam.				March 11

F	G	H	I	J
Includes elections, federal-state relations, civil rights and liberties, crime, the judiciary, education, health care, poverty, urban affairs and population.	Includes formation and debate of U.S. foreign and defense policies, veterans' affairs and defense spending. (Relations with specific foreign countries are usually found under the region concerned.)	Includes business, labor, agriculture, taxation, transportation, consumer affairs, monetary and fiscal policy, natural resources, and pollution.	Includes worldwide scientific, medical and technological developments, natural phenomena, U.S. weather, natural disasters, and accidents.	Includes the arts, religion, scholarship, communications media, sports, entertainment, fashions, fads and social life.

	World Affairs	Europe	Africa & the Middle East	The Americas	Asia & the Pacific
March 12	U.N. Secy. Gen. U Thant reports a danger of a flare-up in Cyprus.	West Germany votes to extend the Nazi crime statutes.	Tunisia opposes Egypt's proposed boycott of West Germany.		
March 13		One thousand Spanish miners attack the police headquarters in Asturias province.	Israel permits the U.S. to inspect its atomic reactor.		Thailand and Malaysia combine their intelligence units.
March 14		Former Soviet Premier Nikita Khrushchev makes his first public appearance since his fall from power in 1964.	Israel agrees to talk with West Germany about possible diplomatic relations.	An Argentine poll indicates that the Peronists are still a strong force.	U.S. planes raid a naval base in North Vietnam.
March 15		Portugal asserts that it will not be driven out of its African colonies.	Some Arab states may reportedly recognize neither German state.		One hundred U.S. planes strike deep into Vietnam.
March 16		Soviet Union agrees to sign an international patent pact.	Arab mobs attack West German property in Iraq and Lebanon.		
March 17	At the U.N. Turkey accuses Cypriote officials of abusing the island's Turkish minority.	French writer Jean-Paul Sartre cancels scheduled lectures in the U.S. because of America's role in Vietnam.	Syria accuses Israel of damaging a water project.		South Vietnamese and Viet Cong forces clash in the Central Highlands.
March 18		Cyprus is reportedly installing Soviet-supplied missiles.	Nigeria holds elections for 54 parliamentary seats.	Cuba foresees a large sugar crop.	Indonesian Communists cut power to U.S. private residences in Jakarta.
March 19		Turkey asks Greece for a parley to break the deadlock on Cyprus.			One hundred ten U.S. planes bomb two bases in North Vietnam.
March 20		Rumania renews debate within the Soviet bloc about national economic roles.	Sudan ousts a minister for slapping a telephone official.	Cuban CP is reportedly tightening control over the armed forces.	
March 21		Greece and Turkey meet for preliminary talks on Cyprus.	Arab guerrillas kill three British soldiers in Yemen.		A joint allied air strike hits Vucon depot in North Vietnam.
March 22			Egypt is reportedly using poisonous gas against royalist forces in Yemen.		U.S. planes bomb radar installations in North Vietnam.
March 23	U.N. expert Wilfred Borrie says population control is essential for economic growth.	Soviet Union says it may send troops to North Vietnam.			U.S. planes pound North Vietnam.
March 24		West Germany reportedly wants to give Israel financial but not military aid.	Reports indicate that 25 protesters have been recently killed in Moroccan riots.		South Vietnamese and Viet Cong troops clash in the Mekong Delta.
March 25		West German Parliament votes to extend the period of prosecution for Nazi crimes until 1970.	Anti-government riots have reportedly ended in Casablanca.		South Vietnamese troops begin an offensive in the Mekong Delta.
March 26	At the U.N. Soviet bloc delegates denounce U.S. policy in Vietnam.	Soviet government shuffles its top economic officials.	Egypt offers the U.S. a temple saved from the Aswan flooding.		U.S. planes strike deep into Vietnam.
	A	B	C	D	E
	Includes developments that affect more than one world region, international organizations and important meetings of major world leaders.	Includes all domestic and regional developments in Europe, including the Soviet Union, Turkey, Cyprus and Malta.	Includes all domestic and regional developments in Africa and the Middle East, including Iraq and Iran and excluding Cyprus, Turkey and Afghanistan.	Includes all domestic and regional developments in Latin America, the Caribbean and Canada.	Includes all domestic and regional developments in Asia and Pacific nations, extending from Afghanistan through all the Pacific Islands, except Hawaii.

U.S. Politics & Social Issues	U.S. Foreign Policy & Defense	U.S. Economy & Environment	Science, Technology & Nature	Culture, Leisure & Life Style	
Pres. Johnson reveals that federal troops may be sent to duty in Selma, Ala.				Speech therapist Arthur Mulligan dies in N.Y.C. at 60.	March 12
Pres. Johnson condemns police tactics in Selma, Ala.	Pres. Johnson says that peace in Vietnam is up to the leaders in Hanoi.		Soviet Union launches a military surveillance satellite.		March 13
Selma Ala. officials stiffen their ban on marches.					March 14
Pres. Johnson calls for civil rights progress and pledges, "we shall overcome" before a joint session of Congress.		U.S. reports that employment is reportedly up by 230,000 jobs.	U.S. officials order a delay in the firing of a two-man Gemini spacecraft.		March 15
Police rout 600 civil rights marchers in Montgomery, Ala.	Under State Secy. George Ball says that France is undermining the U.S. position in Vietnam.			Pianist Vladimir Horowitz announces he is planning to concertize again after a 12-year retirement.	March 16
Selma, Ala. officials arrest ministers picketing the home of Mayor Joseph Smitherman.			Soviet Union launches a manned spacecraft around the earth.		March 17
Pres. Johnson offers to mobilize the Alabama National Guard in order to protect civil rights marchers.			Soviet Astronaut Aleksei Leonev floats in space for 10 minutes.		March 18
Ala. Gov. George Wallace says that the state is too poor to pay for the mobilization of the National Guard.				Norton Simon Foundation buys Rembrandt's *Titus*.	March 19
Pres. Johnson mobilizes the Alabama National Guard to protect civil rights marchers in Selma.	White House says that US Amb.-to-South Vietnam Maxwell Taylor will come to Washington D.C. for talks on March 28.		Soviet Union discloses that spaceship Voskhod Two had to use a parachute in returning to the earth.		March 20
Three thousand two hundred civil rights marchers leave Selma, Ala. for the state capitol at Montgomery.			U.S. launches Ranger 9 toward the moon.	Pope Paul says Mass in Italian in a working class quarter in Rome.	March 21
Soviet Union agrees to purchase a French color television system.	U.S. says it is using non-lethal gas against the Viet Cong.		U.S. Surgeon Gen. Luther Terry warns of the dangers of cigarette smoking.		March 22
Alabama Freedom Marchers pass the midpoint of their march.			Two U.S. astronauts land safely in the Atlantic after operating the world's first maneuverable spacecraft.		March 23
Alabama civil rights marchers reach the outskirts of Montgomery without incident.	State Secy. Dean Rusk defends the use of non-lethal gas in Vietnam.		Ranger 9 sends back photos of the moon before crashing onto its surface.		March 24
Civil rights Freedon March ends at the Ala. state capitol in Montgomery.			Gemini 3 astronauts say their recent flight was almost perfect.	Vatican says it will seek links with atheists.	March 25
Pres. Johnson calls for a war on the Ku Klux Klan.	U.S. State Secy. Dean Rusk discusses the Vietnam situation with Soviet Amb. Anatoly Dobrynin.				March 26

F	G	H	I	J
Includes elections, federal-state relations, civil rights and liberties, crime, the judiciary, education, health care, poverty, urban affairs and population.	Includes formation and debate of U.S. foreign and defense policies, veterans' affairs and defense spending. (Relations with specific foreign countries are usually found under the region concerned.)	Includes business, labor, agriculture, taxation, transportation, consumer affairs, monetary and fiscal policy, natural resources, and pollution.	Includes worldwide scientific, medical and technological developments, natural phenomena, U.S. weather, natural disasters, and accidents.	Includes the arts, religion, scholarship, communications media, sports, entertainment, fashions, fads and social life.

	World Affairs	Europe	Africa & the Middle East	The Americas	Asia & the Pacific
March 27	U.N. officials call for progress in the talks on Cyprus.	Soviet Union announces farm plans aimed at elevating the status of peasants.		Cuba offers arms to North Vietnam.	
March 28		Two-hundred-fifty students end a sit-down strike in Madrid as police free three arrested students.		Reports indicate that urban terrorism is rising in Colombia.	U.S. destroyers begin patrolling the coast of South Vietnam.
March 29		France vetoes a parley on a European meeting.	Saudi Arabian King Faisal names his brother Khaled as his successor.	New earthquake tremors stir fears in Chile.	A bomb kills six people in the U.S. embassy in Saigon.
March 30	U.N. mediator Galo Lasso urges a Cypriote government which includes the minority Turkish population.		Kenya accuses the Soviet Union of training Kenyan pilots without the government's knowledge.	Brazil receives 12 project loans from the U.S.	U.S. and South Vietnamese planes raid key air bases in North Vietnam.
March 31	Soviet Union asks for a disarmament debate at the U.N.	Spain is reportedly seeking Morocco's support in its drive to expel Britain from Gibraltar.			U.S. planes smash a Viet Cong force near Saigon.
April 1		French philosopher Jean-Paul Sartre scores the U.S. role in Vietnam.			South Vietnamese and Viet Cong forces clash near Danang.
April 2	U.N. Secy. Gen. U Thant warns Trukey not to continue to reject U.N. mediator for Cyprus Galo Lasso.	Communists delay traffic to Berlin in reprisal for a scheduled meeting of the West German Parliament in West Berlin.	Kenya charges Communist China with smuggling in arms to dissident forces.		Japan and South Korea conclude three pacts in a step toward a total accord.
April 3			Egypt reportedly will not recognize East Germany.	Canada calls for a temporary halt to the U.S. bombing of North Vietnam.	U.S. planes pound North Vietnam.
April 4		East German guards halt West Berlin Mayor Willy Brandt from driving into Berlin from West Germany.		Argentina agrees to sell wheat to Communist China.	North Vietnamese planes down two U.S. planes in the first air clash between the two countries.
April 5		Communist officials shut the Berlin autobahn for four hours.	Egyptian planes reportedly bomb Qizan, a Saudi border town.		U.S. planes pound North Vietnam.
April 6	At the U.N. Arab delegates call for an economic boycott against Israel.	Communists again close the Berlin autobahn as the West German Parliament meets.	Kenyan students leave the Soviet Union because of alleged racial discrimination.		U.S. officials say that Allied air strikes are improving South Vietnamese morale.
April 7	At the U.N. Soviet bloc delegates accuse Communist China of being "reckless."	Soviet jets fly low over Berlin as the West German Parliament meets.	Reports indicate that Belgian officials are back in the Congo as administrators.		U.S. officials report that Communist China is slowing down Soviet arms shipments across China to North Vietnam.
April 8		Communist officials again block the Berlin autobahn.		Venezuela puts former Pres. Marcos Perez Jimenez on trial.	South Vietnamese and Viet Cong forces clash near Danang.
April 9	U.N. Secy. Gen. U Thant confers with US Amb.-to-UN Adlai Stevenson about Vietnam.	Communist officials block the Berlin autobahn for three hours.	Kenya accuses Communist China of trying to smuggle in arms to dissidents.		Communist China reports a clash with U.S. planes over Hainan, a Chinese island in the South China Sea.
April 10		Former V.P. Richard Nixon visits South Vietnam but is ignored by U.S. embassy officials.		Venezuela arrests three Italians for trying to smuggle money in to Communist guerrillas.	U.S. jets pound North Vietnamese munitions dumps.

A	B	C	D	E
Includes developments that affect more than one world region, international organizations and important meetings of major world leaders.	Includes all domestic and regional developments in Europe, including the Soviet Union, Turkey, Cyprus and Malta.	Includes all domestic and regional developments in Africa and the Middle East, including Iraq and Iran and excluding Cyprus, Turkey and Afghanistan.	Includes all domestic and regional developments in Latin America, the Caribbean and Canada.	Includes all domestic and regional developments in Asia and Pacific nations, extending from Afghanistan through all the Pacific Islands, except Hawaii.

U.S. Politics & Social Issues	U.S. Foreign Policy & Defense	U.S. Economy & Environment	Science, Technology & Nature	Culture, Leisure & Life Style	
Martin Luther King Jr. calls for continued demonstrations throughout Alabama.	U.S. Amb.-to-South Vietnam Maxwell Taylor says he sees some improvement in the South Vietnamese political situation.				March 27
A Selma, Ala. Protestant church is integrated for the first time.				Noted British surgeon Gordon Seagrave dies in Rangoon, Burma at 68.	March 28
Supreme Court rules that a business may be shut to prevent unionism.				Pope Paul urges a Roman Catholic commission to decide a policy for birth control.	March 29
House unit votes for a full investigation of the Ku Klux Klan.	Pres. Johnson says the nation will stay the course in South Vietnam.				March 30
House unit votes to create an agency for the elderly.		Pilots begin a strike at Pan American World Airways after labor talks fail.		Pope Paul has reportedly eliminated derogatory references to Jews and atheists in Holy Week prayers.	March 31
N.Y.C. Mayor Robert Wagner lowers the city's literacy standard for employment hiring.	Pres. Johnson says that U.S. strategy is unchanged in Vietnam despite intensified bombing.	U.S. officials say the 4.7% jobless rate is the lowest rate since 1957.		Beauty expert Helena Rubenstein dies in N.Y.C. at 94.	April 1
	U.S. officials doubt that Soviet leaders will visit the U.S. because of the escalation of the Vietnam War.				April 2
Police say that N.Y.C. subway crime is up 41% over the previous year.	U.S. accuses the Soviet Union of harassing its ships at sea.		U.S. launches a satellite powered by a nuclear reactor.		April 3
		Officials say that smog is increasing along the East Coast.	U.S. officials say that the orbiting nuclear reactor satellite is performing well.		April 4
N.Y.C. Mayor Robert Wagner orders night patrols on subways in order to combat rising crime.		Pres. Johnson offers a farm program with reduced subsidies.			April 5
House begins a debate on medical care for the aged.			U.S. launches a communications satellite.		April 6
Eight hundred N.Y.C. police begin subway patrols in an anti-crime fight.	Pres. Johnson offers unconditional talks on Vietnam.				April 7
House approves a Medicare bill by 313-115.		AFL-CIO says it may leave the International Labor Organization because of communist dominance.		Vatican names Cardinal Konig as its envoy to atheists.	April 8
Congressional panels stiffen the voting rights bill.		Factory jobs hit a postwar peak.			April 9
Both Virginia political parties say that they will run Negroes for the first time since Reconstruction.	Sen. Wayne Morse (D, Ore.) says that the U.S. should pull out of Vietnam.				April 10

F	G	H	I	J
Includes elections, federal-state relations, civil rights and liberties, crime, the judiciary, education, health care, poverty, urban affairs and population.	Includes formation and debate of U.S. foreign and defense policies, veterans' affairs and defense spending. (Relations with specific foreign countries are usually found under the region concerned.)	Includes business, labor, agriculture, taxation, transportation, consumer affairs, monetary and fiscal policy, natural resources, and pollution.	Includes worldwide scientific, medical and technological developments, natural phenomena, U.S. weather, natural disasters, and accidents.	Includes the arts, religion, scholarship, communications media, sports, entertainment, fashions, fads and social life.

	World Affairs	Europe	Africa & the Middle East	The Americas	Asia & the Pacific
April 11		Polish Cardinal Stefan Wyszynski accuses the Polish government of promoting atheism.		Police and students clash briefly at the Univ. of Lima in Peru.	Indonesia says it might improve ties with the U.S. if the U.S. helps in the Indonesian-Malaysian dispute.
April 12	At the U.N. Western delegates call for greater birth control efforts in the lesser developed countries.	Soviets open the Berlin Wall for Easter visits.	Algerian Pres. Ahmed Ben Bella commutes death sentences of two condemned rivals.		North Vietnam spurns a British offer of mediation.
April 13		France calls for slower European integration.	Ghana says that Western nations have turned down a loan appeal.		South Vietnamese and Viet Cong forces clash in the Mekong Delta.
April 14		Soviet Union reports the arrests of illegal gold dealers.	Kenya receives a shipment of Soviet guns.	Mexico arrests 30 leftist extremists.	U.S. planes drop anti-Chinese leaflets over North Vietnam.
April 15		West Germany pays its final installment of reparations to Israel.	Zambian Pres. Kenneth Kuanda accuses Communist China of unwarranted political attacks.	Cuba says that homosexuality will not be tolerated.	
April 16		Turkish Cypriotes protest against discrimination in Nicosia.	Egypt asks for U.S. food aid.		U.S. planes raze six bridges in North Vietnam.
April 17		Soviet Union again says that it may send volunteers to North Vietnam.	Arab guerrillas exchange gunfire with British troops in Aden.		Indonesia is reportedly moving closer to Communist China.
April 18		Turkish Cypriotes protest against the blockade of their neighborhood in Nicosia.	Egyptian Pres. Nasser confers with U.S. officials in Cairo on food aid.		Small-scale rioting takes place in Seoul, South Korea.
April 19	At the U.N. Arab delegates call on the developing nations to break ties with Israel.	Turkey says it plans to expel all Greek nationals.			U.S. troops clash with Viet Cong near Danang.
April 20	U.S. Amb.-to-UN Adlai Stevenson finds hopes dim on arms talks.	Soviet Union cancels all debts owed by collective farms.	Reports indicate that Iraqi troops and planes are moving against the Kurds.		Communist China says it is preparing to send troops to Vietnam.
April 21	U.N. Secy. Gen. U Thant again offers to act as a mediator in the Vietnam conflict.		Election violence takes the lives of 14 in the Sudan.		South Vietnamese and Viet Cong forces clash near Saigon.
April 22		France says it may end its links with SEATO.	Tunisian Pres. Habib Bourguiba calls for negotiations with Israel.		Viet Cong retreat after skirmishing with U.S. Marines.
April 23		France says it will not take part in SEATO's war games.	Egypt calls Tunisian Pres. Habib Bourguiba a traitor.	Cuba accuses Cuban exiles of setting fire to Cuban sugar cane.	U.S. planes raze bridges in North Vietnam.
April 24				A revolt by supporters of former Pres. Juan Bosch collapses in the Dominican Republic.	India accuses Pakistan of major border incursions.
April 25		Soviet Foreign Min. Andrei Gromyko arrives in France for talks.	In Lebanon, about 50,000 Armenians commemorate the 50th anniversary of the Turkish massacres during W.W. II.	Dominican government collapses as army factions battle for power.	India charges Pakistan of mobilizing its troops.
	A	B	C	D	E
	Includes developments that affect more than one world region, international organizations and important meetings of major world leaders.	Includes all domestic and regional developments in Europe, including the Soviet Union, Turkey, Cyprus and Malta.	Includes all domestic and regional developments in Africa and the Middle East, including Iraq and Iran and excluding Cyprus, Turkey and Afghanistan.	Includes all domestic and regional developments in Latin America, the Caribbean and Canada.	Includes all domestic and regional developments in Asia and Pacific nations, extending from Afghanistan through all the Pacific Islands, except Hawaii.

U.S. Politics & Social Issues	U.S. Foreign Policy & Defense	U.S. Economy & Environment	Science, Technology & Nature	Culture, Leisure & Life Style	
Pres. Johnson signs a $1.3 billion education bill.		U.S. auto companies report strong quarterly sales.	Tornadoes kill 150 in the Midwest.		April 11
			Death toll mounts to 239 in U.S. Midwest tornado aftermath.	Pope Paul meets with Italian Socialists in bid to improve relations with the left.	April 12
An Ala. jury indicts three Selma, Ala. residents for the murder of the Rev. James Reeb, a minister from Boston engaged in civil rights activity.	Presidential adviser Henry Cabot Lodge leaves for consultations with U.S. allies in the Pacific.		U.S. scientists say that they have pinpointed the moon's position to within a few feet.		April 13
House hires its first Negro page.	Peace Corps says that it will leave Indonesia.				April 14
	House approves an open-ended fund to aid South Vietnam.	United Steel Workers bars an extension of the current wage pact.			April 15
A U.S. court orders the Dallas County, Tex. sheriff to cease using members of the county posse to police racial demonstrations.	Pres. Johnson cancels upcoming talks with Indian and Pakistani leaders because of the Vietnam situation.		U.S. officials say they plan to explore the ocean bottoms with a small atomic submarine.		April 16
	Pres. Johnson rejects appeals to halt the bombing of North Vietnam.	Auto officials say that 1966 cars will stress power.	U.S. conducts an underground nuclear test.		April 17
	Newspaper publishers report widespread support around the country for Pres. Johnson's Vietnam policy.		Soviet Union conducts an underground nuclear test.	Pope Paul calls for Vietnam negotiations in his Easter message.	April 18
U.S. officials say that the influence of the Ku Klux Klan is growing.	State Secy. Dean Rusk says that the bombing of North Vietnam will continue.			U.S. journalist Joseph Levy dies in N.Y.C. at 64.	April 19
	Pres. Johnson confers with Italian Premier Aldo Moro.		Radar studies show that Mercury is rotating faster than was thought.		April 20
Education officials report that competition for college entrance is becoming increasingly stiff.		U.S. officials fear a steel strike.			April 21
N.Y.C. Mayor Robert Wagner adds 500 police to street patrol in bid to fight growing crime.	U.S. Amb.-to-U.N. Adlai Stevenson says that America's period of "long isolation and brief supremacy" is over.			A bomb explodes in St. Patrick Cathedral in N.Y.C.	April 22
U.S. Senate debates a proposed ban on the poll tax.			Soviet Union launches a communication satellite.		April 23
	Pres. Johnson says that he plans no major changes in Vietnam policy.	U.S. businessmen call for trade with Communist China.	U.S. launches a communication satellite.		April 24
Senate leaders say they will speed action on the voting rights bill.	U.S. officials confirm for the first time that North Vietnamese troops are fighting in the South.				April 25
F	G	H	I	J	
Includes elections, federal-state relations, civil rights and liberties, crime, the judiciary, education, health care, poverty, urban affairs and population.	*Includes formation and debate of U.S. foreign and defense policies, veterans' affairs and defense spending. (Relations with specific foreign countries are usually found under the region concerned.)*	*Includes business, labor, agriculture, taxation, transportation, consumer affairs, monetary and fiscal policy, natural resources, and pollution.*	*Includes worldwide scientific, medical and technological developments, natural phenomena, U.S. weather, natural disasters, and accidents.*	*Includes the arts, religion, scholarship, communications media, sports, entertainment, fashions, fads and social life.*	

	World Affairs	Europe	Africa & the Middle East	The Americas	Asia & the Pacific
April 26		Britain accepts a Soviet plan to seek a Cambodian parley.		U.S. begins evacuating Americans from the Dominican Republic in the wake of civil strife.	India puts forces on alert in wake of border crisis with Pakistan.
April 27		France voices concern over the escalating war in Vietnam.	Egypt withdraws its diplomatic personnel from Tunisia.	A revolt of supporters of former Pres. Juan Bosch again collapses in the Dominican Republic.	South Vietnamese and Viet Cong forces clash in the Central Highlands.
April 28			An Egyptian mob ransacks the Tunisian ambassador's residence.	Pro-Bosch rebels are reportedly holding parts of the Dominican capital.	North Korean jets attack a U.S. plane over the Sea of Japan.
April 29		France and the Soviet Union call for an end to U.S. intervention in Vietnam.	Kenya says that its Soviet arms are old and useless.		U.S. troops skirmish with the Viet Cong near Saigon.
April 30		Britain announces plans to re-nationalize the British steel industry.	Tunisian Pres. Habib Bourguiba urges Egyptian Pres. Nasser to meet with him.	Dominican rebels slay one U.S. Marine.	
May 1	Turkey suggests further talks on Cyprus with Greece.			U.S. troops push slowly into a rebel-held downtown area in Santo Domingo.	Viet Cong reportedly have been given advanced rocketry by the Soviet Union.
May 2			Tunisia accuses Egyptian Pres. Nasser of wanting to become the dictator of the Arab world.	Sniper fire continues in Santo Domingo.	U.S. Navy planes participate in the bombing of North Vietnam.
May 3		Cypriote Pres. Makarios lifts a ban on traffic for Turkish Cypriotes.		U.S. troops open a corridor through rebel-held territory in Santo Domingo.	Cambodia breaks diplomatic relations with the U.S.
May 4	At the U.N. Uruguay criticizes the U.S. intervention in the Dominican Republic.		Moderates win in Bautoland elections in South Africa.	U.S. Marines continue to expand into rebel-held territory in Santo Domingo.	One thousand two hundred more troops land in South Vietnam.
May 5	U.N. orders employees to make economy efforts.			OAS votes 14-5 to send an inter-American peace force to the Dominican Republic.	
May 6		British House of Commons votes 310-306 to nationalize the steel industry.	Egypt condemns the U.S. intervention in the Dominican Republic.	Dominican rebels kill three U.S. Marines.	Nine thousand more U.S. troops land in South Vietnam.
May 7	At the U.N. African delegates condemn the electoral victory of Rhodesian P.M. Ian Smith.		Rhodesian P.M. Ian Smith wins a decisive victory in parliamentary elections.	Sporadic sniper fire continues in Santo Domingo.	North Vietnam downs one U.S. plane.
May 8	At the U.N. African delegates condemn South Africa's apartheid policy.	A Soviet rally hails Stalin for the first time since 1956.	Egyptian and Israeli forces exchange fire along the Gaza Strip.	Dominican military junta says it controls most of the country.	
May 9			Yemeni charter projects a parliamentary regime.	Dominican junta ousts eight right-wing officers in a gesture of conciliation.	Viet Cong and South Vietnamese forces clash near Saigon.
May 10	At the U.N. African delegates score Western investment in South Africa.	Common Market asks for more trade with Eastern Europe.	Egypt condemns two alleged spys to death.	OAS truce unit gets new power in the Dominican Republic.	Five Americans die in Viet Cong attacks.
May 11			Sudanese rightists win in parliamentary elections.		U.S. planes pound Viet Cong forces in South Vietnam.
	A	B	C	D	E
	Includes developments that affect more than one world region, international organizations and important meetings of major world leaders.	Includes all domestic and regional developments in Europe, including the Soviet Union, Turkey, Cyprus and Malta.	Includes all domestic and regional developments in Africa and the Middle East, including Iraq and Iran and excluding Cyprus, Turkey and Afghanistan.	Includes all domestic and regional developments in Latin America, the Caribbean and Canada.	Includes all domestic and regional developments in Asia and Pacific nations, extending from Afghanistan through all the Pacific Islands, except Hawaii.

U.S. Politics & Social Issues	U.S. Foreign Policy & Defense	U.S. Economy & Environment	Science, Technology & Nature	Culture, Leisure & Life Style	
	Defense Secy. Robert McNamara calls North Vietnamese aggression increasingly flagrant.	Steel industry officials agree on major raises for workers.	U.S. scientists urge a landing on Mars in order to seek signs of life.		April 26
	Pres. Johnson defends the bombing of North Vietnam.			U.S. broadcaster Edward Murrow dies in Pawling, N.Y. at 57.	April 27
	Pres. Johnson announces that 405 U.S. Marines have been sent to the Dominican Republic to protect U.S. citizens.		Soviet Union launches a military surveillance satellite.		April 28
Justice Dept. bids schools end segregation by the fall of 1967.	U.S. sends 2,500 airborne troops into the Dominican Republic.		An earthquake kills two in Seattle.		April 29
		United Steel Workers elect I. W. Abel as its next president.	U.S. scientists fear that the introduction of commercial supersonic air travel may bring about substantial climate changes.	Pope Paul calls for a negotiated settlement of the Vietnam War.	April 30
	U.S. officials say that U.S. troops were sent to the Dominican Republic in part to prevent another Cuba.		U.S. launches a military surveillance satellite.		May 1
Senate liberals say they are pushing hard for an end to the poll tax.	U.S. officials say there are now 14,000 U.S. troops in the Dominican Republic.			Pope Paul voices hope for peace in the Dominican Republic.	May 2
Supreme Court backs the legality of the U.S. ban on travel to Cuba.	U.S. urges the OAS to send an inter-American force to the Dominican Republic.			Frank Gilroy's *The Subject was Roses* wins the Pulitzer Prize for drama.	May 3
	Pres. Johnson urges Congress to vote $700 million for the Vietnam War.			U.S. lawyer Mortimer Schwager dies in N.Y.C. at 75.	May 4
	House votes 408-7 to fund the budget for Vietnam.	AFL-CIO Pres. George Meany says the AFL-CIO will stay in the International Labor Organization.	Soviet Mars spacecraft stops transmitting information.		May 5
	Senate votes 88-3 for the Vietnam War budget.			Archeologists unearth 1,900-year-old Indian canals in Arizona.	May 6
	Sen. Robert Kennedy (D, N.Y.) criticizes the U.S. intervention in the Dominican Republic.	U.S. economists agree that the economic outlook is excellent.			May 7
		U.S. officials say that Pres. Johnson is considering a long-term slash in excise taxes.	Soviet Union conducts an underground nuclear test.		May 8
Nine Southern governors call for a slow-down in school integration.			Soviet Union launches a satellite toward the moon.	Pianist Vladimir Horowitz returns to the concert stage after a 12-year absence.	May 9
					May 10
Senate rejects a ban on the poll tax by 49-45.	U.S. presses for a coalition of two major Dominican factions.		An earthquake rocks Alaska but causes little damage.	Pope Paul confers with Lebanese Pres. Charles Helon at the Vatican.	May 11
F	G	H	I	J	
Includes elections, federal-state relations, civil rights and liberties, crime, the judiciary, education, health care, poverty, urban affairs and population.	Includes formation and debate of U.S. foreign and defense policies, veterans' affairs and defense spending. (Relations with specific foreign countries are usually found under the region concerned.)	Includes business, labor, agriculture, taxation, transportation, consumer affairs, monetary and fiscal policy, natural resources, and pollution.	Includes worldwide scientific, medical and technological developments, natural phenomena, U.S. weather, natural disasters, and accidents.	Includes the arts, religion, scholarship, communications media, sports, entertainment, fashions, fads and social life.	

	World Affairs	Europe	Africa & the Middle East	The Americas	Asia & the Pacific
May 12		Indian Pres. Lal Shastri praises Soviet foreign policy while in Moscow.	Iraq breaks its ties with West Germany.	OAS mediators meet with rival factions in Santo Domingo.	Communist China calls for a fall-out shelter program.
May 13	At the U.N. African delegates assail Portugal's rule in Africa.	Britain sends troops to Mauritius to quell rioters.	Israel establishes diplomatic relations with West Germany.	Government planes bomb a rebel radio post in the Dominican Republic.	A huge Communist Chinese rally in Peking condemns the U.S.
May 14	U.N. sends a mission to Santo Domingo in response to dissidents' request.	Italy supports the U.S. intervention in the Dominican Republic.		Dominican junta planes again bomb a rebel radio station.	Communist China conducts its second nuclear test.
May 15	At the U.N. Arab delegates criticize U.S. support of Israel.			Fighting intensifies between the Dominican junta and rebel forces.	South Vietnamese and Viet Cong forces clash near Danang.
May 16			Sudan breaks diplomatic relations with West Germany.	Heavy fighting continues in Santo Domingo.	A munitions explosion kills 21 people in South Vietnam.
May 17		A gas explosion kills 31 miners at a Welsh coal mine.	Algeria rejects a West German aid offer.	U.S. officials and Dominican rebels agree on a government to be led by a Bosch aide.	South Vietnamese and Viet Cong forces clash in the Mekong Delta.
May 18	U.N. Secy. Gen. U Thant urges U.N. action in the Dominican Republic.	Britain's Queen Elizabeth visiting West Germany calls for European unity.	Syria executes an Israeli for allegedly spying in a public square.		U.S. resumes the bombing of North Vietnam after a six-day lull brings no response.
May 19	U.N. experts foresee a growing food deficit.	French Pres. de Gaulle calls for an end to a world allegedly dominated by the two super-powers.	A plane carrying 121 passengers crashes near Cairo.	Dominican junta accepts a truce offer by U.S. officials.	U.S. planes bomb two installations in North Vietnam.
May 20		Major floods threaten central Yugoslavia.		Dominican factions accept a 24-hour truce.	India praises Soviet foreign policy.
May 21	U.N. rejects a Soviet resolution condemning the U.S. intervention in the Dominican Republic.		Tunisia reaffirms its long-standing friendship with the U.S.	Police rout 2,000 Bolivian tin strikers.	South Vietnam arrests 40 alleged anti-government plotters.
May 22	U.N. calls for a cease-fire in the Dominican Republic.			A *de facto* cease-fire begins in the Dominican Republic.	U.S. planes bomb a military base 55 miles from Hanoi.
May 23		Belgian liberals gain in parliamentary elections.	Observers report that heavy fighting is continuing between royalists and republicans in Yemen.	Dominican truce continues as U.S. spurs peace talks.	U.S. officials say that U.S. forces in South Vietnam will rise to 60,000 during June 1965.
May 24		Five hundred thousand West Germans give a warm welcome to British Queen Elizabeth in Stuttgart.		Bolivian authorities and striking tin miners reach an agreement.	Allied troops begin a major offensive around Saigon.
May 25		French police foil a plot to kill French Pres. de Gaulle.		A truce continues between police and striking tin workers in Bolivia.	South Vietnamese and Viet Cong forces clash near Saigon.
May 26	At the U.N. Zambia calls for the admission of Communist China.	France criticizes U.S. intervention in the Dominican Republic.		Bolivian tin miners agree to return to work.	U.S. planes bomb North Vietnam.
May 27	U.N. Secy. Gen. U Thant fears that the OAS peace force will impede U.N. efforts in the Dominican Republic.	British Queen Elizabeth pledges military support for West Berlin, during her trip to West Germany.	Israeli troops attack Jordan in retaliation for guerrilla attacks.		U.S. warships fire on North Vietnam's coast.
	A	**B**	**C**	**D**	**E**
	Includes developments that affect more than one world region, international organizations and important meetings of major world leaders.	*Includes all domestic and regional developments in Europe, including the Soviet Union, Turkey, Cyprus and Malta.*	*Includes all domestic and regional developments in Africa and the Middle East, including Iraq and Iran and excluding Cyprus, Turkey and Afghanistan.*	*Includes all domestic and regional developments in Latin America, the Caribbean and Canada.*	*Includes all domestic and regional developments in Asia and Pacific nations, extending from Afghanistan through all the Pacific Islands, except Hawaii.*

U.S. Politics & Social Issues	U.S. Foreign Policy & Defense	U.S. Economy & Environment	Science, Technology & Nature	Culture, Leisure & Life Style	
House votes for a ban on the poll tax.			A Soviet spacecraft fails to land on the moon.		May 12
N.Y.C. Congressman John Lindsay says he will run for Mayor.					May 13
	U.S. orders a pause in the bombing of North Vietnam.			First woman U.S. Cabinet member Frances Perkins dies in N.Y.C. at 83.	May 14
	Two hundred anti-Vietnam War protesters block traffic on N.Y.C.'s Fifth Avenue.		Soviet Union launches a military surveillance satellite.	Opera star Maria Callas sings Bellini's *Norma* in Paris.	May 15
			A scientist stops a charging bull with electronic impulses sent by wires to its brain.		May 16
	U.S. officials say a full combat role for U.S. troops in Vietnam is imminent.	Pres. Johnson urges speedy approval of his excise tax cut proposal.			May 17
	U.S. calls for a coalition government in the Dominican Republic.				May 18
	Journalists report that the U.S. Senate generally backs Pres. Johnson's Vietnam policy.				May 19
U.S. tells Southern radio and television stations to halt all racial bias.	U.S. backtracks and decides to support the Dominican military junta.			Twenty-seven letters of poet Robert Frost bring $11,500 at an auction.	May 20
	U.S. says it will withdraw 1,700 troops from the Dominican Republic in the near future.				May 21
		U.S. officials report that U.S. tax revenues are $1.5 billion more than anticipated.		A stolen Goya portrait of the Duke of Wellington is returned anonymously to British authorities.	May 22
Bogalusa La. officials decide to repeal all segregation ordinances.	White House tells U.S. diplomatic personnel to serve domestic wines at diplomatic functions.				May 23
Supreme Court voids a mail law curbing communist propaganda.	House begins a debate on a foreign aid bill.		A television satellite links art buyers in New York and London.		May 24
Senate invokes cloture on the voting rights bill in a 70-30 vote.	House approves the foreign aid bill in a 249-148 vote.	Pres. Johnson calls for a law banning billboards along major federal highways.			May 25
Senate approves the voting rights bill by 77-19.		White House officials deny that inflation is increasing.			May 26
		U.S. officials admit that prices rose sharply in April.		Pope Paul says he hopes to visit Poland in 1966 for its millenium anniversary of Catholicism.	May 27

F	G	H	I	J
Includes elections, federal-state relations, civil rights and liberties, crime, the judiciary, education, health care, poverty, urban affairs and population.	Includes formation and debate of U.S. foreign and defense policies, veterans' affairs and defense spending. (Relations with specific foreign countries are usually found under the region concerned.)	Includes business, labor, agriculture, taxation, transportation, consumer affairs, monetary and fiscal policy, natural resources, and pollution.	Includes worldwide scientific, medical and technological developments, natural phenomena, U.S. weather, natural disasters, and accidents.	Includes the arts, religion, scholarship, communications media, sports, entertainment, fashions, fads and social life.

	World Affairs	Europe	Africa & the Middle East	The Americas	Asia & the Pacific
May 28	The US, at the U.N., denies Soviet charges that it is arming South Africa.	French delegates leave the SEATO staff.			South Vietnamese and Viet Cong forces clash in the Central Highlands.
May 29	At the U.N., Israel charges that the Arab countries want to destroy it.	Police clash briefly with students at the Univ. of Barcelona.	Egypt demands that Libya cut its ties with West Germany.	U.S. officials foresee a lengthy impasse in the Dominican Republic.	U.S. officials say that the Viet Cong are increasing their activity in the northern part of South Vietnam.
May 30		France declines an active role in the upcoming NATO exercises.	Portuguese forces capture 14 guerrilla fighters in Mozambique.	Cuba says it wants to sell sugar to the West.	Viet Cong and South Vietnamese troops clash in the Central Highlands.
May 31		Soviet Union pledges more military aid to North Korea.	Jordanian gunfire kills two Israelis near Jerusalem.	Sniper fire kills two people in Santo Domingo.	South Vietnamese forces suffer their worst defeat of the year against the Viet Cong.
June 1		Britain says it may give loans to doctors for new facilities.	Syria accuses Egypt of being too conciliatory toward Israel.	OAS votes to send mediators to the Dominican Republic.	South Vietnamese and Viet Cong forces clash in the Mekong Delta.
June 2			Arab guerrillas stage two attacks against Israel but cause no casualties.		Viet Cong kill two U.S. Marines near Danang.
June 3		West Germany calls for better ties with France.	Lebanon denies allowing Arab guerrillas to attack Israel from its territory.	Canada says it plans to curb uranium sales.	Viet Cong maul a South Vietnamese battalion near Pleiku.
June 4		West Germany supports U.S. policy in Vietnam.	Congolese missionaries report beheadings of Europeans by rebel troops.	OAS mediators begin talks with rival factions in Santo Domingo.	North Vietnamese officials leave for arms talks in the Soviet Union.
June 5			Communist Chinese Premier Chou En-lai criticizes the U.S. after he arrives in Tanzania.	Brazil sees progress in holding down inflation.	Viet Cong maul a South Vietnamese battalion.
June 6		One hundred thousand West Germans cross into East Berlin during a religious holiday.	Communist Chinese Premier Chou En-lai again attacks the U.S. while in Tanzania.	Observers report a cabinet crisis in Argentina.	Eight U.S. Marines die as two helicopters crash in Vietnam.
June 7		Soviet officials say that Stalin's hometown in Soviet Georgia is planning to reopen his home to the public.		Guerrillas murder U.S. consul Allison Wanamaker in Cordoba, Argentina.	U.S. troops clash with the Viet Cong near Danang.
June 8			Tanzania supports Communist China's criticism of the U.S.		Japan says it supports U.S. policy in Vietnam.
June 9	U.S. asks the U.N. to back the OAS role in the Dominican Republic.		South Africa sends economic aid to Basutoland.		Viet Cong kill 14 American troops in a new drive.
June 10		Portuguese Pres. Antonio Salazar decorates 65 soldiers for heroism in fighting in the African colonies.	A coalition cabinet takes power in the Sudan.		South Vietnamese clash with the Viet Cong in the Mekong Delta.
June 11	U.N. backs arms talks which would include Communist China.	French Pres. de Gaulle meets with West German Chancellor Ludwig Erhard in Bonn.	French-speaking African states accuse Ghana of being a base for subversion.	Reports indicate that Ché Guevara has been replaced as Cuba's Minister of Industry.	South Vietnamese military officers take power.
	A	B	C	D	E
	Includes developments that affect more than one world region, international organizations and important meetings of major world leaders.	Includes all domestic and regional developments in Europe, including the Soviet Union, Turkey, Cyprus and Malta.	Includes all domestic and regional developments in Africa and the Middle East, including Iraq and Iran and excluding Cyprus, Turkey and Afghanistan.	Includes all domestic and regional developments in Latin America, the Caribbean and Canada.	Includes all domestic and regional developments in Asia and Pacific nations, extending from Afghanistan through all the Pacific Islands, except Hawaii.

U.S. Politics & Social Issues	U.S. Foreign Policy & Defense	U.S. Economy & Environment	Science, Technology & Nature	Culture, Leisure & Life Style	
	Pres. Johnson urges the OAS to set up machinery to deal with communist subversion.				May 28
Observers report that job recruiters are making a special effort to hire Negro college students.					May 29
The first Negro female college student graduates from the Univ. of Alabama.	State Secy. Dean Rusk declares his support of a plebiscite on the Dominican Constitution.				May 30
	U.S. supports a Brazilian offer of mediation in the Dominican conflict.				May 31
	Pres. Johnson seeks economic aid for Southeast Asia.				June 1
	U.S. calls for elections in the Dominican Republic.	House votes for a $4.8 billion cut in excise taxes.	Soviet Union conducts an underground nuclear test.		June 2
		U.S. officials say that the jobless rate is the lowest since 1957.	U.S. astronaut Edward White floats in space for twenty minutes.		June 3
N.Y.C. officials say they want 17,000 summer jobs for youths.			U.S. Gemini astronauts aboard their satellite make communication and talk with their wives.		June 4
Observers say that Negroes are arming themselves in the South.	U.S. officials acknowledge that U.S. troops are engaged in an active combat role in South Vietnam.	Gemini 4 spacecraft reports no problems.			June 5
Observers report that many Southern schools are pressing for integration so that they will not lose U.S. federal aid.			Gemini 4 spacecraft's computer fails but officials see no serious danger.		June 6
Supreme Court bars curbs on birth control.	Senate approves economic aid to Southeast Asia.		Two Gemini 4 astronauts return safely to earth.		June 7
	Pres. Johnson orders U.S. units to fight with South Vietnamese troops if they seek help.	House unit opposes silver in half dollars.	U.S. officials say that the Gemini 4 astronauts are in good condition.		June 8
		Stocks plunge because of false rumors about the President's health.	U.S. conducts an underground nuclear test.		June 9
	House votes for curbs on the closing of military bases in the U.S.	Senate unit backs a slash in the excise tax.	Observers say that the Soviet satellite heading toward the moon will miss its target.		June 10
					June 11

F	G	H	I	J
Includes elections, federal-state relations, civil rights and liberties, crime, the judiciary, education, health care, poverty, urban affairs and population.	Includes formation and debate of U.S. foreign and defense policies, veterans' affairs and defense spending. (Relations with specific foreign countries are usually found under the region concerned.)	Includes business, labor, agriculture, taxation, transportation, consumer affairs, monetary and fiscal policy, natural resources, and pollution.	Includes worldwide scientific, medical and technological developments, natural phenomena, U.S. weather, natural disasters, and accidents.	Includes the arts, religion, scholarship, communications media, sports, entertainment, fashions, fads and social life.

	World Affairs	Europe	Africa & the Middle East	The Americas	Asia & the Pacific
June 12	At the U.N. Tanzania criticizes minority rule in Rhodesia.			Observers say that Latin American communist countries are staying in the Soviet camp.	South Vietnamese officers continue negotiations for a new government.
June 13		Observers say that the Soviet Union is undecided about pushing for economic reforms.	Tanzania attacks Kenya for rejecting the East African currency unit.	Cuban officials criticize the government for excess spending.	U.S. paratroopers prepare to join the battle at Dong Xoai.
June 14		Yugoslavia calls for the recognition of East Germany by West Germany.			Indonesia and Malaysia report clashes in Borneo.
June 15		Britain calls on North Vietnam to negotiate with the U.S.		Renewed fighting in Santo Domingo leaves 17 dead.	South Vietnamese and Viet Cong forces clash in the Central Highlands.
June 16		Britain says it will allow international inspection of its nuclear plants.		Continued fighting leaves 69 dead in the Dominican Republic.	Reports indicate Indian-Pakistani skirmishes in Kashmir.
June 17	Britain calls for voluntary contributions to reduce the U.N.'s budget.				B-52s leave Guam for South Vietnamese targets for the first time.
June 18	At the U.N. Egypt accuses Israel of trying to provoke a war.	French anti-Gaullists fail to coordinate forces in a unity bid.		A hurricane lashes cities along Mexico's coast.	Air Vice Marshall Nguyen Cao Ky becomes South Vietnamese premier.
June 19	African U.N. delegates criticize South Africa's apartheid policies.		Algerian army ousts Pres. Ahmed Ben Bella.	Police clash briefly with students at the Univ. of Bogota in Colombia.	U.S. planes bomb munition dumps in North Vietnam.
June 20	U.S. eases its stand on U.N. peace force payments.	Soviet Union says Communist China bars joint action to help North Vietnam.	Communist Chinese Premier Chou En-lai meets with Egyptian Pres. Nasser in Cairo.		U.S. planes down a North Vietnamese MiG.
June 21			Algerian troops scatter crowds in Algiers.	Dominicans ignore a call for strikes by the rebel faction.	Cambodian and Thai troops clash along their border.
June 22			Egypt declares its support for the new government in Algeria.		Japan and South Korea resume full diplomatic relations.
June 23		Soviet officials say they will build a huge power center in central Asia.	Kenya bars a rally in support of labor unions.	OAS says it will soon publish a plan for an interim government in the Dominican Republic.	U.S. and Viet Cong forces clash near Saigon.
June 24			Algeria reports foiling a plot by Ben Bella to regain power.	Observers report that tensions are growing between the French and English communities in Quebec.	South Vietnam breaks diplomatic ties with France.
June 25	In a speech at the U.N., Pres. Johnson appeals to the U.N. to press North Vietnam to negotiate.	East Germany imposes new restrictions on inter-German barge traffic.	Algerian police rout students protesting against the new government.	Renewed fighting leaves 16 dead in the Dominican Republic.	Terrorist blasts kill 31 in a floating cafe in Saigon.
June 26	At the U.N. Soviet Union denounces U.S. policy in Vietnam.	Police and students clash briefly at the Univ. of Madrid.	Portuguese troops clash with Angolan guerrillas.	Observers report that social issues are splitting the clergy in Latin America.	Viet Cong overrun a South Vietnamese battalion.
June 27			Indonesian Pres. Sukarno meets with Egyptian Pres. Nasser in Cairo.	Police and students clash briefly at the Univ. of Mexico.	Viet Cong retain their hold on the village of Toumorong in the Central Highlands.
	A	B	C	D	E
	Includes developments that affect more than one world region, international organizations and important meetings of major world leaders.	*Includes all domestic and regional developments in Europe, including the Soviet Union, Turkey, Cyprus and Malta.*	*Includes all domestic and regional developments in Africa and the Middle East, including Iraq and Iran and excluding Cyprus, Turkey and Afghanistan.*	*Includes all domestic and regional developments in Latin America, the Caribbean and Canada.*	*Includes all domestic and regional developments in Asia and Pacific nations, extending from Afghanistan through all the Pacific Islands, except Hawaii.*

U.S. Politics & Social Issues	U.S. Foreign Policy & Defense	U.S. Economy & Environment	Science, Technology & Nature	Culture, Leisure & Life Style	
		New Jersey imposes curbs on water use.	Scientists say that the finding of blue galaxies backs the "big bang" theory in astronomy.		June 12
			U.S. physicists produce anti-matter particles in a complex form.	Religious philosopher Martin Buber dies in Jerusalem at 87.	June 13
Police arrest 472 civil rights demonstrators in Jackson, Miss.	Senate votes for a $3.24 billion foreign aid program.	U.S. employment hits the 60 million mark.	Communist and non-communist space experts meet in Paris.		June 14
Police arrest 200 more protesting Negroes in Jackson, Miss.	Sen. J. W. Fulbright (D, Ark.) calls for a holding action in Vietnam.	Senate approves an excise tax cut by 84-3.			June 15
House approves an agency for urban affairs by 217-184.	U.S. says it is sending 21,000 more troops to Vietnam.		Senate approves a bill requiring a health warning on cigarette packages.		June 16
U.S. tells colleges that they face aid cutoffs if they permit fraternity bias.	Pres. Johnson accuses Dominican rebels of blocking a negotiated settlement.	Pres. Johnson says that the federal budget deficit will be $3.8 billion.		Pope Paul leads a march for Corpus Christi in Rome.	June 17
			Titan 3-C air force missile passes its flight test.		June 18
U.S. officials say they plan to concentrate on school integration for the coming term.			U.S. officials say they plan to try to link two spacecraft scheduled for October flights.		June 19
				Financier Bernard Baruch dies in N.Y.C. at 94.	June 20
Pres. Johnson calls for further tax cuts to help the poor.	White House officials say the Communists must be stopped in South Vietnam.		U.S. launches a military surveillance satellite.		June 21
	Pres. Johnson resumes food aid to Egypt.		House votes for a bill requiring a health warning on cigarette packages.	Movie producer David Selznick dies in Hollywood at 63.	June 22
			Soviet Union launches a communications satellite.	Catholic and Anglican bishops confer in Washington about Church unity.	June 23
U.S. journalist William Buckley enters the race for N.Y.C. mayor.		Stocks dip as inflation fears grow.			June 24
			A military jet crash kills 84 on the West Coast.		June 25
			U.S. launches a communications satellite.		June 26
U.S. officials say that Negro employment is up in the federal government.				U.S. biologist Albert Ebeling dies in Townsend, Vt. at 82.	June 27

F	G	H	I	J
Includes elections, federal-state relations, civil rights and liberties, crime, the judiciary, education, health care, poverty, urban affairs and population.	Includes formation and debate of U.S. foreign and defense policies, veterans' affairs and defense spending. (Relations with specific foreign countries are usually found under the region concerned.)	Includes business, labor, agriculture, taxation, transportation, consumer affairs, monetary and fiscal policy, natural resources, and pollution.	Includes worldwide scientific, medical and technological developments, natural phenomena, U.S. weather, natural disasters, and accidents.	Includes the arts, religion, scholarship, communications media, sports, entertainment, fashions, fads and social life.

	World Affairs	Europe	Africa & the Middle East	The Americas	Asia & the Pacific
June 28		Doctors in Rome go on strike.	Algeria tells the Soviet Union that their ties will be weaker.	Former Pres. Joaquin Balaguer returns to the Dominican Republic.	U.S. planes bomb air fields in North Vietnam.
June 29	At the U.N. South Africa says that its Negro citizens have the highest literacy rate in black Africa.		Former Israeli Premier David Ben-Gurion breaks with the Mapai party and forms his own faction.	Venezuelan troops kill 10 Cuban-backed guerrillas.	U.S. troops launch their first big offensive against the Viet Cong.
June 30		France withdraws from the U.N.'s Korean command.	Communist Chinese Premier Chou En-lai ends his trip to Egypt.		Viet Cong raiders destroy three planes in an airport near Danang.
July 1	At the U.N. Egypt calls for the admission of Communist China.	France threatens to leave the Common Market because of a farm dispute.	Rhodesia cautions Britain not to interfere in its internal affairs.		
July 2				Observers report that progress is being made in a negotiated settlement in the Dominican Republic.	U.S. planes strike within 40 miles of Hanoi.
July 3	At the U.N. the U.S. tries to promote an aid plan for Indochina.	Indonesian Pres. Sukarno confers with French Pres. de Gaulle in Paris.		Argentina vows to crush urban guerrillas.	U.S. planes again strike near Hanoi.
July 4			Observers report friction between Iraqi Pres. Abdel Arif and Iraqi Nasserites.	Reports indicate that Dominican rebels may be stockpiling arms.	B-52s again bomb the Viet Cong from their base on Guam.
July 5	U.N. Secy. Gen. U Thant calls for a global peace corps.	France begins a boycott of Common Market meetings.	Col. Houari Boumedienne assumes the leadership of the Algerian government.	Cuba says its 1965 sugar output will be six million tons.	Viet Cong battle South Vietnamese forces at Bagia.
July 6		France withdraws its delegate from the Common Market.		Dominican junta warns the OAS not to impose a settlement.	U.S. B-52s pound the Viet Cong.
July 7		Spanish Pres. Francisco Franco shuffles his economic advisers.	Yemen arrests 40 supporters of former Premier Ahmed Noman.	Canada says it will buy 125 F-5 jets from the U.S.	Viet Cong again maul South Vietnamese forces near Kontum.
July 8		Hungary reports jailing several Catholic priests.		Peru begins a crackdown on leftist guerrillas.	U.S. reports 23 combat fatalities during the last week in Vietnam.
July 9	U.N. Secy. Gen. U Thant confers with British leaders on Vietnam.	France says it will not join NATO's atom panel.		Brazilian House votes to bar aides of former Pres. João Goulart from office.	Singapore leaders accuse the Malaysian federal government of bias.
July 10	U.S. proposes a global parley on world financial problems.			Dominican factions near a political accord.	U.S. planes bomb air fields in North Vietnam.
July 11					U.S. planes attack North Vietnamese supply dumps.
July 12	U.N. African delegates criticize South Africa's apartheid policy.	France announces an improved A-bomb.	Iraqi government purges ministers said to be pro-Nasser.	Students go on strike in Guayaquil, Ecuador.	U.S. Marines rout Viet Cong near Danang.
July 13		British House of Commons votes to end hangings.	Observers report increased rebel activity in southern Sudan.		U.S. planes pound a suspected Viet Cong jungle post.
	A	B	C	D	E
	Includes developments that affect more than one world region, international organizations and important meetings of major world leaders.	*Includes all domestic and regional developments in Europe, including the Soviet Union, Turkey, Cyprus and Malta.*	*Includes all domestic and regional developments in Africa and the Middle East, including Iraq and Iran and excluding Cyprus, Turkey and Afghanistan.*	*Includes all domestic and regional developments in Latin America, the Caribbean and Canada.*	*Includes all domestic and regional developments in Asia and Pacific nations, extending from Afghanistan through all the Pacific Islands, except Hawaii.*

U.S. Politics & Social Issues	U.S. Foreign Policy & Defense	U.S. Economy & Environment	Science, Technology & Nature	Culture, Leisure & Life Style	
	U.S. announces a major aid program for Ethiopia.		Six nations join in opening the Comsat telephone system.		June 28
N.Y.C. police demonstrate against a proposed civilian review board of police activity.				U.S. journalist Milton King dies in N.Y.C. at 55.	June 29
	U.S. ends economic aid to Taiwan.	U.S. price index climbs 0.3% for the second month in a row.		British author Robert Ruark dies in London at 49.	June 30
	Pres. Johnson orders a speed-up in the development of a supersonic airliner.	U.S. officials say that unemployment held steady during the first part of the year.			July 1
Pres. Johnson calls for a teacher corps in poverty areas.	U.S. lends Turkey $40 million for a Euphrates Dam project.				July 2
	Soviet Union says its missile power exceeds the West's estimates.				July 3
Civil rights leaders call for an integration drive in Bogalusa, La.	Reports indicate that Negro civil rights leaders are unhappy with the expansion of the war in Vietnam.			Pope Paul criticizes youths for wild outbursts at music concerts.	July 4
	CORE passes a resolution calling for a withdrawal from Vietnam but then reverses itself.				July 5
	U.S. recognizes the Algerian government.	U.S. cash receipts rise by $4 billion despite the tax cut.		U.S. Lutheran and Catholic clergy confer on beliefs.	July 6
		General Motors announces seven new safety items for its 1966 cars.	U.S. spacecraft Mariner 4 begins to feel the gravitational pull of Mars.		July 7
A Negro civil rights marcher kills a white man in Bogalusa, La.	Pres. Johnson nominates Henry Cabot Lodge to resume his position as Amb.-to-South Vietnam in place of Maxwell Taylor.			Former dean of Barnard College Virginia Gildersleeve dies in Centerville, Mass. at 87.	July 8
Senate passes a Medicare bill by 68-21.	Sen. Robert Kennedy decries the use of force against political revolutions abroad.				July 9
A federal judge orders the Bogalusa, La. police not to use violence against demonstrating Negroes.	Former V.P. Nixon says he supports U.S. policy in Vietnam.		Soviet Union conducts an underground nuclear test.		July 10
Troopers avert a clash between Negro marchers and white hecklers in Bogalusa, La.	U.S. says it plans an increase in draft calls.		U.S. conducts an underground nuclear test.	U.S. clergymen urge a role for the U.N. in Vietnam.	July 11
					July 12
Pres. Johnson pledges a major effort to help Negroes.	Reports indicate that Pres. Johnson is weighing a call-up of the reserves.	House passes a bill to establish a water resources council.			July 13

F	G	H	I	J
Includes elections, federal-state relations, civil rights and liberties, crime, the judiciary, education, health care, poverty, urban affairs and population.	*Includes formation and debate of U.S. foreign and defense policies, veterans' affairs and defense spending. (Relations with specific foreign countries are usually found under the region concerned.)*	*Includes business, labor, agriculture, taxation, transportation, consumer affairs, monetary and fiscal policy, natural resources, and pollution.*	*Includes worldwide scientific, medical and technological developments, natural phenomena, U.S. weather, natural disasters, and accidents.*	*Includes the arts, religion, scholarship, communications media, sports, entertainment, fashions, fads and social life.*

	World Affairs	Europe	Africa & the Middle East	The Americas	Asia & the Pacific
July 14			Jordan sentences 38 citizens to prison on chargess of spying for Israel.		U.S. jets strike a target in North Vietnam 40 miles from Communist China.
July 15		Presidential envoy Averell Harriman arrives in Moscow for talks on Vietnam.		Ecuadorian junta says it is willing to speed a return to civilian rule.	One thousand eight hundred more U.S. troops arrive in Vietnam.
July 16			Egypt raises prices on state goods and urges its citizens to curb spending.		U.S. planes bomb North Vietnamese air fields.
July 17	At the U.N. India accuses Pakistan of border incidents.	Britain promises an increase in technical aid to Chile.	Arab International Boycott Commission meets in Libya without Tunisia.	Ecuador warns university students not to employ violent tactics when protesting against the government.	U.S. command in South Vietnam asks for additional troops.
July 18			Sixteen government officials resign in an inter-Arab dispute in Aden.	Peruvian police say communist guerrillas are responsible for recent bank robberies.	Viet Cong artillery pounds Bienhoa.
July 19	U.N. Secy. Gen. U Thant discusses the Vietnam War with State Secy. Dean Rusk.	France rejects the monetary talks proposed by the U.S.	Sudan tells rebels to accept amnesty or face penalties.	Police clash briefly with students at the Univ. of Mexico.	South Vietnamese police foil a Viet Cong attempt to assassinate U.S. Amb. Maxwell Taylor.
July 20	Pres. Johnson names Associate Justice Arthur Goldberg to be the U.S. Amb.-to-U.N.	British House of Lords approves a ban on the death penalty for murder.		Dominican factions call on the OAS peace force to leave.	Viet Cong again shell Bienhoa outposts.
July 21		Supporters of former Greek Premier George Papandreou battle police in Athens.	Observers report that the rebellion in the southern Sudan is growing.		U.S. B-52s again bomb near Saigon.
July 22				U.N. officials report sporadic shelling in the Dominican Republic.	U.S. jets wreck a bridge near Communist China.
July 23		Rumania says that no super-power will dictate its foreign policy.	Israel's ruling Mapai party ousts David Ben-Gurion's faction.		Observers report that the Viet Cong are increasing their taxation on guerrillas.
July 24	At the U.N. Pakistan accuses India of border incursions.		Egyptian Pres. Nasser pledges complete equality to Egypt's Christian Coptics.	OAS reports progress in Dominican negotiations.	U.S. planes bomb an arms plant in North Vietnam.
July 25		U.S. and European officials begin talks in Brussels on an advanced nuclear reactor.	Israel plans an increased television service to help offset Arab programs.		U.S. pilots report anti-aircraft missiles near Hanoi.
July 26		France boycotts a meeting of EEC ministers.		Cuban Premier Fidel Castro says he will purge his ''bourgeois'' aides.	Viet Cong maul South Vietnamese forces in the Mekong Delta.
July 27	Seventeen-nation parley on nuclear proliferation resumes in Geneva.	Britain says it will slash its spending to protect the pound.		Mail strike ends in Canada.	U.S. raids two North Vietnamese missile sites.
July 28		Edward Heath becomes Britain's Conservative Party leader.		Guatemala lifts its state of siege as guerrilla activity declines.	Observers report that North Vietnam is increasing preparations for a major war.

A	B	C	D	E
Includes developments that affect more than one world region, international organizations and important meetings of major world leaders.	*Includes all domestic and regional developments in Europe, including the Soviet Union, Turkey, Cyprus and Malta.*	*Includes all domestic and regional developments in Africa and the Middle East, including Iraq and Iran and excluding Cyprus, Turkey and Afghanistan.*	*Includes all domestic and regional developments in Latin America, the Caribbean and Canada.*	*Includes all domestic and regional developments in Asia and Pacific nations, extending from Afghanistan through all the Pacific Islands, except Hawaii.*

U.S. Politics & Social Issues	U.S. Foreign Policy & Defense	U.S. Economy & Environment	Science, Technology & Nature	Culture, Leisure & Life Style	
	Defense Secy. Robert McNamara hints at a call-up of the reserves.	Pres. Johnson orders a panel to assess the nation's water shortage.	U.S. spacecraft Mariner 4 passes near Mars.	US Amb.-to-U.N. Adlai Stevenson dies in London at 65.	July 14
Pres. Johnson bars all wiretapping by federal employees except in matters related to national security.		U.S. economists say they will try to prolong the current economic boom into 1966.	Mariner 4 sends back the first photos of Mars.		July 15
N.Y.C. Negro leaders demand a civilian review board to oversee police behavior.	U.S. withdraws several thousand troops from Europe and sends them to Vietnam.		Mariner 4 photos depict a desolate Mars.	Adlai Stevenson is given a national funeral in Washington, D.C.	July 16
			Mariner 4 photos present a 600 mile panorama of the Martian surface.		July 17
White House officials call for efforts to increase the stability of the Negro family.			Soviet Union puts a rocket into solar orbit.	Japanese Gen. Otozo Yamada dies in Tokyo at 83.	July 18
				Former South Korean Pres. Syngman Rhee dies in Honolulu at 90.	July 19
	Defense Secy. Robert McNamara says that the situation has become worse in Vietnam.			Venezuelan writer Victor Manuel Rivas dies in N.Y.C. at 56.	July 20
House and Senate conferees clear a Medicare bill.	Pres. Johnson begins an intensive analysis of the Vietnam situation with top aides.	U.S. Treasury officials doubt that the Vietnam War will lead to higher taxes.			July 21
House approves additional funds for the anti-poverty drive.	U.S. officials say they are considering a troop increase of up to 200,000 men in Vietnam.		Soviet Union launches a military surveillance satellite.	U.S.'s first space administrator Roy Johnson dies in Stamford, Conn. at 59.	July 22
Senate passes a bill making the assassination of a President a federal crime.	Pres. Johnson indicates he is weighing a draft increase for the Vietnam War.	U.S. fines eight steel firms for price-fixing.			July 23
			U.S. launches a military surveillance satellite.		July 24
	N.Y. Gov. Nelson Rockefeller says he will not run for the presidency in 1968.		Flash floods recede in Colorado.	British actress Irene Browne dies in London at 69.	July 25
Pres. Johnson forms a panel to study crime problems.	U.S. officials report that Pres. Johnson is nearing a decision on Vietnam War escalation.	House unit votes to end a ban on the union shop.			July 26
		General Motors officials report their highest earnings ever.		Canadian industrialist James Young dies in Montreal at 81.	July 27
Pres. Johnson names Abe Fortas to succeed Arthur Goldberg on the Supreme Court.	Pres. Johnson orders 50,000 more men to Vietnam and doubles the draft; Congress expresses its approval.	Pres. Johnson says that the economic impact of Vietnam will be slight.			July 28

F	G	H	I	J
Includes elections, federal-state relations, civil rights and liberties, crime, the judiciary, education, health care, poverty, urban affairs and population.	Includes formation and debate of U.S. foreign and defense policies, veterans' affairs and defense spending. (Relations with specific foreign countries are usually found under the region concerned.)	Includes business, labor, agriculture, taxation, transportation, consumer affairs, monetary and fiscal policy, natural resources, and pollution.	Includes worldwide scientific, medical and technological developments, natural phenomena, U.S. weather, natural disasters, and accidents.	Includes the arts, religion, scholarship, communications media, sports, entertainment, fashions, fads and social life.

	World Affairs	Europe	Africa & the Middle East	The Americas	Asia & the Pacific
July 29	At the U.N. Cambodia accuses Thailand of border incursions.		Algeria signs an oil-gas accord with France.		U.S. planes attack North Vietnamese air fields.
July 30	Turkey calls for a U.N. meeting on the Cyprus problem.	Thousands of backers of former Greek Premier George Papandreou demonstrate in central Athens.			
July 31				Honduras and El Salvador begin negotiations on a deportation accord.	Several thousand Japanese students protest against U.S. use of Okinawa for attacks on North Vietnam.
Aug. 1			Egyptian authorities arrest pro-west publisher, Mustafa Amin.	Chile calls for a linking of Latin America to NATO.	Viet Cong stage strikes at 15 posts near Saigon.
Aug. 2	At the U.N. Iraq accuses Iran of aiding Iraqi Kurds.	Political scuffles continue in the streets of Athens.	Israeli troops slay three Arab guerrillas near Latrum.		Thirty B-52s attack Viet Cong targets.
Aug. 3	At the U.N. Turkey calls for justice for the Turkish Cypriote minority.	West Berlin Mayor Willy Brandt proposes talks with the Soviets.			
Aug. 4	French-speaking U.N. African delegates accuse Ghana of trying to subvert African governments.	Greek deputies topple the cabinet during a wild parliamentary session.	South Africa rules out Negro labor unions.	Police and students clash briefly at the Univ. of Bogota in Colombia.	U.S. planes bomb North Vietnam.
Aug. 5	At the U.N. Britain calls for action to defend the rights of the Cypriote Turkish minority.	Greek Premier George Athansiadas-Novas resigns as protests continue.	Sudan and its southern rebels trade warnings about a possible civil war.		South Korea asserts that North Korea is planning a war of infiltration.
Aug. 6	At the U.N. India and Pakistan accuse each other of border incursions.				India says it will ration grain in the cities.
Aug. 7	At the U.N. Syria accuses Egypt of being too conciliatory toward Israel.	Bulgaria widens economic reforms.	Egypt says that a war against Israel is inevitable.	Police and students clash briefly at the Univ. of Caracas in Venezuela.	Communist China accuses the U.S. of ramming a merchant ship.
Aug. 8				Colombia says it is planning a birth control program.	Singapore cuts its tie with Malaysia.
Aug. 9	At the U.N. Western delegates call for greater birth control efforts in the developing world.	Britain says it will not sell engines for use in Indonesian planes.			Singapore says it plans to seek accords with Asian communist nations.
Aug. 10	U.N. drops the Eichmann kidnapping case from its agenda.	Greek parliamentarian factions weigh strategy as cabinet deadlock persists.			India says that Pakistan is trying to provoke a war in Kashmir.
Aug. 11			Former Israeli P.M. David Ben-Gurion starts his comeback effort at a street rally.	Canada makes a major wheat sale to the Soviet Union.	Indonesia assails Britain for keeping a naval base at Singapore.
Aug. 12		Observers say that Britain wants to leave Aden.			North Vietnam downs a second U.S. jet.
Aug. 13				Peru bombs Andean jungles in drive against pro-communist guerrillas.	India warns Pakistan of a possible war.

A	B	C	D	E
Includes developments that affect more than one world region, international organizations and important meetings of major world leaders.	Includes all domestic and regional developments in Europe, including the Soviet Union, Turkey, Cyprus and Malta.	Includes all domestic and regional developments in Africa and the Middle East, including Iraq and Iran and excluding Cyprus, Turkey and Afghanistan.	Includes all domestic and regional developments in Latin America, the Caribbean and Canada.	Includes all domestic and regional developments in Asia and Pacific nations, extending from Afghanistan through all the Pacific Islands, except Hawaii.

U.S. Politics & Social Issues	U.S. Foreign Policy & Defense	U.S. Economy & Environment	Science, Technology & Nature	Culture, Leisure & Life Style	
			Mariner 4's final photos depict a Mars which resembles the moon.	U.S. physicist Alvin Graves dies in Colorado at 55.	July 29
Pres. Johnson signs the Medicare bill for the elderly.	U.S. officials say they are considering expanding economic ties with Eastern Europe.	Steel union officials say they will strike on Sept. 1 unless their demands are met.	U.S. officials begin intensive tests on a proposed fertility drug.		July 30
Whites attack Negro civil rights marchers in Americus, Ga. and cause minor injuries.			Soviet Union launches a communications satellite.		July 31
Two Americus, Ga. churches bar civil rights workers.				U.S. officials say they plan to explore the Soviet Arctic Sea.	Aug. 1
N.Y.C. says it will recruit Negro teachers ousted from positions in the South.	State Secy. Dean Rusk says North Vietnam holds the key to peace.				Aug. 2
House unit votes for an end to quotas for immigration.	Draft quotas go up sharply for September and October.	House unit votes for a rise in the minimum wage.	Soviet Union conducts an underground nuclear test.		Aug. 3
	Pres. Johnson asks for $1.7 billion more for the Vietnam War.				Aug. 4
Supreme Court nominee Abe Fortas says police must have adequate time to interrogate persons suspected of crimes.		FPC establishes price regulation for natural gas.			Aug. 5
Pres. Johnson signs the 1965 Voting Rights Act.	One thousand Vietnam critics stage a sit-down outside the White House.	U.S. officials warn N.Y.C. it could run out of water during 1966.	Soviet Union launches a military surveillance satellite.		Aug. 6
U.S. suspends literacy tests in seven Southern states.					Aug. 7
U.S. officials move to enroll voters under the 1965 Voting Rights Act.	Washington police arrest 36 anti-war protesters at the White House.			British diplomat Walford Selby dies at 84 in Salisbury, Rhodesia.	Aug. 8
	Pres. Johnson denies that there is a substantial split in U.S. opinion about Vietnam.	Labor Sec. Willard Wirtz urges more jobless pay.			Aug. 9
U.S. voting officials sign up 1,144 Negroes in the first few days of the current voter drive.	Former V.P. Nixon urges intensified raids against North Vietnam.	N.Y.C. presents a plan to bolster water reserves.			Aug. 10
Rioting breaks out in Watts, the Negro neighborhood of Los Angeles.		U.S. says it will send water experts to study shortages in five cities.			Aug. 11
House authorizes $3.3 billion in aid for needy areas.	Vietnam War foes try to halt troop trains in Berkeley, Calif.	Five Lake Erie basin states agree to fight water pollution.		Former Japanese Premier Hayato Ikeda dies in Tokyo at 65.	Aug. 12
Two thousand troops enter Los Angeles during the third day of Negro rioting.	U.S. officials say that they will leave the Congo (Brazzaville) because of mistreatment of the embassy staff.	U.S. says N.Y.C. is facing a very serious water shortage.	U.S. Gemini 5 astronauts begin an 11-day seclusion.		Aug. 13
F	G	H	I	J	
Includes elections, federal-state relations, civil rights and liberties, crime, the judiciary, education, health care, poverty, urban affairs and population.	Includes formation and debate of U.S. foreign and defense policies, veterans' affairs and defense spending. (Relations with specific foreign countries are usually found under the region concerned.)	Includes business, labor, agriculture, taxation, transportation, consumer affairs, monetary and fiscal policy, natural resources, and pollution.	Includes worldwide scientific, medical and technological developments, natural phenomena, U.S. weather, natural disasters, and accidents.	Includes the arts, religion, scholarship, communications media, sports, entertainment, fashions, fads and social life.	

	World Affairs	Europe	Africa & the Middle East	The Americas	Asia & the Pacific
Aug. 14	At the U.N. Pakistan and India accuse each other of border incursions.	Police and students clash briefly at the Univ. of Madrid.	Israeli troops repulse Arab guerrillas near Jerusalem.		Six thousand, four hundred more Marines arrive in Vietnam.
Aug. 15		West Germany says it is willing to renew ties with Arab states.		Police and students clash briefly at the Univ. of Lima in Peru.	Viet Cong bomb a police compound in Saigon.
Aug. 16	At the U.N. the U.S. drops the fight to compel all members to pay dues.	West Germany offers the Congo (Leopoldville) $2.5 million more in aid.	Sudan rules out a break of diplomatic relations with the U.S.		Indonesia says that the U.S. is its major enemy.
Aug. 17	At the U.N. Egypt calls on Britain to leave South Yemen.	Thirty-three thousand Greeks in Athens demonstrate against King Constantine and for former Prime Minister George Papandreou.			
Aug. 18	U.N. debates the Communist Chinese ultimatum demanding that India evacuate Pakistani territory.	King Constantine asks Greek Socialists to form a government.	Observers say that Kenya and Uganda are wary of subversive activities emanating from Tanzania.	Canada hails the 25th anniversary of its defense pact with the U.S.	U.S. Marines trap 2,000 Viet Cong near Saigon. India accuses Communist China of making troop movements along its border.
Aug. 19		Greek police battle supporters of former Prime Minister George Papandreou in Athens.	Israel accepts the credentials of West Germany's first ambassador to the Jewish state.	Observers say that Peru is making progress in its fight against leftist guerrillas.	U.S. Marines kill 600 guerrillas in a two-day battle.
Aug. 20		Fifteen thousand leftists riot as Greece installs a new government.	Egypt says that Israel plans to test a nuclear device in the near future.	Argentina arrests 650 leftists.	
Aug. 21		Police and students clash at the Univ. of Athens.	Egyptian Pres. Nasser leaves for talks in Saudi Arabia.		U.S. planes fire on hundreds of Viet Cong fleeing Chulai.
Aug. 22		Rural crowds hail former Greek Prime Minister George Papandreou.	Egyptian Pres. Nasser and Saudi King Faisal confer on the conflict in Yemen.		U.S. troops clear the route to Kontum.
Aug. 23			Observers report that the Baath party is solidifying its control in Syria.		U.S. troop plane with 71 soldiers crashes near Hong Kong.
Aug. 24		Police and students clash at the Univ. of Athens.	Egyptian Pres. Nasser and Saudi King Faisal agree to a compromise solution to the Yemeni situation.		U.S. planes bomb North Vietnam.
Aug. 25		Portugal releases several hundred political prisoners.			India seizes two Pakistani posts across the Kashmir border.
Aug. 26	At the U.N. Pakistan accuses India of trying to provoke a war.				Indian troops seize a third Pakistani post.
Aug. 27	U.N. Secy. Gen. U Thant consults with U.N. delegates on the Vietnam War.	Greek Prime Minister Elias Tsirimokos tries to stave off a threatened defeat in parliament.	Arab saboteurs blow up an Israeli pipeline near Haifa.		U.S. planes bomb Viet Cong positions.
Aug. 28		Greek deputies oust Prime Minister Elias Tsirimokos in a 159-135 vote.	Saudi Arabia announces a five-year development plan.		Indian army units again cross into Pakistani territory.
	A	B	C	D	E
	Includes developments that affect more than one world region, international organizations and important meetings of major world leaders.	Includes all domestic and regional developments in Europe, including the Soviet Union, Turkey, Cyprus and Malta.	Includes all domestic and regional developments in Africa and the Middle East, including Iraq and Iran and excluding Cyprus, Turkey and Afghanistan.	Includes all domestic and regional developments in Latin America, the Caribbean and Canada.	Includes all domestic and regional developments in Asia and Pacific nations, extending from Afghanistan through all the Pacific Islands, except Hawaii.

U.S. Politics & Social Issues	U.S. Foreign Policy & Defense	U.S. Economy & Environment	Science, Technology & Nature	Culture, Leisure & Life Style	
Death toll mounts to 21 in Negro rioting in Los Angeles.			Soviet Union reports the reception of new moon photos.		Aug. 14
U.S. troops begin to contain rioters in Los Angeles.				U.S. architect H.W. Congdon dies at 89 in Arlington, Vt.	Aug. 15
U.S. authorities put the death toll from the Los Angeles rioting at 33.			A United Air Lines jet crash leaves 30 dead north of Chicago.		Aug. 16
	Pres. Johnson affirms his foreign aid pledges to Latin America.	U.S. Steel Corp. says it is doubling its capital spending plans.		U.S. educator Harry Handler dies in Passaic, N.J. at 84.	Aug. 17
U.S. grants Los Angeles $1.7 million in riot aid.	U.S. says it is considering draft calls for married men without children. U.S. warns Communist China not to attack India. White House says that most excise tax cut benefits will go to consumers. Talks resume on the N.Y.C. newspaper strike.				Aug. 18
House passes a four-year farm subsidy bill.	Former Pres. Eisenhower backs Pres. Johnson's Vietnam policy.				Aug. 19
West Coast police find van loads of riot loot in Los Angeles.		A New Jersey factory plant shuts as drought spreads.	U.S. officials report that the U.S. birth rate continued to decline in 1965.		Aug. 20
			U.S. launches Gemini 5 but a power loss makes its scheduled eight-day mission uncertain.		Aug. 21
One thousand troops bring order to Springfield, Mass. after rioting breaks out.			Power returns to the orbiting Gemini 5 satellite.		Aug. 22
	U.S. officials say they plan to build a jet with West Germany.		Soviet Union launches a communications satellite.	Egyptian nationalist leader Mustafa Nahas dies in Cairo at 86.	Aug. 23
	House Republicans accuse Pres. Johnson of a lack of candor on Vietnam.	United Steel Workers reject a new wage offer.	Gemeni 5 astronauts set a longevity mark on their fourth day in space.		Aug. 24
House approves a bill reforming immigration.	Former V.P. Nixon leaves for a tour of Asian nations.	Pres. Johnson urges steel union and management representatives to reach a settlement.	Pres. Johnson orders the military to construct a spacecraft to be used for possible defense purposes.		Aug. 25
House passes a college aid bill by 367-22.	U.S. says that married men without children will no longer be exempt from the draft.	Pres. Johnson again calls for a negotiated steel settlement.			Aug. 26
		U.S. officials say that cuts in the excise tax have slowed price rises.		Swiss architect Le Corbusier dies at Cap Matin in France at 77.	Aug. 27
			Gemini 5 prepares for an advanced landing in the face of a storm.		Aug. 28

F	G	H	I	J
Includes elections, federal-state relations, civil rights and liberties, crime, the judiciary, education, health care, poverty, urban affairs and population.	Includes formation and debate of U.S. foreign and defense policies, veterans' affairs and defense spending. (Relations with specific foreign countries are usually found under the region concerned.)	Includes business, labor, agriculture, taxation, transportation, consumer affairs, monetary and fiscal policy, natural resources, and pollution.	Includes worldwide scientific, medical and technological developments, natural phenomena, U.S. weather, natural disasters, and accidents.	Includes the arts, religion, scholarship, communications media, sports, entertainment, fashions, fads and social life.

	World Affairs	Europe	Africa & the Middle East	The Americas	Asia & the Pacific
Aug. 29		Police and students clash at the Univ. of Athens.	Israeli troops repulse Arab guerrillas near Latrum.	Santo Domingo rebels clash with OAS peace units.	Anti-government protesters demonstrate in Danang.
Aug. 30		Glacier avalanche buries scores at a Swiss dam site at Saas-Fee.		Dominican junta resigns in favor of an interim government.	India announces taking several Pakistani posts in Kashmir.
Aug. 31		French Pres. de Gaulle meets in Paris with Undersecy. of State George Ball about Vietnam.		Dominican rebels agree to work with the interim Dominican government.	Observers say that the danger of a major war in Kashmir is growing.
Sept. 1	U.S. Amb.-to-U.N. Arthur Goldberg at the U.N., denounces Albanian attacks on the U.S.	Greek King Constantine begins talks with Greek parliamentary leaders.	Arab guerrillas kill another British officer in Aden.		Fighting intensifies between India and Pakistan.
Sept. 2	Observers predict a close vote on Communist Chinese admission to the U.N.	West German-East German talks on Berlin Wall-crossings reach an impasse.			Indian and Pakistani planes battle over Kashmir.
Sept. 3		Britain announces its anti-inflation plan.		Hector Garcia-Godoy becomes the provisional president of the Dominican government.	A record air attack force pounds the Viet Cong.
Sept. 4	U.N. calls for a cease-fire in Kashmir.		Israeli troops blow up 11 Jordanian water pumps in a reprisal raid.		Pakistani troops take the offensive in Kashmir fighting.
Sept. 5			Israel warns Jordan not to allow guerrillas to operate from its territory.		Observers say that superior equipment is giving Pakistan the upper hand in Kashmir fighting.
Sept. 6	U.N. Secy. Gen. U Thant says he plans to visit India and Pakistan in the near future.	Police and students clash at the Univ. of Rome.		Brazil denies rumors of a pact with Argentina concerning anti-guerrilla warfare.	Fighting spreads in Kashmir as Indian troops drive on Lahore and Pakistani troops raid the Punjab.
Sept. 7	U.N. Secy. Gen. U Thant leaves on a peace mission to the Indian sub-continent.	Soviet Union appeals for a cease-fire in the Kashmir fighting.	Arab governments call for a cease-fire in Kashmir fighting.		Indian forces begin an apparent drive toward Karachi.
Sept. 8	U.N. calls for a cease-fire in Kashmir fighting.	Britain halts arms aid to India.		Police and students clash briefly at the Univ. of Mexico.	India attacks Pakistani troops in two new sectors.
Sept. 9	U.N. Secy. Gen. U Thant begins peace talks with leaders in Pakistan.	French Pres. de Gaulle says that after 1969 France will no longer participate in an integrated Western defense system.		Right-wing Gen. Elias Wessin y Wessin leaves the Dominican Republic.	Pakistan pushes back the Indian thrust in the Lahore area.
Sept. 10	U.N. fails to get Pakistan's agreement to a cease-fire.	Greek King Constantine presses his search for a Prime Minister.			Fighting continues to intensify between India and Pakistan.
Sept. 11		French press generally backs French Pres. de Gaulle's stand on NATO.	Tunisia says it will boycott the upcoming meeting of Arab governments.		India says that the Kashmir fighting is at its most intense.
Sept. 12				Dominican government cancels a political rally as sporadic fighting erupts.	Intensive fighting continues between India and Pakistan.
Sept. 13			Twelve Arab League leaders open a conference in Morocco.	Peruvian cabinet resigns.	Heavy fighting continues in West Pakistan.
	A	**B**	**C**	**D**	**E**
	Includes developments that affect more than one world region, international organizations and important meetings of major world leaders.	*Includes all domestic and regional developments in Europe, including the Soviet Union, Turkey, Cyprus and Malta.*	*Includes all domestic and regional developments in Africa and the Middle East, including Iraq and Iran and excluding Cyprus, Turkey and Afghanistan.*	*Includes all domestic and regional developments in Latin America, the Caribbean and Canada.*	*Includes all domestic and regional developments in Asia and Pacific nations, extending from Afghanistan through all the Pacific Islands, except Hawaii.*

U.S. Politics & Social Issues	U.S. Foreign Policy & Defense	U.S. Economy & Environment	Science, Technology & Nature	Culture, Leisure & Life Style	
			Gemini 5 astronauts return safely to earth.	British Gen. George Erskine dies in London at 66.	Aug. 29
The school year begins with widespread integration in the South.	U.S. officials say they are planning daily B-52 raids against North Vietnam.		U.S. Gemini 5 astronauts begin 11 days of tests.		Aug. 30
Congress approves a new cabinet post for urban affairs.			U.S. economist Frank Surface dies on Fire Island at 83.		Aug. 31
	Pres. Johnson praises the Dominican peace pact.	Steel companies add 2¢ in their offer to spur wage talks.			Sept. 1
Miss. Gov. Paul Johnson sends National Guard troops to Natchez to prevent racial violence.	National Student Association calls for a halt to the bombing of North Vietnam.	Pres. Johnson urges a quick steel pact settlement.			Sept. 2
	U.S. declares its neutrality in the Indian-Pakistani conflict.	Pres. Johnson reports an accord on a new steel pact.	U.S. scientists say that the thin air on Mars is ideal for aerial inspection.		Sept. 3
	Pres. Johnson pledges $20 million in Dominican aid.			Pope Paul visits flood-ravaged areas in Rome.	Sept. 4
		Steel Workers Union ratifies a new pact covering three years.		Dr. Albert Schweitzer dies in Gabon at 90.	Sept. 5
Three thousand whites demonstrate in support of segregation in Bogalusa, La.	U.S. calls for an end of the Kashmir fighting.				Sept. 6
	U.S. cuts off arms aid to Pakistan and India.		Hurricane hits the Florida coast as thousands flee.		Sept. 7
	U.S. officials say there are 108,000 U.S. troops in Vietnam.		A Florida hurricane leaves hundreds homeless.		Sept. 8
		U.S. economists foresee economic growth continuing into 1966.	Hurricane Betsy causes 185,000 people to flee homes in southern Louisiana.		Sept. 9
	U.S. officials say they doubt that Communist China will attack India.		Hurricane Betsy leaves 23 dead in three states.	Vatican draft declaration exonerates the Jews of any collective responsibility in the crucifixion of Jesus.	Sept. 10
	Former Pres. Eisenhower sees the ruin of NATO if France pulls out.			Pope Paul calls for an orthodox approach to the teaching of the Eucharist.	Sept. 11
			Soviet Union conducts an underground nuclear test.	Observers say a conservative mood is emerging as Catholic prelates gather for talks.	Sept. 12
	A U.S. trade mission leaves for Poland and Rumania.			U.S. Gen. Lucian Truscott dies in Washington, D.C. at 70.	Sept. 13

F	G	H	I	J
Includes elections, federal-state relations, civil rights and liberties, crime, the judiciary, education, health care, poverty, urban affairs and population.	Includes formation and debate of U.S. foreign and defense policies, veterans' affairs and defense spending. (Relations with specific foreign countries are usually found under the region concerned.)	Includes business, labor, agriculture, taxation, transportation, consumer affairs, monetary and fiscal policy, natural resources, and pollution.	Includes worldwide scientific, medical and technological developments, natural phenomena, U.S. weather, natural disasters, and accidents.	Includes the arts, religion, scholarship, communications media, sports, entertainment, fashions, fads and social life.

	World Affairs	Europe	Africa & the Middle East	The Americas	Asia & the Pacific
Sept. 14			Iran says it may send jet fuel to Pakistan.		Observers say that India wants a cease-fire.
Sept. 15	U.N. Secy. Gen. U Thant leaves India after peace talks.	Police and students clash briefly at the Univ. of Naples.		Congo (Leopoldville) accuses the former French Congo of border intrusions.	Singapore says it may ask for Soviet troop help if Malaysia asks for U.S. troop help.
Sept. 16	U.N. Secy. Gen. U Thant says that both sides want a truce in Kashmir.	Britain unveils a five-year plan to help the economy.		A bomb explodes inside the Central Bank of Argentina.	Pakistan reports halting an Indian offensive at Sial Kot.
Sept. 17		Former Deputy P.M. Stephanos Stephanopoulos becomes Greek prime minister.	Observers say that Iraq has foiled a pro-Egyptian coup attempt.		India says it will not heed a Communist Chinese ultimatum to evacuate Pakistani territory.
Sept. 18					
Sept. 19	U.N. delegates prepare to demand a halt in the Kashmir fighting.	West German Christian Democrats lead in early election returns.	Rhodesian P.M. Ian Smith tells Britain he will never agree to majority rule.		Communist China extends the deadline of its ultimatum to India by three more days.
Sept. 20	U.N. calls for a cease-fire in the Kashmir fighting.	West German Christian Democrats win parliamentary elections with 47.5% of the vote.	Arab guerrillas blow up an Israeli water pipe near the Jordanian border.	Dominican politicians begin an election campaign.	India accuses Communist China of firing at its border guards.
Sept. 21		Britain discovers gas in the North Sea.	Reports indicate that Communist China will build a railroad in Tanzania.		India agrees to a UN-sponsored cease-fire in Kashmir.
Sept. 22	U.N. Secy. Gen. U Thant says he will name an observer team to monitor a Kashmir cease-fire.	Fist fights break out between deputies in the Greek Parliament.		Bolivian miners go on strike.	Pakistan agrees to a cease-fire in Kashmir.
Sept. 23	At the U.N. the U.S. condemns Communist China's ultimatum to India.	Soviet Union criticizes Communist China's ultimatum to India.		Bolivia banishes 15 politicians to rural towns.	India accuses Pakistan of cease-fire violations.
Sept. 24		Greek government survives its first vote of confidence in parliament.		U.S. troops begin withdrawing from the Dominican Republic.	India rules out re-opening talks on the Kashmir territorial question.
Sept. 25	International Monetary Fund says it is considering major monetary reforms.	West German Christian Democrats affirm their support for Chancellor Ludwig Erhard.			India and Pakistan charge each other with cease-fire violations.
Sept. 26		Britain pledges more aid for Aden.	African guerrilla leaders from Portuguese colonies meet in Tanzania.	Violence erupts as former Pres. Juan Bosch returns to the Dominican Republic.	Tensions abate along the Kashmir border.
Sept. 27	U.N. bids India and Pakistan to heed the Kashmir cease-fire.	Soviet Union introduces limited economic reforms.	British authorities close secondary schools in Aden in the wake of rioting.		U.S. planes bomb North Vietnam.
Sept. 28	Pakistan bids the U.N. to send a peace force to Kashmir.	British Labor party rejects Liberals' bid for a coalition.		A student dies as sporadic violence mars the Dominican truce.	India and Pakistan renew fighting in Kashmir.
Sept. 29	At the U.N. France calls for the admission of Communist China.	British P.M. Harold Wilson isolates the Labor Party critics of his foreign policy.	Congolese insurgents repel government troops near Lake Tanganyika.	Cuba says that its citizens are free to leave the country.	India accuses Pakistan of breaking their truce.
	A	**B**	**C**	**D**	**E**
	Includes developments that affect more than one world region, international organizations and important meetings of major world leaders.	*Includes all domestic and regional developments in Europe, including the Soviet Union, Turkey, Cyprus and Malta.*	*Includes all domestic and regional developments in Africa and the Middle East, including Iraq and Iran and excluding Cyprus, Turkey and Afghanistan.*	*Includes all domestic and regional developments in Latin America, the Caribbean and Canada.*	*Includes all domestic and regional developments in Asia and Pacific nations, extending from Afghanistan through all the Pacific Islands, except Hawaii.*

U.S. Politics & Social Issues	U.S. Foreign Policy & Defense	U.S. Economy & Environment	Science, Technology & Nature	Culture, Leisure & Life Style	
Senate approves a four-year farm bill.			U.S. conducts an underground nuclear test.	Vatican council re-opens at St. Peter's.	Sept. 14
	Sen. J.W. Fulbright (D, Ark.) decries the U.S. intervention in the Dominican Republic.			U.S. atomic scientist Samuel Allison dies in Chicago at 64.	Sept. 15
	Sen. Stuart Symington (D, Mo.) calls on Western Europe to pay more for its own defense.				Sept. 16
	Under State Secy. George Ball calls on West European governments to reject nationalism.		Brush fires sweep the Northern California coast.		Sept. 17
	U.S. troops clash with the Viet Cong in a battle 17 miles north of the Binh Province town of Ankhe.				Sept. 18
N.Y.C. launches a drive to recruit Negro teachers.					Sept. 19
			U.S. launches a military surveillance satellite.		Sept. 20
		Pres. Johnson signs a bill creating two national coastal parks.	Soviet Union launches a communications satellite.		Sept. 21
Senate passes a bill placing curbs on immigration from the Western Hemisphere.	U.S. officials say they will increase the Vietnam force to 200,000 men.				Sept. 22
	Senate cuts $50 million from the foreign aid request.	Teamsters union says it will raise money for jailed Pres. Jimmy Hoffa.			Sept. 23
	U.S. says general agreement has been reached with Panama on a new canal treaty.	Negotiations continue in the N.Y.C. newspaper strike.		Soviet philosopher Mikhail Kammair dies in Moscow at 67.	Sept. 24
			Soviet Union launches five satellites with a single rocket.	Observers say that the Vatican will approve a declaration on the need for religious liberty.	Sept. 25
Negro youths kill a white social worker in Los Angeles.				Pope Paul says mass at a gypsy camp in Italy.	Sept. 26
U.S. officials say that school desegregation is up 50% in the South.				Jesuits say that atheists are trying to infiltrate the Catholic Church.	Sept. 27
			U.S. scientists discover their second comet within a week.	Vatican bishops debate the utility of Sigmund Freud.	Sept. 28
House rejects Pres. Johnson's plea for Washington, D.C. home rule.					Sept. 29

F	G	H	I	J
Includes elections, federal-state relations, civil rights and liberties, crime, the judiciary, education, health care, poverty, urban affairs and population	Includes formation and debate of U.S. foreign and defense policies, veterans' affairs and defense spending. (Relations with specific foreign countries are usually found under the region concerned.)	Includes business, labor, agriculture, taxation, transportation, consumer affairs, monetary and fiscal policy, natural resources, and pollution.	Includes worldwide scientific, medical and technological developments, natural phenomena, U.S. weather, natural disasters, and accidents.	Includes the arts, religion, scholarship, communications media, sports, entertainment, fashions, fads and social life.

	World Affairs	Europe	Africa & the Middle East	The Americas	Asia & the Pacific
Sept. 30	At the U.N. Pakistan accuses India of breaking the cease-fire.	Soviet Union says its main ally in Asia is India.	Congolese rebels continue to hold out against government troops.		U.S. planes bomb Viet Cong positions.
Oct. 1		Greece pledges support for the independence of Cyprus.	Rhodesian P.M. Ian Smith says that negotiations with Britain are going nowhere.		Indonesia announces that a plot to depose Pres. Sukarno has been foiled.
Oct. 2	At the U.N. India and Pakistan accuse each other of cease-fire violations.	Greek military commander Gen. George Grivas visits Cyprus.			Pakistan says it will resume fighting if its demands are not met.
Oct. 3		Soviet CP leader Leonid Brezhnev gets the presidium post.	An Arab mob burns a Jewish synagogue in Aden.	Police and students scuffle briefly at the Univ. of Kingston in Jamaica.	Indonesian army begins arrests of officers who tried to depose Pres. Sukarno.
Oct. 4				Cuban Premier Fidel Castro says that guerrilla leader Ché Guevara is fighting abroad.	U.S. planes bomb North Vietnam.
Oct. 5		Conservative Party makes gains in Norwegian voting.	Israel observes Yom Kippur.	Opposition candidates lead in Brazilian voting.	Major clashes break out between the Indonesian army and the Communist Party.
Oct. 6		British P.M. Harold Wilson says he may participate directly in the British-Rhodesian independence talks.	Egyptian Pres. Nasser purges police leaders because of their ignorance of a plot against him.	Supporters of former Pres. Juscelino Kubitschek win Brazilian elections.	Indonesian army units and rebel forces battle in central Java.
Oct. 7		British P.M. Harold Wilson and Rhodesian P.M. Ian Smith confer in London.	British troops rout Arab protesters in Aden.	Police and students scuffle at the Univ. of Lima in Peru.	Observers say that the Indonesian Army clearly has the upper hand in its clashes with Communist Party members.
Oct. 8		Talks on Rhodesian independence collapse in London.			Indonesian mobs raze Communist Party offices in Jakarta.
Oct. 9		In London Rhodesian P.M. Ian Smith warns that Rhodesia will fight for its independence.	British troops arrest Arab guerrilla leaders in Aden.	A student boycott increases tensions in Santo Domingo.	U.S. planes bomb Viet Cong positions.
Oct. 10			British arrest four guerrillas suspected of terrorism in Aden.	Observers report that Peruvian land reform is undercutting the appeal of leftist guerrillas.	South Vietnamese and Viet Cong forces clash near Saigon.
Oct. 11		Britain says it may reduce defense spending.	Congolese government mercenaries capture the last rebel stronghold in the eastern Congo.	Student unrest flares up at the Univ. of Rio de Janeiro.	Indonesian army arrests more Communist Party leaders as the crack-down continues.
Oct. 12	At the U.N. India and Pakistan accuse each other of having started last month's war.	France says it will build 30 missile silos for its nuclear weapons.	British troops scuffle with Arab protesters in Aden.		Cambodia says it wants some form of diplomatic contact with the U.S.
Oct. 13	At the U.N. Arab delegates accuse Israel of mistreating its Arab citizens.		Congolese Pres. Joseph Kasavubu dismisses the 15-month-old government of Premier Moise Tshombe.	Uruguayan unions begin a 72-hour general strike.	India and Pakistan report minor clashes.
Oct. 14	U.N. Secy. Gen. U Thant urges faster troop withdrawals from Kashmir.	British Conservative Party says it favors ending a defense role east of Suez.			Anti-communist Gen. Suharto becomes the head of the Indonesian Army.

A	B	C	D	E
Includes developments that affect more than one world region, international organizations and important meetings of major world leaders.	Includes all domestic and regional developments in Europe, including the Soviet Union, Turkey, Cyprus and Malta.	Includes all domestic and regional developments in Africa and the Middle East, including Iraq and Iran and excluding Cyprus, Turkey and Afghanistan.	Includes all domestic and regional developments in Latin America, the Caribbean and Canada.	Includes all domestic and regional developments in Asia and Pacific nations, extending from Afghanistan through all the Pacific Islands, except Hawaii.

U.S. Politics & Social Issues	U.S. Foreign Policy & Defense	U.S. Economy & Environment	Science, Technology & Nature	Culture, Leisure & Life Style	
Republican leaders condemn the right-wing John Birch Society.		Pres. Johnson says that nuclear power will be the key to future energy needs.			Sept. 30
	House approves a $3.2 billion foreign aid bill.			Vatican deplores all forms of anti-Semitism.	Oct. 1
U.S. says it may cut off federal aid to the Chicago school system because of racial discrimination.			U.S. officials say they are now ahead of the Soviets in space.		Oct. 2
		Pres. Johnson calls for stiffer curbs on auto exhaust.		Pope Paul names the first Negro U.S. bishop, Harold Perry.	Oct. 3
Abe Fortas becomes a member of the Supreme Court.		Interior Secy. Stewart Udall urges greater efforts on desalinization.	Soviet Union launches a rocket toward the moon.		Oct. 4
Civil rights leader Charles Evers prevents a brawl between Negroes and whites in Natchez, Miss.	Senate approves a foreign aid compromise bill.				Oct. 5
					Oct. 6
				Vatican Council disagrees on a stand on nuclear weapons.	Oct. 7
White and Negro students brawl at Chicago's Austin High School.		N.Y.C. newspaper unions reach an accord with publishers on ending the strike.	Soviet Union reports that its moon satellite has failed to reach its target.	U.S. writer Thomas Costain dies in N.Y.C. at 80.	Oct. 8
			Soviet Union conducts an underground nuclear test.	Three plays by Ray Bradbury open in N.Y.C.	Oct. 9
	Several hundred students demonstrate against the Vietnam War in Berkeley, Calif.		U.S. conducts an underground nuclear test.		Oct. 10
		Senate refuses to curb a debate over the union shop issue.			Oct. 11
	U.S. pledges to pressure Rhodesia into making political concessions.			Vivian Beaumont Theater opens at Lincoln Center.	Oct. 12
	U.S. orders the Army to speed the training of 150,000 reservists.			U.S. photographer Dorothea Lange dies in San Francisco at 70.	Oct. 13
	U.S. officials say that the December draft call will be the biggest since the Korean War.		Three French scientists win the Nobel Prize in medicine.	Cézanne's *Maisons a l'Estaque* sets the world's auction record for impressionist paintings.	Oct. 14

F	G	H	I	J
Includes elections, federal-state relations, civil rights and liberties, crime, the judiciary, education, health care, poverty, urban affairs and population.	*Includes formation and debate of U.S. foreign and defense policies, veterans' affairs and defense spending. (Relations with specific foreign countries are usually found under the region concerned.)*	*Includes business, labor, agriculture, taxation, transportation, consumer affairs, monetary and fiscal policy, natural resources, and pollution.*	*Includes worldwide scientific, medical and technological developments, natural phenomena, U.S. weather, natural disasters, and accidents.*	*Includes the arts, religion, scholarship, communications media, sports, entertainment, fashions, fads and social life.*

	World Affairs	Europe	Africa & the Middle East	The Americas	Asia & the Pacific
Oct. 15		Soviet Union says it plans to join talks of the Asian Development Bank members.		Several hundred Cuban refugees leave Cuba for the U.S.	U.S. planes bomb North Vietnam.
Oct. 16	At the U.N. Egypt accuses Iran of cooperating with Israel.	France calls for a complete reorganization of NATO.	Rhodesian officials say they are considering the risk of economic sanctions.		South Vietnamese and Viet Cong forces clash in the Mekong Delta.
Oct. 17		Britain tells Israel that its growing trade with Arab countries will not change its policy in the Middle East.		Several hundred more refugees leave Cuba for the U.S.	U.S. jets bomb a missile base in North Vietnam.
Oct. 18			Rhodesian P.M. Ian Smith says the British Commonwealth has no role to play in independence talks.	Uruguayan unionists seek wage talks with government.	Indonesian Army imposes a ban on the Communist Party.
Oct. 19	At the U.N. Iraq accuses Egypt of being too conciliatory toward Israel.		Observers say that Burundi has foiled an attempted coup.	Dominican troops fight with rebel holdouts.	India says it will not develop its own A-bomb.
Oct. 20			Three Sudanese ministers resign.	Dominican authorities say police will soon begin a house-to-house search for guns.	Observers say that Indonesia is turning away from Communist China.
Oct. 21		British P.M. Harold Wilson says he will visit Rhodesia in an attempt to break independence talks deadlock.		Two hundred fifty Cuban exiles land in Florida.	U.S. planes bomb Viet Cong positions.
Oct. 22	More U.N. monitors leave for Kashmir.	Coalition cabinet in Austria resigns.	African states call on Britain to use force against Rhodesia.	France sends troops to Martinique in wake of political riots.	U.S. planes bomb North Vietnam.
Oct. 23		Observers in Moscow say that Soviet-Sino relations are continuing to deteriorate.	Tunisia says that the Arab states should not ignore the reality of Israel.	Rebel forces kill a provincial governor in the Dominican Republic.	Indonesian Pres. Sukarno orders an end to anti-communist demonstrations.
Oct. 24		British P.M. Harold Wilson leaves for Rhodesia for independence talks.		Observers report serious political differences within the Dominican government.	India acts to crush a movement in Kashmir for a plebiscite.
Oct. 25	United Nations' Children's Fund wins the Nobel Peace Prize.	Soviet Union denounces U.N. Secy. Gen. U Thant's statements on Kashmir.	Eight thousand black Rhodesians cheer British P.M. Harold Wilson as he arrives for independence talks.	Canada makes a major wheat sale to Communist China.	U.S. planes bomb North Vietnam.
Oct. 26		West German Chancellor Ludwig Erhard's cabinet takes the oath of office.		Observers say that U.S.-Canadian relations are not an issue in the upcoming Canadian elections.	Observers say that the Indonesian army is supporting demonstrations against Pres. Sukarno.
Oct. 27		Yugoslavia says it wants ties to the Common Market.	Rhodesian blacks roam Salisbury in a day of protest.	Brazilian Pres. Humberto Castelo Branco assumes additional powers and abolishes parties.	Viet Cong artillery destroys 20 planes at U.S. bases.
Oct. 28		French Foreign Min. Maurice Couve de Murville begins talks with Soviet leaders in Moscow.	Israel attacks two Lebanese border towns in retaliation for guerrilla attacks.	Argentine Pres. Arturo Illia flys to Chile for talks.	Indonesian army arrests 189 Communist Party members.
Oct. 29			Lebanon denounces the recent Israeli attack on several Lebanese border towns.	Dominican police kill four protesters at a union rally.	Viet Cong and South Vietnamese forces clash near Danang.
	A	B	C	D	E
	Includes developments that affect more than one world region, international organizations and important meetings of major world leaders.	Includes all domestic and regional developments in Europe, including the Soviet Union, Turkey, Cyprus and Malta.	Includes all domestic and regional developments in Africa and the Middle East, including Iraq and Iran and excluding Cyprus, Turkey and Afghanistan.	Includes all domestic and regional developments in Latin America, the Caribbean and Canada.	Includes all domestic and regional developments in Asia and Pacific nations, extending from Afghanistan through all the Pacific Islands, except Hawaii.

U.S. Politics & Social Issues	U.S. Foreign Policy & Defense	U.S. Economy & Environment	Science, Technology & Nature	Culture, Leisure & Life Style	
	Hundreds of demonstrations across the nation score U.S. policy in Vietnam.		Soviet Union launches a military surveillance satellite.	Soviet writer Mikhail Sholokhov wins the Nobel Prize for literature.	Oct. 15
	Pentagon says the U.S. is dropping plans for a NATO nuclear fleet.		U.S. launches a military surveillance satellite.		Oct. 16
Justice Dept. says it will investigate anti-draft groups in the U.S.	A Vietnam protest organization says it plans a drive to promote draft evasion.				Oct. 17
Milwaukee Catholic hierarchy declares its support of the civil rights movement.	FBI arrests draft protester David Miller for burning his draft card.		Soviet Union launches a communications satellite.		Oct. 18
Ku Klux Klan head Robert Shelton refuses to answer 73 questions as a congressional inquiry on the Klan begins.					Oct. 19
Congress votes funds for a teacher corps.	Pres. Johnson signs a $3.2 billion foreign aid bill.	Pres. Johnson signs a bill to control auto exhaust.			Oct. 20
Sen. Edward Kennedy abandons his fight to win Senate approval of Francis Morrissey's judicial nomination.	Auto unions declare their support of U.S. Vietnam policy.		Three Americans and a Japanese win the Nobel Prize in physics and chemistry.		Oct. 21
				Philosopher Paul Tillich dies in Chicago at 79.	Oct. 22
Pres. Johnson says he wants rent subsidies for the poor.			Princeton Univ. scientists find data on ultra-violet light emanating from giant stars.		Oct. 23
Observers say that Negro southerners are registering to vote very quickly.	Sen. J.W. Fulbright calls for an end to the U.S. bombing of North Vietnam.				Oct. 24
	U.S. approves a major food grant to Egypt.				Oct. 25
	Selective Service officials say they will begin drafting students and married men.	General Motors earnings break all profit records.			Oct. 26
	Students clash with each other on U.S. Vietnam policy at Manhattan College in N.Y.C.				Oct. 27
	U.S. nears an accord with Cuba on refugees.			Vatican again makes statements absolving Jews of any collective responsibility for the crucifixion of Jesus.	Oct. 28
	U.S. says it may consider an airlift to Zambia if Rhodesia blocks its access to the sea.		U.S. conducts an underground nuclear test in the Aleutians.		Oct. 29

F	G	H	I	J
Includes elections, federal-state relations, civil rights and liberties, crime, the judiciary, education, health care, poverty, urban affairs and population.	Includes formation and debate of U.S. foreign and defense policies, veterans' affairs and defense spending. (Relations with specific foreign countries are usually found under the region concerned.)	Includes business, labor, agriculture, taxation, transportation, consumer affairs, monetary and fiscal policy, natural resources, and pollution.	Includes worldwide scientific, medical and technological developments, natural phenomena, U.S. weather, natural disasters, and accidents.	Includes the arts, religion, scholarship, communications media, sports, entertainment, fashions, fads and social life.

	World Affairs	Europe	Africa & the Middle East	The Americas	Asia & the Pacific
Oct. 30			Observers report that Egypt is withdrawing many of its troops from Yemen.		Viet Cong stage their first major attack against dug-in-Marines.
Oct. 31			Israel and Jordan trade fire in no-man's land.		Police disperse rioting leftists at the Univ. of Singapore.
Nov. 1	U.N. calls on Britain to use force against Rhodesia.			Cuban Premier Fidel Castro says he expects no thaw in U.S.-Cuban relations.	U.S. jets wreck three missile sites in North Vietnam.
Nov. 2	At the U.N. France criticizes the number of alleged useless studies made by that organization.	French Foreign Min. Couve de Murville ends talks with Soviet officials without major progress.	Israeli Premier Levi Eshkol wins a vote of confidence in national elections.	Dominican banks open for the first time in six months.	South Vietnamese and Viet Cong troops clash in the Central Highlands.
Nov. 3		Police and students clash briefly at the Univ. of Madrid.			Pakistan asserts that India is receiving modern Soviet MiGs.
Nov. 4		Pres. de Gaulle calls on voters to re-elect him in upcoming elections.	Former Israeli P.M. David Ben-Gurion says he will continue to oppose P.M. Levi Eshkol.	Brazil increases taxes in order to raise military salaries.	Observers report that the Indian-Pakistani cease-fire is holding.
Nov. 5	At the U.N. the Soviet Union abstains in a vote on immediate withdrawal of Indian-Pakistani forces from each other's territory.		Israeli and Jordanian forces exchange gunfire.	Brazil tells Congress to reduce its deputies by a third.	Indonesia strips Communists of all their powers in parliament.
Nov. 6	At the U.N. African delegates criticize Western investment in South Africa.	Soviet Union says that Communist China will have to make the first step in any policy of reconciliation.	Israeli and Jordanian forces clash along their border.	Cuba agrees to airlift refugees to the U.S.	U.S. planes bomb North Vietnamese air fields.
Nov. 7	U.N. takes up the question of Communist Chinese admission.	Soviet Union displays three new mobile rocket systems.	Tunisia calls on Arab states to negotiate with Israel.		U.S. troops engage in savage combat west of Pleime.
Nov. 8	U.N. delegates clash on the question of Communist Chinese admission.	French Pres. de Gaulle says that he will serve a full term if elected.		Canadian Liberal Party fails to win a majority in parliamentary elections.	U.S. troops maul a Viet Cong battalion near Danang.
Nov. 9			Israeli and Egyptian forces exchange gunfire.	Chilean and Argentine border guards scuffle.	Observers say India is seeking new Soviet arms.
Nov. 10	At the U.N. Soviet Union accuses NATO of trying to provoke a war.		Observers report that Iran is worried about Arab claims on part of its territory.		Senator Ferdinand Marcos takes the lead in Philippine presidential elections.
Nov. 11	U.N. calls on Britain to use force against Rhodesia.	Britain declares economic sanctions against Rhodesia.	Rhodesia declares its independence from Britain.		U.S. planes bomb Viet Cong troops near Saigon.
Nov. 12	U.N. calls on all its members to stop all forms of aid to Rhodesia.		Israel names Teddy Kolleck mayor of Jerusalem.	Sealift of Cuban refugees to the U.S. begins.	Philippine Senator Ferdinand Marcos wins in the presidential election.
Nov. 13	U.N. African delegates call for a trade boycott of Rhodesia.		Zambia declares economic sanctions against Rhodesia.	Hundreds of Cuban refugees arrive at Key West, Florida.	Communist China attacks Indian defense posts at several points.
Nov. 14	U.N. police get equipment to prevent future immolation suicides.	Workers finish restoration of the St. Paul's area in London.		Cuba accuses Cuban exiles of staging attacks with gunboats.	Indonesian troops rout Communist guerrillas in central Java.
	A	B	C	D	E
	Includes developments that affect more than one world region, international organizations and important meetings of major world leaders.	*Includes all domestic and regional developments in Europe, including the Soviet Union, Turkey, Cyprus and Malta.*	*Includes all domestic and regional developments in Africa and the Middle East, including Iraq and Iran and excluding Cyprus, Turkey and Afghanistan.*	*Includes all domestic and regional developments in Latin America, the Caribbean and Canada.*	*Includes all domestic and regional developments in Asia and Pacific nations, extending from Afghanistan through all the Pacific Islands, except Hawaii.*

U.S. Politics & Social Issues	U.S. Foreign Policy & Defense	U.S. Economy & Environment	Science, Technology & Nature	Culture, Leisure & Life Style	
U.S. reviews its farm policy in light of dwindling surpluses.	Twenty-five thousand marchers support U.S. Vietnam policy in N.Y.C.		U.S. launches a communications satellite.		Oct. 30
Former F.B.I. agent Willas Adams says he once bugged the hotel room of Mrs. Franklin Roosevelt during W.W. II.	U.S. calls on Japan to lower its tariff barriers.	Pres. Johnson calls on aluminum producers to rescind recent price increases.		Vatican absolves the Jews of the 1475 "ritual murder" of a boy in Trent.	Oct. 31
First U.S. rural area gets birth control aid in York County, Pa.		U.S. officials say they may sell aluminum to reduce prices.	U.S. nature experts say that few animals were hurt by the recent underground nuclear blast in the Aleutians.		Nov. 1
U.S. Rep. John Lindsay is elected mayor of N.Y.C.					Nov. 2
	Journalists say that most West Coast students back U.S. policy in Vietnam.	U.S. officials state their opposition to curbs on meat imports.		U.S. psychologist Harold Hildreth dies in Washington D.C. at 59.	Nov. 3
		U.S. jobless rate dips to an eight-year low.			Nov. 4
		Alcoa Aluminum Co. announces price increases opposed by Pres. Johnson.			Nov. 5
		U.S. officials say they will sell aluminum to keep down prices.			Nov. 6
		U.S. economists assail recent aluminum price rises.	U.S. conducts an underground nuclear test.		Nov. 7
			A plane crash near Cincinnati leaves 58 dead.	Former Pres. Eisenhower suffers what appears to be a heart attack.	Nov. 8
Roger Laporte immolates himself in an anti-war protest at the U.N.			A power failure snarls the Northeast.	Former Pres. Eisenhower rests after suffering a mild heart attack.	Nov. 9
	U.S. officials say they want the Indian Ocean island of Diego Garcia as a defense base.	Aluminum producers cancel price rises at government insistence.		Former Pres. Eisenhower suffers more pains in his chest.	Nov. 10
	U.S. criticizes Rhodesia's unilateral declaration of independence.		A plane crash near Salt Lake City leaves 41 dead.		Nov. 11
			FAA says it finds no pattern in the three recent 727 plane crashes.	Vatican Council makes a strong anti-war statement.	Nov. 12
			Ninety-one passengers drown as the *Yarmouth Castle* cruise ship burns and sinks off Nassau.	Observers report that the Vatican is considering an appeal to atheists for a dialogue.	Nov. 13
	Republican leader Barry Goldwater says he could support N.Y. Gov. Nelson Rockefeller in a presidential campaign.				Nov. 14

F	G	H	I	J
Includes elections, federal-state relations, civil rights and liberties, crime, the judiciary, education, health care, poverty, urban affairs and population.	Includes formation and debate of U.S. foreign and defense policies, veterans' affairs and defense spending. (Relations with specific foreign countries are usually found under the region concerned.)	Includes business, labor, agriculture, taxation, transportation, consumer affairs, monetary and fiscal policy, natural resources, and pollution.	Includes worldwide scientific, medical and technological developments, natural phenomena, U.S. weather, natural disasters, and accidents.	Includes the arts, religion, scholarship, communications media, sports, entertainment, fashions, fads and social life.

	World Affairs	Europe	Africa & the Middle East	The Americas	Asia & the Pacific
Nov. 15	South Africa spurns the U.N. debate on Rhodesia.	Hundreds of Britons threaten to boycott schools in racially tense Birmingham.	Sudan calls for a ban on all Communist activity.		U.S. planes bomb North Vietnam.
Nov. 16	U.N. Secy. Gen. U Thant calls for a compromise on Vietnam.	Soviet Union accuses the U.S. government of persecuting U.S. Communists.	Four thousand black Rhodesian postal workers refuse to pledge their loyalty to the newly independent regime.	Leftist students attack Sen. Robert Kennedy at the Univ. of Conception in Chile.	Indonesian troops continue their offensive against Communist guerrillas in East Java.
Nov. 17	U.N. votes not to admit Communist China.	Police and students scuffle at the Univ. of Barcelona.	Israeli and Jordanian forces exchange gunfire for several minutes.		South Vietnamese and Viet Cong forces clash in the Mekong Delta.
Nov. 18	U.S. says it is cool to U.N.-sponsored arms talks.	Britain says it will grant independence to British Guiana.		In Brazil State Secy. Dean Rusk calls on Latin Americans to create a hemispheric force.	Viet Cong maul U.S. troops in the Central Highlands.
Nov. 19	U.N. Secy. Gen. U Thant calls for an 18-nation disarmament parley to halt spread of nuclear weapons.	Greek-Cypriote talks end with a pledge of ultimate union with Greece.		Government troops maul communist guerrillas in Peru.	Communist China says it does not want to join the U.N.
Nov. 20		France announces that it will launch its first satellite within a month.	Rhodesian P.M. Ian Smith says that government forces can handle any guerrilla threat.	Chile and Mexico reject the U.S. proposal of a hemispheric force.	U.S. officials foresee a big drive by North Vietnam in the Central Highlands.
Nov. 21		Police and students clash briefly at the Univ. of Rome.	South Africa says it is ready to help Rhodesia.	Brazil permits a limited revival of political activity.	U.S. troops engage in fierce fighting in the Central Highlands.
Nov. 22	U.S. agrees to an arms parley bid by the U.N.	U.S. authorities say no West German pilot could take off in a plane carrying nuclear weapons.	Rhodesian police disperse several hundred protesting blacks.		U.S. planes attack missile sites in the Hanoi area.
Nov. 23	U.N. calls for world arms talks which would include Communist China.	Cypriote Pres. Makarios calls Turkey a barrier to peace talks.	Rhodesian police kill a black protester.		Viet Cong besiege a government camp at Tuyan.
Nov. 24	Twenty-six U.N. nations call for an end to all atomic tests.	Soviet Union sentences U.S. tourist Newcomb Mott to 18 months in prison for crossing the Soviet border without authorization.	Congolese Gen. Joseph Mobutu deposes Pres. Joseph Kasavubu in a bloodless coup.		U.S. officials announce the highest weekly casualty rate for the war—240 U.S. combat fatalities.
Nov. 25	U.N. Arab delegates accuse Israel of trying to provoke a war.	British P.M. Harold Wilson prepares to start new Vietnam peace talks.	Congolese Pres. Joseph Mobutu cancels upcoming elections.	A general strike brings Montevideo, Uruguay to a halt.	India accuses Communist China of border incursions in Sikkim.
Nov. 26		France launches its first satellite into space.	Zambia accuses Rhodesia of sabotaging equipment at its copper mines.		Nuclear carrier *Enterprise* reaches Vietnam.
Nov. 27	At the U.N. Israel defends its right to make retaliatory raids against neighboring Arab countries.				Defense Secy. Robert McNamara arrives in Saigon for military talks.
Nov. 28			Israeli and Egyptian forces clash briefly along the Gaza Strip.	Observers say tensions are growing between Honduras and El Salvador.	Viet Cong maul a South Vietnamese battalion.
Nov. 29	U.N. delegates criticize South Africa's apartheid policy.	British Foreign Min. Michael Stewart arrives in Moscow for Vietnam peace talks.	Dahomey's army stages its second coup within 25 months.	Brazil orders a crack-down on rightist military leaders.	
	A	**B**	**C**	**D**	**E**
	Includes developments that affect more than one world region, international organizations and important meetings of major world leaders.	Includes all domestic and regional developments in Europe, including the Soviet Union, Turkey, Cyprus and Malta.	Includes all domestic and regional developments in Africa and the Middle East, including Iraq and Iran and excluding Cyprus, Turkey and Afghanistan.	Includes all domestic and regional developments in Latin America, the Caribbean and Canada.	Includes all domestic and regional developments in Asia and Pacific nations, extending from Afghanistan through all the Pacific Islands, except Hawaii.

U.S. Politics & Social Issues	U.S. Foreign Policy & Defense	U.S. Economy & Environment	Science, Technology & Nature	Culture, Leisure & Life Style	
Supreme Court limits a law forcing U.S. Communists to register as members of a foreign organization.			Soviet Union launches a military surveillance satellite.		Nov. 15
			Soviet Union launches a military surveillance satellite.		Nov. 16
		U.S. sells copper stocks to reduce the market price.	Birth control pill manufacturers agree to make warnings of possible health risks.		Nov. 17
				Pope Paul begins procedures for beatification of his two immediate predecessors.	Nov. 18
		Treasury Secy. Henry Fowler declares a tougher policy on prices and wages.	U.S. launches a military surveillance satellite.		Nov. 19
	U.S. says it is considering expanding economic curbs against Rhodesia.		Soviet Union launches a communications satellite.		Nov. 20
	Former V.P. Nixon says the Vietnam War will be the major issue in the 1968 elections.			U.S. author Katherine Anthony dies in N.Y.C. at 87.	Nov. 21
				Cassius Clay knocks out Floyd Patterson to keep his heavyweight title.	Nov. 22
	U.S. says it will cut its force in Berlin by 700 men.			Prince Franz Josef of Liechtenstein refuses $6 million for a painting by Leonardo da Vinci.	Nov. 23
		U.S. offers to sell stockpiled wheat to head off a rise in the price of bread.			Nov. 24
	U.S. rejects a U.N. plea for an end to underground nuclear tests.				Nov. 25
	Pres. Johnson backs the right to dissent on Vietnam policy.			Pope Paul reaffirms the Church's birth control prohibitions.	Nov. 26
	About 20,000 demonstrators protest against the war in Vietnam in Washington, D.C.	U.S. aides foresee a $7 billion federal deficit.	Soviet Union conducts an underground nuclear test.	Vatican recovers stolen manuscripts by the Italian poets Petrarch and Tasso.	Nov. 27
			U.S. conducts an underground nuclear test.	U.S. journalist Maurice Kane dies in Silver Spring, Md. at 59.	Nov. 28
	Defense Secy. Robert McNamara says that the Vietnam War will be long and costly.			Russian church leader Metropolitan Nikodim hails the Vatican council.	Nov. 29

F	G	H	I	J
Includes elections, federal-state relations, civil rights and liberties, crime, the judiciary, education, health care, poverty, urban affairs and population.	Includes formation and debate of U.S. foreign and defense policies, veterans' affairs and defense spending. (Relations with specific foreign countries are usually found under the region concerned.)	Includes business, labor, agriculture, taxation, transportation, consumer affairs, monetary and fiscal policy, natural resources, and pollution.	Includes worldwide scientific, medical and technological developments, natural phenomena, U.S. weather, natural disasters, and accidents.	Includes the arts, religion, scholarship, communications media, sports, entertainment, fashions, fads and social life.

	World Affairs	Europe	Africa & the Middle East	The Americas	Asia & the Pacific
Nov. 30		France calls on the U.S. to leave Vietnam.	Egypt accuses moderate Egyptian journalist Mustafa Amin of spying, presumably for the U.S.		India accuses Communist China of building up its border forces.
Dec. 1	North Vietnam rejects a U.N. offer of mediation in peace talks.	Britain says it would send troops to Rhodesia if the Kariba Dam is threatened.	Congolese Pres. Joseph Mobutu says he will rule by decree.	Dominican Republic receives $50 million in U.S. aid.	
Dec. 2	U.N. Asian delegates indicate that the U.N. will have little role as a mediator in the Vietnam conflict.			Cuba says it may send troops to Vietnam.	U.S. planes bomb North Vietnam.
Dec. 3			Zambia says it may ask for U.S. troops to protect the Kariba Dam.		Reports indicate that Communist China is demanding transit fees in dollars for Soviet equipment going to North Vietnam.
Dec. 4	U.S. and 20 other nations sign the Asian Development Bank charter.	Police and students scuffle at the Univ. of Athens.	Observers say the Kariba Dam in Zambia may have been mined by Rhodesia.		Viet Cong and South Vietnamese forces clash in the Mekong Delta.
Dec. 5		Police and students scuffle at the Univ. of Rome.	Rhodesia prepares emergency measures in the face of sanctions.	Argentina and Chile agree to negotiate their territorial differences.	U.S. planes bomb North Vietnam.
Dec. 6		French Pres. de Gaulle fails to win 50% of the vote in presidential elections.	Tanzanian students protest Britain's decision not to send troops to Rhodesia.		U.S. planes bomb North Vietnam.
Dec. 7	U.N. Arab delegates call on the U.S. to disassociate itself from Israel.		Iraqi Kurds report a new offensive by the central government.		Indonesian Pres. Sukarno dares the parliament to oust him.
Dec. 8		Thousands of Soviet citizens demonstrate against the war in Vietnam.	Rhodesia restricts trade with Zambia and Malawi.		India asks for U.S. aid as famine looms.
Dec. 9	U.N. African delegates call on Britain to use force against Rhodesia.	Soviet chief of state Anastas Mikoyan resigns.	Iraq arrests 50 leaders of the banned Communist Party.		U.S. planes bomb Viet Cong positions.
Dec. 10		Soviet Union says it does not intend to put nuclear weapons into orbit.		Uruguay says it plans to cut diplomatic relations with the Soviet Union because of its contacts with internal guerrillas.	Observers say the role of South Vietnamese troops is shrinking as the U.S. build-up continues.
Dec. 11		Police and students clash at the Univ. of Madrid in Spain.	Jordanian and Egyptian soldiers exchange gunfire near Jerusalem.		U.S. Marines battle a huge enemy unit in the Quangtui area.
Dec. 12		Observers say Portugal is trying to develop the island of Timor in the Pacific.		Uruguay warns its unions of possible curbs.	U.S. planes bomb North Vietnam.
Dec. 13		French socialists call for an end to France's nuclear force.	Observers say Egypt will not break diplomatic relations with Britain.	Leftist unions in Uruguay withdraw a strike call in the face of government pressure.	U.S. planes bomb Viet Cong positions.
Dec. 14	U.N. approves a resolution criticizing all forms of discrimination.	Britain says it plans to impose an oil embargo on Rhodesia.			India reports killing 30 Communist Chinese soldiers on the Sikkim border.
	A	B	C	D	E
	Includes developments that affect more than one world region, international organizations and important meetings of major world leaders.	*Includes all domestic and regional developments in Europe, including the Soviet Union, Turkey, Cyprus and Malta.*	*Includes all domestic and regional developments in Africa and the Middle East, including Iraq and Iran and excluding Cyprus, Turkey and Afghanistan.*	*Includes all domestic and regional developments in Latin America, the Caribbean and Canada.*	*Includes all domestic and regional developments in Asia and Pacific nations, extending from Afghanistan through all the Pacific Islands, except Hawaii.*

U.S. Politics & Social Issues	U.S. Foreign Policy & Defense	U.S. Economy & Environment	Science, Technology & Nature	Culture, Leisure & Life Style	
	Two freed U.S. prisoners of war say the U.S. should leave Vietnam.	U.S. officials express concern about rising prices.	Soviet Union conducts an underground nuclear test.		Nov. 30
	U.S. officials say that the pressure to bomb Haiphong harbor is growing.		U.S. conducts an underground nuclear test.		Dec. 1
An all-white jury sentences a segregationist to 10 years in prison for the slaying of a Negro in Anniston, Ala.	Observers say that U.S. labor unions are solidly behind U.S. Vietnam policy.	November figures indicate a slight dip in the jobless rate.			Dec. 2
Natchez, Miss. boycott ends as Negroes gain objectives.	U.S. says it will intensify raids over Laos.		Gemini 7 sends back messages by laser to the earth.	National Council of Churches calls for a halt to the U.S. bombing of Vietnam.	Dec. 3
	U.S. says it will widen curbs on Rhodesian trade.		An airlines crash in Danbury, Conn. leaves three dead.		Dec. 4
		Federal Reserve Board defies Pres. Johnson and raises the discount rate to 41/2%.		Roman Catholic and Eastern Orthodox churches agree to nullify the anathema of 1054, excommunicating the leaders of each Church.	Dec. 5
	Defense Secy. Robert McNamara orders the closing of 149 military bases, largely in the U.S.	Interest rates increase in the wake of Federal Reserve Board price hikes.		Pope Paul ends the right of the Vatican to conduct secret trials.	Dec. 6
			Gemini 7 shifts into a higher orbit.	Roman Catholic and Eastern Orthodox Churches officially renounce the 11th century excommunications.	Dec. 7
	Presidential assistant McGeorge Bundy resigns.	Pollution experts find gains in the Lake Erie clean up.		Pope Paul closes the Vatican Council amid pageantry.	Dec. 8
	U.S. decides to step up food aid to India.			Baseball star Branch Rickey dies in Columbia, Mo. at 83.	Dec. 9
	Sen. Ernest Gruening (D, Alaska) assails U.S. involvement in Vietnam.		U.S. composer Henry Cowell dies in Shady, N.Y. at 68.		Dec. 10
	U.S. says it will give Turkey birth control aid.		Soviet Union launches a military surveillance satellite.	Dallas officials choose architect Philip Johnson to design the Kennedy Memorial.	Dec. 11
Martin Luther King Jr. says the civil rights movement must begin operating in the North.	U.S. says it eventually wants Spain in NATO.		Gemini satellite misfires on pad and fails to take off.		Dec. 12
	Republican Party leaders warn of an "endless" war in Vietnam.				Dec. 13
	Pres. Johnson confers with Pakistani Pres. Ayub Khan in Washington.	American Airlines proposes half fares for youths from 12 to 21.	U.S. launches a military surveillance satellite.		Dec. 14
F	G	H	I	J	
Includes elections, federal-state relations, civil rights and liberties, crime, the judiciary, education, health care, poverty, urban affairs and population.	Includes formation and debate of U.S. foreign and defense policies, veterans' affairs and defense spending. (Relations with specific foreign countries are usually found under the region concerned.)	Includes business, labor, agriculture, taxation, transportation, consumer affairs, monetary and fiscal policy, natural resources, and pollution.	Includes worldwide scientific, medical and technological developments, natural phenomena, U.S. weather, natural disasters, and accidents.	Includes the arts, religion, scholarship, communications media, sports, entertainment, fashions, fads and social life.	

	World Affairs	Europe	Africa & the Middle East	The Americas	Asia & the Pacific
Dec. 15	U.N. extends aid to Palestinian refugees.		Tanzania breaks diplomatic relations with Britain.		U.S. jets smash a big power plant near Haiphong.
Dec. 16	U.N. African delegates walk out during an address by British P.M. Harold Wilson.	Police and students scuffle at the Univ. of Barcelona.			India expresses concern about an alleged build-up of Communist Chinese troops.
Dec. 17		Switzerland freezes Rhodesia's bank assets.	Israeli and Jordanian troops exchange gunfire.	Dominican sugar workers end a four-day strike.	South Vietnamese and Viet Cong troops clash near Danang.
Dec. 18	U.N. African delegates call on Britain to use force against Rhodesia.	French polls predict a de Gaulle victory.	Rhodesia blocks train shipments of oil to Zambia.	Brazil launches its second meteorological rocket.	U.S. planes bomb Viet Cong positions.
Dec. 19	At the U.N. Iraq accuses Iran of fomenting unrest among Iraqi Kurds.	French Pres. de Gaulle wins presidential elections with 54.7% of the vote.	Israeli and Egyptian troops clash along the Gaza Strip.	Dominican government troops clash with rebel forces.	U.S. planes bomb North Vietnam.
Dec. 20	At the U.N. India and Pakistan accuse each other of cease-fire violations.	Spain legalizes strikes.	Yemeni royalists say that current peace talks have failed.	Rival factions continue gun battle in the Dominican Republic.	U.S. planes bomb Viet Cong positions.
Dec. 21		Soviet Union agrees to increase aid to North Vietnam.		Sniper fire continues in Santo Domingo.	North Vietnam downs six U.S. planes.
Dec. 22		Czechoslovakia's CP criticizes itself for serious economic mistakes.	Army seizes power in Dahomey.	Students and police clash briefly at the Univ. of Rio de Janeiro.	U.S. and South Vietnam order a 30-hour holiday truce.
Dec. 23		Police and students scuffle at the Univ. of Rome.	Iraqi Kurds press an offensive despite winter snows.		U.S. troops clash with the Viet Cong near Danang.
Dec. 24		Police and students scuffle at the Univ. of Barcelona.	Algeria decides to widen the autonomy of its collective farms.	Honduras and El Salvador accuse each other of border violations.	Holiday truce holds in South Vietnam.
Dec. 25	U.N. African delegates criticize South Africa's apartheid policy.	France calls for the withdrawal of the U.S. from Vietnam.	Iran accuses Iraq of strafing its border area.	Mexico begins a literacy program on television.	U.S. planes bomb North Vietnam.
Dec. 26		East German border guards kill a German trying to escape to the West.	Rhodesia says it has six-months of oil in stockpiles.		U.S. cancels a scheduled raid by planes against North Vietnam.
Dec. 27		Thirteen die as a gas rig collapses in the North Sea.	Rhodesia begins rationing gasoline.		South Vietnamese officials say that television will begin in January 1966.
Dec. 28	U.N. African delegates call on Britain to use force against Rhodesia.	Police and students clash at the Univ. of Athens.	Israelis and Syrians exchange gunfire.		
Dec. 29		West Germany makes a major credit loan to Israel.	Tunisia calls for Arab negotiations with Israel.	Rival factions exchange gunfire in Santo Domingo.	
Dec. 30	U.N. Arab delegates say that a war with Israel is inevitable.				Ferdinand Marcos begins his presidential term in the Philippines.

A	B	C	D	E
Includes developments that affect more than one world region, international organizations and important meetings of major world leaders.	*Includes all domestic and regional developments in Europe, including the Soviet Union, Turkey, Cyprus and Malta.*	*Includes all domestic and regional developments in Africa and the Middle East, including Iraq and Iran and excluding Cyprus, Turkey and Afghanistan.*	*Includes all domestic and regional developments in Latin America, the Caribbean and Canada.*	*Includes all domestic and regional developments in Asia and Pacific nations, extending from Afghanistan through all the Pacific Islands, except Hawaii.*

U.S. Politics & Social Issues	U.S. Foreign Policy & Defense	U.S. Economy & Environment	Science, Technology & Nature	Culture, Leisure & Life Style	
	Defense Secy. McNamara warns NATO of a Communist Chinese nuclear threat.		Two Gemini spacecraft fly within six feet of each other.	British author Somerset Maugham dies in Nice, France at 91.	Dec. 15
	Eggs and fists fly as pacifists demonstrate against the Vietnam War in Times Square.		Gemini spacecraft splashes down safely in the Pacific Ocean.		Dec. 16
	Pres. Johnson confers with British P.M. Harold Wilson on ways to end the Vietnam War.		Gemini 7 ends its 14-day record flight.		Dec. 17
			Soviet Union conducts an underground nuclear test.		Dec. 18
			Five different international scientific teams say they have identified indications of the primordial flash that occurred when the universe was born.		Dec. 19
	U.S. gives permission to field commanders to pursue enemy troops into Cambodia.				Dec. 20
Little Rock, Ark. integrates its school facilities.	U.S. and Germany agree to abandon plans for a NATO atomic fleet.			U.S. banker Albert Andriesse dies in White Plains, N.Y. at 85.	Dec. 21
	U.S. pledges enough wheat to India to avert a famine.			British broadcaster Richard Dimbeley dies in London at 52.	Dec. 22
	U.S. aides doubt the holiday truce will bring talks.			Pope Paul calls for negotiations in Vietnam.	Dec. 23
			Soviet Union launches a communications satellite.	U.S. lawyer Richard Murphy dies in N.Y.C. at 76.	Dec. 24
				Pope Paul calls for a negotiated settlement in Vietnam.	Dec. 25
		U.S. market for steel shows strength.		Viscount Margesson dies in the Bahamas at 75.	Dec. 26
Observers say that the movement for divorce reform is growing in the U.S.	V.P. Hubert Humphrey begins a tour of the Far East.			U.S. architect Frederick Kiesler dies in N.Y.C. at 75.	Dec. 27
	U.S. tells North Vietnam that the bombing lull is a peace overture.		Soviet Union launches Cosmos 102 and 103.	U.S. scholar Lynn Thorndike dies in N.Y.C. at 83.	Dec. 28
	U.S. Amb.-to-U.N. Arthur Goldberg leaves for talks with the Pope about the Vietnam War.		U.S. scientists say U.S. astronauts can make longer flights without any health danger.	U.S. air pollution foe William Christy dies in Philadelphia at 81.	Dec. 29
U.S. officials say they will investigate the Chicago school system because of discrimination charges.	U.S. labor leader George Meany says that spending for the Vietnam War must not cut into domestic programs.			U.S. film critic Frank Nugent dies in Los Angeles at 57.	Dec. 30

F	G	H	I	J
Includes elections, federal-state relations, civil rights and liberties, crime, the judiciary, education, health care, poverty, urban affairs and population.	*Includes formation and debate of U.S. foreign and defense policies, veterans' affairs and defense spending. (Relations with specific foreign countries are usually found under the region concerned.)*	*Includes business, labor, agriculture, taxation, transportation, consumer affairs, monetary and fiscal policy, natural resources, and pollution.*	*Includes worldwide scientific, medical and technological developments, natural phenomena, U.S. weather, natural disasters, and accidents.*	*Includes the arts, religion, scholarship, communications media, sports, entertainment, fashions, fads and social life.*

	World Affairs	Europe	Africa & the Middle East	The Americas	Asia & the Pacific
Dec. 31		Soviet authorities set a 10 p.m. curfew for unescorted children during vacation period.	Iraqi authorities leave for talks with Saudi officials.		Philippines says it may send troops to Vietnam.

A	B	C	D	E
Includes developments that affect more than one world region, international organizations and important meetings of major world leaders.	Includes all domestic and regional developments in Europe, including the Soviet Union, Turkey, Cyprus and Malta.	Includes all domestic and regional developments in Africa and the Middle East, including Iraq and Iran and excluding Cyprus, Turkey and Afghanistan.	Includes all domestic and regional developments in Latin America, the Caribbean and Canada.	Includes all domestic and regional developments in Asia and Pacific nations, extending from Afghanistan through all the Pacific Islands, except Hawaii.

U.S. Politics & Social Issues	U.S. Foreign Policy & Defense	U.S. Economy & Environment	Science, Technology & Nature	Culture, Leisure & Life Style	
		Bethlehem Steel Co. raises prices by $5 a ton.		U.S. banker William du Pont dies in Wilmington, Del. at 69.	Dec. 31

F	G	H	I	J
Includes elections, federal-state relations, civil rights and liberties, crime, the judiciary, education, health care, poverty, urban affairs and population.	*Includes formation and debate of U.S. foreign and defense policies, veterans' affairs and defense spending. (Relations with specific foreign countries are usually found under the region concerned.)*	*Includes business, labor, agriculture, taxation, transportation, consumer affairs, monetary and fiscal policy, natural resources, and pollution.*	*Includes worldwide scientific, medical and technological developments, natural phenomena, U.S. weather, natural disasters, and accidents.*	*Includes the arts, religion, scholarship, communications media, sports, entertainment, fashions, fads and social life.*

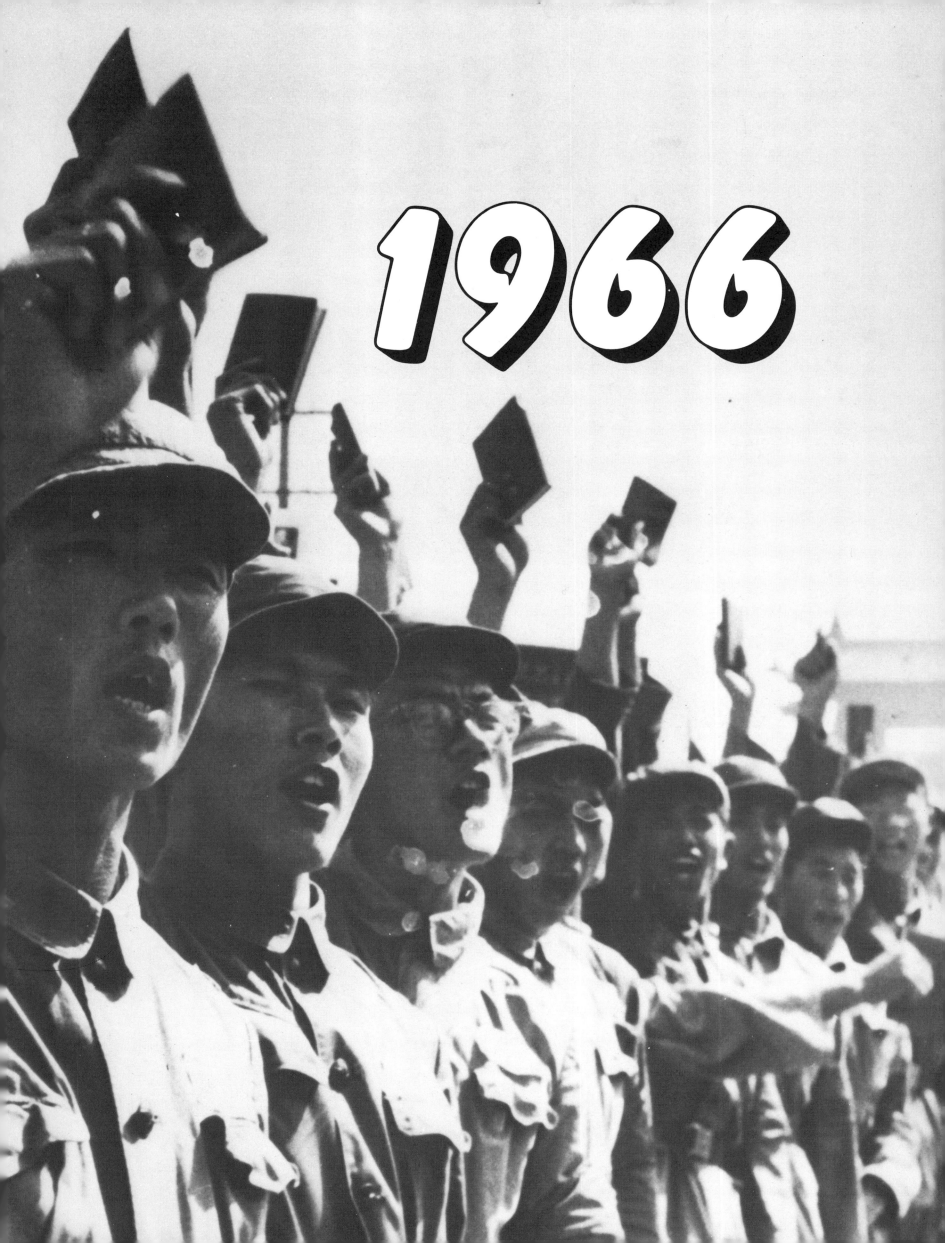

1966

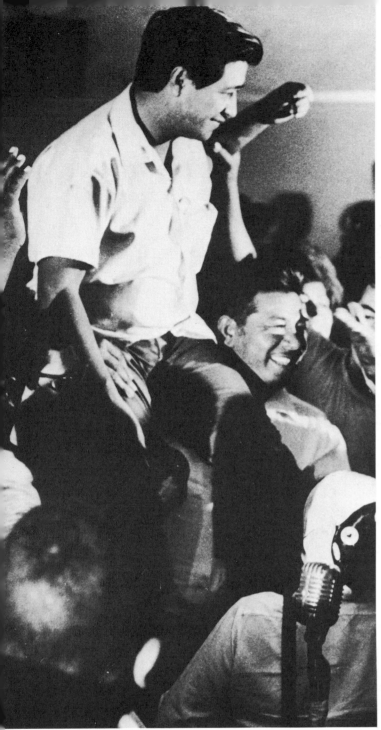

First nighters fill the new Metropolitan Opera House for its opening.

Farm workers hoist Cesar Chavez, head of the AFL-CIO Farm Workers Union, to their shoulders in Delano, Calif., Sept. 1. Chavez' group wins out over the Teamsters to become the bargaining agent for grape pickers on two California ranches.

Vice President Hubert Humphrey, left, and Ambassador At Large W. Averell Harriman visit Indian Prime Minister Indira Gandhi. Chester Bowles, Ambassador to India, stands behind Mrs. Gandhi.

Members of the Red Guard demonstrate in front of the Soviet Embassy in Peiking, holding booklets containing the writings of Mao Tze-tung.

Jim Ryun leads the field in the mile run at the National AAU Track and Field Championships in New York City.

Former Nazi Munitions Minister Albert Speer, left, was released from prison Oct. 1 after serving a 20-year sentence.

Composer Igor Stravinsky conducts the New York Philharmonic.

Chou En-lai arrives June 16 for a visit to Rumania.

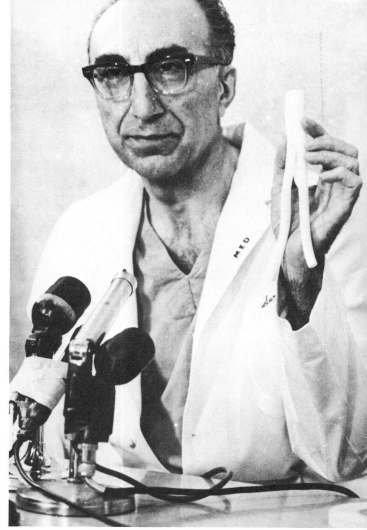

Dr. Michael E. DeBakey implanted a bypass "heart pump" in a patient on May 17.

Ralph Nader testifies before a Senate Public Works Committee during hearings on the auto industry generated by Nader's allegations that the industry had neglected auto safety.

	World Affairs	Europe	Africa & the Middle East	The Americas	Asia & the Pacific
Jan.	UNESCO estimates that 43% to 45% of the world's adults are illiterate.	Indian P.M. Bahadur Shastri dies at the age of 61 in Tashkent (Soviet Union) during the Indian-Pakistani peace negotiations.	Britain completes its infantry withdrawal from Tripoli, Libya. . . .Reports indicate that Iran and Iraq have reached agreement on how to settle their dispute over their Kurdish populations.	Dominican Republic sends right-wing military officers abroad to diplomatic posts.	India and Pakistan sign an accord providing for the withdrawal of all their troops from positions occupied as a result of the 1965 border war. . . .Congress Party elects Indira Gandhi as India's third prime minister.
Feb.	U.N. Security Council votes to debate a U.S. resolution calling for an international conference on the Vietnamese War.	French Pres. de Gaulle announces that France will assume control of all foreign military bases on its territory by Arpil 1969. . . .Britain announces that it will withdraw its troops from Aden in 1968.	Syrian radicals led by Maj. Gen. Salah Jedid take power in a bloody coup. . .Ghanaian military leaders overthrow Pres. Kwame Nkrumah in a violent coup.	Eighteen Latin American nations protest the "subversive aims" of the recent Communist-dominated "Revolutionary Conference" in Havana.	Indonesian Pres. Sukarno says that the anti-Malaysia "confrontation" will continue despite the intention of the Philippines to recognize Malaysia.
March	IMF grants India an emergency loan because of its recent drought.	France formally announces its intention to withdraw from NATO's integrated military command structure but not the Alliance itself. . . .British P.M. Harold Wilson's Labor Party wins a landslide victory in Parliamentary election. . . .West Germany says it wants to begin "dialogues" with Poland and Czechoslovakia.	Kenya orders the expulsion of Soviet, Communist Chinese and Czech officials. . . .Maj. Gen. Hafez Assad becomes Syria's new defense minister.	Army forces Ecuador's ruling junta to relinquish power.	Indonesian Pres. Sukarno turns over all power to the staunchly anti-Communist Gen. Suharto who immediately bans the Indonesian Communist Party. . . .
April	U.N. African delegates criticize Western investment in South Africa.	French Foreign Min. Maurice Couve de Murville says that France is willing to keep its 75,000 troops in West Germany if the West German government so desires.	Rhodesian police clash with African guerrillas for the first time since Rhodesia proclaimed its independence in 1965.	Gen. Artur Costa e Silva is choosen as Brazil's presidential nominee to succeed Pres. Castelo Branco.	South Vietnam's anti-government Buddhist leadership announces an all-out campaign to topple the military regime of Premier Nguyen Ky.
May	U.N. Security Council rejects an African resolution calling for the use of force by Britain against Rhodesia.	West German Chancellor Ludwig Erhard declares that he wants all French military forces to remain in Germany.	Egyptian Pres. Gamal Nasser supports the Yemeni republican claims to the Saudi Arabian border towns of Quian and Najran.	British Guiana becomes independent and adopts the name of Guyana.	South Vietnamese forces retake Danang and other major towns in the Northern provinces from Buddhist dissidents.
June	U.N. Secy. Gen. U Thant criticizes the US raids on the Hanoi-Haiphong oil installations.	U.S. begins to withdraw its military forces from France.	Reports indicate that hundreds of Ibos have been slain in northern Nigeria.	Lt. Gen. Juan Carlos Ongania ousts Argentinian Pres. Arturo Illia in a bloodless coup.	U.S. bombers strike at fuel storage installations near Hanoi and Haiphong. . . .Reports from Communist China indicate that major government purges took place in May.
July	Finance ministers and central bank governors of the ten leading financial nations meet in The Hague to discuss international monetary reform.	France places all of its armed forces assigned to NATO under national control.	A military revolt led by Moslem Hausas overthrows Nigerian Pres. Maj. Gen. Johnson Aguiyi-Ironsi. . . .Katangan gendarmes and white mercenaries seize several cites in the southern Congo (Kinshasa).	U.S. troops begin to withdraw from the Dominican Republic.	South Vietnamese Premier Ky says that he will not be a presidential candidate in the projected 1967 elections.
Aug.	At the U.N., African delegates call for an arms embargo against South Africa.	Three Soviet newspapers say that North Vietnamese pilots are being trained in the Soviet Union to fly supersonic fighters.	Lt. Col. Yakubu Gowan becomes Nigeria's head-of-state.	Argentina suspends the right to strike for labor unions.	Communist Chinese youths called "Red Guards" harass foreigners and ordinary citizens in major Chinese cities. . .Indonesia and Malaysia sign an agreement ending their three-year political confrontation.
Sept.	U.N. Secy. Gen. U Thant criticizes US policy in South Vietnam.	NATO moves its headquarters out of France to Casteau, Belgium.	An assassin stabs South African P.M. Hendrik Verwoerd to death during a Parliamentary session. . . .Ruling National Party elects Justice Min. Balthazar Vorster as South African prime minister.	Last troops of the Latin American peace force leave the Dominican Republic.	Heaviest fighting of the Vietnam War rages south of the demilitarized zone. . .Indonesian Amb.-to-U.S. Lambertus Palar estimates that about 100,000 Indonesians were slain in the aftermath of the aborted 1965 Communist coup.
Oct.	U.N. proclaims the end of South Africa's mandate over South-West Africa (Namibia).	Reports indicate that Hungary's economic situation has improved significantly over the last 10 years.	Lesotho becomes an independent state.	Brazilian voters elect Artur Costa e Silva as president in an unopposed election.	Communist Chinese Red Guards continue their attacks against leading party politicians and extend their criticism to Confucius.
Nov.	U.N. votes 57 to 47 to refuse Communist China admission.	Major flooding causes serious damage in Florence, Italy.	West Bank demonstrators demand that King Hussein take stronger measures agianst Israel. . . .Reports indicate that African guerrillas are making some gains against the Portuguese administration in Angola.	Colombia indicates that it may distribute birth control devices to its citizens.	Savage fighting rages in the Vietnamese Central Highlands between U.S. and Communist forces.
Dec.	U.N. unanimously votes for sanctions against Rhodesia.	West German Parliament elects Kurt Georg Kiesinger as Chancellor. . .French Communists and Socialists agree to work together in the 1967 parliamentary elections.	Rhodesia rejects British terms for ending its rebellion. . . .Jordan refuses to allow Palestinian guerrillas to take up positions near the Israeli border. . . .Jordan accuses Syria of sending saboteurs across its border.	Reports indicate that Brazil is making major economic gains.	A small number of North Korean pilots have reportedly flown planes in North Vietnam.

A	B	C	D	E
Includes developments that affect more than one world region, international organizations and important meetings of major world leaders.	*Includes all domestic and regional developments in Europe, including the Soviet Union, Turkey, Cyprus and Malta.*	*Includes all domestic and regional developments in Africa and the Middle East, including Iraq and Iran and excluding Cyprus, Turkey and Afghanistan.*	*Includes all domestic and regional developments in Latin America, the Caribbean and Canada.*	*Includes all domestic and regional developments in Asia and Pacific nations, extending from Afghanistan through all the Pacific Islands, except Hawaii.*

U.S. Politics & Social Issues	U.S. Foreign Policy & Defense	U.S. Economy & Environment	Science, Technology & Nature	Culture, Leisure & Life Style
Martin Luther King Jr. announces that the Southern Christian Leadership Conference will launch its "first sustained Northern movement" in 1966 and that Chicago will be the target city.	Pres. Johnson announces the resumption of the bombing of North Vietnam. . . .An AP poll of 50 US Senators shows that they are evenly divided about the wisdom of the decision.	Pres. Johnson submits his 1967 fiscal budget to Congress and predicts a $1.8 deficit.	Reports indicate that the US goal of landing a man of the moon by the end of the decade is making steady progress.	Swiss sculptor Alberto Giacometti dies in Chur, Switzerland at 64.
Justice Department files numerous suits for the 1966-1967 academic year against Southern school districts.	Sen. Robert Kennedy (D NY) proposes that the Communist National Liberation Front be admitted to a coalition government in South Vietnam.	Labor Secy. Willard Wirtz announces that February's unemployment figures are the lowest since 1953.	Soviet Union sends two dogs into orbit around the earth.	Elie Abel's account of the 1962 Cuban confrontation, *The Missile Crisis*, is published.
Rioting breaks out in Watts, the black neighborhood in Los Angeles. . . .US Office of Education withholds federal funds from a southern school district for the first time. . . .Birmingham Ala. Mayor Albert Boutwell publicly appeals for qualified black applicants for the city's police force.	Defense Secy. Robert McNamara announces that US military forces in South Vietnam currently total 225,000 and that another 20,000 men will soon be added.	General Motors apologizes to consumer affairs activist Ralph Nader for having initiated an investigation into his private life.	First man-made object to touch another planet, Soviet satellite Venus 3, crashes into Venus.	James Dickey's *Buckdancer's Choice* wins the 1965 National Book Award for poetry.
A federal court outlaws the Mississippi poll tax, the last such tax in the US.	Martin Luther King Jr. calls for a complete pull-out of U.S. troops from South Vietnam.	Labor Department announces that the cost of living for March 1966 is 2.8% above that of March 1965.	World's third heart transplant operation takes place in Houston, Texas.	Richard Morris's *The Peacemakers: The Great Powers and American Independence* wins the Frederic Bancroft Prize for history.
Supreme Court rules that the Fifth Amendment's protection against self-incrimination restricts police interrogation of arrested suspects.	U.S. officials admit for the first time that U.S. troops have fired into Cambodian territory in self-defense.	UAW re-elect Walter Reuther as their president.	U.S. launches Explorer 32 whose mission is to study the various parts of the upper atmosphere.	Arthur Schlesinger's *A Thousand Days* wins the 1965 Pulitzer Prize for history.
Civil rights activist James Meredith is shot during a voter registration march in Mississippi but rejoins the marchers after recuperating from a minor wound.	Anti-Vietnam War New Politics Conference announces that it will begin a search for a presidential candidate for the 1968 elections.	Pres. Johnson says that the problem of inflation is becoming more serious.	Surveyor 1 sends back photos to earth indicating that the moon's surface is safe for a manned craft.	French painter Jean Arp dies in Basel, Switzerland at 78.
Certain civil rights activists criticize the goal of integration for the first time. . .Rioting breaks out in Cleveland and other U.S. cites among young blacks.	Senate Majority leader Mike Mansfield (D Mont.) calls for a reduction of U.S. forces in Europe.	Mexican-American farm workers begin a state-wide march across Texas in protest against the state's minimum wage.	Two U.S. astronauts return to earth in Gemini 10.	Composer Igor Stravinsky conducts a program with the New York Philharmonic.
Martin Luther King Jr. leads a march of 500 blacks through an all-white Chicago neighborhood. . .House of Representatives passes a bill forbidding discrimination in housing for about 40% of the nation's units.	Defense Department issues an October draft call for 46,200 men, the highest monthly figure since May, 1953.	U.S. reports that 1966 appears to be the most inflationary year since 1957.	Reports indicate that 18 Japanese have died so far from diseases related to the 1945 A-bombing of Hiroshima.	A proposed Constitutional amendment to permit voluntary prayer in schools fails to get the necessary two-thirds majority in the Senate.
2,000 National Guardsmen enter San Francisco's black neighborhoods in order to stop rioting.	U.S. Amb. to U.N. Arthur Goldberg assures Jewish leaders that Pres. Johnson is not making U.S. support of Israel dependent on American-Jewish support of the Vietnam War.	California grape pickers elect Cesar Chavez as their chief union bargaining agent.	U.S. spaceship Gemini 11 achieves an unprecedented first orbit "docking" with a target vehicle.	Metropolitan Opera opens its first season in the new opera house at Lincoln Center in N.Y.C.
Reports indicate that Democratic officials are worried about a white "backlash" in reaction to Negro demands.	Pres. Johnson attends a conference of Asian allies in Manilla and visits South Vietnam. . .Reports indicate that few candidates in the upcoming November elections are attacking Pres. Johnson's Vietnam policy.	Treasury Secy. Henry Fowler says that military spending represents a little more than 8% of the GNP.	U.S. doctors report that Vitamin A may inhibit some forms of lung cancer.	Israeli writer Shmuel Agnon wins the Nobel Prize for literature.
Republicans make moderate gains in Congressional and gubernatorial races.	Defense Secy. Robert McNamara says that the Soviet Union may be deploying an anti-ballistic missile system.	Reports indicate that Pres. Johnson will ask for a tax rise in 1967.	U.S. astronauts take photos of the solar eclipse.	Roman Catholic cardinals accuse the Johnson administration of putting pressure on the poor to use birth control.
U.S. Public Health Service says that it may cut funds for segregated Southern hospitals.	U.S. officials acknowledge for the first time that the U.S. planes may have inadvertently bombed Hanoi.	U.S. unemployment rate declines to 3.7%.	U.S. scientists say that weather predictions for two weeks in advance will be possible within 15 years.	A survey indicates that a majority of U.S. Roman Catholics use artificial birth control methods.

F	G	H	I	J
Includes elections, federal-state relations, civil rights and liberties, crime, the judiciary, education, health care, poverty, urban affairs and population.	*Includes formation and debate of U.S. foreign and defense policies, veterans' affairs and defense spending. (Relations with specific foreign countries are usually found under the region concerned.)*	*Includes business, labor, agriculture, taxation, transportation, consumer affairs, monetary and fiscal policy, natural resources, and pollution.*	*Includes worldwide scientific, medical and technological developments, natural phenomena, U.S. weather, natural disasters, and accidents.*	*Includes the arts, religion, scholarship, communications media, sports, entertainment, fashions, fads and social life.*

	World Affairs	Europe	Africa & the Middle East	The Americas	Asia & the Pacific
Jan. 1			Fierce fighting takes place between Iraqi troops and Kurdish guerrillas. . . . Col. Jean Bokassa deposes Pres. David Dacko of the Central African Republic. . . . Rhodesian P.M. Ian Smith offers to resume gasoline shipments to Zambia and to suspend the punitive royalty on coal exports to the neighboring state. . . . Government of Upper Volta arrests several union leaders in a crackdown on political opposition.		V.P. Humphrey confers with Chinese Nationalist Pres. Chiang Kai-shek in Taiwan about the war in Vietnam.
Jan. 2			Zambian Pres. Kenneth Kaunda rejects Rhodesian P.M. Ian Smith's offer for trade liberalization. . . . Upper Volta Pres. Maurice Yameogo decrees a curfew and state of emergency.	Cuban Premier Fidel Castro announces that Communist China will sharply reduce its trade with Cuba this year.	V.P. Humphrey meets with South Korean Pres. Chung Hee Park in Seoul to discuss the Vietnamese situation. . . . Soviet Union charges that the U.S. plans to extend the Vietnam War to Laos and Cambodia.
Jan. 3	Communist-dominated Revolutionary Solidarity Conference begins in Havana, Cuba; disputes immediately erupt between pro-Chinese and pro-Soviet delegations.	Fishing trawlers from the Republic of Ireland and Northern Ireland clash off Ireland's southeastern coast.	Upper Volta union leaders call for a general strike in the country's capital. . . . Dahomey severs diplomatic relations with Communist China due to alleged subversive activities.	Communist-dominated mine union begins a strike in two copper mines in Chile.	Amb.-at-large Averell Harriman confers with Indian P.M. Lal Bahadur Shastri and Pakistani Pres. Mohammed Ayub Khan as part of the administration's "peace drive" in Vietnam. . . . *New York Herald Tribune* reports that some 60,000 Communist Chinese soldiers have recently been shifted to positions along the Sino-Soviet border in Sinkiang Province.
Jan. 4			Rhodesian government reduces the gasoline supplied to commercial bulk users by half in response to the British oil embargo. . . . Iraq accuses Iran of giving sanctuary to Kurdish guerrilla fighters. . . . Central African Republic Pres. Jean Bokassa abolishes the constitution and dissolves the National Assembly. . . . Col. Sangoule Lamizana deposes Pres. Maurice Yameogo in a bloodless coup in Upper Volta.		Talks between India and Pakistan on the Kashmir dispute begin under Soviet sponsorship in Tashkent.
Jan. 5	Chinese Communist delegate Wu Hsueh-tsien charges the Soviet Union with collaborating with the U.S. in a speech before the Revolutionary Solidarity Conference in Havana. . . . U.S. Amb.-to-the-U.N. Arthur Goldberg says the U.S. is ready to withdraw from South Vietnam as soon as its government is "in a position to determine its own future."	France announces that it will keep in step with its Common Market partners by reducing tariffs on their goods by 10%.			Soviet Premier Aleksei Kosygin confers separately with Indian P.M. Lal Shastri and Pakistani Pres. Khan on the Kashmir dispute.
Jan. 6			Iran rejects the Iraqi charges as being "utterly without foundation.". . . Central African Republic Pres. Bokassa ends diplomatic relations with Communist China.	Dominican Republic armed forces seize the government radio station and telecommunications center in Santo Domingo after provisional Pres. Hector Garcia-Godoy strips 34 right-wing officers of their rank and assigns them to diplomatic posts abroad.	Amb.-at-large Averell Harriman confers with Thai Foreign Min. Thanat Khoman in Bangkok. . . . Burmese officials announce a series of nationalization measures aimed at reducing the private sector to about 38% of internal trade.
Jan. 7			Central African Republic Pres. Bokassa says he seized power to foil a plot to disband the army and execute its leaders.	Dominican Republic Armed Forces Min. Francisco Rivera Caminero, one of the military leaders facing expulsion, meets with provisional Pres. Garcia-Godoy in an unsuccessful effort to persuade him to rescind the ouster order.	Amb.-at-large Harriman confers with Japanese Premier Eisaku Sato in Tokyo as part of the continuing U.S. effort to conclude a cease-fire in Vietnam.

A	B	C	D	E
Includes developments that affect more than one world region, international organizations and important meetings of major world leaders.	*Includes all domestic and regional developments in Europe, including the Soviet Union, Turkey, Cyprus and Malta.*	*Includes all domestic and regional developments in Africa and the Middle East, including Iraq and Iran and excluding Cyprus, Turkey and Afghanistan.*	*Includes all domestic and regional developments in Latin America, the Caribbean and Canada.*	*Includes all domestic and regional developments in Asia and Pacific nations, extending from Afghanistan through all the Pacific Islands, except Hawaii.*

U.S. Politics & Social Issues	U.S. Foreign Policy & Defense	U.S. Economy & Environment	Science, Technology & Nature	Culture, Leisure & Life Style	
	U.S. State Dept. postpones all Congressional trips to South Vietnam in the face of widespread disturbances.	N.Y.C. subway and bus workers go on strike. Mayor John Lindsay calls the srike "an act of defiance against eight million people.". . . Gardner Ackley, chairman of Pres. Johnson's Council of Economic Advisers, summons four Bethlehem Steel executives to Washington for a conference on recent price rises.		Pope Paul VI urges the chiefs of states of the major powers to work for an early end to the war in Vietnam.	Jan. 1
Atty. Gen. Nicholas Katzenbach pledges full support of the federal government for voter registration in a speech in Mobile, Ala. . . . Arsonists destroy Negro church near Newton, Ga.					Jan. 2
Atty. Gen. Nicholas Katzenbach meets in Mobile with 12 U.S. Attorneys for Alabama, Georgia, Florida, Louisiana and Mississippi, urging them to promote "fair representation" of blacks on federal juries and among their staff workers.	V.P. Humphrey concludes his five-day tour of the Far East, saying he found no evidence during his trip that North Vietnam is ready to negotiate.	N.Y.C. administration obtains a court order directing the city's transit workers to call off their strike.			Jan. 3
Southern Christian Leadership Conference begins daily marches through Birmingham, Ala. to protest discrimination in voter registration. . . . A House Un-American Activities subcommittee resumes its investigation of the Ku Klux Klan.	U.S. State Department reports that non-communist countries' shipments to North Vietnam have decreased under U.S. pressure.	Transport Workers Union chief Mike Quill goes to jail for defiance of the court order ending the N.Y.C. transit workers strike. . . . A major U.S. steel company, Colorado Fuel and Iron, postpones its scheduled price rise.			Jan. 4
		Administration and steel industry negotiators reach a compromise on increases in the price of structural steel products.			Jan. 5
Chairman John Lewis of the Student Nonviolent Coordinating Committee says SNCC will support "the men in this country who are unwilling to respond to a military draft."				Harold Perry becomes auxiliary bishop of the Roman Catholic archdiocese of New Orleans, the first time since 1875 that a black clergyman has been elevated to a bishopric in the U.S.	Jan. 6
Martin Luther King Jr. announces that his Southern Christian Leadership Conference will launch its "first sustained Northern movement" in Chicago this year. . . . Justice Dept. files suit in Montgomery, Ala. federal court in order to desegregate two Tuskegee restaurants.					Jan. 7

F	G	H	I	J
Includes elections, federal-state relations, civil rights and liberties, crime, the judiciary, education, health care, poverty, urban affairs and population.	*Includes formation and debate of U.S. foreign and defense policies, veterans' affairs and defense spending. (Relations with specific foreign countries are usually found under the region concerned.)*	*Includes business, labor, agriculture, taxation, transportation, consumer affairs, monetary and fiscal policy, natural resources, and pollution.*	*Includes worldwide scientific, medical and technological developments, natural phenomena, U.S. weather, natural disasters, and accidents.*	*Includes the arts, religion, scholarship, communications media, sports, entertainment, fashions, fads and social life.*

	World Affairs	Europe	Africa & the Middle East	The Americas	Asia & the Pacific
Jan. 8		Polish government withdraws the passport of Stefan Cardinal Wyszynski just before his scheduled departure for Rome to attend the 1,000th anniversary of Christianity in Poland. . . . Charles de Gaulle begins his second seven-year term as French President. Michel Debré replaces Valery Giscard d'Estaing as Finance Minister.		Mutinous Dominican Republic Army troops yield their positions to an Inter-American Armed Force.	South Vietnamese forces clash with Communist forces near Saigon.
Jan. 9		A Polish government communique charges that Cardinal Wyszynski had "used his last trip to Rome. . .for political activities damaging. . .the Polish People's Republic."			Amb.-at-large Harriman arrives in Australia and says "Peiping does not want peace, but let's hope sanity prevails in Hanoi and ends this struggle the honorable way."
Jan. 10			Israeli Premier Levi Eshkol announces the formation of an 18-member coalition cabinet. Abba Eban replaces Golda Meir who had served as foreign minister since 1949. . . . Burundi ousts U.S. Amb. Donald Dumont for allegedly contacting anti-government conspirators.		India and Pakistan sign an accord providing for the withdrawal of all their troops from positions occupied as a result of their 1965 border conflict.
Jan. 11	In Cuba, Revolutionary Solidarity Conference's political committee advocates armed force as the only way "to free" the South Arabian protectorates.	Indian P.M. Lal Shastri, 61, dies of a heart attack in Tashkent.	U.S. State Dept. retaliates by asking Burundi to recall its ambassador to Washington.	Floods and landslides kill several hundred people in Rio de Janeiro.	A U.S. military spokesman discloses that a North Vietnamese anti-aircraft battalion is operating in South Vietnam. . . . Pres. Sukarno orders U.S. newsmen to leave Indonesia because of journalistic "lies."
Jan. 12		Soviet Amb.-to-France Valerian Zorin announces that Pres. de Gaulle will visit the Soviet Union in 1966. . . . Soviet newspaper *Izvestia* accuses two Soviet writers, Andrei Sinyavsky and Yuli Daniel, of acting as "tools to fan psychological warfare against the Soviet Union."	Reports indicate that Iran and Iraq have reached agreement on ways to settle their disputes over the Kurds.		A Malaysian exile group in Peiping announces plans "to liberate" Malaysia. . . . *The New York Times* reports that in Indonesia more than 100,000 Communists and their sympathizers have been killed by vigilante groups composed primarily of devout Moslems. . . . V.P. Humphrey and Soviet Premier Aleksei Kosygin arrive in New Delhi for the funeral of Indian P.M. Shastri.
Jan. 13	In Cuba the Revolutionary Solidarity Conference condemns U.S. intervention in the Dominican Republic.		Majority of the delegates at a Commonwealth prime ministers' meeting on Rhodesia uphold Britain's decision not to use force against Rhodesia.		Indonesia recalls its ambassador to Communist China. . . . V.P. Humphrey confers with Soviet Premier Kosygin for two hours in New Delhi.
Jan. 14		French police inspector, Louis Souchon, says that three high government officials were involved in the disappearance and presumed kidnapping of Moroccan leftist Mehdi Ben Barka. . . . Soviet C.P. newspaper *Pravda* charges that two U.S. destroyers off the Soviet Black Sea coast are engaged in "muscle flexing and intelligence operations."			C.P. Central Committee Secy. Aleksandr Shelepin arrives in Hanoi for military assistance talks. . . . In the wake of riots protesting the Declaration of Tashkent, Pakistani Pres. Mohammed Ayub Khan broadcasts an appeal for national unity.
Jan. 15	UNESCO estimates that 43% to 45% of the world's adults are illiterate. . . . Communist-dominated Revolutionary Solidarity Conference ends in Havana with a call to overthrow the "reactionary" regimes of South America.	Soviet C.P. Secy. Leonid Brezhnev and Mongolian C.P. First Secy. Yumzhagin Tsedenbal sign a 20-year mutual assistance treaty in Ulan Bator.			Pres. Sukarno reports that a fact-finding commission estimates that 87,000 people were killed in the aftermath of the abortive 1965 coup in Indonesia. . . . Communist China protests anti-Chinese incidents in Indonesia. . . . State Dept. Secy. Dean Rusk and Amb.-at-large Harriman arrive in Saigon for talks with Premier Cao Ky.
	A	B	C	D	E
	Includes developments that affect more than one world region, international organizations and important meetings of major world leaders.	Includes all domestic and regional developments in Europe, including the Soviet Union, Turkey, Cyprus and Malta.	Includes all domestic and regional developments in Africa and the Middle East, including Iraq and Iran and excluding Cyprus, Turkey and Afghanistan.	Includes all domestic and regional developments in Latin America, the Caribbean and Canada.	Includes all domestic and regional developments in Asia and Pacific nations, extending from Afghanistan through all the Pacific Islands, except Hawaii.

U.S. Politics & Social Issues	U.S. Foreign Policy & Defense	U.S. Economy & Environment	Science, Technology & Nature	Culture, Leisure & Life Style	
Martin Luther King Jr. says: "I would be the last person to condemn someone who on the basis of conscience is a conscientious objector.". . . Roy Wilkins, executive director of the National Association for the Advancement of Colored People, says that the NAACP "disassociates itself" from the SNCC statement.	Senate majority leader Mike Mansfield (D, Mont.) says that in Vietnam "a majority of the population remains under nominal government control but (the) dominance of the countryside rests largely in the hands of the Viet Cong.				Jan. 8
	Prof. Staughton Lynd returns to New York after a 10-day visit to North Vietnam.				Jan. 9
Ga. House of Representatives votes by 184 to 12 not to seat State Rep.-elect Julian Bond because he publicly opposes U.S. policy in Vietnam and backs the avoidance of the draft. . . . Vernon Dahmer, 58, who had been active in voter registration, dies of burns from a Molotov cocktail explosion in Hattiesburg, Miss. In Washington, Atty. Gen. Nicholas Katzenbach announces that an FBI investigation is underway.	White House Press Secy. Bill Moyers acknowledges that a U.S. official recently met with a North Vietnamese representative.	N.Y.C. Mayor John Lindsay criticizes the striking transit workers and says that New York "will not capitulate before the lawless demands of a single power group. It will not allow the power brokers. . .to dictate to this city the terms under which it will exist."		Barbara Tuchman's *The Proud Tower: A Portrait of the World before the War—1890-1914* is published.	Jan. 10
Atty. Gen. Katzenbach announces the development of a "battle plan against crime."	*St. Louis Post-Dispatch* reports that "substantial numbers" of Thai troops have infiltrated into Laos with the knowledge and possible assistance of the U.S. The U.S. State Dept. says the article is "totally without foundation."	AFL-CIO Pres. George Meany says he thinks Mayor Lindsay is "trying very hard to settle this (strike) and is being fair to everyone concerned."		Alberto Giacometti, the Swiss sculptor, dies in Chur, Switzerland at 64.	Jan. 11
	In his State-of-the-Union Message, Pres. Johnson pledges that the U.S. will stay in Vietnam "until aggression has stopped.". . . Leonard Epstein, an official of an American company working in the missile field, asserts that Vadim Isakov, a UNICEF employee, tried to buy advanced missile components.				Jan. 12
Pres. Johnson announces the appointment of Dr. Robert Weaver as Secretary of Housing and Urban Development. Dr. Weaver is the first black cabinet officer.		N.Y.C.'s 12-day subway and bus strike ends.			Jan. 13
					Jan. 14
					Jan. 15

F	G	H	I	J
Includes elections, federal-state relations, civil rights and liberties, crime, the judiciary, education, health care, poverty, urban affairs and population.	*Includes formation and debate of U.S. foreign and defense policies, veterans' affairs and defense spending. (Relations with specific foreign countries are usually found under the region concerned.)*	*Includes business, labor, agriculture, taxation, transportation, consumer affairs, monetary and fiscal policy, natural resources, and pollution.*	*Includes worldwide scientific, medical and technological developments, natural phenomena, U.S. weather, natural disasters, and accidents.*	*Includes the arts, religion, scholarship, communications media, sports, entertainment, fashions, fads and social life.*

	World Affairs	Europe	Africa & the Middle East	The Americas	Asia & the Pacific
Jan. 16		In a sermon in Warsaw, Polish Cardinal Wyszynski denies charges made by the Polish Communist Party that he engaged in disloyal activity when he encouraged Polish bishops to work with West German bishops for reconciliation between the two states.	Maj. Gen. Johnson Aguiyi-Ironsi assumes power in Nigeria and abolishes Parliament.		Communist China denies what it calls Soviet rumors accusing it of impeding the shipment of Soviet military equipment to North Vietnam through China. . . . A joint U.S.-South Vietnamese communique restates South Vietnam's demands that "all aggression" must stop before the Ky government would attend a peace conference.
Jan. 17		A U.S. Air Force plane carrying nuclear weapons crashes in Spain. . . . West German Refugee Affairs Min. Johann-Baptist Gradl says that West Germans would have to make territorial "sacrifices" if they expected progress toward reunification. . . . Foreign Ministers of the six Common Market countries meet in Luxembourg. This is the first joint meeting since July 1, 1965, when France began its boycott of EEC meetings because of its opposition to growing EEC supranationality.	Rhodesian P.M. Ian Smith says that he is willing to reopen negotiations with Britain.		An additional 7,000 U.S. combat troops land in South Vietnam, raising the American force level to nearly 190,000 men.
Jan. 18			Reports from Cairo indicate that Egyptian Pres. Nasser and Saudi Arabian King Faisal have agreed on a plebiscite to determine the type of government in Yemen.		Viet Cong ambushes a South Vietnamese force near Saigon.
Jan. 19	U.N. approves 82 development projects costing about $254.5 million.	French Information Secy., Yvon Bourges, reads a government statement, reportedly drafted by Pres de Gaulle, saying that the Ben Barka abduction had been "organized abroad with the complicity of agents of French special services or police."	Britain completes its infantry withdrawal from Tripoli, Libya. . . . Ali Fitouhi, Iranian ambassador to Lebanon, says that diplomatic relations with Egypt will only resume when Egyptian President Nasser stops "disseminating sedition" to Iran's Arab population.		Congress Party elects Indira Gandhi as India's third prime minister. . . . A report in the Chinese Communist Party newspaper Jenmin Jih Pao indicates that a conflict has developed between army professionals and C.P. members over the control of the Chinese Army.
Jan. 20		Britain bans the import of chrome from Rhodesia. . . . Presiding French judge in the Ben Barka case, Louis Zollinger, says he is convinced that Moroccan Interior Min. Mohammad Oufkir organized the kidnapping. . . . U.S. citizen, Newcomb Mott, dies aboard a Trans-Siberian train that was taking him to a labor camp to which he had been sentenced for illegally crossing the Soviet border.			Silence descends upon the Vietnamese battlefield as a three-day truce marking the Vietnamese New Year begins. . . . Australian P.M. Robert Menzies announces his retirement. Menzies headed the Australian government since 1949.
Jan. 21		Soviet foreign ministry says that Newcomb Mott cut his own throat. . . . Spanish government announces that it will no longer permit military aircraft from NATO nations (except Britain) to fly over Spain to and from Gibraltar.	Despite a series of recent military challenges to his rule, General Johnson Aguiyi-Ironsi announces the formation of a new Nigerian government.	Peru asks for a meeting of the OAS to discuss the recent Communist-dominated conference in Havana.	Indian government estimates that 12 million Indians face probable starvation unless foreign nations donate food.
Jan. 22				Right-wing Dominican army officers leave their country for diplomatic assignments overseas.	Thai authorities accuse Cambodia of shelling a Thai village for the second time in three weeks.
Jan. 23		France and Morocco recall their ambassadors from each other's capitals.			The New York Times reports that U.S. reconnaissance planes have recently spotted a squadron of 25 Chinese MiG's in North Vietnam.

A	B	C	D	E
Includes developments that affect more than one world region, international organizations and important meetings of major world leaders.	Includes all domestic and regional developments in Europe, including the Soviet Union, Turkey, Cyprus and Malta.	Includes all domestic and regional developments in Africa and the Middle East, including Iraq and Iran and excluding Cyprus, Turkey and Afghanistan.	Includes all domestic and regional developments in Latin America, the Caribbean and Canada.	Includes all domestic and regional developments in Asia and Pacific nations, extending from Afghanistan through all the Pacific Islands, except Hawaii.

U.S. Politics & Social Issues	U.S. Foreign Policy & Defense	U.S. Economy & Environment	Science, Technology & Nature	Culture, Leisure & Life Style	
	In an article appearing in *Harper's* magazine, retired Lt. Gen. James Gavin proposes that the U.S. withdraw its forces to "enclaves" along the South Vietnamese coast and negotiate to end the war.				Jan. 16
				Truman Capote's *In Cold Blood* is published.	Jan. 17
					Jan. 18
A U.S. District Judge orders the Alabama Macon County Jury Commission to compile a new jury list which does not discriminate against blacks.					Jan. 19
	Pres. Johnson submits to Congress his proposed Constitutional amendments for making House members' terms four years instead of two and for abolishing the Electoral College. . . . Pres. Johnson calls on North Vietnam to respond positively to the halt in U.S. air raids.				Jan. 20
	Accused spy Vadim Isakov resigns from UNICEF in order to return to the Soviet Union.				Jan. 21
	U.S. State Department calls for a full investigation of the alleged suicide of U.S. citizen Newcomb Mott.				Jan. 22
	Secy. Dean Rusk expresses hope that the U.S.' European allies will send troops to fight in Vietnam.				Jan. 23

F	G	H	I	J
Includes elections, federal-state relations, civil rights and liberties, crime, the judiciary, education, health care, poverty, urban affairs and population.	Includes formation and debate of U.S. foreign and defense policies, veterans' affairs and defense spending. (Relations with specific foreign countries are usually found under the region concerned.)	Includes business, labor, agriculture, taxation, transportation, consumer affairs, monetary and fiscal policy, natural resources, and pollution.	Includes worldwide scientific, medical and technological developments, natural phenomena, U.S. weather, natural disasters, and accidents.	Includes the arts, religion, scholarship, communications media, sports, entertainment, fashions, fads and social life.

	World Affairs	Europe	Africa & the Middle East	The Americas	Asia & the Pacific
Jan. 24					U.S. forces clash with Communist troops near Saigon.
Jan. 25		Soviet leader Leonid Brezhnev is appointed chairman of a commission to work out a new program for collective farms.			Indian and Pakistani troops begin withdrawing from frontier positions that have been held since the end of the 1965 border fighting.
Jan. 26		Radio Moscow suggests that Newcomb Mott might have committed suicide because he felt abandoned by the U.S. embassy in Moscow.			Indian Prime Minister Indira Gandhi and Pakistani Pres. Ayub Khan reaffirm their support of the Tashkent accord.
Jan. 27	U.N. Disarmament Conference reconvenes in Geneva.	British Foreign Secy. Michael Stewart says that Britain's current force of 55,000 men in Singapore, Malaysia and Borneo will be maintained as long as a threat from Indonesia exists.			South Vietnamese and Communist forces clash near Saigon.
Jan. 28			40-50 Moroccan students seize the Moroccan embassy in Algiers and hold it for two hours to protest the Ben Barka abduction.		Rioting and looting break out in the southern Indian state of Kerala during a general strike called to protest a cut in the rice ration.
Jan. 29					President Ho Chi Minh of North Vietnam calls a U.S. offer for unconditional peace talks ". . . an effort to fool public opinion. . ." He says that if the United States really wants peace it will have to recognize the National Front for the Liberation of South Vietnam as ". . . the sole representative of the people of South Vietnam. . ."
Jan. 30		Britain bans all trade with Rhodesia.			South Vietnamese and Communist forces fight in the Mekong Delta.
Jan. 31		West German government indicates that it has payed East Germany about $24 million since 1964 for the release of 2,600 political prisoners. . . . Two coal miners are killed, apparently inadvertently, by policemen during a riot protesting the closing of unprofitable coal mines in Belgium.			South Vietnamese attack a Viet Cong unit near Saigon.
Feb. 1				Queen Elizabeth begins a tour of British Commonwealth countries in the Caribbean.	Chinese and Malays riot for several hours at a job training center in Singapore.

A	B	C	D	E
Includes developments that affect more than one world region, international organizations and important meetings of major world leaders.	Includes all domestic and regional developments in Europe, including the Soviet Union, Turkey, Cyprus and Malta.	Includes all domestic and regional developments in Africa and the Middle East, including Iraq and Iran and excluding Cyprus, Turkey and Afghanistan.	Includes all domestic and regional developments in Latin America, the Caribbean and Canada.	Includes all domestic and regional developments in Asia and Pacific nations, extending from Afghanistan through all the Pacific Islands, except Hawaii.

U.S. Politics & Social Issues	U.S. Foreign Policy & Defense	U.S. Economy & Environment	Science, Technology & Nature	Culture, Leisure & Life Style	
Rev. Martin Luther King Jr. urges Negroes to "go into the highways and byways" in order to encourage voter registration. . . . 25 Negroes block traffic in central Harlem in a rent strike protest. . . . Justice Dept. files suit against the owners of the Choctaw and Delmar Motels in Bogalusa, La. for refusing to accommodate Negroes. . . . Mississippi Supreme Court reverses the grand larceny conviction of M.L. Hopkins, a Negro, on the grounds that no Negroes had been considered to serve on his jury.	Sen. Eugene McCarthy (D Minn.) urges the Foreign Relations Committee to make a "full and complete" study of the effects of the CIA on U.S. foreign relations. . . . Key members of the Senate Foreign Relations Committee voice strong support for continuance of the bombing pause. . . . Defense Secy. Robert McNamara says there is no evidence of Chinese planes in North Vietnam.	Pres. Johnson submits his budget for fiscal 1967 to Congress which foresees a $1-8 billion deficit, the smallest deficit in seven years.			Jan. 24
In Jackson, Miss. U.S. District Judge Harold Cox orders five local restaurants to serve customers regardless of race.					Jan. 25
	An AP poll of 50 U.S. senators shows that 25 favor and 25 oppose a resumption of the bombing of North Vietnam. . . . U.S. government says that it had rejected a suggested exchange of Mott and a Soviet spy.				Jan. 26
	U.S. State Dept. says that Soviet authorities told Mott that his parents and his country had abandoned him "to make him more pliable at the trial."				Jan. 27
	U.S. Sen. J. W. Fulbright (D Ark.) challenges the legality of the U.S. military involvement in South Vietnam.				Jan. 28
					Jan. 29
Southern Regional Council, a nonprofit research organization, reports that 17 people died in the South during 1965 in race-related violence.					Jan. 30
	Pres. Johnson announces the resumption of the bombing of North Vietnam; Ex-Presidents Truman and Eisenhower support the decision, but most governments express their regrets.			*The Fall of Paris: The Siege and the Commune, 1870-1871* by the English historian, Alistair Horne, is published.	Jan. 31
Police remove about 110 Negroes from a deactivated Air Force base in Greenville, Miss. following a two-day protest against bad housing conditions.	Pres. Johnson requests the smallest amount of foreign aid in the program's 18-year history.				Feb. 1
F	G	H	I	J	
Includes elections, federal-state relations, civil rights and liberties, crime, the judiciary, education, health care, poverty, urban affairs and population.	*Includes formation and debate of U.S. foreign and defense policies, veterans' affairs and defense spending. (Relations with specific foreign countries are usually found under the region concerned.)*	*Includes business, labor, agriculture, taxation, transportation, consumer affairs, monetary and fiscal policy, natural resources, and pollution.*	*Includes worldwide scientific, medical and technological developments, natural phenomena, U.S. weather, natural disasters, and accidents.*	*Includes the arts, religion, scholarship, communications media, sports, entertainment, fashions, fads and social life.*	

	World Affairs	Europe	Africa & the Middle East	The Americas	Asia & the Pacific
Feb. 2	U.N. Security Council votes to debate a U.S. resolution calling for an international conference on the Vietnam War.	Cypriote Pres. Makarios and Greek Premier Stephanos Stephanopoulos reaffirm their support of Cyprus' ultimate incorporation into Greece.			1,000 national policemen and 1,000 civil servants join anti-government demonstrators in Hue. . . . Communist China accuses the USSR of supporting alleged U.S. "military encirclement of China."
Feb. 3		Belgian government announces that no coal miners will be dismissed until new jobs are found for them.			South Vietnamese forces clash with the Viet Cong near Saigon.
Feb. 4		Turkisk P.M. Suleyman Demirel declares that Turkey will not accept Cypriote union with Greece.	The New York Times reports that in December 1965 a Soviet delegation to Cairo refused to sell atomic weapons to Egypt but offered a guarantee of nuclear protection if Israel developed a nuclear capability.		U.S. forces maul a Viet Cong battalion near Saigon.
Feb. 5					Communist forces attack a U.S. supply base near Saigon.
Feb. 6				Costa Rican voters elect Jose Trejos Fernandez as president of one of Latin America's few stable democracies. . . . Cuban Premier Fidel Castro accuses Communist China of "betraying" the Cuban revolution.	Viet Cong ambush a South Vietnamese force.
Feb. 7		West German Chancellor Ludwig Erhard meets with Pres. de Gaulle in Paris. . . . East German border guards kill an East German attempting to escape to West Berlin.		Eighteen Latin American states file a formal protest at the U.N. protesting the "subversive aims" of the recent Communist-dominated conference in Havana.	In a major military operation, U.S. troops move into the Central Highlands in a search and destroy mission.
Feb. 8		French Pres. de Gaulle and West German Chancellor Ludwig Erhard end two days of talks in Paris amid signs of continuing differences.	Rhodesia forbids newspapers from mentioning that they have undergone censorship.		India and Pakistan restore phone communications.
Feb. 9			Liberia's Parliament grants Pres. William Tubman emergency powers for 12 months.	Troops fire on student demonstrators in Santo Domingo inciting trade unions to call for strikes.	Viet Cong attack a South Vietnamese force near Saigon.
Feb. 10		French government arrests Maj. Marcel Le Roy of the French counter-intelligence service in connection with the Ben Barka affair. . . . Trial of two Soviet writers accused of "anti-Soviet" agitation begins in Moscow. Fifty to 75 Soviet students sympathetic to the defendants are on hand. In an unusual development both authors deny their guilt during the proceedings.			Indian and Pakistani military commanders agree to reduce their armed forces in Kashmir to the 1949 level. . . . V.P. Humphrey flys to Saigon for a three-day inspection of South Vietnam's rural pacification programs and U.S. troop installations.
Feb. 11		Belgian P.M. Pierre Harmel resigns from a coalition cabinet.	Rhodesian government bans non-Rhodesian Africans from working in Rhodesia.	Dominican Republic students continue to demonstrate for the departure of remaining right-wing military leaders.	South Vietnamese and Communist forces clash near Saigon.
	A	B	C	D	E
	Includes developments that affect more than one world region, international organizations and important meetings of major world leaders.	Includes all domestic and regional developments in Europe, including the Soviet Union, Turkey, Cyprus and Malta.	Includes all domestic and regional developments in Africa and the Middle East, including Iraq and Iran and excluding Cyprus, Turkey and Afghanistan.	Includes all domestic and regional developments in Latin America, the Caribbean and Canada.	Includes all domestic and regional developments in Asia and Pacific nations, extending from Afghanistan through all the Pacific Islands, except Hawaii.

U.S. Politics & Social Issues	U.S. Foreign Policy & Defense	U.S. Economy & Environment	Science, Technology & Nature	Culture, Leisure & Life Style	
House votes to cite seven Ku Klux Klan leaders for contempt of Congress for refusing to supply records. . . . A gunman wounds two white civil rights workers in Kosciusko, Miss.	U.S. State Dept. agrees to sell "a limited number" of advance fighter-bombers to Jordan.			Violinist Jascha Heifetz celebrates his 65th birthday.	Feb. 2
	U.S. State Dept. takes preliminary steps to revoke the passports of seven Americans who recently visited North Vietnam.		A Soviet space vehicle makes the first successful landing on the moon and transmits photos of the lunar surface back to earth.		Feb. 3
Justice Dept. files suit against the St. Louis AFL-CIO construction union for alleged discrimination.	Pres. Johnson announces that major food shipments will be sent to India in face of the threat of starvation.				Feb. 4
	About 100 anti-war veterans try to return medals, discharges and separation papers to Pres. Johnson in Washington. . . . U.S. State Dept. acknowledges the sale of Patton tanks to Israel. . . . Anti-war demonstrations involving about 1,000 people take place in N.Y.C.				Feb. 5
	Pres. Johnson confers in Honolulu with South Vietnamese Premier Cao Ky.				Feb. 6
Justice Dept. files numerous suits for the 1966-1967 academic year against Southern school districts. . . . Justice Dept. files suit against two Mississippi law officers accused of beating five civil rights workers. . . . U.S. Office of Education recommends that federal aid be cut off to several southern school districts because of failure to comply with civil rights legislation.					Feb. 7
	Pres. Johnson gives an optimistic report on the Honolulu conference.	Labor Secy. Willard Wirtz announces that February's unemployment figures are the lowest since 1953.		Vatican says that the office responsible for the censorship of books has been abolished.	Feb. 8
					Feb. 9
A federal court rules in Atlanta that the Ga. House of Representatives violated no "fundamental federal right" in refusing to seat Julian Bond.	In televised hearings on U.S. policy in Vietnam, George Kennan says: "There is more respect to be won in the opinion of the world by a resolute and courageous liquidation of unsound positions than in the most stubborn pursuit of extravagant or unpromising objectives."	About half of Newark N.J.'s public school teachers go on strike. . . . Administration supporters fail to break a filibuster led by Sen. Everett Dirksen against a proposal to repeal Section 14(b) of the Taft-Hartley Act.		Elie Abel's *The Missile Crisis*, an account of the 1962 Cuban confrontation, is published.	Feb. 10
					Feb. 11

F	G	H	I	J
Includes elections, federal-state relations, civil rights and liberties, crime, the judiciary, education, health care, poverty, urban affairs and population.	Includes formation and debate of U.S. foreign and defense policies, veterans' affairs and defense spending. (Relations with specific foreign countries are usually found under the region concerned.)	Includes business, labor, agriculture, taxation, transportation, consumer affairs, monetary and fiscal policy, natural resources, and pollution.	Includes worldwide scientific, medical and technological developments, natural phenomena, U.S. weather, natural disasters, and accidents.	Includes the arts, religion, scholarship, communications media, sports, entertainment, fashions, fads and social life.

	World Affairs	Europe	Africa & the Middle East	The Americas	Asia & the Pacific
Feb. 12		British P.M. Harold Wilson announces that the railroad union has called off its national strike scheduled for Feb. 13.		Cuba announces the conclusion of a Soviet-Cuban trade agreement for 1966. . . . Dominican Pres. Hector Garcia-Godoy orders troops back to their quarters in a bid to ease tensions.	Viet Cong launch a surprise attack against South Vietnamese troops.
Feb. 13				Gunfire kills three more people in fighting between police and demonstrators in the Dominican Republic.	Indonesian Pres. Sukarno says that the anti-Malaysia "confrontation" will continue despite the Philippines' intention to recognize Malaysia. . . . V.P. Humphrey flies to Bangkok and assures Thai leaders that the US has not pressed South Vietnam to negotiate with the Viet Cong.
Feb. 14		A Soviet court sentences Andrei Sinyavsky and Yuli Daniel to seven and five years of hard labor respectively for "anti-Soviet" publications.			Australian currency is converted to a dollars-and-cents decimal system.
Feb. 15		France makes public a letter from Pres. de Gaulle to North Vietnam offering to help negotiate a settlement of the Vietnam War.			Reports from Vientiane, Laos, indicate that North Vietnamese military units are expanding the Ho Chi Minh supply trail in eastern Laos.
Feb. 16		France approves measures implementing its fifth economic plan.	Rhodesia begins to receive oil shipped from South Africa.		U.S. troops clash with Communist forces near Saigon.
Feb. 17		Pres. de Gaulle is reported to have told Pres. Johnson that military intervention in Vietnam is self-defeating.	A French satellite is launched into orbit from a base in Algeria.	Colombian students riot in Bogota after learning of the death of a university professor turned guerrilla leader in a Feb. 15 clash with government troops.	Viet Cong ambush South Vietnamese troops in the Mekong Delta.
Feb. 18					Prime Min. Indira Gandhi confers with four representatives of a movement to win independence for Nagaland, an Indian province.
Feb. 19		Hungary announces that an undisclosed number of persons have been arrested for "conspiring" against the government.			South Vietnamese troops attack a Viet Cong base near Saigon.
Feb. 20			Scheduled round of Yemeni peace talks fails to take place because the royalist delegation allied with Saudi Arabia refuses to attend.		U.S. and Viet Cong forces clash near Saigon.
Feb. 21	British P.M. Harold Wilson begins an official visit to the Soviet Union.	British officials and African leaders of the Bechuanaland Protectorate agree that independence will be granted on Sept. 30. The new country will be known as Botswana. . . . French Pres. de Gaulle announces that France will assume control of all foreign military bases on its territory by April, 1969. . . . De Gaulle declares that France will continue to adhere to the 1949 North Atlantic Treaty and will participate in the alliance's political meetings.	Saudi Arabia appeals for U.S. diplomatic and military aid if Egypt resumes fighting in Yemen.		Indonesian Pres Sukarno dismisses anti-Communist Gen. Abdul Nasuton in a campaign to slow the anti-Communist movement that began after the abortive Oct. 1965 coup.

A	B	C	D	E
Includes developments that affect more than one world region, international organizations and important meetings of major world leaders.	*Includes all domestic and regional developments in Europe, including the Soviet Union, Turkey, Cyprus and Malta.*	*Includes all domestic and regional developments in Africa and the Middle East, including Iraq and Iran and excluding Cyprus, Turkey and Afghanistan.*	*Includes all domestic and regional developments in Latin America, the Caribbean and Canada.*	*Includes all domestic and regional developments in Asia and Pacific nations, extending from Afghanistan through all the Pacific Islands, except Hawaii.*

U.S. Politics & Social Issues	U.S. Foreign Policy & Defense	U.S. Economy & Environment	Science, Technology & Nature	Culture, Leisure & Life Style	
	Pres. Johnson authorizes a blacklist of non-Communist and Polish ships that trade with North Vietnam.				Feb. 12
	State Dept. warns U.S. citizens planning to visit Russia that they might be treated roughly if they got into trouble with Soviet authorities.				Feb. 13
		Newark N.J. school teachers return to work after agreeing to a fact-finding panel. . . . Treasury Secy. Henry Fowler announces that the U.S. 1965 balance of payments deficit was $1.299 billion.			Feb. 14
American Indians in the state of Washington stage a "fish-in" in protest against state laws which forbid net fishing.				National Institute of Arts & Letters awards its Gold Medals to composer Virgil Thomson and sculptor Jacques Lipchitz.	Feb. 15
		U.S. stock market suffers a sharp seven-point loss.		World Council of Churches calls for a cease-fire in Vietnam.	Feb. 16
Justice Dept. reports that seven executions took place in four states during 1965.				Pope Paul announces changes liberalizing the fasting and abstinence rules for Roman Catholics. . . . Hans Hofmann, the German-born abstract expressionist painter, dies in New York at the age of 85.	Feb. 17
	On the last day of nationally televised hearings on Vietnam, State Secy. Dean Rusk defends U.S. policy.	Amalgamated Clothing Workers Union becomes the first AFL-CIO union to question Pres. Johnson's Vietnam policy.			Feb. 18
	Sen. Robert Kennedy proposes that the National Liberation Front, the political arm of the Viet Cong, be "admitted to a share of power and responsibility" in a future coalition government in South Vietnam.				Feb. 19
					Feb. 20
A U.S. District Court charges Deputy Sheriff Wayne Humphries of Mitchell County, Ga. with the beating of a Negro farm worker who had enrolled his children in a previously all-white school. . . . A white motorist fires into a crowd of 150 Negroes picketing a supermarket; five demonstrators are wounded. Later in the day the assailant is arrested. . . . New Jersey Supreme Court rules that a barber's refusal to cut the hair of Negro customers violates anti-discrimination laws.		AFL-CIO Executive Council disagrees with the administration's wage and price guidelines.			Feb. 21

F	G	H	I	J
Includes elections, federal-state relations, civil rights and liberties, crime, the judiciary, education, health care, poverty, urban affairs and population.	Includes formation and debate of U.S. foreign and defense policies, veterans' affairs and defense spending. (Relations with specific foreign countries are usually found under the region concerned.)	Includes business, labor, agriculture, taxation, transportation, consumer affairs, monetary and fiscal policy, natural resources, and pollution.	Includes worldwide scientific, medical and technological developments, natural phenomena, U.S. weather, natural disasters, and accidents.	Includes the arts, religion, scholarship, communications media, sports, entertainment, fashions, fads and social life.

	World Affairs	Europe	Africa & the Middle East	The Americas	Asia & the Pacific
Feb. 22		British Defense Min. Denis Healey announces cuts in defense spending and the projected withdrawal of British troops from Aden in 1968.	Ugandan Prime Min. Milton Obote seizes all government power and arrests five cabinet ministers. . . . UAR Pres. Gamal Nasser threatens to keep his estimated 70,000 troops in Yemen another five years unless an acceptable Yemeni government is established. . . . Pres. Nasser denounces U.S. arms sale to Israel and accuses the West of fostering "right-wing liberation movements, conspiring against the Arab people and placing them within spheres of Western influence."		Communist China charges that Cuban Premier Fidel Castro has "added his voice to the anti-Chinese chorus."
Feb. 23			Syrian radicals led by Maj. Gen. Salah Jedid oust P.M. Salah al-Bitar in a bloody coup.		The New York Times reports that about 96,000 South Vietnamese soldiers deserted in 1965.
Feb. 24		British P.M. Harold Wilson returns to London where he relates that Soviet officials offered to exchange Gerald Brooke, a British lecturer jailed in 1965, for two Soviet spys. Wilson declares that such an exchange would set a dangerous precedent and would lead to additional arrests of British tourists.	Ghanaian military leaders depose Pres. Kwame Nkrumah in a violent coup which reportedly involved the deaths of 11 Russians. . . . A gunman murders South Yemeni Trade Union Congress Pres. Ali Hussein el-Qadhi in Aden.		U.S. forces surprise a Viet Cong force near Saigon.
Feb. 25			Syrian Damascus radio says that the Syrian military junta has named Yussef Zayen as premier.		Indian and Pakistani troops complete their withdrawal from the border positions they seized during the 1965 fighting.
Feb. 26			British troops break up a demonstration of about 1,000 rock-throwing rioters in Aden.	Dominican Pres. Garcia-Godoy grants amnesties to a group of rightists who revolted against the central government in Nov. 1965.	South Vietnamese troops fight a Viet Cong battalion to a standstill.
Feb. 27				Sporadic student unrest takes place in the Dominican Republic.	U.S. troops clash with Viet Cong in the Central Highlands.
Feb. 28		British Foreign Secy. Michael Stewart says that Britain has agreed to bring its dispute with Spain over Gibraltar to the conference table despite Spain's economic pressure against Gibraltar. . . . British P.M. Harold Wilson announces that new elections will be held on March. 31.	Organization of African Unity meets in Addis Ababa and splits over the question of Ghanaian representation.		An Indian ethnic group, the Mizo, launch an armed revolt against Indian rule near the Burmese border.
March 1		East Germany formally applies for U.N. membership for the first time.	Ghana's new government orders the expulsion of Soviet, Chinese Communist and East German technicians and teachers. . . . Maj. Gen Hafez Assad becomes Syria's new defense minister.		
March 2			Guinean Pres. Sékou Touré warmly welcomes ousted Pres. Kwame Nkrumah to Guinea on his return from Moscow.	Alberto Heber Usher succeeds Washington Beltran as president of the National Council in Uruguay.	South Vietnamese forces clash with the Viet Cong near Saigon.

A	B	C	D	E
Includes developments that affect more than one world region, international organizations and important meetings of major world leaders.	Includes all domestic and regional developments in Europe, including the Soviet Union, Turkey, Cyprus and Malta.	Includes all domestic and regional developments in Africa and the Middle East, including Iraq and Iran and excluding Cyprus, Turkey and Afghanistan.	Includes all domestic and regional developments in Latin America, the Caribbean and Canada.	Includes all domestic and regional developments in Asia and Pacific nations, extending from Afghanistan through all the Pacific Islands, except Hawaii.

U.S. Politics & Social Issues	U.S. Foreign Policy & Defense	U.S. Economy & Environment	Science, Technology & Nature	Culture, Leisure & Life Style	
	In a clarifying statement Sen. Robert Kennedy says that he did not propose that the NLF be "automatically" included in a coalition government but that it should not be "automatically excluded."	George Meany announces that the AFL-CIO will contribute $30,000 to a program designed to prepare Negroes for union apprenticeship tests.	Soviet Union sends two dogs into orbit around the earth.	First North American performance of Alberto Ginastera's opera *Don Rodrigo* opens in New York.	Feb. 22
In a 5-4 decision, the Supreme Court overturns breach-of-peace convictions of five Negroes who attempted to integrate a public library in Clinton, La. . . . Nelson Edwards, a Negro who recently integrated an all-white Detroit neighborhood, reports that he has suffered frequent harassment.	Defense Secy. Robert McNamara declares that Communist China "already has named Thailand as its next victim.". . . V.P. Humphrey returns to Washington after a 14-day tour of nine Asian nations.	Pres. Johnson sends Congress a special message on conservation, emphasizing pollution control.			Feb. 23
Birmingham, Ala. Negroes begin a boycott of white merchants practicing discrimination.					Feb. 24
		AFL-CIO Executive Council declares its "unstinting support" of Pres. Johnson's Vietnam policy.			Feb. 25
Ohio Civil Rights Commission charges that systematic discrimination exists in the Cincinnati building trades unions. . . . Talmadge Hayer, a member of the Black Muslims, admits to having murdered Malcolm X.			National Safety Council reports a record 48,500 traffic deaths for 1965.		Feb. 26
	Sen. Robert Kennedy says that the U.S. should realize that the Viet Cong "are going to end up, in some way or another, within the governmental structure of South Vietnam."				Feb. 27
					Feb. 28
Pres. Johnson sends Congress new health proposals which increase government programs.	U.S. Senate rejects an amendment to repeal the 1964 Gulf of Tonkin resolution by 92 to 5.		The first man-made object to touch another planet, unmanned Soviet spaceship Venus 3, crashes into the planet Venus.		March 1
	U.S. acknowledges that one of its hydrogen bombs is missing from the recent B-52 bomber accident in Spain. . . . Defense Secy. Robert McNamara announces that U.S. military forces currently total 215,000 men and that another 20,000 will soon be added.	Pres. Johnson sends Congress proposals to improve mass transportation.			March 2

F	G	H	I	J
Includes elections, federal-state relations, civil rights and liberties, crime, the judiciary, education, health care, poverty, urban affairs and population.	Includes formation and debate of U.S. foreign and defense policies, veterans' affairs and defense spending. (Relations with specific foreign countries are usually found under the region concerned.)	Includes business, labor, agriculture, taxation, transportation, consumer affairs, monetary and fiscal policy, natural resources, and pollution.	Includes worldwide scientific, medical and technological developments, natural phenomena, U.S. weather, natural disasters, and accidents.	Includes the arts, religion, scholarship, communications media, sports, entertainment, fashions, fads and social life.

	World Affairs	Europe	Africa & the Middle East	The Americas	Asia & the Pacific
March 3	U.S., British and French U.N. delegations reject the East German request for U.N. membership.			Dominican Republic Pres. Hector Garcia-Godoy sets June 1 as the date for presidential elections.	Regular Indian troops begin to move into the Mizo's region in order to quell an uprising. . . . U.S. Air Force jets bomb targets in North Vietnam's Red River Valley for the first time since the bombing resumed on January 31.
March 4			U.S., Britain and eight African countries recognize Ghana's new government.		U.S. planes carry out their heaviest attack on North Vietnam since the beginning of the raids in February 1965.
March 5		Soviet newspaper *Izvestia* says that collective farmers will be allowed to maintain private plots.			
March 6		Austrian Chancellor Josef Klaus's People's Party wins an absolute parliamentary majority in national elections.		Guatemalan voters give Julio Cesar Mendez Montenegro a plurality in presidential elections.	U.S. troops clash with the Viet Cong 50 miles from Saigon.
March 7					Communist and South Vietnamese forces battle in the Central Highlands.
March 8		*Le Monde* (Paris) reports that France had a $1.1 billion balance of payments surplus in 1965.			Australia announces it will include 1,500 draftees in the 4,500 reinforcements to be sent to South Vietnam in June.
March 9		French government formally announces its intention to withdraw from NATO's integrated military command but not from the alliance itself. . . . 350 Catalan students stage a sit-in at a Catholic monastery near Barcelona to protest the government-controlled student union.			India's Congress party agrees to the creation of a state for the Sikh minority in Punjab.
March 10		Protesters hurl smoke bombs during the wedding of Crown Princess Beatrix of the Netherlands and German diplomat Claus von Amsberg because of the latter's World War II service.	Kenya orders the expulsion of Soviet, Chinese Communist and Czech officials. . . . Reports from Africa indicate that Guinean Pres. Sékou Touré has pledged to send Guinean forces to Ghana to help restore deposed Pres. Nkrumah.	Cuba sentences five men to long prison terms for allegedly plotting with the CIA to assassinate Premier Castro. . . . Dominican Pres. Garcia-Godoy declares that the "armed forces may be at present the best factor for order that the country has."	South Vietnam's government ousts Lt. Gen. Nguyen Chanh Thi from the National Leadership Committee.
March 11		Spanish police force protesting students to evacuate a Catholic monastery.	Reports indicate that several hundred Soviet technicians will continue to work in Ghana despite previous statements to the contrary.	Chilean leftist politicians lead demonstrators in an attempt to block workers from going to work at Anaconda's El Salvador mine; fighting breaks out in which eight persons are killed, including one policeman.	South Vietnamese forces clash with the Viet Cong in the Mekong Delta.
March 12					Indonesian Pres. Sukarno turns over all government power to the staunchly anti-communist Gen. Suharto who immediately bans the Indonesian Communist Party. . . . New Zealand announces that it will raise its token combat force in South Vietnam to 150 men.

A	B	C	D	E
Includes developments that affect more than one world region, international organizations and important meetings of major world leaders.	Includes all domestic and regional developments in Europe, including the Soviet Union, Turkey, Cyprus and Malta.	Includes all domestic and regional developments in Africa and the Middle East, including Iraq and Iran and excluding Cyprus, Turkey and Afghanistan.	Includes all domestic and regional developments in Latin America, the Caribbean and Canada.	Includes all domestic and regional developments in Asia and Pacific nations, extending from Afghanistan through all the Pacific Islands, except Hawaii.

U.S. Politics & Social Issues	U.S. Foreign Policy & Defense	U.S. Economy & Environment	Science, Technology & Nature	Culture, Leisure & Life Style	
An NAACP-sponsored boycott ends in Natchez, Miss. after town officials promise that two policemen guilty of a racial beating will be discharged. . . . An Alabama federal court rules that the state poll tax is unconstitutional.		Striking railroad men return to work under threat of heavy fines.			March 3
			Soviet Union conducts an underground nuclear test.		March 4
A boycott of Washington, D.C. merchants who refuse to support home rule for the district begins.			U.S. conducts an underground nuclear test.		March 5
			Soviet Union launches a military surveillance satellite.		March 6
Surgeon Gen. William Stewart announces non-discrimination guidelines for hospitals receiving federal funds.	Defense Secy. Robert McNamara says that the U.S. has no intention of diluting its "veto" over the use of nuclear weapons supplied to its allies.				March 7
A federal court orders the state of Mississippi to grant the NAACP a state charter.	Senate Foreign Relations Committee begins hearings designed to better understanding of Communist China.			Lawyers for the recently deceased Michel Monet say that he left his 92 paintings by his father, Claude Monet, to the Académié des Beaux Arts in Paris.	March 8
Pres. Johnson asks Congress for funds to combat the nation's growing crime rate.	U.S. Defense Dept. releases figures on the racial breakdown of combat deaths in Vietnam. The report indicates that Negroes represented about 15% of Army men and about 18% of Army deaths between 1961 and 1965.	General Motors acknowledges having initiated an investigation of Washington lawyer Ralph Nader, a leading consumer affairs activist.			March 9
Three blacks are found guilty of the 1965 murder of Black Muslim leader Malcolm X.					March 10
A federal judge orders the total desegregation of the Macon County, Ala. school system.	V.P. Humphrey says U.S. would accept a Viet Cong role in the South Vietnamese government "if they won their place fairly in free elections."			Jean Lacouture's *Vietnam* is published.	March 11
Birmingham Ala. Mayor Albert Boutwell publicly appeals for qualified Negro applicants for the city's police force.	Thirty-eight state governors, receiving a White House orientation on Vietnam, "wholeheartedly" back the administration's policy.		U.S. launches a communications satellite.		March 12

F	G	H	I	J
Includes elections, federal-state relations, civil rights and liberties, crime, the judiciary, education, health care, poverty, urban affairs and population.	*Includes formation and debate of U.S. foreign and defense policies, veterans' affairs and defense spending. (Relations with specific foreign countries are usually found under the region concerned.)*	*Includes business, labor, agriculture, taxation, transportation, consumer affairs, monetary and fiscal policy, natural resources, and pollution.*	*Includes worldwide scientific, medical and technological developments, natural phenomena, U.S. weather, natural disasters, and accidents.*	*Includes the arts, religion, scholarship, communications media, sports, entertainment, fashions, fads and social life.*

	World Affairs	Europe	Africa & the Middle East	The Americas	Asia & the Pacific
March 13			Kenyan Pres. Jomo Kenyatta ousts V.P. Oginga Odinga, a member of the minority Luo ethnic group, and accuses him of having plotted with Communist officials.		Gen. Suharto announces that Indonesia will continue its "confrontation" with Malaysia. . . . A successful five-hour strike takes place in Danang in protest of Thi's ouster. Supporters claim he was dismissed for fighting "corruption and dictatorship.". . . A Viet Cong unit causes heavy damage during a twenty-minute attack against the U.S. Tansonn-hut Air Base in Saigon.
March 14		Austria and Albania agree to raise the level of their diplomatic missions to the ambassadorial rank.	In a radio broadcast from Guinea, former Pres. Nkrumah appeals to Ghanaians to revolt against the new government.	Fidel Castro charges Communist Chinese leaders of being past the point of "senility.". . . Chilean Pres. Eduardo Frei Montalva denounces labor demonstrations as "a systematic attempt to undermine. . .the authority of the state."	U.S. and Communist forces clash near Saigon.
March 15		West German Chancellor Ludwig Erhard rejects the idea of a separate West German army and supports its current integrated status under NATO.		A general strike called by Chilean labor unions fails to attract widespread backing.	A general work stoppage protesting Gen. Thi's ouster paralyzes Danang.
March 16		*London Times* reports that 25 Soviet intellectuals have recently written to First Secy. Leonid Brezhnev about the dangers of rehabilitating Stalin. . . . *The New York Times* cites sources from the Communist Chinese embassy in Moscow claiming that Soviet troop movements have recently taken place in Mongolia along the Chinese border.	Ivory Coast Pres. Felix Houphouet-Boigny says that his country's troops will block any attempted invasion of Ghana. . . . Soviet Union recognizes the new Ghanaian government.		Buddhist demonstrations spread to Saigon for the first time. . . . At the behest of Gen. Nguyen Cao Ky, Gen. Thi begins a tour of northern cities in an appeal to his supporters to end their protests. . . . Several thousand Australian demonstrators protest Australia's participation in the Vietnamese War.
March 17					
March 18		Fourteen NATO nations reject France's assertion that the alliance is outdated.			Reports from Indonesia indicate that former Pres. Sukarno is under house arrest. . . . Chinese Communist Amb.-to-Indonesia Chung-Ming leaves Jakarta in what is described as the start of a phased Chinese withdrawal.
March 19		Reports indicate that the Soviet Union is installing a missile defense system around Moscow.			Communist and South Vietnamese forces clash near Saigon.
March 20			A gunman murders William Hunn, a British official, in South Yemen.		Viet Cong unit throws bombs in a civilian market near Saigon.
March 21					South Korea agrees to send 20,000 more troops to Vietnam, where another 20,000 men are already fighting.
March 22		A West German newspaper, *Die Welt*, publishes a letter allegedly written by the Soviet C.P. Central Committee which accuses Communist China of wanting to provoke a war between the Soviet Union and the United States.	Pres. Joseph Mobutu of Zaire abolishes Parliament and assumes all legislative powers.	Ecuadorean Chamber of Commerce calls a general strike to protest the increase on duties for foreign goods.	

A	B	C	D	E
Includes developments that affect more than one world region, international organizations and important meetings of major world leaders.	Includes all domestic and regional developments in Europe, including the Soviet Union, Turkey, Cyprus and Malta.	Includes all domestic and regional developments in Africa and the Middle East, including Iraq and Iran and excluding Cyprus, Turkey and Afghanistan.	Includes all domestic and regional developments in Latin America, the Caribbean and Canada.	Includes all domestic and regional developments in Asia and Pacific nations, extending from Afghanistan through all the Pacific Islands, except Hawaii.

U.S. Politics & Social Issues	U.S. Foreign Policy & Defense	U.S. Economy & Environment	Science, Technology & Nature	Culture, Leisure & Life Style	
	V.P. Humphrey urges that U.S. policy towards Communist China should be one of "containment without necessarily isolation.". . . *Ramparts* magazine reports that Michigan State University acted as a cover for the CIA during the 1950's.				March 13
				Leonard Bernstein makes a triumphant debut as opera conductor of Verdi's opera *Falstaff* in Vienna.	March 14
Rioting breaks out in the Watts district of Los Angeles when police try to stop Negro high school students from throwing stones and bricks at local traffic.				James Dickey's *Buckdancer's Choice* wins the 1965 National Book Award for poetry.	March 15
	Republican members of Congress's Joint Economic Committee accuse the administration of underestimating the costs of the Vietnam War.		Two U.S. astronauts stage the first docking (physical joining) of orbiting spacecrafts.		March 16
			The Gemini 8 astronauts, Neil Armstrong and Major David Scott, are forced down into the Pacific after losing control of their craft. They are picked up three hours later by the U.S. Navy destroyer Leonard F. Mason.		March 17
	U.S. government halts virtually all American trade with Rhodesia.			Opera soprano Maria Callas gives up her U.S. citizenship for marital and tax reasons.	March 18
	U.S. signs a cultural exchange pact with the Soviet Union.		Soviet Union launches a military surveillance satellite.		March 19
	State Secy. Dean Rusk criticizes a European plan to construct a steel mill in Communist China. . . . One hundred ninety-eight American scholars call for a rapprochement with Communist China.				March 20
Supreme Court rules that the Constitution does not protect publishers of salacious material.		Pres. Johnson proposes consumer protection measures including a Child Safety Act to protect children from harmful drugs and toys.		Three New York newspapers announce merger plans.	March 21
Labor Secy. Willard Wirtz says that 1,000 federal jobs are unfilled in Los Angeles because of lack of transportation.	Ex-Pres. Eisenhower says that "The draft-card burners should be sent to jail--at least for the war's duration."	U.S. government orders the J.P. Stevens & Co. textile manufacturing firm to rehire 71 workers fired for union activity. . . . Ralph Nader asserts before a Senate committee that 50 to 60 of his friends and family relations were quizzed by private investigators about his private life.		Archbishop of Canterbury, Dr. Arthur Ramsey, arrives in Rome for an historic meeting with Pope Paul VI.	March 22
F	G	H	I	J	
Includes elections, federal-state relations, civil rights and liberties, crime, the judiciary, education, health care, poverty, urban affairs and population.	*Includes formation and debate of U.S. foreign and defense policies, veterans' affairs and defense spending. (Relations with specific foreign countries are usually found under the region concerned.)*	*Includes business, labor, agriculture, taxation, transportation, consumer affairs, monetary and fiscal policy, natural resources, and pollution.*	*Includes worldwide scientific, medical and technological developments, natural phenomena, U.S. weather, natural disasters, and accidents.*	*Includes the arts, religion, scholarship, communications media, sports, entertainment, fashions, fads and social life.*	

	World Affairs	Europe	Africa & the Middle East	The Americas	Asia & the Pacific
March 23	IMF grants India an emergency loan because of the recent drought.				Communist China rejects a Soviet invitation to attend the 23rd Congress of the Soviet Communist Party.
March 24		Greece and Albania agree to resume commercial relations for the first time since 1940. . . . Portugese Premier Antonio de Oliveira Salazar says that the West can no longer expect "automatic cooperation" from Portugal.		Two thousand students in Quito, Ecuador demand a return to civilian rule.	Viet Cong launch a brief terrorist attack against civilians in the Central Highlands.
March 25		East Germany sentences a former SS doctor, Horst Fischer, to death. . . . West German government says it is "prepared to make sacrifices" for German reunification.		Soldiers break up an anti-government rally of several hundred students at the Central University in Quito, Ecuador.	South Vietnamese Premier Ky announces that a convention will be held to draw up a Constitution within two months.
March 26		East German First Secy. Walter Ulbricht invites West German leaders to appear at a public rally in East Berlin for a debate about reunification.			Anti-government demonstrators, including 1,000 South Vietnamese troops, protest in Hue. . . . Chinese Communist chief of state Liu Shao-chi begins a visit to West Pakistan.
March 27			Syrian Baath Party Congress elects its 16-member leadership group.		Liu Shao-chi says that Communist China supports Pakistan in its dispute with India over Kashmir.
March 28	U.S. Amb-to-U.N. Arthur Goldberg says that Communist China's isolation is not "desirable" but self-imposed.	Turkish National Assembly elects Gen. Cevdet Sunay as president to succeed the ailing Gen. Cemal Gursal.			
March 29		West German government says it wants to begin "dialogues" with Poland and Czechoslovakia. . . . Twenty-third Congress of the Soviet Communist Party begins in Moscow with both Communist China and Albania absent.		Army forces Ecuador's ruling junta to relinquish power. . . . Anti-government violence continues in Ecuador despite the announcement of the junta's ouster.	Communist China rejects U.S. proposals for exchanges of scholars and newsmen, saying that improved relations depend upon the U.S. evacuation of Taiwan.
March 30		First Secy. Sharaf Rashidov of the Uzbekistan Republic Communist Party says that large gold deposits have been recently found in Uzbekistan. . . . First Secy. Nikolai Yegorychev of the Moscow C.P. defends "the heroic history of our people" under Stalin before the Congress.		Ecuadorean Army appoints a civilian cabinet of 12 businessmen and professionals.	Communist China accuses Indonesia of engaging in "frantic anti-Chinese activities."
March 31		British P.M. Wilson's Labor Party wins a landslide victory in Parliamentary elections.	South African segregationist party wins the greatest election victory in South Africa's history.		
April 1					Anti-government Buddhist leaders call for a general strike in South Vietnam from their northern stronghold in Hue.
April 2		A tanker explosion kills two workers in Marseilles.	African delegates from 11 countries denounce Rhodesia at a conference in Kenya.		Buddhists demonstrate against the South Vietnamese government in Danang.
	A	B	C	D	E
	Includes developments that affect more than one world region, international organizations and important meetings of major world leaders.	Includes all domestic and regional developments in Europe, including the Soviet Union, Turkey, Cyprus and Malta.	Includes all domestic and regional developments in Africa and the Middle East, including Iraq and Iran and excluding Cyprus, Turkey and Afghanistan.	Includes all domestic and regional developments in Latin America, the Caribbean and Canada.	Includes all domestic and regional developments in Asia and Pacific nations, extending from Afghanistan through all the Pacific Islands, except Hawaii.

U.S. Politics & Social Issues	U.S. Foreign Policy & Defense	U.S. Economy & Environment	Science, Technology & Nature	Culture, Leisure & Life Style	
	Americans for Democratic Action (ADA) call for the de-escalation of the Vietnam War.			William Meredith wins the National Institute of Arts and Letters Award for Poetry. . . . Archbishop of Canterbury, Dr. Arthur Ramsey, meets with Pope Paul VI in the Sistine Chapel. It is the first such official visit in history.	March 23
Justice Dept. files suit against Mississippi's jury selection laws.					March 24
Supreme Court declares the Virginia poll tax is unconstitutional.					March 25
	About 20,000-25,000 demonstrators in N.Y.C. protest against the Vietnamese War.		Soviet Union conducts an underground nuclear test.		March 26
					March 27
Atty. Gen. Nicholas Katzenbach announces the arrest of 13 Ku Klux Klan members in connection with the Jan. 10 slaying of civil rights activist Vernon Dahmer.	Pres. Johnson meets with Indian Prime Min. Gandhi at the White House. The two leaders discuss India's food needs, the Vietnam War and Communist China.				March 28
House passes a bill for rent aid to low income families.		HUD initiates regulations limiting the amounts of hydrocarbons emitted through the exhaust of new cars.		Bernard Fall wins the George Polk Memorial Award in journalism for his reporting from Vietnam.	March 29
FBI arrests 33 men in New York on charges of operating a conspiracy involving fraudulent documents designed to avoid military service. . . . Richmond, Va. school board agrees "to take all reasonable steps to eliminate racial segregation of all facilities."	Defense Secy. McNamara says that the blockading of Haiphong harbor would probably not significantly hinder the North Vietnamese war capacity.			Alan Moorehead's *The Fatal Impact: An Account of the South Pacific 1767-1840*, is published.	March 30
For the first time the U.S. Office of Education withholds federal funds from a southern school district. . . . Three hundred Negroes stage a demonstration in Cordele, Ga. Several of them lower the American flag from the courthouse flagpole and tear it to pieces.		Strikes cripple eight major railroads across the nation.			March 31
	Pres. Johnson claims that 50,000 Communist troops have been put out of action during the last three months in South Vietnam.	Wildcat strikes protesting the gradual reduction of work crews break out in the Port of New York.	Soviet Union launches a communications satellite.		April 1
	U.S. says it will sell jet fighters to Jordan.				April 2

F	G	H	I	J
Includes elections, federal-state relations, civil rights and liberties, crime, the judiciary, education, health care, poverty, urban affairs and population.	*Includes formation and debate of U.S. foreign and defense policies, veterans' affairs and defense spending. (Relations with specific foreign countries are usually found under the region concerned.)*	*Includes business, labor, agriculture, taxation, transportation, consumer affairs, monetary and fiscal policy, natural resources, and pollution.*	*Includes worldwide scientific, medical and technological developments, natural phenomena, U.S. weather, natural disasters, and accidents.*	*Includes the arts, religion, scholarship, communications media, sports, entertainment, fashions, fads and social life.*

	World Affairs	Europe	Africa & the Middle East	The Americas	Asia & the Pacific
April 3	African delegates at the U.N. criticize Britain's refusal to use force against Rhodesia.	A gale kills ten sailors on the Humber River in England.			Indian P.M. Indira Gandhi returns to India after meetings with Western and Soviet leaders.
April 4		A brief anti-government demonstration takes place at the University of Madrid.			Singapore and U.S. agree to exchange ambassadors. . . . Several thousand Buddhist demonstrators clash with police in Saigon. . . . South Vietnamese Premier Nguyen Cao Ky sends 4,000 marines to the Danang airbase for possible use against anti-government demonstrations. . . . Chinese premier Liu Shao-chi begins a visit to Afghanistan.
April 5		Police scuffle with students on the campus of the University of Rome.	Ghana accuses Communist China of sending arms to former President Nkrumah in Guinea.	Canadian House of Commons defeats a bill to abolish the death penalty by a vote of 143-112.	Food riots break out in West Bengal. . . . Anti-government demonstrations continue in Saigon as police throw tear gas grenades at marchers.
April 6		British P.M. Harold Wilson reshuffles his cabinet but changes do not indicate any major turns in policy.	Portugal declares that it will not cooperate with the British oil embargo of Rhodesia.		Rioting breaks out in Hong Kong ostensibly in protest against a proposal to increase fares on ferry boats. . . . Indian leftists call a 24-hour general strike in protest against food distribution policies.
April 7	African delegates criticize South African apartheid policies at the U.N.	U.S. embassy in Madrid announces that the U.S. Navy has found the H-bomb missing since Jan. 17.		Dominican Pres. Hector Garcia-Godoy signs a decree legalizing the pro-Castro 14th of June Movement.	An Indonesian newspaper says that a "peaceful confrontation" with Malaysia is better than a violent one. . . . Violent clashes between police and demonstrators in Calcutta result in three deaths. . . . Police kill one demonstrator during Hong Kong riots.
April 8		Twenty-third Soviet Communist Party congress ends with calls for peaceful co-existence.		A fire kills two people on the cruise ship *Viking Princess* off the coast of Cuba.	Hong Kong riots end after a strict curfew is imposed.
April 9	U.N. Security Council approves Britain's use of force in preventing oil shipments to Rhodesia via Mozambique.	A liberalized press censorship law goes into effect in Spain.	Lebanese Premier Abdullah Yaffi announces the formation of a cabinet.	A small anti-government demonstration takes place on the campus of the University of Rio de Janeiro.	South Vietnam's anti-government Buddhist leadership announces an all-out campaign to topple the military regime of Premier Ky.
April 10			Greece supports the British blockade of a Greek tanker bringing oil to Rhodesia. . . . A British frigate blocks a Greek freighter from docking at Mozambique with a cargo of oil.	Guatemalan Congress elects Julio Cesar Mendez Montenegro as president.	*The New York Times* reports that Communist Chinese leaders have failed to obtain Afghan support for a U.S. withdrawal from Vietnam.
April 11		Police and leftist students clash briefly at the University of Paris.			Indian P.M. Indira Gandhi confers with Kughato Sukhai, a Nagaland official, about the recent unrest in the area. . . . U.S. government confirms reports that the unrest in South Vietnam has begun to impair the war effort.
April 12		Greek P.M. Stephanos Stephanopoulos announces his determination to stay in office despite the loss of a Parliamentary majority.			For the second time in five weeks, U.S. officials report that American losses were higher than South Vietnamese losses (the figures covered the first week in March). . . . Indonesia announces that it will "cease to consider big and moderate-sized businesses as enemies of our state.". . . For the first time Guam-based B-52 bombers attack North Vietnam.

A	B	C	D	E
Includes developments that affect more than one world region, international organizations and important meetings of major world leaders.	Includes all domestic and regional developments in Europe, including the Soviet Union, Turkey, Cyprus and Malta.	Includes all domestic and regional developments in Africa and the Middle East, including Iraq and Iran and excluding Cyprus, Turkey and Afghanistan.	Includes all domestic and regional developments in Latin America, the Caribbean and Canada.	Includes all domestic and regional developments in Asia and Pacific nations, extending from Afghanistan through all the Pacific Islands, except Hawaii.

U.S. Politics & Social Issues	U.S. Foreign Policy & Defense	U.S. Economy & Environment	Science, Technology & Nature	Culture, Leisure & Life Style	
		A court order ends a four-day strike of railroad firemen.	Soviet spacecraft Luna 10 becomes the first man-made object to achieve lunar orbit.		April 3
Job Corps Director Franklyn Johnson agrees to move his organization's training center from downtown St. Petersburg Fla. because of rowdyism. . . . Newport News, Va. Shipbuilding & Drydock Co. agrees to give priority to Negroes for supervisory positions.		Striking railroad firemen return to work after their four-day strike.	Tornadoes kill at least nine people in central Florida.		April 4
	A U.S. government spokesman admits that the planes flying South Vietnamese troops north to put down anti-government demonstrations were piloted by Americans.				April 5
Ala. Gov. George Wallace says that Ala. will refuse to comply with federal guidelines for school desegregation.	Liberal Republican Rippon Society calls for a change in policy towards Communist China.	Schenley Industries, a major grape grower in California, recognizes the National Farm Workers Association as the sole bargaining agent for its agricultural farm workers.			April 6
		Di Giorgia Corp., the largest grape grower in California, announces that it will permit secret ballot union elections for its farm workers, but still refuses to agree to a contract permitting strikes.			April 7
A federal court outlaws the $2.00 Mississippi poll tax, the last such tax in America.			Soviet Union conducts an underground nuclear test.		April 8
	A bomb injures five people at an anti-Vietnamese War organization building in Berkeley, Calif.				April 9
Justice Dept. estimates that Negro voter registration has increased nearly 50% since the August 1965 passage of the Voting Rights Act.	A small anti-Vietnamese War demonstration takes place in N.Y.C.	About 8,000 demonstrators in Calif. urge a boycott of Di Giorgio Corp. agricultural products.	A B-18 airplane crash kills two passengers in Tucson, Ariz.	British novelist Evelyn Waugh, 62, dies in Taunton, Somerset, England.	April 10
	Senate Democratic leader Mike Mansfield (D, Mont.) questions the wisdom of the U.S. committment to South Vietnam.		A train derailment injures 62 passengers at West Roxbury, Mass.	A.E. Hotchner's *Papa Hemingway* is published.	April 11
Atty. Gen. Nicholas Katzenbach orders federal voting examiners to go to Mississippi where local registrars are allegedly still using literacy tests.	U.S. asks France to postpone for one year its Apr. 1, 1967 deadline for the evacuation of U.S. troops.		U.S. launches a communications satellite.		April 12

F	G	H	I	J
Includes elections, federal-state relations, civil rights and liberties, crime, the judiciary, education, health care, poverty, urban affairs and population.	Includes formation and debate of U.S. foreign and defense policies, veterans' affairs and defense spending. (Relations with specific foreign countries are usually found under the region concerned.)	Includes business, labor, agriculture, taxation, transportation, consumer affairs, monetary and fiscal policy, natural resources, and pollution.	Includes worldwide scientific, medical and technological developments, natural phenomena, U.S. weather, natural disasters, and accidents.	Includes the arts, religion, scholarship, communications media, sports, entertainment, fashions, fads and social life.

	World Affairs	Europe	Africa & the Middle East	The Americas	Asia & the Pacific
April 13		Portugese Premier Antonio de Oliveira Salazar criticizes the U.N. resolution empowering Britain to use force to prevent oil shipments to Rhodesia via Mozambique.	A gunman assassinates the acting president of Yemen, Abdullah el-Airiny. . . . Reports from Syria indicate that Khalid Bakdash, an important official of the outlawed Syrian C.P., has returned to Syria after an eight-year self-imposed exile. . . . Zairian armed forces capture the town of Opala from dissident army units. . . . Iraqi Pres. Abdul Salam Arif dies in a helicopter crash near Basra, Iraq.		
April 14		French Foreign Min. Maurice Couve de Murville says that France is willing to keep its 75,000 troops in West Germany if the West German government agrees.	Kenyan V.P. Oginga Odinga resigns from the government.	Hundreds of thousands of Mexicans warmly welcome Pres. Johnson as he arrives in Mexico City for a short visit.	South Vietnam's Premier Ky approves national elections for an assembly within three to five months.
April 15	Arab states at the U.N. accuse Israel of mistreating its Arab minority.		Uganda adopts a new Constitution giving wider powers to the central government.	Pres. Johnson unveils a statue of Abraham Lincoln in Mexico City.	South Vietnamese Unified Buddhist Church promises to halt its agitation if the Parliamentary elections take place on schedule.
April 16		French newspaper *Le Monde* criticizes French Pres. de Gaulle's frequent attacks on U.S. influence in Western Europe.	Iraqi government elects deceased Pres. Abdul Arif's brother, Maj. Gen. Abdel Rahman Arif, as president.		Malaysian P.M. Abdul Rahman offers to hold peace talks with Indonesia if it calls off its guerrilla warfare campaign. . . . About 50,000 workers go on a one-day strike in Saigon in protest against the alleged beating of two textile workers during a work stoppage.
April 17		Forty to fifty thousand Poles cheer Cardinal Wyszynski as he arrives for an outdoor mass in Poznan, Poland.	Reports indicate that Gen. Mustapha Mullah el-Barzani, the leader of Kurdish insurgents, has proposed a one-month truce as a means to begin negotiations.		Thousands of South Vietnamese Roman Catholics protest near Saigon against the government's refusal to quell Buddhist demonstrators. . . . Indonesian artillery fires on a British patrol boat near Singapore but does no damage. . . . Communist China rejects a U.S. offer of university visits for Chinese scholars and scientists.
April 18		Greek P.M. Stephanopoulos regains his Parliamentary majority.		Hearings open in Ottawa about an alleged security scandal involving the Associate Defense Min. Pierre Sevigny.	Thich Tri Quang, chairman of the Unified Buddhist Church, tours the northern provinces and urges a halt to the anti-government unrest. . . . United Buddhist Church of Saigon asserts that the government has broken the Apr. 14 truce pact which promised elections in return for an end to demonstrations.
April 19	African delegates at the UN criticize Western investment in South Africa.		Twenty-nine supporters of former Kenyan V.P. Oginga Odinga resign from the Kenyan government.		
April 20		French officials say that the U.S. has been refusing to deliver nuclear fuel promised under the 1959 agreement since November 1964. . . . West German Defense Min. Kai-Uwe von Hassel says that the American troops in West Germany are "the kernel of European security."	British troops clash with Arab demonstrators in Aden.		A train explosion kills 55 people in the Indian province of Assam. Government officials attribute it to the Nagaland guerrillas. . . . Using tear gas, Saigon police break up a demonstration by thousands of Buddhists.

A	B	C	D	E
Includes developments that affect more than one world region, international organizations and important meetings of major world leaders.	*Includes all domestic and regional developments in Europe, including the Soviet Union, Turkey, Cyprus and Malta.*	*Includes all domestic and regional developments in Africa and the Middle East, including Iraq and Iran and excluding Cyprus, Turkey and Afghanistan.*	*Includes all domestic and regional developments in Latin America, the Caribbean and Canada.*	*Includes all domestic and regional developments in Asia and Pacific nations, extending from Afghanistan through all the Pacific Islands, except Hawaii.*

U.S. Politics & Social Issues	U.S. Foreign Policy & Defense	U.S. Economy & Environment	Science, Technology & Nature	Culture, Leisure & Life Style	
	Martin Luther King's Southern Christian Leadership Conference calls for a complete pull-out of U.S. troops from Vietnam. . . . State Secy. Dean Rusk acknowledges that the U.S. has been preventing French military planes en route to South Pacific test sites from flying over the U.S. on the grounds that the tests violate the 1963 test-ban treaty.			Pope Paul VI and the Most Rev. Arthur Ramsey, Archbishop of Canterbury, express hope of eventual Christian unification. . . . French author Georges Duhamel dies in Valmondois, France at 81.	April 13
Student Nonviolent Coordinating Committee elects Stokely Carmichael as president. . . . Office of Economic Opportunity Director Sargent Shriver is almost shouted down by angry delegates during an address at a "poor people's conference" in Washington. . . . A N.Y. court sentences to life imprisonment the three men convicted of slaying the black Muslim leader, Malcolm X.	House Republican leader Gerald Ford accuses the administration of "the shocking mismanagement" of the Vietnam War, citing an alleged shortage of bombs. . . . U.S. State Dept. discloses that universities requesting permission to invite Communist Chinese scholars and scientists to the U.S. will be allowed to do so.		Sandoz Pharmaceuticals withdraws its market supplies of the psychedelic drug LSD.		April 14
Reports indicate that fewer than one-fourth of U.S. southern school districts have met the U.S. Office of Education's deadline for complying with desegregation guidelines.					April 15
	State Secy. Dean Rusk indicates that the U.S. is seeking ways to diminish tensions with Communist China.		U.S. launches a communications satellite.	Last performance is given in the old New York City opera house on Broadway.	April 16
Dr. Timothy Leary, a former Harvard psychologist, is arrested on drug charges.	The New York Times reports that the U.S. has been refusing to supply France with enriched uranium fuel that was promised in a 1959 agreement.				April 17
	U.S. State Dept. agrees to provide Indonesia with major food credit loans. . . . Sen. Barry Goldwater (R, Ariz.) says that the U.S. should blockade the port of Haiphong and bomb the petroleum depots around Hanoi. . . . House Minority Leader Gerald Ford says that the U.S. will have to send at least another 200,000 troops to Vietnam to achieve a stalemate "in a war that now looks like a war without end."			Drs. William Masters and Virginia Johnson's Human Sexual Response is published.	April 18
Sen. Robert Kennedy criticizes administration budget cuts which he says will hurt the poor.	U.S. Defense Dept. discloses that about 15,000 military personnel will be transferred from Europe to Vietnam. . . . Pres. Johnson signs emergency food legislation for India.		Soviet Union conducts an underground nuclear test.		April 19
U.S. Senate rejects a proposed Constitutional amendment designed to overturn the Supreme Court's "one-man, one-vote" decision.	U.S. announces that it has agreed to sell Israel "tactical" military aircraft.				April 20

F	G	H	I	J
Includes elections, federal-state relations, civil rights and liberties, crime, the judiciary, education, health care, poverty, urban affairs and population.	Includes formation and debate of U.S. foreign and defense policies, veterans' affairs and defense spending. (Relations with specific foreign countries are usually found under the region concerned.)	Includes business, labor, agriculture, taxation, transportation, consumer affairs, monetary and fiscal policy, natural resources, and pollution.	Includes worldwide scientific, medical and technological developments, natural phenomena, U.S. weather, natural disasters, and accidents.	Includes the arts, religion, scholarship, communications media, sports, entertainment, fashions, fads and social life.

	World Affairs	Europe	Africa & the Middle East	The Americas	Asia & the Pacific
April 21		British television for the first time broadcasts the opening of the British Parliament.			A hunger strike begins in the main Buddhist pagoda of Saigon.
April 22		Meeting of foreign ministers of the Central Treaty Organization ends with a call for continued vigilance against "subversive" activities.	Kenyan Home Affairs Min. Daniel Arap Moi confirms reports that Kenya has accused former V.P. Odinga of meeting secretly with Tanzanian officials. . . . Police scuffle with a small group of anti-government demonstrators on the campus of the University of Mexico.		
April 23	At the U.N. the Colombian delegate accuses Cuba of attempted subversion.	Italy and Soviet Union sign an economic agreement.	Reports indicate that Syria is buying more military equipment from the Soviet Union.		For the first time significant numbers of North Vietnamese aircraft challenge American bombers. . . . Henry Cabot Lodge discusses the South Vietnamese internal crisis with Premier Ky.
April 24		German newspaper *Die Welt* criticizes French Pres. de Gaulle's decision to withdraw from the military command structure of NATO.	A mine injures several Israelis near the Jordanian border.	Ten thousand Dominican demonstrators call for the departure of the OAS's 8,000-man peace-keeping force.	U.S. bombers attack Communist troop concentrations in the Central Highlands.
April 25		East German guards shoot down a man trying to escape to West Berlin. . . . French Foreign Min. Couve de Murville begins an official visit to Rumania.	Ramogi Achieng Onenko, a member of former V.P. Odinga's Luo tribe, criticizes the Kenya government for not taking measures against European and Indian businesses.	Reports indicate that members of the OAS are unhappy with the U.S. handling of the Alliance for Progress.	
April 26		An earthquake kills about 10 people in Tashkent, Soviet Central Asia.		Brazilian government chooses Gen. Artur Costa e Silva as its presidential nominee to succeed Pres. Humberto Castelo Branco.	*The New York Times* reports that Communist China has begun penalizing families who have more than three children.
April 27		Spanish university students stage violent demonstrations in Barcelona.	Iraqi Pres. Abdel Arif rejects a Kurdish offer of negotiations.		A Viet Cong terrorist bomb kills civilian construction workers at a Saigon bus stop. . . . Guam-based B-52 bombers attack North Vietnam.
April 28		Soviet Union charges the U.S. of still wanting "to leave the door open for nuclear proliferation among NATO partners," especially West Germany. . . . French Foreign Min. Couve de Murville arrives in Bulgaria for an official state visit. . . . Student protests spread to Bilbao Univ. in Spain.	A mine damages an Israeli army jeep near the Jordanian border.		Albanian Premier Mehmet Shehu arrives in Peiping for a state visit.
April 29	U.N. Secy. Gen. U Thant tells British P.M. Harold Wilson that a majority of the U.N.'s members want "more courageous" action by Britain on the Rhodesian question.	Madrid University students demonstrate in support of Barcelona students.	Rhodesian police clash with African guerrillas for the first time since Rhodesia proclaimed its independence in 1965. Seven guerrillas are reportedly killed. . . . Israeli soldiers raid two villages in Jordan in retaliation for alleged Arab guerrilla attacks on Israel.		4,000 more U.S. troops land in South Vietnam.
	A	B	C	D	E
	Includes developments that affect more than one world region, international organizations and important meetings of major world leaders.	Includes all domestic and regional developments in Europe, including the Soviet Union, Turkey, Cyprus and Malta.	Includes all domestic and regional developments in Africa and the Middle East, including Iraq and Iran and excluding Cyprus, Turkey and Afghanistan.	Includes all domestic and regional developments in Latin America, the Caribbean and Canada.	Includes all domestic and regional developments in Asia and Pacific nations, extending from Afghanistan through all the Pacific Islands, except Hawaii.

U.S. Politics & Social Issues	U.S. Foreign Policy & Defense	U.S. Economy & Environment	Science, Technology & Nature	Culture, Leisure & Life Style	
		Labor Dept. announces that the cost of living for March 1966 is 2.8% above that of March 1965.	Houston doctors place an artificial heart pump in the chest of Marcel De Rudder, a heart attack victim; it is the third such experiment.	Richard Morris's *The Peacemakers: The Great Powers and American Independence* wins the Frederic Bancroft Prize for history.	April 21
		Pres. Johnson says that "disquieting signs are beginning to appear" of growing inflation. . . . Pres. Johnson says it is time to establish "strict safety standards for automobiles.". . . N.Y.C. Mayor John Lindsay fails in his attempts to postpone the merger plans of three city newspapers.	Airplane crash kills 81 passengers near Ardmore, Okla.		April 22
New Bedford, Mass. city council protests Job Corps rowdyism.					April 23
Office of Economic Opportunity Director Sargent Shriver says he has no intention of moving the New Bedford, Mass. Job Corps training center.	A report from a House Armed Services subcommittee criticizes Secy. Robert McNamara's plans not to develop a new strategic bomber.				April 24
	U.S. State Dept. says that it appears that France will not extend its deadline for U.S. troop evacuation. . . . Harvard economist John Kenneth Galbraith calls for the U.S. to pull out of South Vietnam and says "If we were not in Vietnam, all that part of the world would be enjoying the obscurity it so richly deserves."	President's Council of Economic Advisers reports that there may be a slight federal budget surplus for 1966.			April 25
Ala. Gov. George Wallace orders the resegregation of his state's mental hospitals which were desegregated a week earlier.	U.S. State Dept. reiterates previous warnings that Communist Chinese planes fighting over North Vietnam will be pursued to their home base. . . . Chmn. Richard Russell (D, Ga.) of the Senate Armed Services Committee urges an extension of the U.S. bombing of North Vietnam.	U.S. auto industry modifies its opposition to federal standards for car safety.	Heart transplant patient Marcel De Rudder dies of a ruptured lung.		April 26
N.Y. Gov. Nelson Rockefeller signs a bill expanding the grounds of divorce beyond adultery. . . . In a 5-4 ruling the Supreme Court refuses to review a Ga. court decision holding the NAACP liable for damages arising out of a picketing campaign in Savannah, Ga.	*The New York Times* reports that the Johnson administration has decided to ask West Germany to forego indefinitely the nominal ownership of allied nuclear weapons.	ICC approves the merger of the Pennsylvania and New York Central Railroads. . . . United Mine Workers Union ends a two-and-a-half week strike.		Pope Paul meets with Soviet Foreign Min. Andrei Gromyko.	April 27
Pres. Johnson sends Congress legislation forbidding discrimination in the sale and financing of nearly all housing.	A statement from government sources says that only Pres. Johnson will decide if enemy aircraft will be pursued into Communist China. . . . Chmn. J. William Fulbright (D, Ark.) of the Senate Foreign Relations Committee warns that America may be succumbing to the "arrogance of power" which has afflicted other great powers of the past.				April 28
	Rev. Martin Luther King Jr. criticizes the U.S. involvement in South Vietnam.				April 29

F	G	H	I	J
Includes elections, federal-state relations, civil rights and liberties, crime, the judiciary, education, health care, poverty, urban affairs and population.	*Includes formation and debate of U.S. foreign and defense policies, veterans' affairs and defense spending. (Relations with specific foreign countries are usually found under the region concerned.)*	*Includes business, labor, agriculture, taxation, transportation, consumer affairs, monetary and fiscal policy, natural resources, and pollution.*	*Includes worldwide scientific, medical and technological developments, natural phenomena, U.S. weather, natural disasters, and accidents.*	*Includes the arts, religion, scholarship, communications media, sports, entertainment, fashions, fads and social life.*

	World Affairs	Europe	Africa & the Middle East	The Americas	Asia & the Pacific
April 30	Arab U.N. delegates criticize the recent Israeli raid against Jordan.		Israel warns Jordan that retaliatory raids will take place if the Arab guerrilla incidents continue against Israel.		A U.S. spokesman in Saigon says that American military forces currently total 255,000 men in South Vietnam. . . . A record number of U.S. planes bomb North Vietnam.
May 1		Polish Communist Party First Secy. Wladyslaw Gomulka makes a brief appearance at a gathering celebrating the 1,000th anniversary of Poland's conversion to Christianity.	Egyptian Pres. Nasser supports the North Yemeni republican claims to the Saudi Arabian border towns of Qizan and Najran.	Joaquin Balaguer defeats Juan Bosch in presidential election in the Dominican Republic. . . . Dr. Carlos Lleras Restrepo wins Colombian presidential elections.	U.S. troops fire into Cambodian territory during a clash with a Viet Cong unit. It is the first deliberate attack on a target in Cambodia which is confirmed by U.S. sources.
May 2	U.N. Arab delegates criticize former West German Chancellor Konrad Adenauer's trip to Israel.	Students and police clash at Madrid University when students attempt to march on the chancellor's office.	West German ex-Chancellor Adenauer begins a visit to Israel.		Anti-government demonstrators clash with police in Saigon.
May 3		France informs all NATO members that permission for flights over French territory by military aircraft will be subject to monthly instead of yearly review as of June 1. . . . About 300,000 Roman Catholics take part in rites marking Christianity's 1,000th anniversary in Poland.	At an official dinner for Adenauer, Israeli Premier Levi Eshkol declares that there can be no atonement for the Nazi atrocities against the Jews.	Twenty-one Latin American nations disagree about the status of Cuba at a meeting dealing with the denuclearization of the continent.	Rev. Hoang Quynh, leader of South Vietnam's Roman Catholics, warns of the dangers of premature elections.
May 4		Italian Fiat Automobile Co. signs an agreement with the Soviet Union for the construction of a major automobile plant in Russia.	Israeli soldiers clash with Arab guerrillas near the Sea of Galilee.		U.S. bombers attack the southern part of North Vietnam.
May 5		Police break up a demonstration of 2,000 students in Madrid.	Violent demonstrations against Adenauer erupt at Hebrew University in Jerusalem. . . . Syrian Foreign Min. Ibrahim Makhous declares that Syria will blow up the oil pipelines on its territory if Israeli troops invade Syria. . . . North Yemeni republican government asserts that the Saudi Arabian border towns of Quizan and Najran were seized illegally in 1930 and that they will be re-taken by force if necessary.		South Vietnamese committee begins work on drafting an election law in Saigon.
May 6	At Red Cross headquarters in Geneva, U.S. Amb-at-large Averell Harriman expresses concern over North Vietnam's refusal to grant U.S. prisoners "the treatment provided for in the Geneva convention."	Police and students clash on the campus of the University of Madrid.	Former West German Chancellor Adenauer decides to cancel his projected visit to Bar-Llan University near Tel-Aviv because of violent demonstrations.		
May 7		Twelve deputies from Epirus in northwest Greece threaten to withdraw their support if the Greek government does not uphold Greece's territorial claims to northern Epirus, currently in Albania. . . . Rumanian C.P. Gen. Secy. Nicolae Ceausescu vigorously defends Rumania's policy of independence in a speech in Bucharest.	Algerian Pres. Houari Boumedienne announces the nationalization of 11 mines belonging chiefly to French companies. . . . Reports indicate that Algeria has received a large shipment of arms from the Soviet Union.		South Vietnamese Premier Ky declares that he has no intention of resigning after the projected elections of a constituent assembly.
May 8		Polish Cardinal Wyszynski leads a procession carrying a copy of the Black Madonna through Cracow.	Israeli government criticizes demonstrators protesting the visit of former West German Chancellor Konrad Adenauer.	Police and a small group of anti-government demonstrators scuffle on the campus of the University of Buenos Aires.	Buddhist leaders in Danang warn the government that protests will be launched if scheduled elections in the fall are not held as promised.
	A	B	C	D	E
	Includes developments that affect more than one world region, international organizations and important meetings of major world leaders.	Includes all domestic and regional developments in Europe, including the Soviet Union, Turkey, Cyprus and Malta.	Includes all domestic and regional developments in Africa and the Middle East, including Iraq and Iran and excluding Cyprus, Turkey and Afghanistan.	Includes all domestic and regional developments in Latin America, the Caribbean and Canada.	Includes all domestic and regional developments in Asia and Pacific nations, extending from Afghanistan through all the Pacific Islands, except Hawaii.

U.S. Politics & Social Issues	U.S. Foreign Policy & Defense	U.S. Economy & Environment	Science, Technology & Nature	Culture, Leisure & Life Style	
N.Y. Gov. Rockefeller signs a bill providing free medical aid for the poor.	*Washington Post* reports that Secy. McNamara has proposed a new policy of automatic but limited nuclear response to attacks on NATO territory. . . . Melvin Laird, Chmn. of the House Republicans, asserts that the American public is confused by the Vietnam War.				April 30
					May 1
				Arthur Schlesinger's *A Thousand Days* wins the 1965 Pulitzer Prize for history. . . . Isaac Singer's *In My Father's Court* is published.	May 2
Ala. Gov. George Wallace's wife, Lurleen, overwhelmingly wins the state's Democratic gubernatorial primary.	U.S. officials admit for the first time that U.S. troops have fired into Cambodian territory in self-defense.			Lester Bassett wins the first Pulitzer Prize to be given in music in three years.	May 3
		Federal Reserve Board Chmn. William McChesney Martin proposes a tax increase to combat inflation.	U.S. conducts an underground nuclear test.		May 4
	Sen. J. William Fulbright says he regrets having said that "Saigon has become an American brothel."	Pres. Johnson announces a 15% increase in wheat acreage allotment to meet the rise in world demand. . . . Treasury Secy. Henry Fowler says that current inflationary trends might be only temporary and that a tax increase could be an "overcure."		Several U.S. Protestant denominations meet to discuss possible church mergers.	May 5
			Soviet Union conducts an underground nuclear test.		May 6
A Los Angeles policeman accidently kills Leonard Deadwyler, a Negro, during a speeding incident.	Pres. Johnson announces that the U.S. will seek a U.N. treaty barring any nation from asserting sovereignty over the moon or other celestial bodies.				May 7
	State Secy. Dean Rusk expresses confidence that Premier Ky will hold scheduled elections and turn over power to a civilian regime.			Bolshoi ballerina Maya Plisetskaya scores a triumph in N.Y.C.	May 8
F	G	H	I	J	
Includes elections, federal-state relations, civil rights and liberties, crime, the judiciary, education, health care, poverty, urban affairs and population.	*Includes formation and debate of U.S. foreign and defense policies, veterans' affairs and defense spending. (Relations with specific foreign countries are usually found under the region concerned.)*	*Includes business, labor, agriculture, taxation, transportation, consumer affairs, monetary and fiscal policy, natural resources, and pollution.*	*Includes worldwide scientific, medical and technological developments, natural phenomena, U.S. weather, natural disasters, and accidents.*	*Includes the arts, religion, scholarship, communications media, sports, entertainment, fashions, fads and social life.*	

	World Affairs	Europe	Africa & the Middle East	The Americas	Asia & the Pacific
May 9	At the U.N. African delegates criticize South Africa's apartheid policies.	Britain and Rhodesia open exploratory talks in London.			Communist China explodes its third nuclear device.
May 10		Soviet C.P. Gen. Secy. Leonid Brezhnev meets with Rumanian Premier Ceausescu in Bucharest.	Soviet Premier Aleksei Kosygin begins a visit to Egypt. . . . Moroccan King Hassan II protests the recent Algerian nationalization of the Gara Djebilet mine located in territory claimed by Morocco.	Guatemalan Congress elects Mendez Montenegro as president in a run-off election.	Indian Foreign Min. Swaren Singh says that the Communist Chinese nuclear test is in "arrogant defiance" of the world's wishes.
May 11		West Germany extends a major credit to Israel. . . . Barcelona police club and disperse more than 100 Roman Catholic priests protesting at a police station. . . . France recognizes Algeria's right to nationalize the former French mines but asks for financial compensation. . . . European Community adopts financial regulations for a common agricultural program.	An Israeli patrol clashes with Arab guerrillas near the Jordanian border.		In the closest strike to date near to port of Haiphong, U.S. planes attack a missile site.
May 12		West German government affirms that the U.S. presence in Europe is the key to stability.			South Vietnamese troops launch a drive in the Mekong Delta.
May 13		West Germany calls for a resumption of diplomatic relations with the Arab states and says that the recent credit extended to Israel is not for military purchases.	A Rhodesian court convicts 21 African Rhodesians of plotting to overthrow the government and sentences them to five or 10 year prison terms.		Communist China charges that U.S. planes violated its air space on May 12 and shot down a training plane. . . . Rumanian First Deputy Premier Emil Bodnaras leaves Peiping after a day of talks with Communist Chinese Premier Chou En-lai.
May 14		A group of Roman Catholic priests beaten by police in Barcelona appeal to Archbishop Gregorio Modrego y Casaus to publicly denounce the incident.	Arab League meets in Cairo and criticizes the British presence in South Yemen.		U.S. planes attack Communist troop positions in the Central Highlands.
May 15		Spanish Archbishop Modrego, reportedly under government pressure, rejects priests' demands and merely issues a general statement against violence.	Israeli soldiers and Arab guerrillas exchange gunfire near the Jordan River.		After an all-day battle with dissident soldiers, 1,500 South Vietnamese troops seize Danang.
May 16		An official of the Rumanian Foreign Ministry refuses to confirm or deny a report that Rumania has recently sent a note to Warsaw Pact nations saying that the presence of Soviet troops on the territory of member nations is no longer justified.	Syria passes a series of harsh laws against "industrial sabotage" and "labor negligence."		Danang Buddhists say that three monks will burn themselves to death if pro-Ky troops attack their pagoda. . . . U.S. begins an intensive drive against the Viet Cong in the Central Highlands. . . . Thai P.M. Thanom Kittikachorn charges Cambodia with planting land mines in Thailand.

A	B	C	D	E
Includes developments that affect more than one world region, international organizations and important meetings of major world leaders.	Includes all domestic and regional developments in Europe, including the Soviet Union, Turkey, Cyprus and Malta.	Includes all domestic and regional developments in Africa and the Middle East, including Iraq and Iran and excluding Cyprus, Turkey and Afghanistan.	Includes all domestic and regional developments in Latin America, the Caribbean and Canada.	Includes all domestic and regional developments in Asia and Pacific nations, extending from Afghanistan through all the Pacific Islands, except Hawaii.

U.S. Politics & Social Issues	U.S. Foreign Policy & Defense	U.S. Economy & Environment	Science, Technology & Nature	Culture, Leisure & Life Style	
	Sen. Eugene McCarthy (D, Minn.) criticizes the U.S. military involvement in South Vietnam. . . . Sen. Robert Kennedy urges the U.S. to give greater support to "the forces of reform and social justice" in Latin America.				May 9
California Supreme Court rules that a state constitutional amendment nullifying state fair-housing laws is unconstitutional.			Massachusetts repeals its 87-year ban on the dissemination of contraceptives and birth control information.		May 10
	Sen. Edward Kennedy says he has been unsuccessful in his attempts to arrange a prisoner exchange with North Vietnam.				May 11
A U.S. district court rules that a swimming pool operated by the Cambridge, Md. volunteer fire department is a public accommodation and therefore must be integrated.	Sen. Frank Church (D, Ida.) completes a NATO fact-finding tour for the Senate Foreign Relations Committee and declares that the European role in NATO will have to be increased.	Reports indicate that American consumers are becoming more concerned about inflation.		Auberon Waugh's *Who Are The Violets Now** is published.	May 12
Supreme Court rules that the Fifth Amendment's protection against self-incrimination restricts police interrogation of an arrested suspect.	U.S. Defense Secy. Robert McNamara and West German Defense Min. Kai-Uwe von Hassel negotiate about the costs of maintaining U.S. troops in West Germany.	House Interstate Commerce Committee concludes its car safety hearings.			May 13
Student Nonviolent Coordinating Committee (SNCC) decides to exclude whites from policy making positions.	University officials administer the draft deferment examination. . . . U.S. reports that 243 planes have been lost over North Vietnam since the beginning of the bombing in February 1965.				May 14
	About 10,000 demonstrators in Washington pledge their support for Congressional candidates who oppose the war in Vietnam.			Pope Paul expresses his "keen regret" over Poland's refusal to allow him to visit the country during its religious festivities.	May 15
An NAACP report says that "a mere 5.2% of Negro children in the South attend integrated schools" 12 years after the Supreme Court's 1954 desegregation ruling.	Amb.-to-South Vietnam Henry Cabot Lodge, before the House Foreign Relations Committee, supports a troop build-up in Vietnam.	British merchant marines begin a 45-day strike.		Vladimir Nabokov's latest book, *Despair*, is published.	May 16

F	G	H	I	J
Includes elections, federal-state relations, civil rights and liberties, crime, the judiciary, education, health care, poverty, urban affairs and population.	Includes formation and debate of U.S. foreign and defense policies, veterans' affairs and defense spending. (Relations with specific foreign countries are usually found under the region concerned.)	Includes business, labor, agriculture, taxation, transportation, consumer affairs, monetary and fiscal policy, natural resources, and pollution.	Includes worldwide scientific, medical and technological developments, natural phenomena, U.S. weather, natural disasters, and accidents.	Includes the arts, religion, scholarship, communications media, sports, entertainment, fashions, fads and social life.

	World Affairs	Europe	Africa & the Middle East	The Americas	Asia & the Pacific
May 17		*The New York Times* reports that Rumania is pressing for a change in Warsaw Pact strategy that would permit member nations to have a veto over the use of nuclear weapons stationed on their territory. . . . Soviet Union rejects West Germany's March 25 offer to undertake serious negotiations between the two countries.			A Buddhist strike closes down part of Hue.
May 18	In a U.N. debate over the use of force against Rhodesia, Lord Caradon, Britain's U.N. delegate, urges African nations not to press for action which might hinder efforts to bring about a peaceful solution.	A Rumanian Foreign Ministry official declares that the Warsaw Pact is "sufficiently strong to meet present needs.". . . Britain and Spain begin talks on the future of Gibraltar while half of the enclave's inhabitants demonstrate in favor of British rule.	An Egyptian-Soviet communique calls for the withdrawal of U.S. troops from Vietnam.		
May 19		Reports indicate that the Italian Fiat Automobile Co. will manufacture 35,000 cars annually in Poland.	Former Congolese Premier Moise Tshombe is accused of treason by the government of the Congo (Kinshasa).		U.S. troops clash with Communist forces in the Central Highlands.
May 20		Britain and Rhodesia suspend their talks.	Ugandan Pres. Milton Obote demands that the central government's capital be removed from the kingdom of Buganda.		Heavy fighting resumes between pro- and anti-government troops in Danang.
May 21	U.N. Arab delegates criticize the recent sale of U.S. warplanes to Israel.			Shooting incidents take place between Americans and Cubans at the U.S. naval base at Guantanamo, Cuba. Reports indicate that one Cuban is killed.	South Vietnamese and Communist forces clash in the Mekong Delta.
May 22					A Viet Cong unit abducts 35 Vietnamese civilian laborers from the village of Hogiang and kills 19 of them when government forces try to rescue the captives.
May 23	U.N. Security Council rejects an African resolution calling for the use of force against Rhodesia by Britain.	British officials meet with South Arabian Federation officials in London to discuss preliminary arrangements for the granting of independence in 1968.	Ugandan Pres. Milton Obote accuses Mutesa II, the king of Buganda and former Ugandan president, of high treason.		South Vietnamese government troops win complete control of Danang after defeating dissident soldiers.
May 24	U.N. Secy. Gen. U Thant calls for the de-escalation of the Vietnam War.	Police clash with Catalan nationalists in Barcelona.	Nigerian Head of State Maj. Gen. Johnson Aguiyi-Ironsi, an Ibo, abolishes Nigeria's four federal regions in favor of greater centralization. . . . In savage fighting Uganda crushes a growing separatist movement in the kingdom of Buganda.		U.S. planes stage heavy raids over North Vietnam.
May 25		West German Chancellor Ludwig Erhard declares that he wants all French military forces to remain in Germany.	Bugandan leader Mutesa II flees from Uganda.	British Guiana becomes the independent state of Guyana.	Communist China says it will not attend any disarmament conferences. . . . Government troops disperse 2,000 Buddhist protesters in Saigon. . . . Protests in several Australian cities occur in wake of the first death of an Australian conscript in South Vietnam. . . . Peiping radio charges that Li Chi, the C.P.'s chief of propaganda in the capital, is involved in the "anti-party" group.

A	B	C	D	E
Includes developments that affect more than one world region, international organizations and important meetings of major world leaders.	*Includes all domestic and regional developments in Europe, including the Soviet Union, Turkey, Cyprus and Malta.*	*Includes all domestic and regional developments in Africa and the Middle East, including Iraq and Iran and excluding Cyprus, Turkey and Afghanistan.*	*Includes all domestic and regional developments in Latin America, the Caribbean and Canada.*	*Includes all domestic and regional developments in Asia and Pacific nations, extending from Afghanistan through all the Pacific Islands, except Hawaii.*

U.S. Politics & Social Issues	U.S. Foreign Policy & Defense	U.S. Economy & Environment	Science, Technology & Nature	Culture, Leisure & Life Style	
About 500 Los Angeles Negroes riot over the recent slaying of Negro Leonard Deadwyler. They loot liquor stores and assault several journalists. . . . Twenty percent of Tuscaloosa's school children boycott classes in protest against alleged discrimination in the school district system.	U.S. protests to Cambodia about the April 29 deaths of two American soldiers by a Viet Cong unit operating from Cambodia. . . . Secy. Rusk refuses to say if he thinks Premier Ky was justified in taking Danang by force. . . . Sen. Fulbright says that his statement about America's alleged "arrogance of power" applies to "the extent but not the character of the nation's aspirations.". . . Pres. Johnson appeals for "national unity" during a Democratic Party fundraising dinner in Chicago. . . . State Secy. Dean Rusk says that the U.S. is reconsidering its food shipments to Egypt because of its recent anti-American statements.		Doctors in Houston, Tex. implant the first DeBakey bypass heart pump.	Saul Friedlander's *Pius XII and the Third Reich* is published.	May 17
Ten thousand Univ. of Wisconsin students protest against the draft.	Defense Secy. McNamara says that the U.S. should not be a "global gendarme."				May 18
		United Auto Workers re-elect Walter Reuther as their president.	Doctors announce the success of the first transplant of a mitral heart valve in Cleveland, Ohio.		May 19
	U.S. refuses the export to France of a computer required for the French nuclear weapons program.				May 20
One hundred demonstrators picket the Pittsburgh, Pa. school board headquarters to protest segregation in the city schools.		United Auto Workers adopt a resolution deploring "appeasement" in South Vietnam but warning against the dangers of a wider war.		New concert hall opens in Rotterdam replacing the building destroyed by Nazi bombs in 1940.	May 21
Congress of Racial Equality (CORE) announces that as a result of a picketing campaign begun April 6, realtors in central Baltimore have agreed to rent to black Americans. . . . About 200 Negroes attack policemen investigating an auto accident in Bakersfield, Calif.			Soviet Union launches a military surveillance satellite.		May 22
Baltimore Mayor Theodore McKeldin says that CORE is doing "a good job" and that he is "delighted to have them help us" in making racial progress.				Andre Maurois' *Prometheus: The Life of Balzac* is published. . . . Lord Moran's *The Struggle for Survival*, a biography of Winston Churchill, is published.	May 23
	A small anti-Vietnamese War demonstration takes place outside the Pentagon.				May 24
	In arguing against the administration's Vietnamese policies, Sen. J. William Fulbright says: "It seems almost incredible to me that in order to give elections to people that never had an election we are willing to kill thousands of them."	U.S. House rejects proposals to delete coverage of farm workers from a minimum wage bill.	U.S. launches Explorer 32 whose mission is to measure the temperatures, compositions, densities and pressures of various parts of the upper atmosphere.	Bernard Fall's *Vietnam Witness* is published.	May 25

F	G	H	I	J
Includes elections, federal-state relations, civil rights and liberties, crime, the judiciary, education, health care, poverty, urban affairs and population.	Includes formation and debate of U.S. foreign and defense policies, veterans' affairs and defense spending. (Relations with specific foreign countries are usually found under the region concerned.)	Includes business, labor, agriculture, taxation, transportation, consumer affairs, monetary and fiscal policy, natural resources, and pollution.	Includes worldwide scientific, medical and technological developments, natural phenomena, U.S. weather, natural disasters, and accidents.	Includes the arts, religion, scholarship, communications media, sports, entertainment, fashions, fads and social life.

	World Affairs	Europe	Africa & the Middle East	The Americas	Asia & the Pacific
May 26		Polish police disperse a crowd protesting anti-Church government policy in Brzeg, with tear gas and nightsticks. . . . *The New York Times* reports that Spain has offered to coordinate its defense system with Britain if the latter yields substantial sovereignty over Gibraltar.		U.S. turns over Atkinson Air Field in Georgetown, Guyana to the new independent government.	A U.S. military spokesman reports that 146 Americans were killed during May 15-21. This is the highest casualty total to date for a one week period. . . . Buddhist students sack and burn the U.S. cultural center in Hue.
May 27		For the first time since 1948, the Finnish government includes several Communists.	South Arabian Information Min. Abdel-Rahman Girgrah indicates that his country would like continued British protection.	U.S. Defense Department reveals that 11 US-Cuban incidents at Guantanamo have taken place during the last five months.	A split is reported between moderate and militant factions of the United Buddhist Church of South Vietnam. . . . Maj. Gen. Stanley Larsen, commander of U.S. forces in central South Vietnam, estimates that there are about 10,000 North Vietnamese troops massed in Cambodia.
May 28			Reports from Uganda indicate that 600 to 1,200 people were killed during the recent fighting. . . . Nigeria's largest ethnic group, the Hausas, clash with Ibo in northern Nigeria. Reports indicate that the Hausas resent the new Ibo-dominated central government.	Cuban Premier Fidel Castro orders a military alert for all of Cuba.	Viet Cong ambush a South Vietnamese unit near Saigon.
May 29		Riot police disperse a crowd protesting against anti-Church government activity in Gdansk, Poland.		Cuba says it has no intention of seizing the Guantanamo Naval Base.	Officials from Malaysia and Indonesia meet in Thailand to discuss ways of ending Indonesia's confrontation policies toward Malaysia.
May 30		Police clash with a small group of Communist students at the University of Rome.	Israeli artillery pounds Arab guerrilla bases across the Jordanian border.		Two Buddhists burn themselves to death in protest against government policies in South Vietnam.
May 31			Kuwaiti National Assembly confirms P.M. Jaber as crown prince.		Protesting students abandon the radio station in Hue in the face of military threats.
June 1		Cyprus imposes a blockade of the Turkish quarter of Nicosia in reprisal for two explosions outside the guarded zone.		Joaquin Balaguer succeeds Hector Garcia-Godoy as president of the Dominican Republic.	South Vietnamese government and Buddhists agree on the expansion of the ruling National Leadership Committee.
June 2			Reports indicate that hundreds of Ibos have recently been slain in northern Nigeria. . . . Britain and Rhodesia begin exploratory talks in Salisbury on ways to end their dispute.	Several hundred youths demonstrate in Santo Domingo against alleged fraud in the Dominican elections.	Indonesian Foreign Min. Adam Malik announces the formation of a Southeast Asian union that will include Malaysia, Indonesia, Thailand and the Philippines. . . . South Vietnamese regular forces move into Hue in order to restore the central government's control.
June 3	Thailand appeals to the U.N. to send observer teams to the Thai-Cambodian border where alleged skirmishes are taking place.		Sen. Robert Kennedy begins an unofficial speaking tour of South Africa. . . . Kenyan Pres. Jomo Kenyatta is given widespread powers to combat "subversion" by the Senate.	A mysterious slaying of a Panamanian student leader precipitates violent anti-government riots in Panama City.	Reports from China indicate that a major purge called the great proletarian Cultural Revolution took place in May. . . . South Korean troops wipe out a Viet Cong unit in the Central Highlands.
June 4		Polish government warns people not to gather around the Black Madonna in public places.			Massive demonstrations sweep through the streets of Peiping in support of the latest purges. . . . Four more Buddhists burn themselves to death, bringing to nine the number of self-immolations since May 29.

A	B	C	D	E
Includes developments that affect more than one world region, international organizations and important meetings of major world leaders.	*Includes all domestic and regional developments in Europe, including the Soviet Union, Turkey, Cyprus and Malta.*	*Includes all domestic and regional developments in Africa and the Middle East, including Iraq and Iran and excluding Cyprus, Turkey and Afghanistan.*	*Includes all domestic and regional developments in Latin America, the Caribbean and Canada.*	*Includes all domestic and regional developments in Asia and Pacific nations, extending from Afghanistan through all the Pacific Islands, except Hawaii.*

U.S. Politics & Social Issues	U.S. Foreign Policy & Defense	U.S. Economy & Environment	Science, Technology & Nature	Culture, Leisure & Life Style	
In Fayette, Miss., K.D. Dennis, a white, shoots and wounds Charles Knight, a Negro. . . . Pres. Johnson urges Congress to enact a new law controlling political campaign expenditures.	Pres. Johnson denounces minority rule in southern Africa at a gathering of African diplomats at the White House. . . .				May 26
350 Negroes protest the previous day's shooting in Fayette, Miss. at the county courthouse.					May 27
	Seventy-five demonstrators picket the N.Y.C. offices of the Dow Chemical Co. in protest against the firm's manufacture of Napalm for use in Vietnam.				May 28
	Sen. George McGovern (D, S.D.) says that the U.S. involvement in South Vietnam is a serious error.		U.S. launches a military surveillance satellite.		May 29
			U.S. launches an unmanned lunar probe, Surveyor 1.		May 30
NAACP sues the U.S. Steel Corp.'s plant near Birmingham, Ala. for alleged job discrimination.		Supreme Court bars a merger of two grocery store chains even though there is no proof that the merger would reduce competition.		New York Metropolitan Opera performs in Paris for the first time since 1912.	May 31
White House Conference on Civil Rights begins in Washington.	Sen. Gale McGee (D, Wy.) defends the administration's policy in Vietnam.				June 1
CORE's national director, Floyd McKissick, calls for a U.S. pull-out of South Vietnam at the White House Conference on Civil Rights.	Pres. Johnson congratulates Dominican provisional Pres. Garcia-Godoy for having "led the Dominican people from the turbulence of civil strife to the tranquility of free elections."		Surveyor I lands gently on the moon's surface and sends back photos indicating that it is safe for a manned craft.		June 2
Twenty of the 270 graduating seniors of Amherst College walk out of commencement exercises as Defense Secy. McNamara is presented with an honorary degree.			U.S. launches the Gemini 9 spacecraft, America's 11th manned orbital mission.		June 3
					June 4

F	G	H	I	J
Includes elections, federal-state relations, civil rights and liberties, crime, the judiciary, education, health care, poverty, urban affairs and population.	Includes formation and debate of U.S. foreign and defense policies, veterans' affairs and defense spending. (Relations with specific foreign countries are usually found under the region concerned.)	Includes business, labor, agriculture, taxation, transportation, consumer affairs, monetary and fiscal policy, natural resources, and pollution.	Includes worldwide scientific, medical and technological developments, natural phenomena, U.S. weather, natural disasters, and accidents.	Includes the arts, religion, scholarship, communications media, sports, entertainment, fashions, fads and social life.

	World Affairs	Europe	Africa & the Middle East	The Americas	Asia & the Pacific
June 5				Dominican Pres. Joaquin Balaguer says that the OAS Inter-American Peace Force might have to remain to assure stability.	A U.S. military spokesman says that 256 U.S. planes have been lost over North Vietnam since Feb. 7, 1965. . . . South Vietnamese government dismisses Hue's police chief for having failed to prevent attacks on the U.S. consulate on June 1.
June 6			Sen. Robert Kennedy denounces apartheid before 18,000 people at the University of Capetown. A five minute ovation follows his speech.	Police kill two students in violent clashes in Panama.	Ten civilians are added to South Vietnam's ruling committee of 10 generals.
June 7			Large crowds respond enthusiastically to Sen. Robert Kennedy in South Africa as he continues his speaking tour.		In one of the biggest battles of the war, heavy fighting rages between U.S. and North Vietnamese troops in Kontum province in the Central Highlands. . . . East Pakistanis demanding autonomy riot in Dacca; police kill 11 demonstrators. . . . Communist Chinese press attacks an army official, Lo Jui-ching, for the first time.
June 8		Reports indicate that COCOM (Coordinating Committee), a 15-nation grouping of Japan and all NATO countries except Iceland, has rejected a U.S. proposal to restrict computer sales to communist nations.	Reports indicate that the Soviet Union has discontinued work on a hydroelectric dam in Ghana. . . . Cheering crowds greet Sen. Robert Kennedy in Soweto, Johannesburg's black district.	Nicaraguan Pres. Rene Schick Gutierrez says he is willing to have his country used as a base for an attack on Cuba, "at any time."	Heavy fighting continues in Kontum province in Vietnam. . . . Buddhist leader Tri Quang starts a hunger strike in Hue to protest U.S. support of the Ky government.
June 9		Police clash briefly with a small group of protesting students on the campus of the University of Barcelona.	Ghana charges the Soviet Union and East Germany with having set up an extensive spy system under former Pres. Kwame Nkrumah.		Buddhist leader Tri Quang announces that military traffic will be permitted to use the Hue-Phubai road during the day.
June 10		British politician Enoch Powell criticizes the government's immigration policies for being too liberal.	Ugandan Pres. Milton Obote announces the dissolution of the Kingdom of Buganda.		South Vietnamese Premier Ky sends about 400 combat police into Hue in a renewed effort to wrest control of the city from Buddhist and military dissidents.
June 11			National elections begin in Kenya.	Minor student unrest continues in the Dominican Republic.	Reports indicate that the only remaining issue between Indonesia and Malaysia is the status of the Malaysian states of Sabah and Sarawak.
June 12			South Arabian Foreign Min. Mohammad Farid says that he will ask the U.S. to guarantee his country's defense in view of Britain's refusal to do so.	Police and demonstrating students clash briefly in Panama City.	About 15,000 Roman Catholics demonstrate in favor of the Ky government in Saigon.

A	B	C	D	E
Includes developments that affect more than one world region, international organizations and important meetings of major world leaders.	Includes all domestic and regional developments in Europe, including the Soviet Union, Turkey, Cyprus and Malta.	Includes all domestic and regional developments in Africa and the Middle East, including Iraq and Iran and excluding Cyprus, Turkey and Afghanistan.	Includes all domestic and regional developments in Latin America, the Caribbean and Canada.	Includes all domestic and regional developments in Asia and Pacific nations, extending from Afghanistan through all the Pacific Islands, except Hawaii.

U.S. Politics & Social Issues	U.S. Foreign Policy & Defense	U.S. Economy & Environment	Science, Technology & Nature	Culture, Leisure & Life Style	
James Meredith, the Negro student who helped integrate the University of Mississippi in 1962, begins a 220-mile voting rights march from Memphis, Tenn. to Jackson, Miss. to encourage Negroes to register to vote.			U.S. astronaut Eugene Cernan spends a record two hours and nine minutes outside Gemini 9.		June 5
N.J. Supreme Court rules that a Negro convicted of manslaughter is entitled to a new trial because the presiding judge used a derogatory racial epithet. . . . James Meredith is shot and wounded during his voting rights march. . . . Police arrest Aubrey James Norvell, a white resident of Memphis, for the Meredith shooting.			Gemini 9 parachutes safely into the Atlantic Ocean.		June 6
Former movie star Ronald Reagan wins the Republican gubernatorial nomination in California. . . . Leaders of America's three leading civil rights organizations, Martin Luther King (SCLC), Floyd McKissick (CORE) and Stokely Carmichael (SNCC), vow to continue the Meredith march.				French painter Jean Arp, 78, dies in Basel, Switzerland.	June 7
Mississippi state NAACP field secretary, Charles Evers, announces that the six-month boycott of white merchants in Fayette, Miss. has ended following agreement by city officials to a list of Negro demands. . . . New York Univ. seniors and faculty members, numbering 130-200, walk out of commencement exercises as Defense Secy. McNamara is presented with an honorary degree.					June 8
			Soviet Union launches a communications satellite.		June 9
A Negro organization announces that it intends to monitor alleged police abuses in Watts, the major Negro district of Los Angeles.			Soviet Union conducts an underground nuclear test.		June 10
A National Conference for New Politics holds its first meeting in New York. The organization opposes the war in Vietnam and supports civil rights and anti-poverty action. . . . Job Corps trainees stone passing cars in Edison, N.J.	Defense Secy. McNamara announces that 18,000 U.S. troops will be sent to Vietnam within 45 days.				June 11
Police find the body of Ben Chester White, 65, a Negro, near Natchez, Miss. . . . An incident between a policeman and a Puerto Rican youth sets off rioting in the Puerto Rican district of Chicago. . . . A National Industrial Conference Board study indicates that gains are being made in the hiring of Negroes although firms are having difficulty finding qualified applicants for many positions.	New Politics Conference announces that it will begin a search for a presidential candidate in 1968.			Polish conductor Herman Scherchen dies in Florence at 76.	June 12

F	G	H	I	J
Includes elections, federal-state relations, civil rights and liberties, crime, the judiciary, education, health care, poverty, urban affairs and population.	*Includes formation and debate of U.S. foreign and defense policies, veterans' affairs and defense spending. (Relations with specific foreign countries are usually found under the region concerned.)*	*Includes business, labor, agriculture, taxation, transportation, consumer affairs, monetary and fiscal policy, natural resources, and pollution.*	*Includes worldwide scientific, medical and technological developments, natural phenomena, U.S. weather, natural disasters, and accidents.*	*Includes the arts, religion, scholarship, communications media, sports, entertainment, fashions, fads and social life.*

	World Affairs	Europe	Africa & the Middle East	The Americas	Asia & the Pacific
June 13		Soviet Premier Kosygin begins an official visit to Finland.			Police with tear gas disperse about 500 demonstrating Buddhist monks in South Vietnam.
June 14		Police and striking workers clash in Amsterdam. . . . Common Market agrees on tariff reduction porposals to be presented at the current trade negotiation session in Geneva.	In Nairobi, Kenya, Sen. Robert Kennedy says that a majority of black South Africans oppose economic sanctions against South Africa because they would also suffer the adverse economic repercussions.		Three thousand demonstrators riot in Saigon.
June 15		Radical students join striking workers in clashes with police in Amsterdam. . . . First Deputy Chmn. Rainer Barzel of the West German Christian Democrats says that there might "be a place for Soviet troops" in a reunified Germany. . . . *The New York Times* reports that Rumanian Foreign Min. Corneliu Manescu refused to endorse a Warsaw Pact declaration condemning West Germany as the chief "troublemaker" in Europe during a June 11 foreign ministers meeting.	Syrian and Israeli forces fight a three-hour sea and air battle in and around the Sea of Galilee.		Government troops clash with rioters in Saigon.
June 16		West German Chancellor Ludwig Erhard says that Barzel's statement is a "personal expression of opinion.". . . Communist Chinese Premier Chou En-lai arrives in Rumania for official talks.			Government troops begin to remove Buddhist protest altars from Saigon streets.
June 17		Reports indicate that Polish Cardinal Wyszynski has thanked the West German episcopate for its "Christian sympathy" during Poland's religious celebrations.	Britain and its African colony of Basutoland agree that on Oct. 4, 1966 independence will come into effect.		A young Buddhist girl burns herself to death in Saigon.
June 18	Arab U.N. delegates accuse Israel of provoking the recent Israeli-Syrian clash.	Polish Cardinal Wyszynski discloses that police seized the touring portrait of the Black Madonna during the previous week.	Reports indicate that Kenya is calm despite the recent political dispute by leaders of the country's two largest ethnic groups.		South Vietnam devalues the piaster in an anti-inflation measure. . . . Chinese Communist Premier Chou En-lai says that his country is in the midst of a "cultural revolution directed against a handful of anti-socialist intellectuals."
June 19		Soviet Union denounces the recent proposals for reunification by West German leader Rainer Barzel.		OAS proposes some minor charter reforms.	Pro-government South Vietnamese troops end the Buddhist resistance in Hue. . . . Reports indicate that the Communist Chinese press is giving increased prominence to Defense Min. Lin Piao.
June 20		British Prime Min. Wilson raises the possibility of communist influence as a source of difficulty in settling the merchant marine strike. . . . Cypriote government re-imposes the blockade of the Turkish quarter of Nicosia for no apparent reason. . . . French Pres. Charles de Gaulle begins a visit to the Soviet Union. . . . Communist Chinese Premier Chou En-lai praises the Rumanian people for their successful "fight against external control."		Canada agrees to sell a large quantity of wheat to the Soviet Union.	Government troops arrest militant Buddhist leader Tri Quang and fly him to Saigon.

A	B	C	D	E
Includes developments that affect more than one world region, international organizations and important meetings of major world leaders.	Includes all domestic and regional developments in Europe, including the Soviet Union, Turkey, Cyprus and Malta.	Includes all domestic and regional developments in Africa and the Middle East, including Iraq and Iran and excluding Cyprus, Turkey and Afghanistan.	Includes all domestic and regional developments in Latin America, the Caribbean and Canada.	Includes all domestic and regional developments in Asia and Pacific nations, extending from Afghanistan through all the Pacific Islands, except Hawaii.

U.S. Politics & Social Issues	U.S. Foreign Policy & Defense	U.S. Economy & Environment	Science, Technology & Nature	Culture, Leisure & Life Style	
Angry crowds break windows and stone cars in Chicago's Puerto Rican district. . . . Job Corps administration announces that its requirements for accepting trainees will be raised because of persistent rowdyism by many of its present members. . . . A Texas state court rules that Jack Ruby, the convicted slayer of Lee Harvey Oswald, is sane.			U.S. launches a military surveillance satellite.		June 13
Minor outbreaks of violence result in 31 arrests in Chicago's Puerto Rican district. . . . Police arrest three members of the Ku Klux Klan in connection with the recent slaying of Ben Chester White.					June 14
Chicago's Puerto Rican district appears calm and back to normal. . . . U.S. Conference of Mayors urges the administration to put domestic problems on an equal footing with the Vietnamese War.	U.S. State Dept. announces the resumption of full-scale economic aid to India and Pakistan which had been stopped because of the 1965 war.				June 15
Oklahoma City Negroes demonstrate for the desegregation of a privately owned amusement park.				Critics choose Peter Weiss's *Marat/Sade* as the best play of the 1965-66 season.	June 16
Newsmen covering the James Meredith voter registration march discover a poisonous snake which had been placed in their truck.					June 17
					June 18
Sen. Robert Kennedy says that he will support Pres. Johnson for re-election in 1968. . . . Rock throwing and fist fights erupt between Negro and Puerto Rican youths in Jersey City, N.J.	On his return to the U.S., Sen. Robert Kennedy again denounces apartheid but cautions that it took the U.S. "such a long period of time to accomplish what's right that we should keep this in mind in any criticisms of South Africa."			Prof. Pierre Montet, who discovered remains of Egyptian colony at Byblos, Syria, and other important Egyptian archeological items, dies in Paris at 80.	June 19
A "march for decent welfare" takes place in Cleveland, Ohio. . . . Supreme Court rules that taking a blood sample from a driver for use as evidence of drunken driving does not violate the Fifth Amendment. . . . In an interview Martin Luther King says: "It is absolutely necessary for the Negro to gain power" but that such power should be shared with whites.					June 20

F	G	H	I	J
Includes elections, federal-state relations, civil rights and liberties, crime, the judiciary, education, health care, poverty, urban affairs and population.	Includes formation and debate of U.S. foreign and defense policies, veterans' affairs and defense spending. (Relations with specific foreign countries are usually found under the region concerned.)	Includes business, labor, agriculture, taxation, transportation, consumer affairs, monetary and fiscal policy, natural resources, and pollution.	Includes worldwide scientific, medical and technological developments, natural phenomena, U.S. weather, natural disasters, and accidents.	Includes the arts, religion, scholarship, communications media, sports, entertainment, fashions, fads and social life.

	World Affairs	Europe	Africa & the Middle East	The Americas	Asia & the Pacific
June 21		Police clash with demonstrating Basques in the Spanish province of Asturias.			U.S. bombers pound Communist postions in North Vietnam.
June 22	U.N. Secy. Gen. U Thant urges Cypriote Pres. Makarios to lift the blockade of the Turkish quarter.	French spokesmen say that Pres. de Gaulle has told First Secy. Brezhnev that the U.S. and USSR tend to counterbalance each other's inclination towards hegemony.	At a U.S. press conference, King Faisal says: "Unfortunately, Jews support Israel and we consider those who provide assistance to our enemies as our own enemies."		Government troops take Quangtri, the only remaining anti-government Buddhist stronghold in northern South Vietnam.
June 23		Cypriote Pres. Makarios ends the blockade of the Turkish quarter.			Government troops seize the principal Buddhist stronghold in Saigon, the Secular Affairs Institute.
June 24		Communist Chinese Premier Chou En-lai arrives in Albania for official talks.		OAS Council approves a resolution calling for the withdrawal of the 8,200-man OAS peace force from the Dominican Republic within three months.	Government troops thwart a Buddhist protest march in Hue.
June 25			King Faisal clarifies his June 22 statement by saying, "We are not against the religion of the Jews but against the Zionists and the Jews who help the Zionists.". . . Fourteen French speaking African states agree on a program of economic cooperation.		Premier Ky visits Hue and asks its residents "to forget the misunderstandings of the past."
June 26			Pres. Jomo Kenyatta wins a decisive victory over former V.P. Oginga Odinga in Kenyan national elections.		
June 27		French Communist Party lauds Pres. de Gaulle's attempts to reduce U.S. influence in Western Europe.	Reports indicate that sporadic violence is still taking place against Ibos in northern Nigeria.		
June 28	African U.N. delegates call on Britain to use force against Rhodesia.			A three-man military junta headed by Lt. Gen. Juan Carlos Ongania ousts Argentinian Pres. Arturo Illia.	
June 29	U.N. Secy. Gen. U Thant criticizes the U.S. raids on the Hanoi-Haiphong oil installations. . . . British P.M. Harold Wilson expresses regret over the extension of the U.S. air attacks and disassociates Britain from them.	East Germany rejects its original proposal of having public debates between East and West German leaders. . . . Reports indicate that French Pres. de Gaulle has rejected a Soviet request to recognize East Germany.	Iraqi Pres. Abdel Rahman Arif announces that the leader of Iraq's Kurds, Mustapha Mullah el-Barzani, has agreed to a 12-point peace proposal.	Lt. Gen. Juan Carlos Ongania is sworn in as the president of Argentina. . . . Canadian P.M. Lester Pearson expresses his regret over the recent U.S. bombing extension.	For the first time American bombers strike at fuel storage installations near Hanoi and Haiphong. . . . North Vietnam says that it has put captured American pilots "on display" for crowds in Hanoi. . . . Philippine Foreign Secy. Narciso Ramos calls on SEATO to help his government in its campaign against the Communist-led Huk guerrilla movement in Central Luzon.
	A	B	C	D	E
	Includes developments that affect more than one world region, international organizations and important meetings of major world leaders.	Includes all domestic and regional developments in Europe, including the Soviet Union, Turkey, Cyprus and Malta.	Includes all domestic and regional developments in Africa and the Middle East, including Iraq and Iran and excluding Cyprus, Turkey and Afghanistan.	Includes all domestic and regional developments in Latin America, the Caribbean and Canada.	Includes all domestic and regional developments in Asia and Pacific nations, extending from Afghanistan through all the Pacific Islands, except Hawaii.

U.S. Politics & Social Issues	U.S. Foreign Policy & Defense	U.S. Economy & Environment	Science, Technology & Nature	Culture, Leisure & Life Style	
After two days without any incidents, the Meredith voter registration march encounters violence in Philadelphia, Miss. from a mob of 300 stone-throwing whites. Local police do not intervene to prevent the attacks. . . . About 600 Negroes riot in Pompano Beach, Fla. after a minor racial incident at a supermarket.	Saudi Arabia's King Faisal begins a state visit to the United States with a meeting with Pres. Johnson.	National Farm Workers Association and Schenley Industries sign a one-year contract providing for a wage increase and a union shop.			June 21
In the aftermath of Puerto Rican rioting in Chicago, Claudio Flores, a community leader, becomes a member of the Mayor's Commission on Human Relations.	House Armed Services Committee begins public hearings on alleged inequities in the military draft. . . .				June 22
A mob of Negro youths throws stones at passing cars and breaks the windows of a supermarket in Cleveland, Ohio.	N.Y.C. Mayor John Lindsay and N.Y. Gov. Nelson Rockefeller cancel scheduled dinners for King Faisal because of the alleged "anti-Semitic" tone of some of his remarks.			Film version of Edward Albee's *Who's Afraid of Virginia Woolf* opens. Richard Burton and Elizabeth Taylor play the lead roles.	June 23
James Meredith re-joins the voter registration march after recovering from gunshot wounds. . . . Police arrest eight whites for attempting to block the integration of a beach on Chicago's South Side. . . . A Cleveland Negro community leader, Bertram Gardner, urges police to close his neighborhood's bars and patrol in integrated cars.	Pres. Johnson endorses proposals for an all-Asian conference to settle the Vietnamese War and denies that the U.S. plans to build permanent bases in South Vietnam and Thailand.			N.Y. Gov. Nelson Rockefeller signs a bill enabling a citizens' committee to try to save the old Metropolitan Opera House in New York.	June 24
	U.S. military officials in Saigon say that Viet Cong-held territory is being sprayed with a poisonous plant killer in order to deprive the guerrillas of food.				June 25
Miss. march begun by James Meredith ends in front of the state capitol in Jackson, Miss.			Dr. Maurice Hilleman and Dr. Eugene Buynak in West Point, Pa. announce the development of a live-virus vaccine against mumps.	U.S. soprano Jane Marsh becomes the first American winner of the Tchaikovsky Competition in Moscow since Van Cliburn.	June 26
Justice Dept. files suit against officials in Philadelphia, Miss. for not preventing the June 21 harassment of the Meredith voter registration marchers.	Harvard Univ. Prof. Henry Kissinger cautions the U.S. about forcing West Germany into an anti-French policy or attempting to build a Bonn-Washington alliance within NATO. Such a policy, he believes, would require the continued presence of large U.S. forces in Europe at a time when mutual U.S.-Soviet withdrawals might be possible.				June 27
A gun battle breaks out between whites and Negroes at a gas station in Cordele, Ga.		N.Y. Gov. Nelson Rockefeller signs a bill repealing most of the state's full-crew railroad laws which had created superfluous jobs.			June 28
		Major U.S. banks raise the prime rate for business loans from 5.5% to 5.75%.			June 29

F	G	H	I	J
Includes elections, federal-state relations, civil rights and liberties, crime, the judiciary, education, health care, poverty, urban affairs and population.	Includes formation and debate of U.S. foreign and defense policies, veterans' affairs and defense spending. (Relations with specific foreign countries are usually found under the region concerned.)	Includes business, labor, agriculture, taxation, transportation, consumer affairs, monetary and fiscal policy, natural resources, and pollution.	Includes worldwide scientific, medical and technological developments, natural phenomena, U.S. weather, natural disasters, and accidents.	Includes the arts, religion, scholarship, communications media, sports, entertainment, fashions, fads and social life.

	World Affairs	Europe	Africa & the Middle East	The Americas	Asia & the Pacific
June 30		U.S. begins the withdrawal of its military forces from France.	Iraqi Pres. Abdel Rahman Arif crushes an attempted coup d'etat led by Brig. Gen. Arif Abdel Razzak.		
July 1		France places all its armed forces assigned to NATO under national control. . . . Italian Foreign Min. Amintore Fanfani expresses his reservations about the U.S. raids on North Vietnamese oil installations.	OAU urges Britain to use force against Rhodesia. . . . Congolese Pres. Joseph Mobutu issues a decree changing the European names of his country's cities to African names.	Britain announces that Barbados will become independent on Nov. 30, 1966. . . . American troops begin to withdraw from the Dominican Republic. . . . Police arrest a number of Jewish shopkeepers and close their stores in Argentina. . . . Julio Cesar Mendez Montenegro is sworn in as Guatemalan president, ending three years of army rule. In his inaugural address he stresses his desire for an accord with Guatemala's communist guerrillas.	Indian demonstrators in several cities protest the American raids on the Hanoi-Haiphong area.
July 2		France explodes its first nuclear bomb since March 1963.	Israeli troops clash briefly with Arab infiltrators in northern Israel.		Indonesian Foreign Min. Adam Malik says that Britain has promised to withdraw its troops from Malaysia after the Indonesian-Malaysian peace agreement is ratified. . . . India says that Pakistan has nearly doubled its armed forces in Pakistani Kashmir since the 1965 border fighting. . . . Reports indicate that much of the population of Hanoi is being evacuated to the countryside.
July 3		British cabinet Minister Frank Cousins resigns in protest against the government's wage and price restraint program.		Lt. Gen. Rene Barrientos Ortuno wins the presidential election in Bolivia.	
July 4		A 30-pound concrete block is dropped on the roof of a car containing Queen Elizabeth II and Prince Philip in Belfast, Ireland; neither one is injured.			Rear Adm. James Reedy says that half of the Hanoi-Haiphong area's petroleum installations have been destroyed by U.S. raids.
July 5		British Parliament approves the reintroduction of a bill abolishing criminal penalties for homosexual acts between consenting adults.			U.S. pilots report that North Vietnam's anti-aircraft defenses are improving rapidly. . . . Australian P.M. Harold Holt declares his support of the bombing extension of North Vietnam.
July 6		French Premier Georges Pompidou visits London for talks on Britain's possible entry into the Common Market. . . . Warsaw Pact members declare their readiness to send "volunteers" to North Vietnam.	Kamuzu Banda is inaugurated as first president of Malawi.		
July 7		British House of Commons upholds P.M. Harold Wilson's qualified support of U.S. policy in Vietnam.	Rhodesian P.M. Ian Smith accuses Britain of having intensified its economic sanctions against Rhodesia while exploratory talks are still in progress.		Pentagon reports that North Vietnamese jets are using air-to-air missiles for the first time against U.S. planes.
	A	B	C	D	E
	Includes developments that affect more than one world region, international organizations and important meetings of major world leaders.	Includes all domestic and regional developments in Europe, including the Soviet Union, Turkey, Cyprus and Malta.	Includes all domestic and regional developments in Africa and the Middle East, including Iraq and Iran and excluding Cyprus, Turkey and Afghanistan.	Includes all domestic and regional developments in Latin America, the Caribbean and Canada.	Includes all domestic and regional developments in Asia and Pacific nations, extending from Afghanistan through all the Pacific Islands, except Hawaii.

U.S. Politics & Social Issues	U.S. Foreign Policy & Defense	U.S. Economy & Environment	Science, Technology & Nature	Culture, Leisure & Life Style	
Two hundred and fifty welfare beneficiaries demonstrate for greater welfare payment in N.Y.C.	Rep. Gerald Ford (R, Mich.) says that the U.S. should have bombed the Hanoi-Haiphong oil installations "months ago.". . . In a speech in Omaha, Neb., Pres. Johnson warns that U.S. air strikes "will continue to impose a growing burden" on North Vietnam.				June 30
At the opening of the CORE national convention, Stokely Carmichael denounces "white liberals" and calls integration "irrelevant.". . . A Boston court sentences David O'Brien to a term not exceeding four years for having burned his draft card.		N.Y. Gov. Nelson Rockefeller signs a bill mandating the first income tax on N.Y.C. residents.			July 1
CORE national director Floyd McKissick says Negroes must not surrender the right of self-defense.					July 2
Much of the criticism at CORE's national convention centers on Negroes who "work for the establishment.". . . A night of rioting begins when Negro youths throw rocks at a police car in Omaha, Neb. . . . HEW Secy. John Gardner announces termination of federal aid to five southern school districts because they refuse to comply with desegregation guidelines.				U.S. composer Deems Taylor dies in New York at 80.	July 3
CORE national convention approves a resolution endorsing the concept of black power. . . . Omaha officials call in the National Guard to quell rioting Negro youths. . . . NAACP's Pres. Roy Wilkins attacks CORE's espousal of self-defense.		Mexican-American farm workers begin a statewide march across Texas to protest the current minimum wage.			July 4
NAACP dissociates itself from the black power faction of the civil rights movement.	Pres. Johnson estimates that about 86% of North Vietnam's petroleum storage capacity has been hit in the recent raids.				July 5
Omaha's Negro district is calm for the first time in several nights. . . . In an allusion to the black power movement, V.P. Humphrey reaffirms the goal of integration at the NAACP's national convention.				Ford Foundation announces extensive grants to support U.S. symphony orchestras.	July 6
		Despite government charges of corruption, the Teamsters Union re-elects by acclamation Pres. James Hoffa.			July 7

F	G	H	I	J
Includes elections, federal-state relations, civil rights and liberties, crime, the judiciary, education, health care, poverty, urban affairs and population.	Includes formation and debate of U.S. foreign and defense policies, veterans' affairs and defense spending. (Relations with specific foreign countries are usually found under the region concerned.)	Includes business, labor, agriculture, taxation, transportation, consumer affairs, monetary and fiscal policy, natural resources, and pollution.	Includes worldwide scientific, medical and technological developments, natural phenomena, U.S. weather, natural disasters, and accidents.	Includes the arts, religion, scholarship, communications media, sports, entertainment, fashions, fads and social life.

	World Affairs	Europe	Africa & the Middle East	The Americas	Asia & the Pacific
July 8		Warsaw Pact nations invite West Europeans to join them in a European security conference.	Prince Charles Ndinzeye deposes his absent father, King Mwambutsa, in a bloodless coup in Burundi.		North Vietnam says that angry Vietnamese crowds have demanded "punishments" for captured American pilots. . . . South Vietnamese Chief of State Nguyen Van Thieu calls for a land invasion of North Vietnam.
July 9		Soviet Union charges that U.S. air strikes against Haiphong endanger Soviet ships.	Egyptian Pres. Gamal Nasser says that the Arab countries will never accept Israel as a neighbor.		South Vietnamese government dismisses five generals from the army because of alleged participation in the March-June Buddhist anti-government campaign.
July 10				Canada signs an agreement with the Soviet Union providing for direct air service between the two countries.	Communist Chinese news agency confirms the ouster of propaganda head Lu Ting-yi.
July 11		Soviet Union, protesting U.S. policy in Vietnam, announces that it will not participate in the eighth annual U.S.-Soviet track meet.		Police and student demonstrators scuffle on the campus of the University of Buenos Aires.	
July 12		Indian P.M. Indira Gandhi arrives in Moscow for talks with Premier Aleksei Kosygin.	Repatriation of Hausa and Ibo troops to their respective native areas begins in Nigeria.	Argentinian Pres. Juan Carlos Ongania assures representatives of the Jewish community that "extremists, whether of the right or left, will be fought."	A U.S. Air Force spokesman reports that 110 U.S. planes have been lost in Vietnam since Jan. 1, 1961.
July 13		West German newspaper *Die Welt* criticizes French Pres. de Gaulle's systematic campaign to undercut U.S. influence in Western Europe.	A land mine kills two Israelis in northern Israel.		
July 14		Welsh nationalists win their first seat in the British House of Commons.	Israeli jets carry out a 25-minute daylight raid eight miles inside Syria in retaliation for the previous day's land-mine killing.		A force of over 8,500 U.S. Marines and 2,500 South Vietnamese troops launches a massive drive in Quangtri Province. . . . Philippine Pres. Ferdinand Marcos agrees to send 2,000 troops to South Vietnam.
July 15	Arab U.N. delegates criticize Israel's recent reprisal raid.	Reports indicate that the withdrawal of U.S. troops from France is proceeding normally.		U.S. recognizes the new Argentinian government.	
July 16	U.N. Secy. Gen. U Thant urges North Vietnam "to exercise restraint in its treatment of American prisoners."	British P.M. Harold Wilson arrives in Moscow for official talks.	Nigeria becomes the first English-speaking African nation to become an associate member of the Common Market.	Guatemala's Communist leaders reject the new government's offer to negotiate.	Communist China says that Chmn. Mao recently swam 15 kilometers in an hour and five minutes in the Yangtze River.
July 17				Reports indicate that the 28 Guatemalan leftists missing since their arrest in March and April were shot by the former military government.	North Vietnamese Pres. Ho Chi Minh orders a "partial" mobilization of the country.
July 18	International Court of Justice dismisses a suit challenging South Africa's right to govern South-West Africa.				A crowd of religious pilgrims tramples 17 people to death during a rush for shelter from a torrential rain storm in Lucknow, India. . . . Communist China offers its territory as a possible haven for North Vietnamese military forces.

A	B	C	D	E
Includes developments that affect more than one world region, international organizations and important meetings of major world leaders.	Includes all domestic and regional developments in Europe, including the Soviet Union, Turkey, Cyprus and Malta.	Includes all domestic and regional developments in Africa and the Middle East, including Iraq and Iran and excluding Cyprus, Turkey and Afghanistan.	Includes all domestic and regional developments in Latin America, the Caribbean and Canada.	Includes all domestic and regional developments in Asia and Pacific nations, extending from Afghanistan through all the Pacific Islands, except Hawaii.

U.S. Politics & Social Issues	U.S. Foreign Policy & Defense	U.S. Economy & Environment	Science, Technology & Nature	Culture, Leisure & Life Style	
About 1,000 inmates of the Maryland Penitentiary in Baltimore riot in protest against alleged poor living conditions.		A strike shuts down 60% of U.S. domestic airlines service.			July 8
				New York City Ballet opens its Saratoga Performing Arts Center.	July 9
Martin Luther King talks of making Chicago "an open city" before a predominantly Negro crowd in Chicago. . . . A voter registration march begins in Bogalusa. La.					July 10
Martin Luther King meets with Chicago Mayor Richard Daley for talks on the city's segregated housing.			Soviet Union conducts an underground nuclear test.		July 11
Rioting erupts on Chicago's West Side Negro district; several hundred people are arrested.	Pres. Johnson assures Communist China that the U.S. seeks a "peace of conciliation" and not of "conquest" in Asia.				July 12
Roving Negro mobs trade gunfire with police on Chicago's West Side.					July 13
Several hundred policemen begin to restore order on Chicago's West Side as looting decreases.					July 14
National Guardsmen enter Chicago's West Side with orders of "shoot to kill" if attacked. Their presence reduces violent incidents dramatically. . . . Fighting breaks out between Negroes, whites and Puerto Ricans in an area of Brooklyn, N.Y. where their three neighborhoods meet.					July 15
Scattered violence takes place after police arrest a Negro woman in Troy, N.Y.					July 16
Fighting breaks out between Negroes and Puerto Ricans in Brooklyn, N.Y. Two people suffer gunshot wounds and two others suffer knife wounds. . . . Four thousand Negroes demonstrate in Washington, D.C. for home rule for the District of Columbia.					July 17
Shooting, looting and fire-bombing sweep through Cleveland's Negro district.			Gemini 10 manned spaceship sets a record for distance above the earth's surface.		July 18

F	G	H	I	J
Includes elections, federal-state relations, civil rights and liberties, crime, the judiciary, education, health care, poverty, urban affairs and population.	Includes formation and debate of U.S. foreign and defense policies, veterans' affairs and defense spending. (Relations with specific foreign countries are usually found under the region concerned.)	Includes business, labor, agriculture, taxation, transportation, consumer affairs, monetary and fiscal policy, natural resources, and pollution.	Includes worldwide scientific, medical and technological developments, natural phenomena, U.S. weather, natural disasters, and accidents.	Includes the arts, religion, scholarship, communications media, sports, entertainment, fashions, fads and social life.

	World Affairs	Europe	Africa & the Middle East	The Americas	Asia & the Pacific
July 19	In what is reported to be the first official contact between the U.S. and Mongolia, Max Finger, counselor of the U.S. mission to the U.N., offers $25,000 in flood relief to Lutun Chuluunbaatar, counselor of the Mongolian mission.	France explodes a nuclear bomb.		Argentina begins talks with Britain about the future of the Falkland Islands.	Two North Vietnamese ambassadors say that all captured American pilots will be tried as "war criminals."
July 20		British P.M. Harold Wilson announces drastic cuts in domestic spending in order to fight inflation.	An Israeli patrol skirmishes with Arab guerrillas near the Syrian border.		
July 21		French Pres. de Gaulle visits West Germany for talks with Chancellor Ludwig Erhard.			
July 22			Zambia announces that it will resume copper shipments through Rhodesia.	Haiti and the Dominican Republic resume diplomatic relations which were severed in 1963 over a dispute involving political refugees.	U.S. bombers pound Communist supply roads in North Vietnam.
July 23			Zambian Pres. Kenneth Kaunda announces that his country will partially boycott the British Commonwealth in protest against Britain's refusal to use stronger measures against Rhodesia. . . . An 800-man force of Katangan gendarmes and white mercenaries seize the city of Kisangani (formerly Stanleyville).	Argentinian Pres. Juan Carlos Ongania bans the satirical political weekly *Tia Vicenta*.	North Vietnamese Pres. Ho Chi Minh says that there is "no trial in view" for American pilots. . . . A 27-man air force unit from Thailand arrives in Saigon. It is the fifth allied nation to become involved in the fighting.
July 24		Common Market countries agree on major farm commodity prices.	Congolese Pres. Joseph Mobutu orders an investigation of charges by Katangan gendarmes that they have not been paid for months.		
July 25	Finance ministers and central bank governors of the ten leading financial nations meet in The Hague to discuss international monetary reform. . . . U.N. Secy. Gen. U Thant arrives in Moscow for talks with the Soviet government.	British Defense Min. Denis Healey says Britain will have to withdraw part of its forces from Germany unless other countries contribute more for the costs involved. . . . British Parliament approves a bill renationalizing the steel industry.	An airlift evacuates 44 whites from Kisangani in the Congo to Kinshasa in wake of the Katangan army mutiny.		South Vietnamese Pres. Ky urges an allied invasion of North Vietnam, even at the risk of a military confrontation with Communist China.
July 26				Guatemalan Congress approves a decree granting immediate amnesty to political prisoners arrested since Nov. 1, 1960.	U.S. troops clash with the Viet Cong in the Central Highlands.
July 27		Former Belgian Premier Paul-Henri Spaak resigns his Parliamentary seat and retires from political life.	Sudanese Parliament elects Saadik el Mahdi as prime minister.		India and the U.S. agree to set aside plans to establish an Indian-American education foundation.
July 28		Police break up a small anti-government demonstration in Barcelona, Spain.	Congo charges that ex-Premier Moise Tshombe and Belgium are linked with the Katangan mutineers.	Sporadic student unrest takes place in Santo Domingo.	
July 29			A military revolt led by Moslem Hausas overthrows Nigerian Pres. Maj. Gen. Johnson Aguiyi-Ironsi.	Argentina seizes the country's eight national universities in an effort to suppress anti-government activity.	
	A	B	C	D	E
	Includes developments that affect more than one world region, international organizations and important meetings of major world leaders.	Includes all domestic and regional developments in Europe, including the Soviet Union, Turkey, Cyprus and Malta.	Includes all domestic and regional developments in Africa and the Middle East, including Iraq and Iran and excluding Cyprus, Turkey and Afghanistan.	Includes all domestic and regional developments in Latin America, the Caribbean and Canada.	Includes all domestic and regional developments in Asia and Pacific nations, extending from Afghanistan through all the Pacific Islands, except Hawaii.

U.S. Politics & Social Issues	U.S. Foreign Policy & Defense	U.S. Economy & Environment	Science, Technology & Nature	Culture, Leisure & Life Style	
National Guard withdraws from Chicago's West Side. . . . Cleveland Mayor Ralph Locher tours the riot area and orders its bars to be closed during the evening. . . . Neighborhood residents complain about unruly behavior by Job Corps trainees in Excelsior Springs, Mo. Officials at the center admit problems but maintain progress is being made.					July 19
Several hundred National Guardsmen move into Cleveland's Negro district as rioting and looting continue.	Pres. Johnson warns North Vietnam not to put American pilots on trial.				July 20
One person is killed in Brooklyn, N.Y., as racial strife continues.	U.S. launches its 41st nuclear submarine.		Gemini 10 returns safely to earth with its two U.S. astronauts.		July 21
One thousand additional policemen patrol the racial battle ground in Brooklyn, N.Y.	During a highly charged Senate debate on the foreign aid authorization bill, Sen. J. William Fulbright attacks the Vietnam War and asks "whether anyone ever thought of asking the Asians if they really wanted to join the Great Society.". . . State Secy. Dean Rusk warns that the bombing of North Vietnam's port of Haiphong could lead to "a larger war very quickly."				July 22
N.Y.C. Mayor John Lindsay meets with representatives of the three clashing Brooklyn factions.	Pres. Johnson makes speeches in three mid-western states about the importance of seeing things through in Vietnam.			Composer Igor Stravinsky conducts the New York Philharmonic. . . . World Council of Churches adopts a resolution criticizing the "growing American military presence in Vietnam."	July 23
For the first time since July 18, Cleveland's Negro district is calm.			Soviet Union launches a communications satellite.		July 24
		U.S. stock market registers its greatest loss since the assassination of Pres. John F. Kennedy.			July 25
John Williamson, the chief counsel of the National Association of Real Estate Boards, says he is against the proposed open housing bill before Congress.	U.S. State Dept. declares that the U.S. is not seeking a wider war in Vietnam.			About 75,000 New Yorkers attend an open-air concert of Beethoven's *Eroica Symphony*.	July 26
FBI chief J. Edgar Hoover reports that the U.S. crime rate has risen 46% in the past five years although population has risen only 8%.	Senate Majority Leader Mike Mansfield (D, Mont.) calls for a reduction of U.S. forces in Europe.				July 27
				London Symphony begins a series of concerts in Florida.	July 28
A N.Y. court sentences Terry Sullivan to one-year's imprisonment for having torn up his draft card.	British P.M. Harold Wilson confers with Pres. Johnson about Britain's financial problems.			Opera stage director Edward Craig dies in Florence at 94.	July 29
F	G	H	I	J	
Includes elections, federal-state relations, civil rights and liberties, crime, the judiciary, education, health care, poverty, urban affairs and population.	Includes formation and debate of U.S. foreign and defense policies, veterans' affairs and defense spending. (Relations with specific foreign countries are usually found under the region concerned.)	Includes business, labor, agriculture, taxation, transportation, consumer affairs, monetary and fiscal policy, natural resources, and pollution.	Includes worldwide scientific, medical and technological developments, natural phenomena, U.S. weather, natural disasters, and accidents.	Includes the arts, religion, scholarship, communications media, sports, entertainment, fashions, fads and social life.	

	World Affairs	Europe	Africa & the Middle East	The Americas	Asia & the Pacific
July 30	U.N. Secy. Gen. U Thant says that "the general feeling in Moscow" is that any possible peace initiative for the Vietnam War will have to come from those "doing the fighting."		Zaire orders the expulsion of Pierre Marchal, the Belgian counsel general, for his alleged involvement in the Katangan mutiny. . . . Two Yemeni-based Egyptian jets strafe government buildings in Bahrein, a British protectorate.		U.S. bomber offensive against North Vietnam is extended to the demilitarized zone separating North and South Vietnam.
July 31			Zambia announces a five-year plan for the construction of a rail link to the Tanzanian coast which would make Zambia less dependent on Rhodesia.	Argentina suspends all university and high school classes in order to permit the reorganization of their administrations.	South Vietnamese Premier Ky says he will not be a presidential candidate in the projected 1967 elections.
Aug. 1		Protestant and Catholic demonstrators scuffle in Northern Ireland.	Lt. Col. Yakubu Gowon becomes Nigeria's head-of-state.	Inter-American Development Bank creates a fund loan to help economic integration in South America.	A Chinese Communist Party newspaper, *Chiehfang Chun Pao*, says that a pro-Mao faction advocating the ascendency of politics in the armed forces has defeated a faction emphasizing military affairs.
Aug. 2	At the U.N. African delegates criticize South Africa's apartheid policies.		Portuguese army command in Mozambique says that the fight against African guerrillas is going well.	Brazil imposes a one-year wage freeze.	
Aug. 3	U.N. rejects a censure motion against Israel for its July 14 raid against Syria.	Soviet newspaper *Soviet Sport* expresses doubt about Chmn. Mao's July 16 swimming feat. It says that 65 minutes for 15 kilometers is considerably better than the world's record and it invites Mao to participate in the next international swimming competition.	Body of deposed Nigerian head of state Maj. Gen. Johnson Aguiyi-Ironsi is reportedly found in Nigeria.	Nicaraguan Pres. Rene Schick Gutierrez dies of a heart attack.	Cambodia accuses the U.S. of having bombed a frontier village on Aug. 2. . . . Singapore joins the IMF. . . . A U.S. Marine sweep called Operation Prairie begins just south of the demilitarized zone.
Aug. 4					U.S. military sources in Saigon estimate 1966 combat losses at 2,691 killed and 15,012 wounded.
Aug. 5		Police scuffle with protesting Basque students in Spain.		Sixty-five professors at the Roman Catholic Univ. of Buenos Aires protest the closing of Argentina's high schools and state universities.	
Aug. 6			Iraq Pres. Abdul Salam Arif names Naji Talib to form a new cabinet.	Lt. Gen. Rene Barrientos Ortuno is inaugurated president of Bolivia.	India and Pakistan decide not to resume the negotiations emanating from the 1965 war.
Aug. 7		Police scuffle with Communist demonstrators in Rome.	An Israeli patrol ambushes Arab infiltrators near the Sea of Galilee.	Dr. Carlos Lleras Restrepo is inaugurated as president of Colombia.	North Vietnam shoots down seven U.S. aircraft.
Aug. 8			Israel and Syria exchange prisoners who have been in captivity from between one and 12 years. Two of the four Israeli prisoners are taken to mental hospitals as a result of having suffered extensive torture.		Indian Defense Min. Yeshwantrao Chavan accuses Communist China of arming Pakistan "at a fantastic rate."

A	B	C	D	E
Includes developments that affect more than one world region, international organizations and important meetings of major world leaders.	Includes all domestic and regional developments in Europe, including the Soviet Union, Turkey, Cyprus and Malta.	Includes all domestic and regional developments in Africa and the Middle East, including Iraq and Iran and excluding Cyprus, Turkey and Afghanistan.	Includes all domestic and regional developments in Latin America, the Caribbean and Canada.	Includes all domestic and regional developments in Asia and Pacific nations, extending from Afghanistan through all the Pacific Islands, except Hawaii.

U.S. Politics & Social Issues	U.S. Foreign Policy & Defense	U.S. Economy & Environment	Science, Technology & Nature	Culture, Leisure & Life Style	
About 250 Negro demonstrators march into a white Chicago neighborhood in protest against segregated housing. . . . Police break up a fight between Job Corps members and local youths in Kalamazoo, Mich. . . . A night of looting again takes place in Omaha, Neb. . . . Puerto Ricans clash with police in Perth Amboy, N.J.				Alexander Ernst von Falkenhausen, 88, German military commander of Belgium and northern France during World War II, cies in Nassau, West Germany.	July 30
	Reports indicate that Pres. Johnson has promised to purchase $100 million worth of aircraft equipment from the British Rolls-Royce, Ltd.				July 31
Charles Joseph Whitman climbs to the top of the Univ. of Texas's 27-story tower and shoots 44 people before being gunned down. A total of 14 people die as a result of the 90-minute shooting rampage.					Aug. 1
In the wake of the Univ. of Texas massacre, Pres. Johnson calls for the prompt enactment of gun control legislation.		Major U.S. steel companies announce a 2.1% price increase.	Eighteen Japanese reportedly have died so far from diseases related to the 1945 A-bombing of Hiroshima.		Aug. 2
Tex. Gov. John Connally still opposes gun control despite the recent Univ. of Texas shooting rampage. . . . About 50 Negro youths loot stores in Minneapolis, Minn.					Aug. 3
Southern Regional Council in Atlanta says that registration of eligible Negro voters in six Southern states has risen from 30% to 46% since the passage of the Voting Rights Act of 1965.	Defense Dept. issues an October draft call for 46,200 men, the highest monthly figure since May, 1953. . . . House Foreign Affairs subcommittee on Europe issues a report saying that the U.S. is partly responsible for the crisis in NATO because of its tendency "to dictate rather than lead."	Gardner Ackley, the chairman of the President's Council of Economic Advisers, criticizes the recent steel price hike.	Soviet Union conducts an underground nuclear test.		Aug. 4
Congressional Quarterly says that the American Medical Assn. was the top spending lobby for 1965. . . . Rev. Martin Luther King leads a march of 600 demonstrators through a white working-class district of Chicago.		*Wall Street Journal* says that France has the second highest gold reserves in the world with the U.S. in first place.			Aug. 5
Five thousand demonstrators march in N.Y.C. to protest the Vietnam War.				Luci Baines Johnson, 19, the President's younger daughter, marries Patrick John Nugent, 23.	Aug. 6
White and Negro teenage gangs clash in Lansing, Mich. Police arrest 31 people.					Aug. 7
Police disperse a voter registration rally in Grenada, Miss. with tear gas. . . . Negroes begin a boycott of white merchants in Edwards, Miss. after town officials reject demands for basic services. . . . SCLC calls for a guaranteed income for poor families.	Ex-V.P. Richard Nixon calls for a substantial increase in military strength in Vietnam.	Agriculture Secy. Orville Freeman authorizes a 15% increase in the 1967 wheat acreage allotment. It is the second 15% increase in four months.			Aug. 8
F	G	H	I	J	
Includes elections, federal-state relations, civil rights and liberties, crime, the judiciary, education, health care, poverty, urban affairs and population.	*Includes formation and debate of U.S. foreign and defense policies, veterans' affairs and defense spending. (Relations with specific foreign countries are usually found under the region concerned.)*	*Includes business, labor, agriculture, taxation, transportation, consumer affairs, monetary and fiscal policy, natural resources, and pollution.*	*Includes worldwide scientific, medical and technological developments, natural phenomena, U.S. weather, natural disasters, and accidents.*	*Includes the arts, religion, scholarship, communications media, sports, entertainment, fashions, fads and social life.*	

	World Affairs	Europe	Africa & the Middle East	The Americas	Asia & the Pacific
Aug. 9		U.S. Amb.-to-France Charles Bohlen says that coverage of the Vietnamese War on French television is anti-American in tone.	Iraqi Pres. Abdel Rahman Arif tells new ministers that the Iraqi economy must make room for both the public and private sector.	Argentina raises the price of gasoline by 30%.	Pakistani Pres. Mohammed Ayub Khan says that Pakistan must build up its armed forces in order to match "India's military machine."
Aug. 10	At the U.N. Arab delegates accuse Israel of trying to provoke a war.	Britain freezes wages and prices.	Nigeria confirms that army mutineers killed former Pres. Johnson Aguiyi-Ironsi during the July 29 coup.	Police scuffle with a small group of anti-government demonstrators at the Univ. of Rio de Janeiro.	Thai Premier Thanom Kittikachorn publicly acknowledges for the first time Thailand's cooperation with the U.S. in the Vietnam War.
Aug. 11	At the U.N. Israel warns Arab states to stop allowing guerrillas to infiltrate into Israel.	Pres. de Gaulle's criticism of the U.S. is called popular with French voters.	Israel reports killing three Arab infiltrators.		Indonesia and Malaysia sign an agreement ending their three-year political confrontation.
Aug. 12			Two grenades explode in Salisbury, Rhodesia injuring several people.	Students in major cities protest the closing of Argentina's universities.	North Korea declares its independence from both Communist China and the Soviet Union by asserting that it will follow its own unique path. . . . Communist Chinese Central Committee endorses a step-up in the "great proletarian cultural revolution.". . . Indonesian Foreign Min. Adam Malik proposes a joint Indonesian-Malaysian force to combat Communist guerrillas operating along their mutual border.
Aug. 13		Ten thousand East German soldiers parade at a ceremony marking the fifth anniversary of the construction of the Berlin Wall.	Egyptian soldiers remain bogged down in Yemen.		Cambodian Prince Norodom Sihanouk cancels the upcoming visit by Amb.-at-large Averell Harriman because of alleged U.S. air strikes against Cambodia on July 31 and Aug. 2.
Aug. 14		Reports indicate that West Germany would like better relations with East European governments.		Chile, Ecuador, Peru, Colombia and Venezuela meet in Bogota, Colombia to discuss the economic integration of Latin America.	Recent U.S. troop arrivals in South Vietnam bring the total American military force to about 292,000.
Aug. 15		Britain announces that it will begin to withdraw its 10,000-man force from Malaysia because of the recent Indonesian-Malaysian agreement.	Syrian and Israeli planes battle for three hours.		Recent South Korean troop arrivals bring their total forces in South Vietnam to 41,500.
Aug. 16			An Iraqi air force pilot defects to Israel by flying his Soviet-built MiG-21 to an undisclosed Israeli airbase.	Argentina offers to restore most university privileges abolished by the July 29 decree.	Viet Cong guerrillas burn down 120 homes in Quangngai Province after herding the residents out of the buildings. . . . United Buddhist Church urges its followers to boycott the Sept. 11 elections in South Vietnam.
	A	**B**	**C**	**D**	**E**
	Includes developments that affect more than one world region, international organizations and important meetings of major world leaders.	*Includes all domestic and regional developments in Europe, including the Soviet Union, Turkey, Cyprus and Malta.*	*Includes all domestic and regional developments in Africa and the Middle East, including Iraq and Iran and excluding Cyprus, Turkey and Afghanistan.*	*Includes all domestic and regional developments in Latin America, the Caribbean and Canada.*	*Includes all domestic and regional developments in Asia and Pacific nations, extending from Afghanistan through all the Pacific Islands, except Hawaii.*

U.S. Politics & Social Issues	U.S. Foreign Policy & Defense	U.S. Economy & Environment	Science, Technology & Nature	Culture, Leisure & Life Style	
House of Representatives passes a bill forbidding discrimination in housing for about 40% of the nation's units. . . . Rioting and looting break out in Detroit's Negro district after police try to arrest several law-breakers.		Washington Post reports that France has converted about $1.5 billion in U.S. dollars into gold during the last 18 months.			Aug. 9
NAACP's Roy Wilkins says that civil rights forces are not happy with the limitations of the open housing bill. . . . Police arrest 30-40 whites and Negroes as violence intensifies in Detroit. . . . Martin Luther King says that the most significant event of the past year is the spread of the civil rights movement to the North. . . . A federal court orders five Louisiana counties to add 13,000 Negroes to their voter rolls.					Aug. 10
Census Bureau reports that 1,700,000 non-white families and 6,300,000 white families fell into the poverty category in 1965. . . . Senate Democratic leader Mike Mansfield (Mont.) says that the only way to end the Senate filibuster against the administration's civil rights bill is for Senate Minority Leader Everett Dirksen to join with civil rights forces.	SCLC urges a de-escalation of the Vietnamese War.				Aug. 11
Civil rights demonstrators continue their protests against alleged housing discrimination in Chicago. . . . Violence subsides in Detroit but 1,500 Negroes clash with police in Muskegon, Michigan.			Soviet Union launches a military surveillance satellite.		Aug. 12
Gangs of Negro youths stone passing cars in Ypsilanti, Mich. . . . Philadelphia police raid four civil rights meeting places and find sticks of dynamite in one of them.	U.S. Gen. William Westmoreland, commander of U.S. forces in Vietnam, meets with Pres. Johnson.				Aug. 13
Philadelphia police arrest several SNCC officials in connection with the dynamite cache found on Aug. 13.	Pres. Johnson declares that a Communist military take-over in South Vietnam is no longer possible. . . . Senate Foreign Relations Committee Chmn. J. William Fulbright (D, Ak.) says that the CIA must be subjected to more outside control.				Aug. 14
Executive Reorganization subcommittee of the Senate Government Operations Committee begins hearings on the problems of the cities. . . . Philadelphia police arrest John Jenkins, a construction worker, and charge him with theft of dynamite.		Daily newspaper New York Herald Tribune ends publication.		Gunther Schuller becomes the president of the New England Conservatory of Music.	Aug. 15
Sen. Robert Kennedy criticizes the administration's policies for the cities as being inadequate.	House Un-American Activities Committee begins hearings on Americans who allegedly aid the Viet Cong. Shouting matches and forcible ejections mark much of the testimony.	Major U.S. banks increase their prime interest rate to 6%.			Aug. 16

F	G	H	I	J
Includes elections, federal-state relations, civil rights and liberties, crime, the judiciary, education, health care, poverty, urban affairs and population.	Includes formation and debate of U.S. foreign and defense policies, veterans' affairs and defense spending. (Relations with specific foreign countries are usually found under the region concerned.)	Includes business, labor, agriculture, taxation, transportation, consumer affairs, monetary and fiscal policy, natural resources, and pollution.	Includes worldwide scientific, medical and technological developments, natural phenomena, U.S. weather, natural disasters, and accidents.	Includes the arts, religion, scholarship, communications media, sports, entertainment, fashions, fads and social life.

	World Affairs	Europe	Africa & the Middle East	The Americas	Asia & the Pacific
Aug. 17		French police raid a camp in southern France which is allegedly a recruiting center for African white mercenaries.			North Korea accuses Communist China of "Trotskyism" and aligns itself with the Soviet Union. . . . Indonesian demonstrators demand the resignation of Pres. Sukarno.
Aug. 18			Arab demonstrators clash with British troops in Aden.	Seventy-four Argentinian students start a hunger strike in Buenos Aires.	Communist Chinese youths called "Red Guards for the Cultural Revolution" harass foreigners and ordinary citizens in major cities. . . . Australian troops fight their first major engagement of the war. Seventeen are killed. . . . Peiping radio says that Communist Chinese Defense Min. Lin Piao has been elevated to second place in the Chinese leadership.
Aug. 19		An earthquake rocks eastern Turkey killing more than 2,000 people.			Pro and anti-Sukarno demonstrators clash in Indonesia.
Aug. 20	At the U.N. Western nations say that population control is essential for economic progress.	Police scuffle with anti-government demonstrators in Paris.	Israeli soldiers and Arab infiltrators exchange gunfire near the Sea of Galilee.		Reports indicate that North Vietnam has enlarged and improved the Ho Chi Minh trail through Laos to South Vietnam during the last 18 months. . . . Recent troop arrivals raise U.S. troop strength to 297,000 men.
Aug. 21					India adopts a five-year economic program.
Aug. 22			Britain and Rhodesia begin a third round of exploratory talks in Salisbury.		Red Guards denounce beauticians and tailors for their "bourgeois" customs. . . . Indonesian Gen. Amir Machmud, commander of the Jakarta military district, appeals to students to "cooperate with the armed forces in maintaining peace and eliminating communist elements."
Aug. 23			Two grenades explode in Salisbury, Rhodesia injuring several people.		A Viet Cong mine kills seven crew members on a U.S. freighter in the Longtao River near Saigon. . . . Red Guards desecrate Christian churches in Peiping.
Aug. 24			Conflicting border claims create tension between Algeria and Morocco.		Red Guards begin breaking into private homes in order to destroy jewelry, books and other items deemed to be "Western." . . . U.S. planes fly a record 146 missions over North Vietnam.
Aug. 25	At the U.N. African delegates criticize Western investments in South Africa.		Britain breaks off talks with Rhodesia because of its opposition to Rhodesia Constitutional amendments proposed by P.M. Ian Smith.		Red Guards pillage Peiping's Convent of the Sacred Heart and expel its eight elderly Western nuns.

A	B	C	D	E
Includes developments that affect more than one world region, international organizations and important meetings of major world leaders.	Includes all domestic and regional developments in Europe, including the Soviet Union, Turkey, Cyprus and Malta.	Includes all domestic and regional developments in Africa and the Middle East, including Iraq and Iran and excluding Cyprus, Turkey and Afghanistan.	Includes all domestic and regional developments in Latin America, the Caribbean and Canada.	Includes all domestic and regional developments in Asia and Pacific nations, extending from Afghanistan through all the Pacific Islands, except Hawaii.

U.S. Politics & Social Issues	U.S. Foreign Policy & Defense	U.S. Economy & Environment	Science, Technology & Nature	Culture, Leisure & Life Style	
Atty. Gen. Nicholas Katzenbach says that there is no indication that the Los Angeles and Cleveland riots "were planned, controlled or run by extreme left-wing elements."			U.S. sends Pioneer 7 space probe around the sun.		Aug. 17
In replying to Sen. Robert Kennedy's charges of inadequate funding for cities, HEW Secy. John Gardner says, "We should be particularly wary of the old American habit of spending a lot of money to still our anxieties.". . . V.P. Humphrey visits Cleveland's Negro district which was rocked by rioting in July.			U.S. spacecraft Lunar Orbiter 1 begins sending back photos of the moon's surface.		Aug. 18
Civil rights workers picket the homes of two Milwaukee judges who belong to the Fraternal Order of Eagles, a national fraternity which excludes Negro members. . . . James Forman, national director of SNCC, says that he has "some very good evidence that police planted the dynamite" that was recently confiscated in Philadelphia. . . . Labor Secy. Willard Wirtz says that many new jobs are located in the suburbs and not the central cities.	Anti-Vietnam activist Jerry Rubin is ejected for disorderly conduct from the House Un-American Activities Committee's hearings on private American support of the Viet Cong.	Airline mechanics and ground workers end a 43-day old strike.			Aug. 19
				Most U.S. Roman Catholics reportedly use artificial means of birth control.	Aug. 20
Martin Luther King leads a march of 500 Negroes through an all-white Chicago neighborhood.	Pres. Johnson confers with Canadian P.M. Lester Pearson.	Labor Secy. Willard Wirtz calls the recent steel price increases inflationary.		A proposed Constitutional amendment to permit voluntary prayer in schools fails to get the necessary two-thirds majority in the Senate.	Aug. 21
Angry crowds pelt 175 civil rights marchers with rocks and bottles in South Deering, an all-white Chicago neighborhood.	State Secy. Dean Rusk says that if the U.S. withdraws from Vietnam "we can await the great catastrophe that surely awaits at the end of the trail."	1966 appears to be the most inflationary year since 1957.			Aug. 22
Police arrest 38 civil rights workers for parading without a permit in Homer, La.	Defense Secy. Robert McNamara announces plans to try and use the 600,000 young men who are annually rejected for military service because they lack the most elementary educational skills.	Pres. Johnson instructs officials to undertake a major study of rising medical costs.			Aug. 23
Pres. Johnson signs a bill requiring the humane treatment of animals used in medical research. . . . Ill. Gov. Otto Kerner says he will mobilize the National Guard for Dr. Martin Luther King's projected civil rights demonstration on Aug. 28 in Cicero. . . . Pres. Johnson says that his administration has done more for urban problems than has any previous administration.			Soviet Union launches spacecraft Luna II.	Gen. Tadeusz Bor-Komorowski, 71, leader of the 1944 Warsaw revolt, dies near Betchley, England.	Aug. 24
		N.Y. Federal Reserve Bank reports that the U.S. stock of monetary gold fell $75 million in the week ending Aug. 25.	U.S. conducts an underground nuclear test.		Aug. 25

F	G	H	I	J
Includes elections, federal-state relations, civil rights and liberties, crime, the judiciary, education, health care, poverty, urban affairs and population.	Includes formation and debate of U.S. foreign and defense policies, veterans' affairs and defense spending. (Relations with specific foreign countries are usually found under the region concerned.)	Includes business, labor, agriculture, taxation, transportation, consumer affairs, monetary and fiscal policy, natural resources, and pollution.	Includes worldwide scientific, medical and technological developments, natural phenomena, U.S. weather, natural disasters, and accidents.	Includes the arts, religion, scholarship, communications media, sports, entertainment, fashions, fads and social life.

	World Affairs	Europe	Africa & the Middle East	The Americas	Asia & the Pacific
Aug. 26				Canadian railroad workers strike for higher wages.	U.S. planes fly a record 156 missions over North Vietnam. . . . Red Guards break into Peiping's Central Art Gallery and destroy Chinese and Western art objects. . . . Viet Cong kill government officials, policemen and ordinary citizens in terrorist attacks in South Vietnam as the national election campaign gets under way.
Aug. 27		Reports indicate that the French C.P. is supporting Pres. de Gaulle's anti-NATO policies.	Israeli soldiers clash with Arab infiltrators near the Gaza Strip.	Argentinian police use tear gas to break up an unauthorized outdoor class of 500 students of architecture at the University of Buenos Aires.	A spokesman for the Viet Cong reiterates that the U.S. must withdraw its forces from South Vietnam before peace talks can begin. . . . Viet Cong hand grenade attacks kill two South Vietnamese civilians near Saigon.
Aug. 28		Three Soviet newspapers say that North Vietnamese pilots are being trained in the Soviet Union to fly supersonic fighters.		Argentina supends the right to strike for labor unions.	Red Guards attack East German diplomats near the Soviet Embassy.
Aug. 29	At the U.N. Israel says that Arab guerrillas are encouraged by major Arab countries.	Police scuffle with protesting Protestants and Catholics in Belfast.			Reports indicate that nearly one-tenth of the South Vietnamese Army deserted during the first half of 1966. . . . Thousands of Red Guards demonstrate in front of the Soviet embassy.
Aug. 30			Zambian Pres. Kenneth Kaunda says he will not attend the coming meeting of the British Commonwealth nations because of British P.M. Wilson's "lukewarm" reaction to the Rhodesian Smith regime.		North Vietnam and Communist China sign an aid agreement.
Aug. 31		British workers demonstrate against Britain's liberal immigration policy.	Israel opens its Parliament in a new building in Jerusalem.		Chinese Defense Min. Lin Piao addresses a rally of 500,000 Red Guards in Peiping. . . . U.S. planes attack North Vietnamese patrol boats in the Gulf of Tonkin. . . . Viet Cong hand grenade attacks kill eight civilians near Saigon.
Sept. 1	U.N. Secy. Gen. U Thant announces that he will not seek a second five-year term.	Police scuffle with anti-government demonstrators in Paris.		Venezuela becomes the tenth member of the Latin American Free Trade Association.	French Pres. Charles de Gaulle, in a speech in Cambodia, urges the U.S. to withdraw from Vietnam.
Sept. 2	At the U.N. Israel accuses the Arab countries of trying to provoke a war.				A Viet Cong land mine kills six South Vietnamese civilians near Saigon.
Sept. 3		Reports indicate that West European allies share French Pres. de Gaulle's doubts about the willingness of the U.S. to defend Western Europe.	An Israeli patrol clashes with Arab infiltrators near Jerusalem.	Police scuffle with striking workers in Rosario, Argentina.	U.S. and Communist forces clash in the Central Highlands.
Sept. 4	At the U.N. Arab delegates accuse Israel of trying to provoke a war.	Italian Communists are seen becoming independent of Russia.	An Israeli patrol clashes with Arab infiltrators near the Gaza Strip.		
	A	B	C	D	E
	Includes developments that affect more than one world region, international organizations and important meetings of major world leaders.	Includes all domestic and regional developments in Europe, including the Soviet Union, Turkey, Cyprus and Malta.	Includes all domestic and regional developments in Africa and the Middle East, including Iraq and Iran and excluding Cyprus, Turkey and Afghanistan.	Includes all domestic and regional developments in Latin America, the Caribbean and Canada.	Includes all domestic and regional developments in Asia and Pacific nations, extending from Afghanistan through all the Pacific Islands, except Hawaii.

U.S. Politics & Social Issues	U.S. Foreign Policy & Defense	U.S. Economy & Environment	Science, Technology & Nature	Culture, Leisure & Life Style	
Civil rights leaders and Chicago officials agree on a program to end *de facto* housing discrimination in Chicago. . . . Negro youths throw Molotov cocktails at passing cars in Waukegan, Ill.					Aug. 26
Reports indicate that civil rights leaders intend to measure the new accord on Chicago housing desegregation by the following standard: at least 1% Negro occupancy in all Chicago neighborhoods by Apr. 30, 1967. . . . Racial violence continues in Waukegan, Ill.					Aug. 27
Police arrests total 80 in wake of recent Negro rioting in Waukegan, Ill.			Soviet spacecraft Luna II achieves orbit around the moon.		Aug. 28
A Los Angeles judge sentences Sam Henry to life imprisonment for the murder of Larry Gomez during the March rioting in Watts.					Aug. 29
Justice Department files suit to prevent the state of Alabama from paying tuition for white students attending segregated private schools. . . . Racial violence rocks Benton Harbor, Mich.	Pres. Johnson says that the U.S. cannot assume that Communist China's militant declarations are "only rhetoric."	Texas Gov. John Connally meets with striking Mexican-American farm workers.			Aug. 30
Mich. Gov. George Romney places more than 500 National Guardsmen on riot alert. . . . New Orleans public school desegregation advances to the seventh grade under a grade-a-year plan.	Former V.P. Nixon says that "if Vietnam falls, the Pacific will be transformed into a Red ocean, and the road will be open to a third world war.". . . Senate majority leader Mike Mansfield introduces a resolution calling for "substantial cuts" in U.S. forces stationed in Europe.				Aug. 31
Justice Dept. files suit against Marion County General Hospital of Columbia, Miss. because of alleged discrimination. . . . Benton Harbor, Mich. returns to normal but rioting breaks out in Dayton, Ohio.					Sept. 1
Ala. Gov. George Wallace signs into law a bill declaring U.S. school desegregation guidelines unconstitutional. . . . Ill. Gov. Otto Kerner orders the mobilization of 2,000 National Guardsmen in preparation for a civil rights march in Cicero, Ill. . . . Dayton, Ohio returns to normal after rioting with only scattered incidents marring the calm.	State Department announces the expulsion of Soviet embassy official Valentin Revin for trying to buy military secrets.	Calif. grape pickers elect Cesar Chavez as their chief union bargaining agent.			Sept. 2
	Reports indicate that organized labor generally supports Pres. Johnson's Vietnam policy.				Sept. 3
250 civil rights activists demonstrate against housing discrimination in Cicero, Ill.					Sept. 4

F	G	H	I	J
Includes elections, federal-state relations, civil rights and liberties, crime, the judiciary, education, health care, poverty, urban affairs and population.	Includes formation and debate of U.S. foreign and defense policies, veterans' affairs and defense spending. (Relations with specific foreign countries are usually found under the region concerned.)	Includes business, labor, agriculture, taxation, transportation, consumer affairs, monetary and fiscal policy, natural resources, and pollution.	Includes worldwide scientific, medical and technological developments, natural phenomena, U.S. weather, natural disasters, and accidents.	Includes the arts, religion, scholarship, communications media, sports, entertainment, fashions, fads and social life.

	World Affairs	Europe	Africa & the Middle East	The Americas	Asia & the Pacific
Sept. 5	At the U.N. African delegates criticize South Africa's apartheid policies.	Protestant and Catholic demonstrators scuffle in Belfast.	Reports indicate that Arabs living on the West Bank of the Jordan River are still unhappy with King Hussein's rule.		South Vietnamese and Communist forces clash in the Mekong Delta.
Sept. 6		Representatives of the 23 British Commonwealth nations meet in London.	An assassin stabs to death South African P.M. Hendrik Verwoerd during a session of Parliament. . . . Syria says that it has crushed a coup attempt organized by Michel Aflak, one of the original founders of the Arab Baath Party.		
Sept. 7		French Amb.-to-NATO Pierre de Leusse says that France will continue to participate in certain NATO defense projects.	South African Justice Min. Balthazar Vorster says that Verwoerd's slaying appears to have been the deed of only one deranged individual acting independently. . . . Syrian army units exchange gun fire in the northern city of Aleppo.		Reports from Hong Kong indicate that the mayor of Canton, Tseng Sheng, was recently roughed up by Red Guards after he asked them to be polite to foreign visitors. . . . Nearly 4,000 U.S. troops land in South Vietnam, raising the total number to about 308,000 men.
Sept. 8			Syria orders a nine o'clock pm curfew for Damascus.	Canada announces the one-year postponement of the introduction of a universal medical care program.	Communist China says it has absolutely no intention of talking with the U.S. about peace in Vietnam.
Sept. 9		NATO moves its headquarters out of France to Casteau, Belgium.	Egyptian Premier Zakaria Mohieddin resigns because Pres. Nasser did not want to adopt his policy of trying to attract Western capital. . . . Syrian Labor Federation Pres. Khalid al-Jundi says that anti-communist Col. Salim Hatoum was the leader of the latest conspiracy.		Reports from Saigon indicate that the U.S. is planning to triple its crop destruction campaign in Viet Cong-held territory. . . . Cambodia accuses the U.S. of having bombed its territory on Sept. 7.
Sept. 10		Reports indicate that there may be major oil deposits in the North Sea.	Syria says that Col. Salim Hatoum has escaped to Jordan.		Viet Cong mortar attack kills two civilians near Saigon.
Sept. 11			A land mine injures three Israeli soldiers near the Syrian border.		Indonesian Amb.-to-US Lambertus Palar estimates that about 100,000 Indonesians were slain in the aftermath of the aborted 1965 Communist coup. . . . Communist Chinese newspaper *Jenmin Jih Pao* warns government officials not to oppose the Red Guards. . . . France explodes a nuclear bomb in the Pacific. . . . South Vietnamese voters choose an Assembly that will draft a new Constitution and pave the way for a civilian government in 1967.
Sept. 12			Ghana dismisses all judges who were appointed by former Pres. Kwame Nkrumah.		South Vietnamese government says that about 80% of its citizens voted in the Sept. 11 election. . . . Five hundred U.S. planes carry out the heaviest raids of the war. . . . Tokoyo newspaper *Asahi* says that Communist Chinese troops were recently called out to control a crowd of 100,000 protesters demonstrating against the Red Guards.

A	B	C	D	E
Includes developments that affect more than one world region, international organizations and important meetings of major world leaders.	Includes all domestic and regional developments in Europe, including the Soviet Union, Turkey, Cyprus and Malta.	Includes all domestic and regional developments in Africa and the Middle East, including Iraq and Iran and excluding Cyprus, Turkey and Afghanistan.	Includes all domestic and regional developments in Latin America, the Caribbean and Canada.	Includes all domestic and regional developments in Asia and Pacific nations, extending from Afghanistan through all the Pacific Islands, except Hawaii.

U.S. Politics & Social Issues	U.S. Foreign Policy & Defense	U.S. Economy & Environment	Science, Technology & Nature	Culture, Leisure & Life Style	
		Mexican-American farm workers end their two-month state-wide march for a higher minimum wage in Austin, Tex., the state capital.			Sept. 5
In a meeting with Bernard Donovan, Superintendent of N.Y.C. schools, Negro parents demand "total community control" of a new school in East Harlem. . . . Rioting breaks out in Atlanta after a Negro is arrested for suspected car theft. . . . Senate Minority Leader Everett Dirksen reiterates his opposition to the open housing provision in the administration's civil rights bill. . . . Ala. Gov. George Wallace's son attends a newly desegregated school. . . . Pvt. Dennis Mora receives a three-year prison sentence at hard labor for refusing to go to South Vietnam.	Senate Minority Leader Everett Dirksen opposes Sen. Mike Mansfield's resolution calling for cuts in U.S. forces in Europe. . . . Pres. Johnson reportedly complains at a meeting with Jewish War Veterans about a lack of support for his Vietnam policy on the part of American Jewish leaders.		U.S. and the Soviet Union begin to exchange photos taken by their weather satellites.	Dr. William Claire Menninger, 66, president of the Menninger Foundation (psychiatric clinic in Topeka) dies in Topeka, Kansas.	Sept. 6
Prominent Negro leaders in Atlanta criticize SNCC Chmn. Stokely Carmichael for inciting Negroes to riot on Sept. 6.	U.S. Senate passes a foreign aid bill.				Sept. 7
Atlanta police arrest Stokely Carmichael on charges of incitement to riot.	Pres. Johnson says the question of cuts in U.S. forces in Europe should be handled in consultation with "our allies."	In an anti-inflation move, Pres. Johnson asks Congress to suspend the 7% business tax credit for new investment for 16 months.			Sept. 8
Privates James Johnson and David Samas receive five-year sentences at hard labor for refusing to go to South Vietnam.		Pres. Johnson signs the administration's Traffic Safety Act.		*Science* magazine reports that one-third of American women in their early twenties are using birth control pills.	Sept. 9
About 400 Atlanta Negroes throw bottles and bricks at passing cars after a Negro is shot to death by a white motorist.			Soviet Union conducts an underground nuclear test.		Sept. 10
Several hundred Atlanta Negroes attack white pedestrians with bottles and bricks.					Sept. 11
Police break up an armed confrontation between Negroes and whites in Bogalusa, La. . . . A white mob attacks Negro children trying to integrate a Grenada, Miss. school. . . . Several Atlanta Negroes throw bottles and bricks at policemen and newsmen. . . . Sixty parents picket a new school in East Harlem and demand a Negro principal.		For the second time in eight weeks, Pres. Johnson vetoes a bill "because it is inflationary."	US spaceship Gemini II achieves an unprecedented first orbit "docking" with a target vehicle.		Sept. 12
F	G	H	I	J	
Includes elections, federal-state relations, civil rights and liberties, crime, the judiciary, education, health care, poverty, urban affairs and population.	Includes formation and debate of U.S. foreign and defense policies, veterans' affairs and defense spending. (Relations with specific foreign countries are usually found under the region concerned.)	Includes business, labor, agriculture, taxation, transportation, consumer affairs, monetary and fiscal policy, natural resources, and pollution.	Includes worldwide scientific, medical and technological developments, natural phenomena, U.S. weather, natural disasters, and accidents.	Includes the arts, religion, scholarship, communications media, sports, entertainment, fashions, fads and social life.	

	World Affairs	Europe	Africa & the Middle East	The Americas	Asia & the Pacific
Sept. 13	U.S. and European countries agree on steps for increased financial cooperation.	French Pres. de Gaulle returns to Paris after his 19-day world tour.	Ruling National Party elects Justice Min. Balthazar Vorster as South African prime minister.	Canada asserts that the federal government, not the provincial governments, is responsible for the national economy.	Communist Chinese Red Guards harangue foreigners and ordinary citizens in major Chinese cities. . . . U.S. Navy pilot Lt. Dieter Dengler, who recently escaped Communist captivity in North Vietnam, says that American prisoners are often beaten, shot at and hung upside down on trees.
Sept. 14		Majority of the British Commonwealth nations advocate the use of force against Rhodesia.	South African P.M. Balthazar Vorster pledges to continue his country's apartheid policy.	Dominican guerrillas kill two American soldiers in Santo Domingo.	
Sept. 15		Sweden reportedly opposes U.S. policy in Vietnam.	Tanzanian Pres. Julius Nyerere criticizes British P.M. Wilson for not taking more forceful measures against Rhodesia.		Communist Chinese newspaper *Jenmin Jih Pao* says that the Cultural Revolution will be temporarily suspended because of the fall harvest. . . . Indonesian Foreign Min. Adam Malik says that the government is continuing to investigate Pres. Sukarno's role in the 1965 coup attempt but has not yet found any evidence implicating him.
Sept. 16		Soviet newspaper *Pravda* denounces Communist China's Red Guard campaign.			Communist China charges that the U.S. has recently bombed Chinese territory.
Sept. 17			An Israeli patrol clashes with Arab infiltrators near the Syrian border.	Police clash with anti-government protesting students in Panama City.	
Sept. 18	U.N. Secy. Gen U Thant criticizes U.S. policy in South Vietnam.				Communist China charges that U.S. planes attacked Chinese territory on Sept. 5,9 and 17.
Sept. 19	U.N. approves the admission of Guyana.			Last American troops leave the Dominican Republic.	Heaviest fighting of the Vietnam War rages south of the demilitarized zone. . . . Thousands of demonstrating students in Jakarta accuse Pres. Sukarno of having engineered the 1965 attempted Communist coup. . . . Guam-based B-52 bombers carry out heavy raids over North Vietnam.
Sept. 20	U.N. elects Afghan Abdul Rahman Pazhwak as its president.			Last troops of the Latin American peace force leave the Dominican Republic.	

A	B	C	D	E
Includes developments that affect more than one world region, international organizations and important meetings of major world leaders.	Includes all domestic and regional developments in Europe, including the Soviet Union, Turkey, Cyprus and Malta.	Includes all domestic and regional developments in Africa and the Middle East, including Iraq and Iran and excluding Cyprus, Turkey and Afghanistan.	Includes all domestic and regional developments in Latin America, the Caribbean and Canada.	Includes all domestic and regional developments in Asia and Pacific nations, extending from Afghanistan through all the Pacific Islands, except Hawaii.

U.S. Politics & Social Issues	U.S. Foreign Policy & Defense	U.S. Economy & Environment	Science, Technology & Nature	Culture, Leisure & Life Style	
Julian Bond, who has been twice refused a seat in the Georgia Legislature, again wins the Democratic nomination in his old district. . . . Negro leader A.Z. Young calls for armed resistance to white violence in Bogalusa, La. . . . Justice Dept. files suit against Grenada, Miss. officials for inadequate police protection of black school children. . . . Pres. Johnson fails to convince Sen. Everett Dirksen to support the administration's civil rights bill.					Sept. 13
A federal jury convicts Robert Shelton, imperial wizard of the United Klans of America, of contempt of Congress because of his refusal to produce Klan membership records. . . . Bogalusa School Board Pres. Alcous Stewart announces plans to appeal a federal district court order to speed up school integration. . . . One hundred and fifty state troopers and FBI agents escort Negro school children to Grenada, Miss. schools.	US Amb.-to-UN Arthur Goldberg assures Jewish leaders that Pres. Johnson is not making U.S. support of Israel dependent on American-Jewish support of the Vietnam War.		US spaceship Gemini II sets an altitude record for a manned flight.	Nikolai Cherkasov who starred in Sergei Eisenstein's films *Ivan the Terrible* and *Alexander Nevsky*, dies in Leningrad at 63.	Sept. 14
	Pres. Johnson confers with Philippine Pres. Ferdinand Marcos at the White House.		U.S. spaceship Gemini II returns safely to earth.		Sept. 15
Bogalusa, La. City Atty. Robert Rester calls for an investigation of the Deacons for Defense, a Negro group promoting armed resistance to alleged white injustices. . . . U.S. district Judge Claude Clayton sentences Grenada Town Constable, Grady Carroll, to four months in jail for not protecting Negro school children.	State Secy. Dean Rusk says that the U.S. will continue to oppose Communist Chinese membership in the U.N.			Metropolitan Opera opens its season in the new opera house at Lincoln Center, N.Y.C.	Sept. 16
FBI agents arrest 13 whites in connection with the recent disorders in Grenada, Mississippi.	Administration's leading dove, State Dept. Undersecretary George Ball, resigns.		Soviet Union launches a military surveillance satellite.		Sept. 17
Rev. C.B. Burt, a white Methodist minister, criticizes the "bestiality" of the white mobs in Grenada, Miss.		Soviet Union launches a weather satellite.			Sept. 18
Stanley Lisser, the white principal of a new school in East Harlem, announces that he wants to be reassigned to a new school district. The Board of Education immediately announces the appointment of Beryl Banfield, a Negro. She refuses the post and backs Lisser. . . . Administration withdraws its civil rights bill from Senate consideration after the failure of two attempts to impose cloture. U.S. concedes that its planes might have recently strayed over Communist China.	U.S. concedes that its planes might have recently strayed over Communist China.			Pope Paul appeals for an end to the war in Vietnam.	Sept. 19
Teachers threaten to boycott the East Harlem school in protest against the removal of Lisser. . . . Three hundred prominent white citizens publish a statement decrying the recent violence in Grenada. . . .	U.S. Defense Dept. says that the American crop destruction program is a military necessity in Vietnam.	U.S. auto companies raise their prices by about 4%.			Sept. 20
F	G	H	I	J	
Includes elections, federal-state relations, civil rights and liberties, crime, the judiciary, education, health care, poverty, urban affairs and population.	Includes formation and debate of U.S. foreign and defense policies, veterans' affairs and defense spending. (Relations with specific foreign countries are usually found under the region concerned.)	Includes business, labor, agriculture, taxation, transportation, consumer affairs, monetary and fiscal policy, natural resources, and pollution.	Includes worldwide scientific, medical and technological developments, natural phenomena, U.S. weather, natural disasters, and accidents.	Includes the arts, religion, scholarship, communications media, sports, entertainment, fashions, fads and social life.	

	World Affairs	Europe	Africa & the Middle East	The Americas	Asia & the Pacific
Sept. 21			An Israeli patrol clashes with Arab guerrillas near the Jordanian border.		
Sept. 22	At the UN US Amb.-to-UN Arthur Goldberg says that the U.S. will halt the bombing of North Vietnam if it can be assured, privately or publicly, that the gesture will be reciprocated.	British Institute of Strategic Studies says that the Soviet Union is deploying an anti-ballistic missile system around Moscow and Leningrad.	Egyptian troops reportedly are still bogged down in Yemen.		Cambodia accuses the U.S. of having bombed its territory on Sept. 21.
Sept. 23					Reports from Danang indicate that another North Vietnamese army unit has recently crossed into South Vietnam. . . . North Vietnam denounces the latest U.S. de-escalation proposal. . . . U.S. military discloses that U.S. planes are defoliating dense jungle areas just south of the demilitarized zones.
Sept. 24		Italian government is reportedly worried about unemployment among university graduates.	Rhodesia's ruling party gives P.M. Ian Smith a unanimous vote of confidence.		France explodes a nuclear bomb in the Pacific. . . . Indonesia begins widespread security checks on government employees, students and teachers.
Sept. 25	World Bank says that it granted 37 loans in the fiscal year ending June 30, 1966.	A Soviet foreign trade report shows an increase in Soviet trade with Communist China despite the deterioration of relations between the two countries.	Israel says that Arab guerrillas from Jordan damaged an electric transformer near the Dead Sea.		Communist and South Vietnamese forces clash in the Mekong Delta.
Sept. 26			Botswana police arrest seven armed guerrillas in the northern part of the country.	Police scuffle with anti-government demonstrators in the Dominican Republic.	
Sept. 27	During a U.N. General Assembly debate, Thailand's Foreign Min. Thanat Khoman criticizes U.N. Secy. Gen. U Thant's peace proposals for failing to demand concessions from North Vietnam.				U.S. halts air strikes in part of the demilitarized zone.
Sept. 28		French Foreign Min. Maurice Couve de Murville calls on the U.S. to make a "new move" toward a political solution of the Vietnam War.			
Sept. 29	At the U.N. General Assembly Turkish Foreign Min. Ihsan Caglayangil supports latest U.S. peace proposals.		A Syrian land mine injures seven Israeli workers in Israel.		U.S. reports a record 970 casualties in the Sept. 18-24 period.
Sept. 30	At the U.N. General Assembly the Netherlands' Foreign Min. Joseph Luns criticizes those who demand unilateral U.S. de-escalation of the Vietnamese War.	Soviet Union reveals plans to increase greatly wholesale prices.	Botswana becomes Africa's 39th independent state.		
Oct. 1		Polish Communists are told to "purify" their ranks by top officials.		Haiti fears that a recent hurricane has left 1,000 dead.	Soviet bloc officials stage a walk-out at a Peiping rally.
	A	B	C	D	E
	Includes developments that affect more than one world region, international organizations and important meetings of major world leaders.	*Includes all domestic and regional developments in Europe, including the Soviet Union, Turkey, Cyprus and Malta.*	*Includes all domestic and regional developments in Africa and the Middle East, including Iraq and Iran and excluding Cyprus, Turkey and Afghanistan.*	*Includes all domestic and regional developments in Latin America, the Caribbean and Canada.*	*Includes all domestic and regional developments in Asia and Pacific nations, extending from Afghanistan through all the Pacific Islands, except Hawaii.*

U.S. Politics & Social Issues	U.S. Foreign Policy & Defense	U.S. Economy & Environment	Science, Technology & Nature	Culture, Leisure & Life Style	
Principal Stanley Lisser retains his position and opens the new East Harlem school on the first day of classes.		Pres. Johnson says he regrets the recent auto price increases. . . . Treasury Dept. reports that the Vietnamese War is costing about $1.2 billion a month.		Louisville Symphony conductor Robert Whitney announces his retirement at 61.	Sept. 21
				Philadelphia Orchestra members go on strike.	Sept. 22
Police arrest 11 Negro and white demonstrators protesting the reinstatement of Lisser.	Defense Secy. Robert McNamara says that the U.S. does not intend to reduce the number of nuclear weapons assigned to NATO.	Pres. Johnson signs a bill extending minimum wage coverage to an additional 8,100,000 employees, including certain farm workers.	US conducts an underground nuclear test.		Sept. 23
			U.S. launches a weather satellite.		Sept. 24
About 400 Atlanta Negroes pelt police with stones after an officer attempted to make a routine arrest.					Sept. 25
	West German Chancellor Ludwig Erhard confers with Pres. Johnson in Washington.				Sept. 26
Racial violence breaks out in San Francisco's Negro areas after a policeman shoots a car thief.	Reports indicate that the Johnson-Erhard talks are concentrating on West German financial support of U.S. forces in West Germany. . . . White House announces that Pres. Johnson will attend an Asian conference on Vietnam to be held in Manila.				Sept. 27
Two thousand National Guardsmen enter San Francisco's Negro neighborhoods to stop rioting. . . . Segregationist Lester Maddox defeats Ellis Arnall, a racial moderate, in a run-off for the Democratic nomination for Governor in Georgia.	Former V.P. Richard Nixon calls Pres. Johnson's efforts to end the Vietnamese War a "pathetic exercise in instant diplomacy."	American Airlines mechanics decide not to strike 30 minutes before a strike deadline.			Sept. 28
Cyril Magnin, president of San Francisco's Chamber of Commerce, begins to organize a job search for Negro youths.					Sept. 29
	Ex-Pres. Dwight Eisenhower says that he favors using "as much force as we need to win" the war in Vietnam.				Sept. 30
Army reports that two out of three Negroes fail the mental exam and are rejected by the draft.		U.S. announces plans to study the flow of the Gulf Stream.	Soviet Union launches a military surveillance satellite.		Oct. 1

F	G	H	I	J
Includes elections, federal-state relations, civil rights and liberties, crime, the judiciary, education, health care, poverty, urban affairs and population.	*Includes formation and debate of U.S. foreign and defense policies, veterans' affairs and defense spending. (Relations with specific foreign countries are usually found under the region concerned.)*	*Includes business, labor, agriculture, taxation, transportation, consumer affairs, monetary and fiscal policy, natural resources, and pollution.*	*Includes worldwide scientific, medical and technological developments, natural phenomena, U.S. weather, natural disasters, and accidents.*	*Includes the arts, religion, scholarship, communications media, sports, entertainment, fashions, fads and social life.*

	World Affairs	Europe	Africa & the Middle East	The Americas	Asia & the Pacific
Oct. 2		Soviet Union says that its missile advisers in North Vietnam have been subjected to U.S. bomber raids.	Reports indicate that 300 Ibo tribesmen have been recently killed by Nigerian mobs.		U.S. reports killing 150 Viet Cong.
Oct. 3		Soviet Union announces major new aid programs for North Vietnam.		Brazilian voters elect Artur Costa e Silva in an unopposed presidential election.	U.S. planes bomb Communist positions in the Central Highlands.
Oct. 4		British P.M. Harold Wilson calls for wage and price controls in order to bolster Britain's deteriorating economy.	Lesotho becomes an independent nation.		U.S. planes bomb the Ho Chi Minh trail.
Oct. 5	U.N. Secy. Gen. U Thant reportedly is trying to convince North Vietnam to negotiate with the U.S.			Hurricane Inez buffets Cuba.	U.S. authorities report that U.S. forces suffered twice as many casualties as South Vietnamese forces during the week of Sept. 25-Oct.1.
Oct. 6		Britain calls for a simultaneous halt of the U.S. bombing of North Vietnam and of the North Vietnamese infiltration of South Vietnam.			
Oct. 7	At the U.N. General Assembly, Yugoslav Foreign Min. Marko Nikezic says that the U.S. must make the first move to end the Vietnam War.	Soviet Union orders the expulsion of all Communist Chinese students.	First reported Arab infiltrators of the Israeli section of Jerusalem plant land mines in front of several apartments.	Panama expresses optimism about upcoming negotiations with the U.S. on the status of the Panama Canal.	
Oct. 8			An Israeli patrol skirmishes with Arab guerrillas near the Syrian border.		South Vietnam tentatively agrees to the political demands of dissident Montagnard tribesmen in the Central Highlands. . . . U.S. officials report a pilot shortage because of losses over North Vietnam.
Oct. 9		Soviet Union says U.S. attacks against North Vietnam are the biggest obstacle to wider cooperation between the two super powers.	A land mine kills four Israeli soldiers near the Syrian border.		
Oct. 10	Swedish Foreign Min. Torsten Nilsson tells the U.N. General Assembly that "a veritable poll of international opinion" supports unilateral U.S. action to de-escalate the Vietnamese War.				Defense Secy. McNamara arrives in South Vietnam for an official visit amid reports that U.S. military officers will ask him for more troops.
Oct. 11			Jordanian King Hussein warns that if a war breaks out between Israel and Syria he will join Syria.		U.S. planes bomb Communist positions in the Central Highlands.
Oct. 12	U.S. Amb.-to-U.N. Arthur Goldberg proposes a U.N. commission empowered to organize a vote of self-determination for South-West Africa. . . . At the U.N. Egyptian Foreign Min. Mahmoud Riad calls on the U.S. to end the bombing of North Vietnam.	Police skirmish with protesting anti-government students in West Berlin.			
Oct. 13	At the U.N. 12 Arab states back Syria in its dispute with Israel.	Soviet Union accuses Communist China of blocking efforts to aid North Vietnam.			A record 173 U.S. planes attack North Vietnam. . . . U.S. casualties between Oct. 2-8 reportedly were higher than South Vietnamese casualties for the third consecutive week.
	A	B	C	D	E
	Includes developments that affect more than one world region, international organizations and important meetings of major world leaders.	Includes all domestic and regional developments in Europe, including the Soviet Union, Turkey, Cyprus and Malta.	Includes all domestic and regional developments in Africa and the Middle East, including Iraq and Iran and excluding Cyprus, Turkey and Afghanistan.	Includes all domestic and regional developments in Latin America, the Caribbean and Canada.	Includes all domestic and regional developments in Asia and Pacific nations, extending from Afghanistan through all the Pacific Islands, except Hawaii.

U.S. Politics & Social Issues	U.S. Foreign Policy & Defense	U.S. Economy & Environment	Science, Technology & Nature	Culture, Leisure & Life Style	
N.Y.C. Negroes seek greater control of neighborhood schools.		All 50 U.S. states agree to set water pollution curbs.	Gales cause major property damage in Florida.		Oct. 2
	Seventy-five thousand more U.S. soldiers will be sent to South Vietnam during 1967 than originally planned.	Reports indicate that the government will have a balanced budget during the last part of 1966.			Oct. 3
Senate Republicans call Pres. Johnson's anti-poverty program a "boondoggle."	Pres. Johnson confers with French Foreign Min. Maurice Couve de Murville about France's criticism of NATO.		Hurricane Inez batters Florida's coast.	Pope Paul calls for peace in Vietnam.	Oct. 4
	Senate begins an investigation of charges that U.S. food aid to South Vietnam is being sold on the black market.				Oct. 5
	Pres. Johnson announces that he is inviting all allied countries fighting in South Vietnam to attend the upcoming Manila Conference.	Pres. Johnson predicts that 1967 will be as good a business year as 1966 was.			Oct. 6
	Pres. Johnson calls for better relations with East Europe.				Oct. 7
	U.S. allows a Yale University religious group to send medical help to North Vietnam.		Soviet Union launches a weather satellite.		Oct. 8
Congress takes up a bill granting home rule to the District of Columbia.			Hurricane Inez begins moving towards Texas.		Oct. 9
Supreme Court agrees to review a 1963 conviction of Dr. Martin Luther King Jr. for staging a demonstration despite a court injunction.	Pres. Johnson meets with Soviet Foreign Min. Andrei Gromyko at the White House.	U.S. reports that there is a growing skilled labor shortage.		Pope Paul turns down U.S. Cardinal Spellman's offer to resign.	Oct. 10
	U.S. reports that negotiations with the Soviet Union on the treaty to bar the spread of nuclear weapons are going well.		U.S. officials say that the scheduled lunar manned landing will be broadcast live.		Oct. 11
Senate Republicans criticize the administration's anti-poverty bill.		Commerce Secy. John Connor says that he does not think that government controls will be needed to regulate the economy.			Oct. 12
	At a news conference Pres. Johnson rejects suggestions that the U.S. suspend air attacks on North Vietnam.			Two Americans, Charles Huggins & Francis Rous, win the Nobel Prize for medicine.	Oct. 13

F	G	H	I	J
Includes elections, federal-state relations, civil rights and liberties, crime, the judiciary, education, health care, poverty, urban affairs and population.	Includes formation and debate of U.S. foreign and defense policies, veterans' affairs and defense spending. (Relations with specific foreign countries are usually found under the region concerned.)	Includes business, labor, agriculture, taxation, transportation, consumer affairs, monetary and fiscal policy, natural resources, and pollution.	Includes worldwide scientific, medical and technological developments, natural phenomena, U.S. weather, natural disasters, and accidents.	Includes the arts, religion, scholarship, communications media, sports, entertainment, fashions, fads and social life.

	World Affairs	Europe	Africa & the Middle East	The Americas	Asia & the Pacific
Oct. 14	At the U.N. Israel accuses Syria of working for the complete destruction of the Jewish state.	Britain vetoes two recent union settlements because of their inflationary impact.		Guatemala reportedly is considering a land reform program.	U.S. reports that there are 325,000 U.S. troops in South Vietnam.
Oct. 15		Soviet Union says that better ties are impossible with the U.S. as long as the Vietnamese War goes on.	Beirut Intra Bank closes its doors because of lack of liquidity.		Communist Chinese Red Guards denounce Confucius.
Oct. 16		East European Communist leaders begin to arrive in Moscow for the upcoming conference of Communist nations.	Lebanon shuts all banks for a three-day period.		
Oct. 17	Cambodian Amb.-to-UN Huot Sambath calls on the U.S. to withdraw from South Vietnam.	British officials say that the Soviet Union may be interested in acting as a mediator in the Vietnamese War.	All Lebanese banks close in response to the recent bankruptcy of one of Lebanon's major banks.	A brief clash takes place between police and a small group of protesting students in Lima, Peru.	U.S. planes bomb the southeastern sector of the demilitarized zone for the first time since Sept. 27.
Oct. 18	At the U.N. Saudi Arabia assails N.Y.C. as the U.N. site because of the city's large Jewish population.		Both U.S. and Soviet financial interests are bidding to take over Lebanon's biggest bank.		Pres. Johnson visits American Samoa and lauds its high standard of living.
Oct. 19	At the U.N. Britain scores South Africa's continued presence in South-West Africa.		An Israeli patrol kills three Arab infiltrators.		
Oct. 20			Business reportedly has yet to return to normal in Lebanon in the wake of the recent bankruptcy of a leading Lebanese bank.		Pres. Johnson, speaking in Canberra, hails Australia's aid in the Vietnam War.
Oct. 21		An avalanche kills at least 131 people in Alberfan, Wales.			
Oct. 22	At the UN the U.S. says that economic sanctions against South Africa would be counter-productive.	Reports indicate that Hungary's economic situation has improved significantly over the last 10 years.	Israeli soldiers kill several Arab infiltrators at the Jordanian border.		Pres. Johnson receives a warm welcome in Brisbane, Australia.
Oct. 23				Chile buys 24 British jet fighters.	Pres. Johnson receives an enthusiastic welcome in Manila.
Oct. 24	At the U.N. the U.S. announces that it will increase its food grant program.	Spain shuts down access roads to Gibraltar.	Reports indicate that Egyptian troops are still bogged down in Yemen.	Peru criticizes the recent purchase of British jets by Chile.	U.S. planes bomb the Ho Chi Minh supply trail.
Oct. 25		Soviet bloc reportedly is advising North Vietnam to be less intransigent about negotiating with the U.S.	Yemen executes seven former government aides.		U.S. and its Pacific allies pledge to leave South Vietnam six months after North Vietnam abandons the war.
Oct. 26		France is reportedly cool toward an offer by Poland and Czechoslovakia to establish an international nuclear control zone in Europe.	Israeli soldiers and Arab guerrillas skirmish for several hours.		Pres. Johnson pays a surprise visit to South Vietnam and talks with combat troops.

A	B	C	D	E
Includes developments that affect more than one world region, international organizations and important meetings of major world leaders.	Includes all domestic and regional developments in Europe, including the Soviet Union, Turkey, Cyprus and Malta.	Includes all domestic and regional developments in Africa and the Middle East, including Iraq and Iran and excluding Cyprus, Turkey and Afghanistan.	Includes all domestic and regional developments in Latin America, the Caribbean and Canada.	Includes all domestic and regional developments in Asia and Pacific nations, extending from Afghanistan through all the Pacific Islands, except Hawaii.

U.S. Politics & Social Issues	U.S. Foreign Policy & Defense	U.S. Economy & Environment	Science, Technology & Nature	Culture, Leisure & Life Style	
Senate leaders reject a proposal to tie cost-of-living increases directly to Social Security benefits.		General Electric Co. reaches agreement with 11 unions to avert a strike which would have impeded the U.S. effort in Vietnam.			Oct. 14
		Pres. Johnson signs a bill creating the Department of Transportation.	Soviet Union conducts an underground nuclear test in Central Asia.		Oct. 15
Pres. Johnson makes a campaign appearance in Doylestown, Pa. . . . Reports indicate that Democratic officials are worried about a white "backlash" in reaction to Negro demands.					Oct. 16
	Pres. Johnson leaves for the seven-nation conference on Vietnam in Manila.	Pres. Johnson invokes the Taft-Hartley Act to stop scattered strikes against General Electric which threaten the U.S. war effort in Vietnam.	Soviet Union launches a military surveillance satellite.		Oct. 17
		Supreme Court orders a three-month delay in merger plans between the Pennsylvania and New York Central railroads.	U.S. conducts an underground nuclear test.		Oct. 18
Negro youths assault five white teachers at a high school in Oakland, Calif.	Reports indicate that few candidates in the upcoming November elections are attacking Pres. Johnson's Vietnam policy.	A labor union for Roman Catholic priests opens a national office in Santa Monica, Calif.			Oct. 19
Congress passes a compromise anti-poverty bill.				Israeli writer Shmuel Agnon wins the Nobel Prize for literature.	Oct. 20
Mississippi Negroes accuse state officials of impeding the voter registration drive.	House approves a measure encouraging easier U.S. trade with Eastern Europe.	U.S. Treasury Dept. estimates that the nation's economic growth will soon level off at 4%.	Soviet Union launches Luna 12 satellite.		Oct. 21
U.S. Senate approves a bill financing federal electoral campaigns with public funds.		Treasury Secy. Henry Fowler says that military spending represents a little more than 8% of the GNP.			Oct. 22
Sen. Robert Kennedy says that some Negro civil rights leaders are inciting racial hatred against whites.		*The New York Times* survey indicates that big business is unhappy with Pres. Johnson's handling of the economy for the first time since he became president.	International Cancer Congress opens in Tokyo.		Oct. 23
			U.S. doctors report that Vitamin A may inhibit some forms of lung cancer.		Oct. 24
		Labor officials reportedly fear that the "white backlash" may hurt Congressmen who support labor legislative positions.	U.S. launches a military surveillance satellite.		Oct. 25
School desegregation is seen making slow but steady progress in the South.			U.S. scientists duplicate the photosynthesis process in Calif.	Pianist Andre Watts makes his N.Y. debut.	Oct. 26

F	G	H	I	J
Includes elections, federal-state relations, civil rights and liberties, crime, the judiciary, education, health care, poverty, urban affairs and population.	Includes formation and debate of U.S. foreign and defense policies, veterans' affairs and defense spending. (Relations with specific foreign countries are usually found under the region concerned.)	Includes business, labor, agriculture, taxation, transportation, consumer affairs, monetary and fiscal policy, natural resources, and pollution.	Includes worldwide scientific, medical and technological developments, natural phenomena, U.S. weather, natural disasters, and accidents.	Includes the arts, religion, scholarship, communications media, sports, entertainment, fashions, fads and social life.

	World Affairs	Europe	Africa & the Middle East	The Americas	Asia & the Pacific
Oct. 27	U.N. proclaims the end of South Africa's mandate over South-West Africa (Namibia).	For the first time in 18 months, France will not be able to buy U.S. gold because of a lack of U.S. dollars caused by the U.S. troop withdrawal from France.	A bomb derails an Israeli freight train near the Jordanian border.	Chile says that Latin American nations must establish a plan to curb armaments.	Communist China announces that it has successfully fired a guided missile with a nuclear warhead.
Oct. 28	U.N. Secy. Gen. U Thant scores the recent Communist Chinese nuclear test.	French Pres. de Gaulle denounces the U.S. presence in South Vietnam.			
Oct. 29			Ghana seizes the foreign minister of Guinea.		North Vietnamese units down three U.S. helicopters in South Vietnam.
Oct. 30		Albania reaffirms its support of Communist China in its dispute with the Soviet Union.	Guinea places U.S. Ambassador Robinson McIlvaine under house arrest. . . . Arab guerrillas destroy an Israeli water pipeline at the Jordanian border.		Pres. Johnson receives a tumultuous reception in South Korea.
Nov. 1	African U.N. delegates criticize South Africa's continued control of South-West Africa.	Soviet C.P. First Secy. Leonid Brezhnev defends his policy of limited cooperation with the West.			North Koreans kill eight U.S. soldiers at the demilitarized zone.
Nov. 2	At the U.N. only Cuba and Albania refuse to back a resolution supporting a treaty to stop the spread of nuclear weapons.	West German Chancellor Ludwig Erhard says that he will resign if he isn't given more support from his party.		Colombia says that it has decided to construct an interoceanic waterway.	North Koreans continue their harassing tactics at the demilitarized zone.
Nov. 3		Strikes shut down British Motor Corp.			Communist China ridicules Pres. Johnson's statement that it is pursuing a dangerous course by developing nuclear weapons.
Nov. 4	At the U.N. the Soviet Union blocks a resolution urging Israel and Syria to de-escalate their border skirmishes.	Major flooding causes serious damage in Florence, Italy.			U.S. and North Korean representatives meet in a tense negotiating session at the demilitarized zone.
Nov. 5		Recent floods damage some Florence, Italy paintings.	Ghana releases captive Guinean envoys.		South Vietnamese forces kill a reported 150 Viet Cong near the Cambodian border.
Nov. 6		Communist Chinese representatives walk out of a rally celebrating the 49th anniversary of the Bolshevik Revolution in Moscow.	Reports indicate that African guerrillas are gaining in Angola against the Portuguese.		North Vietnamese ambush 40 U.S. troops in South Vietnam.
Nov. 7		Communist Chinese representatives again walk out of celebrations of the 49th anniversary of the Bolshevik Revolution in Moscow.	Egypt and Syria stress new unity aim.		Indian demonstrators march to protest the slaughter of cows for food.
Nov. 8		Reports indicate that West German Christian Democrats will replace Chancellor Ludwig Erhard.	Pres. Sékou Touré of Guinea orders U.S. Peace Corps out of the country.		An outnumbered U.S. unit repulses a Viet Cong force but sustains heavy casualties.
Nov. 9	At the U.N. Arab delegates warn Israel that its alleged attacks on its Arab neighbors are risking a war.	Kurt-Georg Kiesinger reportedly is the leading candidate to succeed West German Chancellor Erhard.			Constituent Assembly criticizes South Vietnamese Premier Nguyen Cao Ky for the first time.
Nov. 10		British P.M. Harold Wilson says he thinks his country will enter the European Economic Community.			Viet Cong use non-poisonous gas for the first time.
	A	B	C	D	E
	Includes developments that affect more than one world region, international organizations and important meetings of major world leaders.	Includes all domestic and regional developments in Europe, including the Soviet Union, Turkey, Cyprus and Malta.	Includes all domestic and regional developments in Africa and the Middle East, including Iraq and Iran and excluding Cyprus, Turkey and Afghanistan.	Includes all domestic and regional developments in Latin America, the Caribbean and Canada.	Includes all domestic and regional developments in Asia and Pacific nations, extending from Afghanistan through all the Pacific Islands, except Hawaii.

U.S. Politics & Social Issues	U.S. Foreign Policy & Defense	U.S. Economy & Environment	Science, Technology & Nature	Culture, Leisure & Life Style	
			U.S. communications satellite system, Comsat, opens link with Asia.		Oct. 27
V.P. Humphrey tries to unite a divided Democratic Party in Florida.	A poll of Congressmen indicates that about 60% of them support the current U.S. policy in Vietnam.	Reports indicate that many shoppers are switching from butter to margarine because of rising prices.		Beale Street in Memphis, Tenn. becomes a national landmark.	Oct. 28
Republican Party officials see a chance to make dramatic electoral gains in the South.	Pres. Johnson assures Asian allies that the U.S. will not allow Communist China to threaten them with nuclear weapons.		Soviet Union's Luna 12 duplicates recent photos of U.S. satellites.	Pope Paul reaffirms the Catholic Church's traditional opposition to artificial birth control.	Oct. 29
Seven Negro candidates will be running in the upcoming elections in Lowndes County, Ala. for the first time.				Chicago police recover a stolen painting by Correggio.	Oct. 30
Autopsy slides of late Pres. John Kennedy's body are turned over to the National Archives.	Pres. Johnson says that the U.S. will not give in to the Communists in South Vietnam.	Reports indicate that housewives are more demanding buyers at supermarkets in the face of rising inflation.			Nov. 1
	Pres. Johnson returns to Washington after completing his Asian trip.	Borden Co. takes its powdered milk off the market because of possible bacterial "contamination"?			Nov. 2
Pres. Johnson reportedly won't make a pre-election tour of the country.	Reports indicate preparations for an intensified bombing campaign against North Vietnam.	Attorneys for jailed Teamsters Pres. Jimmy Hoffa say that they will continue their appeals.	U.S. launches a military surveillance satellite.		Nov. 3
Pres. Johnson bitterly criticizes former V.P. Nixon and calls him a "chronic campaigner."	Pres. Johnson says that the upcoming elections will not affect the country's Vietnam policy.	October price index dips slightly.			Nov. 4
N.Y. Gov. Nelson Rockefeller calls for more stringent penalties for drug addicts.	Defense Secy. Robert McNamara says that fewer troops will be sent to South Vietnam during 1967.	Major electricity blackouts are called still possible in the U.S.			Nov. 5
Pres. Johnson urges voters to reject any "white backlash."	Former V.P. Nixon accuses Defense Secy. McNamara of "pre-election fakery."				Nov. 6
Commentators predict Republican gains in upcoming Congressional voting.			Soviet Union launches a communications satellite.	Roman Polanski's film *Cul-de-Sac* opens in New York.	Nov. 7
Republicans make moderate gains in Congressional and gubernatorial races.			U.S. postpones the launching of Gemini 12 for one day.	Pope Paul announces plans for cooperation with Protestants on Biblical translations.	Nov. 8
	U.S. is considering reducing its aid to Guinea.		Experts hope for mumps vaccine in 1967.		Nov. 9
U.S. plans to train Negroes in the South in order to cut migration rate to the North.	Defense Secy. McNamara says that the Soviet Union may be deploying an anti-ballistic missile system.		Soviet Union launches a military surveillance satellite.		Nov. 10
F	G	H	I	J	
Includes elections, federal-state relations, civil rights and liberties, crime, the judiciary, education, health care, poverty, urban affairs and population.	*Includes formation and debate of U.S. foreign and defense policies, veterans' affairs and defense spending. (Relations with specific foreign countries are usually found under the region concerned.)*	*Includes business, labor, agriculture, taxation, transportation, consumer affairs, monetary and fiscal policy, natural resources, and pollution.*	*Includes worldwide scientific, medical and technological developments, natural phenomena, U.S. weather, natural disasters, and accidents.*	*Includes the arts, religion, scholarship, communications media, sports, entertainment, fashions, fads and social life.*	

	World Affairs	Europe	Africa & the Middle East	The Americas	Asia & the Pacific
Nov. 11	U.N. Secy Gen. U Thant calls for an unconditional end to the U.S. bombing of North Vietnam.	West German Christian Democratic candidate Kurt-Georg Kiesinger says that Allied authorities exonerated him long ago on Nazi-association charges during World War II.			Reports indicate that the South Vietnamese government may soon undergo a shake-up.
Nov. 12			Israel downs one Jordanian plane over their common border.		Soviet bloc officials walk out of a meeting with Communist Chinese authorities in Peiping.
Nov. 13		London demonstrators march in support of Rhodesia.	A fierce battle breaks out between Israeli and Jordanian artillery forces.	Colombia indicates that it may distribute birth control devices to its citizens.	Viet Cong pound U.S. troops in the Central Highlands in one of the fiercest attacks of the war.
Nov. 14		Bugarian Premier Todor Zhivkov calls for a world Communist meeting to consider the "heresy" of Communist China.			U.S. planes stage heavy raids over North Vietnam.
Nov. 15	At the U.N. Israel blames Syria for recent border harassment.	Soviet leader Leonid Brezhnev repeats Bulgaria's call for a meeting of all Communist parties to deal with Communist China.		Police clash with a small group of students on the campus of the University of Buenos Aires.	Communist China modifies its recent threats to intervene in the Vietnamese War.
Nov. 16	At the U.N. the U.S. joins other countries in condemning Israel for its recent reprisal raid against Jordan.	Police clash with a small group of protesting students at the University of Barcelona.	Reports indicate that Zambia is increasing its trade with Rhodesia despite its stated goal of reducing it.		Heavy fighting breaks out just south of the demilitarized zone in South Vietnam.
Nov. 17		Soviet Union offers to help in the construction of a steel mill in Austria.	Reports indicate that Spain may be granting Spanish Equatorial Africa its independence.		U.S. planes pound Communist positions along the Ho Chi Minh trail.
Nov. 18	At the U.N. Italy suggests that Communist China be asked if it wants membership.	West German officials block a rally of ultranationalists in Munich.			U.S. planes stage heavy raids over the Ho Chi Minh trail.
Nov. 19	Arab U.N. delegates warn Israel that it is risking a coordinated war by its Islamic neighbors.	Reports indicate that European Communist parties are divided on how to react to Communist China.			U.S. destroyers shell a radar site in North Vietnam.
Nov. 20		West German rightists make gains in voting in Bavaria.	Arabs vote to cut investment links with Ford and Coca-Cola companies because of their ties with Israel.		Savage fighting rages in the Central Highlands between U.S. and Communist forces.
Nov. 21	At the U.N. Jordan says that Israel is trying to provoke a war.	Soviet Union reportedly is moving more troops to its border with Communist China.		Haiti discounts rumors of an imminent invasion by exiles.	U.S. planes pound Communist positions in the Central Highlands.
Nov. 22	Communist China indicates that it is not interested in U.N. membership.	Spain proposes liberalization reforms for Parliamentary voting.			
Nov. 23	At the U.N. Canada suggests that provisions be made to seat both Communist and Nationalist Chinese delegations.		Jordanian students in the Arab sector of Jerusalem demand that Israel be attacked immediately.		

A	B	C	D	E
Includes developments that affect more than one world region, international organizations and important meetings of major world leaders.	Includes all domestic and regional developments in Europe, including the Soviet Union, Turkey, Cyprus and Malta.	Includes all domestic and regional developments in Africa and the Middle East, including Iraq and Iran and excluding Cyprus, Turkey and Afghanistan.	Includes all domestic and regional developments in Latin America, the Caribbean and Canada.	Includes all domestic and regional developments in Asia and Pacific nations, extending from Afghanistan through all the Pacific Islands, except Hawaii.

U.S. Politics & Social Issues	U.S. Foreign Policy & Defense	U.S. Economy & Environment	Science, Technology & Nature	Culture, Leisure & Life Style	
	Opening day of a Washington, D.C. conference on U.S. draft reform produces heated disagreements.		U.S. launches the final flight of the Gemini program.	Two U.S. Protestant groups--the Methodist and Evangelical Churches--vote to merge.	Nov. 11
	Pres. Johnson signs a food aid bill which excludes countries which trade with North Vietnam.	U.S. engineers reduce the flow of Niagara Falls in an erosion study.	U.S. astronauts take photos of the solar eclipse.		Nov. 12
	Pres. Johnson says he plans to travel to Europe in the coming year.		U.S. astronaut Edwin Aldrin takes a "space walk" outside his orbiting Gemini spacecraft for two hours and nine minutes.		Nov. 13
Supreme Court upholds the trespass conviction of 32 Florida civil rights demonstrators.		AFL-CIO endorses the administration's Vietnam policy.	U.S. astronaut Edwin Aldrin goes for his third "space walk" in three days.	Roman Catholic cardinals accuse the Johnson administration of pressuring the poor to use birth control.	Nov. 14
			Two U.S. astronauts, Capt. James Lovell Jr. and Edwin Aldrin Jr. splash down in the Pacific in spacecraft Gemini 12.		Nov. 15
		Reports indicate that the President's economic advisers are pushing for a tax increase.		Pope Paul criticizes Roman Catholic progressives.	Nov. 16
	U.S. officials indicate that the U.S. build-up in Thailand may soon tail off.	Housing starts have fallen to their lowest level in twenty years.		Recent prices for Pablo Picasso's paintings rise dramatically.	Nov. 17
	State Secy. Dean Rusk rules out a bombing pause during the Christmas season.	General Motors announces a production cut-back.	Lunar Orbiter 2 sends back photos of the moon.		Nov. 18
N.Y. Gov. Nelson Rockefeller calls for Republican moderates to set the tone in the 1968 Presidential election.			Soviet Union launches a communications satellite.		Nov. 19
N.Y.C. officials say that they will press for a plan to give the poor food stamps to be used in the purchase of food.	U.S. officials indicate that the 1967 U.S. troop total for South Vietnam will be about 475,000.				Nov. 20
	U.S. State Dept. says that it is considering supplying Jordan with military equipment.			U.S. Roman Catholic bishops support the U.S. presence in Vietnam but warn against the dangers of escalation.	Nov. 21
N.Y.C. officials announce plans for a civilian review board to monitor police despite the proposal's recent defeat in a referendum.	U.S. denies that the Soviet Union has discussed its border problems with Communist China in recent US-Soviet talks.	U.S. auto makers recall about 500,000 cars because of possible defects.			Nov. 22
A former aide to the late Pres. John Kennedy, Theodore Sorensen, says that Sen. Robert Kennedy should not challenge Pres. Johnson in the upcoming 1968 elections under any circumstances.		Labor Dept. reports that consumer prices are continuing to inch upwards.	Pres. Johnson praises the Gemini 12 crew in a White House ceremony.	Ireland's second president, Sean O'Kelly, dies in Dublin at 84.	Nov. 23
F	G	H	I	J	
Includes elections, federal-state relations, civil rights and liberties, crime, the judiciary, education, health care, poverty, urban affairs and population.	*Includes formation and debate of U.S. foreign and defense policies, veterans' affairs and defense spending. (Relations with specific foreign countries are usually found under the region concerned.)*	*Includes business, labor, agriculture, taxation, transportation, consumer affairs, monetary and fiscal policy, natural resources, and pollution.*	*Includes worldwide scientific, medical and technological developments, natural phenomena, U.S. weather, natural disasters, and accidents.*	*Includes the arts, religion, scholarship, communications media, sports, entertainment, fashions, fads and social life.*	

	World Affairs	Europe	Africa & the Middle East	The Americas	Asia & the Pacific
Nov. 24	U.N. calls for a complete suspension of nuclear tests.	Reports indicate that unemployment is rising in Britain.	West Bank Jordanians demonstrate against King Hussein and demand that he take stronger measures against Israel.		U.S. planes bomb the Ho Chi Minh trail.
Nov. 25	U.N. Security Council criticizes Israel's Nov. 13 raid against Jordan.		Jordanian troops repress West Bank Arab demonstrators demanding action against Israel.		U.S. planes pound Communist positions in the Central Highlands.
Nov. 26		Soviet Union denounces Communist Chinese leader Mao Tse-tung in a bitter attack.	Jordanian King Hussein says that citizens living near Israel will be given arms to protect themselves.		Australian voters give strong support to P.M. Henry Holt and his policy of backing the U.S. in the Vietnamese War.
Nov. 27	At the U.N. African delegates criticize Western investment in South Africa.		Reports indicate that Egyptian Pres. Gamal Nasser's policy of pan-Arabism is becoming less popular in the Middle East.	Early returns show Uruguay's center-left party leading the country's conservative party.	U.S. troops clash with Communist forces in the Central Highlands.
Nov. 28		Hungarian C.P. leader Janos Kadar verbally attacks Communist China.	Jordan says that "outside Arab sources" paid the recent West Bank demonstrators.		South Vietnamese troops clash with Communist forces in the Mekong Delta.
Nov. 29	U.N. votes 57 to 47 to refuse Communist China admission.		Israel reports the downing of two Egyptian jets.		South Vietnam says that its troops will observe brief truces during Christmas and New Years.
Nov. 30	Reports indicate that Secy. Gen. U Thant will remain at his post.	British P.M. Harold Wilson leaves London for new talks with Rhodesian P.M. Ian Smith.			
Dec. 1		West German Parliament elects Kurt-Georg Kiesinger as Chancellor.	Jordan accuses Syria of sending saboteurs across its border.	Reports indicate that economic conditions are continuing to deteriorate in Haiti.	Viet Cong defections set record during November according to U.S. sources.
Dec. 2	U.N. Secy. Gen. U Thant agrees to accept another four-year term.	Soviet Union warns against a renaissance of fascism in West Germany.			U.S. bombers make their second closest strike to Hanoi.
Dec. 3		A bill submitted to the Spanish Parliament offers religious liberty.	Rhodesian P.M. Ian Smith ends talks with British P.M. Harold Wilson with no hint of success.		Viet Cong attack Saigon's airport.
Dec. 4		Flood damage in Florence, Italy is extremely heavy.			Viet Cong renew raids on Saigon's airport.
Dec. 5	Britain asks the U.N. to apply sanctions against Rhodesia.	Soviet Union holds military training program for citizens who live along the Chinese border.	Rhodesia rejects Britain's terms for ending its rebellion.		Communist China warns Portuguese authorities on Macao not to crack down on pro-Mao demonstrators.
Dec. 6	Members of the British Commonwealth begin to apply economic sanctions against Rhodesia.	French bases will not be made available to U.S. forces in case of an emergency.	Rhodesian P.M. Ian Smith defends his rejection of Britain's proposals in a radio address in Salisbury.		
Dec. 7		Britain's Conservative Party condemns P.M. Harold Wilson's attempts to encourage economic sanctions against Rhodesia.	Syria calls on all Jordanians to overthrow the government of King Hussein.		U.S. planes bomb the Ho Chi Minh supply route.

A	B	C	D	E
Includes developments that affect more than one world region, international organizations and important meetings of major world leaders.	Includes all domestic and regional developments in Europe, including the Soviet Union, Turkey, Cyprus and Malta.	Includes all domestic and regional developments in Africa and the Middle East, including Iraq and Iran and excluding Cyprus, Turkey and Afghanistan.	Includes all domestic and regional developments in Latin America, the Caribbean and Canada.	Includes all domestic and regional developments in Asia and Pacific nations, extending from Afghanistan through all the Pacific Islands, except Hawaii.

U.S. Politics & Social Issues	U.S. Foreign Policy & Defense	U.S. Economy & Environment	Science, Technology & Nature	Culture, Leisure & Life Style	
	U.S. officials indicate that they favor stronger economic ties with Eastern Europe.			U.S. scientists appeal to Pope Paul to change the Church's anti-birth control policies.	Nov. 24
Pres. Johnson approves $1-billion in aid to children of poor families.	U.S. urges a world food fund to combat emergencies.	N.Y.C. declares a pollution emergency as a heavy smog covers the city.			Nov. 25
		Smog emergency ends in N.Y.C. in wake of a cool air mass.	U.S. launches a military surveillance satellite.		Nov. 26
		Reports indicate that Pres. Johnson will ask for a tax rise in 1967.			Nov. 27
	U.S. raises its diplomatic relations with Hungary and Bulgaria to the ambassadorial level.	U.S. releases funds to bolster the sagging construction industry.			Nov. 28
N.Y.C. merchants decry the growing welfare load in the city.	State Dept. predicts that Communist China will soon set off another nuclear test.			Sigmund Freud's and William C. Bullitt's book on Woodrow Wilson is published.	Nov. 29
Justice Department says that it is reviewing all past cases involving eavesdropping.	U.S. announces a joint development project with West Germany for a vertical take-off fighter.		Orbiter 2 transmits best photos of the moon to date.		Nov. 30
Thousands of Berkeley, Calif. students boycott classes to protest the recent arrests of 10 students demonstrating against Navy recruiters on campus.	U.S. offers to exchange seed samples with Communist China.				Dec. 1
U.S. Public Health Service says that it may cut funds for Southern hospitals because of segregation.		U.S. unemployment rate declines to 3.7%.		A survey indicates that a majority of U.S. Roman Catholics use artificial birth control.	Dec. 2
	Pres. Johnson holds a friendly meeting with Mexican Pres. Gustavo Ordaz at the US-Mexican border.	Conservationists announce plans to defeat a proposed airport for the N.J. marshlands.			Dec. 3
Big city mayors are increasingly critical of the nation's space program.		N.Y.C. Mayor John Lindsay calls the city's air pollution "unacceptable."	U.S. launches a military communications satellite.		Dec. 4
Supreme Court voids Georgia's refusal to seat State Rep. Julian Bond because he advocates draft resistance.		UAW Pres. Walter Reuther says the union will exert its independence from the AFL-CIO on certain basic issues.			Dec. 5
	Pres. Johnson says that he will ask Congress for $9-$10-billion more for the Vietnam War.	Johnson administration provides funds to help the sagging housing industry.		A vandal slashes three paintings in the Capitol in Washington, D.C.	Dec. 6
	State Dept. acknowledges that U.S. helicopter pilots are flying Thai troops into anti-guerrilla combat in northeast Thailand.			Vatican opens its 1846-1878 archives to scholars.	Dec. 7
F	G	H	I	J	
Includes elections, federal-state relations, civil rights and liberties, crime, the judiciary, education, health care, poverty, urban affairs and population.	Includes formation and debate of U.S. foreign and defense policies, veterans' affairs and defense spending. (Relations with specific foreign countries are usually found under the region concerned.)	Includes business, labor, agriculture, taxation, transportation, consumer affairs, monetary and fiscal policy, natural resources, and pollution.	Includes worldwide scientific, medical and technological developments, natural phenomena, U.S. weather, natural disasters, and accidents.	Includes the arts, religion, scholarship, communications media, sports, entertainment, fashions, fads and social life.	

	World Affairs	Europe	Africa & the Middle East	The Americas	Asia & the Pacific
Dec. 8	U.N. reaches agreement on the first international treaty governing the exploration of space.			Drafting of a stricter press law stirs concern in Argentina.	U.S. planes pound Communist positions south of the demilitarized zone.
Dec. 9	At the U.N. Zambia castigates Britain for only applying selective economic sanctions against Rhodesia.	Soviet Union begins allowing some of its citizens who have relatives abroad to emigrate.			Communists down three U.S. planes over both Vietnams.
Dec. 10	At the U.N. African delegates call for strict economic sanctions against Rhodesia.				Viet Cong step up terrorist action in the Saigon area with a number of grenade attacks on civilians.
Dec. 11			Jordan refuses to allow Palestinian guerrillas to take up positions near the Israeli border.		South Vietnamese forces clash with the Viet Cong in the Mekong Delta.
Dec. 12	At the U.N. U.S. supports economic sanctions against Rhodesia.	Britain publishes details on plans to convert currency to a decimal system. . . . Soviet Union sends 100 new supersonic fighter-planes to North Vietnam.	Northern Nigeria experiences economic problems in wake of the recent flight of Ibo merchants.		About 100 Viet Cong guerrillas ambush a U.S. unit 65 miles from Saigon.
Dec. 13	At the U.N. Britain opposes a proposed blockade of South Africa.	West German Chancellor Kurt-Georg Kiesinger emphasizes the importance of good relations with France.	Egyptian Pres. Nasser agres to allow former Saudi King Ibn Saud to live in Egypt.		
Dec. 14		Soviet Union backs an oil embargo of Rhodesia.		Venezuelan troops clear striking students from the University of Caracas.	U.S. planes pound the Ho Chi Minh supply trail.
Dec. 15		Soviet Union announces that it is increasing its defense spending.			South Vietnamese and Viet Cong forces clash in the Mekong Delta.
Dec. 16	U.N. unanimously votes for economic sanctions against Rhodesia.	Madrid metal workers' union goes on strike for the first time under the Franco government. . . . NATO countries call for more contact between the two Germanies.			U.S. planes attack the Ho Chi Minh supply trail.
Dec. 17	U.N. backs a pact to bar arms in space.		Israel reports a minor border skirmish with Arab guerrillas near the Syrian border.	Police clash with demonstrating students on the campus of the University of Buenos Aires.	U.S. says that Viet Cong's 1966 defection rate was greater than South Vietnam's.
Dec. 18	At the U.N. African delegates call on Britain to use force against Rhodesia.	Reports indicate that West German Chancellor Kurt-Georg Kiesinger is trying to smooth over US-French differences.			U.S. planes attack industrial installations near Hanoi.
Dec. 19	At the U.N. Arab delegates accuse Israel of mistreating its Arab citizens.	Police and protesting students scuffle at the University of Madrid.	Syria accuses Jordan of curbing guerrilla attacks against Israel.	Brazil reports major economic gains.	U.S. planes pound Communist positions in the Central Highlands.
Dec. 20	U.N. Secy Gen. U Thant reportedly may be a secret mediator between the U.S. and North Vietnam.	French Communists and Socialists agree to work together in the 1967 Parliamentary elections.			

A	B	C	D	E
Includes developments that affect more than one world region, international organizations and important meetings of major world leaders.	Includes all domestic and regional developments in Europe, including the Soviet Union, Turkey, Cyprus and Malta.	Includes all domestic and regional developments in Africa and the Middle East, including Iraq and Iran and excluding Cyprus, Turkey and Afghanistan.	Includes all domestic and regional developments in Latin America, the Caribbean and Canada.	Includes all domestic and regional developments in Asia and Pacific nations, extending from Afghanistan through all the Pacific Islands, except Hawaii.

U.S. Politics & Social Issues	U.S. Foreign Policy & Defense	U.S. Economy & Environment	Science, Technology & Nature	Culture, Leisure & Life Style	
Sen. Robert Kennedy accuses black power advocates of hurting the civil rights cause.	Pres. Johnson says that he will seek Senate approval of the proposed U.N. treaty governing space exploration.			Pope Paul appeals to all sides to extend the upcoming Christmas truce in Vietnam.	Dec. 8
	State Dept. says that North Vietnam has rejected a proposed prisoner exchange.	U.S. reports that wholesale prices declined during November.		National Council of Churches urges the administration to show "more candor" in its reports on Vietnam.	Dec. 9
FBI head J. Edgar Hoover says that former Atty. Gen. Robert Kennedy worked on a number of illegal wiretap cases.			Soviet Union conducts an underground nuclear test.	Mrs. John Kennedy expresses dismay over William Manchester's book, *The Death of a President*, an account of the assassination of her husband, because of some personal material included.	Dec. 10
Ford Foundation decides to increase backing for educational television.	U.S. Navy is reported pressing for an extension of the bombing of North Vietnam.		U.S. conducts an underground nuclear test.		Dec. 11
					Dec. 12
	U.S. agrees to sell advanced fighter aircraft to Iran.	Federal government is seen assuming a much more aggressive policy in fighting air pollution.		Mrs. John Kennedy will go to court to halt publication of William Manchester's book on the late President Kennedy's assassination.	Dec. 13
	U.S. officials acknowledge for the first time that the U.S. may have bombed Hanoi inadvertently.	U.S. reports that industrial production fell in November.	Two U.S. scientists say that animal skin is sensitive to light.		Dec. 14
	U.S. asserts that no civilian targets have been hit in Hanoi.	U.S. officials predict a slower economic growth rate over the next three years.		Cartoonist Walt Disney, a pioneer in film animation, dies in Los Angeles at 65.	Dec. 15
				Mrs. John Kennedy sues author William Manchester to stop publication of his book on the assassination of her husband.	Dec. 16
			U.S. conducts an underground nuclear test.		Dec. 17
N.Y.C. says that it has run out of funds to combat adult illiteracy.					Dec. 18
				Author William Manchester says that his book on the assassination of Pres. Kennedy contains no indiscretions.	Dec. 19
N.Y.C. Negroes say that they want more control over their local schools.		Port Authority of New York says it still wants an airport in the New Jersey marshlands despite conservationists' objections.	U.S. conducts an underground nuclear test in Nevada.		Dec. 20

F	G	H	I	J
Includes elections, federal-state relations, civil rights and liberties, crime, the judiciary, education, health care, poverty, urban affairs and population.	*Includes formation and debate of U.S. foreign and defense policies, veterans' affairs and defense spending. (Relations with specific foreign countries are usually found under the region concerned.)*	*Includes business, labor, agriculture, taxation, transportation, consumer affairs, monetary and fiscal policy, natural resources, and pollution.*	*Includes worldwide scientific, medical and technological developments, natural phenomena, U.S. weather, natural disasters, and accidents.*	*Includes the arts, religion, scholarship, communications media, sports, entertainment, fashions, fads and social life.*

	World Affairs	Europe	Africa & the Middle East	The Americas	Asia & the Pacific
Dec. 21	At the U.N. U.S. Amb.-to-U.N. Arthur Goldberg says that the U.S. poses no conditions for any peace talks in the Vietnamese War.	A Soviet court sentences a U.S. tourist to three years in a labor camp for exchanging money on the black market.		Police clash with a small group of anti-government demonstrators at the University of Mexico City.	Reports indicate that a small number of North Korean pilots have flown planes in North Vietnam.
Dec. 22		Unemployment is reportedly rising in Britain.	Guinea may be easing its hostile attitude toward the US.		India says that the Soviet Union is sending grain to help combat drought conditions.
Dec. 23			Jordanian King Hussein reportedly is holding his ground against demands by West Bank citizens for stiffer measures against Israel.		A 48-hour cease-fire begins in Vietnam.
Dec. 24		French newspaper *Le Monde* hails improved West German-French ties.	Isolated attacks continue against Ibos in northern Nigeria.		Thailand presses its drive against Communist guerrillas in the northeast.
Dec. 25		Polish Cardinal Stefan Wyszynski says that he rejects government demands to close some Catholic seminaries.			
Dec. 26		European Economic Community rejects Spain's application because it is not a democracy.			Full-scale fighting resumes as the Christmas truce ends in South Vietnam.
Dec. 27	At the U.N. a Swedish expert on population says that urban living reduces human fertility.			Cuban government agrees to allow U.S. citizens living in Cuba to join relatives in the U.S.	Allied troops launch a major operation in the Mekong Delta.
Dec. 28		Spain remains hopeful about eventual membership in the Common Market despite its recent rejection.	Guinea curbs the political activities of former Ghanaian Pres. Kwame Nkrumah.	A medium-size earthquake strikes Chile's copper region.	Communist China explodes its fifth nuclear device.
Dec. 29			Jordan accuses Syria of sabotage attacks.	Argentinian Cabinet resigns amid talk of a major governmental shakeup.	A call for a general strike in Saigon by labor officials is generally ignored.
Dec. 30	U.N. Secy. Gen. U Thant calls for an early end to the Vietnamese War.	Reports indicate that British P.M. Harold Wilson is coming under heavy pressure from his left-wing to disassociate himself from U.S. policy in Vietnam.			
Dec. 31	At the U.N. African delegates criticize South Africa's apartheid policies.	Yugoslavia protests U.S. suspension of surplus food sales.	An Israeli patrol skirmishes with Arab infiltrators.		A second 48-hour holiday truce begins in Vietnam.

A	B	C	D	E
Includes developments that affect more than one world region, international organizations and important meetings of major world leaders.	Includes all domestic and regional developments in Europe, including the Soviet Union, Turkey, Cyprus and Malta.	Includes all domestic and regional developments in Africa and the Middle East, including Iraq and Iran and excluding Cyprus, Turkey and Afghanistan.	Includes all domestic and regional developments in Latin America, the Caribbean and Canada.	Includes all domestic and regional developments in Asia and Pacific nations, extending from Afghanistan through all the Pacific Islands, except Hawaii.

U.S. Politics & Social Issues	U.S. Foreign Policy & Defense	U.S. Economy & Environment	Science, Technology & Nature	Culture, Leisure & Life Style	
	U.S. State Secy. Dean Rusk calls on the Soviet Union not to deploy an anti-ballistic missile system.				Dec. 21
Negro organizations charge that urban renewal programs ignore the residents that they displace.	U.S. makes major food grants to India.			Pope Paul calls on all sides in the Vietnamese War to compromise.	Dec. 22
	U.S. says it will begin to ship grain to Pakistan to alleviate a bad harvest.	United Steelworkers Union officials call on wildcat strikers in Indiana to return to work.		U.S. Roman Catholic Cardinal Spellman arrives for Christmas in Vietnam.	Dec. 23
U.S. Negroes oppose any attempt to bar Harlem Congressman Adam Clayton Powell from taking his seat because of financial improprieties.			Second Soviet rocket lands on the moon.		Dec. 24
Administration officials reportedly believe that anti-poverty programs are proving to be politically unpopular.	Sen. John Stennis (D, Miss.) praises the administration's Vietnam policy.		U.S. East Coast digs out of a major snow storm.	Newsweek magazine says that Pres. Johnson is unhappy about parts of William Manchester's book on the assassination of Pres. Kennedy.	Dec. 25
A survey of N.Y. Democratic officials indicates that at least half of them would prefer that Pres. Johnson not run in the 1968 presidential election.	U.S. officials acknowledge that U.S. planes may have sometimes inadvertently struck civilian targets in North Vietnam.	Danger of pollution to agriculture is reportedly on the rise.		Choreographer Paul Taylor's Orbs opens the N.Y.C. Ballet season.	Dec. 26
	U.S. says that fewer troops will be sent to Vietnam during 1967 than were sent during 1966.	Teamsters Union plans to seek wage increases above the federal guidelines.		Representatives of the Kennedy family and of author William Manchester reach a temporary accord on their dispute over the upcoming book about the Kennedy assassination.	Dec. 27
	Pres. Johnson reportedly is satisfied that the bombing of North Vietnam is directed only at military targets.		U.S. scientists say that weather predictions of about two weeks in advance will be possible within 15 years.		Dec. 28
A New Orleans court upholds a lower court decision mandating the desegregation of city schools.	U.S. offers major credits to Poland.	UAW accuses the AFL-CIO of living in the past.			Dec. 29
A U.S. spokesman says that Pres. Johnson strongly supports anti-poverty programs even if they are politically unpopular.			Soviet Union conducts an underground nuclear test.	The harpsichord's popularity in the musical world is seen increasing.	Dec. 30
	Pres. Johnson announces the selection of Boeing and General Electric to design the U.S. supersonic airliner.				Dec. 31

F	G	H	I	J
Includes elections, federal-state relations, civil rights and liberties, crime, the judiciary, education, health care, poverty, urban affairs and population.	Includes formation and debate of U.S. foreign and defense policies, veterans' affairs and defense spending. (Relations with specific foreign countries are usually found under the region concerned.)	Includes business, labor, agriculture, taxation, transportation, consumer affairs, monetary and fiscal policy, natural resources, and pollution.	Includes worldwide scientific, medical and technological developments, natural phenomena, U.S. weather, natural disasters, and accidents.	Includes the arts, religion, scholarship, communications media, sports, entertainment, fashions, fads and social life.

1967

President Johnson confers with West German Foreign Minister Willy Brandt on Feb. 9, during Brandt's visit to Washington.

A square block in Detroit in flames during the July race riots.

King Hussein of Jordan, left, and Egyptian President Abdel Nasser sign a joint defense pact in Cairo on May 30.

French President Charles De Gaulle visiting Expo 67 in Montreal.

Fighting continues on the Syrian battlefront despite a cease-fire agreement with Israel made June 10.

Demonstrators in front of the Pentagon protesting the Vietnam war on Oct. 21.

Sen. Robert Kennedy addresses supporters June 5 at the Ambassador Hotel in Los Angeles moments before he is shot and mortally wounded.

Thurgood Marshall, the first Negro Supreme Court Justice, is sworn in on Sept. 1.

English composer Benjamin Britten rehearses singers who will take part in the premiere of his opera *Gloriana* on Nov. 22.

The Shah of Iran crowns his wife, Empress Farah, after crowning himself Oct. 26 in Teheran.

	World Affairs	Europe	Africa & the Middle East	The Americas	Asia & the Pacific
Jan.	A U.N. subcommission votes to suppress a report alleging acts of racial discrimination in certain developing countries because it would offend those countries in question.	Rumania is the first East European country to establish full diplomatic ties with West Germany.	Reports indicate that Egyptian planes bombed a Saudi border village several times.	In a growing trend towards centralization, the Brazilian Congress adopts a new constitution extending the power of the federal government.	A virtual civil war between Communist Chinese Red Guards and dissident workers spreads to Peking. . . .U.S. troops' strength reaches 404,000 in South Vietnam.
Feb.	South African mission to the U.N. criticizes the Jan. 18 UNESCO report on apartheid by pointing out the Negro literacy in South Africa is ten times higher than in the rest of Africa.	Reports indicate that the Soviet Union has informed Warsaw Pact members that it will withdraw 50,000 troops from Eastern Europe for deployment along the Soviet-Chinese border.	Competing Arab nationalist forces clash with British troops and with each other in Aden. . . .Tanzanian Pres. Julius Nyerere proclaims the nationalization of all banks.	Fourteen Latin American nations sign a treaty banning nuclear weapons from Latin America.	Communist Chinese Red Guards harass Soviet diplomatic personnel in Peking. . . .Soviet Union decides to repatriate dependents of its diplomatic personnel in Communist China.
March	A U.N. commission on Human Rights refers consideration of the problem of continued slavery in the Arab world to a sub-commission.	France launches its first nuclear-powered submarine. . . .German Social Democrats elect Helmut Schmidt as their parliamentary leader.	Clashes continue between British troops and Arab residents of Aden. . . .Residents of French Somaliland (Djibouti) vote for "increased autonomy" but not complete independence from France.	Arthur da Costa e Silva is inaugurated as Brazil's 22d president. . . .Bolivia asserts that Communist Ché Guevara is leading anti-government guerrillas.	Reports indicate that violent clashes took place between pro and anti-Mao forces in Canton on March 4 which left more than 100 killed or wounded.
April	At the International Planned Parenthood Federation Conference, Dr. Oscar Harkavy says that Taiwan is the only country to date which has successfully organized large-scale family planning in the developing world.	A Greek military junta assumes power in Greece.	Reports indicate that Nigeria's eastern region, called Biafra, is considering seceeding from the rest of the country. . . .Yemen expels all U.S. officials.	Bolivian troops capture French leftist author Regis Debray who has been accompanying Bolivian guerrillas.	U.S. planes bomb the port of Haiphong for the first time.
May	After three years of discussions, the 53 Kennedy Round tariff-cutting nations reach an agreement which reduces industrial tariffs by about one-third.	A poll indicates that 74% of West Germans interviewed favor direct contacts between East and West German leaders.	Nigeria's Eastern Region secedes and declares its independence as the Republic of Biafra. . . .Egyptian Pres. Nasser forces U.N. troops to leave the Sinai whereupon he blockades the Gulf of Aquaba and sends more than 50,000 Egyptian troops into the Sinai Peninsula.	Venezuela says that Cubans are fighting with Venezuelan guerrillas, Cuban Premier Fidel Castro confirms the charge.	U.S. planes bomb the center of Hanoi for the first time. . . .Savage fighting takes place between U.S. and North Vietnamese troops at Khesanh. . . .Two Soviet destroyers scrape the U.S. destroyer *Walker* in the Sea of Japan for allegedly being too close to Soviet territory.
June	U.N. Relief Commissioner Laurence Michelmore says that at least 100,000 Arabs have left the Israeli-conquered West-Bank of the Jordan River.	British Foreign Min. George Brown announces that Britian will grant the South Arabian Federation of Aden its independence on Jan. 9, 1968.	Israel attacks Egypt, Jordan and Syria and conquers large amounts of territories from each country.	Bolivian army kills 21 miners in clashes and occupies tin mines.	Communist China announces that it has successfully tested its first hydrogen bomb. . . .South Korean Pres. Chung Hee Park's political party wins a majority of parliamentary seats in an election marked by controversy.
July	U.N. Gen. Assembly demands that Israel rescind the measures taken to reunify the city of Jerusalem under Israeli administration.	A British government White Paper calls for the complete withdrawal of British troops from Singapore and Malaysia by 1975.	Fighting breaks out between troops of the Nigerian federal government and the secessionist region of Biafra. . . .Israeli and Egyptian forces regularly exchange artillery barrages across the Suez Canal.	In an emotionally charged speech in Montreal, French Pres. Charles de Gaulle calls for an independent Quebec.	Communist Chinese Red Guards continue to harass foreign diplomats in Peking despite efforts by the government to put a break on the Cultural Revolution.
Aug.	U.N. Secy. Gen. U Thant appoints Dr. Ernesto Thalman to undertake a fact-finding mission in Jerusalem to determine the effects of Israel's annexation of the former Jordanian sector of the city.	Greek government indicts Greek leftist politician Andreas Papandreou on charges of high treason.	Egyptian Pres. Gamal Abdel Nasser and Saudi King Faisal announce the formation of a three-nation committee to supervise the withdrawal of Egyptian troops from Yemen.	Foreign Ministers of 11 Latin American countries meet to discuss proposals for setting up a Latin American common market.	Philippeans, Malaysia, Singapore, Thailand and Indonesia form an economic grouping called the Association of South East Asian Nations (ASEAN). . . .Red Guards set fire to the British chancery in Peking and harass British diplomatic personal.
Sept.	World Bank reports that for the sixth consecutive year there has been practically no increase in foreign aid from the industrial countries.	In line with his aim to reduce the influence of the U.S. and Russia, French Pres. Charles de Gaulle visits Poland and calls for a more independent attitude in Eastern Europe.	Arab leaders pledge no negotiations with Israel at the end of the Khartoum Conference. . . .First Israeli settlement is established in Arab territory captured during the June 1967 war.	Fighting intensifies between government and guerrilla forces in Bolivia.	South Vietnamese Gen. Nguyen Van Thieu wins presidential elections.
Oct.	In the U.N. Gen Assembly, Rumania pursues its independent course by asserting that the time has come for all foreign troops to leave Europe, including those of the Soviet Union.	Greek Public Order Min. Pavlos Totomis announces that former Premier George Papandreou has been released from house detention. . . .Turkey threatens to intervene militarily in Cyprus unless the fighting between the Greek and Turkish communities ends.	Kenya and Somalia sign an agreement providing for efforts to end their border dispute. . . .Intermittant fighting intensifies between Egypt and Israel as Egypt sinks an Israeli destroyer and Israel bombs oil refineries in Alexandria.	Bolivian army crushes a guerrilla movement and kills its prominant Communist leader Ernesto Ché Guevara.	Indonesia and Communist China complete the withdrawal of their diplomatic missions from each other's country. . . .Secondary schools reopen in Communist China amid signs that the country's leaders are trying to discourage the aggressive campaign by young militants known as Red Guards.
Nov.	U.N. Security Council unanimously passes a British resolution calling for an eventual withdrawal of Israeli forces from captured Arab territories and for an end to the Arabs' state of belligerancy against Israel.	Heavy gold speculation continues on European markets amid speculation that the U.S. will suspend the gold convertability of the dollar.	Britain grants independence to the South Arabian Federation and withdraws its troops. The newly independent country adopts the name of South Yemen amid signs that it is considering aligning itself with the Soviet Union.	Bolivian army captures the remnants of communist Ché Guevara's guerrilla band.	Fierce fighting continues in South Vietnam particularly around Dakto near the demilitarized zone. . . .Tension between Communist China and Britain over the status of Hong Kong decreases.
Dec.	Delegates of the Organization for Economic Cooperation and Development agree in principle to a plan under which the developed nations would grant special tariff concessions to the developing nations.	A call for a revolt against the ruling military junta by Greek King Constantine fails and the King flies to exile in Rome.	Soviet military and diplomatic personnel establish a major presence in the newly independent country of South Yemen.	Uruguayan Pres. Oscar Daniel Gestido dies in Montevideo at 66.	Australian P.M. Harold Holt disappears while swimming off an Australian beach and his body is never found.

A	B	C	D	E
Includes developments that affect more than one world region, international organizations and important meetings of major world leaders.	Includes all domestic and regional developments in Europe, including the Soviet Union, Turkey, Cyprus and Malta.	Includes all domestic and regional developments in Africa and the Middle East, including Iraq and Iran and excluding Cyprus, Turkey and Afghanistan.	Includes all domestic and regional developments in Latin America, the Caribbean and Canada.	Includes all domestic and regional developments in Asia and Pacific nations, extending from Afghanistan through all the Pacific Islands, except Hawaii.

U.S. Politics & Social Issues	U.S. Foreign Policy & Defense	U.S. Economy & Environment	Science, Technology & Nature	Culture, Leisure & Life Style
U.S. Public Health Service ends its funding of Alabama programs because of noncompliance with the 1964 Civil Rights Act. . . .Justice Dept. files its first public accomodations suit against a restaurant which refused to serve Negroes.	U.S. acknowledges a tacit understanding between the Johnson administration and Communist China involving a Chinese pledge not to enter the Vietnamese War if the U.S. doesn't invade North Vietnam.	U.S. automobile manufacturers say that they will be unable to meet six to 10 of the government's 23 proposed safety standards for the 1968 model autos.	A Smithsonian Astrophysical Observatory spokesman says that a tenth satellite of the planet Saturn has been discovered by Dr. Audouin Dollfus of France.	Random House publishes Sen. J. William Fulbright's critique of U.S. foreign policy The Arrogance of Power.
In the first government suit against an employer the Justice Department sues the Dillon Supply Co. of Raleigh, N.C. for racial discrimination.	Defense Secy. Robert McNamara denies that he thinks that the bombing of North Vietnam is ineffective. . . .Dr. Martin Luther King Jr. assails U.S. policy in Vietnam.	AFL-CIO Pres. George Meany endorses Pres. Johnson for re-election in 1968.	National Safety Council reports that a record 52,000 Americans were killed in 1966 traffic accidents.	Two American University professors announce that 700 pages of manuscripts and drawings by Leonardo da Vinci have been found in the Spanish Library in Madrid.
Justice Dept. reports that only one person was executed by civil authorities in the U.S. during 1966.	Sen. Robert Kennedy calls for a halt to the bombing of North Vietnam. . . .Pres. Johnson announces that the Soviet Union is ready to enter into arms control negotiations.	Teamsters Union Pres. James Hoffa begins an eight-year sentence for jury tampering.	Dr. Maimon Cohen of the Buffalo N.Y. State University School of Medicine reports evidence linking the hallucinogenic drug LSD to hereditary cell damage.	Random House publishes Marshall McLuhan's The Medium is the Massage . Lopert Pictures releases Ingmar Bergman's Persona .
U.S. Supreme Court refuses to delay the desegregation of public schools in six Southern states by the fall.	V.P. Humphrey says that the U.S. must realize that Western Europe is now an equal partner.	U.S. Commerce Dept. reports that personal income has risen to record levels.	U.S. announces that eight possible landing sites have been selected for the scheduled manned space flight to the moon.	Wesleyan Universtiy Press publishes James Dickey's Poems 1957-1967 .
U.S. Supreme Court declares unconstitutional voter-approved amendment to the California Constitution which gives property owners "absolute discretion" in resale and rental of housing.	Defense Secy. Robert McNamara says that "very little progress" has been made in talks with the Soviet Union about curtailing an anti-missile defense system.	UAW Pres. Walter Reuther acknowledges that his union once received $50,000 from the CIA for international union activities.	A U.S. Public Health Service survey asserts that there is a strong relationship between smoking and certain physical ailments such as heart disease.	U.S. painter Edward Hopper dies in New York at 84.
Worst outbreak of racial violence since the 1965 Watts Los Angeles riots erupts in Newark, N.J. as Negro youths loot stores and smash windows. . . .Pres. Johnson appoints Thurgood Marshall, the first Negro, to the Supreme Court.	Pres. Johnson meets with Soviet Premier Aleksei Kosygin in Glassboro, N.J.	Consumer critic Ralph Nader criticizes the federal safety agency for failing to support work on an experimental crash-proof car.	American Medical Association goes on record as favoring the liberalization of U.S. abortion laws.	Harper & Row publishes Martin Luther King Jr.'s Where Do We Go From Here: Chaos or Community?
Worst U.S. riot in the 20th century breaks out in Detroit as thousands of Negro looters roam streets. Pres. Johnson orders federal troops to put down disorders.	U.S. sends three transport planes to the Congo (Kinshasa) to help the government put down an invasion of white mercenaries and Katangese tribesmen.	National Association of Manufacturers warns that the fiscal 1968 budget will be large enough to have a negative effect on the economy unless taxes are increased.	U.S. launches Orgo 4 satellite whose mission is to study the relationship between the sun and the earth's environment during a period of increased solar activity.	Pope Paul arrives in Turkey and prays in an Eastern Orthodox church the first time a Catholic Pope has done so.
A growing schism between black power leaders and white liberals dominates the first convention of the National Conference for a New Politics.	State Secy. Robert McNamara says that he does not believe that the bombing of North Vietnam "has in any significant way affected their war-making capability."	Gardner Ackley, chairman of the President's Council of Economic Advisers, warns that a failure to increase taxes will end the chances of price stability. . . .American Bankers Association declares its support of a tax increase.	U.S. continues its lunar space program with several satellite launchings.	Belgian surrealist painter Rene Magritte dies in Brussels at 68.
Defense Secy. Robert McNamara says that the Pentagon will declare off-limits all segregated housing located near military installations throughout the U.S.	Defense Secy. Robert McNamara announces that the U.S. will deploy: an anti-missile ballistic system.	Two hundred sixty university economists endorse the administration's proposed tax increase.	U.S. launches Biosatellite 2 which contains thousands of biological specimens.	U.S. author Carson McCullers and British poet Siegfried Sassoon die. . . . Monthly Review Press publishes Regis Debray's Revolution in the Revolution?
Negro State Rep. Carl Stokes wins the Democratic nomination for mayor of Cleveland, O. in what appears to be a trend toward greater Negro electoral participation.	At least 55,000 demonstrators march against the Vietnamese War in Washington, D.C. . . .A Louis Harris poll indicates that public support for the Vietnam War has dropped to 58% from 72% in July.	Federal Highway Administration proposes 10 new auto safety standards.	Soviet satellite Venera 4 lands on Venus.	Jiri Menzel's film Closely Watched Trains is released in New York.
Sen. Eugene McCarthy (D, Minn.) announces that he will enter five or six Democratic presidential primaries in 1968 to further the campaign for a negotiated settlement of the Vietnamese War.	Anti-Vietnamese War demonstrators increase their harassment of administration spokesmen and manage to force the cancellation of a scheduled speech by Pres. Johnson in Syracuse, N.Y.	U.S. Surgeon General announces the formation of a task force to alert the public about the dangers of cigarette smoking.	U.S. launches the Saturn 5 rocket which is believed to be the most powerful space booster ever launched.	Russian-born sculptor Ossip Zadkine dies in Paris at 77.
Louisville, Ky. passes an open-housing bill. . . .U.S. Supreme Court reverses the murder conviction of Wallace Satterfield because he was not warned of his rights until immediately before his confession.	Presidential candidate Eugene McCarthy says that the U.S. should begin to vacate part of South Vietnam.	UAW Pres. Walter Reuther confirms his union's boycott of the AFL-CIO convention.	South African surgeons perform the world's first human heart transplant operation on Louis Washkansky who survives for 18 days.	N.Y. Film Critics award for the best motion picture of 1967 goes to In the Heat of the Night . . . .Luchino Visconti's film The Stranger is released in New York.
F	G	H	I	J
Includes elections, federal-state relations, civil rights and liberties, crime, the judiciary, education, health care, poverty, urban affairs and population.	Includes formation and debate of U.S. foreign and defense policies, veterans' affairs and defense spending. (Relations with specific foreign countries are usually found under the region concerned.)	Includes business, labor, agriculture, taxation, transportation, consumer affairs, monetary and fiscal policy, natural resources, and pollution.	Includes worldwide scientific, medical and technological developments, natural phenomena, U.S. weather, natural disasters, and accidents.	Includes the arts, religion, scholarship, communications media, sports, entertainment, fashions, fads and social life.

	World Affairs	Europe	Africa & the Middle East	The Americas	Asia & the Pacific
Jan. 1		*Elephtheria*, a Greek newspaper, accuses ex-Prime Minister Panayotis Kanellopoulos of participation in an alleged right-wing conspiracy. . . . Queen Elizabeth II awards Dr. Anna Freud, the daughter of Sigmund Freud, the title of Commander of the Order of the British Empire for her distinguished work in psychology. . . . Austrian Socialist Party elects Bruno Kreisky as its leader.	Syrian and Israeli forces clash in the Galilee border region.	In a reference to U.S. investment, Canadian P.M. Lester Pearson says that while Canada welcomes foreign capital it must be "responsive to Canadian policy."	Viet Cong announces that it will observe a seven-day cease-fire during Tet, the lunar New Year, from Feb. 8 to Feb. 15. . . . Maoist forces claim to have seized control of the main cities in Sinkiang Province.
Jan. 2		About 13,000 electrical workers go on strike in Madrid in protest against the arrest of their labor leaders. The strike ends the same day, however, when the labor leaders are released from jail. . . . Spain sentences novelist Issac Montero to six months imprisonment for writing about his experiences with government censorship.			Maoist forces claim to have seized the entire administrative apparatus of Heilungkiang Province.
Jan. 3		An assassin kills ex-Algerian National Liberation Front Secy. Gen. Mohammed Khider in Madrid.	Sporadic fighting takes place between Syria and Israel along their border.		Portuguese authorities bar pro-Nationalist Chinese residents of Macao from displaying the Nationalist flag.
Jan. 4		French CP attacks the policies of Communist China at its 18th congress. . . . Soviet Union emphatically denies Yugoslav reports of armed clashes on the Soviet-Chinese border.	Kenyan Pres. Jomo Kenyatta names Daniel Arap Moi as vice president.		Nguyen Van Tien, a member of the National Liberation Front's Central Committee, says that the NLF is independent of North Vietnam.
Jan. 5		Britain warns Spain not to interfere with British aircraft using Gibraltar. . . . Spain and Rumania establish relations at the consular and commercial level. It is the first arrangement for formal relations between Spain and an East European communist country since the end of the Spanish Civil War in 1936.	Skirmishes take place between Syria and Israel. . . . Egypt reportedly bombs the Yemeni village of Kitaf with poison gas.		Red Guard posters allege that Mao Tsetung was forced out of his presidential post in 1958 by a faction led by chief of state Liu Shao-chi. . . . A North Vietnamese diplomat, Mai Van Bo, says that if the United States stops its bombing of North Vietnam unconditionally "this fact will be examined and studied by the (Hanoi) government."
Jan. 6		French Communist George Marchais says that 56 pro-Peking members of the French CP have been expelled since 1964. . . . East Germany announces that it will charge international (rather than the lower domestic) rates for postal and phone service with West Germany.	Portuguese army reports killing 243 African guerrillas on Dec. 25, 1966.	Venezuela announces that it has arrested six Castroite terrorists.	Dissident workers and pro-Mao Red Guards clash in Nanking. . . . U.S. and South Vietnam launch a major drive in the Mekong Delta. . . . Japanese officials say that the December, 1966 Communist Chinese nuclear test has produced the highest level of radioactivity ever recorded in Japan.
Jan. 7	Evgen Vacek, a Czech U.N. employee, is allowed to resign and return to Prague after U.S. officials show U.N. Secy. Gen. U Thant evidence about Vacek's spy activities.		Syria and Israel clash along their borders.		Pro- and anti-Mao forces fight in Canton. . . . Outlawed Thai CP publicly announces its support of the pro-communist Thailand Popular Front.
	A	B	C	D	E
	Includes developments that affect more than one world region, international organizations and important meetings of major world leaders.	*Includes all domestic and regional developments in Europe, including the Soviet Union, Turkey, Cyprus and Malta.*	*Includes all domestic and regional developments in Africa and the Middle East, including Iraq and Iran and excluding Cyprus, Turkey and Afghanistan.*	*Includes all domestic and regional developments in Latin America, the Caribbean and Canada.*	*Includes all domestic and regional developments in Asia and Pacific nations, extending from Afghanistan through all the Pacific Islands, except Hawaii.*

U.S. Politics & Social Issues	U.S. Foreign Policy & Defense	U.S. Economy & Environment	Science, Technology & Nature	Culture, Leisure & Life Style	
	State Secy. Dean Rusk says that the unrest in China "may give Hanoi somewhat more freedom of action" than they have had in the past.				Jan. 1
Afro-American Baptist Ministers Conference of Greater New York expresses its support of Rep. Adam Clayton Powell. . . . Federal officials arrest 72 armed men who reportedly were planning an invasion of Haiti. . . . Ronald Reagan becomes California's 33rd governor.					Jan. 2
NAACP Executive Secy. Roy Wilkins expresses his support for Rep. Adam Clayton Powell. . . . Reports indicate that the Columbia Broadcasting System payed the Haitian invasion expedition more than $1,000 to take three CBS cameramen along with them. . . . NAACP announces that of its six new board members five are considered moderates. . . . Equal Employment Opportunity Commission says that Negroes have made substantial gains in employment in Southern textile mills since the passage of the 1964 Civil Rights Act.	State Dept. criticizes a Dec. 25, 1966 *New York Times* article about alleged civilian casualties in North Vietnam in wake of U.S. bombing.	American automobile manufacturers say they will be unable to meet six to ten of the government's 23 proposed safety standards for the 1968 model autos.	A Smithsonian Astrophysical Observatory spokesman says that a 10th satellite of the planet Saturn was discovered by Dr. Audouin Dollfus of France's Meudon Observatory in December 1966.	Jack Ruby, 55, convicted slayer of Pres. Kennedy's alleged assassin, Lee Harvey Oswald, dies in Dallas, Texas of a blood clot.	Jan. 3
American Newspaper Publishers Association issues a report defending press coverage of crime news and opposing "restriction or censorship at the source of news." . . . U.S. officials release all members of the Haitian military expedition on bail except for its leader, Rolando Masferrer Rojas.				Pope Paul VI bans jazz masses and other alleged distortions of the liturgy.	Jan. 4
In his inaugural address California Gov. Ronald Reagan attacks crime and high government spending.	Pres. Johnson suspends virtually all U.S. trade with Rhodesia. . . . FBI reports that 450 people were convicted of violating military draft laws in 1966.	California health officials report that radioactive fallout levels of the previous week were the highest since 1962 because of the Communist Chinese nuclear explosion in December 1966.	For the first time a carbon dioxide jet is used to clear an atherosclerotic coronary artery during an operation in N.Y.C.	Harold Pinter's play *The Homecoming* opens in New York.	Jan. 5
Justice Dept. files suits against four Southern restaurants which have refused to serve Negroes.		Commerce Dept. names a panel to investigate the possibility of developing an electrically powered car.			Jan. 6
Council of Elected Negro Democrats of N.Y. expresses its support of Rep. Adam Clayton Powell.					Jan. 7
F	**G**	**H**	**I**	**J**	
Includes elections, federal-state relations, civil rights and liberties, crime, the judiciary, education, health care, poverty, urban affairs and population.	*Includes formation and debate of U.S. foreign and defense policies, veterans' affairs and defense spending. (Relations with specific foreign countries are usually found under the region concerned.)*	*Includes business, labor, agriculture, taxation, transportation, consumer affairs, monetary and fiscal policy, natural resources, and pollution.*	*Includes worldwide scientific, medical and technological developments, natural phenomena, U.S. weather, natural disasters, and accidents.*	*Includes the arts, religion, scholarship, communications media, sports, entertainment, fashions, fads and social life.*	

	World Affairs	Europe	Africa & the Middle East	The Americas	Asia & the Pacific
Jan. 8		Three Algerian exile leaders accuse Algerian Pres. Houari Boumedienne of organizing the assassination of Gen. Mohammed Khider. . . . French CP praises Pres. de Gaulle "for the improvement of French-USSR relations" and for his stand on Vietnam.			Chinese Communist Premier Chou En-lai calls for moderation in the current phase of the Cultural Revolution. . . . Fighting between dissident workers and Red Guards spreads to Peking. . . . Additional troops join the US-South Vietnamese drive into the Mekong Delta.
Jan. 9		Greek political leader Andreas Papandreou agrees to support the Paraskevopoulos caretaker government and thus ends a feud that threatened to split his father's Center Union Party.	Israeli tanks participate in the Syrian border clashes for the first time.		U.S. flies to Hong Kong 48 Chinese Communist fishermen who were rescued by a U.S. destroyer during a storm in December 1966.
Jan. 10	U.N. Secy. Gen. U Thant says that he has certain basic differences with U.S. policy in Vietnam. He does not believe that Vietnam is vital to Western interests.		Syria accuses Israel of trying to provoke a larger confrontation.		*Hsinhua*, the Chinese Communist news agency, reports that a "large number" of Shanghai textile workers have left their posts and have been "taken-in" by anti-Mao elements. . . . Red Guard posters in Peking attack Chou En-lai.
Jan. 11		Spanish government seizes the weekly magazine *Actualidad Espanola* because of a critical article.	Israel accuses Syria of using heavy weapons which violate the 1949 armistice agreement. . . . A former Yemeni republican official says he saw Egyptian planes stage gas attacks in Yemen on Dec. 11, 1966.		A regularly scheduled meeting between the U.S. and Communist China in Warsaw is canceled at Chinese request. . . . North Vietnam demands that Thai authorities stop permitting the U.S. to use Thailand's air bases for their attacks on Vietnam.
Jan. 12		East Germany announces that it will extend permission for West Germans to visit East Berlin for two more months. . . . West Germany announces that restrictions on several thousand categories of East European goods will be abolished.			Peking radio announces that forces loyal to Mao have captured the Shanghai railway administration after several days of struggle.
Jan. 13	U.N. delegates from seven Asian nations criticize U Thant's views about Vietnam and assert that South Vietnam is "essential" to their own security.	West German Chancellor Kurt-Georg Kiesinger and French Pres. Charles de Gaulle confer in Paris.	Lt. Col. Etienne Eyadema deposes Togolese Pres. Nicholas Grunitzky.		Nationalist China reports downing two Communist Chinese MiGs near Quemoy. It is the first alleged air clash since 1961. . . . U.S. planes fly a record 549 single mission attacks over South Vietnam. . . . New Chinese Communist security measures make it a crime to criticize Chmn. Mao, Defense Min. Lin Piao or the Cultural Revolution.
Jan. 14		Reports indicate that the Kiesinger-de Gaulle meeting has helped to revitalize the 1963 French-West German treaty which had lost much of its meaning under former West German Chancellor Ludwig Erhard. . . . Greek parliament gives Prime Minister Ioannis Paraskevopoulos's caretaker government a vote of confidence.	A mine wounds three Israelis near the Lebanese border. . . . Nigeria officially confirms the death of Maj. Gen. Johnson Aguiyi-Ironsi during the July 1966 mutiny.		Japanese correspondents report that Communist Chinese chief of state Liu Shao-chi has withdrawn the "self-criticism" he allegedly made in October 1966. . . . William Baggs, the American correspondent of the *Miami News*, reports seeing a street in Hanoi which had been bombed by American planes. . . . A record 144 U.S. soldiers were killed during January 8-14.

A	B	C	D	E
Includes developments that affect more than one world region, international organizations and important meetings of major world leaders.	*Includes all domestic and regional developments in Europe, including the Soviet Union, Turkey, Cyprus and Malta.*	*Includes all domestic and regional developments in Africa and the Middle East, including Iraq and Iran and excluding Cyprus, Turkey and Afghanistan.*	*Includes all domestic and regional developments in Latin America, the Caribbean and Canada.*	*Includes all domestic and regional developments in Asia and Pacific nations, extending from Afghanistan through all the Pacific Islands, except Hawaii.*

U.S. Politics & Social Issues	U.S. Foreign Policy & Defense	U.S. Economy & Environment	Science, Technology & Nature	Culture, Leisure & Life Style	
NY Democratic state chmn. John Burns expresses his support for Rep. Adam Clayton Powell. . . . *New York Times* reports that the number of jobs the National Urban League finds annually has increased over the last five years from 2,000 to 40,000 in 1966.				Pope Paul VI reaffirms the Roman Catholic ban on divorce.	Jan. 8
Justice Dept. files its first public accommodations suit against a restaurant which has refused to serve Negroes in Maryland. . . . *Congressional Quarterly* reports that the average age of House members is 50.8 years and the average age of Senate members is 57.7 years. . . . Justice Dept. files suit against the school board election of Madison Parish, La. on the grounds that local officials discriminated against Negro voters.	Agency for International Development says that no more than 5-6% of U.S. economic aid to South Vietnam has been stolen.	A Civil Service Commission report shows that Negroes constitute 13.9% of the federal payroll. . . . A federal study says that the sulphur dioxide air pollution in New York is the worst in the country.		Representatives of the Roman Catholic and Anglican churches confer in Gazzada, Italy about steps toward eventual unification. . . . Putnam's Sons publishes Vladimir Nabokov's *Speak Memory*	Jan. 9
Congress bars Rep. Adam Clayton Powell from taking his House seat pending an investigation into alleged corruption charges.	Reports indicate that the Johnson administration has ordered a temporary halt to the bombing of the Yenvien railroad yards near Hanoi because of alleged civilian casualties. . . . In his State of the Union Message Pres. Johnson asks Congress to enact a 6% tax boost to pay for the Vietnamese War. . . . Three American women who visited North Vietnam at the end of December 1966 report their findings at a news conference in New York.				Jan. 10
Newly elected Georgia Governor Lester Maddox urges respect for federal authority in his inaugural address despite his arch-segregationist past. . . . Justice Department files three desegregation suits against two Mississippi and one Louisiana school district.	U.S. State Secy. Dean Rusk takes issue with U Thant's statement that Vietnam is not vital to Western interests.	Pres. Johnson cancels the increased tariff rates imposed on sheet glass in 1962.		Pope Paul VI reaffirms the doctrine of papal infallibility in an address in St. Peter's Basilica.	Jan. 11
Federal government threatens to stop its funding of Alabama welfare and mental health programs because of the state's refusal to comply with desegregation guidelines. . . . California Gov. Ronald Reagan announces sharp tuition hikes for Univ. of California students.			U.S. launches an Air Force satellite.		Jan. 12
U.S. Public Health Service ends its funding of Alabama programs because of noncompliance with the 1964 Civil Rights Act.			Boston doctors replace a shattered larynx with a new tube and valve made of skin taken from the patient's thigh.	Harvard Professor Bryan Patterson announces the discovery of a two-and-a-half-million-year-old bone fragment from an early ancestor of modern man.	Jan. 13
Office of Economic Opportunity (OEO) announces that it is distributing $26 million in grants for adult education.	Four hundred sixty-two Yale Univ. faculty members urge Pres. Johnson to halt the bombing of North Vietnam.			Dr. Louis Leakey announces the discovery of 20 million-year-old skull fragments of the oldest known representative of the line that probably developed into man but was not itself manlike.	Jan. 14

F	G	H	I	J
Includes elections, federal-state relations, civil rights and liberties, crime, the judiciary, education, health care, poverty, urban affairs and population.	*Includes formation and debate of U.S. foreign and defense policies, veterans' affairs and defense spending. (Relations with specific foreign countries are usually found under the region concerned.)*	*Includes business, labor, agriculture, taxation, transportation, consumer affairs, monetary and fiscal policy, natural resources, and pollution.*	*Includes worldwide scientific, medical and technological developments, natural phenomena, U.S. weather, natural disasters, and accidents.*	*Includes the arts, religion, scholarship, communications media, sports, entertainment, fashions, fads and social life.*

	World Affairs	Europe	Africa & the Middle East	The Americas	Asia & the Pacific
Jan. 15	U.N. Secy. Gen. U Thant appeals to Israel and Syria to negotiate their border dispute.	West German Chancellor Kurt-Georg Kiesinger says that despite differences with France over NATO, the nature of the Soviet threat to West Europe and British entry into the Common Market, "the fullest possible use of the Franco-German Treaty" will be made.	Congolese government (Kinshasa) decrees the seizure of all properties of Union Miniere du Haut-Katanga in the Congo.		U.S. resumes air strikes against the Hanoi area for the first time since December 1966. . . . Provisional People's Consultation Congress will investigate Indonesian Pres. Sukarno's alleged role in the attempted 1965 communist coup.
Jan. 16		France and Britain agree to produce jointly a military jet plane. . . . British P.M. Harold Wilson begins a tour of six Common Market capitals to assess Britain's prospects for Common Market membership.	Syria and Israel agree to discuss their border dispute.	Lynden Oscar Pindling becomes the Bahamas' first Negro prime minister.	U.S. planes bomb petroleum installations in North Vietnam. . . . Peking radio reports that "a handful of reactionary port authorities" still control Shanghai. . . . Peking television says it will discontinue all broadcasts until the end of the Cultural Revolution.
Jan. 17		Thirteen thousand workers stage a one-hour sit-down strike in four electrical plants in Madrid. . . . Top Soviet leaders arrive in Poland for talks about the Vietnamese War and Communist China. . . . Britian says it will reduce its armed forces on Malta over the next four years.		Chilean senate votes to deny permission for Pres. Eduardo Frei Montalva to visit the U.S.	The Mekong River drive, launched Jan. 6, has become the largest allied offensive of the war, using 16,000 troops. . . . Reports indicate that Wu Leng-hsi, the editor of the Chinese Communist Party's newspaper, has been recently purged. . . . American journalist William Baggs reports that most of the North Vietnamese city, Phuly, has been destroyed by U.S. bombing. . . . South Vietnam suggests an extension of the February Tet truce to North Vietnam.
Jan. 18	UNESCO publishes a report on apartheid in South Africa.	British Liberal Party elects Jeremy Thorpe as its new leader.	Israeli and Jordanian forces exchange gun-fire at the Gulf of Aqaba. . . . U.S. planes arrive in Jordan with the first shipment of American heavy arms.	Canadian P.M. Lester Pearson rejects a petition demanding that Canada halt all arms shipments to the U.S. until it withdraws from Vietnam.	Reports indicate that Shanghai Mayor Tsao Ti-chiu has been publicly humiliated at a "mass criticism" meeting. . . . U.S. Amb-to-Thailand Graham Martin says that U.S. forces in Thailand number 35,300. . . . South Vietnamese Premier Nguyen Cao Ky arrives in Australia where he is greeted by anti-war demonstrators. . . . Vietnamese Communists reject a truce extension because the offer was not made to the Viet Cong as well.
Jan. 19		Leaders of Spain's official government labor unions urge the government to liberalize their economic policies.			Reports indicate that the Red Guards have seized Peking's police headquarters and the People's University. . . . Communist China warns Thailand not to send combat troops to Vietnam or to permit the stationing of U.S. B-52s on Thai territory. . . . Ex-Mexican Amb.-to-U.S. Luis Quitanilla says that the bombing destruction that he has seen during a recent trip to North Vietnam confirms earlier reports by Harrison Salisbury, a managing editor of *The New York Times* . . . . North Korea sinks a South Korean navy patrol boat. . . . A coal mine explosion kills 19 miners in New Zealand.
Jan. 20	A U.N. sub-commission votes to suppress a report alleging acts of discrimination in various countries because it would offend the countries in question.	Yugoslavia makes known its opposition to an international conference of Communist parties.		Cuba executes Enrique Gonzalez Rodriguez, an alleged U.S. CIA agent.	South Korea places its navy on combat alert. . . . Communist Chinese Defense Min. Lin Piao calls for the purge of "bourgeois reactionary" elements in the army's Cultural Revolution Committee.

A	B	C	D	E
Includes developments that affect more than one world region, international organizations and important meetings of major world leaders.	*Includes all domestic and regional developments in Europe, including the Soviet Union, Turkey, Cyprus and Malta.*	*Includes all domestic and regional developments in Africa and the Middle East, including Iraq and Iran and excluding Cyprus, Turkey and Afghanistan.*	*Includes all domestic and regional developments in Latin America, the Caribbean and Canada.*	*Includes all domestic and regional developments in Asia and Pacific nations, extending from Afghanistan through all the Pacific Islands, except Hawaii.*

U.S. Politics & Social Issues	U.S. Foreign Policy & Defense	U.S. Economy & Environment	Science, Technology & Nature	Culture, Leisure & Life Style	
State of Arkansas issues a report describing the Tucker Prison Farm as the site of "torture, brutality, extortion and gross wrong-doings.". . . Stokely Carmichael, chairman of the Student Nonviolent Coordinating Committee (SNCC), announces that he will not seek re-election at the organization's next annual meeting.	Sen. Russell Long (D, La.) urges an increase in the bombing of North Vietnam. . . . A French correspondent reports in *U.S. News & World Report* that Communist China has set three conditions for its staying out of the Vietnamese War: that the U.S. not invade Communist China; not invade North Vietnam; not bomb the Red River dikes in North Vietnam. The US is seen agreeing to them.	Three congressional leaders predict that Congress will make significant cuts in the administration's programs.			Jan. 15
Lurleen Wallace, the wife of former Gov. George Wallace, becomes governor of Alabama. . . . Lucius Amerson becomes the sheriff of Tuskegee, Ala. He is the first Negro southern sheriff in this century.	U.S. acknowledges a tacit understanding between the Johnson administration and Communist China: China will not enter the Vietnamese War if the U.S. refrains from invading China or North Vietnam.	Rep. Benjamin Rosenthal (D, NY) introduces legislation to create a cabinet-level consumers' department.		Mrs. John F. Kennedy, Harper & Row Inc. and author William Manchester end their legal dispute over Manchester's *The Death of A President*, his account of the Kennedy assassination.	Jan. 16
	Seventy-nine Catholics parade in front of Francis Cardinal Spellman's N.Y. residence to protest his support of the Vietnamese War.		Blizzards and extreme cold cause at least eight deaths in Wisconsin and Minnesota.	Demolition of the old N.Y. Metropolitan Opera house begins as last minute efforts to save it fail.	Jan. 17
Student Nonviolent Coordinating Committee (SNCC) Chmn. Stokely Carmichael says that white liberals should "raise funds and organize whites in the suburbs to support the Negro cause." . . . A Massachusetts court convicts Albert DeSalvo, the confessed "Boston strangler" for sex offenses involving four women.	Rev. Reinhold Niebuhr, retired vice president of the Union Theological Seminary in New York, calls for an end to the Vietnamese War.		U.S. launches eight communications satellites.		Jan. 18
Rep. Adam Clayton Powell announces that NAACP lawyers will press his legal fight for his congressional seat. . . . U.S. orders the Shelby County (Tenn.) school board to desegregate its facilities.	Sen. John Stennis (D,Miss.) proposes an increase in the bombing of North Vietnam and of U.S. personnel in South Vietnam. . . . Senate Republican leader Everett Dirksen criticizes the administration's efforts to increase East-West trade.			Houghton Mifflin publishes Arthur Schlesinger's *The Bitter Heritage: Vietnam and American Democracy 1941-1966*.	Jan. 19
Calif. Board of Regents votes to dismiss Clark Kerr, president of the Univ. of California, who has been under attack by Gov. Ronald Reagan. . . . AEC releases a statement justifying its selection of the Weston, Ill., site for an atom smasher despite the town's lack of a fair-housing ordinance.		Treasury Dept. says that U.S. military spending in 1966 was $12 billion higher than in 1965.			Jan. 20

F	G	H	I	J
Includes elections, federal-state relations, civil rights and liberties, crime, the judiciary, education, health care, poverty, urban affairs and population.	Includes formation and debate of U.S. foreign and defense policies, veterans' affairs and defense spending. (Relations with specific foreign countries are usually found under the region concerned.)	Includes business, labor, agriculture, taxation, transportation, consumer affairs, monetary and fiscal policy, natural resources, and pollution.	Includes worldwide scientific, medical and technological developments, natural phenomena, U.S. weather, natural disasters, and accidents.	Includes the arts, religion, scholarship, communications media, sports, entertainment, fashions, fads and social life.

	World Affairs	Europe	Africa & the Middle East	The Americas	Asia & the Pacific
Jan. 21	U.N. Disarmament Committee reconvenes in Geneva.	Britain approves the construction of a fertilizer plant to be built in Cuba.			Peking posters report the suicides of two important CP officials. . . . Fighting between Red Guards and peasant-worker militia breaks out in Kiangsi Province. . . . A Viet Cong mine kills journalist Bernard Fall, the author of seven books on Vietnam. . . . Communist Chinese Red Guards say that an important North Korean official has been purged.
Jan. 22		Spanish police raid the Montserrat Abbey near Barcelona and confiscate leaflets and mimeograph machines. . . . Soviet authorities quickly break up a demonstration of 50 Soviet intellectuals in Moscow. . . . Soviet authorities close an exhibit of abstract art in Moscow.		Brazilian Congress adopts a new constitution extending the power of the federal government. . . . Nicaraguan National Guard troops clash with followers of the opposition Conservative Party.	Radio broadcasts from Nanchang, the capital of Kiangsi, say that the anti-Mao peasant-worker militia has overwhelmed the Red Guards. . . . Red Guards clash with anti-Maoist forces in the capital of Inner Mongolia. . . . Indian P.M. Indira Gandhi announces that India has agreed to restrict its trade with North Vietnam and Cuba in return for U.S. grain. . . . Red Guards charge that the Japanese CP has adopted a "revisionist" line.
Jan. 23				Nicaraguan National Guard halts fighting.	Premier Ky arrives in New Zealand and encounters 350 hooting demonstrators at the official welcome.
Jan. 24		One thousand four hundred and seventy-five British scientists and university teachers call on the British government to reverse its support of U.S. policy in Vietnam. . . . Soviet Pres. Nikolai Podgorny arrives in Italy for a state visit. . . . A French government commission urges the legalization of the sale of contraceptive pills.	A South African commission reports that Dimitrio Tsafendas acted alone in the 1966 slaying of Premier Hendrik Verwoerd.	Nicaragua shuts three opposition radio stations and the opposition newspaper La Prensa.	Thailand accuses Communist China of directing guerrillas in northeast Thailand.
Jan. 25		U.S. says that its bilateral talks with Communist China in Warsaw will be suspended until June 7 at the request of China. . . . Communist Chinese students returning from studies in Western Europe fight with Soviet policemen in Red Square. . . . A British court sentences Colin Jordan to 18 months in prison for inciting race hatred in a pamphlet called The Colored Invasion.	Britain decides not to extradite the ex-Ghanaian Amb.-to-U.K. Kwesi Armah who has been charged with the theft of government funds.	A gunfire exchange kills one person in Nicaragua.	Chinese Communist publication, Chieh-fang Chun Pao, urges the Chinese Army to support the "revolutionary" committees even if they are in the minority.
Jan. 26				Nicaraguan government arrests Pedro Joaquin Chamorro Cardenal, the editor of the opposition newspaper, La Prensa	Reports indicate that the Red Guards have paraded Railroad Min. Lu Cheng-tsao through Peking with a dunce cap on his head. . . . A continuous demonstration begins in front of the Soviet embassy in Peking to protest alleged harassment of Chinese students in Moscow on Jan. 25. . . . Maoist forces claim to have seized Kiangsi Province.

A	B	C	D	E
Includes developments that affect more than one world region, international organizations and important meetings of major world leaders.	Includes all domestic and regional developments in Europe, including the Soviet Union, Turkey, Cyprus and Malta.	Includes all domestic and regional developments in Africa and the Middle East, including Iraq and Iran and excluding Cyprus, Turkey and Afghanistan.	Includes all domestic and regional developments in Latin America, the Caribbean and Canada.	Includes all domestic and regional developments in Asia and Pacific nations, extending from Afghanistan through all the Pacific Islands, except Hawaii.

U.S. Politics & Social Issues	U.S. Foreign Policy & Defense	U.S. Economy & Environment	Science, Technology & Nature	Culture, Leisure & Life Style	
A Calif. court convicts Mario Savio, former leader of the Free Speech Movement, of creating a public nuisance during a sit-in against Navy recruiters on the Berkeley campus of the Univ. of California.	U.S. intelligence sources indicate that North Vietnamese civilian areas have been damaged as well as military targets.				Jan. 21
A. Philip Randolph, president of the AFL-CIO Brotherhood of Sleeping Car Porters, charges that Rep. Adam Clayton Powell has been "denied due process."	Senate Foreign Relations Committee Chmn. J.W. Fulbright suggests that South Vietnamese Premier Nguyen Cao Ky be replaced if he refuses to negotiate with the National Liberation Front. . . . Detectives arrest 23 demonstrators who display posters of maimed Vietnamese civilians during a mass in St. Patrick's Cathedral, N.Y.C.				Jan. 22
Pres. Johnson proposes that Social Security benefits and welfare payments be increased for the elderly. . . . Office of Economic Opportunity announces a major grant to the Chicago Head Start program. . . . Thousands of Univ. of California students protest recent tuition hikes.	U.S. announces that an aircraft carrier will dock at Capetown, South Africa on the way back from Vietnam. . . . A plan to end the Vietnamese War appears in *The Arrogance of Power*, a book by Senate Foreign Relations Committee Chmn. J.W. Fulbright. . . . Defense Secy. Robert McNamara says that North Vietnam doubled its troop strength in South Vietnam during 1966. . . . Senate Foreign Relations Committee opens hearings on the controversial Consular Convention between the U.S. and the Soviet Union. The treaty would provide full diplomatic immunity for consular employees. . . . Defense Secy. McNamara says that the U.S. and the USSR must limit their anti-ballistic missile systems. . . . Defense Secy. McNamara tells the Senate Armed Services Committee that the bombing of North Vietnam probably has not reduced the rate of infiltration into South Vietnam.	In a negotiation session of the Kennedy Round of tariff cutting, the U.S. and the Common Market still face a deadlock. The U.S. wants tariff cuts on its agricultural produce and the Common Market wants tariff reductions for its chemical products.			Jan. 23
U.S. Senate defeats an attempt to weaken the Senate filibuster rule requiring a two-thirds vote to shut off debate.		Pres. Johnson submits his fiscal 1968 budget to Congress with an estimated deficit of $2.1 billion.		Random House publishes J. William Fulbright's *The Arrogance of Power*.	Jan. 24
In San Juan SNCC Chmn. Stokely Carmichael leads a demonstration of 250 Puerto Ricans against the Vietnamese War and for Puerto Rican independence.	Reports indicate that U.S. pilots have been barred from bombing within a five mile radius of the center of Hanoi.		Soviet Union launches a satellite.	Houghton Mifflin publishes Sigmund Freud's and William Bullitt's *Thomas Woodrow Wilson*.	Jan. 25
	Fifty American Rhodes Scholars in Britain express doubt about the wisdom of the Vietnamese War in a letter to Pres. Johnson. . . . Maj. Gen. Jerry Page is relieved as commandant of the Air War College in Montgomery, Ala. and is ordered to Okinawa to take command of the 313th Air Division.	Pres. Johnson submits his economic report to Congress. It claims that the unemployment rate has fallen from 7% in early 1961 to less than 4% in 1966.	U.S. launches a weather satellite, Essa 4.		Jan. 26

F	G	H	I	J
Includes elections, federal-state relations, civil rights and liberties, crime, the judiciary, education, health care, poverty, urban affairs and population.	Includes formation and debate of U.S. foreign and defense policies, veterans' affairs and defense spending. (Relations with specific foreign countries are usually found under the region concerned.)	Includes business, labor, agriculture, taxation, transportation, consumer affairs, monetary and fiscal policy, natural resources, and pollution.	Includes worldwide scientific, medical and technological developments, natural phenomena, U.S. weather, natural disasters, and accidents.	Includes the arts, religion, scholarship, communications media, sports, entertainment, fashions, fads and social life.

	World Affairs	Europe	Africa & the Middle East	The Americas	Asia & the Pacific
Jan. 27	Representatives from 60 countries sign a treaty banning mass destruction weapons in space.	Spanish university students launch violent demonstrations in major Spanish cities to protest rising prices and the suppression of civil liberties. . . . Malta denounces the British decision to reduce its defense forces there. . . . French policemen prevent Communist Chinese students from marching on the Soviet embassy.	Egyptian planes reportedly bomb the Saudi Arabian village of Najran near the Yemeni border. . . . Zambian Foreign Min. Simon Kapwepwe calls U.N. imposed sanctions on Rhodesia ineffective.		Communist Chinese CP paper *Jenmin Jih Pao* calls alleged harassment of Chinese students in Moscow a "violent provocation.". . . Peking posters report that more than 100 people were killed on Jan. 25 in Sinkiang during intense fighting. . . . Biggest operation of the Vietnam War, Operation Cedar Falls, ends. . . North Korea rebukes Maoist forces for spreading "false propaganda" about an alleged coup attempt.
Jan. 28		Yugoslav Pres. Tito arrives in the Soviet Union for a visit. . . . Soviet Union charges that "Nazism and militarism" are on the rise in West Germany. . . . Sen. Robert Kennedy expresses his support of Pres. Johnson's Vietnam policies upon arriving in Great Britain. . . . Hundreds of students riot at the Univ. of Madrid because of the presence of police on campus.	Egyptian planes reportedly strike the Saudi Arabian village of Najran again.		Three U.S. helicopters and patrol boats accidentally kill 31 Vietnamese citizens when they mistake them for members of the Viet Cong.
Jan. 29		Maltese demonstrate against the British decision to reduce its defense forces on the island. . . . Soviet Union says that its economy grew by 8.6% during 1966.		Bombs explode outside of six Yugoslav embassies and consulates in the U.S. and Canada.	Peking posters forbid the Chinese army from humiliating officials by parading them through the streets with paper dunce caps on their heads. . . . Japanese Premier Eisaku Sato's Liberal Democratic Party retains its majority position in parliamentary elections. . . . Peking posters say that Premier Chou En-lai has ordered all Chinese students studying abroad to return home to participate in the Cultural Revolution.
Jan. 30		Soviet Pres. Nikolai Podgorny confers with Pope Paul. It is the first meeting between a Roman Catholic Pontiff and a communist head of state. . . . Maltese Parliament begins debate about the possibility of expelling all British armed forces. . . . In Paris Sen. Robert Kennedy says that Gen. de Gaulle will "play an important role" in any successful effort to end the Vietnamese War. . . . Seven hundred Univ. of Madrid students clash with police. The authorities finally close the university.	Fishermen in Dahomey reportedly attack government tax collectors and policemen.	Bank of Montreal reports that Canadian unemployment has dropped from a high of 11% in 1961 to 3 1/2% in 1966.	Peking posters report that fighting has spread to Szechwan Province and that "dozens" of people have been killed. . . . Maoist forces claim to have seized control of the main city in Shantung Province.
Jan. 31		Rafael Guijarro Moreno, a Univ. of Madrid student, dies after leaping from a window while police were searching his room for evidence of communist involvement. . . . Malta grounds all British Air Force planes. . . . West Germany and Rumania agree to establish full diplomatic relations.			U.S. troop strength reaches 404,000 in South Vietnam.
Feb. 1		Malta impounds a shipload of British cargo. . . . Britain agrees to give Zambia technical aid in order to reduce its economic dependence on Rhodesia. . . . France protests the treatment of French diplomat Robert Richard who was forced to stand for more than seven hours in the cold because of an alleged traffic violation in Peking. . . . Fifteen thousand Barcelona Univ. students strike in sympathy with their colleagues in Madrid and Valencia.			U.S. forces accidentally bomb a South Vietnamese hamlet.

A	B	C	D	E
Includes developments that affect more than one world region, international organizations and important meetings of major world leaders.	*Includes all domestic and regional developments in Europe, including the Soviet Union, Turkey, Cyprus and Malta.*	*Includes all domestic and regional developments in Africa and the Middle East, including Iraq and Iran and excluding Cyprus, Turkey and Afghanistan.*	*Includes all domestic and regional developments in Latin America, the Caribbean and Canada.*	*Includes all domestic and regional developments in Asia and Pacific nations, extending from Afghanistan through all the Pacific Islands, except Hawaii.*

U.S. Politics & Social Issues	U.S. Foreign Policy & Defense	U.S. Economy & Environment	Science, Technology & Nature	Culture, Leisure & Life Style	
Office of Economic Opportunity announces major grants to Indians in Arizona, New Mexico and Montana. . . . Negroes end a 10-month boycott of white businesses in Port Gibson, Miss. after winning concessions.	The New York Times reports that the Jan. 26 dismissal of Major Gen. Jerry Page may have been due to remarks he made at a secret seminar for senior Air Force Reserve officers in December 1966 where he allegedly discussed reports of bomb shortages in Vietnam.		A flash fire kills three U.S. astronauts in their spacecraft at Cape Kennedy.	French Marshal Alphonse-Pierre Juin, who opposed Pres. de Gaulle's Algerian policy in 1960, dies in Paris at 78.	Jan. 27
					Jan. 28
SNCC Chmn. Stokely Carmichael says that Negroes should withdraw from the Democratic Party and form their own party. . . . A U.S. district court convicts Bobby Baker of corruption charges. Baker had worked for Pres. Johnson when he was Senate Majority Leader.					Jan. 29
A N.Y. Court rules that local draft boards of the Selective Service System cannot punish registrants who publicly protest the Vietnamese War by reclassifying them into 1-A status, the category most likely to be drafted.	Senate Foreign Relations Committee begins hearings on American foreign policy.	Pres. Johnson urges Congress to authorize federal and regional regulation of air pollution controls.		Lippincott publishes Hell in a Very Small Place: The Siege of Dienbienphu by Bernard Fall. . . . Publishers' Weekly reports that the leading mass-market paperback book in 1966 was J.R.R. Tolkien's The Hobbit and the Fellowship of the Ring. . . . Farrar Straus & Giroux publishes Robert Lowell's Near the Ocean.	Jan. 30
Several U.S. Negro leaders criticize the proposed stopover of the carrier Franklin D. Roosevelt at Capetown, South Africa. . . . Civil rights leaders challenge the AEC's choice of Weston, Ill. for its atom smasher despite the town's lack of a fair-housing ordinance. . . . Calif. Gov. Ronald Reagan slashes the Univ. of California's budget by 29%.	At the Senate Foreign Relations Committee hearings, former Amb.-to-Japan Edwin Reischauer calls the bombing of North Vietnam a "psychological blunder" which will not force the country to negotiate. . . . Pres. Johnson urges Congress to expand veterans' benefits. . . . U.S. historian Arthur Schlesinger challenges the view that North Vietnam is acting as "the spearhead" of a Communist Chinese plan of expansion.	Federal government issues 20 new safety standards for motor vehicles.		West German church leader Bishop Otto Dibelius, who was suspended from his position as head of the Berlin diocese for rejecting Nazi doctrines, dies in West Berlin at 86.	Jan. 31
House Democrats deprive Rep. John Bell Williams (D, Miss.) of his chairmanship for having supported the Republican presidential ticket in 1964.	Anti-Vietnamese War church leaders meet with Defense Secy. Robert McNamara.	Consumer affairs advocate Ralph Nader denounces the new auto safety standards for being too lenient.		Grove Press publishes Jean Genet's Miracle of the Rose . . . . Brandon Films releases La Guerre Est Finie.	Feb. 1

F	G	H	I	J
Includes elections, federal-state relations, civil rights and liberties, crime, the judiciary, education, health care, poverty, urban affairs and population.	Includes formation and debate of U.S. foreign and defense policies, veterans' affairs and defense spending. (Relations with specific foreign countries are usually found under the region concerned.)	Includes business, labor, agriculture, taxation, transportation, consumer affairs, monetary and fiscal policy, natural resources, and pollution.	Includes worldwide scientific, medical and technological developments, natural phenomena, U.S. weather, natural disasters, and accidents.	Includes the arts, religion, scholarship, communications media, sports, entertainment, fashions, fads and social life.

	World Affairs	Europe	Africa & the Middle East	The Americas	Asia & the Pacific
Feb. 2		Soviet newspaper *Izvestia* charges that Communist China has hindered the transport of Soviet aid to North Vietnam. . . . Reports indicate that the Soviet Union has informed the Warsaw Pact that it will withdraw 50,000 troops from Eastern Europe for redeployment along the Soviet-Chinese border. . . . Left-wing Greek politician Andreas Papandreou warns that the U.S., NATO and the Greek monarchy are plotting to involve Greece in a sell-out over Cyprus. . . . Almost all Univ. of Valencia students boycott classes to protest a Feb. 1 police raid on the campus.	For the first time in eight years, Israeli and Syrian representatives discuss their border dispute.	Nicaragua allows an opposition newspaper to resume publication but its publisher Pedro Joaquin Chamorro Cardenal remains in prison.	U.S. launches a major drive called Operation Gadsten 70 miles northwest of Saigon.
Feb. 3		East Germany says that it is "deplorable" that Rumania did not demand West German recognition of East Germany as a precondition for the establishment of relations. . . . Four thousand Univ. of Saragossa students go on strike in sympathy with their Valencia colleagues.		Canadian P.M. Lester Pearson announces the creation of a royal commission on the status of women in Canada.	Communist Chinese diplomats clash with Soviet policemen at the Chinese embassy in Moscow. . . . Peking radio says that anti-Maoist forces are staging a comeback in Shansi Province.
Feb. 4			U.S. cancels shore leaves for the sailors on the aircraft carrier *Franklin D. Roosevelt* in Capetown, South Africa.		Soviet Union begins an emergency airlift of the dependents of its diplomatic personnel in Peking. . . . Maoist forces say that they have set up a "people's commune" in Shanghai.
Feb. 5	U.N. report asserts that Afghanistan, Morocco and Lebanon are not taking strong enough action to eliminate the illicit cultivation of the opium poppy.		A South Arabian Federation official is shot to death in Aden.	Brig. Gen. Anastasio Somoza Debayle wins the presidential election in Nicaragua.	Soviet Union's airlift of the dependents of its diplomatic personnel in Peking continues. . . . Allied forces begin to defoliate the southern part of the demilitarized zone.
Feb. 6		Soviet Premier Aleksei Kosygin arrives in London for talks. . . . Soviet students in Moscow protest attacks on Soviet citizens in Peking. . . . Spanish university students go on strike in Valladolid and Grenada.	Tanzanian Pres. Julius Nyerere proclaims the nationalization of all banks in Tanzania. . . . Israel sentences Israeli editor Shmuel Mor to one year in prison for publishing charges about Israeli involvement in the Moroccan Ben Barka affair.		Communist Chinese demonstrators spit and swear at departing Soviet diplomatic dependents. . . . New Zealanders accidentally kill four Australians in South Vietnam.
Feb. 7		Soviet students clash with Communist Chinese diplomatic personnel in Moscow. . . . Italian CP denounces Maoist ideology.	UPI reports that the Soviet Union will supply Iran with Soviet arms. . . . Tanzania orders restrictions on currency movement to neighboring Kenya and Uganda.	Canada reports a slight trade surplus for 1966.	Communist China tells the Soviet Union it can no longer guarantee the safety of its diplomatic personnel in Peking. . . . Communist Chinese theoretical journal *Hung Chi* says that Chief of State Liu Shao-chi and CP Gen. Secy. Teng Hsiao-ping are "counter-revolutionary revisionists."
Feb. 8	West German Foreign Min. Willy Brandt arrives in the U.S. for an official visit.			Brazil devalues the cruzeiro.	*Toronto Globe & Mail* reports that two important Communist Chinese Army officials have been dismissed. . . . U.S. suspends bombing of North Vietnam as Tet truce begins.
Feb. 9	Moroccan King Hassan II meets with Pres. Johnson and State Secy. Dean Rusk in Washington.	West German Foreign Min. Willy Brandt says his country hopes to have normal relations with Eastern Europe. . . . Soviet Premier Kosygin says that West Germany must "give up the hope of. . .ever obtaining nuclear weapons." . . . Common Market countries adopt a plan to harmonize their value-added taxes. . . . Six thousand five hundred workers in an electrical plant go on strike in Madrid.	Egyptian planes reportedly kill 70 people in a poison gas attack on the southern Yemeni village of Beni Salamah.	A series of earthquakes rock Colombia and kill 100 people.	U.S. Defense Dept. concedes that a U.S. Navy plane recently flew over Communist China's Hainan Island. . . . Reports indicate that Poland and Hungary are evacuating their diplomatic personnel from Peking. . . . Japanese CP daily *Akahata* denounces Maoist ideology.

A	B	C	D	E
Includes developments that affect more than one world region, international organizations and important meetings of major world leaders.	Includes all domestic and regional developments in Europe, including the Soviet Union, Turkey, Cyprus and Malta.	Includes all domestic and regional developments in Africa and the Middle East, including Iraq and Iran and excluding Cyprus, Turkey and Afghanistan.	Includes all domestic and regional developments in Latin America, the Caribbean and Canada.	Includes all domestic and regional developments in Asia and Pacific nations, extending from Afghanistan through all the Pacific Islands, except Hawaii.

U.S. Politics & Social Issues	U.S. Foreign Policy & Defense	U.S. Economy & Environment	Science, Technology & Nature	Culture, Leisure & Life Style	
Office of Economic Opportunity awards a grant to a program for farm workers in Arizona.	Pres. Johnson says that the proposed Consular Convention poses "no problem" for the nation's security. . . . Pres. Johnson discounts reports of North Vietnamese peace feelers. . . . Pres. Johnson announces the immediate allocation of two million tons of U.S. grain to India.			Columbia Pictures releases Anatole Litvak's *The Night of the Generals* with Peter O'Toole.	Feb. 2
Office of Economic Opportunity awards a grant for housing for the poor in Washington, D.C. . . . Ark. Gov. Winthrop Rockefeller fires four officials at the Ark. Tucker Prison Farm because of a report condemning the prison's conditions.	American Legion says that the proposed Consular Convention would grant a "license to spy."	United Auto Workers Pres. Walter Reuther resigns from the executive council of the AFL-CIO thereby increasing the rift between himself and AFL-CIO Pres. George Meany.			Feb. 3
	Presidential Asst. Walt Rostow confirms contacts between U.S. and North Vietnamese officials.	New tentative federal standards would limit hydrocarbon pollution from automobiles.	U.S. launches Lunar Orbiter 3 whose mission is to send back photos of the lunar surface in order to help select a site for a manned landing on the moon.	A spokesman for U.S. Roman Catholic Cardinal Spellman says: "The vast majority of Americans and their clergymen are in support of. . .American policy in Vietnam."	Feb. 4
Adlai E. Stevenson Institute of International Affairs is formally established at the Frank Lloyd Wright Robie House in Chicago.	On his return to the U.S., Sen. Robert Kennedy says that American influence is diminishing in Western Europe because of both Gen. de Gaulle and the Vietnamese War.			Yale University's Bollingen Prize for poetry goes to Robert Penn Warren.	Feb. 5
Pres. Johnson calls on Congress to enact the Safe Streets & Crime Control Act of 1967. . . . A Boston court sentences Gary Hicks to three years in prison for failing to report to his local draft board for a physical examination.	Sen. Robert Kennedy reports to Pres. Johnson on informal discussions he held with West European leaders during his recent trip.			Henry Morgenthau, former U.S. Treasury Secy. (1934-1945), dies in Poughkeepsie, N.Y. at 75.	Feb. 6
			Colo. Dr. Thomas Marchioro reports that antilymphocyte, a serum produced in horses, greatly increases the safety of kidney transplant operations. . . . Soviet Union launches a satellite.	Pope Paul appeals for an extension of the Tet truce cease-fire.	Feb. 7
Pres. Johnson announces the expansion of the Head Start program. . . . Office of Economic Opportunity awards a grant to the Seminole Indians of Florida. . . . Sen. John Pastore (D, R.I.) says that the approval of the AEC's site at Weston, Ill. might hinge on the enactment of a fair housing ordinance.	Sen. Robert Kennedy calls for a new and less hostile U.S. policy toward Communist China.		Lunar Orbiter 3 successfully enters orbit around the moon. . . . Heavy snow storms kill 18 people in New England. . . . France launches a satellite.		Feb. 8
More than 3,000 Univ. of California students and faculty members march on the State Capitol in Sacramento to protest budget cuts and tuition proposals.	State Secy. Dean Rusk restates the U.S. position that the bombing of North Vietnam will continue until North Vietnam shows some willingness to de-escalate the war.	Auto Workers Pres. Walter Reuther says the AFL-CIO is "becoming increasingly the comfortable complacent custodian of the status quo."	National Safety Council reports that a record 52,000 Americans were killed in 1966 traffic accidents.	Twenty-eight U.S. religious leaders urge Pres. Johnson to extend the Tet truce.	Feb. 9

F	G	H	I	J
Includes elections, federal-state relations, civil rights and liberties, crime, the judiciary, education, health care, poverty, urban affairs and population.	*Includes formation and debate of U.S. foreign and defense policies, veterans' affairs and defense spending. (Relations with specific foreign countries are usually found under the region concerned.)*	*Includes business, labor, agriculture, taxation, transportation, consumer affairs, monetary and fiscal policy, natural resources, and pollution.*	*Includes worldwide scientific, medical and technological developments, natural phenomena, U.S. weather, natural disasters, and accidents.*	*Includes the arts, religion, scholarship, communications media, sports, entertainment, fashions, fads and social life.*

	World Affairs	Europe	Africa & the Middle East	The Americas	Asia & the Pacific
Feb. 10	South African mission to the U.N. criticizes the Jan. 18 UNESCO report on apartheid by pointing out that black literacy in South Africa is ten times higher than in the rest of Africa. . . . U.N. Secy. Gen. U Thant calls for an indefinite extension of the Tet truce.	West German Foreign Min. Willy Brandt endorses the proposed non-proliferation treaty barring the spread of nuclear weapons.	Rioting breaks out in the South Arabian Federation of Aden. . . . Tanzania assumes control of the country's eight largest flour-milling firms.		
Feb. 11		Soviet Union announces that all Chinese citizens traveling in the Soviet Union will have to have visas as of Feb. 12, 1967. . . . About 800 employees of an electrical plant go on strike in Santander, Spain.	British troops clash with Arab nationalists in Aden. . . . Tanzanian Pres. Julius Nyerere announces the nationalization of eight of the country's leading export-import firms.		Communist China announces that all Soviet citizens will have to have a visa to travel in China as of Feb. 12, 1967. . . . Communist Chinese People's Liberation Army assumes virtual control of Peking.
Feb. 12			South Arabian Federation Information Min. Abdulrahman Girgirah accuses Egypt of fomenting trouble in Aden.		U.S. resumes the bombing of North Vietnam as Tet truce ends.
Feb. 13		High-ranking North Korean government officials confer with Soviet leaders in Moscow.	Israeli and Syrian soldiers clash near the Sea of Galilee.	Canada denies entry to Dr. Timothy Leary, founder of the LSD religious cult.	Peking posters announce that pro-Mao forces have seized power in the capital of Tibet. . . . Indonesia's Supreme Court accuses Pres. Sukarno of "prior knowledge" of the abortive 1965 communist coup.
Feb. 14		*Manchester Guardian* reports that Soviet Premier Aleksei Kosygin asked North Vietnam to de-escalate its military activities in return for a cessation of U.S. bombing but that North Vietnam refused.	Israeli and Syrian soldiers clash along their common border.	Fourteen Latin American nations sign a treaty banning nuclear weapons from Latin America.	Nanking radio calls for hard work in "disaster areas" to "overcome spring famine." . . . A Peking poster lists 24 military leaders who have been allegedly either denounced or purged for their opposition to the Cultural Revolution.
Feb. 15					Nationwide voting begins in India.
Feb. 16					Communists in Vietnam down a record 13 U.S. helicopters. . . . Peking radio reports that pro-Mao army troops have defeated anti-Maoists in Fukien Province. . . . Peking posters say that anti-Mao forces have mobilized the army to suppress Maoist forces in Szechwan Province.
Feb. 17		Spain and the Soviet Union sign a shipping agreement establishing regular service between the two countries.	Congo (Kinshasa) settles its copper production dispute with Belgian companies.		Peking posters report more than 100 deaths fighting in Tibet. . . . Japanese Parliament formally re-elects P.M. Eisaku Sato.

A	B	C	D	E
Includes developments that affect more than one world region, international organizations and important meetings of major world leaders.	Includes all domestic and regional developments in Europe, including the Soviet Union, Turkey, Cyprus and Malta.	Includes all domestic and regional developments in Africa and the Middle East, including Iraq and Iran and excluding Cyprus, Turkey and Afghanistan.	Includes all domestic and regional developments in Latin America, the Caribbean and Canada.	Includes all domestic and regional developments in Asia and Pacific nations, extending from Afghanistan through all the Pacific Islands, except Hawaii.

U.S. Politics & Social Issues	U.S. Foreign Policy & Defense	U.S. Economy & Environment	Science, Technology & Nature	Culture, Leisure & Life Style	
Thirty-eight states ratify the 25th Amendment specifying the procedure for the performance of a President's duties in case of disablement.	U.S. State Dept. expresses concern over an alleged Communist build-up in South Vietnam during the truce period. . . . State Secy. Dean Rusk pledges renewed wheat assistance to Morocco.				Feb. 10
Ten thousand Univ. of California students and faculty members boo and jeer at Gov. Ronald Reagan when he defends his budget cuts.	State Dept. confirms that U.S. is continuing to supply its forces during the Tet truce period.				Feb. 11
	Sen. Jacob Javits (R, N.Y.) calls for "an unconditional cessation" of the U.S. bombing of North Vietnam.			Mrs. Neville Chamberlain, widow of the former British prime minister, dies in London at 84.	Feb. 12
National Student Association acknowledges that it has received more than $3 million from foundations acting as conduits for the U.S. Central Intelligence Agency since 1952. . . . U.S. Supreme Court refuses to review the case of David Miller who was convicted for burning his draft card. . . . Supporters of Rep. Adam Clayton Powell fail to persude Negroes to stage a one-day protest strike.	Sen. Robert Kennedy expresses his regret over the resumption of the bombing of North Vietnam. . . . Five hundred Harvard Univ. students demonstrate against U.S. Amb.-to-U.N. Arthur Goldberg.			Two American Univ. professors announce that 700 pages of manuscripts and drawings by Leonardo da Vinci have been found in the Spanish Library in Madrid.	Feb. 13
Weston, Ill. passes a fair housing ordinance prohibiting discriminatory practices by real estate brokers and salesmen.	Three university scientists deliver a petition to the White House bearing the signatures of 5,000 U.S. scientists protesting the use of chemical warfare in Vietnam. . . . U.S. State Dept. confirms the CIA financing of overseas student activities and defends it as a necessary means of offsetting the influence of communist student groups. . . . Defense Dept. says that U.S. Negro soldiers suffered about 5% proportionately higher combat fatalities than whites during 1966 in Vietnam.	U.S. Treasury Dept. reports that U.S. 1966 balance of payments deficit was $1.4 billion.	Soviet Union launches a satellite.	Mrs. Arnold Schoenberg, widow of the late composer, dies in Los Angeles at 68.	Feb. 14
Pres. Johnson calls on Congress to pass legislation ending housing bias by 1969. . . . Pres. Johnson appoints a commission to investigate the alleged CIA role in subsidizing various organizations dealing with education, law and journalism overseas.	Defense Secy. McNamara denies reports that he thinks the bombing of North Vietnam is ineffective. . . . U.S. State Dept. forbids a U.S. Navy ship from docking at Durban, South Africa. . . . Twenty-five hundred women demonstrate against the Vietnam war in front of the Pentagon.	A wildcat strike idles the General Motors Mansfield, O. plant.	France launches a satellite.	William Christian Bullitt, first U.S. ambassador to the Soviet Union and co-author (with Sigmund Freud) of a psychological study of Woodrow Wilson, dies in Neuilly, France at 76.	Feb. 15
		Pres. Johnson proposes new consumer protection measures. . . . National Highway Safety Agency proposes federal standards for highway safety programs.			Feb. 16
		A N.J. chemical plant blast kills 11 people.			Feb. 17

F	G	H	I	J
Includes elections, federal-state relations, civil rights and liberties, crime, the judiciary, education, health care, poverty, urban affairs and population.	Includes formation and debate of U.S. foreign and defense policies, veterans' affairs and defense spending. (Relations with specific foreign countries are usually found under the region concerned.)	Includes business, labor, agriculture, taxation, transportation, consumer affairs, monetary and fiscal policy, natural resources, and pollution.	Includes worldwide scientific, medical and technological developments, natural phenomena, U.S. weather, natural disasters, and accidents.	Includes the arts, religion, scholarship, communications media, sports, entertainment, fashions, fads and social life.

	World Affairs	Europe	Africa & the Middle East	The Americas	Asia & the Pacific
Feb. 18		Eleven former Spanish coal miners stage a sit-in strike to protest their 1964 dismissal for illegal labor activities.	Israeli soldiers kill a Syrian soldier inside the Israeli border.		Viet Cong carry out mortar attacks in the vicinity of two provincial capitals. . . . Indonesia says that Communist supporters of Pres. Sukarno have launched a terrorist campaign in Jogjakarta, Java.
Feb. 19			Reports indicate that Iran currently considers Egyptian Pres. Gamal Abdel Nasser more of a threat than the Soviet Union. . . . A dynamite charge fails to damage an Israeli water pipeline near the Jordanian border.		
Feb. 20		Other Spanish miners in the province of Asturias go on strike in sympathy with the 11 former coal miners, dismissed in 1964 for illegal labor activities.			U.S. planes bomb a North Vietnamese truck convoy in North Vietnam. . . . Pres. Sukarno surrenders his remaining executive powers to Gen. Suharto, *de facto* ruler of Indonesia. . . . An earthquake kills 26 people in Indonesia.
Feb. 21	U.N. reports that the U.S. has contributed 43% of the U.N. budget since its founding in 1945.	French Pres. de Gaulle condemns the war in Vietnam as a "detestable conflict."	Israel denies that Moroccan agents asked Israeli agents to assist in the Ben Barka kidnapping.	OAS foreign ministers approve a proposal, 15-1, to reduce Latin American arms spending.	Reports indicate that Mao Tse-tung has ordered the Red Guards to cease their political activity, Feb. 11, among troops based in Sinkiang Province. . . . Indian P.M. Indira Gandhi suffers major reverses as nationwide elections end. . . . Peking posters accuse North Korean Central Committee Chmn. Kim Il Song of "sabotaging the struggle of the Vietnamese people.". . . Ex-Indian Defense Min. and leading Indian leftist V.K. Krishna Menon loses his race for a seat in Parliament.
Feb. 22		Hungarian First Secy. Janos Kadar says that his country is ready to establish diplomatic relations with West Germany.	Ghana accuses the Soviet Union, Communist China and Cuba of trying to help former Pres. Kwame Nkrumah to return to power.	Donald Burns Sangster becomes prime minister of Jamaica.	Twenty-five thousand U.S. and South Vietnamese troops launch the largest offensive of the war, Operation Junction City. . . . In Paris, North Vietnamese diplomat Mai Van Bo says that only a permanent bombing halt would make negotiations possible.
Feb. 23		West German Foreign Min. Willy Brandt says that he sees "nothing standing in the way of further talks" with Hungary.	Chad announces that it killed 50 guerrillas on Feb. 22 near the Sudanese border.	OAS Council approves the admission of Trinidad and Tobago.	Reinforcements bring U.S. troop strength in South Vietnam to 414,000. . . . In *Hung Chi*, the Chinese CP theoretical journal, Mao Tse-tung orders Red Guards to stop attacks on government and party officials.
Feb. 24		Spanish cabinet approves a text liberalizing the country's religious laws. . . . West Germany announces that it will "include Yugoslavia in the area of its policy of detente" even though diplomatic relations have been suspended since 1957 when Yugoslavia recognized East Germany. . . . Six thousand three hundred Spanish miners go on strike in sympathy with the 11 former coal miners who were dismissed in 1964 for illegal labor activities.			Maoist forces set up a "people's commune" in Shanghai which warns against "anarchism (and) small group mentality."

A	B	C	D	E
Includes developments that affect more than one world region, international organizations and important meetings of major world leaders.	Includes all domestic and regional developments in Europe, including the Soviet Union, Turkey, Cyprus and Malta.	Includes all domestic and regional developments in Africa and the Middle East, including Iraq and Iran and excluding Cyprus, Turkey and Afghanistan.	Includes all domestic and regional developments in Latin America, the Caribbean and Canada.	Includes all domestic and regional developments in Asia and Pacific nations, extending from Afghanistan through all the Pacific Islands, except Hawaii.

U.S. Politics & Social Issues	U.S. Foreign Policy & Defense	U.S. Economy & Environment	Science, Technology & Nature	Culture, Leisure & Life Style	
The New York Times reports that the American Newspaper Guild has received $1 million in CIA grants since 1960. . . . Asst. Treasury Secy. Robert Wallace warns U.S. banks that they will lose federal deposits if they discriminate against Negroes in hiring practices. . . . New Orleans Dist. Atty. James Garrison confirms reports that he is conducting a public investigation of the assassination of Pres. John Kennedy.				Dr. J. Robert Oppenheimer, who directed the development and testing of the first atomic bomb, dies in Princeton, N.J. at 62.	**Feb. 18**
					Feb. 19
	At the Senate Foreign Relations Committee hearings U.S. historian Henry Steele Commager says the U.S. has "greatly overextended" its power abroad. . . . Pres. Johnson reiterates his demand for North Vietnamese reciprocity if the bombing is to be stopped.			National Gallery of Art in Washington announces the purchase of Leonardo da Vinci's painting *Ginevra dei Benci*.	**Feb. 20**
	Sen. Robert Kennedy says that all relevant government agencies have participated in CIA funding decisions and that the CIA should not be treated as a scapegoat.	AFL-CIO Pres. George Meany says that his relations with Pres. Johnson have been "very good.". . . Pres. Johnson asks Congress to enact a proposed Patent Reform Act of 1967.		New Directions publishes Tennessee Williams' *A Novella* and *Four Short Stories*.	**Feb. 21**
David Ferrie, a prime suspect in the Garrison assassination investigation, is found dead in New Orleans. New Orleans coroner, Nicholas Chetta, declares that Ferrie died of natural causes. Dist. Atty. James Garrison calls his death a suicide.	Hundreds of Univ. of Wisconsin students demonstrate against the presence on campus of representatives of the Dow Chemical Co.			United Artists releases Peter Brook's film *Marat/Sade*.	**Feb. 22**
Select House Committee investigating Rep. Adam Clayton Powell recommends that he be seated but publicly censured by the House Speaker. . . . Office of Economic Opportunity awards a grant to the Jacarilla Apache Tribe of New Mexico.	A U.S. army court sentences Harry Muir to two years at hard labor for refusing to serve in Vietnam. . . . Congressional leaders announce that no special investigation of the CIA will be held.	AFL-CIO Pres. George Meany endorses Pres. Johnson for re-election in 1968. . . . UAW Pres. Walter Reuther warns of a possible takeover of the Mansfield, O. local union by the central UAW leadership. The wildcat strike ends later that day. . . . U.S. Senate increases the national debt limit to $336 billion.			**Feb. 23**
Office of Economic Opportunity awards a grant to the Upward Bound program in N.Y.C. . . . Negro demonstrators march in Louisville, Ky.'s affluent East Side for the first time. . . . New Orleans Dist. Atty. James Garrison announces that his staff has "solved" the Kennedy assassination case but that months will be needed "to work on details of evidence."	Defense Secy. McNamara denies that he disagrees with State Secy. Rusk about the wisdom of bombing North Vietnam. . . . AFL-CIO says that it opposes stopping the bombing of North Vietnam until there is "a matching act of de-escalation."	AFL-CIO Pres. George Meany says that he will investigate charges that the CIA has supported some AFL-CIO unions.			**Feb. 24**

F	G	H	I	J
Includes elections, federal-state relations, civil rights and liberties, crime, the judiciary, education, health care, poverty, urban affairs and population.	*Includes formation and debate of U.S. foreign and defense policies, veterans' affairs and defense spending. (Relations with specific foreign countries are usually found under the region concerned.)*	*Includes business, labor, agriculture, taxation, transportation, consumer affairs, monetary and fiscal policy, natural resources, and pollution.*	*Includes worldwide scientific, medical and technological developments, natural phenomena, U.S. weather, natural disasters, and accidents.*	*Includes the arts, religion, scholarship, communications media, sports, entertainment, fashions, fads and social life.*

	World Affairs	Europe	Africa & the Middle East	The Americas	Asia & the Pacific
Feb. 25				Guerrillas capture a Bolivian army patrol.	*Jenmin Jih Pao*, the Chinese CP daily, says that the Red Guards agree that the Cultural Revolution "is by no means a revolution of dismissing people from office."
Feb. 26			An assassin kills Adeni Legislative Council member Sayed Mohammad Hassan in Aden.	Conference of foreign ministers of 20 countries of the OAS concludes in Buenos Aires.	U.S. warships shell the demilitarized zone.
Feb. 27		Britain, West Germany and the U.S. meet in London to discuss troop withdrawals from West Germany.	A bomb kills six people in Aden.	Brazil suspends the political rights of 44 labor leaders and local politicians. . . . Britain grants independence to seven small Caribbean islands which chose to remain "associated states" whose defense and foreign affairs will still be run by Britain.	Viet Cong use heavy Soviet rockets for the first time against U.S. forces. . . . U.S. planes mine the rivers of southern North Vietnam.
Feb. 28		A Roman Catholic-Jewish joint service in Madrid is the first such service held in Spain. . . . Three British-controlled banks nationalized by Tanzania on Feb. 6 say that they will withdraw their British employees from Tanzania. . . . Spanish authorities issue a warrant for the arrest of Marcelin Camacho, a top leader of the illegal "workers commission" movement.	Competing Arab nationalist forces clash in Aden. . . . West Germany and Jordan resume full diplomatic relations which had been severed in 1965 when West Germany recognized Israel.	An administrative reform bill centralizes power still further in Brazil.	Communist mortars attack U.S. positions near the demilitarized zone.
March 1	U.N. Secy. Gen. U Thant discusses the Vietnamese War with three North Vietnamese representatives in Rangoon. . . . U.N. reports that per capita food production has dropped to pre-W.W. II levels in Asia and Africa. . . . Moroccan King Hassan II asks the U.N. to send a disarmament team to visit Algeria and Morocco to suggest minimum armament levels.	NATO Council unanimously adopts an Italian proposal to study means of closing the "technological gap" between Western Europe and the U.S. . . . Spanish labor leader Marcelin Camacho gives himself up to the police.	British forces kill two Arab demonstrators in Aden.	Oscar Diego Gestido is inaugurated as president of Uruguay.	Communist shore guns open fire on three U.S. war ships.
March 2		France completes the first stage of its missile testing program with the launching of a solid-fueled rocket.	Cuba announces cuts in the number of employees in the Domestic Trade Ministry in what may be a political purge or an attack on "bureaucracy."		U.S. positions come under heavy attack near the demilitarized zone.
March 3		Britain, West Germany and the U.S. meet in London to discuss troop withdrawals from West Germany.			

A	B	C	D	E
Includes developments that affect more than one world region, international organizations and important meetings of major world leaders.	*Includes all domestic and regional developments in Europe, including the Soviet Union, Turkey, Cyprus and Malta.*	*Includes all domestic and regional developments in Africa and the Middle East, including Iraq and Iran and excluding Cyprus, Turkey and Afghanistan.*	*Includes all domestic and regional developments in Latin America, the Caribbean and Canada.*	*Includes all domestic and regional developments in Asia and Pacific nations, extending from Afghanistan through all the Pacific Islands, except Hawaii.*

U.S. Politics & Social Issues	U.S. Foreign Policy & Defense	U.S. Economy & Environment	Science, Technology & Nature	Culture, Leisure & Life Style	
	Dr. Martin Luther King Jr. assails U.S. policy in Vietnam.				Feb. 25
Washington Post reports that Dist. Atty. James Garrison's assassination probe is focusing on anti-Castro Cuban refugees.					Feb. 26
In the first government suit against an employer, the Justice Dept. sues the Dillon Supply Co. of Raleigh, N.C. for racial discrimination. . . . Office of Economic Opportunity awards a grant to the Upward Bound program in Chicago. . . . Pres. Johnson reiterates his support for Washington, D.C. home rule. . . . A federal jury indicts 19 men in connection with the 1964 murders of civil rights workers Michael Schwerner, Andrew Goodman and James Chaney. It indicts 12 men in connection with the January 1966 murder of black leader Vernon Dahmer. . . . A bomb kills black activist Wharlest Jackson in Natchez, Miss. . . . U.S. Supreme Court rules that union members can sue their unions in state courts for failure to properly handle their grievances against employers.	Pres. Johnson, in a news conference, praises the McNamara-Rusk working relationship. . . . Pres. Johnson denies that the latest U.S. military measures in Vietnam constitute an escalation of the war.	AFL-CIO urges the elimination of draft inequities and opposes student deferments.	Soviet Union launches a satellite.	Continental Films releases LeRoi Jones's *Dutchman*.	Feb. 27
Pres. Johnson appoints acting Atty. Gen. Ramsey Clark as Attorney General. . . . Local government leaders post a reward for information leading to the conviction of the murderers of Wharlest Jackson.				Dial Press publishes Anatoly Kuznetsov's *Babi Yar* . . . . George Polk Memorial Award for excellence in journalism goes to Harrison Salisbury of *The New York Times* for his news mission to North Vietnam.	Feb. 28
New Orleans Dist. Atty. James Garrison orders the arrest of businessman Clay Shaw in connection with the Kennedy assassination probe. . . . Justice Dept. files a school desegregation suit against Polk County, Fla. . . . Office of Economic Opportunity director Sargent Shriver announces that Volunteers in Service to America (VISTA) will enlist an estimated 8,000 volunteers for work with the poor and the elderly. . . . House votes to exclude Rep.-elect Adam Clayton Powell from the 90th Congress. . . . A U.S. court sentences retired American Lt. Col. William Whalen to 15 years in prison for stealing classified information.	State Secy. Rusk and Defense Secy. McNamara appear before newsmen and reiterate that they agree about Vietnam policy.			Random House publishes Marshall McLuhan's *The Medium is the Message*	March 1
A leading House liberal Morris Udall (D, Ariz.) says that Rep. Adam Clayton Powell had escaped expulsion for "a long time" because he is a Negro. . . . Natchez, Tenn. community leaders brief Natchez Negroes on the progress of their investigation of the murder of Wharlest Jackson.	Pres. Johnson announces that Soviet Premier Aleksei Kosygin has "confirmed the willingness of the Soviet government to discuss means of limiting the arms race.". . . Sen. Robert Kennedy calls for a halt of the bombing of North Vietnam.				March 2
U.S. Court of Appeals reverses the 1965 conviction of the U.S. CP for failing to register with the government as an agent of the Soviet Union. . . . Maryland House of Delegates approves a bill repealing the state law banning interracial marriages.	Two hundred members of the faculty and staff of Columbia Univ. Teachers College urge the President to stop the bombing of North Vietnam.		Soviet Union launches a satellite.	St. Martin's Press publishes Robert Blake's *Disraeli* . . . . Yale Univ. announces that philanthropist Paul Mellon has donated his library on alchemy and the occult to the university.	March 3

F	G	H	I	J
Includes elections, federal-state relations, civil rights and liberties, crime, the judiciary, education, health care, poverty, urban affairs and population.	*Includes formation and debate of U.S. foreign and defense policies, veterans' affairs and defense spending. (Relations with specific foreign countries are usually found under the region concerned.)*	*Includes business, labor, agriculture, taxation, transportation, consumer affairs, monetary and fiscal policy, natural resources, and pollution.*	*Includes worldwide scientific, medical and technological developments, natural phenomena, U.S. weather, natural disasters, and accidents.*	*Includes the arts, religion, scholarship, communications media, sports, entertainment, fashions, fads and social life.*

	World Affairs	Europe	Africa & the Middle East	The Americas	Asia & the Pacific
March 4		A Baptist church opens with public ceremonies in Spain. It is the 240th authorized Protestant church. . . . In a televised election eve address de Gaulle appeals to the French electorate to return a Gaullist majority to the Assembly.			Viet Cong maul the 173rd Airborne Brigade.
March 5		French left makes gains in National Assembly elections.		Col. Fidel Sanchez Hernandez wins presidential elections in El Salvador.	Indonesian authorities say that government troops clashed with 80 Communists March 5 on Java.
March 6	An international study of 12 industrial nations indicates that math achievement levels are highest in Japan and lowest in the U.S.				Svetlana Stalina, the only daughter of the late Joseph Stalin, asks for U.S. asylum at the U.S. embassy in New Delhi.
March 7		Alexei Rumyantsev, editor of the Soviet CP economic weekly, says that the Soviet Union intends to introduce the profit system in all industrial enterprises by the end of 1968. . . . French Communists and Socialists form a single slate of candidates to contest the Gaullists in the second-round balloting, March 12.	An Arab mob sets fire to the headquarters of a rival political group in Aden.		
March 8					Travelers arriving in Hong Kong from Canton, China say that more than 100 people have been killed or wounded since March 4 in fighting near Canton. . . . A radio broadcast from Honan Province says that Maoists have "smashed" an anti-Mao force.
March 9		Left-wing Greek politician Andreas Papandreou asserts that forces within Greece are plotting to either rig the scheduled May elections or to prevent them from taking place.			U.S. reports a record 232 American combat deaths for the week of Feb. 26-March 4. . . . Maoist forces set up a "people's commune" in Peking.
March 10		Malta rejects a new British proposal easing the effects of defense cuts on Malta's economy. . . . Spain's Council of Ministers authorizes the election of about one-sixth of the Spanish Parliament. Currently its members are appointed.	Jon Kimche, the editor of the British Zionist journal *Jewish Observer & Middle East Review*, is fired for refusing to withdraw an article about Israel's unemployment problems.		U.S. planes bomb the North Vietnamese Thainguyen iron and steel complex for the first time.
March 11		France's National Student Union severs relations with the International Student Conference because of its alleged ties to the CIA.			Communist China deports two Soviet diplomats for alleged "persecution" of Chinese employees of the Soviet embassy. . . . U.S. First Infantry Division fights in one of the heaviest battles of Operation Junction City. . . . Abdul Qawaee Mackawee, the head of the Adeni radicals, says from Cairo that his organization will intensify its violence in Aden.
March 12		Malta accepts the same British proposal that it rejected on March 10.			Indonesian Congress unanimously approves a resolution formally stripping Pres. Sukarno of all his power.

A	B	C	D	E
Includes developments that affect more than one world region, international organizations and important meetings of major world leaders.	Includes all domestic and regional developments in Europe, including the Soviet Union, Turkey, Cyprus and Malta.	Includes all domestic and regional developments in Africa and the Middle East, including Iraq and Iran and excluding Cyprus, Turkey and Afghanistan.	Includes all domestic and regional developments in Latin America, the Caribbean and Canada.	Includes all domestic and regional developments in Asia and Pacific nations, extending from Afghanistan through all the Pacific Islands, except Hawaii.

U.S. Politics & Social Issues	U.S. Foreign Policy & Defense	U.S. Economy & Environment	Science, Technology & Nature	Culture, Leisure & Life Style	
Miss. NAACP field chief leads a silent march through Natchez in memory of Wharlest Jackson. . . . A fire destroys a Negro church in Grenada, Miss.	Federation of American Scientists urges a de-escalation of the Vietnamese War.				March 4
NAACP executive director Roy Wilkins attends Wharlest Jackson's funeral and says that despite the killing, moderation is becoming "noticeable" in rural Miss.	Former V.P. Richard Nixon says that Sen. Robert Kennedy's "proposals are not new. . . and have the effect of prolonging the war.". . . A U.S. staff report warns that the withdrawal of a large number of U.S. and British forces from Western Europe could have a demoralizing effect on NATO.		Dr. Donald Louria of N.Y.C.'s Bellevue Hospital reports that more than 130 users of LSD have been admitted to Bellevue as mental patients in the past 18 months.	Mohammed Mossadegh, former prime minister of Iran (1951-1953), dies in Teheran at 86.	March 5
A U.S. district court fines the captain of a Soviet fishing trawler seized for fishing in U.S. waters. . . . N.Y. Gov. Nelson Rockefeller calls for an election on April 11 to fill Adam Clayton Powell's seat.		A second wildcat strike protests the suspension of several Mansfield, O. plant employees.		Lopert Pictures Corp. releases Ingmar Bergman's *Persona* .. . . Hungarian composer Zoltan Kodaly dies in Budapest at 84.	March 6
Civil Rights activist James Meredith says he will run against Adam Clayton Powell in the special election for his congressional seat.		Teamsters Pres. James Hoffa begins an eight-year sentence for jury tampering.	France launches a small monkey into space.	Alice B. Toklas, author, friend and companion of Gertrude Stein, dies in Paris at 89.	March 7
Office of Economic Opportunity awards a grant for various programs for the elderly. . . . Adam Clayton Powell files suit to regain his congressional seat.	U.S. historian Arthur Schlesinger charges that the administration "does not want to negotiate" an end to the war in Vietnam.	UAW Pres. Walter Reuther orders the seizure of the Mansfield, O. local union because of wild-cat strikes.	U.S. launches Oso 3 whose mission is to provide data on the sun and its influence on the earth's atmosphere.	Bernard Malamud's *The Fixer* wins the 18th annual National Book Award for fiction. . . . Columbia Pictures releases Franco Zeffirelli's *The Taming of the Shrew* .	March 8
	Thailand acknowledges for the first time that the U.S. is using Thai bases for air attacks on North Vietnam.	Pres. Johnson sends Congress his fiscal 1968 oceanic projects. . . . Pres. Johnson recommends the restoration of the 7% tax credit for business investment.			March 9
Office of Economic Opportunity awards 26 grants to Upward Bound projects.	V.P. Humphrey says that Sen. Robert Kennedy is "surely entitled to his point of view on Vietnam (and has) never broken with the President on our fundamental involvement there."	Mansfield, O. General Motors plant is almost back to normal strength.	Soviet Union launches a satellite.		March 10
					March 11
A fire destroys a former Episcopal church in Hayneville, Miss. which had been used by an anti-poverty organization.	In a *New York Times* advertisement 6,766 college and public school teachers call for an end of the bombing of North Vietnam.				March 12
F	G	H	I	J	
Includes elections, federal-state relations, civil rights and liberties, crime, the judiciary, education, health care, poverty, urban affairs and population.	*Includes formation and debate of U.S. foreign and defense policies, veterans' affairs and defense spending. (Relations with specific foreign countries are usually found under the region concerned.)*	*Includes business, labor, agriculture, taxation, transportation, consumer affairs, monetary and fiscal policy, natural resources, and pollution.*	*Includes worldwide scientific, medical and technological developments, natural phenomena, U.S. weather, natural disasters, and accidents.*	*Includes the arts, religion, scholarship, communications media, sports, entertainment, fashions, fads and social life.*	

	World Affairs	Europe	Africa & the Middle East	The Americas	Asia & the Pacific
March 13	Reports indicate that Botswana has told U.N. Secy. Gen. U Thant that its dependence on the Rhodesian railroad for transportation of its exports is so great that it cannot take part in the U.N. economic sanctions on Rhodesia. . . . U.N. Secy. Gen. U Thant reports that Switzerland and Botswana have failed to comply with the U.N.'s economic sanctions on Rhodesia. . . . Algerian Rep.-to-U.N. Benabdelkader Azzout rejects Moroccan King Hassan's plea for a U.N. role in North African disarmament.		Congo (Kinshasa) sentences ex-P.M. Moise Tshombe, in exile in Spain, to death in absentia. . . . Malawi and South Africa sign a trade agreement allowing certain products of Malawi to enter South Africa duty free. . . . Israeli government says that 35,000 unemployed people have registered with labor exchanges. . . . Lt. Col. Odumegwu Ojukwu, the Nigerian military commander of the Eastern Region, warns that the East might secede if attacked militarily or "economically."		Ruling Indonesian Pres. Suharto says that because of Pres. Sukarno's failing health he will "be treated as president but (will be) without any power.". . . Chinese CP daily *Jenmin Jih Pao* virtually calls off the Cultural Revolution in the countryside when it says that power should not be seized during the spring farming season.
March 14		Soviet Union accuses Communist China of hindering Soviet freight trains enroute to North Vietnam. . . . Austrian Chancellor Josef Klaus arrives in the Soviet Union for a visit designed to gain Soviet permission to join the Common Market. . . . West German Social Democrats elect Helmut Schmidt as their parliamentary leader.	About 300 demonstrators protesting unemployment in Israel stone the City Hall of Tel Aviv.	Cuban Premier Fidel Castro accuses "certain communist countries" of establishing relations with oligarchic Latin American governments.	One hundred thousand demonstrators protest against Chief of State Liu Shao-chi and CP Gen. Secy. Teng Hsiao-ping in Peking.
March 15		Italy uncovers a spy ring involving 300 people trying to obtain intelligence on NATO bases and operations for the Soviet Union.		Artur da Costa e Silva, 64, is inaugurated as Brazil's 22nd president.	Communists attack a U.S. air base in Danang. . . . Reports indicate that the Communist Chinese Army has taken over the police stations in Sinkiang Province.
March 16		An Athens court convicts 15 Greek army officers of conspiring "to commit acts of high treason.". . . Common Market Statistical Office says that trade between Eastern Europe and the Common Market countries doubled between 1958 and 1965. . . . Speaking in Lisbon on the sixth anniversary of the outbreak of guerrilla warfare in Angola, Portuguese Foreign Min. Alberto Franco Nogueira declares that the African province has "returned to normal.". . . A Madrid court clears Father Victor Manuel Arbeloa Muro of charges of insulting the government's National Movement. Arbeloa had written articles condemning atrocities committed by both sides during the Spanish Civil War.	Israel claims to have slain two of five Arab infiltrators in the northern Negev.	Brazilian Pres. Artur da Costa e Silva admits that there is "a profound cleavage of inequality" in Brazil.	U.S. marines suffer heavy losses near the Laotian border.
March 17		Traditional Serbo-Croatian rivalry flares up when 19 croatian groups demand the dissolution of Croatia's linguistic union with Serbia.	Parliamentary elections are inconclusive in Sierra Leone. . . . Nigeria says that regional governments will be given veto power over all federal decisions affecting foreign policy and finance.		Communist shore guns in Vietnam damage a U.S. destroyer.
March 18		An oil tanker, the *Torrey Canyon*, runs aground at the western entrance of the English Channel spilling oil.			South Vietnamese Assembly adopts the draft of a new constitution providing for a democratically elected civilian government. . . . U.S. reports a record 211 combat deaths in Vietnam for the March 12-18 period. . . . Soviet Union expels two Communist Chinese diplomats in apparent retaliation for the March 11 Chinese expulsions. . . . AP reports that the Communist Chinese Army has assumed control of industrial production in six provinces.
	A	**B**	**C**	**D**	**E**
	Includes developments that affect more than one world region, international organizations and important meetings of major world leaders.	Includes all domestic and regional developments in Europe, including the Soviet Union, Turkey, Cyprus and Malta.	Includes all domestic and regional developments in Africa and the Middle East, including Iraq and Iran and excluding Cyprus, Turkey and Afghanistan.	Includes all domestic and regional developments in Latin America, the Caribbean and Canada.	Includes all domestic and regional developments in Asia and Pacific nations, extending from Afghanistan through all the Pacific Islands, except Hawaii.

U.S. Politics & Social Issues	U.S. Foreign Policy & Defense	U.S. Economy & Environment	Science, Technology & Nature	Culture, Leisure & Life Style	
Adam Clayton Powell declares from the Bahamas that he will return to New York on Palm Sunday, March 19, despite an order for his arrest. . . . Civil rights activist James Meredith withdraws from the special election for Adam Clayton Powell's seat under pressure from Negro politicians. . . . A bomb severely damages the Head Start office in Liberty, Miss. . . . Twenty-four Negroes file suit against the Campbell Soup Co. of Columbia, S.C. for alleged job discrimination. . . . AFL-CIO American Newspaper Guild announces that it is ending its relationship with certain foundations from which it has received funds for international programs because of their alleged ties to the CIA.	*Time* magazine reports that the Feb. 6 meeting between Pres. Johnson and Sen. Robert Kennedy involved a heated exchange which was marked by profanity. . . . Pres. Johnson asks Congress for a 30% increase in aid to Latin America.		France launches a small monkey into space.		March 13
Pres. Johnson submits plans for continuing the anti-poverty program. . . . Perry Russo testifies before a three-judge panel in New Orleans that he overheard David Ferrie, a "Leon Oswald" and Clem Bertrand (whom he identified in the court room as Clay Shaw) discuss plans for the assassination of Pres. Kennedy on three different occasions.	Both the White House and Sen. Robert Kennedy deny the accuracy of the *Time* magazine article on a Robert Kennedy-Pres. Johnson meeting but when Kennedy is asked if Pres. Johnson said that he had no political future because of his Vietnam stand, Kennedy replies, "I don't want to talk about that."				March 14
National Farmers Union calls for a boycott of new farm equipment to protest low farm income. . . . Justice Dept. reports that only one person was executed by civil authorities in the U.S. during 1966. . . . Labor Secy. Willard Wirtz announces a project to provide a comprehensive job-placement service for the unemployed in the slums of eight major cities.	Pres. Johnson defends his Vietnam War policies before the Tennessee General Assembly.				March 15
	Pres. Johnson proposes a draft lottery to replace current selective service procedures. . . . Senate ratifies the U.S.-Soviet consular convention. . . . *The New York Times* reports that Pres. Johnson has approved an invitation for South Vietnamese Pres. Ky to attend the coming Guam conference despite advice to the contrary from the U.S. embassy in Saigon.		Dr. Maimon Cohen of the N.Y. State University School of Medicine, Buffalo, reports evidence linking the hallucinogenic drug LSD to hereditary cell damage. . . . Soviet Union launches a satellite.	Universal Pictures releases Charlie Chaplin's film, *A Countess from Hong Kong*.	March 16
Adam Clayton Powell cancels plans to return to N.Y. . . . Three New Orleans judges rule that there is sufficient evidence to try Clay Shaw, one of Dist. Atty. Garrison's prime suspects in his investigation of the assassination of Pres. Kennedy.	Sen. Robert Kennedy says that Pres. Johnson "has been an outstanding President of the United States."	UAW Pres. Walter Reuther says that the UAW does not want to leave the AFL-CIO despite its recent criticism of that body.	Blizzards and floods kill 28 people along the U.S. East Coast.		March 17
					March 18

F	G	H	I	J
Includes elections, federal-state relations, civil rights and liberties, crime, the judiciary, education, health care, poverty, urban affairs and population.	*Includes formation and debate of U.S. foreign and defense policies, veterans' affairs and defense spending. (Relations with specific foreign countries are usually found under the region concerned.)*	*Includes business, labor, agriculture, taxation, transportation, consumer affairs, monetary and fiscal policy, natural resources, and pollution.*	*Includes worldwide scientific, medical and technological developments, natural phenomena, U.S. weather, natural disasters, and accidents.*	*Includes the arts, religion, scholarship, communications media, sports, entertainment, fashions, fads and social life.*

	World Affairs	Europe	Africa & the Middle East	The Americas	Asia & the Pacific
March 19		Forty members of the Serbian Writers' Association demand that Serbs living in Croatia be allowed to use Serbian and that their children be educated in Serbian.	Residents of French Somaliland (Djibouti) vote for "increased autonomy" but not complete independence from France.		Peking posters refer to Premier Chou En-lai as Chmn. Mao's "close comrade-in-arms", a phrase previously reserved exclusively for Defense Min. Lin Piao. . . . Chinese CP's Central Committee orders the army to assume command of the country's industrial and mining enterprises.
March 20			About 2,000 French Somaliland residents favoring complete independence from France riot in Djibouti. . . . Israel's coalition government turns back a vote of no-confidence by 62-41.		One thousand five hundred to two thousand U.S. marines disembark from ships just south of the demilitarized zone. . . . Reports from Peking indicate that the Communist Chinese Army has taken over many government buildings in Tibet.
March 21	U.N. Commission on Human Rights refers consideration of the problem of continued slavery in the world to a subcommission.	Executive committees of the Serbian and Croatian Communist parties criticize Serbian and Croatian nationalist tendencies. . . . Austrian Chancellor Josef Klaus leaves the Soviet Union without having succeeded in gaining its permission to allow Austria to join the Common Market.			Heavy fighting rages throughout South Vietnam in one of the bloodiest days of the war.
March 22	U.N. Commission on Human Rights votes 20-7 for an appeal to the General Assembly to establish a permanent high commissioner's office on human rights. The U.S. supports the proposal; the Soviet Union opposes it.	French Pres. de Gaulle says that France will continue to rule French Somaliland despite the Feb. 20 riots.	A gunman attempts to shoot Senegalese Pres. Leopold Sedar Senghor but is overpowered by police.	The New York Times reports that the Cuban Health Ministry has taken steps to implement a birth control program.	U.S. officials announce that Thailand has agreed to allow U.S. B-52s on its territory for bombing raids against Communist targets in North and South Vietnam.
March 23			Senegal charges that the March 22 assassination attempt on Pres. Senghor was organized by supporters of ex-P.M. Mamadou Dia.	Guerrillas ambush a Bolivian Army patrol.	
March 24		Huge oil slicks from the Torrey Canyon begin to coat the beaches of Cornwall.	Army seizes power in Sierra Leone in a bloodless coup.	Measles kill 50 Indians in Mexico.	Viet Cong puts out of action most of the vehicles in a 121-truck South Vietnamese convoy.
March 25		Two thousand demonstrators in London protest the U.S. Vietnam policy.			Communist gunners damage a U.S. warship from the South Vietnamese coast line for the first time. . . . U.S. reports a record 274 combat deaths for the March 19-25 period. . . . A jaundice epidemic kills 30 people in Gaya, India.
March 26		Yugoslav Pres. Tito criticizes alleged Serbian and Croatian nationalist agitation. . . . Soviet Union warns Indonesia that their relations will suffer if its anticommunist campaign continues.	Army dissolves the House of Representatives in Sierra Leone.		
March 27		Soviet news agency Tass reports that the government is studying two plans for the introduction of the profit system in agriculture. . . . Yugoslav Pres. Tito again criticizes Serbian and Croatian nationalists but opposes "Draconian measures" against them.		Bolivia announces that new guerrilla fighting has taken the lives of seven troops.	U.S. Navy planes bomb fuel depots near Haiphong.

A	B	C	D	E
Includes developments that affect more than one world region, international organizations and important meetings of major world leaders.	Includes all domestic and regional developments in Europe, including the Soviet Union, Turkey, Cyprus and Malta.	Includes all domestic and regional developments in Africa and the Middle East, including Iraq and Iran and excluding Cyprus, Turkey and Afghanistan.	Includes all domestic and regional developments in Latin America, the Caribbean and Canada.	Includes all domestic and regional developments in Asia and Pacific nations, extending from Afghanistan through all the Pacific Islands, except Hawaii.

U.S. Politics & Social Issues	U.S. Foreign Policy & Defense	U.S. Economy & Environment	Science, Technology & Nature	Culture, Leisure & Life Style	
				Peter Watkins' film *The War Game* is released. . . . Peppercorn-Wormser Films releases *Falstaff* with Orson Welles.	March 19
Justice Dept. files a school desegregation suit against Dale County, Ala.	Pres. Johnson confers with top South Vietnamese leaders in Guam. . . . Britain, West Germany and the U.S. meet in Washington to discuss troop withdrawals from West Germany.				March 20
	U.S. Senate votes for financing of the war in Vietnam by 77-3. . . . U.S. State Dept. confirms a recent exchange of letters between Pres. Johnson and North Vietnamese Pres. Ho Chi Minh. . . . Pres. Johnson returns to Washington after his two-day meeting in Guam with South Vietnamese leaders.	Consumer advocate Ralph Nader criticizes the federal National Traffic Safety Agency for an alleged lack of initiative.		A N.Y. court dismisses Mrs. Ernest Hemingway's suit to prohibit the sale of A.E. Hotchner's book *Papa Hemingway* .	March 21
A Montgomery, Ala. court orders the state's officials to begin the desegregation of all public schools. . . . A New Orleans grand jury indicts Clay Shaw, charging that he was a party to a conspiracy, along with Lee Harvey Oswald and David Ferrie, to murder Pres. Kennedy.			Soviet Union launches a satellite.		March 22
	Newly elected Sen. Edward Brooke (R, Mass.) reverses his former stand after a trip to Vietnam and supports current U.S. policy.				March 23
Vacationing college students riot in Ft. Lauderdale, Fla.				Sen. Robert Kennedy's wife, Ethel, gives birth to their 10th child.	March 24
A U.S. district court fines the captain of a second Soviet fishing trawler seized for fishing in U.S. waters. . . . Vacationing college students riot in Ocean Drive Beach, S.C. Police arrest 150.	Rev. Martin Luther King Jr. leads an anti-Vietnam War march of 5,000 demonstrators in Chicago.		In the *British Medical Journal* two British neurologists say that "there is an apparent association" between oral contraceptives and disabling strokes.		March 25
Vacationing college students riot in Hollywood, Calif.	V.P. Humphrey begins a tour of West European capitals to explain U.S. foreign policy. . . . Sen. Stuart Symington (D, Mo.) says that during a recent trip to Southeast Asia a U.S. fighter pilot told him that North Vietnamese pilots are "becoming more aggressive."			Harold Pinter's *The Homecoming* wins the 21st annual Perry Award for the best N.Y. play of the 1966-1967 season.	March 26
Sen. Robert Kennedy's press secretary says that he has "no plans" to enter any presidential primaries in 1968.	U.S. Senate Preparedness Investigating Subcommittee recommends an escalation of the air war against North Vietnam.				March 27

F	G	H	I	J
Includes elections, federal-state relations, civil rights and liberties, crime, the judiciary, education, health care, poverty, urban affairs and population.	Includes formation and debate of U.S. foreign and defense policies, veterans' affairs and defense spending. (Relations with specific foreign countries are usually found under the region concerned.)	Includes business, labor, agriculture, taxation, transportation, consumer affairs, monetary and fiscal policy, natural resources, and pollution.	Includes worldwide scientific, medical and technological developments, natural phenomena, U.S. weather, natural disasters, and accidents.	Includes the arts, religion, scholarship, communications media, sports, entertainment, fashions, fads and social life.

	World Affairs	Europe	Africa & the Middle East	The Americas	Asia & the Pacific
March 28	U.N. Secy. Gen U Thant proposes a three-point plan to end the Vietnamese War. U.S. and South Vietnam accept the plan with qualifications but North Vietnam rejects it.			Bolivia asserts that its guerrillas are organized by Ché Guevara, one of Cuban Pres. Fidel Castro's top aides.	A private U.S. yacht carrying eight U.S. pacifists and $10,000 worth of medical supplies for North Vietnam arrives in Haiphong.
March 29		France launches its first nuclear powered submarine.	Malawi's Pres. Hastings Kamuzu Banda attacks African critics of his country's cooperation with South Africa, claiming they allegedly trade with South Africa in secret.		
March 30		Greek caretaker government of P.M. Ioannis Paraskevopoulos resigns over a dispute between its two principal parliamentary backers.			Red Guard posters say that Premier Chou En-lai should never be criticized.
March 31		One thousand demonstrators in Rome protest U.S. Vietnamese policy as V.P. Humphrey confers with Italian Premier Aldo Moro. . . . Soviet Defense Min. Rodion Malinovsky dies in Moscow at 68.	Nigerian Eastern Region issues an edict ordering all tax revenues paid in the East to go directly to the regional government.		For the first time *Hung Chi* the Chinese theoretical journal, openly attacks Communist China's head of state, Liu Shao-chi.
April 1	U.N. Secy. Gen. U Thant suggests that the U.S. should initiate a unilateral truce.			Bolivian Pres. Rene Barrientos Ortuno flies to the guerrilla combat area.	South Vietnam's new constitution goes into effect when Chief of State Nguyen Van Thieu signs the document.
April 2			Sierra Leone decrees five-year jail terms for publishers whose newspapers allegedly defamed government leaders. . . . For the first time in its history, Israel reports a monthly trade surplus (for February). . . . Riots break out as a three-man U.N. mission visits Aden.	Christian Democratic party of Chilean Pres. Eduardo Frei Montalva wins 36.5% of the vote in municipal elections, more than twice the number of votes of any other party.	Hundreds of thousands of Red Guards, soldiers and school children bang drums, clash cymbals and chant "down with Liu Shao-chi" in central Peking.
April 3	A letter bomb burns Nicolas Rodriquez Astiarzarain, the acting chief of Cuba's U.N. mission in N.Y.C.	Twenty thousand workers go on a brief work stoppage in Bilboa, Spain. . . . French National Assembly re-elects Gaullist Jacques Chaban-Delmas as Speaker. . . . Eighteenth congress of the West German Free Democratic Party begins with signs of a split between reformist and more conservative members.	Ruling National Reformation Council lifts martial law in Sierra Leone. . . . Israeli and Syrian forces exchange gun fire.		U.S. rejects a Philippine request that it turn over the Sangley Point naval air station at Manila Bay to the Philippine Navy. . . . Hundreds of thousands of Communist Chinese demonstrators demand the overthrow of head of state Liu Shao-chi.
April 4	U.N. Secy. Gen. U Thant begins a tour of five Asian countries.	More than 5,000 workers and students clash with police in Bilboa, Spain. . . . Both left- and right-wing students riot in Athens. . . . Spain increases government control over the press. . . . About 120 Dutch sailors and marines assault Dutch beatniks in Amsterdam.	Nigerian federal government suspends all national flights to the Eastern Region.		U.S. reports that the 500th U.S. plane lost over North Vietnam since the bombing began in August 1964 was downed on April 2.
April 5			Nigeria's Eastern Region appeals to all Easterners living outside their native region to return home.		North and South Korean troops skirmish along the dimilitarized zone in Korea.
April 6		French Pres. Charles de Gaulle renames George Pompidou as prime minister.			Communist forces make major gains just south of the demilitarized zone in Vietnam.
	A	**B**	**C**	**D**	**E**
	Includes developments that affect more than one world region, international organizations and important meetings of major world leaders.	*Includes all domestic and regional developments in Europe, including the Soviet Union, Turkey, Cyprus and Malta.*	*Includes all domestic and regional developments in Africa and the Middle East, including Iraq and Iran and excluding Cyprus, Turkey and Afghanistan.*	*Includes all domestic and regional developments in Latin America, the Caribbean and Canada.*	*Includes all domestic and regional developments in Asia and Pacific nations, extending from Afghanistan through all the Pacific Islands, except Hawaii.*

U.S. Politics & Social Issues	U.S. Foreign Policy & Defense	U.S. Economy & Environment	Science, Technology & Nature	Culture, Leisure & Life Style	
Students at the predominantly Negro Texas Southern Univ. bar doors to university buildings to protest the administration's refusal to recognize the Friends of SNCC organization.				In his fifth encyclical letter, Pope Paul supports land expropriation for and by the poor when required for the "common good."	March 28
A U.S. court in New Orleans affirms an earlier court order upholding the legality of the revised federal school desegregation guidelines. . . . Pres. Johnson orders a halt to covert financing of private and voluntary organizations by federal agencies.				Harper & Row publishes Alan Moorehead's *The March to Tunis* .	March 29
Ga. State Rep. Julian Bond and CORE Director Floyd McKissick announce plans for a "third force" political organization for U.S. Negroes.		National Traffic Safety Agency orders a public hearing on one of its new safety standards.			March 30
Sen. Robert Kennedy says he will work for Pres. Johnson in the 1968 election.	Eighteen anti-war demonstrators picket the Selective Service headquarters in Washington, D.C.			McGraw-Hill publishes Joseph Wechsberg's *The Murderers Among Us: The Wiesenthal Memoirs* .	March 31
	Pres. Johnson signs a bill for emergency food aid to India.	Arbitrators announce the terms of the three-year contract between the AFL-CIO United Farm Workers Organizing Committee and the Di Giorgio Fruit Corp.			April 1
Southern Education Reporting Service reports that 16% of the Negro students in the South are attending desegregated schools.	Harvard Univ. economist John Kenneth Galbraith calls for a suspension of the bombing of North Vietnam.				April 2
	U.S. Senate Foreign Relations Committee rejects Pres. Johnson's request for increased aid to Latin America.	AFL-CIO Pres. George Meany announces the end of the federation's eleven-month boycott of Di Giorgio products.			April 3
Chicago Mayor Richard Daley easily wins a fourth term.	Rev. Martin Luther King Jr. intensifies his criticism of U.S. policy in Vietnam and urges young men to declare themselves conscientious objectors. . . . Sen. Mark Hatfield (R, Ore.) says that the Johnson administration "has lost the capacity to solve" the Vietnamese War.		FDA announces an investigation into the possible hallucinogenic effects of smoking dried banana peel. . . . British Health Min. M.K. Robinson says that oral contraceptives slightly increase the risk of blood clots "but that the risk is small and less than that which arises from ordinary pregnancy.". . . Soviet Union launches a satellite.		April 4
Texas Legislature passes its first major civil rights bill since Reconstruction when it forbids discrimination by state officials. . . . At his formal arraignment in New Orleans, Clay Shaw pleads not guilty to charges of participating in a conspiracy to murder Pres. Kennedy.	Peace groups launch a campaign in N.Y.C. high schools to encourage youths to register as conscientious objectors.	UAW Pres. Walter Reuther calls for a "national crusade...to organize the unorganized."	Britain launches its first satellite designed and built entirely in Britain from Vandenberg Air Force base in the U.S.		April 5
Boston police arrest William Baird at his own insistence for violating a Mass. law forbidding the distribution of birth control devices.	NATO's nuclear planning group meets in Washington.		NASA announces that eight possible landing sites have been selected on the basis of Lunar Orbiter 3 photos for a manned visit to the moon.		April 6
F	G	H	I	J	
Includes elections, federal-state relations, civil rights and liberties, crime, the judiciary, education, health care, poverty, urban affairs and population.	Includes formation and debate of U.S. foreign and defense policies, veterans' affairs and defense spending. (Relations with specific foreign countries are usually found under the region concerned.)	Includes business, labor, agriculture, taxation, transportation, consumer affairs, monetary and fiscal policy, natural resources, and pollution.	Includes worldwide scientific, medical and technological developments, natural phenomena, U.S. weather, natural disasters, and accidents.	Includes the arts, religion, scholarship, communications media, sports, entertainment, fashions, fads and social life.	

	World Affairs	Europe	Africa & the Middle East	The Americas	Asia & the Pacific
April 7		Virulent demonstrations against U.S. Vietnamese policy take place in Paris as V.P. Humphrey confers with Pres. de Gaulle.	Israel claims shooting down six Syrian MiGs. Syria concedes the loss of four planes.		Reports indicate that acting Indonesian Pres. Suharto has announced plans to expand the Indonesian Army to deal with alleged communist subversion. . . . South Vietnamese Premier Nguyen Cao Ky flys to Quangtri to inspect the damage caused by the recent Communist attack in northern South Vietnam.
April 8					South Vietnam proposes a one-day battle front truce on May 23 to mark the anniversary of Buddha's birth. . . . A U.S. spokesman says that American civilians will be removed from Quangtri and Hue because of recent Communist attacks.
April 9		French coast receives its first oil pollution from the *Torrey Canyon* oil tanker wreck. . . . One thousand demonstrators in Stockholm, Sweden protest against U.S. Vietnam War policy.		International Planned Parenthood Federation opens its eighth conference in Santiago, Chile.	U.S. troops clash with the Viet Cong in the Mekong Delta. . . . Viet Cong threaten the First Cavalry Division's base at Ankhe.
April 10				Bolivian officials discover an abandoned guerrilla camp.	South Korea announces the deaths of four North Korean infiltrators. . . . First B-52 bombers land in Thailand. . . . Clashes continue between the Viet Cong and U.S. troops in the Mekong Delta. . . . Japanese newspaper *Yomiuri* reports that top Communist officials have voted 6-5 to condemn Chinese Chief-of-State Liu Shao-chi and CP Gen. Secy. Teng Hsiao-ping. . . . Communist China orders the expulsion of a Yugoslav journalist for his "distorted and slanderous" reporting of the Cultural Revolution.
April 11		Marshall Andrei Grechko becomes defense minister of the Soviet Union. . . . Croatian CP expels 11 members for openly participating in the recent nationalist dispute.	Syrian mortars pound an Israeli settlement.	Jamaican P.M. Donald Burns Sangster dies of a brain hemorrhage at 55. . . . Bolivia declares martial law in the southeastern part of the country.	U.S. troops battle the Viet Cong in the Mekong Delta. . . . U.S. officials report that the Soviet Union and Communist China have reached an agreement on expediting the shipment of Soviet supplies to North Vietnam through Communist China. . . . An earthquake kills 37 people in Indonesia.
April 12	Pres. Johnson and the heads of 18 Latin American states meet in Uruguay for an OAS meeting.	Two thousand left-wing building workers riot in Athens. . . . Spain notifies Britain that its aircraft will not be allowed to fly over Spanish territory within an approximately 40-mile-wide strip surrounding Gibraltar. . . . West Germany calls for expanded cooperation between the two German governments.	Israeli and Syrian forces clash north of the Sea of Galilee.		Communists raid the U.S. Marine base at Chulai.
April 13		British government says that it intends "to uphold to the full our right to use the airfield at Gibraltar."		In a move to give the province of Quebec greater autonomy, the Quebec Legislative Assembly approves the creation of a new Ministry of Intergovernmental Affairs.	North and South Korean troops skirmish for two hours. . . . Communists blow up two bridges between Danang and Quangtri. . . . Reports indicate that Communist Chinese Premier Chou En-lai denounced Chief-of-State Liu Shao-chi at an April 6 rally.

A	B	C	D	E
Includes developments that affect more than one world region, international organizations and important meetings of major world leaders.	*Includes all domestic and regional developments in Europe, including the Soviet Union, Turkey, Cyprus and Malta.*	*Includes all domestic and regional developments in Africa and the Middle East, including Iraq and Iran and excluding Cyprus, Turkey and Afghanistan.*	*Includes all domestic and regional developments in Latin America, the Caribbean and Canada.*	*Includes all domestic and regional developments in Asia and Pacific nations, extending from Afghanistan through all the Pacific Islands, except Hawaii.*

U.S. Politics & Social Issues	U.S. Foreign Policy & Defense	U.S. Economy & Environment	Science, Technology & Nature	Culture, Leisure & Life Style	
U.S. court sentences Pres. Johnson's former Senate aide Robert Baker to a one to three year jail sentence. . . . At Fisk University in Nashville, Tenn. SNCC Chmn. Stokely Carmichael says: "If we don't get changes, we are going to tear this country apart." . . . Justice Dept. files a school desegregation suit against Ben Hill County, Ga.				Harper & Row publishes William Manchester's *The Death of a President: November 20-November 25, 1963.*	April 7
Negro students riot at Fisk Univ. in Nashville after police eject a Negro from the University Dinner Club at the request of the Negro management.	Reports indicate that West Germany, Italy and Turkey have asked to be given the authority to fire tactical nuclear weapons in time of war. Currently only the U.S. President has such authorization.				April 8
Negroes fire rifles at passing cars in Nashville, Tenn.	Former Republican presidential candidate Barry Goldwater declares his support of Pres. Johnson's Vietnam policies. . . . Sen. Robert Kennedy says that even though the war protesters are in a minority in the U.S. their demonstrations are curbing Pres. Johnson's handling of the war.				April 9
Negro students continue to riot at Fisk University. . . . U.S. Supreme Court upholds a lower court decision to reverse the convictions of two Louisiana Negro rapists because Negroes were excluded from their 1950 jury. . . . NAACP rejects Dr. Martin Luther King's suggestion that the civil rights and peace movements merge.				*A Man for All Seasons* wins the 39th annual Oscar award for the best film of 1966.	April 10
Fisk Univ. Pres. James Lawson says that most of the rioters are "outside agitators" brought to Nashville by SNCC. . . . Adam Clayton Powell wins a special election for his former congressional seat by a margin of almost 7 to 1.				U.S. National Conference of Catholic Bishops launches a campaign against the movement to liberalize abortions. . . . Random House publishes William Faulkner's *The Wishing Tree.*	April 11
Negroes demonstrate after Louisville, Ky. rejects an open-housing ordinance. . . . Dr. Martin Luther King Jr. denies that he advocates a merger of the civil rights and peace movements.	U.S. announces that it will no longer sell weapons to India and Pakistan in an effort to slow the arms race between them. . . . U.S. rejects a Common Market demand for minimum world grain prices during a bargaining session of the Kennedy Round of tariff-cutting negotiations.	Pres. Johnson signs legislation delaying a nationwide rail strike.	Soviet Union launches a satellite.	One of Communist China's foremost musicians, Ma Szu-tsung, discloses in New York that he defected in December 1966.	April 12
White mobs attack Negro marchers in Louisville, Ky. . . . Justice Dept. files a school desegregation suit against Altheimer School district in Arkansas.			Japan fails to launch its fourth-stage Lambda rocket for the third consecutive time.	Luis Anastasio Somoza de Bayle, president of Nicaragua 1956-1963, dies in Managua, Nicaragua at 45. . . . Random House publishes Ira Levin's *Rosemary's Baby.*	April 13

F	G	H	I	J
Includes elections, federal-state relations, civil rights and liberties, crime, the judiciary, education, health care, poverty, urban affairs and population.	*Includes formation and debate of U.S. foreign and defense policies, veterans' affairs and defense spending. (Relations with specific foreign countries are usually found under the region concerned.)*	*Includes business, labor, agriculture, taxation, transportation, consumer affairs, monetary and fiscal policy, natural resources, and pollution.*	*Includes worldwide scientific, medical and technological developments, natural phenomena, U.S. weather, natural disasters, and accidents.*	*Includes the arts, religion, scholarship, communications media, sports, entertainment, fashions, fads and social life.*

	World Affairs	Europe	Africa & the Middle East	The Americas	Asia & the Pacific
April 14	At the International Planned Parenthood Federation Conference, Dr. Oscar Harkavy says that Taiwan is the only country to date which has successfully organized large-scale family planning.	Greek Premier Panayotis Kanellopoulos dissolves Parliament and schedules elections for May 28. . . . Hungarian National Assembly appoints economist Jeno Fock as premier in anticipation of major economic reforms scheduled for Jan. 1, 1968.			U.S. sends reinforcements to northern South Vietnam.
April 15		Soviet Union will introduce the profit system in 390 of the country's 12,000 state farms in 1967. . . . Israel signs a long-term trade agreement with Rumania in Bucharest.	Fighting erupts between two Arab groups competing for power in anticipation of Britain's scheduled departure from Aden in 1968.		South Vietnamese Premier Nguyen Cao Ky announces the start of construction of a fortified barrier just south of the demilitarized zone.
April 16		Soviet and Iranian authorities agree on a joint development plan for certain Iranian oil resources.		Rumors continue to circulate that Ché Guevara is active in the Bolivian guerrilla movement.	U.S. Brig. Gen. Michael Ryan says that the proposed barrier south of the demilitarized zone is more in the nature of an improved surveillance system. . . . Viet Cong guerrillas murder South Vietnamese government officials 40 miles east of Saigon.
April 17		British Economic Affairs Min. Michael Stewart announces that the government will modify but still extend its freeze on wages and prices for an additional year. . . . Congress of East German Socialist Unity opens in East Berlin.	Ghana suppresses an attempted coup by 122 soldiers.	Quebec provincial government cabinet orders that all food packages be labeled in French.	A Viet Cong grenade wounds nine U.S. soldiers in Saigon. . . . South Korea reports having sunk a North Korean boat about to land spies in South Korea. . . . Peking wall posters condemn Chinese CP Gen. Secy. Teng Hsiao-ping.
April 18		In East Berlin Soviet CP Gen. Secy. Brezhnev calls for a world conference of Communist parties. . . . *London Times* reports that Gibraltar has agreed to import laborers from Malta.			U.S. planes carry out their tenth attack on the Thainguyen iron and steel complex.
April 19		A Yugoslav court convicts dissident writer Mihajlo Mihajlov to four-and-a-half years in prison for publishing "hostile" propaganda. . . . Former West German Chancellor Konrad Adenauer dies in Rhondorf, West Germany at 91. . . . France announces that it has successfully conducted the first test-firing of an intercontinental ballistic missile which will be used by the French submarine fleet. . . . Yugoslav Federal Assembly adopts several measures which appear to decentralize the federal government's power. . . . Belgium expels Soviet *Tass* correspondent Anatoli Ogorodnikov for spying.	Nigeria's Eastern Region takes over all federal services within its territory. . . . An Arab gunman slays a former labor minister in Aden.	Bolivian government troops capture French Communist author Regis Debray who has been accompanying Bolivian guerrillas.	A smallpox epidemic kills 900 people in India. . . . U.S. planes carry out heavy raids against the Xuanmai troop training center south of Hanoi.
April 20		Soviet Union calls Adenauer "a knight of the Cold War (who) supported and inspired a policy of revenge-seeking.". . . Two French parliamentarians, Rene Ribiere and Gaston Deferre, fight a duel after a heated argument in the French Assembly. Neither man is hurt. . . . A Leningrad court sentences Volker Wilhelm Schaffhauser, a West German student, to four years in a labor camp for attempting to distribute anti-Soviet literature for a Soviet emigre group while he was visiting Russia.	Nigeria's Supreme Military Council meets in Lagos without the Eastern Commander Lt. Col. Chukwuemeka Odumegwu Ojukwu to decide on measures dealing with the Eastern Region's latest moves.	Cuban Premier Fidel Castro says that Ché Guevara is "in excellent health and ready for an armed guerrilla fight."	U.S. planes bomb the port of Haiphong for the first time. . . . Four hundred Jakarta Chinese businessmen close their shops in protest against the alleged murder of a Chinese by Indonesian police.

A	B	C	D	E
Includes developments that affect more than one world region, international organizations and important meetings of major world leaders.	Includes all domestic and regional developments in Europe, including the Soviet Union, Turkey, Cyprus and Malta.	Includes all domestic and regional developments in Africa and the Middle East, including Iraq and Iran and excluding Cyprus, Turkey and Afghanistan.	Includes all domestic and regional developments in Latin America, the Caribbean and Canada.	Includes all domestic and regional developments in Asia and Pacific nations, extending from Afghanistan through all the Pacific Islands, except Hawaii.

U.S. Politics & Social Issues	U.S. Foreign Policy & Defense	U.S. Economy & Environment	Science, Technology & Nature	Culture, Leisure & Life Style	
Justice Dept. files suit against an electrical workers union in Columbus, Ohio. . . . Negro community begins a boycott of Louisville, Ky.'s white merchants. . . . Tennessee Campbell County School Board dismisses Gary Scott for teaching that man has descended from a lower order of animals.	Former V.P. Nixon says that Democratic critics of the Vietnamese War are giving "aid and comfort to the enemy.". . . U.S. rejects a Soviet bid to purchase a two-man research submarine.				April 14
In *Newsweek* magazine Hugh Aynesworth charges that New Orleans Dist. Atty. James Garrison offered Alvin Beaubouef, a friend of David Ferrie, $3,000 to testify that he had overheard the planning of the Kennedy assassination. . . . Ivy League colleges announce a new policy of admitting students on the basis of "student diversity" rather than geographic balance.	One hundred thousand protesters demonstrate in Washington, D.C. against the war in Vietnam.				April 15
Negro riots break out in the Hough section of Cleveland; several stores are looted. . . . Four escaped Negro prison convicts surrender to Georgia Gov. Lester Maddox after waiting 30 minutes in a reception line to see him.	State Secy. Dean Rusk says that the "communist apparatus" is behind the peace movement although not "all those who have objections to the war in Vietnam are communists."				April 16
U.S. Supreme Court refuses to delay the desegregation of all public schools in six Southern states by the fall. . . . Five hundred whites jeer Negro marchers in Louisville, Ky.	In Saigon former V.P. Nixon says that the defeat of the Communists is "inevitable."		U.S. launches lunar probe Surveyor 3.	London Independent Producers releases Joseph Losey's film *Accident*.	April 17
Police use tear gas to disperse white mobs in Lousiville, Ky.			A survey indicates that 15% of Princeton Univ. undergraduates have taken marijuana or LSD.	Vatican reaffirms its traditional stand against contraception.	April 18
White teenagers hurl stones at Negro marchers in Louisville, Ky.			Surveyor 3 lands successfully on the moon.	Dr. Charles Sellers' *James K. Polk, Continentalist: 1843-1846* wins the 1967 Bancroft Prize for history. . . . Reports indicate a majority of the members of the Papal Commission of Birth Control favor artificial means of contraception. . . . Harper & Row publishes Harrison Salisbury's *Behind the Lines-Hanoi.*	April 19
Police disperse nearly 600 white hecklers with tear gas in Louisville, Ky. . . . NAACP Executive Director Roy Wilkins denounces the Rev. Martin Luther King's warnings of summer violence as "dangerous."			U.S. launches a weather satellite, Essa 5.		April 20

F	G	H	I	J
Includes elections, federal-state relations, civil rights and liberties, crime, the judiciary, education, health care, poverty, urban affairs and population.	Includes formation and debate of U.S. foreign and defense policies, veterans' affairs and defense spending. (Relations with specific foreign countries are usually found under the region concerned.)	Includes business, labor, agriculture, taxation, transportation, consumer affairs, monetary and fiscal policy, natural resources, and pollution.	Includes worldwide scientific, medical and technological developments, natural phenomena, U.S. weather, natural disasters, and accidents.	Includes the arts, religion, scholarship, communications media, sports, entertainment, fashions, fads and social life.

	World Affairs	Europe	Africa & the Middle East	The Americas	Asia & the Pacific
April 21	A special session of the U.N. General Assembly begins its deliberations on the future of South-West Africa.	A Greek military coup overthrows the interim government of Premier Panayotis Kanellopoulos.			U.S. planes destroy North Vietnamese railroad cars carrying petroleum.
April 22		Reports indicate that Greek King Constantine has refused to sign a decree declaring martial law.	Nigerian federal government warns that stern measures will be taken to "protect the federation's revenue and other commercial interests."		
April 23		Thousands file past the closed coffin of former West German Chancellor Konrad Adenauer in Bonn.		Government troops clash with guerrillas in Bolivia.	Ex-Defense Min. and leading Indian leftist, V.K. Krishna Menon, loses his race for a parliamentary seat.
April 24		Greek Interior Min. Stylianos Patakos issues rules banning long hair for boys and miniskirts for girls. . . . Twenty-four European Communist parties meet in Karlovy Vary, Czechoslovakia. Rumania and Yugoslavia boycott the conference.	A military guard wounds Togolese Pres. Etienne Eyadema in the left arm.	Manitoba Legislative Assembly votes unanimously to restore the right of the French community's schools to use French as a language of instruction in the arts subjects for half a school day.	Indonesia orders the ouster of Communist China's top diplomatic representatives from Jakarta. . . . Fierce fighting rages at Khesanh between U.S. and North Vietnamese troops. . . . For the first time U.S. planes bomb two MiG bases north of Hanoi. . . . One hundred demonstrators jeer at V.P. Humphrey after a speech on Vietnam before the Texas Legislature.
April 25		Pres. Johnson and other major world leaders attend the state funeral of former West German Chancellor Konrad Adenauer. . . . Britain announces that it has referred its airspace dispute with Spain to the International Civil Aviation Organization. . . . Hungarian CP First Secy. Janos Kadar holds out the possibility of diplomatic relations with West Germany.	Swaziland, a landlocked British colony surrounded by South Africa and Mozambique, becomes a self-governing protectorate.	Bolivian government troops clash with guerrillas.	U.S. troops launch an all-out drive against entrenched Communist troops at Khesanh.
April 26		Greek King Constantine, who reportedly opposed the April 21 military coup, attends a cabinet meeting of the new government in the royal palace. . . . Thirty-eight French beaches are now polluted by the huge oil slick from the Torrey Canyon tanker wreck. . . . In a news conference Svetlana Stalina, the daughter of the late Joseph Stalin, says that in the Soviet Union Jews suffer from discrimination in employment.	Three thousand Yemenis attack the U.S. Agency for International Development in Aden.		U.S. planes attack a major bridge north of Hanoi.
April 27		In an attempt to democratize itself, Yugoslav CP says that it must embrace "all social forces which accept the Socialist foundations of society."	Yemeni republican government announces that it has decided unilaterally to end the U.S. aid program.		Agence France-Presse reports that the entire western section of Haiphong has been devastated by U.S. air strikes.
April 28		The New York Times reports that Spanish authorities have arrested nearly 100 labor and student leaders in Vizcaya as of April 27. . . . Britain, West Germany and the U.S. meet in London to discuss troop withdrawals from West Germany. . . . France and West Germany agree on joint development and construction of an experimental synchronous communications satellite.	U.S. announces that it will withdraw the Agency for International Development mission from Yemen.		U.S. planes attack North Vietnam in one of the heaviest raids of the war.

A	B	C	D	E
Includes developments that affect more than one world region, international organizations and important meetings of major world leaders.	Includes all domestic and regional developments in Europe, including the Soviet Union, Turkey, Cyprus and Malta.	Includes all domestic and regional developments in Africa and the Middle East, including Iraq and Iran and excluding Cyprus, Turkey and Afghanistan.	Includes all domestic and regional developments in Latin America, the Caribbean and Canada.	Includes all domestic and regional developments in Asia and Pacific nations, extending from Afghanistan through all the Pacific Islands, except Hawaii.

U.S. Politics & Social Issues	U.S. Foreign Policy & Defense	U.S. Economy & Environment	Science, Technology & Nature	Culture, Leisure & Life Style	
Louisville police arrest Martin Luther King Jr. for defying an injunction against protest marches, but he is allowed to meet with city leaders to find a solution to the housing complaints.	After his recent trip to Western Europe, V.P. Humphrey says that the U.S. must abandon the "old senior-junior relationships" in which the U.S. was the senior partner.		Tornadoes sweep through northern Illinois, leaving 52 dead.	After almost two months in Europe, Svetlana Stalina arrives in New York.	April 21
	Sen. Charles Percy (R, Ill.) criticizes the administration's policy which allegedly allows "our men to die at the rate of 150 to 250 a month. . .in search of a total victory which cannot, in my judgment, really be achieved."	UAW delegates give their union's executive board authority to take the UAW out of the AFL-CIO.	Surveyor 3 begins digging on the moon with its mechanical scoop.		April 22
	Rev. Martin Luther King Jr. calls for increased opposition to the Vietnamese War in an address in Cambridge, Mass.	U.S. Commerce Dept. reports that personal income has risen to record levels.			April 23
U.S. Office of Education announces that it is ordering universities in the Southeastern Conference to desegregate their sports programs or forfeit federal aid. . . . An article in the May 6 issue of the *Saturday Evening Post* cites evidence tending to discredit the testimony of New Orleans Dist. Atty. James Garrison's principal witness, Perry Russo.	Sen. John Tower (R, Tex.) praises the recent attack on the MiG bases in North Vietnam.		Crash of a Soviet spaceship kills cosmonaut Col. Vladimir Koarov.	Wesleyan University Press publishes James Dickey's *Poems 1957-1967.*	April 24
More than 200 whites hold a silent "pray-in" for racial progress in front of the Louisville, Ky. City Hall. . . . Negro shareholders walk out of the annual Eastman Kodak Co. meeting to protest the company's alleged repudiation of an agreement to hire and train more Negroes. . . . Colo. Gov. John Love signs a bill liberalizing his state's abortion statute. . . . Justice Dept. files a school desegregation suit against Loudoun County, Va.	U.S. ratifies a U.N. treaty banning weapons of mass-destruction from outer space. . . . Sen. Robert Kennedy attacks the administration's Vietnam policy. . . . U.S. Amb-to-South Vietnam Henry Cabot Lodge resigns and is replaced by Ellsworth Bunker.				April 25
U.S. Supreme Court rules that its limitations on police interrogation and confessions must also be observed in military courts. . . . Justice Dept. files a school desegregation suit against Northampton County, N.C.			Italy launches its second satellite.	Gen. Secy. Eugene Blake of the World Council of Churches calls on the U.S. to stop the bombing of North Vietnam.	April 26
On a tour to promote a possible 1968 presidential candidacy, ex-Gov George Wallace encounters pickets in Pittsburgh, Pa. . . . U.S. Court of Appeals upholds the civil rights conspiracy convictions of two Alabama Ku Klux Klansmen.	Reports indicate that Defense Secy. McNamara has received a letter signed by 1,000 seminarians asking that conscientious objection to a particular war be made possible.		Soviet Union launches a satellite.		April 27
Calif. Senate Judiciary Committee approves a bill liberalizing the circumstances in which abortions are legal. . . . Former Ala. Gov. George Wallace makes a political visit to Cleveland, Ohio. . . . A U.S. Senate subcommittee asks Pres. Johnson to invoke emergency measures to fight malnutrition in the U.S. South. . . . Virginia restaurant owner Roy McKoy is convicted of contempt of court for refusing to comply with a court order mandating the desegregation of his restaurant.	A joint session of the U.S. Congress responds enthusiastically to an address by Gen. William Westmoreland. . . . In the first high-level U.S. comment on the Greek military coup, State Secy. Rusk says that the U.S. is "awaiting concrete evidence that the new Greek government will make every effort to re-establish democratic institutions."		U.S. launches five satellites into orbit.		April 28

F	G	H	I	J
Includes elections, federal-state relations, civil rights and liberties, crime, the judiciary, education, health care, poverty, urban affairs and population.	*Includes formation and debate of U.S. foreign and defense policies, veterans' affairs and defense spending. (Relations with specific foreign countries are usually found under the region concerned.)*	*Includes business, labor, agriculture, taxation, transportation, consumer affairs, monetary and fiscal policy, natural resources, and pollution.*	*Includes worldwide scientific, medical and technological developments, natural phenomena, U.S. weather, natural disasters, and accidents.*	*Includes the arts, religion, scholarship, communications media, sports, entertainment, fashions, fads and social life.*

	World Affairs	Europe	Africa & the Middle East	The Americas	Asia & the Pacific
April 29		Greek government abolishes the Greek pro-Communist party.	U.S. officials begin to leave Yemen.		U.S. planes attack Chinese-North Vietnamese rail links. . . . Communist China rejects a U.S. offer to make drugs available to aid in halting reported epidemics.
April 30		Spain warns its citizens not to take part in any May Day demonstrations. . . . Forty-nine parliamentary members of the Turkish Republican People's Party (RPP) resign their seats to protest the party's growing left-wing orientation.	Kenyan Defense Min. Njoroge Mungai begins a tour of Middle East countries in an effort to end the reported supply of arms to Somalia. . . . A bomb kills six Arab school children traveling in a bus on the West Bank of the Jordan River.		Communist troops repel U.S. troops on Hill 881 in perhaps the heaviest fighting of the war.
May 1	WHO reports that heart disease is the major cause of death in the industrial countries.	Greek Interior Min. Stylianos Patakos orders the distribution of municipal land to landless farmers. . . . Thousands of Spanish demonstrators march in May Day parades.	U.S. reduces its personnel in Yemen to 13 employees. . . . Gen. Anastasio Somoza Debayle Jr. is sworn in as president of Nicaragua. . . . A general strike shuts down the port of Aden. . . . Kenyan V.P. Daniel Arap Moi leaves for talks in Egypt with Pres. Nasser about Egyptian arms shipments to Somali guerrillas in Kenya.		
May 2		US and Britain announce that they will redeploy up to 41,500 troops from West Germany to their home bases starting Jan. 1, 1968. . . . British P.M. Harold Wilson announces that Britain will again seek admission to the Common Market.	Liberia elects Pres. William Tubman to his sixth presidential term. . . . Kenya issues a report detailing alleged guerrilla warfare by neighboring Somalia.	U.N. Economic Commission for Latin America reports that population increases have wiped out the economic gains made by the area during recent years.	
May 3		Spain deports three U.S. students enrolled at the Univ. of Madrid for taking part in demonstrations.		Canadian government reports that per capita income rose 7% during 1966.	South Korean voters re-elect Pres. Chung Hee Park to his second term as president. . . . Communist China accuses the U.S. of having bombed the southern Chinese town of Ningming.
May 4		A Greek government spokesman says that left-wing politician Andreas Papandreou will stand on trial within five days on charges of involvement in the alleged leftist army officers' Aspida conspiracy. . . . Greek government bans left-wing parties.	Representatives of 12 West African states agree to form a common market.	A course to train 32 Latin American doctors and medical researchers in family planning begins at the Univ. of Salvador in Buenos Aires. . . . A bomb kills Dominican Sen. Rafael Casimiro Castro.	U.S. Marines resume the assault on Hill 881 at Khesanh.
May 5	U.S. rejects a Common Market offer of a 10% guaranteed access to its grain markets during a bargaining session of the Kennedy Round of tariff-cutting negotiations. . . . U.N. Security Council again meets in an effort to resolve the Middle East crisis.	Denmark and Norway condemn the army coup in Greece.	A Ghanaian military court sentences the two leaders of the April 17 attempted coup, Lt. Samuel Arthur and Lt. Moses Yeboah, to death. . . . Arab gunners shell the Israeli town of Ramin from Lebanese territory. . . . About 200 South African Jewish students demonstrate in front of a beer hall near Johannesburg to protest alleged neo-Nazi activities by German-born youths.	Reports indicate that acting Indonesian Pres. Suharto has carried out major changes in the Indonesian Army's high command.	U.S. troops capture Hill 881 after vicious fighting.
	A	**B**	**C**	**D**	**E**
	Includes developments that affect more than one world region, international organizations and important meetings of major world leaders.	*Includes all domestic and regional developments in Europe, including the Soviet Union, Turkey, Cyprus and Malta.*	*Includes all domestic and regional developments in Africa and the Middle East, including Iraq and Iran and excluding Cyprus, Turkey and Afghanistan.*	*Includes all domestic and regional developments in Latin America, the Caribbean and Canada.*	*Includes all domestic and regional developments in Asia and Pacific nations, extending from Afghanistan through all the Pacific Islands, except Hawaii.*

U.S. Politics & Social Issues	U.S. Foreign Policy & Defense	U.S. Economy & Environment	Science, Technology & Nature	Culture, Leisure & Life Style	
Former Ala. Gov. George Wallace makes a political visit to Terre Haute, Indiana.	Gen. William Westmoreland visits ex-Pres. Eisenhower who reiterates his support for the Vietnamese War. . . . About 9,000 people march in two N.Y.C. parades supporting the war in Vietnam.				April 29
	Despite the reported Sino-Soviet agreement on aid to North Vietnam, Communist China declares that it will not take "any united action" with the Soviet Union on the Vietnamese War. . . . Rev. Martin Luther King again calls on draft-age men who oppose the war to declare themselves conscientious objectors.		Tornadoes kill 52 people in southern Minnesota.		April 30
	U.S. Navy Vice Adm. Hyman Rickover denounces the growing reliance on cost-effectiveness studies for decisions on weapons systems.		A U.S. Public Health Service survey asserts that there is a strong relationship between smoking and certain physical ailments such as heart disease.	Bernard Malamud's *The Fixer* wins the Pulitzer Prize for fiction.	May 1
Gary, Indiana Democrats nominate a Negro attorney, Richard Hatcher, as candidate for mayor. . . . Ky. Gov. Edward Breathitt announces that he will call out the National Guard to prevent civil rights demonstrations at the upcoming Kentucky Derby. . . . At a Senate Internal Security Subcommittee hearing Cleveland detective John Ungvary says that the 1966 Cleveland riots were planned by black nationalist groups. . . . Two Negroes file a job discrimination suit against Philip Morris Inc.	Reports indicate that Gen. William Westmoreland, commander of U.S. forces in Vietnam, has asked Pres. Johnson for 600,000 troops.	Pres. Johnson signs a bill delaying a nationwide railroad strike for 47 more days.		British poet W. H. Auden wins the National Medal for literature.	May 2
A federal district court declares unconstitutional the Alabama statute countering the federal guide-lines for school desegregation. . . . Rev. Martin Luther King Jr. arrives in Louisville, Ky. . . . Office of Economic Opportunity Director Sargent Shriver announces a $1 million emergency grant for a four-month food stamp program in the U.S. South.	House Republican leader Gerald Ford says that Pres. Johnson's determination to fight communism in Vietnam has the House's "overwhelming" support. . . . Pres. Johnson says that he has no immediate plans to act on Westmoreland's request for a substantial increase in American forces in Vietnam. . . . Joint Chiefs of Staff Chmn. Earle Wheeler says that there is "no military justification for any reduction of military forces in Central Europe.". . . Wheeler criticizes the delay in the deployment of an anti-missile defense system.	Pres. Johnson reaffirms his support for the proposed six percent tax surcharge.			May 3
	Sen. J. William Fulbright apologizes for "any embarrassment" to certain members of Congress whom he referred to as being closely tied to "the military-industrial complex" in a recent newspaper interview.		U.S. launches Lunar Orbiter 4 whose mission is to provide photos of the moon's surface.		May 4
About 85 demonstrators march in Louisville, Ky. for open housing.	Sen. Robert Kennedy says that Democrats will have "to shape a fresh set of goals and programs" for the future.				May 5

F	G	H	I	J
Includes elections, federal-state relations, civil rights and liberties, crime, the judiciary, education, health care, poverty, urban affairs and population.	*Includes formation and debate of U.S. foreign and defense policies, veterans' affairs and defense spending. (Relations with specific foreign countries are usually found under the region concerned.)*	*Includes business, labor, agriculture, taxation, transportation, consumer affairs, monetary and fiscal policy, natural resources, and pollution.*	*Includes worldwide scientific, medical and technological developments, natural phenomena, U.S. weather, natural disasters, and accidents.*	*Includes the arts, religion, scholarship, communications media, sports, entertainment, fashions, fads and social life.*

	World Affairs	Europe	Africa & the Middle East	The Americas	Asia & the Pacific
May 6		Greek government announces that municipal and communal elections are abolished.		The New York Times reports that 16 U.S. Special Forces advisers are currently training Bolivian troops in counter-guerrilla warfare.	North Vietnam displays captured U.S. pilots in Hanoi.
May 7		British poet Stephen Spender resigns as contributing editor for the magazine Encounter because of its alleged former support by the CIA.		Members of the Dominican Revolutionary Party, formerly led by ex-Pres. Juan Bosch, resign from the National Congress.	
May 8		In an apparent effort to improve Britain's chances for Common Market membership, British P.M. Harold Wilson says that his country might not purchase U.S. Poseidon missiles to replace the Polaris missiles currently being installed in several British submarines.	A land mine blows up an Israeli military vehicle.		Communists assault the U.S. base camp at Conthien. . . . South Korean police arrest three left-of-center politicians.
May 9		NATO defense ministers make official their agreement on a "flexible response" strategy of countering aggression as opposed to "massive retaliation.". . . U.S. officials confirm that West Germany has asked to be given a veto power over the firing of nuclear weapons from West German soil. . . . Greek Interior Min. Stylianos Patakos announces that about half of the 6,138 political prisoners held on the island of Yioura will be released within 10 days.	Ghana executes the April 17 coup leaders, Lt. Moses Yeboah and Lt. Samuel Arthur.	Brazil signs a treaty banning nuclear weapons from Central and South America and the Caribbean. . . . Dominican Pres. Joaquin Balaguer says that recent terrorist activity in his country is the work of "communist agents.". . . Government troops clash with guerrillas in Bolivia.	
May 10		British House of Commons votes 488-62 to support the government's decision to seek Common Market membership.		Reports indicate that the Indonesian cabinet has stripped ex-Pres. Sukarno of his title of chief-of-state. . . . Guatemala's Roman Catholic bishops express their "deepest concern and anxiety" about growing right-wing terrorism.	Two Soviet destroyers scrape the U.S. destroyer Walker in the Sea of Japan. . . . U.S. Navy planes pound the port of Haiphong.
May 11	U.N. Secretariat reports that Britain earned $173 million and the U.S. $101 million from their investments in South Africa for 1965.	Britain formally applies for full membership to the Common Market.	U.N. Secy. Gen. U Thant deplores the Arab raids against Israel.	Reports indicate that a severe heat wave has killed at least 70 Mexican children in recent weeks.	U.S. officials report 274 combat deaths during the April 30-May 6 period. Two-thirds of the deaths occurred at the battle of Khesanh. . . . Civilian-operated pacification program in South Vietnam is turned over to the American military command. . . . Two Soviet destroyers again scrape the U.S. destroyer Walker in the Sea of Japan allegedly because the ship was too near the Soviet coast. . . . Pro-Communist rioting breaks out in Hong Kong.
May 12			Saudi Arabia charges that Egyptian planes attacked the Saudi border town of Najran on May 11. . . . A South-West African court sentences black nationalist Gerson Veil to five years at hard labor for alleged sabotage.	Venezuela reports that it intercepted a small guerrilla landing party, including four Cubans, on May 8.	Viet Cong attack two U.S. air bases at Bienhoa near Saigon. . . . Philippine government report on the Huk communist guerrilla movement says they control areas of Central Luzon.

A	B	C	D	E
Includes developments that affect more than one world region, international organizations and important meetings of major world leaders.	Includes all domestic and regional developments in Europe, including the Soviet Union, Turkey, Cyprus and Malta.	Includes all domestic and regional developments in Africa and the Middle East, including Iraq and Iran and excluding Cyprus, Turkey and Afghanistan.	Includes all domestic and regional developments in Latin America, the Caribbean and Canada.	Includes all domestic and regional developments in Asia and Pacific nations, extending from Afghanistan through all the Pacific Islands, except Hawaii.

U.S. Politics & Social Issues	U.S. Foreign Policy & Defense	U.S. Economy & Environment	Science, Technology & Nature	Culture, Leisure & Life Style	
Rev. Martin Luther King confirms reports that civil rights leaders have canceled plans to interrupt the Kentucky Derby. . . . N.J. Supreme Court rules that a defective child's "right to life" takes precedence over its parents' desire to prevent its birth by abortion. . . . Reports indicate that Univ. of Pennsylvania trustees have decided to terminate contracts for U.S. Army and Air Force chemical and biological warfare research projects at the school.		Interior Secy. Stewart Udall proposes regulations for leasing government-owned oil-shale lands for research and development.			May 6
	Economist John Kenneth Galbraith announces that Pres. Johnson has asked the State Dept. "to make some representation" to the Greek government on behalf of Andreas Papandreou.	UAW Pres. Walter Reuther acknowledges that his union once received $50,000 from the CIA for international union activities.			May 7
About 75 Negroes and whites march through Louisville, Ky. in an open-housing demonstration. . . . New Orleans Dist. Atty. James Garrison announces that he has begun to investigate the CIA and FBI which he charges are withholding evidence about the Kennedy assassination.	U.S. protests the public display of American pilots in North Vietnam as a violation of the Geneva convention.	AFL-CIO Pres. George Meany says that his organization has never received any money from the CIA.	U.S. satellite Orbiter 4 enters a high elliptical orbit around the moon. . . . A more liberal abortion law goes into effect in North Carolina.		May 8
	Pres. Johnson asserts that the Democratic Party could win an "overwhelming mandate" in 1968 if the administration's Vietnam policy is supported. . . . Dr. John Foster, director of defense research and engineering for the Defense Dept. says that an "area defense" against incoming missiles is feasible through use of X-rays from thermonuclear explosions.	U.S. Senate passes the administration's bill restoring the seven percent investment tax credit.			May 9
Negroes riot at Jackson State College, a Negro college in Jackson Miss., when two Negro policemen arrest an automobile speeder on campus.	A nationwide "teach-in" against the Vietnamese War takes place in more than 80 colleges. . . . Defense Dept. announces that the General Dynamics Corp. will produce the F-111 military jet plane.				May 10
Jackson, Miss. Mayor Allen Thompson visits the Jackson State campus and succeeds in dispersing a student mob by promising to withdraw police from the campus. . . . Court order banning night marches in Louisville is changed to allow open-housing demonstrations between 6:00 p.m. and 8:30 p.m. . . . A federal court dismisses a job discrimination suit filed by Negroes against the Monsanto Co. and the Oil, Chemical and Atomic Workers Union. . . . Students at Howard Univ., Washington, D.C., boycott classes to protest administrative action against students who prevented Selective Service Director Lewis Hershey from speaking in March.	U.S. Senate passes a bill extending the military draft by 70-2. . . . Three hundred twenty-one Columbia Univ. faculty members urge Pres. Johnson to "extricate" the U.S. from the Vietnamese War. . . . Defense Secy. McNamara says that the U.S. may curtail military aid to Greece unless constitutional rule is restored.		U.S. satellite Lunar Orbiter 4 begins taking photos of the moon's surface and transmits them back to earth.		May 11
H. Rap Brown replaces Stokely Carmichael as chairman of SNCC. . . . Jackson State College Pres. John Peoples says that 90% of the rioters were "unscrupulous outsiders.". . . Campbell County Board of Education, Tenn. reinstates Gary Scott who was dismissed on April 14 for teaching that man has descended from a lower order of animals.		Business economists of the large U.S. companies forecast a federal deficit of $15-$18 billion for fiscal 1968.	Soviet Union launches a satellite.	University of Plano (Tex.) Press publishes Moise Tshombe's *My Fifteen Months in Government* . . . . Swedish actress Pia Degermark wins the Cannes Film Festival's best actress award for her role in *Elvira Madigan*.	May 12
F	**G**	**H**	**I**	**J**	
Includes elections, federal-state relations, civil rights and liberties, crime, the judiciary, education, health care, poverty, urban affairs and population.	*Includes formation and debate of U.S. foreign and defense policies, veterans' affairs and defense spending. (Relations with specific foreign countries are usually found under the region concerned.)*	*Includes business, labor, agriculture, taxation, transportation, consumer affairs, monetary and fiscal policy, natural resources, and pollution.*	*Includes worldwide scientific, medical and technological developments, natural phenomena, U.S. weather, natural disasters, and accidents.*	*Includes the arts, religion, scholarship, communications media, sports, entertainment, fashions, fads and social life.*	

	World Affairs	Europe	Africa & the Middle East	The Americas	Asia & the Pacific
May 13			Legislative Assembly of French Somaliland votes to change the name of the country to the French Afar Territory. . . . Yemen indicts two U.S. AID mission officials on charges of having carried out a bazooka attack against military installations in Taiz.		North Vietnamese howitzers hit U.S. positions near Conthien and Giolinh. . . . Pro-Communist rioting continues in Hong Kong.
May 14		An Athens newspaper lists 2,500 people known to be held by the government.	Egypt alerts its troops and begins moving them into the Sinai Peninsula.		*Chicago Daily News* publishes an interview in which Communist Chinese Premier Chou En-lai allegedly says that his country will send troops to North Vietnam if it is invaded by the U.S.
May 15	After three years of bargaining, the 53 nations participating in the Kennedy Round tariff-cutting negotiations reach an agreement which reduces industrial tariffs by about one-third.	Greece announces that it is abrogating its border agreement with Yugoslavia which permits citizens of the two countries living in the border area to have free movement across the border.	Egyptian and Syrian military commanders meet to coordinate military strategy and tactics. . . . Sudanese Premier Saadik el Mahdi loses a vote of confidence in the Constituent Assembly.	Government troops clash with guerrillas in Venezuela.	Heavy fighting rages along the demilitarized zone.
May 16		French Pres. Charles de Gaulle again rejects Britain's renewed application for Common Market membership. . . . Italian Foreign Min. Amintore Fanfani concludes an official visit to Moscow by signing consular, tourism and agricultural agreements with Soviet authorities. . . . French printers and newspaper workers go on strike.	Yemen releases two U.S. AID mission officials indicted May 13 on charges of having carried out a bazooka attack against military installations in Taiz.	Venezuelan Foreign Min. Ignacio Iribarren Borges says that his country will ask the OAS to again take up the problem of Cuban subversion in Latin American countries.	Communist China denies that the interview cited in the *Chicago Daily News* story ever took place. . . . Massive anti-British demonstrations throughout Communist China culminate when a Chinese mob sacks the home of British consul Peter Hewitt in Shanghai. . . . North Vietnamese artillery attack U.S. planes along the demilitarized zone.
May 17		Britain declares that it "fully supports the Hong Kong government in fulfilling its duty.". . . Yugoslav Parliament re-elects Marshal Tito to another presidential term. . . . Greece announces the dismissal of hundreds of army officers. . . . Four major French trade unions stage a 24-hour strike.	Two U.S. AID mission officials held by the government leave Yemen for Ethiopia.		North Vietnamese gunners pound U.S. positions along the demilitarized zone.
May 18		Eight Soviet technicians arrive in Brazil to begin work on a Brazilian petrochemical complex.	Sudanese Constituent Assembly elects Mohammed Ahmed Mahgoub as premier. . . . Egypt demands that U.N. troops leave their positions in the Sinai Peninsula. . . . South African police intercept a guerrilla band crossing into South-West Africa from Zambia.	Cuba acknowledges sending guerrillas to Venezuela and says that such action is justified since it is part of the "fight against imperialism."	A force of 5,500 U.S. and South Vietnamese troops invade part of the demilitarized zone separating North and South Vietnam.
May 19	U.N. General Assembly votes 85-2 to establish an 11-member U.N. Council for South-West Africa to administer the territory until its independence.	For the first time since the Communist takeover in 1947, Hungarian voters are given the choice between two rival candidates in nine of the 349 parliamentary seats. . . . Soviet Union ratifies a U.N. treaty banning weapons of mass-destruction from outer space. . . . Yuri Andropov, Soviet CP secretary responsible for relations with foreign Communist parties, becomes chairman of the State Security Committee (KGB).	U.N. accedes to Egypt's demand to withdraw its troops from the Gaza Strip and Sharm el Sheikh at the southern tip of the Sinai Peninsula.		U.S. planes bomb the center of Hanoi for the first time.
May 20		*Torrey Canyon* tanker oil slick now coats the western shores of Brittany. French and British volunteers handwash thousands of endangered birds which risk asphyxiation from the oil slick.	Reports indicate that Egypt has deployed about 58,000 troops along its border with Israel and that Israeli tanks have also moved to the border zone.		U.S. planes bomb the Hoalac MiG airfield near Hanoi. . . . Several thousand demonstrators march on the Soviet embassy in Peking shouting "down with Soviet revisionism."
	A	**B**	**C**	**D**	**E**
	Includes developments that affect more than one world region, international organizations and important meetings of major world leaders.	*Includes all domestic and regional developments in Europe, including the Soviet Union, Turkey, Cyprus and Malta.*	*Includes all domestic and regional developments in Africa and the Middle East, including Iraq and Iran and excluding Cyprus, Turkey and Afghanistan.*	*Includes all domestic and regional developments in Latin America, the Caribbean and Canada.*	*Includes all domestic and regional developments in Asia and Pacific nations, extending from Afghanistan through all the Pacific Islands, except Hawaii.*

U.S. Politics & Social Issues	U.S. Foreign Policy & Defense	U.S. Economy & Environment	Science, Technology & Nature	Culture, Leisure & Life Style	
	About 70,000 pro-war demonstrators march in N.Y.C.				May 13
Labor Secy. Willard Wirtz orders the federal government to refuse bids from contractors who fail to certify that there is no racial discrimination in their companies.	A Protestant weekly magazine *Christian Century* criticizes evangelist Billy Graham for supporting the Vietnamese War.				May 14
U.S. Supreme Court rules that children are entitled to the same procedural protections afforded by the Bill of Rights to adults. . . . Senate allocates money for the 1968 Peace Corps program.	Sen. John Sherman Cooper (R, Ky.) urges the administration to limit its bombing of North and South Vietnam to infiltration routes. . . . U.S. Defense Dept. says that a U.S. plane might have crashed in Communist China earlier in the day.			U.S. painter Edward Hopper dies in New York at 84. . . . New Directions publishes the *Selected Letters of Dylan Thomas*.	May 15
A Houston policeman is killed during a riot at the predominantly Negro Texas Southern Univ. by sniper fire during a campus riot. . . . House Appropriations subcommittee releases testimony of FBI Dir. J. Edgar Hoover charging that SNCC Chmn. Stokely Carmichael has been associated with the Revolutionary Action Movement (RAM), an organization dedicated to the overthrow of "the capitalist system.". . . Rev. Martin Luther King Jr. says that SCLC has chosen Cleveland, O. for civil rights action during the coming summer.	Sen. Joseph Clark (D, Pa.) urges the administration to institute an indefinite cease-fire in Vietnam.				May 16
A conference of anti-Castro Cuban exile leaders is held in Los Angeles. . . . Police begin arresting students and searching dormitories for arms at Texas Southern Univ.	NAACP announces its support for a lottery system draft. . . . U.S. State Dept. announces that Hungarian charge d'affaires in Washington, Janos Radvanyi, has been granted political asylum in the U.S.		Soviet Union launches a satellite.	*The New York Times* journalist Harrison Salisbury wins the Sidney Hillman Foundation Award for his reports from North Vietnam.	May 17
Tenn. Gov. Buford Ellington signs a bill repealing the law prohibiting "any theory that denies the story of (the) divine creation of man as taught in the Bible."	Defense Secy. McNamara says that "very little progress" has been made in talks with the Soviet Union about curtailing an anti-missile defense system.			Oxford University Press publishes Arnold Toynbee's *Acquaintances*.	May 18
Justice Dept. files desegregation suits against the Decatur and Webster County school systems in Ga.				Interior Secy. Stewart Udall, a Mormon, challenges his church's doctrine holding Negroes to be the subject of a "divine curse."	May 19
A former CIA employee, Thomas Braden, says that a CIA agent was the editor of the European magazine, *Encounter*, during a certain period.	Joint Chiefs of Staff Chmn. Gen. Earle Wheeler urges that a decision be taken to build an anti-missile defense system "within the next few months."				May 20

F	G	H	I	J
Includes elections, federal-state relations, civil rights and liberties, crime, the judiciary, education, health care, poverty, urban affairs and population.	Includes formation and debate of U.S. foreign and defense policies, veterans' affairs and defense spending. (Relations with specific foreign countries are usually found under the region concerned.)	Includes business, labor, agriculture, taxation, transportation, consumer affairs, monetary and fiscal policy, natural resources, and pollution.	Includes worldwide scientific, medical and technological developments, natural phenomena, U.S. weather, natural disasters, and accidents.	Includes the arts, religion, scholarship, communications media, sports, entertainment, fashions, fads and social life.

	World Affairs	Europe	Africa & the Middle East	The Americas	Asia & the Pacific
May 21		Greece scores the European communist states for "hypocritically" protesting the suspension of constitutional rights in Greece.	Israel completes partial mobilization of its reserves while Egypt announces the total mobilization of its reserves.	Army Maj. Richard Pearce defects to Cuba in a small private plane.	Police arrest more pro-communist demonstrators in Hong Kong.
May 22		A three-man delegation of European Socialists arrives in Greece to intercede for the political prisoners. . . . Fourth Congress of the Soviet Writers' Union opens in Moscow amid recurring reports of unrest in Soviet artistic circles. . . . A fire kills 322 people in the second largest department store in Brussels. . . . No evidence of arson is seen although Communist youths had been intermittently picketing an American sales promotion display in the store since May 13.	Egyptian Pres. Gamal Abdel Nasser threatens to halt all Israeli shipping through the Gulf of Aqaba.	Quebec Premier Daniel Johnson announces that his province and the French government have agreed to cooperate on several cultural and financial projects.	Communist China says it will intervene in the Vietnamese War if North Vietnam asks it to do so. . . . North Korean bombs kill two U.S. soldiers in their barracks near the demilitarized zone.
May 23		A West German poll indicates that 74% of West Germans favor direct contacts between East and West German leaders. . . . Greek government confirms that the body of Jikiforos Mandelaras, a defense counsel in the recent Aspida treason trial of alleged leftist military officers, was found washed up on the island of Rhodes.	Israeli Premier Levi Eshkol warns that an Egyptian blockade of the Gulf of Aqaba would constitute "an act of aggression" against Israel.		Reports indicate that the first phase of the allied drive into the demilitarized zone has ended and that allied troops have withdrawn to positions just south of the buffer area. . . . Intensity of combat abates but fighting continues during the 24-hour truce in honor of Buddha's birthday in South Vietnam.
May 24	U.N. Secy. Gen. U Thant confers with Egyptian Pres. Nasser in Cairo about the Middle East crisis.	Israeli Foreign Min. Abba Eban meets with French Pres. de Gaulle about the Middle East crisis.	A force of 20,000 Saudi Arabian troops crosses into Jordan.		
May 25		Soviet Air Force defector Vasily Ilyich Epatko crash-lands his plane in Hochstadt, West Germany.			
May 26			Iraq says that its troops are moving into Syria to reinforce Syrian troops poised on the Israeli border.		
May 27		Greek police arrest two more political leaders.	Reports indicate that Egypt has shifted some of its 35,000-man force in Yemen to the Sinai Peninsula.	Two thousand armed strikers clash with police in Guadeloupe. . . . Colombia signs a $100 million loan agreement with the U.S. . . . Cuba charges that a U.S. helicopter from the Guantanamo naval base violated Cuban airspace and landed on Cuban soil for six minutes.	Communist China demands that Mongolia publicly apologize for an alleged attack on Chinese nationals in Ulan Bator on May 21. . . . North Korean gunboats attack South Korean fishing boats.
May 28			Egyptian Pres. Nasser rules out a negotiated peace in the Middle East until Palestinian Arabs are returned to their homeland in Israel.		North Korean gunboats again attack South Korean fishing boats.
May 29	U.N. Secy. Gen. U Thant appeals to the Greek government "on humanitarian grounds on behalf of the political detainees.". . . U.N. Israeli delegate Gideon Rafael assails the blockade of the Gulf of Aqaba.		Egyptian Pres. Nasser tells the National Assembly that the blockade of the Gulf of Aqaba has Soviet support. . . . Egyptian and Israeli troops clash along their common border.		Viet Cong blow up the Hue Hotel.
	A	**B**	**C**	**D**	**E**
	Includes developments that affect more than one world region, international organizations and important meetings of major world leaders.	Includes all domestic and regional developments in Europe, including the Soviet Union, Turkey, Cyprus and Malta.	Includes all domestic and regional developments in Africa and the Middle East, including Iraq and Iran and excluding Cyprus, Turkey and Afghanistan.	Includes all domestic and regional developments in Latin America, the Caribbean and Canada.	Includes all domestic and regional developments in Asia and Pacific nations, extending from Afghanistan through all the Pacific Islands, except Hawaii.

U.S. Politics & Social Issues	U.S. Foreign Policy & Defense	U.S. Economy & Environment	Science, Technology & Nature	Culture, Leisure & Life Style	
	Joint Chiefs of Staff Chairman Earl Wheeler says that the U.S. has "no intention of invading North Vietnam."				May 21
U.S. Supreme Court rules that alien homosexuals can be deported under the 1952 Immigration and Nationality Act which bars entry to "persons afflicted with a psychopathic personality.". . . New Orleans Dist. Atty. James Garrison declares that Lee Harvey Oswald did not kill Pres. Kennedy but that former employees of the CIA, "a large number of them Cubans", were responsible.	U.S. State Dept. advises U.S. citizens not to visit Israel and its neighboring Arab states in view of the growing crisis. . . . In a Memorial Day proclamation, Pres. Johnson appeals to North Vietnam to accept a negotiated settlement of the Vietnamese War.		Soviet Union launches a satellite. . . . U.S. launches a communication satellite into orbit.	U.S. Negro lyricist Langston Hughes dies in N.Y. at 65. . . . Knopf publishes Henry Steele Commager's *The Search for a Usable Past*.	May 22
	Sen. Thruston Morton (R, Ky.) appeals to Pres. Johnson to eschew a policy of "total military victory" in Vietnam. . . . Pres. Johnson declares that the U.S. considers the Gulf of Aqaba "to be an international waterway.". . . An unnamed State Dept. official says that the U.S. would attack Communist China if it intervened in the Vietnamese War on a massive scale.				May 23
House defeats, 197-168, a proposal to distribute certain federal education funds through the state departments of education instead of directly to impoverished school districts. Opponents of the proposal included the administration and civil rights groups.			U.S. launches Explorer 34 whose mission is to measure solar and galactic cosmic rays within and at the boundary of the earth's magnetosphere.	National Institute of Arts and Letters awards its gold medal for history and biography to Arthur Schlesinger Jr.	May 24
	Israeli Foreign Min. Abba Eban meets with Pres. Johnson in Washington.				May 25
	Israeli Foreign Min. Abba Eban again confers with Pres. Johnson in Washington. . . . U.S. Defense Dept. says that a Navy plane might have strayed into Communist China but it does not specify a date.			Vatican decrees that Roman Catholic sacraments can be given to Protestants and members of Eastern Orthodox churches under special circumstances.	May 26
					May 27
					May 28
U.S. Supreme Court declares unconstitutional a voter-approved amendment to the California Constitution which gives property owners "absolute discretion" in resale and rental of housing.			Esro 2, a satellite built by ten European nations, fails to enter orbit.	G.W. Pabst, the Austrian film director of *The Three-Penny Opera*, dies in Vienna at 82. . . . Scribners publishes *By-Line: Ernest Hemingway*, a collection of the author's newspaper articles over four decades.	May 29
F	G	H	I	J	
Includes elections, federal-state relations, civil rights and liberties, crime, the judiciary, education, health care, poverty, urban affairs and population.	Includes formation and debate of U.S. foreign and defense policies, veterans' affairs and defense spending. (Relations with specific foreign countries are usually found under the region concerned.)	Includes business, labor, agriculture, taxation, transportation, consumer affairs, monetary and fiscal policy, natural resources, and pollution.	Includes worldwide scientific, medical and technological developments, natural phenomena, U.S. weather, natural disasters, and accidents.	Includes the arts, religion, scholarship, communications media, sports, entertainment, fashions, fads and social life.	

	World Affairs	Europe	Africa & the Middle East	The Americas	Asia & the Pacific
May 30	Egypt's U.N. delegate Mohamad Awad El Kony asserts that the Strait of Tiran which controls access to the Gulf of Aqaba is in Egyptian territorial waters and can be blocked at will.	Reports indicate that Turkey has given the Soviet Union permission to send 10 warships through the Dardanelles into the Mediterranean.	Egypt and Jordan sign a defense pact and the Jordanian Army is placed under Egyptian command. . . . Nigeria's Eastern Region secedes from the rest of Nigeria and declares its independence as the Republic of Biafra.		U.S. bombers carry out their ninth raid against the Hoalac MiG air base.
May 31	U.N. Security Council meets in an effort to solve the Middle East crisis.		Nigeria's federal government cuts all telecommunications and postal services with the Eastern Region.		
June 1		Common Market countries reach agreement on trade of major agricultural products.	Kenyan Pres. Jomo Kenyatta announces that Somali guerrillas who surrender within a month will not be prosecuted. . . . Gen. Moshe Dayan is appointed Israeli defense minister.	Finance Min. Mitchell Sharp presents the second largest budget in Canadian history--$740 million.	U.S. reports a record 313 Vietnam War combat deaths for the period May 21-27. . . . U.S. consul in Macao advises U.S. citizens to leave because of pro-Communist demonstrations.
June 2		Soviet Union accuses the U.S. of bombing the Soviet ship *Turkestan*. . . . Soviet Union charges that U.S. jets bombed a Soviet merchant ship in the port of Haiphong on the morning of June 2. . . . Police kill a demonstrator during riots protesting the visit of the Shah of Iran in West Berlin. . . . U.S. authorities in West Germany grant political asylum in the U.S. to Soviet Air Force pilot Vasily Ilyich Epatko.	Syrian and Israeli troops clash along their common border.		Fighting rages between U.S. and North Vietnamese troops near Danang.
June 3			Israeli Defense Min. Moshe Dayan says that Israel is in no need of military allies "to help fight its battle."		Fierce fighting continues between U.S. and North Vietnamese troops near Danang.
June 4					
June 5	Soviet Union and the U.S. assure each other on the "hot line" that they do not intend to intervene militarily in the Arab-Israeli war.	A French court convicts eight people for complicity in the October 1965 abduction and probable murder in France of Moroccan opposition leader Mehdi Ben Barka. . . . France announces the suspension of shipments of military equipment and spare parts to the Middle East. . . . *The New York Times* prints a letter from Soviet author Aleksandr Solzhenitsyn denouncing censorship in the Soviet Union. . . . Soviet Union reaffirms that the U.S. bombed the Soviet ship *Turkestan*.	Israel attacks Egypt and Jordan, wiping out the Egyptian air force in several hours and driving deep into Jordan and the Sinai Peninsula.		France explodes a low-yield nuclear device in the Pacific.
June 6	U.N. Security Council unanimously adopts a resolution calling for an immediate cease-fire between Israel and the Arab states.	Soviet Union demands the withdrawal of Israeli troops from Egyptian territory.	Israel continues its rout of Egyptian forces in the Sinai but it meets fierce Jordanian resistance in the Old City of Jerusalem. Egyptian Pres. Nasser closes the Suez Canal to all shipping and severs relations with the U.S. and Britain.		
June 7	U.N. Security Council again calls for a cease-fire in the Middle East War.	West Berlin students negotiate directly with East German authorities for permission to allow a student convoy to pass through East Germany to attend a West German student demonstrator's funeral in Hamburg.	Israel assumes virtual control of the Sinai Peninsula and the Arab section of Jerusalem. Reports indicate that fighting has begun on the Syrian-Israeli border.	Bolivian Pres. Rene Barrientos Ortuno declares a state of siege after secondary school students in La Paz demonstrate against the government.	
	A	B	C	D	E
	Includes developments that affect more than one world region, international organizations and important meetings of major world leaders.	*Includes all domestic and regional developments in Europe, including the Soviet Union, Turkey, Cyprus and Malta.*	*Includes all domestic and regional developments in Africa and the Middle East, including Iraq and Iran and excluding Cyprus, Turkey and Afghanistan.*	*Includes all domestic and regional developments in Latin America, the Caribbean and Canada.*	*Includes all domestic and regional developments in Asia and Pacific nations, extending from Afghanistan through all the Pacific Islands, except Hawaii.*

U.S. Politics & Social Issues	U.S. Foreign Policy & Defense	U.S. Economy & Environment	Science, Technology & Nature	Culture, Leisure & Life Style	
			U.S. traffic fatalities during the Memorial Day week-end total a record 608.		May 30
FBI Director J. Edgar Hoover charges civil rights leaders with issuing an "open invitation" to violence by naming cities where summer violence is expected.	State Secy. Dean Rusk addresses an International Conference on Water for Peace in Washington.				May 31
	U.S. announces that it will remove all American dependents from Biafra.		Soviet Union launches a satellite.		June 1
Rioting breaks out in Boston at a city Welfare Dept. building and spreads to the city's Negro neighborhood. Negro mobs set fires, loot stores and throw rocks and bottles at policemen. . . . Justice Dept. files a desegregation suit against the Houston Independent School District.					June 2
Boston Mayor John Collins says that the rioting is "the worst manifestation of disrespect for the rights of others this city has ever seen."	U.S. denies that it bombed the Soviet ship *Turkestan*.			Belgian symphonic conductor Andre Cluytens dies in Paris at 62.	June 3
Roving bands of Negro youths continue to set fires and loot stores in Boston.				Arthur Miller's *Death of a Salesman* wins the Emmy award for best television drama of the 1966-1967 season.	June 4
About 40 armed Mexican-Americans take control of the new Mexican town of Tierra Amarilla briefly before fleeing into the mountains.	U.S. State Dept. says that it will "steer an even-handed course" during the Middle East hostilities.	An electrical power failure cuts off electricity for up to three hours for about 13 million residents of parts of Pa., Md. and N.J.	Soviet Union launches a satellite.		June 5
	U.S. government refutes Egypt's charges that American planes attacked Egypt.		Soviet Union launches a satellite.		June 6
Justice Dept. files a school desegregation suit against Montgomery County, Miss.	A U.S. court convicts Air Force Sgt. Herbert Boeckenhaupt to 30 years in prison for conspiring to reveal U.S. defense secrets to the Soviet Union.	For the first time since W.W. II., the House rejects a bill to increase the permanent ceiling on the national debt.		Humorist Dorothy Parker dies in New York at 73.	June 7
F	G	H	I	J	
Includes elections, federal-state relations, civil rights and liberties, crime, the judiciary, education, health care, poverty, urban affairs and population.	Includes formation and debate of U.S. foreign and defense policies, veterans' affairs and defense spending. (Relations with specific foreign countries are usually found under the region concerned.)	Includes business, labor, agriculture, taxation, transportation, consumer affairs, monetary and fiscal policy, natural resources, and pollution.	Includes worldwide scientific, medical and technological developments, natural phenomena, U.S. weather, natural disasters, and accidents.	Includes the arts, religion, scholarship, communications media, sports, entertainment, fashions, fads and social life.	

	World Affairs	Europe	Africa & the Middle East	The Americas	Asia & the Pacific
June 8	Soviet Amb.-to-UN Nikolai Fedorenko condemns Israel for its attack on the Arab states.		Egypt accepts the U.N.'s cease-fire order. . . . Israeli planes accidentally attack a U.S. electronics ship, the *Liberty*, about 15 miles north of the Sinai Peninsula.	Four government officials resign in Argentina to protest a pending law that will grant oil concessions to foreign companies.	In a fiercely contested election marked by violence, South Korean Pres. Chung Hee Park's Democratic Republican Party wins a majority of the National Assembly seats. . . . U.S. reports 218 Vietnam War combat fatalities for the period of May 28-June 3.
June 9	An international treaty to recognize the "right of each landlocked state of free access to the sea" comes into force. . . . U.N. Security Council unanimously adopts a resolution calling for an immediate cease-fire between Israel and Syria.	Reports indicate that West Berlin police chief Erich Dusing has been fired. . . . Talks between Spain and Britain about the future of Gibraltar break down. . . . Reports indicate that 79 Soviet writers have signed a petition deploring the failure of the Soviet Writers' Congress to take up the question of censorship.	Syria agrees to a cease-fire. . . . Malawi's Pres. Hastings Kamuzu Banda proposes that the U.S. help finance a rail link between his country and Mozambique. . . . Egyptian Pres. Nasser announces his resignation whereupon many Egyptians demonstrate in favor of his staying on.		
June 10	Syrian Amb.-to-U.N. George Tomeh charges that Israel is still attacking Syria. Israel denies the charges.	Soviet Union severs diplomatic relations with Israel.	Egyptian Pres. Nasser agrees to remain president.		Communist mortars fire on allied troops in the Central Highlands city of Pleiku.
June 11	Syria again accuses Israel of truce violations during the U.N. Security Council session.		Egyptian Pres. Nasser fires top ranking military officers. . . . Israel reports 679 combat fatalities during the recent fighting.		U.S. and South Korean troops report inflicting heavy casualties on North Vietnamese troops.
June 12	U.N. passes a resolution calling on Syria and Israel to prohibit any "forward military movement."	Turkey and Russia sign an agreement for the construction of a Soviet-built oil refinery in Izmir, Turkey. . . . Algerian Foreign Min. Abdelazziz Bouteflika meets with Soviet officials in Moscow. . . . Poland and Hungary sever diplomatic relations with Israel.	A land mine kills three Israeli civilians in the Gaza Strip. . . . Israeli Premier Levi Eshkol declares that his country will retain at least part of the territory that it has won.		South Korean students demanding new parliamentary elections clash with police in Seoul. . . . U.S. troops attack three Viet Cong battalions 50 miles north of Saigon. . . . India's Central Intelligence Department reports that the U.S. CIA gave money to several Indian political parties before last February's elections although the amount was inferior to the aid given by communist countries. . . . Indian mobs attack the Communist Chinese embassy in New Delhi after Chinese mobs attack the Indian embassy in Peking.
June 13		Yugoslavia severs diplomatic relations with Israel.		Quebec Premier Daniel Johnson denies charges that his Union Nationale party sought political arrangements with two Quebec separatist groups in the 1966 elections.	Communist China expels two staff members of the Indian embassy in Peking.
June 14	U.N. Security Council defeats a Soviet draft resolution calling for the condemnation of Israel and the withdrawal of its forces behind the 1949 armistice line.	Reports indicate that the Soviet Union will continue to supply the Arab countries with military aid. . . . Britain announces that it will allow Gibraltar to decide its own future in a referendum.	Israel says that it holds 5,499 Arab prisoners. Reports indicate that the Arabs hold 16 Israeli prisoners.		South Korean students demonstrate against the alleged rigging of the June 8 National Assembly elections. . . . South Vietnamese troops overwhelm a Viet Cong battalion in the Mekong Delta. . . . India expels two members of the Communist Chinese embassy in retaliation for the June 13 expulsions. . . . Communist Chinese Red Guards kick and beat two departing Indian officials at Peking airport.

A	B	C	D	E
Includes developments that affect more than one world region, international organizations and important meetings of major world leaders.	*Includes all domestic and regional developments in Europe, including the Soviet Union, Turkey, Cyprus and Malta.*	*Includes all domestic and regional developments in Africa and the Middle East, including Iraq and Iran and excluding Cyprus, Turkey and Afghanistan.*	*Includes all domestic and regional developments in Latin America, the Caribbean and Canada.*	*Includes all domestic and regional developments in Asia and Pacific nations, extending from Afghanistan through all the Pacific Islands, except Hawaii.*

U.S. Politics & Social Issues	U.S. Foreign Policy & Defense	U.S. Economy & Environment	Science, Technology & Nature	Culture, Leisure & Life Style	
Senate passes a bill requiring that a state have no more than a 10% variance in population between its largest and smallest congressional districts.	Pres. Johnson informs the Soviet Union on the "hot line" that U.S. Sixth Fleet planes are going to the aid of the stricken *Liberty* and are not entering combat.				June 8
Pres. Johnson names a cabinet-level committee to study Mexican-American problems.				Doubleday publishes *At Ease: Stories I Tell to Friends* by Dwight Eisenhower. . . . Doubleday publishes Roger Hilsman's *To Move a Nation: The Politics of Foreign Policy in the Administration of John F. Kennedy* . . . . Queen Elizabeth II issues the title of Commander of the Order of the British Empire to actor and director Richard Attenborough.	June 9
Police capture Reies Lopez Tijerina, the leader of the Mexican-American band which captured the town of Tierra Amarilla on June 5.	Pres. Johnson announces with "deepest reluctance and regret" the resignation of Deputy Defense Secy. Cyrus Vance.				June 10
The New York Times reports that two Louisiana convicts have asserted that New Orleans Dist. Atty. James Garrison's office offered them their freedom if they would cooperate in the assassination probe. . . . Violence erupts in the Negro sections of Tampa, Fla. after police shoot and kill a Negro robbery suspect. Negro mobs set fires and loot stores.			Reports from New York indicate that calf valves in human heart surgery have been successfully used.	Dr. Wolfgang Kohler, a founder of the Gestalt school of psychology, dies in Enfield, New Hampshire, at 80.	June 11
U.S. Supreme Court strikes down a Virginia law banning marriages between whites and nonwhites. . . . The worst outbreak of racial violence since the 1965 Watts Los Angeles riots erupts in Newark, N.J. Negro youths loot stores and smash windows in the downtown area. . . . Florida Gov. Claude Kirk orders 500 National Guardsmen to Tampa.	Reports indicate that the U.S. has warned Israel not to evict Arabs from the occupied areas of Jordan.	A government report warns that "danger to environmental quality. . .is among the most important domestic problems today."	Soviet Union launches satellite Venera 4 whose target is the planet Venus.	Knopf publishes Mikhail Sholokhov's *One Man's Destiny* . . . . Harper & Row publishes Martin Luther King Jr.'s *Where Do We Go From Here: Chaos or Community?*	June 12
Tampa Mayor Nick Nuccio meets with Negro leaders but rejects their demands for suspension of Patrolman Calvert, the policeman who killed the Negro robbery suspect on June 11. . . . Pres. Johnson appoints Thurgood Marshall as the first Negro to the Supreme Court. . . . Snipers open fire on police in Newark's Negro neighborhoods.		Pres. Johnson signs a bill restoring the seven percent tax credit on business investments.			June 13
In Cleveland the Rev. Martin Luther King Jr. says that the Southern Christian Leadership Conference is asking the city's bread industry for more and better jobs for Negroes. . . . One hundred Negro youths patrol the Negro sections of Tampa and help to maintain calm. . . . Leaders of nine civil rights organizations announce that they plan to concentrate their efforts on Cleveland, Ohio for the coming summer. . . . N.J. Gov. Richard Hughes visits Newark and says that he is "shocked and horrified (at the) holiday atmosphere" in the riot areas as looting continues.	Bilateral talks between the U.S. and Communist China resume in Warsaw after having been recessed since Jan. 25.		U.S. launches Mariner 5 whose mission is to orbit the sun.		June 14

F	G	H	I	J
Includes elections, federal-state relations, civil rights and liberties, crime, the judiciary, education, health care, poverty, urban affairs and population.	Includes formation and debate of U.S. foreign and defense policies, veterans' affairs and defense spending. (Relations with specific foreign countries are usually found under the region concerned.)	Includes business, labor, agriculture, taxation, transportation, consumer affairs, monetary and fiscal policy, natural resources, and pollution.	Includes worldwide scientific, medical and technological developments, natural phenomena, U.S. weather, natural disasters, and accidents.	Includes the arts, religion, scholarship, communications media, sports, entertainment, fashions, fads and social life.

	World Affairs	Europe	Africa & the Middle East	The Americas	Asia & the Pacific
June 15		Spanish press denounces British plans for a referendum in Gibraltar.	Jordanian King Hussein dismisses the anti-Nasser chief of the royal cabinet, Wasfi al-Tell.		South Vietnamese Premier Nguyen Cao Ky says that 600,000 U.S. troops will be needed to cope with what he calls the increasing buildup of North Vietnamese troops. . . . South Korean Pres. Chung Hee Park admits that there were some irregularities during the June 8 elections and promises that those guilty of wrong-doing will be punished.
June 16		Canadian External Affairs Min. Paul Martin and French Pres. de Gaulle discuss mutual relations in Paris.	Agence France Presse reports that Egyptian troops have begun to withdraw from Yemen.		Indian students break into the Communist Chinese embassy in New Delhi and attack staff members.
June 17	Soviet Premier Aleksei Kosygin arrives in New York for a special session of the U.N. General Assembly.		Foreign Ministers of 13 Arab states meet in Kuwait to plan joint political strategy in the wake of the Middle East war.		Communist China announces that it has successfully tested its first hydrogen bomb. . . . Several hundred Chinese attack the Indian embassy in Peking.
June 18					Indian P.M. Indira Gandhi refers to the Communist Chinese hydrogen bomb test as "a matter of anxiety."
June 19	U.N. Security Council votes unanimously to extend operations of the U.N. Cyprus force. . . . Soviet Premier Kosygin delivers a blistering attack against Israel in the U.N. and demands that it withdraw from the recently conquered Arab territory.	Polish CP First Secy. Wladyslaw Gomulka warns Polish Jews not to support Israel. . . . British Foreign Min. George Brown announces that Britain will grant the South Arabian Federation of Aden its independence on Jan. 9, 1968. . . . British P.M. Harold Wilson confers with French Pres. de Gaulle in Paris about Britain's terms for Common Market membership.	Jordanian King Hussein appeals to other Arab leaders to adopt a realistic policy and accept the defeat by Israel as "a turning point for the better.". . . Yemeni Royalist sources report that the Egyptian garrison at Sana, Yemen's capital, has been withdrawn.	OAS votes to investigate Venezuela's charges of Cuban subversion.	U.S. troops clash with Viet Cong units 19 miles south of Saigon. . . . Five thousand South Koreans riot in Seoul to protest the alleged rigging of the June 8 National Assembly elections.
June 20	Laurence Michelmore, commissioner of the U.N. Relief and Works Agency, says that at least 100,000 Arabs have left the Israeli conquered West Bank of the Jordan River for the East Bank which is still controlled by Jordan.	British P.M. Harold Wilson continues discussions with French Pres. de Gaulle in Paris. . . . Dutch parliamentarian Oscar Boetes says that he is a member of a secret group that has helped 10-20 U.S. servicemen stationed in West Germany to desert through Amsterdam to France during the past year.	Violence increases in the South Arabian Federation state of Aden following a British announcement that the federation will be granted its sovereignty on Jan. 9, 1968 but that British military forces will remain in the area, at least temporarily. . . . Israel makes public what are described as captured Egyptian documents showing detailed plans for a surprise military strike against Israel although with no specific date for launching the attack.		Fighting continues between U.S. troops and the Viet Cong 19 miles south of Saigon.
June 21	At the U.N. British Foreign Min. George Brown cautions Israel against annexing the Old City of Jerusalem.	Unconfirmed reports indicate that the Soviet Writers' Union has rejected the manuscript of Soviet author Aleksandr Solzhenitsyn's *The First Circle* but is willing to publish another of his novels, *The Cancer Ward* . . . . Soviet Union protests to Communist China about two of its trade officials being allegedly beaten by Red Guards in the town of Mukden. . . . French Pres. Charles de Gaulle accuses Israel of having started the war in the Middle East.	British troops clash with Arab gunmen in Aden.		

	A	B	C	D	E
	Includes developments that affect more than one world region, international organizations and important meetings of major world leaders.	Includes all domestic and regional developments in Europe, including the Soviet Union, Turkey, Cyprus and Malta.	Includes all domestic and regional developments in Africa and the Middle East, including Iraq and Iran and excluding Cyprus, Turkey and Afghanistan.	Includes all domestic and regional developments in Latin America, the Caribbean and Canada.	Includes all domestic and regional developments in Asia and Pacific nations, extending from Afghanistan through all the Pacific Islands, except Hawaii.

U.S. Politics & Social Issues	U.S. Foreign Policy & Defense	U.S. Economy & Environment	Science, Technology & Nature	Culture, Leisure & Life Style	
Tampa City Council votes the members of the youth patrol a citation for their role in restoring peace. . . . Calif. Gov. Ronald Reagan signs a bill liberalizing the state's abortion laws.					June 15
A team of doctors tells a Senate subcommittee that nutritional and medical conditions in Mississippi are "shocking.". . . Atty. Gen. Ramsey Clark issues rules prohibiting wiretapping and other forms of electronic eavesdropping by federal agencies except in "investigations related to...national security."			Soviet Union launches Cosmos 166.		June 16
Sniper fire and looting decline in intensity but still continue in Newark, N.J.					June 17
Police arrest Stokely Carmichael, former chairman of SNCC, in Atlanta for failure to move when requested by an officer. . . . Dr. Richard Weinberg of Newark City Hospital says that some 700 people have been treated during the rioting.					June 18
An NBC telecast charges that New Orleans Dist. Atty. James Garrison has intimidated potential witnesses and offered them bribes to secure their cooperation in his assassination probe. . . . U.S. Conference of Mayors opens with a call for more federal funds for the cities. . . . House passes a bill making it a federal crime to cross state lines to incite a riot.	Pres. Johnson says that "troops must be withdrawn" (from the Israeli occupied Arab territories) but not without reciprocal action to establish peace.				June 19
A federal court convicts heavyweight boxer Cassius Clay (Muhammad Ali) of violating Selective Service laws by refusing to be drafted. . . . House passes a bill making it a federal crime to "cast contempt" upon the U.S. flag "by publicly mutilating, defacing, or trampling upon it." Enactment of the bill is in reaction to recent flag-burning incidents by anti-war demonstrators. . . . Atlanta Negroes throw rocks at policemen.	U.S. formally apologizes to the Soviet Union for what it calls an inadvertent American air strike on the Soviet ship *Turkestan* June 2 off the North Vietnamese port of Campha.		Dr. Milford Rouse, incoming president of the American Medical Association, urges the organization to combat the "threat" of government planning in the medical field.		June 20
U.S. Conference of Mayors votes, 69-54, to reject a proposal to require approval of anti-poverty programs by "responsible local agencies of government.". . . Police arrest 15 Negro members of the Revolutionary Action Movement (RAM) on charges of plotting to murder moderate civil rights leaders.	U.S. State Dept. announces the lifting of restrictions on travel by U.S. citizens to Israel and four Arab countries.	A bill raising the national debt limit passes the House by a vote of 217-196.	American Medical Association goes on record as favoring the liberalization of U.S. abortion laws.	Farrar Straus & Giroux publishes Edmund Wilson's *Galahad, I Thought of Daisy* and *A Prelude* . . . . Pres. Johnson's daughter, Luci Johnson Nugent, gives birth to a boy in Austin, Tex.	June 21

F	G	H	I	J
Includes elections, federal-state relations, civil rights and liberties, crime, the judiciary, education, health care, poverty, urban affairs and population.	*Includes formation and debate of U.S. foreign and defense policies, veterans' affairs and defense spending. (Relations with specific foreign countries are usually found under the region concerned.)*	*Includes business, labor, agriculture, taxation, transportation, consumer affairs, monetary and fiscal policy, natural resources, and pollution.*	*Includes worldwide scientific, medical and technological developments, natural phenomena, U.S. weather, natural disasters, and accidents.*	*Includes the arts, religion, scholarship, communications media, sports, entertainment, fashions, fads and social life.*

	World Affairs	Europe	Africa & the Middle East	The Americas	Asia & the Pacific
June 22	At the U.N. Israeli Foreign Min. Abba Eban says that Israel will not accept the internationalization of Jerusalem.		Israeli Arabs are allowed to visit the Islamic holy sites in the Old City of Jerusalem for the first time. Under Jordanian rule they had been forbidden to do so.	Quebec Associate Education Min. Marcel Masse urges an amendment to the federal constitution allowing Canadian provinces to sign foreign agreements.	U.S. planes pound the North Vietnamese Namdinh power plant. . . . North Vietnamese nearly wipe out a 130-man U.S. brigade in Kontun Province. Eighty Americans are reported killed and 34 are reported wounded.
June 23	At the U.N. Rumanian Premier Ion Maurer supports Israel's call for direct Arab-Israeli negotiations and refrains from condemning Israel as an aggressor.	Scotland's high court sentences an East German-born bartender, Peter Dorschel, to seven years imprisonment for attempting to gather information for the Soviet Union on the U.S. Holy Loch nuclear submarine base.	Israel denies that Arabs are being forced to leave the Israeli-occupied part of Jordan.		U.S. planes again attack a North Vietnamese power plant at Namdinh.
June 24			Israel reveals further details of the alleged Egyptian surprise attack plans against Israel. . . . Western travelers in Egypt report seeing large shipments of Soviet military equipment arriving in the port of Alexandria.	Government troops and armed miners clash in the tin mining district of Bolivia, killing 21 miners.	Communist China assails the Johnson-Kosygin summit conference.
June 25			Israel reports finding large quantities of Communist Chinese arms in the Gaza Strip.	Bolivian Army occupies three mines and orders striking miners to return to work.	
June 26	At the U.N. Jordanian King Hussein accuses Israel of deliberately starting the Middle East War. . . . Soviet Premier Kosygin leaves New York for discussions with Cuban Premier Fidel Castro in Havana.	At a meeting of the Common Market Council of Ministers, French Foreign Min. Maurice Couve de Murville strongly opposes a proposal by the other foreign ministers that Britain be allowed to present its case for membership.		Pres. Johnson and Pres. Marco Robles of Panama announce agreement on the texts of new treaties governing the Panama Canal.	Chinese students in Rangoon attack several Burmese teachers who attempted to end a sit-in at a Chinese school.
June 27	U.N. Secy. Gen. U Thant submits a report to the General Assembly defending his May 18 decision to withdraw U.N. troops from the Sinai Peninsula at the request of Egyptian Pres. Nasser. . . . At the U.N. Colombian Amb.-to-UN Julio Cesar Turbay-Ayala says that the General Assembly cannot ignore the existence of Israel, as the Arabs would wish, because Israel was the "creation of the United Nations."	Fourth Congress of the Czechoslovak Writers' Union opens in Prague.	Two Israeli prisoners are exchanged for 425 Egyptian captives.		France explodes a low-yield nuclear device in the Pacific. . . . Burmese demonstrators go on a rampage through the Chinese quarter of Rangoon. . . . South Vietnamese Premier Nguyen Cao Ky says that the number of government troops will be increased to 685,000.
June 28	At the U.N. General Assembly, Israeli Foreign Min. Abba Eban reiterates that Israel intends to maintain Jerusalem as a united city under Israeli administration.	Britain announces plans to send an additional 700 troops to Aden to cope with the spreading violence. . . . At the Czechoslovak Writers' Union, certain speakers criticize their government's domestic and foreign policies.	Israel formally merges the Old City of Jerusalem which was conquered in early June with the Israeli sector of the city.		Burmese demonstrators protest outside the Chinese embassy in Rangoon as anti-Chinese riots continue.
June 29		Additional speakers attack the Czech government's domestic and foreign policies at the Czechoslovak Writers' Union. . . . Italy announces that it opposes Austrian Common Market membership until Austria proves that its territory is not being used to harbor terrorists.	Arabs and Israelis move freely throughout Jerusalem without incident during the first day of unrestricted movement in the city.	From his Bolivian prison cell, French leftist Regis Debray says that he did not see Ché Guevara among the Bolivian guerrillas.	Communist China suspends all shipments of food to Hong Kong. . . . About 2,000 Burmese riot and attack the Chinese neighborhood of the town of Magwe.
	A	B	C	D	E
	Includes developments that affect more than one world region, international organizations and important meetings of major world leaders.	Includes all domestic and regional developments in Europe, including the Soviet Union, Turkey, Cyprus and Malta.	Includes all domestic and regional developments in Africa and the Middle East, including Iraq and Iran and excluding Cyprus, Turkey and Afghanistan.	Includes all domestic and regional developments in Latin America, the Caribbean and Canada.	Includes all domestic and regional developments in Asia and Pacific nations, extending from Afghanistan through all the Pacific Islands, except Hawaii.

U.S. Politics & Social Issues	U.S. Foreign Policy & Defense	U.S. Economy & Environment	Science, Technology & Nature	Culture, Leisure & Life Style	
Defense Secy. Robert McNamara announces that all segregated housing within a three-and-a-half mile radius of Andrews Air Force Base, Md. will be off-limits as of July 1 for all military families. . . . A Georgia court sentences Stokely Carmichael to 50 days in jail or a $53 fine.	U.S. agrees to process and supply the enriched uranium required for a Swedish nuclear reactor.				June 22
U.S. Senate votes 92-5 to censure Sen. Thomas Dodd (D, Conn.) for using funds obtained "from the public through political testimonials. . .for his personal benefit.". . . Eastman Kodak Co. and a civil rights organization reach an agreement about job training and placement for Rochester Negroes. . . . Justice Dept. sues H.K. Porter Co. in Birmingham, Ala., charging job discrimination. . . . N.J. Gov. Richard Hughes says he has no evidence that "outside agitators" played a role in the Newark riots.	Soviet Premier Aleksei Kosygin meets with Pres. Johnson in Glassboro, N.J. . . . U.S. State Dept. announces that it has canceled all technical assistance to Egypt.			Pope Paul reaffirms the Roman Catholic Church's traditional requirement of priestly celibacy. . . . Farrar Straus & Giroux publishes Clara Malraux's *Memoirs*, the story of her life with French writer Andre Malraux.	June 23
James Meredith, the first Negro admitted knowingly by the Univ. of Mississippi (in 1962), resumes his "march against fear" in Mississippi which had been interrupted on June 6 when he was shot.					June 24
	Soviet Premier Aleksei Kosygin and Pres. Johnson continue discussions in Glassboro, N.J.				June 25
William Gurvich, one of New Orleans Dist. Atty. James Garrison's key investigators, resigns and declares that he has found "no truth" in Garrison's allegation of a conspiracy in the murder of Pres. John Kennedy.	U.S. Defense Dept. announces that a U.S. plane recently strayed off course and was shot down over Communist China.		Pres. Johnson signs a bill authorizing the construction of an atom smasher in Weston, Ill.	Norton publishes Fawn Brodie's *The Devil Drives*, a life of Sir Richard Burton. . . . Pope Paul again calls for the internationalization of Jerusalem. . . . Houghton Mifflin publishes John Kenneth Galbraith's *The New Industrial State* .	June 26
Pres. Johnson receives an enthusiastic welcome at the Junior Chamber of Commerce Convention in Baltimore, Md. In his speech he praises America's unprecedented living standards. . . . Former investigator William Gurvich says that New Orleans Dist. Atty. James Garrison has become so "obsessed" with his assassination probe that he considered raiding the local FBI office for further evidence. . . . Young Negroes in Buffalo riot after a Negro youth reportedly throws a stone at a passing bus and hits a passenger.	Pres. Johnson announces a $5 million emergency relief fund for Arab refugees.	Consumer protection advocate Ralph Nader criticizes the federal safety agency for failing to support work on an experimental crashproof car. . . . Transportation Dept. issues 13 standards for highway safety programs.			June 27
U.S. Atty. Robert Morgenthau says that two Cosa Nostra "families" control 90% of the commercial garbage disposal industry in Westchester County, north of N.Y.C.	U.S. AEC announces that it will liberalize restrictions on the sale of radioactive isotopes to certain communist countries. . . . Pres. Johnson expresses opposition to Israel's merger of Jerusalem. . . . Pres. Johnson confers with King Hussein of Jordan.				June 28
Sporadic looting and gunfire continue in Buffalo's Negro neighborhoods.					June 29

F	G	H	I	J
Includes elections, federal-state relations, civil rights and liberties, crime, the judiciary, education, health care, poverty, urban affairs and population.	Includes formation and debate of U.S. foreign and defense policies, veterans' affairs and defense spending. (Relations with specific foreign countries are usually found under the region concerned.)	Includes business, labor, agriculture, taxation, transportation, consumer affairs, monetary and fiscal policy, natural resources, and pollution.	Includes worldwide scientific, medical and technological developments, natural phenomena, U.S. weather, natural disasters, and accidents.	Includes the arts, religion, scholarship, communications media, sports, entertainment, fashions, fads and social life.

	World Affairs	Europe	Africa & the Middle East	The Americas	Asia & the Pacific
June 30	At the U.N. General Assembly, 18 Latin American countries submit a draft resolution calling for the withdrawal of Israeli forces from all Arab territories and for an end to the state of belligerency between Israel and the Arab states. . . . Forty-six nations sign the documents comprising the Kennedy Round tariff-cutting accord concluded on May 15.	Czech Pres. Antonin Novotny attacks writers who have criticized past CP policy. . . . Soviet Union accuses the U.S. of bombing the Soviet ship *Mikhail Frunze* on June 29. . . . USSR Young Communist League newspaper assails overly zealous censorship officials.	South Africa deports apartheid foe, the Rev. Clarence Crowther. . . . France shuts down its space center in the Algerian Sahara. . . . A plane carrying ex-Congolese Premier Moise Tshombe is hijacked over Spain and flown to Algeria.	Soviet Premier Aleksei Kosygin leaves Havana after talks with Cuban Premier Castro.	Communist China's food embargo of Hong Kong continues. . . . Reports indicate that the South Vietnamese Armed Forces Council has forced Premier Nguyen Cao Ky to withdraw his candidacy for the presidential elections scheduled Sept. 3.
July 1		Three European executive bodies—the Common Market, Euratom and the Coal and Steal Community—merge into a single 14-member European commission. . . . Soviet Premier Aleksei Kosygin confers in Paris with French Pres. de Gaulle. . . . French National Assembly passes a bill legalizing the prescription sale of birth control devices and pills by pharmacists.	Both Egypt and Israel report clashes along the Suez Canal.	Chilean armed forces and police take over the postal and telegraph services to break a ten-day strike.	South Korean Pres. Chung Hee Park begins his second four-year term. . . . South Vietnamese Premier Ky announces his withdrawal from the upcoming presidential election scheduled for Sept. 3.
July 2		East German voters for the first time have a choice of candidates in parliamentary elections for about 15% of the seats. . . . Soviet poet Andrei Voznesensky denounces press censorship at the end of a public poetry reading.	Egypt reportedly kills Yemeni villagers in a poison gas attack. . . . Sporadic fighting continues between Israel and Egypt along the Suez Canal. . . . Israel announces that Arab residents of the West Bank of the Jordan River who fled the fighting of the Middle East War will be permitted to return to their homes.		North Vietnamese troops launch a surprise attack on U.S. troops near Conthien in northern South Vietnam.
July 3		Jordanian King Hussein meets with British P.M. Wilson in London.	British troops re-enter Aden's crater district from which they had been expelled on June 20. . . . Police arrest seven members of the French Somali pro-independence Parti du Movement Populaire in Djibouti. . . . Egypt and Israel exchange artillery barrages along the Suez Canal. . . . Egypt reportedly kills Yemeni villagers in poison gas attack.		Japanese news agency *Jiji* says that Communist China may have conducted its second hydrogen bomb test early on July 3. . . . South Korean police arrest 630 demonstrators in Seoul during a protest against the alleged rigging of the June 8 National Assembly elections. . . . Fighting rages between U.S. and North Vietnamese troops near Conthien.
July 4	U.N. General Assembly declares invalid Israel's June 28th reunification of the city of Jerusalem.	West Germany charges that South Korean authorities abducted 14 Koreans living in West Germany. . . . British House of Commons repeals all criminal penalties for homosexual acts between consenting male adults. . . . Jordanian King Hussein confers with French Pres. de Gaulle in Paris.	Israel claims the downing of two Egyptian planes over the Israeli-held town of Sudr in the Sinai. . . . A Congolese government delegation confers with Algerian authorities in Algiers and requests that ex-Premier Moise Tshombe be extradited to the Congo (Kinshasha).		Fierce fighting continues between U.S. and North Vietnamese troops near Conthien.
July 5		Reports indicate that the 13-nation European Organization for Nuclear Research (CERN) and the Soviet Union signed an agreement on July 4 providing for joint development and use of a Soviet nuclear accelerator.	South Arabian Federation Supreme Council appoints Information Min. Hussein Ali Bayoomi as the federation's first prime minister. . . . Katangese gendarmes and white mercenaries launch an armed rebellion against the Congolese (Kinshasha) government of Pres. Joseph Mobutu in eastern Orientale and Kivu Provinces. . . . Kenya expels five British farmers for naming their cattle after members of Pres. Jomo Kenyatta's cabinet. . . . Jordanian Premier Saad Juma urges former West Bank Arabs to return to their homes.	British Queen Elizabeth II ends a tour of Canada in which she avoided the province of Quebec because of possible French-Canadian nationalist disturbances. . . . *The New York Times* reports that Bolivia has asked Argentina to send troops to help in the fight against Bolivian guerrillas, but that Argentina declined the request for the time being.	U.S. and North Vietnamese troops battle at Conthien and Dongha.
July 6	U.N. Security Council convenes in an emergency session to discuss the Congolese fighting.	Jordanian King Hussein confers with Pope Paul in Rome.	Fighting breaks out between troops of the Nigerian federal government and of the secessionist Eastern Region which has proclaimed itself the Republic of Biafra. . . . Egyptian government issues a budget which cuts public expenditures by 25%.		North Vietnamese artillery pounds U.S. Marines near Conthien.

A	B	C	D	E
Includes developments that affect more than one world region, international organizations and important meetings of major world leaders.	*Includes all domestic and regional developments in Europe, including the Soviet Union, Turkey, Cyprus and Malta.*	*Includes all domestic and regional developments in Africa and the Middle East, including Iraq and Iran and excluding Cyprus, Turkey and Afghanistan.*	*Includes all domestic and regional developments in Latin America, the Caribbean and Canada.*	*Includes all domestic and regional developments in Asia and Pacific nations, extending from Afghanistan through all the Pacific Islands, except Hawaii.*

U.S. Politics & Social Issues	U.S. Foreign Policy & Defense	U.S. Economy & Environment	Science, Technology & Nature	Culture, Leisure & Life Style	
Thousands of welfare recipients demonstrate in cities and towns across the country to protest alleged inadequacies in the welfare system. . . . Looting and sniper fire disrupt a temporary calm in Buffalo as Negro and white leaders confer.		Gov. Ronald Reagan approves the largest state budget in the history of the state of California.			June 30
Seventeen of the nation's 25 Democratic governors, meeting in St. Louis, issue a statement strongly supporting Pres. Johnson.			U.S. launches six military satellites.		July 1
A Gallup Poll indicates that Pres. Johnson and Mich. Gov. George Romney (R) are about equally popular. . . . Buffalo Urban League reports that 750 Negro youths have signed up for jobs in wake of recruiting on July 1-2.	A House Inter-American Affairs Subcommittee report accuses Cuba of supporting guerrilla movements in Colombia, Guatemala, Venezuela, and Bolivia. . . . Reports indicate that Gen. William Westmoreland, commander of U.S. troops in Vietnam, has asked for at least 70,000 more men.				July 2
					July 3
Organized crime fighter Rev. Martin Duffy says that Mt. Vernon, N.Y. is controlled "by a vicious group of gangsters.". . . James Meredith ends his 162-mile "march against fear" in Canton, Miss.					July 4
Congressional Quarterly reports that the AFL-CIO was the top spending lobby for 1966. . . . Justice Dept. files a school desegregation suit against Tunica County, Miss.		FCC orders a cut of about three percent in annual AT&T charges.			July 5
Justice Dept. reports that more than half of the eligible Negro voters in five Southern states are registered to vote.	U.S. announces its support of the Congolese government and dispatches three cargo planes to help suppress the rebellion.	Joint Economic Committee predicts that the 1967 expenditures on the Vietnamese War will probably exceed the President's original estimate.			July 6

F	G	H	I	J
Includes elections, federal-state relations, civil rights and liberties, crime, the judiciary, education, health care, poverty, urban affairs and population.	*Includes formation and debate of U.S. foreign and defense policies, veterans' affairs and defense spending. (Relations with specific foreign countries are usually found under the region concerned.)*	*Includes business, labor, agriculture, taxation, transportation, consumer affairs, monetary and fiscal policy, natural resources, and pollution.*	*Includes worldwide scientific, medical and technological developments, natural phenomena, U.S. weather, natural disasters, and accidents.*	*Includes the arts, religion, scholarship, communications media, sports, entertainment, fashions, fads and social life.*

	World Affairs	Europe	Africa & the Middle East	The Americas	Asia & the Pacific
July 7	Congolese U.N. Amb.-to-U.N. Theodore Idzumbir criticizes Belgium, Portugal and Spain for allegedly permitting anti-Congolese conspirators to operate on their soil.		Congolese and Katangese forces clash in southern Congolese areas amid conflicting reports of military success. . . . Israeli Premier Levi Eshkol says that Israel's military victory was primarily the work of Maj. Gen. Itzhak Rabin.		Defense Secy. McNamara begins a tour of South Vietnam.
July 8	U.N. Security Council meets in an emergency session on the Middle East crisis.		Israel claims sending jets across the Suez Canal to knock out Egyptian tanks and artillery which have been shelling Israeli positions. . . . Foreign diplomats report that Congolese troops fighting the Katangese rebellion went on a rampage in Bukavu and killed 60 people including five Europeans.		U.S. military officers brief Defense Secy. McNamara in South Vietnam.
July 9	At a U.N. Security Council session, the Soviet Union demands the immediate withdrawal of Israeli troops from Arab occupied territory.	Soviet Union unveils two swing-wing supersonic aircraft for the first time.	A land mine kills an Israeli soldier along the Suez Canal.		Defense Secy. McNamara flies by helicopter to the vicinity of the demilitarized zone with Gen. William Westmoreland, commander of U.S. troops in South Vietnam. . . . A typhoon kills more than 300 people in Japan.
July 10	U.N. Security Council approves the stationing of U.N. observers on the Suez cease-fire line to supervise the truce. . . . International Atomic Energy Agency reports an "unexpectedly large" number of orders were placed in 1966 for the construction of nuclear power plants throughout the world.	Paris newspapers say that French leftist Regis Debray has admitted seeing Ché Guevara with the Bolivian guerrillas.	Arab gunmen kill one Arab and wound two British soldiers in Aden. . . . Israel reaffirms its June 27th decision to reunify the city of Jerusalem.		Defense Secy. McNamara tours the Mekong Delta by helicopter.
July 11	U.N. Secy. Gen. U Thant announces the establishment of a $5.5 million Trust Fund for Population Activities.	Common Market agrees on terms for negotiating a preferential trade agreement with Spain.	Israel claims downing an Egyptian plane over the Sinai Peninsula. . . . Israel gives its conditional approval of the stationing of U.N. observers along the Suez cease-fire line.	Ruling Christian Democratic party of Chile issues a declaration recognizing the right of guerrillas to fight against governments that "ignore the people's rights and offer no electoral solutions."	U.N. Korean command reports that 15 North Koreans and at least 14 South Koreans were killed in nine incidents occurring in the week ending July 5. . . . Defense Secy. McNamara meets with South Vietnamese Chief of State Nguyen Van Thieu and Premier Nguyen Cao Ky.
July 12	U.N. General Assembly reconvenes in an emergency session.	West German Chancellor Kurt-Georg Kiesinger and French Pres. de Gaulle confer in Bonn.	Congolese troops pursue dissident forces fleeing south in a truck convoy. . . . Israel claims the sinking of two Egyptian motor torpedo boats.		
July 13		French Pres. de Gaulle declares that the US's "enormous power. . . automatically leads to the extension of U.S. "hegemony" over others. He adds, however, that the U.S. is "our natural friend."	Reports indicate that Jordanian King Hussein has begun a major reorganization of his country's armed forces.		
July 14	U.N. General Assembly demands that Israel rescind the measures it has taken to reunify the city of Jerusalem under a single administration.	British House of Commons passes a liberalized abortion law.	Egyptian artillery pounds the East Bank of the canal and Israeli planes attack positions on the West Bank.		
July 15		French Pres. Charles de Gaulle leaves for an official trip to Canada.	Egyptian planes reportedly kill Yemeni villagers in a poison gas attack. . . . Israel reports seven combat fatalities in the July 14th fighting. . . . Presidents of Egypt, Algeria, Syria, Iraq and the Sudan meet in Cairo.		U.S. planes bomb the southern part of North Vietnam.

A	B	C	D	E
Includes developments that affect more than one world region, international organizations and important meetings of major world leaders.	Includes all domestic and regional developments in Europe, including the Soviet Union, Turkey, Cyprus and Malta.	Includes all domestic and regional developments in Africa and the Middle East, including Iraq and Iran and excluding Cyprus, Turkey and Afghanistan.	Includes all domestic and regional developments in Latin America, the Caribbean and Canada.	Includes all domestic and regional developments in Asia and Pacific nations, extending from Afghanistan through all the Pacific Islands, except Hawaii.

U.S. Politics & Social Issues	U.S. Foreign Policy & Defense	U.S. Economy & Environment	Science, Technology & Nature	Culture, Leisure & Life Style	
A U.S. court orders the reinstatement of 71 textile workers of the J.P. Stevens Co. who were discharged for union activity.	Senate Democratic leader Mike Mansfield charges "that a longer duration of the war is in the offing and that the prospects for peace may well have diminished accordingly."				July 7
	Sen. J.W. Fulbright says that the U.S. is waging a "savage and unsuccessful war against poor people in a small and backward nation.". . . Three American C-130 cargo planes leave for the Congo.			British actress Vivien Leigh, 53, dies in London. . . . Fatima Jinnah, who ran against Mohammed Ayub Khan in the 1965 Pakistani presidential elections, dies in Karachi at 74.	July 8
	U.S. State Dept. says that the cargo planes sent to the Congo will have "a non-combat" status.				July 9
NAACP opens its 58th annual convention in Boston. . . . Oklahoma Supreme Court rules that the state's anti-miscegenation law is unconstitutional.	Several U.S. Senators condemn Pres. Johnson's decision to dispatch three transport planes to the Congo.				July 10
At the NAACP's annual convention, Sen. Edward Brooke (R, Mass.), a Negro, warns against any effort to exclude whites from the civil rights movement. . . . U.S. deports Cuban exile leader Felipe Rivero, the head of a group which has allegedly threatened to bomb the Cuban pavilion at Montreal's Expo 67 fair.	Senate Democratic leader Mike Mansfield warns against further escalation of the Vietnamese War. . . . U.S. State Dept. expresses "increasing concern" about Soviet military shipments to Egypt.			Vatican newspaper reports that Albania has closed its last Roman Catholic church.	July 11
NAACP Labor Secy. Herbert Hill says that his organization plans to file suits to cut off public funds from construction projects where Negroes are denied jobs.	Defense Secy. McNamara discusses his trip to South Vietnam with Pres. Johnson on his return to Washington.	HEW Secy. John Gardner supports cigarette labeling, stating that smoking is "clearly hazardous to health."			July 12
	Pres. Johnson says that the U.S. has decided upon a relatively modest increase in troop levels in South Vietnam. . . . Pres. Johnson calls on Israel to permit a "maximum number" of Arab refugees to return to their homes on the West Bank of the Jordan River.	National Association of Manufacturers warns that the fiscal 1968 budget will be large enough to have "severely damaging effects on the economy" unless taxes are increased.			July 13
At the NAACP annual convention a group of militants demands that the organization change its "middle-class" image.	State Secy. Rusk indicates that the U.S. will resume arms shipments to the Middle East.		U.S. launches Surveyor 4.	Sen. Edward Kennedy's wife, Joan, gives birth to their third child.	July 14
NAACP avoids either endorsing or attacking the Vietnamese War. . . . Newark's death toll now stands at 14 blacks and one white detective.					July 15

F	G	H	I	J
Includes elections, federal-state relations, civil rights and liberties, crime, the judiciary, education, health care, poverty, urban affairs and population.	Includes formation and debate of U.S. foreign and defense policies, veterans' affairs and defense spending. (Relations with specific foreign countries are usually found under the region concerned.)	Includes business, labor, agriculture, taxation, transportation, consumer affairs, monetary and fiscal policy, natural resources, and pollution.	Includes worldwide scientific, medical and technological developments, natural phenomena, U.S. weather, natural disasters, and accidents.	Includes the arts, religion, scholarship, communications media, sports, entertainment, fashions, fads and social life.

	World Affairs	Europe	Africa & the Middle East	The Americas	Asia & the Pacific
July 16		Soviet newspaper *Pravda* blasts Communist Chinese leadership in a bitter editorial.	An Israeli military spokesman says that his country has been operating small boats in the Suez Canal "both because it is a good way to move supplies from one point to another and because we want to retain that right. We don't want it to become a no-man's area or a waterway for Egyptian use only.". . . Five Arab presidents meeting in Cairo vow "to eliminate the consequences of imperialist Israeli aggression in the Arab homeland."		Reports indicate that tens of thousands of Chinese have held massive swimming rallies in celebration of the first anniversary of Chmn. Mao's celebrated swim in the Yangtze River. . . . North Koreans kill three U.S. soldiers near the dimilitarized zone.
July 17			U.N. soldiers take positions on both sides of the Suez Canal to supervise the U.N. truce between Israel and Egypt.		
July 18		A British government White Paper calls for the complete withdrawal of its troops in Singapore and Malaysia by 1975.	First authorized repatriation of Arab refugees from the East to the West Bank of the Jordan River starts.	Former Brazilian Pres. Candido Castelo Branco, 66, dies in an air crash near Forteleza, Brazil. He was Brazil's president between 1964 and 1967.	U.S. planes bomb North Vietnamese troops in the southern part of North Vietnam.
July 19		An article in the Soviet newspaper *Pravda* says that hundreds of Chinese demonstrators tried to cross the Soviet-Chinese border early in 1967.	A bomb thought to be thrown by Biafran sympathizers kills at least five people in a suburb of Lagos.		
July 20		West German police confiscate a neo-Nazi magazine. . . . A three-hour gun battle takes place between Greeks and Turks at Ayios Theodoros on Cyprus.	National Liberation Front of Aden reports kidnapping one of the purported appointees of a proposed caretaker government.	French Pres. Charles de Gaulle arrives at the French territorial island of St. Pierre, south of the Newfoundland coast.	
July 21	General Assembly votes to adjourn "temporarily" and return discussion of the Arab-Israeli dispute to the Security Council.		*The New York Times* reports that Nigerian Ibo refugees claim to have seen federal troops slay civilians. . . . Congo (Kinshasha) reports having bombed mercenary positions in Bukavu. . . . Algeria agrees to extradite ex-Premier Moise Tshombe to the Congo.		
July 22		An earthquake kills 83 people in Turkey.			
July 23			Egyptian planes reportedly kill Yemeni villagers in a poison gas attack. . . . Egyptian Pres. Nasser appeals to the Egyptian people for total mobilization to cope with the economic hardships resulting from the June 5 war.	Sixty and a half percent of Puerto Rican voters approve its commonwealth status. . . . Following a call for violent action by Chilean Communist and Castroite groups, the Chilean government orders legal action against their leaders. . . . In a reversal of the usual order of state visits, French Pres. Charles de Gaulle arrives in the city of Quebec rather than the federal capital of Ottawa.	

A	B	C	D	E
Includes developments that affect more than one world region, international organizations and important meetings of major world leaders.	Includes all domestic and regional developments in Europe, including the Soviet Union, Turkey, Cyprus and Malta.	Includes all domestic and regional developments in Africa and the Middle East, including Iraq and Iran and excluding Cyprus, Turkey and Afghanistan.	Includes all domestic and regional developments in Latin America, the Caribbean and Canada.	Includes all domestic and regional developments in Asia and Pacific nations, extending from Afghanistan through all the Pacific Islands, except Hawaii.

U.S. Politics & Social Issues	U.S. Foreign Policy & Defense	U.S. Economy & Environment	Science, Technology & Nature	Culture, Leisure & Life Style	
A Negro mob beats a Plainfield, N.J. policeman to death. . . . NAACP Executive Dir. Roy Wilkins backs the use of troops to quell riots. . . . Heavy sniper fire continues in Newark, N.J. bringing the death toll to 24.		A nationwide railroad strike begins.	U.S. loses radio contact with Surveyor 4 just as it is about to land on the moon.		July 16
	U.S. pediatrician Dr. Benjamin Spock says he may run as a peace candidate in the 1968 elections.			Jazz saxophonist John Coltrane dies in Huntington, N.Y. at 41 of a liver ailment. . . . George Braziler publishes Stanley Weintraub's *Beardsley: A Biography.*	July 17
Fire bombs and sniper fire take place in the Negro neighborhoods of Cairo, Ill.	In Washington Israeli Amb.-to-U.S. calls on the American government to give Israel "the opportunity" to obtain American arms.	Congress passes a bill to halt the nationwide railroad strike. . . . Pres. Johnson repeats his call for a six percent surcharge on income taxes.	U.S. officals give up trying to re-establish radio contact with Surveyor 4.		July 18
Ill. Gov. Otto Kerner calls in the National Guard as rioting continues in Cairo, Ill. . . . A Virginia court permanently enjoins the state from enforcing the racial restrictions of the will of Indiana Williams, founder of Sweet Briar College.	State Secy. Rusk again says that the U.S. is considering a resumption of military shipments to the Middle East.		U.S. launches Explorer 35. . . . Soviet Union launches Cosmos 178.		July 19
About 1,000 Negro leaders meet in Newark, N.J. for a National Conference on Black Power. . . . House votes down an administration bill for a rat extermination program.					July 20
National Conference on Black Power demands the recall of Newark Mayor Hugh Addonizio.		Treasury Dept. reports a $9.9 billion deficit for the 1967 fiscal year.		Black South African civil rights leader Albert John Luthuli dies near Groutville, South Africa. He was between 67 and 69 years of age.	July 21
National Conference on Black Power demands that all Negroes arrested during the Newark, N.J. riot be released from jail. . . . California Fair Employment Practices Commission orders a Los Angeles operating engineers union to hire a Negro business agent.	Gen. Maxwell Taylor and presidential adviser Clark Clifford leave Washington for a tour of the Far East.		Explorer 35 enters lunar orbit. . . . Soviet Union launches Cosmos 179.	U.S. poet Carl Sandburg dies in Flat Rock, N.C. at 89.	July 22
Worst U.S. riot in the 20th century breaks out in Detroit. Thousands of looters roam the streets. . . . National Conference on Black Power ends on a militant note with delegates approving a series of resolutions aimed at establishing a separate course for black America.					July 23

F	G	H	I	J
Includes elections, federal-state relations, civil rights and liberties, crime, the judiciary, education, health care, poverty, urban affairs and population.	*Includes formation and debate of U.S. foreign and defense policies, veterans' affairs and defense spending. (Relations with specific foreign countries are usually found under the region concerned.)*	*Includes business, labor, agriculture, taxation, transportation, consumer affairs, monetary and fiscal policy, natural resources, and pollution.*	*Includes worldwide scientific, medical and technological developments, natural phenomena, U.S. weather, natural disasters, and accidents.*	*Includes the arts, religion, scholarship, communications media, sports, entertainment, fashions, fads and social life.*

	World Affairs	Europe	Africa & the Middle East	The Americas	Asia & the Pacific
July 24	U.S. and the Soviet Union submit a draft treaty to the U.N. Disarmament Committee to prevent the further spread of nuclear weapons.	Norway applies for full membership in the Common Market. . . . West Germany comments favorably on the U.S.-Soviet draft treaty to prevent the further spread of nuclear weapons.	Nigerian federal troops claim to have captured four white mercenaries. . . . Twenty-five Moslem leaders meet in East Jerusalem (the Old City) and issue a manifesto challenging the authority of the Israeli Ministry of Religious Affairs to deal with Moslem religious activities.	In an emotionally charged speech at the city hall of Montreal, French Pres. Charles de Gaulle calls for a "free Quebec."	Gen. Maxwell Taylor and presidential adviser Clark Clifford confer with U.S. and South Vietnamese officials in Saigon. . . . Red Guards break into the office of a Japanese trading company in Peking and subject several of its employees to a five-hour "trial" on espionage charges. . . . For the first time since May, fighting breaks out in the demilitarized zone.
July 25			Reports indicate that a campaign has begun to encourage the Arab population of the Israeli-occupied West Bank of the Jordan River to defy Israeli rule.	Canadian P.M. Lester Pearson leads a chorus of denunciations of de Gaulle's use of the French Canadian separatist slogan "Quebec libre" ("free Quebec").	Gen. Maxwell Taylor and presidential adviser Clark Clifford continue discussions with U.S. and South Vietnamese officials in Saigon.
July 26		An earthquake kills 112 people in Turkey.		French Pres. Charles de Gaulle leaves Canada a day before his scheduled visit to Ottawa.	Monsoon floods leave 100,000 homeless in Pakistan.
July 27	Red Cross charges that Egypt used poison gas attacks on May 10, 17 and 18 against pro-royalist villages in Yemen.			Chile begins moving police reinforcements and arms into the southern part of the country in order to counter a recent series of bombing incidents.	Gen. Maxwell Taylor and presidential adviser Clark Clifford fly to Thailand for discussions about the Vietnamese War.
July 28		Sweden applies for associate membership in the Common Market. . . . British labor government puts 90% of the country's steel industry back under public ownership.	Pressures and threats by two radical political groups force South Arabian Federation Premier-designate Hussein Ali Bayoomi to abandon his attempts to form a caretaker government pending independence.		Gen. Maxwell Taylor and presidential adviser Clark Clifford confer with Thai P.M. Thanom Kittikachorn in Bangkok.
July 29		Heavy fighting breaks out between Greeks and Turks at Ayios Theodoros on Cyprus.	Israeli Foreign Min. Abba Eban says that Israel is prepared to reach a separate agreement with Egypt on the Suez Canal issue.		A fire kills 129 crewmen on the U.S. aircraft carrier *Forrestal*.
July 30			Reports indicate that Egypt has threatened to withdraw all of its remaining 25,000 troops from Yemen if the republican regime does not share the cost of maintaining them.		Gen. Maxwell Taylor and presidential adviser Clark Clifford arrive in Australia for talks on the Vietnamese War.
July 31	A letter circulating in the U.N. Security Council from Congolese Foreign Min. Justin Bomboko charges that pro-Moise Tshombe mercenaries are being recruited in Belgium "to stir up further trouble in the Congo."	France declares that it intends to aid the people of Quebec in gaining "the objectives of liberation that they themselves have set."	Israeli authorities seize four signers of the July 24 Arab manifesto issued from East Jerusalem and banish them to northern Israeli towns.	Organization of Latin American Solidarity opens in Havana, Cuba. . . . *The New York Times* reports a nighttime curfew has been imposed in Haiti for an indefinite period.	Gen. Maxwell Taylor and presidential adviser Clark Clifford arrive in New Zealand for talks on the Vietnamese War.
Aug. 1			Several skirmishes take place along the Israeli-Jordanian border.	Canadian Trade Min. Robert Winters announces that the Soviet Union will buy $150 million of Canadian wheat.	Gen Ne Win, chairman of the Burmese Revolutionary Council, lifts the martial law in Rangoon which had been imposed after anti-Chinese rioting.
	A	**B**	**C**	**D**	**E**
	Includes developments that affect more than one world region, international organizations and important meetings of major world leaders.	*Includes all domestic and regional developments in Europe, including the Soviet Union, Turkey, Cyprus and Malta.*	*Includes all domestic and regional developments in Africa and the Middle East, including Iraq and Iran and excluding Cyprus, Turkey and Afghanistan.*	*Includes all domestic and regional developments in Latin America, the Caribbean and Canada.*	*Includes all domestic and regional developments in Asia and Pacific nations, extending from Afghanistan through all the Pacific Islands, except Hawaii.*

U.S. Politics & Social Issues	U.S. Foreign Policy & Defense	U.S. Economy & Environment	Science, Technology & Nature	Culture, Leisure & Life Style	
Pres. Johnson orders federal troops to Detroit to put down the rampant looting. . . . SNCC chmn. H. Rap Brown calls on Cambridge, Md., Negroes to "burn down the city.". . . Justice Dept. files a job discrimination suit against two railroad unions.				Universal Pictures releases Peter Watkins' film *Privilege*.	July 24
Sen. Robert Kennedy says that the situation in the central cities "is rapidly becoming the gravest domestic crisis since the War Between the States.". . . Fires and violence break out in the Negro neighborhood of Cambridge, Md. . . . Congressional leaders of both parties call for an investigation of the continued civil disorders in U.S. cities. . . . Detroit Mayor Jerome Cavanagh comes under sharp attack from both Negroes and whites for not adopting a firmer policy toward rioters. The city's Negro newspaper says "if the police had stopped looting when it centered on one. . . block. . . the riot could have been prevented."				Pope Paul arrives in Turkey and prays in an Eastern Orthodox church. It is the first time a Roman Catholic Pope has prayed in such a church.	July 25
Four leading Negro leaders including the Rev. Martin Luther King Jr. appeal for an end to the riots in Negro urban areas. . . . National Guard uses tear gas to disperse Negro mobs in Cambridge, Md. . . . Heavy sniper fire continues in Detroit raising the death toll to 29 Negroes and seven whites.	U.S. Rep. William Widnall tries to promote an investigation of U.S. arms sales but abandons it because of lack of interest.		Soviet Union launches Cosmos 180.		July 26
SNCC Chmn. H. Rap Brown, in a speech in Washington, D.C., calls on Negroes to arm themselves. . . . Rioting and sniper fire decrease in Detroit.	U.S. State Dept., without specifically mentioning Egypt, condemns the gas attacks on Yemeni royalists.			Brandon Films releases Pier Paolo Pasolini's *The Hawks and the Sparrows*.	July 27
A Negro looter is shot to death in Detroit, raising the death toll to 39.			U.S. launches Orgo 4 satellite whose mission is to study the relationship between the sun and the earth's environment during a period of increased solar activity.		July 28
					July 29
Federal troops begin to withdraw from Detroit but 7,000 National Guardsmen remain on duty.				German industrialist Alfried Krupp dies in Essen, West Germany at 59.	July 30
Office of Economic Opportunity Director Sargent Shriver says that "all America is responsible for the racial riots."	Sen. J.W. Fulbright introduces a resolution to prevent the executive branch from making "national commitments" to a foreign power without congressional consent.				July 31
President's new Special Advisory Commission on Civil Disorders meets for the first time.			U.S. launches Lunar Orbiter 5.		Aug. 1

F	G	H	I	J
Includes elections, federal-state relations, civil rights and liberties, crime, the judiciary, education, health care, poverty, urban affairs and population.	*Includes formation and debate of U.S. foreign and defense policies, veterans' affairs and defense spending. (Relations with specific foreign countries are usually found under the region concerned.)*	*Includes business, labor, agriculture, taxation, transportation, consumer affairs, monetary and fiscal policy, natural resources, and pollution.*	*Includes worldwide scientific, medical and technological developments, natural phenomena, U.S. weather, natural disasters, and accidents.*	*Includes the arts, religion, scholarship, communications media, sports, entertainment, fashions, fads and social life.*

	World Affairs	Europe	Africa & the Middle East	The Americas	Asia & the Pacific
Aug. 2		Hungarian government hangs three men accused of persecuting Jews and Communists during W.W. II.	Skirmishes continue along the Israeli-Jordanian border.		Indonesian newspapers report the arrests or dismissals of six police and military officials following the discovery of an alleged plot to return former Pres. Sukarno to power. . . . France explodes a low-yield nuclear device in the Pacific. . . . Gen. Maxwell Taylor and presidential adviser Clark Clifford arrive in South Korea for talks on the Vietnamese War. . . . A Thai government radio whose mission is to counter Communist propaganda begins broadcasts.
Aug. 3		French Armed Forces Min. Pierre Messmer announces that France will test its first hydrogen bomb in July 1968. . . . West German Foreign Min. Willy Brandt begins a tour of Rumania.	Israel announces an agreement with Egypt to accept a U.N. proposal for the "stopping of movements of boats" of both nations in the canal for one month and for a halt in all military activity in the waterway.	Reports indicate that the U.S. has blocked a sale of U.S. financed British jets to Peru.	Gen. Maxwell Taylor and presidential adviser Clark Clifford continue discussions in South Korea on the Vietnamese War. . . . U.S. planes fly 197 missions against North Vietnam, the highest total for a single day since Oct. 14, 1966.
Aug. 4			Thirteen Arab governments announce their agreement on the convening of a summit conference although they do not mention a specific date.		Reports indicate that thousands of Red Guards in Peking have demanded that Chief-of-State Liu Shao-chi be tried in "a people's court.". . . U.S. planes pound two North Vietnamese military bases in the Hanoi area.
Aug. 5					Maori Queen Te Ata calls for the full integration of schools for Maori tribesmen and whites in New Zealand.
Aug. 6		Two Turkish Cypriote villagers are shot to death on Cyprus. Police arrest two Greek Cypriote suspects.	Israel and Jordan reach agreement on a repatriation application that will permit the resumption of the return of Arab refugees who fled their homes on the Israeli-occupied West Bank of the Jordan River.	Cuba displays six allegedly captured Cuban exiles at the Organization of Latin American Solidarity Conference. . . . Hijackers force a Colombian airlines DC-4 to land in Havana.	U.S. planes attack the Hanoi-Haiphong area. . . . South Vietnamese civilian election candidates cancel their campaign because of a dispute with the country's military rulers.
Aug. 7			East Jerusalem Arabs stage a one-day strike to protest Israeli control of the former Jordanian sector. . . . Israeli Defense Min. Moshe Dayan charges that Egypt has violated the U.N. agreement of the previous week forbidding military activity in the Suez Canal. . . . Jordanian Finance Min. Abdel Wahab Majali calls on former West Bank refugees on the East Bank of the Jordan River to return to their former homes. . . . East Jerusalem Arabs stage a one-day general strike. . . . Trial of 37 Africans accused of "terrorism" in South-West Africa begins in Pretoria, South Africa.	Cuba grants political asylum to hijackers of a Colombian DC-4 and allows the plane to return to Colombia.	Nine of the 10 South Vietnamese candidates hold a protest meeting in Saigon about the government's election practices.
Aug. 8		Reports indicate that Rumania has agreed to allow Rumanian citizens of German origins to join their families in West Germany.		Reports indicate that four Latin American communist delegations have threatened to walk out of the Organization of Latin American Solidarity Conference if a resolution condemning the Soviet Union's trade with South American "dictatorships" is adopted.	Five non-communist Asian nations merge their countries into an economic grouping called the Association of Southeast Asian Nations (ASEAN). . . . Chief of State Nguyen Van Thieu appeals to South Vietnamese civilian candidates to resume their campaign.
Aug. 9			Biafran troops capture Benin, the capital of Nigeria's mid-western region. . . . White mercenaries and Katangese gendarmes recapture the eastern Kivu Province capital of Bukavu from Congolese (Kinshasha) government troops.	Reports indicate that a resolution condemning Soviet trade with Latin American "dictatorships" has been adopted by a 15-3 vote at the Organization of Latin American Solidarity Conference.	Tens of thousands of Chinese demonstrate outside the Mongolian embassy in Peking.

A	B	C	D	E
Includes developments that affect more than one world region, international organizations and important meetings of major world leaders.	Includes all domestic and regional developments in Europe, including the Soviet Union, Turkey, Cyprus and Malta.	Includes all domestic and regional developments in Africa and the Middle East, including Iraq and Iran and excluding Cyprus, Turkey and Afghanistan.	Includes all domestic and regional developments in Latin America, the Caribbean and Canada.	Includes all domestic and regional developments in Asia and Pacific nations, extending from Afghanistan through all the Pacific Islands, except Hawaii.

U.S. Politics & Social Issues	U.S. Foreign Policy & Defense	U.S. Economy & Environment	Science, Technology & Nature	Culture, Leisure & Life Style	
For the first time since the rioting began, no major incidents are reported from Detroit. . . . Cambridge, Md. police chief Bryce Kinnamon says that the "sole reason" for the July 28 riot in his city was an inflammatory speech made by H. Rap Brown, SNCC chairman.	Joint Atomic Energy Committee warns that Communist China "could possibly" be capable of launching an intercontinental nuclear missile attack by the early 1970s.			United Artists releases Norman Jewison's film *In the Heat of the Night*.	**Aug. 2**
	Pres. Johnson announces plans to increase U.S. troop strength in Vietnam by at least 45,000 men.	Pres. Johnson asks Congress to impose a 10 percent surcharge on income taxes.			**Aug. 3**
			A six-nation European satellite fails to function properly upon take-off and crashes to the ground.	Alberto Bayo, the Spanish Civil War general who trained Fidel Castro in guerrilla tactics, dies in Havana at 68.	**Aug. 4**
	Gen. Maxwell Taylor and presidential adviser Clark Clifford meet with Pres. Johnson after returning to Washington from a tour of the Far East. . . . U.S. State Dept. announces an easing of travel restrictions on Soviet diplomats accredited to the embassy in Washington.		U.S. satellite Lunar Orbiter 5 enters its lunar orbit.		**Aug. 5**
			Lunar Orbiter 5 begins its photo mission of the moon.		**Aug. 6**
A Michigan court charges two Negro youths with the Aug. 7 murder of a Detroit policeman. . . . A Michigan court charges two white Detroit policemen with the July 26 murder of two Negro youths at the Algiers Motel during the July riots. . . . U.S. Civil Rights Commission calls for stricter enforcement of the federal desegregation guidelines.				McGraw-Hill publishes Heinrich Boll's *Irish Journal*.	**Aug. 7**
Rev. Martin Luther King Jr. announces the cancellation of a boycott against Sealtest Dairy Products of Cleveland, Ohio after they agree to provide more jobs for Negroes.					**Aug. 8**
	In Washington U.S. officials announce that the final death toll of the July 29 U.S. aircraft carrier *Forrestal* fire is 134. . . . Before the Senate Preparedness Subcommittee, Adm. Grant Sharp, commander of U.S. forces in the Pacific, warns that a bombing halt in Vietnam would be disastrous.			British playwright Joe Orton, 34, is bludgeoned to death in London by a friend, Kenneth Halliwell.	**Aug. 9**

F	G	H	I	J
Includes elections, federal-state relations, civil rights and liberties, crime, the judiciary, education, health care, poverty, urban affairs and population.	Includes formation and debate of U.S. foreign and defense policies, veterans' affairs and defense spending. (Relations with specific foreign countries are usually found under the region concerned.)	Includes business, labor, agriculture, taxation, transportation, consumer affairs, monetary and fiscal policy, natural resources, and pollution.	Includes worldwide scientific, medical and technological developments, natural phehomena, U.S. weather, natural disasters, and accidents.	Includes the arts, religion, scholarship, communications media, sports, entertainment, fashions, fads and social life.

	World Affairs	Europe	Africa & the Middle East	The Americas	Asia & the Pacific
Aug. 10	U.N. Council for South-West Africa is officially installed at U.N. headquarters.		Israeli Defense Min. Moshe Dayan declares that Israel cannot maintain its security if it relinquishes all the Arab territory that it captured during the June 5-10 war. . . . White mercenary leader Jean Schramme demands that Congolese Pres. Joseph Mobutu form a "government that represents all the people—not just one tribe."		
Aug. 11			Yugoslav Pres. Tito confers with Egyptian Pres. Gamal Abdel Nasser.	Cuban Communist Premier Fidel Castro renews his attack on communist countries trading with Latin American countries "fighting and murdering guerrillas."	U.S. planes attack within ten miles of the Communist Chinese border for the first time.
Aug. 12				Catholic Univ. students begin a strike in Santiago, Chile. . . . *The New York Times* reports that Peru has recently rejected a U.S. loan proposal because of its austerity provisions.	Communist China assails the new ASEAN economic association formed on Aug. 8 as a "counter-revolutionary alliance.". . . U.S. planes bomb bridges crossing the Canal des Rapides near Hanoi.
Aug. 13		A Czech family of eight flees Czechoslovakia into Austria under heavy fire which wounds several members.			U.S. planes bomb the Kikung River bridge in North Vietnam ten miles from Communist China.
Aug. 14			About 2,000 members of the Congolese Popular Revolutionary Movement attack the Belgian embassy in Kinshasha. . . . Israeli Foreign Min. Abba Eban reiterates his government's decision to retain the territories that Israel has conquered until a peace settlement is reached in direct Arab-Israeli negotiations.		U.S. planes bomb Langson Bridge in North Vietnam. . . . Tens of thousands of Chinese demonstrators protest outside of the Soviet embassy in Peking.
Aug. 15	U.N. Secy. Gen. U Thant appoints Dr. Ernesto Thalman to undertake a fact-finding mission in Jerusalem to determine the effects of Israel's annexation of the former Jordanian sector of the city.				
Aug. 16		Charles Jordan, a U.S. official of an American Jewish agency, is reported missing from his Prague hotel.	Congolese Pres. Joseph Mobutu reprimands Congolese Popular Revolutionary Movement members for their Aug. 14 attack on the Belgian embassy in Kinshasha. . . . Reports indicate that Biafran units have invaded the western region of Nigeria.		South Vietnamese civilian candidates resume their campaign. . . . South Korean port authorities report that the Greek freighter *Vamvakas* had to flee Shanghai on Aug. 12 because of Red Guard attacks.
	A	B	C	D	E
	Includes developments that affect more than one world region, international organizations and important meetings of major world leaders.	*Includes all domestic and regional developments in Europe, including the Soviet Union, Turkey, Cyprus and Malta.*	*Includes all domestic and regional developments in Africa and the Middle East, including Iraq and Iran and excluding Cyprus, Turkey and Afghanistan.*	*Includes all domestic and regional developments in Latin America, the Caribbean and Canada.*	*Includes all domestic and regional developments in Asia and Pacific nations, extending from Afghanistan through all the Pacific Islands, except Hawaii.*

U.S. Politics & Social Issues	U.S. Foreign Policy & Defense	U.S. Economy & Environment	Science, Technology & Nature	Culture, Leisure & Life Style	
A civil rights march protesting the lack of job opportunities for Negroes begins in Bogalusa, La. . . . President's Advisory Commission on Civil Disorders urges prompt action to increase the number of Negroes in the National Guard. . . . FBI reports an 11.4% increase in serious crimes committed in 1966 in comparison with 1965.	Twenty-one House Republicans introduce a resolution urging the reconsideration of the Tonkin Gulf resolution.				Aug. 10
	U.S. Senators from both parties voice concern about the fairness of the upcoming South Vietnamese elections.	Federal Highway Administration announces modifications of the car-safety standard for interior design.			Aug. 11
					Aug. 12
Two carloads of Negroes fire on a crowd of whites in Hammond, La. for no apparent reason. . . . Muhammad Ali (Cassius Clay), deposed heavyweight champion, serves as parade marshall for a three-hour integrated parade through the Watts section of Los Angeles.	Sen. Thruston Morton (R, Ky.) calls for a de-escalation of the Vietnamese War.				Aug. 13
SNCC newsletter denounces Zionism and charges that Israelis are committing atrocities against Arabs. . . . A grand jury in Cambridge, Md. indicts H. Rap Brown on charges stemming from the city's July 24-25 riots. . . . Census Bureau reports that the poor comprise 41% of the nonwhite population and 12% of the white population. . . . Tenth annual convention of Martin Luther King's Southern Christian Leadership Conference calls for a massive civil disobedience campaign in Northern cities. . . . Nearly 800 Negroes stage a "poor people's march" from the Negro Masonic Temple in Jackson, Miss. to the state capitol.		Gardner Ackley, chairman of the President's Council of Economic Advisers, warns that a failure to increase taxes will end the chances of price stability.			Aug. 14
Martin Luther King Jr. says that he will lead demonstrations to disrupt Northern cities in an effort to get federal funds. . . . Major civil rights leaders denounce SNCC's Aug. 14 attack on Israel and its Jewish supporters. . . . Fifteen whites break through a police escort and attack 20 Negro marchers in Holden, La. . . . Martin Luther King Jr. proposes a plan for a massive civil disobedience campaign to disrupt federal activities in Washington.	NASA Director James Webb says that the Soviet Union will probably have more powerful rocket boosters than the U.S. "for a number of years to come.". . . West German Chancellor Kurt-Georg Kiesinger confers with Pres. Johnson in Washington.			Belgian surrealist painter Rene Magritte dies in Brussels at 68.	Aug. 15
Seventy-five whites attack 25 Negro protest marchers in Satsuma, La. . . . Sporadic racial disorders take place in Syracuse, N.Y. . . . Martin Luther King Jr. calls on SCLC delegates "to drive the nation to a guaranteed annual income."	U.S. Senate Foreign Relations Committee begins hearings on the extent of U.S. foreign commitments. . . . Gov. George Romney (R, Mich.) says that he thinks that the Vietnamese War should be a major issue in the 1968 election campaign.	Thirty-four thousand, four hundred U.S. farmers meeting in Des Moines, Ia., agree to withhold all their products from market, if necessary, in a campaign to raise farm prices.			Aug. 16

F	G	H	I	J
Includes elections, federal-state relations, civil rights and liberties, crime, the judiciary, education, health care, poverty, urban affairs and population.	Includes formation and debate of U.S. foreign and defense policies, veterans' affairs and defense spending. (Relations with specific foreign countries are usually found under the region concerned.)	Includes business, labor, agriculture, taxation, transportation, consumer affairs, monetary and fiscal policy, natural resources, and pollution.	Includes worldwide scientific, medical and technological developments, natural phenomena, U.S. weather, natural disasters, and accidents.	Includes the arts, religion, scholarship, communications media, sports, entertainment, fashions, fads and social life.

	World Affairs	Europe	Africa & the Middle East	The Americas	Asia & the Pacific
Aug. 17	Soviet Union charges that anti-Soviet demonstrations are making a "mockery" of relations between Communist China and Russia. . . . Reports indicate that British P.M. Harold Wilson has defended the recent extension of the U.S. bombing of North Vietnam.		In the Congo (Kinshasha), the radio of the rebel-held capital of Bukavu charges that Burundi is helping the federal government to organize an attack on Bukavu.	In a broadcast over Havana radio, civil rights activist Stokely Carmichael calls on U.S. Negroes to arm for "total revolution."	Communist Chinese demonstrators break into the Soviet embassy compound in Peking and set fire to files.
Aug. 18			Rhodesia reports killing eight guerrillas. . . . Kenyan soldiers clash with Somali guerrillas.	Organization of Latin American Solidarity Conference calls on U.S. Negroes to use direct revolutionary action to achieve their goals.	
Aug. 19			Rhodesia says that 30 armed guerrillas entered its territory from Zambia during the previous weekend. . . . Arab guerrilla attacks kill three British airmen in Aden. . . . Reports indicate that Nigeria has received jet fighter planes from the Soviet Union.		
Aug. 20		Body of Charles Jordan, a U.S. official of an American Jewish agency, is found in the Vltava River.	A Biafran bomber raids the Kano airport in northern Nigeria.	About 700 members of rival factions of a Mexican coconut-growers union wage a 20-minute gun-battle in which 23 people are killed.	
Aug. 21		Greek government arrests Greek composer Mikis Theodorakis.		Nearly 600 Catholic Univ. students end a 10-day sit-in at several of their school's buildings in Santiago, Chile. . . . Bolivian Pres. Rene Barrientos says that his country might be willing to exchange French Marxist Regis Debray for anti-communist prisoners held in communist countries.	
Aug. 22			Nigerian federal government accuses the U.S. of "thinly disguised support" for Biafra. . . . Rwandan Pres. Gregoire Kayibanda rejects an appeal of white mercenary leader Jean Schramme to bring his troops into Rwanda. . . . Assembly of Mauritius votes unanimously to ask Britain to grant it its independence during 1967.		Red Guards sack and set fire to the British chancery in Peking. . . . U.S. command in Saigon says that North Vietnam shot down six U.S. planes on Aug. 21.
Aug. 23			Rhodesia reports killing five African guerrillas from Zambia. . . . Tunisian Pres. Habib Bourguiba reiterates his plea for an end to the Arab countries' state of belligerency against Israel.		Reports indicate that Ceylon has restricted people of Chinese origin in their travels to and from Ceylon because of alleged Communist Chinese subversive activities. . . . Red Guards continue their pillage of the British chancery in Peking and force British diplomats to kneel and bow before them. . . . Communist Chinese Public Security Min. Hsieh Fu-chih tells Peking Red Guards to return to school and stop engaging in "civil wars."
Aug. 24			Reports indicate that the National Liberation Front of Aden has seized control of one of their country's provinces. . . . Arab guerrillas wound three Israeli soldiers near Jerusalem. . . . Rhodesian planes strafe guerrilla positions in the Wankie area. . . . *The New York Times* reports that Ethiopia has stepped up its campaign against Eritrean secessionists in the wake of the Arab defeat in the recent Middle East War.	In Canada Ontario Premier John Robarts announces that his province will establish secondary schools in which French will be the language of instruction.	U.S. Thailand-based jets bomb four North Vietnamese railroad yards.

A	B	C	D	E
Includes developments that affect more than one world region, international organizations and important meetings of major world leaders.	Includes all domestic and regional developments in Europe, including the Soviet Union, Turkey, Cyprus and Malta.	Includes all domestic and regional developments in Africa and the Middle East, including Iraq and Iran and excluding Cyprus, Turkey and Afghanistan.	Includes all domestic and regional developments in Latin America, the Caribbean and Canada.	Includes all domestic and regional developments in Asia and Pacific nations, extending from Afghanistan through all the Pacific Islands, except Hawaii.

U.S. Politics & Social Issues	U.S. Foreign Policy & Defense	U.S. Economy & Environment	Science, Technology & Nature	Culture, Leisure & Life Style	
Martin Luther King Jr. says that the SCLC will oppose Pres. Johnson in the 1968 elections unless he de-escalates the Vietnamese War. . . . Louisiana Gov. John McKeithen calls up 650 National Guardsmen to protect Negro marchers. . . . Syracuse, N.Y. Mayor William Walsh imposes a curfew as police use tear gas to disperse about 200 Negroes attacking police cars.	U.S. Senate passes a foreign aid bill by 60-26.				Aug. 17
White hecklers throw bottles and eggs at Negro marchers in Denham Springs, La. . . . Syracuse Mayor William Walsh announces a four-hour reduction in the city curfew.		Pres. Johnson calls for collective bargaining rights for U.S. farmers.		Doubleday publishes Daphne du Maurier's *Vanishing Cornwall.*	Aug. 18
N.Y.C. police arrest H. Rap Brown on federal charges of carrying a gun across state lines while under indictment. . . . An open housing ordinance is introduced in the Milwaukee Common Council.				Historian Isaac Deutscher dies in Rome at 60.	Aug. 19
Syracuse, N.Y. Mayor William Walsh lifts his city's curfew as conditions return to normal.					Aug. 20
	U.S. Defense Dept. reports the downing of a U.S. plane over Communist China on Aug. 11. . . . Former V.P. Richard Nixon favors the use of "massive pressure" against North Vietnam but rules out the use of nuclear weapons.	At House Ways and Means Committee hearings, Pres. W. P. Gullander of the National Association of Manufacturers supports the administration's 10% surtax proposal.			Aug. 21
SNCC chmn. H. Rap Brown is released on bail. . . . U.S. Senate defeats a proposal by Sen. Edward Kennedy to cut funding for a civilian marksmanship training program by a vote of 67-23.	U.S. Senate passes by 84-3 a bill funding the Vietnamese War. . . . Pres. Johnson meets with the Shah of Iran at the White House.				Aug. 22
France pledges a "considerable increase" in its aid to the Canadian Province of Quebec.	White House announces that 20 leading Americans will observe the upcoming South Vietnamese elections.	At House Ways & Means Committee hearings, AFL-CIO Pres. George Meany says that any tax increase should be "at least twice as great" on corporations than on individuals.		In a statement on the Middle East situation, the World Council of Churches says that "no nation should be allowed to keep or annex the territory of another by armed force."	Aug. 23
	Reports indicate that the U.S. has appealed to Israel to extend the Aug. 31 deadline for the return of Arab refugees to their homes on the West Bank of the Jordan River.	A group of 113 business executives declare their support of a tax increase.	Soviet Union launches Cosmos 173.	U.S. industrialist Henry Kaiser dies in Honolulu at 85.	Aug. 24
F	**G**	**H**	**I**	**J**	
Includes elections, federal-state relations, civil rights and liberties, crime, the judiciary, education, health care, poverty, urban affairs and population.	*Includes formation and debate of U.S. foreign and defense policies, veterans' affairs and defense spending. (Relations with specific foreign countries are usually found under the region concerned.)*	*Includes business, labor, agriculture, taxation, transportation, consumer affairs, monetary and fiscal policy, natural resources, and pollution.*	*Includes worldwide scientific, medical and technological developments, natural phenomena, U.S. weather, natural disasters, and accidents.*	*Includes the arts, religion, scholarship, communications media, sports, entertainment, fashions, fads and social life.*	

	World Affairs	Europe	Africa & the Middle East	The Americas	Asia & the Pacific
Aug. 25		Britain and the Soviet Union agree to install a direct telecommunication link between their two governments. . . . A Greek military court convicts 31 opponents of the military government.	Israeli troops dynamite five Arab buildings near Jerusalem in retaliation for the Aug. 24 attack on an Israeli patrol. . . . Egypt arrests 50 top-ranking military and civilian officials, accused of planning a coup d'etat against Egyptian Pres. Nasser. . . . Rhodesian Deputy P.M. John Wrathall warns Zambia that his country will take retaliatory action unless the guerrilla infiltration from Zambia stops.	Argentinian Pres. Juan Carlos Ongania signs a law prohibiting communists from certain positions and activities.	North Vietnam announces further civilian evacuations from Hanoi.
Aug. 26	Financial leaders of 10 leading industrial countries agree to a monetary reform plan.	Greece indicts Greek leftist Andreas Papandreou on charges of high treason.	U.N. envoy Dr. Ernesto Thalman receives a protest petition during a meeting with Arab leaders in Jerusalem. . . . Israel reports shooting down an Egyptian fighter-bomber over the Sinai. . . . Rhodesia reports killing 24 African guerrillas in two weeks of clashes.		North Vietnam downs a record 16 U.S. planes during the Aug. 20-26 period.
Aug. 27		Three out of four East Germans escape from Czechoslovakia to Austria. The fourth is killed by a Czech border guard.	Zambia denies that it is supporting the anti-Rhodesian guerrilla movement. . . . National Liberation Front of Aden seizes government buildings in a provincial capital.		*The New York Times* reports that North Vietnamese MiGs are using Communist Chinese air space as a "sanctuary" to escape air clashes with U.S. planes. . . . Viet Cong attacks shell South Vietnamese cities and kill several hundred civilians.
Aug. 28		British P.M. Harold Wilson assumes control of Britain's Department of Economic Affairs.		Foreign ministers of 11 Latin American countries meet to discuss proposals for setting up a Latin American common market. . . . Argentinian General Confederation of Labor announces that it will not recognize the authority of Argentinian Pres. Juan Carlos Ongania because he is not a constitutional president.	North Vietnamese artillery pounds three U.S. Marine outposts just south of the demilitarized zone.
Aug. 29			Leaders of 13 Arab states meet in Khartoum, Sudan. . . . Reports indicate that a previously arranged cease-fire has collapsed in Yemen.		Soviet Union reportedly has been distributing leaflets in Asian capitals warning of the danger of Communist Chinese nuclear attack in the area. . . . Viet Cong guerrillas blow up nine bridges in South Vietnam.
Aug. 30	At a U.N. Disarmament Committee meeting, Brazil and Nigeria propose that the nuclear non-proliferation pact permit non-nuclear signatories to conduct nuclear explosions for earth-moving purposes.		In speeches at the Khartoum Conference, Egyptian Pres. Nasser and Jordanian King Hussein indicate the need for a political solution of the Arab-Israeli conflict. . . . Kenyan economic planning and development minister accuses Communist China of "gross interference" in Kenya's domestic affairs.		Viet Cong guerrillas storm a jail in the northern city of Quangngai and free 1,200 prisoners most of whom who are also guerrillas.
Aug. 31			Egyptian Pres. Gamal Abdel Nasser and Saudi King Faisal announce the formation of a three-nation committee to supervise the withdrawal from Yemen of Egyptian troops.	Bolivian army reportedly wipes out a nine-man guerrilla group.	Indonesia and Malaysia resume full diplomatic relations which were severed in 1963.
Sept. 1	A U.N. Special Committee votes 16-2 to condemn Britain's plans to hold a referendum in Gibraltar.	Soviet authorities convict three Soviet intellectuals including biologist Vladimir Bukovsky on charges of staging an illegal demonstration on Jan. 22, 1967.	Arab leaders at the conclusion of the Khartoum Conference commit themselves to no peace with Israel, no negotiations with Israel and no recognition of Israel.		Cambodian chief-of-state Norodom Sihanouk dissolves the Cambodian-China Friendship Association because of alleged Communist Chinese subversive activities. . . . North Vietnamese Premier Pham Van Dong reiterates his government's stand that an unconditional halt in U.S. raids on the North is the prerequisite to peace negotiations. . . . Shanghai Municipal Revolutionary Committee orders the army to confiscate the weapons of Maoist revolutionaries.
	A	B	C	D	E
	Includes developments that affect more than one world region, international organizations and important meetings of major world leaders.	*Includes all domestic and regional developments in Europe, including the Soviet Union, Turkey, Cyprus and Malta.*	*Includes all domestic and regional developments in Africa and the Middle East, including Iraq and Iran and excluding Cyprus, Turkey and Afghanistan.*	*Includes all domestic and regional developments in Latin America, the Caribbean and Canada.*	*Includes all domestic and regional developments in Asia and Pacific nations, extending from Afghanistan through all the Pacific Islands, except Hawaii.*

U.S. Politics & Social Issues	U.S. Foreign Policy & Defense	U.S. Economy & Environment	Science, Technology & Nature	Culture, Leisure & Life Style	
George Lincoln Rockwell, founder and leader of the American Nazi Party, is shot to death in Arlington, Va. by a former aide.	At the Senate Preparedness Subcommittee hearings, State Secy. McNamara says that he does not believe that the bombing of North Vietnam "has in any significant way affected their war-making capability."				Aug. 25
A New Orleans federal court rules that Louisiana's program of tuition grants for students in private schools is designed to maintain a segregated school system and is therefore unconstitutional. . . . A civil rights commission reports that progress in improving the Watts section of Los Angeles since the 1965 riot has been "encouraging but far from satisfying."	National Chairman of Americans for Democratic Action John Kenneth Galbraith calls for the de-escalation of the Vietnam War. . . . Sen. Joseph Tydings (D, Md.) says that the increasing U.S. military commitment to South Vietnam is a mistake.				Aug. 26
	National Committee for an Effective Congress warns that a "clash" is developing between "a rising Senate" and Pres. Johnson. . . . Western States Democratic Conference unanimously approves a resolution supporting Pres. Johnson's policies in Vietnam.				Aug. 27
Thousands of Negro and white demonstrators march in Milwaukee in support of open housing. . . . More than 1,000 welfare recipients picket the HEW Dept. building in Washington, D.C. to protest welfare restrictions in the recently passed House Social Security bill.	A Louis Harris public opinion survey reports that public backing for U.S. involvement in the Vietnamese War has dropped from 72% to 61% in the past six weeks. . . . U.S. Defense Dept. acknowledges technical problems with the M-16 rifle and reports that it is being re-evaluated.	American Bankers Association declares its support of a tax increase.			Aug. 28
Congressional leaders charge that the Johnson administration is "losing the war against crime."				U.S. historian Sidney Fay dies in Lexington, Mass. at 91.	Aug. 29
		Republic Steel Corp. announces a 1.8% price hike for steel bars.		U.S. abstract painter Ad Reinhardt dies in New York at 53.	Aug. 30
A growing schism between black power leaders and white liberals dominates the first convention of the National Conference for a New Politics.	U.S. Senate Preparedness Investigating Subcommittee calls unanimously for an intensification of bombing attacks against North Vietnam and for the closing of the port of Haiphong.	Council of Economic Advisers Chmn. Gardner Ackley calls the Aug. 30 steel price hike "distressing."	U.S. conducts an underground nuclear test. . . . Soviet Union launches Cosmos 174.		Aug. 31
Negro leaders decide to meet without white delegates at the National Conference for a New Politics.		Pres. Johnson expresses his regret about the Aug. 30 steel price hike.		British poet Siegfried Sassoon dies in Wiltshire, England at 80. . . . Soviet writer Ilya Ehrenburg dies in Moscow at 76.	Sept. 1

F	G	H	I	J
Includes elections, federal-state relations, civil rights and liberties, crime, the judiciary, education, health care, poverty, urban affairs and population.	Includes formation and debate of U.S. foreign and defense policies, veterans' affairs and defense spending. (Relations with specific foreign countries are usually found under the region concerned.)	Includes business, labor, agriculture, taxation, transportation, consumer affairs, monetary and fiscal policy, natural resources, and pollution.	Includes worldwide scientific, medical and technological developments, natural phenomena, U.S. weather, natural disasters, and accidents.	Includes the arts, religion, scholarship, communications media, sports, entertainment, fashions, fads and social life.

	World Affairs	Europe	Africa & the Middle East	The Americas	Asia & the Pacific
Sept. 2			Nigeria's military commander Maj. Gen. Yakubu Gowan says that his country will not negotiate with Biafran military leader Lt. Col. Chukwuemeka Ojukwu.		Viet Cong terrorist raids against South Vietnamese civilians intensify.
Sept. 3		*London Times* reports that more than 300 Czech intellectuals have issued a 1,000-word manifesto accusing the Czech Communist Party of conducting "a witch-hunt."	Kuwait decides to resume oil shipments to Britain and the U.S. which had been under a boycott since the beginning of the Arab-Israeli war.	Foreign ministers of 11 Latin American countries end their discussions without reaching substantial agreement about setting up a common market.	Communist China announces that it is withdrawing from the International Red Cross. . . . South Vietnamese presidential candidate Nguyen Van Thieu and vice presidential candidate Nguyen Cao Ky win national elections in South Vietnam. . . . A Hong Kong official says that Communist Chinese exports to the British colony declined sharply in the June-August period in comparison to the same period in 1966.
Sept. 4			Four Soviet destroyers and two submarines arrive in the Egyptian port of Alexandria. . . . East Jerusalem Arab schools close down to protest Israeli rule.	Foreign ministers of 11 Latin American countries hold their first meeting with representatives of the Central American states.	South Vietnamese Constituent Assembly Speaker Phan Khac Suu says that seven of the 10 civilian candidates in the Sept. 3 elections have filed protests about alleged fraudulent practices in the balloting. . . . Tokyo newspaper reports that Communist Chinese Premier Chou En-lai has ordered Peking demonstrators not to enter foreign diplomatic missions.
Sept. 5			Britain recognizes the National Liberation Front as the sole representative of the people of the South Arabian Federation.		Fierce fighting rages south of Danang between U.S. and North Vietnamese troops. . . . Peking authorities order the army to prevent the unauthorized arming of civilians. . . . Communist Chinese Party Chmn. Mao Tse-tung's wife Chiang Ching scores the extremism associated with the Cultural Revolution. . . . Indian Foreign Min. Mohamed Ali Currim Chagla resigns in protest against the government's decision to replace English with Indian regional languages in universities.
Sept. 6		French Pres. Charles de Gaulle begins a tour of Poland, the first East European communist country he has visited.	Bukavu radio says that supporters of white mercenaries have captured the Congolese towns of Lubutu and Punia and are pressing north toward Kisangani, capital of Orientale Province. . . . Israel reports the Egyptian shelling of their positions on the East Bank. . . . Egyptian newspaper *Al Ahram* informs the Egyptian public for the first time that their country lost a "sizeable amount" of military equipment in the war with Israel.		South Vietnamese troops throw back a four-hour Viet Cong assault against the city of Tamky.
Sept. 7		Two East German soldiers flee successfully to West Germany near Bad Hersfeld. . . . French Pres. Charles de Gaulle speaks for the need of "independence" for European countries during his Polish tour. . . . Soviet CP Gen. Secy. Leonid Brezhnev declares that Chinese CP Chmn. Mao Tse-tung can "no longer be called a communist." . . . Hungary and the Soviet Union sign a 20-year treaty of friendship.	Israel reports gun fire exchanges along the Israeli-Jordanian border.		North Vietnamese kill 20 U.S. Marines in clashes just south of the demilitarized zone.
Sept. 8		Hundreds of thousands of Poles welcome Pres. de Gaulle in Cracow.	South Africa announces the arrest of an alleged Soviet spy Yuri Nikolayevich Loginov.		U.S. planes bomb railroad and truck bridges north of Hanoi.
Sept. 9		French Pres. de Gaulle pays a solemn visit to the former Nazi concentration camp at Auschwitz. . . . Greek and Turkish officials discuss the Cyprus issue in Turkey.		Canadian Conservatives elect Robert Stanfield to replace former Canadian prime minister John Diefenbaker (1957-1963).	Monsoon rains kill at least 210 people in India.
	A Includes developments that affect more than one world region, international organizations and important meetings of major world leaders.	**B** Includes all domestic and regional developments in Europe, including the Soviet Union, Turkey, Cyprus and Malta.	**C** Includes all domestic and regional developments in Africa and the Middle East, including Iraq and Iran and excluding Cyprus, Turkey and Afghanistan.	**D** Includes all domestic and regional developments in Latin America, the Caribbean and Canada.	**E** Includes all domestic and regional developments in Asia and Pacific nations, extending from Afghanistan through all the Pacific Islands, except Hawaii.

U.S. Politics & Social Issues	U.S. Foreign Policy & Defense	U.S. Economy & Environment	Science, Technology & Nature	Culture, Leisure & Life Style	
Negro leaders reject conciliatory gestures by whites at the National Conference for a New Politics.					Sept. 2
White majority agrees to give Negro delegates half the convention votes at the National Conference for a New Politics.					Sept. 3
	Sen. Robert Kennedy says that he hopes that the South Vietnamese election will lead to negotiations with North Vietnam and the South Vietnamese National Liberation Front. . . . Gov. George Romney says that he underwent "a brainwashing" during his 1965 trip to South Vietnam.		U.S. traffic fatalities during the Labor Day weekend total 609.		Sept. 4
				Lester Barlow, the inventor of aerial bombs and torpedoes used in W.W. I, dies at 80 in Stamford, Conn.	Sept. 5
U.S. Socialist leader Norman Thomas deplores the approval of an alleged policy of "black apartheid" by the National Conference for a New Politics. . . . Pres. Johnson nominates Walter Washington to be the first commissioner of the newly organized municipal government of Washington, D.C.	Twenty-two U.S. observers of the Sept. 3 South Vietnamese elections meet with Pres. Johnson and declare that the elections were generally honest.	UAW begins a strike against the Ford Motor Co.		Brace & World publishes Mary McCarthy's *Vietnam.*	Sept. 6
Defense Secy. Robert McNamara says that the Pentagon will declare off-limits all segregated housing located near military installations throughout the U.S.	Defense Secy. McNamara announces plans to build a fortified barrier just south of the demilitarized zone to curb the flow of North Vietnamese arms and men into the South.		U.S. launches Biosatellite 2 which contains thousands of biological specimens. . . . U.S. conducts an underground nuclear test.	Oxford University Press publishes Mohammad Ayub Khan's *Friends Not Masters.*	Sept. 7
					Sept. 8
				Random House publishes William Styron's *The Confessions of Nat Turner.*	Sept. 9

F	G	H	I	J
Includes elections, federal-state relations, civil rights and liberties, crime, the judiciary, education, health care, poverty, urban affairs and population.	Includes formation and debate of U.S. foreign and defense policies, veterans' affairs and defense spending. (Relations with specific foreign countries are usually found under the region concerned.)	Includes business, labor, agriculture, taxation, transportation, consumer affairs, monetary and fiscal policy, natural resources, and pollution.	Includes worldwide scientific, medical and technological developments, natural phenomena, U.S. weather, natural disasters, and accidents.	Includes the arts, religion, scholarship, communications media, sports, entertainment, fashions, fads and social life.

	World Affairs	Europe	Africa & the Middle East	The Americas	Asia & the Pacific
Sept. 10	U.N. Gen. Assembly votes 73-19 to condemn Britain's recent referendum in Gibraltar.	Greek and Turkish officials discuss the Cyprus issue in Greece but report no progress. . . . Pres. de Gaulle refers to Gdansk, the former German city of Danzig, as "profoundly and extraordinarily Polish.". . . Gibraltarians vote overwhelmingly to retain British sovereignty.	Reports indicate that Egyptian troops have begun to withdraw from Yemen.		U.S. planes bomb the North Vietnamese port of Campha for the first time.
Sept. 11		French Pres. de Gaulle confers with Polish CP First Secy. Wladyslaw Gomulka in Warsaw.	Organization of African Unity meets in Kinshasha, the capital of the Congo.		Communist forces open artillery fire on Indian positions in Sikkim.
Sept. 12			Israel and Egypt exchange gun fire across the Suez Canal.		Indian and Communist Chinese troops exchange intermittent artillery fire at Natu La. . . . Hundreds of Saigon students demonstrate to protest the results of the Sept. 3 elections.
Sept. 13			Israel and Egypt continue gun fire exchanges across the Suez Canal. . . . Egyptian newspaper *Al Ahram* describes the alleged Aug. 25 military plot in detail and accuses former deputy supreme commander Marshall Abdel Hakim Amer of being the plot's leader. . . . Organization of African Unity unanimously adopts a statement demanding that the white mercenaries leave the Congo (Kinshasha) or face possible military action by African states.		Communist Chinese forces continue their shelling of Indian positions at Natu La.
Sept. 14					Six defeated civilian candidates announce the formation of an "opposition front" in South Vietnam. . . . Communist Chinese shelling is so light that Indian forces are instructed to hold their fire.
Sept. 15		Two hundred protesting students forcibly enter the West Berlin city hall before being rejected.	A bomb derails an Israeli freight train near the West Bank city of Tulkarem. . . . Reports indicate major clashes between royalist and republican forces in Yemen.	Cuba reports having signed an agreement with the Soviet Union to collaborate in the "peaceful uses" of atomic energy.	No shelling takes place on the Communist Chinese-Indian border. . . . Viet Cong attacks U.S. ships on the Rachba River.
Sept. 16	U.N. Secy Gen. U Thant discloses unconfirmed reports that North Vietnam has been promised foreign military personnel.		Israeli authorities impose a curfew in the Tulkarem area in response to the Sept. 15 attack. . . . South Africa says that the mission of alleged Soviet spy, Yuri Nikolayevich Loginov, included estimating Rhodesia's dependence on South Africa.		U.S. and South Vietnamese troops inflict major casualties on the Viet Cong in the Mekong Delta.
Sept. 17		Reports indicate that France has notified other NATO members that, beginning Jan. 1 1968, permission for overflights of French territory will be granted on an annual basis instead of the monthly basis which has been in effect since June 1966.	Zambian Pres. Kenneth Kuanda says that the Organization of African Unity has approved plans for providing safe-conduct from the Congo for the 150 white mercenaries still in Bukavu.		Viet Cong attack the provincial capital of Tamky for the second time in less than two weeks.
Sept. 18				Bolivia announces the arrest of 15 people accused of aiding the guerrillas.	U.S. planes bomb military targets in Haiphong.

A	B	C	D	E
Includes developments that affect more than one world region, international organizations and important meetings of major world leaders.	Includes all domestic and regional developments in Europe, including the Soviet Union, Turkey, Cyprus and Malta.	Includes all domestic and regional developments in Africa and the Middle East, including Iraq and Iran and excluding Cyprus, Turkey and Afghanistan.	Includes all domestic and regional developments in Latin America, the Caribbean and Canada.	Includes all domestic and regional developments in Asia and Pacific nations, extending from Afghanistan through all the Pacific Islands, except Hawaii.

U.S. Politics & Social Issues	U.S. Foreign Policy & Defense	U.S. Economy & Environment	Science, Technology & Nature	Culture, Leisure & Life Style	
Violence breaks out in the Negro district of East St. Louis, Ill. after an inflammatory speech by civil rights activist H. Rap Brown.		Two hundred sixty university economists endorse the administration's proposed tax increase.	U.S. AEC announces that the U.S. has created the heaviest isotope "definitely observed by man."	White House announces the engagement of Pres. Johnson's daughter Lynda Bird Johnson and Captain Charles Robb.	Sept. 10
Justice Dept. files suit against Noxubee County, Miss. for interfering with court-ordered school desegregation. . . . Negroes loot stores and set fires in East St. Louis, Ill.		Sen. Robert Kennedy charges that the cigarette industry is "peddling a deadly weapon. . .for financial gain."	Soviet Union launches Cosmos 175.		Sept. 11
East St. Louis, Ill. Negroes drag white motorists from their cars and beat them.	Senate passes the appropriations bill for the Defense Dept. in fiscal 1968 by a vote of 74-3.	AFL-CIO Executive Council urges a massive effort to revitalize urban America. . . . Seven of eight economists endorse a tax increase at House Ways and Means Committee hearings.	Soviet Union launches Cosmos 176.		Sept. 12
Police arrest six East St. Louis, Ill. Negroes on charges of disorderly conduct in wake of racial disorders. . . . Illinois religious leaders appeal to the state legislature to enact a statewide open-housing law.	Senate Appropriations Subcommittee releases testimony revealing technical problems in the developmental models of the F-111 combat plane.	Former Treasury Secy. Robert Roosa declares his support of a tax increase.		Varian Fry, the leader of a group which helped Marc Chagall and Jacques Lipchitz flee German-occupied France, dies in Easton, Conn. at 59.	Sept. 13
Violence flares for more than five hours on Chicago's South Side after a rally sponsored by the radical SNCC organization. . . . Pres. Johnson urges the enactment of gun control laws during a speech at the convention of the International Association of Chiefs of Police.		Federal Reserve Board Chmn. William McChesney Martin endorses a tax increase.	Reports indicate that U.S. satellite Biosatellite 2's wheat seedlings have grown in less than two days of weightlessness "as much. . .as the same plants normally grow in three days on earth."		Sept. 14
A U.S. district court declares Kentucky's sedition laws unconstitutional.				Monthly Review Press publishes Regis Debray's Revolution in the Revolution? . . . . G.P. Putnam's Sons publishes Norman Mailer's Why Are We in Vietnam?	Sept. 15
	U.S. State Dept. says that it has known that volunteer North Korean pilots and Communist Chinese engineers are in North Vietnam. . . . Sen. J. William Fulbright criticizes the proposed anti-ballistic missile system.		Soviet Union launches Cosmos 177.		Sept. 16
Negative public reaction to Gov. George Romney's Sept. 4 "brainwashing" statement is reflected in a Louis Harris survey in which Romney badly trails Pres. Johnson.			Soviet Union launches a satellite.		Sept. 17
Hartford, Conn. whites attack Negro and Puerto Rican protest marchers with rocks and bottles. . . . A Virginia court frees SNCC chmn. H. Rap Brown after five days in jail.	Defense Secy. McNamara announces that the U.S. will deploy an anti-ballistic missile system.		U.S. launches Surveyor 5.	Metropolitan Opera opens its 83rd season with a production of La Traviata starring soprano Montserrat Caballe.	Sept. 18
F	G	H	I	J	
Includes elections, federal-state relations, civil rights and liberties, crime, the judiciary, education, health care, poverty, urban affairs and population.	Includes formation and debate of U.S. foreign and defense policies, veterans' affairs and defense spending. (Relations with specific foreign countries are usually found under the region concerned.)	Includes business, labor, agriculture, taxation, transportation, consumer affairs, monetary and fiscal policy, natural resources, and pollution.	Includes worldwide scientific, medical and technological developments, natural phenomena, U.S. weather, natural disasters, and accidents.	Includes the arts, religion, scholarship, communications media, sports, entertainment, fashions, fads and social life.	

	World Affairs	Europe	Africa & the Middle East	The Americas	Asia & the Pacific
Sept. 19			Arab merchants stage a general strike in the West Bank town of Nablus. . . . Egypt reports the arrest of 181 military officers and civilians for security reasons since the outbreak of the June Arab-Israeli war.		A bomb causes heavy damage at the Chinese Nationalist embassy in Saigon.
Sept. 20	U.N. Secy. Gen. U Thant appeals to the Ivory Coast and Guinea to exchange prisoners.		A dynamite charge blasts an Israeli factory near Hadera. . . . Witnesses begin to testify at the South African trial of 37 African guerrillas.		
Sept. 21		Delegates of the European Organization for Nuclear Research (CERN) tacitly agree to recruit a team to build a nuclear accelerator.	Israel charges that Egyptian artillery shelling killed four Israelis.		First Thai combat troops arrive in South Vietnam. . . . U.S. planes pound the port of Haiphong. . . . U.S. reports 236 combat deaths in South Vietnam for the period of Sept. 10-16.
Sept. 22		*Tass* reports that top Polish officials are meeting top Soviet officials in Moscow.	Egyptian newspaper *Al Ahram* reports that 23 Israelis were killed during the Sept. 21 shelling across the Suez Canal.	Bolivian Gen. Alfredo Ovando Candia, the armed forces commander, says that his troops have succeeded in scattering guerrillas in recent weeks.	
Sept. 23		North Vietnam and the Soviet Union sign an agreement in Moscow for 1968 military and economic assistance.	Israeli authorities intensify their search for hidden arms on the West Bank of the Jordan River.	Argentinian Foreign Min. Nicanor Costa Mendez says that his country will support the use of armed force against Cuban Premier Castro if the OAS decides on such action.	
Sept. 24	World Bank reports that for the sixth consecutive year there has been practically no increase in foreign aid from the industrial countries.		Israeli Premier Levi Eshkol announces plans for resettlement of a former Israeli farm community on the West Bank of the Jordan River. . . . Arab merchants of the West Bank town of Nablus again defy Israeli authorities and stage another general strike.	A meeting of 21 Latin American foreign ministers adopts several resolutions condemning Cuban subversion.	Demonstrations protesting alleged abuses in the Sept. 3 elections take place in Saigon, Danang and Hue.
Sept. 25	Israeli Foreign Min. Abba Eban tells the U.N. General Assembly that a permanent Middle East settlement can only come about through direct negotiations between Israel and the Arabs.	Soviet space scientist Leonid Sedov hints that the Soviet Union may be willing to cooperate with other countries on major space projects.	Guinea and the Ivory Coast agree to an exchange of prisoners. . . . Arab guerrillas dynamite an Israeli factory at Givat Habiba. . . . Witnesses say that the 37 African guerrillas on trial in South Africa were trained in the Soviet Union, Egypt, Tanzania and part of South-West Africa.		U.S. planes bomb the demilitarized zone.
Sept. 26	At the U.N. General Assembly, Uruguayan Foreign Min. Hector Luisi says that a North Atlantic civilization threatens to turn the developing countries into an "external proletariat.". . . At a U.N. Disarmament Committee meeting, Egyptian delegate Hussein Khallaf calls for including in the proposed nuclear non-proliferation treaty a pledge by the nuclear powers that they would not use their nuclear weapons as a form of blackmail against the non-nuclear signatories.	Britain, France and West Germany agree to develop a short-to-medium-distance air bus.	Two rival nationalist groups of the South Arabian Federation agree to a cease-fire.	Bolivian authorities open the military trial of Regis Debray to the press.	U.S. planes continue their attacks on the demilitarized zone between the two Vietnams. . . . Laotian Premier Souvanna Phouma says that there are 40,000 North Vietnamese troops in Laos.
Sept. 27		Czechoslovak CP Central Committee expels three dissident writers from the Communist Party.	Israeli settlers arrive at Kfar Etzion, the former Israeli farm community on the West Bank of the Jordan River. . . . Israeli authorities find three hand grenades outside the home of Premier Levi Eshkol.	Bolivian authorites adjourn indefinitely the trial of guerrilla leader Regis Debray.	U.S. planes pound North Vietnamese positions in the demilitarized zone.

A	B	C	D	E
Includes developments that affect more than one world region, international organizations and important meetings of major world leaders.	*Includes all domestic and regional developments in Europe, including the Soviet Union, Turkey, Cyprus and Malta.*	*Includes all domestic and regional developments in Africa and the Middle East, including Iraq and Iran and excluding Cyprus, Turkey and Afghanistan.*	*Includes all domestic and regional developments in Latin America, the Caribbean and Canada.*	*Includes all domestic and regional developments in Asia and Pacific nations, extending from Afghanistan through all the Pacific Islands, except Hawaii.*

U.S. Politics & Social Issues	U.S. Foreign Policy & Defense	U.S. Economy & Environment	Science, Technology & Nature	Culture, Leisure & Life Style	
Negroes loot stores and smash windows in Dayton, Ohio.	U.S. arms control official Adrian Fisher says that the proposed American anti-ballistic missile (ABM) system is meant to protect the country from Communist Chinese attack.				Sept. 19
House allocates money for a rat-control program.			US satellite Surveyor 5 lands on the moon.	Gillio Pontecorvo's film *The Battle of Algiers* is released in New York.	Sept. 20
Justice Dept. files four civil rights suits against public accommodation places. . . . New Orleans Dist. Atty. James Garrison says that Sen. Robert Kennedy has obstructed his assassination probe to protect his political career.	At the Senate Foreign Relations Committee hearings, Sen. Charles Percy (R, Ill.) recommends that the President report annually to Congress on "our national commitments."				Sept. 21
	Pres. Johnson defends his Vietnam policy before a gathering of 200 leaders of various ethnic groups at the White House.		U.S. conducts an underground nuclear test.		Sept. 22
	National board of the Americans for Democratic Action rejects a statement opposing Pres. Johnson's renomination by a vote of 73-12.		Hurricane Beulah appears to have spent its course but leaves 46 fatalities in its wake.		Sept. 23
	UAW Pres. Walter Reuther calls for an end to the bombing of North Vietnam. . . . National board of the Americans for Democratic Action pledges support to the 1968 presidential candidate who offers "the best prospect for a settlement of the Vietnam conflict."				Sept. 24
				Houghton Mifflin publishes Jonathan Kozol's *Death at an Early Age*.	Sept. 25
Louise Day Hicks, an opponent of mandatory busing for school desegregation, wins 28% of the Boston primary vote in the mayoral race.	Sen. Clifford Case (R, N.J.) says that Pres. Johnson's "misuse" of the Tonkin Gulf resolution has caused "a crisis of confidence."				Sept. 26
	U.S. criticizes the Israeli move into Kfar Etzion, the former Israeli farm community on the West Bank of the Jordan River. . . . Sen. Thruston Morton (R, Ky.) says that Pres. Johnson has been "brainwashed (by the) military-industrial complex."		U.S. launches communications satellite Pacific 2. . . . U.S. conducts an underground nuclear test.	Prince Felix Youssoupoff, the former Russian nobleman who led the 1916 plot to assassinate Gregory Rasputin, dies in Paris at 81. . . . Delacorte-Seymour Lawrence publishes Miguel Angel Asturias' *Mulata*.	Sept. 27

F	G	H	I	J
Includes elections, federal-state relations, civil rights and liberties, crime, the judiciary, education, health care, poverty, urban affairs and population.	*Includes formation and debate of U.S. foreign and defense policies, veterans' affairs and defense spending. (Relations with specific foreign countries are usually found under the region concerned.)*	*Includes business, labor, agriculture, taxation, transportation, consumer affairs, monetary and fiscal policy, natural resources, and pollution.*	*Includes worldwide scientific, medical and technological developments, natural phenomena, U.S. weather, natural disasters, and accidents.*	*Includes the arts, religion, scholarship, communications media, sports, entertainment, fashions, fads and social life.*

	World Affairs	Europe	Africa & the Middle East	The Americas	Asia & the Pacific
Sept. 28	At the U.N. General Assembly, French Foreign Min. Maurice Couve de Murville says that U.S. actions in Vietnam endanger world peace.	NATO's seven-nation Nuclear Planning Group meets in Ankara, Turkey. . . . Greek government arrests newspaper publisher Helen Vlachos in Athens.	Israeli authorities announce that former Jordanian Jerusalem Gov. Anwar el-Khatib will be allowed to return to Jerusalem. . . . Israeli authorities say that captured Arab guerrillas have admitted being trained in Syria and Algeria.		U.S. planes bomb North Vietnamese positions in the demilitarized zone. . . . Laos reports killing 70 North Vietnamese soldiers in an ambush. . . . Peking radio reports that a public rally recently sentenced seven people to death on political or criminal grounds.
Sept. 29	At the U.N. General Assembly, Albanian Amb.-to-U.N. Halim Budo accuses the U.S. and the Soviet Union of trying to dominate the world.	Reports from the NATO Nuclear Planning Group indicate that Turkey is pressing for the use of nuclear land mines along its border with the Soviet Union.		P.M. Fidel Castro declares that small businesses in Cuba will eventually be nationalized leaving only small farms in the private sector.	Two hundred Buddhist monks stage an anti-government march in Danang. . . . U.S. planes bomb the Hoalac MiG base near Hanoi. . . . North Vietnam reports the arrival of civil rights activist Stokely Carmichael on Aug. 25.
Sept. 30			Algeria frees two aides of former Congolese Premier Moise Tshombe but not Tshombe himself.		South Vietnamese police break up a demonstration protesting the Sept. 3 elections in Saigon. . . . U.S. planes bomb missile sites in North Vietnam.
Oct. 1			An Israeli military court sentences Moustapha Yousef Ahmed Hemayes to life in prison for belonging to a guerrilla group.		U.S. planes bomb the port of Campha in North Vietnam.
Oct. 2		Thousands of French farmers demonstrate throughout France for the first time since 1963.	Reports indicate that Egyptian civilians are continuing to flee the city of Suez because of artillery duels between Egypt and Israel.		
Oct. 3	At the U.N. General Assembly, Dutch Foreign Min. Joseph Luns proposes that the U.N. adopt a global aid plan to coordinate all activities designed to assist the developing countries. . . . At a U.N. Disarmament Committee meeting, Swedish delegate Alva Myrdal asserts that the U.S. decision to deploy an anti-ballistic missile system "leads us in a pessimistic direction."	Jordanian King Hussein arrives in Moscow for official talks.			South Vietnamese Constituent Assembly validates the Sept. 3 national elections by a vote of 58-43.
Oct. 4	At the U.N. General Assembly, Botswana's External Affairs Min. M.P.K. Nwako says that his country does not agree with South Africa's apartheid system but favors diplomatic relations with South Africa as "a step in the right direction."	British Labor Party conference calls on the Labor government to disassociate itself completely from U.S. policy in Vietnam. . . . Jordanian King Hussein continues discussions with a Soviet delegation headed by Pres. Nikolai Podgorny.	Israeli Premier Levi Eshkol says that Jordanian King Hussein has approached him through intermediaries to determine whether there is a basis for negotiations between their two countries. . . . Yemeni mobs kill nine Egyptian soldiers in Sana, the capital of Yemen. . . . Egypt announces plans for providing food and shelter for refugees fleeing the city of Suez.		U.S. commanders in Saigon report that the North Vietnamese artillery siege of the U.S. Marine base at Conthien has been broken. . . . U.S. planes attack North Vietnamese targets close to the Communist Chinese border.
Oct. 5	At the U.N. General Assembly, Thai Foreign Min. Thanat Khoman says that the Vietnamese War will only end when North Vietnam is convinced of the futility of its alleged aggression.	A Soviet-Jordanian communique makes no mention of Soviet assistance. . . . British Foreign Min. George Brown urges Labor Party convention delegates to endorse the Labor government's Common Market bid.			U.S. Defense Dept. reports 141 combat deaths for the Sept. 24-30 period. . . . India announces that it suffered 251 casualties in the recent clashes with Communist China.

A	B	C	D	E
Includes developments that affect more than one world region, international organizations and important meetings of major world leaders.	Includes all domestic and regional developments in Europe, including the Soviet Union, Turkey, Cyprus and Malta.	Includes all domestic and regional developments in Africa and the Middle East, including Iraq and Iran and excluding Cyprus, Turkey and Afghanistan.	Includes all domestic and regional developments in Latin America, the Caribbean and Canada.	Includes all domestic and regional developments in Asia and Pacific nations, extending from Afghanistan through all the Pacific Islands, except Hawaii.

U.S. Politics & Social Issues	U.S. Foreign Policy & Defense	U.S. Economy & Environment	Science, Technology & Nature	Culture, Leisure & Life Style	
A pilot project to rehabilitate 1,000 housing units in a Chicago Negro neighborhood without displacing the families is announced.	Pres. Johnson says that there can be no military solution to the problems of Southeast Asia.	U.S. Agriculture Dept. estimates that U.S. cigarette consumption has increased substantially during 1967.			Sept. 28
Three hundred elected Negro officials attend the first National Conference of Negro Elected Officials at the Univ. of Chicago.	Sen. Jacob Javits (R, N.Y.) says that the U.S. commitment in Vietnam "represents a serious imbalance in our national foreign policy."			U.S. author Carson McCullers dies in Nyack, N.Y. at 50.	Sept. 29
					Sept. 30
					Oct. 1
	A Louis Harris poll indicates that public support for the Vietnam War has dropped to 58% from 72% in July. . . . U.S. State Dept. claims that the increased U.S. aerial offensive which started Aug. 11 has slowed the flow of war supplies from Communist China to North Vietnam.				Oct. 2
Negro State Rep. Carl Stokes wins the Democratic nomination for mayor of Cleveland, Ohio.	Sen. Republican leader Everett Dirksen chides Republican critics of Pres. Johnson's Vietnam policy.	House votes down, 213-205, a Republican proposal to cut federal spending by $5 billion. . . . House Ways & Means Committee votes, 20-5, to postpone action on the administration's proposed 10% tax surcharge.	Soviet Union launches a communications satellite.	Folk singer Woody Guthrie dies in New York at 55. . . . British conductor Sir Malcolm Sargent dies in London at 72. . . . Harold Pinter's play *The Birthday Party* opens in New York.	Oct. 3
Lawyers' Committee for Civil Rights Under Law announces plans to recruit and train Negro servicemen to serve as policemen in civilian life.					Oct. 4
	Twenty-three U.S. Senators introduce a resolution urging Pres. Johnson to intensify efforts to have Asian countries contribute more to the Vietnamese War.				Oct. 5

F	G	H	I	J
Includes elections, federal-state relations, civil rights and liberties, crime, the judiciary, education, health care, poverty, urban affairs and population.	Includes formation and debate of U.S. foreign and defense policies, veterans' affairs and defense spending. (Relations with specific foreign countries are usually found under the region concerned.)	Includes business, labor, agriculture, taxation, transportation, consumer affairs, monetary and fiscal policy, natural resources, and pollution.	Includes worldwide scientific, medical and technological developments, natural phenomena, U.S. weather, natural disasters, and accidents.	Includes the arts, religion, scholarship, communications media, sports, entertainment, fashions, fads and social life.

	World Affairs	Europe	Africa & the Middle East	The Americas	Asia & the Pacific
Oct. 6	At the U.N. Gen. Assembly, Lebanese Foreign Min. Georges Hakim says that guarantees of a renunciation of the use of force and of security for all states in the Middle East could follow an Israeli withdrawal from occupied areas.		Israeli authorities report the reopening of six more Arab schools in East Jerusalem which had been closed since Sept. 4 in protest against Israeli rule. . . . Reports from Lebanon indicate that Jordanian King Hussein has proposed an Israeli withdrawal from Arab territory in exchange for an end to Arab belligerency against Israel. . . . Red Cross announces that white mercenary leader Jean Schramme has accepted the Sept. 17 Organization of African Unity offer to permit his force to leave the Congo peacefully under international supervision.		U.S. paratroopers clash with North Vietnamese troops in northern South Vietnam. . . . Burma announces that starting Nov. 1 it will no longer pay the living expenses of the Communist Chinese aid technicians working in Burma.
Oct. 7		Greek Public Order Min. Pavlos Totomis announces that ex-Premier George Papandreou has been released from house detention.	Jordanian King Hussein chooses Bahjat al-Talhouni, a supporter of Egyptian Pres. Nasser, as prime minister.		U.S. paratroopers again clash with North Vietnamese in savage fighting in northern South Vietnam.
Oct. 8					U.S. 101st Airborne Division troops fight their way out of North Vietnamese encirclement in northern South Vietnam.
Oct. 9		Soviet Union launches a rocket carrying French meteorological equipment.		Reports indicate that guerrilla leader Ché Guevara may have been killed by the Bolivian army.	U.S. command announces that about 4,000 troops have been recently flown to the northern part of South Vietnam. . . . Indonesia announces that it plans to suspend ties with Communist China.
Oct. 10	At the U.N. Gen. Assembly, Rumanian Deputy Foreign Min. Mircea Malitza says that European states are moving toward normal ties and that the time has come for all foreign troops to leave the continent. . . . Reports indicate that the U.S., the Soviet Union and European countries have agreed to computerize and share their atomic energy research. . . . At a U.N. Disarmament Committee meeting, Soviet delegate Aleksei Roshchin charges that West Germany is impeding progress toward the conclusion of a non-proliferation treaty.	France announces that it will provide Chile with an atomic reactor.		Bolivian army confirms the death of guerrilla leader Ché Guevara.	Communist Chinese Premier Chou En-lai acknowledges that the Cultural Revolution has adversely affected China's production.
Oct. 11	At the U.N. Gen. Assembly, Iraqi Amb.-to-U.N. Adnan Pachachi calls on the U.N. to force Israel to withdraw from occupied Arab territories.		Israeli Premier Levi Eshkol says that the Soviet Union has replaced 80% of the planes, tanks and artillery that Egypt lost in the June 1967 war.	Bolivian Gen. Alfredo Ovando Candia says that Ché Guevara has been buried but he does not indicate where.	A land mine seriously wounds a Hong Kong resident at the Mankamto crossing point.
Oct. 12	At the U.N. Gen. Assembly, Saudi Arabian Amb.-to-U.S. Ibrahim Al-Sowayel warns that there will be turmoil in the Middle East as long as Israel exists.	French farmers barricade major roads and a railroad line in protest over agricultural profits.	Israeli police officials announce the arrest of 24 members of El Fatah, an Arab guerrilla organization.	Bolivian Pres. Rene Barrientos Ortuno says that Ché Guevara has been cremated.	A British army spokesman confirms that British positions on the Hong Kong-Communist Chinese border have been fortified by land mines. . . . U.S. planes bomb Haiphong shipyards.
Oct. 13	At the U.N. Gen. Assembly, Australian Foreign Min. Paul Hasluck defends U.S. policy in Vietnam.	North Atlantic Council, NATO's highest political body, moves from Paris to Belgium.	Ahmed Shukairy, head of the Palestine Liberation Front, declares that Arab guerrilla raids on the West Bank of the Jordan River are only "the first phase of a popular Palestinian war."		Laos displays 19 captured North Vietnamese soldiers to support charges of North Vietnamese intervention.
	A	**B**	**C**	**D**	**E**
	Includes developments that affect more than one world region, international organizations and important meetings of major world leaders.	*Includes all domestic and regional developments in Europe, including the Soviet Union, Turkey, Cyprus and Malta.*	*Includes all domestic and regional developments in Africa and the Middle East, including Iraq and Iran and excluding Cyprus, Turkey and Afghanistan.*	*Includes all domestic and regional developments in Latin America, the Caribbean and Canada.*	*Includes all domestic and regional developments in Asia and Pacific nations, extending from Afghanistan through all the Pacific Islands, except Hawaii.*

U.S. Politics & Social Issues	U.S. Foreign Policy & Defense	U.S. Economy & Environment	Science, Technology & Nature	Culture, Leisure & Life Style	
	Sen. Frank Lausche (D, O.) denounces critics of the administration's Vietnam policy.			Doubleday & Co. publishes Mrs. Medgar Evers' *For Us, the Living.* . . . Doubleday publishes Matthew Ridgeway's *The Korean War.*	Oct. 6
				British political scientist Sir Norman Angell dies in Surrey, England at 94.	Oct. 7
Democrats announce that their 1968 Convention will take place in Chicago in August.	A Gallup Poll indicates that 48% of Americans want to reduce the scale of fighting in Vietnam, 37% want to increase it and 28% approve the current level of hostilities. . . . U.S. historian Arthur Schlesinger assails the administration's "obsession" with a military victory in Vietnam.			Former British P.M. Clement Atlee (1945-1951) dies in London at 94.	Oct. 8
U.S. Supreme Court refuses to review a March 29 lower court decision ordering the desegregation of the school systems of six Southern states. . . . U.S. Supreme Court refuses to reconsider the contempt-of-court convictions of the Rev. Martin Luther King Jr. and other civil rights leaders emanating from the 1963 protest marches in Birmingham, Ala.	Sen. Hugh Scott (R, Pa.) warns Republicans not to make Vietnam into a political issue.			French author Andre Maurois dies in Paris at 82. . . . Holt, Rinehart & Winston publishes Sen. Eugene McCarthy's *The Limits of Power.*	Oct. 9
			A treaty banning mass-destructive weapons stationed in space comes into force.		Oct. 10
	House Speaker John McCormack (D, Mass.) defends the administration's Vietnam policy.		Soviet Union launches Cosmos 181.		Oct. 11
A federal court rules unconstitutional three Kentucky state laws under which civil rights activists were arrested during open-housing demonstrations in the spring.	State Secy Dean Rusk declares that the U.S. is fighting for its own security in Vietnam and that Communist China poses a threat to world peace.	Federal Highway Administration proposes 10 new auto safety standards.		Warner Bros. releases John Huston's film *Reflections in a Golden Eye.*	Oct. 12
NAACP files a discrimination suit against the Ohio Bureau of Unemployment Compensation.	Former Pres. Eisenhower defends the administration's Vietnam policy.				Oct. 13

F	G	H	I	J
Includes elections, federal-state relations, civil rights and liberties, crime, the judiciary, education, health care, poverty, urban affairs and population.	*Includes formation and debate of U.S. foreign and defense policies, veterans' affairs and defense spending. (Relations with specific foreign countries are usually found under the region concerned.)*	*Includes business, labor, agriculture, taxation, transportation, consumer affairs, monetary and fiscal policy, natural resources, and pollution.*	*Includes worldwide scientific, medical and technological developments, natural phenomena, U.S. weather, natural disasters, and accidents.*	*Includes the arts, religion, scholarship, communications media, sports, entertainment, fashions, fads and social life.*

	World Affairs	Europe	Africa & the Middle East	The Americas	Asia & the Pacific
Oct. 14			Israeli and Jordanian forces exchange artilley fire for two hours.		More than 500 North Vietnamese troops launch a heavy assault against U.S. positions near Conthien. . . . Communist Chinese authorities kidnap British police inspector Frank Knight from the Hong Kong side of the Hong Kong-Communist Chinese border.
Oct. 15			Six Arab guerrillas attack an Israeli community before fleeing back to Jordan.	Cuban Premier Fidel Castro says that the news of Guevara's death is "sadly true."	U.S. planes bomb the major North Vietnamese infiltration route through Laos.
Oct. 16		Turkey threatens to intervene militarily in Cyprus unless the fighting stops.	Israel captures 11 Syrian-trained Arab infiltrators in the Israeli-occupied West Bank of the Jordan River.	Bolivian military sources claim that there are only six guerrillas still at large.	New Zealand and Australia announce plans to increase their forces in Vietnam.
Oct. 17					An outnumbered U.S. infantry division fights off a North Vietnamese regiment during an all-day battle. . . . Thai army takes command of the anti-guerrilla drive in the northeast.
Oct. 18		A fierce storm leaves 21 dead in northern Europe.	Israeli Premier Levi Eshkol rebukes Defense Min. Moshe Dayan for critical statements he is reported to have made about Eshkol at a National Religious Party meeting.		Thailand announces that it has sent troops to its northern provinces in order to counter a Communist Chinese border force.
Oct. 19		British Conservative Party conference overwhelmingly endorses a call for the government to negotiate with Rhodesia.			North Korean artillery kills two South Korean soldiers.
Oct. 20		Reports indicate that the world's most powerful atom smasher located near Moscow has begun operations.	Egyptian newspaper *Al Ahram* admits for the first time that U.S. and British warplanes did not assist Israel in the June 1967 war as was previously alleged. . . . *The New York Times* reports that Biafra has set up a private mission in Lisbon.		
Oct. 21		Demonstrations against U.S. policy in Vietnam take place in major European cities. . . . A Greek court martial convicts 27 people of having formed an alleged communist terrorist group.	Egypt sinks the Israeli destroyer *Eilat* ; 47 Israelis are killed and 91 are wounded.		North Vietnamese Defense Min. Vo Nguyen Giap says that his country is ready to pay "any price" to win the war.
Oct. 22			Israeli Premier Levi Eshkol says that the attack on the *Eilat* was a violation of international navigation laws and of the truce agreement. . . . White mercenary leader Jean Schramme denies that he plans to leave the Congo.		U.S. planes bomb the North Vietnamese naval base at Nuidong for the first time.

A	B	C	D	E
Includes developments that affect more than one world region, international organizations and important meetings of major world leaders.	Includes all domestic and regional developments in Europe, including the Soviet Union, Turkey, Cyprus and Malta.	Includes all domestic and regional developments in Africa and the Middle East, including Iraq and Iran and excluding Cyprus, Turkey and Afghanistan.	Includes all domestic and regional developments in Latin America, the Caribbean and Canada.	Includes all domestic and regional developments in Asia and Pacific nations, extending from Afghanistan through all the Pacific Islands, except Hawaii.

U.S. Politics & Social Issues	U.S. Foreign Policy & Defense	U.S. Economy & Environment	Science, Technology & Nature	Culture, Leisure & Life Style	
				French writer Marcel Ayme dies in Paris at 65.	Oct. 14
				Jiri Menzel's film *Closely Watched Trains* is released.	Oct. 15
Four to five hundred demonstrators picket the Northern California Draft Induction Center in Oakland, Calif. . . . Six hundred poor people from New York gather on the Washington Mall and demonstrate for increased anti-poverty spending. . . . U.S. Supreme Court reverses the murder conviction of Alabama Negro Johnny Coleman because the county where the trial was held has rarely sat Negroes on trial juries.	Sen. Eugene McCarthy (D, Minn.) charges that State Secy. Rusk has raised the "yellow peril specter" in his Oct. 12 reference to Communist China's huge and aggressive population.		Soviet Union launches Cosmos 182.	Tom Stoppard's play *Rosencrantz and Guildenstern Are Dead* opens in New York. . . . Harper & Row publishes Svetlana Stalina's *Twenty Letters to a Friend.*	Oct. 16
			Soviet Union conducts an underground nuclear test.	Henry Pu Yi, the last Manchu emperor of China (1908-1912), dies in Peking at 61.	Oct. 17
About 1,000 University of Wisconsin students demonstrate against recruiters of the Dow Chemical Co. which manufactures napalm used in Vietnam.	House Armed Services subcommittee charges that the Army's M-16 rifle is dangerous to use because of its frequent malfunctions.		Soviet satellite Venera 4 lands on Venus. . . . U.S. conducts an underground nuclear test. . . . Soviet Union launches Cosmos 183. . . . Three scientists win the Nobel Prize in medicine for discovering links between the human eye and the brain.	John Schlesinger's Film *Far From the Madding Crowd* is released.	Oct. 18
Chicago police clash with 100 demonstrators who try to break into the city's draft induction center.				Guatemalan author Miguel Angel Asturias wins the Nobel Prize for literature.	Oct. 19
About 300 Columbia Univ. students demonstrate for an end to CIA and military recruiting on campus. . . . A federal jury convicts seven whites of conspiracy in the 1964 murder of three civil rights workers near Philadelphia, Miss.	Republican Governors refuse to endorse Pres. Johnson's policy in Vietnam.			Former Japanese Premier Shigeru Yoshida (1946-1954) dies in Oisi Japan at 89.	Oct. 20
Equal Employment Opportunity Commission reports that Negro female white collar workers outnumber Negro male white collar workers by almost 2-1. . . . At least 55,000 demonstrators march against the Vietnamese War in Washington D.C.	U.S. Vice Adm. William Ellis says that the Soviet Union is building its first aircraft carrier.				Oct. 21
	Rep. Morris Udall (D, Ariz) says that the U.S. should start bringing troops home from South Vietnam.	UAW negotiators reach agreement with the Ford Motor Co. on a new contract.	Soviet Union launches a communications satellite.		Oct. 22

F	G	H	I	J
Includes elections, federal-state relations, civil rights and liberties, crime, the judiciary, education, health care, poverty, urban affairs and population.	Includes formation and debate of U.S. foreign and defense policies, veterans' affairs and defense spending. (Relations with specific foreign countries are usually found under the region concerned.)	Includes business, labor, agriculture, taxation, transportation, consumer affairs, monetary and fiscal policy, natural resources, and pollution.	Includes worldwide scientific, medical and technological developments, natural phenomena, U.S. weather, natural disasters, and accidents.	Includes the arts, religion, scholarship, communications media, sports, entertainment, fashions, fads and social life.

	World Affairs	Europe	Africa & the Middle East	The Americas	Asia & the Pacific
Oct. 23			Reports indicate that State Secy. Rusk cautioned Israeli Foreign Min. Abba Eban not to take retaliatory action against the sinking of the *Eilat* during their talks in Washington.		U.S. planes carry out heavy attacks on the Hanoi-Haiphong area. . . . Reports indicate that Communist Chinese schools have begun to reopen after having been closed since the summer of 1966 to enable the students to participate in the Cultural Revolution.
Oct. 24	U.N. Security Council convenes amid mounting fears of an escalation of the Middle East fighting.		Israeli guns pound Egyptian oil refineries at the port of Suez.		U.S. planes strike the North Vietnamese Phucyen airfield for the first time.
Oct. 25					Jakarta radio reports that Indonesia has closed its embassy in Peking. . . . U.S. planes bomb the North Vietnamese Phucyen airfield for the second consecutive day.
Oct. 26	British Amb.-to-U.N. Lord Caradon announces that Britain will uphold the Latin American A-ban treaty by signing a protocol attached to the treaty calling for respect of the treaty's provisions by the nuclear powers.	Greece charges Greek composer Mikis Theodorakis with leading the left-wing Patriotic Front. Mohammed Riza Pahlevi formally crowns himself in a ceremony in Teheran. . . . Reports indicate that the Nigerian federal government has hired British, Egyptian and South African fighter pilots.			U.S. planes bomb a thermal power plant in Hanoi.
Oct. 27		Spanish students and police clash in Madrid.	U.S. planes hit a military barracks in Hanoi for the first time. . . . Israeli Gen. Moshe Dayan says that Israel still considers the cease-fire agreement in effect despite the latest round of fighting.		
Oct. 28		Clashes continue between Spanish students and police in Madrid.	Kenya and Somalia sign an agreement providing for efforts to end their border conflict.		
Oct. 29				Mexican Pres. Gustavo Diaz Ordaz participates in the distribution of two-and-a-half million acres of land to peasant families.	U.S. planes pound the North Vietnamese Hoalac MiG airbase. . . . V.P. Hubert Humphrey arrives in South Vietnam.
Oct. 30			Israeli Premier Levi Eshkol says that his country will "consolidate her position" in the Arab territories captured in the Arab-Israeli war. . . . Congolese troops attack the white mercenary-Katangese force at Bukavu. . . . A South African court adjourns the preliminary hearing of five South African journalists accused of publishing false information on jail conditions to give the prosecution more time to prepare its case.		U.S. planes pound several North Vietnamese air bases. . . . U.S. V.P. Humphrey visits U.S. soldiers in South Vietnam.

A	B	C	D	E
Includes developments that affect more than one world region, international organizations and important meetings of major world leaders.	Includes all domestic and regional developments in Europe, including the Soviet Union, Turkey, Cyprus and Malta.	Includes all domestic and regional developments in Africa and the Middle East, including Iraq and Iran and excluding Cyprus, Turkey and Afghanistan.	Includes all domestic and regional developments in Latin America, the Caribbean and Canada.	Includes all domestic and regional developments in Asia and Pacific nations, extending from Afghanistan through all the Pacific Islands, except Hawaii.

U.S. Politics & Social Issues	U.S. Foreign Policy & Defense	U.S. Economy & Environment	Science, Technology & Nature	Culture, Leisure & Life Style	
U.S. Supreme Court reverses a lower court ruling which barred from the U.S. Danish nudist magazines for male homosexuals. . . . U.S. Supreme Court rules that N.Y.S. is required to provide indigent defendants with free transcripts of preliminary hearings. . . . U.S. Supreme Court refuses to review the conviction and $5 fine of LeRoy Garber, a member of the Amish sect, for refusing to send his child to school on religious grounds.	Pres. Johnson defends his Vietnamese War policies at a conference of the International Federation of Commercial, Clerical and Technical Employes.		Soviet Union conducts an underground nuclear test.		Oct. 23
	U.S. eases its ban on arms shipments to the Middle East and announces that it will send Israel and five Arab countries military equipment.				Oct. 24
			U.S. conducts an underground nuclear test. . . . Soviet Union launches Cosmos 184 and 185.		Oct. 25
	Sen. Eugene McCarthy calls for the resignation of State Secy. Rusk. . . . Mexican Pres. Gustavo Diaz Ordaz arrives in Washington for an official visit.		U.S. launches its fourth Orbiting Solar Observatory.	Pope Paul and Eastern Orthodox Patriarch Athenagoras pray side by side in St. Peter's Basilica.	Oct. 26
A Federal court rules that Mississippi can change its qualifications for political candidates without violating the 1965 Voting Rights Act. . . . FBI agents arrest three people for pouring duck blood on records at the Baltimore Selective Service headquarters.	Former V.P. Richard Nixon says that the U.S.'s "vital strategic interests" are involved in Vietnam. . . . In an address before Congress, Mexican Pres. Gustavo Diaz Ordaz asks the U.S. not to increase the restrictions on its imports.		Soviet Union launches Cosmos 186.		Oct. 27
	Republican 1964 presidential candidate Barry Goldwater castigates the recent Pentagon peace demonstrators. . . . At El Paso, Texas, Pres. Johnson and Mexican Pres. Gustavo Diaz Ordaz make a formal transfer of a strip of land between the two countries.		Soviet Union launches Cosmos 187.		Oct. 28
					Oct. 29
	In a major editorial shift, *Life* magazine calls for a pause of the bombing of North Vietnam.		Soviet Union successfully links Cosmos 186 and Cosmos 188. . . . Soviet Union launches Cosmos 189.	Harvard University Press publishes Henry Bragdon's *Woodrow Wilson* . . . . Farrar Straus & Giroux publishes Isaac Bashevis Singer's *The Manor* . . . . Louisiana State University Press publishes *The Faulkners of Mississippi* .	Oct. 30

F	G	H	I	J
Includes elections, federal-state relations, civil rights and liberties, crime, the judiciary, education, health care, poverty, urban affairs and population.	*Includes formation and debate of U.S. foreign and defense policies, veterans' affairs and defense spending. (Relations with specific foreign countries are usually found under the region concerned.)*	*Includes business, labor, agriculture, taxation, transportation, consumer affairs, monetary and fiscal policy, natural resources, and pollution.*	*Includes worldwide scientific, medical and technological developments, natural phenomena, U.S. weather, natural disasters, and accidents.*	*Includes the arts, religion, scholarship, communications media, sports, entertainment, fashions, fads and social life.*

	World Affairs	Europe	Africa & the Middle East	The Americas	Asia & the Pacific
Oct. 31	At a U.N. Disarmament Committee meeting, Brazil submits an amendment making it easier for the non-nuclear signatories to withdraw from the treaty.				Indonesia and Communist China complete the withdrawal of their diplomatic personnel from each other's country. . . . Reports indicate that a Communist Chinese Shanghai newspaper launched an attack against Chinese CP Gen. Secy. Teng Hsiao-ping a week ago. . . . Chief of State Nguyen Van Thieu is inaugurated as first president of South Vietnam's second republic.
Nov. 1			Reports indicate that another white mercenary-Katangese force has invaded the Congo's Katanga Province from Portuguese Angola. . . . Two rival nationalist groups of the South Arabian Federation (Aden) announce that they will negotiate jointly with Britain.		U.S. V.P. Humphrey flies to the bitterly contested northern provinces of South Vietnam. . . . Reports indicate that Britain and Communist China are negotiating their differences over the status of Hong Kong.
Nov. 2	During U.N. Security Council debate, Israeli Foreign Min. Abba Eban says that an Israeli military pull-back prior to a peace settlement is "irrational.". . . U.S. Amb.-to-U.N. Arthur Goldberg says that the Johnson administration favors the participation of the Viet Cong's National Liberation Front in any U.N. Security Council discussions about the Vietnamese War.	Britain announces that it will advance the date of the South Arabian Federation's independence. . . . *London Times* reports that thousands of churches in Albania have been turned into communist youth centers.	Renewed fighting breaks out between the two rival nationalist groups of the South Arabian Federation despite their Nov. 1 accord.		U.S. V.P. Humphrey confers with Malaysian P.M. Abdul Rahman in Kuala Lumpur. . . . Peking radio announces that a "revolutionary committee" has been established in Inner Mongolia.
Nov. 3	U.N. Gen Assembly votes 92-2 to ask Britain again to put an end to the Smith government in Rhodesia.	Soviet CP Gen. Secy. Leonid Brezhnev gives the major speech during festivities celebrating the 50th anniversary of the Bolshevik Revolution. . . . Greece makes public a law abolishing the use of juries for political trials after Dec 1.	Israel reports the capture of an important commander of the El Fatah Arab guerrilla group.		Savage fighting breaks out between U.S. and North Vietnamese troops around Dakto near the Cambodian border. . . . South Korea reports North Korean attacks on South Korean fishing boats.
Nov. 4			White mercenaries and Katangese gendarmes end their armed revolt and flee to neighboring Rwanda. . . . Fighting continues between two rival nationalist groups in the South Arabian Federation.		U.S. V.P. Humphrey confers with acting Pres. Suharto in Jakarta.
Nov. 5	Red Cross confirms from Geneva that the Congolese rebel force has crossed into Rwanda and surrendered its arms.		Jordanian King Hussein asserts that the Arab states are willing to recognize Israel's right to exist but only after it has withdrawn from Arab territory. . . . A bloodless coup overthrows Yemeni Pres. Abdullah al-Salal.		U.S. planes bomb the North Vietnamese Phucyen air base for the second time.
Nov. 6			Jordanian King Hussein says that his views on Arab policy toward Israel reflect those of Egyptian Pres. Nasser. . . . *Toronto Globe & Mail* newspaper estimates that 20,000 Nigerians and Biafrans have died in the civil war.		Communist China hails the 50th anniversary of the Bolshevik Revolution but asserts that the "center of world revolution" has shifted from Moscow to Peking. . . . U.S. planes bomb a military depot near Hanoi for the first time.
Nov. 7	U.N. Gen. Assembly votes unanimously on a draft Declaration on the Elimination of Discrimination Against Women.	Greek Public Order Min. Pavlos Totomis says that Greek composer Mikis Theodorakis is in a prison hospital "recovering from some stomach trouble."	Jordanian King Hussein urges Israel to match "the new and positive approach of the Arabs" toward a Middle East settlement. . . . Israeli troops kill seven Arab infiltrators near Hebron, an Arab West Bank town.		U.S. planes bomb North Vietnamese railroad facilities near the Communist Chinese border.

A	B	C	D	E
Includes developments that affect more than one world region, international organizations and important meetings of major world leaders.	*Includes all domestic and regional developments in Europe, including the Soviet Union, Turkey, Cyprus and Malta.*	*Includes all domestic and regional developments in Africa and the Middle East, including Iraq and Iran and excluding Cyprus, Turkey and Afghanistan.*	*Includes all domestic and regional developments in Latin America, the Caribbean and Canada.*	*Includes all domestic and regional developments in Asia and Pacific nations, extending from Afghanistan through all the Pacific Islands, except Hawaii.*

U.S. Politics & Social Issues	U.S. Foreign Policy & Defense	U.S. Economy & Environment	Science, Technology & Nature	Culture, Leisure & Life Style	
	Sen. Edward Kennedy (D, Mass.) urges the U.S. to place less emphasis on military measures in South Vietnam.				Oct. 31
Atty. Gen. Ramsey Clark says that the Justice Dept. will hold training sessions for city officials on the prevention and control of civil disturbances.				McGraw-Hill publishes Yael Dayan's *Israel Journal*.	Nov. 1
A statistical report says that Negroes comprise 11% of the U.S. population. . . . Negro youths loot stores and set fires in Winston-Salem, N.C. . . . Pres. Johnson announces a pilot plan to attract big business to poor Negro neighborhoods.	U.S. Deputy State Undersecy. (for political affairs) Foy Kohler expresses U.S. concern over the Katangese intrusion to Portuguese Amb.-to-US Vasco Vieira Garin. . . . Selective Service Director Lewis Hershey confirms a policy decision to require the early induction of draft-prone people who interfere with draft procedures.	U.S. Surgeon General announces the formation of a task force to alert the public about the dangers of cigarette smoking.	Soviet Union launches a satellite.		Nov. 2
An Alabama federal court rules that Alabama's teacher-choice and tuition-grant laws are unconstitutional. . . . Pres. Johnson predicts that the U.S. will soon revolt against the lawlessness and crime in the country. . . . Winston-Salem, N.C. Mayor M.C. Benton imposes a curfew as disorders continue.	Defense Secy. McNamara says that the Soviet Union might be developing a method of nuclear attack from orbit. . . . Defense Secy. McNamara announces that the limited anti-ballistic missile system that the U.S. is deploying is called the "Sentinel System."		Soviet Union launches Cosmos 190.		Nov. 3
Police arrest 20 people for curfew violations in Winston-Salem, N.C.	Senate Democratic leader Mike Mansfield calls for renewed efforts by the U.S. to extricate itself from "this miserable venture" in Vietnam.				Nov. 4
National Guardsmen begin to leave Winston-Salem, N.C. as the city returns to normal.					Nov. 5
U.S. Supreme Court declares unconstitutional the loyalty oath requirement for public employees and officeholders in the state of Maryland. . . . A Louis Harris poll reports that Pres. Johnson trails six potential Republican opponents. . . . U.S. Supreme Court rules 6-2 not to consider the question of the legality of the Vietnamese War.		House passes a bill establishing a National Commission on Product Safety.		Little, Brown & Co. publishes George Kennan's *Memoirs: 1925-1950*.	Nov. 6
U.S. voters elect two Negro mayors, Carl Stokes in Cleveland, Ohio and Richard Hatcher in Gary, Ind.		Senate passes a bill establishing a National Commission on Product Safety.	U.S. launches lunar probe Surveyor 6.		Nov. 7

F	G	H	I	J
Includes elections, federal-state relations, civil rights and liberties, crime, the judiciary, education, health care, poverty, urban affairs and population.	Includes formation and debate of U.S. foreign and defense policies, veterans' affairs and defense spending. (Relations with specific foreign countries are usually found under the region concerned.)	Includes business, labor, agriculture, taxation, transportation, consumer affairs, monetary and fiscal policy, natural resources, and pollution.	Includes worldwide scientific, medical and technological developments, natural phenomena, U.S. weather, natural disasters, and accidents.	Includes the arts, religion, scholarship, communications media, sports, entertainment, fashions, fads and social life.

	World Affairs	Europe	Africa & the Middle East	The Americas	Asia & the Pacific
Nov. 8			British Commonwealth Secy. George Thomson confers with Rhodesian P.M. Ian Smith in Salisbury.		Cambodian Chief of State Norodom Sihanouk demands that the U.S. recognize his country's border claims which conflict with Thai border claims. . . . U.S. planes bomb railroad tracks near Hanoi.
Nov. 9		A British court sentences Michael Abdul Malik to one year in prison for inciting race hatred during an anti-white speech.	Reports indicate that Algeria has informed Egypt that it would not denounce a peace settlement reached with Israel. . . . Talks continue between British Commonwealth Secy. George Thomson and Rhodesian P.M. Ian Smith in Salisbury.		South Vietnamese Pres. Thieu adds only two new members to his pre-election cabinet. . . . A Communist Chinese radio broadcast says that two men have been executed before a crowd of 100,000 chanting Maoists.
Nov. 10	At the U.N. Security Council, Portuguese delegate Bonifacio de Miranda denies Portugal's involvement in the recent attacks on the Congo.		Talks conclude between British Commonwealth Secy. George Thomson and Rhodesian P.M. Ian Smith in Salisbury.		Reports indicate that the U.S. may have agreed to give ground-to-air missiles to Thailand in exchange for the dispatch of 10,000 more Thai troops to South Vietnam. . . . A Communist Chinese broadcast says that four "counter-revolutionary" criminals have been executed publicly.
Nov. 11			Britain agrees to negotiate with the the Adenese National Liberation Front, one of the two rival nationalist groups in the South Arabian Federation.		Viet Cong release three U.S. Army prisoners in Cambodia.
Nov. 12		Portuguese government reports that its troops have disarmed and detained 75 whites and 213 Congolese who have recently fled from Katanga into Angola. . . . Speculators trade heavily on the pound and force the British Treasury to put up millions of its reserves to maintain the price of the pound.			
Nov. 13			A bazooka shell hits an Israeli army camp near Hebron on the West Bank of the Jordan River.		A Japanese pacifist group says that four U.S. sailors have deserted the U.S. aircraft carrier *Intrepid* in Tokyo.
Nov. 14	At the U.N. Security Council, Portuguese delegate Bonifacio de Miranda again denies Portugal's involvement in the recent attacks on the Congo.	British Foreign Min. George Brown announces that Britain will grant the South Arabian Federation its independence by Nov. 30, instead of Jan. 9, 1968, as originally planned. . . . In the House of Commons, British Commonwealth Secy. George Thomson says that the chances of resolving the controversy with Rhodesia are slim.	A bomb damages an Israeli auto assembly plant in Nazareth.		First U.S. general, Bruno Hochmuth, is killed in South Vietnam in a helicopter crash.
Nov. 15	U.N. Security Council censures Portugal for allegedly permitting Angolan territory to be used as a base for attacking the Congo.	Turkish and Greek Cypriotes clash in two towns on Cyprus.	Yemen reports that Egypt has agreed to continue its financial aid to the republic until June 1968.		

A	B	C	D	E
Includes developments that affect more than one world region, international organizations and important meetings of major world leaders.	Includes all domestic and regional developments in Europe, including the Soviet Union, Turkey, Cyprus and Malta.	Includes all domestic and regional developments in Africa and the Middle East, including Iraq and Iran and excluding Cyprus, Turkey and Afghanistan.	Includes all domestic and regional developments in Latin America, the Caribbean and Canada.	Includes all domestic and regional developments in Asia and Pacific nations, extending from Afghanistan through all the Pacific Islands, except Hawaii.

U.S. Politics & Social Issues	U.S. Foreign Policy & Defense	U.S. Economy & Environment	Science, Technology & Nature	Culture, Leisure & Life Style	
	Jordanian King Hussein confers with Pres. Johnson at the White House.		U.S. conducts an underground nuclear test.		Nov. 8
Predominantly Negro Central State Univ. in Wilberforce, Ohio expels militant civil rights activist Michael Warren for allegedly threatening the university's Negro president.	American Association of University Professors protests the new Selective Service policy of drafting people who interfere with draft procedures. . . . Four hundred fifty Yale Univ. faculty members appeal in an advertisement to Pres. Johnson to stop the bombing of North Vietnam.		U.S. launches the Saturn-5 rocket which is believed to be the most powerful space booster ever launched.	Hill & Wang publishes *Not Yet Uhuru*, the autobiography of Kenyan politician Oginga Odinga.	Nov. 9
Institute for Defense Analysis suggests a wider range of non-lethal weapons for the nation's police force.	Pres. Johnson defends his Vietnam policy during visits to U.S. military bases in the U.S. South. . . . U.S. Amb.-to-South Vietnam Ellsworth Bunker arrives in Washington for talks with Pres. Johnson and other officials.		U.S. launches weather satellite Essa 6.		Nov. 10
Pres. Johnson signs a bill extending the Appalachian Regional Development Act.	John Kenneth Galbraith, chairman of Americans for Democratic Action, says the U.S. cannot win in Vietnam since it is a nationalist conflict. . . . Pres. Johnson defends his Vietnam policy on board the U.S. aircraft carrier *Enterprise* near San Diego.		U.S. Commerce Dept. reports that the 1964 Alaskan earthquake was the strongest ever recorded in North America.		Nov. 11
A Gallup Poll reports that 50% of those interviewed consider the Vietnam War to be the country's major problem.	Pres. Johnson cancels a speech scheduled for Nov. 13 in Syracuse because of a threatened anti-war demonstration. . . . Pres. Johnson attends church services in Williamsburg, Va. where the Rev. Cotesworth Lewis questions U.S. policy in Vietnam during the sermon. . . . Vietnam critic Lt. Gen. James Gavin says that the U.S. should begin to de-escalate the war.				Nov. 12
U.S. Supreme Court rules unanimously that states are required to provide counsel for indigent probationers in proceedings to revoke probation or to reimpose suspended sentences. . . . Police and several hundred students clash at Central State Univ. in Wilberforce, Ohio.	US Amb.-to-South Vietnam Ellsworth Bunker confers with Pres. Johnson at the White House.			Houghton Mifflin publishes Randolph Churchill's *Winston Churchill, Vol. II.*	Nov. 13
University officials suspend classes at Central State Univ., Wilberforce, Ohio.	Hundreds of anti-war demonstrators clash with police in New York during a protest against State Secy. Rusk's presence at a dinner.				Nov. 14
N.Y.S. Commission for Human Rights finds Local 501 of the International Brotherhood of Electrical Workers and Local 38 of the Sheet Metal Workers guilty of discrimination against Negroes.	U.S. commander in South Vietnam William Westmoreland arrives in Washington for consultations with the President and other officials. . . . U.S. pledges the eventual return of the Bonin Islands to Japan.				Nov. 15

F	G	H	I	J
Includes elections, federal-state relations, civil rights and liberties, crime, the judiciary, education, health care, poverty, urban affairs and population.	*Includes formation and debate of U.S. foreign and defense policies, veterans' affairs and defense spending. (Relations with specific foreign countries are usually found under the region concerned.)*	*Includes business, labor, agriculture, taxation, transportation, consumer affairs, monetary and fiscal policy, natural resources, and pollution.*	*Includes worldwide scientific, medical and technological developments, natural phenomena, U.S. weather, natural disasters, and accidents.*	*Includes the arts, religion, scholarship, communications media, sports, entertainment, fashions, fads and social life.*

	World Affairs	Europe	Africa & the Middle East	The Americas	Asia & the Pacific
Nov. 16					Britain reopens part of its diplomatic mission in Peking. . . . U.S. planes attack a shipyard in the port of Haiphong for the first time.
Nov. 17	U.N. Gen. Assembly votes, 82-7, with 21 abstentions, to condemn Portugal's "colonial war" in its African territories.	Reports indicate that Turkey has called on Greece to remove its troops from Cyprus.			
Nov. 18		Britain devalues the pound by 14.3%.	U.S. civil rights activist Stokely Carmichael reportedly ridicules African guerrilla leaders while in Tanzania.		
Nov. 19			Yemen reports the arrival of Soviet aircraft.		Savage battle at Dakto between U.S. and North Vietnamese troops centers on Hill 875.
Nov. 20		Four U.S. sailors who sought asylum in Japan on Oct. 24 turn up in Moscow and denounce U.S. policy in Vietnam. . . . NATO Secy. Gen. Manlio Brosio says that the Soviet Union is aiming at "a European concert orchestrated and dominated" by Moscow.	Israeli and Jordanian forces clash along their border.		A Communist Chinese broadcast says that 12 people were tried and convicted on Nov. 19 for undermining the Cultural Revolution. . . . British police inspector Frank Knight escapes from his Communist Chinese captors and returns to Hong Kong. . . . AP correspondents say that there is a Viet Cong base in Cambodia. . . . U.S. paratroop battalion reinforces beleaguered American troops at Dakto. . . . India launches its first rocket.
Nov. 21	U.S. dollar comes under heavy attack in major European money markets.	Britain lifts the restrictions which were imposed on the movement of Communist Chinese diplomats Aug. 22. . . . An Athens military court sentences eight Greeks to prison terms on charges of plotting to overthrow the military regime. . . . Negotiations open in Geneva between Britain and the Adenese National Liberation Front, one of the two rival nationalist groups in the South Arabian Federation. . . . Gold buying on the European gold markets is extremely heavy.	Israel launches an air strike against Jordan. It is the first Israeli air strike since the June war.		Heavy Communist fire prevents U.S. troops from taking Hill 875 at Dakto. . . . Indian government ousts the opposition United Front regimes in the states of West Bengal and Hariana.
Nov. 22	U.N. Secy. Gen U Thant expresses concern about military preparations being taken by Greece and Turkey in the Cyprus dispute. . . . U.N. Security Council unanimously passes a British resolution calling for an eventual withdrawal of Israeli forces from captured Arab territories and for an end to the Arabs' state of belligerency with Israel. . . . A U.N. Gen. Assembly committee denounces South Africa's main trading partners. . . . Delegates to GATT assemble at Geneva for their annual meeting.	Reports indicate that Greece has rejected Turkey's demand that it remove its troops from Cyprus. . . . British Defense Min. Denis Healey says that the reduced spending called for in the latest austerity measures must not change "the broad structure of our forces" abroad. . . . Four U.S. sailors again denounce American policy in Vietnam at an anti-war rally.			U.S. troops pull back from Hill 875 at Dakto to await reinforcements. . . . Reports indicate that British journalist Anthony Grey is still under house arrest in Peking.
	A	**B**	**C**	**D**	**E**
	Includes developments that affect more than one world region, international organizations and important meetings of major world leaders.	Includes all domestic and regional developments in Europe, including the Soviet Union, Turkey, Cyprus and Malta.	Includes all domestic and regional developments in Africa and the Middle East, including Iraq and Iran and excluding Cyprus, Turkey and Afghanistan.	Includes all domestic and regional developments in Latin America, the Caribbean and Canada.	Includes all domestic and regional developments in Asia and Pacific nations, extending from Afghanistan through all the Pacific Islands, except Hawaii.

U.S. Politics & Social Issues	U.S. Foreign Policy & Defense	U.S. Economy & Environment	Science, Technology & Nature	Culture, Leisure & Life Style	
HUD Secy. Robert Weaver announces the selection of 63 cities as participants in the model cities program.	In the aftermath of the Nov. 14 demonstration against State Secy. Rusk, Students for a Democratic Society staff member Robert Gottlieb says that foreign policy decision makers will be pursued wherever they go. . . . U.S. commander in South Vietnam, William Westmoreland, confers with Pres. Johnson at the White House. . . . Senate Foreign Relations Committee approves, 14-0, a resolution to curb the commitment of U.S. armed forces.			Random House publishes Stokely Carmichael's *Black Power*.	Nov. 16
Rochester civil rights organization announces that the Eastman Kodak Co. has decided to institute a program to develop locally owned businesses in Negro neighborhoods. . . . Police and Negro high school students clash in Philadelphia.	Pres. Johnson assails the violent tactics of some anti-war demonstrators.			Doubleday publishes Bernard Fall's *Last Reflections on a War*.	Nov. 17
Sen. Robert Kennedy says he has "no plans" to make a presidential bid in 1968.	Delegates to the convention of the Young Democratic Clubs of America adopt a resolution backing the administration's policies in Vietnam but also urging consideration of a bombing pause.	Pres. Johnson affirms his determination to maintain the current value of the dollar.			Nov. 18
NAACP calls for the ouster of Philadelphia Police Commissioner Frank Rizzo for alleged improper police actions in the Nov. 17 racial disorders.	Gen. William Westmoreland defends the bombing of North Vietnam on NBC-TV's *Meet the Press*.			Dr. Casimir Funk, who discovered vitamins, dies in Albany, N.Y. at 83.	Nov. 19
	Senate Democratic leader Mike Mansfield (Mont.) advocates direct negotiations between South Vietnam and the National Liberation Front.	Pres. Johnson signs a bill establishing a National Commission on Product Safety.		Knopf publishes Edwin Reischauer's *Beyond Vietnam*.	Nov. 20
Fighting breaks out between Negro and white Chicago high school students. . . . House allocates money for the 1968 Peace Corps program. . . . U.S. Commerce Department estimates that the U.S. population has reached 200 million.	At the National Press Club in Washington, U.S. commander in Vietnam Gen. William Westmoreland says that he is "absolutely certain" that the enemy is losing the war. . . . U.S. lodges a protest with the Soviet Union for "assisting, harboring and exploiting" the four U.S. sailors who denounced American Vietnam policy on Nov. 20.	Pres. Johnson signs a compromise air pollution bill.	Soviet Union launches Cosmos 191.		Nov. 21
Central State Univ. President Rembert Stokes says that students responsible for recent campus disorders will not be expelled from the university. . . . Philadelphia Mayor James Tate backs Philadelphia Police Commissioner Frank Rizzo. . . . U.S. Civil Rights Commission issues a report calling for an attack on slum problems as the nation's "first priority."	Pres. Johnson appoints former U.S. Deputy Defense Secy. Cyrus Vance as his special aid in the Cypriote crisis. . . . At a Pentagon briefing U.S. Commander in Vietnam Gen. William Westmoreland says that the battle around Dakto is "the beginning of a great defeat for the enemy."				Nov. 22

F	G	H	I	J
Includes elections, federal-state relations, civil rights and liberties, crime, the judiciary, education, health care, poverty, urban affairs and population.	*Includes formation and debate of U.S. foreign and defense policies, veterans' affairs and defense spending. (Relations with specific foreign countries are usually found under the region concerned.)*	*Includes business, labor, agriculture, taxation, transportation, consumer affairs, monetary and fiscal policy, natural resources, and pollution.*	*Includes worldwide scientific, medical and technological developments, natural phenomena, U.S. weather, natural disasters, and accidents.*	*Includes the arts, religion, scholarship, communications media, sports, entertainment, fashions, fads and social life.*

	World Affairs	Europe	Africa & the Middle East	The Americas	Asia & the Pacific
Nov. 23			Egyptian Pres. Nasser calls for an Arab summit meeting to discuss the Nov. 22 U.N. resolution.		
Nov. 24	U.N. Secy Gen. U Thant stresses the need to remove Greek and Turkish troops from Cyprus. . . . GATT delegates agree to pay "special attention" to the needs of the developing nations.	Gold buying on the European gold markets continues to be extremely heavy.	An Organization of African Unity peace mission backs the Nigerian federal government in its fight against Biafra. . . . France confirms having signed an oil exploration pact with Iraq.		Nationalist China announces that its guerrillas destroyed eight Communist Chinese MiGs on the Chinese mainland Nov. 19.
Nov. 25	U.N. Security Council urges restraint on all sides in the Cyprus dispute.	U.S. and the Soviet Union reach an agreement on measures restricting intensive fishing by Soviet vessels along the American east coast.			Fierce fighting resumes at Dakto between North Vietnamese and U.S. troops.
Nov. 26		Gold buying on the European markets declines as major European nations affirm their intention to maintain the value of gold at its current $35 an ounce value. . . . A Greek military court convicts 24 people of plotting to overthrow the government. . . . Heavy rains leave at least 138 people dead in Portugal.	British troops begin to leave the South Arabian Federation.		North Vietnamese artillery fire pounds U.S. troops near Dakto. . . . A Nationalist Chinese magazine reports that 11 of the 17 members of the Cultural Revolution Group have been purged since January.
Nov. 27	World's major banking nations affirm their intention to maintain the value of gold at the current rate of $35 an ounce.	French Pres. de Gaulle, in a press conference, again rejects Britain's Common Market bid. He also refers to the Jewish people as "sure of itself and dominating."	Israeli authorities destroy several buildings in retaliation for the Arab slaying of an Israeli youth in a neighboring Jewish town. . . . Yemeni royalists claim that the airport of their capital, Sana, "is now at the mercy of our guns."		For the first time in several weeks, fighting breaks out at Conthien just south of the demilitarized zone. . . . A dam break kills at least 138 people in Indonesia.
Nov. 28	U.N. General Assembly rejects a resolution calling for the seating of Communist China and the expulsion of Nationalist China by a vote of 58-45.		Britain grants independence to the South Arabian Federation. . . . Israeli officials report the arrests of 18 Arabs in connection with the slaying of an Israeli youth in a neighboring Jewish town. . . . Gabonese Pres. Leon Mba dies in Paris at 65.		U.S. officials concede that the heavy fighting at Dakto is hurting the U.S. pacification program.
Nov. 29	International Monetary Fund approves a British request for a standby credit.	Roy Jenkins succeeds James Callaghan as British Chancellor of the Exchequer. . . . Jacob Kaplan, the grand rabbi of France, accuses French Pres. de Gaulle of "giving the highest possible sanction to a campaign of discrimination."	Reports indicate that the Israeli Army has leveled 800 buildings in Jiftliq, an alleged Arab guerrilla base. . . . British troops complete their evacuation of the South Arabian Federation.		U.S. commander in Vietnam Gen. William Westmoreland returns to Saigon after his visit to Washington. . . . Communist China lifts the Aug. 30 restrictions which were imposed on the movement of British diplomats.
Nov. 30	Britain informs the U.N. General Assembly that it has ceded certain islands off the Arabian peninsula to Oman and others to South Yemen. . . . Delegates of the Organization for Economic Cooperation & Development meet in Paris.	Student riots break out at Madrid Univ. . . . An earthquake kills 20 people on the Yugoslav-Albanian border.	National Liberation Front Pres. Qahtan Mohamed al-Shaabi is proclaimed president of the South Arabian Federation whose name is changed to the People's Republic of South Yemen.		U.S. troops beat back a heavy Viet Cong assault 80 miles north of Saigon near the Cambodian border. . . . Reports indicate that Britain and Communist China have reached an accord easing tensions on the Hong Kong border.
Dec. 1	OECD delegates agree in principle to a plan under which the developed nations would grant special tariff concessions to the developing nations.	Reports indicate that Greece and Turkey have signed an agreement resolving the immediate issue in their current confrontation over Cyprus. . . . Authorities decide to close Madrid University.	South Yemen challenges the British cession of the Kuria Muria Islands to Oman. . . . Israel says that Egypt shot down two of its patrol planes earlier in the day. . . . Kenya, Tanzania and Uganda formally inaugurate the East African Community.		Thailand extends martial law to five additional provinces to combat a growing Communist guerrilla movement.

A	B	C	D	E
Includes developments that affect more than one world region, international organizations and important meetings of major world leaders.	*Includes all domestic and regional developments in Europe, including the Soviet Union, Turkey, Cyprus and Malta.*	*Includes all domestic and regional developments in Africa and the Middle East, including Iraq and Iran and excluding Cyprus, Turkey and Afghanistan.*	*Includes all domestic and regional developments in Latin America, the Caribbean and Canada.*	*Includes all domestic and regional developments in Asia and Pacific nations, extending from Afghanistan through all the Pacific Islands, except Hawaii.*

U.S. Politics & Social Issues	U.S. Foreign Policy & Defense	U.S. Economy & Environment	Science, Technology & Nature	Culture, Leisure & Life Style	
	The New York Times reports that military authorities in Washington are worried about reports of supplies reaching Communist forces in South Vietnam via Cambodia.		Soviet Union launches Cosmos 192.	Randon House publishes John O'Hara's The Instrument.	Nov. 23
		U.S. reaffirms its intention to buy and sell gold at $35 an ounce.		Doubleday publishes Robert Kennedy's To Seek a Newer World.	Nov. 24
Gallup Poll reports that 41% approve of Pres. Johnson's performance while 49% disapprove.			Soviet Union launches Cosmos 193.	Russian-born sculptor Ossip Zadkine dies in Paris at 77.	Nov. 25
	Sen. Robert Kennedy says that South Vietnamese troops are not making the effort that they should be making.				Nov. 26
A Louis Harris Poll shows Sen. Robert Kennedy favored 52% to 32% over Pres. Johnson. . . . University officials re-open classes at Central State Univ. in Wilberforce, Ohio.	Reports indicate that presidential aide Cyrus Vance has suggested that Greece and Turkey remove from Cyprus those troops not authorized by the 1960 independence accord.	House passes a bill strengthening the 1953 Flammable Fabrics Act.		Mrs. Pierre Mendes-France, wife of the former French prime minister, dies in Paris at 56.	Nov. 27
Rev. Martin Luther King Jr. announces that Cleveland, Ohio Pick-N-Pay Supermarkets have agreed to hire 300 Negroes. . . . Detroit passes an open-housing bill.	Former Pres. Eisenhower advocates a limited U.S. invasion of North Vietnam.				Nov. 28
	Defense Secy. McNamara accepts an offer of the presidency of the World Bank.	C.L. Haggerty, president of the AFL-CIO Building Trades Department, appeals to all member unions to admit qualified Negro journeymen and to begin training programs for poor Negroes.			Nov. 29
Sen. Eugene McCarthy (Minn.) announces that he will enter five or six Democratic presidential primaries in 1968 to further the campaign for a negotiated settlement of the Vietnamese War. . . . A Gallup Poll reports that only in the East does Pres. Johnson's performance meets with more than 50% approval.	Senate unanimously passes a resolution urging Pres. Johnson to seek U.N. Security Council action on the Vietnamese War.			Former V.P. Richard Nixon announces the engagement of his younger daughter, Julie, to former Pres. Dwight Eisenhower's grandson, David Eisenhower.	Nov. 30
	Reports from Washington indicate that the U.S. and South Vietnam have been in contact with Viet Cong representatives.	UAW Pres. Walter Reuther confirms his union's boycott of the AFL-CIO convention. . . . Senate passes a bill strengthening the 1953 Flammable Fabrics Act. . . . U.S. Steel Corp. announces price rises.			Dec. 1

F	G	H	I	J
Includes elections, federal-state relations, civil rights and liberties, crime, the judiciary, education, health care, poverty, urban affairs and population.	Includes formation and debate of U.S. foreign and defense policies, veterans' affairs and defense spending. (Relations with specific foreign countries are usually found under the region concerned.)	Includes business, labor, agriculture, taxation, transportation, consumer affairs, monetary and fiscal policy, natural resources, and pollution.	Includes worldwide scientific, medical and technological developments, natural phenomena, U.S. weather, natural disasters, and accidents.	Includes the arts, religion, scholarship, communications media, sports, entertainment, fashions, fads and social life.

	World Affairs	Europe	Africa & the Middle East	The Americas	Asia & the Pacific
Dec. 2	U.N. Secy. Gen. U Thant announces the establishment of nine new U.N. observation posts along the Suez Canal to help maintain the Israeli-Egyptian cease-fire.	Classes at Madrid Univ. remain suspended.			South Vietnamese Pres. Nguyen Van Thieu advocates South Vietnamese pursuit and attack of Communist troops inside Cambodia during battles with the Viet Cong.
Dec. 3		Governments of Cyprus, Greece and Turkey inform U.N. Secy Gen. U Thant that they have accepted a mutually agreed upon pact.	South Yemen declares its right to use "all possible means" to recover the Kuria Muria Islands. . . . Brig. Gen. Chaim Bar-Lev becomes Israeli chief-of-staff.		Viet Cong attack a government headquarters at Binhson, 330 miles north of Saigon.
Dec. 4		British State Min. (for foreign affairs) Fred Mulley welcomes Pres. Johnson's Dec. 2 announcement and says that Britain will also open up to inspection most of its nuclear activities. . . . Classes re-open and rioting resumes at Madrid Univ.	Yemeni government concedes for the first time that fighting is raging around Sana.		U.S. and South Vietnamese troops maul a Viet Cong battalion in the Mekong Delta.
Dec. 5	U.N. Gen. Assembly unanimously welcomes the Treaty for the Prohibition of Nuclear Weapons in Latin America.	A general strike virtually paralyzes Madrid Univ.	North Yemeni royalists claim to have shot down a Soviet plane.		South Vietnam says that it will oppose the presence of the National Liberation Front in any U.N. discussions. . . . Viet Cong demolish a Montagnard refugee camp with hand grenades and flamethrowers.
Dec. 6		A West German aircraft company announces that 11 European aircraft companies have agreed to form a holding company for the development of space rockets.	South Yemen expresses concern about royalist military successes in North Yemen but adds that it will not intervene militarily.	Uruguayan Pres. Oscar Daniel Gestido dies in Montevideo at 66.	U.S. Marine base comes under the heaviest shelling since Sept. 25.
Dec. 7	U.N. General Assembly votes, 91-2, with 17 abstentions, to condemn colonial economic exploitation "contrary to the interests of the indigenous population."	France announces that it will begin to build an atomic power plant on the Rhone in 1968.	Israeli forces wipe out an Arab guerrilla base near the West Bank town of Nablus.		Fierce fighting rages near Bongson, 140 miles south of Danang.
Dec. 8		Reports indicate that Soviet CP Gen. Secy. Leonid Brezhnev is flying to Prague in order to prevent the ouster of Czech Pres. Antonin Novotny. . . . Soviet scientist Boris Nikolayevich says that the Soviet Union has concluded treaties for the establishment of space tracking stations in Egypt, Mali and other countries. . . . U.S. dependents begin to return to Cyprus.	Jordan accuses Israel of expelling 200 Jordanians from the West Bank to the East Bank on Dec. 7. . . . Jordan returns the body of Israeli pilot David Nevo shot down over Jordan on Nov. 21.		South Vietnamese troops trap two Viet Cong battalions in the Mekong Delta.
Dec. 9		Rumanian Parliament unanimously confirms CP Gen. Secy. Nicolae Ceausescu as president.	Israeli authorities say that an autopsy of the body of an Israeli pilot shot down over Jordan on Nov. 21 indicates that he was beaten and stabbed to death.		National Liberation Front of South Vietnam denies that it has sought to send representatives to the U.N.

	A	B	C	D	E
	Includes developments that affect more than one world region, international organizations and important meetings of major world leaders.	Includes all domestic and regional developments in Europe, including the Soviet Union, Turkey, Cyprus and Malta.	Includes all domestic and regional developments in Africa and the Middle East, including Iraq and Iran and excluding Cyprus, Turkey and Afghanistan.	Includes all domestic and regional developments in Latin America, the Caribbean and Canada.	Includes all domestic and regional developments in Asia and Pacific nations, extending from Afghanistan through all the Pacific Islands, except Hawaii.

U.S. Politics & Social Issues	U.S. Foreign Policy & Defense	U.S. Economy & Environment	Science, Technology & Nature	Culture, Leisure & Life Style	
Sen. Eugene McCarthy says that there is "no conspiracy, collusion or common plan" between Sen. Robert Kennedy and himself.	Pres. Johnson announces that if the nuclear nonproliferation treaty is passed, the U.S. will open up to inspection all nuclear activities with the exception of those "with direct national security significance."	President's Council of Economic Advisers Chmn. Gardner Ackley deplores the Dec. 1 steel price hikes.		Roman Catholic archbishop of New York Francis Cardinal Spellman dies in New York at 78.	Dec. 2
	Yale Univ. Pres. Kingman Brewster strongly opposes the early drafting of those violators of the Selective Service Act who are eligible for the draft.		A team of South African surgeons headed by Dr. Christiaan Barnard successfully performs the world's first human heart transplant on Louis Washkansky. . . . Soviet Union launches Cosmos 194.		Dec. 3
U.S. Supreme Court affirms a lower court decision declaring unconstitutional the Alabama tuition grant law.	Pres. Johnson defends his Vietnam policy before a group of about 400 businessmen at the White House. . . . Antiwar demonstrations take place throughout the country.	U.S. Federal Reserve Board Chmn. William McChesney Martin says that the U.S. should repeal the law requiring gold backing for 25% of the nation's paper money supply. . . . AFL-CIO Pres. George Meany expresses strong support for the administration's Vietnam policy.	Sloan-Kettering Institute doctors report favorable results in a new form of drug therapy in the treatment of leukemia. . . . U.S. launches a satellite which will measure electro-density in the atmosphere.		Dec. 4
Senate passes a bill barring discrimination against workers between 40- and 65-years-old because of their age.	Police arrest 264 demonstrators at a N.Y.C. induction center. . . . Voters defeat a proposal calling for the "prompt return home" of U.S. forces in Vietnam by 57% to 37% in a Cambridge, Mass. referendum. . . . Presidential envoy Cyrus Vance confers with Pres. Johnson about the Cyprus negotiations.		South African Dr. Christiaan Barnard says that he is "perfectly satisfied" with heart transplant patient Louis Washkansky's condition. . . . U.S. Air Force launches a satellite.		Dec. 5
House passes a bill barring discrimination against workers between the ages of 40 and 65 because of their age.	About 2,500 anti-war demonstrators disrupt traffic in N.Y.C.	Pres. Johnson repeats appeals to industry and labor to hold down price and wage increases. . . . House and Senate pass a bill strengthening the federal meat inspection system.	First U.S. attempt to transplant a human heart ends in failure at Maimonides Hospital in Brooklyn, New York.		Dec. 6
Justice Dept. files job discrimination suits against two Cincinnati labor unions.	Police arrest 300 anti-war demonstrators trying to block an induction center in N.Y.C. . . . Sen. Edward Kennedy (D, Mass.) attacks the policy of early drafting of those violators of the Selective Service Act who are eligible for the draft. . . . House Senate and House Republican leaders charge the administration with not fully exploiting opportunities to end the Vietnamese War. . . . V.P. Humphrey says that South Vietnam is in contact with individual members of the National Liberation Front.	Labor Secy. Willard Wirtz gives a speech, at the AFL-CIO convention, about the necessity for wage and price restraint.			Dec. 7
	State Secy. Rusk says that there is "dissension" between Northerners and Southerners in the National Liberation Front. . . . N.Y.C. police arrest 140 demonstrators on the final day of the "Stop-the-Draft-Week" demonstrations. . . . Senate Foreign Relations Committee Chmn. J. W. Fulbright calls the Vietnam War "immoral and unnecessary." . . . State Secy. Rusk at the AFL-CIO convention defends the administration's Vietnam policy.		Slight symptoms of immunological rejection appear in heart transplant patient Louis Washkansky's body. . . . First Negro U.S. astronaut Maj. Robert Lawrence dies when his training flight plane crashes.		Dec. 8
President's National Advisory Commission on Rural Poverty asserts that rural poverty is so widespread that it constitutes "a national disgrace.". . . New Orleans Dist. Atty. James Garrison says that Pres. John Kennedy was killed by a man who fled through the Dallas drainage system.	Selective Service Director Lewis Hershey and Atty. Gen. Ramsey Clark say that violators of the Selective Service Act face early induction or legal action. . . . V.P. Humphrey calls on Democratic critics of the administration's Vietnam policy to "clearly enunciate" alternatives.		Reports indicate that doctors have successfully suppressed symptoms of immunological rejection in heart transplant patient Louis Washkansky's body by intensified drug treatments.	Pres. Johnson's elder daughter, Lynda Bird Johnson, marries Marine Capt. Charles Robb at the White House.	Dec. 9
F	G	H	I	J	
Includes elections, federal-state relations, civil rights and liberties, crime, the judiciary, education, health care, poverty, urban affairs and population.	Includes formation and debate of U.S. foreign and defense policies, veterans' affairs and defense spending. (Relations with specific foreign countries are usually found under the region concerned.)	Includes business, labor, agriculture, taxation, transportation, consumer affairs, monetary and fiscal policy, natural resources, and pollution.	Includes worldwide scientific, medical and technological developments, natural phenomena, U.S. weather, natural disasters, and accidents.	Includes the arts, religion, scholarship, communications media, sports, entertainment, fashions, fads and social life.	

	World Affairs	Europe	Africa & the Middle East	The Americas	Asia & the Pacific
Dec. 10		A fierce storm leaves 23 dead in northern Europe.			South Vietnamese troops batter the remnants of two Viet Cong battalions in the Mekong Delta.
Dec. 11	U.N. Gen. Assembly votes, 96-0, with 11 abstentions, to continue the office of the U.N. High Commissioner for Refugees for five more years. . . . U.N. Secy. Gen. U Thant charges that the Greek Cypriote National Guard used "disproportionate force" in trying to restore order in a Cypriote village containing both Greeks and Turks. . . . International Monetary Fund reports a decline in world trade during the third quarter of 1967.	Extremely heavy gold buying hits the European gold markets.	Arab Foreign Ministers meeting in Cairo agree to hold a summit conference of Arab heads of state in January 1968.		An earthquake kills at least 200 people in India.
Dec. 12	U.N. Security Council recommends the admission of South Yemen.	NATO's Defense Planning Committee adopts a three-stage "flexible response" defense strategy. . . . Extremely heavy gold buying continues on the European gold markets.	U.N. envoy Gunnar Jarring begins a trip to the Middle Eastern confrontation states to determine peace prospects. . . . An Israeli army patrol exchanges gunfire with Arab guerrillas near Lydda in Israel. . . . North Yemeni Maj. Gen. Hassan al-Amri charges that the U.S. is the only country supplying arms to royalists in the current civil war.	Canada announces that it will sell 78.4 million bushels of wheat to Communist China.	
Dec. 13	U.N. General Assembly votes, 89-2, to ask the Security Council to take more effective measures to end apartheid.	Britain reports its November balance-of-trade deficit to be $530.4 million. . . . Greek King Constantine broadcasts an appeal for his countrymen to join him in toppling the ruling military junta, but the Greek army appears to be in control of the situation.	Egypt says that it would start work to reopen the Suez Canal if Israel withdraws from the Sinai Peninsula.		More Australian troops arrive in South Vietnam, bringing their total force strength to 8,200 men. . . . *The New York Times* reports that the administration is considering giving U.S. commanders permission to carry out "hot pursuit" of the enemy into Cambodia. . . . Following a heated five-day debate, the Indian Parliament passes a bill retaining English as an official language until each of the states that currently opposes the use of Hindi is willing to accept Hindi as the official language.
Dec. 14	A South Vietnamese National Liberation Front document advocating a coalition government circulates among U.N. delegates. . . . U.N. General Assembly votes, 81-2, with 18 abstentions, to call on the U.N.'s specialized agencies to extend aid to peoples struggling for "liberation."	Greek King Constantine flies to exile in Rome. . . . British P.M. Harold Wilson says that diplomatic recognition of the Greek military government is now out of the question after the exile of Greek King Constantine. . . . Rumanian Pres. Nicolae Ceausescu confers with top Soviet leaders in Moscow.	Western diplomatic sources report a Soviet airlift to North Yemen during the last three weeks.		U.S. planes bomb the Longbien bridge in Hanoi.
Dec. 15		French Senate demands that a National Assembly bill legalizing the sale of birth control devices be amended to raise from 18 to 24 the legal age at which women could purchase them. . . . Diplomatic observers describe the joint Soviet-Rumanian communique issued at the end of government talks as "cold.". . . Greek King Constantine meets with Greek Foreign Min. Panayotis Pipinelis in Rome. . . . Heavy gold buying continues on the European gold markets.	Reports indicate that Israel has begun to round up members of an Arab sabotage organization. . . . Algeria says that troops supporting Pres. Houari Boumedienne crushed an attempted coup on Dec. 14.		Fighting resumes in the Bongson area. . . . U.S. planes bomb the Canal des Rapides bridge near Hanoi.
Dec. 16	U.N. General Assembly votes, 110-2, to call on South Africa to halt the trial of 37 South-West Africans accused of guerrilla activities. . . . Reports indicate that Communist China and East Germany have raised the level of the South Vietnamese National Liberation Front's representatives in their respective capitals.	Greek King Constantine meets with a Greek government delegation for five hours. . . . Gold buying declines on the European markets as major European nations affirm their intention to maintain the value of gold at its current $35-an-ounce value.			Fighting continues in the Bongson area. . . . Czechoslovak news agency says that 20 people were sentenced to death at a Dec. 11 public trial in Hunan Province in Communist China.

A	B	C	D	E
Includes developments that affect more than one world region, international organizations and important meetings of major world leaders.	*Includes all domestic and regional developments in Europe, including the Soviet Union, Turkey, Cyprus and Malta.*	*Includes all domestic and regional developments in Africa and the Middle East, including Iraq and Iran and excluding Cyprus, Turkey and Afghanistan.*	*Includes all domestic and regional developments in Latin America, the Caribbean and Canada.*	*Includes all domestic and regional developments in Asia and Pacific nations, extending from Afghanistan through all the Pacific Islands, except Hawaii.*

U.S. Politics & Social Issues	U.S. Foreign Policy & Defense	U.S. Economy & Environment	Science, Technology & Nature	Culture, Leisure & Life Style	
	Sen. Eugene McCarthy (D, Minn.) says that the U.S. should begin to vacate part of South Vietnam. . . . Reports indicate that the U.S. Navy has started a campaign to warn U.S. sailors not to join "anti-war peace groups."		U.S. conducts an underground nuclear test. . . . Heart transplant patient Louis Washkansky undergoes cobalt therapy treatment.		Dec. 10
U.S. Supreme Court declares unconstitutional a provision of a 1950 law making it a crime for Communist Party members to work at defense facilities. . . . U.S. Supreme Court upholds a lower court decision requiring the J.P. Stevens Co. to reinstate 71 workers illegally discharged for union activity. . . . Police arrest civil rights activist Stokely Carmichael on his return to New York after a four month trip abroad.		AFL-CIO overwhelmingly backs Pres. Johnson's Vietnam policy. . . . House votes to cut fiscal 1968 spending by $4.1 billion. . . . AFL-CIO convention reelects Pres. George Meany to another two-year term.			Dec. 11
Milwaukee passes an open-housing bill. . . . Senate passes a tougher District of Columbia criminal code. . . . Pres. Johnson assails House Republicans for allegedly always supporting "the status quo.". . . Administrative Office of the U.S. Courts reports that draft law violation convictions increased from 372 in fiscal 1966 to 748 in fiscal 1967.	Pres. Johnson thanks AFL-CIO George Meany for his union's support of U.S. Vietnam policy. . . . Sen. Edward Kennedy (D, Mass.) estimates that total civilian war casualties in South Vietnam are running at a rate of about 150,000 a year.	Senate votes to cut spending by $4.1 billion in fiscal 1968 budget. . . . At the AFL-CIO convention NAACP Dir. Roy Wilkins warns against reliance on voluntary compliance for reducing bias.			Dec. 12
House passes a tougher District of Columbia criminal code.	U.S. Defense Dept. official says that the U.S. is developing a spacecraft which could carry nuclear weapons. . . . U.S. denies North Yemeni charges that it is supplying arms to royalist forces.		U.S. launches spacecraft Pioneer 8.		Dec. 13
	U.S. State Dept. says that the Greek military junta has lost its claim to legitimacy after the exile of Greek King Constantine.	Pres. Johnson signs a bill strengthening the 1953 Flammable Fabrics Act.	Stanford Univ. scientists announce the artificial production of DNA or deoxyribonucleic acid.		Dec. 14
Pres. Johnson signs a bill barring discrimination against workers between the ages of 40 and 65 because of their age.	State Secy. Rusk says that the U.S. will "wait for a while" before deciding whether to recognize the Greek military government.	Congress adjourns without having enacted the administration's 10% income tax surcharge request. . . . UAW and the General Motors Corp. agree on a new three-year contract. . . . Pres. Johnson signs a bill strengthening the federal meat inspection system.	U.S. conducts an underground nuclear test.		Dec. 15
Louisville, Ky. passes an open-housing bill.			South African doctors report that heart transplant patient Louis Washkansky has developed double pneumonia. . . . Soviet Union launches Cosmos 195.		Dec. 16

F	G	H	I	J
Includes elections, federal-state relations, civil rights and liberties, crime, the judiciary, education, health care, poverty, urban affairs and population.	Includes formation and debate of U.S. foreign and defense policies, veterans' affairs and defense spending. (Relations with specific foreign countries are usually found under the region concerned.)	Includes business, labor, agriculture, taxation, transportation, consumer affairs, monetary and fiscal policy, natural resources, and pollution.	Includes worldwide scientific, medical and technological developments, natural phenomena, U.S. weather, natural disasters, and accidents.	Includes the arts, religion, scholarship, communications media, sports, entertainment, fashions, fads and social life.

	World Affairs	Europe	Africa & the Middle East	The Americas	Asia & the Pacific
Dec. 17			A Yemeni royalist radio announces that its troops are launching an attack on Sana, the capital of Yemen. . . . Dissident army officers overthrow Pres. Christophe Soglo of Dahomey.		Australian P.M. Harold Holt disappears while swimming off an Australian beach. . . . U.S. planes bomb the Kep and Phucyen MiG bases in North Vietnam.
Dec. 18		British P.M. Harold Wilson announces that Britain will continue its three-year-old embargo of arms to South Africa.	A provisional government forms in Dahomey headed by Maj. Maurice Kouandete. . . . Six of the 10 members of the Palestine Liberation Organization Executive Committee demand the resignation of their chairman, Ahmed Shukairy. . . . Mohsan al-Aini resigns as premier of North Yemen.		U.S. bombs the Longbien bridge in North Vietnam. . . . Australia announces the presumed death by drowning of P.M. Harold Holt.
Dec. 19	U.N. General Assembly votes unanimously to adopt an international treaty on the rescue and return of astronauts. . . . U.N. General Assembly's Special Political Committee votes, 42-38, to appoint a U.N. custodian for Arab property in Israeli-held territory.	A Greek official representing the ruling military junta meets with Greek King Constantine in Rome to negotiate his possible return to Greece. . . . France again blocks efforts of other Common Market countries to open negotiations with Britain on Common Market membership. . . . Reports from Bonn indicate that Israel will buy 75% of the steel for the Elath-Ashdod oil pipeline from West Germany.	Former Pres. Christophe Soglo of Dahomey takes refuge in the French embassy in Cotonou, the country's capital. . . . Israel and Rumania sign a trade agreement in Tel-Aviv. . . . Britain announces that it will renew diplomatic relations with Egypt.		Reports indicate that the U.S. has granted American pilots permission to fly through a previously restricted area of North Vietnam along the Communist Chinese border. . . . U.S. planes bomb the Hanoi area for the sixth straight day.
Dec. 20		Greek King Constantine announces that his only condition for his return to his country is a government announcement of a firm timetable for "the re-establishment of a normal democratic political life."	Israel deports two Arabs active in anti-Israeli demonstrations to Jordan.		New U.S. reinforcements raise U.S. force total to 474,300 in South Vietnam.
Dec. 21			Israel announces the smashing of an Arab sabotage organization.		World leaders including Pres. Johnson attend Australian P.M. Harold Holt's funeral. . . . U.S. forces launch an offensive in and around the demilitarized zone.
Dec. 22		*The New York Times* reports the sentencing to long prison terms of four Soviet intellectuals. . . . French Pres. de Gaulle pardons former Gen. Edmond Jouhaud who served five years of a life sentence for attempting to overthrow the French government during the Algerian war.	Israeli newspaper *Maariv* reports that recently captured Arab guerrillas have confessed their plans to stir up trouble in East Jerusalem and Bethlehem during Christmas observances.		U.S. planes carry out heavy raids in the demilitarized zone. . . . South Vietnam announces that it has sentenced the former mayor of Danang to 10 years in prison for participating in the Buddhist revolts of May 1966.
Dec. 23					Pres. Johnson flies to South Vietnam and visits U.S. troops.
Dec. 24		Greek government releases leftist politician Andreas Papandreou from prison.	Iraq and the Soviet Union sign an agreement for Soviet development of Iraqi oil deposits.		A tenuous Christmas truce goes into effect in South Vietnam. . . . U.S. announces that it has detected the seventh Communist Chinese atmospheric nuclear test in Sinkiang Province.
Dec. 25		Reports indicate the Greek King Constantine may return to Greece from his exile in Rome.			South Vietnamese truce ends and U.S. planes resume their strikes against North Vietnam.
Dec. 26		Greek Public Order Ministry Secy. Gen. Ioannis Ladas says that the more than 2,500 prisoners on the islands of Leros and Yioura will not benefit from the current amnesty.			U.S. authorities report 108 enemy-initiated incidents during the Dec. 24 truce.
	A	**B**	**C**	**D**	**E**
	Includes developments that affect more than one world region, international organizations and important meetings of major world leaders.	*Includes all domestic and regional developments in Europe, including the Soviet Union, Turkey, Cyprus and Malta.*	*Includes all domestic and regional developments in Africa and the Middle East, including Iraq and Iran and excluding Cyprus, Turkey and Afghanistan.*	*Includes all domestic and regional developments in Latin America, the Caribbean and Canada.*	*Includes all domestic and regional developments in Asia and Pacific nations, extending from Afghanistan through all the Pacific Islands, except Hawaii.*

U.S. Politics & Social Issues	U.S. Foreign Policy & Defense	U.S. Economy & Environment	Science, Technology & Nature	Culture, Leisure & Life Style	
					Dec. 17
U.S. Supreme Court reverses the murder conviction of Wallace Satterfield because he was not warned of his rights until immediately before his confession. . . . U.S. Supreme Court rules, 7-1, that police must obtain judicial warrants to use electronic eavesdropping (not wiretapping) devices.	Oakland, Calif. police arrest 218 of about 750 anti-war demonstrators who try to block the armed forces induction center in the city. . . . Retired U.S. Marine Corps commandant Gen. David Shoup says that American vital interests are not at stake in Vietnam. . . . U.S. State Dept. says that U.S. diplomats in Greece are conducting routine business with the military government.	Pres. Johnson signs a bill passed by the House and Senate to cut spending by $4.1 billion for the fiscal 1968 budget.		Luchino Visconti's film *The Stranger* is released.	Dec. 18
	U.S. reaffirms its ban on arms sales to South Africa.		Soviet Union launches Cosmos 196.		Dec. 19
A federal court sentences seven whites to prison terms for conspiracy in the 1964 murder of three civil rights workers near Philadelphia, Miss.					Dec. 20
Michigan House of Representatives defeats an open-housing bill by 55-47.			Louis Washkansky, the first human to live with a transplanted heart, dies in South Africa.		Dec. 21
	Former Pres. Dwight Eisenhower urges continued public support for the Vietnamese War. . . . In its Dec. 22 issue, *Time* magazine says that the U.S. should seek a "diplomatic compromise" in Vietnam rather than a "military victory."			Dr. Oscar Creech, co-inventor of the heart-lung machine technique for treatment of malignant diseases, dies in New Orleans at 51.	Dec. 22
					Dec. 23
					Dec. 24
					Dec. 25
Defense Secy. McNamara cracks down on operators of rental housing who discriminate against Negro servicemen.		U.S. Commerce Dept. reports the U.S. balance of trade surplus to be $296 million in November 1967.	Soviet Union launches Cosmos 197.		Dec. 26

F	G	H	I	J
Includes elections, federal-state relations, civil rights and liberties, crime, the judiciary, education, health care, poverty, urban affairs and population.	*Includes formation and debate of U.S. foreign and defense policies, veterans' affairs and defense spending. (Relations with specific foreign countries are usually found under the region concerned.)*	*Includes business, labor, agriculture, taxation, transportation, consumer affairs, monetary and fiscal policy, natural resources, and pollution.*	*Includes worldwide scientific, medical and technological developments, natural phenomena, U.S. weather, natural disasters, and accidents.*	*Includes the arts, religion, scholarship, communications media, sports, entertainment, fashions, fads and social life.*

	World Affairs	Europe	Africa & the Middle East	The Americas	Asia & the Pacific
Dec. 27			Israel reports the slaying of two Arab guerrillas in the Gaza Strip.		South Vietnamese troops maul a Viet Cong battalion near Quangtri.
Dec. 28		Turkish Cypriote leaders form a "transitional administration" that is to have "jurisdiction over all Turks living in Turkish zones."	A mine kills an Israeli soldier in the Gaza Strip.		U.S. Marines suffer heavy losses against North Vietnamese troops in Quangnam Province.
Dec. 29		Four U.S. Navy men who deserted in Japan on Oct. 24 arrive in Stockholm, Sweden. . . . Cypriote Pres. Makarios assails Turkish Cypriote attempts to set up their own administration.		Brazil announces that it will devalue its currency on Jan. 2, 1968.	U.S. command reports 15,812 combat fatalities during 1967 in South Vietnam.
Dec. 30					South Vietnam announces the extension of the allies' proposed New Year's truce 12 hours beyond the 24 hours originally planned. . . .
Dec. 31					Communists ambush a U.S. Army patrol in one of the first reported major violations of the Viet Cong New Year's truce.

A	B	C	D	E
Includes developments that affect more than one world region, international organizations and important meetings of major world leaders.	Includes all domestic and regional developments in Europe, including the Soviet Union, Turkey, Cyprus and Malta.	Includes all domestic and regional developments in Africa and the Middle East, including Iraq and Iran and excluding Cyprus, Turkey and Afghanistan.	Includes all domestic and regional developments in Latin America, the Caribbean and Canada.	Includes all domestic and regional developments in Asia and Pacific nations, extending from Afghanistan through all the Pacific Islands, except Hawaii.

U.S. Politics & Social Issues	U.S. Foreign Policy & Defense	U.S. Economy & Environment	Science, Technology & Nature	Culture, Leisure & Life Style	
Pres. Johnson signs a bill for a tougher District of Columbia criminal code.					Dec. 27
Chicago Police Superintendent James Conlisk says that six Chicago policemen have been involved in Ku Klux Klan activity for which they will be disciplined.		U.S. Federal Reserve Board reports that the U.S. gold stock has declined by $270 million during the first 11 months of 1967.		N.Y. Film Critics award for the best motion picture of 1967 goes to *In the Heat of the Night.*	Dec. 28
Chicago Tribune article says that New Orleans Dist. Atty. James Garrison was under psychiatric care from 1950 to 1955.					Dec. 29
					Dec. 30
					Dec. 31

F	G	H	I	J
Includes elections, federal-state relations, civil rights and liberties, crime, the judiciary, education, health care, poverty, urban affairs and population.	Includes formation and debate of U.S. foreign and defense policies, veterans' affairs and defense spending. (Relations with specific foreign countries are usually found under the region concerned.)	Includes business, labor, agriculture, taxation, transportation, consumer affairs, monetary and fiscal policy, natural resources, and pollution.	Includes worldwide scientific, medical and technological developments, natural phenomena, U.S. weather, natural disasters, and accidents.	Includes the arts, religion, scholarship, communications media, sports, entertainment, fashions, fads and social life.

1968

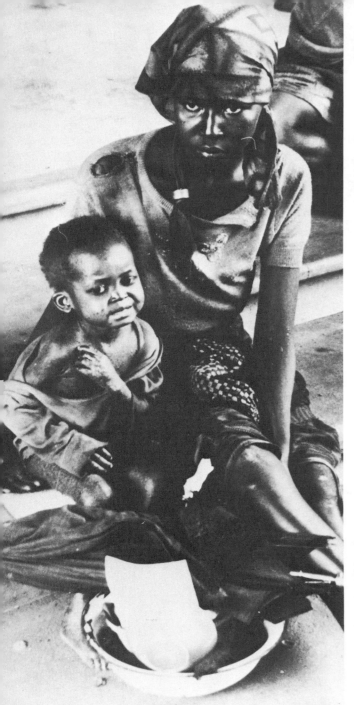

Two starvation victims of the Nigerian civil war await treatment in Biafra.

Police chase protesters out of Grant Park in Chicago during the August Democratic National Convention.

The Beatles, one of the decades most popular rock groups.

Richard M. Nixon wins the Republican nomination for president in Miami on Aug. 9.

Students and police clash in Paris in May. Students have been protesting university regulations and alleged police brutality.

American soldiers fighting in the Mekong Delta.

Mrs. Martin Luther King and two of her children at the funeral of her slain husband Apr. 9.

Aristotle Onassis and the former Mrs. Jaqueline Kennedy after their wedding Oct. 20 on the island of Scorpios.

The Gateway Arch in St. Louis, which is dedicated in May.

Apollo 8 is recovered from the Pacific Ocean December 27 after it and three astronauts orbited the moon ten times.

	World Affairs	Europe	Africa & the Middle East	The Americas	Asia & the Pacific
Jan.	U.S. and the Soviet Union submit a revised and completed draft treaty to prevent the spread of nuclear weapons to the U.N. Disarmament Committee.	Czechoslovak CP elects Alexander Dubcek to succeed Antonin Novotny as CP first secretary amid signs of a political liberalization movement.	Britain announces plans to withdraw from the Persian Gulf countries by 1971 despite their offer to finance the cost of maintaining its troops in the area.	Cuban Communist Party denounces pro-Soviet Cuban Communists for allegedly trying to overthrow Premier Fidel Castro.	North Korean patrol boats capture U.S. intelligence ship, *Pueblo* . . . .Communist troops launch the heaviest offensive of the Vietnamese War and capture several major towns.
Feb.	U.N. Relief & Works Agency (UNRWA) announces that about 67,000 of the 77,000 refugees in nine Jordan River Valley camps have fled eastward to Amman because of border fighting.	Several major European countries recognize the Greek military junta despite misgivings about its authoritarian character.	Nine Persian Gulf emirates agree to form a union when Britain withdraws its military forces from the area in 1971. . . .Major fighting continues between royalist and republican forces in North Yemen.	Canadian Justice Min. Pierre Elliot Trudeau announces that he is a candidate to succeed P.M. Lester Pearson for the leadership of the Liberal Party.	Fierce fighting rages throughout South Vietnam as allied forces push Communist troops out of major cities.
March	Seven active members of the London Gold Pool agree to establish a two-tier pricing system for gold, a private market price and an inter-governmental price.	Anti-government demonstrations and strikes erupt throughout Poland. . . .Liberalization drive gains momentum in Czechoslovakia as Pres. Antonin Novotny is forced to resign.	Fifteen thousand Israeli troops carry out a day-long retaliatory raid in Jordan. It is their first major ground thrust into Arab territory since the June 1967 war.	Panamanian National Assembly votes Pres. Marco Aurelio Robles out of office but with the support of the National Guard, he ignores the vote.	A major allied offensive puts Communist forces on the defensive for the first time since the launching of their Jan. 31 offensive.
April	U.N. Security Council passes a resolution calling on Israel to cancel a military parade scheduled for May 2 in Jerusalem.	Czechoslovak state prosecutor's office announces that an investigation is under way into the death of former Foreign Min. Jan Masaryk in 1948. . . .Student riots break out in major West German cities after an assassin seriously injures West German student leader Rudi Dutschke.	Intermittant shelling continues between Israel, Egypt and Jordan. . . .Sudan reports more than 100 casualties in recent clashes with Ethiopian guerrillas.	Pierre Elliot Trudeau succeeds retiring Lester Pearson as Canadian prime minister.	North Vietnam and the U.S. establish public diplomatic contact for the first time but fail to agree on a site for peace talks.
May	International Red Cross appeals for emergency food aid for the Nigerian seccessionist province, Biafra.	Press censorship ends in Czechoslovakia. . . .Student demonstrations and strikes bring France to a virtual standstill.	Nigerian and Biafran representatives meet for the first time but report no progress in their peace negotiations.	Five South American countries agree on proposals for the joint development of the Rio Plata area.	Communists launch a major offensive throughout South Veitnam and take over part of Saigon.
June	U.N. General Assembly approves the nuclear non-proliferation treaty.	Gaullist candidates win a smashing victory in French National Assembly elections. . . .Soviet troops remain in Czechoslovakia after the end of Warsaw Pact troop exercises.	*The New York Times* reports that the Israeli cabinet has agreed on a plan formulated by Labor Min. Yigal Allon calling for Israeli settlements along the Jordan River in territory captured during the June 1967 war.	Canada's Liberal Party led by P.M. Pierre Elliott Trudeau wins a decisive victory. . . . Uruguay declares a limited martial law emergency in the face of widespread strikes.	Savage fighting takes place around the U.S. base at Khesanh. . . .No progress is reported at the Paris peace talks.
July	Sixty-two nations sign the nuclear non-proliferation treaty.	Soviet Politburo and the Czechoslovak Presidium meet in Cierna, Czechoslovakia as Soviet pressure mounts against the Czech liberalization drive. . . .French National Assembly votes a general amnesty for all convicted persons of fugitives in the Algerian War.	Diplomatic sources in Cairo say that Egypt would be willing to permit israeli cargo vessels to use the Suez Canal if Israeli troops pull back from the East Bank of the canal. . . .Reports indicate widespread starvation in Biafra because of the civil war.	Violent clashes take place between students, police and federal troops in Mexico City.	South Vietnamese Pres. Nguyen Van Thieu says that the U.S. may be able to begin to withdraw soldiers in 1969.
Aug.	U.N. Security Council condemns the invasion of Czechoslovakia by a vote of 10-2.	Soviet Union and four other East European countries invade Czechoslovakia to crush its liberalization drive. . . .France explodes its first thermonuclear bomb and becomes the world's fifth thermonuclear nation. . . .Portugese Pres. Antonio de Oliveira Salazar suffers a serious heart attack.	Peace talks between Nigeria and Biafra show little signs of progress. . . .Nigerian government fires on planes bringing food supplies to starving Biafrans.	Serious clashes continue between students and federal troops in Mexico City.	Heavy fighting continues between allied forces and Communist troops in South Vietnam.
Sept.	International Red Cross estimates that 8,000-10,000 people are starving to death every day in Biafra.	Under heavy Soviet pressure, Czechoslovak government officials are forced to curtail drastically their country's liberalization drive.	Sporadic shelling continues between Israel, Egypt and Jordan. . . .Somalia renounces its territorial claims to Djibouti.	Violent clashes continue between police and students in Mexico City and leave at least 17 dead.	Communist China charges that Soviet aircraft have violated its north-eastern border.
Oct.	At the U.N. Laos charges that North Vietnam has carried the Vietnamese War into Laos.	Under intense Soviet pressure, Czechoslovak leaders agree publicly to abandon the remnants of their liberalization drive and to allow Soviet troops to remain in their country for an indefinite period.	Reports indicate that the new Syrian cabinet represents a victory for the nationalist wing of the Baath party which favors more cooperation with Arab countries and less dependence on the Soviet Union.	A military coup led by Gen. Juan Velasco Alvarado overthrows Peruvian Pres. Fernando Terry. . . . A military coup ousts Panamanian Pres. Arnulfo Arias and Col. Omar Torrijos becomes National Guard commander and *de facto* political leader.	*The New York Times* reports that 40% of the cadres in Shanghai, China have been made to do manual work.
Nov.	U.N. Gen. Assembly votes 58-44 against a resolution to seat Communist China and expel Nationalist China.	Fierce speculation batters the French franc. . . .Czechoslovak government forbids almost all tavel to the West.	Widespread rioting breaks out in Egypt and all universities are closed.	Reports indicate that the new Peruvian government plans to nationalize a major portion of U.S. property.	North Korea releases the 82 surviving members of U.S. ship *Pueblo*. . . . South Vietnamese Pres. Nguyen Van Thieu agrees to participate in the Paris peace talks after a boycott of several weeks.
Dec.	U.N. votes, 60-22, to establish a committee to investigate Israeli human rights practices in the occupied territories.	Disputes over the shape of the conference table dominate the opening sessions of the expanded Paris peace talks.	Israeli commandos destroy 13 civilian planes during a raid on Beirut airport.	Guyanan P.M. Forbes Burnham decisively defeats Marxist Cheddi Jagan. . . .Brazilian government suspends congress after its criticism of military rulers. . . .Rafael Caldera Rodriquez wins an authentically democratic presidential election in Venezuela.	U.S. reports that American combat deaths have passed 30,000 in South Vietnam.
	A	B	C	D	E
	Includes developments that affect more than one world region, international organizations and important meetings of major world leaders.	*Includes all domestic and regional developments in Europe, including the Soviet Union, Turkey, Cyprus and Malta.*	*Includes all domestic and regional developments in Africa and the Middle East, including Iraq and Iran and excluding Cyprus, Turkey and Afghanistan.*	*Includes all domestic and regional developments in Latin America, the Caribbean and Canada.*	*Includes all domestic and regional developments in Asia and Pacific nations, extending from Afghanistan through all the Pacific Islands, except Hawaii.*

U.S. Politics & Social Issues	U.S. Foreign Policy & Defense	U.S. Economy & Environment	Science, Technology & Nature	Culture, Leisure & Life Style
Atty. Gen Ramsey Clark reports that 952 men were convicted for violating the Selective Service laws in 1967.	Pres. Johnson nominates Clark Clifford as defense secretary.	HEW Secy. John Gardner proposes new federal standards to reduce the amount of car-exhaust pollutants.	U.S. launches a working model of the lunar landing craft that will be used for the first manned American expedition to the moon.	Houghton Mifflin publishes David Halberstam's book on the Vietnamese War, *One Very Hot Day* .
Former V.P. Richard Nixon and former Alabama Gov. George Wallace announce their candidacies for president.	Outgoing Defense Secy. Robert McNamara says that the Soviet Union more than doubled its force of land-based intercontinental ballistic missiles in 1967.	AFL-CIO Building & Construction Trades Department announces that it will actively recruit and then train Negro apprentices.	World's only surviving heart transplant patient Philip Blaiberg is reported to be in normal condition after "an episode of rejection."	Catalan poet Jaime Sabartes dies in Paris at 86.
In the New Hampshire presidential primary, Pres. Johnson polls 48% in a write-in vote against 42% for Sen. Eugene McCarthy. . . .Sen. Robert Kennedy announces his candidacy for president.	Pres. Johnson announces that he will neither seek nor accept the nomination for another term as president. He also unilaterally orders a bombing halt of North Vietnam except for the part right above the demilitarized zone.	UAW Pres. Walter Reuther says that his union will withdraw from the AFL-CIO if it doesn't agree to his plans to modernize the labor federation.	Both the Soviet Union and the U.S. continue launchings of satellites which can inspect each other's territory.	George Kennan's *Memoirs* wins the 1967 National Book Award.
Rioting breaks out in major U.S. cities after an assassin kills the Rev. Martin Luther King Jr. . . .Pres. Johnson signs a bill prohibiting racial discrimination in the sale or rental of about 80% of the nation's housing. . . .V.P. Hubert Humphrey and N.Y. Gov. Nelson Rockefeller enter the presidential race.	Defense Secy. Clark Clifford says that the administration does not intend to go beyond a ceiling of 549,500 troops in South Vietnam.	Senate passes a bill combining the administration-requested 10% surcharge with a mandatory $6 billion reduction in federal spending.	Soviet Union and the U.S. continue their underground nuclear testing programs.	Lopert Pictures releases Ingmar Bergman's film *Hour of the Wolf* in N.Y.C. . . .Knopf publishes John Updike's *Couples*
Sen. Robert Kennedy wins the Indiana and Nebraska Democratic primaries but loses to Sen. Eugene McCarthy in the Oregon Democratic primary. . . .U.S. Supreme Court rules that interrogators must warn prison inmates of their rights before asking incriminating questions.	U.S. begins peace talks with North Vietnam in Paris but reports indicate little progress.	A Senate-House conference committee approves a bill coupling a $6 billion federal spending reduction with a 10% income tax surcharge.	U.S. rocket launches a European scientific research satellite.	U.S. composer George Crumb wins the Pulitzer Prize for music. . . .Dutch painter Kees van Dongen dies in Monte Carlo at 91.
Martin Luther King Jr.'s alleged assassin James Earl Ray, is arrested in London.	Reports indicate that the U.S. and the Soviet Union are ready to take serious steps towards negotiating an arms limitation agreement.	House passes a bill combining a 10% tax surcharge and a $6 billion cut in federal spending.	In Houston Tex. Sam Willoughby receives the heart of a ram in an unsuccessful effort to prolong his life.	Marcel Breuer wins the 1968 Gold Medal of the American Institute of Architects.
Senate Judiciary Committee blocks gun-control legislation. . . .Negroes riot in Gary, Ind. and Cleveland, Ohio.	Pres. Johnson announces that the U.S. and the Soviet Union have agreed to begin talks on limiting and reducing their arsenals of offensive and defensive nuclear weapons.	Administration urges "utmost restraint" in wage and price decisions by business and labor.	U.S. launches a satellite whose mission is to record atmospheric densities.	Roman Catholic Church's traditional prohibition against birth control by artificial means is reaffirmed in a papal encyclical. . . .Atheneum publishes J.J. Servan Schreiber's *The American Challenge* .
Democrats nominate V.P. Hubert Humphrey and Republicans nominate Richard Nixon as their presidential candidates. . . .Violent clashes take place between anti-war demonstrators and police at the Democratic convention in Chicago.	Pres. Johnson says that the U.S. will make no further moves to de-escalate the Vietnamese War until North Vietnam makes a serious move toward peace.	Commerce Department reports that the U.S. balance-of-international-payments deficit was $150 million for the second quarter of 1968.	Trevor De Wee receives the heart of a pig in a South African heart transplant operation.	Many European and North American Roman Catholics take issue with the Pope's reaffirmation of the Church's ban against artificial birth control means.
No major policy differences develop between presidential candidates Richard Nixon and Hubert Humphrey.	London Institute of Strategic Studies reports that the Soviet Union will have as many intercontinental missiles as the U.S. by the end of 1968.	Inflation rate continues to increase gradually in the U.S.	Soviet Union and the U.S. continue their underground nuclear testing programs.	Harper & Row publishes Aleksandr Solzhenitsyn's *One Day in the Life of Ivan Denisovich* .
Sen. Eugene McCarthy endorses Vice Pres. Humphrey for President. . . .Pres. Johnson withdraws his nomination of Supreme Court Justice Abe Fortas to be Chief Justice of the United States because of a Senate Filibuster.	Pres. Johnson announces that he is suspending the bombing of all parts of North Vietnam as of Nov. 1.	Pres. Johnson signs a bill designed to protect the public from radiation emissions from electronic products.	U.S. launches Apollo 7, the spacecraft designed to carry the first Americans to the moon.	Dial Press publishes [Aleksandr Solzhenitsyn's *The Cancer Ward* . . . . Mrs. Jacqueline Kennedy, the widow of Pres. John Kennedy, marries Greek shipping magnate Aristotle Onassis.
Richard Nixon is elected 37th president of the U.S.	U.S. halts all military bombardment of North Vietnam. . . .U.S. officials confirm that America's Pakistani base on the Afghanistan border will be closed in 1969.	U.S. officials see no let-up in the continuing American balance-of-payments deficit.	U.S. officials announce that America will try to orbit three astronauts around the moon before Christmas.	Holt, Rhinehart & Winston publishes Andre Malraux's *Anti-Memoirs* .
Acting Pres. S.I. Hayakawa closes San Francisco State College because of continuing student disorders. . . .N.Y. Negro secondary students riot in the Ocean Hill-Brownsville district where parents are trying to gain local control of public schools.	Two U.S. destroyers cruise the Black Sea, over the protests of the Soviet Union. . . . The U.S. announces that it will lift the ban against cultural exchanges with the Soviet Union, Poland, Bulgaria and Hungary imposed in September as an expression of the U.S. condemnation of the Czechoslovak invasion.	Pres.-elect Nixon chooses Dr. Paul McCracken to be chairman of the Council of Economic Advisers.	U.S. astronauts circle the moon and return to earth safely.	Ingmar Bergman's film *Shame*— opens in New York. . . . Hungarian conductor Georg Solti becomes musical director of the Chicago Symphony.
F	G	H	I	J
Includes elections, federal-state relations, civil rights and liberties, crime, the judiciary, education, health care, poverty, urban affairs and population.	*Includes formation and debate of U.S. foreign and defense policies, veterans' affairs and defense spending. (Relations with specific foreign countries are usually found under the region concerned.)*	*Includes business, labor, agriculture, taxation, transportation, consumer affairs, monetary and fiscal policy, natural resources, and pollution.*	*Includes worldwide scientific, medical and technological developments, natural phenomena, U.S. weather, natural disasters, and accidents.*	*Includes the arts, religion, scholarship, communications media, sports, entertainment, fashions, fads and social life.*

	World Affairs	Europe	Africa & the Middle East	The Americas	Asia & the Pacific
Jan. 1	First stage of the Kennedy Round tariff-cutting accord goes into effect.	Grand rabbi of France Jacob Kaplan meets with French Pres. de Gaulle.	Biafran military units report heavy fighting at the port of Calabar in Biafra. . . . Guinea re-elects Pres. Sekou Toure in an uncontested election.		North Vietnamese Foreign Min. Nguyen Duy Trinh says that his government will start talks if the U.S. unconditionally stops the bombing of North Vietnam. Previously, North Vietnam has said that talks could, rather than "will", take place after a bombing halt.
Jan. 2		Reports indicate that Soviet forces stationed in Mongolia include tank and anti-aircraft units.	Israel and Jordan clash along their Jordan River border.	Cuban Premier Fidel Castro announces the rationing of petroleum because of a slow-down in Soviet deliveries.	U.S. officials report that the New Year's cease-fire was "the worst truce ever" because of the numerous Communist violations.
Jan. 3		A US-French-Belgian research company forms to explore the uses of nuclear explosives for peaceful purposes. Greek government dismisses four top bankers from their posts.	Nigeria introduces new currency notes in an effort to prevent Biafra from using Nigerian currency for foreign purchases.	Bolivian Pres. Rene Barrientos Ortuno says that Bolivia might be willing to exchange French leftist Regis Debray for Cuban Maj. Huber Matos, currently serving a 20-year sentence in Cuba. . . . Cuban authorities issue ration coupons for car owners.	U.S. troops maul Communist forces south of Danang. . . . Nambac, a Laotian town, falls to Communist forces.
Jan. 4			Nigeria arrests U.S. artist Larry Rivers and French film maker Pierre-Dominique Gaisseau on suspicion of being white mercenaries working for Biafra. . . . Kenyan Pres. Jomo Kenyatta appoints V.P. Daniel Arap Moi as leader of of government business in the National Assembly.	Several SNCC representatives attend the opening of an International Cultural Congress in Havana, Cuba.	Reports indicate that North Vietnam has asked Laos, Burma and Cambodia if preliminary peace talks could take place in their capitals.
Jan. 5		Czechoslovak CP elects Alexander Dubcek to succeed Antonin Novotny as CP first secretary.	Nigerian military leader Maj. Gen. Yakubu Gowon offers to halt federal military operations if Biafra responds positively.	A delegation of French-speaking Arcadians leaves Canada for a visit to France.	U.S. command announces that U.S. troops' total in South Vietnam is 486,000.
Jan. 6		Grand Rabbi of France Jacob Kaplan says his fears of a new wave of anti-Semitism in France were dispelled by his Jan 1 meeting with French Pres. de Gaulle. . . . Toronto Telegram reports that at least 15 Ukranian intellectuals were sentenced to long prison terms during the winter of 1965-1966.	Israel and Jordan clash along their Jordan River border. . . . Israeli Defense Min. Moshe Dayan says that the position of the Soviet Union will be the determining factor in any Egyptian decision about whether or not to attack Israel.	Bolivian Pres. Rene Barrientos Ortuno says that Bolivia lost 57 soldiers in clashes with Che Guevara's guerrillas.	North Vietnamese kill 20 U.S. troops near Danang.
Jan. 7		Reports indicate that 52 Soviet intellectuals have signed a protest note deploring trials which are not open to the public.	Clashes continue between Israel and Jordan along their border.		North Vietnamese kill 16 U.S. Marines near Hue.
Jan. 8		A trial of four Soviet intellectuals begins in Moscow. . . . U.S. and Communist Chinese officials confer in Warsaw in the 134th meeting since 1955. . . . France confirms that it is preparing to withdraw 5,000 troops from West Germany.	Israeli-Jordanian clashes intensify as both sides use heavy artillery. . . . Nigeria releases U.S. artist Larry Rivers and French film maker Pierre-Dominique Gaisseau.	Bolivian Pres. Rene Barrientos Ortuno says that communist guerrillas are shifting their activities to the cities of Latin America.	Two major U.S.-Viet Cong clashes take place near Saigon.
	A	B	C	D	E
	Includes developments that affect more than one world region, international organizations and important meetings of major world leaders.	Includes all domestic and regional developments in Europe, including the Soviet Union, Turkey, Cyprus and Malta.	Includes all domestic and regional developments in Africa and the Middle East, including Iraq and Iran and excluding Cyprus, Turkey and Afghanistan.	Includes all domestic and regional developments in Latin America, the Caribbean and Canada.	Includes all domestic and regional developments in Asia and Pacific nations, extending from Afghanistan through all the Pacific Islands, except Hawaii.

U.S. Politics & Social Issues	U.S. Foreign Policy & Defense	U.S. Economy & Environment	Science, Technology & Nature	Culture, Leisure & Life Style	
	Sen. Eugene McCarthy expresses hope for a "reasonable--not perfect--negotiated settlement" of the war.	Pres. Johnson announces mandatory restraints on corporate investment abroad and other measures to protect the dollar.		Viking Press publishes James Joyce's *Giacomo Joyce*. . . . British poet Cecil Day Lewis becomes Britain's poet laureate.	**Jan. 1**
			National Safety Council reports 363 fatalities in traffic accidents over the New Year's holiday week-end. . . . South African doctors perform the world's third heart transplant operation on Dr. Philip Blaiberg.	Pope Paul appoints 34 non-Italian clergymen to policymaking positions in the Roman Curia in what is seen as part of a papal effort to internationalize the church's central administration.	**Jan. 2**
Sen. Eugene McCarthy announces that he will enter the New Hampshire presidential primary.		HEW Secy. John Gardner proposes new federal standards to reduce the amount of car-exhaust pollutants.		Vatican weekly fears that the U.S. may extend its fighting to include Laos and Cambodia.	**Jan. 3**
A N.J. court sentences Negro playwright LeRoi Jones to two-and-a-half to three years in prison for illegal possession of firearms during the 1967 Newark riots.	State Secy. Rusk says that the U.S. is in the process of evaluating North Vietnam's Jan. 1 statement concerning possible peace talks. . . . Sen. Robert Kennedy says that the U.S. should respond favorably to North Vietnam's offer to negotiate.		A live-virus vaccine against mumps is licensed for distribution by Merck, Sharp & Dohme.		**Jan. 4**
A federal grand jury indicts pediatrician Dr. Benjamin Spock for counseling violations of the Selective Service law. . . . Sen. Eugene McCarthy concedes that a word of support from either Robert or Edward Kennedy would help his campaign prospects.	House Armed Services Committee Chmn. Mendel Rivers urges Pres. Johnson not to consider a bombing halt of North Vietnam until North Vietnam returns U.S. prisoners.		National Archives makes public the agreement governing access to the autopsy photos and X-rays of Pres. John Kennedy's body.	Viking Press publishes Iris Murdoch's *The Nice and the Good*. . . . Thomas Crowell publishes Nora Levin's *The Holocaust: The Destruction of European Jewry, 1933-1945*.	**Jan. 5**
A Gallup Poll says that Sen. Eugene McCarthy would get about 12% of the vote if he headed an independent peace party ticket.					**Jan. 6**
	Israeli Prime Minister Levi Eshkol confers with Pres. Johnson in Texas. . . . Asst. State Secy. William Bundy expresses doubt as to whether a bombing halt would result in genuine peace talks.		U.S. launches Surveyor 7, the last unmanned American lunar probe.		**Jan. 7**
Sen. Robert Kennedy says that he does not think his support of Sen Eugene McCarthy would "further the cause" of anti-war protests. Israeli Premier Levi Eshkol and Pres. Johnson conclude talks in Texas.				Pope Paul urges the U.S. and North Vietnam to negotiate their differences.	**Jan. 8**

F	G	H	I	J
Includes elections, federal-state relations, civil rights and liberties, crime, the judiciary, education, health care, poverty, urban affairs and population.	*Includes formation and debate of U.S. foreign and defense policies, veterans' affairs and defense spending. (Relations with specific foreign countries are usually found under the region concerned.)*	*Includes business, labor, agriculture, taxation, transportation, consumer affairs, monetary and fiscal policy, natural resources, and pollution.*	*Includes worldwide scientific, medical and technological developments, natural phenomena, U.S. weather, natural disasters, and accidents.*	*Includes the arts, religion, scholarship, communications media, sports, entertainment, fashions, fads and social life.*

	World Affairs	Europe	Africa & the Middle East	The Americas	Asia & the Pacific
Jan. 9		Portugal reports that 34 Portugese troops died in Portuguese Guinea and 11 troops died in Angola and Mozambique during December 1967. . . . France and the Soviet Union announce an agreement to place French scientific equipment aboard a Soviet lunar probe. . . . Soviet authorities deny ex-Maj. Gen. Pyotr Grigorenko permission to attend the current trial of four Soviet intellectuals. . . . France makes public an exchange of letters between Pres. Charles de Gaulle and Israeli ex-Premier David Ben-Gurion dealing with de Gaulle's Nov. 27, 1967, comments about the Jewish people.	Israel announces that work has started on restoring the former Jewish quarter of the Old City of Jerusalem.	Cuba reports that a package from New York exploded and injured five postal workers.	Sweden grants asylum to four U.S. sailors who deserted their ship in Japan in October 1967.
Jan. 10		Spanish authorities close the Political & Economic Science College at Madrid Univ. . . . Reports indicate that 31 Soviet intellectuals have appealed for a public trial for the four Soviet intellectuals on closed trial since Jan. 8.	Israel and Jordan clash along their border. . . . Israel extends compulsory military service from 30 months to 36.		North Vietnam reiterates that it will start peace talks if the U.S. unconditionally halts the bombing of North Vietnam.
Jan. 11		Greek junta leader George Papadopoulos addresses a group of naval cadets in Athens with the cry, "Long live the King." . . . Britain reports that its 1967 balance of trade deficit amounts to nearly $3 billion. . . . At least 1,000 Madrid Univ. students demonstrate. . . . An Amnesty International representative reports being barred from the Soviet Jan. 8 trial of four Soviet intellectuals.	Israel expropriates 838 acres of the former Jordanian sector of Jerusalem.	Bahamian Premier Lynden Pindling proposes that Britain grant the Bahamas complete internal independence. . . . French officials announce that France will help to finance a French-language newspaper in New Brunswick, Canada.	U.S. troops clash with the Viet Cong in the Mekong Delta.
Jan. 12		East German government adopts a penal code increasing the use of the death penalty for political offenses. . . . Soviet authorities convict four intellectuals of "anti-Soviet" activity. A Spanish court sentences five union leaders to four-month prison terms for illegal union activity. . . . Reports from Belgrade indicate that 400 members of the Yugoslav CP have been recently expelled.	Israel and Egypt begin to exchange war prisoners captured during the June 1967 war. . . . Sporadic clashes take place between Israel and Jordan. . . . Zambia deports five South African policemen who were arrested there in December 1967. . . . A three-nation Arab commission fails to bring together North Yemeni royalist and republican forces.	Cuban Premier Fidel Castro expresses interest in exchanging political prisoners for the remains of guerrilla leader Che Guevara's body.	U.S. and Cambodia announce measures to help Cambodia avoid involvement in the Vietnamese War.
Jan. 13		More than 100 Portugese lawyers telegraph the justice ministry protesting the incarceration of Portugese opposition leader Mario Soares.	Israel and Jordan exchange machine gun fire briefly across the Jordan River. . . . Three-nation Arab commission appeals to Syria, Saudi Arabia, the Soviet Union and Iran not to interfere in the internal affairs of North Yemen.		AP reports increased movement of North Vietnamese troops into South Vietnam.
Jan. 14		Greek King Constantine indicates that Greece's top officers want him to return from his Italian exile but that the ruling junta's junior officers seem to be opposed. . . . Fifteen Western intellectuals send a message of support to Soviet intellectuals convicted in Moscow.			Laotian authorities report that the North Vietnamese are extending the Ho Chi Minh trail in eastern Laos.
Jan. 15	Congo (Kinshasa) is the first foreign government to resume recognition of Greece.	Flemish students riot in Louvain, Belgium, after the French faculty announces that it plans to remain at the university.			South Vietnamese Pres. Nguyen Van Thieu expresses "regret" that the U.S. has taken the lead in "peace efforts" in Vietnam.

A	B	C	D	E
Includes developments that affect more than one world region, international organizations and important meetings of major world leaders.	Includes all domestic and regional developments in Europe, including the Soviet Union, Turkey, Cyprus and Malta.	Includes all domestic and regional developments in Africa and the Middle East, including Iraq and Iran and excluding Cyprus, Turkey and Afghanistan.	Includes all domestic and regional developments in Latin America, the Caribbean and Canada.	Includes all domestic and regional developments in Asia and Pacific nations, extending from Afghanistan through all the Pacific Islands, except Hawaii.

U.S. Politics & Social Issues	U.S. Foreign Policy & Defense	U.S. Economy & Environment	Science, Technology & Nature	Culture, Leisure & Life Style	
Top civil rights leaders meet in Washington, D.C.	US Amb.-to-India Chester Bowles begins talks with Cambodian officials about the strained relations between U.S. and Cambodia.		U.S. Spacecraft Surveyor 7 lands on the moon.		Jan. 9
Signs of tension emerge between radical and moderate civil rights leaders at their meeting in Washington, D.C.			World's fifth heart transplant patient dies in Brooklyn, N.Y.	Harper & Row publishes Harold Macmillan's *The Blast of War 1939-1945*.	Jan. 10
		U.S. Agriculture Dept. says that the number of U.S. farms declined by three percent during 1967.	U.S. launches Geos 2 whose mission is to provide more accurate information on the size and shape of the earth.	Farrar Straus & Giroux publishes Alec Waugh's *My Brother Evelyn and Other Portraits*.	Jan. 11
Atty. Gen. Ramsey Clark reports that 952 men were convicted for violating the Selective Service laws in 1967. . . . Michigan Gov. George Romney opens his presidential campaign in New Hampshire.	Sen. Eugene McCarthy accuses the administration of being "afraid to negotiate" a solution to the Vietnamese War.			Simon & Schuster publishes Martin Buber's *A Believing Humanism*.	Jan. 12
U.S. Selective Service System reports that 316 Negroes were added to local draft boards during 1967.	V.P. Humphrey defends the administration's Vietnam policy before the Democratic State Central Committee and receives enthusiastic applause.				Jan. 13
	Sen. Eugene McCarthy's attack on the administration's Vietnam policy receives a lukewarm reaction before the Democratic State Central Committee. . . . Senate Republican leader Everett Dirksen reaffirms his support of the administration's Vietnam policy.				Jan. 14
U.S. Supreme Court upholds a lower court decision that the Louisiana program of tuition grants for students in private segregated schools is unconstitutional.	Five thousand women demonstrate against the Vietnamese War on Capitol Hill in Washington, D.C. . . . . U.S. State Dept. asserts that it will not recognize the Jan. 11 expropriation by Israel of Jordanian territory in Jerusalem. . . . State Secy. Rusk assures South Vietnam that the U.S. will not act independently of it in seeking to end the conflict. . . . Former Pres. Dwight Eisenhower reiterates his support of the administration's Vietnam policy.			Houghton Mifflin publishes David Halberstam's *One Very Hot Day*.	Jan. 15
F	G	H	I	J	
Includes elections, federal-state relations, civil rights and liberties, crime, the judiciary, education, health care, poverty, urban affairs and population.	*Includes formation and debate of U.S. foreign and defense policies, veterans' affairs and defense spending. (Relations with specific foreign countries are usually found under the region concerned.)*	*Includes business, labor, agriculture, taxation, transportation, consumer affairs, monetary and fiscal policy, natural resources, and pollution.*	*Includes worldwide scientific, medical and technological developments, natural phenomena, U.S. weather, natural disasters, and accidents.*	*Includes the arts, religion, scholarship, communications media, sports, entertainment, fashions, fads and social life.*	

	World Affairs	Europe	Africa & the Middle East	The Americas	Asia & the Pacific
Jan. 16		British P.M. Harold Wilson says that Britain will pull out of Bahrein and Sharjah on the Persian Gulf by the end of 1971. . . . Finnish voters re-elect Dr. Urho Kekkonen as president. . . . Greek leftist politician Andreas Papandreou leaves Greece.	Mali National Assembly resigns and delegates all power to Pres. Modibo Keita.	Gunmen kill two U.S. military attaches of the U.S. embassy in Guatemala.	*The New York Times* reports that North Vietnam is massing a large troop force in Laos for a possible onslaught against the U.S. Marine base at Khesanh.
Jan. 17		Reports indicate that Pavel Litvinov, grandson of the late Soviet foreign minister, lost his job as a university lecturer on Jan. 3. Litvinov has apparently been active among Soviet dissidents.	Bahrein and Saudi Arabia announce that they will build a causeway linking Bahrein Island, in the Persian Gulf, with the Arabian Peninsula.		U.S. troops clash with the Viet Cong in northern South Vietnam.
Jan. 18	U.S. and the Soviet Union submit a revised and complete draft treaty to prevent the further spread of nuclear weapons to the U.N. Disarmament Committee. . . . U.N. Security Council votes to extend the stay of its peace-keeping force on Cyprus for another three months.	Portuguese police arrest liberal Catholic leader Francisco Sousa Tavares. . . . Soviet Foreign Ministry warns foreign correspondents not to attend a news conference scheduled by the mother and wife of two Soviet intellectuals convicted on Jan. 12. . . . British House of Commons defeats a Conservative motion opposing the government's decision to withdraw its main forces from the Far East by the end of 1971. . . . Britain, France and the U.S. announce publicly their willingness to relinquish their remaining W.W. II occupation rights.	Mobs in Nigeria's secessionist province, Biafra, set fire to buildings owned by British companies. . . . Israel announces the appointment of Maj. Gen. Itzhak Rabin as Israeli ambassador to the U.S. . . . Israeli authorities impose a curfew in Gaza to facilitate a weapons search.	Cuba announces the downing of a small U.S. plane over its territory.	U.S. troops maul North Vietnamese near Conthien.
Jan. 19	Colombia and the Soviet Union resume diplomatic relations after a lapse of 20 years.	Greek police arrest Christos Lambrakis, owner of five Athens publications. . . . Portuguese police arrest newspaper columnist Urbano Tavares Rodrigues.	Anti-British demonstrations take place in Biafra.		South Vietnamese Pres. Nguyen Van Thieu says that North Vietnam must stop its infiltration of South Vietnam if a bombing pause is to take place. . . . Heavy fighting erupts around Dakto for the first time since November 1967.
Jan. 20			Fighting breaks out between Indians and Africans on the island of Mauritius. . . . Eight Palestinian groups announce the formation of a joint military command in Cairo. . . . Israeli authorities lift the curfew in Gaza imposed on Jan. 18.	French Pres. de Gaulle promises a delegation of French-speaking Arcadians from Canada that France will not "neglect" them as it allegedly has done in the past.	Heavy fighting continues around Dakto.
Jan. 21			Reports indicate that Persian Gulf countries have offered to finance the entire cost of maintaining Britain's military presence. . . . Ruling Israeli Mapai party formally merges with the Rafi and Ahdut Haavoda parties to form the Israeli Labor Party. . . . Ethnic fighting continues on the island of Mauritius.	A U.S. Roman Catholic order announces that seven of its missionaries working in Guatemala have been expelled by the government because of their alleged cooperation with leftist forces.	North Vietnamese launch an attack against U.S. Marine base at Khesanh.
Jan. 22		A U.S. bomber with four unarmed hydrogen bombs crashes in Greenland. Personnel only find fragments of the destroyed bombs. . . . British P.M. Harold Wilson arrives in Moscow for an official visit. . . . Five hundred and fifty-five U.S. intellectuals send a petition to Soviet authorities asking for an amnesty for recently convicted Soviet intellectuals.	British governor Sir John Rennie of Mauritius requests British troops to quell ethnic fighting.		U.S. and South Vietnamese troops withdraw from Khesanh. . . . Laotian troops set up defensive positions about 60 miles from their capital Vientiane to block a Communist offensive.
Jan. 23		British P.M. Harold Wilson confers with top Soviet officals in Moscow. . . . U.S. and other governments move to resume normal diplomatic relations with Greece.	Israel and Egypt end their prisoner exchanges, having traded 4,481 Egyptians for 11 Israelis. . . . British troops arrive from Singapore and help to restore order on Mauritius.	Alliance for Progress reports that Latin America failed to achieve its 2.5% per capita GNP increase during 1967.	North Korean patrol boats capture U.S. intelligence ship *Pueblo* . . . . North Vietnamese shell the U.S. Marine base at Khesanh.
	A	**B**	**C**	**D**	**E**
	Includes developments that affect more than one world region, international organizations and important meetings of major world leaders.	*Includes all domestic and regional developments in Europe, including the Soviet Union, Turkey, Cyprus and Malta.*	*Includes all domestic and regional developments in Africa and the Middle East, including Iraq and Iran and excluding Cyprus, Turkey and Afghanistan.*	*Includes all domestic and regional developments in Latin America, the Caribbean and Canada.*	*Includes all domestic and regional developments in Asia and Pacific nations, extending from Afghanistan through all the Pacific Islands, except Hawaii.*

U.S. Politics & Social Issues	U.S. Foreign Policy & Defense	U.S. Economy & Environment	Science, Technology & Nature	Culture, Leisure & Life Style	
	U.S. State Dept. "regrets" Britain's decision to withdraw its forces from the Persian Gulf, Singapore and Malaysia.		Soviet Union launches Cosmos 199.	Jay Allen's play *The Prime of Miss Jean Brodie* opens in New York.	Jan. 16
H. Carl Moultrie, president of the Washington chapter of the NAACP says that he has been instructed by the national board not to become involved in any movement that includes civil rights leader Stokely Carmichael.	Pres. Johnson says that the Vietnamese War is costing the country $25 billion a year.		U.S. launches a satellite into polar orbit.		Jan. 17
	Pres. Johnson orders a 10% reduction in U.S. overseas staffs as part of an effort to reduce the American balance-of-payment deficit. . . . Negro singer Eartha Kitt denounces the Vietnamese War in front of Mrs. Lyndon Johnson at a White House conference on juvenile delinquency.		U.S. conducts an underground test in Nevada. . . . U.S. AEC announces that it will reduce the amount of plutonium produced for nuclear weapons by shutting down two nuclear reactors.	Random House publishes *John Gielgud Directs Richard Burton in Hamlet*.	Jan. 18
	Pres. Johnson nominates Clark Clifford as defense secretary. . . . Sen. George Aiken (R, Vt.) says that "we are fighting nationalists first in Vietnam."		U.S. conducts an underground nuclear test in Nevada.	William Morrow publishes LeRoi Jones's *Black Music*.	Jan. 19
			Soviet Union launches Cosmos 200.		Jan. 20
	Sen. Robert Kennedy accuses the administration of insisting upon "unconditional surrender" from North Vietnam.		U.S. Food & Drug Administration reports that intrauterine birth control devices are highly effective and involve only an extremely small element of risk.	Washington, D.C.'s 19th century Ford's Theater re-opens.	Jan. 21
U.S. Supreme Court upholds a lower court decision declaring unconstitutional a verse prayer recited by kindergarten children even though the word God was deleted. . . . U.S. Supreme Court rules that it is legal to require teachers to swear allegiance to state and federal Constitutions.	U.S. Defense Dept. announces that there is "no danger of a nuclear explosion at the crash site" in Greenland since the weapons were "unarmed."		U.S. launches a working model of the lunar landing craft that will be used for the first manned American expedition to the moon.		Jan. 22
	Sen. J.W. Fulbright says that the over-extended U.S. commitment in Vietnam makes incidents like the capture of the *Pueblo* more possible. . . . Seventeen Republican congressional leaders call for an escalation of the Vietnamese War.				Jan. 23

F	G	H	I	J
Includes elections, federal-state relations, civil rights and liberties, crime, the judiciary, education, health care, poverty, urban affairs and population.	*Includes formation and debate of U.S. foreign and defense policies, veterans' affairs and defense spending. (Relations with specific foreign countries are usually found under the region concerned.)*	*Includes business, labor, agriculture, taxation, transportation, consumer affairs, monetary and fiscal policy, natural resources, and pollution.*	*Includes worldwide scientific, medical and technological developments, natural phenomena, U.S. weather, natural disasters, and accidents.*	*Includes the arts, religion, scholarship, communications media, sports, entertainment, fashions, fads and social life.*

	World Affairs	Europe	Africa & the Middle East	The Americas	Asia & the Pacific
Jan. 24	U.N. Commission on Narcotic Drugs adopts a resolution calling on all governments to prohibit the use of LSD (Lysergic Acid Diethylamide) except in medical institutions.	U.S. Amb.-to the Soviet Union appeals to Soviet officials to persuade North Korean leaders to release the *Pueblo* and its crew. . . . Australia resumes diplomatic relations with Greece. . . . Spain warns the U.S. that it might deny American warships the right to use Spanish Mediterranean ports if they do not stop using Gibraltar as a port-of-call.			North Vietnam shoots down three U.S. planes.
Jan. 25	U.N. Security Council unanimously calls on South Africa to release the 35 South-West Africans currently on trial on charges of terrorism.	Britain resumes diplomatic relations with Greece.	Jordanian gunfire kills two Israeli soldiers. . . . Israel agrees to allow Egypt to raise two sunken vessels in the southern end of the Suez Canal to enable stranded foreign ships to the north to leave the waterway. . . . American Joint Distribution Committee reports that 24,200 Jews have left Arab countries since the 1967 war.		North Vietnamese troops ambush a U.S. convoy near Khesanh.
Jan. 26	U.N. Security Council convenes at U.S. request to discuss the *Pueblo* affair. . . . U.N. Children's Fund (UNICEF) announces an additional authorization of emergency aid to Arab refugees in Jordan and Syria.	British ship *Kingston Peridot* sinks with crew of 20 in savage seas.	Zambia demands more British foreign aid to compensate for the cost of supporting economic sanctions against Rhodesia. . . . Egyptian journalist Mohammed Heykal says that the U.N. Gunnar Jarring Mission "has not achieved any progress." Israeli submarine *Dakar* is reported missing in the eastern Mediterranean.		
Jan. 27		Soviet Union estimates that its population is about 237 million. . . . Greece releases composer Mikis Theodorakis from prison. . . . French submarine *Minerve* is reported missing in the Mediterranean. . . . *The New York Times* reports that U.S. ships are temporarily staying out of Spain's Mediterranean ports.			North Vietnam announces that it will free several U.S. captives as a humanitarian gesture in honor of Tet, the lunar new year. . . . U.S. military sources in Seoul say that the U.S. has been building up its air strength in the Korean area since the seizure of the *Pueblo*.
Jan. 28		Avalanches in the Swiss Alps leave at least 11 dead.	Egypt begins a survey in preparation of the removal of sunken vessels in the Suez Canal.	Cuban CP Central Committee reports that pro-Soviet Cuban Communists will be tried as "traitors to the revolution."	
Jan. 29	International Red Cross representatives arrive in Greece for a visit to Greek political prisoners on the islands of Leros and Yioura.	Greece releases 86 political prisoners.	Israeli authorities arrest 71 suspected Arab guerrillas. . . . South Africa begins the eviction of more than 12,000 black Africans from a declared white area near Dundee.	Cuban CP Central Committee reports that pro-Soviet Cuban Communists have been urging the Soviet Union to use economic pressure to control Premier Castro.	
Jan. 30	UNESCO says that the gap between the rich and poor nations widened between 1960-1965.	Polish authorities ban a play because of passages which could be interpreted as being critical of the Soviet Union. . . . West German Free Democrats adopt a resolution demanding an end to the U.S. bombing of North Vietnam.	Egypt and Israel exchange gunfire across the Suez Canal. . . . As a result of the artillery clash, Egypt announces that it will not try to clear the Suez Canal of sunken vessels.	Cuban CP Central Committee accuses Cuban Communist Anibal Escalante of maintaining secret contacts with Soviet diplomats.	Communist troops launch the heaviest offensive of the Vietnamese War. Nearly all major South Vietnamese cities are assaulted.
Jan. 31		Eighteen-nation Council of Europe votes to expel or suspend Greece from membership if parliamentary democracy is not restored by the spring of 1969. . . . Amnesty International representative Anthony Marreco charges that Greek political prisoners have been tortured. . . . French Navy declares the submarine *Minerve* to be lost. . . . West Germany and Yugoslavia resume diplomatic relations after a 10-year break.	Kenyan Prime Min. Jomo Kenyatta announces that Kenya and Somalia have resumed diplomatic relations.	Cuban CP Central Committee says that Cuban Communist Anibal Escalante has admitted to secret contacts with Soviet diplomats and has asked to be confined to the Yarey People's Poultry Farm. . . . Colombia reports that it has almost eliminated a pro-Castro guerrilla force.	A Viet Cong suicide squad seizes and holds the U.S. Embassy in Saigon for six hours. Communists take Hue, Dalat, Kontum and Quangtri in northern South Vietnam.

A	B	C	D	E
Includes developments that affect more than one world region, international organizations and important meetings of major world leaders.	Includes all domestic and regional developments in Europe, including the Soviet Union, Turkey, Cyprus and Malta.	Includes all domestic and regional developments in Africa and the Middle East, including Iraq and Iran and excluding Cyprus, Turkey and Afghanistan.	Includes all domestic and regional developments in Latin America, the Caribbean and Canada.	Includes all domestic and regional developments in Asia and Pacific nations, extending from Afghanistan through all the Pacific Islands, except Hawaii.

U.S. Politics & Social Issues	U.S. Foreign Policy & Defense	U.S. Economy & Environment	Science, Technology & Nature	Culture, Leisure & Life Style	
Pres. Johnson appeals to Congress to enact his 1967 civil rights proposals.	State Secy. Rusk says that the seizure of the *Pueblo* is "in the category of actions to be construed as an act of war."				Jan. 24
HEW Secy. John Gardner resigns.	Pres. Johnson orders nearly 15,000 Air Force and Navy reservists to active duty in the wake of the *Pueblo* affair. . . . Pres. Johnson's nominee for Defense Secy., Clark Clifford, states his opposition to a halt of the bombing of North Vietnam "under the current military and political circumstances.". . . Sen. Edward Kennedy urges a "confrontation" with the South Vietnamese government over the question of "corruption."		Soviet Union launches Cosmos 184.	Macmillan Co. publishes Arthur Koestler's *The Ghost in the Machine*.	Jan. 25
	U.S. State Dept. denounces North Korean threats to punish the *Pueblo's* crew.		U.S. conducts a low-yield nuclear test in Nevada.		Jan. 26
Pres. Johnson recommends that tax concessions be used to help solve the problem of getting insurance on slum property.	Sen. Birch Bayh (D, Ind.) says that the U.S. should withdraw from South Vietnam if the South Vietnamese government does not demonstrate a capacity for self-government within a year.				Jan. 27
	U.S. Defense Dept. officially confirms the American build-up in the Korean area. . . . Sen. Edward Kennedy again criticizes the alleged wide-spread corruption in South Vietnam.				Jan. 28
Three human skeletons are found in wooden coffins on the Cummins State Prison Farm in Arkansas. . . . Office of Economic Opportunity announces substantial cutbacks and administrative retrenchment for the balance of fiscal 1968.		Pres. Johnson submits a record federal budget to Congress.		Little, Brown & Co. publishes Gore Vidal's *Myra Breckinridge*.	Jan. 29
Negro prisoner Reuben Johnson says that he has witnessed the murders of 12 prisoners during his 32 years at the Cummins State Prison Farm in Arkansas.	U.S. Senate unanimously confirms the nomination of Clark Clifford as Defense Secretary.				Jan. 30
A former Cummins State Prison Farm inmate Pershing Mills says that he witnessed the murders of five prisoners by prison guards.					Jan. 31

F	G	H	I	J
Includes elections, federal-state relations, civil rights and liberties, crime, the judiciary, education, health care, poverty, urban affairs and population.	*Includes formation and debate of U.S. foreign and defense policies, veterans' affairs and defense spending. (Relations with specific foreign countries are usually found under the region concerned.)*	*Includes business, labor, agriculture, taxation, transportation, consumer affairs, monetary and fiscal policy, natural resources, and pollution.*	*Includes worldwide scientific, medical and technological developments, natural phenomena, U.S. weather, natural disasters, and accidents.*	*Includes the arts, religion, scholarship, communications media, sports, entertainment, fashions, fads and social life.*

	World Affairs	Europe	Africa & the Middle East	The Americas	Asia & the Pacific
Feb. 1	Second U.N. Conference on Trade and Development (UNCTAD) opens in New Delhi, India.	West German Free Democratic Party elects Walter Scheel as its new leader.			South Vietnamese Pres. Nguyen Van Thieu declares a nationwide state of martial law as savage fighting continues throughout South Vietnam. . . . Viet Cong launch major attacks in the Mekong Delta.
Feb. 2	At the second U.N. Conference on Trade and Development, nearly all delegations from the communist and developing countries walk out as the South African delegate rises to address the conference.			Quebec Natural Resources Min. Paul Allard announces in Paris that France has agreed to his proposal to set up a joint French-Quebec Committee for geological and mining research.	
Feb. 3					North Vietnamese forces continue to hold most of Kontum in the Central Highlands.
Feb. 4			Israeli navy abandons the search for its missing submarine *Dakar*.		
Feb. 5		Reports indicate that 101 Greek Army officers have been dismissed since King Constantine's Dec. 13, 1967 attempt to topple the ruling junta.	First black African diplomat to be accredited to South Africa, Joe Kachingwe of Malawi, arrives in Capetown.		North Vietnamese artillery pounds Hill 861, the U.S. strongpoint at Khesanh.
Feb. 6	At the second U.N. Conference on Trade and Development, nearly all delegations from the communist and the developing countries walk out as the South African delegate rises to address the conference.	About one quarter of the Labor Party members of Parliament urge British P.M. Harold Wilson to withdraw British support of U.S. policy in Vietnam. . . . Reports indicate a wave of protests in the Soviet Union against the Jan. 8 trial of four Soviet intellectuals. . . . Sweden grants asylum to six American soldiers opposed to U.S. policy in Vietnam. . . . Scheduled publication of Aleksandr Solzhenitsyn's *The Cancer Ward* in a Soviet literary magazine is cancelled by Soviet officials.	A major battle begins between royalist and republican forces around the North Yemeni capital of Sana.		U.S. reports a record 546 combat fatalities for the previous week.
Feb. 7	At the second U.N. Conference on Trade and Development, nearly all Arab and African delegates walk out as the Israeli delegate rises to address the conference.	Belgian cabinet resigns after failing to reconcile differences between Dutch-speaking Flemings and French-speaking Wallons.		*The New York Times* reports that a group of British engineers have arrived in Cuba to work on a fertilizer plant. . . . Six Latin American nations comprising the Andean Group establish a $100 million development fund.	

A	B	C	D	E
Includes developments that affect more than one world region, international organizations and important meetings of major world leaders.	Includes all domestic and regional developments in Europe, including the Soviet Union, Turkey, Cyprus and Malta.	Includes all domestic and regional developments in Africa and the Middle East, including Iraq and Iran and excluding Cyprus, Turkey and Afghanistan.	Includes all domestic and regional developments in Latin America, the Caribbean and Canada.	Includes all domestic and regional developments in Asia and Pacific nations, extending from Afghanistan through all the Pacific Islands, except Hawaii.

U.S. Politics & Social Issues	U.S. Foreign Policy & Defense	U.S. Economy & Environment	Science, Technology & Nature	Culture, Leisure & Life Style	
Former V.P. Richard Nixon officially declares his candidacy for the Republican presidential nomination.	Outgoing Defense Secy. Robert McNamara says that the Soviet Union more than doubled its force of land-based intercontinental ballistic missiles in 1967.	Pres. Johnson again stresses the necessity of a tax increase.		McGraw-Hill publishes Desmond Morris' *The Naked Ape* . . . . Peter Nichols' *A Day in the Life of Joe Egg* opens in N.Y.C. . . . Japanese conductor Seiji Ozawa is named music director of the San Francisco Symphony.	Feb. 1
	Pres. Johnson asserts that the Communist offensive in South Vietnam is "a complete failure."		U.S. Public Health Service reports that cigarette smoking has increased among U.S. youths.		Feb. 2
					Feb. 3
	Defense Secy. McNamara says that there is a possibility that the *Pueblo* might have intruded into North Korean waters during a period of radio silence between Jan. 10 and Jan. 21.				Feb. 4
Pres. Johnson calls for a slight increase in funding for the Office of Education. . . . Former V.P. Richard Nixon says that Pres. Johnson should not have suspended the bombing of North Vietnam before the recent Communist offensive. . . . Negro students protest against the segregation of a local bowling alley in Orangeburg, S.C. . . . Ark. Gov. Winthrop Rockefeller asks the state Legislature to authorize a reform of the state prison system. . . . Negro and white students clash at Hillhouse High School in New Haven, Conn.	Sen. Jacob Javits (R, N.Y.) says that there is a "fundamental stalemate in Vietnam.". . . Sen. Edward Kennedy says that the South Vietnamese government should "stop the sale of deferments" which enables the wealthy to avoid military service. . . . U.S. reaffirms its support of the Nigerian federal government.		Stein & Day publishes Russian singer Chaliapin's autobiography, *Chaliapin, An Autobiography as Told to Maxim Gorky*. Random House publishes Arthur Morse's *While Six Million Died*.		Feb. 5
Negro students continue their demonstrations against a segregated bowling alley in Orangeburg, S.C. . . . Negro and white students clash at Lee High School in New Haven, Conn.	Defense Dept. discloses that the acquisition of sites for and the construction of the Sentinel anti-ballistic-missile (ABM) system has been halted until a one-month review of all "major weapons systems" has been completed.		Soviet Union launches Cosmos 201.	Coward-McCann publishes Jack Kerouac's *Vanity of Duluoz*.	Feb. 6
The New York Times reports that at least 70 of the 254 deaths reported at the Cummins State Prison Farm since 1936 have resulted from violence. . . . Pres. Johnson proposes a series of measures dealing with crime. . . . Justice Dept. files suit against two pipefitters unions because of alleged discrimination against Negroes. . . . Police and Negro students clash at South Carolina State College in Orangeburg, S.C.	State Secy. Rusk discloses during a closed meeting with more than 100 Congressmen that Pres. Johnson sent a foreign envoy to North Vietnam in January. . . . At the Senate Foreign Relations Committee hearings, the subject of tactical nuclear weapons is mentioned in connection with the defense of the U.S. Marine base at Khesanh.			American Opera Society presents the U.S. premiere of Haydn's *Orfeo ed Euridice*.	Feb. 7

F	G	H	I	J
Includes elections, federal-state relations, civil rights and liberties, crime, the judiciary, education, health care, poverty, urban affairs and population.	*Includes formation and debate of U.S. foreign and defense policies, veterans' affairs and defense spending. (Relations with specific foreign countries are usually found under the region concerned.)*	*Includes business, labor, agriculture, taxation, transportation, consumer affairs, monetary and fiscal policy, natural resources, and pollution.*	*Includes worldwide scientific, medical and technological developments, natural phenomena, U.S. weather, natural disasters, and accidents.*	*Includes the arts, religion, scholarship, communications media, sports, entertainment, fashions, fads and social life.*

	World Affairs	Europe	Africa & the Middle East	The Americas	Asia & the Pacific
Feb. 8	U.N. Secy. Gen. U Thant confers with Nguyen Hoa, the North Vietnamese consul general in India. . . . At the second U.N. Conference on Trade and Development, U.N. Gen. Secy. U Thant says that the period since the first UNCTED conference in 1964 has been largely one of "frustrated hopes."		North Yemeni republican forces lift the royalist siege of Sana, the country's capital. . . . Israeli and Jordanian tanks engage in a five-hour artillery duel across the Jordan River.		Fighting rages north of Khesanh.
Feb. 9					Reports indicate that the Cambodian government is fighting communist guerrillas in its territory. . . . U.S. planes carry out their first raids on the Hanoi and Haiphong areas within a month.
Feb. 10	Cypriote U.N. delegate Zenon Rossides demands that Turkey make clear whether it still claims the right to intervene militarily in Cyprus.		A North Yemeni spokesman confirms the royalist setback around Sana but says it is only temporary.		
Feb. 11	U.N. Secy Gen. U Thant arrives in Moscow for a visit.		Israeli and Jordanian forces exchange gunfire across the Jordan River.	For the first time since 1954, opposition parties are allowed to campaign in a federal election in Paraguay.	Allied troops make steady progress in their drive to clear Communist troops out of Hue.
Feb. 12		Sweden and the Soviet Union sign an agreement providing for an exchange of scientists particularly in the area of physics.	Israeli Premier Levi Eshkol warns Jordan about artillery attacks on Israeli forces. . . . Zambian Pres. Kenneth Kaunda reveals that he resigned on Feb. 4 because of "tribal wranglings" but was persuaded to resume his office.		U.S. troops maul a Viet Cong force near the northern coastal town of Quangngai.
Feb. 13	U.N. Secy. Gen. U Thant confers with British P.M. Harold Wilson in London.		Israeli Defense Min. Moshe Dayan holds the Jordanian government responsible for Jordanian-based guerrilla attacks on Israel.		U.S. troops clash with the Viet Cong in the suburbs of Saigon.
Feb. 14	U.N. Secy. Gen. U Thant confers with French Pres. de Gaulle and North Vietnamese diplomat Mai Van Bo in Paris.	Italy says that two North Vietnamese representatives met with Italian Foreign Min. Amintore Fanfani Feb. 4-6 and that the results of the talks have been communicated to Washington. . . . Soviet ambassador to East Germany Pyotr Abrasimov warns the U.S. that continuing West German political activity in West Berlin violates the city's four-power status.	Israel charges that Jordanian artillery recently covered the retreat of Arab guerrillas back into Jordan.		U.S. planes pound Communist troops in Hue.
Feb. 15		West German Chancellor Kurt Kiesinger meets with French Pres. de Gaulle in Paris.	Israel and Jordan exchange heavy artillery fire across the Jordan River. . . . Damascus radio announces that Maj. Gen. Ahmed Sweidani has been replaced as Syrian chief of staff by Maj. Gen. Mustafa Tlas.		Allied artillery continues to shell Communist positions in Hue.

A	B	C	D	E
Includes developments that affect more than one world region, international organizations and important meetings of major world leaders.	Includes all domestic and regional developments in Europe, including the Soviet Union, Turkey, Cyprus and Malta.	Includes all domestic and regional developments in Africa and the Middle East, including Iraq and Iran and excluding Cyprus, Turkey and Afghanistan.	Includes all domestic and regional developments in Latin America, the Caribbean and Canada.	Includes all domestic and regional developments in Asia and Pacific nations, extending from Afghanistan through all the Pacific Islands, except Hawaii.

U.S. Politics & Social Issues	U.S. Foreign Policy & Defense	U.S. Economy & Environment	Science, Technology & Nature	Culture, Leisure & Life Style	
Former Ala. Gov. George Wallace announces his third party presidential candidacy. . . . Three Negro youths die in a confrontation with police at South Carolina State College in Orangeburg, S.C.	British P.M. Harold Wilson meets with Pres. Johnson at the White House. . . . Senate Foreign Relations Committee Chmn. Sen. J.W. Fulbright sends a letter to State Secy. Rusk asking whether nuclear weapons are being introduced into South Vietnam. . . . Sen. Robert Kennedy calls for political compromise in Vietnam since "a total military victory is not within sight."				Feb. 8
South Carolina Gov. Robert McNair orders National Guardsmen to seal off the campus of South Carolina State College in Orangeburg, S.C.	British P.M. Harold Wilson and Pres. Johnson continue talks at the White House.		World's only surviving heart transplant patient Philip Blaiberg is reported to be in normal condition after "an episode of rejection."		Feb. 9
Governor's Select Commission on Civil Disorders in New Jersey charges that National Guardsmen and local officials used "excessive and unjustified force" against Negroes during the 1967 Newark riot. . . . Justice Dept. announces that it is investigating the shooting of three Negroes on Feb. 8 in a clash with police at South Carolina State College in Orangeburg, S.C.					Feb. 10
Former V.P. Richard Nixon says that "peace in the Pacific is the issue" in the presidential elections. . . . Eight hundred local Negroes call for the removal of the National Guard from Orangeburg, S.C.	Senate Democratic leader Mike Mansfield says that it should not be the U.S.'s purpose to insure that a political structure "be enshrined over the smoldering ruins of a devastated Vietnam."				Feb. 11
Justice Dept. files a school desegregation suit against Franklin County, Miss. . . . Deputy state medical examiner Dr. Rodney Carlton reports evidence of violence on one of the three skeletons discovered on Jan. 29 at the Cummins State Prison Farm. . . . A strike by largely Negro sanitation workers takes place in Memphis, Tenn.	U.S. government officials confirm that Pres. Johnson sent a foreign envoy to Hanoi in January to determine North Vietnam's conditions for starting negotiations.			Hollywood Foreign Press Association chooses *In the Heat of the Night* as the best dramatic film of 1968. . . . Ramparts publishes Eldridge Cleaver's *Soul on Ice*.	Feb. 12
Justice Dept. supports a private suit against discrimination in patient facilities and medical care in the Orangeburg, S.C., hospital.	A Gallup Poll reports public approval of Pres. Johnson's handling of the war has declined to 35%.	AFL-CIO Building and Construction Trades Dept. announces that it will actively recruit and then train Negro apprentices.			Feb. 13
Justice Dept. files two school desegregation suits in Baldwin and Crisp Counties in Georgia. . . . Negro students protest against poor elementary school conditions in Social Circle, Ga.	U.S. announces that it will resume arms shipments to Jordan. . . . State Secy. Dean Rusk says that North Vietnam has rejected all U.S. proposals for starting negotiations to end the war in Vietnam. . . . Joint Chiefs of Staff Chmn. Gen. Earle Wheeler refuses to speculate about the use of tactical nuclear weapons in South Vietnam.				Feb. 14
Justice Dept. files a school desegregation suit against the Screven County, Ga. board of education. . . . Prison consultant Austin McCormick tells the Arkansas Legislature that they have "the worst prison system in the country.". . . About 2,500 Negro students throughout North and South Carolina and Virginia demonstrate against the Feb. 8 slayings in Orangeburg, S.C. . . . U.S. State Dept. announces that the U.S. and Mexico have agreed to implement a fishing agreement.					Feb. 15

F	G	H	I	J
Includes elections, federal-state relations, civil rights and liberties, crime, the judiciary, education, health care, poverty, urban affairs and population.	*Includes formation and debate of U.S. foreign and defense policies, veterans' affairs and defense spending. (Relations with specific foreign countries are usually found under the region concerned.)*	*Includes business, labor, agriculture, taxation, transportation, consumer affairs, monetary and fiscal policy, natural resources, and pollution.*	*Includes worldwide scientific, medical and technological developments, natural phenomena, U.S. weather, natural disasters, and accidents.*	*Includes the arts, religion, scholarship, communications media, sports, entertainment, fashions, fads and social life.*

	World Affairs	Europe	Africa & the Middle East	The Americas	Asia & the Pacific
Feb. 16	U.S. Amb.-to-U.N. Arthur Goldberg tells the Security Council that it should take vigorous action to obtain the release of the South-West Africans currently on trial in South Africa on charges of terrorism.	Soviet Union renews its threat to harass West Berlin by low-flying jet aircraft if committees of the Bonn Bundestag hold meetings in the city.	Israel and Jordan continue their artillery fire across the Jordan River. . . . In a nationwide broadcast Jordanian King Hussein warns Arab guerrillas not to use Jordan as a base for attacks on Israel because of Israeli reprisals.	Canadian Justice Min. Pierre Elliott Trudeau announces that he is a candidate to succeed P.M. Lester Pearson for the leadership of the Liberal Party.	Entrenched Communist troops hold off allied troops in Hue. . . . North Vietnam releases three U.S. airmen. They are the first U.S. captives to be freed.
Feb. 17		Holland resumes diplomatic relations with Greece.			Indian doctors perform the world's sixth heart transplant in Bombay.
Feb. 18		*The New York Times* reports that the Greek government had told King Constantine that he is no longer welcome in the Greek embassy in Rome.	Two of the largest seven Trucial states on the Persian Gulf Dubai and Abu Dhabi announce merger plans. . . . A Jordanian official discloses that Jordanian security forces have recently seized arms and ammunitions in raids on Arab guerrilla bases in Jordan.		Viet Cong launch a coordinated artillery attack on allied positions from the Central Highlands to the Mekong Delta.
Feb. 19		British officials and a Swazi delegation meet in London to discuss the arrangements under which Swaziland will become a sovereign state. . . . A Warsaw court sentences a Polish writer to three years in prison for having written a satiric operetta. Reports from Prague indicate that national parliamentary elections will not be held in 1969.	Arab guerrilla group El Fatah spurns Jordanian King Hussein's Feb. 16 warning not to use Jordan as a guerrilla base. . . . North and South Yemen claim that their troops are attacking royalist forces in North Yemen. . . . Jerusalem Mayor Teddy Kollek complains that Israeli efforts to integrate the Arab and Jewish sections of Jerusalem socially and psychologically have been a "total failure."		Viet Cong shell U.S. Tansonnhut air base. . . . Communists blow up a gasoline storage depot in Saigon.
Feb. 20	U.N. Relief and Works Agency (UNRWA) and Jordan are establishing a refugee camp near Amman.	An earthquake leaves at least 19 dead on two Aegean Islands.	A military tribunal sentences several Egyptian officers to long prison terms for their alleged negligence in the June 1967 war. . . . An Arab bazooka shell hits an Israeli settlement east of the Sea of Galilee. . . . South African Defense Min. Pieter Botha warns Britain that it won't be able to use South African military facilities if the British embargo on arms shipments to South Africa continues.		Allied bombers pound Communist troops near Tansonnhut air base. . . . Lloyds Register of Shipping reports that Japan led the world in merchant ship production on 1967.
Feb. 21	U.N. Relief and Works Agency (UNRWA) announces that about 67,000 of the 77,000 refugees in nine Jordan River Valley camps have fled eastward to Amman because of the recent border fighting.	Soviet scientist Boris Vasilyevich Timofeyev reports finding "shells of algae" in carbon-containing meteorites. . . . One hundred and fifty thousand Germans attend a pro-American demonstration in West Berlin. . . . Swedish Education Min. Olof Palme heads an anti-war demonstration in Stockholm.	Arab saboteurs damage Israeli water and fuel pipes.		U.S. planes raid North Vietnamese positions in Hue.
Feb. 22				Chilean police arrest five guerrillas who fought with the late Che Guevara in Bolivia as they cross the border into Chile. . . . Three bombs explode at U.S. business military installations in Puerto Rico but cause little damage.	Laotian Premier Souvanna Phouma charges that North Vietnam has a force of 40,000 men in Laos. . . . U.S. Marines advance slowly against tenacious Communist defenders entrenched in Hue.
Feb. 23		Several hundred student radicals storm the rector's office at the Univ. of Rome.	Governments of South Africa and Lesotho announce their agreement in principle to the joint construction of a series of dams and power stations.	Argentine Amb.-to-the Organization of American States Eduardo Roc rejects U.S. attempts to bring the issue of arms sales to Latin America before the OAS. . . . A police bomb expert is injured while attempting to defuse a bomb on the Shell Oil Co. pipeline in Puerto Rico.	Communist troops probe U.S. Marine base at Khesanh.
	A	**B**	**C**	**D**	**E**
	Includes developments that affect more than one world region, international organizations and important meetings of major world leaders.	*Includes all domestic and regional developments in Europe, including the Soviet Union, Turkey, Cyprus and Malta.*	*Includes all domestic and regional developments in Africa and the Middle East, including Iraq and Iran and excluding Cyprus, Turkey and Afghanistan.*	*Includes all domestic and regional developments in Latin America, the Caribbean and Canada.*	*Includes all domestic and regional developments in Asia and Pacific nations, extending from Afghanistan through all the Pacific Islands, except Hawaii.*

U.S. Politics & Social Issues	U.S. Foreign Policy & Defense	U.S. Economy & Environment	Science, Technology & Nature	Culture, Leisure & Life Style	
National Security Council abolishes draft deferments for all graduate students except those in certain specialties.	Pres. Johnson says that he does not think that North Vietnam is more ready to negotiate now than it has been in the past. . . . U.S. Defense Dept. discloses that U.S. planes intercepted two Soviet bombers off the Newfoundland coast on Feb. 9, but that the Soviet planes "evidenced no hostile intentions."			Catalan poet Jaime Sabartes dies in Paris at 86.	Feb. 16
Black power advocates H. Rap Brown and Stokely Carmichael address a rally in Oakland, Calif.	U.S. State Dept. expresses its concern about increased Communist activity in Laos.				Feb. 17
Black Power advocates H. Rap Brown and Stokely Carmichael address a rally in Los Angeles, Calif.	Pres. Johnson meets with former Pres. Dwight Eisenhower in California.				Feb. 18
		AFL-CIO Pres. George Meany says that binding arbitration should be considered for many labor disputes. . . . U.S. airlines agree to reduce domestic fares by 50% for foreign visitors.		Holt, Rinehart & Winston publishes Soviet Marshal Vasili Chuikov's *The Fall of Berlin*.	Feb. 19
Police arrest civil rights activist H. Rap Brown in New York. . . . Negro students clash with police at predominantly-Negro Alcorn Agricultural and Mechanical College in Lorman, Miss.	Senate Foreign Relations Committee begins hearings on the 1964 North Vietnamese attacks on two U.S. destroyers which led to the Tonkin Gulf resolution.	AFL-CIO categorically supports Pres. Johnson's Vietnam policy.	Soviet Union launches Cosmos 202 & Cosmos 203.	Putnam publishes Simone de Beauvoir's *Les Belles Images*.	Feb. 20
Arkansas Legislature authorizes a reform of the state prison system.	A bomb explodes at the Soviet embassy in Washington. . . . U.N. Secy. Gen. U Thant confers with Pres. Johnson in Washington.	AFL-CIO Pres. George Meany strongly praises Pres. Johnson's policy toward organized labor.	U.S. conducts a low-intermediate-yield test in Nevada.	Lord Florey, the discoverer of the practical uses of penicillin, dies in London at 69.	Feb. 21
Pres. Johnson proposes a housing program for low and moderate-income Americans.					Feb. 22
Virginia judge Robert Merhige rules that civil rights activist H. Rap Brown has violated the travel restrictions of his bond. . . . Police and demonstrators supporting striking sanitation workers clash in Memphis, Tenn.	Naval commander Capt. John Herrick says that he has "no doubt" that both his ship, the *Maddox*, and the other destroyer, the *Turner Joy*, did nothing to provoke the 1964 North Vietnamese attacks in the Gulf of Tonkin.	Lloyds of London reports that the number of ships launched in 1967 set a record for the second straight year.			Feb. 23

F	G	H	I	J
Includes elections, federal-state relations, civil rights and liberties, crime, the judiciary, education, health care, poverty, urban affairs and population.	Includes formation and debate of U.S. foreign and defense policies, veterans' affairs and defense spending. (Relations with specific foreign countries are usually found under the region concerned.)	Includes business, labor, agriculture, taxation, transportation, consumer affairs, monetary and fiscal policy, natural resources, and pollution.	Includes worldwide scientific, medical and technological developments, natural phenomena, U.S. weather, natural disasters, and accidents.	Includes the arts, religion, scholarship, communications media, sports, entertainment, fashions, fads and social life.

	World Affairs	Europe	Africa & the Middle East	The Americas	Asia & the Pacific
Feb. 24	U.S. Secy. Gen. U Thant says that if the U.S. stops the bombing of North Vietnam "meaningful talks" to end the Vietnamese War will take place much earlier than expected.		Egypt Interior Min. Sharaway Gomaa says that 23 people have been wounded in recent anti-government demonstrations. . . . Arab mortar shells hit an Israeli settlement north of the Sea of Galilee. . . . Ghana orders the release of 95 political prisoners.	Chile deports five guerrillas who fought with the late Che Guevara. They intend to go to Cuba.	After nearly a month of vicious fighting, South Vietnamese troops capture the Imperial Palace in the walled Citadel of Hue. . . . U.S. mission in Saigon admits for the first time that the Communists' Tet offensive has dealt a major blow to the allies' pacification program.
Feb. 25		Cypriot voters re-elect Archbishop Makarios as president. . . . Reports from Prague indicate that anti-liberal Maj. Gen. Jan Sejna has fled the country and requested permanent residence in the U.S.	Senegalese voters re-elect Pres. Leopold Senghor who ran unopposed. . . . Egypt decrees the retrial of several military officers convicted on charges of negligence in the June 1967 war in response to public pressure for stiffer sentences.	Two bombs explode along the Shell Oil Co. pipeline in Puerto Rico but cause little damage.	Soviet Premier Aleksei Kosygin arrives in India for a state visit. . . . South Vietnamese Pres. Nguyen Van Thieu visits Hue.
Feb. 26	Secy. Gen. U Thant proposes that a fact-finding mission be sent to the Middle East to investigate the conditions of civilians in the Arab areas occupied by Israel. . . . U.S. and Japan sign an agreement providing for the sale of enriched uranium by the U.S. to Japan.		South Africa convicts 30 South-West Africans on charges of terrorism. . . . Israeli Foreign Min. Abba Eban confirms Israel's approval of U.N. Middle East peace envoy Gunnar Jarring's proposal for direct Arab-Israeli talks.		U.S. troops sight three Communist armored vehicles 50 miles from Saigon. Such heavy equipment has never before been seen so close to the South Vietnamese capital.
Feb. 27		Britain curbs the right of Asians to move to Britain.	Nine Persian Gulf emirates agree to form a union when Britian withdraws its military forces from the area by the end of 1971.	Argentinian government arrests Gen. Adolfo Candido Lopez, a frequent critic of the ruling military junta.	Burma releases 127 political prisoners. . . . AP reports that Communist forces are inching their way forward around the U.S. base at Khesanh.
Feb. 28	France says that it has "specific information" supporting U.N. Secy. Gen. U Thant's contention that a U.S. bombing halt of North Vietnam is a "necessary and sufficient" condition for starting negotiations. . . . Greek government deposes Bishop Panteleimon of Salonika.		Israel changes the designation of Arab areas captured in June 1967 from "enemy territory" to "militarily occupied territory." . . . Saudi Arabian King Faisal says that his government will aid North Yemeni royalist forces in view of the alleged intervention of Syria, the Soviet Union and South Yemen in the North Yemeni civil war.	Argentina releases from jail Jorge Antonio Vago, editor of the banned magazine *Prensa Confidencial*. . . . Panamanian Christian Democrats initiate impeachment procedures against Pres. Marco Aurelio Robles.	Heavy fighting takes place in the Central Highlands.
Feb. 29		Greece protests Sweden's and Denmark's hostile attitude toward the ruling Greek junta.	Jordan hangs two Jordanians convicted of spying for Israel.		Sporadic fighting takes place in Hue as allied troops mop up Communist forces.
March 1	A giant wave of speculation hits the world's gold markets.	Portugal releases opposition leader Mario Soares from prison. . . . Warsaw branch of the Polish Writers' Union passes a resolution criticizing government censorship.	Arab guerrillas slay an Israeli Druse near Jerusalem. . . . Bolivia expresses its "concern" over Chile's Jan. 24 deportation of five guerrillas who fought with the late Che Guevara.		South Vietnamese House of Representatives rejects Pres. Nguyen Van Thieu's request for emergency economic powers.
March 2		Reports indicate that nearly 1,000 Greek government employees have been dismissed during the last week ostensibly because they support King Constantine. . . . A bomb explodes on the second floor of the U.S. consulate in Turin.	South African bureau of statistics estimates that the country's population is made up of almost 13 million blacks, three-and-a-half million whites, almost two million coloreds and about one half million Asians. . . . Israeli authorities begin a major roundup of Arab suspects. . . . Israeli Premier Levi Eshkol affirms Israel's readiness to meet with the Arabs and he does not insist upon direct talks.		Allied forces clash with Communist troops in the northern suburbs of Saigon.

A	B	C	D	E
Includes developments that affect more than one world region, international organizations and important meetings of major world leaders.	*Includes all domestic and regional developments in Europe, including the Soviet Union, Turkey, Cyprus and Malta.*	*Includes all domestic and regional developments in Africa and the Middle East, including Iraq and Iran and excluding Cyprus, Turkey and Afghanistan.*	*Includes all domestic and regional developments in Latin America, the Caribbean and Canada.*	*Includes all domestic and regional developments in Asia and Pacific nations, extending from Afghanistan through all the Pacific Islands, except Hawaii.*

U.S. Politics & Social Issues	U.S. Foreign Policy & Defense	U.S. Economy & Environment	Science, Technology & Nature	Culture, Leisure & Life Style	
N.Y. Gov. Nelson Rockefeller says that he would accept a presidential draft by the Republican National Convention but he adds that he does not expect it. . . . Pres. Johnson announces that 60 major business executives have joined a program to help find jobs for the hard-core unemployed.		AFL-CIO rejects Pres. Johnson's Council of Economic Advisers' guideline recommendations.			Feb. 24
About 100 local Negro ministers call for a boycott of certain downtown businesses in Memphis, Tenn.			U.S. Public Health Service reports that U.S. 1967 birth rate was a record low.		Feb. 25
Agriculture Dept. reports that 20% of U.S. households have nutritionally "poor" diets. . . . Negro students return to South Carolina State College in Orangeburg, S.C.	Senate Democratic leader Mike Mansfield calls for the halt of the bombing of North Vietnam.	AFL-CIO pledges its cooperation in the search for jobs for the hard-core unemployed "even to the extent of waiving conditions" of qualifications.		Atheneum publishes James Watson's *The Double Helix*.	Feb. 26
Pres. Johnson sends a special farm message to Congress.	Pres. Johnson defends his Vietnam policy in Dallas, Tex.				Feb. 27
Gov. George Romney (R, Mich.) announces his withdrawal as a candidate for President.	U.S. State Dept. ends travel restrictions on U.S. citizens for Syria. . . . Reports indicate that the U.S. has cancelled all nuclear-armed airborne alert flights as a result of the Jan. 22 crash in Greenland.				Feb. 28
In a controversial report the President's National Advisory Commission on Civil Disorders blames "white racism" for being chiefly responsible for the poverty and frustration in the Negro neighborhoods where violence has exploded in recent years. The report also says that the nation is moving toward two "separate and unequal" societies.	Former Amb.-to-Soviet Union George Kennan calls the U.S. intervention in Vietnam a "massive miscalculation."		U.S. conducts a low-yield nuclear test in Nevada.	Dr. Hugo Benioff, seismologist who designed instruments for measuring movements of earth's crust, dies in Mendocino, Calif. at 68.	Feb. 29
Howard Univ. students disrupt their school's Charter Day ceremony in Washington, D.C. . . . . Reports indicate that the police throughout the nation are stockpiling weapons in preparations for summer riots.	Clark Clifford is sworn in as the new U.S. Defense Secretary.				March 1
Justice Dept. reports that 789 people were convicted of draft evasion in the year ending June 30, 1967. . . . Virginia Supreme Court upholds the legality of civil rights activist H. Rap Brown's July 1967 arrest in Alexandria, Va. . . . National board of the American Civil Liberties Union (ACLU) votes, 26-20, to defend persons under indictment for counseling draft-evasion.		UAW Pres. Walter Reuther says that his union will withdraw from the AFL-CIO if it doesn't agree to his plans to modernize the labor federation.	Soviet Union launches a spacecraft named Zond (Probe).		March 2

F	G	H	I	J
Includes elections, federal-state relations, civil rights and liberties, crime, the judiciary, education, health care, poverty, urban affairs and population.	*Includes formation and debate of U.S. foreign and defense policies, veterans' affairs and defense spending. (Relations with specific foreign countries are usually found under the region concerned.)*	*Includes business, labor, agriculture, taxation, transportation, consumer affairs, monetary and fiscal policy, natural resources, and pollution.*	*Includes worldwide scientific, medical and technological developments, natural phenomena, U.S. weather, natural disasters, and accidents.*	*Includes the arts, religion, scholarship, communications media, sports, entertainment, fashions, fads and social life.*

	World Affairs	Europe	Africa & the Middle East	The Americas	Asia & the Pacific
March 3			Egyptian Pres. Gamal Nasser blames recent disturbances on "reactionary elements." . . . Israel reports having killed 50 Arab infiltrators trying to cross the Jordan River to the West Bank in the previous ten days. . . . Israeli authorities destroy the residence of a suspected Arab guerrilla leader in Jerusalem. Several adjacent structures are also damaged.		U.S. planes and artillery pound Communist troops in northern South Vietnam.
March 4		Czechoslovak CP presidium recommends the end of press censorship. . . . British officials say that the current foot-and-mouth livestock epidemic was probably caused by lamb imported from Argentina.	Egyptian Pres. Nasser concedes in a *Look* magazine interview (published March 3) that he had been mistaken in charging that U.S. planes helped Israel during the June 1967 war. . . . Israel reports the seizure of two suspected commanders of the Arab guerrilla organization El Fatah. . . . Rhodesia's High Court rejects the clemency appeals of condemned black African guerrillas.	Canadian P.M. Lester Pearson announces that Canada has suspended relations with Gabon because it issued a diret invitation to the province of Quebec to attend an international education conference. . . . Panamanian Pres. Marco Aurelio Robles dismisses his entire cabinet.	Communist artillery attack inflicts heavy casualties in South Vietnamese cities.
March 5		Reports from Prague indicate that Jiri Hendrych, an opponent of liberal reform, has been dismissed from his post as Czech CP Secretary for Ideological Affairs.	Saudi Arabian King Faisal accuses Israel of dishonoring Moslem shrines in East Jerusalem.		Communist mortar pounds five provincial South Vietnamese capitals.
March 6		Greek government deposes Archbishop Iakovos of Attica. . . . British Commonwealth Secy. George Thomson assails the Jan. 6 execution of black African guerrillas in Rhodesia.	Rhodesia executes three black African guerrillas on murder charges. . . . Jerusalem Mayor Teddy Kollek, an Israeli, criticizes the Israelis for extending to East Jerusalem their military practice of blowing up the homes of suspected Arab guerrillas.	Panamanian Pres. Marco Aurelio Robles refuses to appear before a special assembly commission investing corruption charges against him.	India announces that Kenyan Asians with British passports will not be allowed to live in India without special permits. . . . U.S. planes pound Communist positions around Khesanh.
March 7	U.N. Committee on Colonialism censures Rhodesia for the March 6 execution of black African guerrillas.		Egyptian Foreign Min. Mahmoud Riad tells U.N. Middle East peace envoy Gunnar Jarring that Egypt "categorically" refuses to meet Israeli representatives in Cyprus. . . . Jerusalem Mayor Teddy Kollek visits an Arab neighborhood where several buidings have been recently damaged by the destruction of the home of a suspected Arab guerrilla leader. He apologizes for the incident and offers immediate compensation for the damage.	Canadian P.M. Lester Pearson threatens to cut ties with France if it invites Quebec to an educational conference. . . . Panamanian Pres. Marco Aurelio Robles denies that he has violated the country's constitution.	South Vietnamese troops take a heavy toll of Communist forces around Dongha. . . . Cambodiam Chief of State Norodom Sihanouk charges that Asian Communists are using Cambodian guerrillas to overthrow his government. . . . Indonesia and Malaysia anncunce a friendship accord. Republican presidential candidate Richard Nixon urges tougher measures to quell domestic rioters. Two hundred black students from South Carolina State College burst in on the General Assembly at the State Capitol in Columbia, S.C. and present a list of eight grievances.
March 8		Norway announces its intention to remain in NATO. . . . Students protesting political repression clash with police at Warsaw University. . . . Greek left-wing politician Andreas Papandreou arrives in the U.S. . . . Cypriot Pres. Makarios orders the removal of all Greek police and Greek road blocks in the Nicosia area, giving Turkish Cypriots freedom of movement for the first time in four years.	About 150 people are reported missing after a large mudslide in the eastern Congo (Kinshasa).		South Vietnamese troops clash with North Vietnamese forces at Khesanh.

A	B	C	D	E
Includes developments that affect more than one world region, international organizations and important meetings of major world leaders.	*Includes all domestic and regional developments in Europe, including the Soviet Union, Turkey, Cyprus and Malta.*	*Includes all domestic and regional developments in Africa and the Middle East, including Iraq and Iran and excluding Cyprus, Turkey and Afghanistan.*	*Includes all domestic and regional developments in Latin America, the Caribbean and Canada.*	*Includes all domestic and regional developments in Asia and Pacific nations, extending from Afghanistan through all the Pacific Islands, except Hawaii.*

U.S. Politics & Social Issues	U.S. Foreign Policy & Defense	U.S. Economy & Environment	Science, Technology & Nature	Culture, Leisure & Life Style	
					March 3
V.P. Hubert Humphrey says that the President's National Advisory Commission on Civil Disorders' warning that the U.S. is moving toward two "separate and unequal" societies is "open to some challenge." . . . Pres. Johnson proposes the training of more health workers. . . . Martin Luther King Jr. announces that the "nonviolent poor people's march on Washington" will begin April 22.	U.S. State Dept. calls Egyptian Pres. Nasser's March 4 remarks an "encouraging development."		U.S. launches geophysical satellite Ogo 5.		**March 4**
U.S. Supreme Court upholds the right of police to seize evidence without a search warrant. . . . Republican presidential aspirant Richard Nixon pledges that if elected he will end the war in Vietnam. . . . Police arrest 121 strike leaders after a sit-in at the Memphis Tenn. City Hall. . . . White House press secretary George Christian says that V.P. Humphrey's questioning of the conclusions of the President's National Advisory Commission on Civil Rights reflects his own thinking and not necessarily that of the administration.			U.S. launches Explorer 37. . . . Soviet Union launches Cosmos 204 and 205.		**March 5**
Pres. Johnson proposes programs to help the American Indian.	U.S. State Dept. deplores the March 6 executions of black African guerrillas in Rhodesia.		Carbon monoxide poisoning kills at least 21 miners in Belle Isle, La.	George Kennan's *Memoirs* wins the 1967 National Book Award. . . . Stein & Day publishes Leslie Fiedler's *The Return of the Vanishing American.*	**March 6**
	White House confirms that it is re-examining its military needs in Vietnam but has not yet decided whether more troops will be necessary.				**March 7**
A U.S. court-martial convicts Capt. Dale Noyd of refusing to train pilots scheduled for duty in Vietnam.		Pres. Johnson urges intensified efforts to curb pollution. . . . U.S. Treasury reports that U.S. gold losses in 1967 were $1,169,600,000.		Pope Paul appoints the Most Rev. Terence Cooke as auxiliary bishop of New York.	**March 8**

F	G	H	I	J
Includes elections, federal-state relations, civil rights and liberties, crime, the judiciary, education, health care, poverty, urban affairs and population.	*Includes formation and debate of U.S. foreign and defense policies, veterans' affairs and defense spending. (Relations with specific foreign countries are usually found under the region concerned.)*	*Includes business, labor, agriculture, taxation, transportation, consumer affairs, monetary and fiscal policy, natural resources, and pollution.*	*Includes worldwide scientific, medical and technological developments, natural phenomena, U.S. weather, natural disasters, and accidents.*	*Includes the arts, religion, scholarship, communications media, sports, entertainment, fashions, fads and social life.*

	World Affairs	Europe	Africa & the Middle East	The Americas	Asia & the Pacific
March 9		The New York Times reports that as many as 10,000 Communist Party and government officials have been ousted in Rumania. . . . Clashes continue between students and police at Warsaw University.			U.S. troops maul Communist forces near Tamky.
March 10	Major industrial nations reaffirm their determination to support the $35-per-ounce gold price.		Congolese radio (Brazzaville) reports that an Angolan guerrilla movement, Movimento Popular de Libertacao de Angola (MPLA), has held its first regional assembly inside Angola. . . . African guerrillas attack 17 U.S. tourists in Rhodesia. Three require hospitalization.		Communist artillery rocks U.S. bases in northern South Vietnam.
March 11	International Monetary Fund reports that the rate of increase of global exports declined in 1967 in comparison with the four previous years. . . . U.N. Secy. Gen. U Thant assails the March 6 execution of black African guerrillas in Rhodesia.	Tens of thousands of Poles fight with police in central Warsaw. . . . Students in Cracow, Poland express their solidarity with striking students in Warsaw. . . . Two U.S. deserters in Sweden return to their base in West Germany.	Rhodesia executes two black African guerrillas on murder charges. . . . Rhodesia commutes the death sentences of more than 30 African guerrillas.		Communists pound the U.S. base at Danang.
March 12		University of Rome opens for the first time since March 1. . . . Swedish Premier Tage Erlander declares that Sweden will continue to oppose American policy in Vietnam. . . . A U.S. deserter in Sweden returns to West Germany. . . . Three U.S. soldiers who deserted their posts in West Germany are granted permission to remain in France.	Egyptian Pres. Nasser reiterates his government's refusal not to negotiate with Israel. . . . Britain's former Indian Ocean colony of Mauritius becomes an independent state within the Commonwealth.		U.S. planes carry out one of their heaviest raids against Communist positions around Khesanh.
March 13		British officials announce the end of the foot-and-mouth livestock epidemic which has killed an estimated 422,000 cattle, sheep and pigs. . . . Three thousand students in Cracow, Poland demonstrate against the government.		Argentina reaffirms its determination to gain sovereignty over the Falkland Islands.	Allied spokesmen disclose that U.S. and South Vietnamese forces launched a combined operation March 7 in the Mekong Delta.
March 14	A giant wave of speculation hits the world's gold markets.	Students in Cracow, Poland boycott classes.	Five African guerrillas are sentenced to death for bringing weapons into Rhodesia.	Panamanian National Assembly votes to impeach Pres. Marco Aurelio Robles. . . . Cuban Premier Castro announces plans for "eradicating" all private businesses.	Reports indicate that North Vietnamese troops have been sighted in the Mekong Delta for the first time. . . . Indian P.M. Indira Gandhi says that she is not satisfied with the proposed nuclear non-proliferation treaty.
March 15		At the request of the U.S., Britain closes the London gold market. . . . Czechoslovak National Assembly dismisses Interior Min. Josef Kudrna. . . . Michael Stewart replaces George Brown as British Foreign Secy. . . . Canadian House of Commons approves a three percent surcharge on personal and corporate income taxes.	Somali Premier Mohamed Ibrahim Egal announces that U.N. geologists have discovered major uranium deposits in Somalia.	Panamanian Pres. Marco Aurelio Robles says he will ignore the March 14 impeachment vote of the National Assembly.	Fifty thousand allied military troops begin a drive against Communist forces.

A	B	C	D	E
Includes developments that affect more than one world region, international organizations and important meetings of major world leaders.	Includes all domestic and regional developments in Europe, including the Soviet Union, Turkey, Cyprus and Malta.	Includes all domestic and regional developments in Africa and the Middle East, including Iraq and Iran and excluding Cyprus, Turkey and Afghanistan.	Includes all domestic and regional developments in Latin America, the Caribbean and Canada.	Includes all domestic and regional developments in Asia and Pacific nations, extending from Afghanistan through all the Pacific Islands, except Hawaii.

U.S. Politics & Social Issues	U.S. Foreign Policy & Defense	U.S. Economy & Environment	Science, Technology & Nature	Culture, Leisure & Life Style	
Republican presidential candidate Richard Nixon says he will not elaborate on his plans to end the Vietnamese War because he is unwilling to reveal "his bargaining positions in advance."	In reaction to the bombing of Arab homes in East Jerusalem, the U.S. State Dept. reminds Israel of its obligation to abide by the Geneva Convention's provisions for protection of people in occupied territories. . . . Senate Democratic leader Mike Mansfield calls for a full re-evaluation of U.S. foreign policy.		Reports indicate that the Soviet satellite Zond which was launched March 2 has returned to earth.	Pope Paul expresses "sorrow" about the March 6 execution of black African guerrillas in Rhodesia.	March 9
A pastoral letter read at all the masses in St. Patrick's Cathedral in N.Y. supports the March 3 conclusions of the President's National Advisory Commission blaming "white racism" as the underlying cause of racial riots.	Former Presidential aide McGeorge Bundy states his opposition to further increases in U.S. forces in Vietnam. . . . A Gallup Poll reports that 49% of those interviewed thought the U.S. made a mistake in sending troops to fight in Vietnam.				March 10
Senate passes a bill barring discrimination in the sale or rental of about 80% of the nation's housing and returns the bill to the House. U.S. Supreme Court affirms a lower court ruling that Alabama must desegregate its prisons. . . .	State Secy. Rusk testifies before a largely hostile Senate Foreign Relations Committee.			Twentieth Century Fund publishes Gunnar Myrdal's Asian Drama.	March 11
Charles Griffen, a white, defeats black civil rights activist Charles Evers by a 2-1 margin in a Mississippi congressional race. . . . In the New Hampshire presidential primary, Pres. Johnson polls 48% of a write-in vote against 42% for Sen. Eugene McCarthy. Former V.P. Richard Nixon wins 79% of the Republican vote.	State Secy. Rusk continues to defend the administration's Vietnam policy before the Senate Foreign Relations Committee.	Advisory Committee to the U.S. Treasury on International Monetary Arrangements warns that a failure to enact a tax increase would "endanger world-wide confidence in the dollar." . . . AFL-CIO agrees to hold a special convention to discuss UAW Pres. Walter Reuther's reform proposals if the UAW accepts the convention's findings.	U.S. conducts an underground nuclear test in Nevada.		March 12
Leaders of the Poor People's Campaign begin to erect their shantytown on the Washington, D.C. Mall. . . . Sen. Robert Kennedy says that he is reassessing the possibility of running against Pres. Johnson. . . . Pres. Johnson sends Congress special proposals to curb crime and improve housing in Washington, D.C. . . . . Police arrest nine marchers demonstrating their support of striking sanitation workers in Memphis, Tenn.		UAW Pres. Walter Reuther calls the AFL-CIO's March 12 proposals "unacceptable."	An Army nerve gas kills at least 6,400 sheep in Utah.		March 13
Republican presidential candidate Richard Nixon calls for a greater role for South Vietnamese soldiers in the Vietnamese War. . . . Sen. Robert Kennedy says that he cannot support Pres. Johnson for renomination. . . . NAACP Director Roy Wilkins expresses his support at a large rally in Memphis, Tenn. of striking sanitation workers.	U.S. State Dept. cautions South Vietnam against carrying out threats to invade North Vietnam. . . . U.S. Senate completes action on legislation to eliminate the requirement that 25% of U.S. currency be backed by gold.		Soviet Union launches Cosmos 206. . . . U.S. conducts an underground nuclear test in Nevada.	Art historian Erwin Panofsky dies in Princeton, N.J. at 75.	March 14
An AP survey indicates that most Democratic state chairmen support the renomination of Pres. Johnson.	Former Pres. Dwight Eisenhower reiterates he supports the administration's Vietnam policy.				March 15

F	G	H	I	J
Includes elections, federal-state relations, civil rights and liberties, crime, the judiciary, education, health care, poverty, urban affairs and population.	Includes formation and debate of U.S. foreign and defense policies, veterans' affairs and defense spending. (Relations with specific foreign countries are usually found under the region concerned.)	Includes business, labor, agriculture, taxation, transportation, consumer affairs, monetary and fiscal policy, natural resources, and pollution.	Includes worldwide scientific, medical and technological developments, natural phenomena, U.S. weather, natural disasters, and accidents.	Includes the arts, religion, scholarship, communications media, sports, entertainment, fashions, fads and social life.

	World Affairs	Europe	Africa & the Middle East	The Americas	Asia & the Pacific
March 16	London Gold Pool members meet in Washington.	Left-wing and right-wing students clash at the Univ. of Rome. . . . In a Polish Journalists Association resolution, the epithets "cosmopolitan and Zionist" are reintroduced. . . . Czechoslovak CP First Secy. Alexander Dubcek promises the "democratization" of political life. . . . Swedish Foreign Ministry reiterates its opposition to U.S. policy in Vietnam.	Clashes take place between Rhodesian security forces and African guerrillas.		South Korea announces that its one-and-a-half million military reservists have been formed into a militia to cope with increased North Korean infiltration.
March 17	Seven active members of the London Gold Pool agree to establish a two-tier pricing system for gold, a private market price and an inter-governmental price.	Police clash with anti-Vietnamese War demonstrators in London.	Clashes continue between Rhodesian security forces and African guerrillas. . . . Fighting breaks out between Africans and Indians on Mauritius.	Right-wing guerrillas kidnap the Most Rev. Mario Casariego, the Roman Catholic archbishop of Guatemala.	
March 18	A U.N. body studying jurisdiction over the world's seabeds meets in New York.	Polish steelworkers in Nowa Huta join Cracow students in a solidarity strike. . . . University authorities again close the Univ. of Rome. . . . West German Foreign Min. Willy Brandt calls for recognition of the Oder-Neisse line as Germany's eastern frontier "pending a peace settlement.". . . As gold trading resumes in Europe, price fluctuates between $37 and $40 an ounce. . . . Reports indicate that Czechoslovak Pres. Antonin Novotny's son has been prevented from leaving the country because of corruption charges. . . . Britain and Spain resume their negotiations about the status of Gibraltar.	Israeli Defense Min. Moshe Dayan says that Arab saboteurs based in Jordan constitute the principle threat to Israel. . . . Fighting continues between Africans and Indians on Mauritius. . . . Rhodesia reports that its planes have bombed guerrilla positions in the Rhodesian bush.	Antigua declares a state of emergency after 10 days of strikes.	Heavy Communist shelling pounds Khesanh.
March 19	Jordanian Amb.-to-U.N. Muhammed el-Farra charges that Israel is contemplating a massive thrust into Jordan. . . . The New York Times reports that the six European Gold Pool members have tacitly agreed not to withdraw gold from the U.S. monetary stock during "the period of financial stress created by the Vietnam War."	Polish CP leader Wladislaw Gomulka restates his offer to allow any Jew to emigrate to Israel. . . . U.S. and Danish officials announce that the Greenland crash site of the B-52 bomber carrying four hydrogen bombs has been cleared of any dangerous radiation. . . . Sweden grants asylum to eight U.S. Army men who deserted their posts in West Germany.	Extreme right wing of Premier Ian Smith's ruling Rhodesian Front announces it is going into opposition.	Labor rioting erupts on the island of Antigua.	South Vietnamese troops uncover a large arms cache near the Tansonnhut Air Base. . . . U.S. planes bomb North Vietnamese forces around Khesanh.
March 20	U.N. Economic Commission says that Eastern Europe recorded major growth in 1967.	France grants residence and work permits to five U.S. Army deserters. . . . Portugal re-arrests opposition leader Mario Soares. . . . Greek navy defector Constantine Marotis-Lanas says that Greek political prisoners are being tortured. . . . Czechoslovak CP Central Committee recommends the resignation of Czech Pres. Antonin Novotny.	South Yemen reports suppressing an attempted coup by dissident army elements.	The New York Times reports that the Brazilian Interior Ministry has accused 134 former employees of the Indian Protective Service of abusing Brazilian Indians. . . . Labor rioting continues on the island of Antigua.	U.S. planes carry out one of their heaviest raids in more than a month over North Vietnam.
March 21	U.N. Security Council convenes at the request of Jordan.	Portugese authorities bannish opposition leader Dr. Mario Soares to the island of Sao Tome off the West African coast. . . . German Social Democratic Party re-elects Willy Brandt as its leader. . . . Czech National Assembly committee meeting recommends the resignation of Czech Pres. Antonin Novotny.	Fifteen thousand Israeli troops carry out a day-long retaliatory raid in Jordan. It is their first major ground thrust into Arab territory since the June 1967 war.	Antiguan government lifts the state of emergency but all commercial establishments remain closed.	U.S. planes pound North Vietnamese air bases.
March 22	At the U.N. Security Council debate, Israeli Amb. Yosef Tekoah says that the March 21 Israeli thrust into Jordan has led to the discovery of a huge guerrilla base containing large quantities of arms and amunition.	Czechoslovak CP presidium announces a rehabilitation program for 30,000 victims of Stalinism. . . . Czech Pres. Antonin Novotny resigns.	Israel and Jordan exchange sporadic fire across the Jordan River.	Cuba and the Soviet Union sign an agreement for increased trade.	U.S. planes bomb the North Vietnamese Haiguong chemical plant for the first time.

A	B	C	D	E
Includes developments that affect more than one world region, international organizations and important meetings of major world leaders.	Includes all domestic and regional developments in Europe, including the Soviet Union, Turkey, Cyprus and Malta.	Includes all domestic and regional developments in Africa and the Middle East, including Iraq and Iran and excluding Cyprus, Turkey and Afghanistan.	Includes all domestic and regional developments in Latin America, the Caribbean and Canada.	Includes all domestic and regional developments in Asia and Pacific nations, extending from Afghanistan through all the Pacific Islands, except Hawaii.

U.S. Politics & Social Issues	U.S. Foreign Policy & Defense	U.S. Economy & Environment	Science, Technology & Nature	Culture, Leisure & Life Style	
Sen. Robert Kennedy announces his candidacy for the Democratic presidential nomination.	Pres. Johnson says that if the Communists refuse to negotiate in Vietnam then "we shall win a settlement on the battlefield."		Soviet Union launches Cosmos 207.		March 16
Sen. Robert Kennedy says that he would have "great reservations" about supporting Pres. Johnson if the Democrats renominate him.				Dr. Ira Altshuler, a pioneer in music therapy for the mentally ill, dies in Livonia, Mich. at 74.	March 17
HEW Dept. issues a policy statement extending its school desegregation guidelines to northern schools. . . . Sen. Robert Kennedy opens his presidential campaign with a stinging attack on Pres. Johnson's Vietnam policy. . . . He concedes his share of the responsibility for initial U.S. policy in Vietnam in the early 1960s but adds that "past error is no excuse for its own perpetuation."	Pres. Johnson calls for "a total national effort" to win the Vietnamese War.	U.S. Commerce Department reports that U.S. profits in 1967 declined from the 1966 record profits.			March 18
Howard Univ. students take control of the administrative building on their Washington, D.C. campus. . . . Senators Robert Kennedy and Eugene McCarthy agree to run a joint slate in Washington, D.C. . . . . Martin Luther King Jr. announces that he will call for "a massive outpouring of hundreds of people" in Washington June 15 for a special protest day.	Pres. Johnson reaffirms his determination to "prevail" in Vietnam.			Anton Chekhov's *The Cherry Orchard* opens at the Lyceum Theatre in New York.	March 19
	Former Pres. Truman expresses his general support of Pres. Johnson's foreign and domestic policies.			Little, Brown publishes Brian Crozier's *Franco* . . . . French conductor Pierre Boulez becomes guest conductor of the Cleveland Orchestra.	March 20
N.Y. Gov. Nelson Rockefeller announces that he is not campaigning "directly or indirectly for the presidency."	Pres. Johnson says that the U.S. will not "break under frustration" in Vietnam.		Soviet Union launches Cosmos 208.		March 21
Former U.S. Rep. Adam Clayton Powell surrenders to N.Y.C. police. . . . Pres. Johnson nominates Wilbur Cohen to succeed John Gardner as HEW Dept. Secy.	Pres. Johnson announces the appointment of Gen. William Westmoreland, U.S. commander in Vietnam, as Army Chief-of-Staff.		Soviet Union launches Cosmos 209. . . . U.S. conducts an underground nuclear test in Nevada.	Doubleday publishes Sen. Edward Kennedy's *Decisions for a Decade*.	March 22

F	G	H	I	J
Includes elections, federal-state relations, civil rights and liberties, crime, the judiciary, education, health care, poverty, urban affairs and population.	Includes formation and debate of U.S. foreign and defense policies, veterans' affairs and defense spending. (Relations with specific foreign countries are usually found under the region concerned.)	Includes business, labor, agriculture, taxation, transportation, consumer affairs, monetary and fiscal policy, natural resources, and pollution.	Includes worldwide scientific, medical and technological developments, natural phenomena, U.S. weather, natural disasters, and accidents.	Includes the arts, religion, scholarship, communications media, sports, entertainment, fashions, fads and social life.

	World Affairs	Europe	Africa & the Middle East	The Americas	Asia & the Pacific
March 23		Leaders of most Eastern European communist nations meet in Dresden and call on Czechoslovak CP First Secy. Alexander Dubcek to explain his recent liberal reforms.	Jordanian King Hussein declares that his government is not responsible for the security of Israel and therefore will do nothing to inhibit guerrillas operating from Jordan.		U.S. planes bomb the Catbi airfield in North Vietnam.
March 24	U.N. Security Council unanimously adopts a resolution condemning Israel for its March 21 thrust into Jordan.		Elections for the Lebanese Chamber of Deputies begin. . . . Jordan and Israel exchange sporadic fire across the Jordan River.	Panamanian National Assembly votes Pres. Marco Aurelio Robles out of office but, with the support of the National Guard, Robles ignores the move. . . . Panamanian National Assembly elects First V.P. Max Delvalle as president.	U.S. planes bomb the Hanoi area in two separate raids.
March 25	Iceland joins GATT.	Police prevent student radicals from reoccupying the Univ. of the Sacred Heart in Milan, Italy. . . . Hungarian P.M. Jeno Fock confers with French leaders in Paris. He is the first Hungarian P.M. to visit France since W.W.II.	Four French-speaking West African states-Mali, Mauritania, Senegal and Guinea-conclude negotiations for the formation of the Organization of Senegal River States. . . . Sporadic artillery fire continues between Israel and Jordan.	Panamanian politicians Max Delvalle and Marco Aurelio Robles both claim to be the legitimate president.	Allied troops maul Communist forces about 28 miles from Saigon.
March 26		Czechoslovak CP First Secy. Alexander Dubcek admits that certain reservations were expressed at the March 23 meeting of Eastern European communist countries about the recent liberal reforms in Czechoslovakia. . . . Warsaw Univ. students demand the reinstatement of six professors dismissed for allegedly inciting demonstrations.	South Yemen announces the purging of 150 army officers in the wake of the March 20 attempted coup.	Montreal business and professional leaders launch a drive to offset recent gains by French-Canadian separatists. . . . Panamanian National Guard prevents Max Delvalle and opposition deputies from entering the National Assembly building.	
March 27		British Foreign Secy. Michael Stewart pledges that the Falkland Islands will not be transferred to Argentina unless the islanders favor such a move. . . . Soviet Col. Yuri Gagarin, the first man to make an orbital flight, dies in a jet plane crash. . . . Czechoslovakia issues a formal protest to East Germany about the latter's alleged interference in Czechoslovakia's internal affairs. . . . West German Chancellor Kurt Kiesinger says that the dispute over Germany's eastern border should not prevent a reconciliation between Germany and Poland.	Reports indicate that massacres have taken place between rival Angolan guerrilla groups.	Sporadic disorders occur in Panama City.	Indonesian Assembly elects Acting Pres. Gen. Suharto to a five-year term as president. . . . U.S. planes bomb the North Vietnamese Langgiai rail yard near the Chinese border.
March 28		Soviet newspaper *Pravda* denies that Russia and other East European communist countries tried to restrain Czechoslovakia's reform movement during the March 23 meeting of communist countries in Dresden. . . . Polish officials close six departments of Warsaw University.	Israel returns 12 Jordanian soldiers captured during the March 21 raid into Jordan in exchange for the bodies of three Israeli soldiers. . . . U.S. and Jordan sign an agreement for the resumption of American arms sales.	Clashes between students and police in Rio de Janeiro result in the death of one student.	

A	B	C	D	E
Includes developments that affect more than one world region, international organizations and important meetings of major world leaders.	Includes all domestic and regional developments in Europe, including the Soviet Union, Turkey, Cyprus and Malta.	Includes all domestic and regional developments in Africa and the Middle East, including Iraq and Iran and excluding Cyprus, Turkey and Afghanistan.	Includes all domestic and regional developments in Latin America, the Caribbean and Canada.	Includes all domestic and regional developments in Asia and Pacific nations, extending from Afghanistan through all the Pacific Islands, except Hawaii.

U.S. Politics & Social Issues	U.S. Foreign Policy & Defense	U.S. Economy & Environment	Science, Technology & Nature	Culture, Leisure & Life Style	
HEW Dept Secy. nominee Wilbur Cohen says that the vast majority of people on welfare are incapable of doing the most elementary work tasks. . . . In a Gallup Poll, Sen. Robert Kennedy leads Pres. Johnson by 44%-41% among Democratic voters.					March 23
The New York Times survey indicates that Pres. Johnson could win 65% of the votes at the Democratic National Convention.					March 24
Maryland General Assembly approves a bill liberalizing conditions under which abortion is legal. . . . Sen. Eugene McCarthy withdraws from his March 19 agreement to run a joint slate of delegates in Washington, D.C. with Sen. Robert Kennedy. . . . A Louis Harris poll indicates that only about half of McCarthy's voter support was specifically an anti-war vote; the other half was a general protest vote which included people in favor of escalating the war. . . . HEW Secy.-designate Wilbur Cohen says the report of the National Advisory Commission on Civil Disorders attributing Negro riots to "white racism" is "oversimplified.". . . Negro youths battle with police in Memphis, Tenn. Larry Payne, 16, is killed during the melee. . . . Sen. Robert Kennedy says that "each person has to examine his own conscience and do what he thinks is right" when faced with the prospect of military service in Vietnam.					March 25
Martin Luther King Jr. says that his projected march on Washington will include the construction of "a shanty-town."					March 26
Students at predominantly Negro Bowie State College in Bowie, Md. demonstrate for better housing. . . . An AP survey reveals that 14 of 24 Democratic governors favor Pres. Johnson while only two are leaning toward Senators Kennedy or McCarthy. . . . Former V.P. Richard Nixon says that the problems of the cities "should not blind us to the problems of that other country-rural America.". . . Sen. Robert Kennedy says "we must return local control to the peoples themselves (since the) solutions of the 1930s are not the solutions of today."				Harcourt, Brace & World publishes Robert Gutman's *Richard Wagner* . . . . Harper & Row publishes William Gass' *In the Heart of the Heart of the Country*.	March 27
Students at premominantly Negro Bowie State College in Bowie, Md. continue to demonstrate for better housing. . . . Sen. Robert Kennedy criticizes former V.P. Richard Nixon's proposals for dealing with the Vietnamese War on the grounds that they offer no change from current policies.				Paul Eriksson publishes Maxim Gorky's *Untimely Thoughts*.	March 28

F	G	H	I	J
Includes elections, federal-state relations, civil rights and liberties, crime, the judiciary, education, health care, poverty, urban affairs and population.	*Includes formation and debate of U.S. foreign and defense policies, veterans' affairs and defense spending. (Relations with specific foreign countries are usually found under the region concerned.)*	*Includes business, labor, agriculture, taxation, transportation, consumer affairs, monetary and fiscal policy, natural resources, and pollution.*	*Includes worldwide scientific, medical and technological developments, natural phenomena, U.S. weather, natural disasters, and accidents.*	*Includes the arts, religion, scholarship, communications media, sports, entertainment, fashions, fads and social life.*

	World Affairs	Europe	Africa & the Middle East	The Americas	Asia & the Pacific
March 29	Nine of the 10 leading financial nations meet in Stockholm to discuss monetary reform.	Czechoslovakia asks for the return of the gold taken out of its territory by the retreating Germans in W.W. II which was confiscated by the U.S. . . . Soviet CP Gen. Secy. Leonid Brezhnev says that intellectuals who step out of line will be punished. . . . A Polish newspaper accuses W.W.II Polish Jews of having "closely cooperated" with the Germans.	Israel and Jordan engage in a six-hour artillery duel across the Jordan River. . . . A mine kills four Israeli farm workers near the Sea of Galilee.	Clashes continue between students and police in Rio de Janeiro. . . . Cuba proclaims that total centralization is the new basis of the country's economic policy.	
March 30	U.N. Security Council convenes in an emergency session to discuss the latest fighting in the Middle East. . . . Nine of the 10 leading financial nations (with France in dissent) endorse a plan to create a new form of monetary reserves to supplement gold, dollars and pounds.	In a secret vote the Czechoslovak National Assembly elects Gen. Ludvig Svoboda as president. . . . Soviet astronaut Yuri Gagarin receives a full state funeral and his ashes are interned in the Kremlin wall.	Police close the main campus of Haile Selassie University in Addis Ababa, Ethiopia after students protest a fashion show featuring Western clothing.	Cuba announces the virtual rationing of food staples.	U.S. troops push out from their base at Khesanh but are driven back by intense Communist fire.
March 31	U.N. Economic Commission says that Latin America's per capita rate of economic growth during 1967 was only 1.5%.	Polish Deputy Politburo member Piotr Jaroszewicz charges "world Zionism" with conspiring to mobilize Jews against Poland.	Arab guerrillas fire on an Israeli patrol near the West Bank town of Hebron. . . . Voters in Dahomey approve a constitution making the country a one-party state for five years. . . . Guinean Pres. Sekou Toure says that he favors Guinea and Mali becoming a single state.		Soviet Union protests to Communist China about the detention of a Soviet tanker carrying supplies to North Vietnam.
April 1		Reports indicate that West Germany has agreed to reimburse Britain for about 85% of the costs of maintaining British troops in West Germany. . . . London gold market opens for the first time since March 15. . . . Soviet Union assails Pres. Johnson for not having ordered a complete halt to the bombing of North Vietnam. . . .	Ethiopian students and police clash in Addis Ababa.	Inter-American Development Bank reports that Latin America registered a 5% economic growth rate in 1967. . . . Panamanian Supreme Court begins deliberations on the validity of the impeachment and conviction of Pres. Marco Aurelio Robles. . . . Brazilian federal troops are mobilized to quell demonstrating students in Rio de Janeiro.	U.S. air strikes against North Vietnam range as far as 205 miles north of the demilitarized zone.
April 2		Czechoslovak student weekly hints that former Czechoslovak Foreign Min. Jan Garrigue Masaryk might have been murdered by the Soviet secret police. . . . British Treasury reports that Britain's gold and foreign exchange reserves fell by the equivalent of $48 million in March.	Three African states-Congo (Kinshasa), Chad and the Central African Republic-officially form the Union of Central African states. . . . Clashes continue between Ethiopian police and students in Addis Ababa. . . . Soviet Premier Aleksei Kosygin arrives in Iran for an official visit.	Canada announces a new program to increase the use of the French language in the Canadian armed forces. . . . Britain makes public a plan for an association between Guatemala and British Honduras.	Pakistani Pres. Ayub Khan announces that the country's wheat crop has increased 14% from 1967. . . . North Vietnam calls Pres. Johnson's decision to restrict the bombing of North Vietnam "fraudulent."
April 3		French Pres. Charles de Gaulle hails Pres. Johnson's decision to limit the bombing of North Vietnam. . . . France reports that its gold and foreign exchange reserves increased by the equivalent of $8.5 million in March. . . . Czechoslovak state prosecutor's office announces that an investigation is under way into the death of former Foreign Min. Jan Garrigue Masaryk.	Biafra announces that it is prepared to negotiate without conditions with the Nigerian federal government. . . . Clashes continue between Ethiopian police and students in Addis Ababa.	Clashes continue between students and police in Rio de Janeiro.	North Vietnam and the U.S. agree to establish direct diplomatic contact. . . . Soviet Union repeats protests to Communist China about the detention of a Soviet tanker carrying supplies to North Vietnam.
April 4	In a U.N. Security Council debate, Jordan opposes the stationing of U.N. troops along the Jordan River.	Czechoslovak CP Central Committee announces major changes in the make-up of the party presidium.			U.S. helicopters mount bruising raids against Communist positions around Khesanh.

A	B	C	D	E
Includes developments that affect more than one world region, international organizations and important meetings of major world leaders.	*Includes all domestic and regional developments in Europe, including the Soviet Union, Turkey, Cyprus and Malta.*	*Includes all domestic and regional developments in Africa and the Middle East, including Iraq and Iran and excluding Cyprus, Turkey and Afghanistan.*	*Includes all domestic and regional developments in Latin America, the Caribbean and Canada.*	*Includes all domestic and regional developments in Asia and Pacific nations, extending from Afghanistan through all the Pacific Islands, except Hawaii.*

U.S. Politics & Social Issues	U.S. Foreign Policy & Defense	U.S. Economy & Environment	Science, Technology & Nature	Culture, Leisure & Life Style	
Sen. Robert Kennedy says that there is "a double standard" for U.S. health care which benefits the wealthy. . . . Bowie State College Md. students seize the administrative building on their campus. . . . Several hundred demonstrators march in support of striking sanitation workers in Memphis, Tenn.				Macmillan publishes Che Guevara's *Venceremos*.	March 29
Maryland Gov. Spiro Agnew refuses to meet with Bowie State College students until they relinquish control of occupied buildings. . . . Sen. Robert Kennedy says that the U.S. public wants a Vietnamese settlement in which "something still remains of the country of Vietnam and of our own hopes for domestic progress." . . . A Gallup Poll says that the public's approval of Pres. Johnson's performance is at a record low of 36%.	Canada and the U.S. agree to extend the North American Air Defense Command for another five years.				March 30
	Pres. Johnson announces that he will neither seek nor accept nomination for another term as president. He also says that he has unilaterally ordered a bombing halt of North Vietnam except for the part right above the demilitarized zone.			Concert pianist Elly Ney dies in Tutzig, West Germany at 85.	March 31
U.S. Supreme Court rules that one-man, one-vote doctrine applies to local units of government.	Sen. Robert Kennedy and Sen. Eugene McCarthy praise Pres. Johnson's decision to restrict the bombing of North Vietnam.				April 1
Sen. Eugene McCarthy wins the Wisconsin Democratic primary with 57.6% of the vote. . . . Sen. Eugene McCarthy says that he has asked many Democratic leaders not to make commitments to a presidential candidate until later in the campaign. . . . HEW Dept. Secy.-designate Wilbur Cohen calls the report of the National Advisory Commission on Civil Disorders a "valuable contribution."	State Secy. Dean Rusk states his opposition to a coalition government in South Vietnam. . . . Sen. Robert Kennedy says that the U.S. should re-examine its entire position in Vietnam. . . . U.S. explains that there will be no bombing of North Vietnam north of the 20th Parallel which is 225 miles north of the demilitarized zone.	Senate passes a bill combining the administration-requested 10% surcharge with a mandatory $6 billion reduction in federal spending.			April 2
Pres. Johnson meets with Sen. Robert Kennedy at the White House.			Soviet Union launches Cosmos 210.	MGM releases Stanley Kubrick's *2001: A Space Odyssey* in New York.	April 3
An assassin kills the Rev. Martin Luther King Jr. . . . About 60 Cornell University Negro students hold the Economics Department chairman captive for six hours to protest an alleged racist remark by a university professor.			U.S. launches an unmanned Apollo spacecraft but brings it back to earth because of mechanical trouble. . . . Tornadoes and blizzards leave at least 18 dead in the central regions of the U.S.	Brandon Films releases Paolo Pasolini's *Accatone* in New York.	April 4

F	G	H	I	J
Includes elections, federal-state relations, civil rights and liberties, crime, the judiciary, education, health care, poverty, urban affairs and population.	*Includes formation and debate of U.S. foreign and defense policies, veterans' affairs and defense spending. (Relations with specific foreign countries are usually found under the region concerned.)*	*Includes business, labor, agriculture, taxation, transportation, consumer affairs, monetary and fiscal policy, natural resources, and pollution.*	*Includes worldwide scientific, medical and technological developments, natural phenomena, U.S. weather, natural disasters, and accidents.*	*Includes the arts, religion, scholarship, communications media, sports, entertainment, fashions, fads and social life.*

	World Affairs	Europe	Africa & the Middle East	The Americas	Asia & the Pacific
April 5		Soviet Union expresses its full support of North Vietnam's decision to begin diplomatic talks with the U.S.	South African government introduces a parliamentary bill which would establish legislative councils for seven different ethnic groups in South-West Africa. . . . Iran and the Soviet Union make known their opposition to the proposed British-sponsored Arab Persian Gulf federation.	No clashes take place between students and police in Rio de Janeiro for the first time in more than a week.	U.S. declares that the siege of Khesanh is officially lifted.
April 6		Czechoslovak Premier Jozef Lenart announces the resignation of his cabinet. . . . Amnesty International representative Anthony Marreco repeats charges that Greek political prisoners have been tortured.	Rhodesian P.M. Ian Smith announces the lifting of press censorship imposed in November 1965. . . . Zambia charges that Portugese planes bombed three Zambian villages on March 22. . . . France agrees to sell Iraq 54 Mirage fighter-bombers.	Canadian Liberal Party elects Justice Min. Pierre Elliott Trudeau as its leader. . . . Brazilian bishop Jose Castro Pinto and 14 priests issue a statement critical of the ruling military regime.	Nearly 1,000 U.S. relief troops are flown into Khesanh. Racial disorders rock Washington and Chicago.
April 7			Soviet Union and Iran express similiar views on the Middle East, Southeast Asia and European security in a joint communique.	Brazilian Pres. Arthur da Costa e Silva says that the government will not declare a state of siege in spite of student agitation.	
April 8		Czechoslovak National Assembly approves a new cabinet. . . . Greek Press Secy. Michael Sideratos rejects charges that Greek political prisoners have been tortured.	Representatives of Zambia, Tanzania and Communist China meet in Dar es Salaam to discuss the projected Tanzam railroad. . . . Several dozen Israeli helicopter-borne soldiers cross 18 miles into Jordan in pursuit of Arab guerrillas.		South Vietnamese troops launch a drive to recapture the Langvei Special Forces Camp. . . . Main allied relief column arrives in Khesanh.
April 9		Czechoslovak CP publishes its "action program" concerning political reforms.	Egyptian Pres. Nasser discounts the possibility of talks with Israel. . . . Iraq announces its rejection of foreign bids to develop its sulphur deposits. . . . Ethiopian Emperor Haile Selaisse orders more than 2,000 striking students to return to classes.	Quebec government receives a reminder from France about the forthcoming education conference in Paris. . . . Brazilian authorities issue formal charges against 120 former employees of the government Indian agency for mistreating Brazilian Indians.	
April 10			Egypt declares its full support of the Palestinian resistance movement. . . . Iraq announces its rejection of foreign bids to develop its North Rumailia oil fields. . . . Four African nations that severed diplomatic relations with Britain in December 1965 over Rhodesia resume ties with Britain.		South Vietnamese Pres. Nguyen Van Thieu requests unlimited mobilization powers. . . . Reports indicate that North Vietnamese troops and equipment are continuing to infiltrate into South Vietnam on an unabated scale since the March 31 partial bombing halt.
April 11		An assassin seriously injures West German student leader Rudi Dutschke in West Berlin. Student riots break out in major West German cities. . . . *London Times* prints signed statements allegedly smuggled out of a Greek prison camp telling of conditions of "inhuman isolation and moral torture."	Reports indicate that Syria is suppressing one of the three major Arab guerrilla groups operating from its territory-- the Popular Front for the Liberation of Palestine.		
April 12		West Berlin police keep an estimated 2,000 students from storming the city hall. . . . Polish press accuses Jewish officials who emigrated to Israel in 1956 of passing secret military information to the Jewish state.	U.S. says it will not return the Czechoslovak gold confiscated from the Germans in W.W. II until compensation is paid for the U.S. property nationalized in 1948.	Quebec Education Min. Jean-Guy Cardinal says that he will lead the Quebec delegation to the forthcoming education conference in Paris.	
April 13		Police arrest 230 students in West Berlin. . . . East German Interior Min. Friedrich Dickel announces that top West German officials will not be allowed to travel to West Berlin by land routes.			

A	B	C	D	E
Includes developments that affect more than one world region, international organizations and important meetings of major world leaders.	Includes all domestic and regional developments in Europe, including the Soviet Union, Turkey, Cyprus and Malta.	Includes all domestic and regional developments in Africa and the Middle East, including Iraq and Iran and excluding Cyprus, Turkey and Afghanistan.	Includes all domestic and regional developments in Latin America, the Caribbean and Canada.	Includes all domestic and regional developments in Asia and Pacific nations, extending from Afghanistan through all the Pacific Islands, except Hawaii.

U.S. Politics & Social Issues	U.S. Foreign Policy & Defense	U.S. Economy & Environment	Science, Technology & Nature	Culture, Leisure & Life Style	
Racial disorders break out in major cities in the wake of Martin Luther King's assassination.				Knopf publishes John Updike's *Couples*.	April 5
	U.S. commander in Vietnam Gen. William Westmoreland confers with Pres. Johnson at the White House.		U.S. launches two satellites which will measure cosmic radiation in space.		April 6
Racial disorders continue in Washington and Chicago. . . . Negro students hold Tuskegee Institute trustees captive for 12-13 hours to protest their refusal to adopt student demands for reform.	U.S. commander in Vietnam Gen. William Westmoreland and Pres. Johnson continue their discussions at the White House.		Soviet Union launches Luna 14.	Pope Paul devotes part of his Palm Sunday sermon to the assassination of Martin Luther King Jr.	April 7
U.S. Supreme Court refuses to bar court-ordered blood transfusions for children of Jehovah's Witnesses. . . . Racial disorders hit Cincinnati, Pittsburgh and Nashville, Tenn. Duke University students demonstrate in support of striking university employees.	U.S. receives a North Vietnamese note proposing diplomatic contacts in Pnompenh, Cambodia.			Dutton publishes Lawrence Durrell's *Tunc*. . . . Harold Babcock, the discoverer of the reversal of the sun's magnetic field, dies in Pasadena, Calif. at 86.	April 8
Racial disorders break out in Kansas City.	U.S. rejects a North Vietnamese suggestion to have diplomatic talks in Pnompenh, Cambodia. . . . Reports indicate that the U.S. has restricted its bombing of North Vietnam to the area between the demilitarized zone and the 19th Parallel.		Soviet Union launches Cosmos 211.	Lopert Pictures releases Ingmar Bergman's *Hour of the Wolf* in N.Y.C.	April 9
House passes a Senate-passed civil rights bill prohibiting racial discrimination in the sale or rental of about 80% of the nation's housing. . . . Four to five hundred Colgate Univ. students and faculty members stage a sit-in in the main university administrative building to protest discriminatory fraternity housing practices.			U.S. conducts an underground nuclear test in Nevada.	U.S. Oscar award for the best 1967 film goes to *In the Heat of the Night*. . . . Swiss art historian Sigfried Giedion dies in Zurich at 74.	April 10
A Humphrey-for-President campaign office opens in Washington, D.C. . . . Pres. Johnson signs a bill prohibiting racial discrimination in the sale or rental of about 80% of the nation's housing. . . . Duke University students continue their demonstrations in support of university reforms and striking university employees.	Defense Secy. Clark Clifford announces a call-up of 24,500 military reservists to be used in Vietnam but says that the administration does not intend to go beyond a ceiling of 549,500 troops. . . . North Vietnam proposes that preliminary diplomatic talks be held in Warsaw. . . . U.S. restates its position that diplomatic talks with North Vietnam should be held in a "neutral" city.			Oxford University Press publishes Gunther Schuller's *Early Jazz*.	April 11
					April 12
Sen. Robert Kennedy says that the U.S. must abandon the idea that "foreign commitments take precedence over the welfare of our own people."					April 13

F	G	H	I	J
Includes elections, federal-state relations, civil rights and liberties, crime, the judiciary, education, health care, poverty, urban affairs and population.	*Includes formation and debate of U.S. foreign and defense policies, veterans' affairs and defense spending. (Relations with specific foreign countries are usually found under the region concerned.)*	*Includes business, labor, agriculture, taxation, transportation, consumer affairs, monetary and fiscal policy, natural resources, and pollution.*	*Includes worldwide scientific, medical and technological developments, natural phenomena, U.S. weather, natural disasters, and accidents.*	*Includes the arts, religion, scholarship, communications media, sports, entertainment, fashions, fads and social life.*

	World Affairs	Europe	Africa & the Middle East	The Americas	Asia & the Pacific
April 14		Several thousand students clash with police in West Berlin.	Jordanian gunfire from the east bank of the Jordan River kills an Israeli soldier.		
April 15		Violent demonstrations take place in several major West German cities. . . . Five British Parliament members begin an investigatory tour around Athens. . . . Greek government places former Greek Prime minister George Papandreou under house arrest.	Israel says that it has smashed an Arab guerrilla attempt to establish bases in the Nablus area.		North Vietnam shoots down four U.S. planes over its territory.
April 16		Czechoslovak CP newspaper *Rude Pravo* charges that former Foreign Min. Jan Garrigue Masaryk was murdered for political reasons. . . . Supreme Court of the Russian Republic upholds the sentences of the January trial of Soviet intellectuals.			North Vietnamese forces resume the shelling of the U.S. base at Khesanh.
April 17		West German Klaus Frings dies of a wound caused by a flying object during a March 15 riot in Munich. . . . *London Times* reports that 34 students have been expelled from Warsaw University. . . . Former Greek P.M. George Papandreou appeals to the "free world" to join in a boycott against the current Greek military regime.	Soviet Premier Aleksei Kosygin arrives in Pakistan for a visit.	Canadian embassy in Moscow rejects a Soviet note accusing Lt. Col. Jean Watson, a Canadian official, of activities bordering on espionage.	Defense committee of the South Vietnamese House of Representatives rejects Pres. Nguyen Van Thieu's April 10 request for unlimited mobilization powers. . . . Communist artillery continues to shell the U.S. base at Khesanh.
April 18	Israel agrees to a fact-finding U.N. mission to investigate the conditions of civilians in the Arab areas occupied by Israel if the mission also examines the Jewish communities living in Arab countries.	West German Rudiger Schrenk dies of a wound caused by a flying object during a March 15 riot in Munich. . . . Greece releases 100 political prisoners. . . . A Greek government official says that punitive action will not be taken against former Greek Premier George Papandreou because of his April 17 statement. . . . Polish CP Secy. Jozef Kepa admits that the current anti-Zionist campaign has degenerated to the "filthy defaming of people."	Nigeria says that it is willing to meet with Biafran representatives. . . . Israel expropriates 29 acres near the Wailing Wall in the Old City in Jerusalem. . . . Noncommissioned army officers in Sierra Leone stage a successful coup d'etat.		U.S. planes carry out their heaviest raids in 1968 over North Vietnam.
April 19		NATO's seven-member Nuclear Planning Group announces their rejection of an anti-ballistic missile system in Europe for the time being. . . . Czechoslovak Bedrich Pokorny, who was involved in the 1948 investigation of former Foreign Min. Jan Masaryk's death, is found dead in a forest near Brno. . . . At ceremonies marking the 25th anniversary of the Warsaw ghetto uprising, a Polish government official compares Israeli soldiers with German Nazis.	Zambian Pres. Kenneth Kaunda announces nationalizations of many private and foreign businesses.		North Vietnam rejects all sites proposed by the U.S. for preliminary peace talks. . . . U.S. planes carry out another massive raid against North Vietnam.
April 20	Secy. Gen. U Thant expresses concern about the effects of Israel's scheduled military parade in Jerusalem on May 2.	British politician Enoch Powell says Britain should curtail the immigration of nonwhites and encourage those already in Britain to leave the country. . . . Greek P.M. George Papadopoulos warns the U.S. that continuing to suspend heavy armaments to Greece could be harmful for both countries.	Reports indicate that five Jordanian political parties banned since 1957 including the Moslem Brotherhood and the Communists have been allowed to form a coalition. . . . Pakistani Pres. Ayub Khan reportedly has unsuccessfully pressed the Soviet Union for a reduction of Soviet arms shipments to India.	Pierre Elliott Trudeau succeeds retiring Lester Pearson as Canadian prime minister.	

A	B	C	D	E
Includes developments that affect more than one world region, international organizations and important meetings of major world leaders.	Includes all domestic and regional developments in Europe, including the Soviet Union, Turkey, Cyprus and Malta.	Includes all domestic and regional developments in Africa and the Middle East, including Iraq and Iran and excluding Cyprus, Turkey and Afghanistan.	Includes all domestic and regional developments in Latin America, the Caribbean and Canada.	Includes all domestic and regional developments in Asia and Pacific nations, extending from Afghanistan through all the Pacific Islands, except Hawaii.

U.S. Politics & Social Issues	U.S. Foreign Policy & Defense	U.S. Economy & Environment	Science, Technology & Nature	Culture, Leisure & Life Style	
Justice Dept. officials acknowledge that the methods of riot control following Martin Luther King's death were based on the minimum use of gunfire.			Soviet Union launches Cosmos 212.	Pope Paul appeals to both sides in Vietnam to accept a truce.	April 14
Chicago Mayor Richard Daley instructs Chicago police to "shoot to kill" arsonists and to "shoot to maim or cripple" looters in future rioting.			Soviet Union launches Cosmos 213.	Macmillan publishes Michael Harrington's *Toward a Democratic Left*.	April 15
In reaction to Chicago Mayor Richard Daley's April 15 "shoot to kill" instructions, N.Y.C. Mayor John Lindsay says, "We happen to think that protection of life. . . is more important than protecting property.". . . A settlement is reached in the Memphis, Tenn. sanitationmen's strike, the cause which brought the Rev. Martin Luther King Jr. to the city. . . . A U.S. jury finds the Rev. Philip Berrigan guilty of impeding Selective Service procedures.	Pres. Johnson confers in Honolulu with Vietnam War U.S. military commanders.		*The New York Times* reports that the budget for the U.S. space program is steadily decreasing.		April 16
U.S. Atty. Gen. Ramsey Clark repudiates Chicago Mayor Richard Daley's April 15 "shoot to kill" instructions. . . . Mayor Daley modifies his instructions and says that arsonists and looters "should be restrained if possible by minimum force."	Sen. Robert Kennedy says that "American foreign policy has become identified with power, and in that obsession we have forgotten our purposes.". . . Pres. Johnson confers with South Korean Pres. Chung Hee Park.	Commerce Dept. reports that the U.S. GNP rose at a record annual rate during 1968's first quarter.			April 17
N.Y. Gov. Nelson Rockefeller proposes that $150 billion be invested in the next decade "to save and rebuild" the nation's cities. . . . Civil rights activist H. Rap Brown is released from jail after eight weeks in various state and federal prisons for bond violations.	Pres. Johnson briefs former Pres. Dwight Eisenhower about recent developments in the Vietnamese War. Sen. Robert Kennedy says that the U.S. should not quibble about the site for preliminary peace negotiations with North Vietnam.	A nationwide telephone strike begins but has little effect because of the automation of the telephone system.	U.S. conducts an underground nuclear test in Nevada. . . . Soviet Union launches Cosmos 214.	Bancroft Prize (1967) for U.S. history goes to Bernard Bailyn's *The Ideological Origins of the American Revolution*.	April 18
	Sen. Eugene McCarthy says that NATO is no longer useful.	Federal Reserve Board Chmn. William McChesney Martin says that the U.S. "is in the midst of the worst financial crisis since 1931.". . . A N.Y. federal judge invalidates the 1966 elections of the National Maritime Union.	A tornado leaves 11 dead in Arkansas. . . . Soviet Union launches Cosmos 215.		April 19
			Soviet Union launches Cosmos 216.	Concert pianist Alexander Borovsky dies in Waban, Mass. at 79. . . . Ramu, the Indian youth known as the "wolf boy," dies from a chronic respiratory infection and epileptic fits at 25 in Lucknow, India.	April 20

F	G	H	I	J
Includes elections, federal-state relations, civil rights and liberties, crime, the judiciary, education, health care, poverty, urban affairs and population.	*Includes formation and debate of U.S. foreign and defense policies, veterans' affairs and defense spending. (Relations with specific foreign countries are usually found under the region concerned.)*	*Includes business, labor, agriculture, taxation, transportation, consumer affairs, monetary and fiscal policy, natural resources, and pollution.*	*Includes worldwide scientific, medical and technological developments, natural phenomena, U.S. weather, natural disasters, and accidents.*	*Includes the arts, religion, scholarship, communications media, sports, entertainment, fashions, fads and social life.*

	World Affairs	Europe	Africa & the Middle East	The Americas	Asia & the Pacific
April 21		British Conservative Party dismisses Enoch Powell as their defense spokesman for having suggested that Britain should encourage its non-white population to leave the country. . . . Soviet authorities arrest 300 Crimean Tartars for assembling to celebrate the birth of Lenin.	Jordanian Foreign Min. Abdel Moneim Rifai says that the Arab states are prepared to start "indirect negotiations" with Israel if it declares its intention to impliment the U.N. Security Council's Resolution 242. . . . A mine kills two Israeli Arabs near Mount Tabor.	Quebec separatist leaders plan to launch a political party within six months.	South Vietnamese forces are placed on alert in Saigon in anticipation of Communist attacks. . . . Soviet Premier Aleksei Kosygin confers with Indian P.M. Indira Gandhi on his way back to Moscow.
April 22	U.N. Secretariat announces that it will send a fact-finding mission to the Middle East to investigate the condition of civilians in the Arab areas occupied by Israel. . . . U.S. Britain and the Soviet Union sign an agreement pledging international cooperation in the rescue of endangered astronauts.	Five British Parliament members say that they have found no evidence of large-scale torture of political prisoners in Greece. . . . Warsaw University officials warn that the school will remain closed until October if student demonstrations continue.		Quebec attends the opening of an education conference in Paris.	South Vietnamese forces are placed on alert in the region surrounding Saigon in anticipation of Communist attacks.
April 23		More than 2,000 London dock workers walk off their jobs in support of British politician Enoch Powell.	Reports indicate that the Soviet Union is supplying Egypt with short-range ground-to-ground missiles for the first time. . . . Biafran military leader Lt. Col. Chukwuemeka Odumegwu Olukwu calls on Nigeria to accept a cease-fire.	Canadian P.M. Pierre Trudeau dissolves Parliament and calls a June 25 general election.	South Vietnamese Foreign Min. Tran Van Do says that his country has warned the U.S. not to restrict the bombing of North Vietnam indefinitely.
April 24	U.N. votes membership for the Indian Ocean island of Mauritius.	Czechoslovak Premier Oldrich Cernik says that the "existing realities" of a divided Germany should be recognized. . . . Czechoslovak Premier Oldrich Cernik presents his government's economic reform measures to the National Assembly. . . . About 600 London meat workers march to the House of Commons in support of British politician Enoch Powell.	Nine West African countries sign an agreement to form a West African Regional Group. . . . Zambian Pres. Kenneth Kaunda says that he does not intend to nationalize all private businesses in Zambia. . . . Ghana orders the release of 70 political prisoners.		U.S. planes carry out a heavy raid over North Vietnam. Ford Foundation announces a major grant to the city of Gary, Ind. to help Negro Mayor Richard Hatcher. Trinity College trustees promise $15,000 for a scholarship program to be matched by student fundraising. . . . Negroes and student radicals continue to occupy five Columbia Univ. buildings.
April 25	Jordan asks the U.N. Security Council to convene to discuss Israel's scheduled military parade in Jerusalem on May 2.		Nigeria rejects the Biafran offer of a cease-fire but says that it is willing to begin negotiations without conditions. . . . A Jordanian cabinet realignment ousts two ministers who opposed the operation of Arab guerrillas bands from Jordanian soil. . . . Israeli police break up an unauthorized demonstration of Arab women in East Jerusalem. . . . Algerian Pres. Houri Boumedienne escapes serious injury as gunmen open fire on his limousine in Algiers.	Quebec Premier Daniel Johnson confirms reports that Gabon has asked Quebec's aid for a hospital or a diagnostic center. . . . Negro youths break store windows and throw Molotov cocktails in Hamilton, Bermuda.	U.S. and North Vietnamese representatives confer in Vientiane, Laos about the choice of a site for preliminary talks. . . . West Pakistani autonomists demonstrate against the integration of West Pakistan's provinces into one unit.

A	B	C	D	E
Includes developments that affect more than one world region, international organizations and important meetings of major world leaders.	Includes all domestic and regional developments in Europe, including the Soviet Union, Turkey, Cyprus and Malta.	Includes all domestic and regional developments in Africa and the Middle East, including Iraq and Iran and excluding Cyprus, Turkey and Afghanistan.	Includes all domestic and regional developments in Latin America, the Caribbean and Canada.	Includes all domestic and regional developments in Asia and Pacific nations, extending from Afghanistan through all the Pacific Islands, except Hawaii.

U.S. Politics & Social Issues	U.S. Foreign Policy & Defense	U.S. Economy & Environment	Science, Technology & Nature	Culture, Leisure & Life Style	
Former V.P. Nixon says that the current U.S. "economic crisis. . . . rules out any vast outpouring of federal funds into the cities this year."	Sen. Eugene McCarthy says that Senate Democratic leader Mike Mansfield might be a good replacement for State Secy. Dean Rusk.			Tom Stoppard's *Rosencrantz and Guildenstern Are Dead* wins the Tony Award for the best play of the New York 1967-1968 season.	April 21
Sen. Robert Kennedy says that the inflation rate in the U.S. is unacceptable. . . . Trinity College (Hartford, Conn.) students hold their president captive in his office for three hours to force acceptance of an enlarged scholarship program for Negroes and courses on Afro-American culture and history. . . . U.S. Supreme Court upholds the legality of the 1964 Mississippi anti-picketing law.	Defense Secy. Clark Clifford says that the South Vietnamese are now capable of beginning to ensure their own security. . . . Sen. Eugene McCarthy says that the U.S. military establishment influences "almost every aspect of our national life."		Soviet Union launches communications satellite Molniya-1.	Atheneum publishes David Schoenbrun's *Vietnam* . . . . Overseas Press Club presents its prize for distinguished achievement in foreign journalism to Eric Pace for his writing on the 1967 Arab-Israeli war.	April 22
U.S. government makes public a letter from Pres. Johnson to Defense Secy. Clark Clifford praising the "wise and restrained use of force" by federal troops in the rioting following Martin Luther King's assassination. . . . Negroes and student radicals occupy five Columbia Univ. buildings to protest the university's decision to build a gymnasium in a nearby city park. . . . U.S. Supreme Court upholds the right of states and cities to ban reading material from minors. . . . Justice Dept. reports that 46 people were killed in the rioting that followed the assassination of the Rev. Martin Luther King Jr. . . . Sen. Eugene McCarthy wins 76 1/2% of the vote in the Democratic presidential primary in Pennsylvania in which he was the only candidate. . . . Trinity College students continue their demonstrations in support of a scholarship program for Negroes.			U.S. conducts an underground nuclear test in Nevada.		April 23
	Sen. Robert Kennedy says that the U.S. should intervene militarily in other countries only in the most serious of circumstances.		Soviet Union launches Cosmos 217. . . . Soviet Union conducts an underground nuclear test in Central Asia.	Pantheon publishes Staughton Lynd's *Intellectual Origins of American Radicalism.*	April 24
V.P. Humphrey says that there is no place in U.S. politics for "the Stokely Carmichaels" or white extremists. . . . In its first suit against a Northern school system, Justice Dept. charges discrimination in faculty and staff assignments in a suburban Chicago school. . . . Negroes and student radicals seize two more Columbia Univ. buildings. . . . Former V.P. Nixon says that U.S. Negroes need "more black ownership, black pride. . .and black power. . .in the constuctive sense of that often misapplied term."	Former State Undersecy. George Ball replaces Arthur Goldberg as U.S. Amb.-to-U.N.	U.S. Commerce Dept. reports a $157.7 deficit in the U.S. balance-of-international trade in March.	Soviet Union launches Cosmos 218.	U.S. historian Caryle Buley, author of *The Old Northwest: Pioneer Period, 1815-1840,* dies in Indianapolis, Ind. at 74. . . . Tom Stoppard's *Rosencrantz and Guildenstern Are Dead* wins the N.Y. Drama Critics Circle award for the best play of the 1967-1968 season.	April 25

F	G	H	I	J
Includes elections, federal-state relations, civil rights and liberties, crime, the judiciary, education, health care, poverty, urban affairs and population.	*Includes formation and debate of U.S. foreign and defense policies, veterans' affairs and defense spending. (Relations with specific foreign countries are usually found under the region concerned.)*	*Includes business, labor, agriculture, taxation, transportation, consumer affairs, monetary and fiscal policy, natural resources, and pollution.*	*Includes worldwide scientific, medical and technological developments, natural phenomena, U.S. weather, natural disasters, and accidents.*	*Includes the arts, religion, scholarship, communications media, sports, entertainment, fashions, fads and social life.*

	World Affairs	Europe	Africa & the Middle East	The Americas	Asia & the Pacific
April 26		French State Secy. for International Cooperation says that the six-man Quebec delegation is attending the education conference in the capacity of observers. . . . About 500 students from the London School of Economics demonstrate against British politician Enoch Powell. . . . East Germany bars West Berlin Mayor Klaus Schutz from traveling to Bonn in his capacity as Bundesrat president. . . . Rumanian CP Central Committee charges former CP First Secy. Gheorghe Gheorghiu-Dej, who died in March 1965, with direct responsibility for the 1946 execution of Stefan Foris, the CP's wartime secy. gen.	Israeli Defense Min. Moshe Dayan says that the Jordan Valley will become a battlefield unless Jordan curbs Arab guerrillas operating from its territory.	Negro youths continue to roam through the streets of Hamilton, Bermuda. . . . Uruguay's Foreign Min. Hector Luisi resigns after severe criticism in the Senate.	South Vietnamese Pres. Nguyen Van Thieu advocates a cease-fire during peace negotiations.
April 27	U.N. Security Council passes a resolution calling on Israel to cancel a military parade scheduled for May 2 in Jerusalem.	Quebec Education Min. Jean-Guy Cardinal insists that his delegation at the education conference in Paris is to be treated on the basis of "full equality with other countries."	Rhodesia reports a fresh outbreak of guerrilla infiltration from Zambia.	Bermuda police restore calm to Hamilton.	Pakistani government bans public demonstrations in the Peshawar district of West Pakistan. . . . U.S. and North Vietnamese representatives confer in Vientiane, Laos about the site for preliminary talks. . . . North Korean troops attack U.N. forces near the demilitarized zone.
April 28		Three allied powers protest East Germany's decision to bar West Berlin Mayor Klaus Schutz from traveling to Bonn in his capacity as Bundesrat president. . . . *The New York Times* reports that Turkey no longer seeks the emplacement of nuclear land mines along its border with the Soviet Union. . . . About 2,000 British students demonstrate against British politician Enoch Powell.	Sudan reports more than 100 casualties in recent clashes with Ethiopian guerrillas. . . . An Israeli patrol kills 13 Arab guerrillas on the occupied West Bank of the Jordan River.	Uruguay's Labor Min. Guzman Acosta y Lara resigns after severe criticism in the Senate.	U.S. and North Vietnamese representatives confer in Vientiane, Laos about the site for preliminary talks but no progress is reported.
April 29			Egyptian Pres. Nasser asserts that another war with Israel is inevitable.		
April 30			Israeli and Jordanian forces clash along the Jordan River. . . . Reports indicate that Jordanian King Hussein has appealed to Egyptian Pres. Nasser to continue discussions with U.N. peace envoy Gunnar Jarring.		US mission in Saigon says that Communist troops executed more than 1,000 civilians in Hue during the Tet offensive.
May 1	Sixteen of the U.S.'s major trading partners agree to a one-year acceleration of their tariff cuts on American exports and to a one-year deferment of reciprocal tariff reductions by the U.S.	Greek military junta places two former ministers under arrest.			South Vietnam arrests peace advocate Truong Dinh Dzu.
May 2	A U.N. Security Council resolution deplores the Israeli military parade in Jerusalem.	Six French students occupy a lecture hall at the University of Paris's suburban Nanterre campus. . . . Greek military junta places a former vice president of parliament under arrest. . . . British Commonwealth Secretariat announces that Nigeria and Biafra have agreed to hold preliminary discussions in London.	Israeli armed forces stage a military parade in Jerusalem in celebration of the 20th anniversary of the country's independence.		U.S. says that it has cut off a major North Vietnamese infiltration route in the Ashau Valley.
May 3		Czechoslovak CP First Secy. Alexander Dubcek arrives in Moscow for talks about the current liberalization campaign. . . . French police clash with more than 1,000 students in the Latin Quarter of Paris.	Tanzanian Parliament grants Pres. Julius Nyerere the right to ban any newspaper. . . . South African Parliament abolishes representation for the country's mixed-race population.	Reports indicate that Canada has expressed its regret to France that it did not seek Quebec's participation in the recent education conference in Paris through the Canadian federal government.	North Vietnam and the U.S. agree on Paris as the site for their preliminary talks.
	A	**B**	**C**	**D**	**E**
	Includes developments that affect more than one world region, international organizations and important meetings of major world leaders.	*Includes all domestic and regional developments in Europe, including the Soviet Union, Turkey, Cyprus and Malta.*	*Includes all domestic and regional developments in Africa and the Middle East, including Iraq and Iran and excluding Cyprus, Turkey and Afghanistan.*	*Includes all domestic and regional developments in Latin America, the Caribbean and Canada.*	*Includes all domestic and regional developments in Asia and Pacific nations, extending from Afghanistan through all the Pacific Islands, except Hawaii.*

U.S. Politics & Social Issues	U.S. Foreign Policy & Defense	U.S. Economy & Environment	Science, Technology & Nature	Culture, Leisure & Life Style	
White House announces the creation of a government-sponsored but independent Urban Institute. . . . Radical students hold administrative personnel captive for several hours at Ohio State University in Columbus. . . . Sen. John Stennis (D, Miss.) states his opposition to the proposed Poor People's Campaign. . . . Sen. Robert Kennedy says that non-professionals should be trained to dispense medical care in the U.S. . . . Defense Secy. Clark Clifford announces the establishment of a riot-control command center in the Pentagon. . . . Columbia Univ. announces that it has suspended work on its controversial gymnasium located in a city park.			Soviet Union launches Cosmos 219. . . . U.S. conducts an underground nuclear test in Nevada.		April 26
Columbia University's board of trustees denounces students occupying the university's buildings. . . . V.P. Hubert Humphrey announces his candidacy for the Democratic nomination for president.	An estimated 87,000 demonstrators march against the Vietnamese War in N.Y.C.				April 27
Columbia Univ. faculty votes 466-40 to condemn the student occupation of the university's buildings. . . . V.P. Humphrey says that if elected President he could not promise not to send U.S. troops abroad in case of communist expansion.			In Paris Clovis Roblain becomes the world's seventh human heart transplant patient.	Walter Reade Organization releases Sergei Bondarchuk's film *War and Peace*.	April 28
Delegates from the Poor People's Campaign meet with Agriculture Secy. Orville Freeman and discuss alleged malnutrition in the U.S.	Former U.S. Amb.-to-U.N. Arthur Goldberg denies that there is a rift between himself and Pres. Johnson.		Sen. Warren Magnuson's (D, Wash.) office announces the discovery of relics of the earliest known human being in the Americas who probably lived 11,000 to 12,000 years ago.	Farrar, Straus & Giroux publishes Hermann Hesse's *The Journey to the East*.	April 29
N.Y.C. police clear the Columbia Univ. buildings of protesting students. . . . N.Y. Gov. Nelson Rockefeller enters the race for the Republican presidential nomination.			World's seventh heart transplant patient, Clovis Roblain, dies in Paris.	Atlantic-Little, Brown publishes Pauline Kael's *Kiss Kiss Bang Bang*.	April 30
	Sen. Robert Kennedy says that as the strongest nation in the world, the U.S., should not be concerned over whether it would "lose face" by agreeing to North Vietnamese proposals about a site for diplomatic talks.			British historian Sir Harold Nicolson dies in Kent, England at 81.	May 1
Caravans drawn by mules start from various parts of the country toward Washington, D.C. as the Poor People's Campaign begins. . . . In his first campaign trip after announcing his presidential candidacy, V.P. Humphrey calls for "a new and complete national commitment to human rights."	State Secy. Rusk says that U.S.-North Korean negotiations are stalemated over the release of the *Pueblo*.		In Palo Alto, Calif., Joseph Rizor becomes the world's eighth heart transplant patient.	N.Y. City Ballet presents the first performance of George Balanchine's *Requiem Canticles*.	May 2
Pres. Johnson says that government officials have made "extensive preparations" for the Poor People's Campaign.			Everett Thomas becomes the world's ninth human heart recipient in an operation in Houston, Tex. . . . Frederick West becomes the world's 10th human heart transplant patient in an operation in London.		May 3

F	G	H	I	J
Includes elections, federal-state relations, civil rights and liberties, crime, the judiciary, education, health care, poverty, urban affairs and population.	*Includes formation and debate of U.S. foreign and defense policies, veterans' affairs and defense spending. (Relations with specific foreign countries are usually found under the region concerned.)*	*Includes business, labor, agriculture, taxation, transportation, consumer affairs, monetary and fiscal policy, natural resources, and pollution.*	*Includes worldwide scientific, medical and technological developments, natural phenomena, U.S. weather, natural disasters, and accidents.*	*Includes the arts, religion, scholarship, communications media, sports, entertainment, fashions, fads and social life.*

	World Affairs	Europe	Africa & the Middle East	The Americas	Asia & the Pacific
May 4		National Union of French Students and the National Union of University Teachers issue a call for student-teacher strikes. . . . French newspaper *Le Monde* quotes Soviet Gen. Aleksei Yepishev as saying that if "a group of faithful Communists" in Czechoslovakia appealed for help, the Soviet army is "ready to do its duty."			South Vietnam says that it has no objections to the selection of Paris for the site of the preliminary U.s.-North Vietnamese talks but that it has reservations about the talk in general.
May 5		Reports indicate major tensions between Soviet leaders and Czechoslovak CP first secy. Alexander Dubcek during their talks in Moscow.	Israeli authorities report the shelling of a Galilee village from Lebanon.		Communist forces launch a coordinated attack on South Vietnamese cities.
May 6		French police clash with more than 10,000 students in the Latin Quarter of Paris. . . . Czech Foreign Min. Jiri Hajek arrives in Moscow for talks with Soviet Foreign Min. Andrei Gromyko.	Israeli authorities allow Arab residents to leave two West Bank towns which are on strike against the Israeli occupation. . . . Representatives of Nigeria and Biafra start peace negotiations in London.		Heavy fighting rages in South Vietnamese cities.
May 7		Student demonstrations spread to major provincial French universities. . . . Soviet news agency *Tass* charges that the Czechoslovak investigation into the Masaryk affair is designed to stir up "anti-Soviet moods."	Tunisia decides to break ties with Syria. . . . Algeria announces that former Algerian Army Maj. Amar Mellah has been arrested and charged with being the prinicpal instigator of the April 25 assassination attempt against Pres. Houri Boumedienne. . . . *London Times* reports that all of Sierra Leone's army and police officers are still in jail following the April 18 coup.		Heavy fighting continues in Saigon.
May 8		Britain agrees to sell Peru six Canberra bombers. . . . Reports from Warsaw indicate that Soviet troops are moving toward Czechoslovakia. . . . French Pres. de Gaulle warns students not to provoke further violence.	Nigeria and Biafra decide to use Kampala, Uganda as the site for their peace negotiations.		Communist forces seize several buildings in the Cholon district of Saigon.
May 9			Algerian national oil and gas concern, Sonatrach, takes over 14 foreign-owned oil and gas distribution companies.	British Honduras P.M. George Price rejects Britain's plan for an association between Guatemala and British Honduras.	An estimated 1,000 Communist troops continue fighting in and around the Cholon district in Saigon. . . . U.S. State Dept. confirms that the North Koreans have shifted the captured *U.S.S. Pueblo* from Wonsan harbor to another location.
May 10		Greek military junta lifts censorship for one Athens newspaper *Eleftheros Kosmos* as an experiment. West German students demonstrate against a proposed law allowing the West German government to curtail civil liberties in times of national danger. . . . North Vietnam and the U.S. begin peace talks in Paris. An estimated 30,000 French students gather outside the Sorbonne in Paris and demand the removal of police from university buildings.		Canadian P.M. Pierre Trudeau says that Canada should increase its contacts with Communist China.	Allied planes bomb Communist troops entrenched in Saigon.
May 11		French Premier Georges Pompidou announces the release of students arrested by the police. . . . West German students continue demonstrations against a proposed law allowing the West German government to curtail civil liberties in times of national danger. . . . Portugese police arrest newspaper editor Dr. Raul Rego for remarks critical of the Salazar regime.	In its first broadcast the Arab guerrilla operation Al Fatah announces that its ultimate aim is to free all of Palestine and not just to end the Israeli occupation of Arab areas seized in June 1967.	Canada charges that Soviet police used physical violence against Canadian embassy official Lt. Col. Jean Watson.	Sporadic enemy resistance flares up in the Cholon district of Saigon.
	A	B	C	D	E
	Includes developments that affect more than one world region, international organizations and important meetings of major world leaders.	Includes all domestic and regional developments in Europe, including the Soviet Union, Turkey, Cyprus and Malta.	Includes all domestic and regional developments in Africa and the Middle East, including Iraq and Iran and excluding Cyprus, Turkey and Afghanistan.	Includes all domestic and regional developments in Latin America, the Caribbean and Canada.	Includes all domestic and regional developments in Asia and Pacific nations, extending from Afghanistan through all the Pacific Islands, except Hawaii.

U.S. Politics & Social Issues	U.S. Foreign Policy & Defense	U.S. Economy & Environment	Science, Technology & Nature	Culture, Leisure & Life Style	
					May 4
		Nationwide telephone strike ends.	James Cobb becomes the world's 11th heart transplant patient in an operation in Houston, Tex. . . . World's eighth human heart transplant patient Joseph Rizor dies in Palo Alto, Calif.		May 5
U.S. Supreme Court rules that interrogators must warn prison inmates of their rights before asking incriminating questions. . . . Poor People's Campaign caravan travels through Selma, Ala.		House Ways & Means Chmn. Wilbur Mills endorses a tax increase of $10 billion coupled with reductions in federal spending.		U.S. composer George Crumb wins the Pulitzer Prize for Music. . . . New American Library publishes Norman Mailer's *The Armies of the Night.*	May 6
Sen. Robert Kennedy defeats Sen. Eugene McCarthy in the Indiana Democratic presidential primary with 42% of the vote against 27%.		UAW delegates re-elect Walter Reuther as UAW president.	John Stuckwish becomes the world's 12th heart transplant patient in Houston, Tex. . . . Soviet Union launches Cosmos 220.	Alabama Gov. Lurleen Wallace dies of cancer in Montgomery, Ala., at 41.	May 7
Poor People's Campaign southern caravan reaches Birmingham, Ala. with 400-500 participants.	Pres. Johnson meets with Thai P.M. Thanom Kittikachorn in Washington.	UAW convention greets V.P. Humphrey with a two-minute ovation.	World's 11th heart transplant patient James Cobb dies in Houston, Tex.		May 8
A Poor People's Campaign caravan leaves Boston.	West Germany and the U.S. discuss the costs of maintaining American troops in West Germany. . . . Pres. Johnson and Thai Premier Thanom Kittikachorn continue their talks in Washington.	A Senate-House conference committee approves a bill coupling a $6 billion federal spending reduction with a 10% income tax surcharge. . . . UAW convention greets Sen. Robert Kennedy with a 45-second ovation. . . . UAW Pres. Walter Reuther says that the U.S. labor movement must be revitalized.	Elie-Joseph Reynes becomes the world's 13th heart transplant patient in an operation in Montpellier, France.		May 9
U.S. National Park Service issues a 37-day renewable permit to allow the Poor People's Campaign to erect its plywood-and-canvas shantytown in Washington D.C. . . . Participants in the Poor People's Campaign leave Los Angeles.	West Germany and the U.S. continue their talks in Washington about the costs of maintaining American troops in West Germany.	UAW Pres. Walter Reuther says that the AFL-CIO is unable to deal adequately with modern corporate organization.	World's 13th heart transplant patient Elie-Joseph Reynes dies in Montpellier, France.		May 10
Poor People's Campaign marchers begin to arrive in Washington, D.C. . . . Sen. Robert Kennedy proposes a minimum income tax to prevent certain wealthy individuals from escaping all taxation.			British anthropologist Louis Leakey announces that he has found evidence that pre-human hominids in Africa used crude stone hammers.	Howard Nemerov wins the Theodore Roethke Memorial Poetry Award.	May 11

F	G	H	I	J
Includes elections, federal-state relations, civil rights and liberties, crime, the judiciary, education, health care, poverty, urban affairs and population.	*Includes formation and debate of U.S. foreign and defense policies, veterans' affairs and defense spending. (Relations with specific foreign countries are usually found under the region concerned.)*	*Includes business, labor, agriculture, taxation, transportation, consumer affairs, monetary and fiscal policy, natural resources, and pollution.*	*Includes worldwide scientific, medical and technological developments, natural phenomena, U.S. weather, natural disasters, and accidents.*	*Includes the arts, religion, scholarship, communications media, sports, entertainment, fashions, fads and social life.*

	World Affairs	Europe	Africa & the Middle East	The Americas	Asia & the Pacific
May 12		Univ. of Paris re-opens without the presence of police. . . . Greek military junta declares that it will no longer censor Greek magazines. . . . West German students continue demonstrations in Bonn against a proposed law allowing the West German government to curtail civil liberties in times of national danger.	Lebanon charges that Israel has shelled a Lebanese border village. . . . Israel and Lebanon exchange mortar fire across their cease-fire line.	Brazilian Justice Min. Luis Gama e Silva says that there is a connection between the purchase of large tracts of former Indian land and the mistreatment of Brazilian Indians. . . . Arnulfo Arias wins a three-way presidential race in Panama.	Reports indicate that all Communist forces have withdrawn from Saigon.
May 13	U.N. Secy. Gen. U Thant calls for an unconditional cessation of the U.S. bombing of North Vietnam.	Widespread strikes take place in France in support of higher wages and protesting French students. . . . North Vietnam and the U.S. begin talks on substantive matters for the first time in Paris. . . . At least 200,000 demonstrators march against the French government in Paris.	Fighting breaks out against the government in South Yemen.	Canadian P.M. Pierre Trudeau calls for a halt to the U.S. bombing of North Vietnam.	Viet Cong attack a U.S. Special Forces camp 55 miles from Saigon.
May 14	International Red Cross appeals for emergency food relief for Biafra.	A wave of wildcat sit-in strikes sweeps through French factories. . . . Soviet Union calls Czechoslovakia's first president, Thomas Masaryk, an "absolute scoundrel." The Czechoslovak press condemns the accusation as an "insult without parallel."	Ivory Coast recognizes the Republic of Biafra.		Saigon residents begin to return to the neighborhoods which they fled when the Communist urban offensive began May 5.
May 15		Poland says that Warsaw Pact maneuvers are taking place in Poland near the Czechoslovak border. . . . North Vietnam and the U.S. meet in Paris but report no progress.	Egypt indicates that it would consider a peace settlement that could precede the withdrawal of Israeli troops from Arab areas captured in June 1967.		South Vietnamese and Communist soldiers clash around Saigon. . . . U.S. planes pound North Vietnam south of the 19th Parallel.
May 16		French Socialist leader Francois Mitterrand calls for the resignation of the Gaullist government. . . . A petition signed by more than 1,000 people protesting the incarceration of Portugese opposition leader Mario Soares is presented to the secretary of the presidency in Lisbon.	South Yemen announces that it has crushed the revolt which broke out on May 13. . . . Reports indicate that most of the civilians of Port Harcourt in Biafra have abandoned the city in the face of advancing Nigerian troops. . . . Western diplomats in Cairo say that Egypt is prepared to end its state of belligerency with Israel and let Israeli ships use the Strait of Tiran if Israel pledges to leave the captured Arab territories.	Canada estimates that its population was 20.7 million as of April 1.	U.S. planes attack the Vinh airfield in North Vietnam. . . . Clashes continue between South Vietnamese and Communist forces around Saigon.
May 17		West German Chancellor Kurt-Georg Kiesinger says that West Germany will not be provoked by East Germany into taking rash measures. . . . A NATO guided-missile firing range opens on Crete. . . . Striking workers close down Orly and Le Bourget international airports in Paris. . . . Soviet Premier Aleksei Kosygin arrives in Czechoslovakia for an official visit.	Israel officials say that they insist upon the demilitarization of the Sinai Peninsula and the recognition of their country by the Arab states before they will return the captured territories.		
May 18		French Pres. de Gaulle cuts short his trip to Rumania and returns to France. . . . North Vietnam and the U.S. meet in Paris but report no progress.			
May 19		West German Chancellor Kurt-Georg Kiesinger says that French Pres. de Gaulle has assured him that France will not renounce the NATO treaty in 1969 unless something unforeseen develops. . . . An estimated 10,000 Czech students stage an anti-Soviet rally in Prague. . . . Soviet Union agrees to help Pakistan build an electrical complex.	Nigeria announces that its army has captured Port Harcourt, the main port of Biafra.	Foreign ministers of five South American countries meet to discuss joint development of the Rio Plata.	U.S. troops battle North Vietnamese forces around Khesanh.
	A	B	C	D	E
	Includes developments that affect more than one world region, international organizations and important meetings of major world leaders.	Includes all domestic and regional developments in Europe, including the Soviet Union, Turkey, Cyprus and Malta.	Includes all domestic and regional developments in Africa and the Middle East, including Iraq and Iran and excluding Cyprus, Turkey and Afghanistan.	Includes all domestic and regional developments in Latin America, the Caribbean and Canada.	Includes all domestic and regional developments in Asia and Pacific nations, extending from Afghanistan through all the Pacific Islands, except Hawaii.

U.S. Politics & Social Issues	U.S. Foreign Policy & Defense	U.S. Economy & Environment	Science, Technology & Nature	Culture, Leisure & Life Style	
Mrs. Martin Luther King, Jr. leads a march of welfare mothers in Washington, D.C. . . . Ford Foundation announces grants for projects aimed at increased understanding between the police and local communities.			Jean-Marie Boulogne becomes France's third heart transplant patient in an operation in Marseilles.		May 12
		Treasury Secy. Henry Fowler endorses a bill with a $6 billion spending cut and a 10% income tax surcharge. . . . AFL-CIO announces that it will suspend the UAW union unless it pays its dues.		McGraw-Hill publishes Vladimir Nabokov's *King, Queen, Knave.*	May 13
Sen. Robert Kennedy defeats Sen. Eugene McCarthy in the Nebraska Democratic presidential primary by 52%-31%. In the Republican primary, former V.P. Nixon wins 70% of the vote.		Commerce Dept. reports that the U.S.'s balance-of-payments deficit in the first quarter of 1968 was about $600 million.			May 14
			Despite assertions to the contrary, Dr. Cyrus Gordon of Brandeis University claims that inscriptions on a stone prove that the Phoenicians landed in Brazil in the Sixth Century BC. . . . World's 12th heart transplant patient John Stuckwish dies in Houston, Tex.		May 15
	GAO reports that a certain amount of the U.S. development loans made to Brazil have been wasted because of a ''lack of effective administration.''	AFL-CIO suspends the UAW for failure to pay dues.	U.S. launches a European satellite whose mission is to study the polar ionosphere.		May 16
A Washington, D.C. Court rules that landlords have no legal right to evict tenants in retaliation for reporting housing code violations.			U.S. conducts an underground nuclear test in Nevada.	Farrar, Straus & Giroux publishes Mihajlo Mihajlov's *Russian Themes.*	May 17
Negro gangs loot and riot in Cambridge, Md. after police slay Daniel Henry, a Negro.	Sen. Robert Kennedy suggests that the South Vietnamese government begin negotiations with the National Liberation Front.		U.S. launches a weather satellite which is destroyed after a flight of 120 seconds because it was dangerously off-course.	Doubleday publishes Bruce Page's *The Philby Conspiracy.*	May 18
Americans for Democratic Action reaffirm their support of Sen. Eugene McCarthy. . . . Negroes throw stones at firemen fighting fires in Cambridge, Md. . . . In the midst of spreading strikes, French workers occupy the Paris Opera.					May 19

F	G	H	I	J
Includes elections, federal-state relations, civil rights and liberties, crime, the judiciary, education, health care, poverty, urban affairs and population.	Includes formation and debate of U.S. foreign and defense policies, veterans' affairs and defense spending. (Relations with specific foreign countries are usually found under the region concerned.)	Includes business, labor, agriculture, taxation, transportation, consumer affairs, monetary and fiscal policy, natural resources, and pollution.	Includes worldwide scientific, medical and technological developments, natural phenomena, U.S. weather, natural disasters, and accidents.	Includes the arts, religion, scholarship, communications media, sports, entertainment, fashions, fads and social life.

	World Affairs	Europe	Africa & the Middle East	The Americas	Asia & the Pacific
May 20		Reports from Bonn indicate that Hungarian CP First Secy. Janos Kadar has refused to participate in Warsaw Pact maneuvers near the Czechslovak border. . . . Most normal work activity in France grinds to a halt. Trains, planes and most public transportation no longer function. Shoppers feverishly stockpile provisions. . . . Portugese police release newspaper editor Dr. Raul Rego from prison. . . . Polish press agency says that the anti-Zionist campaign has caused several foreign companies to cancel their contracts with the Polish government.	Zambia recognizes the Republic of Biafra. . . . Biafran troops launch a counterattack against Nigerian forces.	A force of perhaps 20 to 30 Haitian exiles invade Haiti. . . . Five South American countries agree on proposals for the joint development of the Rio Plata area. . . . Britain abandons its plan for an association between Guatemala and British Honduras.	
May 21	U.N. Security Council adopts a resolution opposing Israel's administrative unification of the Jordanian and Israeli sectors of Jerusalem.		A land mine kills two Israeli farmers near the Gaza Strip.	Haitian coast guard vessel shells the small May 20 invasion force. . . . U.S. suspends loans to Peru because of recent purchases of French Mirage jet fighters. . . . Panamanian National Guard recognizes the validity of Arnulfo Arias's election.	
May 22		Gaullist government of French P.M. Georges Pompidou narrowly survives a parliamentary effort to overthrow it. . . . North Vietnamese and U.S. representatives meet in Paris but report no progress.	Israeli Foreign Min. Abba Eban says that Israel will ignore the May 21 U.N. resolution opposing the administrative unification of Jerusalem.	In New York, Haitian Coalition Secy. Gen. Raymond Joseph says that his group knew about the May 20 invasion but did not direct it. . . . Bermudian voters elect members of the predominantly white United Bermuda Party to 30 or the 40 Assembly seats in the island's first universal suffrage election.	
May 23		Violent street fighting between police and students erupts again in the Latin Quarter of Paris. . . . Five hundred student demonstrators occupy the Free University of Brussels.	Anti-Israeli demonstrations take place in the Gaza Strip. . . . Peace talks begin between Nigeria and Biafra in Uganda.	Haitian government reports that the May 20 invasion force has taken over a small village near Cap-Haitian.	
May 24		Soviet Union orders the expulsion of Canadian embassy official Lt. Col. Jean Watson. . . . French Pres. de Gaulle calls for a national referendum in June and threatens to resign if he does not win massive support.		Canada orders the expulsion of a junior Soviet embassy attache in retaliation to the expusion of a Canadian embassy official in Moscow. . . . Uruguay imposes severe economic restrictions to cut electric consumption in half.	
May 25		Soviet Premier Aleksei Kosygin ends his consultations in Czechoslovakia amid reports that Warsaw Pact exercises will be held soon on Czech soil. . . . A French youth dies of knife wounds as violent clashes between police and students continue in Paris. . . . South Vietnamese troops battle Communist forces just north of Saigon. . . . The New York Times reports that Belgian factory workers have reacted with indifference to student bids for their support.	Nigeria and Biafra agree to allow Ugandan Foreign Min. Sam Odaka to participate in their talks. . . . AP reports widespread civilian massacres in the Nigerian civil war. . . . Israeli authorities break up an anti-Israeli demonstration.		
May 26		British newspaper, The Observer, publishes an article about Britain's chemical and biological warfare experiments.	Israeli authorities exchange gunfire with Arab civilians in the Gaza Strip. . . . Nigeria says that one of its negotiators in the peace talks with Biafra, Johnson Banjo, has been missing since May 22. . . . Sudanese Umma Mahdist Party renominates P.M. Mohamed Ahmed Mahgoub.	Reports indicate that the survivors of the May 20 invasion of Haiti are fleeing through the countryside.	South Vietnamese troops fight a small contingent of Communist forces.

A	B	C	D	E
Includes developments that affect more than one world region, international organizations and important meetings of major world leaders.	Includes all domestic and regional developments in Europe, including the Soviet Union, Turkey, Cyprus and Malta.	Includes all domestic and regional developments in Africa and the Middle East, including Iraq and Iran and excluding Cyprus, Turkey and Afghanistan.	Includes all domestic and regional developments in Latin America, the Caribbean and Canada.	Includes all domestic and regional developments in Asia and Pacific nations, extending from Afghanistan through all the Pacific Islands, except Hawaii.

U.S. Politics & Social Issues	U.S. Foreign Policy & Defense	U.S. Economy & Environment	Science, Technology & Nature	Culture, Leisure & Life Style	
National Guardsmen disperse Negroes with tear gas in Cambridge, Md. . . . U.S. Supreme Court upholds equal treatment by the law for illegitimate children. . . . U.S. Supreme Court upholds the legality of peaceful picketing at private suburban shopping centers.				Atheneum publishes George Painter's *Andre Gide*.	**May 20**
CBS-TV broadcasts a documentary called *Hunger In America*.	Pres. Johnson asks Congress for a supplemental $3.9 billion for the Vietnamese War.				**May 21**
New Orleans court sentences civil rights militant H. Rap Brown to five years in prison for violating the Federal Firearms Act. . . . Sen. Eugene McCarthy says that until "very recently" Sen. Robert Kennedy has approved of the Vietnam War.		House and Senate pass a truth-in-lending bill.			**May 22**
Senate passes an anti-crime bill. . . . U.S. government agencies announce a $10 million program to provide food and medical aid for the poor.		U.S. Treasury says that total U.S. monetary reserves dropped $86 million in April.			**May 23**
Poor People's Campaign leader Jesse Jackson announces the evacuation of about 200 inhabitants of the campaign's shantytown-Resurrection City-because of bad weather.			Soviet Union launches Cosmos 221.		**May 24**
Leaders of non-Negro groups in the Poor People's Campaign bitterly denounce the treatment they have received from Negro leaders. . . . Sen. Robert Kennedy proposes a $1 billion subsidized loan program to help businesses locate in rural and urban poverty areas.					**May 25**
Remaining National Guardsmen leave Cambridge, Md. as state of emergency is lifted.					**May 26**

F	G	H	I	J
Includes elections, federal-state relations, civil rights and liberties, crime, the judiciary, education, health care, poverty, urban affairs and population.	*Includes formation and debate of U.S. foreign and defense policies, veterans' affairs and defense spending. (Relations with specific foreign countries are usually found under the region concerned.)*	*Includes business, labor, agriculture, taxation, transportation, consumer affairs, monetary and fiscal policy, natural resources, and pollution.*	*Includes worldwide scientific, medical and technological developments, natural phenomena, U.S. weather, natural disasters, and accidents.*	*Includes the arts, religion, scholarship, communications media, sports, entertainment, fashions, fads and social life.*

	World Affairs	Europe	Africa & the Middle East	The Americas	Asia & the Pacific
May 27	U.N. Security Council meets to discuss the recent attempt to invade Haiti.	North Vietnamese and U.S. representatives meet in Paris but report no progress.	A U.N. report says that the 1967 war dealt a sharp setback to the economies of the Arab states. . . . Israeli troops disperse demonstrating Arab high school students in the Gaza Strip.		
May 28		Greek Premier George Papadopoulos announces the restoration of the rights of peaceful assembly and free association.	Israeli military authorities seal off the Gaza Strip to Arab traffic to counter anti-Israeli demonstrations. . . . Israel pays the U.S. more than $3 million in compensation for the sinking of the *U.S. Liberty* on June 8, 1967. . . . Jordanian police fight off an attempt by armed Arab guerrillas to rescue a fellow guerrilla under interrogation by police.		Sporadic fighting takes place in Saigon.
May 29	U.N. Security Council unanimously approves a resolution calling for a trade embargo of Rhodesia.	Greek military junta dismisses 30 judges. . . . Reports indicate that French Pres. de Gaulle is in West Germany conferring with army generals about the unrest in France. . . . United Socialist Party votes to withdraw from Italy's coalition government.	Israeli Foreign Min. Abba Eban says that Israel will only return the 1967 captured territories when the Arab states are ready to sign peace treaties with his country. . . . *The New York Times* reports that Communist China has agreed to help build a railroad from Mali to Guinea. . . . Senegalese students seize the Univ. of Dakar in protest against cuts in student stipends.	Canadian P.M. Pierre Elliott Trudeau proposes that Canada diversify its bilateral links to include Europe and the developing nations.	Sporadic fighting continues in Saigon.
May 30		Italian CP calls for massive demonstrations to express solidarity with French students and workers. . . . French Pres. de Gaulle dissolves the National Assembly and calls for new elections to be held within the 40-day statutory period.	Reports indicate that the U.S. has begun air-lifting arms to Jordan.		South Vietnam eases newspaper censorship in force since the February Tet Offensive. . . . Increased fighting between South Vietnamese and Communist forces rages in the Cholon district of Saigon.
May 31		Signs point to a back-to-work trend among France's 10 million striking workers. . . . France imposes temporary but stiff controls on the outflow of privately owned French francs. . . . In Paris North Vietnamese negotiators reject U.S. demands for military reciprocity in exchange for a halt to the bombing of North Vietnam.	Biafra breaks off peace talks with Nigeria and accuses it of negotiating in bad faith. . . . Senegalese Pres. Leopold Senghor declares a state of emergency as several labor unions declare a general strike in support of student demands.		
June 1		Police and students clash in Turin, Italy.			Fierce fighting continues in the Cholon district of Saigon.
June 2		Yugoslav students demonstrate in Belgrade for better living conditions and the dismissal of the city's police chief. . . . Ruling Justice Party wins 38 of the 53 contested seats in Turkey. . . .			

A	B	C	D	E
Includes developments that affect more than one world region, international organizations and important meetings of major world leaders.	Includes all domestic and regional developments in Europe, including the Soviet Union, Turkey, Cyprus and Malta.	Includes all domestic and regional developments in Africa and the Middle East, including Iraq and Iran and excluding Cyprus, Turkey and Afghanistan.	Includes all domestic and regional developments in Latin America, the Caribbean and Canada.	Includes all domestic and regional developments in Asia and Pacific nations, extending from Afghanistan through all the Pacific Islands, except Hawaii.

U.S. Politics & Social Issues	U.S. Foreign Policy & Defense	U.S. Economy & Environment	Science, Technology & Nature	Culture, Leisure & Life Style	
U.S. Supreme Court rules that "freedom of choice" plans in the South are illegal if they do not bring about integration as well as other plans would. . . . Agriculture Secy. Orville Freeman calls the May 21 CBS-TV documentary "Hunger In America" a "one-sided and dishonest presentation.". . . Sen. Robert Kennedy states his support of gun control laws in Roseburg, Ore. . . . U.S. Supreme Court upholds the right of states to regulate fishing by American Indians.		Commerce Department reports a $248 million surplus in the U.S. balance-of-international trade in April.		Morrow publishes Tom Wicker's *JFK and LBJ* . . . . Stein & Day publishes Geoffrey Ashe's *Gandhi.*	May 27
Sen. Eugene McCarthy (45%) scores an upset victory over Sen. Robert Kennedy (39%) in the Oregon Democratic presidential primary. . . . Police prevent 150 demonstrators from the Poor People's Campaign from entering the Agriculture Dept.	U.S. peace negotiator in Paris Cyrus Vance confers with Pres. Johnson in Washington. . . . Pres. Johnson sends Congress a message urging more free world trade.	AFL-CIO International Ladies Garment Workers Union endorses V.P. Humphrey for president.		Random House publishes *Lion in the Garden. Interviews with William Faulkner, 1926-1962.* . . . National Institute of Arts & Letters awards its Gold Metal for Poetry to W.H. Auden. . . . Dutch painter Kees van Dongen dies in Monte Carlo at 91.	May 28
Sen. Robert Kennedy says that his candidacy will stand or fall on the results of the California primary. . . . House Public Works Committee approves a bill prohibiting the use of federal property in the District of Columbia for overnight campsites. . . . Pres. Johnson calls for the granting of the vote to 18-year-olds. . . . Louisville, Ky. Mayor Kenneth Schmied meets with Negro youths after a looting spree of the town's business district.			U.S. submarine *Scorpion* is reported missing.		May 29
Three to four hundred demonstrators from the Poor People's Campaign protest at the Supreme Court building. . . . U.S. Supreme Court extends the right to trial by jury to criminal defendants in all but "petty" cases. . . . Former V.P. Nixon says that the U.S. Supreme Court has given a "green light criminal elements" in the U.S.	U.S. commander in South Vietnam William Westmoreland confers with Pres. Johnson in Texas.		Soviet Union launches Cosmos 222.		May 30
Nearly 500 demonstrators from the Poor People's Campaign take over an auditorium in the HEW Dept. and demand to meet with HEW Secy. Wilbur Cohen.				U.S. literary critic Edmund Wilson wins the Aspen Award for outstanding contribution to the humanities. . . . Macmillan publishes Alfred Steinberg's *Sam Johnson's Boy.*	May 31
Senator Robert Kennedy and Sen. Eugene McCarthy participate in an informal television debate.			Soviet Union launches Cosmos 223.	Deaf, dumb and blind writer Helen Keller dies in Westport, Conn. at 87.	June 1
					June 2

F	G	H	I	J
Includes elections, federal-state relations, civil rights and liberties, crime, the judiciary, education, health care, poverty, urban affairs and population.	Includes formation and debate of U.S. foreign and defense policies, veterans' affairs and defense spending. (Relations with specific foreign countries are usually found under the region concerned.)	Includes business, labor, agriculture, taxation, transportation, consumer affairs, monetary and fiscal policy, natural resources, and pollution.	Includes worldwide scientific, medical and technological developments, natural phenomena, U.S. weather, natural disasters, and accidents.	Includes the arts, religion, scholarship, communications media, sports, entertainment, fashions, fads and social life.

	World Affairs	Europe	Africa & the Middle East	The Americas	Asia & the Pacific
June 3		Police and students clash on the campus of the University of Rome.			South Vietnamese officials report that recent fighting in Saigon has resulted in 125,000 refugees.
June 4		Police and students clash on the campuses of major Italian universities. . . . French Finance Ministry discloses that France's gold and foreign exchange reserves dropped by $306 million during May.	Senegalese striking workers return to work after the government releases union leaders. . . . Israel and Jordan engage in a day-long clash near the Sea of Galilee.		Viet Cong rockets strike Saigon and the surrounding area.
June 5		At the Paris peace talks, the U.S. protests Communist rocket attacks against Saigon, and North Vietnam demands a complete halt in the U.S. bombing of the North. . . . Italy's ruling coalition government resigns because of the withdrawal of the United Socialist Party. . . . British Treasury reports that Britain's foreign exchange and gold reserves fell by $26.4 million in May.	Arabs stage general strikes in Jerusalem to mark the first anniversary of the 1967 war.		
June 6		Public services return to normal in Paris.	Nigerian military leader Maj. Gen. Yakubu Gowon orders an investigation into alleged atrocities by federal troops. . . . Israeli police clash with Arab demonstrators in Jerusalem.	Guatemalan authorities reportedly believe that guerrilla leader Cesar Montes was killed in a clash with government troops on May 11. . . . Canadian P.M. Pierre Trudeau voices his opposition to the theory that Canada is composed of an English "nation" and a French "nation" during a speech in the province of Quebec.	
June 7		Violent clashes between workers and police occur in the nationalized Renault automobile assembly plant in Flins near Paris.	Clashes continue between Israeli police and Arab demonstrators in Jerusalem.		France conducts an atmospheric test in the Pacific. . . . Communist rockets bombard churches and hospitals as well as military installations in Saigon.
June 8		Scotland Yard detectives arrest Martin Luther King Jr's alleged assassin James Earl Ray at Heathrow Airport in London.	Arab Conference for the Boycott of Israel agrees to permit agricultural products from the Israeli-occupied West Bank of the Jordan River to enter Arab countries.	Quebec Premier Daniel Johnson says that Quebec must control its own culture and education.	
June 9		In a nationwide television address, Yugoslav Pres. Tito promises to respond to student grievances.	Nigeria asserts that its troops have cleared out all Biafran troops from Port Harcourt. . . . Jordan reports that Saudi Arabia has pledged $36 million for arms purchases for the Jordanian Army.		
June 10		During a clash between police and antigovernment demonstrators in Paris, a student is pushed into the Seine where he drowns. . . . West Germany and the U.S. agree that West Germany will pay for most of the costs of maintaining U.S. troops in West Germany. . . . A three-week national election campaign begins in France.			Cambodian Chief of State Prince Sihanouk releases two U.S. Army soldiers who were captured May 25 just inside the Cambodian border.

A	B	C	D	E
Includes developments that affect more than one world region, international organizations and important meetings of major world leaders.	Includes all domestic and regional developments in Europe, including the Soviet Union, Turkey, Cyprus and Malta.	Includes all domestic and regional developments in Africa and the Middle East, including Iraq and Iran and excluding Cyprus, Turkey and Afghanistan.	Includes all domestic and regional developments in Latin America, the Caribbean and Canada.	Includes all domestic and regional developments in Asia and Pacific nations, extending from Afghanistan through all the Pacific Islands, except Hawaii.

U.S. Politics & Social Issues	U.S. Foreign Policy & Defense	U.S. Economy & Environment	Science, Technology & Nature	Culture, Leisure & Life Style	
More than 400 demonstrators from the Poor People's Campaign stage a seven-hour camp-in on the steps of the Justice Department. . . . U.S. Supreme Court rules, 6-3, that jurors cannot be excluded from murder trial juries because of their objections to capital punishment. . . . U.S. Supreme Court rules that public school teachers cannot be dismissed for publicly criticizing school systems.				Dial Press publishes James Baldwin's *Tell Me How Long the Train's Been Gone.* . . . An actress shoots and critically wounds pop artist Andy Warhol in New York.	June 3
Sen. Robert Kennedy defeats Sen. Eugene McCarthy in California's Democratic presidential primary. . . . Atty. Gen. Ramsey Clark meets with Poor People's Campaign delegates.	Pres. Johnson appeals to the Soviet Union to join the U.S. and other nations "in the spirit of Glassboro" to help achieve world peace.		Soviet Union launches Cosmos 224.		June 4
Sen. Robert Kennedy is seriously wounded in Los Angeles by a gunman after winning the California Democratic Primary.			U.S. Navy announces that the U.S. submarine *Scorpion* is "presumed lost."	Simon & Schuster publishes Larry Collins and Dominique Lapierre's *Or I'll Dress You in Mourning.*	June 5
Sen. Robert Kennedy dies of gunshot wounds inflicted by Sirhan Sirhan. . . . Negro leader Bayard Rustin announces that he is suspending his activities as coordinator of the scheduled June 19 demonstration by the Poor People's Campaign amid signs of growing disputes within the campaign's leadership.			U.S. conducts an underground nuclear test in Nevada.	British journalist Randolph Churchill, the son of Sir Winston Churchill, dies in London at 57.	June 6
Los Angeles grand jury hears testimony that an unidentified woman was seen talking to Robert Kennedy's assassin Sirhan Sirhan seconds before the slaying took place. . . . Negro leader Bayard Rustin resigns from the Poor People's Campaign. . . . Body of Sen. Robert Kennedy lies in state in St. Patrick's Cathedral in New York.					June 7
During a requiem mass for the late Robert Kennedy, Sen. Edward Kennedy delivers a eulogy in a strong but at times shaking voice in which he quotes his brother's favorite passage, "Some men see things as they are and say why. I dream of things that never were and say why not."					June 8
					June 9
U.S. Supreme Court upholds the right of policemen to stop and frisk people for weapons. . . . Administration sends Congress its proposals to ban the mail-order sale of guns and ammunition.	U.S. commander in South Vietnam Gen. William Westmoreland says that an allied military victory "in a classic sense" is impossible in Vietnam because of the self-imposed constraints limiting the U.S. war effort.			Norton publishes Anthony Burgess's *Enderby.*	June 10

F	G	H	I	J
Includes elections, federal-state relations, civil rights and liberties, crime, the judiciary, education, health care, poverty, urban affairs and population.	Includes formation and debate of U.S. foreign and defense policies, veterans' affairs and defense spending. (Relations with specific foreign countries are usually found under the region concerned.)	Includes business, labor, agriculture, taxation, transportation, consumer affairs, monetary and fiscal policy, natural resources, and pollution.	Includes worldwide scientific, medical and technological developments, natural phenomena, U.S. weather, natural disasters, and accidents.	Includes the arts, religion, scholarship, communications media, sports, entertainment, fashions, fads and social life.

	World Affairs	Europe	Africa & the Middle East	The Americas	Asia & the Pacific
June 11		Police and students continue to clash in the Latin Quarter of Paris. . . . East Germany announces a number of new regulations governing travel by West German citizens between West Germany and West Berlin.	The body of Nigerian peace negotiator, Johnson Banjo, is found in Kampala, Uganda. There is evidence that he was murdered.		
June 12	U.N. General Assembly approves the nuclear non-proliferation treaty.	West Germany protests the June 11 East German travel regulations. . . . At the Paris peace talks, the U.S. protests Communist rocket attacks against Saigon and North Vietnam demands a complete halt of the U.S. bombing of the North. . . . Soviet Union launches Cosmos 225 and Cosmos 226.	Israeli Defense Min Moshe Dayan says that Israel has suffered 578 killed and wounded since the end of the June 1967 war.	Argentine police clear protesting students out of the main building of the University of La Plata.	
June 13				Uruguay declares a limited martial law emergency in reaction to wide-spread strikes.	Reports indicate that South Vietnamese legislators are demanding the resumption of the bombing of North Vietnam if the shelling of Saigon continues.
June 14		U.S. turns over a military radar and communications station to the Turkish general staff. . . . East German CP newspaper Neues Deutschland says that West Germany faces "new unpleasant surprises" as long as it claims to represent "the entire German nation."	Israel and Egypt fight a two-and-a-half hour artillery and tank duel across the Suez Canal.		
June 15		West German Foreign Min. Willy Brandt says that his country will "represent its own interests in Berlin" through direct contact with the Soviet Union. . . . Reports indicate that the Soviet government is allowing members of four Moslem minorities to end their exile and return to their native territories.	Israel and Lebanon exchange mortar fire across their cease-fire line.		U.S. troops take a heavy toll of Communist troops around Khesanh.
June 16		Reports indicate that a split has developed in the West German government about whether to take a hard or soft line in response to recent East German actions on Berlin.	An Israeli plan permitting Arabs to visit the West Bank of the Jordan River for brief periods goes into effect. . . . Jordan reports that since the 1967 war about 400,000 Arabs have fled to Jordan from the Israeli occupied territories.		
June 17		Britain activates a $1.4 billion drawing from the International Monetary Fund. . . . British House of Commons votes to impose stricter sanctions on Rhodesia. . . . Czechoslovakia and North Vietnam sign an agreement in Prague providing more Czech aid.	Arab guerrillas kill an Israeli soldier on the Golan Heights. . . . Israel and Jordan trade artillery salvos across the Jordan River.		

A	B	C	D	E
Includes developments that affect more than one world region, international organizations and important meetings of major world leaders.	Includes all domestic and regional developments in Europe, including the Soviet Union, Turkey, Cyprus and Malta.	Includes all domestic and regional developments in Africa and the Middle East, including Iraq and Iran and excluding Cyprus, Turkey and Afghanistan.	Includes all domestic and regional developments in Latin America, the Caribbean and Canada.	Includes all domestic and regional developments in Asia and Pacific nations, extending from Afghanistan through all the Pacific Islands, except Hawaii.

U.S. Politics & Social Issues	U.S. Foreign Policy & Defense	U.S. Economy & Environment	Science, Technology & Nature	Culture, Leisure & Life Style	
Four armed convicts take 25 hostages in the Atlanta, Georgia Federal Prison. . . . Calif. Gov. Ronald Reagan says that in most instances civil disorders have been encouraged by "demagogic" statements by prominent people. . . . Close associates of Sen. Edward Kennedy report that he will neither run for the presidency nor accept a vice presidential nomination. . . . Sen. Eugene McCarthy meets with Pres. Johnson at the White House for a briefing.	Pres. Johnson meets with the Shah of Iran in Washington.		Soviet Union conducts an underground nuclear test in Central Asia.		June 11
Sen. Eugene McCarthy announces the resumption of his presidential campaign. . . . In the first suit against state agencies for job discrimination, Justice Dept. charges eight Alabama state agencies with discriminating against Negroes. . . . Postmaster Gen. Marvin Watson announces new postal requirements governing the mailing of firearms. . . . About 250 demonstrators begin a vigil outside the Agriculture Dept. in support of demands for broader food distribution to the poor.	Reports indicate that the U.S. has promised the Shah of Iran modern arms on easy credit terms.			Art historian Sir Herbert Reed dies near Malton, England at 74. . . . Roman Polanski's film *Rosemary's Baby* opens in New York.	June 12
Sen. Eugene McCarthy says that he thinks the U.S. public would accept a unilateral withdrawal of U.S. forces from Vietnam.	Pres. Johnson renews his appeal for Soviet cooperation at White House ceremonies marking the exchange of the instruments of ratification of the U.S.-Soviet consular treaty.		In Houston, Tex. Sam Willoughby receives the heart of a ram in an unsuccessful effort to prolong his life until a human donor could be found. . . . U.S. puts eight military reconnaissance satellites into orbit.		June 13
A federal jury in Boston convicts pediatrician Dr. Benjamin Spock of conspiring to aid, abet, and counsel registrants to violate the Selective Service law. . . . France announces that the development of the French nuclear force will be delayed for one or two years because of the economic problems emanating from the recent political troubles.	State Secy. Rusk discusses the Berlin situation with Soviet officials in Washington.				June 14
Kennedy family, in a brief television message, thanks the American people for its expression of sympathy after the death of Robert Kennedy.			U.S. conducts an underground nuclear test in Nevada.		June 15
House Agriculture Committee Chmn. W.R. Poage issues a study indicating that there have been no verified cases of starvation in the U.S.				Greek Orthodox Church's governing body calls abortion "a sinful act."	June 16
Senate passes a bill making it a federal crime to desecrate the U.S. flag. . . . U.S. Supreme Court rules, in a 5-4 vote, that jailing chronic alcoholics for public drunkeness is not a violation of their constitutional rights. . . . U.S. Supreme Court rules that federal aid cannot be withheld from dependent children whose mothers maintain illicit sexual relations.	Pres. Johnson reaffirms U.S. support of West Berlin.			Chief Rabbi of Moscow, Yehuda Levin, arrives in the U.S. for a visit.	June 17

F	G	H	I	J
Includes elections, federal-state relations, civil rights and liberties, crime, the judiciary, education, health care, poverty, urban affairs and population.	*Includes formation and debate of U.S. foreign and defense policies, veterans' affairs and defense spending. (Relations with specific foreign countries are usually found under the region concerned.)*	*Includes business, labor, agriculture, taxation, transportation, consumer affairs, monetary and fiscal policy, natural resources, and pollution.*	*Includes worldwide scientific, medical and technological developments, natural phenomena, U.S. weather, natural disasters, and accidents.*	*Includes the arts, religion, scholarship, communications media, sports, entertainment, fashions, fads and social life.*

	World Affairs	Europe	Africa & the Middle East	The Americas	Asia & the Pacific
June 18		British House of Lords vetoes the House of Commons' measure imposing stricter sanctions on Rhodesia. . . . West German Foreign Min. Willy Brandt declares that the new East German rules governing traffic between West Germany and West Berlin do not pose an immediate crisis.	*The New York Times* reports that the Israeli cabinet has agreed on a plan formulated by Labor Min. Yigal Allon calling for Israeli settlements along the Jordan River. . . . *The New York Times* reports that more than 300 Egyptian pilots are undergoing an intensive one-year training program in the Soviet Union.	Widespread strikes bring the economy of Uruguay to a virtual standstill.	U.S. troops inflict heavy casualties on Communist troops around Khesanh.
June 19	U.N. Security Council adopts a resolution welcoming pledges from the U.S., the Soviet Union and Britain to act "immediately" through the Council in the event of a nuclear attack or threat of such an attack on non-nuclear weapon states.				South Vietnamese Pres. Nguyen Van Thieu signs a general mobilization measure.
June 20		Warsaw Pact troops hold joint military exercises in Czechoslovakia. . . . Britain withdraws from a project for the construction of the world's largest atom smasher because of financial reasons. . . . West German leaders pledge to continue the policy of seeking closer relations with East Europe despite East Germany's latest restrictions on travel to Berlin.		Reports indicate that Guatemala has lifted the nationwide state of siege in effect since March 18. . . . Brazilian students seize a building on the University of Rio de Janeiro campus to protest poor education facilities and alleged U.S. interference in Brazilian education programs.	U.S. reports that American combat deaths in Vietnam have risen over 25,000.
June 21		West Germany bars an official East German delegation from crossing into Bavaria in its first retaliatory action since the start of the latest Berlin dispute. . . . Rival electoral campaign workers clash in Paris' Latin Quarter.		Brazilian students roam Rio streets hurling rocks at police and buildings. One policeman is reported killed.	
June 22			Israeli Premier Levi Eshkol declares that the Jordan River must remain Israel's "security border."	Brazilian police arrest 200 demonstrating students in Brasilia.	Communist forces maul a South Vietnamese battalion outside of Saigon.
June 23		Gaullist candidates run extemely well in the first round of voting for the French National Assembly.	Israel and Jordan trade artillery fire across the Jordan River. . . . Israel and Egypt fight an 85-minute artillery duel across the Suez Canal.	Brazilian authorities suspend classes at the Univ. of Rio de Janeiro.	U.S. planes bomb the southern panhandle of North Vietnam.
June 24		A North Vietnames delegation arrives in Moscow for talks. . . . NATO officials meet in Iceland.		About 1,000 Quebec separatists riot in Montreal against the presence of P.M. Pierre Trudeau at the St. Jean Baptiste Day parade. . . . Five hundred Brazilian teachers and clergymen sign a petition condemning police violence against students.	*Baltimore Sun* reports that the U.S. is withdrawing from Khesanh.
June 25		Sen. Giovanni Leone is sworn in as premier of a minority Christian Democratic government in Italy. . . . NATO officials of the North Atlantic Council warn of Soviet penetration in the Mediterranean.		Canada's Liberal Party led by P.M. Pierre Trudeau wins a decisive victory. . . . About 150 Brazilian professors and priests picket the Education Ministry in Rio in support of student demands.	*The New York Times* reports that slightly more than half of the members of the 1965 Central Committee of the Chinese CP have been purged. . . . Communist forces down two U.S. helicopters near Saigon.
	A	**B**	**C**	**D**	**E**
	Includes developments that affect more than one world region, international organizations and important meetings of major world leaders.	*Includes all domestic and regional developments in Europe, including the Soviet Union, Turkey, Cyprus and Malta.*	*Includes all domestic and regional developments in Africa and the Middle East, including Iraq and Iran and excluding Cyprus, Turkey and Afghanistan.*	*Includes all domestic and regional developments in Latin America, the Caribbean and Canada.*	*Includes all domestic and regional developments in Asia and Pacific nations, extending from Afghanistan through all the Pacific Islands, except Hawaii.*

U.S. Politics & Social Issues	U.S. Foreign Policy & Defense	U.S. Economy & Environment	Science, Technology & Nature	Culture, Leisure & Life Style	
Sen. Eugene McCarthy wins at least 52 of N.Y.'s 123 elected delegates in the state's Democratic primary. . . . U.S. Supreme Court rules that racial discrimination is illegal in all sales and rentals of residential and other property.			Soviet Union launches Cosmos 227.		June 18
Pres. Johnson signs the omnibus crime bill. . . . American Civil Liberties Union announces that Los Angeles attorney Russell Parsons will defend Robert Kennedy's assassin Sirhan Sirhan.	U.S. State Dept. reports no progress in the negotiations for the release of the U.S. ship *Pueblo.*			N.Y.C. Hunter College audience jeers chief Rabbi of Moscow Yehuda Levin when he denies that there is no widespread anti-Semitism in the Soviet Union.	June 19
Washington police arrest demonstrators blocking the entrance of the Agriculture Department.		House passes a bill combining a 10% tax surcharge and a $6 billion cut in federal spending.			June 20
More than 300 protesters march outside of the Agriculture Dept. in Washington, D.C.		Senate passes a bill combining a 10% tax surcharge and a $6 billion cut in federal spending.	Soviet Union launches Cosmos 228.		June 21
V.P. Humphrey and Sen. Eugene McCarthy appear separately before the Democratic Party convention in St Paul, Minn.					June 22
Sen. Eugene McCarthy announces that he plans to meet with North Vietnamese officials in Paris. . . . Minnesota Democratic Party rejects a McCarthy plank calling for the complete halt to the bombing of North Vietnam. . . . Negro youths shoot a white visitor in the knee and rob four others at the Poor People's Campaign shantytown. . . . Interior Dept.'s permit for the Poor People's Campaign shantytown expires.				*Inadmissible Evidence,* a film based on John Osborne's play, opens in New York.	June 23
House passes a bill making it a federal crime to desecrate the U.S. flag. . . . Pres. Johnson asks Congress to require the licensing of every privately owned gun. . . . Washington police arrest 124 residents of the Poor People's Campaign shanty town when they refuse to leave the campsite.				Pope Paul appeals to both sides in Vietnam to accept a truce. . . . Dr. Hattie Alexander, the developer of a treatment for children's meningitis, dies in New York at 67. . . .	June 24
Civil rights activist the Rev. Ralph Abernathy is sentenced to 20 days in jail for leading on unlawful assembly at the foot of Capitol Hill.				Francois Truffaut's film *The Bride Wore Black* opens in New York.	June 25

F	G	H	I	J
Includes elections, federal-state relations, civil rights and liberties, crime, the judiciary, education, health care, poverty, urban affairs and population.	*Includes formation and debate of U.S. foreign and defense policies, veterans' affairs and defense spending. (Relations with specific foreign countries are usually found under the region concerned.)*	*Includes business, labor, agriculture, taxation, transportation, consumer affairs, monetary and fiscal policy, natural resources, and pollution.*	*Includes worldwide scientific, medical and technological developments, natural phenomena, U.S. weather, natural disasters, and accidents.*	*Includes the arts, religion, scholarship, communications media, sports, entertainment, fashions, fads and social life.*

	World Affairs	Europe	Africa & the Middle East	The Americas	Asia & the Pacific
June 26		Reports from Paris indicate that France has agreed to deliver 25 disassembled planes to Israel despite its arms embargo on the Middle East confrontation states. . . . Yugoslav Pres. Tito warns that further purges may take place in the country's CP.		About 10,000 protesters demonstrate against the Brazilian government in Rio. . . . Uruguay freezes all prices and wages except for salaries of public officials.	U.S. troops take a heavy toll of North Vietnamese forces around the Demilitarized Zone.
June 27		Soviet authorities liberalize divorce procedures. . . . Soviet Union says that it is ready to discuss arms control measures with the U.S.	Twelve Soviet technicians arrive in Ghana to resume work on Soviet projects.	Argentine police and students clash on the eve of the second anniversary of the military coup which brought the Ongania government to power.	U.S. command in South Vietnam confirms that U.S. troops are withdrawing from Khesanh.
June 28	U.N. Middle East peace envoy meets with Soviet Premier Aleksei Kosygin in Moscow.		An Israeli patrol reports repulsing an Arab guerrilla unit crossing the Jordan River.	Bomb explode outside of three government buildings in Buenos Aires but cause no injuries.	Reports from Washington indicate that Communist China has barred use of its rail lines to ship war supplies to North Vietnam in recent days.
June 29		French Pres. de Gaulle asks voters to give him a decisive victory in the June 30 national elections.			South Vietnamese troops find huge quantities of Communist weapons and ammunition outside of Saigon.
June 30		Dr. Kristjan Eldjarn, who campaigned on an anti-NATO platform, is elected president of Iceland. . . . Soviet Union forces down a U.S. airliner over or near the Kurile Islands north of Japan. . . . Warsaw Pact troop exercises end in Czechoslovakia but Soviet forces remain on Czech soil. . . . Gaullist candidates win a smashing victory in the final round of voting for the French National Assembly.			
July 1	Sixty-two nations sign the nuclear nonproliferation treaty. . . . 18 member nations of the General Agreement on Tariffs and Trade (GATT) carry out tariff reductions with the exception of France which imposes temporary import quotas.	Soviet Union issues a nine-point disarmament and arms control plan.		Cuba publishes the text of guerrilla leader Che Guevara's diary. . . . Canadian free medical service goes into effect. . . . In response to government demands for Mexican equity in all foreign firms, a U.S. subsidiary, General Electric de Mexico, puts 10% of its stock on public sale to Mexicans.	Reports indicate that Communist China has refused a U.N. invitation to attend a U.N. conference in Geneva. . . . U.S. troops inflict heavy casualties on Communist troops around Khesanh.
July 2		Soviet Union releases the U.S. airliner forced down on June 30 after the U.S. acknowledged that the plane inadvertently violated Soviet airspace. . . . British Treasury reports that Britain's foreign exchange and gold reserves fell by $62.4 million in June.	Nigeria denies Biafran charges that it is blocking food and medicine shipments to Biafra.	Widespread strikes bring the economy of Uruguay to a virtual standstill.	U.S. and North Vietnamese troops clash below the demilitarized zone.
July 3		At the Paris peace talks, North Vietnam confirms that it intends to release three captured U.S. pilots.	Nigeria turns down a British offer of emergency relief aid because of London's alleged backing of Biafra. . . . British director of famine relief Leslie Kirkley reports from Biafra that about 400 children are dying every day of starvation. . . . Reports indicate that Egyptian Pres. Mahmoud Riad has said "We recognize the realities and one of the realities is Israel. Now we want peace."		U.S. troops discover hidden Soviet and Communist Chinese rockets near Saigon.
July 4		France announces the successful testing of two new long-range ballistic missiles. . . . A Soviet-North Vietnamese communique says that the Soviet Union will continue to provide military support to North Vietnam. . . . Egyptian Pres. Nasser arrives in the Soviet Union for talks on the Middle East.	Rhodesian government dismisses Internal Affairs Min. William Harper, a leader of the right-wing opposition.		

A	B	C	D	E
Includes developments that affect more than one world region, international organizations and important meetings of major world leaders.	Includes all domestic and regional developments in Europe, including the Soviet Union, Turkey, Cyprus and Malta.	Includes all domestic and regional developments in Africa and the Middle East, including Iraq and Iran and excluding Cyprus, Turkey and Afghanistan.	Includes all domestic and regional developments in Latin America, the Caribbean and Canada.	Includes all domestic and regional developments in Asia and Pacific nations, extending from Afghanistan through all the Pacific Islands, except Hawaii.

U.S. Politics & Social Issues	U.S. Foreign Policy & Defense	U.S. Economy & Environment	Science, Technology & Nature	Culture, Leisure & Life Style	
U.S. officials impound the mules of the Poor People's Campaign caravan on the grounds that they are not being properly cared for. . . . Pres. Johnson announces the resignation of Supreme Court Chief Justice Earl Warren.			Soviet Union launches Cosmos 229.	Marcel Breuer wins the 1968 Gold Medal of the American Institute of Architects.	June 26
Pres. Johnson asks Congress to approve a constitutional amendment to lower the voting age to 18.				Harcourt, Brace & World publishes Mikhail Bulgakov's *The Heart of a Dog.*	June 27
Backers of Sen. Eugene McCarthy walk out of a N.Y. Democratic State Committee meeting over a dispute about at-large delegates.			U.S. conducts an underground nuclear test in Nevada.	Knopf publishes John Hersey's *The Algiers Motel Incident.* . . . Putnam publishes William Buckley's *The Jeweler's Eye.*	June 28
Sen. Eugene McCarthy protests "arbitrary actions" denying him "a fair distribution" of delegates in many states.	Pres. Johnson declares that it is time to begin talks on limiting offensive and defensive nuclear weapons.				June 29
Sen. Eugene McCarthy says that it is conceivable that he could back N.Y. Gov. Nelson Rockefeller for the presidency over V.P. Humphrey.					June 30
	Pres. Johnson announces that the U.S. and the Soviet Union have agreed to begin talks on limiting and reducing their arsenals of offensive and defensive nuclear weapons. . . . U.S. calls on the Soviet Union to release the American plane downed on June 30.		Soviet Union conducts an underground nuclear test in Central Asia.	Psychologist Edwin Boring dies in Cambridge, Mass. at 81. . . . Random House publishes David Kraslow's and Stuart Loory's *The Secret Search for Peace in Vietnam.*	July 1
Key Congressional figure Rep. Carl Albert (D, Okla.) states his opposition to all major gun control bills.	*The New York Times* reports that Japanese radar indicates that the U.S. plane forced down by the Soviet Union because of an alleged overflight of Soviet territory was intercepted over international waters. . . . U.S. expresses regret over the violation of Soviet airspace by a U.S. plane on June 30.		Anthropologist Dr. Elwyn Simons announces the discovery of a five to 10 million-year-old hominid's jaw in India.	*Ramparts* magazine publishes the text of Cuban guerrilla leader Che Guevara's diary.	July 2
Pres. Johnson, citing a sniper slaying in New York's Central Park earlier in the day, calls for gun control legislation.					July 3
Calif. Gov. Ronald Reagan says that many U.S. citizens carry guns "because they have lost faith in (the) government's ability to protect them." . . . Antiwar demonstrators heckle V.P. Humphrey during a speech in Philadelphia.			U.S. launches a radio astronomy satellite.	Beacon Press publishes William Styron's *The Confessions of Nat Turner.*	July 4

F	G	H	I	J
Includes elections, federal-state relations, civil rights and liberties, crime, the judiciary, education, health care, poverty, urban affairs and population.	Includes formation and debate of U.S. foreign and defense policies, veterans' affairs and defense spending. (Relations with specific foreign countries are usually found under the region concerned.)	Includes business, labor, agriculture, taxation, transportation, consumer affairs, monetary and fiscal policy, natural resources, and pollution.	Includes worldwide scientific, medical and technological developments, natural phenomena, U.S. weather, natural disasters, and accidents.	Includes the arts, religion, scholarship, communications media, sports, entertainment, fashions, fads and social life.

	World Affairs	Europe	Africa & the Middle East	The Americas	Asia & the Pacific
July 5			Nigeria warns relief agencies that unauthorized flights over its territory will be shot down. . . . Israeli officials say that they will never agree to the return of U.N. forces in the absence of a peace treaty between Egypt and Israel.		U.S. Marines fight a day-long battle near Giolinh.
July 6	U.N. Secy. Gen. U Thant confers with U.S. and North Vietnamese officials in Paris.		Jordan strips eight Arab judicial officials of their civil service status for cooperating with Israeli authorities in the West Bank. . . . Egyptian government spokesman Mohammed el-Zayyat says that Egypt would be willing to permit the return of U.N. peace-keeping forces to Egyptian territory once Israel has given back the areas conquered in 1967.	Pres. Johnson meets with the presidents of five Central American countries in El Salvador.	South Vietnam warns that it will not accept an unconditional cease-fire.
July 7		European central banks meet in Basel to discuss a proposed loan to Britain.	Egyptian government spokesman Mohammed el-Zayyat denies that Egypt is ready to recognize Israel. . . . Tanzanian Pres. Julius Nyerere promises to accelerate the country's drive towards socialism.	Pres. Johnson tours El Salvador.	France resumes its nuclear testing program in the Pacific. . . . A U.S. Navy spokesman discloses that allied forces have intensified their patrols on the Saigon River. . . . Japanese Liberal-Democratic Party maintains its majority in the House of Councilors in a vote which is interpreted as a rebuff of the Socialist party's anti-American platform.
July 8	In the U.N. Security Council, Cambodia claims that two U.S. helicopters bombed a rice field just inside Cambodia on June 29. . . . U.N. Middle East peace envoy Gunnar Jarring meets with Israeli and Arab representatives in London.	Britain announces that it has been given a major credit by 12 central banks. . . . Greek military junta sentences three naval officers to prison for allegedly plotting to overthrow the government. . . . Czechoslovakia decides not to attend the upcoming meeting of communist countries in Warsaw.	Diplomatic sources in Cairo say that Egypt would be willing to permit Israeli cargo vessels to use the Suez Canal if Israeli troops pull back from the East Bank of the canal.		U.S. forces fight three sharp engagements near Saigon.
July 9	U.N. Middle East peace envoy Gunnar Jarring continues discussions with Israeli and Arab representatives in London.	Polish Communist ideologist Zenon Kliszko calls for an end to the anti-Zionist campaign. . . . Director of Poland's anti-Semitic campaign Lt. Gen. Mieczyslaw is appointed to the Polish Politburo. . . . A U.S. newspaper, the international *Herald Tribune*, goes on sale for the first time in forty years in Moscow.	Israel reports the killing of four Arab guerrillas. . . . Reports indicate that only 1,000 Arabs to date have decided to accept the Israeli proposal for visits to the West Bank of the Jordan River.	Leaders of Quebec's three major separatist groups fail to agree on merger plans. . . . Six South American countries of the Andean Group meet to discuss plans for greater economic integration.	U.S. Marines capture an arms supply dump north of Conthien.
July 10	U.N. Middle East peace envoy Gunnar Jarring meets with U.N. Secy. Gen. U Thant in Geneva.	British House of Commons passes a bill outlawing racial discrimination by a vote of 182-44. . . . Pres. Charles de Gaulle appoints Maurice Jacques Couve de Murville to replace Georges Pompidou as prime minister of France. . . . At the Paris peace talks, both sides report no progress. . . . Egyptian Pres. Gamal Nasser leaves the Soviet Union after extensive talks on the Middle East.	U.N. Truce Organization asserts that Egypt initiated hostilities during a recent Egyptian-Israeli artillery exchange.		South Vietnamese Pres. Nguyen Van Thieu says that the U.S. may be able to begin to withdraw soldiers in 1969. . . . South Vietnamese troops throw back about 200 Viet Cong trying to penetrate Saigon's outer defenses.
July 11		Greek military junta makes public a constitution designed to facilitate a return civilian rule. . . . Soviet P.M. Aleksei Kosygin arrives in Sweden for a state visit. . . . French National Assembly re-elects Jacques Chaban-Delmas as its president. . . . Soviet newspaper *Pravda* draws a parallel between the "counter-revolutionaries" in Czechoslovakia and those accused of the same charge in Hungary during 1956.			U.S. Marines clash with North Vietnamese troops near Conthien.

A	B	C	D	E
Includes developments that affect more than one world region, international organizations and important meetings of major world leaders.	Includes all domestic and regional developments in Europe, including the Soviet Union, Turkey, Cyprus and Malta.	Includes all domestic and regional developments in Africa and the Middle East, including Iraq and Iran and excluding Cyprus, Turkey and Afghanistan.	Includes all domestic and regional developments in Latin America, the Caribbean and Canada.	Includes all domestic and regional developments in Asia and Pacific nations, extending from Afghanistan through all the Pacific Islands, except Hawaii.

U.S. Politics & Social Issues	U.S. Foreign Policy & Defense	U.S. Economy & Environment	Science, Technology & Nature	Culture, Leisure & Life Style	
			Soviet Union launches Cosmos 230.	Doubleday publishes Robert Graves' translation of *The Rubaiyyat of Omar Khayaam*.	July 5
	Defense Dept. announces that it has agreed to sell additional batteries of Hawk anti-aircraft missiles to Israel.				July 6
Pres. Johnson signs a bill making it a federal crime to desecrate the U.S. flag. . . . Sen. Eugene McCarthy cancels his plans to meet with North Vietnamese officials in Paris.	Former V.P. Nixon says that the economic blockade of Cuba must be tightened.				July 7
	Rumania and the U.S. agree to expand contacts in the fields of science and technology.			Atheneum publishes Hugh Sidey's *A Very Personal Presidency*.	July 8
Former V.P. Nixon says that a manditory jail sentence should be given to any felon using a gun while engaging in any serious federal crime. . . . House Rules Committee approves Pres. Johnson's bill to ban mail order sales of rifles and ammunition.				Random House publishes Jean Lacouture's *Ho Chi Minh*. . . . Atheneum publishes Anthony Storr's *Human Agression*.	July 9
Senate Judiciary Committee blocks gun control legislation. . . . Pediatrician Dr. Benjamin Spock is given a two-year sentence for conspiring to aid, abet and counsel men to avoid the draft.	Sen. Eugene McCarthy advocates delaying the deployment of the Sentinel missile defense system.		Soviet Union launches Cosmos 231.		July 10
	Pres. Johnson appeales to Nigerian and Biafran authorities to allow food supplies to be delivered. . . . Defense Secy. Clark Clifford says that the Communists may be preparing a new series of attacks in South Vietnam during the current lull in battle activity.		U.S. launches a satellite whose mission is to record atmospheric densities.		July 11

F	G	H	I	J
Includes elections, federal-state relations, civil rights and liberties, crime, the judiciary, education, health care, poverty, urban affairs and population.	Includes formation and debate of U.S. foreign and defense policies, veterans' affairs and defense spending. (Relations with specific foreign countries are usually found under the region concerned.)	Includes business, labor, agriculture, taxation, transportation, consumer affairs, monetary and fiscal policy, natural resources, and pollution.	Includes worldwide scientific, medical and technological developments, natural phenomena, U.S. weather, natural disasters, and accidents.	Includes the arts, religion, scholarship, communications media, sports, entertainment, fashions, fads and social life.

	World Affairs	Europe	Africa & the Middle East	The Americas	Asia & the Pacific
July 12		Egyptian Pres. Nasser confers with Yugoslav Pres. Tito in Belgrade.	Reports from Washington indicate that U.S. officials blame both Nigerian and Biafran authorities for the deadlock in transporting food. . . . Nigeria announces that it is willing to open a land corridor into Biafra for food transport.		
July 13	U.N. Secy. Gen. U Thant says that he is confident that North Vietnam will make a "definite move towards peace" if the U.S. stops the bombing of North Vietnam.	Greek military junta arrests former P.M. Constantine Kollias.			
July 14		Soviet Union and four East European countries meet in a hastily convoked conference in Warsaw. . . . Sweden and the Soviet Union issue a joint communique calling for the end of the U.S. bombing of North Vietnam. . . . Greek military junta issues a decree permitting the government to proclaim a civil mobilization at any time.			Defense Secy. Clark Clifford arrives in South Vietnam for a visit. . . . South Vietnamese troops find Communist arms caches near Saigon.
July 15		U.S. Sixth Fleet arrives in Istanbul. . . . Czech Lt. Gen. Vaclav Prchlik calls for a rotation of the top command of the Warsaw Pact forces which would include non-Soviet figures. . . . British House of Commons votes 298-242 to impose stricter sanctions on Rhodesia.	Ruling Rhodesian Front Party backs P.M. Ian Smith's government by a vote of 95-2. . . . U.S. Amb.-to-U.N. George Ball gives Israeli Premier Levi Eshkol a letter from Pres. Johnson urging Israel to undertake indirect negotiations with the Arabs.	The New York Times says that Cuban guerrilla leader Che Guevara was betrayed by a Soviet spy working within his group.	France conducts an atmospheric test in the Pacific.
July 16	U.N. Disarmament Committee reconvenes in Geneva.	Soviet Union and four Eastern European countries warn Czechoslovakia that its liberalization drive is "completely unacceptable.". . . Anti-U.S. demonstrations take place in Istanbul.		U.S. Amb.-to-U.N. George Ball makes a helicopter tour of the Golan Heights.	Allied forces repulse a Communist attack 50 miles from Saigon.
July 17		Longest session to date four-and-a-half hours--takes place at the Paris peace conference but neither side reports any progress.	Ruling Rhodesian Front Party recommends that Rhodesia declare itself a republic. . . . A military coup overthrows the government of Iraqi Pres. Abdel Rahman Arif. . . . Israeli authorities lift a curfew for the West Bank of the Jordan River in force since the June 1967 war. . . . Israel reports killing 17 Arab guerrillas near the Dead Sea. . . . After two-and-a-half years of military rule, Dahomey returns to civilian government.	Widespread strikes bring the economy of Uruguay to a virtual standstill.	Defense Secy. Clark Clifford says that he expects a major enemy offensive in Vietnam within two months. . . . Cambodian forces seize a U.S. patrol boat just on the Cambodian side of the border with South Vietnam.
July 18		Czechoslovak CP First Secy. Alexander Dubcek appeals to the Czechoslovak people to rally around the government's liberal elements. . . . Belgium Parliament votes to stop all further arms deliveries to Nigeria. . . . Turkish demonstrators rough up U.S. servicemen in Ankara.	Biafran leader Lt. Col. Chukwuemeka Ojukwu says that he would agree to land routes into Biafra for emergency food shipments but that an airlift is the only way to save millions of lives.		South Vietnamese Pres. Thieu says that he is not going to the upcoming conference with Pres. Johnson in Hawaii "to surrender to the Communists.". . . U.S. planes bomb North Vietnamese surface-to-air-missile sites for the first time.
July 19	GATT nations criticize France for not consulting with its trading partners before imposing temporary import quotas.	Soviet Union issues a summons to the Czechoslovak Presidium to meet with the Soviet Politburo in Russia.	Israel reports killing one Arab guerrilla in the Jordan Valley. . . . Representatives of Nigeria and Biafra meet in Niger and agree to hold peace talks in Ethiopia. . . . Rhodesia says that a South African policeman has been killed in the latest guerrilla attack.	Bolivian Interior Min. Antonio Arguedas crosses into Chile and asks for political asylum.	
July 20		Latest deadline for the withdrawal of Soviet troops from Czech soil passes with Soviet forces still in place.	Representatives of Nigeria and Biafra continue exploratory talks in Niger. . . . Biafran government reports wide-spread starvation in its territory.	Clashes between Bolivian police and protestors leave a military officer dead.	
	A	B	C	D	E
	Includes developments that affect more than one world region, international organizations and important meetings of major world leaders.	Includes all domestic and regional developments in Europe, including the Soviet Union, Turkey, Cyprus and Malta.	Includes all domestic and regional developments in Africa and the Middle East, including Iraq and Iran and excluding Cyprus, Turkey and Afghanistan.	Includes all domestic and regional developments in Latin America, the Caribbean and Canada.	Includes all domestic and regional developments in Asia and Pacific nations, extending from Afghanistan through all the Pacific Islands, except Hawaii.

U.S. Politics & Social Issues	U.S. Foreign Policy & Defense	U.S. Economy & Environment	Science, Technology & Nature	Culture, Leisure & Life Style	
	U.S. announces that it is donating $1.3 million worth of food to the victims of the Nigerian civil war. . . . V.P. Humphrey says that the U.S. should redefine its national interest which "does not run to maintaining the status quo wherever it is challenged."				July 12
	N.Y. Gov. Nelson Rockefeller proposes a Vietnam peace plan.				July 13
				World Council of Churches says that it is trying to organize charter flights to Biafra with emergency food provisions.	July 14
		First direct airline service between the U.S. and the Soviet Union opens.		Atheneum publishes Jean-Jacques Servan Schreiber's *The American Challenge*. . . . World Council of Churches votes to raise more money for its relief activities in Nigeria and Biafra.	July 15
Supreme Court Justice Abe Fortas begins testimony before the Senate Judiciary Committee.			Soviet Union launches Cosmos 232.	Atlantic-Little, Brown publishes Robert Gittings's *John Keats*. . . . World Council of Churches Fourth Assembly supports the right of individuals to refuse to participate in "particular wars" on grounds of conscience.	July 16
Supreme Court Justice Abe Fortas admits that he has defended the administration's Vietnam Policy in talks with important civic leaders.	Sen. Eugene McCarthy says that the OAS trade embargo of Cuba should be phased out.				July 17
Former Pres. Dwight Eisenhower endorses Richard Nixon for the Republican presidential nomination.	Defense Secy. Clark Clifford denies a report that he has persuaded South Vietnamese Pres. Thieu to agree to a complete halt to the bombing of North Vietnam.		Soviet Union launches Cosmos 233.	Nobel Prize winner Dr. Corneille Jean Francois Heymans dies in Knokke, Belgium at 76.	July 18
House rejects a proposal to license guns by a vote of 172-68.	Pres. Johnson confers with South Vietnamese Pres. Nguyen Van Thieu in Honolulu. . . . U.S. State Dept. says that it has apologized for the U.S. patrol boat intrusion into Cambodian waters on July 17.			Atheneum publishes Harold Nicolson's *The Later Years, 1945-1962*.	July 19
Vice Pres. Humphrey and Sen. Eugene McCarthy agree to a nationally televised debate.	Calif. Gov. Ronald Reagan says that the US's national interest is at stake in Vietnam.			U.S. banker and historian Bray Hammond dies in Thetford, Vt. at 81.	July 20

F	G	H	I	J
Includes elections, federal-state relations, civil rights and liberties, crime, the judiciary, education, health care, poverty, urban affairs and population.	*Includes formation and debate of U.S. foreign and defense policies, veterans' affairs and defense spending. (Relations with specific foreign countries are usually found under the region concerned.)*	*Includes business, labor, agriculture, taxation, transportation, consumer affairs, monetary and fiscal policy, natural resources, and pollution.*	*Includes worldwide scientific, medical and technological developments, natural phenomena, U.S. weather, natural disasters, and accidents.*	*Includes the arts, religion, scholarship, communications media, sports, entertainment, fashions, fads and social life.*

	World Affairs	Europe	Africa & the Middle East	The Americas	Asia & the Pacific
July 21		Reports from Prague indicate that the Soviet Union has renewed its demand that Czechoslovakia allow the stationing of Warsaw Pact troops along its border area with West Germany.	Iraqi Foreign Min. Nasser el-Hani says that Iraq will not resume relations with the U.S. . . . Reports indicate that Nigeria and Biafra have agreed upon an agenda for their peace talks.	A Chilean official says that Bolivian Interior Min. Antonio Arguedas has admitted giving photostats of the Che Guevara diary to Cuban agents in Bolivia.	Viet Cong terrorist bombs kill eight civilians outside movie theaters in Saigon.
July 22	Soviet physicist Andrei Sakharov foresees a convergence of the Soviet and American political systems. . . . Reports indicate that a heavy concentration of Soviet troops has been sighted near the Czechoslovak border in Poland. . . . French National Assembly votes a general amnesty for all convicted persons or fugitives in the Algerian war. . . . In a dramatic reversal of its position, the Soviet Politburo agrees to meet with the Czechoslovak Presidium in Czechoslovakia. . . . Bulgaria reports that the Albanian ambassador has been expelled.		Biafra reportedly has denied that agreement has been reached on an agenda for peace talks. . . . Iraqi Foreign Min. Nasser el-Hani says that agreements with a French oil firm are still in force despite the July 17 coup. . . . Israel reports killing six Arab guerrillas in the Jordan Valley. . . . Rhodesian P.M. Ian Smith thanks tribal leaders for their help in combatting guerrilla infiltration from Zambia.	Bolivian Pres. Rene Barrientos declares Bolivia to be under a state of siege because of recent protests.	Upon his return to South Vietnam, South Vietnamese Pres. Thieu says that the Honolulu Conference produced no major policy changes. . . . Viet Cong terrorist bomb kills four civilians in a Saigon cafe.
July 23	Soviet Defense Ministry announces that it will conduct major troop maneuvers near the Czechoslovak border. . . . Britain highest court, the Privy Council, rules unanimously that Rhodesia's 1965 declaration of independence is illegal. . . . London Times reports that Professor G. Petrovic, editor of the Zagreb review Praxis, has been expelled from the Yugoslav CP for supporting left-wing students.		Three Arab guerrillas hijack an Israeli commercial airliner and force it to land in Algeria.		
July 24		House of Commons votes, 244-52, to censure Laborite member Tam Dalyell for "gross contempt of the House" for leaking secret information on Britain's germ warfare research program to the British newspaper, The Observer. . . . At the Paris peace talks, U.S. negotiator W. Averell Harriman calls on North Vietnam to recognize that the government of South Vietnam must play a part in any peace settlement. . . . Students and police clash in Istanbul. . . . Soviet Union grants a $66 million credit to Pakistan.	Egyptian Pres. Nasser confirms rumors that he is in poor health and that he will soon go to the Soviet Union for medical treatment.	Chile grants asylum to Bolivian Interior Min. Antonio Arguedas.	
July 25	Jordan complains to U.N. Secy. Gen. U Thant that Israel is planning to deport 50,000 inhabitants of the Gaza Strip.	Czech Presidium removes anti-Soviet Lt. Gen. Vaclav Prchlik in a concession to the Soviet Union. . . . Clashes continue between students and police in Istanbul.		Bolivian Pres. Rene Barrientos' cabinet resigns after the Social Democratic Party withdraws its two cabinet members.	U.S. reports 157 U.S. combat deaths for the period of July 14-20 in Vietnam.
July 26	Israeli mission to the U.N. denies that its government is trying to pressure Gaza Strip inhabitants into leaving.	Czechoslovak liberal weekly Literarni Listy publishes a lengthy petition supporting the Czech liberalization movement.	Egyptian Pres. Nasser flies to the Soviet Union. . . . Rhodesian P.M. Ian Smith begins talks with South African P.M. Balthazar Vorster in Pretoria, South Africa. . . . Preliminary peace talks between Nigeria and Biafra end with little sign of progress.	Students and police clash in Mexico City.	A Viet Cong terrorist bomb blows up the plant of the Chinese newspaper A Chau in Saigon.
July 27		Moscow newspapers say that the Soviet Air Force has joined the current war games.	Rhodesian P.M. Ian Smith ends talks with South African P.M. Balthazar Vorster in Pretoria, South Africa. . . . South Yemeni dissident forces cut their country's main road.	Bolivian Pres. Rene Barrientos names an all-military cabinet as a "temporary emergency measure."	U.S. planes bomb Communist forces near the Cambodian border.
July 28		Ninth World Youth Festival opens in Bulgaria.	South Yemen says that an armed revolt has broken out against the government.		

A	B	C	D	E
Includes developments that affect more than one world region, international organizations and important meetings of major world leaders.	Includes all domestic and regional developments in Europe, including the Soviet Union, Turkey, Cyprus and Malta.	Includes all domestic and regional developments in Africa and the Middle East, including Iraq and Iran and excluding Cyprus, Turkey and Afghanistan.	Includes all domestic and regional developments in Latin America, the Caribbean and Canada.	Includes all domestic and regional developments in Asia and Pacific nations, extending from Afghanistan through all the Pacific Islands, except Hawaii.

U.S. Politics & Social Issues	U.S. Foreign Policy & Defense	U.S. Economy & Environment	Science, Technology & Nature	Culture, Leisure & Life Style	
		Administration urges "utmost restraint" in wage and price decisions by business and labor.		Pope Paul confirms that the Vatican is sending food relief to Biafra. . . . German conductor Joseph Keilberth dies in Munich at 60.	July 21
					July 22
A small band of black nationalists gun down three policemen in Cleveland. . . . United Auto Workers and International Brotherhood of Teamsters forms an alliance. . . . Sen. Eugene McCarthy accuses the Johnson administration of being "inflexible" on Vietnam.	Pres. Johnson defends his Vietnam policy at the Governors Conference in Cincinnati.			Paul Almond's film *Isabel* opens in New York.	July 23
Negro Mayor Carl Stokes of Cleveland confers with local Negro leaders about recent racial disorders. . . . House passes a bill banning the interstate mail order sale of guns.		U.S. Treasury says that total U.S. monetary reserves dropped $285 million in June.			July 24
Cleveland Negro Mayor Carl Stokes sends National Guardsmen back into Negro neighborhoods in the midst of continued looting.	N.Y. Gov Nelson Rockefeller says that the long-term foreign policy goal of the U.S. should be to shift "from a relationship of conflict to one of cooperation with the Soviet Union."				July 25
Black militant Ahmed Evans is arraigned in Cleveland and charged with the July 23 slaying of three Cleveland policemen. . . . Sen. Edward Kennedy announces that he will not accept the Democratic vice presidential nomination.					July 26
Cleveland Negro Mayor Carl Stokes says that the July 23 slayings of three Cleveland policemen was a premeditated attack. . . . Violence breaks out in Gary, Ind. after two policemen try to arrest two Negro rape suspects.					July 27
Negro Mayor Richard Hatcher orders a curfew in Gary, Ind. as looting and arson spread.				German chemist Dr. Otto Hahn, the discoverer of nuclear fission, dies in Gottingen, Germany at 89.	July 28
F	G	H	I	J	
Includes elections, federal-state relations, civil rights and liberties, crime, the judiciary, education, health care, poverty, urban affairs and population.	Includes formation and debate of U.S. foreign and defense policies, veterans' affairs and defense spending. (Relations with specific foreign countries are usually found under the region concerned.)	Includes business, labor, agriculture, taxation, transportation, consumer affairs, monetary and fiscal policy, natural resources, and pollution.	Includes worldwide scientific, medical and technological developments, natural phenomena, U.S. weather, natural disasters, and accidents.	Includes the arts, religion, scholarship, communications media, sports, entertainment, fashions, fads and social life.	

	World Affairs	Europe	Africa & the Middle East	The Americas	Asia & the Pacific
July 29		Soviet Politburo and the Czechoslovak Presidium meet in Cierna, Czechoslovakia near the Soviet border.	Nigerian government announces that it has captured the Biafran divisional headquarters of Ahoada. . . . Jordan forbids Arab refugees from the Gaza Strip from moving to Jordan on the grounds that it would ease Israel's occupation burdens and strain the Jordanian economy. . . . International Red Cross cancels its food emergency flights to Biafra because of technical difficulties in arranging for landings.	In Brazil a spokesman for Cardinal Jaime DeBarros Camara of Rio de Janeiro says that the recent papal decision on birth control must be accepted. . . . Mt. Arena, a volcano, erupts in Costa Rica.	
July 30		Reports indicate that Czech Pres. Ludvig Svoboda has made an impassioned defense of his country's liberalization program before officials from other communist countries.	Reports indicate that South Yemen has declared a general mobilization to fight the current insurgency movement.	Violent clashes take place between students, police and federal troops in Mexico City.	
July 31	UNESCO approves a policy under which it will grant funds for birth control projects.	Reports indicate that the Soviets have tried to split the Czechoslovak delegation between conservatives and liberals. . . . At the Paris peace talks, North Vietnam rejects State Secy. Rusk's call for North Vietnamese restraint in exchange for a complete halt to the bombing of North Vietnam. . . . France issues a statement of support for Biafra by calling for self-determination.	Reports indicate that left-wing elements have gained the upper hand in the Iraqi government.	Mexico City Mayor Alfonso Corona del Rosal orders the withdrawal of troops from the National University of Mexico.	
Aug. 1		Bulgarian plainclothesmen assault Western journalists taking pictures of Maoist followers at the ninth World Youth Festival in Bulgaria. . . . Talks between Czechoslovakia, the Soviet Union and four other Communist countries end in Cierna, Czechoslovakia.	Congolese (Brazzaville) Pres. Alphonse Massamba-Debat dissolves the National Assembly. . . . Rhodesian security forces kill nine African guerrillas.	About 50,000 students stage a peaceful march in Mexico City.	U.S. combat reinforcements push U.S. troop totals to 541,000.
Aug. 2	U.N. Secy. Gen. U Thant charges that Israel has prevented the dispatch of a U.N. fact-finding mission to the Middle East by demanding a broadening of its inquiry to include the conditions of Jews in Arab countries.		Congolese (Brazzaville) Pres. Alphonse Massamba-Debat broadcasts an appeal for national unity.	Clashes between students and police result in two deaths in Bolivia.	
Aug. 3		Reports indicate that the Soviet Union and four East European countries have agreed to allow Czechoslovakia to continue its liberalization course. . . . Bulgarian plainclothesmen assault Maoist student leader Karl Wolff at the ninth World Youth Festival in Bulgaria.	A left-wing military coup over throws Congolese (Brazzaville) Pres. Alphonse Massamba-Debat.	Mexican authorities accuse the Mexican CP of instigating the current unrest.	
Aug. 4		Czechoslovak CP First Secy. Alexander Dubcek in a TV speech, tells the Czech people that the country's liberalization process will continue. . . . Bulgaria blames the New Left student radicals for the recent violence at the ninth World Youth Festival.	Congolese (Brazzaville) Pres. Alphonse Massamba-Debat is recalled and charged with the formation of a new government. . . . Israeli planes strike a guerrilla base ten miles inside of Jordan.	Bolivian Pres. Rene Barrientos authorizes the opening of parliament after an all-night negotiation session with political leaders. . . . Mexican CP denies that it is responsible for the current unrest.	About 3,000 U.S. and South Vietnamese troops are helicoptered into the Ashau Valley near Hue.
Aug. 5		French Students' Union announces that its delegates have been expelled from the ninth World Youth Festival in Bulgaria.	International Red Cross resumes its emergency relief flights to Biafra.	French leftist Regis Debray denies a July 15 *New York Times* story that Cuban guerrilla leader Che Guevara was betrayed by a Soviet spy working within his group. . . . Univ. of Guatemala students begin boycotting classes.	
	A	**B**	**C**	**D**	**E**
	Includes developments that affect more than one world region, international organizations and important meetings of major world leaders.	*Includes all domestic and regional developments in Europe, including the Soviet Union, Turkey, Cyprus and Malta.*	*Includes all domestic and regional developments in Africa and the Middle East, including Iraq and Iran and excluding Cyprus, Turkey and Afghanistan.*	*Includes all domestic and regional developments in Latin America, the Caribbean and Canada.*	*Includes all domestic and regional developments in Asia and Pacific nations, extending from Afghanistan through all the Pacific Islands, except Hawaii.*

U.S. Politics & Social Issues	U.S. Foreign Policy & Defense	U.S. Economy & Environment	Science, Technology & Nature	Culture, Leisure & Life Style	
A Gallup Poll shows Richard Nixon ahead of major Democratic candidates while a Harris Poll shows him trailing them. . . . Sniper fire resounds in the Negro neighborhoods of Gary, Ind.			World's first woman-to-woman heart transplant operation takes place in Houston, Tex.	Roman Catholic Church's traditional prohibition on birth control by artificial means is reaffirmed in a papal encyclical.	July 29
Order returns to Gary, Ind. as looting and sniper fire appear to have stopped.	Former Pres. Dwight Eisenhower says that the U.S. must not accept "a camouflaged surrender" in Vietnam. . . . State Secy. Rusk expresses his "bitter disappointment" over North Korea's refusal to release the crew of the U.S. ship, *Pueblo* . . . . State Secy. Rusk urges both sides in the Nigerian civil war to use military restraint.	United Steelworkers Union agrees on a new three-year contract providing a package increase of about six percent. . . . U.S. Commerce Dept. reports an $87.2 million deficit in the U.S. balance-of-international trade in June.	Soviet Union launches Cosmos 234. . . . U.S. conducts an undergrount test in Nevada.	Most Rev. Dr. Michael Ramsey, Archbishop of Canterbury, says that the Roman Catholic position on birth control is "widely different from that of the Anglican community."	July 30
	Pres. Johnson asserts that the Communists are preparing a massive offensive in South Vietnam.	Pres. Johnson criticizes recent settlement United Steel Workers Union agreement wage and steel company price hikes.		*The Heart Is a Lonely Hunter*, a film based on Carson McCullers' book, opens in New York. Pope Paul defends his recent decision on birth control to visitors at his summer retreat.	July 31
Pres. Johnson signs a bill providing for large numbers of housing units for low and middle income families.			Census Bureau reports that 1967 U.S. birth rate was a record low.		Aug. 1
House and Senate pass a bill extending federal poultry inspection standards to poultry sold within a state.				Seven Dutch Roman Catholic bishops criticize the Pope's birth control ban.	Aug. 2
			Trevor De Wee receives the heart of a pig in a heart transplant operation in South Africa. . . . Heart transplant patient Everett Thomas returns to work in Texas.	Soviet commander in the battle of Stalingrad, Marshal Konstantine Rokossovsky, dies in Moscow at 71.	Aug. 3
				Viennese pianist Paul Ulanowsky dies in New York at 60.	Aug. 4
Republican National Convention opens in Miami.				Simon & Schuster publishes Drew Pearson's *The Case Against Congress*.	Aug. 5

F	G	H	I	J
Includes elections, federal-state relations, civil rights and liberties, crime, the judiciary, education, health care, poverty, urban affairs and population.	*Includes formation and debate of U.S. foreign and defense policies, veterans' affairs and defense spending. (Relations with specific foreign countries are usually found under the region concerned.)*	*Includes business, labor, agriculture, taxation, transportation, consumer affairs, monetary and fiscal policy, natural resources, and pollution.*	*Includes worldwide scientific, medical and technological developments, natural phenomena, U.S. weather, natural disasters, and accidents.*	*Includes the arts, religion, scholarship, communications media, sports, entertainment, fashions, fads and social life.*

	World Affairs	Europe	Africa & the Middle East	The Americas	Asia & the Pacific
Aug. 6			Israeli ground forces pursue Arab guerrillas into Jordan for the first time since April 8.		
Aug. 7		At the Paris peace talks, U.S. Amb. Averell Harriman announces that the U.S. will soon release 14 North Vietnamese captive seamen.		Leftist guerrillas in Uruguay kidnap businessman Ulises Pereira Reverbel.	
Aug. 8			Arab guerrilla group Al Fatah warns Israeli civilians of possible commando attacks. . . . The New York Times reports that Biafran guerrillas have launched successful raids behind Nigerian lines. East Jerusalem Arabs stage a general strike.		U.S. forces mistakenly kill 72 South Vietnamese civilians in a ground and air attack.
Aug. 9		Yugoslav Pres. Tito arrives in Czechoslovakia to demonstrate his support of the Czech government in its confrontation with the Soviet Union.	Peace talks between Nigeria and Biafra shows little signs of progress in Addis Ababa, Ethiopia. . . . Palestine Liberation Organization (PLO) reports that "mutineers" have seized the PLO's chief of staff Brig. Gen. Abdel Razek Yahia in Damascus.	A student strike begins at Mexico City's two main universities. . . . Hundreds of students clash with police in Uruguay, when security forces enter Univ. of Montevideo to search for the kidnapped businessman.	
Aug. 10		Soviet Union announces that Warsaw Pact maneuvers are now taking place near Czechoslovakia's borders.	International Red Cross again suspends its emergency relief flights to Biafra because of recent anti-aircraft fire by the federal Nigerian government.		Reports indicate that Indonesia has killed or captured 2,000 members of the Communist Party since April 1968. . . . A U.S. plane mistakenly kills eight American soldiers.
Aug. 11		In a rebuttal to the July 22 essay by Soviet physicist Andrei Sakharov, Soviet newspaper Izvestia says that the struggle between communism and capitalism will intensify in the future. . . . Yugoslav Pres. Tito leaves Czechoslovakia. . . . A Hungarian court sentences U.S. citizen Henrietta Blueye to six months in jail for trying to help an East German to escape to the West.		Univ. of Guatemala officials agree to student demands that required attendance be abolished. . . . Leftist guerrillas in Uruguay release kidnapped businessman Ulises Pereira Reverbel.	U.S. forces mistakenly wound four American Marines.
Aug. 12		Yugoslav dissident Milovan Djilas says that he completely agrees with Pres. Tito's support of Czechoslovak liberalization.	Two Syrian air force pilots land in Israel by mistake and are arrested as prisoners of war. . . . The New York Times reports that Biafran guerrillas have continued their successful raids behind Nigerian lines.	Peruvian Pres. Fernando Belaunde Terry reaches an agreement increasing Peru's control over its oil wells but stopping short of complete nationalization. . . . Canadian P.M. Pierre Trudeau calls for the implementation of a bill establishing equality between French and English languages in the federal courts and public services.	Heavy fighting erupts in the Mekong Delta.
Aug. 13	International Federation of Airline Pilots' Association announces plans to halt all flights between Western Europe and Algeria to force the release of 14 crewmen and passengers of the July 23 hijacked Israeli airliner.	Britain reports that its trade deficit for July was $347.2 million. . . . A bomb explodes near the car of Greek Premier George Papadopoulos but does not injure him. Police immediately arrest suspect Alexandros Panaghoulis.	Swedish Count Carl-Gustav von Rosen flies in ten tons of food and medicine to Biafra by a secret route. . . . Biafran units reoccupy Ikot Ekpene with little Nigerian opposition.	Students demonstrate against the government in Mexico City.	Heavy fighting continues in the Mekong Delta.
Aug. 14	Algeria threatens counter-actions along with other Arab countries if it is boycotted by the international pilots association.	Portugese Pres. Antonio de Oliveira Salazar collapses in his home presumably of a heart attack. . . . At the Paris peace talks, North Vietnam presses for a complete halt to the bombing of its territory.	Zambia bans the country's opposition United Party after riots in the copperbelt zone. . . . International Red Cross announces a a plan to fly food to Biafra.	A Uruguayan student dies from wounds suffered on Aug. 12 in a clash with police.	South Vietnamese troops discover three Viet cong munition factories in the Mekong Delta.

A	B	C	D	E
Includes developments that affect more than one world region, international organizations and important meetings of major world leaders.	Includes all domestic and regional developments in Europe, including the Soviet Union, Turkey, Cyprus and Malta.	Includes all domestic and regional developments in Africa and the Middle East, including Iraq and Iran and excluding Cyprus, Turkey and Afghanistan.	Includes all domestic and regional developments in Latin America, the Caribbean and Canada.	Includes all domestic and regional developments in Asia and Pacific nations, extending from Afghanistan through all the Pacific Islands, except Hawaii.

U.S. Politics & Social Issues	U.S. Foreign Policy & Defense	U.S. Economy & Environment	Science, Technology & Nature	Culture, Leisure & Life Style	
			U.S. launches a military reconnaissance satellite. . . . Former Pres. Dwight Eisenhower suffers his sixth heart attack. . . . Pres. Johnson begins to undergo a series of medical exams. . . . *Washington Post* says that Cosmos 234 is the Soviet Union's 100th military reconnaissance satellite.	Stein & Day publishes *The Complete Bolivian Diaries of Che Guevara and Other Captured Documents.* . . . Former Pres. Dwight Eisenhower suffers another heart attack but is reported to be in a "stable" condition.	Aug. 6
Police arrest 52 Negroes as looting breaks out in Miami's Negro areas. . . . Republican 1968 platform stresses the need for an honorable negotiated peace in Vietnam.		U.S. Steel Corp. raises prices by about two and a half percent.	*The New York Times* reports that the U.S. satellite launched Aug. 6 "may be able to hover over a target area eight to nine hours." An explosion kills nine miners in a mine near Greenville, Ky.		Aug. 7
Richard Nixon wins the Republican Party's nomination for president and Maryland Gov. Spiro Agnew is chosen as his running mate.			Japan's first heart transplant operation takes place. . . . U.S. launches two satellites whose missions are to study the atmosphere during high solar activity.		Aug. 8
	Sen. Eugene McCarthy says that the U.S. should postpone the scheduled testing of multiple warheads.		Soviet Union launches Cosmos 235.		Aug. 9
Sen. George McGovern (S.D.) announces that he is an active candidate for the Democratic presidential nomination. . . . Pres. Johnson briefs Republican nominees Nixon and Agnew on world affairs.			U.S. launches a satellite whose mission is to study hurricanes and other storms.	Mexican Roman Catholic bishops endorse the Pope's birth control ban.	Aug. 10
				Pope Paul defends his position against artificial birth control.	Aug. 11
	U.S. imposes stricter economic sanctions on Rhodesia.	Pres. Johnson vetoes a bill forbidding cotton purchases from countries without diplomatic relations with the U.S.		Pope Paul appeals to both sides to to give "proper priority" to humanitarian aid in the Nigerian civil war. . . . *Hunger*, a film based on Knut Hamsun's novel of the same name, opens in New York.	Aug. 12
	U.S. official Robert Moore meets with relief agency officials to discuss U.S. relief efforts for Biafra.	U.S. Treasury Dept. announces tariffs on French imports to counter the June 26 temporary French import quotas.	Heart transplant patient Louis Fierro returns to work in Houston, Tex.		Aug. 13
	Sen. George McGovern says that he would oppose a platform endorsing the administration's Vietnam policies.				Aug. 14

F	G	H	I	J
Includes elections, federal-state relations, civil rights and liberties, crime, the judiciary, education, health care, poverty, urban affairs and population.	*Includes formation and debate of U.S. foreign and defense policies, veterans' affairs and defense spending. (Relations with specific foreign countries are usually found under the region concerned.)*	*Includes business, labor, agriculture, taxation, transportation, consumer affairs, monetary and fiscal policy, natural resources, and pollution.*	*Includes worldwide scientific, medical and technological developments, natural phenomena, U.S. weather, natural disasters, and accidents.*	*Includes the arts, religion, scholarship, communications media, sports, entertainment, fashions, fads and social life.*

	World Affairs	Europe	Africa & the Middle East	The Americas	Asia & the Pacific
Aug. 15		Rumanian Pres. Nicolae Ceausescu visits Czechoslovakia to demonstrate his support of the Czech government in its confrontation with the Soviet Union.	Nigeria rejects the Red Cross's food relief plan because of fears that Biafra might use the flights to bring in arms.		Allied troops take a heavy toll of Communist troops near the demilitarized zone.
Aug. 16	U.N. Security Council unanimously adopts a resolution condemning Israel for its Aug. 4 military incursion into Jordan.	After a lapse of three weeks, the Soviet Union resumes its criticism of the Czechoslovak press.	Various international agencies including UNICEF and the World Council of Churches say that the Nigerian civil war is the biggest emergency since W.W.II.		
Aug. 17	International Federation of Airline Pilots' Association V.P. Vitali Nicolayev announces that his organization's scheduled boycott of Algeria has been cancelled following assurances by the Algerian government that the crew and passengers of the Israeli airliner will be released.	Rumanian Pres. Nicolae Ceausescu leaves Czechoslovakia after having received an enthusiastic reception from the Czech people.	International Red Cross "deplores" Nigeria's rejection of its plan.		An estimated 600 Communist troops infiltrate the provincial capital of Tayninh.
Aug. 18			Grenade explosions injure 10 people in the Jewish section of Jerusalem and cause Israeli youths to storm the Arab sector of the city where they throw rocks.	Canadian P.M. Pierre Elliott Trudeau says that Canada will not be bound by American guarantees of an immediate NATO response to a Communist military threat against West Germany.	Communist artillery offensive opens against South Vietnamese towns. . . . Communist troops attack government installations in Tayninh.
Aug. 19			A captured Nigerian officer in Owerri says that 30 Soviet advisers have been with his company for two months. . . . International Red Cross resumes relief flights to Biafra after suspending them for several days because of Nigerian attacks on aircraft. . . . Israeli Defense Min. Moshe Dayan visits the Arab sector of Jerusalem where he denounces the Aug. 18 Israeli rioters.		Communist forces withdraw from Tayninh after creating havoc.
Aug. 20		An estimated 200,000 troops of five Warsaw Pact nations invade Czechoslovakia under cover of darkness.	Lebanese newspaper *An Nahar* reports that 158 Syrian Army officers have defected to Iraq.	Argentine Pres. Juan Carlos Ongania dismisses the chiefs of the Army, Navy and Air Force.	
Aug. 21		Czechoslovaks do not resist the Warsaw Pact invasion militarily but students sit in front of tanks and raise barricades. . . . At the Paris peace talks, North Vietnam asserts that Pres. Johnson's stand is counter to that of many U.S. politicians.	A bomb shatters windows but causes no injuries outside of the U.S. consulate in East Jerusalem.		U.S. troops kill more than 100 Communists in a rubber plantation 44 miles from Saigon.
Aug. 22	U.N. Security Council condemns the invasion of Czechoslovakia by a vote of 10-2.	An estimated 20,000 Czechoslovaks demonstrate against the Warsaw Pact invasion in central Prague.	An Israeli patrol kills five Al Fatah members near Jericho. . . . East Jerusalem Arabs stage a strike to protest the Aug. 18 Israeli riot but the walkout is only partially observed.		Saigon comes under Communist rocket attack for the first time in two months.
Aug. 23		Soviet agents force Czech Pres. Ludvig Svoboda to fly to Moscow for talks.		Cuban Premier Castro concedes that there is no legal justification for the invasion of Czechoslovakia but he supports the action in order to block "counterrevolutionaries."	Communist artillery attack rocks South Vietnamese provincial capitals.
Aug. 24		Soviet soldiers kill three young men distributing anti-Soviet leaflets in Prague. . . . France explodes its first thermonuclear bomb and becomes the world's fifth thermonuclear nation.	Nigeria begins what is described as a "final offensive" against the secessionist state of Biafra.		Savage fighting takes place at the U.S. Special Forces Camp at Duclap as North Vietnamese overrun one-third of the base.
	A	B	C	D	E
	Includes developments that affect more than one world region, international organizations and important meetings of major world leaders.	Includes all domestic and regional developments in Europe, including the Soviet Union, Turkey, Cyprus and Malta.	Includes all domestic and regional developments in Africa and the Middle East, including Iraq and Iran and excluding Cyprus, Turkey and Afghanistan.	Includes all domestic and regional developments in Latin America, the Caribbean and Canada.	Includes all domestic and regional developments in Asia and Pacific nations, extending from Afghanistan through all the Pacific Islands, except Hawaii.

U.S. Politics & Social Issues	U.S. Foreign Policy & Defense	U.S. Economy & Environment	Science, Technology & Nature	Culture, Leisure & Life Style	
	Defense Secy. Clark Clifford says that substantive negotiations could begin at the Paris peace talks if North Vietnam informs the U.S. that they have reduced the level of combat and will continue to do so.				Aug. 15
		Commerce Department reports that U.S. balance-of-international payments deficit was $150 million for the second quarter of 1968.	Former Pres. Eisenhower suffers his seventh heart attack. . . . Two new U.S. missiles-the Navy's Poseidon and the Air Force's Minuteman-are successfully test-fired. . . . U.S. launches a weather satellite into near-polar orbit. . . . U.S. launches a record 12 satellites into polar orbit.		Aug. 16
				The New York Times survey shows that Roman Catholic hierarchies of Poland, South America and southern Europe widely support the Pope's birth control ban.	Aug. 17
		Pres. Johnson signs a bill extending federal poultry inspection standards to poultry sold within a state.	In Houston, Tex., Marie Giannaris becomes the world's second child heart transplant patient.		Aug. 18
	Pres. Johnson says that the U.S. will make no further moves to de-escalate the Vietnamese War until North Vietnam makes a serious move toward peace. . . . Sen. George McGovern says that there must be a massive de-escalation of the Vietnamese War.			Farrar, Straus & Giroux publishes Tom Wolfe's The Electric Kool-Aid Acid Test.	Aug. 19
	Pres. Johnson meets with the National Security Council after the invasion of Czechoslovakia.				Aug. 20
V.P. Humphrey calls off his scheduled debate with Sen. Eugene McCarthy.	Sen. Edward Kennedy calls for an unconditional halt to the bombing of North Vietnam. . . . Pres. Johnson criticizes the Warsaw Pact invasion of Czechoslovakia.				Aug. 21
	State Secy. Rusk says that the U.S. is not planning any "retaliatory actions" against the Warsaw Pact nations which invaded Czechoslovakia.			Pope Paul arrives in Colombia for a visit. It is the first time a pope has traveled to South America. . . . Anglican church votes that deaconesses share the same status as deacons.	Aug. 22
	U.S. State Dept. denounces talk that the Czechoslovak invasion was made possible by a tacit understanding between the U.S. and the Soviet Union about respective spheres of influence.			Houghton Mifflin publishes Noel Barber's A Sinister Twilight. The Fall of Singapore.	Aug. 23
			World's 34th heart transplant operation takes place in Richmond, Va. . . . . Internal Revenue Service says that the number of U.S. cigarettes smoked declined by .28%.		Aug. 24
F	**G**	**H**	**I**	**J**	
Includes elections, federal-state relations, civil rights and liberties, crime, the judiciary, education, health care, poverty, urban affairs and population.	Includes formation and debate of U.S. foreign and defense policies, veterans' affairs and defense spending. (Relations with specific foreign countries are usually found under the region concerned.)	Includes business, labor, agriculture, taxation, transportation, consumer affairs, monetary and fiscal policy, natural resources, and pollution.	Includes worldwide scientific, medical and technological developments, natural phenomena, U.S. weather, natural disasters, and accidents.	Includes the arts, religion, scholarship, communications media, sports, entertainment, fashions, fads and social life.	

	World Affairs	Europe	Africa & the Middle East	The Americas	Asia & the Pacific
Aug. 25		About 10 clandestine Czech radio stations are broadcasting throughout the country. . . . Soviet police arrest five dissidents protesting the invasion of Czechoslovakia in Red Square.	Israel and Jordan duel with tanks and artillery across the Jordan River.		U.S. Special Forces lead allied reinforcements for the U.S. camp at Duclap.
Aug. 26		British P.M. Harold Wilson denounces the invasion of Czechoslovakia but says it should not deter the West from seeking detente with the Soviet Union.	Israel claims that two of its soldiers were killed in an ambush along the Suez Canal.	Canadian External Affairs Min. Mitchell Sharp announces that nearly one-third of the recruits to the Canadian foreign service over the past three years were French-speaking.	
Aug. 27	Eight nonaligned nations of the U.N. Disarmament Committee denounce France and Communist China for carrying out atmospheric nuclear tests.	Pres. Ludvig Svoboda and CP First Secy. Alexander Dubcek return to Prague after talks in Moscow where at one point Svoboda is said to have threatened to commit suicide.		Students demonstrate against the government in the center of Mexico City.	
Aug. 28	U.N. Disarmament Committee adjourns after having called for a study of chemical and biological warfare.	At the Paris peace talks, North Vietnam says that the elaborate security precautions taken at the Democratic Convention demonstrate how unpopular the war is. . . . Czech Pres. Ludvig Svoboda confirms that the withdrawal of occupation forces will take "several months.". . . France sends 20 planeloads of paratroopers to aid Chad in putting down a serious guerrilla movement in the northern part of the country.	A bomb injures six Israelis in Jerusalem.	Terrorists assassinate US Amb.-to-Guatemala John Mein. . . . Students and police clash in front of the National Palace in Mexico City.	
Aug. 29		Czechoslovak National Assembly Pres. Josef Smrkovsky announces that press censorship will be reimposed.	In an effort to counter reports of federal troops massacring Ibo tribesmen, the Nigerian government invites foreign representatives to observe the conduct of their troops.	Guatemalan Pres. Julio Cesar Mendez imposes a 30-day state of siege. . . . New banking regulations require that two-thirds of the shares of Peruvian banks be held by Peruvian citizens.	
Aug. 30			Savage fighting takes place between the two principal religious sects of North Yemen in Sana, the country's capital.	French-speaking high school students near Montreal occupy their town's high school to protest the school board's decision to make English the school's only language of instruction.	Communist forces overrun U.S. Special Forces Camp at Hathanh.
Aug. 31			A severe earthquake shakes northeastern Iran. . . . Algeria releases the remaining crewmen and passengers on the July 23 hijacked Israeli airliner. . . . Fighting occurs between regular army units and dissident forces in the Congo (Brazzaville). . . . Reports indicate that at least 3,000 North Yemenis have died in the recent internecine fighting.		
Sept. 1		Czechoslovak Presidium is reshuffled.	A second earthquake rocks northeastern Iran. Authorities estimate that 18,000-22,000 people have died. . . . An anti-Egyptian speech by Tunisia causes an uproar at the meeting of foreign ministers of the Arab League in Cairo.	Mexican Pres. Gustavo Diaz Ordaz says he will not allow students to disrupt the opening of Olympic Games in Mexico City on Oct. 12.	
Sept. 2		Prague radio reports that three Czechoslovak literary journals have been banned.	Israel says it will free 16 Arab guerrilla captives. . . . Tunisian delegate Tayeb Sahabani walks out of the Arab League's foreign ministers conference when he is prevented from completing his speech.		U.S. troops recapture U.S. Special Forces Camp at Hathanh.
	A	B	C	D	E
	Includes developments that affect more than one world region, international organizations and important meetings of major world leaders.	Includes all domestic and regional developments in Europe, including the Soviet Union, Turkey, Cyprus and Malta.	Includes all domestic and regional developments in Africa and the Middle East, including Iraq and Iran and excluding Cyprus, Turkey and Afghanistan.	Includes all domestic and regional developments in Latin America, the Caribbean and Canada.	Includes all domestic and regional developments in Asia and Pacific nations, extending from Afghanistan through all the Pacific Islands, except Hawaii.

U.S. Politics & Social Issues	U.S. Foreign Policy & Defense	U.S. Economy & Environment	Science, Technology & Nature	Culture, Leisure & Life Style	
					Aug. 25
FBI reports that the number of serious crimes was up 16% in 1967. . . . Democratic Convention opens in Chicago in a tense atmosphere.	U.S. State Dept. says that it will contribute another 10,000 tons of food to Biafra.			Alfred Knopf publishes Joseph Heller's play *We Bombed in New Haven* . . . . Paul Newman's film *Rachel, Rachel* opens in New York.	Aug. 26
Police use tear gas to disperse 3,000 anti-war demonstrators in Chicago and make 140 arrests. . . . Sen. Ernest Gruening, 81, who opposed the war in Vietnam, is defeated in his bid for re-election in the Alaska primary.			U.S. conducts an underground nuclear test in Nevada. . . . Soviet Union launches Cosmos 236. and Cosmos 237.		Aug. 27
Democratic Convention nominates V.P. Humphrey as its presidential candidate as violent street battles between police and students rage in Chicago.			Soviet Union launches Cosmos 238.	Harper & Row publishes Robert McNamara's *The Essence of Security*.	Aug. 28
Democratic Convention nominates Sen. Edmund Muskie of Maine as its vice presidential candidate.			Former Pres. Eisenhower is taken off the critical list. . . . U.S. conducts an underground nuclear test in Nevada.		Aug. 29
Chicago police carry out a dawn raid on McCarthy headquarters because of objects allegedly thrown at them from the windows.				Belgian Roman Catholics say that each individual has the right to accept or reject artificial birth control.	Aug. 30
	U.S. State Dept. says that the European balance-of-power has been upset by the Warsaw Pact invasion of Czechoslovakia.			British historian Dr. George Peabody Gooch dies in Beaconsfield, England at 94. . . . A Gallup Poll indicates that U.S. Catholics oppose the Pope's birth control ban by 54%-28%.	Aug. 31
					Sept. 1
				French actor-director Jean-Louis Barrault discloses that he has been fired from the directorship of the French theater known as the Odean because of his indulgent attitude towards its seizure by striking workers in May 1968.	Sept. 2

F	G	H	I	J
Includes elections, federal-state relations, civil rights and liberties, crime, the judiciary, education, health care, poverty, urban affairs and population.	*Includes formation and debate of U.S. foreign and defense policies, veterans' affairs and defense spending. (Relations with specific foreign countries are usually found under the region concerned.)*	*Includes business, labor, agriculture, taxation, transportation, consumer affairs, monetary and fiscal policy, natural resources, and pollution.*	*Includes worldwide scientific, medical and technological developments, natural phenomena, U.S. weather, natural disasters, and accidents.*	*Includes the arts, religion, scholarship, communications media, sports, entertainment, fashions, fads and social life.*

	World Affairs	Europe	Africa & the Middle East	The Americas	Asia & the Pacific
Sept. 3		An earthquake strikes northwestern Turkey and kills at least 15 people. . . . Reports from Prague indicate that Soviet soldiers have withdrawn from key buildings in major cities.	A mine kills three Israeli soldiers on the Golan Heights.		
Sept. 4	U.N. World Health Organiztion reports that 200,000 people died in auto accidents in 1966.	Press censorship is reimposed in Czechoslovakia. . . . At the Paris peace talks, North Vietnam criticizes the Democratic and Republican platform planks on Vietnam.	Three bombs kill one Israeli and injure 71 others in central Tel Aviv. . . . International Red Cross begins an airlift of starving Biafran children out of Biafra.	Immigrant parents keep their children home from St. Leonard's elementary schools near Montreal to protest the school board's decision to gradually eliminate the English language.	
Sept. 5					
Sept. 6		Soviet First Deputy Foreign Min. Vasily Kuznetsov visits Prague and confers with Czechoslovak leaders.	Israeli authorities report the arrest of 19 Arabs believed to be responsible for the recent bombings. . . . Governing Rhodesian Front votes 217-206 to approve proposals for a new constitution which hard-line apartheid supporters opposed.	Mexican government rejects students' demands for the elimination of the riot police. . . . Mexico signs an agreement allowing the International Atomic Energy Agency to have complete jurisdiction over its nuclear program.	Using women and children as shields, a Viet Cong force attacks U.S. troops 26 miles from Saigon.
Sept. 7				Brazilian parliamentary member Marcio Moreira Alves criticizes the Brazilian government for its suppression of civil liberties.	
Sept. 8			Heavy artillery fire causes major casualties on both sides of the Suez Canal.		North Vietnamese kill a South Vietnamese general, Brig. Gen. Truong Quang An.
Sept. 9		Central banks conclude a $2 billion credit plan to support the British pound. . . . Austrian border authorities report that Soviet officers have manned at least three of the Czechoslovak border crossings with Austria. . . . French Pres. de Gaulle condemns the Soviet occupation of Czechoslovakia but says that efforts to seek a political detente with Russia must continue.	In Tunis the trial begins of demonstrators who attacked Jewish neighborhoods in June 1967.		
Sept. 10		Czechoslovak Premier Oldrich Cernik confers with top Soviet officials in Moscow. . . . Czechoslovak Interior Ministry confirms the suicide of Jan Zaruba, a deputy interior minister who reportedly killed himself rather than turn over ministry papers to the Soviet secret police.			
Sept. 11	U.N. Security Council approves Swaziland's membership in the U.N.	Most Soviet tanks and military units withdraw from the center of Prague. . . . At the Paris peace talks, both sides air conflicting battlefield claims. . . . Reports indicate that Italy and Greece have assured Yugoslavia that they will not rekindle old border disputes in the face of current Soviet pressure.	Apartheid supporter Lord Graham resigns as Rhodesian minister of external affairs. . . . Reports indicate that the Congo (Kinshasa) has informed Algeria that it has no objections to the release of former Congolese Premier Moise Tshombe.	Canadian P.M. Pierre Trudeau criticizes France for sending an official to a French-speaking community in Manitoba without notifying the federal government.	Communist troops launch a major assault on the provincial capital of Tayninh.

A	B	C	D	E
Includes developments that affect more than one world region, international organizations and important meetings of major world leaders.	*Includes all domestic and regional developments in Europe, including the Soviet Union, Turkey, Cyprus and Malta.*	*Includes all domestic and regional developments in Africa and the Middle East, including Iraq and Iran and excluding Cyprus, Turkey and Afghanistan.*	*Includes all domestic and regional developments in Latin America, the Caribbean and Canada.*	*Includes all domestic and regional developments in Asia and Pacific nations, extending from Afghanistan through all the Pacific Islands, except Hawaii.*

U.S. Politics & Social Issues	U.S. Foreign Policy & Defense	U.S. Economy & Environment	Science, Technology & Nature	Culture, Leisure & Life Style	
					Sept. 3
Former V.P. Nixon draws an enthusiastic and orderly crowd in Chicago. . . . N.Y.C. police allegedly attack several Black Panthers in a Brooklyn criminal court.				*London Times* prints a letter from Pope Paul calling for unity in the face of divisions over the question of artificial birth control.	Sept. 4
			Soviet Union conducts an underground nuclear test in Central Asia. . . . Soviet Union launches Cosmos 239.	Charles Scribners publishes Arthur Larson's *Eisenhower*.	Sept. 5
			U.S. conducts an underground nuclear test in Nevada.	West German Roman Catholic conference criticizes the Pope's birth control ban. . . . Soviet stage designer Nikolai Akimov dies in Moscow at 67.	Sept. 6
					Sept. 7
V.P. Humphrey accuses Richard Nixon of being "sort of a Cold War warrior.". . . A Calif. court convicts Black Panther founder Huey Newton of manslaughter in the October 1967 slaying of an Oakland policeman.			France conducts its second hydrogen bomb test at its Pacific testing grounds.		Sept. 8
V.P. Humphrey says that the U.S. can start to remove troops from South Vietnam in late 1968 or early 1969.					Sept. 9
A Gallup Poll reports that 50% of the union members interviewed in the South favor George Wallace over Humphrey (29%) or Nixon (16%). . . . Two Oakland, Calif. policemen are jailed for firing bullets into Black Panther's headquarters.	Officials deny reports that the U.S. plans to apologize to North Korea for the alleged intrusion of the U.S.S. *Pueblo* into North Korean waters. . . . Pres. Johnson urges Western Europe to take a larger share of its defense burden.				Sept. 10
	Republican presidential nominee Richard Nixon says that he favors the nuclear non-proliferation treaty but wants it implemented "at a future time" when Soviet intentions can be better gauged.			Harper & Row publishes Aleksandr Solzhenitsyn's *One Day in the Life of Ivan Denisovich*.	Sept. 11

F	G	H	I	J
Includes elections, federal-state relations, civil rights and liberties, crime, the judiciary, education, health care, poverty, urban affairs and population.	*Includes formation and debate of U.S. foreign and defense policies, veterans' affairs and defense spending. (Relations with specific foreign countries are usually found under the region concerned.)*	*Includes business, labor, agriculture, taxation, transportation, consumer affairs, monetary and fiscal policy, natural resources, and pollution.*	*Includes worldwide scientific, medical and technological developments, natural phenomena, U.S. weather, natural disasters, and accidents.*	*Includes the arts, religion, scholarship, communications media, sports, entertainment, fashions, fads and social life.*

	World Affairs	Europe	Africa & the Middle East	The Americas	Asia & the Pacific
Sept. 12			Seventy-four-member right-wing Salisbury Central Branch withdraws from the ruling Rhodesian Front.		
Sept. 13		Czechoslovak National Assembly votes 275-2 to reimpose "preventive censorship.". . . European Migration Committee reports that more than 25,000 Czechs have left their country since the Aug. 21 Soviet invasion.	Rhodesian High Court upholds the legality of P.M. Ian Smith's government.		Allied troops make a major thrust into the southern half of the demilitarized zone.
Sept. 14		Under intense Soviet pressure Czechoslovak Foreign Min. Jiri Hajek submits his resignation which Pres. Ludvig Svoboda rejects. . . . Czech CP First Secy. Alexander Dubcek appeals to Czechoslovaks not to provoke incidents with the occupying Warsaw Pact troops.	Nigeria requisitions two Red Cross planes for military uses.		Allied troops defend Tayninh against Communist forces.
Sept. 15					
Sept. 16	U.N. Secy. Gen. U Thant calls for a complete halt to the U.S. bombing of North Vietnam.	Portugese Pres. Antonio de Oliveira Salazar sinks into a coma.	Advancing Nigerian troops claim the capture of the Biafran city of Owerri.		Communist China charges that Soviet aircraft have violated its northeastern border. . . . Communist forces attack a U.S. military unit near Tayninh.
Sept. 17					U.S. planes bomb targets in and around the demilitarized zone.
Sept. 18	U.N. Security Council adopts a resolution calling on Israel and the Arabs to respect the Council's cease-fire.	Soviet Union asserts its right to intervene in West Germany "to halt the dangerous activity of neo-Nazism.". . . Britain reports its August trade deficit to have been $276 million. . . . Rumania rehabilitates 14 victims of 1950s Stalinist trials. . . . At the Paris peace talks, both sides report no progress.	Deposed King of North Yemen Mohammad al-Badr returns to his country after two years of exile in Saudi Arabia.	Federal troops seize the National Univ. in Mexico City. . . . Quebec Cultural Affairs Min. Jean-Noel Tremblay says that The French language will be required for all business transactions in Quebec. . . . Police use tear gas to disperse students manning barricades around the University of Montevideo, Uruguay.	U.S. planes continue bombing targets in and around the demilitarized zone. . . . Philippine Pres. Ferdinand Marcos asserts his country's dominion over Malaysia's Borneo state of Sabah.
Sept. 19		Under intense Soviet pressure Czech Pres. Ludvig Svoboda accepts the resignation of Czech Foreign Min. Jiri Hajek.	Egyptian Gov. Hamid Mahmoud reports that thousands of Egyptian civilians have fled the city of Suez because of the recent fighting.	Soldiers turn back Mexican students trying to retake the campus of the National Univ.	Malaysia suspends diplomatic relations with the Philippines.
Sept. 20		A Czechoslovak magazine poll indicates the overwhelming popularity of Czech CP First Secy. Alexander Dubcek. . . . Reports from Prague indicate that the Soviet Union is pressing for the removal of Czechoslovak CP First Secy. Alexander Dubcek. . . . Hungarian Premier Jeno Fock defends his country's economic reform program.	Somalia renounces its former claims to the French colony of Djibouti.	Police gunfire kills two students at the Univ. of Montevideo, Uruguay.	U.S. officials in Saigon say that the American defoliation of selected areas of South Vietnam is "a complete success.". . . U.S. planes pound targets in the demilitarized zone.
Sept. 21		Czechoslovak Premier Alexander Cernik says that Warsaw Pact troops will begin "a gradual departure from Czechoslovakia within several days."		Reports from Peru indicate that slum settlers surrounding Lima have won the right to obtain formal titles to their lots.	

A	B	C	D	E
Includes developments that affect more than one world region, international organizations and important meetings of major world leaders.	Includes all domestic and regional developments in Europe, including the Soviet Union, Turkey, Cyprus and Malta.	Includes all domestic and regional developments in Africa and the Middle East, including Iraq and Iran and excluding Cyprus, Turkey and Afghanistan.	Includes all domestic and regional developments in Latin America, the Caribbean and Canada.	Includes all domestic and regional developments in Asia and Pacific nations, extending from Afghanistan through all the Pacific Islands, except Hawaii.

U.S. Politics & Social Issues	U.S. Foreign Policy & Defense	U.S. Economy & Environment	Science, Technology & Nature	Culture, Leisure & Life Style	
House passes a bill establishing a Redwood National Park in northern California.	London Institute of Strategic Studies reports that the Soviet Union will have as many intercontinental missiles as the U.S. by the end of 1968. . . . Republican presidential nominee Richard Nixon calls for the suspension of aid and credits to countries dealing with North Vietnam.		U.S. conducts an underground nuclear test in Nevada.		Sept. 12
Republican vice presidential candidate Spiro Agnew uses the word "Polack" in referring to Americans of Polish ancestry.					Sept. 13
	Reports indicate that Pres. Johnson has decided against selling Israel 50 F-4 Phantom jets for the time being. . . .		Soviet Union launches Cosmos 240.		Sept. 14
	V.P. Humphrey says that the U.S. should sell F-4 Phantom jets to Israel.		Soviet Union launches an unmanned lunar probe.		Sept. 15
	Reports indicate that the U.S. is ready to increase its forces in West Germany in response to the invasion of Czechoslovakia.		Soviet Union launches Cosmos 241.	N.Y. Metropolitan Opera opens its 84th season with Francesco Cilea's *Adriana Lecouvreur*.	Sept. 16
A Gallup Poll indicates that 56% of a national sample approved of the way the Chicago police handled the demonstrators at the Democratic Convention while 31% disapproved. . . . Calif. Gov. Ronald Reagan tries to prevent a series of lectures by Negro author Eldridge Cleaver at the Univ. of Calif. at Berkeley.			U.S. conducts an underground nuclear test in Nevada.		Sept. 17
Senate passes a bill by 70-17 to ban the mail order purchase of rifles and handguns.	V.P. Humphrey urges immediate Senate ratification of the nuclear non-proliferation treaty.		Soviet Union's lunar probe flies around the moon. . . . U.S. fails to place a communications satellite into synchronous orbit.		Sept. 18
V.P. Humphrey says that he will make peace in Vietnam his chief goal if elected president. . . . Senate passes a bill establishing a Redwood National Park in northern California.	U.S. says that it recognizes Sabah as part of the Malaysian Federation. . . . Pres. Johnson calls for a sustained effort in Vietnam.				Sept. 19
Republican presidential nominee Richard Nixon draws an impressive crowd in downtown Philadelphia. . . . Calif. Board of Regents decides to allow Negro author Eldridge Cleaver to give one guest lecture but not an entire series of lectures at the Univ. of Calif. at Berkeley.	U.S. says that it is neutral in the Malaysian-Philippine dispute over the state of Sabah.		Soviet Union launches Cosmos 242.	U.S. astronomer Dr. Dinsmore Alter dies in Oakland, Calif. at 80.	Sept. 20
In a jocular reference to a reporter of Japanese ancestry, Republican vice presidential candidate Spiro Agnew uses the term "fat Jap."			Soviet Union's lunar probe splashes down in the Indian Ocean.		Sept. 21
F	G	H	I	J	
Includes elections, federal-state relations, civil rights and liberties, crime, the judiciary, education, health care, poverty, urban affairs and population.	*Includes formation and debate of U.S. foreign and defense policies, veterans' affairs and defense spending. (Relations with specific foreign countries are usually found under the region concerned.)*	*Includes business, labor, agriculture, taxation, transportation, consumer affairs, monetary and fiscal policy, natural resources, and pollution.*	*Includes worldwide scientific, medical and technological developments, natural phenomena, U.S. weather, natural disasters, and accidents.*	*Includes the arts, religion, scholarship, communications media, sports, entertainment, fashions, fads and social life.*	

	World Affairs	Europe	Africa & the Middle East	The Americas	Asia & the Pacific
Sept. 22		Reports indicate that hundreds of Soviet civilian personnel have been seen moving into Prague.	Fighting continues around the Biafran town of Owerri between Nigerian and Biafran forces.	Uruguayan government closes down all Montevideo universities and secondary schools.	South Vietnamese troops engage North Vietnamese forces trying to escape the demilitarized zone.
Sept. 23	U.N. Secy. Gen. U Thant speculates that a majority of the General Assembly would support a halt to the U.S. bombing of North Vietnam.	Reports indicate that Czechoslovak CP First Secy. Alexander Dubcek and Soviet First Deputy Foreign Min. Vasily Kuznetsov have failed to agree on an agenda for scheduled talks in Moscow. . . . Greece releases former Premier George Papandreou from detention.	Reports from Amman indicate that Jordanian King Hussein is interested in indirect negotiations with Israel to avert a possible outbreak of war.	Mexican students use firearms on a large scale for the first time in their battles with police. . . . Canadian P.M. Pierre Elliott Trudeau says that he has no intention of abolishing the British monarchy in Canada.	South Vietnamese troops take a heavy toll of North Vietnamese forces near the demilitarized zone.
Sept. 24	U.N. decides to allow Haiti to continue to vote despite its being two years in arrears in paying its U.N. dues. . . . U.N. Secy. Gen. U Thant denies that he plans to encourage any member state to place the Vietnam question on the Assembly's agenda.	Czechoslovak CP First Secy. Alexander Dubcek cancels his scheduled trip to Moscow. . . . Czechoslovak newspaper *Rude Pravo* publishes a letter in which 50 Czech economists laud the government for upholding its plans for a new system of economic management. . . . Yugoslav Premier Mika Spiljak says that military readiness must be increased in the wake of the Czechoslovak invasion.		Clashes between Mexican police and students result in at least 17 deaths in recent weeks. . . . Uruguay orders the expulsion of three Soviet embassy employees who are believed to have worked with striking students.	Philippine Pres. Ferdinand Marcos instructs his Foreign Office to arrange talks with Malaysia about the Philippine claim to the Malaysian state of Sabah.
Sept. 25		Soviet news agency *Tass* accuses the Czech press of continuing to publish "anti-Socialist propaganda.". . . At the Paris peace talks, discussions focus on the strength and legitimacy of the South Vietnamese government.	Reports indicate that Arab refugees are no longer leaving Israeli-occupied areas and going to Jordan. . . . Israeli Defense Min. Moshe Dayan believes that the chances of war are increasing because of the intensification of Arab guerrilla attacks.		
Sept. 26		Soviet Union justifies its invasion of Czechoslovakia with a new argument: that the Soviets have the right to intervene in any communist country when "right-wing anti-socialist forces" threaten to undermine it.	Israeli P.M. Levi Eshkol warns that continued Arab forays into Israel could precipitate war.	Quebec Premier Daniel Johnson dies at 53, presumably of a heart attack.	
Sept. 27	U.N. Security Council votes, 12-0, to approve a resolution again calling on Israel to permit a U.N. representative to study the conditions of Arab areas held by Israel since the June 1967 war.	Dr. Marcelo Caetano replaces gravely ill Portugese Pres. Salazar and hints that his rule will be more democratic. . . . France vetoes British entry into the Common Market for the third time. . . . A consortium of European nuclear companies is formed.	International Red Cross estimates that 8,000-10,000 people are starving to death every day in Biafra. . . . Reports indicate that Arab aid to the Eritrean secessionist movement in Ethiopia has declined since the June 1967 war with Israel.	Five thousand Mexico City students demonstrate against the seizure of the National Univ. in Mexico City. . . . Canada's Roman Catholic bishops neither condemn nor support artificial birth control. . . . Canadian P.M. Pierre Trudeau rejects demands to send food shipments to Biafra but says private shipments could be made.	Four thousand U.S. Marines sweep into the demilitarized zone.
Sept. 28		French Pres. de Gaulle meets with West German Chancellor Kurt-Georg Kiesinger in Bonn.			Intelligence reports from Saigon indicate that Communist military activity in the area of Cambodia closest to Saigon has tripled since November 1967.
Sept. 29		Reports from Vienna indicate that Albania has made diplomatic overtures to Yugoslavia as a result of their common distrust of Bulgaria.	Reports from Biafra indicate that it has appealed to Communist China for help.		

A	B	C	D	E
Includes developments that affect more than one world region, international organizations and important meetings of major world leaders.	Includes all domestic and regional developments in Europe, including the Soviet Union, Turkey, Cyprus and Malta.	Includes all domestic and regional developments in Africa and the Middle East, including Iraq and Iran and excluding Cyprus, Turkey and Afghanistan.	Includes all domestic and regional developments in Latin America, the Caribbean and Canada.	Includes all domestic and regional developments in Asia and Pacific nations, extending from Afghanistan through all the Pacific Islands, except Hawaii.

U.S. Politics & Social Issues	U.S. Foreign Policy & Defense	U.S. Economy & Environment	Science, Technology & Nature	Culture, Leisure & Life Style	
Anti-war hecklers disrupt V.P. Humphey's speech in Cleveland.					Sept. 22
Republican vice presidential candidate Spiro Agnew apologizes for his use of the terms "Polack" and "fat Jap.". . . V.P. Humphrey promises to "reassess the entire situation in Vietnam" if elected. . . . A Harris poll says that Nixon is leading Humphrey by 39%-31%.			Soviet Union launches Cosmos 243. . . . Oceanographer Dr. Albert Enget says that he has found the "oldest remnants of life"--Three-and-a-half billion-year-old sea fossils in South Africa.		Sept. 23
Republican presidential candidate Richard Nixon opposes reducing the number of U.S. troops in Vietnam. . . . Berkeley students demand that Negro author Eldridge Cleaver be allowed to give a series of lectures.			U.S. conducts an underground nuclear test in Nevada.	English and Welsh Roman Catholic bishops support artificial birth control. . . . Austrian Roman Catholic bishops say that worshippers using artificial contraceptives do not have to attend confession before being admitted to communion.	Sept. 24
Republican presidential nominee Richard Nixon charges that V.P. Humphrey's talk of an early return of some U.S. troops from Vietnam might undermine the U.S. negotiation position in the Paris peace talks. . . . Republican and Southern Democratic Senators begin a filibuster against Pres. Johnson's nomination of Supreme Court Justice Abe Fortas to be Chief Justice of the United States. . . . Democratic Vice presidential candidate Edmund Muskie invites an anti-war heckler to share the podium at Washington & Jefferson College.	U.S. reports that fiscal 1968 economic aid totaled $2.17 billion, with South Vietnam the leading recipient.			Atlantic-Little, Brown publishes George Kennan's *Democracy and the Student Left.*	Sept. 25
U.S. Amb.-to-U.N. George Ball resigns to join the Humphrey campaign.					Sept. 26
Black Panther founder Huey Newton is sentenced to two to 15 years imprisonment.				Doubleday & Co. publishes John Barth's *Lost in the Funhouse.*	Sept. 27
A Gallup Poll says that Nixon is leading Humphrey by 43%-28%.			*London Times* reports that archeologists have found "the earliest known potters' workshop in the Aegean area."		Sept. 28
About 150 anti-war demonstrators disrupt a Humphrey rally in Seattle.	Defense Secy. Clark Clifford says that the U.S. should maintain nuclear superiority over the Soviet Union.				Sept. 29

F	G	H	I	J
Includes elections, federal-state relations, civil rights and liberties, crime, the judiciary, education, health care, poverty, urban affairs and population.	*Includes formation and debate of U.S. foreign and defense policies, veterans' affairs and defense spending. (Relations with specific foreign countries are usually found under the region concerned.)*	*Includes business, labor, agriculture, taxation, transportation, consumer affairs, monetary and fiscal policy, natural resources, and pollution.*	*Includes worldwide scientific, medical and technological developments, natural phenomena, U.S. weather, natural disasters, and accidents.*	*Includes the arts, religion, scholarship, communications media, sports, entertainment, fashions, fads and social life.*

	World Affairs	Europe	Africa & the Middle East	The Americas	Asia & the Pacific
Sept. 30	World Bank Pres. Robert McNamara announces a new emphasis on population control as his organization's lending program.	Austrian Pres. Franz Jonas arrives in Yugoslavia to discuss closer cooperation between the two countries in the wake of the invasion of Czechoslovakia.		In Quebec French Premier Maurice Couve de Murville confers with Canadian P.M. Pierre Trudeau and says that policy differences between France and the Canadian government have been exaggerated. . . . Federal troops withdraw from the National University in Mexico City.	U.S. battleship *New Jersey* shells the demilitarized zone.
Oct. 1		West German demonstrators break up the right-wing National Democratic Party's first rally in Bonn. . . . A top Soviet official says that economic decentralization will continue through 1971-1975.	*Manchester Guardian* reports a major French airlift to Biafra. . . . Conflicting reports say that the Biafran town of Owerri is held by both Nigerian and Biafran troops.	Arnulfo Arias is inaugurated as Panamanian President.	Malaysia rejects a Philippine offer to discuss conflicting claims to the Malaysian state of Sabah.
Oct. 2	U.S. State Secy. Dean Rusk condemns the Soviet invasion of Czechoslovakia at the U.N.	West German right-wing National Democratic Party announces the cancellation of all of its public meetings "until restoration of democratic order."	An Israeli patrol kills eight Arab guerrillas near Jericho.	About 185 children of Canadian immigrant parents begin to attend elementary school classes in private homes in St. Leonard to avoid classes taught in French.	
Oct. 3	In the U.N. General Assembly, Guyana accuses Venezuela of occupying Guyana's half of Ankoka island.	British Labor Party conference passes a resolution calling for a halt to further negotiations with the white minority government of Rhodesia. . . . Czechoslovak leaders meet Soviet leaders in Moscow.	A team of international observers says that it has found no evidence of genocide against the Ibos of Biafra.	A military coup overthrows Peruvian Pres. Fernando Belaunde Terry. Gen. Juan Velasco Alvarado becomes president.	U.S. planes carry out the heaviest raids on North Vietnam since July 2.
Oct. 4	In the U.N. General Assembly, Pakistani Foreign Affairs Min. Mian Arshad Husain says that security must be guaranteed for non-nuclear states.	Under intense Soviet pressure Czechoslovak leaders agree publicly to abandon the remnants of their liberalization drive and to allow Soviet troops to remain in their country for an indefinite period. . . . British Labor Party conference turns down a demand for the wholesale nationalization of industry.		New military junta in Peru annuls a recent agreement with the International Petroleum Corp. concerning ownership of Peru's oil wells. . . . Bolivian Pres. Rene Barrientos Ortuno appoints a largely civilian cabinet to replace an all-military one.	U.S. officials publicly quote Cambodian leaders for the first time admitting that Communist forces are using Cambodian territory for attacks on South Vietnam.
Oct. 5		Three hundred Catholic demonstrators clash with police in Londonderry, Northern Ireland. . . . About 100 Portugese students clash with police in Lisbon. Commentators say that such a demonstration would not have been allowed in the past. . . . Czechoslovakia newspapers carry articles denouncing the Soviet news media for spreading "lies" about developments in Czechoslovakia.	American Jewish Committee reports that Egypt has forbidden the departure of its 1,000 remaining Jews of which about one quarter are in jail. . . . An Israeli patrol kills two Arab guerrillas near the Golan Heights.		U.S. planes try to clear the way for an allied relief column going to Anduc. . . . South Vietnamese politician Maj. Gen. Duong Van Minh returns to Saigon after four years of exile in Thailand.
Oct. 6		Reports from Vienna indicate that Albania has reinforced its coastal defenses with Chinese help. . . . Police and Roman Catholic demonstrators clash in Londonderry, Northern Ireland.	Fighting continues around the Biafran town of Owerri between Nigerian and Biafran forces.	Quebec Liberal Party convention pledges that it will make French the "priority language" in Quebec but will also guarantee English-speaking residents to send their children to schools of their choice.	Hundreds of allied forces are sent to relieve pressure on the U.S. Special Forces camp at Anduc. . . . U.S. forces are reported to have launched a drive to relieve allied outposts at Anduc and Thuongduc near Danang.
Oct. 7	In the U.N. General Assembly, France criticizes the U.S. intervention in Vietnam.	Finnish Foreign Min. Ahti Karjalainen condemns the Czechoslovak invasion.			

A	B	C	D	E
Includes developments that affect more than one world region, international organizations and important meetings of major world leaders.	Includes all domestic and regional developments in Europe, including the Soviet Union, Turkey, Cyprus and Malta.	Includes all domestic and regional developments in Africa and the Middle East, including Iraq and Iran and excluding Cyprus, Turkey and Afghanistan.	Includes all domestic and regional developments in Latin America, the Caribbean and Canada.	Includes all domestic and regional developments in Asia and Pacific nations, extending from Afghanistan through all the Pacific Islands, except Hawaii.

U.S. Politics & Social Issues	U.S. Foreign Policy & Defense	U.S. Economy & Environment	Science, Technology & Nature	Culture, Leisure & Life Style	
V.P. Humphrey says that if elected president he will stop the bombing of North Vietnam if it agrees to restore the demilitarized zone.				Knopf publishes Muriel Spark's *The Public Image* .	Sept. 30
Senate passes a higher education bill.				French painter Marcel Duchamp dies in Neuilly, France at 81.	Oct. 1
Pres. Johnson withdraws his nomination of Supreme Court Justice Abe Fortas to be Chief Justice of the United States. . . . Pres. Johnson signs a bill establishing a Redwood National Park in northern California.	U.S. Senate rejects by a vote of 45-25 a proposal to delete funds for an antiballistic missile system.		Soviet Union launches Cosmos 244.	Fifty-five English Roman Catholic priests say that artificial birth control is not wrong.	Oct. 2
Presidential candidates Nixon and Humphrey reject the use of nuclear weapons in Vietnam. . . . Presidential candidate Richard Nixon says that George Wallace "isn't fit to be president" because of some of his extreme positions.			U.S. launches a European satellite whose mission is to study solar and cosmic radiation. . . . Soviet Union launches Cosmos 245. . . . U.S. conducts a nuclear underground test in Nevada.		Oct. 3
					Oct. 4
Americans for Democratic Action endorses the Humphrey-Muskie ticket.			Soviet Union launches a communications satellite. . . . U.S. launches an intelligence satellite.		Oct. 5
The New York Times endorses V.P. Humphrey.				Tony Richardson's film *The Charge of the Light Brigade* opens in New York.	Oct. 6
Democratic vice presidential candidate Edmund Muskie's criticism of presidential candidate George Wallace is greeted by silence at the International Association of Iron Workers convention. . . . *The New York Times* survey indicates that the Democrats will maintain control of the Congress despite Republican gains. . . . Negro author Eldridge Cleaver gives a lecture entitled "The Roots of Racism" on the Univ. of Calif., Berkeley campus.			Soviet Union launches Cosmos 246.	Macmillan publishes Robert Conquest's *The Great Terror.*	Oct. 7

F	G	H	I	J
Includes elections, federal-state relations, civil rights and liberties, crime, the judiciary, education, health care, poverty, urban affairs and population.	Includes formation and debate of U.S. foreign and defense policies, veterans' affairs and defense spending. (Relations with specific foreign countries are usually found under the region concerned.)	Includes business, labor, agriculture, taxation, transportation, consumer affairs, monetary and fiscal policy, natural resources, and pollution.	Includes worldwide scientific, medical and technological developments, natural phenomena, U.S. weather, natural disasters, and accidents.	Includes the arts, religion, scholarship, communications media, sports, entertainment, fashions, fads and social life.

	World Affairs	Europe	Africa & the Middle East	The Americas	Asia & the Pacific
Oct. 8	West German Foreign Min. Willy Brandt and Soviet Foreign Min. Andrei Gromyko meet at the Soviet Mission to the U.N. in New York. It is the first formal conference between the two countries' foreign ministers since 1962.	Soviet Premier Aleksei Kosygin meets with Finnish Pres. Urho Kekkonen in the Gulf of Finland.		Colombia announces the Oct. 5 death of guerrilla chief Ciro Castano Trujillo. . . . Students seize several buildings at various universities throughout Quebec.	
Oct. 9		A trial of five Soviet dissidents who protested the Soviet invasion of Czechoslovakia opens in Moscow. . . . Three hundred people, including eight Soviet army officers opposed to Czech liberalization, hold a meeting in Prague amid signs that a pro-Soviet opposition group is forming. . . . About 1,500 Roman Catholic students stage a street sit-in in Belfast to protest alleged police brutality in the recent Londonderry clashes. . . . At the Paris peace talks, North Vietnam repeats its demand for a complete halt to the bombing of its territory. . . . Soviet Premier Aleksei Kosygin and Finnish Pres. Urho Kekkonen continue talks in the Gulf of Finland. . . . Reports indicate that a Czechoslovak delegation arrived in Moscow Oct. 8 to negotiate a treaty legalizing the stationing of Soviet troops on Czech soil.	British P.M. Wilson and Rhodesian P.M. Ian Smith meet in Gibraltar. . . . A hand grenade injures 48 Israelis at the Tomb of the Patriarchs in the West Bank town of Hebron.	Peruvian government officially seizes the holdings of the International Petroleum Corp.	
Oct. 10		Finnish Pres. Urho Kekkonen denies reports of Soviet military pressure on his country.			
Oct. 11	At the U.N. Albania attacks both the Soviet Union and the U.S.	British Conservative Party says that it would reverse the Labor government's decision to remove Britain's military presence east of Suez. . . . French National Assembly adopts a bill decentralizing the university system. . . . A Soviet court sentences five dissidents who protested the invasion of Czechoslovakia to terms of up to five years.		Quebec separatist movements meet in Quebec City to negotiate a merger. . . . A military coup ousts Panamanian Pres. Arnulfo Arias. Col. Omar Torrijos becomes National Guard commander. . . . Canadian students occupy Montreal's Ecole des Beaux Arts in Montreal.	U.S. troops engage about 300 Communist forces 27 miles from Saigon.
Oct. 12		Reports from Prague indicate that the main speaker at the Oct. 9 pro-Soviet meeting was Antonin Kapek, an ousted candidate member of the Czechoslovak CP Presidium. British Conservative Party leader Edward Heath scores the right-wing views of Enoch Powell.	Spanish Equatorial Guinea becomes the independent state of Equatorial Guinea.	Two leftist gunmen kill U.S. Army Capt. Charles Chandler in Sao Paulo, Brazil. . . . Panamanian National Guard commander Col. Omar Torrijos accuses deposed Pres. Arias of having tried to set up a dictatorship. . . . A Canadian study shows that 40% of the market value of all equities listed on Canadian stock markets are foreign owned.	
Oct. 13		Soviet CP cinema official says that many Western films have been banned.	British P.M. Wilson and Rhodesian P.M. Ian Smith report "some progress" at the conclusion of their talks but admit that fundamental differences remain.	Deposed Panamanian Pres. Arnulfo Arias, in a message broadcast over a clandestine radio, calls on his countrymen to rise against the ruling military junta.	*The New York Times* reports that 40% of the cadres in Shanghai, China have been made to do manual work. . . . Communist mortars fire on South Vietnamese forces from within Cambodian territory.
Oct. 14	At the U.N. Yugoslavia condemns the Czechoslovak invasion.	North Vietnam's chief negotiator at the Paris peace talks, Le Duc Tho, leaves for Hanoi as rumors circulate that North Vietnam is reviewing its position.		A new Quebec separatist party, the Parti Quebecois, headed by Rene Levesque emerges from the convention of French-Canadian separatist movements. . . . Brazilian police arrest Jose Luis Andrade Maciel on charges of masterminding the Oct. 12 killing of U.S. Army Capt. Charles Chandler in Sao Paulo, Brazil.	

A	B	C	D	E
Includes developments that affect more than one world region, international organizations and important meetings of major world leaders.	Includes all domestic and regional developments in Europe, including the Soviet Union, Turkey, Cyprus and Malta.	Includes all domestic and regional developments in Africa and the Middle East, including Iraq and Iran and excluding Cyprus, Turkey and Afghanistan.	Includes all domestic and regional developments in Latin America, the Caribbean and Canada.	Includes all domestic and regional developments in Asia and Pacific nations, extending from Afghanistan through all the Pacific Islands, except Hawaii.

U.S. Politics & Social Issues	U.S. Foreign Policy & Defense	U.S. Economy & Environment	Science, Technology & Nature	Culture, Leisure & Life Style	
Sen. Eugene McCarthy says he will support V.P. Humphrey only if he accepts a new government in South Vietnam and new reforms for the Democratic Party.	Pres. Johnson protests deep cuts in his foreign aid authorization bill.		*Washington Post* reports that Cosmos 244 is the 13th test flight of a Soviet Fractional Orbital Bombardment System, a system for dropping nuclear bombs from orbit.	Franco Zeffirelli's film *Romeo and Juliet* opens in New York.	Oct. 8
Mounted policemen break up a group of about 400 anti-war demonstrators awaiting V.P. Humphrey. . . . V.P. Humphrey rejects Sen. Eugene McCarthy's Oct. 8 conditions for his support.	Pres. Johnson directs State Secy. Rusk to start negotiations with Israel on its request to buy U.S. fighter-bombers.			An Australian court rules that an accused murderer is insane because he has an extra Y chromosome.	Oct. 9
House passes a bill by a vote of 160-149 to ban the mail order purchase of rifles and handguns.					Oct. 10
House and Senate pass a bill increasing penalties for possession of illegal drugs.		House and Senate pass a bill designed to protect the public from electronic products' radiation emissions.	U.S. launches Apollo 7, the spacecraft designed to carry the first Americans to the moon. . . . Soviet Union launches Cosmos 247.		Oct. 11
	Ford Foundation Pres. McGeorge Bundy states his support of an unconditional halt in the bombing of North Vietnam and a substantial withdrawal of U.S. forces from South Vietnam in 1969.			Counsel for Sacco and Vanzetti, Michael Angelo Musmanno, dies in Pittsburgh at 71.	Oct. 12
Presidential candidate Richard Nixon says that Western European countries should carry more of the defense burden.				Yugoslav dissident Milovan Djilas arrives in the U.S. for a stay at Princeton University.	Oct. 13
				Farrar, Straus & Giroux publish Isaac Bashevis Singer's *The Seance and Other Stories* . . . . A French court gives a reduced sentence to a murderer because he has an extra Y chromosome.	Oct. 14

F	G	H	I	J
Includes elections, federal-state relations, civil rights and liberties, crime, the judiciary, education, health care, poverty, urban affairs and population.	*Includes formation and debate of U.S. foreign and defense policies, veterans' affairs and defense spending. (Relations with specific foreign countries are usually found under the region concerned.)*	*Includes business, labor, agriculture, taxation, transportation, consumer affairs, monetary and fiscal policy, natural resources, and pollution.*	*Includes worldwide scientific, medical and technological developments, natural phenomena, U.S. weather, natural disasters, and accidents.*	*Includes the arts, religion, scholarship, communications media, sports, entertainment, fashions, fads and social life.*

	World Affairs	Europe	Africa & the Middle East	The Americas	Asia & the Pacific
Oct. 15	At the U.N. Philippine Foreign Affairs Secy. Narciso Ramos says that the Philippine-Malaysian dispute over Sabah province should be referred to the International Court of Justice.	East German Interior Min. Friedrich Dickel demands the banning of West German right-wing National Democratic Party in West Berlin. . . . Yugoslav Foreign Min. Marko Nikezic confers with French Premier Maurice Couve de Murville in Paris amid talk of possible Yugoslav arms purchases.		Quebec Education Min. Jean-Guy Cardinal warns striking students that they risk losing one semester of studies.	U.S. officials in Saigon report that North Vietnamese forces seemed to have retreated from areas surrounding South Vietnamese cities. . . . Reports indicate that Communist China is no longer attacking Yugoslavia's reform communism.
Oct. 16	At the U.N. Laotian Finance Min. Sisouk Na Champassak charges that North Vietnam has carried the Vietnamese War into Laos.	West German right-wing National Democratic Party announces the dissolution of its West Berlin branch apparently under pressure from West Berlin authorities. . . . Soviet Premier Aleksei Kosygin flies to Prague to sign a treaty authorizing the "temporary stay" of Soviet troops in Czechoslovakia. . . . In Paris U.S. State Undersecy. Nicholas Katzenbach urges Western European nations to assume a more active role in world affairs. . . . U.S. delegate William Jorden reports some "movement" at the Paris peace talks.	Israeli and Jordanian forces exchange artillery fire.		
Oct. 17		Western European Union Assembly adopts a resolution supporting a "hot line" phone communication between the NATO Council and the Warsaw Pact. . . . U.S. State Undersecy. Nicholas Katzenbach arrives in Yugoslavia to demonstrate U.S. support in the wake of the invasion of Czechoslovakia.	Israel reports the slaying of six Arab guerrillas.	Singapore executes two Indonesians for allegedly planting a bomb in a Singapore building in 1965.	
Oct. 18		Reports from Moscow indicate that former Soviet Premier Georgi Malenkov has returned from exile.			
Oct. 19		Reports from Prague indicate that the Soviet Union is demanding a purge of the liberal members of the Czechoslovak CP.		Mexico announces that the writer Octavio Paz has been dismissed as its ambassador to India because of his recent criticism of the government's handling of the student unrest.	Peking radio confirms Western accounts of a possible breakthrough in the Paris peace talks.
Oct. 20		Yugoslav Pres. Tito tells a crowd of 100,000 that Yugoslavia will resist militarily if invaded.			
Oct. 21	At the U.N. Cambodian Amb. Huot Sambath charges that the U.S. is continuing to operate inside Cambodia.	Hungarian troops begin their gradual withdrawal from central Czechoslovakia.		Some 6,000 university and junior college students march in Montreal to publicize their demands for better university facilities.	U.S. military authorities release 14 North Vietnamese prisoners of war.
Oct. 22		Czechoslovak Academy of Sciences denounces the Soviet invasion.	Reports indicate that the Soviet Union is supplying Nigeria with MiG fighters.	Deposed Panamanian Pres. Arnulfo Arias leaves Panama for asylum in the United States. . . . Most junior college classes resume after officials agree to meet student demands in Quebec.	Communist forces shell the U.S. base at Dongha for the first time in 56 days.
Oct. 23		At the Paris peace talks, U.S. Amb. Averell Harriman asserts that the National Liberation Front "was born in Hanoi in 1960." . . . Italian socialists hold a national congress in Rome.	Violent anti-Israeli demonstrations take place in the occupied West Bank towns of Ramallah, Jenin and Nablus.	A government report indicates that French-Canadians in Quebec earn less than English-speaking Quebec residents equal educational qualifications. . . . Peruvian Pres. Gen. Juan Velasco Alvarado announces that the suspension of constitutional guarantees will continue for an additional thirty days.	U.S. troops take a heavy toll of Communist forces near Danang.
	A	B	C	D	E
	Includes developments that affect more than one world region, international organizations and important meetings of major world leaders.	Includes all domestic and regional developments in Europe, including the Soviet Union, Turkey, Cyprus and Malta.	Includes all domestic and regional developments in Africa and the Middle East, including Iraq and Iran and excluding Cyprus, Turkey and Afghanistan.	Includes all domestic and regional developments in Latin America, the Caribbean and Canada.	Includes all domestic and regional developments in Asia and Pacific nations, extending from Afghanistan through all the Pacific Islands, except Hawaii.

U.S. Politics & Social Issues	U.S. Foreign Policy & Defense	U.S. Economy & Environment	Science, Technology & Nature	Culture, Leisure & Life Style	
Republican vice presidential candidate Spiro Agnew says that the young and the poor cannot take the lead in solving their own problems.	Pres. Johnson reaffirms U.S. support for Yugoslav independence in the wake of the Czechoslovak invasion.			Dial Press publishes Aleksandr Solzhenitsyn's *The Cancer Ward*.	Oct. 15
Pres. Johnson signs a higher education bill.				Three Americans jointly win the Nobel Prize in medicine.	Oct. 16
Presidential candidate Richard Nixon says that the U.S. should begin to move toward volunteer armed forces.	*The New York Times* reports that the U.S. has offered to halt the bombing of North Vietnam if North Vietnam promises to decrease attacks on South Vietnamese cities.			Japanese author Yasunari Kawabata wins the Nobel Prize in literature.	Oct. 17
Vice presidential candidate Spiro Agnew says, "to some extent, if you've seen one city slum you've seen them all."		Pres. Johnson signs a bill designed to protect the public from radiation emissions from electronic products.			Oct. 18
Presidential candidate Richard Nixon says that the U.S. should encourage regional defense associations to lessen the need of direct U.S. intervention.			Soviet Union launches Cosmos 248.		Oct. 19
V.P. Humphrey issues a statement supporting birth control.			Soviet Union launches Cosmos 249.	Scandinavian Roman Catholic bishops say that each individual has the right to accept or reject artificial birth control. Jacqueline Kennedy, the widow of Pres. John Kennedy, marries Greek shipping magnate Aristotle Onassis.	Oct. 20
A Gallup Poll shows Richard Nixon leading Hubert Humphrey by 43%-31%.	U.S. officials say that shipments of major military equipment to Greece will be resumed.			Coward-McCann publishes John Le Carre's *A Small Town in Germany*. Liberal Spanish cleric Dom Aurelio Maria Escarre dies in Barcelona at 60.	Oct. 21
Pres. Johnson signs a gun control bill but calls it inadequate.				Knopf publishes Arthur Schlesinger's *The Birth of the Nation*.	Oct. 22
N.Y.C. police arrest nine Cuban exiles charged with bombing offices of countries trading with Cuba.				Harcourt, Brace & World publishes *The Collected Essays, Journalism and Letters of George Orwell*.	Oct. 23

F	G	H	I	J
Includes elections, federal-state relations, civil rights and liberties, crime, the judiciary, education, health care, poverty, urban affairs and population.	*Includes formation and debate of U.S. foreign and defense policies, veterans' affairs and defense spending. (Relations with specific foreign countries are usually found under the region concerned.)*	*Includes business, labor, agriculture, taxation, transportation, consumer affairs, monetary and fiscal policy, natural resources, and pollution.*	*Includes worldwide scientific, medical and technological developments, natural phenomena, U.S. weather, natural disasters, and accidents.*	*Includes the arts, religion, scholarship, communications media, sports, entertainment, fashions, fads and social life.*

	World Affairs	Europe	Africa & the Middle East	The Americas	Asia & the Pacific
Oct. 24		Former governor-general of Algeria Jacques Soustelle returns to France after six years of exile abroad. . . . Reports indicate that Czechoslovakia has decided not to implement a worker-management plan because of Soviet pressure.			
Oct. 25	A U.N. General Assembly resolution calls on Britain to use force against Rhodesia.	French Pres. de Gaulle visits Turkey and obliquely suggests that it reduce its military participation in NATO. . . . Czechoslovak CP leader Alexander Dubcek says that the country will have to move faster to meet Soviet demands. . . . More than 1,000 students seize the London School of Economics in order to use it as "a sanctury" in the event of violence during the upcoming anti-Vietnam War demonstration. . . . *London Times* reports that Hungary has agreed to settle its debt to foreign holders of 1924 bonds.	A mine kills three Israeli soldiers in the Jordan Valley.	U.S. extends formal recognition to the military government of Peru. . . . Peruvian government says that it plans to expand trade with Communist countries.	
Oct. 26		British students vote to end the occupation of the London School of Economics. . . . A group of 50 prominent Portugese leaders petition Pres. Marcelo Caetano to investigate the death of a university student imprisoned for political reasons.	Egypt and Israel exchange gunfire across the Suez Canal. . . .		Communist troops launch their first major ground assault in South Vietnam in a month.
Oct. 27		Czechoslovak Parliament passes a law giving Slovakia greater autonomy. . . . Fifty thousand protestors demonstrate in London against the Vietnamese War.	Arab guerrillas kill two Israeli soldiers in the extreme north of Israel.		U.S. planes bomb the Tayninh area.
Oct. 28		East German news agency reports that youths have been givern jail sentences of up to 27 months for portesting against the Czechoslovak invasion. . . . Thousands of Czechoslovaks in Prague demonstrate against the Soviet invasion. . . . Italian socialists end a national congress divided over renewing the center-left alliance with the Christian Democrats.	East Jerusalem Arabs demonstrate against Israeli rule. . . . Israeli authorities impose a curfew on Jericho after a pro-Egyptian march by 150 school children. Reports indicate that the new Syrian cabinet represents a victory for the nationalist wing of the Baath party which favors more cooperation with Arab countries and less dependence on the Soviet Union.		U.S. planes continue their bombardment of the Tayninh area.
Oct. 29		Israeli Defense Min. Moshe Dayan warns Egypt of retaliation if it "continues th violate the cease-fire."			U.S. planes bomb Communist positions in the demilitarized zone.
Oct. 30			Israeli authorities deport Mayor Nadim Zaro of the West Bank town of Ramallah to Jordan because of anti-Israeli activities.		
Oct. 31		Czech pastors call for the end of the Soviet occupation. . . . *Jane's All the World's Aircraft,* 1968-69 edition, reports that the Soviet Union launched at least 12 orbit bombardment systems in 1967-1968. . . . Police disperse several hundred Portuguese students protesting the death of student activist Daniel Campos de Sousa Teixeira.	Israeli commandos destroy targets 200 miles from the Suez Canal in a helicopter raid along the Nile River.	Reports indicate that Canadian P.M. Pierre Trudeau has offered federal funds to the opposition parties for research assistance. . . .	Communist CP announces that Chief-of-State Liu Shao-chi has been expelled from the party.
Nov. 1	U.N. Security Council meets to discuss the latest Egyptian-Israeli commando raids.	Former Greek P.M. George Papandreou dies at 80 of a bleeding ulcer in Athens.			U.S. halts all military bombardment of North Vietnam.

A	B	C	D	E
Includes developments that affect more than one world region, international organizations and important meetings of major world leaders.	Includes all domestic and regional developments in Europe, including the Soviet Union, Turkey, Cyprus and Malta.	Includes all domestic and regional developments in Africa and the Middle East, including Iraq and Iran and excluding Cyprus, Turkey and Afghanistan.	Includes all domestic and regional developments in Latin America, the Caribbean and Canada.	Includes all domestic and regional developments in Asia and Pacific nations, extending from Afghanistan through all the Pacific Islands, except Hawaii.

U.S. Politics & Social Issues	U.S. Foreign Policy & Defense	U.S. Economy & Environment	Science, Technology & Nature	Culture, Leisure & Life Style	
Presidential candidate Richard Nixon rejects the notion of "parity" or equality of nuclear forces between the Soviet Union and the U.S. . . . Pres. Johnson signs a bill increasing penalties for possession of illegal drugs.	Pres. Johnson says that the U.S. is still waiting for a reply from North Vietnam promising a de-escalation of the war in return for a complete halt of the U.S. bombing.			Dutton publishes Francoise Sagan's *The Heart-Keeper.* . . . World Publishing publishes Norman Mailer's *Miami and the Siege of Chicago.*	Oct. 24
Presidential candidate Richard Nixon calls for a national standard for welfare payments.				Austrian actor Rudolf Forster dies in Vienna at 84.	Oct. 25
Pres. Johnson attacks the Republicans as "wooden soldiers of the status quo."			Soviet Union launches manned spacecraft Soyuz 3.		Oct. 26
Presidential candidate Richard Nixon says that he is against imposing a coalition government on South Vietnam.				Austrian physicist Lise Meitner dies in London at 89.	Oct. 27
Civil rights leader Dr. Ralph Abernathy endorses V.P. Humphrey for president. Rice Univ. announces that Pres. Johnson will conduct seminars on campus during 1969.	Pres. Johnson confers in Washington with Gen. Creighton Abrams, new commander of U.S. forces in South Vietnam.			Viking Press publishes Saul Bellow's *Mosby's Memoirs and Other Stories.*	Oct. 28
Sen. Eugene McCarthy endorses V.P. Humphrey for president.	Pres. Johnson continues discussions with Gen. Creighton Abrams, commander of U.S. forces in South Vietnam.				Oct. 29
			Soviet spacecraft Soyuz 3 returns safely to earth. U.S. conducts an underground nuclear test in Nevada.	U.S. physicist Luis Walter Alvarez wins the Nobel Prize in physics.	Oct. 30
Presidential candidates Nixon, Humphrey and Wallace support Pres. Johnson's decision to stop the bombing of North Vietnam.	Pres. Johnson announces that he is suspending the bombing of North Vietnam as of Nov. 1.		Soviet Union launches Cosmos 250 and Cosmos 251.		Oct. 31
Congressional Quarterly reports that Pres. Johnson was supported on 75% of the key roll-call votes in the second session of the 90th Congress.	*The New York Times* reports that U.S. decided to seek North Vietnamese military restraint after a bombing halt instead of before during a series of meetings which ended Sept. 17.		Soviet Union launches Cosmos 252.		Nov. 1
F	G	H	I	J	
Includes elections, federal-state relations, civil rights and liberties, crime, the judiciary, education, health care, poverty, urban affairs and population.	Includes formation and debate of U.S. foreign and defense policies, veterans' affairs and defense spending. (Relations with specific foreign countries are usually found under the region concerned.)	Includes business, labor, agriculture, taxation, transportation, consumer affairs, monetary and fiscal policy, natural resources, and pollution.	Includes worldwide scientific, medical and technological developments, natural phenomena, U.S. weather, natural disasters, and accidents.	Includes the arts, religion, scholarship, communications media, sports, entertainment, fashions, fads and social life.	

	World Affairs	Europe	Africa & the Middle East	The Americas	Asia & the Pacific
Nov. 2		*New York Times* reports that 2,000 Jews have emigrated from Poland since March.	Egyptian Pres. Nasser announces the formation of a civil guard to defend against Israeli commando attacks west of the Suez Canal. . . . Israeli authorities impose a curfew in Bethlehem for the first time since the city's capture in the June 1967 war.		South Vietnamese Pres. Nguyen Van Thieu announces that his government will not attend the Paris peace talks if the National Liberation Front is represented by a separate delegation.
Nov. 3		Fifty thousand Greeks defy martial law and demonstrate against the government in central Athens.	Jordanian soldiers and Palestinian commandoes clash near Amman.	Panamanian students and professors clash with the National Guard in anti-government protests in Panama City.	A U.S. plane accidently bombs a Marine Corps unit killing six Marines.
Nov. 4			Jordanian security forces suppress an anti-government demonstration of 10,000.	Peruvian newspapers stage a 24-hour general strike in protest against recent press restrictions.	
Nov. 5			Israeli P.M. Levi Eshkol declares that Israel considers the Jordan River as its security frontier in any peace agreement it might negotiate with Jordan.		
Nov. 6		Several hundred Czechs demonstrate in Prague against the Soviet invasion of Czechoslovakia.	Israeli Defense Min. Moshe Dayan suggests the West Bank town of Hebron and the adjacent occupied area be merged into a single economic unit with Jerusalem and Beersheba. . . . A Rhodesian court sentences five black Africans to life in prison for entering Rhodesia armed.		
Nov. 7	A U.N. General Assembly resolution calls on Britain to use force against Rhodesia.	Czech police break up an anti-Soviet demonstration of 2,000 in Prague with clubs and tear gas. . . . Anti-Nazi Beate Klarsfeld slaps West German Chancellor Kurt-Georg Kiesinger in the face because of his former membership in the Nazi party.			U.S. authorities report 150 combat fatalities for the Oct. 27-Nov. 2 period. . . . North Korean patrol boats capture four South Korean fishing boats. . . . Anti-government student rioting breaks out in Pakistan.
Nov. 8		Czech government suspends two magazines because of articles critical of the Soviet occupation.	Egyptian sources report that the Soviet Amb. Sergei Vinogradov has said the Aswan Dam "will be defended, even if we have to defend it ourselves."		North Korean patrol boats capture ten South Korean fishing boats.
Nov. 9				Reports indicate that Peru plans to nationalize mountainous farmland belonging to a U.S. mining firm.	South Vietnam suspends two newspapers critical of the government.
Nov. 10		Portugese opposition leader Mario Soares returns to Portugal from his eight-month exile. . . . Reports indicate that Soviet officers have been spat upon by participants in an anti-Soviet demonstration in Czechoslovakia.	British Union Jack is lowered for the last time in Rhodesia.		Communists shell U.S. Marine positions inside the demilitarized zone for the first time since Nov. 1.
Nov. 11	Rumania formally applies for GATT membership. It is the first Communist government to apply for full membership.	Soviet Premier Aleksei Kosygin invites former Defense Secy. Robert McNamara to Moscow and suggests that arms control talks should begin between the two countries.	New Rhodesian flag is raised at government installations.		Cambodian Chief of State Prince Norodom Sihanouk says that allied forces have attacked his country in the previous five days.
	A	B	C	D	E
	Includes developments that affect more than one world region, international organizations and important meetings of major world leaders.	Includes all domestic and regional developments in Europe, including the Soviet Union, Turkey, Cyprus and Malta.	Includes all domestic and regional developments in Africa and the Middle East, including Iraq and Iran and excluding Cyprus, Turkey and Afghanistan.	Includes all domestic and regional developments in Latin America, the Caribbean and Canada.	Includes all domestic and regional developments in Asia and Pacific nations, extending from Afghanistan through all the Pacific Islands, except Hawaii.

U.S. Politics & Social Issues	U.S. Foreign Policy & Defense	U.S. Economy & Environment	Science, Technology & Nature	Culture, Leisure & Life Style	
A consensus is growing that V.P. Humphrey is rapidly narrowing the gap between himself and Richard Nixon.				Dutch Roman Catholic episcopate upholds the Dutch bishops' decision leaving use of artificial contraceptives up to the individual.	Nov. 2
V.P. Humphrey speaks before an enthusiastic crowd of 58,000 in Texas.					Nov. 3
V.P. Humphrey draws an enthusiastic crowd of 100,000 in Los Angeles. . . . Left-wing students occupy administrative buildings at San Fernando Valley State College in Calif.					Nov. 4
Richard Nixon is elected 37th President of the United States. . . . Student disturbances take place at George Washington Univ., Washington, D.C.					Nov. 5
Student unrest breaks out at San Francisco College when Negro students demand admission of all Negro applicants regardless of qualifications.				French conductor Charles Munch dies in Richmond, Va. at 77. . . . Former Lebanese P.M. Sami es-Solh dies in Beirut at 79.	Nov. 6
					Nov. 7
Negro students protest alleged inadequacies in Hyde County, N.C. school integration plan.			U.S. launches spacecraft Pioneer 9 whose mission is to gather data on solar plasma.		Nov. 8
				French Roman Catholic bishops declare that it is up to the individual to decide whether to use artificial contraceptives.	Nov. 9
Students announce plans to burn puppies in napalm at Grossmont College, El Cajon, Calif.			Soviet Union launches spaceship Zond 6.		Nov. 10
One hundred students occupy the administrative building of the Univ. of Connecticut in Storrs to press amnesty demands for students arrested in anti-Dow Chemical Co. demonstrations on Oct. 30. . . . Grossmont College students call off plans to burn puppies in napalm.	Pres.-elect Richard Nixon says that Pres. Johnson can speak for the next administration about major foreign policy matters.				Nov. 11
F	G	H	I	J	
Includes elections, federal-state relations, civil rights and liberties, crime, the judiciary, education, health care, poverty, urban affairs and population.	Includes formation and debate of U.S. foreign and defense policies, veterans' affairs and defense spending. (Relations with specific foreign countries are usually found under the region concerned.)	Includes business, labor, agriculture, taxation, transportation, consumer affairs, monetary and fiscal policy, natural resources, and pollution.	Includes worldwide scientific, medical and technological developments, natural phenomena, U.S. weather, natural disasters, and accidents.	Includes the arts, religion, scholarship, communications media, sports, entertainment, fashions, fads and social life.	

	World Affairs	Europe	Africa & the Middle East	The Americas	Asia & the Pacific
Nov. 12	Former Spanish colony of Equatorial Guinea becomes the U.N.'s 126th member.	Bank of France raises its discount rate to shore up the French franc. . . . In Warsaw Soviet CP Gen. Secy. Leonid Brezhnev calls for "an even mightier offensive against the West.". . . NATO Supreme Commander Gen. Lyman Lemnitzer calls for improved NATO defenses in the wake of the Czechoslovak invasion. . . . Thousands of high school and university students boycott classes in major Italian cities to press demands for educational reforms.		Canadian P.M. Pierre Trudeau says that Canada will make no new contributions to NATO until the country has completed a review of its defense posture. . . . French-Canadian student demonstrations close Chicoutimi Junior College.	U.S. reports the loss of its first plane over South Vietnam since the halt of the bombing of North Vietnam. . . . South Vietnam says that it wants written assurances from North Vietnam about the peace talks agenda.
Nov. 13		Student demonstrators halt traffic in Rome.			South Vietnam criticizes Defense Secy. Clark Clifford's warning that the U.S. might procede without the South Vietnamese government in the Paris peace talks. . . . A Laotian official says that two North Vietnamese regiments have recently crossed into Laos from South Vietnam.
Nov. 14		At the Polish CP meeting in Warsaw, Italian communists call for autonomy for national communists movements. . . . NATO Defense Planning Committee announces plans for substantial increases in NATO's conventional military strength. . . . About 12 million Italian workers stage a strike for better wages. . . . Yale Univ. says that it will admit female undergraduate students for the first time starting in 1969.		Canadian Party leader Robert Stanfield accuses the Trudeau government of bringing Canada into disrepute by delaying a firm statement on NATO policy.	South Vietnamese government suspends the *Saigon Daily News* for printing details of Defense Secy. Clifford's recent criticism of the South Vietnamese government.
Nov. 15		Czech government places police on alert in case of anti-Soviet demonstrations. . . . Fierce speculation hits the French franc.		Canadian P.M. Pierre Trudeau denies a report that Canada will increase its financial contributions to NATO. . . . French-Canadian student demonstrations close two colleges in Quebec. . . . Canada announces a major wheat sale to Communist China.	
Nov. 16		British and Rhodesian officials report minor progress but major differences remain unresolved. . . . Polish leader of the anti-Semitic wing of the Communist Party Gen. Mieczyslaw Moczar is denied full membership on the Politburo. . . . Right-wing Conservative Party member Enoch Powell renews his efforts to halt immigration of non-whites to Britain.		Quebec and France agree to expand cultural, educational and technical cooperation.	
Nov. 17		Czech government forbids an anti-Soviet demonstration in Prague. . . . Czechoslovak CP First Secy. Alexander Dubcek urges a compromise between Soviet demands and his progressive programs.			South Korea reports that 17 North Korean infiltrators have been killed recently.
Nov. 18		Britain says that it is shipping some armaments to Nigeria. . . . France announces that a Nov. 16 strategic submarine missile test was successful. . . . Yugoslav Defense Min. Gen. Nikolai Ljubicic says that the country's defense budget will be increased in 1969. . . . Fierce speculation batters the French franc. . . . Roman Catholic demonstrators fight with police on the steps of Londonderry's City Hall in Northern Ireland. . . . Czechoslovak CP First Secy. Alexander Dubcek obliquely confirms reports that he met secretly with Soviet CP Gen. Secy. Leonid Brezhnev on Nov. 15 in Warsaw. . . . Czech students in Bohemia and Moravia begin a university strike.	*Newsweek* magazine reports that French mercenaries are training Biafran soldiers.	In an apparent reversal of his earlier position, Canadian P.M. Pierre Trudeau says that Canada has deferred plans to reduce its NATO air division in face of the invasion of Czechoslovakia.	North and South Vietnamese troops engage in heavy fighting around Danang.

A	B	C	D	E
Includes developments that affect more than one world region, international organizations and important meetings of major world leaders.	Includes all domestic and regional developments in Europe, including the Soviet Union, Turkey, Cyprus and Malta.	Includes all domestic and regional developments in Africa and the Middle East, including Iraq and Iran and excluding Cyprus, Turkey and Afghanistan.	Includes all domestic and regional developments in Latin America, the Caribbean and Canada.	Includes all domestic and regional developments in Asia and Pacific nations, extending from Afghanistan through all the Pacific Islands, except Hawaii.

U.S. Politics & Social Issues	U.S. Foreign Policy & Defense	U.S. Economy & Environment	Science, Technology & Nature	Culture, Leisure & Life Style	
Univ. of Connecticut students evacuate occupied administrative building after use of police is threatened. . . . U.S. Supreme Court strikes down a 1928 Arkansas law forbidding the teaching of the theory of the evolution of man from lower animal orders.	Defense Secy. Clark Clifford warns South Vietnam that if it doesn't partici- pate in the Paris peace talks, the U.S. will proceed without it.		U.S. officials announce that the U.S. will try to place three astronauts around the moon before Christmas. . . . Results of the first U.S. study of the effects of birth control pills shows a link with increased death rates from diseases of the veins.		Nov. 12
A policeman and Black Panther member are wounded in a shoot-out in Berkeley, Calif.	Pres.-elect Nixon names H.R. Halder- man as special assistant to the presi- dent.		Soviet Union launches Cosmos 253.		Nov. 13
Student disturbances take place at Colo- rado State University, Fort Collins, Colo.	Pres.-elect Nixon names John Ehrlich- man as counsel to the President. U.S. government offers $500,000 to three religious agencies to help charter a transport plane to fly relief supplies into Biafra.		Soviet spaceship Zond 6 circles the moon.		Nov. 14
A Miami court finds nine Cuban exiles guilty of conspiring to damage ships of countries that trade with Cuba.	Pres.-elect Nixon names Ron Ziegler as special assistant to the president in charge of press relations. . . . State Secy. Rusk says that Austria and Yugo- slavia are in the area of "NATO security interests."				Nov. 15
Police patrol Bluefield State College in West Virginia after Negro students at- tack the student union building.			Soviet Union launches a space station.		Nov. 16
			Soviet spaceship Zond 6 returns safely to earth.		Nov. 17
Student disturbances occur at St. Cloud State College, St. Cloud, Minn.	U.S. urges Israel to allow the return of all Arab refugees who fled the West Bank in the 1967 war.				Nov. 18

F	G	H	I	J
Includes elections, federal-state rela- tions, civil rights and liberties, crime, the judiciary, education, health care, pover- ty, urban affairs and population.	*Includes formation and debate of U.S. foreign and defense policies, veterans' affairs and defense spending. (Relations with specific foreign countries are usual- ly found under the region concerned.)*	*Includes business, labor, agriculture, taxation, transportation, consumer af- fairs, monetary and fiscal policy, natural resources, and pollution.*	*Includes worldwide scientific, medical and technological developments, natural phenomena, U.S. weather, natural disas- ters, and accidents.*	*Includes the arts, religion, scholarship, communications media, sports, enter- tainment, fashions, fads and social life.*

	World Affairs	Europe	Africa & the Middle East	The Americas	Asia & the Pacific
Nov. 19	U.N. General Assembly votes, 58-44, against a resolution to seat Communist China and expel Nationalist China.	French government orders budget cuts to defend the French franc. . . . Reports from Czechoslovakia indicate that factory workers are supporting student demands for a liberalization program.	A bloodless coup overthrows Pres. Modibo Keita of Mali. . . . Israel announces that it will allow an additional 7,000 Arab refugees to return to the West Bank.	About 200 social science students occupy their faculty headquarters at the Univ. of Ottawa.	
Nov. 20		Six hundred Czech factory workers go on an all-day strike against the Soviet occupation. . . . Foreign exchange markets close in Europe to halt intense speculation. . . . Key industrial nations end their meeting on ways to deal with the recent wave of speculation. . . . About 2,000 Lisbon students demonstrate for greater freedoms.	Sierra Leone P.M. Siaka Probyn Stevens declares a state of emergency following ethnic clashes.	Simon Fraser College students take over administrative headquarters in Vancouver, Canada.	Reports from Laos indicate the entrance of four North Vietnamese battalions on Nov. 15.
Nov. 21		British Atty. Gen. Sir Elwyn Jones says that he is considering investigating whether right-wing conservative Enoch Powell has violated the Race Relations Act which prohibits encouragement of racial violence. Greek government grants a stay of execution to Alexandros Panaghoulis who attempted to assassinate Greek P.M. George Papadopoulos on Aug 13.	Reports from Mali indicate that the state socialism of deposed Pres. Modibo Keita is being discarded. . . . Major anti-government demonstrations erupt in Mansura, Egypt, 75 miles from Cairo. . . . The New York Times reports that the Jordanian government and Arab guerrillas have worked out an agreement to avoid confrontations. . . . Nigeria and the Soviet Union sign a major economic assistance agreement.		U.S. artillery fires into the demilitarized zone for the first time since Nov. 1. . . . Major fighting occurs between allied and Communist forces in the Danang area.
Nov. 22		U.S. and Rumania sign an agreement for the exchange of information on the peaceful uses of atomic energy. . . . British Atty. Gen. Sir Elwyn Jones decides against investigating Enoch Powell for possible violation of the Race Relations Act.	New Mali Pres. Moussa Traore says his country is open to private capital. . . . A bomb kills 12 people and injures 55 in the Israeli section of Jerusalem.	Mexican National Student Strike Council decides to call off its strike because it is no longer effective.	North Korea releases the 82 surviving members of the U.S. ship Pueblo.
Nov. 23		West German newspaper Bild-Zeitung says that West Germany is now the most powerful country in Western Europe because of its financial strength. . . . Pres. de Gaulle stuns the financial world by announcing that he will not devalue the French franc.	Student riots break out in Alexandria, Egypt. . . . Israeli authorities place the West Bank town of Nablus under a curfew because of recent protests.	Reports indicate that striking student leaders have been expelled from French-Canadian colleges in Quebec.	A Laotian official says that North Vietnamese forces are entering Laos from South Vietnam as well as from North Vietnam.
Nov. 24		The New York Times reports that the Soviet Union maintains a tight control over all nuclear warheads in East Germany.	Egypt orders the closing of all universities in the wake of student unrest.		
Nov. 25		France puts into effect strict foreign exchange controls. . . . Soviet Union promises to provide North Vietnam with large amounts of military equipment. . . . Northern Ireland announces the replacement of the Londonderry mayor and governing council by an appointed commission that is expected to be more impartial in its dealings with the Catholic and Protestant populations. . . . Czechoslovak government forbids virtually all travel to the West.	Israel deports eight Arabs to Jordan which brings to 31 the number of West Bank Arabs forced to leave because of anti-Israeli activities. . . . Tax riots erupt in the Western Nigerian town of Ishara. . . . Egyptian government closes the secondary schools in Alexandria.	McGill Univ. students occupy a university department building to press their demands for greater university representation.	
Nov. 26		French P.M. Couve de Murville presents the government's latest austerity measures. . . . Czechoslovak cultural organizations express their support for the liberalization program. . . . U.S. and Rumania sign a two-year cultural exchange agreement.	In a new move to curb terrorist raids, Israeli announces that all vehicular traffic over the Jordan River will be prohibited. . . . Tax riots erupt in the Western Nigerian town of Ibadan.		South Vietnam says that it will participate in the Paris peace talks. . . . Communist China proposes that its representatives meet with those of the incoming Nixon administration. . . . Allied troops enter the demilitarized zone for the first time since Nov. 1.
	A	B	C	D	E
	Includes developments that affect more than one world region, international organizations and important meetings of major world leaders.	Includes all domestic and regional developments in Europe, including the Soviet Union, Turkey, Cyprus and Malta.	Includes all domestic and regional developments in Africa and the Middle East, including Iraq and Iran and excluding Cyprus, Turkey and Afghanistan.	Includes all domestic and regional developments in Latin America, the Caribbean and Canada.	Includes all domestic and regional developments in Asia and Pacific nations, extending from Afghanistan through all the Pacific Islands, except Hawaii.

U.S. Politics & Social Issues	U.S. Foreign Policy & Defense	U.S. Economy & Environment	Science, Technology & Nature	Culture, Leisure & Life Style	
U.S. Supreme Court rules that the postponement of public rallies without allowing the demonstrators an opportunity to object is unconstitutional. . . . HEW Dept. proposes a new regulation that would virtually end investigations of welfare applicants before they receive relief. . . . Black Panthers allegedly attack San Francisco policemen.	Pres. Johnson calls for a sustained effort in Vietnam.		Biologists Marshall Nirenberg and Har Gobind Khorana win the 1968 Albert Lasker Medical Research Awards for their clarification of the genetic code.		Nov. 19
			Soviet Union launches Cosmos 254. . . . Explosions trap 78 miners below the surface in a mine near Mannington, W. Va.		Nov. 20
Negro students ransack the administrative building of Oshkosh State University in Wisconsin.	U.S. signs an agreement apologizing for the alleged intrusion of the U.S. ship *Pueblo* into North Korean waters to gain the release of the crew but simultaneously publicly disavows the statement.	Pres. Johnson creates a seven-man National Water Commission to plan the nation's long-range conservation efforts.		Holt, Rinehart & Winston Inc. publishes Andre Malraux's *Anti-Memoirs*.	Nov. 21
	U.S. officials confirm that the U.S. Pakistani base on the Afghanistan border will be closed in 1969.		U.S. conducts a nuclear underground test in Nevada.	Portegese bishops announce their support of an encyclical banning artificial birth control. . . . Funk & Wagnalls publishes Jim Bishop's *The Day Kennedy Was Shot*.	Nov. 22
	Pueblo Cmndr. Lloyd Bucher says that both he and his crew members were often beaten by their North Korean captors.				Nov. 23
					Nov. 24
	State Secy. Rusk tells Soviet Amb. Anatoly Dobrynin that the U.S. would like to start arms control talks as soon as possible.			Little, Brown publishes William Manchester's *The Arms of Krupp*. . . . U.S. novelist Upton Sinclair dies in Bound Brook, N.J. at 90.	Nov. 25
In the wake of racial disturbances at Bluefield State College in West Virginia, officials decide to close all dormatories. . . . A Gallup Poll says that 43% of those questioned approve of Pres. Johnson's handling of the presidency.				Houston's Alley Theater Co. opens in its new building in Houston, Tex.	Nov. 26

F	G	H	I	J
Includes elections, federal-state relations, civil rights and liberties, crime, the judiciary, education, health care, poverty, urban affairs and population.	Includes formation and debate of U.S. foreign and defense policies, veterans' affairs and defense spending. (Relations with specific foreign countries are usually found under the region concerned.)	Includes business, labor, agriculture, taxation, transportation, consumer affairs, monetary and fiscal policy, natural resources, and pollution.	Includes worldwide scientific, medical and technological developments, natural phenomena, U.S. weather, natural disasters, and accidents.	Includes the arts, religion, scholarship, communications media, sports, entertainment, fashions, fads and social life.

	World Affairs	Europe	Africa & the Middle East	The Americas	Asia & the Pacific
Nov. 27		Protest demonstrations erupt among Albanians living in Yugoslavia.		Univ. of Ottawa students end their strike after gaining greater participation in administrative affairs.	Japanese Liberal-Democratic Party re-elects Premier Eisaku Sato as its president. . . . *The New York Times* says that the Nov. 26 Communist Chinese proposal for a peaceful co-existence agreement was the first such public call.
Nov. 28		Czech government demands the suspension of a Soviet propaganda newspaper *Pravy* distributed in Czechoslovakia. . . . Bank of France reports that total French reserves have dropped by more than $3 billion since May. . . . In Spain Bishop Jose Maria Cirarda of Bilboa announces a series of liberal reforms which may indicate that the Vatican is unhappy with the conservative Franco regime.			North Vietnamese attack government positions in Laos. . . . North Vietnamese radio says that the country's delegation at the Paris peace talks will not talk with representatives of the South Vietnamese government.
Nov. 29	U.N. General Assembly condemns Portugal's colonial policy in Africa.		Nixon headquarters confirms that former Pa. Gov. William Scranton will visit the Middle East on a fact-finding mission.	Canadian P.M. Pierre Trudeau says that Canada's major problem is the economic disparities between its different regions. . . . Venezuelan terrorists machine gun to death two security guards in preelection violence.	U.S. reports 160 combat deaths for the Nov. 17-23 period. . . . Fighting continues between government and North Vietnamese troops in Laos.
Nov. 30		Protestant and Catholic demonstrators clash in Armagh, Northern Ireland. . . . Soviet newspapers attack "anti-socialist" Czechoslovak forces for the first time in almost a month. . . . Yugoslav Pres. Tito says that his country is ready to defend itself against the Soviet Union.			
Dec. 1		Britain, West Germany and Holland agree to build a centrifuge separation plant to produce low-cost enriched-uranium reactor fuel.	Israeli and Jordanian forces trade the heaviest artillery fire since the June 1967 war.	Rafael Caldera Rodriguez wins an authentically democratic presidential election in Venezuela.	
Dec. 2	U.N. General Assembly condemns South Africa's apartheid policy.	Police and striking farm workers clash in Avola, Sicily, resulting in the deaths of two workers.	Iraq troops stationed in Jordan shell an Israeli border settlement. . . . Israeli planes attack the Jordanian town of Irbid, about 40 miles north of Amman.		
Dec. 3		Police serve a summons on the Rev. Ian Paisley, leader of Northern Ireland's militant Protestants, for contributing to the Nov. 30 disturbances in Armagh. . . . Disorders occur in Italian cities in reaction to the Dec. 2 slayings of two farm workers.	Iraq troops stationed in Jordan exchange artillery fire with Israeli forces. . . . Israeli planes strike targets in Jordan.		*Washington Post* reports that the Soviet Union has invited Nationalist Chinese journalists to visit. . . . Reports from Laos indicate that Communist Chinese troops are building a road in northern Laos.
Dec. 4		Three major Italian labor unions strike for higher wages in Rome.	Israeli jets carry out their third air strike against Jordan in three days.	Mexican National Student Strike Council officially ends its four month-old strike by high school and university students.	
Dec. 5		Striking workers halt public transportation in Rome.		About 3,000 Quebec high school students demonstrate for a unilingual French school system.	

A	B	C	D	E
Includes developments that affect more than one world region, international organizations and important meetings of major world leaders.	Includes all domestic and regional developments in Europe, including the Soviet Union, Turkey, Cyprus and Malta.	Includes all domestic and regional developments in Africa and the Middle East, including Iraq and Iran and excluding Cyprus, Turkey and Afghanistan.	Includes all domestic and regional developments in Latin America, the Caribbean and Canada.	Includes all domestic and regional developments in Asia and Pacific nations, extending from Afghanistan through all the Pacific Islands, except Hawaii.

U.S. Politics & Social Issues	U.S. Foreign Policy & Defense	U.S. Economy & Environment	Science, Technology & Nature	Culture, Leisure & Life Style	
A Calif. court issues a warrant for the arrest of Negro author Eldridge Cleaver for violation of parole.					Nov. 27
				Random House publishes John O'Hara's *And Other Stories*.	Nov. 28
Black Panthers allegedly attack a Jersey City police station.	Hungary announces that its universities are open to students from the West.		Soviet Union launches Cosmos 255. . . . Officials give up trying to find the 78 miners trapped in the Nov. 20 mine explosion near Mannington, W. Va.		Nov. 29
HEW Dept. issues a new regulation requiring local welfare departments to provide legal assistance for clients.			Soviet Union launches Cosmos 256.		Nov. 30
A special panel of the National Commission on the Causes and Prevention of Violence criticizes the Chicago police force for their alleged brutality in the handling of demonstrators during the Democratic Convention. . . . Newark, N.J. Black Panther headquarters is fire-bombed.					Dec. 1
Officials re-open Bluefield State College in West Virginia as a commuter college because of racial disorders in dormatories. . . . N.Y.C. Negro students riot in the Ocean Hill-Brownsville district where parents are trying to gain local control of the public schools.	Pres.-elect Nixon confers with his Middle East envoy former Pa. Gov. William Scranton. . . . Pres.-elect Nixon announces that Prof. Henry Kissinger will be his special assistant for national security affairs.				Dec. 2
			Soviet Union launches Cosmos 257.		Dec. 3
	Defense Secy. Clark Clifford says that he hopes arms control talks can begin with the Soviet Union before the end of the Johnson administration. . . .	Pres.-elect Nixon chooses Dr. Paul McCracken to be chairman of the Council of Economic Advisers.	*Washington Post* says that Soviet satellites 248, 249 and 252 may be able to destroy U.S. orbiting satellites.	In an emotional speech at St. Peter's, Pope Paul criticizes priests and bishops dissenting from his ban on artificial birth control.	Dec. 4
N.Y.C. Afro-American Teachers Associations calls on striking students to return to class. . . . Police use tear gas to keep students from breaking into San Francisco State College administrative building.	U.S. State Department condemns Biafra's refusal to allow daytime relief flights to land at the major Uli-Ihiala airstrip.		U.S. launches a European satellite whose mission is to study solar winds.		Dec. 5
F	G	H	I	J	
Includes elections, federal-state relations, civil rights and liberties, crime, the judiciary, education, health care, poverty, urban affairs and population.	Includes formation and debate of U.S. foreign and defense policies, veterans' affairs and defense spending. (Relations with specific foreign countries are usually found under the region concerned.)	Includes business, labor, agriculture, taxation, transportation, consumer affairs, monetary and fiscal policy, natural resources, and pollution.	Includes worldwide scientific, medical and technological developments, natural phenomena, U.S. weather, natural disasters, and accidents.	Includes the arts, religion, scholarship, communications media, sports, entertainment, fashions, fads and social life.	

	World Affairs	Europe	Africa & the Middle East	The Americas	Asia & the Pacific
Dec. 6		French CP causes a stir when it says that each Communist party must take into consideration national "particularities." . . . Rome returns to normal as striking workers resume work. . . . In a surprise move East and West Germany agree to enlarge their trade relations.			
Dec. 7					
Dec. 8		South Vietnamese Vice Pres. Nguyen Cao Ky arrives in France for the Paris peace talks.			
Dec. 9		Soviet Union denies that it is trying to establish a naval base in Algeria. . . . U.S. and South Vietnamese delegations hold their first working sessions at the Paris peace talks. . . . Reports from Rumania indicate that it is still undecided about allowing Warsaw Pact military exercises on its territory in the spring of 1969.		Canadian government commission recommends reforms allowing children to learn both French and English.	France and Japan sign an agreement for the cooperative development of high-speed breeder-reactors.
Dec. 10			Israeli and Egyptian jets clash over the Sinai Peninsula for the first time since the 1967 war.		
Dec. 11		Northern Ireland P.M. Terence O'Neill dismisses Protestant militant William Craig from his position as Home Affairs Minister.			U.S. and North Vietnamese troops clash in the demilitarized zone.
Dec. 12		Thousands of industrial workers in Sicily stage a strike for higher wages. . . . U.S. and South Vietnamese delegations consult in Paris.		Brazilian Chamber of Deputies votes not to permit parliamentary critic Marcio Moreira Alves to be tried for criticism of the national government.	U.S. planes carry out heavy raids against Communist targets on the northern approaches to Saigon.
Dec. 13	U.N. General Assembly defeats a resolution expelling South Africa from the U.N. Conference on Trade & Development.	Sicilian workers continue their strike for higher wages.		Brazilian government suspends congress after its criticism of military rulers.	U.S. planes continue raids against Communist targets north of Saigon.
Dec. 14		French government threatens to expel disruptive students after rash of disorders on Dec. 13.		Brazilian police begin widespread arrests of former top government officials.	Allied forces are alerted for a possible Communist attacks on Saigon.
Dec. 15		U.S. and South Vietnamese delegations consult in Paris. . . . Switzerland agrees to join a project for the construction of Europe's largest nuclear accelerator.	Israel accuses Jordan of shelling an Israeli village.	AP reports that two U.S. missionary priests have been arrested in Brazil for alleged "subversive" activities.	
	A	**B**	**C**	**D**	**E**
	Includes developments that affect more than one world region, international organizations and important meetings of major world leaders.	*Includes all domestic and regional developments in Europe, including the Soviet Union, Turkey, Cyprus and Malta.*	*Includes all domestic and regional developments in Africa and the Middle East, including Iraq and Iran and excluding Cyprus, Turkey and Afghanistan.*	*Includes all domestic and regional developments in Latin America, the Caribbean and Canada.*	*Includes all domestic and regional developments in Asia and Pacific nations, extending from Afghanistan through all the Pacific Islands, except Hawaii.*

U.S. Politics & Social Issues	U.S. Foreign Policy & Defense	U.S. Economy & Environment	Science, Technology & Nature	Culture, Leisure & Life Style	
Student disturbances take place at Washington University, St. Louis, Mo. . . .					Dec. 6
Negro students at Brown University demand mandatory 11% Negro enrollment.			U.S. launches satellite Stargazer whose mission is to gather data on extremely hot young stars.		Dec. 7
A fire destroys the administrative building of San Fernando Valley State College in Calif. Officials report evidence of arson.				*The Fixer*, a film based on Bernard Malamud's novel of the same name, opens in New York.	Dec. 8
Rockefeller Foundation announces that State Secy. Dean Rusk will be an associate during 1969. . . . Students and police clash at San Francisco State College.	Pres.-elect Nixon's Middle East envoy William Scranton calls for a "more evenhanded" U.S. approach to the Middle East. . . . Two U.S. destroyers begin a scheduled five-day cruise in the Black Sea.	American Farm Bureau Federation convention meets in Kansas City.		Swiss theologian Karl Barth dies in Basle at 82. . . . *The Birthday Party*, a film based on Harold Pinter's play of the same name opens in New York.	Dec. 9
Student disturbances take place at Radcliffe College, Cambridge, Mass.		Dominant theme at American Farm Bureau Federation convention is opposition to the national boycott of California table grapes.	Soviet Union launches Cosmos 288.		Dec. 10
Agriculture Dept. announces a liberalization of the food stamp program.	Pres.-elect Nixon announces the names of his twelve cabinet members led by State Secy. William Rogers. . . . Pres.-elect Nixon's press spokesman, Ronald Ziegler dissociates Nixon from Middle East envoy William Scranton's call for a "more evenhanded" U.S. policy in the Middle East.				Dec. 11
Negro students boycott schools in Worth County, Ga. in response to alleged week-long detention of two Negro children.				Actress Tallulah Bankhead dies in New York at 65.	Dec. 12
Acting Pres. S.I. Hayakawa closes San Francisco State College because of continuing student disorders. . . . Minority students smash windows and beat whites at San Mateo College after a political rally.	U.S. and Mexico officially exchange several hundred acres of border territory.		U.S. FDA warns against the "unrestricted use" of artificial sweeteners. . . . A *Science* magazine article reports that a Boston research team says that marijuana has no serious negative effects.	Dr. Froelich Rainey, director of the University Museum of the University of Pennsylvania, announces that the site of the Greek city of Sybaris has been found.	Dec. 13
N.Y.C. Board of Education proposes a school decentralization plan giving more authority to local school boards.	Israeli Defense Min. Moshe Dayan meets with Pres.-elect Nixon in New York. . . . *The New York Times* reports that the U.S. is drawing up a contingency plan for a $20 million relief operation in Biafra.		Soviet Union launches Cosmos 289.		Dec. 14
V.P. Humphrey accepts a teaching position at Macalester College in Minnesota.	Defense Secy. Clark Clifford blames South Vietnam for the delaying the procedural talks in Paris.		U.S. launches Essa 8 weather satellite.		Dec. 15

F	G	H	I	J
Includes elections, federal-state relations, civil rights and liberties, crime, the judiciary, education, health care, poverty, urban affairs and population.	*Includes formation and debate of U.S. foreign and defense policies, veterans' affairs and defense spending. (Relations with specific foreign countries are usually found under the region concerned.)*	*Includes business, labor, agriculture, taxation, transportation, consumer affairs, monetary and fiscal policy, natural resources, and pollution.*	*Includes worldwide scientific, medical and technological developments, natural phenomena, U.S. weather, natural disasters, and accidents.*	*Includes the arts, religion, scholarship, communications media, sports, entertainment, fashions, fads and social life.*

	World Affairs	Europe	Africa & the Middle East	The Americas	Asia & the Pacific
Dec. 16	U.N. General Assembly condemns South Africa's presence in South-West Africa (Namibia.)	Spanish Jews celebrate the first opening of a synagogue in Spain in 600 years. . . . In Paris South Vietnamese V.P. Nguyen Cao Ky criticizes Defense Secy. Clark Clifford's placing blame on South Vietnam for delaying procedural talks. . . . *Newsweek* magazine publishes excerpts from *The Black Book,* an account of the Soviet invasion of Czechoslovakia by the Institute of History of the Czech Academy of Sciences.	Jordan accuses Israel of attacking Jordanian targets south of the Dead Sea.	Guyanan P.M. Forbes Burnham decisively defeats Marxist Cheddi Jagan.	U.S. releases seven North Vietnamese civilian seamen captured Oct. 22, 1967.
Dec. 17		U.S. and South Vietnamese delegations consult in Paris.			
Dec. 18	U.N. calls on Britain to grant independence to the territory of Oman.	West German cabinet defers a decision asking for a ban on the right-wing National Democratic Party.			
Dec. 19	U.N. votes, 60-22, to establish a committee to investigate Israeli human rights practices in the occupied territories.	Czechoslovakia expels *Newsweek* correspondent Allan Tillier.		Venezuelan guerrillas assassinate the police chief of a small village 35 miles from Caracas.	U.S. reports that American combat deaths have passed 30,000 in South Vietnam. . . . U.S. planes attack North Vietnamese anti-aircraft positions west of Donghoi in South Vietnam.
Dec. 20		Greek government reprieves Alexandros Panaghoulis, the attempted assassin of Greek P.M. George Papadopoulos.	Israeli planes bomb targets in the Jordan Valley.	Brazil removes censors from international cable offices.	
Dec. 21		For the first time at the Paris peace talks, South Vietnamese V.P. Nguyen Cao Ky says that South Vietnam recognizes the "reality" of the National Liberation Front.	An Israeli patrol clashes with Arab guerrillas near Jericho.		
Dec. 22		South Vietnamese V.P. Nguyen Cao Ky leaves Paris for consultations in Saigon. . . . *The New York Times* reports that the Soviet Union and Bulgaria have agreed on long-term plans for the integration of their economies.		Reports indicate that former Brazilian Pres. Juscelino Kubitschek has been released from jail after being held several days.	
Dec. 23		Albanians living in Yugoslavia protest against the central government.	Soviet Foreign Min. Andrei Gromyko confers with Egyptian Pres. Gamal Nasser in Cairo.	Brazilian police arrest Alberto Dines, editor-in-chief of the *Jornal do Brazil.*	In Saigon South Vietnamese Vice Pres. Ky says for the first time that South Vietnam will deal with the National Liberation Front but only after North Vietnamese troops have left the South.
Dec. 24			Soviet Foreign Min. Andrei Gromyko and Egyptian Pres. Nasser continue discussions in Cairo.		
Dec. 25		Yugoslav press agency reports the expulsion of two Albanian elementary school teachers in the Yugoslav province bordering Albania because of their participation in anti-government demonstrations.			

A	B	C	D	E
Includes developments that affect more than one world region, international organizations and important meetings of major world leaders.	*Includes all domestic and regional developments in Europe, including the Soviet Union, Turkey, Cyprus and Malta.*	*Includes all domestic and regional developments in Africa and the Middle East, including Iraq and Iran and excluding Cyprus, Turkey and Afghanistan.*	*Includes all domestic and regional developments in Latin America, the Caribbean and Canada.*	*Includes all domestic and regional developments in Asia and Pacific nations, extending from Afghanistan through all the Pacific Islands, except Hawaii.*

U.S. Politics & Social Issues	U.S. Foreign Policy & Defense	U.S. Economy & Environment	Science, Technology & Nature	Culture, Leisure & Life Style	
FBI says that nationally reported crime in the first nine months of 1968 was 19% higher than in the corresponding period in 1967.	Pres.-elect Nixon's press spokesman Ronald Ziegler announces that FBI Director J. Edgar Hoover has agreed to remain in his position at Nixon's request.	*Wall Street Jouranl* reports that ehe U.S. intends to increase sharply import duties on West European agricultural and industrial products if the Common Market imposes a proposed $60-per-ton soybean tax.	Soviet Union launches Cosmos 260.		Dec. 16
	Israeli jets bomb targets in the Jordan Valley.			Hungarian conductor Georg Solti becomes musical director of the Chicago Symphony.	Dec. 17
FBI arrests 32 people in Chicago on charges that they obtained fraudulent National Guard papers to avoid the draft.	U.S. announces the tentative approval of two missile sites for the Sentinel anti-ballistic missile system (ABM).		Soviet Union conducts an underground nuclear test. . . . US launches communications spacecraft Intelsat 3A		Dec. 18
			U.S. conducts an underground nuclear test in Nevada.	U.S. socialist spokesman Norman Thomas dies in Huntington, N.Y. at 84.	Dec. 19
Wisconsin State Univ. board of regents expels 90 Negro students for the Nov. 21 ransacking of Oshkosh State Univ.	U.S. announces that that the Moscow State Symphony will begin an American tour in February 1969. Its earlier scheduled tour was cancelled because of the invasion of Czechoslovakia.		Soviet Union launches Cosmos 261.	U.S. author John Steinbeck dies in New York at 66.	Dec. 20
			U.S. launches Apollo 8 and its three astronauts whose mission is to fly around the moon.	Scots author of *Tunes of Glory*, James Kennaway, dies in an auto accident in London at 40.	Dec. 21
					Dec. 22
				Ingmar Bergman's film *Shame* opens in New York.	Dec. 23
	U.S. Defense Dept. says that it has established a court of inquiry to investigate North Korea's capture of the U.S. ship *Pueblo*.		For the first time in history, men circle the moon as Apollo 8's astronauts enter lunar orbit.		Dec. 24
Boston Negro high school students riot over demands to form student unions.			Apollo 8 astronauts continue their lunar orbits.		Dec. 25

F	G	H	I	J
Includes elections, federal-state relations, civil rights and liberties, crime, the judiciary, education, health care, poverty, urban affairs and population.	*Includes formation and debate of U.S. foreign and defense policies, veterans' affairs and defense spending. (Relations with specific foreign countries are usually found under the region concerned.)*	*Includes business, labor, agriculture, taxation, transportation, consumer affairs, monetary and fiscal policy, natural resources, and pollution.*	*Includes worldwide scientific, medical and technological developments, natural phenomena, U.S. weather, natural disasters, and accidents.*	*Includes the arts, religion, scholarship, communications media, sports, entertainment, fashions, fads and social life.*

	World Affairs	Europe	Africa & the Middle East	The Americas	Asia & the Pacific
Dec. 26		At the Paris peace talks, Communist delegates insist upon a round table while allied delegates hold out for two separate tables. . . . Two Arab guerrillas attack an Israeli commercial jetliner in Athens.			
Dec. 27					Communist China conducts its eighth nuclear test.
Dec. 28			Israeli commandos destroy 13 civilian planes in Beirut airport in retaliation for the Dec. 26 attack on an Israeli jetliner. . . .		
Dec. 29			Arab guerrillas shell five Israeli settlements in apparent retaliation for the Dec. 28 Israeli attack on the Beirut airport.		
Dec. 30					
Dec. 31	U.N. Security Council condemns the Dec. 28 Israeli attack on the Beirut airport.	British novelist E.M. Forster is awarded the Order of Merit.	Arab guerrillas shell an Israeli settlement in the upper Galilee.		

A	B	C	D	E
Includes developments that affect more than one world region, international organizations and important meetings of major world leaders.	Includes all domestic and regional developments in Europe, including the Soviet Union, Turkey, Cyprus and Malta.	Includes all domestic and regional developments in Africa and the Middle East, including Iraq and Iran and excluding Cyprus, Turkey and Afghanistan.	Includes all domestic and regional developments in Latin America, the Caribbean and Canada.	Includes all domestic and regional developments in Asia and Pacific nations, extending from Afghanistan through all the Pacific Islands, except Hawaii.

U.S. Politics & Social Issues	U.S. Foreign Policy & Defense	U.S. Economy & Environment	Science, Technology & Nature	Culture, Leisure & Life Style	
			Soviet Union launches Cosmos 262.		Dec. 26
	U.S. announces its agreement to sell Israel 50 F-4 Phantom jets.				Dec. 27
					Dec. 28
	U.S. condemns the Dec. 28 Israeli attack on the Beirut airport.				Dec. 29
FBI reports that 1968 was the first year in which no executions took place in the U.S.				First U.N. Secy. Gen. Trygve Halvdan Lie dies in Geilo, Norway at 72.	Dec. 30
					Dec. 31

F	G	H	I	J
Includes elections, federal-state relations, civil rights and liberties, crime, the judiciary, education, health care, poverty, urban affairs and population.	Includes formation and debate of U.S. foreign and defense policies, veterans' affairs and defense spending. (Relations with specific foreign countries are usually found under the region concerned.)	Includes business, labor, agriculture, taxation, transportation, consumer affairs, monetary and fiscal policy, natural resources, and pollution.	Includes worldwide scientific, medical and technological developments, natural phenomena, U.S. weather, natural disasters, and accidents.	Includes the arts, religion, scholarship, communications media, sports, entertainment, fashions, fads and social life.

1969

An aerial view of the crowd at the Woodstock Festival in Bethel, N.Y., held on Aug. 16.

French composer Pierre Boulez, who is appointed this year to succeed Leonard Bernstein as music director of the N.Y. Philharmonic starting in 1971.

Sirhan Sirhan, center, accused assassin of Robert Kennedy, at his trial in Los Angeles Jan. 8.

American astronaut Edwin E. Aldrin poses on the moon July 31 after the successful landing of Apollo 11.

Two performers from *Oh, Calcutta*, a new off-Broadway musical that features nudity.

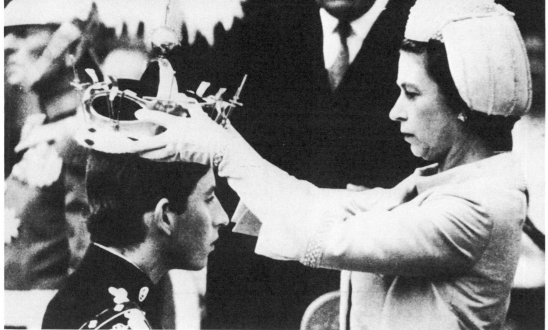

Queen Elizabeth invests her son, Prince Charles, as Prince of Wales at Caernarvon Castle July 1.

Golda Meir is sworn in as Premier of Israel on March 17.

Three of the "Chicago 8" preparing to go on trial in Chicago for inciting riots during the Democratic National Convention. They are, left to right, Jerry Rubin, David T. Dellinger, and Abby Hoffman.

President Nixon meets with South Korean chief executive Nguyen Wan Thieu on Midway Island June 8.

Two Jews accused of spying for Israel are executed in Bagdad Jan. 28.

	World Affairs	Europe	Africa & the Middle East	The Americas	Asia & the Pacific
Jan.	U.N.'s Children's Fund reports that about two million people have starved to death during the Nigerian civil war.	In Prague Czech student Jan Palach burns himself to death publicly to protest the Soviet invasion of Czechoslovakia. . . .France confirms that it has banned all sales of military equipment to Israel.	Fourteen Iraqis, including nine Jews, are hanged publicly in Baghdad after being convicted as Israeli spys.	Canadian P.M. Pierre Trudeau says that he cannot "preclude" the possibility of Canada's withdrawal from NATO.	Philippean Pres. Ferdinand Marcos says that his country will have to reassess its dependence on the U.S. in light of the imminent reduction of U.S. forces in Asia.
Feb.	International Red Cross flights resume to starving Biafrans.	French Pres. de Gaulle announces that a referendum will soon be held on proposed reforms granting expanded regional autonomy.	Israeli Premier Levi Eshkol dies of heart attack. . . .Israeli jets attack positions in Syria for the first time since the 1967 war. . . .Al Fatah guerrilla leader Yasir Arafat is elected chairman of the Palestine Liberation Organization (PLO).	Brazil suspends all interim elections and increases government control over legislators.	Pakistani Pres. Mohammad Ayub Khan annoues that he will not be a candidate in the 1970 presidential elections.
March	U.N. Security Council votes to condemn South Africa's continued control of Namibia.	Soviet troops reportedly clash with Communist Chinese forces in a major engagement along their frontier. . . .Spain grants an amnesty to all persons accused of criminal acts during the Spanish Civil War.	Golda Meir is sworn in as Israel's fourth prime minister. . . .Reports from Beirut indicate that Syrian Defense Min. Hafez al-Assad has seized power in Damascus.	Venezuela's first peaceful transition of political power take place when Rafael Rodriquez becomes the country's 43rd president. . . .Peru seizes two more U.S. fishing boats in its campaign to extend its maritime territorial zone.	Communist Chinese troops reportedly clash with Soviet forces along their border. . . .Pakistani Pres. Mohammad Ayub Khan resigns from office after months of anti-government unrest.
April	U.N. Secy. Gen. U Thant says that "a virtual state of active war" exists between Egypt and Israel.	Charles de Gaulle resigns as president of France after French voters reject his regional reform plan. . . .In a culmination of the anti-reform drive backed by the Soviet Union, Slovak CP First Secy. Gustav Husak replaces Czechoslovak CP First Secy. Alexander Dubcek.	Jordanian King Hussein makes the first public pledge by an Arab leader that Israeli ships will be allowed to use the Suez Canal as part of a peace settlement. . . .France sends a contingent of soldiers to the Central African Republic to protect the Bokassa government.	Venezuelan Foreign Min. Aristedes Calvani says that some Venezuelan guerrilla leaders are apparently still closely tied to Cuban Communists.	About 150,000 people demonstrate throughout Japan for the return of Okinawa.
May	At the U.N. African delegates criticize Western arms sales to South Africa.	Reports from Moscow indicate that Soviet and Communist Chinese forces have clashed several times during a recent one-week period.	Lebanese army troops and Palestinian guerrillas clash near the Israeli border.	Presidential envoy Nelson Rockefeller confronts several anti-U.S. demonstrations during his tour of Latin American capitals.	Chinese and Malaysian ethnic groups clash in Malaysia. . . .Allied forces capture Apbia Mountain in the Ashau Valley after one of the bloodiest battles of the war.
June	Nigeria denounces attempts by the International Red Cross to relieve starving Biafrans. . . .International Red Cross estimates that 1.5 million Biafrans have starved to death.	Former French Premier George Pompidou overwhelmingly defeats Alain Poher in presidential elections.	Reports indicate that the Lebanese government is urging Arab guerrillas to withdraw from Lebanon.	Honduras and El Salvador break-off diplomatic relations as tensions mount between the two countries.	Reports indicate that South Vietnamese officials are deeply worried by imminent U.S. troop withdrawals.
July	International Red Cross accuses Nigeria of obstructing efforts to help starving Biafrans.	Italian government falls after Socialists withdraw from their coalition with Christian Democrats.	Israel launches the first air assault against Egyptian ground installations along the Suez Canal since the 1967 war.	Fighting breaks out between Honduras and El Salvador.	Communist China charges that Soviet armed personnel have recently intruded across the Armur River frontier.
Aug.	U.N. condemns Israel's Aug. 11 raid against Lebanon.	British troops take over responsibility for security in Northern Ireland. . . .Pres. Nixon receives a tumultuous welcome in Rumania. . . .Czech government suppresses demonstrations protesting the 1968 Soviet invasion.	Israel stages raids against Lebanese and Egyptian territory. . . .An Australian tourist causes minor damage to the Al Aksa Mosque in Jerusalem when he tries to start a fire. . . .Several hundred Communist Chinese technicians arrive in Tanzania.	Brazilian Pres. Arthur da Costa e Silva suffers a serious stroke.	Communists launch heaviest offensive in three months as battle lull comes to an end in South Vietnam.
Sept.	International Red Cross gains Nigerian approval for relief flights to Biafra after months of suspension.	West German Chancellor Kurt-Georg Kiesinger's Christian Democrats narrowly defeat Willy Brandt's Social Democrats, but Brandt indicates that he may try to from a coalition government with the Free Democrats.	Libyan military ousts the monarchy and proclaims a republic.	Brazil flies 15 guerrillas to Mexico to obtain the release of kidnapped U.S. Ambassador C. Burke Elbrick.	North Vietnamese leader Ho Chi Minh dies at 79.
Oct.	International Monetary Fund votes to create special drawing rights to help foster world trade.	West German Parliament elects Willy Brandt as the country's fourth chancellor.	A policeman assassinates Somali Pres. Ali Shermarke. . . .Lebanese troops engage in fierce battles with Palestinian guerrillas.	Canadian P.M. Pierre Elliott Trudeau calls on France to repudiate policies which encourage Quebec separatism.	Communist Chinese are reportedly extending their road building network in northern Laos.
Nov.	U.N. reports that 100 million people have been vaccinated in Africa against smallpox in the last three year years.	West Germany signs the treaty banning the spread of nuclear weapons.	Saudi Arabian and South Yemeni forces clash along their border.	Jamaica launches a family planning campaign.	North Vietnam says that it is willing to talk to the U.S. in private.
Dec.	GATT administration reports that Western Europe has replaced the U.S. as the "mainspring" of world economic expansion.	Greece defies West European countries by ruling out an early return to civilian rule.	Egyptian Pres. Gamal Abdel Nasser walks out of a conference of Arab leaders because of Saudi Arabian refusals to increase financial support for Arab armies.	A military coup ousts Gen. Omar Torrijos in Panama while he is on a trip to Mexico.	Japanese Liberal Party scores a resounding victory in parliamentary elections. . . .Singapore urges that the U.S. not allow a Communist victory in South Vietnam.

A	B	C	D	E
Includes developments that affect more than one world region, international organizations and important meetings of major world leaders.	Includes all domestic and regional developments in Europe, including the Soviet Union, Turkey, Cyprus and Malta.	Includes all domestic and regional developments in Africa and the Middle East, including Iraq and Iran and excluding Cyprus, Turkey and Afghanistan.	Includes all domestic and regional developments in Latin America, the Caribbean and Canada.	Includes all domestic and regional developments in Asia and Pacific nations, extending from Afghanistan through all the Pacific Islands, except Hawaii.

U.S. Politics & Social Issues	U.S. Foreign Policy & Defense	U.S. Economy & Environment	Science, Technology & Nature	Culture, Leisure & Life Style
Senate Democrats vote, 31-26, to oust Senate Majority Whip Sen. Russell Long (la.) in favor of Sen. Edward Kennedy (Mass.).	Richard Nixon becomes the 37th President of the United States.	An investigating team of law students organized by consumer advocate Ralph Nader charges the Federal Trade Commission with gross incompetence, including alcoholism and "spectacular lassitide."	U.S. astronauts Neil Armstrong and Edwin Aldrin are choosen to be the first men to land on the moon.	National Society of Film Critics votes Ingmar Bergman's *Shame* the best film of 1968.
Pres. Nixon declares his support of University of Notre Dame Pres. Theodore Hesburgh's "get tough" policy for dealing with campus disorders.	Pres. Nixon says that his upcoming European trip is aimed at revitalizing the Atlantic Alliance.	Pres. Nixon sets up a study group to deal with possible economic problems arising from the eventual end of the Vietnamese War.	U.S. launches a satellite whose mission is to study the possibility of life on Mars.	German philosopher Karl Jaspers dies in Basel, Switzerland at 86.
James Earl Ray pleads guilty to the murder of Dr. Martin Luther King Jr.	Pres. Nixon announces his decision to proceed with an anti-ballistic missile system.	Pres. Nixon asks Congress to extend the 10% income tax surcharge for one year.	Three U.S. astronauts test flight the Apollo spacecraft which will land the first Americans on the moon.	Dwight David Eisenhower, 34th President of the United States and supreme allied commander in Europe during World War II, dies in Washington, D.C. at 78.
In a landmark decision U.S. Supreme Court rules that residency requirements for welfare benefits are illegal. . . .Harvard University militant students seize the main administration building. . . .Negro students seize the Cornell University student union with guns.	U.S. Defense Dept. says that the U.S. reconnaissance plane downed on April 14 by North Korea was over international war waters.	U.S. Federal Reserve announces a rise in its discount rate to six percent, the highest rate in 40 years.	Houston doctors perform the world's first total human eye transplant.	Knopf publishes John Cheever's *Bullet Park* .
Supreme Court Justice Abe Fortas resigns from the Supreme Court because of financial improprieties. . . .NAACP Dir. Roy Wilkens criticizes the impracticality of black studies programs when Negro communities are in desperate need of tangible skills.	Navy Secy. John Chafee announces that no disciplinary action will be taken against the members of the *U.S.S. Pueblo* .	U.S. economists see no early end to the inflationary spiral.	U.S. manned spacecraft comes within nine miles of the moon's surface.	McGraw Hill publishes Vladimir Nabokov's *Ada* .
Warren Burger becomes the Chief Justice of the U.S. Supreme Court.	Pres. Nixon announces that 25,000 U.S. troops will be withdrawn from South Vietnam this year after consultations with South Vietnamese Pres. Nguyen van Thieu on Midway Island.	Interest rates continue to rise on the credit markets.	U.S. scientists report evidence of gravity waves passing through the earth.	French composer Pierre Boulez becomes the director of the New York Philharmonic.
Sen. Edward Kennedy reports to Edgartown, Mass., police that a car which he was driving plunged into a pond with a female passenger.	Nixon confers with Asian allies in Manilla and bids them to contribute more to their own military defense.	Federal government registers its first budget surplus in seven years.	U.S. astronauts Neil Armstrong and Edwin Aldrin land on the moon and walk on its surface.	German-born architect Walter Gropius dies in Boston at 86.
Pres. Nixon asks for welfare reforms which require either training or work for many recipients.	Pres. Nixon defers a decision about further troop withdrawals from South Vietnam because of the latest Communist offensive.	U.S. economic officials say that peace in Vietnam will not produce major economic dividends.	U.S. Apollo astronauts leave quarantine and are reportedly in excellent health.	N.Y.C. landmarks panel bars a skyscraper over Grand Central Station.
NAACP announces a major suit against discrimination in the construction industry.	Pres. Nixon announces a withdrawal of about 35,000 U.S. troops from South Vietnam.	Treasury Dept. offers notes at eight percent interest, a 110-year high.	FDA says that birth control pills are safe.	U.S. Episcopal church leaders vote $200,000 in reparations for Negroes.
Supreme Court rules that segregated school systems must complete integration plans "at once.". . .Reports indicte that fear of crime is the major issue in municipal elections.	White House announces that arms talks with the Soviet Union will begin on Nov. 17 in Helsinki, Finland. . . .Vice Pres. Spiro Agnew calls anti-war demonstrators "effete snobs."	Pres. Nixon says that he will continue to push for austerity measures to cool off the economy.	Scientist report progress on vaccines against meningitis and rubella.	Samuel Beckett wins the Nobel Prize in literature.
V.P. Spiro Agnew accuses the television networks of distorting the news. . . .Senate votes, 55-45, against Pres. Nixon's Supreme Court nominee Clement Haynsworth.	U.S. Army charges Lt. William Calley with the murders of at least 109 South Vietnamese civilians on or about March 16, 1968. . . .Two hundred fifty thousand war protesters stage a peaceful rally in Washington.	Labor Dept. says that widespread corruption may exist in the United Mine Workers Union.	U.S. Apollo 12 astronauts land on the moon and walk on its surface for several hours.	Joseph Kennedy, the father of the late Pres. John Kennedy, dies in Hyannisport, Mass. at 81.
Capt. Ernest Medina denies that he ordered or saw an alleged March 16, 1968 massacre by U.S. troops of South Vietnamese civilians at Mylai.	U.S. eases curbs on trade with Communist China. . . .Pres. Nixon announces a withdrawal of 50,000 U.S. troops from South Vietnam by April 15, 1970. . . .House passes the smallest foreign aid bill since W.W. II.	Senete votes to outlaw cigarette advertising on television and radio after Dec. 31, 1970.	Reports indicate that a growing number of U.S. doctors see links between changes in body chemistry and mental depression.	Vatican proposes closer ties to Jews including possible joint prayer ceremonies. . . .N.Y. film critics vote for Gosta Gavras's *Z* as the best picture of 1969.
F	G	H	I	J
Includes elections, federal-state relations, civil rights and liberties, crime, the judiciary, education, health care, poverty, urban affairs and population.	*Includes formation and debate of U.S. foreign and defense policies, veterans' affairs and defense spending. (Relations with specific foreign countries are usually found under the region concerned.)*	*Includes business, labor, agriculture, taxation, transportation, consumer affairs, monetary and fiscal policy, natural resources, and pollution.*	*Includes worldwide scientific, medical and technological developments, natural phenomena, U.S. weather, natural disasters, and accidents.*	*Includes the arts, religion, scholarship, communications media, sports, entertainment, fashions, fads and social life.*

	World Affairs	Europe	Africa & the Middle East	The Americas	Asia & the Pacific
Jan. 1	Eleven member nations of GATT reduce import duties on hundreds of goods in a second round of tariff cuts.	French Pres. Charles de Gaulle forcefully condemns the December 1968 Israeli raid on Beirut airport.	Tanzania begins a drive to rid the country of miniskirts and bell-bottom trousers. . . . Israeli forces exchange fire with Lebanese troops and Arab guerrillas in Lebanon. . . . Biafra calls for a limited truce in the Nigerian civil war.	Canadian P.M. Pierre Trudeau acknowledges that his government's current review of defense policy is causing a morale problem in the Canadian armed forces.	Viet Cong release three U.S. Army prisoners in South Vietnam.
Jan. 2	U.N. Children's Fund reports that about two million people have starved to death during the Nigerian civil war.	Protestants and Catholics brawl in Belfast, Northern Ireland.	Israel says that the Israeli town of Kiryat Shmona has been attacked with rockets from Lebanon for the second time in three days.	Canadian P.M. Pierre Elliott Trudeau says that he cannot "preclude" the possibility of Canada's withdrawal from NATO. . . . Peru decrees that all foreign banks there must be controlled by Peruvians. . . . A guerrilla group seizes a village in Guyana. . . . Brazilian officials detain the correspondent of the French newspaper Le Monde for writing an article critical of the Justice Ministry.	Indonesia reports the deaths of 65 Communist guerrillas in recent action. . . . A Viet Cong mine kills 12 South Vietnamese civilians.
Jan. 3		Police disperse a mob of Roman Catholics trying to break up a Protestant meeting in Londonderry, Northern Ireland. . . . Soviet Union announces that it has constructed an experimental nuclear breeder reactor.		The New York Times reports that several prominent Brazilian journalists have been interrogated at length in recent weeks by government officials. . . . Guyanese army units drive guerrillas from the village of Letham.	
Jan. 4	A Protestant and Catholic relief organization announces that it has flown 1,000 relief flights to Biafra since operations began in April 1968.	Protestant extremists attack a Roman Catholic march in Northern Ireland. . . . French newspaper Le Monde reports that important French army officers have recommended that the U.S. be asked to help in developing France's atomic weapons.	About 25,000 Lebanese university students go on strike to protest alleged government incompetence in the face of the December 1968 Israeli attack on Beirut airport. . . . Spain returns its North African enclave of Ifni, which was seized in 1934, to Morocco.		
Jan. 5	International Red Cross charges that Nigerian planes attacked its hospital in Biafra.			Guyanese P.M. Forbes Burnham charges that Venezuela is helping Guyanese guerrillas. . . . A bomb explodes near a Montreal secondary school but causes no injuries.	
Jan. 6		First contingent of U.S. troops to be deployed to West Germany by rapid trans-Atlantic airlift arrives near Frankfurt.	Equatorial Guinea bans International Red Cross flights to starving Biafrans. . . . Kenya begins a drive to force the country's Indian merchants out of business and into exile. . . . Israel and Jordan exchange gunfire for forty minutes across the Jordan River. . . . Lebanon says that villagers aged 18 to 50 in areas bordering Israel have been asked to report for military training.	More than 80 Cubans break through Cuban border guards and are given refuge at the U.S. Guantanamo naval station. . . . A bomb explodes near the home of Montreal Police Director Jean-Paul Gilbert but causes no injuries.	
Jan. 7		France confirms that it has banned all sales of military equipment to Israel. . . . Soviet Union and France agree to double their trade in 1970-1974.		Quebec Premier Jean-Jacques Bertrand says that he would prefer a presidential system for Quebec within a loose confederation of Canadian states.	
Jan. 8		In a move to gain greater control over its universities, East Germany is reported to have begun a program to link curriculum to jobs in industry. . . . A French government official asserts that "Israeli influences are making themselves felt in circles close to the news media."		Brazilian officials release the correspondent of the French newspaper Le Monde after holding her for six days. . . . Police arrest two youths in connection with the Jan. 5 and 6 bombings in Montreal.	
	A	**B**	**C**	**D**	**E**
	Includes developments that affect more than one world region, international organizations and important meetings of major world leaders.	*Includes all domestic and regional developments in Europe, including the Soviet Union, Turkey, Cyprus and Malta.*	*Includes all domestic and regional developments in Africa and the Middle East, including Iraq and Iran and excluding Cyprus, Turkey and Afghanistan.*	*Includes all domestic and regional developments in Latin America, the Caribbean and Canada.*	*Includes all domestic and regional developments in Asia and Pacific nations, extending from Afghanistan through all the Pacific Islands, except Hawaii.*

U.S. Politics & Social Issues	U.S. Foreign Policy & Defense	U.S. Economy & Environment	Science, Technology & Nature	Culture, Leisure & Life Style	
				Pope Paul expresses sympathy to Lebanon for the December 1968 Israeli attack on Beirut airport.	Jan. 1
A black power gunman forces a U.S. jet to fly to Cuba. . . . A Calif. court sentences John Kangas to four months in prison for burning an American flag.					Jan. 2
Senate Democrats vote, 31-26, to oust Senate Majority Whip Sen. Russell Long (La.) in favor of Sen. Edward Kennedy (Mass.).	State Secy. Dean Rusk voices concern about pressure within the U.S. for withdrawal of U.S. troops from Europe.				Jan. 3
	Pres.-elect Nixon names Elliot Richardson to be Undersecretary of State.				Jan. 4
	Pres.-elect Nixon names Henry Cabot Lodge as chief U.S. negotiator at the Paris talks on the Vietnamese War.	An investigating team of law students organized by consumer advocate Ralph Nader charges the Federal Trade Commission with gross incompetence, including alcoholism and "spectacular lassitude" among its employees.	Soviet Union launches a satellite designed to land on Venus in mid-May.	U.S. poets Karl Shapiro and John Berryman win the Bollingen Prize in poetry.	Jan. 5
San Francisco State College, the recent scene of violent demonstrations, opens for the first time in three weeks.				National Society of Film Critics votes Ingmar Bergman's *Shame* the best film of 1968.	Jan. 6
Trial of Sirhan Bishara Sirhan, accused murderer of Sen. Robert Kennedy, opens in Los Angeles. . . . Johnson administration begins a drive to recruit more Negroes for the National Guard.	U.S. announces that it will increase its food aid to Biafra and Nigeria.				Jan. 7
An escaped convict murders two FBI agents in Washington, D.C.	U.S. State Dept. denies that it has made cash payments to Cuba for the return of hijacked aircraft.			*London Times* reports that nearly 1,000 of 9,000 Dutch Roman Catholic priests have resigned, mainly because of the celibacy requirement. . . . Dutch Roman Catholic Church criticizes the Pope's opposition to birth control. . . . Pres. Johnson breaks ground for the Joseph Hirshhorn Museum in Washington.	Jan. 8
F	G	H	I	J	
Includes elections, federal-state relations, civil rights and liberties, crime, the judiciary, education, health care, poverty, urban affairs and population.	Includes formation and debate of U.S. foreign and defense policies, veterans' affairs and defense spending. (Relations with specific foreign countries are usually found under the region concerned.)	Includes business, labor, agriculture, taxation, transportation, consumer affairs, monetary and fiscal policy, natural resources, and pollution.	Includes worldwide scientific, medical and technological developments, natural phenomena, U.S. weather, natural disasters, and accidents.	Includes the arts, religion, scholarship, communications media, sports, entertainment, fashions, fads and social life.	

	World Affairs	Europe	Africa & the Middle East	The Americas	Asia & the Pacific
Jan. 9		A Norwegian gunboat seizes three Russian and two East German trawlers off its coastline. . . . Czechoslovak Union of Metal Workers calls for the democratic election of the federal Assembly's chairman.	Last remaining bridge between Israel and Jordan is blown up during a gunfire duel between both countries.		Japanese police are called in to separate battling student groups at Tokyo University. . . . Reports indicate that the wives and children of Soviet officials have returned to Peking after months of repatriation.
Jan. 10		Sweden says that it will extend full diplomatic recognition to North Vietnam. . . . Nineteen women whose husbands or sons are in jail begin a sit-in in a Madrid church. . . . West German Foreign Min. Willy Brandt and Soviet Ambassador Semyon Tsarapkin meet in Bonn to resume talks suspended in July 1968.		Reports indicate that Brazilian Interior Min. Alfonso Albuquerque Lima has declared that the military government and not Congress will choose Brazil's next two presidents. . . . Four Montreal students confess to storing dynamite in a secret cache.	Japanese student radicals try to disrupt a meeting between student moderates and the administration of Tokyo University.
Jan. 11		Roman Catholic demonstrators rampage through the town of Newry, 40 miles from Belfast. . . . Czech Trade Union of Printers refuses to print the first issue of a doctrinaire Communist government publication.	Israeli jets attack Jordanian artillery positions.	About 125 students at the French-language University of Moncton in New Brunswick occupy administration buildings to force more federal aid grants.	Viet Cong carry out extensive mortar attacks against South Vietnamese cities and cause heavy civilian casualties.
Jan. 12	At the U.N. Arab delegates accuse Israel of trying to provoke a war.	Thousands of London demonstrators protest Britain's immigration policies.	Israel confirms that it has recalled its ambassador to France for consultations about the French arms embargo. . . . The New York Times reports that petroleum production has begun in the Cabinda district of Angola.	Right-wing Dominican Gen. Elias Wessin y Wessin returns to the Dominican Republic after three years of exile in the U.S.	
Jan. 13		Under heavy pressure Czechoslovak editors agree to new self-censorship demands.		Peru announces that it has taken over 18 cattle ranches owned primarily by a U.S. corporation. . . . Canada is represented at the international conference of French-language education ministers in Kinshasha, the Congo, by a combined provincial-federal delegation.	U.S. forces fight off a Viet Cong attack at Cantho in the Mekong Delta.
Jan. 14	European and Japanese steel producers announce agreement on the limitations of steel exports to the U.S.	Czech correspondent in New York Karel Kral says that he has decided not to return to Prague for fear of punitive government actions. . . . France says that it will come to the aid of Lebanon if it is attacked by Israel.	Guinean Pres. Sekou Toure says that he has uncovered a coup planned with French backing. Kenya warns the local press not to highlight the campaign to force Indian merchants out of business.	Reports indicate that National Guard Commander Omar Torrijos holds the real political power in Panama.	Viet Cong attack a 50-truck U.S. convoy about 60 miles from Saigon. . . . South Vietnamese Premier Tran Van Huong says that U.S. forces can begin a gradual withdrawal from South Vietnam.
Jan. 15		About 2,000 students and workers demonstrate in the center of Prague against the Soviet invasion.			A Communist Laotian force destroys a government ammunition depot on Laos.
Jan. 16		In Prague student Jan Palach publicly sets himself on fire to protest the Soviet invasion of Czechoslovakia. . . . In Paris U.S. and North Vietnamese officials agree on the shape of the conference table for expanded talks which will include South Vietnam and the National Liberation Front.	Israeli jets attack targets in Jordan.	Argentina publishes a decree strengthening Argentinian banks facing competition from foreign banks. . . . Brazil removes three Supreme Court justices. It is believed to be the first time in Brazilian history that the executive has directly intervened in the judicial branch in such a way. . . . Canadian P.M. Pierre Elliott Trudeau meets with Pope Paul and says that diplomatic relations with the Vatican are possible.	The New York Times reports that a massive migration from town to country took place during Communist China's recent Cultural Revolution.
Jan. 17		Czech students at Charles University issue a statement in honor of their comrade Jan Palach.			A Viet Cong mine damages two U.S. vessels in South Vietnam. . . . Japan's 1968 balance-of-payments surplus reaches a record high. . . . Anti-government student demonstrations break out in Dacca, Pakistan.

A	B	C	D	E
Includes developments that affect more than one world region, international organizations and important meetings of major world leaders.	Includes all domestic and regional developments in Europe, including the Soviet Union, Turkey, Cyprus and Malta.	Includes all domestic and regional developments in Africa and the Middle East, including Iraq and Iran and excluding Cyprus, Turkey and Afghanistan.	Includes all domestic and regional developments in Latin America, the Caribbean and Canada.	Includes all domestic and regional developments in Asia and Pacific nations, extending from Afghanistan through all the Pacific Islands, except Hawaii.

U.S. Politics & Social Issues	U.S. Foreign Policy & Defense	U.S. Economy & Environment	Science, Technology & Nature	Culture, Leisure & Life Style	
A U.S. university student forces a U.S. jet to fly to Cuba.			U.S. astronauts Neil Armstrong and Edwin Aldrin are chosen to be the first men to land on the moon. . . . A two-year U.S. Air Force study concludes that unidentified flying objects (UFOs) are not extraterrestrial spaceships.		Jan. 9
Justice Dept. sues the Georgia Power Co. for job discrimination. . . . U.S. hijacker Willis Jessie returns to America from his Cuban exile because of political disillusionment.		Justice Dept. files a suit against four major automobile manufacturers for delaying the installation of anti-pollution devices.	Soviet Union launches a satellite designed to land on Venus in mid-May.	Grove Press publishes Juan Bosch's *Pentagonism*.	Jan. 10
An Ecuadorian forces a Peruvian plane to fly to Cuba.				Three hundred twenty-two French priests demand the abolition of the celibacy rule.	Jan. 11
			Soviet Union launches Cosmos 263.		Jan. 12
Supreme Court rules that a South Carolina textile plant was illegally closed in an effort to avoid unionization. . . . U.S. Supreme Court rules that college draft deferments are legal. . . . Pres.-elect Nixon meets with six Negro leaders and pledges to support their objectives.	It is announced that Dr. John Foster will continue as director of research and engineering for the Defense Department.		National Research Council reports that the 50,000 traffic accident deaths annually represent the fourth leading cause of death in the U.S.		Jan. 13
HEW Secy. Robert Finch says that he is opposed to a guaranteed-income proposal. . . . Convicted U.S. spy Morton Sobell is released from prison after serving 17 years of a 30-year sentence.		Commerce Dept. reports that the U.S. GNP grew by 9% in 1968.			Jan. 14
Justice Department files suits against four South Carolina school districts.		In his sixth and last budget sent to Congress, Pres. Johnson proposes a $3.5 billion reduction in spending for the Vietnamese War.	U.S. conducts two underground nuclear tests in Nevada.		Jan. 15
An HEW official reports that the department has charged Louisiana with operating a segregated college system. . . . Senate votes 53-45 against the modification of the filibuster rule.			Soviet Union performs the first "docking" of manned vehicles in space and the first transfer of personnel between orbiting spaceships.	Viking Press publishes Iris Murdoch's *Bruno's Dream*.	Jan. 16
Roy Cohn, former aide to the late Sen. Joseph McCarthy, is indicted on charges of bribery, conspiracy and extortion. . . . Justice Dept. files a job discrimination suit against the Owens-Corning Fiberglass Corp. of South Carolina.	Pres. Johnson says that his biggest disappointment on leaving office is the failure to achieve peace in Vietnam.				Jan. 17

F	G	H	I	J
Includes elections, federal-state relations, civil rights and liberties, crime, the judiciary, education, health care, poverty, urban affairs and population.	Includes formation and debate of U.S. foreign and defense policies, veterans' affairs and defense spending. (Relations with specific foreign countries are usually found under the region concerned.)	Includes business, labor, agriculture, taxation, transportation, consumer affairs, monetary and fiscal policy, natural resources, and pollution.	Includes worldwide scientific, medical and technological developments, natural phenomena, U.S. weather, natural disasters, and accidents.	Includes the arts, religion, scholarship, communications media, sports, entertainment, fashions, fads and social life.

	World Affairs	Europe	Africa & the Middle East	The Americas	Asia & the Pacific
Jan. 18				In an apparent protest against the Jan. 16 dismissal of three Brazilian Supreme Court justices, Supreme Court Pres. Antonio Goncalves de Oliveira resigns.	U.S. reports the capture of more than 1,200 Viet Cong suspects. . . . Japanese police begin to clear some 400 militant leftist students from an occupied building at Tokyo University.
Jan. 19		Czech student Jan Palach dies of self-inflicted burns.		Antonio Carlos Lafayette de Andrada becomes Brazilian Supreme Court President.	Japanese police continue to clear militant leftist students from an occupied building at Tokyo University.
Jan. 20		Soviet Union again indicates that it is interested in arms limitation talks. . . . More than 100,000 Czechoslovak students gather in Prague to honor Jan Palach.	Israeli soldiers reportedly kill an Arab woman while breaking up a demonstration in Rafeh in the Gaza Strip.		Pakistani students battle police in anti-government demonstrations in Dacca.
Jan. 21		Czech regional trade unions express their support for the reinstitution of the country's liberalization drive.	Israeli Defense Min. Moshe Dayan apologizes to Arab officials for the Jan. 20 killing of an Arab woman by Israeli soldiers.	Antonio Carlos Lafayette de Andrada resigns without explanation from his post as Brazilian Supreme Court President. . . . Striking government workers riot in Montevideo, Uruguay.	A Viet Cong rocket kills two U.S. soldiers in South Vietnam after hitting a tank landing ship.
Jan. 22		An Athens military court sentences two people to prison terms for attempting to overthrow the military government. . . . A Spanish military court sentences four youths to long prison terms for attempted arson at the Univ. of Madrid. . . . Hunger strikes in support of Jan Palach's protest against the Soviet invasion spread in several Czech cities.	Africa's first desalination plant is inaugurated by Mauritanian Pres. Ould Daddah.		U.S. reports the discovery of a tunnel complex belonging to the Viet Cong in South Vietnam. . . . Laos orders the Laotian Communist representative to leave Vientiane.
Jan. 23		French students seize administrative offices at the Sorbonne.		Venezuelan guerrillas take temporary control of a Caracas slum.	U.S. troops overrun an abandoned village held by Communist forces near Quangngai.
Jan. 24		Reports indicate that the Spanish government is taking a harder line against dissident forces. . . . Czech CP First Secy. Alexander Dubcek warns citizens not to provoke authorities during the scheduled funeral of student martyr Jan Palach on Jan. 25. . . . Italy announces that it has decided to recognize Communist China.	Kenyan students occupy Nairobi Univ. to protest the government's refusal to allow opposition leader Oginga Odinga to speak.	A U.S. Navy deserter forces a Florida plane to take him to Cuba. . . . Quebec and France sign three letters of agreement on scientific and economic matters.	Indian Pres. Zakir Hussain presents Mrs. Martin Luther King Jr. with the Jawaharlal Nehru Award. . . . Student rioting results in three deaths in Dacca, Pakistan.
Jan. 25		British Conservative Party leader Edward Heath calls for tighter curbs on non-white immigration into Britain. . . . Jan Palach, who burned himself to death to protest the Soviet occupation, is given a hero's burial in Prague. . . . At the Paris peace talks, U.S. proposes the restoration of the neutrality of the demilitarized zone between the two Vietnams.	Sierra Leone releases some 200 political prisoners under arrest since November 1968.	Canadian Postmaster General Eric Kierans says that NATO has become obsolete.	After two months of seclusion, Communist CP Chmn. Mao Tse-tung attends a massive rally in Peking.
Jan. 26		Czech police disperse demonstrators trying to place a portrait of student martyr Jan Palach in Prague's central square.	Tanzania announces a plan to stem the flow of people from the country to the cities.		Viet Cong mines kill seven U.S. Marines in South Vietnam. Police kill three curfew violators in Dacca, Pakistan.
	A	B	C	D	E
	Includes developments that affect more than one world region, international organizations and important meetings of major world leaders.	Includes all domestic and regional developments in Europe, including the Soviet Union, Turkey, Cyprus and Malta.	Includes all domestic and regional developments in Africa and the Middle East, including Iraq and Iran and excluding Cyprus, Turkey and Afghanistan.	Includes all domestic and regional developments in Latin America, the Caribbean and Canada.	Includes all domestic and regional developments in Asia and Pacific nations, extending from Afghanistan through all the Pacific Islands, except Hawaii.

U.S. Politics & Social Issues	U.S. Foreign Policy & Defense	U.S. Economy & Environment	Science, Technology & Nature	Culture, Leisure & Life Style	
	In his final report to Congress, Defense Secy. Clark Clifford says that the Soviet inter-continental missile force has grown from 250 in mid-1966 to 900 in September 1968.				Jan. 18
	U.S. officially protests the detention of a recently captured fishing boat by Peru.				Jan. 19
Richard Nixon is inaugurated as the 37th President of the United States. . . . U.S. Supreme Court rules that states and cities cannot erect special barriers to the passage of open-housing laws. . . . Justice Dept. files a job discrimination suit against longshoremen's unions of Brownsville, Tex.	U.S. Navy's Court of Inquiry into the 1968 capture of the *U.S.S. Pueblo* opens with Cmdr. Lloyd Bucher as its first witness.			Daniel Cohn-Bendit's *Obsolete Communism* is published in New York. . . . Robert Kennedy's *Thirteen Days* is published in New York.	Jan. 20
Following a nationwide trend Harvard University establishes a degree program in Afro-American studies. . . . HEW officials uphold a school desegregation plan for Henry County, Va.	*U.S.S. Pueblo* Cmdr. Lloyd Bucher asserts that he was 18-20 miles from the nearest North Korean land point when he was captured. . . . On his first full day in office, Pres. Nixon meets with the National Security Council to discuss Vietnam and arms limitation talks.				Jan. 21
		Paul Volcker is appointed undersecretary for monetary affairs.	AEC reports the completion and testing of the world's largest super-conducting magnet. . . . U.S. launches a satellite which will study solar flares.	John Eisenhower's *The Bitter Woods*, an account of the Battle of the Bulge, is published in New York.	Jan. 22
Professor Patrick Moynihan of Harvard is appointed presidential assistant for urban affairs. . . . Fire bombing and rock throwing break out in Jacksonville, Fla. after a white man is acquitted of murder in the 1968 death of a Negro.	U.S. urges Britain not to sell advanced fighter jets to Malaysia. . . . *U.S.S. Pueblo* Cmdr. Lloyd Bucher says that he was beaten into unconsciousness by his North Korean captors and that he saw an alleged South Korean spy whose eye had been gouged out.		Soviet Union launches Cosmos 264.	Ralph Martin's *Jennie: The Life of Lady Randolph Churchill* is published.	Jan. 23
				Miguel Angel Asturias's *Strong Wind* is published in New York.	Jan. 24
					Jan. 25
Civil rights leader Edwin Pratt is shot to death in Seattle, Wash.		More than 3,000 coal miners demand action against black lung disease at a demonstration in Charleston, W. Va.		Pope Paul says that he cannot approve of the suicides by Czech youths but that he admires their spirit of self-sacrifice. . . . Noonday Press publishes Susan Sontag's *Trip to Hanoi*.	Jan. 26

F	G	H	I	J
Includes elections, federal-state relations, civil rights and liberties, crime, the judiciary, education, health care, poverty, urban affairs and population.	Includes formation and debate of U.S. foreign and defense policies, veterans' affairs and defense spending. (Relations with specific foreign countries are usually found under the region concerned.)	Includes business, labor, agriculture, taxation, transportation, consumer affairs, monetary and fiscal policy, natural resources, and pollution.	Includes worldwide scientific, medical and technological developments, natural phenomena, U.S. weather, natural disasters, and accidents.	Includes the arts, religion, scholarship, communications media, sports, entertainment, fashions, fads and social life.

	World Affairs	Europe	Africa & the Middle East	The Americas	Asia & the Pacific
Jan. 27	International Red Cross says that it has abandoned attempts to resume flights to Biafra from Equatorial Guinea.	Police again clash with demonstrators trying to post a photo of student martyr Jan Palach in Prague's central square. . . . Two militant Protestant leaders are sentenced to three months in prison in Armagh, Northern Ireland for participating in an unlawful assembly during a Catholic civil rights march.	Police clear out student protesters from Nairobi University. . . . Fourteen Iraqis, including nine Jews, are hanged publicly in Baghdad after being convicted as Israeli spies.	Canadian Defense Min. Leo Cadieux says that NATO is still essential to Canadian security interests.	Philippine Pres. Ferdinand Marcos says that his country will have to reassess its dependence on the U.S. in light of the imminent reduction of U.S. forces in Asia. . . . Police kill one member of a mob trying to set fire to a government building in Pakistan.
Jan. 28	International Red Cross says that Dahomey has agreed to allow it to use its territory for food relief flights to starving Biafrans. . . . International Commission of Jurists says that it is "very perturbed" about the Jan. 27 hangings in Iraq.	In another indication of the end of Czech liberalization, Czech Interior Min. Jan Pelnar announces that security forces will crack down on dissidents. . . . Italy becomes the 86th country to sign the nuclear non-proliferation treaty.		Uruguay accuses Argentinian forces of landing on a contested island in the Rio de la Plata.	Australia announces a major wheat deal with Communist China. . . . Violence breaks out between police and anti-government demonstrators in Peshawar, Pakistan.
Jan. 29		Britain says that all major seaports will be nationalized.			
Jan. 30	A U.N. report shows faster rate of industrial growth in the developing nations than in the industrial nations during the early 1960s.	At the Paris peace talks, North Vietnam and the National Liberation Front reject the U.S. proposal to restore the neutrality of the demilitarized zone. . . . About 400 West German students go on a rampage in Cologne and smash windows of the U.S. Information Center. . . . Reports indicate that Hungary has formed two joint stock companies with France.	Congo (Kinshasha) and Congo (Brazzaville) agree to restore economic relations. . . . Beirut newspaper Al Kifah says that Iraq should not have held the Jan. 27 executions in public.	London Times reports that Argentina has signed an agreement with West Germany for the construction of two submarines.	
Jan. 31	Second round of Kennedy tariff cuts goes into effect.	French Pres. de Gaulle begins a tour of Brittany to counter a separatist movement.	Egyptian newspaper Al Ahram says that Iraq should not have held the Jan. 27 executions in public.	Canadian External Affairs Min. Mitchell Sharp condemns the signing of a Quebec-France satellite agreement because of lack of prior notification to the federal government.	Westinghouse announces that it will build an atomic reactor for South Korea.
Feb. 1	International Red Cross flights resume to starving Biafrans.	Seven thousand Protestant militants demonstrate against the moderate policies of the government of Northern Ireland.		Venezuelan guerrillas take control of the town of Zazarida for several hours. . . . Peru establishes diplomatic relations with the Soviet Union.	U.S. troops fight off an assault by 500 North Vietnamese troops.
Feb. 2		French Pres. de Gaulle announces that a referendum will soon be held on proposed reforms granting expanded regional autonomy.	Several thousand Arab school girls rampage through the streets of Gaza in protest against Israeli rule.		Viet Cong vow to launch a new offensive in South Vietnam.
Feb. 3		Spanish government closes a steel plant in Bilbao after a two-day strike.	Israeli Premier Levi Eshkol suffers a heart attack. . . . Al Fatah guerrilla leader Yasir Arafat is elected chairman of the newly formed executive committee of the Palestine Liberation Organization (PLO). . . . Central African Republic and Chad agree to end the one-month blockade between them. . . . Dr. Eduardo Chivambo Mondlane, leader of the Mozambique Liberation Front (Frelimo) is assassinated in Dar es Salaam.	Alliance for Progress reports a healthy 5.4% increase in the GNP for Latin America during 1968. . . . London Times reports that Brazil has opened the first of two power plants which will supply enough electricity for half of the country's population.	
Feb. 4				Venezuelan guerrillas occupy a town of 40,000 for half an hour.	In a trend designed to reduce the importance of U.S. forces, U.S. transfers 300 helicopters to South Vietnam.

A	B	C	D	E
Includes developments that affect more than one world region, international organizations and important meetings of major world leaders.	Includes all domestic and regional developments in Europe, including the Soviet Union, Turkey, Cyprus and Malta.	Includes all domestic and regional developments in Africa and the Middle East, including Iraq and Iran and excluding Cyprus, Turkey and Afghanistan.	Includes all domestic and regional developments in Latin America, the Caribbean and Canada.	Includes all domestic and regional developments in Asia and Pacific nations, extending from Afghanistan through all the Pacific Islands, except Hawaii.

U.S. Politics & Social Issues	U.S. Foreign Policy & Defense	U.S. Economy & Environment	Science, Technology & Nature	Culture, Leisure & Life Style	
Pres. Nixon visits parts of Washington, D.C. destroyed during rioting.			AEC announces that a compact nuclear power plant designed to produce electricity for moon-based astronauts is now operating.	Harper & Row publishes Harrison Salisbury's *The 900 Days. The Siege of Leningrad*.	Jan. 27
Two U.S. escaped convicts force a U.S. plane to fly them to Cuba. . . . Senate votes, 50-42, against the modification of the filibuster rule.					Jan. 28
HEW Secy. Robert Finch upholds a cutoff of federal funds from five southern school districts.	White House announces plans for Pres. Nixon to visit Western Europe for talks with allied leaders.			Pope Paul deplores the public hangings held in Iraq on Jan. 27. . . . Former CIA Director Allen Dulles dies in Washington, D.C. at 75. . . . Random House publishes David Halberstam's *The Unfinished Odyssey of Robert Kennedy*.	Jan. 29
A federal court rules that Mississippi's program of tuition grants to private schools is unconstitutional. . . . Yale Univ. faculty votes to deprive officer training courses of academic credit. . . . Howard Univ. Medical School freshman class votes to boycott classes because of the administration's refusal to agree to their demands.	Defense Secy. Melvin Laird warns against a rejection of the Sentinel anti-ballistic missile system. . . . Pres. Nixon directs the Defense Department to develop a plan to shift toward a volunteer army. . . . Joseph Sisco is appointed Assistant Secretary of State for the Middle East.		U.S. launches a Canadian satellite.		Jan. 30
A court order upholds a plan for the total desegregation of Mt. Vernon, N.Y. public schools through busing. . . . A hijacker forces a U.S. plane to fly him to Cuba.	U.S. and the Soviet Union reach an agreement lowering the Soviet king crab catch in the eastern Bering Sea.	U.S. removes countervailing duties temporarily imposed on French imports.		Putnam publishes Jules Witcover's *Eighty-Five Days. The Last Campaign of Robert Kennedy*.	Jan. 31
	U.S. Navy turns over 60 heavily armed river patrol boats to the South Vietnamese Navy.				Feb. 1
				British horror movie actor Boris Karloff dies in Midhurst, England at 81. . . . U.S. historian Wallace Notestein dies in New Haven, Conn. at 90.	Feb. 2
Two men and two women force a U.S. plane to fly them to Cuba. . . . Ten thousand people demonstrate in front of the Iraqi U.N. mission to protest the Jan. 27 public hangings of alleged Israeli spies.		Pres. Nixon sets up a study group to deal with economic problems arising from the eventual end of the Vietnamese War.			Feb. 3
Harvard Univ. faculty votes to deprive officer training courses of academic credit.			Department of Interior is considering using underground nuclear explosions to increase natural gas production.	Choreographer George Balanchine divorces his fifth wife. . . . Southern liberal journalist Ralph McGill dies in Atlanta at 70.	Feb. 4

F	G	H	I	J
Includes elections, federal-state relations, civil rights and liberties, crime, the judiciary, education, health care, poverty, urban affairs and population.	*Includes formation and debate of U.S. foreign and defense policies, veterans' affairs and defense spending. (Relations with specific foreign countries are usually found under the region concerned.)*	*Includes business, labor, agriculture, taxation, transportation, consumer affairs, monetary and fiscal policy, natural resources, and pollution.*	*Includes worldwide scientific, medical and technological developments, natural phenomena, U.S. weather, natural disasters, and accidents.*	*Includes the arts, religion, scholarship, communications media, sports, entertainment, fashions, fads and social life.*

	World Affairs	Europe	Africa & the Middle East	The Americas	Asia & the Pacific
Feb. 5		Millions of Italian workers stage a 24-hour strike for higher pensions. . . . West German cabinet authorizes the start of legal proceedings to ban an extreme right-wing newspaper.	A freighter with private donations of food supplies from the West arrives at the Portuguese island of Sao Tome off Biafra. . . . Arabs stage anti-Israeli demonstrations in occupied West Bank towns.	Venezuelan guerrillas ambush a government patrol. . . . Reports indicate that Costa Rica is undertaking a serious birth control program. . . . A hijacker forces a Colombian plane to fly him to Cuba.	Pakistani Pres. Ayub Khan says that he has invited opposition leaders to meet with him to discuss the current unrest.
Feb. 6		No progress is reported at the Paris peace talks. . . . Reports indicate that Yugoslavia and Rumania have agreed to increase defense cooperation in the wake of the Soviet invasion of Czechoslovakia.	Arab guerrilla leader Yasir Arafat announces plans to shift a large part of his guerrilla force from Egypt and Syria to Jordan. . . . Arabs continue anti-Israeli demonstrations in occupied West Bank towns.	Peru announces that it is seizing the remaining assets of the U.S.-owned International Petroleum Co.	Students and police clash in Lahore, Pakistan.
Feb. 7		Soviet Union announces that measures will be imposed to stop the pollution of Lake Baikal in Siberia. . . . *The New York Times* reports that Turkey is permitting Soviet submarines to start their passage through the Bosporus in darkness despite the 1936 Montreux Convention forbidding it.	AP and UPI correspondents report the bombing of a Biafran marketplace by Nigerian planes.	Venezuelan air force attacks guerrillas in their mountain hideout. . . . Brazil forces five state legislatures to recess.	Viet Cong kill two U.S. civilian employees 19 miles west of Saigon.
Feb. 8		Italian CP reiterates its demand that Italy withdraw from NATO.			A government spokesman says that South Vietnamese troops overran a Viet Cong camp on Feb. 7 in the Mekong Delta.
Feb. 9	Central bankers of the major financial powers meet to discuss a program to prevent currency speculation from leading to devaluation.	East Germany announces that it will prohibit West German politicians from crossing its territory for the March 5 presidential election in West Berlin.			Reports indicate that at least 33 Pakistanis have been killed during anti-government demonstrations in recent months. . . . South Vietnam reports the discovery of the largest Viet Cong arms cache to date.
Feb. 10		East Germany begins to enforce tighter controls on travel in and out of Berlin. . . . Yugoslavia and West Germany sign their first trade agreement since establishing diplomatic relations.		Canadian External Affairs Min. Mitchell Sharp says that Canada will soon begin negotiations with Communist China about possible diplomatic relations. . . . A federal-provincial constitutional conference opens in Ottawa with heavy criticism by premiers from the Western provinces.	Ex-Air Marshal Mohammad Khan pledges to try to guarantee the safety of Pakistani Pres. Ayub Khan if he resigns.
Feb. 11		Yugoslavia approves a law creating territorial defense units throughout the country.	Israeli Defense Min. Moshe Dayan tells Arab West Bank residents that they may demonstrate in schoolyards but not in central parts of cities.	A hijacker forces a Venezuelan plane to fly him to Cuba. . . . Students at St. George Williams University in Montreal smash a $1 million computer to protest alleged "racism."	
Feb. 12		Millions of workers participate in a one-day strike in Italy. . . . Sporadic walkouts take place in a number of French factories.	Israel reports a sharp increase in Egyptian sniping along the Suez Canal.		U.S. announces the beginning of a large drive against Communist troops in northern South Vietnam.

A	B	C	D	E
Includes developments that affect more than one world region, international organizations and important meetings of major world leaders.	Includes all domestic and regional developments in Europe, including the Soviet Union, Turkey, Cyprus and Malta.	Includes all domestic and regional developments in Africa and the Middle East, including Iraq and Iran and excluding Cyprus, Turkey and Afghanistan.	Includes all domestic and regional developments in Latin America, the Caribbean and Canada.	Includes all domestic and regional developments in Asia and Pacific nations, extending from Afghanistan through all the Pacific Islands, except Hawaii.

U.S. Politics & Social Issues	U.S. Foreign Policy & Defense	U.S. Economy & Environment	Science, Technology & Nature	Culture, Leisure & Life Style	
	Anti-Vietnamese War university intellectuals meet with National Security adviser Henry Kissinger in Washington. . . . Pres. Nixon urges the Senate to approve the nuclear non-proliferation treaty.		U.S. launches a military observation satellite.		Feb. 5
Pres. Nixon expresses concern about the skeptical attitude towards him on the part of the Negro community.	Defense Dept. reports that construction of the Sentinel anti-ballistic missile system will be halted for a one-month policy review. . . . Pres. Nixon says that his upcoming European trip is aimed at revitalizing the Atlantic alliance. . . . U.S. announces that it will study the feasibility of using nuclear blasts to dig a harbor in northwestern Australia.				Feb. 6
Pres. Nixon meets with NAACP Director Roy Wilkins as part of his attempts to build links with the Negro community. . . . Harvard Negro students disrupt a class on poverty because it is allegedly "racist."		Justice Dept. files a suit against a Baltimore slaughter house because of pollution violations.	Soviet Union launches Cosmos 265.		Feb. 7
A Gallup Poll says that 59% of those interviewed approve of Pres. Nixon's performance after one week in office, while only 5% disapprove. . . . Great Neck, N.Y. school board approves an experimental plan to bus in minority students from N.Y.C.					Feb. 8
					Feb. 9
A hijacker, claiming that he has a sick father in Cuba, forces a U.S. plane to fly him to Havana.		HEW Secy. Robert Finch announces guidelines for the control of air pollution.	A California dentist says that wisdom teeth have been transplanted in mouths with a 92% success rate.	Houghton Mifflin publishes Samuel Eliot Morison's *Harrison Gray Otis 1765-1848* . . . Knopf publishes Eric Goldman's *The Tragedy of Lyndon Johnson.*	Feb. 10
	U.S. State Dept. says that it has informed Canada of its concern about Canada's possible recognition of Communist China. . . . U.S. State Dept. announces that an agreement has been reached with Cuba allowing passengers on hijacked planes to return on the planes in which they came instead of waiting for a U.S. plane to be sent from America to pick them up.		First transplant of a human larynx takes place in Belgium. . . . France cancels a plan to orbit a French satellite by means of a Soviet rocket because of economic reasons.		Feb. 11
In an attempt to discourage widespread campus disorders, N.Y. State Senate passes a bill to bar state financial aid to any college student convicted of a crime on a college campus.	*The New York Times* reports, citing Pentagon officials, that the Soviet Union has installed about 75 anti-missile launchers around Moscow.	*Wall Street Journal* reports that U.S. company profits increased substantially during the last quarter of 1967.		Harper & Row publishes Eric Hoffer's *Working and Thinking on the Waterfront.*	Feb. 12

F	G	H	I	J
Includes elections, federal-state relations, civil rights and liberties, crime, the judiciary, education, health care, poverty, urban affairs and population.	*Includes formation and debate of U.S. foreign and defense policies, veterans' affairs and defense spending. (Relations with specific foreign countries are usually found under the region concerned.)*	*Includes business, labor, agriculture, taxation, transportation, consumer affairs, monetary and fiscal policy, natural resources, and pollution.*	*Includes worldwide scientific, medical and technological developments, natural phenomena, U.S. weather, natural disasters, and accidents.*	*Includes the arts, religion, scholarship, communications media, sports, entertainment, fashions, fads and social life.*

	World Affairs	Europe	Africa & the Middle East	The Americas	Asia & the Pacific
Feb. 13		Italian CP again scores the Soviet invasion of Czechoslovakia. . . . British P.M. Harold Wilson and West German Chancellor Kurt-Georg Kiesinger end two days of talks in Bonn.	Al Fatah officials assert that Israeli Defense Min. Moshe Dayan has offered to meet with Arab guerrilla leader Yasir Arafat.	A bomb explodes at the Montreal Stock Exchange but causes only minor injuries.	Twenty-five thousand Pakistani workers demonstrate for higher wages in Lahore. . . . Thai Foreign Min. Thanat Khoman says that the 48,000 U.S. troops in his country will probably be withdrawn after the end of the Vietnamese War.
Feb. 14		Reports indicate that East Germany and the Soviet Union have begun unannounced maneuvers west of Berlin.	Israeli jets bomb Jordanian positions south of the Sea of Galilee.	Mexico announces that it has begun negotiations with Cuba for the return of hijackers forcing planes to fly to Havana. . . . A bomb explodes outside the U.S. embassy in Lima, Peru. . . . A Peruvian Navy gunboat attacks two U.S. fishing vessels off the coast of Peru and damages one of them.	Pakistani Pres. Ayub Khan agrees to free a number of political prisoners.
Feb. 15		East German border guards tighten security checks and cause delays of more than an hour at the border between the two Germanies.			Anti-government unrest continues in Lahore, Pakistan.
Feb. 16		Twenty thousand Turks demonstrate against a visit by the U.S. Sixth Fleet.	Arab guerrilla leader Yasir Arafat confers with Jordanian King Hussein in what is reported to be their first meeting.		Allied troops suspend fighting in observance of the Tet Lunar New Year.
Feb. 17		East Germany assures West German businessmen that they will have no border crossing problems for the upcoming Leipzig Fair in March.	Nearly 200 schoolgirls stage a sit-down demonstration against Israeli rule in the West Bank town of Ramallah.	Peru and the Soviet Union sign their first trade agreement.	Allied troops continue to observe the Tet Lunar New Year truce.
Feb. 18		Arab terrorists attack an Israeli plane in Zurich but cause little damage before their capture.	Israeli police remove about 400 rioting girls from a secondary school in the West Bank town of Bethlehem.	*The New York Times* reports that backing for Peru's anti-U.S. policies is spreading in Latin America.	Pakistani police fire on anti-government demonstrators in Dacca. . . . U.S. military spokesman says that there was no major fighting during the Feb. 16-17 Tet truce despite numerous minor incidents.
Feb. 19		London School of Economics reopens after being closed almost a month in wake of student disorders.	*Washington Post* reports that Zambia is negotiating the purchase of an anti-aircraft system from Britain.	Chile announces a balance-of-payments surplus for 1968 because of high copper prices. . . . Peruvian politician Victor Raul Haya de la Torre returns to Peru after an 11-month exile.	
Feb. 20		British Defense Min. Denis Healey calls on the Nixon administration to reaffirm the U.S. commitment to defend Western Europe.	Iraq executes eight more people as alleged spies for Israel; all are Moslems.	Canadian External Affairs Min. Mitchell Sharp says that formal contacts have been made with Communist Chinese officials in connection with possible diplomatic relations. . . . Sharp also reaffirms his country's commitment to NATO.	
Feb. 21		Madrid Univ. opens after being closed for almost a month in wake of student unrest. . . . Authorities close the University of Rome after weeks during which students occupied buildings.	Tanzanian Pres. Julius Nyerere releases Sheik Muhammed Shamte Hamadi, the former prime minister of Zanzibar, from a five-year detention sentence. . . . An Arab bomb kills two Israelis in a supermarket in Jerusalem.		Pakistani Pres. Ayub Khan announces that he will not be a candidate in the 1970 presidential elections.
Feb. 22		*The New York Times* reports that West Germany is developing a fast-breeder reactor.		Peru increases its offer of compensation for an expropriated U.S. oil company. . . . A bomb explodes in the basement of the Liberal Party's Reform Club in Montreal. . . . Roman Catholic Church of Brazil calls for the democratization of political life.	

A	B	C	D	E
Includes developments that affect more than one world region, international organizations and important meetings of major world leaders.	Includes all domestic and regional developments in Europe, including the Soviet Union, Turkey, Cyprus and Malta.	Includes all domestic and regional developments in Africa and the Middle East, including Iraq and Iran and excluding Cyprus, Turkey and Afghanistan.	Includes all domestic and regional developments in Latin America, the Caribbean and Canada.	Includes all domestic and regional developments in Asia and Pacific nations, extending from Afghanistan through all the Pacific Islands, except Hawaii.

U.S. Politics & Social Issues	U.S. Foreign Policy & Defense	U.S. Economy & Environment	Science, Technology & Nature	Culture, Leisure & Life Style	
State police break up a sit-in by students protesting a Dow Chemical Co. recruiter at the University of Massachusetts. . . . HEW Secy. Robert Finch cuts off federal school aid to three Southern school districts because of inadequate desegregation programs. . . . Stanford University ends academic credit for officers training.			First heart transplant operation is performed in West Germany.	Houghton Mifflin publishes *The Collected Short Prose of James Agee*. . . . U.S. poet Richard Eberhart wins the Academy of American Poets fellowships.	Feb. 13
		A 57-day dock strike ends in the Port of New York.	First West German heart transplant patient dies in Munich.		Feb. 14
					Feb. 15
		Commerce Dept. reports that the major reason for the improved U.S. balance-of-payments status is the repatriation of funds from abroad by U.S. corporations.		A poll indicates that 68% of Dutch priests favor the abolition of celibacy.	Feb. 16
University of Notre Dame Pres. Theodore Hesburgh announces a "get-tough" policy for dealing with campus disorders.	U.S. naval court of inquiry begins to focus its investigation on the *U.S.S. Pueblo* crew's 11-month imprisonment and torture.	Commerce Department reports an increase in housing starts in January.			Feb. 17
About 1,000 West Virginia coal miners go on strike to underline their demands for a black lung compensation bill. . . . Ray Bliss resigns as chairman of the Republican National Committee.	Senate Foreign Relations Committee opens hearings on the proposed anti-ballistic missile system. . . . *U.S.S. Pueblo* crew member Lt. Frank Schumacher says that his captors threatened him with death unless he signed a confession.				Feb. 18
	U.S.S. Pueblo crew member Lt. Timothy Harris breaks down and weeps as he recalls his temptation to commit suicide.	Treasury Secy. David Kennedy says that a tight monetary policy will be followed to fight inflation.	Heart, liver, kidneys and corneas of an unidentified man are transplanted to six different patients in N.Y.C.		Feb. 19
Pres. Nixon recommends changes in the presidential election system in order to ensure that the candidate with the highest vote total becomes President.	Most members of the Senate Foreign Relations Committee criticize the proposed anti-ballistic missile system. . . . Several crew members of the *U.S.S. Pueblo* say that they were frequently beaten during their captivity.	AFL-CIO approves the idea of a national union of policemen.	First inter-hospital transfer of a heart takes place in New York.	Simone de Beauvoir's *The Woman Destroyed* is published in N.Y.C. . . . Little, Brown & Co. publishes Herbert Ehrmann's *The Case That Will Not Die: Commonwealth vs. Sacco and Vanzetti*.	Feb. 20
				Random House publishes Philip Roth's *Portnoy's Complaint*. . . . Farrar, Straus & Giroux publishes Edmund Wilson's *The Duke of Palermo And Other Plays*.	Feb. 21
	Senate Armed Services Committee opens public hearings on the proposed anti-ballistic missile system. . . . U.S. bars the entry of leftist Mexican writer Carlos Fuentes.	AFL-CIO criticizes the concept of "black capitalism."			Feb. 22

F	G	H	I	J
Includes elections, federal-state relations, civil rights and liberties, crime, the judiciary, education, health care, poverty, urban affairs and population.	*Includes formation and debate of U.S. foreign and defense policies, veterans' affairs and defense spending. (Relations with specific foreign countries are usually found under the region concerned.)*	*Includes business, labor, agriculture, taxation, transportation, consumer affairs, monetary and fiscal policy, natural resources, and pollution.*	*Includes worldwide scientific, medical and technological developments, natural phenomena, U.S. weather, natural disasters, and accidents.*	*Includes the arts, religion, scholarship, communications media, sports, entertainment, fashions, fads and social life.*

	World Affairs	Europe	Africa & the Middle East	The Americas	Asia & the Pacific
Feb. 23		Soviet Defense Ministry newspaper compares Communist Chinese leader Mao Tse-tung with Adolf Hitler.	Arab guerrilla leader George Habash claims responsibility for the Jan. 21 bomb explosion in Jerusalem.	A bomb damages the Selective Service office in Isabela, Puerto Rico.	Communist forces shell at least 18 provincial capitals in a new offensive.
Feb. 24			Israel jets attack a position in Syria for the first time since the 1967 war.		Communist offensive lessens somewhat but a number of towns are still shelled.
Feb. 25	General Agreement on Tariffs & Trade (GATT) estimates that world exports increased by 11% in 1968.	Jan Zajic commits suicide by fire in Prague in protest against the Soviet occupation of Czechoslovakia.	Reports indicate that Tanzania has decided to end its participation in the U.S. Peace Corps. . . . A bomb heavily damages the British Consulate in East Jerusalem.	Quebec separatists are suspected of planting a bomb which explodes at a book store in Montreal.	Australia and New Zealand announce that their troops will remain in Malaysia after the departure of British troops. . . . Communist forces attack U.S. positions just south of the demilitarized zone.
Feb. 26		Soviet Union criticizes Czechoslovakia's hopes for increased trade with the West.	Israeli P.M. Levi Eshkol dies of a heart attack in Jerusalem.	Brazil suspends all interim elections and increases government control over legislators.	Communist troops assault two major installations in the Saigon area.
Feb. 27		West Germany and Hungary sign a trade agreement.		Brazil issues a decree facilitating expropriation of large estates in connection with a land reform program. . . . Eleven Puerto Rico University students are sentenced to six to 14 months in jail for instigating 1967 riots.	For the first time in six months, U.S. troops spot Communist forces within six miles of Saigon.
Feb. 28		Soviet Union threatens to impose traffic restrictions on shipments from West Berlin to West Germany because of the March 5 scheduled presidential election in West Berlin.		Uruguay and the Soviet Union announce the signing of a trade agreement. . . . Canadian police uncover a huge arms cache near Montreal.	
March 1	U.N. Human Rights Commission votes, 13-1, to condemn Israeli rule in the Arab-occupied territories.	Communist border guards seal off one of the two main auto routes into West Berlin.	Reports from Beirut indicate that Syrian Defense Min. Hafez al-Assad has seized power in Damascus. . . . Israeli police announce the arrest of 40 Arabs suspected of being involved in the Feb. 21 supermarket explosion in Jerusalem.		Allies launch a major drive in the Ashau Valley. . . . Communist Laotian forces attack a government garrison at Na Khang.
March 2		Soviet Union says that it cannot guarantee the safety of flights coming into West Berlin.	Reports indicate that Syrian security chief Abdel Kerim al-Jundi has committed suicide in the wake of Defense Min. Assad's seizure of power.		*Free China Weekly* reports that foreign investment is booming in Taiwan. . . . A clash reportedly takes place between the Soviet Union and Communist China involving troops, tanks and artillery. . . . Communist Laotian forces capture a government garrison at Na Khang.
March 3		An East European source says that East Germany and Poland pushed hard for a decision to invade Czechoslovakia in August 1968.	Leadership committee of the ruling Labor Party nominates Golda Meir, 70, to serve as interim prime minister. . . . Ethiopian officials close the national university at Addis Ababa.		Four Communist rockets hit Saigon and kill 12 citizens.
	A	**B**	**C**	**D**	**E**
	Includes developments that affect more than one world region, international organizations and important meetings of major world leaders.	Includes all domestic and regional developments in Europe, including the Soviet Union, Turkey, Cyprus and Malta.	Includes all domestic and regional developments in Africa and the Middle East, including Iraq and Iran and excluding Cyprus, Turkey and Afghanistan.	Includes all domestic and regional developments in Latin America, the Caribbean and Canada.	Includes all domestic and regional developments in Asia and Pacific nations, extending from Afghanistan through all the Pacific Islands, except Hawaii.

U.S. Politics & Social Issues	U.S. Foreign Policy & Defense	U.S. Economy & Environment	Science, Technology & Nature	Culture, Leisure & Life Style	
	Senate Armed Services Committee holds final days of public hearings on the proposed anti-ballistic missile system. . . . Pres. Nixon begins his European trip with a stop in Brussels where he consults with P.M. Gaston Eyskens.			Former Saudi King Ibn Saud dies in Athens at 67.	Feb. 23
Pres. Nixon affirms his support of Univ. of Notre Dame Pres. Theodore Hesburgh's "get-tough" policy for dealing with campus disorders. . . . U.S. Supreme Court agrees to decide if a state has the right to sterilize a mentally retarded person. . . . Supreme Court rules that states cannot forbid prisoners from giving legal aid to illiterate fellow inmates . . . Univ. of Pennsylvania students occupy the administration building in their drive to end military recruitment on campus.	Pres. Nixon arrives in London for talks. . . . U.S.S. Pueblo crew member Monroe Goldman says that he was beaten for 13 consecutive hours while naked by his North Korean captors.		U.S. launches a satellite to study the possibility of life on Mars.	Praeger publishes Hans Morgenthau's A New Foreign Policy for the United States.	Feb. 24
Univ. of Pennsylvania students leave an occupied administrative building after being read a court injunction banning such sit-ins. . . . A gunman forces a U.S. plane to fly to Cuba.	Pres. Nixon consults with British P.M. Harold Wilson and other British public and private officials in London. . . . Several U.S.S. Pueblo crew members report severe beatings while naked by their North Korean captors.		Soviet Union launches Cosmos 266.	George Polk Award in journalism goes to David Kraslow and Stuart Loory for articles on Pres. Johnson's secret peace talks.	Feb. 25
Striking miners bring the West Virginia coal industry to a virtual standstill. . . . Rogers Morton becomes the new chairman of the Republican National Committee.	Pres. Nixon arrives in West Germany for talks.		Soviet Union launches Cosmos 267. . . . U.S. launches a weather satellite.	German philosopher Karl Jaspers dies in Basel, Switzerland at 86.	Feb. 26
	Several U.S.S. Pueblo crew members say that they were invited to visit Russia by North Korean women. . . . Pres. Nixon receives a tumultuous welcome in West Berlin.		U.S. launches a satellite which will study the possibility of life on Mars.	Random House publishes Eldridge Cleaver's Post-Prison Writings and Speeches.	Feb. 27
	Pres. Nixon confers at length with French Pres. de Gaulle in Paris.	Commerce Dept. reports that U.S. exports exceeded U.S. imports during January.		McGraw Hill publishes J.J. Servan-Schreiber's The Spirit of May.	Feb. 28
New Orleans businessman Clay Shaw is acquitted of conspiring to assassinate Pres. John Kennedy.	Pres. Nixon meets informally with a wide range of French citizens including prominent socialists.				March 1
	Pres. Nixon confers with Pope Paul in Rome.			Ronald Neame's film The Prime of Miss Jean Brodie is released.	March 2
New York University expels Robert Kirkman for leading violent invasions of meeting halls.			Three U.S. astronauts blast off on a test flight with the Apollo spacecraft which will land the first Americans on the moon.	Little, Brown & Co. publishes Bruce Catton's Grant Takes Command.	March 3

F	G	H	I	J
Includes elections, federal-state relations, civil rights and liberties, crime, the judiciary, education, health care, poverty, urban affairs and population.	Includes formation and debate of U.S. foreign and defense policies, veterans' affairs and defense spending. (Relations with specific foreign countries are usually found under the region concerned.)	Includes business, labor, agriculture, taxation, transportation, consumer affairs, monetary and fiscal policy, natural resources, and pollution.	Includes worldwide scientific, medical and technological developments, natural phenomena, U.S. weather, natural disasters, and accidents.	Includes the arts, religion, scholarship, communications media, sports, entertainment, fashions, fads and social life.

	World Affairs	Europe	Africa & the Middle East	The Americas	Asia & the Pacific
March 4				Canadian P.M. Pierre Elliott Trudeau says that he has sent mineral resource maps to all provincial premiers. . . . Police arrest a self-styled "Marxist revolutionary" for illegal possession of dynamite in Montreal.	After nearly two weeks of relative calm, a new wave of violence erupts in Pakistan. . . . Viet Cong mortar shell hits a South Vietnamese prison near Danang and kills five prisoners.
March 5		Defying the Communist ban on holding West German elections in Berlin, West German electors elect Gustav Heinemann as president of West Germany.	Israel announces the arrest of 80 Arabs suspected of conducting guerrilla operations in Israel.	Panama frees about 100 political prisoners, leaving about 400 still under arrest.	
March 6		Reports indicate that France has filed a countersuit against the Common Market commission's suit against special French export subsidies.	Nine Persian Gulf states ratify the settlement of a border dispute between the area's two most powerful states--Dibai and Abu Dhabi.		U.S. reports the deaths of 453 Americans during the first week of the Communist drive begun in February.
March 7		House of Lords approves without debate a bill permitting doctors to end the lives of incurably sick patients on their specific request.	Students in Addis Ababa begin a boycott of schools despite an appeal by Emperor Haile Selassie. . . . Rhodesia commutes the death sentences of 49 convicted African guerrillas.	Canadian P.M. Pierre Elliott Trudeau says that the question of Arctic jurisdiction between the U.S. and Canada is a difficult one.	U.S. forces throw back three Communist attacks against U.S. positions around Saigon.
March 8		For the first time Czechoslovakia officially honors the Czechoslovak Jews killed in Auschwitz.	Israel and Egypt engage in their heaviest artillery duel in four and a half months.	Argentina proposes to negotiate a trade agreement with the Common Market.	U.S. reports an incursion of 100 U.S. Marines into Laos.
March 9	U.N. observer Lt. Gen. Odd Bull reports that Egypt and not Israel initiated the March 8 artillery duel.		Reports from Spain indicate that Pres. Francisco Macias Nguemo has assumed dictatorial powers in Equatorial Guinea. . . . Israel and Egypt continue their heavy artillery duel across the Suez Canal.	Police kill eight squatters in a clash near Santiago, Chile.	At a news conference in Danang, Defense Secy. Melvin Laird says he will ask Congress to increase the budget for the Vietnam War for the next fiscal year.
March 10		A major work stoppage takes place in France to support higher wages.		Reports indicate that Ecuador and the Soviet Union will probably establish diplomatic relations. . . . Ecuador and the Soviet Union sign a trade agreement.	Japan announces that it now tops West Germany as the world's third largest industrial power.
March 11		Yugoslav Pres. Tito denounces Soviet attempts to dominate Yugoslavia. . . . Major work stoppage continues in France.	Israel and Egypt exchange artillery fire across the Suez Canal.	In Venezuela's first peaceful transition of political power, Rafael Caldera Rodriguez becomes the country's 43rd president. . . . Police are placed on alert in Chile because of tensions growing out of the March 9 police-squatter confrontation.	Communist mortars attack a number of South Vietnamese cities, wounding many civilians.
March 12		Czechoslovak CP ousts several of its liberal members.	Egyptian-Israeli artillery duel continues across the Suez Canal.	Peru signs trade agreements with a number of East European countries. . . . Student unrest results in at least seven deaths in Colombia. . . . Chilean Senate is called into special session to discuss the March 9 police-squatter confrontation.	Five- to six-hundred Communist troops attack a U.S. infantry unit in the northern part of South Vietnam.
March 13		French Pres. de Gaulle meets with West German Chancellor Kurt-Georg Kiesinger in Paris.	Palestine Liberation Organization (PLO) criticizes acceptance by Arab states of a U.N. resolution implicitly recognizing the legitimacy of the State of Israel. . . . Egyptian-Israeli artillery duel continues across the Suez Canal.	Brazilian government strips another 95 politicians of their political rights. . . . Colombian government imposes a curfew in the wake of student unrest. . . . U.S. oil companies accept Ecuador's demands for higher royalty payments.	

A	B	C	D	E
Includes developments that affect more than one world region, international organizations and important meetings of major world leaders.	Includes all domestic and regional developments in Europe, including the Soviet Union, Turkey, Cyprus and Malta.	Includes all domestic and regional developments in Africa and the Middle East, including Iraq and Iran and excluding Cyprus, Turkey and Afghanistan.	Includes all domestic and regional developments in Latin America, the Caribbean and Canada.	Includes all domestic and regional developments in Asia and Pacific nations, extending from Afghanistan through all the Pacific Islands, except Hawaii.

U.S. Politics & Social Issues	U.S. Foreign Policy & Defense	U.S. Economy & Environment	Science, Technology & Nature	Culture, Leisure & Life Style	
	Scientists at some 30 U.S. campuses participate in a one-day "research stoppage" to protest alleged government misuse of science in defense-oriented projects.				March 4
Pres. Nixon establishes an Office of Minority Business Enterprise. . . . A gunman forces a U.S. plane to fly to Cuba.	Anti-war hecklers disrupt a speech by Sen. J. William Fulbright (D, Ark.) in New York, despite his opposition to the Vietnamese War.		Soviet Union launches Cosmos 268 and 269.	Little, Brown & Co. publishes Anthony Powell's *The Military Philosophers.*	March 5
	U.S. Army deserter Edwin Arnett is sentenced to four years at hard labor.		Soviet Union launches Cosmos 270.		March 6
	Senate Armed Services Committee reports 250 convictions for desertions during 1968.		Soviet Union conducts an underground nuclear test.	Farrar, Straus & Giroux publishes Hermann Hesse's *Gertrude* .	March 7
West Virginia Legislature passes a black lung compensation bill.		Interior Secy. Walter Hickel announces a drive against alligator poachers.			March 8
				Walter Reade releases Rudolf Noelte's film *The Castle* .	March 9
James Earl Ray pleads guilty to the murder of Dr. Martin Luther King Jr. . . . U.S. Supreme Court posthumously clears the Rev. Martin Luther King Jr. of a conviction for parading without a permit in Birmingham, Ala. in 1965. . . . Supreme Court rules that the joint commercial operation of two competing newspapers violates antitrust laws. . . . U.S. Supreme Court declines to delay the induction of five graduate students who sought deferments through the end of the academic year.	*U.S.S. Pueblo* Commander Lloyd Bucher says that he often saw North Koreans pull apart live birds and toads during his captivity.	Labor Department reports that unemployment is at the lowest level since October 1953.		National Book Award for poetry goes to John Berryman.	March 10
West Virginia Governor signs a black lung compensation bill.					March 11
U.S. authorities arrest ten Haitians and two Americans in connection with a secret military training base for Haitian exiles in Florida.				Harcourt, Brace & World publishes Kingsley Amis's *I Want It Now* . . . . Harper & Row publishes Anthony Sampson's *Anatomy of Europe* .	March 12
	U.S.S. Pueblo Commander Lloyd Bucher says that the Navy provided inadequate equipment to destroy secret papers.	Interior Secy. Walter Hickel meets with Florida Gov. Claude Kirk to discuss measures against alligator poachers.	Three U.S. astronauts return safely to earth after having flight-tested their Apollo spacecraft.		March 13

F	G	H	I	J
Includes elections, federal-state relations, civil rights and liberties, crime, the judiciary, education, health care, poverty, urban affairs and population.	*Includes formation and debate of U.S. foreign and defense policies, veterans' affairs and defense spending. (Relations with specific foreign countries are usually found under the region concerned.)*	*Includes business, labor, agriculture, taxation, transportation, consumer affairs, monetary and fiscal policy, natural resources, and pollution.*	*Includes worldwide scientific, medical and technological developments, natural phenomena, U.S. weather, natural disasters, and accidents.*	*Includes the arts, religion, scholarship, communications media, sports, entertainment, fashions, fads and social life.*

	World Affairs	Europe	Africa & the Middle East	The Americas	Asia & the Pacific
March 14		A West German court sentences Josef Bachmann, the assassin of leftist student leader Rudi Dutschke, to seven years at hard labor. . . . Italian police eject students occupying the University of Pavia. . . . *The New York Times* reports a threatened hunger strike among Soviet dissidents. . . . French Pres. de Gaulle and West German Chancellor Kurt-Georg Kiesinger continue talks in Paris.	Israeli jets attack Arab guerrilla bases in Jordan.		
March 15			Reports indicate that Kenya has stopped its expulsion of Indian merchants. . . . Israeli police announce the arrest of three Arabs in connection with the recent bombing of Hebrew University in Jerusalem.	Uruguay lifts many of the restrictions imposed during the state of emergency declared in June 1968.	A clash resumes between the Soviet Union and China involving troops, tanks and artillery. . . . North Koreans kill one U.S. soldier in a border skirmish.
March 16		About 300 right-wing students riot in Milan and attack left-wing book stores.	Israeli jets attack Arab guerrilla bases in Jordan. . . . Jordanian King Hussein confers in Cairo with Egyptian Pres. Nasser.	Chilean Communists gain an absolute majority in the country's largest labor union. . . . A hijacker forces a Colombian plane to fly to Cuba.	U.S. troops exchange gunfire with two North Korean infiltrators. . . . Thai troops maul a Viet Cong unit near Saigon.
March 17			Israeli jets attack Arab guerrilla bases in Jordan. . . . Golda Meir is sworn in as Israel's fourth prime minister. . . . Reports indicate that Syria has permitted the stationing of 6,000 Iraqi troops on its territory.	Student unrest breaks out into open violence in Sincelejo, Colombia. . . . Cuba becomes the first government to recognize the National Liberation Front of South Vietnam.	U.S. flys 700 paratroopers to South Korea in a simulated counter-attack.
March 18	U.N. Disarmament Committee reconvenes in Geneva.		Egyptian-Israeli artillery duel resumes across the Suez Canal.	Colombian Pres. Carlos Lleras Restrepo warns of a crackdown against student unrest.	Reports indicate that North Korea changed its top military leadership in December 1968. . . . Allied troops launch a major drive around Saigon.
March 19		Soviet poet Yevgeni Yevtushenko scores Communist Chinese Chmn. Mao.		Brazil devalues the cruzeiro. . . . A small force of British paratroopers takes over the tiny Caribbean island of Anguilla to prevent it from seceding from a Caribbean island federation. . . . Peru seizes two more U.S. fishing boats.	Communists fire ten rockets into Danang.
March 20	U.N. Security Council votes to condemn South Africa's continued control of Namibia. . . . International Atomic Energy Agency reports that demands for uranium are rising sharply because of the construction of nuclear power plants.	West Germany announces that it will import more goods from Eastern Europe during 1969.	Syrian Baathist Party convenes in an effort to settle a factional dispute between Defense Min. Hafez al-Assad and Pres. Nureddin al-Attassi.	Brazilian security forces arrest 20 alleged Communists.	U.S. reports 351 combat fatalities for the March 9-15 period.
March 21			Israel concedes the downing of one of its jets by Jordanian aircraft fire. . . . Ghana releases the captains and one crewman of the two Soviet fishing trawlers seized in October 1968. . . . Equatorial Guinea asks Spanish personnel to remain in their former colony.	Uruguayan security forces arrest Jorge Manera Lluveras, an alleged leader of the urban guerrilla force, Tupamaros.	Communist troops attack a U.S. artillery base near Saigon.
March 22			Israeli official says that its new policy is to destroy Arab guerrilla bases instead of waiting for attacks and then retaliating.		
March 23			Egyptian and Israeli patrols clash along the Suez Canal.	*Le Monde* of Paris reports that Brazilian Pres. Arthur da Costa e Silva has issued a decree setting procedures for the sequestration of the properties of persons accused of malfeasance in public office.	
	A	**B**	**C**	**D**	**E**
	Includes developments that affect more than one world region, international organizations and important meetings of major world leaders.	*Includes all domestic and regional developments in Europe, including the Soviet Union, Turkey, Cyprus and Malta.*	*Includes all domestic and regional developments in Africa and the Middle East, including Iraq and Iran and excluding Cyprus, Turkey and Afghanistan.*	*Includes all domestic and regional developments in Latin America, the Caribbean and Canada.*	*Includes all domestic and regional developments in Asia and Pacific nations, extending from Afghanistan through all the Pacific Islands, except Hawaii.*

U.S. Politics & Social Issues	U.S. Foreign Policy & Defense	U.S. Economy & Environment	Science, Technology & Nature	Culture, Leisure & Life Style	
	Pres. Nixon announces his decision to proceed with an anti-ballistic missile system. . . . Pres. Nixon says that in view of the Communists' recent offensive, there is no prospect of U.S. troop reductions in "the foreseeable future.". . . Pres. Nixon says that $2.5 billion has been cut from the January Defense Dept. budget request.			U.S. artist Ben Shahn dies in New York at 70.	March 14
			Soviet Union launches Cosmos 271.		March 15
					March 16
Two U.S. planes are forced to fly hijackers to Cuba.	Sen. George McGovern (D, S.D.) attacks the administration's Vietnam policy for not withdrawing more U.S. troops.	Commerce Dept. reports that 1968 fourth-quarter corporate profits reached record levels.		Census Bureau says that the U.S. population grew more slowly in 1968 than in any other year since 1940.	March 17
					March 18
A Chicago court convicts 10 people for interfering with police during the 1968 Democratic Convention.		House votes to raise the national debt limit.			March 19
A federal jury indicts eight policemen and eight demonstrators in connection with the disorders during the 1968 Democratic National Convention.	Defense Secy. Melvin Laird stresses the Soviet threat in defending the administration's anti-ballistic missile system before a congressional committee. . . . Sen. Edward Kennedy (D, Mass.) urges the U.S. to have normal relations with Communist China.	Commerce Dept. reports that orders for durable goods have jumped to record levels.	U.S. conducts an underground nuclear test.	Knopf publishes Christopher Lasch's The Agony of the American Left. . . . National Catholic Office for Motion Pictures names Rachel, Rachel as the best film of 1968.	March 20
	Defense Secy. Melvin Laird again stresses the Soviet threat in defending the administration's anti-ballistic missile system before a second congressional committee.		U.S. conducts an underground nuclear test.	Doubleday publishes Bernard Fall's Anatomy of a Crisis: The Laotian Crisis of 1960-1961.	March 21
Pres. Nixon says that the universities should handle the problem of campus unrest themselves and not depend on intervention by the federal government.					March 22
				U.S. diplomatic historian Bernadotte Schmitt dies in Alexandria, Va. at 82.	March 23

F	G	H	I	J
Includes elections, federal-state relations, civil rights and liberties, crime, the judiciary, education, health care, poverty, urban affairs and population.	Includes formation and debate of U.S. foreign and defense policies, veterans' affairs and defense spending. (Relations with specific foreign countries are usually found under the region concerned.)	Includes business, labor, agriculture, taxation, transportation, consumer affairs, monetary and fiscal policy, natural resources, and pollution.	Includes worldwide scientific, medical and technological developments, natural phenomena, U.S. weather, natural disasters, and accidents.	Includes the arts, religion, scholarship, communications media, sports, entertainment, fashions, fads and social life.

	World Affairs	Europe	Africa & the Middle East	The Americas	Asia & the Pacific
March 24		British Foreign Secy. Michael Stewart defends the dispatch of British troops to Anguilla. . . . Spanish political leader Francisco Franco says that he will not slow the departure of Spanish personnel fleeing chaotic conditions in Equatorial Guinea.	Trial opens in Algeria of 56 defendants charged with conspiring to assassinate Pres. Houari Boumedienne. . . . Egyptian-Israeli artillery duel resumes across the Suez Canal. . . . Reports indicate that Israeli Foreign Min. Abba Eban and Jordanian King Hussein held an unsuccessful negotiating session in London in late 1968.	Last military official resigns from the Bolivian cabinet. . . . *London Times* reports that Brazilian government has tightened press censorship.	
March 25		Soviet leader Mikhail Suslov makes the first public derogatory remark about Stalin since 1964 when he blames "the cult of Stalin" for setting back the Comintern. . . . Protestant militant Ian Paisley begins serving a six-month prison term in Northern Ireland.		Reports indicate that about 280 British paratroopers remain on the Caribbean island of Anguilla. . . . Twenty-two Peruvian priests threaten to resign after their archbishop dismisses three priests for involvement in political demonstrations.	Pakistani Pres. Mohammad Ayub Khan resigns from office after months of anti-government unrest. . . . U.S. troops maul North Vietnamese forces about 45 miles from Saigon.
March 26		Czechoslovakia announces that it has eased restrictions on foreign tourists. . . . Sir Learie Nicholas Constantine becomes the first Negro member of the British House of Lords.	*Washington Post* reports the presence of Zambian troops near the Rhodesian border. . . . South Africa sentences 11 black Africans to jail for guerrilla activity. . . . Israeli jets pound Jordanian targets.	Venezuela lifts its six-year ban on the Communist Party. . . . Peruvian Archbishop Carlos Maria Jurgens Byrne announces the reinstatement of three dismissed Peruvian priests.	North and South Korean forces clash briefly at their border.
March 27	U.N. Security Council takes up the March 26 Israeli attack on Jordan in wake of alleged civilian casualties.	Bulgaria warns artists not to deviate from the Party line.			Communist forces kill 14 U.S. troops near the demilitarized zone. . . . Pakistan arrests 21 workers suspected of instigating strikes.
March 28		Greek poet George Seferis attacks the Greek military junta in a written statement. . . . Spanish government grants an amnesty to all persons accused of criminal acts during the Spanish Civil War. . . . In a further display of independence, Rumania refuses to sign a Soviet-backed resolution attacking the West at a conference on Nazi criminals. . . . Czechoslovakia's victory over a Soviet ice hockey team sets off widespread anti-Soviet demonstrations in Prague.	Reports indicate that almost all Spanish personnel have left Equatorial Guinea. . . . Tunisia signs a trade accord with the Common Market. . . . Israeli police clash with Arab protesters demonstrating against alleged maltreatment of Arab guerrilla suspects in Jerusalem.	Nicaragua agrees to rescind duties imposed on goods from other Central American countries.	Pakistani radio announces that local military commanders can make their own laws when dealing with local disturbances.
March 29		Czech demonstrators ransack the Prague offices of Aeroflot, the Soviet airline.		About 6,000 students demonstrate for the conversion of Montreal's McGill University into a French-language institution.	Saigon comes under sporadic Communist shelling.
March 30		Guerrillas blow up a power station near Belfast, Northern Ireland. . . . West German students smash windows at a U.S. Army headquarters.	Israeli jets attack Jordanian positions south of the Sea of Galilee.	Britain and the Caribbean island of Anguilla sign an agreement resolving their dispute.	South Vietnamese official discloses the discovery of two mass graves near Hue. . . . Pakistan announces the arrest of two East Pakistani labor leaders.
March 31		Government of Northern Ireland mobilizes 1,000 part-time policemen to guard against sabotage. . . . Soviet press charges that liberal Czech politician Josef Smrkovsky took part in the March 29 anti-Soviet demonstrations in Prague.		Brazilian Pres. Arthur da Costa e Silva pledges presidential elections for 1970. . . . Argentinian Pres. Juan Carlos Ongania criticizes U.S. protectionism.	Sporadic shelling of Saigon resumes. . . . In Karachi Pakistani students return to classes for the first time in five months.
April 1	U.N. Security Council condemns the March 26 Israeli attack on Jordan.	Soviet news agency *Tass* says that Rumanian troops took part in Warsaw Pact exercises in Bulgaria during the previous week. . . . Reports indicate that Czech Pres. Ludvig Svoboda is standing firm against Soviet pressure to change the composition of the current government.	Israel reports that another Arab saboteur network around Jerusalem has been smashed.	Bolivian Pres. Rene Barrientos Ortuno confirms reports that U.S. Central Intelligence Agency personnel helped train units fighting Communist guerrilla leader Ernesto (Ché) Guevara.	
	A	**B**	**C**	**D**	**E**
	Includes developments that affect more than one world region, international organizations and important meetings of major world leaders.	*Includes all domestic and regional developments in Europe, including the Soviet Union, Turkey, Cyprus and Malta.*	*Includes all domestic and regional developments in Africa and the Middle East, including Iraq and Iran and excluding Cyprus, Turkey and Afghanistan.*	*Includes all domestic and regional developments in Latin America, the Caribbean and Canada.*	*Includes all domestic and regional developments in Asia and Pacific nations, extending from Afghanistan through all the Pacific Islands, except Hawaii.*

U.S. Politics & Social Issues	U.S. Foreign Policy & Defense	U.S. Economy & Environment	Science, Technology & Nature	Culture, Leisure & Life Style	
Supreme Court rules that it is not unconstitutional for more money to be spent on public schools in wealthier districts than in poorer ones.	Pres. Nixon confers with Canadian P.M. Pierre Elliott Trudeau about the effects of the U.S. anti-ballistic missile system on Canada.		U.S. announces that it will not attempt the scheduled May landing on the moon.	Former Congo (Kinshasa) Pres. Joseph Kasavubu dies in the Lower Congo. He was reported to be in his fifties. . . . Macmillan publishes Bruno Bettelheim's *The Children of the Dream*. . . . Soviet cellist Vsevolod Lezhnev defects to the U.S.	March 24
Supreme Court rules that police must warn suspects of their rights immediately after arrest and not just before questioning at a police station. . . . U.S. Supreme Court orders a new election in Greene County, Ala. because Negro candidates were kept off the ballot. . . . Supreme Court overturns a state order limiting picketing of striking employees of a Florida railroad. . . . A hijacker forces a U.S. plane to fly him to Cuba.	U.S. emphasizes the need for private talks with the Communists for progress in Vietnam. . . . Pres. Nixon continues discussions with Canadian P.M. Pierre Elliott Trudeau.			U.S. journalist Max Eastman dies in Barbados at 86.	March 25
	U.S. announces agreement with Spain for a five-year extension of the pact granting the U.S. military bases in Spain.	Pres. Nixon asks Congress to extend the 10% income tax surcharge for one year. . . . Senate votes to raise the national debt limit.		Mikos Jancso's film *The Red and the White* is released.	March 26
	State Secy. William Rogers says that the U.S. will withdraw all of its troops from South Vietnam as soon as North Vietnam does the same.				March 27
				Dwight David Eisenhower, 34th President of the United States and Supreme Allied Commander in Europe during World War II, dies in Washington, D.C. at 78. . . . Overseas Press Club Award 1969 goes to Peter Rehak for his reporting of the Soviet invasion of Czechoslovakia. . . . A poll indicates that 72% of Dutch Roman Catholics feel that priests should be allowed to marry.	March 28
			U.S. announces that it has abandoned plans to excavate a harbor with nuclear explosives in Australia.		March 29
				French Pres. Charles de Gaulle visits the bier of former Pres. Eisenhower.	March 30
	A Gallup Poll indicates that 44% of those interviewed support Pres. Nixon's handling of the war and 26% disapprove.			Leaders from all over the world attend the last religious services for former Pres. Eisenhower. . . . Delacorte Press publishes Kurt Vonnegut's *Slaughterhouse Five*.	March 31
Supreme Court rules that labor unions can fine members who exceed daily production quotas. . . . Negro Councilman Thomas Bradley leads Los Angeles incumbent Mayor Sam Yorty in the first round of voting for mayor.	Defense Secy. Melvin Laird announces further cuts in the 1970 defense budget.				April 1

F	G	H	I	J
Includes elections, federal-state relations, civil rights and liberties, crime, the judiciary, education, health care, poverty, urban affairs and population.	Includes formation and debate of U.S. foreign and defense policies, veterans' affairs and defense spending. (Relations with specific foreign countries are usually found under the region concerned.)	Includes business, labor, agriculture, taxation, transportation, consumer affairs, monetary and fiscal policy, natural resources, and pollution.	Includes worldwide scientific, medical and technological developments, natural phenomena, U.S. weather, natural disasters, and accidents.	Includes the arts, religion, scholarship, communications media, sports, entertainment, fashions, fads and social life.

	World Affairs	Europe	Africa & the Middle East	The Americas	Asia & the Pacific
April 2		Bowing to Soviet pressure, Czechoslovakia imposes new press curbs.	Iran ends diplomatic ties with Lebanon because of its refusal to extradite an Iranian official wanted for alleged corruption. . . . Ghanaian political leader Joseph Ankrah resigns after admitting having accepted bribes.		
April 3		No progress is reported at the Paris peace talks. . . . Czechoslovak leader Alexander Dubcek warns that further anti-Soviet demonstrations could lead to increased Soviet intervention in the country's life.	Ethiopian police kill one student in Addis Ababa.	*Washington Post* reports that peace talks between leftist guerrillas and the Venezuelan government have already begun. . . . Canadian P.M. Pierre Elliott Trudeau says that Canada will reduce the size of its military force in Europe.	U.S. combat fatalities in Vietnam surpass the combat fatalities incurred during the Korean War.
April 4		Soviet Adm. Sergei Gorshkov denies that Soviet vessels in the Atlantic Ocean will be shifted to the Pacific to meet a possible Chinese threat. . . . Liberal Czech journalist Josef Vohnout is fired from his post as chairman of the Czech Press and Information office.	Israel and Egypt exchange artillery fire across the Suez Canal.		North Vietnamese suffer heavy loses in an attack against a U.S. artillery base near Godauha.
April 5		*London Times* reports that censors have been installed in all major daily newspapers in Czechoslovakia.		Anguillan political leader P.R. Webster lashes out at his island's forced federation with St. Kitts.	Viet Cong inflict heavy casualties near Kontum.
April 6		Soviet newspaper accuses the Czech government of opening two strip-tease clubs.		West German Foreign Min. Willy Brandt arrives in Canada for discussions about planned Canadian force reductions in Europe.	
April 7			Algeria sentences three defendants to death for allegedly conspiring to murder Pres. Houari Boumedienne.		Viet Cong kill 11 American soldiers about 100 miles from Saigon.
April 8	In a major shift in policy, U.S. proposes to the U.N. Disarmament Conference that the International Atomic Energy Agency verify all cut-offs in the production of nuclear weapons materials.	Czechoslovak CP Presidium says it will discipline any writers who contravene Party policy.	Arab guerrillas and Israeli forces clash at the adjacent Israeli and Jordanian ports of Elath and Aquba.		U.S. soldiers ambush a Viet Cong force 17 miles from Saigon. . . . Indian Foreign Min. Dinesh Singh says that his country supports the Soviet Union in its border dispute with Communist China.
April 9		Greek ruling junta restores the right of assembly. . . . French Foreign Min. Michel Debré affirms France's loyalty to the Atlantic Alliance. . . . French Independent Republican Party leader Valery Giscard d'Estaing criticizes Pres. de Gaulle's regional reform bill.	Israeli and Jordanian forces engage in two sharp clashes across the Jordan River.	Venezuela says that it is ready to talk with leftist guerrillas. . . . Leading Chilean Christian Democrat Radomiro Tomic says that he will not be a contender for the party's 1970 presidential nomination. . . . In Argentina 251 priests issue a statement criticizing the Church hierarchy for not taking enough measures toward promoting social justice.	
April 10		French Pres. de Gaulle says that he will resign if his regional reform bill is rejected in the scheduled April 27 referendum. . . . Institute of Strategic Studies in London predicts that the Soviet Union will have more intercontinental missiles deployed than will the U.S. by mid-1969. . . . NATO announces that the largest Mediterranean maneuvers in recent years will begin on April 20.	Reports indicate that Jordanian troops have arrested two Arab guerrillas believed responsible for the April 8 attack on the Israeli port of Elath.	Canadian External Affairs Min. Mitchell Sharp announces that Communist China has responded favorably to Canada's bid for the start of talks on possible diplomatic relations.	Communist forces launch an artillery attack against military and civilian targets throughout South Vietnam.

A	B	C	D	E
Includes developments that affect more than one world region, international organizations and important meetings of major world leaders.	*Includes all domestic and regional developments in Europe, including the Soviet Union, Turkey, Cyprus and Malta.*	*Includes all domestic and regional developments in Africa and the Middle East, including Iraq and Iran and excluding Cyprus, Turkey and Afghanistan.*	*Includes all domestic and regional developments in Latin America, the Caribbean and Canada.*	*Includes all domestic and regional developments in Asia and Pacific nations, extending from Afghanistan through all the Pacific Islands, except Hawaii.*

U.S. Politics & Social Issues	U.S. Foreign Policy & Defense	U.S. Economy & Environment	Science, Technology & Nature	Culture, Leisure & Life Style	
				Pope Paul criticizes the widespread dissent in the Catholic Church. . . . Body of former Pres. Dwight Eisenhower is buried in Abiline, Kan.	April 2
Illinois National Guardsmen arrest about 200 Negro youths engaged in vandalism.		U.S. Federal Reserve announces a rise in its discount rate to 6%, the highest rate in 40 years. . . . Commerce Dept. reports new factory orders are at a record high.		Paramount Pictures releases *Goodbye Columbus* . . . . Pope Paul says that there is "practically schismatic ferment" in the Catholic Church.	April 3
Memphis, Tenn. policemen bring scattered looting under control.		Pres. Nixon announces the relaxation of some restrictions on U.S. lending and investment abroad.	For the first time in medical history, an artificial heart is placed in a patient during an operation on Haskell Karp in Skokie, Ill.		April 4
One thousand marchers pay tribute to the late Martin Luther King Jr. in Montgomery, Ala.	More than 20,000 N.Y.C. demonstrators march against the Vietnamese War.				April 5
					April 6
U.S. Supreme Court says that even a difference of six percent population between voting districts is a violation of the one-man, one-vote principle.	State Secy. William Rogers says that the deadline requiring imposition of economic sanctions against Peru has been indefinitely extended.	Pres. Nixon signs a bill raising the national debt limit.			April 7
Pres. Nixon orders the release of funding to renovate areas destroyed by ghetto rioting.	Pres. Nixon confers with Jordanian King Hussein.				April 8
Harvard University militant students seize the main administration building.	Senate Democratic leader Mike Mansfield (D, Mont.) calls for an immediate withdrawal of 50,000 U.S. troops from South Vietnam.				April 9
Harvard University calls in police to clear the administration building of students who are demanding an end to military recruiting on campus.					April 10

F	G	H	I	J
Includes elections, federal-state relations, civil rights and liberties, crime, the judiciary, education, health care, poverty, urban affairs and population.	*Includes formation and debate of U.S. foreign and defense policies, veterans' affairs and defense spending. (Relations with specific foreign countries are usually found under the region concerned.)*	*Includes business, labor, agriculture, taxation, transportation, consumer affairs, monetary and fiscal policy, natural resources, and pollution.*	*Includes worldwide scientific, medical and technological developments, natural phenomena, U.S. weather, natural disasters, and accidents.*	*Includes the arts, religion, scholarship, communications media, sports, entertainment, fashions, fads and social life.*

	World Affairs	Europe	Africa & the Middle East	The Americas	Asia & the Pacific
April 11		Soviet Union again proposes that border talks, which were broken off in 1964, be resumed with Communist China. . . . Czechoslovak CP leader Gustav Husak attacks liberal elements in the Czechoslovak government. . . . About 5,000 shopkeepers clash with police in Bourgoin, France.	Jordanian King Hussein makes the first public pledge by an Arab leader that Israeli ships will be allowed to use the Suez Canal as part of a peace settlement.	British diplomat Lord Caradon returns to Anguilla for another attempt to mediate its dispute with St. Kitts.	
April 12		Italian prisoners riot in the Turin jail. . . . Within a period of two hours, Czechoslovakia issues and then retracts an announcement that the Soviet Union is sending troop reinforcements.	Israeli Premier Golda Meir repeats Israeli demands for direct Arab-Israeli negotiations.	The New York Times reports unrest among Colombian priests because of lack of independence in the Church hierarchy.	
April 13		Italian police drive prisoners back into their cells in Turin. . . . Soviet press strongly criticizes the Italian CP for attacking the Soviet invasion of Czechoslovakia. . . . Czechoslovakia announces that it will participate in new Warsaw Pact exercises.	Iraq hangs four Iraqi Moslems accused of spying for the U.S. Central Intelligence Agency.	St. Kitts-Nevis-Anguillan P.M. Robert Bradshaw maintains his opposition to the break-away move by Anguilla.	
April 14	U.S. and Soviet representatives meet in Vienna to exchange information on the peaceful uses of nuclear explosions.	Rioting Italian prisoners take hostages in Milan's jail. . . . Portuguese P.M. Marcello Caetano begins a visit to his country's African territories.	Israeli and Egyptian forces engage in the sharpest clashes across the Suez Canal since March 8.	A state of emergency is proclaimed on the tiny British-ruled Caribbean island of Montserrat after an attack by 20 persons on the local police station.	
April 15	South Africa draws $66.2 million in foreign exchange from the International Monetary Fund.	The New York Times reports that several top Yugoslav generals were purged following the 1968 invasion of Czechoslovakia. . . . Italian police launch an assault on rioting prisoners in Milan and free hostages.		British administrator of the island of Montserrat says that the April 14 attack on the local police station was not a sign of hostility toward British rule. . . . Bolivian Gen. Cesar Ruiz announces that no further press interviews with jailed French leftist Regis Debray will be allowed.	North Korea downs a U.S. reconnaissance plane.
April 16		French small shop-keepers stage their second one-day strike in less than a month in protest against the spread of large retail businesses.	France sends a contingent of soldiers to the Central African Republic to protect the Bokassa government.		
April 17	U.N. Secy. Gen. U Thant praises U.S. restraint in reacting to North Korea's downing of a U.S. reconnaissance plane.	In a culmination of the anti-reform drive backed by the Soviets, Slovak. CP First Secy. Gustav Husak replaces Czechoslovak CP First Secy. Alexander Dubcek.	Lebanese Communist newspaper al Nida reports that Iraq is curbing the activities of Arab commandoes stationed there.	Nicaragua announces the seizure of two U.S. fishing boats.	
April 18		Soviet Union warmly praises the new Czechoslovak leader Gustav Husak. . . . West German Social Democratic Party adopts a platform which includes possible recognition of East Germany.		Reports indicate that leftist Venezuelan guerrillas may be ready for a cease-fire. . . . Reports indicate that the Bolivian government has lifted the state of emergency imposed in the wake of labor unrest.	Communist forces kill seven U.S. troops in a day-long battle 50 miles north of Saigon.
April 19		Reports from London indicate that the new Czechoslovak leader Gustav Husak is a moderate conservative but not a Stalinist.	Iran declares void the 1937 agreement granting Iraq control of the Shatt-al-Arab River. . . . Egyptian commandoes attack Israeli positions on the Suez Canal's East Bank.		
April 20					After three days of relative calm, Communist forces carry out heavy rocket attacks against civilian and military targets in South Vietnam.
	A	B	C	D	E
	Includes developments that affect more than one world region, international organizations and important meetings of major world leaders.	Includes all domestic and regional developments in Europe, including the Soviet Union, Turkey, Cyprus and Malta.	Includes all domestic and regional developments in Africa and the Middle East, including Iraq and Iran and excluding Cyprus, Turkey and Afghanistan.	Includes all domestic and regional developments in Latin America, the Caribbean and Canada.	Includes all domestic and regional developments in Asia and Pacific nations, extending from Afghanistan through all the Pacific Islands, except Hawaii.

U.S. Politics & Social Issues	U.S. Foreign Policy & Defense	U.S. Economy & Environment	Science, Technology & Nature	Culture, Leisure & Life Style	
Harvard University classroom attendance is at 20-30% of normal in the wake of continuing unrest.		AFL-CIO denounces UAW Pres. Walter Reuther.	Soviet scientist Lev Artsimovich says that important progress has been made toward producing electric power from atomic explosions.		April 11
					April 12
			Longest-surviving U.S. heart transplant patient Fred Everman dies in Arlington, Va. . . . Houston doctors report the successful operation of a preservation chamber for vital organs in its first test with a human heart and lungs.		April 13
Nearly 6,000 Harvard University students vote by a narrow margin to continue their strike for three more days.	Pres. Nixon implies that the Alliance for Progress placed too much emphasis on what the U.S. could do for Latin America instead of what could be done in partnership.			Last surviving son of Mahatma Gandhi, Ramdas Gandhi, dies in Bombay at 73.	April 14
	Congressional reaction to the April 14 downing of the U.S. reconnaissance plane is largely cautious.				April 15
	U.S. Defense Dept. says that the U.S. reconnaissance plane downed on April 14 by North Korea was over international waters.				April 16
Sirhan Bishara Sirhan is found guilty of the murder of Sen. Robert Kennedy.		Commerce Department reports that the U.S. GNP is now over $900 billion.		Farrar, Straus & Giroux publishes *The Complete Poems* of Randall Jarrell.	April 17
Negro students set fires to back demands for automatic admission to Brooklyn College, N.Y.C. for any Negro student regardless of qualifications.	Pres. Nixon says that there are no immediate plans to reduce U.S. forces in South Vietnam.			Harvard University Press publishes *Franklin Roosevelt and Foreign Affairs*, edited by Edgar Nixon.	April 18
About 100 Negro students seize the Cornell University student union with guns to force the dropping of disciplinary measures against three Negro students.	U.S. transfers 20 jet bombers to South Vietnam as part of its policy of shifting the burden of the war to the Asian nation.				April 19
Cornell Dean of Faculty Robert Miller agrees to drop disciplinary measures against three Negro students.				Brandon Films releases Max Ophul's film *Lola Montes*.	April 20
F	G	H	I	J	
Includes elections, federal-state relations, civil rights and liberties, crime, the judiciary, education, health care, poverty, urban affairs and population.	*Includes formation and debate of U.S. foreign and defense policies, veterans' affairs and defense spending. (Relations with specific foreign countries are usually found under the region concerned.)*	*Includes business, labor, agriculture, taxation, transportation, consumer affairs, monetary and fiscal policy, natural resources, and pollution.*	*Includes worldwide scientific, medical and technological developments, natural phenomena, U.S. weather, natural disasters, and accidents.*	*Includes the arts, religion, scholarship, communications media, sports, entertainment, fashions, fads and social life.*	

	World Affairs	Europe	Africa & the Middle East	The Americas	Asia & the Pacific
April 21		British troops begin to guard public utilities in Northern Ireland. . . . Portuguese P.M. Marcello Caetano ends his visit to Portugal's African territories.	Egyptian commandoes attack Israeli positions on the canal's East Bank.		A U.S. Navy task force begins moving into the Sea of Japan as a warning to North Korea.
April 22	U.N. Secy. Gen. U Thant says that "a virtual state of active war" exists between Egypt and Israel.	Poland sentences student leader Irena Lasota to 18 months in jail. . . . New press censorship measures are announced by the Czech government.	Iran sends several freighters which refuse to pay tolls up the Shatt-al-Arab River in defiance of Iraqi demands. . . . Egyptian commandoes attack Israeli positions on the canal's East Bank.	In an apparent effort to assert Canadian sovereignty over the Northwest Territories, Gov. Gen. Roland Michener begins a tour of the area.	
April 23		Bank of London and South America announces a major loan to Hungary.		Foreign ministers of five South American nations sign a treaty for the joint development of the Rio de la Plata basin.	A U.S. helicopter gunship accidentally kills five South Vietnamese soldiers.
April 24		West German cabinet agrees to submit a bill to the Bundestag abolishing a statute of limitations on Nazi war crimes. . . . Hungarian officials, during a radio broadcast, admit that poverty still exists in their country. . . . Officials report no progress at the Paris peace talks.	Lebanese Premier Rashid Karami resigns in the wake of clashes between security forces and demonstrators demanding an end to government restrictions against guerrillas using Lebanon as a base for attacks on Israel.	Venezuelan Foreign Min. Aristedes Calvani says that some Venezuelan guerrilla leaders are apparently still closely tied to Cuban Communists.	U.S. B-52 bombers carry out one of their heaviest raids in South Vietnam.
April 25		Irish guerrillas blow up another water main supplying Belfast. . . . French Pres. de Gaulle again states that he will resign if his regional reform plan is rejected.	Iran sends another two freighters which refuse to pay tolls up the Shatt-al-Arab River in defiance of Iraqi demands. . . . Arab guerrilla organization Al Fatah demands an end to restrictions on guerrillas operating from Lebanon.		U.S. B-52 bombers pound Communist targets in the Central Highlands.
April 26				Peruvian Pres. Juan Velasco says that his country has taken emergency measures to counter the effects of possible economic sanctions by the U.S.	U.S. forces kill more than 200 Communist troops in one of the bloodiest battles of the war.
April 27		Reports indicate that Latvian student Llya Reus has committed suicide in protest against the Soviet invasion of Czechoslovakia. . . . French voters reject Pres. de Gaulle's regional reform plan by a margin of 52%-48%.		Bolivian Pres. Rene Barrientos Ortuno dies in a helicopter crash. . . . Cuban official Carlos Rafael Rodriguez praises Peru's nationalization of U.S. property.	
April 28		Charles de Gaulle resigns as president of France. . . . Renewed monetary speculation hits the French franc but central bank intervention keeps the situation under control.	An Arab mine kills an Israeli worker in the El Hamma region. . . . Israeli newspapers express satisfaction about French Pres. de Gaulle's resignation while Arab newspapers express their regrets.		About 150,000 people demonstrate throughout Japan for the return of Okinawa. . . . U.S. troops engage in six hours of hand-to-hand combat near the Cambodian border.
April 29		Former French Premier George Pompidou announces his candidacy for the upcoming presidential elections. . . . Belgium, the Netherlands and Luxembourg agree to abolish virtually all internal frontier controls.	Israeli commandoes blow up a power station 200 miles into Egyptian territory.	Venezuelan Defense Min. Martin Garcia Villasmil says that there is no direct evidence of Cuban support of Venezuelan guerrillas since November 1968. . . . Venezuela resumes diplomatic relations with Czechoslovakia.	

A	B	C	D	E
Includes developments that affect more than one world region, international organizations and important meetings of major world leaders.	Includes all domestic and regional developments in Europe, including the Soviet Union, Turkey, Cyprus and Malta.	Includes all domestic and regional developments in Africa and the Middle East, including Iraq and Iran and excluding Cyprus, Turkey and Afghanistan.	Includes all domestic and regional developments in Latin America, the Caribbean and Canada.	Includes all domestic and regional developments in Asia and Pacific nations, extending from Afghanistan through all the Pacific Islands, except Hawaii.

U.S. Politics & Social Issues	U.S. Foreign Policy & Defense	U.S. Economy & Environment	Science, Technology & Nature	Culture, Leisure & Life Style	
Cornell faculty votes overwhelmingly to reject demands for nullification of the reprimands against three Negro students. . . . In a landmark decision U.S. Supreme Court rules that residency requirements for welfare benefits are illegal. . . . Supreme Court declines to rule on laws which make it a crime to burn or deface the flag.				Scribner's publishes Carlos Baker's *Ernest Hemingway*. . . . Pier Paolo Pasolini's film *Teorema* is released.	April 21
Supreme Court rules that fingerprints obtained in mass arrests for the purpose of investigation cannot be used as evidence. . . . City College of New York Pres. Gordon Gallagher closes the school after Negro and Puerto Rican students lock themselves inside the college's gates.			Houston doctors perform the world's first total human eye transplant.	British Navy Capt. Robin Knox-Johnson completes the first solo sea voyage around the world. . . . U.S. translator Rolfe Humphries dies in Redwood City, Calif. at 74.	April 22
Cornell faculty capitulates to Negro demands after Negroes gain the backing of some 8,000 white students. . . . A Los Angeles jury decides that Sen. Robert Kennedy's murderer Sirhan Bishara Sirhan should be executed.					April 23
	Defense Secy. Melvin Laird announces the closing of 36 military installations.			Bancroft Prize for History goes to Dr. Winthrop Jordan's book *White Over Black: American Attitudes Toward the Negro, 1550-1812*.	April 24
City College of New York engineering students continue to attend classes despite the closing of the school.	Defense Secy. Melvin Laird defends the administration's proposed anti-ballistic missile system.		Houston Ophthalmological Society criticizes an April 22 eye transplant operation for being a premature surgical operation.		April 25
A Negro economic organization headed by James Forman demands "reparations" from U.S. churches.					April 26
Negro civil rights leader Bayard Rustin criticizes the impracticality of black studies programs when Negro communities are in desperate need of practical skills.	Defense Dept. announces a reduction in the naval task force mobilized to protect U.S. reconnaissance flights off North Korea.				April 27
U.S. Supreme Court decides to rule on the legality of speeding up the induction process for men who return their draft cards in protest against the Vietnamese War. . . . Pres. Nixon proposes self-government for Washington, D.C.	Pres. Nixon expresses his "deep regret" about Pres. de Gaulle's resignation. . . . A Louis Harris poll indicates that 47% of those interviewed support the proposed anti-ballistic missile system while 26% are against it.			Knopf publishes John Cheever's *Bullet Park*.	April 28
Pres. Nixon urges college officials to take a tough line against student demonstrators who break the law.	A Congressional hearing discloses an apparent $2.1 billion overcost for the new C-5A jet transport plane.				April 29
F	**G**	**H**	**I**	**J**	
Includes elections, federal-state relations, civil rights and liberties, crime, the judiciary, education, health care, poverty, urban affairs and population.	*Includes formation and debate of U.S. foreign and defense policies, veterans' affairs and defense spending. (Relations with specific foreign countries are usually found under the region concerned.)*	*Includes business, labor, agriculture, taxation, transportation, consumer affairs, monetary and fiscal policy, natural resources, and pollution.*	*Includes worldwide scientific, medical and technological developments, natural phenomena, U.S. weather, natural disasters, and accidents.*	*Includes the arts, religion, scholarship, communications media, sports, entertainment, fashions, fads and social life.*	

	World Affairs	Europe	Africa & the Middle East	The Americas	Asia & the Pacific
April 30	Egypt files a protest with the U.N. about the April 29 Israeli raid deep into its territory.		Israeli Premier Golda Meir says that the April 29 raid into Egypt was in retaliation for recent Egyptian commando raids.	Venezuela resumes diplomatic relations with Hungary.	Cambodian Prince Sihanouk goes back on a previous decision to seek diplomatic relations with the U.S.
May 1		Soviet-bloc countries, with the exception of East Germany, celebrate May Day with peace-oriented celebrations.	Ghana announces the lifting of the ban on political parties.		
May 2		Reports indicate that more than 1,000 Czech liberals have been arrested by police.	Arab guerrillas kill three Israeli soldiers on the Golan Heights.	*Time* magazine estimates that there are only 200-300 active guerrillas in Venezuela.	A helicopter crash kills 12 U.S. soldiers in South Vietnam.
May 3				Venezuelan CP meets for the first time since its legalization.	Laotian government reports the capture of a Communist stronghold on the Plaines des Jarres.
May 4		Socialist leader Francois Mitterand says that he will not run in the upcoming French presidential elections.	Israeli jets strike Arab guerrilla bases in Jordan.		A helicopter crash kills eight U.S. soldiers in South Vietnam.
May 5		Socialist Gaston Defferre is chosen to oppose George Pompidou in the upcoming French presidential elections. . . . British P.M. Harold Wilson restates his determination to bring his country into the Common Market.	A Palestinian guerrilla kills a Lebanese soldier as Lebanese forces try to curb guerrilla activity near the Israeli border.	OAS Secy. Gen. Galo Plaza Lasso begins a trip to Europe in an attempt to diversify Latin American trade.	Malaysian P.M. Abdul Rahman accuses Communists of being behind the latest ethnic unrest.
May 6		Moscow radio accuses Communist Chinese leader Mao Tse-tung of having killed thousands of Chinese. . . . Czechoslovak Presidium adopts stricter press censorship measures.	Lebanese troops kill two members of the Syrian-backed Saiqa guerrilla organization near the Israeli border.		A helicopter crash kills two U.S. crewmen in South Vietnam.
May 7		Czechoslovak Academy of Science demands an end to rapidly growing press censorship. . . . Soviet Union accuses Communist China of seizing Soviet artillery destined for North Vietnam. . . . Soviet police arrest former military officer Pyotr Grigoryevich Grigorenko for his criticism of governmental repression.	Israeli jets strike Arab guerrilla bases in Jordan.		
May 8			Arab guerrilla leader Yasir Arafat confers with Lebanese officials on ways to stop Lebanese-Palestinian clashes in Southern Lebanon.		

A	B	C	D	E
Includes developments that affect more than one world region, international organizations and important meetings of major world leaders.	Includes all domestic and regional developments in Europe, including the Soviet Union, Turkey, Cyprus and Malta.	Includes all domestic and regional developments in Africa and the Middle East, including Iraq and Iran and excluding Cyprus, Turkey and Afghanistan.	Includes all domestic and regional developments in Latin America, the Caribbean and Canada.	Includes all domestic and regional developments in Asia and Pacific nations, extending from Afghanistan through all the Pacific Islands, except Hawaii.

U.S. Politics & Social Issues	U.S. Foreign Policy & Defense	U.S. Economy & Environment	Science, Technology & Nature	Culture, Leisure & Life Style	
Several hundred Negro and Puerto Rican students vandalize the president's office at Brooklyn College.			U.S. conducts two underground nuclear tests. . . . Univ. of Chicago anthropologist Clark Howell announces the discovery of two man-like jaws in Ethiopia which appear to be almost four million years old.	Dial publishes H. Rap Brown's *Die Nigger Die*.	April 30
Negro students vandalize buildings at Queens College in New York after being refused complete control of their remedial programs.	Sen. George Aiken (R, Vt.) urges the U.S. to begin an immediate withdrawal from South Vietnam.			Viking publishes Lewis Chester's *An American Melodrama. The Presidential Campaign*.	May 1
N.Y.C. police restore order at Queens College. . . . HEW Dept. rules that a black-only program at Antioch College does not violate the 1964 Civil Rights Act.				German Nazi Franz von Papen dies in Obersasbach West Germany at 89.	May 2
				Indian Pres. Dr. Zakir Hussain dies in New Delhi at 72.	May 3
Negro civil rights activist James Forman disrupts a N.Y.C. church service and demands "economic reparations.". . . Negro Supreme Court Justice Thurgood Marshall says that black militants who violate the law must pay the consequences. . . . *Life* magazine reports that Supreme Court Justice Abe Fortas accepted but later returned a $20,000 fee from financier Louis Wolfson who was imprisoned April 25 for violating securities laws.				British poet Sir Osbert Sitwell dies in Montagnana, Italy at 76.	May 4
Sen. Edward Kennedy (D, Mass.) says that the corruption charges against Supreme Court Justice Abe Fortas are extremely serious.				Simon & Schuster publishes Herbert Mathews' *Fidel Castro*. . . . McGraw-Hill publishes Vladimir Nabokov's *Adai* . . . . Farrar, Straus & Giroux publishes Bernard Malamud's *Pictures of Fidelman*. . . . Pulitzer Prize for Poetry goes to George Oppen.	May 5
Negro and Puerto Rican students attack firemen called in to fight fires set at Brooklyn College. . . . Chapel Hill, N.C. elects a Negro mayor.	Navy Secy. John Chafee announces that no disciplinary action will be taken against the members of the *U.S.S. Pueblo*. . . . Peruvian envoy Marco Fernandez Baca discusses his country's nationalization of a U.S. oil firm with Pres. Nixon. . . . A study commissioned by Sen. Edward Kennedy says that the proposed U.S. anti-ballistic missile system would be inefficient to the point of being useless.				May 6
City College of New York is again ordered closed after Negro students attack white students. . . . Sen. Robert Taft (R, Ohio) says that Supreme Court Justice Abe Fortas may have to be impeached.			U.S. conducts an underground nuclear test.	A first printing copy of the Declaration of Independence is sold for $404,000 in Philadelphia.	May 7
				New York City Ballet star Suzanne Farrell resigns because of personal differences with its director George Balanchine.	May 8

F	G	H	I	J
Includes elections, federal-state relations, civil rights and liberties, crime, the judiciary, education, health care, poverty, urban affairs and population.	*Includes formation and debate of U.S. foreign and defense policies, veterans' affairs and defense spending. (Relations with specific countries are usually found under the region concerned.)*	*Includes business, labor, agriculture, taxation, transportation, consumer affairs, monetary and fiscal policy, natural resources, and pollution.*	*Includes worldwide scientific, medical and technological developments, natural phenomena, U.S. weather, natural disasters, and accidents.*	*Includes the arts, religion, scholarship, communications media, sports, entertainment, fashions, fads and social life.*

	World Affairs	Europe	Africa & the Middle East	The Americas	Asia & the Pacific
May 9		West Germany decides against an upward re-evaluation of the mark.	Israel discloses that Israeli commandoes have been regularly crossing into Jordan during the past year.		U.S. troops kill more than 100 Communist soldiers near Danang.
May 10		Reports from Moscow indicate that Soviet and Communist Chinese forces have clashed several times during the past week.	Israel reports the slaying of four Arab guerrilla infiltrators.		
May 11				Presidential envoy Nelson Rockefeller begins a tour of Latin American capitals.	Communist forces launch an important offensive throughout South Vietnam.
May 12		Interim French Pres. Alain Poher announces his candidacy for the upcoming presidential elections.	An Arab guerrilla broadcast from Cairo says that no progress has been made in talks with Lebanese officials.		Reports indicate that Communist China has agreed to navigation talks with the Soviet Union. . . . Communist artillery continues to pound South Vietnamese military and civilian targets throughout the country.
May 13		British P.M. Harold Wilson dismisses James Callaghan from the cabinet because of his opposition to the government's labor reform bill.			Five Communist rockets strike the Tansonnhut airport in Saigon.
May 14		French presidential candidate George Pompidou indicates that he may be more receptive toward British Common Market membership than was Pres. de Gaulle.	Israel reports the deaths of three soldiers by Egyptian shelling.	Canadian Parliament approves a bill liberalizing abortions and decriminalizing private homosexual acts. . . . Presidential envoy Nelson Rockefeller visits Honduras for talks.	Malaysian P.M. Abdul Rahman suspends the constitution in the wake of unrest between the Chinese and Malay communities.
May 15		Czechoslovakia bans two more liberal magazines as its methodical campaign to crush the remnants of the reform movement continues.		Latin American officials meet in Chile to formulate a common economic policy for presentation to the Nixon administration.	
May 16			Washington Post reports that British officials blame the French for deliberately scuttling chances for peace negotiations in the Nigerian civil war by sending arms to Biafra in September 1968.	Presidential envoy Nelson Rockefeller visits Nicaragua for talks.	Malaysian P.M. Abdul Rahman declares emergency rule as ethnic unrest continues.
May 17		About 130 conservative Czech journalists denounce reform writers.	Al Fatah guerrillas attack a fortified Israeli position on the West Bank of the Jordan River for the first time since the June 1967 war.	In a possible modification of its revolutionary policy, Cuban official Carlos Rafael Rodriguez says that Cuba's support of guerrilla warfare is mainly "ideological."	Malaysian P.M. Abdul Rahman blames Chinese "secret societies" for the recent rioting.
May 18		In his first public appearance since his downfall, Alexander Dubcek calls for better relations with the Soviet Union.			Allied forces drive off a Communist attack after five hours of intense fighting 38 miles from Saigon.
May 19		Czech Premier Oldrich Cernik warns against the dangers of "anti-Sovietism."		Panamanian leaders tell presidential envoy Nelson Rockefeller that the scheduled elections in 1970 will be free ones.	

A	B	C	D	E
Includes developments that affect more than one world region, international organizations and important meetings of major world leaders.	Includes all domestic and regional developments in Europe, including the Soviet Union, Turkey, Cyprus and Malta.	Includes all domestic and regional developments in Africa and the Middle East, including Iraq and Iran and excluding Cyprus, Turkey and Afghanistan.	Includes all domestic and regional developments in Latin America, the Caribbean and Canada.	Includes all domestic and regional developments in Asia and Pacific nations, extending from Afghanistan through all the Pacific Islands, except Hawaii.

U.S. Politics & Social Issues	U.S. Foreign Policy & Defense	U.S. Economy & Environment	Science, Technology & Nature	Culture, Leisure & Life Style	
					May 9
Sen. Walter Mondale (Minn.) becomes the first Democratic member of Congress to suggest that Supreme Court Justice Abe Fortas resign.					**May 10**
Newsweek magazine reports that Pres. Nixon is trying to force Supreme Court Justice Abe Fortas to resign.					**May 11**
NAACP Director Roy Wilkins says that black studies programs are silly when Negro communities are in desperate need of practical skills. . . . Sen. James Allen (Ala.) becomes the second Democratic Senator to call for the resignation of Supreme Court Justice Abe Fortas.	Pentagon research director John Foster defends the computerization of the proposed anti-ballistic missile system as being capable of handling various attacks.	Trade unions officials boo Housing Secy. George Romney when he charges that their high wages are hampering the nation's building program.		Farrar, Straus & Giroux publishes Flannery O'Connor's *Mystery and Manners*. . . . Houghton Mifflin publishes Arthur Schlesinger's *The Crisis of Confidence. Ideas, Power and Violence in America.*	**May 12**
A former staunch Fortas backer, Sen. Joseph Tydings (D, Md.) calls on the Supreme Court Justice to resign. . . . Civil rights activist Charles Evers is elected mayor of Fayette, Miss.					**May 13**
Los Angeles Times reports that Supreme Court Justice Fortas's agreement with the Wolfson foundation provided him with $20,000 a year for life.					**May 14**
Supreme Court Justice Abe Fortas resigns from the Supreme Court.		AFL-CIO elects Joseph Kirkland to its second most important post.			**May 15**
			Soviet satellite Venera 5 completes its trip to Venus.	British actor Lewis Casson dies in London at 93. . . . Knopf publishes Doris Lessing's *The Four-Gated City.*	**May 16**
			Soviet satellite Venera 6 completes its trip to Venus.		**May 17**
			U.S. launches the last manned spacecraft before the scheduled trip to the moon.		**May 18**
One person dies as police clear non-students from the Berkeley University campus.	Sen. J. William Fulbright calls for the rejection of what he terms the U.S. foreign policy of "chronic. . . intervention."		Sen. Edward Kennedy urges a slowdown in the U.S. space program after the scheduled landing on the moon.	Random House publishes Jane Jacobs' *The Economy of Cities*. . . . Farrar, Straus & Giroux publishes Robert Lowell's *Notebook 1967-68*. . . . Viking publishes Graham Greene's *Collected Essays* . . . . U.S. jazz composer for the tenor sax Coleman Hawkins dies in New York at 64.	**May 19**
F	G	H	I	J	
Includes elections, federal-state relations, civil rights and liberties, crime, the judiciary, education, health care, poverty, urban affairs and population.	*Includes formation and debate of U.S. foreign and defense policies, veterans' affairs and defense spending. (Relations with specific foreign countries are usually found under the region concerned.)*	*Includes business, labor, agriculture, taxation, transportation, consumer affairs, monetary and fiscal policy, natural resources, and pollution.*	*Includes worldwide scientific, medical and technological developments, natural phenomena, U.S. weather, natural disasters, and accidents.*	*Includes the arts, religion, scholarship, communications media, sports, entertainment, fashions, fads and social life.*	

	World Affairs	Europe	Africa & the Middle East	The Americas	Asia & the Pacific
May 20					Allied forces capture Apbia Mountain in the Ashau Valley after one of the bloodiest battles of the war.
May 21	UNESCO votes to postpone a decision for one year on continued "consultative" status for the Jewish organization B'nai B'rith.		Israeli forces cross into Jordan to destroy Arab guerrilla bases.		Laotian government troops advance into the Plaine de Jarres.
May 22			Biafran planes bomb Port Harcourt.		
May 23				Peru decides against going through with the scheduled visit of presidential envoy Nelson Rockefeller.	U.S. reports at least 50 combat fatalities in the fight for Apbia Mountain.
May 24	U.N. Association of the U.S. recommends that the U.N. appoint a commissioner of population.		Biafran planes bomb Port Benin.		South Vietnam reports heavy losses in battles fought in the Saigon area on May 23.
May 25			Nigeria announces that retaliatory air raids have been staged against two Biafran airstrips.		Violence flares up between Malaysia's Chinese and ethnic communities.
May 26					Reports indicate that anti-Communist forces are making some headway in Laos.
May 27				Presidential envoy Nelson Rockefeller arrives in Colombia for talks. . . .	U.S. and Laotian forces are coordinating their attacks on North Vietnamese supply lines.
May 28				Police arrest about 100 anti-U.S. demonstrators in Bogota, Colombia.	U.S. abandons recently won Apbia Mountain in South Vietnam.
May 29				Street fights break out in Cordoba, Argentina between students and workers and the police as the government prepares itself for nationwide strikes and violence. Three people are known dead and many are injured.	
May 30				Labor riots break out in the Caribbean island of Curacao. . . . Anti-U.S. demonstrators refuse Presidential envoy Nelson Rockefeller's offer of discussions in Quito, Equador.	South Vietnamese Pres. Nguyen Van Thieu reiterates that he will never accept a coalition government with Communist forces.
May 31				About 500 Dutch marines fly into Curacao to restore order. . . . Presidential envoy Nelson Rockefeller shortens his stay in Bolivia because of political demonstrations.	

A	B	C	D	E
Includes developments that affect more than one world region, international organizations and important meetings of major world leaders.	Includes all domestic and regional developments in Europe, including the Soviet Union, Turkey, Cyprus and Malta.	Includes all domestic and regional developments in Africa and the Middle East, including Iraq and Iran and excluding Cyprus, Turkey and Afghanistan.	Includes all domestic and regional developments in Latin America, the Caribbean and Canada.	Includes all domestic and regional developments in Asia and Pacific nations, extending from Afghanistan through all the Pacific Islands, except Hawaii.

U.S. Politics & Social Issues	U.S. Foreign Policy & Defense	U.S. Economy & Environment	Science, Technology & Nature	Culture, Leisure & Life Style	
	White House announces that Pres. Nixon will meet with South Vietnamese Pres. Nguyen Van Thieu on Midway Island on June 8. . . . Sen. Edward Kennedy denounces the fight for Apbia Mountain as a "senseless" offensive operation.				May 20
Judge Herbert Walker sentences Sirhan Sirhan to death for the murder of Robert Kennedy despite a clemency plea from Sen. Edward Kennedy.			U.S. manned spacecraft enters lunar orbit.	McGraw Hill publishes Whitney Young's *Beyond Racism*. . . . Harcourt, Brace & World publishes Gunter Grass's *Speak Out*.	May 21
University officials close predominantly Negro North Carolina Agricultural and Technical State University after police find the body of a dead student.			U.S. manned spacecraft comes within nine miles of the moon's surface.	U.S. diplomat Angus Ward dies in Coin, Spain at 75.	May 22
Police face isolated sniper fire at North Carolina Agricultural and Technical State University.				Costa-Gavras' film *Z* wins first prize at the Cannes Film Festival.	May 23
Calm returns to North Carolina Agricultural and Technical State University after several days of disorders.	Former U.S. Amb. and Paris peace talks representative Averell Harriman calls for an immediate withdrawal of 50,000 U.S. troops from South Vietnam. . . . U.S. State Dept. expresses its regrets about Peru's decision not to receive the visit of presidential envoy Nelson Rockefeller.			U.S. manned spacecraft heads back towards earth.	May 24
National Guardsmen leave North Carolina Agricultural and Technical State University.				United Artists releases John Schlesinger's film *Midnight Cowboy*.	May 25
Judge Arthur Faquin denies James Earl Ray's request for a new trial.			U.S. manned spacecraft lands safely in the Pacific Ocean.	Knopf publishes Michael Crichton's *The Andromeda Strain*.	May 26
					May 27
					May 28
					May 29
				Irish nationalist Robert Briscoe dies in Dublin at 74.	May 30
			Soviet Union conducts an underground test.		May 31

F	G	H	I	J
Includes elections, federal-state relations, civil rights and liberties, crime, the judiciary, education, health care, poverty, urban affairs and population.	*Includes formation and debate of U.S. foreign and defense policies, veterans' affairs and defense spending. (Relations with specific foreign countries are usually found under the region concerned.)*	*Includes business, labor, agriculture, taxation, transportation, consumer affairs, monetary and fiscal policy, natural resources, and pollution.*	*Includes worldwide scientific, medical and technological developments, natural phenomena, U.S. weather, natural disasters, and accidents.*	*Includes the arts, religion, scholarship, communications media, sports, entertainment, fashions, fads and social life.*

	World Affairs	Europe	Africa & the Middle East	The Americas	Asia & the Pacific
June 1		Czechoslovak liberals lose party posts in a broad purge. . . . George Pompidou wins the first round of France's presidential election.		Venezuela asks presidential envoy Nelson Rockefeller to postpone his visit because of possible violence.	U.S. troops clash with the Viet Cong in the Mekong Delta.
June 2		French Communist Party tells its voters not to vote in the final round of presidential elections next week. . . . Soviet newspaper *Pravda* says that Soviet youths are spoiled.		Labor leaders vow new strikes in Argentina.	
June 3		Pro-Soviet Czech officials continue to replace liberals in Prague.		Chilean students demonstrate against the upcoming visit of presidential envoy Nelson Rockefeller.	Japan says that U.S. may keep its naval base in Okinawa after the island is returned to Japanese sovereignty.
June 4				Latin American foreign ministers agree on joint economic proposals to be made to the Nixon administration.	Reports indicate that the National Liberation Front of South Vietnam has rejected South Vietnamese Pres. Thieu's offers to negotiate in secret.
June 5	U.N. meets to discuss recent skirmishes on Cyprus.	Reports indicate that Spain has agreed to an extension of U.S. bases on its territory.	An Israeli patrol clashes with Egyptian infiltrators along the Suez Canal.		U.S. planes bomb Communist positions near the demilitarized zone.
June 6		Rumania says that Communist parties shouldn't criticize Communist China.	Reports indicate that Amman, Jordan is making dramatic economic progress.		Communist artillery pounds Danang.
June 7	At the U.N. Arab delegates call for an Israeli withdrawal from captured Arab territory.	Soviet leader Leonid Brezhnev says that Communist China is a threat to world peace.			
June 8		Reports indicate that the Soviet Union is making steady progress in developing multiple-warhead missiles.	Israel says that it will allow more West Bank refugees to return to their homes.		U.S. planes bomb Communist positions in the Mekong Delta.
June 9		Rumania asserts that it will maintain its independent course.	Iraq bitterly criticizes the U.S.'s Middle East policy.		South Vietnamese Pres. Thieu says that he is still opposed to a coalition government with the Communists.
June 10		Bulgaria denounces Communist China.			
June 11		Italian Communists score lack of democracy in the Soviet Union.	An Israeli patrol clashes with Arab guerrillas along the Jordan River.	Chilean Foreign Min. Gabriel Valdes presents the economic suggestions of Latin American countries to Pres. Nixon.	
June 12	At the U.N., African delegates criticize Western investment in South Africa.		Israel claims killing 13 infiltrators along the Suez Canal.		
June 13		British House of Commons votes for easier divorce procedures.	Soviet Foreign Min. Andrei Gromyko leaves Cairo after talks with Pres. Nasser.		Laotian officials admit that U.S. planes are transporting government troops in Laos.
	A	B	C	D	E
	Includes developments that affect more than one world region, international organizations and important meetings of major world leaders.	*Includes all domestic and regional developments in Europe, including the Soviet Union, Turkey, Cyprus and Malta.*	*Includes all domestic and regional developments in Africa and the Middle East, including Iraq and Iran and excluding Cyprus, Turkey and Afghanistan.*	*Includes all domestic and regional developments in Latin America, the Caribbean and Canada.*	*Includes all domestic and regional developments in Asia and Pacific nations, extending from Afghanistan through all the Pacific Islands, except Hawaii.*

U.S. Politics & Social Issues	U.S. Foreign Policy & Defense	U.S. Economy & Environment	Science, Technology & Nature	Culture, Leisure & Life Style	
	Pentagon warns arms contractors that unrealistically low bids to buy a program will no longer be tolerated.		Soviet Union launches a communications satellite.		June 1
Pres. Nixon asks Congress for a two-year extension of the anti-poverty program.	Reports indicate that Pres. Nixon has decided to move nuclear weapons out of Okinawa.			Ireland promises tax exemptions for artists.	June 2
Pres. Nixon criticizes violent tactics of student demonstrators.	Reports indicate that Pres. Nixon will soon make an announcement of the first withdrawal of U.S. troops from South Vietnam.				June 3
Gallup Poll indicates that Pres. Nixon's popularity is still high.	Pres. Nixon criticizes an alleged trend towards "isolationism" in the U.S.		U.S. launches a communications satellite.		June 4
Tough federal legislation dealing with campus disorders is reportedly making progress on Capitol Hill.	State Secy. William Rogers says that the U.S. is not irrevocably committed to any one government in South Vietnam.				June 5
	State Secy. William Rogers says that continued testing of multiple-warhead missiles could endanger arms talks.			Mourners in Washington, D.C. mark the death of Sen. Robert Kennedy.	June 6
An aide to black militant Malcolm X, Kenyatta 37X, is shot and killed in N.Y.C.	Pres. Nixon leaves for talks with South Vietnamese Pres. Thieu.		U.S. astronauts say that the manned moon landing is on schedule.		June 7
Police have set up community relations boards across the nation to improve race relations.	Pres. Nixon announces that 25,000 U.S. soldiers will be withdrawn from South Vietnam this year after conferring with South Vietnamese Pres. Thieu on Midway Island.	Grape pickers go on strike in Coachella Valley, Calif.			June 8
Harvard University expells 16 students who were involved in the seizure of university buildings two months ago.	Defense Secy. Melvin Laird says that more U.S. troops may be withdrawn from Vietnam later in the year.	Interest rates continue to rise on the credit markets.			June 9
	Pres. Nixon calls on North Vietnam to reciprocate his troop withdrawals.	Treasury Secy. David Kennedy says that a reduction in taxes will lead to serious inflation.	Pentagon cancels its scheduled manned orbiting laboratory program.	French composer Pierre Boulez becomes the director of the New York Philharmonic. . . . For the first time since the Reformation, a Catholic Pope, Pope Paul, visits Geneva.	June 10
	Congressional leaders indicate that Pres. Nixon's foreign aid requests will be cut.	Pres. Nixon meets with his economic advisers to discuss the possibility of a surtax extension.		U.S. labor leader John L. Lewis dies in Washington, D.C. at 89.	June 11
Nixon administration officials are urging universities to take a firm stand against student protesters who break the law.		House committee approves Pres. Nixon's request for a one-year extension of tax surcharge.		Stuttgart Ballet presents *The Taming of the Shrew* in New York.	June 12
Southern Baptists reject Negro demands for reparations.	Pres. Nixon hints at new Latin American policies after talks with Colombian Pres. Carlos Lleras Restrepo.	Justice Dept. announces that it has filed an antitrust suit against the U.S. Steel Corp.			June 13
F	G	H	I	J	
Includes elections, federal-state relations, civil rights and liberties, crime, the judiciary, education, health care, poverty, urban affairs and population.	*Includes formation and debate of U.S. foreign and defense policies, veterans' affairs and defense spending. (Relations with specific foreign countries are usually found under the region concerned.)*	*Includes business, labor, agriculture, taxation, transportation, consumer affairs, monetary and fiscal policy, natural resources, and pollution.*	*Includes worldwide scientific, medical and technological developments, natural phenomena, U.S. weather, natural disasters, and accidents.*	*Includes the arts, religion, scholarship, communications media, sports, entertainment, fashions, fads and social life.*	

	World Affairs	Europe	Africa & the Middle East	The Americas	Asia & the Pacific
June 14					U.S. planes bomb Communist positions in the Central Highlands.
June 15		Former French P.M. George Pompidou overwhelmingly defeats Alain Poher in presidential elections.	Israel begins to evict Arab residents from a small urban renewal area near the Jewish Wailing Wall.	Reports indicate that Japan is investing heavily in Latin America.	Communist troops attack artillery bases in the Ashau Valley.
June 16	At the U.N. Colombia advocates the seating of Communist China.	Reports indicate that uncensored literature is still circulating on the black market in Czechoslovakia.		Brazil arrests hundreds of students to block demonstrations against presidential envoy Nelson Rockefeller.	Thai troops rout a Viet Cong force.
June 17	Nigeria denounces the International Red Cross's attempts to relieve starvation in Biafra.	Britain says that it wants to reopen negotiations for its admission to the Common Market.	Arab artillery kills a U.S. tourist near the Dead Sea in Israel.	Presidential envoy Nelson Rockefeller talks with Brazilian officials.	Reports indicate that North Vietnamese troops have reoccupied Apbia Mountain, the scene of a bitter fight in May 1969.
June 18		Britain agrees to abandon tough labor legislation in return for a promise by trade unions to reduce strikes.	Israeli jets bomb targets deep in Jordan.	Seven Brazilian students in Rio de Janeiro discuss alleged political repression with presidential envoy Nelson Rockefeller.	Reports indicate that South Vietnamese officials are deeply worried by U.S. troop withdrawals.
June 19				Potential violence causes presidential envoy Nelson Rockefeller to avoid Montevideo, Uruguay.	
June 20	International relief officials estimate that 1.5 million Biafrans have starved to death.	Jacques Chaban-Delmas becomes French Prime Minister. . . . Spain signs an accord with the U.S. to extend American base rights on Spanish territory.		Urban guerrillas set fire to a General Motors building in Montevideo, Uruguay.	Reports indicate that Taiwan is making significant economic progress.
June 21		Police scuffle with a small group of anti-government demonstrators at the University of Rome.	Israeli commandoes kill 15 Egyptians in an attack on an Egyptian radar post.	Reports indicate that Cuba has almost completely stopped its attempts to undermine Latin American governments.	Intense fighting erupts near South Vietnam's demilitarized zone between allied and Communist troops.
June 22	At the U.N. Arab delegates decry the latest Israeli air force raids.	Maurice Schumann, an advocate of European union, becomes French foreign minister.	Israeli jets bomb guerrilla bases in Jordan.	Presidential envoy Nelson Rockefeller ends his third Latin American trip.	
June 23	U.N. Secy. Gen. U Thant warns of threats to the world's environment.		Israeli commandoes sabotage Jordan's largest irrigation project.		
June 24		A mysterious poison kills millions of fish in the Rhine.	Arab saboteurs damage the Israeli oil refinery at Haifa.	Peru announces a major land reform program.	U.S. planes attack the Ho Chi Minh supply road.
June 25			Reports indicate that fighting between African and Arab ethnic groups in Chad is serious.		Reports indicate that the Viet Cong is concentrating on winning rural areas in South Vietnam.
June 26	At the U.N. Arab delegates accuse Israel of trying to provoke a war.		Chile says that it will soon demand a controlling interest in U.S.-owned copper mines.	Honduras and El Salvador break diplomatic relations.	Communists continue to shell U.S. forces at Benhet.
June 27		Common Market agrees on an aid plan for Africa.	Israeli Defense Min. Moshe Dayan hints that Israel plans to keep much of the West Bank.		
June 28		Reports indicate that Soviet leaders will visit Rumania in late July.			Communist forces pound U.S. Army base at Benhet.
	A	B	C	D	E
	Includes developments that affect more than one world region, international organizations and important meetings of major world leaders.	Includes all domestic and regional developments in Europe, including the Soviet Union, Turkey, Cyprus and Malta.	Includes all domestic and regional developments in Africa and the Middle East, including Iraq and Iran and excluding Cyprus, Turkey and Afghanistan.	Includes all domestic and regional developments in Latin America, the Caribbean and Canada.	Includes all domestic and regional developments in Asia and Pacific nations, extending from Afghanistan through all the Pacific Islands, except Hawaii.

U.S. Politics & Social Issues	U.S. Foreign Policy & Defense	U.S. Economy & Environment	Science, Technology & Nature	Culture, Leisure & Life Style	
Reports indicate that summer jobs for poor youths are on the rise.	U.S. is reportedly on the verge of improving its relations with Peru.		U.S. scientists report evidence of gravity waves passing through the earth.		June 14
Negro college graduates reportedly are being besieged by job offers.					June 15
Supreme Court rules that the House violated the Constitution in excluding Rep. Adam Clayton Powell.				Field Marshal Earl Alexander of Tunis dies in Slough, England, at 77. . . . Composer Igor Stravinsky is hospitalized in New York.	June 16
	Police eject 100 war protesters from the Pentagon.		Soviet Union conducts an underground nuclear test.		June 17
	Former Defense Secy. Clark Clifford calls for the withdrawal of all U.S. troops from Vietnam within one year.	House passes a bill strengthening health warnings on cigarette packages.			June 18
Pres. Nixon supports the FBI's occasional use of wiretaps.	U.S. officials say that negotiations with North Vietnam over U.S. prisoners have gone nowhere.		Soviet Union conducts an underground nuclear test.	New York's Joffrey Ballet scores a triumph in Vienna.	June 19
	Administration officials say that there is no set timetable for the withdrawal of U.S. troops from Vietnam.				June 20
Civil rights leader Ralph Abernathy is held on riot charges in Charleston, S.C.	Reports indicate that the U.S. is shaping a plan to give Viet Cong political power in South Vietnam.		U.S. officials say that if all goes well the manned lunar landing will take place on July 21.		June 21
	Senate opposition to the U.S. anti-ballistic missile system is reportedly waning.				June 22
Warren Burger becomes the Chief Justice of the U.S. Supreme Court.			Missouri tornadoes kill six.	Pope Paul says that dissent in the Church has gone too far.	June 23
Senate votes to double the food stamp program.				Stuttgart Ballet presents a new production of *Giselle* in New York.	June 24
	U.S. transfers 64 river gunboats to South Vietnam.			New York Metropolitan Opera stages a new production of *Rigoletto*.	June 25
	U.S. names permanent negotiators for Soviet-U.S. arms talks.	Federal Reserve Board moves to slow the use of Eurodollars by U.S. banks.			June 26
	Pres. Nixon confers with Canadian P.M. Pierre Elliott Trudeau.	House approves an extension of the 10% tax surcharge.	Rehearsals begin at Cape Kennedy for the scheduled moon landing.	Pantheon publishes Julio Cortazar's *Cronopios and Famas*.	June 27
U.S. Eskimos press land claims in Alaska.	White House announces that Pres. Nixon will visit Rumania in early August.		U.S. launches a monkey into 30-day orbit around the earth.		June 28
F	G	H	I	J	
Includes elections, federal-state relations, civil rights and liberties, crime, the judiciary, education, health care, poverty, urban affairs and population.	Includes formation and debate of U.S. foreign and defense policies, veterans' affairs and defense spending. (Relations with specific foreign countries are usually found under the region concerned.)	Includes business, labor, agriculture, taxation, transportation, consumer affairs, monetary and fiscal policy, natural resources, and pollution.	Includes worldwide scientific, medical and technological developments, natural phenomena, U.S. weather, natural disasters, and accidents.	Includes the arts, religion, scholarship, communications media, sports, entertainment, fashions, fads and social life.	

	World Affairs	Europe	Africa & the Middle East	The Americas	Asia & the Pacific
June 29		Police and protesting students scuffle briefly in Paris's Latin Quarter.	Algeria reports that former Congolese Premier Moise Tshombe has died of a heart attack in an Algerian prison.	Argentinian protests flare up as presidential envoy Nelson Rockefeller's visit approaches.	
June 30			Israeli P.M. Golda Meir warns that reprisals will continue as long as Arab states attack Israel.		U.S. planes bomb Communist positions around Benhet.
July 1	International Red Cross accuses Nigeria of obstructing efforts to help starving Biafrans.		Israel moves its national police headquarters from Tel-Aviv in a move to consolidate its hold over the newly united city.	Presidential envoy Nelson Rockefeller receives a warm welcome in Haiti.	South Vietnamese trucks reach the besieged allied base at Benhet with supplies.
July 2		Reports from Moscow indicate that the U.S. informed the Soviet Union about Pres. Nixon's upcoming visit to Rumania before it was announced publicly.	Israel claims the downing of four Egyptian planes as violent clashes continue to increase along the Suez Canal.		U.S. officials say that the siege of Benhet has ended.
July 3	U.N. criticizes Israeli plans to extend land annexations in Jerusalem.			Dominican Republic announces that three demonstrators were killed during the recent stay of presidential envoy Nelson Rockefeller.	
July 4		Italian Socialists end their ties with Italy's ruling Christian Democrats.	Israel says that it intends to keep the Gaza Strip permanently.	OAS confers about the recent skirmishes between Honduras and El Salvador.	Pakistan says that it intends to end English as the country's official language.
July 5	U.N. Secy Gen. U Thant warns that another Middle Eastern war is possible.	Italian government falls as socialists leave government coalition.	Panel of leading architects backs Israeli plans to build a park around the Old City of Jerusalem.		U.S. planes pound Communist positions in the Central Highlands.
July 6		Common Market countries agree to reopen negotiations with Britain over its application for membership.	Iraq receives a major credit from the Soviet Union.		Fighting increases sharply in Vietnam indicating that the recent lull in enemy activity may be over.
July 7	U.N. Secy. Gen. U Thant says that "open warfare" has been resumed along the Suez Canal.	Soviet Union says that a naval squadron will visit Cuba during the end of July.	Reports indicate that Israel completely dominates the air skirmishes with Egypt.	Canada approves a bill putting French on an equal footing with English for federal government activities.	U.S. planes pound Communist positions in the Mekong Delta.
July 8		Reports indicate that the Soviet Union is intensifying its jamming of Western broadcasts to Eastern Europe.	Israel downs seven Syrian jets over Syrian territory.		Communist China charges that Soviet armed personnel have recently intruded across the Armur River frontier.
July 9		Rumania rejects Soviet objections to Pres. Nixon's upcoming trip.		Brazil's Amazon highway is going ahead on schedule.	Communist forces kill nine U.S. soldiers south of Danang.
July 10		Soviet Union warns Communist China about the use of force in settling their border dispute.			U.S. officials announce the lowest weekly U.S. casualty rate in six months.
July 11			South Africa fines a journalist for his articles on the country's prison conditions.	Argentinian rightists are reportedly seeking a purge of Church officials considered too liberal.	U.S. planes pound Communist positions along the Ho Chi Minh supply trial.
July 12		Soviet Union charges that Communist China has broken off border negotiations.		Reports indicate that labor plans a series of long strikes in Argentina.	Communist and South Vietnamese forces clash near the demilitarized zone.
	A	**B**	**C**	**D**	**E**
	Includes developments that affect more than one world region, international organizations and important meetings of major world leaders.	Includes all domestic and regional developments in Europe, including the Soviet Union, Turkey, Cyprus and Malta.	Includes all domestic and regional developments in Africa and the Middle East, including Iraq and Iran and excluding Cyprus, Turkey and Afghanistan.	Includes all domestic and regional developments in Latin America, the Caribbean and Canada.	Includes all domestic and regional developments in Asia and Pacific nations, extending from Afghanistan through all the Pacific Islands, except Hawaii.

U.S. Politics & Social Issues	U.S. Foreign Policy & Defense	U.S. Economy & Environment	Science, Technology & Nature	Culture, Leisure & Life Style	
	U.S. officials say that Pres. Nixon will stress Asian self-defense measures during his upcoming trip to the region.		Soviet Union launches a weather satellite.		June 29
Senate unit bars free food stamps.	Pres. Nixon sets up a panal to explore alleged waste in the Pentagon.				June 30
A federal judge orders Chicago to integrate its public housing projects.		Federal government registers its first budget surplus in seven years.		New York's Lincoln Center completes its fund drive.	July 1
	State Secy. William Rogers says that Communist infiltration of South Vietnam has recently declined.	A poll indicates that most Americans oppose the surcharge tax extension.			July 2
Nixon administration says that minor exceptions will be made in current school desegregation plans for school districts with bona fide problems.	State Dept. announces the end of the embargo of credit sales to Peru and Ecuador.				July 3
		Construction of a highway to northern Alaska stirs fears of conservationists.	Gales in Ohio kill six.		July 4
			U.S. astronauts express confidence about the upcoming moon flight.	German architect Walter Gropius dies in Boston at 86.	July 5
	Hudson Institute publishes a book defending the U.S. anti-ballistic missile system.		Soviet Union launches a military surveillance satellite.		July 6
			Gale winds continue to batter Ohio.		July 7
	Senate begins debate on the proposed U.S. anti-ballistic missile system.	Nixon Administration asks Congress to broaden unemployment coverage.			July 8
Justice Dept. tells Waterbury, Conn. that it must correct racial imbalance in its school system. Justice Dept. tells the Chicago school system to implement its integration plans more quickly.	Pentagon is considering giving Turkey 100 new tanks.	U.S. scientists report a possible link between cancer and pesticides.			July 9
Justice Dept. sues two more Southern school districts for failure to implement desegregation plans.		U.S. stock market drops to a 15-month low.		An exhibition on Russian choreographer Sergei Diaghilev opens in Strasbourg, France.	July 10
	U.S. reconnaissance planes follow the Soviet naval force heading toward Cuba.	Treasury Dept. announces higher interest rates on savings bonds.		Art dealers report that German faience is gaining in popularity.	July 11
	U.S. officials stress that America is neutral in the Soviet-Communist Chinese border dispute.				July 12

F	G	H	I	J
Includes elections, federal-state relations, civil rights and liberties, crime, the judiciary, education, health care, poverty, urban affairs and population.	Includes formation and debate of U.S. foreign and defense policies, veterans' affairs and defense spending. (Relations with specific foreign countries are usually found under the region concerned.)	Includes business, labor, agriculture, taxation, transportation, consumer affairs, monetary and fiscal policy, natural resources, and pollution.	Includes worldwide scientific, medical and technological developments, natural phenomena, U.S. weather, natural disasters, and accidents.	Includes the arts, religion, scholarship, communications media, sports, entertainment, fashions, fads and social life.

	World Affairs	Europe	Africa & the Middle East	The Americas	Asia & the Pacific
July 13		Rioting erupts in Northern Ireland between Protestants and Catholics.	Israel and Egypt engage in a three-hour artillery duel.	Brazil agrees to increase trade with Portugal.	Communist guerrillas throw bombs into a civilian market near Saigon.
July 14				Reports indicate that border fighting is increasing between El Salvador and Honduras.	U.S. troops begin pulling out of the Mekong Delta.
July 15		Reports indicate that Britain is cool to the idea of a European parliament.		Honduras and El Salvador continue an artillery duel along their border.	U.S. planes bomb Communist positions in the Central Highlands.
July 16	U.N. Reports that aid to developing countries increased sharply during 1968.	Reports indicate that France may be reconsidering its objection to Britain's joining the Common Market.		Reports indicate that the war between Honduras and El Salvador is abating because of a lack of war material for both sides.	Indian P.M. Indira Gandhi forces Finance Min. Morarji Desai out of her cabinet.
July 17		Spain confirms reports that Prince Juan Carlos of Borbon will succeed Francisco Franco as chief of state.		Reports indicate skirmishes along the border of El Salvador and Honduras.	Reports indicate major tensions between India and Nepal.
July 18	Pres. Nixon urges more funding for birth control programs.		A brief skirmish takes place between Egyptians and Israelis along the Suez Canal.	Both Honduras and El Salvador accept an OAS peace plan.	Reports of U.S. nerve gas stored on Okinawa raise a storm in Japan.
July 19		Spain reportedly is permitting more labor activity than in the past.	Reports indicate that Israel is planning to keep much of the territory conquered in 1967.		India nationalizes its 14 largest banks.
July 20			Israel launches the first air assault against Egyptian ground installations along the Suez Canal since the 1967 war.	Seven Soviet warships dock in Cuba.	Vietnam's combat lull enters its fifth week.
July 21					U.S. planes bomb Communist targets in the Central Highlands.
July 22			Israeli planes strike Egyptian artillery positions along the Suez Canal.	El Salvador demands that Honduras pay reparations for war damages.	Indian P.M. Indira Gandhi appears to be a winner in a fierce party struggle.
July 23		Prince Juan Carlos of Borbon is formally invested as Spain's future King.	Egyptian Pres. Nasser attacks the U.S. for its support of Israel.		
July 24	After five years of negotiating, 10 leading Western nations have reached agreement on creating the first international reserve currency unit.		Egyptian and Israeli forces clash along the Suez Canal for the third time within one week.		Reports indicate that Communist guerrillas are operating in northern Burma.
July 25		Reports indicate that East Germany is taking a harder line on negotiations with West Germany than is the Soviet Union.	Israeli fighters strike Egyptian artillery positions for the fourth time within one week.		Laos denies Communist charges that there are 12,000 U.S. troops in its territory.
July 26			Israeli planes bomb Egyptian positions along the Suez Canal.	Sporadic sniping continues along the border between Honduras and El Salvador.	Reports indicate that the Nationalist Chinese on Taiwan are reducing the size of their army.
	A	B	C	D	E
	Includes developments that affect more than one world region, international organizations and important meetings of major world leaders.	Includes all domestic and regional developments in Europe, including the Soviet Union, Turkey, Cyprus and Malta.	Includes all domestic and regional developments in Africa and the Middle East, including Iraq and Iran and excluding Cyprus, Turkey and Afghanistan.	Includes all domestic and regional developments in Latin America, the Caribbean and Canada.	Includes all domestic and regional developments in Asia and Pacific nations, extending from Afghanistan through all the Pacific Islands, except Hawaii.

U.S. Politics & Social Issues	U.S. Foreign Policy & Defense	U.S. Economy & Environment	Science, Technology & Nature	Culture, Leisure & Life Style	
			Soviet Union launches an unmanned spacecraft toward the moon.		July 13
Pres. Nixon says that he will submit welfare reforms to Congress.	White House announces that Pres. Nixon will also meet with British P.M. Harold Wilson during his upcoming world trip.		Three U.S. astronauts scheduled to fly to the moon say that they have no fear of the flight.		July 14
Welfare protesters threaten to disrupt a N.Y.C. Chase Manhattan bank.	State Dept. says that use of U.S. arms in the conflict between Honduras and El Salvador is "regrettable."				July 15
		White House rules out wage and price controls as a means of dealing with inflation.	U.S. manned spaceflight Apollo 11 blasts off for moon trip.		July 16
Senate report urges broader health plan coverage.		Television broadcasters plan to curb ads for cigarettes because of health dangers.	U.S. manned spacecraft passes the half-way point on its trip to the moon.		July 17
A car driven by Sen. Edward Kennedy runs off the highway in Chappaquidick, Mass. and plunges into a pond, killing a woman passenger.				Bolshoi Ballet presents the western premiere of *Spartacus* in New York.	July 18
Sen. Edward Kennedy reports to Edgartown, Mass. police that a car which he was driving plunged into a pond with a woman passenger.	White House names a panel to investigate corruption in the Pentagon.		U.S. manned spacecraft prepares for lunar landing as officials report no problems.		July 19
	U.S. rules out recognition of Biafra.	Coral-eating starfish are said to endanger Pacific islands.	U.S. astronauts Neil Armstrong and Edwin Aldrin leave their spacecraft and walk on the moon.		July 20
	U.S. acts to relax curbs on trade with Communist China.	House unit backs cut in allowance for oil depletion.	Two U.S. astronauts lift-off from the moon.		July 21
				Vatican reports that Pope Paul will soon make the first Papal visit to Africa.	July 22
	Reports indicate a very close vote on funding for proposed anti-ballistic missile system.	Labor Dept. reports substantial consumer price rises in June.		Bolshoi Ballet dances *Carmen Suite* in London.	July 23
Sen. Edward Kennedy enters a court plea answering charges that he left the scene of an accident.			U.S. astronauts return safely to earth as the nation celebrates their successful moon walk.		July 24
Sen. Edward Kennedy says that his failure to immediately report his July 18 accident involving one fatality was "indefensible."	Pres. Nixon, speaking in Guam, says that U.S. allies must contribute more to their own defense.		U.S. astronauts seem to be in excellent health after their moon trip.		July 25
	Pres. Nixon confers with Asian allies in Manila and bids them to contribute more to their own defense.		U.S. scientists examine first moon rock samples.		July 26

F	G	H	I	J
Includes elections, federal-state relations, civil rights and liberties, crime, the judiciary, education, health care, poverty, urban affairs and population.	Includes formation and debate of U.S. foreign and defense policies, veterans' affairs and defense spending. (Relations with specific foreign countries are usually found under the region concerned.)	Includes business, labor, agriculture, taxation, transportation, consumer affairs, monetary and fiscal policy, natural resources, and pollution.	Includes worldwide scientific, medical and technological developments, natural phenomena, U.S. weather, natural disasters, and accidents.	Includes the arts, religion, scholarship, communications media, sports, entertainment, fashions, fads and social life.

	World Affairs	Europe	Africa & the Middle East	The Americas	Asia & the Pacific
July 27	Leading architects call for a plan to save Venice from being engulfed by the sea.	Reports indicate that the Soviet Union is disturbed by the enthusiastic reaction of East Europeans to the Apollo space flight.	Egyptian commandoes attack Israeli positions along the Suez Canal.		Reports indicate that Communist forces are making steady advances in Laos.
July 28	U.N. Secy. Gen. U Thant denies reports that he plans to resign.	Soviet Union reports a shortage of skilled workers.	Egypt and Israel exchange a small number of prisoners of war.		Communist China criticizes Pres. Nixon's Asian trip.
July 29			Israeli and Egyptian patrols skirmish along the Suez Canal.	El Salvador says that it will withdraw its troops from Honduras.	U.S. Asian allies indicate uneasiness about the current U.S. withdrawal from South Vietnam.
July 30	At the U.N. Arab delegates castigate Israel for its attacks on Egypt.		Israeli planes attack an Arab guerrilla base in Lebanon.		Pres. Nixon pays an unscheduled visit to South Vietnam.
July 31					Pres. Nixon arrives in India.
Aug. 1		Reports indicate that Czechoslovak liberals are facing frequent harassment in their jobs.			Pres. Nixon leaves Pakistan after talks with Pakistani leaders.
Aug. 2		Pres. Nixon receives a tumultuous welcome in Rumania.	Egyptian and Israeli patrols skirmish along the Suez Canal.		
Aug. 3	At the U.N. Arab delegates accuse Israel of trying to provoke a war.	Renewed rioting breaks out in Belfast between Catholics and Protestants.	Israel declares that it will retain large parts of the Sinai Peninsula permanently.		
Aug. 4		Belfast police battle opposing mobs during the night.	Israeli Defense Min. Moshe Dayan says that Soviet advisers are helping Egyptian armed forces.		Cambodia resumes diplomatic relations with the U.S.
Aug. 5		Italian Christian Democrats form a minority coalition.			
Aug. 6		Rumania criticizes Soviet attempts to impose uniformity on the Communist movement.	Reports indicate that South Yemen is on the verge of a civil war.	Argentina closes down a political magazine critical of the government.	Reports indicate that North Vietnamese infiltration of the South is still low.
Aug. 7		Soviet Union criticizes Pres. Nixon's recent visit to Rumania.	Portugal warns Zambia on aid to Angolan guerrillas.		Viet Cong indicates that it may consider working with non-Communist elements.
Aug. 8		France devalues the franc. . . . Soviet Union announces an agreement with Communist China on river navigation.			
Aug. 9		France prepares to ease inflationary effects of Aug. 9 devaluation.			

A	B	C	D	E
Includes developments that affect more than one world region, international organizations and important meetings of major world leaders.	Includes all domestic and regional developments in Europe, including the Soviet Union, Turkey, Cyprus and Malta.	Includes all domestic and regional developments in Africa and the Middle East, including Iraq and Iran and excluding Cyprus, Turkey and Afghanistan.	Includes all domestic and regional developments in Latin America, the Caribbean and Canada.	Includes all domestic and regional developments in Asia and Pacific nations, extending from Afghanistan through all the Pacific Islands, except Hawaii.

U.S. Politics & Social Issues	U.S. Foreign Policy & Defense	U.S. Economy & Environment	Science, Technology & Nature	Culture, Leisure & Life Style	
			U.S. scientists say that moon rocks are igneous.		July 27
	Pres. Nixon, in a speech given in Bangkok, reassures Thailand that the U.S. will help in its defense.		U.S. scientists discover many small glass-like particles in the moon rocks.		July 28
	Reports indicate that Pres. Nixon has told Asian allies that they can count on U.S. financial support but not combat troops in the future.	Senate continues to bottle up Pres. Nixon's request for an extension of the income tax surcharge.	British medical journal says that there may be a link between birth control pills and cancer.		July 29
Sen. Edward Kennedy announces that he will remain in the U.S. Senate despite the controversy surrounding his auto accident.		U.S. Steel Co. raises its steel prices.	U.S. Mariner 6 sends back radio signals about the nature of Mars.	Russian novelist Anatoly Kuznetsov defects to London.	July 30
Mass. state officials request an inquest into the July 18 auto accident of Sen. Edward Kennedy.	White House says that it plans major cuts in defense spending.	House unit recommends major tax relief for all income categories.	U.S. Mariner 6 transmits close-up photos of Mars.	Pope Paul begins his African tour in Uganda.	July 31
U.S. sues Georgia in an attempt to speed school integration.	U.S. is said to be testing enemy intentions in South Vietnam by limiting big offensives.		First laser rays are returned to earth by the reflector left by Apollo spacecraft on the moon.	Pope Paul attacks racial discrimination in a speech in Uganda.	Aug. 1
House liberals seek a larger tax cut for middle income people.				Pope Paul returns to Italy from his African trip. . . . Russian writer Anatoly Kuznetsov renounces all of his published works because of the ill effects of government censorship.	Aug. 2
			U.S. scientists ask for unmanned probes of outer planets.	Reports indicate that Pope Paul was very pleased with his recent trip to Africa.	Aug. 3
Mass. state prosecutor renews a request for an inquest in the July 18 accident involving Sen. Edward Kennedy.	Pres. Nixon meets with congressional leaders to discuss his new Asian policy of encouraging more military self-reliance.	U.S. reports that unemployment increased to 3.6% in July.			Aug. 4
Pres. Nixon says that he wants cities to manage federal job aid independent of states.	U.S. believes that the Soviet Union is testing multiple warhead missiles.	Treasury Dept. seeks a big tax increase on oil companies.	U.S. spacecraft Mariner 7 sends back best photos of Mars to date.		Aug. 5
Pres. Nixon asks for a job safety review board.			Moon dust samples show signs of organic matter.		Aug. 6
	Reports indicate that an anti-Pentagon coalition is growing in Congress.	House passes a major tax reform bill opposed by oil-producing states.	U.S. research submarine finds major turbulence in the Gulf Stream.		Aug. 7
Pres. Nixon asks for welfare reforms which require either training or work for recipients.	Sen. J. William Fulbright (D, Ark.) criticizes U.S. pledges to aid Thailand in case of an attack.	Soviet Union launches a military surveillance satellite.			Aug. 8
N.Y.C. Mayor John Lindsay praises Pres. Nixon's welfare proposals.	Defense Secy. Melvin Laird backs Senate curb on chemical war agents.	Treasury Dept. hints that the recent House tax cut bill went too far.		Police find bodies of five brutally murdered persons including actress Sharon Tate in Los Angeles.	Aug. 9

F	G	H	I	J
Includes elections, federal-state relations, civil rights and liberties, crime, the judiciary, education, health care, poverty, urban affairs and population.	Includes formation and debate of U.S. foreign and defense policies, veterans' affairs and defense spending. (Relations with specific foreign countries are usually found under the region concerned.)	Includes business, labor, agriculture, taxation, transportation, consumer affairs, monetary and fiscal policy, natural resources, and pollution.	Includes worldwide scientific, medical and technological developments, natural phenomena, U.S. weather, natural disasters, and accidents.	Includes the arts, religion, scholarship, communications media, sports, entertainment, fashions, fads and social life.

	World Affairs	Europe	Africa & the Middle East	The Americas	Asia & the Pacific
Aug. 10	U.N. Secy. Gen. U Thant again denies reports that he plans to resign.		Israeli jets attack a major Jordanian irrigation project.		Communist troops kill 19 U.S. Marines near the demilitarized zone.
Aug. 11		European currency markets are relatively stable despite the devaluation of the French franc.	Israeli planes attack Arab guerrilla camps in Lebanon.		
Aug. 12	World Bank raises its lending rate from six and a half to seven percent.	Common Market suspends France from its uniform agricultural price support system.	Jordanian P.M. Abdel Moneim Rifai resigns.		Communists launch heaviest offensive in three months as lull comes to an end in South Vietnam.
Aug. 13		Soviet Union accuses Communist China of provoking recent border clashes.	Artillery battles erupt along the Suez Canal.	Canadian P.M. Pierre Elliott Trudeau announces budget cuts in anti-inflation campaign.	Communist China says that the Soviet Union is responsible for recent border clashes.
Aug. 14	Irish Republic urges the U.N. to act in Northern Ireland.	British troops move into Northern Ireland to separate Protestant and Catholic rioters.			Allies launch a counter-offensive in Vietnam.
Aug. 15		Britain begins airlifting more troops into Northern Ireland.		Reports indicate that Brazilian guerrillas are shifting their attacks to urban areas. . . . Canada refuses to allow a shipment of U.S. poison gas to enter the country.	Communist China accuses the Soviet Union of mobilizing its troops near their common border.
Aug. 16	At the U.N. Arab delegates say that Israel is trying to provoke a war.	Shots and fires plague Belfast for the third consecutive night.			Most war material reportedly is still going to U.S. forces in South Vietnam despite attempts to "Vietnamize" the war.
Aug. 17		Northern Ireland rejects the Irish Republic's calls for coalition rule.	Two hundred Communist Chinese technicians arrive in Tanzania.		
Aug. 18	U.N. Secy. Gen. U Thant says that he may seek observer teams to help police enforce the troubled truce at the Israeli-Lebanese border.	Northern Irish government plans to form a civic committee to improve Catholic-Protestant relations.			
Aug. 19	U.N. refuses to investigate conditions of Jews living in Arab countries.	British troops take over responsibility for security in Northern Ireland.	Israeli and Egyptian patrols clash along the Suez Canal.		Communist China accuses the Soviet Union of having provoked 429 border incidents.
Aug. 20	U.N. rejects Irish Republic's call for U.N. action in Northern Ireland.	Protestant militants accuse Britain of yielding too much power to Catholics in Northern Ireland.	Israel reports that "open-bridges" policy across the Jordan River is working.		South Vietnam arrests more than 100 citizens on spy charges.
Aug. 21		Czech government suppresses demonstrations protesting the 1968 Soviet invasion.	A fire damages the Al Aksa Mosque in Jerusalem.		U.S. suffers highest weekly death toll in two months in South Vietnam.
Aug. 22		Five thousand Czech protesters clash with riot police in Bruno as demonstrations against the Soviet invasion continue.	Israel arrests an Australian tourist in connection with the Aug. 21 burning of part of the Mosque of Al-Aksa in Jerusalem.	Peru nationalizes an $80-million U.S. industry.	Fighting near Danang enters its sixth day.
Aug. 23	At the U.N. African delegates criticize South Africa's apartheid policies.	Reports indicate that the anti-Soviet demonstrations in Czechoslovakia may speed the fall of liberal Alexander Dubcek.	Egyptian Pres. Nasser says that war against Israel is a "sacred duty."		
	A	**B**	**C**	**D**	**E**
	Includes developments that affect more than one world region, international organizations and important meetings of major world leaders.	*Includes all domestic and regional developments in Europe, including the Soviet Union, Turkey, Cyprus and Malta.*	*Includes all domestic and regional developments in Africa and the Middle East, including Iraq and Iran and excluding Cyprus, Turkey and Afghanistan.*	*Includes all domestic and regional developments in Latin America, the Caribbean and Canada.*	*Includes all domestic and regional developments in Asia and Pacific nations, extending from Afghanistan through all the Pacific Islands, except Hawaii.*

U.S. Politics & Social Issues	U.S. Foreign Policy & Defense	U.S. Economy & Environment	Science, Technology & Nature	Culture, Leisure & Life Style	
Reports indicate that Calif. Gov. Ronald Reagan's tough stand on campus disorders is popular with voters.			U.S. ends quarantine of moon astronauts who are reportedly in excellent health.		Aug. 10
	Anti-Pentagon coalition in Congress continues to criticize the defense budget.	Ford raises 1970 truck prices by five percent.	Soviet Union conducts an underground nuclear test.		Aug. 11
		U.S. lowers the price of its wheat sales abroad.			Aug. 12
			Millions of New Yorkers welcome U.S. astronauts.	*Twelfth Night* opens at the Delacorte Theater in New York.	Aug. 13
	White House says that the recent Communist drive in South Vietnam may affect Pres. Nixon's upcoming decisions on troop withdrawals.	Treasury Dept. says that the recent tax relief bill passed by Congress may be inflationary.	U.S. launches a military surveillance satellite.		Aug. 14
	Reports indicate that many Irish-Americans are unhappy with the British airlift of troops into Northern Ireland.			Tens of thousands of young people pour into Bethel, New York for a rock festival.	Aug. 15
U.S. mayors welcome Pres. Nixon's plans for revenue sharing.			Justice Dept. expresses concern about lack of uniformity in drug abuse laws across the nation.	Three hundred thousand youths attend a rock festival in Bethel, New York.	Aug. 16
	Reports indicate that the military is considering biracial councils to improve race relations.		Two hundred thousand flee a fierce hurricane along the Mississippi coast.	Rock festival ends without major incidents in Bethel, New York.	Aug. 17
Pres. Nixon nominates Clement Haynsworth to the Supreme Court.	U.S. may support a U.N. resolution condemning Israeli raids against Lebanon.		Hurricane causes major property damage in Mississippi.		Aug. 18
White House denies that Pres. Nixon's welfare reform program will end the food stamp program.			Hurricane leaves at least 170 dead in Mississippi.		Aug. 19
			Mississippi faces an epidemic threat because of hurricane damage.		Aug. 20
	U.S. calls on North Vietnam to duplicate American troop withdrawals.		Mississippi death toll may exceed 300 in wake of recent hurricane.	World Council of Churches rejects call by Negroes for reparations.	Aug. 21
		U.S. reports that consumer prices rose .5% during July.	Virginia flooding leaves at least 80 dead.		Aug. 22
U.S. officials indicate that major urban rioting by Negroes may be over.	Pres. Nixon defers a decision about further troop withdrawals from South Vietnam because of a recent communist offensive.		U.S. launches a weather satellite.		Aug. 23
F	G	H	I	J	
Includes elections, federal-state relations, civil rights and liberties, crime, the judiciary, education, health care, poverty, urban affairs and population.	*Includes formation and debate of U.S. foreign and defense policies, veterans' affairs and defense spending. (Relations with specific foreign countries are usually found under the region concerned.)*	*Includes business, labor, agriculture, taxation, transportation, consumer affairs, monetary and fiscal policy, natural resources, and pollution.*	*Includes worldwide scientific, medical and technological developments, natural phenomena, U.S. weather, natural disasters, and accidents.*	*Includes the arts, religion, scholarship, communications media, sports, entertainment, fashions, fads and social life.*	

	World Affairs	Europe	Africa & the Middle East	The Americas	Asia & the Pacific
Aug. 24	At the U.N. Arab delegates accuse Israel of desecrating Islamic holy shrines in the occupied territories.	A bomb meant for an Israeli trade exhibit kills an Arab saboteur in Ankara, Turkey.	Israel denounces the alleged Arab campaign of villification since the recent fire in the Mosque of Al-Aksa.		V.V. Giri becomes the President of India.
Aug. 25		Minor skirmishing continues in Northern Ireland.	Iraq hangs 15 alleged spys including two Jews.		Thailand says that it wants U.S. troops to remain in the country.
Aug. 26	U.N. condemns Israel's Aug. 11 raid against Lebanon.		Israelis discover rocket launchers near Jerusalem.		
Aug. 27		France plans to borrow from the International Monetary Fund to defend the franc.			Japanese report finding major oil deposits in the East China Sea in territory which is claimed by several nations.
Aug. 28		Soviet Union says that it would automatically use nuclear weapons in a war against Communist China.	Israeli commandoes strike deep into Egyptian territory and destroy a radar station.	Police skirmish with anti-government demonstrators at the University of Mexico City.	U.S. planes bomb Communist positions in the Central Highlands.
Aug. 29	U.N. 1970's budget is up six percent over 1969.	Britain urges that Northern Ireland's Catholic minority be given more political power.	Syria admits U.S. tourists for the first time since the 1967 war.		Reports indicate that Communist China is moving more troops to its border with the Soviet Union.
Aug. 30		Czechoslovakia calls on political refugees from the Soviet invasion to return home.	Syria frees 105 passengers but keeps six Israeli passengers after a hijacked U.S. plane lands in Damascus.		Communist China reportedly is building a road to Pakistan.
Aug. 31		Reports indicate that West German Christian Democrats may be losing support among voters.	Syria announces that it is freeing four of six Israeli passengers from the recently hijacked U.S. plane.	Brazilian Pres. Costa e Silva suffers a stroke.	
Sept. 1	International Pilots Association insists that Syria free Israeli passengers held from the recently hijacked U.S. plane.		Libyan military ousts the monarchy and proclaims a republic.	Peru begins talks again with the U.S. on financial compensation for recently expropriated U.S. companies.	
Sept. 2		Turkey reports a major trade deficit.	Arab guerrilla rockets kill two Israelis in northern Israel.	Three Brazilian military leaders assume command of the government in the wake of Pres. Costa e Silva's illness.	Reports indicate that Communist Chinese labor units are no longer in North Vietnam.
Sept. 3		France invokes austerity measures to defend the franc.			North Vietnamese leader Ho Chi Minh dies at 79.
Sept. 4			Libyan military continues to consolidate its rule.	Gunmen kidnap U.S. Amb.-to-Brazil Burke Elbrick.	North Vietnam proclaims a week of mourning for deceased leader Ho Chi Minh.
Sept. 5		Sporadic violence takes place between Protestants and Catholics in Belfast.	Israel says that it plans to continue increased retaliatory raids in Lebanon.	Brazil agrees to free 15 guerrillas in return for the release of U.S. Ambassador Burke Elbrick.	Communist China assures North Vietnam that aid will continue.
Sept. 6	At the U.N. Arab delegates criticize recent Israeli attacks on Lebanon.	British troops scuffle with demonstrators in Belfast.		Brazil flys 15 guerrillas to Mexico to obtain the release of U.S. Amb. Burke Elbrick.	Reports indicate that Indian-Nepalese ties remain delicate.
	A	**B**	**C**	**D**	**E**
	Includes developments that affect more than one world region, international organizations and important meetings of major world leaders.	*Includes all domestic and regional developments in Europe, including the Soviet Union, Turkey, Cyprus and Malta.*	*Includes all domestic and regional developments in Africa and the Middle East, including Iraq and Iran and excluding Cyprus, Turkey and Afghanistan.*	*Includes all domestic and regional developments in Latin America, the Caribbean and Canada.*	*Includes all domestic and regional developments in Asia and Pacific nations, extending from Afghanistan through all the Pacific Islands, except Hawaii.*

U.S. Politics & Social Issues	U.S. Foreign Policy & Defense	U.S. Economy & Environment	Science, Technology & Nature	Culture, Leisure & Life Style	
U.S. officials see pupil integration doubling in the South this year.			Lunar rocks indicate that the moon's surface has changed little in recent times.		Aug. 24
N.Y.C. suburban Nassau County passes an open-housing law.	U.S. officials say that Pres. Nixon's delayed cut-back of U.S. troop withdrawals is a warning to North Vietnam.	U.S. economic officials say that peace in Vietnam will not produce major economic dividends.			Aug. 25
About half the staff lawyers in the Justice Dept. protest alleged slow down of school integration program by the Nixon administration.	U.S. begins talks on troop cut-backs in Thailand.	U.S. reportedly will spur competition to produce a low-pollution vehicle for the 1990s.		N.Y.C. landmarks panel bars a skyscraper over Grand Central Station.	Aug. 26
Reports indicate that funds for areas damaged by urban riots are often misused.	U.S. State Department says that North Vietnam may be again slowing down its infiltration of the South.	U.S. officials see no let-up in the inflation rate.			Aug. 27
Negroes call off protests against alleged discrimination in the Pittsburgh construction industry after obtaining demands.	U.S. reassures Thailand that any troop withdrawals will not be precipitous.				Aug. 28
White construction workers protest jobs given to Negroes in Pittsburgh.	Pres. Nixon says that the U.S. will always stand by Israel.				Aug. 29
Exact fare rules cut bus robberies in major cities.	U.S. criticizes Syrian decision to hold six Israeli passengers from hijacked U.S. plane.	AFL-CIO Pres. George Meany calls for price controls as best way to slow inflation.			Aug. 30
Campus violence spurs tough legislation against law-breakers in many states.		Visitors are reportedly straining the facilities of the U.S. national parks.		Pope Paul deplores the burning of the Mosque of Al-Aksa in Jerusalem.	Aug. 31
Reports indicate that school integration in the South is increasing dramatically as the school year opens.	U.S. reports that American personnel in Libya are safe.	Federal Reserve says that a Vietnam peace would release $8-billion.			Sept. 1
Hartford, Conn. imposes a curfew as Negro youths riot.			Reports indicate that some western residents are concerned about underground nuclear testing in Nevada.		Sept. 2
NAACP announces a major suit against discrimination in the construction industry.	U.S. officials see little change in North Vietnamese policies despite Ho's death.	U.S. officials warn water pollution violators that they face federal suits.		U.S. Episcopal Church leaders vote $200,000 in reparations for Negroes.	Sept. 3
Alabama legislature backs Gov. George Wallace's call to parents to enroll their children in all-white schools.		Pres. Nixon introduces a tax reform bill which would aid high-income brackets.	FDA says that birth control pills are safe.		Sept. 4
	Undersecy. of State Elliot Richardson says that the U.S. will continue to press for improved ties with Communist China.		Soviet Union conducts an underground nuclear test.		Sept. 5
	U.S. recognizes new Libyan junta.		Soviet Union launches a military surveillance satellite.		Sept. 6

F	G	H	I	J
Includes elections, federal-state relations, civil rights and liberties, crime, the judiciary, education, health care, poverty, urban affairs and population.	Includes formation and debate of U.S. foreign and defense policies, veterans' affairs and defense spending. (Relations with specific foreign countries are usually found under the region concerned.)	Includes business, labor, agriculture, taxation, transportation, consumer affairs, monetary and fiscal policy, natural resources, and pollution.	Includes worldwide scientific, medical and technological developments, natural phenomena, U.S. weather, natural disasters, and accidents.	Includes the arts, religion, scholarship, communications media, sports, entertainment, fashions, fads and social life.

	World Affairs	Europe	Africa & the Middle East	The Americas	Asia & the Pacific
Sept. 7	U.N. Secy. Gen. U Thant calls for an end to the Nigerian civil war.		Reports indicate that the Lebanese political system is under serious strain because of the influx of Arab refugees who fled the West Bank of the Jordan River during the 1967 war.	Brazilian guerrillas release U.S. ambassador Burke Elbrick.	Soviet and Communist Chinese officials attend funeral ceremonies of North Vietnamese Pres. Ho Chi Minh in Hanoi.
Sept. 8	At the U.N. 14 countries call for a debate on the seating of Communist China.	Arab guerrillas toss bombs into Israeli offices in Bonn, Brussels and The Hague.	Saudi authorities arrest more than 200 military officers in an alleged plot against the government.	Brazil says it will take tougher measures against urban guerrillas.	Reports indicate that Malaysia is keeping a close watch out for any increased Communist guerrilla activity.
Sept. 9	At the U.N. Arab states blame Israel for the Aug. 21 fire at Al Aksa mosque in Jerusalem.		Israeli tanks cross the Suez Canal in a 10-hour assault.	Brazil decrees the death penalty for "political terrorism."	South Vietnam steps up its military operations while the U.S. and Communist forces reduce activities following the death of Ho Chi Minh.
Sept. 10		Soviet Union gives details of alleged Communist Chinese intrusions into its territory.	Israeli jets continue raids along the Suez Canal.		U.S. resumes pre-truce level of military activity in South Vietnam.
Sept. 11		In a surprise move Communist Chinese leader Chou En-lai confers with Soviet Premier Aleksei Kosygin in Moscow.	Israel reports downing 11 Egyptian jets in the heaviest air combat since the 1967 war.		Reports indicate that the Communist Chinese Army has increased its forces significantly in the wake of the recent frontier clashes with the Soviet Union.
Sept. 12	U.N. Secy. Gen. U Thant calls on the Big Four to intensify Middle East peace-making efforts.	West Germany urges a ban on biological warfare.	Israeli jets continue their bombing raids along the Suez Canal.		Communist China is said to be moving a nuclear plant away from its Soviet frontier.
Sept. 13	International Red Cross gains Nigerian approval for relief flights to Biafra after months of suspension.	Street fighting flares in Ulster.	Israelis maintain pressure on Egypt in a new air strike.		Viet Cong launch an artillery attack against a South Vietnamese civilian village which leaves more than 100 dead.
Sept. 14	U.N. discusses the Aug. 21 Al Aksa mosque incident.	Greek opposition leaders in exile are coalescing around former P.M. George Papadopoulos who lives in Paris.	Israeli jets attack Egyptian positions along the Suez Canal for the fourth consecutive day.	Reports indicate that Brazilian Pres. Arthur da Costa e Silva is permanently paralyzed.	Reports indicate that Communist infiltration of the Mekong Delta has increased since the U.S. pullout.
Sept. 15	U.N. Secy. Gen. U Thant asks for a voice for Communist China in current arms negotiations.	West Germany says that it will de-emphasize the role of the tank in a shift to an explicit defensive strategy.	Reports indicate that the Libyan military are in firm control of the country following their Sept. 1 coup.	Brazilian political leaders meet to choose a new president.	
Sept. 16	At the U.N. State Secy. William Rogers asks the Soviet Union for help in ending the Vietnamese War.	Soviet Union has reportedly stopped its criticism of Communist China since the recent talks between Premier Aleksei Kosygin and Communist Chinese leader Chou En-lai.	Israeli jets again pound Egyptian positions along the Suez Canal.		Viet Cong slay 24 civilians in a terrorist assault near Saigon.
Sept. 17	Reports indicate that U.N. Secy. Gen. U Thant is seeking the admission of Communist China to the U.N.	France says it will take a hard line against threatened strikes by Communist unions.	Israeli jets again strike Arab targets in Egypt and Jordan.	Argentina imposes martial law in Rosario after hours of labor demonstrations for higher wages.	
Sept. 18	At the U.N. Pres. Nixon offers to meet with Communist Chinese leaders to end the Vietnamese War.	Reports from Moscow indicate that Communist China has halted its alleged border harassment since the recent meeting between Soviet Premier Aleksei Kosygin and Communist Chinese leader Chou En-lai.		Canada says that the Northwest Passage is open to all countries.	
Sept. 19	U.N. Secy. Gen. U Thant indicates that he is pessimistic about progress in disarmament talks.	Soviet Union reiterates that Israel must leave the occupied Arab territories.	Newly independent state of Swaziland indicates that it has no choice but to pursue good relations with South Africa.	Cuba indicates that it may begin extraditing hijackers.	

A	B	C	D	E
Includes developments that affect more than one world region, international organizations and important meetings of major world leaders.	Includes all domestic and regional developments in Europe, including the Soviet Union, Turkey, Cyprus and Malta.	Includes all domestic and regional developments in Africa and the Middle East, including Iraq and Iran and excluding Cyprus, Turkey and Afghanistan.	Includes all domestic and regional developments in Latin America, the Caribbean and Canada.	Includes all domestic and regional developments in Asia and Pacific nations, extending from Afghanistan through all the Pacific Islands, except Hawaii.

U.S. Politics & Social Issues	U.S. Foreign Policy & Defense	U.S. Economy & Environment	Science, Technology & Nature	Culture, Leisure & Life Style	
	U.S. is undecided about accepting the Viet Cong's truce bid during funeral ceremonies for Ho Chi Minh.			Senate Minority Leader Everett Dirksen dies in Washington at 73.	Sept. 7
	U.S. asks Mexico for more help in combatting drug smuggling.				Sept. 8
	Senate rejects a proposal to limit the purchase by the Defense Department of the new C-5A supertransport planes.		Soviet Union launches a weather satellite.		Sept. 9
	Reports indicate that the anti-Pentagon congressional coalition is trying to reduce funds for naval aircraft carriers.	U.S. oil companies bid $900 million for Alaskan oil leases.	U.S. is reducing medical research grants by 20%.		Sept. 10
	Reports indicate that the U.S. has suspended B-52 raids across South Vietnam in a peace initiative.	General Motors lifts 1970 car prices by 3.9%.	Study of satellite photos of Mars shows a region with terrain unlike that of the earth and the moon.		Sept. 11
U.S. civil rights leaders charge that the Nixon administration has retreated in the fight for desegregation.	Pres. Nixon orders resumption of B-52 raids in South Vietnam after the enemy shows no signs of reciprocating the bombing halt.				Sept. 12
Disputes over sex education in the schools are seen splitting many U.S. communities.	Reports indicate that Pres. Nixon is planning a pull-out of 35,000 troops from Vietnam.				Sept. 13
			A government report warns of the dangers of links between cancer and heavy cigarette smoking.		Sept. 14
			Pres. Nixon backs a manned space flight to Mars but rejects a crash program.		Sept. 15
Whites and blacks exchange gunfire in Cairo, Ill.	Pres. Nixon announces a withdrawal of about 35,000 U.S. troops from South Vietnam.				Sept. 16
	Senate votes a resolution preventing use of U.S. troops in Thailand and Laos.	Treasury Dept. offers notes at eight percent, a 110-year high.			Sept. 17
N.Y.C. reports that more people are applying for welfare but that few are being accepted.	Sen. Edward Kennedy says that the U.S. should pull out of South Vietnam more quickly.	Senate group asks for the repeal of the seven percent business tax credit.			Sept. 18
N.Y.C. officials deny that they are deliberately discouraging the acceptance of new welfare applicants.	Pres. Nixon announces a 50,000-man cut in planned draft calls for the rest of the year.				Sept. 19
F	G	H	I	J	
Includes elections, federal-state relations, civil rights and liberties, crime, the judiciary, education, health care, poverty, urban affairs and population.	Includes formation and debate of U.S. foreign and defense policies, veterans' affairs and defense spending. (Relations with specific foreign countries are usually found under the region concerned.)	Includes business, labor, agriculture, taxation, transportation, consumer affairs, monetary and fiscal policy, natural resources, and pollution.	Includes worldwide scientific, medical and technological developments, natural phenomena, U.S. weather, natural disasters, and accidents.	Includes the arts, religion, scholarship, communications media, sports, entertainment, fashions, fads and social life.	

	World Affairs	Europe	Africa & the Middle East	The Americas	Asia & the Pacific
Sept. 20	General Assembly votes to take up the Mideast question.	Soviet-bloc countries announce plans for maneuvers in Poland.		Reports indicate that Mexican farmers are growing more marijuana for export.	Five U.S. allies with combat troops in Vietnam indicate that they will not make troop cuts.
Sept. 21		Soviet press criticizes the large amounts of advertising in the U.S. press.	Israeli jets strike Egyptian positions across the Suez Canal.	An airplane crash kills 40 passengers near Mexico City.	North Vietnam denounces the recent U.S. troop withdrawal announcement as a trick.
Sept. 22	At the U.N. Jordan criticizes the recent U.S. plane sale to Israel.	Soviet Union informs the U.S. that it is not yet ready to meet for arms talks.	Reports indicate that Israel has agreed to allow Jordan to repair a major irrigation canal on its territory if it stops artillery attacks against Israel.		Enemy gunfire downs three U.S. helicopters in South Vietnam.
Sept. 23	At the U.N. Arab delegates denounce U.S. support of Israel.	Soviet Union denies that it has any knowledge about the health of Communist Chinese leader Mao Tse-tung.	Israel maintains its air offensive along the Suez Canal as jets attack Egyptian positions.		Reports indicate that Japan is planning to improve its coastal defenses.
Sept. 24	U.N. takes up the question of Caribbean islands still ruled by European countries.	West Germany closes money markets until after the upcoming elections.	Israeli planes strike Egypt and Jordan.		Battle activity in South Vietnam remains low but Viet Cong terrorism is on the increase.
Sept. 25	U.N. authorities say that economic sanctions against South Africa are not working.	Fifty-five thousand workers demonstrate for higher wages in Italy.	Libya says that it wants greater control over the U.S. Air Force base on its territory.		Combat lull continues in South Vietnam.
Sept. 26		An uneasy calm prevails on European money markets in anticipation of upcoming West German elections.	A bomb kills one Israeli in a Jerusalem suburb.	A military junta overthrows Bolivian Pres. Luis Adolfo Siles Salinas in a bloodless coup.	U.S. troops find two Viet Cong bases near Saigon.
Sept. 27		West Germany holds parliamentary elections.	Moroccan King Hassan criticizes some Arab guerrilla activity as detrimental to the Arab cause.	Reports indicate that ethnic relations in Quebec between English and French communities are still bad.	South Vietnamese Pres. Thieu says that his country will still need U.S. help by the end of 1970.
Sept. 28		West German Chancellor Kurt-Georg Kiesinger's Christian Democrats narrowly defeat Willy Brandt's Social Democrats but Brandt indicates that he may try to form a coalition government with Free Democrats.	Libya indicates unhappiness with the U.S. military presence on its soil.	City of Toronto opens a new science center.	US B-52 raids continue in South Vietnam despite the combat lull.
Sept. 29	World bankers applaud the re-opening of West German financial markets.	West Germany re-opens its financial markets.	Earthquakes cause minor damage in South Africa.	Reports indicate that Mexico is unhappy with U.S. efforts to induce more stringent controls on Mexican drug production.	U.S. troops clash with Communist forces in the Central Highlands.
Sept. 30		West German political leaders Willy Brandt and Walter Scheel open coalition talks in Bonn.			South Vietnamese and Communist forces clash in the Mekong Delta.
Oct. 1	World Bank says that wealthy nations should give more money to the developing countries.	West German Social Democrats and Free Democrats near full accord on coalition rule.	New Libyan government begins erasing all road signs in English.	Mexican students stage a rally commemorating the slaying of student colleagues in 1968.	Five-hundred thousand Chinese hail Communist Chinese leader Mao Tse-tung in Peking.
Oct. 2		Spain liberalizes its labor laws.	U.S. Peace Corps begins to leave Libya under pressure from new government.	Mexico blocks demonstrations marking deaths in 1968 protests.	U.S. military command reports the lowest Vietnam War fatality level in two years.
	A	B	C	D	E
	Includes developments that affect more than one world region, international organizations and important meetings of major world leaders.	*Includes all domestic and regional developments in Europe, including the Soviet Union, Turkey, Cyprus and Malta.*	*Includes all domestic and regional developments in Africa and the Middle East, including Iraq and Iran and excluding Cyprus, Turkey and Afghanistan.*	*Includes all domestic and regional developments in Latin America, the Caribbean and Canada.*	*Includes all domestic and regional developments in Asia and Pacific nations, extending from Afghanistan through all the Pacific Islands, except Hawaii.*

U.S. Politics & Social Issues	U.S. Foreign Policy & Defense	U.S. Economy & Environment	Science, Technology & Nature	Culture, Leisure & Life Style	
Reports indicate that states and cities are not heeding Pres. Nixon's plea for a construction slow-down to combat inflation.	U.S. officials pledge to step up the fight against the use of marijuana in Vietnam.				Sept. 20
U.S. opens an anti-drug drive along the Mexican border.	Senate majority leader Mike Mansfield (D, Mont.) urges faster troop withdrawals from Asia.				Sept. 21
	Defense Dept. announces that it will cut the strength of the Air Force and the Marines in an economy move.	U.S. reports that August consumer prices rose 0.4%.			Sept. 22
Labor Dept. orders construction unions to meet rough hiring quotas for minority workers on federal projects.	Pres. Nixon says that he backs development of a supersonic transport plane.				Sept. 23
U.S. finds that more than half of New Yorkers on welfare are ineligible for assistance.	Reports indicate that pressure on Pres. Nixon to speed troop withdrawals from Vietnam is growing in Congress.				Sept. 24
Pres. Nixon asks Congress to link Social Security benefits to the cost-of-living.	Pres. Nixon confers with Israeli P.M. Golda Meir at the White House.				Sept. 25
Pres. Nixon says that he backs a "middle course" on school desegregation.	Pres. Nixon urges the U.S. public to give him time to end the Vietnamese War on "honorable terms."				Sept. 26
	U.S. presses Japan to allow the visit of a nuclear freighter.		Soviet Union conducts an underground nuclear test.		Sept. 27
The New York Times says that new campus disorders should not be tolerated this academic year.	Defense Secy. Melvin Laird has reportedly shifted some budget-making power from civilians to military officers at the Pentagon.				Sept. 28
N.Y.C. Negroes reportedly have gained more control of local public schools.					Sept. 29
Cleveland Negro Mayor Carl Stokes is nominated for a second term by Democratic voters.	U.S. announces plans for a withdrawal of 6,000 troops from Thailand.	AFL-CIO assails the administration's attempts to slow inflation by restraining economic activity.	U.S. orders a curb on codeine-based cough syrups because of health hazards.		Sept. 30
Several U.S. Senators criticize Pres. Nixon's nominee to the Supreme Court, Clement Haynsworth, because of possible financial improprieties.					Oct. 1
	House turns back an attempt to block funding for the U.S. anti-ballistic missile system.		U.S. conducts an underground nuclear test in Alaska.		Oct. 2

F	G	H	I	J
Includes elections, federal-state relations, civil rights and liberties, crime, the judiciary, education, health care, poverty, urban affairs and population.	Includes formation and debate of U.S. foreign and defense policies, veterans' affairs and defense spending. (Relations with specific foreign countries are usually found under the region concerned.)	Includes business, labor, agriculture, taxation, transportation, consumer affairs, monetary and fiscal policy, natural resources, and pollution.	Includes worldwide scientific, medical and technological developments, natural phenomena, U.S. weather, natural disasters, and accidents.	Includes the arts, religion, scholarship, communications media, sports, entertainment, fashions, fads and social life.

	World Affairs	Europe	Africa & the Middle East	The Americas	Asia & the Pacific
Oct. 3	International Monetary Fund votes to create "special drawing rights" to help foster world trade.	West German Social Democrats and Free Democrats agree to form a coalition government.	Israeli and Egyptian patrols clash along the Suez Canal.		Enemy downs three U.S. helicopters over South Vietnam.
Oct. 4	U.N. Secy. Gen. U Thant discusses the Middle East situation with his aides.	For the first time a public rally in Lisbon criticizes the continuing guerrilla warfare between Portuguese troops and African nationalists in Angola.	Israeli jets pound Egyptian positions along the Suez Canal.		Combat lull continues in South Vietnam.
Oct. 5	At the U.N. African delegates criticize South Africa's continued control of South-West Africa.	Portuguese police disperse an anti-government demonstration.	Israel and Egypt resume their shelling along the Suez Canal.	Reports indicate that Luis Echeverria will be Mexico's next president.	In a change of position, South Vietnamese Pres. Thieu indicates that he is willing to start cease-fire talks with Communist forces.
Oct. 6	Reports indicate that the U.S. and the Soviet Union have reached an accord prohibiting nuclear arms on the Seabed.	East Germany makes a guarded offer of good relations with the new West German government of Willy Brandt.	Israeli authorities begin trial of Michael Rohan who is accused of setting the Aug. 21 fire in Al Aksa mosque in Jerusalem.		
Oct. 7	U.S. and Soviet Union submit a treaty to U.N. banning nuclear weapons on the Seabed.	Police clash with East German youths near the Berlin Wall.		Montreal police go on strike for higher pay.	Communist China announces agreement with the Soviet Union to hold negotiations over their border dispute.
Oct. 8				Montreal police return to work after looters take advantage of their strike.	Laotian Premier Souvanna Phouma says that he is confident that the U.S. will continue to help defend Laos.
Oct. 9		Czechoslovakia announces a ban on travel to the West.	Reports indicate that Tanzanian Pres. Julius Nyerere is reducing his criticism of the Western countries.		U.S. combat fatalities are lowest since 1966.
Oct. 10	At the U.N. Jordan claims an ancient Jewish scroll acquired by Israel after the 1967 war.	Police and striking workers clash in Rome.		Colombia begins a crack-down on guerrilla kidnappings.	North Vietnam is reportedly stepping up its military activity in Laos.
Oct. 11	U.N. announces a $2.7-million budget deficit.	British troops fire warning shots at violent demonstrators in Belfast.	Tanzania arrests six opposition politicians.		
Oct. 12		Britain sends 600 more soldiers to Northern Ireland.	A new rightist party fields 50 candidates in South African elections.		
Oct. 13		French workers clash with police in Paris.			South Vietnamese and Communist forces clash in the Central Highlands.
Oct. 14		Portugal protests Sweden's support of African guerrillas in Angola.	An Israeli patrol clashes with Arab infiltrators near the Dead Sea.		Malaysia criticizes Communist China's support of North Vietnam.
Oct. 15		Czechoslovak Assembly replaces Alexander Dubcek as its chairman.	A policeman assassinates Somali Pres. Ali Shermarke.	Canada establishes diplomatic ties with the Vatican.	Communist China reportedly has 20,000 road construction workers in Laos.
Oct. 16			Israeli jets attack Egyptian and Jordanian positions.	Canadian P.M. Pierre Elliott Trudeau calls on France to repudiate policies which encourage Quebec separatism.	North Vietnam proposes that the U.S. and Viet Cong negotiate alone.
	A	B	C	D	E
	Includes developments that affect more than one world region, international organizations and important meetings of major world leaders.	Includes all domestic and regional developments in Europe, including the Soviet Union, Turkey, Cyprus and Malta.	Includes all domestic and regional developments in Africa and the Middle East, including Iraq and Iran and excluding Cyprus, Turkey and Afghanistan.	Includes all domestic and regional developments in Latin America, the Caribbean and Canada.	Includes all domestic and regional developments in Asia and Pacific nations, extending from Afghanistan through all the Pacific Islands, except Hawaii.

U.S. Politics & Social Issues	U.S. Foreign Policy & Defense	U.S. Economy & Environment	Science, Technology & Nature	Culture, Leisure & Life Style	
			U.S. launches a weather satellite.	Reports indicate that researchers are making progress in deciphering the ancient Mayan language.	Oct. 3
	U.S. refuses to confirm or deny rumors of secret talks with North Vietnam.		U.S. launches a military surveillance satellite.		Oct. 4
				Vatican opens talks with Church officials on dealing with dissent within the Church.	Oct. 5
	U.S. officials discount claims of progress in Vietnamese peace talks.	U.S. reports that unemployment has risen to four percent, the highest rate since 1967.		Pope Paul defends the principle of Papal supremacy during a talk in Rome.	Oct. 6
		White House says that a four percent unemployment rate is "acceptable."		Maj. Gen. Fred Walker, U.S. W.W. II commander at Salerno, dies in Washington, D.C. at 82.	Oct. 7
Key Republican senators indicate that they will vote against Pres. Nixon's Supreme Court nominee Clement Haynsworth.	U.S. officials say that Communist China may be easing its long-standing enmity toward the U.S.	House votes to limit funding for water pollution curbs.		In a church conference in Rome, dissident Roman Catholic priests call for curbs on the Papacy's power.	Oct. 8
Senate unit narrowly votes, 10-7, to endorse Supreme Court nominee Clement Haynsworth.	Defense Secy. Melvin Laird says that the U.S. is speeding the shift of the burden of the war to the South Vietnamese Army.	Senate unit bars tax on interest from local bonds.			Oct. 9
	Former V.P. Hubert Humphrey says that Pres. Nixon's Vietnam policy is on "the right path."	Senate unit bars cut in taxes for high-income group.			Oct. 10
Chicago police arrest 103 demonstrating radical youths.	Presidents of 79 U.S. universities bid Pres. Nixon to step up the Vietnam pull-out.			Pope Paul pledges to consider a greater role for Church bishops.	Oct. 11
Reports indicate that fear of crime is the major issue in municipal elections.	State Secy. William Rogers says that the critics of Pres. Nixon's Vietnam policy are making negotiations impossible.		Soviet Union launches Soyuz 7 spacecraft containing three astronauts.	Pope Paul says that his relation with Church bishops is the most important problem confronting the Vatican.	Oct. 12
	Pres. Nixon vows not to be swayed by growing Vietnam War protests.	U.S. Senate unit backs a repeal of the unlimited charitable deduction tax law.	Soviet Union launches its third manned Soyuz spacecraft in as many days.	Roman Catholic bishops criticize Papal centralization in a meeting with Pope Paul.	Oct. 13
Justice Dept. sues the Waterbury, Conn. school system for racial segregation.	U.S. officials continue their attacks on antiwar demonstrators.		Soviet Union conducts an underground nuclear test in Siberia.		Oct. 14
	About 22,000 demonstrators protest against the Vietnamese War in Washington, D.C.			French W.W. II collaborationist Armand Achille-Fould dies in France at 79.	Oct. 15
	Defense Secy. Melvin Laird hints that a "residual force" of U.S. troops will remain in Vietnam indefinitely.	Pres. Nixon says that he will continue to push for austerity measures to cool off the economy.	Three Americans win the Nobel Prize in medicine for work on reproductive mechanism of viruses.		Oct. 16

F	G	H	I	J
Includes elections, federal-state relations, civil rights and liberties, crime, the judiciary, education, health care, poverty, urban affairs and population.	Includes formation and debate of U.S. foreign and defense policies, veterans' affairs and defense spending. (Relations with specific foreign countries are usually found under the region concerned.)	Includes business, labor, agriculture, taxation, transportation, consumer affairs, monetary and fiscal policy, natural resources, and pollution.	Includes worldwide scientific, medical and technological developments, natural phenomena, U.S. weather, natural disasters, and accidents.	Includes the arts, religion, scholarship, communications media, sports, entertainment, fashions, fads and social life.

	World Affairs	Europe	Africa & the Middle East	The Americas	Asia & the Pacific
Oct. 17		France rules out early talks with Britain about possible Common Market membership.	Violence flares up in western Nigeria as residents protest against proposed tax hikes.	Bolivia nationalizes the U.S.-owned Bolivia Gulf Oil Corp.	
Oct. 18	U.N. reports a rise in world illiteracy because of the high birth rate in developing nations.	Soviet negotiators leave for border talk negotiations with Communist China in Peking.	Reports indicate that Tunisian Pres. Habib Bourguiba is seriously sick.	Bolivia says that it nationalized the US-owned Gulf Oil Corp. because of its excessive profits.	North Koreans kill four U.S. soldiers near the demilitarized zone.
Oct. 19	At the U.N. Arab delegates accuse Israel of trying to provoke a war.	Two East Germans hijack a Polish jet and force it to fly to West Berlin.			
Oct. 20		Police scuffle with Protestant demonstrators in Belfast.	Israeli jets bomb Egyptian positions along the Suez Canal.		
Oct. 21		West German Parliament elects Willy Brandt as the country's fourth Chancellor.	Reports indicate that Belgians are returning to work in the Congo (Kinshasha).	Chilean government troops put down two rebellious regiments demanding higher pay.	Anti-Vietnam war rioters bring Tokyo close to paralysis.
Oct. 22	At the U.N. African delegates criticize U.S. investment in South Africa.	Czech government says that Soviet soldiers are doing industrial work in Czechoslovakia.	Lebanese Premier Rashid Karami resigns after Lebanese troops clash with Palestinian guerrillas in southern Lebanon.	Chilean Pres. Eduardo Frei Montalva says that the Oct. 21 army revolt was an attempted coup.	
Oct. 23		Reports indicate that three Soviet naval officers were arrested last June for advocating the liberalization of Soviet society.	Lebanon reports that a large number of Syrian troops are massing near its borders.	Canadian P.M. Pierre Elliott Trudeau reaffirms Canadian sovereignty in the Arctic.	U.S. weekly casualty rate in Vietnam is the lowest in three years.
Oct. 24		Reports indicate that the Soviet Union has agreed to begin arms talks with the U.S.	Israel says that it will act if Syria invades Lebanon.		Communist-led state government of Kerala, India, falls because of corruption charges.
Oct. 25	U.N. celebrates its 24th birthday in a subdued mood.	Soviet Union calls on the major powers not to intervene in Lebanon.	A Palestinian guerrilla force based in Syria crosses into Lebanon and takes several villages within six miles of the Syrian border.	Dominican Republic reports a bumper agricultural harvest.	
Oct. 26		British troops scuffle with Catholic demonstrators in northern Ireland.	Reports indicate that there is a lull in the fighting in Lebanon.		Russian has reportedly replaced French as North Vietnam's second language.
Oct. 27		Soviet Union calls for better relations with West Germany.	Lebanon is reportedly near an agreement with Palestinian guerrillas about the use of its territory for attacks on Israel.		South Vietnamese and Communist forces clash in the Cental Highlands.
Oct. 28	At the U.N. Arab delegates criticize recent Israeli air attacks against Egypt and Jordan.	West German Chancellor Willy Brandt offers to improve ties with East Germany.	Palestinian guerrilla leader Yasir Arafat calls on the Lebanese populace to oppose their government's policy of restricting guerrilla operations against Israel.		Communist Chinese are reportedly extending their road building network in northern Laos.
Oct. 29		Reports indicate that Spanish moderates are gaining the upper hand in the government's cabinet.	Egypt says that it is willing to act as a mediator between Lebanon and Palestinian guerrillas.	Peru is reportedly seeking to attract foreign investment.	
Oct. 30			Lebanese troops fight a 12-hour battle with Palestinian guerrillas.		North Vietnam rejects a U.S. bid for private talks.

A	B	C	D	E
Includes developments that affect more than one world region, international organizations and important meetings of major world leaders.	Includes all domestic and regional developments in Europe, including the Soviet Union, Turkey, Cyprus and Malta.	Includes all domestic and regional developments in Africa and the Middle East, including Iraq and Iran and excluding Cyprus, Turkey and Afghanistan.	Includes all domestic and regional developments in Latin America, the Caribbean and Canada.	Includes all domestic and regional developments in Asia and Pacific nations, extending from Afghanistan through all the Pacific Islands, except Hawaii.

U.S. Politics & Social Issues	U.S. Foreign Policy & Defense	U.S. Economy & Environment	Science, Technology & Nature	Culture, Leisure & Life Style	
	Defense Secy. Melvin Laird reportedly seeks the halt in U.S. production of biological agents for use in war.	White House announces that Arthur Burns will replace William Martin as Federal Reseve Board's head.	Soviet satellite Soyuz 7 returns back safely.		Oct. 17
	Nixon administration says that it plans to cut military spending over the next five years.				Oct. 18
Nixon administration seeks softer penalties for marijuana users.	V.P. Spiro Agnew calls anti-war demonstrators "effete snobs."		U.S. launches a weather satellite.	Italian soprano Magda Olivero makes her New York debut in Francesco Cilèa's *Adriana Lecouvreur.*	Oct. 19
	Vietnamese war critic Sen. J. William Fulbright (D, Ark.) says that Pres. Nixon is sincere in his desire to end the war.	*The New York Times* criticizes the Nixon administration's tight-money policies.	Hurricane Laurie heads toward the Louisiana coast.	International Labor Organization wins the 1969 Nobel Peace Prize.	Oct. 20
			U.S. launches a military surveillance satellite.	U.S. novelist Jack Kerouac dies in St. Petersburg, Fla. at 47.	Oct. 21
	U.S. Senate votes to liberalize trade with Eastern Europe and the Soviet Union.			Pope Paul says that he agrees with bishops who are asking for decentralization in the Church.	Oct. 22
	Pres. Nixon confers with the Shah of Iran at the White House.			Samuel Beckett wins the 1968 Nobel Prize in literature.	Oct. 23
U.S. says that it plans to increase funds for family planning.		Reports indicate that pollution of the Long Island Sound has doubled within 10 years.	Soviet Union conducts an underground nuclear test.		Oct. 24
	White House announces that arms talks with the Soviet Union will begin on Nov. 17 in Helsinki, Finland.		Soviet Union has reportedly dropped plans to land men on the moon.		Oct. 25
A survey indicates that 20% of Cornell University students approve the use of violence for obtaining social demands.		Thirteen unions go on strike against General Electric across the U.S.	U.S. launches a weather satellite.		Oct. 26
	Pentagon announces plans to cut back the number of U.S. bases abroad.	Nationwide strikes cripple General Electric.		Pope Paul promises to give Church bishops a greater role in policy making.	Oct. 27
	Sen. J. William Fulbright (D, Ark.) accuses the administration of conducting a clandestine war in Laos.			Roman Catholic bishops appeal for Church unity in the wake of recent disputes with the Pope.	Oct. 28
Supreme Court rules that segregated school systems must complete integration plans "at once."	Reports indicate that the U.S. is ready to return Okinawa to Japan.	House passes a tough measure requiring coal mine owners to adopt strict safety measures.			Oct. 29
Pres. Nixon vows to enforce a Supreme Court decision mandating immediate desegregation of schools.		Pres. Nixon proposes new legal powers for consumer protection.	Scientists report progress on vaccines against meningitis and rubella.	Knopf publishes Ray Bradbury's *I Sing the Body Electric.*	Oct. 30
F	G	H	I	J	
Includes elections, federal-state relations, civil rights and liberties, crime, the judiciary, education, health care, poverty, urban affairs and population.	*Includes formation and debate of U.S. foreign and defense policies, veterans' affairs and defense spending. (Relations with specific foreign countries are usually found under the region concerned.)*	*Includes business, labor, agriculture, taxation, transportation, consumer affairs, monetary and fiscal policy, natural resources, and pollution.*	*Includes worldwide scientific, medical and technological developments, natural phenomena, U.S. weather, natural disasters, and accidents.*	*Includes the arts, religion, scholarship, communications media, sports, entertainment, fashions, fads and social life.*	

	World Affairs	Europe	Africa & the Middle East	The Americas	Asia & the Pacific
Oct. 31		Soviet bloc countries call for an all-European security conference.	Lebanese troops continue to battle Palestinian forces in Lebanon.		South Vietnamese Pres. Thieu makes an emotional appeal to the South Vietnamese people for sacrifices and self-reliance.
Nov. 1		Spain is reportedly seeking closer ties with Western Europe.	Clashes continue between Palestinian guerrillas and Lebanese troops in Lebanon.	Venezuelan army clears Caracas University of protesting students.	Communists seize an artillery post in South Vietnam.
Nov. 2	At the UN Arab delegates accuse Israel of trying to provoke a war.	Rumania calls on foreign troops to leave the European countries.	Lebanon reaches a cease-fire pact with Palestinian guerrillas.		Allied troops withdraw from three bases in the Central Highlands under Communist pressure.
Nov. 3	U.N. opens its debate on Communist Chinese membership.		Reports indicate that Lebanon has agreed to allow Palestinian guerrillas to use its territory.	Canada announces that it will reduce its use of the pesticide DDT by 90% next year.	Communist forces stage three artillery attacks in South Vietnam.
Nov. 4		Soviet writers' union ousts Alexander Solzhenitsyn.			
Nov. 5			Egyptian guerrillas stage a raid against Israeli forces.	Venezuelan guerrillas kill at least 10 government troops in an ambush.	
Nov. 6			Egyptian Pres. Nasser says that negotiations with Israel are out of the question.		U.S. is reportedly holding back its troops in battle areas as much as possible.
Nov. 7			Lebanon says it will seek aid from Arab states in wake of the recent accord with Palestinians.		
Nov. 8				Reports indicate that Canada is seeking increased trade with Communist China.	South Vietnam reportedly expects a big rice crop.
Nov. 9	At the U.N. Egypt denounces U.S. support of Israel.		Egyptian ships shell Israeli positions in the northern Sinai. . . . Biafran air raids are reportedly hampering Nigeria's oil production.		
Nov. 10			Israel reports having destroyed all Egyptian ground-to-air missiles along the Suez Canal.		U.S. officials report a big jump in enemy activity in South Vietnam during the last week.
Nov. 11	U.N. votes against expelling Nationalist China and seating Communist China.			Canadian P.M. Pierre Elliott Trudeau confers with U.N. Secy. Gen. U Thant on the legal status of the Arctic.	Reports indicate that the South Vietnamese government is managing to curb Viet cong terrorist attacks against Saigon's citizens.
Nov. 12		West Germany says that it will sign the treaty barring the spread of nuclear weapons.	Palestinian guerrillas reportedly control 14 refugee camps in Lebanon.	Soviet Defense Min. Andrei Grechko arrives in Cuba for talks.	
Nov. 13		Britain tells Libya that it is willing to withdraw its military forces.	Israeli planes attack Jordan.		

A	B	C	D	E
Includes developments that affect more than one world region, international organizations and important meetings of major world leaders.	Includes all domestic and regional developments in Europe, including the Soviet Union, Turkey, Cyprus and Malta.	Includes all domestic and regional developments in Africa and the Middle East, including Iraq and Iran and excluding Cyprus, Turkey and Afghanistan.	Includes all domestic and regional developments in Latin America, the Caribbean and Canada.	Includes all domestic and regional developments in Asia and Pacific nations, extending from Afghanistan through all the Pacific Islands, except Hawaii.

U.S. Politics & Social Issues	U.S. Foreign Policy & Defense	U.S. Economy & Environment	Science, Technology & Nature	Culture, Leisure & Life Style	
Civil rights officials press their school desegregation suits in the wake of the Supreme Court's recent decision.	Pres. Nixon calls for less Latin American dependence on the U.S.		Soviet Union conducts an underground nuclear test.		Oct. 31
Negro students end their sit-in at Vassar College after the administration agrees to fund a black studies program.	Pres. Nixon is reportedly doing well in survey polls.				Nov. 1
				William Freedman, who broke the Japanese war code in W.W. II, dies in Washington, D.C. at 78.	Nov. 2
Sixty Yale students hold the university's business manager captive because of a recent dismissal of a Negro employee for negligence.	In a nationwide address Pres. Nixon asks for public support of his phased withdrawal from South Vietnam.				Nov. 3
Liberal Mayor John Lindsay wins re-election in N.Y.C.	Pres. Nixon declares that the "silent majority" supports his Vietnam policy.	U.S. Consumer Federation of America denounces Pres. Nixon's consumer protection program as inadequate.	Soviet Union launches Cosmos 308.		Nov. 4
Harvard University Negro students occupy a dormitory construction project to back up demands that more minority workers be employed on it.		U.S. Senate unit votes to bar cigarette ads on television after the end of 1970.		U.S. sculptor Thomas Jones dies in Hyannis, Mass. at 77.	Nov. 5
A U.S. court orders school integration in Mississippi by Dec. 31.	U.S. officials believe that a pull-out of U.S. troops from South Vietnam is possible by mid-1971.		British scientists say that radar will be used to trace the profile of the Antarctic.	Doubleday publishes Victor Serge's *Men in Prison.*	Nov. 6
Four hundred students demonstrate for more jobs for Negroes in construction projects at Tufts University.		U.S. reports that the jobless rate for October was 3.9%.	Soviet Union launches a weather satellite.	New Deal's chief trust buster Thurman Arnold dies in Alexandria, Va. at 78.	Nov. 7
	U.S. says that it plans to bring the issue of North Vietnam's treatment of U.S. soldiers before the U.N.	U.S. officials are reportedly worried about the effects of food additives.			Nov. 8
Reports indicate that school desegregation is proceeding peacefully in the South.	U.S. historian George Kennan urges a quick U.S. withdrawal from Vietnam.	Consumer critic Ralph Nader praises the Nixon administration for releasing the results of auto safety compliance tests.		U.S. astronomer and discoverer of the planet Pluto, Vesto Slipher, dies in Flagstaff, Ariz. at 93.	Nov. 9
Police disperse rioting Negro youths in Memphis, Tenn.	V.P. Spiro Agnew denounces anti-war demonstrators as "the strident minority."	U.S. reports that 10% of car component tests have failed federal safety standards.			Nov. 10
U.S. Indians demand, in talks with U.S. officials in Washington, more federal support.	Hundreds of nationwide Veterans' Day demonstrations take place in support of Pres. Nixon's Vietnam policy.		Countdown for the U.S. second manned moon-landing flight is going smoothly.		Nov. 11
	House unit votes funds for the proposed anti-ballistic missile system.	Senate votes $1-billion to fight water pollution.			Nov. 12
V.P. Spiro Agnew accuses the television networks of distorting the news.	Pres. Nixon pays separate visits to the House and Senate to express appreciation for support of his Vietnam policy.		Three U.S. astronauts report that they are ready for their upcoming moon trip.	Pakistan's first Pres. Gen. Iskander Mirza dies in London at 70.	Nov. 13

F	G	H	I	J
Includes elections, federal-state relations, civil rights and liberties, crime, the judiciary, education, health care, poverty, urban affairs and population.	Includes formation and debate of U.S. foreign and defense policies, veterans' affairs and defense spending. (Relations with specific foreign countries are usually found under the region concerned.)	Includes business, labor, agriculture, taxation, transportation, consumer affairs, monetary and fiscal policy, natural resources, and pollution.	Includes worldwide scientific, medical and technological developments, natural phenomena, U.S. weather, natural disasters, and accidents.	Includes the arts, religion, scholarship, communications media, sports, entertainment, fashions, fads and social life.

	World Affairs	Europe	Africa & the Middle East	The Americas	Asia & the Pacific
Nov. 14	Eighteen industrial nations submit plans to help developing countries by cutting tariffs.	France announces plans to build atom plants based on a U.S. design.			South Vietnamese and Communist forces clash in the Central Highlands.
Nov. 15			French troops are reportedly engaged in frequent combat in Chad.		Pakistani workers go on strike throughout West Pakistan.
Nov. 16	At the U.N. African delegates attack South Africa's apartheid policies.	Hungary criticizes "inhuman methods" employed by the Czech government in its purges of liberals.	Israeli P.M. Golda Meir says that she supports Pres. Nixon's Vietnam policy.	Cuba attacks intellectuals who do not support the government.	
Nov. 17	U.S. and the Soviet Union begin arms talks in Helsinki in a cordial mood.		Israeli jets bomb three areas in Jordan.		Indian P.M. Indira Gandhi turns back attempts to topple her government.
Nov. 18			Sniper fire continues across the Suez Canal.		
Nov. 19	An international research team says that oulays for arms spending are soaring in developing nations.	Hungary stresses the need for expanded trade contacts with the West.	An Arab terrorist throws a bomb at an Israeli bank in Jerusalem, killing an Arab bystander.		South Vietnamese and Communist troops clash in the Mekong Delta.
Nov. 20		West Germany says that it is willing to pay 24 million marks a year for the return of the British Sixth Brigade.	First clash between the Lebanese Army and Palestinian commandoes takes place since their Nov. 2 Cairo agreement.		Communist China is reportedly building an extensive civil defense program.
Nov. 21		Soviet Union announces that it will observe Stalin's Dec. 21 birthday for the first time in 13 years.		Uruguayan guerrillas free a kidnapped banker after a payment of $60,000 as a donation to a hospital serving Montevideo's poor.	South Vietnam denies reports that U.S. troops massacred Vietnamese civilians in the village of Songmy on March 18, 1968.
Nov. 22		Seven Soviet writers protest curbs on Soviet author Alexander Solzhenitsyn.	Israeli police break up an Israeli mob marching towards the Arab quarter of Acre who were angered by recent sabotage strikes near Haifa.	Canada announces a major program to reduce water pollution.	North Vietnam says that it is willing to talk to the U.S. in private.
Nov. 23		Soviet Union has reportedly asked its Soviet bloc countries to begin buying oil from Arab countries.	Eight more Iraqis, including one Jew, have reportedly been secretly executed for allegedly spying for Israel.		U.S. is reportedly intensifying its raids against Communist supply trails in Laos.
Nov. 24		Portuguese National Assembly opens with indications of greater political diversity.	Egyptian planes attack Israeli targets in the northern Sinai.		
Nov. 25		West Germany is reportedly actively seeking improved ties with Poland.	Former Lebanese P.M. Rashid Karami forms a new cabinet.		
Nov. 26		Flooding covers the square in front of St. Mark's Basilica in Venice.	Israeli jets attack artillery in Jordan.		South Vietnam announces that its weekly casualty rate is the highest in 18 months.
Nov. 27	At the U.N. Arab delegates accuse Israel of territorial expansionism.	Two Arab guerrillas throw a grenade into the El Al terminal in Athens which injures 15.	Israel reports downing two Egyptian jets over the Suez Canal.		U.S. weekly casualty rate is the highest in two months in South Vietnam.
	A	B	C	D	E
	Includes developments that affect more than one world region, international organizations and important meetings of major world leaders.	Includes all domestic and regional developments in Europe, including the Soviet Union, Turkey, Cyprus and Malta.	Includes all domestic and regional developments in Africa and the Middle East, including Iraq and Iran and excluding Cyprus, Turkey and Afghanistan.	Includes all domestic and regional developments in Latin America, the Caribbean and Canada.	Includes all domestic and regional developments in Asia and Pacific nations, extending from Afghanistan through all the Pacific Islands, except Hawaii.

U.S. Politics & Social Issues	U.S. Foreign Policy & Defense	U.S. Economy & Environment	Science, Technology & Nature	Culture, Leisure & Life Style	
U.S. officials announce plans to speed-up school integration in the South in accordance with the recent Supreme Court decision.	U.S. begins reducing forces in the Philippines.			U.S. Catholic bishops approve broad changes in the liturgy.	Nov. 14
White House says that V.P. Agnew's criticism of the news media reflects Pres. Nixon's thinking.	Two-hundred fifty thousand war protesters stage a peaceful rally in Washington.		U.S. manned spacecraft Apollo 12 enters lunar orbit.	U.S. architect Buckminster Fuller gives a lecture on planetary planning in New Delhi.	Nov. 15
			U.S. spacecraft Apollo 12 reports no problems as it heads toward the moon.	Pope Paul renews his call for a world food fund.	Nov. 16
		U.S. officials report a decline in industrial output in October.	U.S. spacecraft Apollo 12 begins its descent toward the moon.	Joseph Kennedy, the father of the late Pres. John Kennedy, is reportedly gravely ill in Hyannisport, Mass.	Nov. 17
Sixty chanting black militants break up a luncheon of 1,500 for N.Y.C.'s master plan.	State Secy. William Rogers expresses pessimism about the direction of the peace negotiations with North Vietnam.	Pres. Nixon urges aid to industries which have been hurt by imports.	Apollo 12 astronauts make final preparations for their moon landing.	Joseph Kennedy, the father of the late Pres. John Kennedy, dies in Hyannisport, Mass. at 81.	Nov. 18
	Congress clears a bill permitting a draft lottery.		U.S. Apollo 12 astronauts land on the moon and go for a walk of several hours.		Nov. 19
V.P. Spiro Agnew attacks the communications media as being politically biased.	Reports indicate that the U.S. and Japan have agreed on the terms for the return of Okinawa.		Two U.S. Apollo 12 astronauts blast off from the moon and re-enter their command ship.		Nov. 20
	Reports indicate that curbs on U.S. forces stationed in Japan will be eased after the scheduled return of Okinawa.		Apollo 12 leaves its lunar orbit and heads for home.		Nov. 21
A Gallup Poll indicates that 68% of those interviewed approved of Pres. Nixon's performance during the mid-November anti-war demonstrations in Washington.			Harvard University reports that a gene has been isolated for the first time.		Nov. 22
South Carolina Negroes say that they are forming a new political party.		The New York Times calls for federal aid to help the financially troubled New Haven Railroad.	Two U.S. Apollo 12 astronauts hold a press conference from their space-ship.		Nov. 23
	U.S. Army announces that Lt. William Calley has been charged with the murders of at least 109 South Vietnamese civilians on or about March 16, 1968.		Apollo 12 astronauts splash-down safely in the Pacific Ocean.	U.S. country-western musician Spade Cooley dies in Oakland, Calif. at 59.	Nov. 24
CBS Pres. Frank Stanton says that V.P. Spiro Agnew is trying to intimidate the television networks.	Pres. Nixon orders the destruction of germ warfare stocks.	Senate rejects a proposal to end the surtax this year.	U.S. Apollo 12 astronauts pass post-flight tests.		Nov. 25
U.S. veteran Varnado Simpson says that he killed 10 South Vietnamese civilians on March 16, 1968 at Songmy.	Pres. Nixon signs a bill creating a draft lottery.		Soviet Union conducts an underground nuclear test.		Nov. 26
			Soviet Union launches a military surveillance satellite.		Nov. 27

F	G	H	I	J
Includes elections, federal-state relations, civil rights and liberties, crime, the judiciary, education, health care, poverty, urban affairs and population.	Includes formation and debate of U.S. foreign and defense policies, veterans' affairs and defense spending. (Relations with specific foreign countries are usually found under the region concerned.)	Includes business, labor, agriculture, taxation, transportation, consumer affairs, monetary and fiscal policy, natural resources, and pollution.	Includes worldwide scientific, medical and technological developments, natural phenomena, U.S. weather, natural disasters, and accidents.	Includes the arts, religion, scholarship, communications media, sports, entertainment, fashions, fads and social life.

	World Affairs	Europe	Africa & the Middle East	The Americas	Asia & the Pacific
Nov. 28	U.N. opposes a wide curb on the pesticide DDT for the developing nations.	West Germany signs the treaty banning the spread of nuclear weapons.		Police and a small group of anti-government demonstrators scuffle at the University of Mexico City.	
Nov. 29	U.N. reports that 100 million people have been vaccinated in Africa against smallpox in the last three years.	Italian Communist Party ousts four Stalinists.	Reports indicate that Saudi Arabian and South Yemini forces have clashed in recent weeks.	Jamaica is reportedly launching a family planning campaign.	
Nov. 30		Austria and Italy reach a settlement of their long-standing border dispute.	Israeli jets strike Egyptian positions along the Suez Canal.		
Dec. 1		France indicates that it is still opposed to British entry into the Common Market.	South Yemeni and Saudi Arabian air forces battle over their common border.		Communist Chinese schools are still reportedly stressing political indoctrination as opposed to a conventional curriculum.
Dec. 2		Common Market countries agree on talks with Britain about possible membership.	Archeologists discover a depiction of a 2,200-year-old Menorah of the Second Temple period in Jerusalem.	Reports indicate that Brazilian student leader Charles Schreier may have died while undergoing government interrogation.	Malaysia reviews the citizenship status of 250,000 ethnic Chinese and Indian citizens.
Dec. 3	Administration of GATT reports that Western Europe has replaced the U.S. as the "mainspring" of world economic expansion.	NATO approves rules for the defensive use of tactical nuclear weapons.	Israeli commandoes attack a guerrilla base in South Lebanon.		
Dec. 4	At the U.N. the U.S. criticizes Arab and Israeli spokesmen for their "violent" attacks on each other.	Soviet bloc countries, in a meeting, issue cautious praise for the new West German government under Willy Brandt.	Tunisia suffers major flood damage.	Honduras and El Salvador agree to meet for border talks.	
Dec. 5	U.N. says that defoliant chemicals used in Vietnam may be linked to birth defects.	West Germany says that it considers the recent Soviet bloc statement about the possibility of improved relations to be "conciliatory."	Syria releases two Israeli passengers from an Aug. 29, 1969 hijacked plane in return for 13 Arab prisoners.		
Dec. 6	U.N. talks begin on housing funds for the developing nations.		Egypt returns two Israeli pilots to Israel in return for 58 Egyptian prisoners.		Ten U.S. soldiers die in a helicopter crash in South Vietnam.
Dec. 7		Soviet Union agrees to begin talks with West Germany toward an agreement to renounce the use of force.	Five government ministers lose in Kenyan elections.	Cuba announces that four Cuban exiles have been executed for alleged spy activity for the U.S.	Japanese P.M. Eisaku Sato asks for support of his pro-U.S. policy as the Japanese electoral campaign begins.
Dec. 8	Price of free market gold drops close to $35 level.		Syrian and Israeli tanks fight a one-hour battle in the Golan Heights.		Communist forces launch 44 artillery attacks against allied installations in South Vietnam.
Dec. 9		Reports indicate that the liberalization of Portuguese political life is continuing.	Saudi Arabia has reportedly authorized its forces to cross into South Yemeni territory in clashes with South Yemeni forces.		Communist forces are reportedly maintaining their high level of activity in the Mekong Delta.
	A	**B**	**C**	**D**	**E**
	Includes developments that affect more than one world region, international organizations and important meetings of major world leaders.	Includes all domestic and regional developments in Europe, including the Soviet Union, Turkey, Cyprus and Malta.	Includes all domestic and regional developments in Africa and the Middle East, including Iraq and Iran and excluding Cyprus, Turkey and Afghanistan.	Includes all domestic and regional developments in Latin America, the Caribbean and Canada.	Includes all domestic and regional developments in Asia and Pacific nations, extending from Afghanistan through all the Pacific Islands, except Hawaii.

U.S. Politics & Social Issues	U.S. Foreign Policy & Defense	U.S. Economy & Environment	Science, Technology & Nature	Culture, Leisure & Life Style	
Reports indicate that Puerto Ricans are becoming more active politically in major U.S. cities.		Labor Dept. says that widespread corruption may exist in the United Mine Workers Union.	Soviet Union launches a weather satellite.		Nov. 28
Reports indicate that more Americans are using Swiss bank accounts in order to avoid taxation.		United Mine Workers Union Pres. Tony Boyle denies that there is widespread corruption in the union hierarchy.			Nov. 29
	Reports indicate that the U.S. paid Thailand $1-billion to send a division to fight in South Vietnam between 1965 and 1971.	Reports indicate that major unions will be seeking higher wages in order to offset recent sharp rises in the cost of living.	U.S. conducts an underground nuclear test.	U.S. psychiatrist James McCartney dies in Westhampton, N.Y. at 71.	Nov. 30
A federal court orders 16 southern school districts to integrate by the fall of 1970.	First draft lottery in a generation is held in Washington, D.C.	Senate votes to reduce the depletion allowance for oil and gas producers to 23%.			Dec. 1
U.S. court declines to issue an injunction barring publicity in the news media about the alleged Songmy massacre.	House vote indicates that a vast majority supports Pres. Nixon's Vietnam policy.				Dec. 2
	House panel cuts the Pentagon's requested budget by $5.3 billion.	House unit votes for a 15% rise in Social Security pensions.		Soviet civil war hero Marshal Kliment Voroshilov dies in Moscow at 88.	Dec. 3
Capt. Ernest Medina denies that he ordered or saw an alleged March 16, 1968 massacre of South Vietnamese civilians at Mylai by U.S. troops. . . . Two Black Panthers die in a fatal shoot-out with police in Chicago.	U.S. is reportedly annoyed by an alleged lack of consultation from West Germany about its recent overtures toward the Soviet bloc.				Dec. 4
170 Negro students seize the main administration building at Harvard University in protest against alleged discrimination in hiring of Negro workers on campus.		Senate approves a $6.5-billion rise in Social Security benefits.		German aviation pioneer Claude Dornier dies in Zug, Switzerland at 85.	Dec. 5
NAACP says that it will mount a nationwide campaign against suburban zoning laws.			U.S. launches a military surveillance satellite.		Dec. 6
			Reports indicate that a growing number of U.S. doctors see links between changes in body chemistry and depression.	British actor Eric Portman dies in Cornwall at 68.	Dec. 7
Los Angeles police battle Black Panther members in a four-hour gun battle.	Pres. Nixon pledges penalties for anyone found guilty of murder of South Vietnamese citizens at Songmy.	Pres. Nixon threatens to veto a tax reform bill because of increases in Social Security benefits judged to be inflationary.			Dec. 8
A U.S. court rules that New York State's limitation on Medicaid payments is illegal.	House passes the smallest foreign aid bill since W.W. II.				Dec. 9

F	G	H	I	J
Includes elections, federal-state relations, civil rights and liberties, crime, the judiciary, education, health care, poverty, urban affairs and population.	Includes formation and debate of U.S. foreign and defense policies, veterans' affairs and defense spending. (Relations with specific foreign countries are usually found under the region concerned.)	Includes business, labor, agriculture, taxation, transportation, consumer affairs, monetary and fiscal policy, natural resources, and pollution.	Includes worldwide scientific, medical and technological developments, natural phenomena, U.S. weather, natural disasters, and accidents.	Includes the arts, religion, scholarship, communications media, sports, entertainment, fashions, fads and social life.

	World Affairs	Europe	Africa & the Middle East	The Americas	Asia & the Pacific
Dec. 10		Czechoslovakia urges West Germany to disavow the 1938 Munich Pact.	Israel criticizes U.S. State Secy. William Rogers' recent plans for Middle East peace talks which provide for eventual Israeli withdrawal from territories occupied during the 1967 war.	British Columbia is reportedly undertaking a major campaign against water pollution.	U.S. planes bomb Communist supply lines in Laos.
Dec. 11		Soviet Union says that nudity is a sign of Western "decadence."	Israel downs three Syrian jets over Damascus.		
Dec. 12		Greece withdraws from the Council of Europe because of accusations of human rights violations.			U.S. planes bomb Communist supply lines in Laos.
Dec. 13		Britain discloses plans to leave Libya by March 1970.		Brazil denies that its Indian population along the Amazon is being severely mistreated.	Singapore urges the U.S. not to pull out of Vietnam too hastily.
Dec. 14		Rumania calls on other Soviet bloc countries to initiate ties with West Germany.	Egyptian commandoes cross the Suez Canal and capture an Israeli captain.		Laos acknowledges the presence of Communist Chinese troops in northern Laos.
Dec. 15		Greece defies West European countries by ruling out an early return to civilian rule.	Israel accuses Egypt of having tortured two recently released Israeli pilots.		Communist and South Vietnamese forces clash in the Mekong Delta.
Dec. 16		Soviet Union is reportedly maintaining its traditional high military spending despite a lag in economic growth.	Israeli Defense Min. Moshe Dayan says that 516 Arab homes have been demolished as punishment for suspected guerrilla activity.	A military coup ousts General Omar Torrijos Herrara in Panama during his trip to Mexico.	Communists launch a brief rocket attack against the center of Saigon.
Dec. 17		Reports indicate that a power struggle is taking place between moderate and extreme conservatives in Czechoslovakia.	Israeli jets bomb the Suez area.		Communist troops maul South Vietnamese forces in the Mekong Delta.
Dec. 18		Reports indicate that Czechoslovak liberals are still being purged by party conservatives.	Egyptian Pres. Nasser and Saudi King Faisal confer in Egypt in an effort to improve their ties.		Communist and South Vietnamese forces clash in the Mekong Delta.
Dec. 19				U.S. companies sign their first trade agreement with Peru since the 1968 coup.	Fierce fighting erupts near the Cambodian border between U.S. and Communist forces.
Dec. 20	At the U.N. Arab delegates accuse the U.S. of encouraging Israeli air strikes against Egypt.	Soviet Union reports a lack of progress on border talks with Communist China.	Ugandan Pres. Milton Obote reportedly has survived an assassination attempt.		U.S. bombers strike Communist supply lines in the Ashau Valley.
Dec. 21		The two German states agree on talks in mid-January 1970 concerning possible diplomatic ties.	Arab world leaders meet in Rabat, Morocco.		Communist troops launch attacks in the Mekong Delta.
Dec. 22	U.S. and Soviet Union agree to open full-scale arms talks in Vienna on April 16, 1970.	Poland agrees to open major diplomatic talks with West Germany.	Israeli commandoes strike across the Suez Canal.		U.S. planes bomb Communist supply lines in Laos.
	A	B	C	D	E
	Includes developments that affect more than one world region, international organizations and important meetings of major world leaders.	*Includes all domestic and regional developments in Europe, including the Soviet Union, Turkey, Cyprus and Malta.*	*Includes all domestic and regional developments in Africa and the Middle East, including Iraq and Iran and excluding Cyprus, Turkey and Afghanistan.*	*Includes all domestic and regional developments in Latin America, the Caribbean and Canada.*	*Includes all domestic and regional developments in Asia and Pacific nations, extending from Afghanistan through all the Pacific Islands, except Hawaii.*

U.S. Politics & Social Issues	U.S. Foreign Policy & Defense	U.S. Economy & Environment	Science, Technology & Nature	Culture, Leisure & Life Style	
		Henry Ford vows an "intensified effort" to curb auto pollution.		Vatican proposes closer ties to Jews, including possible joint prayer ceremonies.	Dec. 10
Harvard University suspends 75 Negro students after they occupy the dean's office.	Pres. Nixon confers with former Pres. Lyndon Johnson.		British panel links some birth control pills to a risk of blood clotting.		Dec. 11
Democratic House liberals succeed in blocking a Republican move to shift control of poverty programs to the states.		Senate votes to outlaw cigarette advertising on television and radio after Dec. 31, 1970.	U.S. launches a weather satellite.		Dec. 12
Supreme Court orders six southern school districts to complete school desegregation by Feb. 1.				Metropolitan Opera officials announce that the season will open on Dec. 29 after striking workers agree to return to work.	Dec. 13
		House unit holds detergents to be a major pollution factor.		Massachusetts Institute of Technology Professor Max Millikan dies in Boston at 56.	Dec. 14
	Pres. Nixon announces a withdrawal of 50,000 U.S. troops from South Vietnam by April 15, 1970.	House approves a 15% pension rise for itself effective Jan. 1.		World's oldest fossilized flea is found in Australia.	Dec. 15
	White House says that it agrees with the recent Senate resolution against the use of U.S. troops in Laos.				Dec. 16
Justice Dept. indicts Newark Mayor Hugh Addonizio on extortion charges.			Pres. Nixon calls on Congress to hold down the federal budget.		Dec. 17
Pres. Nixon says that he will veto anti-poverty funds passed by Congress because of their inflationary impact.	U.S. says that it will triple the number of South Vietnamese troops to be trained in the U.S.		Soviet Union conducts an underground nuclear test.		Dec. 18
Justice Dept. designates a special grand jury to investigate the fatal shooting of two Black Panthers on Dec. 4 in Chicago.	U.S. eases curbs on trade with Communist China.	Congressional conferees agree on a 15% pension increase.	Soviet Union launches a military surveillance satellite.		Dec. 19
	U.S. is reportedly pushing for Israeli withdrawals from occupied Arab territories.				Dec. 20
	Top U.S. industrialists have reportedly told the Nixon administration that they are losing business in the Arab world because of U.S. support of Israel.			French resistance leader Gen. Georges Catroux dies in Paris at 92.	Dec. 21
	U.S. State Secy. William Rogers defends U.S. Middle East policy before Jewish leaders.				Dec. 22
F	G	H	I	J	
Includes elections, federal-state relations, civil rights and liberties, crime, the judiciary, education, health care, poverty, urban affairs and population.	Includes formation and debate of U.S. foreign and defense policies, veterans' affairs and defense spending. (Relations with specific foreign countries are usually found under the region concerned.)	Includes business, labor, agriculture, taxation, transportation, consumer affairs, monetary and fiscal policy, natural resources, and pollution.	Includes worldwide scientific, medical and technological developments, natural phenomena, U.S. weather, natural disasters, and accidents.	Includes the arts, religion, scholarship, communications media, sports, entertainment, fashions, fads and social life.	

	World Affairs	Europe	Africa & the Middle East	The Americas	Asia & the Pacific
Dec. 23		Soviet Union is reportedly reacting negatively to recent U.S. Middle East peace plans.	Egyptian Pres. Nasser walks out of the Moroccan conference of Arab leaders because of Saudi refusals to increase financial support of Arab armies.		Viet Cong begin a three-day holiday truce.
Dec. 24			Arab leaders leave Rabat, Morocco after talks collapse.		Violations mark the Christmas truce in South Vietnam.
Dec. 25			Israeli jets raid the Suez Canal area for more than eight hours.	Reports indicate that São Paulo, Brazil is facing major urban problems because of its strong economic growth.	U.S. planes resume operations because of alleged Communist truce violations.
Dec. 26	At the U.N. African delegates criticize South Africa's apartheid policy.	Spanish opposition politicians are reportedly becoming bolder in their criticism.	Israeli planes attack the Suez area in a three-and-a-half-hour raid.		U.S. planes bomb Communist supply routes in the Ashau Valley.
Dec. 27		Reports indicate that Rumania's steel industry is making impressive progress.	Egypt, Sudan and Libya announce plans to hold regular meetings.		Japanese liberal party scores a resounding victory in parliamentary elections.
Dec. 28		Archeologists discover an ancient temple of Aphrodite in Turkey.	Israeli planes raid Egypt and Jordan.		Viet Cong kill seven U.S. troops near Saigon.
Dec. 29		Soviet Union says that U.S. curbs on trade hurt U.S. business interests.	Israeli P.M. Golda Meir hints at future austerity measures.		South Vietnam closes two newspapers because they criticize the government.
Dec. 30					Communist and South Vietnamese forces clash in the Mekong Delta.
Dec. 31		Czechoslovakia announces another purge of party liberals.	South African P.M. John Vorster rules out any relaxation of his country's apartheid policy in sports.		V.P. Spiro Agnew arrives in South Vietnam for a one-day visit.

A	B	C	D	E
Includes developments that affect more than one world region, international organizations and important meetings of major world leaders.	Includes all domestic and regional developments in Europe, including the Soviet Union, Turkey, Cyprus and Malta.	Includes all domestic and regional developments in Africa and the Middle East, including Iraq and Iran and excluding Cyprus, Turkey and Afghanistan.	Includes all domestic and regional developments in Latin America, the Caribbean and Canada.	Includes all domestic and regional developments in Asia and Pacific nations, extending from Afghanistan through all the Pacific Islands, except Hawaii.

U.S. Politics & Social Issues	U.S. Foreign Policy & Defense	U.S. Economy & Environment	Science, Technology & Nature	Culture, Leisure & Life Style	
	U.S. State Secy. William Rogers reports that Communist infiltration into South Vietnam has dipped.	An oil leak in the Santa Barbara Channel is polluting nearby beaches.		Former Honduran dictator Gen. Tiburcio Carias Andino (1933-1948) dies in Honduras at 94.	Dec. 23
White House will provide meals for more poor school children.		U.S. stores report large Christmas sales.	U.S. conducts an underground nuclear test.	U.S. pianist Clarence Adler dies in N.Y.C. at 83.	Dec. 24
				Bolshoi Ballet performs a controversial *Swan Lake* in Moscow.	Dec. 25
	Pentagon will reportedly cut armed forces by 200,000 over next several years.				Dec. 26
		Pres. Nixon may propose a new excise tax to balance the budget in fiscal 1971.	U.S. launches a weather satellite.		Dec. 27
N.Y.C. Puerto Rican militants seize a church in East Harlem to demand space for a free breakfast program.	Reports indicate that U.S. foreign aid will continue to decline.			Rafael Leonidas Trujillo Jr., the son of the late Dominican dictator, dies in Madrid at 40.	Dec. 28
Pres. Nixon says that the U.S. should not get involved with campus disorders.		White House announces that Pres. Nixon will sign the 1969 mine safety bill.		N.Y. film critics vote *Z* as the best picture of 1969.	Dec. 29
	U.S. gives North Vietnam a list of missing U.S. troops.	Pres. Nixon vows to balance the budget despite Congressional funding plans.	Reports indicate that the Soviet Union is cutting back on its space program for economic reasons.	Boston Museum of Fine Arts acquires a major collection of East Mediterranean gold objects.	Dec. 30
Justice Dept. asks the Supreme Court to give six Southern school systems until next fall to desegregate.			Soviet Union conducts an underground nuclear test.		Dec. 31

F	G	H	I	J
Includes elections, federal-state relations, civil rights and liberties, crime, the judiciary, education, health care, poverty, urban affairs and population.	*Includes formation and debate of U.S. foreign and defense policies, veterans' affairs and defense spending. (Relations with specific foreign countries are usually found under the region concerned.)*	*Includes business, labor, agriculture, taxation, transportation, consumer affairs, monetary and fiscal policy, natural resources, and pollution.*	*Includes worldwide scientific, medical and technological developments, natural phenomena, U.S. weather, natural disasters, and accidents.*	*Includes the arts, religion, scholarship, communications media, sports, entertainment, fashions, fads and social life.*

INDEX

INDEX

The index refers to all daily entries, which are keyed to dates and column letters rather than to page numbers. Headings are arranged in letter-by-letter alphabetical order. Subject headings (e.g., AGRICULTURE, ARMAMENTS) refer to events in the U.S. unless otherwise indicated by a cross-reference or relevant subhead. For subject entries in foreign countries, see country names.

AMERICAN Institute of
Physics
7/5/64I

AMERICAN Institute of Physics
4/27/60I

AMERICAN Institute of Public
Opinion (Gallup Poll)
(Princeton, N.J.)
1/14/60J, 2/16/60F,
4/14/60J, 11/7/60F,
12/10/60F, 12/24/60J,
1/17/61F, 2/20/61H,
3/29/61F, 5/30/61I,
8/13/61F, 11/4/61F,
12/26/61J, 12/28/61J,
1/21/62F, 8/11/62F,
9/18/62F, 10/3/62F,
11/11/62F, 1/19/63F,
6/14/63G, 7/18/63F,
12/14/63F, 12/26/63J,
2/4/64F, 2/7/64J, 11/2/64F,
7/2/67F, 10/8/67G,
11/12/67F, 11/25/67F,
11/30/67F, 1/6/68F,
2/13/68G, 3/10/68G,
3/23/68F, 3/30/68F,
7/29/68F, 8/31/68J,
9/10/68F, 9/17/68F,
9/28/68F, 10/21/68F,
11/26/68F, 2/8/69F,
3/31/69G, 6/4/69F,
11/22/69F

AMERICAN Iron & Steel Institute
5/24/62H

AMERICAN Jewish Committee
1/10/60J, 11/9/62J,
8/15/64D

AMERICAN Jewish Congress
1/30/60B, 2/11/60G,
2/28/60G, 1/15/61J,
10/19/61J, 4/15/62F

AMERICAN Jewish Yearbook
(book)
7/26/62A

AMERICAN Joint Distribution
Committee
1/25/68C

AMERICAN Journal of Sociology (magazine)
11/26/64F

AMERICAN League
8/2/60J, 10/18/60J,
11/23/60J, 7/20/62J,
10/21/63J, 11/7/63J,
9/9/64J

AMERICAN Legion
8/26/60G, 10/18/60F,
9/12/63G, 2/3/67G

AMERICAN Meat Institute
8/1/60H

AMERICAN Medical Associa-
tion (AMA)
5/5/60F, 1/11/61F, 3/11/61I,
6/1/61J, 7/6/61H, 7/28/61H,
7/28/61I, 9/8/61I, 5/21/62F,
5/23/62F, 6/22/62I,
6/26/62I, 6/27/62I, 7/5/62F,
7/17/63I, 9/11/63F, 2/6/64I,
8/5/66F, 6/20/67I
Abortion
6/21/67I
Medicare
12/2/64F, 2/7/65I
Smoking
6/24/64I, 12/4/64I

AMERICAN Melodrama. The
Presidential Campaign
(book)
5/1/69J

AMERICAN Merchant Marine
Institute
8/22/60H

AMERICAN Meteorological Society
1/20/60I

AMERICAN Motors Corp.
1/5/60H

AMERICAN Motors Corp.
8/26/61H, 2/10/62F

AMERICAN Nazi Party
8/30/60F

AMERICAN Newspaper Guild
2/19/62J, 2/18/67F,
3/13/67F

AMERICAN Newspaper Publ-
ishers Association
4/23/63H, 1/4/67F

AMERICAN Opera Society
2/7/68J

AMERICAN Opinion (magazine)
12/1/64F

AMERICAN Physical Society
3/15/62I, 1/24/63I, 4/22/63I

AMERICAN Poets, Academy of
2/13/69J

AMERICAN Public Health Association
10/7/64I

AMERICAN Republican Army
6/18/61F

AMERICAN Scientists, Federation of
2/4/60G

AMERICANS for Constitutional
Action
4/10/60F

AMERICANS for Democratic
Action (ADA)
5/14/61G, 10/1/61F,
9/5/64G, 3/23/66G,
8/26/67G, 9/23/67G,
9/24/67G, 11/11/67G,
5/19/68F, 10/5/68F, 5/5/69J

AMERICAN States, Organization of (OAS)—See Organization of American States (OAS)
Armed Forces & Defense
2/21/67D
Arm Sales
2/23/68D
Bolivia
9/3/62D, 6/17/63D
Canada
12/18/64D
Charter
6/19/66D
Chile
8/11/64D, 9/6/64D
Communists & Communism
5/28/65G
Communists & Communism
(International)
6/5/63D, 7/3/63D, 7/8/63D
Conferences
2/26/67D, 4/12/67A
Cuba
4/26/61D, 5/17/61G,
7/13/61D, 11/1/61D,
12/24/61D, 1/3/62D,
1/18/62D, 1/22/62D,
1/30/62D, 1/31/62D,
2/2/62D, 2/3/62D, 2/7/62D,
2/27/62D, 3/23/62D,
10/23/62D, 2/22/63D,
4/23/63D, 7/6/64D,
7/22/64D, 7/26/64D,
8/3/64D, 9/8/64D,
9/23/67D, 7/17/68G

Dominican Republic
2/9/60D, 2/15/60D,
1/4/61D, 1/19/61D,
6/5/61D, 6/8/61D,
6/15/61D, 6/16/61D,
9/12/61D, 11/21/61D,
1/4/62D, 5/6/63D, 5/8/63D,
5/9/63D, 5/13/63D,
5/3/65G, 5/5/65D,
5/10/65D, 5/12/65D,
5/27/65A, 6/1/65D,
6/4/65D, 6/9/65A,
6/23/65D, 7/6/65D,
7/20/65D, 7/24/65D,
8/29/65D, 4/24/66D,
6/5/66D, 6/24/66D
El Salvador
7/4/69D, 7/18/69D
Foreign Trade
5/5/69D
Guatemala
3/20/62D
Haiti
5/2/63D, 5/8/63D, 5/9/63D,
5/13/63D, 6/12/63D,
8/19/63D
Honduras
7/4/69D, 7/18/69D
Mexico
6/3/61D
Nicaragua
2/16/61D
Panama
1/29/64D
Panama Canal Zone
1/10/64D, 1/11/64D,
1/15/64D, 1/17/64D,
1/31/64D, 2/4/64D,
2/16/64D, 3/12/64D,
3/17/64D, 4/3/64D
Peru
1/21/66D
Resolutions
8/10/62D
Trinidad & Tobago
2/23/67D
United States
1/2/64G, 3/16/64D,
4/25/66D
Venezuela
12/3/63D, 2/24/64D,
4/4/64D, 5/16/67D,
6/19/67D

AMERICAN Stock Exchange
5/15/61H, 1/5/62H,
1/22/62H, 9/24/64H

AMERICAN Telephone & Tele-
graph Co. (AT&T)
10/21/60I, 5/10/61I,
6/18/61F, 7/10/62I,
7/26/62H, 12/27/62H,
5/7/63I, 3/17/64H, 7/5/67H

AMERICAN Tobacco Co.
1/5/64H

AMERICAN University
2/13/67J

AMERICUS, Ga.
7/31/65F, 8/1/65F

AMERSON, Lucius
1/16/67F

AMHERST College
12/9/64G, 6/3/66F

AMIN, Mustafa
8/1/65C, 11/30/65C

AMINI, Ali
5/5/61C, 5/11/61C,
5/16/61C, 1/28/62C,
7/19/62C

AMINO Acid
10/27/61I

AMIS, Kingsley
3/12/69J

AMISH Sect
10/23/67F

AMNESTY International
1/11/68B, 1/31/68B,
4/6/68B

AMOEDA, Julio
1/28/60D

AMRI, Hassan al-
12/12/67C

AMU, Abdul
2/5/62J

AMUSEMENT Parks
Desegregation
6/16/66F

AN, Truong Quang
9/8/68E

ANACONDA Co.
2/11/60H

ANACONDA Copper Co.
3/11/66D

ANATOMY of a Crisis: The
Laotian Crisis of 1960-1961
(book)
3/21/69J

ANATOMY of a Murder (book)
7/15/60J

ANATOMY of Europe (book)
3/12/69J

ANDERS, Edward
4/29/64I

ANDERSON, Elmer
7/3/61F

ANDERSON, Gary
10/16/64J

ANDERSON, George
5/6/63G

ANDERSON, Jack
3/28/63F

ANDERSON, Marian
7/4/63J

ANDERSON, Mary
1/29/64F

ANDERSON, Robert B.
11/26/60G

ANDERSON, Rudolf
10/27/62D

ANDES Mountains
3/14/62I

AND Other Stories (book)
11/28/68J

ANDRADE Maciel, Jose Luis
10/14/68D

ANDRE Gide (book)
5/20/68J

ANDREW, Prince (Great Britain)
3/22/60B

ANDREW, Jan
4/2/61J

ANDREWS, Julie
12/3/60J

ANDREWS Air Force Base, Md.
6/22/67F

ANDRIE, Ivo
10/26/61J

ANDRIESSE, Albert
12/21/65J

ANDROMEDA Strain, The
(book)
5/26/69J

ANDROPOV, Yuri
5/19/67B

ANDY Williams Show, The (program)
5/26/63J

ANESTHESIA
6/9/61I

ANGELL, Sir Norman
10/7/67J

ANGLICAN Church—See En-
gland, Church of
1/17/61J, 2/25/65J,
6/23/65J, 1/9/67J, 7/30/68J,
8/22/68J

ANGOLA
6/28/62B, 8/12/63C
Algeria
12/18/61C
Casualties
1/9/68B
China (Communist), People's
Republic of
1/3/64C
Communists & Communism
1/3/64C
Congo, Republic of the (Leopoldville) (formerly Belgian
Congo)
6/4/61C, 8/29/62C,
6/29/63C, 11/15/67A
Demonstrations & Riots
10/13/60C, 2/7/61C
Ghana
5/24/61C
Government & Politics
4/5/62C, 12/15/62C,
6/29/63C
Guerrilla Warfare
12/18/61C, 6/26/65C,
11/6/66C, 3/16/67B,
3/10/68C, 3/27/68C,
10/4/69B, 10/14/69B
Human Rights
4/20/61C
Independence
1/30/62C
Nationalist Groups
7/18/63C
Petroleum
1/12/69C
Portugal
3/8/60C, 6/30/61A,
6/30/61B, 7/25/61C,
8/28/61C, 11/28/61C,
1/30/62C
Portuguese Troops
5/5/61C
Rebellions & Revolutions
3/8/60C, 3/16/61C,
4/13/61C, 4/28/61C,
5/3/61B, 7/1/61C,
10/10/61C, 8/7/62C
Sweden
10/14/69B
Tunisia
5/4/61C
Union of Soviet Socialist Republics (USSR)
3/15/61C
United Nations (U.N.)
3/15/61C, 3/27/61B,
4/20/61C, 6/9/61C,
6/30/61A, 7/25/61C,
11/28/61C, 1/15/62A
United States
3/15/61C, 3/27/61B,
5/4/61C
Zambia
8/7/69C

ANGOLATIN America
Ghana
5/12/61C

ANGUILLA
4/11/69D, 4/13/69D

2/13/60C, 2/14/60A,
2/15/60C, 8/27/60G,
1/5/61C
Test Suspension
11/24/66A
Turkey
9/29/67B
Underground Devices
8/24/62I
Underground Tests
1/27/60A, 2/17/60G,
5/3/60A, 5/7/60G,
7/27/60A, 8/16/60G,
9/27/60A, 9/5/61A,
10/10/61A, 1/26/63A,
2/8/63G, 2/11/63A,
3/18/63B, 3/19/63C,
4/15/63C, 7/16/63A,
7/25/63A, 10/26/63G,
11/3/63B, 8/24/64G,
10/11/64A, 10/22/64G,
11/5/64H, 1/15/65I,
1/19/65G, 1/25/65B,
2/13/65I, 4/17/65I, 4/18/65I,
5/8/65I, 6/2/65I, 6/9/65I,
7/10/65I, 7/11/65I, 8/3/65I,
9/12/65I, 9/14/65I, 10/9/65I,
10/10/65I, 10/29/65I,
11/1/65I, 11/7/65I,
11/25/65G, 11/27/65I,
11/28/65I, 11/30/65I,
12/1/65I, 3/4/66I, 3/5/66I,
3/26/66I, 4/8/66I, 4/19/66I,
5/4/66I, 5/6/66I, 6/10/66I,
7/11/66I, 8/4/66I, 8/25/66I,
9/10/66I, 9/23/66I,
10/15/66I, 10/18/66I,
12/10/66I, 12/11/66I,
12/17/66I, 12/20/66I,
12/30/66I, 8/31/67I, 9/7/67I,
9/22/67I, 9/27/67I,
10/17/67I, 10/18/67I,
10/23/67I, 10/25/67I,
11/8/67I, 12/10/67I,
12/15/67I, 1/18/68I,
1/19/68I, 3/12/68I, 3/14/68I,
4/10/68I, 4/18/68I, 4/23/68I,
4/24/68I, 4/26/68I, 5/17/68I,
6/6/68I, 6/11/68I, 6/15/68I,
6/28/68I, 7/1/68I, 7/30/68I,
8/27/68I, 8/29/68I, 9/5/68I,
9/6/68I, 9/12/68I, 9/17/68I,
9/24/68I, 10/3/68I,
10/30/68I, 11/22/68I,
12/18/68I, 12/19/68I,
1/15/69I, 3/7/69I, 3/20/69I,
3/21/69I, 4/30/69I, 5/7/69I,
5/31/69I, 6/17/69I, 6/19/69I,
9/2/69I, 9/5/69I, 9/27/69I,
10/2/69I, 10/14/69I,
10/24/69I, 10/31/69I,
11/26/69I, 11/30/69I,
12/18/69I, 12/24/69I,
12/31/69I
United Nations (U.N.)
9/21/61A, 10/27/61A,
10/28/61A, 11/6/61A,
12/4/61A, 9/9/62I,
11/6/62A, 8/31/64I,
11/24/65A, 11/24/66A,
8/30/67A, 6/12/68A,
6/19/68A
**United States Bases &
Troops**
6/2/69G
U.S. Policy
3/27/62G,
Venus
4/1/64I
Vietnam War
2/7/68G, 2/8/68G,
2/14/68G, 10/3/68F
Weapons Freeze Proposal
2/18/64A, 8/27/64A

**Weapons Production Curtail-
ment**
7/2/63G
**ATOMIC Energy Commission
(AEC)**
1/30/60G, 5/14/60H,
8/15/60H, 8/27/60G,
9/6/60H, 1/30/61G, 6/3/61I,
6/10/61H, 7/19/61G,
9/4/61A, 9/5/61A, 9/6/61A,
9/22/61A, 12/11/61A,
1/20/67F, 2/8/67F
Appointments
3/28/64F
Appropriations
9/30/61H, 9/26/62H,
8/30/64H
Nuclear Power
11/22/62H
ATOMIC Scientists, Bulletin of
(newspaper)
1/1/62I
ATOMS
3/15/62I
ATOMS for Peace Award
4/5/60I, 7/30/63I
ATTASSI, Farhan
2/23/65C
ATTASSI, Nureddin al-
3/20/69C
ATTENBOROUGH, Richard
6/9/67J
ATTORNEYS, U.S.
1/3/66F
AUBURN University
9/25/62F
AUBURN University
1/4/64F
AUDEN, W.H.
5/2/67J, 5/28/68J
AUGUSTIN, Remy
1/12/61D
AURES Mountains
7/1/64C, 7/13/64C
AURIOL, Vincent
7/2/60B
AUSCHWITZ
9/9/67B, 3/8/69B
AUSTRALIA
10/9/68J
Accidents & Disasters
12/17/67E
Arms Sales
2/9/65G
Atomic Energy & Weapons
7/28/63A, 9/5/63A, 2/6/69G
**China (Communist), People's
Republic of**
2/6/61E, 5/11/61E,
1/28/69E
Deaths
12/18/67E, 12/21/67E
Demonstrations & Riots
1/18/67E
**European Economic Com-
munity (EEC) (Common Mar-
ket)**
7/14/61B
Foreign Trade
2/6/61E
Government & Politics
2/2/60E, 1/20/66E
Grain
2/6/61E, 5/11/61E,
1/28/69E
Greece
1/24/68B
Harbors
3/29/69I

Holt, Henry
11/26/66E
Malaysia, Federation of
2/25/69E
Monetary System
2/14/66E
Protests & Rallies
5/25/66E
Sports
12/1/62J, 1/11/63J
United States
10/22/66E
**United States Bases &
Troops**
5/9/63G
Vietnam, South
8/3/62E, 6/8/64E
Vietnam War
1/9/65E, 3/8/66E, 3/16/66E,
5/25/66E, 7/5/66E,
8/18/66E, 10/20/66E,
11/26/66E, 1/18/67E,
2/6/67E, 10/13/67A,
10/16/67E, 12/13/67E
AUSTRIA
Albania
3/14/66B
**Birth Control & Family Plan-
ning**
9/24/68J
Czechoslovakia
9/9/68B
Deaths
5/29/67J, 8/4/68J,
10/25/68J, 10/27/68J
Elections
11/18/62B
**European Economic Com-
munity (EEC) (Common Mar-
ket)**
12/15/61B, 7/28/62B,
3/21/67B, 6/29/67B
Foreign Trade
1/4/60B
Government & Politics
4/2/64B, 10/22/65B,
3/6/66B, 1/1/67B
Hungary
10/31/64B
Italy
7/17/60A, 10/27/60B,
1/28/61B, 3/2/61B,
6/25/61B, 11/30/69B
**North Atlantic Treaty Organi-
zation (NATO)**
11/15/68G
Steel Industry
11/17/66B
Terrorism
6/29/67B
**Union of Soviet Socialist Re-
publics (USSR)**
6/30/60B, 7/8/60A,
11/17/66B, 3/14/67B,
3/21/67B
United Nations (U.N.)
7/17/60A
Yugoslavia
11/26/60B, 9/30/68B

AUTOMATION—See Labor—Automation

AUTOMOBILE Industry—See
also Traffic Accidents
Contracts
8/22/61H, 11/2/61H,
9/9/64H, 9/18/64H,
10/22/67H, 12/15/67H
Deaths
10/25/60I
Electric
1/6/67H
Imports
1/7/63H

Labor
3/20/64H, 10/21/65G,
5/19/66H, 2/23/67H,
3/6/67H, 3/8/67H, 3/10/67H
Management
1/5/60H, 10/4/60H,
11/9/60H
New Models
4/17/65H
Numbers
12/1/60H
Plant Closings
12/9/63H
Pollution Control
10/3/65H, 10/20/65H,
3/29/66H, 2/4/67H,
1/3/68H, 1/10/69H,
8/26/69H, 12/10/69H
Prices
9/20/66H, 9/21/66H
Production
9/9/60H, 2/1/64H, 7/5/64H,
11/18/66H
Profit-Sharing
8/26/61H
Recalls
11/22/66H
Registration
5/27/61H
Safety
2/24/61H, 2/15/63H,
1/26/65H, 7/7/65H,
4/22/66H, 4/26/66H,
5/13/66H, 1/3/67H,
1/31/67H, 2/1/67H,
3/21/67H, 6/27/67H,
8/11/67H, 10/12/67H,
11/9/69H, 11/10/69H
Sales
1/13/61H, 1/7/63H,
4/11/65H
Seat Belts
12/13/63H
Small Cars
4/10/62H
Strikes & Settlements
9/11/61H, 9/20/61H,
10/3/61H, 10/15/61H,
2/8/62H, 10/8/62H,
9/25/64H, 10/5/64H,
10/25/64H, 2/15/67H,
9/6/67H
Tariffs
1/15/65D
Wages & Hours
4/15/61H

AUTOMOBILE Racing
8/14/60J
Accidents & Disasters
12/11/60J, 10/11/64J
Australian Grand Prix
11/18/62J, 2/10/63J
Belgian Grand Prix
6/18/61J, 6/14/64J
British Grand Prix
7/22/60J, 7/21/62J
Daytona 500
2/26/61J
Deaths
6/19/60J, 5/12/61J,
9/10/61J, 9/10/62J,
5/30/64J, 7/2/64J, 8/22/64J
Grand National Stock Car
7/21/63J
Grand Prix of Austria
8/23/64J
Indianapolis 500
5/30/60J, 5/30/61J,
5/30/62J, 5/30/64J
Italian Grand Prix
9/10/61J, 9/16/62J

Le Mans
6/11/61J, 6/16/63J,
6/21/64J
Le Mans
6/26/60J
Monte Carlo Grand Prix
1/24/60J, 6/3/62J
Monte Carlo Rally
1/25/62J
Pacific Grand Prix
10/23/60J
Records & Achievements
8/5/63J, 7/17/64J,
10/27/64J
Stock Car
2/14/60J
Stock Car Race
9/4/61J
U.S. Grand Prix
10/4/64J
Women
9/2/63J
AVALANCHES
1/10/62I, 8/30/65B,
10/21/66B, 1/28/68B
AVANCE
1/7/60D
AVERY, Milton Clark
1/3/65J
AVERY, Sewell Lee
10/31/60H
**AVIATION & Aviation Indus-
try**—See also Aircraft, Military; Airplane Accidents; Air-
ports; Helicopters; Hijackings;
Jet Planes; names of plane
types
Acquisitions & Mergers
8/11/60H, 6/19/63H
Air Rights
4/25/67B
Air Routes
3/14/61H
Air Traffic Control
1/12/60H
Antitrust & Monopolies
6/30/61H, 2/13/62H
Awards & Honors
3/13/61I
Deaths
1/30/60I, 3/6/60I, 4/14/60I,
7/1/60J, 12/10/60I,
12/26/60I, 12/5/69J
Discrimination
4/22/63F
Fares
9/9/61H, 12/14/65H,
2/19/68H
International
3/26/61B, 8/21/61B,
7/15/68H
Mercury Project
10/10/63I
Mergers & Acquisitions
1/23/62H
Passenger Service
2/12/63H
Pilots
3/15/60H
Records & Achievements
1/3/60I, 5/12/63I
Safety
3/3/60H, 6/24/64H
Strikes & Settlements
3/18/60H, 6/7/60H,
6/17/60H, 9/4/60H,
2/23/61H, 3/31/65H,
7/8/66H, 8/19/66H,
9/28/66H
Supersonic Planes
6/24/63H, 2/29/64H,
4/30/65I, 7/1/65G,
12/31/66G, 7/9/67B

Vietnam, South
6/7/64E, 4/17/66E,
6/12/66E
Vietnam War
11/12/65J, 12/23/65J,
12/25/65J, 1/1/66J,
11/21/66J, 1/17/67G,
1/22/67G, 2/4/67J
Vital Statistics
10/24/60J, 5/5/61J, 5/4/62J
Women
9/14/64J
World War II
11/18/64B, 11/19/64B
Yugoslavia
10/17/60B

CATHOLIC University (Chile)
8/12/67D, 8/21/67D

CATHOLIC Welfare Confer-
ence, National
12/14/61F

CATROUX, Gen. Georges
12/21/69J

CATTON, Bruce
2/4/60J, 3/3/69J

CAU, Jean
11/20/61J

CAUDLE, T. Lamar
5/4/60F

CAVANAUGH, Jerome
6/23/63F, 7/25/67F

CAWLEY, Rex
9/13/64J

CAYETTE, André
9/7/60J

CEZANNE, Paul
10/14/65J

CEAUSESCU, Nicolae
5/7/66B, 5/10/66B,
12/9/67B, 12/14/67B,
8/15/68B, 8/17/68B

CELEBREZZE, Anthony
7/14/62F, 9/7/62F,
9/17/62H, 10/25/62H

CELLER, Emanuel
5/8/61F, 5/9/61F, 5/10/61F,
6/26/62F

CELTIC Ash (horse)
6/11/60J

CEMETERIES
7/19/60G, 8/12/60F

CENSORSHIP—See under spe-
cific subjects; e.g., Radio Industry; under country names

CENSUS—See Population &
Census Reports

CENTAUR, The (book)
3/10/64J

CENTER for the Study of
Democratic Institutions
1/29/62H

CENTRAL African Federa-
tion—See also Nyasaland;
Rhodesia
Constitution
12/18/60C
Government & Politics
10/11/60C
Great Britain
10/11/60C

CENTRAL African Republic
4/2/68C
Armed Forces & Defense
1/7/66C
Chad
2/3/69C

China (Communist), People's
Republic of
1/6/66C
Coups & Attempted Coups
1/1/66C
France
4/16/69C
Government & Politics
1/4/66C, 1/7/66C

CENTRAL African States,
Union of
4/2/68C

CENTRAL America—See Latin
America

CENTRAL American Bank for
Economic Integration
11/3/60D

CENTRAL American States,
Organization of
12/14/62D

CENTRAL Intelligence Agency
(CIA)
1/30/60D, 5/9/60G,
6/1/60G, 6/30/60E,
11/10/60G, 2/12/64F,
1/24/66G, 3/13/66G,
8/14/66G, 2/13/67F,
2/14/67G, 2/21/67G,
2/24/67H, 3/13/67F,
5/7/67B, 5/7/67H, 5/8/67H
Algeria
5/1/61B
Appointments
9/27/61G, 1/31/62G
Bay of Pigs Invasion
4/17/61D, 4/21/61D,
5/2/61G
Bolivia
4/1/69D
Cuba
2/11/61G, 11/21/62D,
2/6/63G, 8/16/63D,
10/30/63D, 5/22/64D,
3/10/66D, 1/20/67D,
5/22/67F
Deaths
1/29/69J
Ghana
2/5/64C
India
6/12/67E
Investigation of
2/15/67F, 2/23/67G,
3/13/67F, 3/29/67F,
5/20/67F
Iraq
4/13/69C
Kennedy Assassination
2/13/64F, 5/8/67F
Labor
2/24/67H, 5/7/67H, 5/8/67H
Press
2/18/67F
Student Funding
3/11/67B
Students
10/20/67F
Union of Soviet Socialist Republics (USSR)
1/9/64B
U-2 Incident
3/6/62G
Vietnam, South
9/2/63E, 9/9/63E, 10/5/63G
Vietnam War
8/22/64G

CENTRAL State University
(Ohio)
11/9/67F, 11/13/67F,
11/14/67F, 11/22/67F,
11/27/67F

CENTRAL Treaty Organization
(CENTO)
4/30/60C, 4/29/63E,
4/30/63E, 4/22/66B

CENTRAL University (Ecuador)
3/25/66D

CENTRAL University (Venezuela)
12/2/60D

CERDAN, Marcel
6/14/60J

CERLETTI, Ugo
7/25/63I

CERNAN, Eugene
10/18/63I, 6/5/66I

CERNIK, Alexander
9/21/68B

CERNIK, Oldrich
4/24/68B, 9/10/68B,
5/19/69B

CEYLON
Assassinations & Assassination Attempts
5/10/61E
China (Communist), People's
Republic of
8/23/67E
Church-State Relations
12/1/60E
Communists & Communism
7/27/60E
Demonstrations & Riots
4/26/61E
Elections
10/4/61E
Executions
5/10/61E, 7/6/62E
Foreign Aid
2/8/63E
Foreign Investments
9/11/64A
Foreign Population
8/23/67E
Government & Politics
3/21/60E, 4/23/60E,
7/21/60E
Languages & Linguistics
1/10/61E, 3/1/61E
Nationalization of Industry
2/8/63E

CEZANNE, Paul
8/13/61J

CHABAN-DELMAS, Jacques
4/3/67B, 7/11/68B,
6/20/69B

CHACHARIS, George
2/24/62F, 12/12/62F

CHAD
4/2/68C, 6/25/69C
Central African Republic
2/3/69C
France
8/28/68B, 11/15/69C
Guerrilla Warfare
2/23/67C, 8/28/68B

CHAFEE, John
5/6/69G

CHAFFEE, Roger
10/18/63I

CHAGALL, Marc
10/22/60J, 9/13/67J

CHAGLA, M.C.
2/9/61E, 9/5/67E

CHALIAPIN, An Autobiography
as told to Maxim Gorky
(book)
2/5/68J

CENTRAL Treaty Organization
(CENTO)

CHALLE, Maurice
4/23/60C, 4/22/61B,
4/24/61B, 4/26/61B,
5/31/61B

CHALLENGE of Ideas, The
(film)
7/13/61G

CHALMERS, Rene
8/18/63D

CHAM, Thich Tham
1/3/65E

CHAMBERLAIN, Mrs. Neville
2/12/67J

CHAMBERLAIN, Wilt
3/13/60J, 3/25/60J,
8/10/60J, 3/2/62J, 3/19/63J

CHAMBER of Commerce, Ju-
nior
1/2/62J, 6/27/67F

CHAMBER of Commerce, U.S.
3/8/60H, 7/6/61H,
4/30/62H, 5/31/62H,
6/29/62H, 2/15/63H,
3/16/63H

CHAMBERS, Whittaker (Jay
David)
7/9/61C

CHAMORRO Cardenal, Pedro
Joaquin
1/26/67D, 2/2/67D

CHAMPASSAK, Sisouk Na
10/16/68A

CHAN, Song Yo
6/16/62E

CHANCE, Dean
11/9/64J

CHANDLER, Charles
10/12/68D, 10/14/68D

CHANEY, James
6/22/64F, 6/25/64F,
8/5/64F, 8/7/64F, 12/4/64F,
1/10/65F, 1/16/65F,
2/27/67F, 10/20/67F,
12/20/67F

CHANG, John
8/19/60E, 8/23/60E,
5/16/61E, 5/17/61E,
5/20/61E, 7/4/61E,
8/16/62E, 9/27/62E

CHANG Do Young
5/16/61E, 5/20/61E,
7/3/61E, 1/10/62E

CHAPEL Hill, N.C.
2/8/64F, 5/6/69F

CHAPLIN, Charlie
3/16/67J

CHAPLIN, Ralph
3/23/61F

CHARGE of the Light Brigade,
The (film)
10/6/68J

CHARITY—See Philanthropy

CHARLES, Bob
7/13/63J

CHARLES Sumner and the
Coming of the Civil War
(book)
5/1/61J

CHARLESTON, S.C.
9/3/63F

CHARLES University (Cze-
choslovakia)
1/17/69B

CHASE Manhattan Bank
11/1/60H, 7/15/69F

CHATEAUGAY (horse)
5/4/63J, 5/18/63J, 6/8/63J

CHATTANOOGA, Tenn.
7/9/63F

CHAU, A (newspaper)
7/26/68E

CHAUDET, Paul
12/14/61B

CHAVAN, Y.B.
9/2/63E, 8/8/66E

CHAVEZ, Cesar
9/2/66H

CHEBAB, Fouad
7/20/60C

CHEEVER, John
4/28/69J

CHEHAB, Fouad
12/31/61C

CHEKOV, Anton
3/19/68J

CHEMICAL Industry
Accidents & Disasters
2/17/67I
Employment Discrimination
5/11/67F
Strikes & Settlements
8/4/63H

CHEMICAL Warfare
5/15/62A, 3/9/63E,
12/11/63A, 3/22/65C,
3/22/65G, 3/24/65G,
1/5/67C, 1/11/67C,
2/9/67C, 2/14/67G,
7/2/67C, 7/3/67C,
7/15/67C, 7/23/67C,
7/27/67A, 7/27/67G,
3/13/68I, 5/26/68B,
8/28/68A, 7/18/69E,
8/9/69G, 8/15/69D,
12/5/69A
Research & Development
5/6/67F

CHEMISTRY
5/9/61I
Awards & Honors
11/3/60I, 11/1/62I, 4/1/63I,
10/21/65I
Elements
4/22/63I

CHEN Cheng
8/1/61E, 8/2/61G, 3/5/65J

CHEN Yi
2/2/61E, 4/2/61E, 5/16/61A,
7/9/61A, 8/4/61E,
10/11/61E, 7/7/63A,
10/28/63E, 11/20/63E,
6/24/64E

CHERKASOV, Nikolai
9/14/66J

CHERRY Orchard, The (play)
3/19/68J

CHESS
1/2/60J, 4/17/60J, 5/7/60J,
11/7/60J, 1/2/61J, 5/12/61J,
10/4/61J, 1/6/62J, 1/3/63J,
5/20/63J, 8/24/63J,
12/30/63J, 8/27/64J,
11/24/64J

CHESSMAN, Caryl Whittier
2/19/60F, 5/2/60F

CHESTER, Lewis
5/1/69J

CHETTA, Nicholas
2/22/67F

CHIANG Ching
9/5/67E

Gutowski, Bob
8/2/60J

Hahn, Otto
7/28/68J

Hall, David M.
1/29/60F

Hammarskjold, Dag
9/18/61A, 9/29/61A

Hammerstein 2d, Oscar
8/23/60J

Hammett, Samuel Dashiell
1/10/61J

Hammond, Bray
7/20/68J

Hand, Learned
8/18/61F

Handler, Harry
8/17/65J

Hansberry, Lorraine
1/12/65J

Hansen, Hans C.
2/19/60B

Harper, Fowler
1/8/65J

Hart, Luke
2/19/64J

Hart, Moss
12/20/61J

Hawkins, Coleman
5/19/69J

Haynes, George E.
1/8/60F

Hemingway, Ernest
7/2/61J

Hennings, Jr., Thomas C.
9/13/60F

Hesse, Hermann
8/9/62J

Heymans, Corneille Jean
Francois
7/18/68J

Hilda Doolittle (H.D.)
9/27/61J

Hildreth, Harold
11/3/65J

Hino, Ashihoi
1/24/60J

Hisamuddin Alam Shah, Sultan Sir (Malaya)
9/1/60E

Ho Chi Minh
9/3/69E, 9/4/69E, 9/7/69E

Hochmuth, Bruno
11/14/67E

Hofmann, Hans
2/17/66J

Holden, Charles
5/1/60J

Holt, Harold
12/18/67E

Holt, Henry
12/21/67E

Hoover, Herbert C.
10/20/64F

Hopper, Edward
5/15/67J

Hornsby, Rogers
1/5/63J

Horstemeyer, Bill
8/22/64J

Hoskins, John
3/30/64G

Houtery, Eugene
7/18/62I

Hubbs, Ken
2/15/64J

Huber, Max
1/1/60A

Hughes, Langston
5/22/67J

Humphries, Rolfe
4/22/69J

Hussain, Zakir
5/3/69J

Huxley, Aldous
11/22/63J

Ibanez del Campo, Carlos
4/28/60D

Ikeda, Hayato
8/12/65J

Jaspers, Karl
2/26/69J

Jinnah, Fatima
7/8/67J

Johnson, Daniel
9/26/68D

Johnson, Roy
7/22/65J

John XXIII, Pope
6/3/63J

Jones, Bassett
1/24/60I

Jones, Sir Harold Spencer
11/4/60I

Jones, Thomas
11/5/69J

Jordan, Charles
8/20/67B

Juin, Alphonse-Pierre
1/27/67J

Jundi, Abdel Kerim al-
3/2/69C

Kagawa, Toyohiko
4/23/60E

Kaiser, Henry
8/24/67J

Kane, Maurice
11/28/65J

Karloff, Boris
2/2/69J

Kasavubu, Joseph
3/24/69J

Kassim, Abdul Karim
2/9/63C

Kauffman, George S.
6/2/61J

Kefauver, Estes
8/10/63F

Keilberth, Joseph
7/21/68J

Keith, William
1/17/65J

Keller, Helen
6/1/68J

Kelly, Robert
1/13/65J

Kennaway, James
12/21/68J

Kennedy, Joseph
11/18/69J

Kennedy, Patrick Bouvier
8/9/63F

Kenyatta 37X
6/7/69F

Kerouac, Jack
10/21/69J

Kerr, Robert S.
1/1/63F

Kesselring, Albert
7/16/60B

Khan, Prince Aly
5/11/60E

Kiesler, Frederick
12/27/65J

King, Milton
6/29/63J

Klots, Allen
1/1/65J

Kluckhohn, Clyde
7/29/60J

Klunder, Bruce
4/7/64F

Knabenshue, Roy
3/6/60I

Koarov, Vladimir
4/24/67I

Kodaly, Zoltan
3/6/67J

Kohler, Wolfgang
6/11/67J

Kovacs, Ernie
1/13/62J

Kraus, Ezra Jacob
2/28/60I

Kreisler, Fritz
1/29/62J

Krupp, Alfried
7/30/67J

Kurchatov, Igor Vasilevich
2/7/60I

Laklifi, Abderrahmane
7/30/60B

Lambrakis, Gregory
5/22/63B

Lange, Dorothea
10/13/65J

La Rocca, Dominick James
2/22/61J

Laughton, Charles
12/15/62J

Lawrence, Robert
12/8/67I

Leasher, Glenn
9/10/62J

Le Corbusier
8/27/65J

Lee Ki Poong
4/28/60E

Leigh, Vivian
7/8/67J

Levy, Joseph
4/19/65J

Lewis, Clarence Irving
2/3/64J

Lewis, John L.
6/11/69J

Lie, Trygve
12/30/68J

Lipscomb, Gene
5/10/63J

Lloyd, Frank
8/10/60J

Long, Earl Kemp
9/5/60F

Low, David
9/19/63J

Luciano, Charles (Lucky)
1/26/62F

Lumumba, Patrice
2/13/61C

Luthuli, Albert John
7/21/67J

Mabach, Karl
2/7/60I

MacArthur, Douglas
4/5/64G

MacDonald, Dave
5/30/64J

Mack, Russell V.
3/28/60F

Magritte, Rene
8/15/67J

Maher Pasha, Aly
8/23/60C

Majali, Hazza
8/29/60C

Malinin, Mikhail Sergeevich
1/24/60B

Malinovsky, Rodion
3/31/67B

Margai, Sir Milton Augustus
Strieby
4/27/64C

Margesson, Viscount
12/26/65J

Marquand, John P.
7/16/60J

Martinez Barrio, Diego
1/1/62B

Marx, Chico (Leonard)
10/11/61J

Marx, Harpo
9/28/64J

Marx, Robert
9/5/60G

Maugham, W. Somerset
12/15/65J

Maurois, Andre
10/9/67J

Mba, Leon
11/28/67C

McCartney, James
11/30/69J

McCullers, Carson
9/29/67J

McGill, Ralph
2/4/69J

Mees, Charles Edward Kennet
8/15/60I

Meitner, Lise
10/27/68J

Mendes-France, Mrs. Pierre
11/27/67J

Menninger, William Claire
9/6/66J

Metalious, Grace
2/25/64J

Millikan, Max
12/14/69J

Mimmi, Marcello Cardinal
3/6/61J

Mirza, Iskander
11/13/69J

Mitchell, Samuel
2/22/60I

Mitropoulos, Dimitri
11/2/60J

Mohr, Charles
4/17/60J

Monroe, Marilyn
8/5/62J, 8/17/62J

Montet, Pierre
6/19/66J

Moore, Davey
3/25/63J

Moore, William
4/23/63F

Morgenthau, Henry
2/6/67J

Moses, (Anna Mary Robertson) Grandma
12/13/61J

Mossadegh, Mohammed
3/5/67J

Muench, Aloisius Joseph
Cardinal
2/15/62J

Mulligan, Arthur
3/12/65J

Munch, Charles
11/6/68J

Muniz, Joao Carlos
6/18/60D

Murillo, Gerardo
8/15/64J

Murphy, Richard
12/24/65J

Murrow, Edward R.
4/27/65J

Musmanno, Michael Angelo
10/12/68J

Nahas, Mustafa
8/23/65J

Namier, Sir Lewis B.
8/21/60J

Nehru, Jawaharlal
5/27/64A, 5/27/64E,
5/28/64E

Nelson, Harold R.
4/3/60I

Neuberger, Richard L.
3/9/60F

Ney, Elly
3/31/68J

Nicolson, Sir Harold
5/1/68J

Nishio, Toshizo
10/26/60E

Noddack, Walter
12/7/60I

Norodom Suramarit, King
(Cambodia)
4/3/60E

Notestein, Wallace
2/2/69J

Nugent, Frank
12/30/65J

Nutter, Donald
1/25/62F

O'Casey, Sean
9/18/64J

O'Connor, Flannery (Mary)
8/3/64J

Odets, Clifford
8/15/63J

O'Kelly, Sean
11/23/66J

Oppenheimer, J. Robert
2/18/67J

Orton, Joe
8/9/67J

Oswald, Lee Harvey
11/24/63F

Ottley, Roi
10/1/60J

Pabst, G.W.
5/29/67J

Palach, Jan
1/19/69B

Pankhurst, Estelle Sylvia
9/27/60J

Panofsky, Erwin
3/14/68J

Pant, Govind Ballabh
3/7/61E

Papandreou, George
11/1/68B

Papanicolaou, George Nicholas
2/19/62I

Paret, Benny (Kid)
4/3/62J

Parker, Dorothy
6/7/67J

Pasternak, Boris L.
5/30/60J

Pauker, Ana
6/14/60B

Paul, King (Greece)
3/6/64B

Pearson, 2nd, Frederick S.
1/17/60J

Penn, Lemuel
7/11/64F

Perkins, Frances
5/14/65J

Piaf, Edith
10/11/63J

Picado, Teodoro
6/1/60D

Pieck, Wilhelm
9/7/60B

Pokorny, Bedrich
4/19/68B

Pollitt, Harry
6/27/60B

Porter, Cole
10/15/64J

Portman, Eric
12/7/69J

Post, Emily
9/25/60J

Prather, Victor
5/4/61I

Pratt, Edwin
1/26/69F

Pu Yi, Henry
10/17/67J

DEFENSE Contracts—See under ARMED Forces & Defense

DEFFERRE, Gaston
4/20/67B,
5/5/69B

DEFIANT Ones, The (film)
7/10/61J

DE GAULLE, Charles
1/13/60B, 9/5/61C,
2/14/68A, 5/14/69B
Agriculture
3/18/60B
Algeria
1/19/60C, 1/20/60C,
1/24/60C, 1/25/60C,
1/26/60C, 1/28/60C,
1/29/60C, 1/30/60C,
1/31/60C, 2/1/60B, 2/1/60C,
2/3/60C, 2/5/60C, 2/8/60C,
2/9/60C, 2/10/60C,
2/11/60B, 2/29/60C,
3/3/60C, 3/7/60C,
3/14/60C, 4/23/60C,
4/25/60B, 5/13/60C,
5/30/60C, 6/14/60C,
6/20/60C, 7/6/60C,
9/5/60C, 10/21/60C,
11/4/60C, 11/7/60C,
11/10/60C, 11/14/60C,
11/16/60C, 11/19/60C,
12/9/60C, 12/10/60C,
12/14/60C, 12/15/60B,
12/20/60C, 12/26/60B,
12/28/60B, 12/31/60C,
1/4/61B, 1/6/61B, 1/8/61B,
1/9/61B, 1/11/61B,
2/27/61C, 4/22/61B,
4/23/61B, 4/26/61B,
5/8/61B, 5/10/61C,
6/27/61C, 6/28/61C,
7/7/61C, 8/30/61C,
9/12/61C, 9/30/61B,
10/2/61C, 10/30/61C,
1/4/62C, 1/22/62C,
1/26/62C, 2/5/62C,
3/18/62B, 3/19/62C,
3/23/62C, 3/26/62B,
4/8/62B, 5/23/62C, 6/8/62B,
7/3/62C, 1/27/67J,
12/22/67B
Algiers
9/27/61C, 12/29/61C
Arab-Israeli Conflict
5/24/67B, 6/21/67B
Armed Forces & Defense
8/17/61B
Arms Control & Disarmament
8/15/60A, 2/19/62A,
2/28/62B, 10/30/64A
Assassinations & Assassination Attempts
9/5/61B, 5/19/62B,
8/22/62B, 2/11/63B,
2/15/63B, 3/4/63B,
3/11/63B, 5/25/63B
Atomic Energy & Weapons
2/13/60B, 2/27/60A,
4/7/60B, 2/5/62B, 5/15/62B,
12/27/62B, 7/29/63A,
8/6/63B
Berlin
5/31/61B, 10/24/61B,
12/9/61B
Cambodia
3/24/64E
Canada
4/18/60D, 6/16/67B,
7/15/67B, 7/20/67D,
7/23/67D, 7/24/67D,
7/26/67D

China (Nationalist), Republic of
2/10/64E
Civil Rights
10/10/64D
Cold War
9/9/68B
Communists & Communism
1/8/67B
Congo, Republic of the (Leopoldville) (formerly Belgian Congo)
12/2/64C
Days of May
5/8/68B
Elections
3/4/67B, 6/23/68B
Europe
5/16/62B
Europe, West
7/9/64B, 7/23/64B,
11/6/64B
European Economic Community (EEC) (Common Market)
5/9/62B, 6/13/62B,
1/14/63B, 1/15/63B,
1/20/63B, 1/21/63B,
1/24/63G, 1/30/63B,
2/11/63B, 12/16/64B,
5/16/67B, 6/19/67B,
6/20/67B, 11/27/67B
Far East
1/31/64E, 2/1/64E, 2/7/64E,
6/10/64E, 6/26/64E,
7/23/64E, 7/24/64E
Foreign Relations
9/29/63B, 12/31/64B,
5/19/65B
France
5/17/62B
French Somaliland
3/22/67B
Germany
7/12/61B, 9/21/61B
Germany, East
6/29/66B
Germany, West
5/20/61B, 9/9/62B,
1/22/63B, 1/23/63B,
11/22/63B, 12/3/63B,
2/15/64B, 7/4/64B,
12/7/64B, 1/20/65B,
6/11/65B, 2/7/66B, 2/8/66B,
7/21/66B, 1/13/67B,
1/14/67B, 7/12/67B,
5/29/68B, 9/28/68B,
3/13/69B, 3/14/69B
Government & Politics
7/2/60B, 9/12/61B,
9/25/61B, 10/3/61B,
4/14/62B, 4/27/62B,
5/23/62B, 9/20/62B,
10/4/62B, 10/5/62B,
10/10/62B, 10/26/62B,
10/28/62B, 11/7/62B,
11/25/62B, 11/27/62B,
11/4/65B, 11/8/65B,
12/6/65B, 12/18/65B,
12/19/65B, 1/8/66B,
4/6/67B, 5/24/68B,
5/30/68B, 6/29/68B,
6/30/68B, 7/10/68B,
1/31/69B, 2/2/69B, 4/9/69B,
4/10/69B, 4/25/69B,
4/27/69B, 4/28/69B,
4/28/69C, 4/28/69G
Great Britain
3/13/60B, 4/7/60B,
1/29/61B, 6/2/62B,
12/16/62B, 1/15/63B,
1/25/63B, 1/24/65B,
2/18/65B
Greece
5/19/63B

Health
4/17/64B
Indonesia
7/3/65B
Israel
1/1/69B
Jews
11/27/67B, 11/29/67B,
1/1/68B, 1/6/68B, 1/9/68B
Jordan, Hashemite Kingdom of
7/4/67B
Laos
5/20/64E, 5/23/64E
Latin America
3/15/64D, 3/20/64D,
9/21/64D, 9/25/64D,
10/10/64D
Mali Federation (Senegal, Sudan)
1/18/60C
Mexico
3/18/64D
Military Bases
2/21/66B
Monetary System
11/23/68B
Morocco
1/19/66B
North Atlantic Treaty Organization (NATO)
8/11/60B, 9/5/60B,
10/7/60B, 10/8/60B,
5/9/61B, 7/21/62B,
1/14/63B, 2/4/63B,
2/14/63B, 6/25/63B,
12/7/64B, 9/9/65B,
9/11/65B, 2/21/66B,
4/24/66B, 8/27/66B,
9/3/66B, 5/19/68B
Pardons
12/15/63B
Poland
9/6/67B, 9/7/67B, 9/8/67B,
9/9/67B, 9/10/67B,
9/11/67B
Rumania
5/18/68B
Speeches
5/31/60A
Strikes & Settlements
3/3/63B
Summit Conferences & Proposals
4/23/60A, 4/24/60A,
5/14/60B, 5/17/60A
Travel
4/7/60B, 4/18/60D,
5/19/63B, 9/21/64D,
9/25/64D, 10/10/64D,
9/13/66B, 7/20/67D,
7/23/67D, 7/24/67D,
7/26/67D, 9/6/67B, 9/7/67B,
9/8/67B, 9/9/67B, 9/10/67B,
9/11/67B, 5/18/68B
Tunisia
9/5/61C
Turkey
10/25/68B
Union of Soviet Socialist Republics (USSR)
3/24/60B, 2/1/63B,
1/12/66B, 6/20/66B,
6/22/66B, 7/1/67B
United Nations (U.N.)
4/11/61A
United States
1/6/60G, 5/31/61B,
8/6/63B, 6/10/64E,
4/16/66B, 6/27/66B,
7/13/66B, 8/11/66B,
2/5/67G, 4/7/67B,
7/13/67B, 2/28/69G,
3/30/69J

Vietnam
8/29/63E, 9/2/63E
Vietnam, South
2/11/64E
Vietnam War
8/31/65B, 2/15/66B,
2/17/66B, 9/1/66E,
10/28/66B, 1/30/67B,
2/21/67B, 4/3/68B

DE Geer, Derek Jan
11/28/60B

DEGERMARK, Pia
5/12/67J

DEGRAFFENRIED, Ryan
5/1/62F

DELACORTE Theater (N.Y.C.)
8/13/69J

DELAWARE
7/19/60F, 9/1/60F

DE LEUSSE, Pierre
9/7/66B

DELGADO, Francisco
10/5/60E

DELOUVRIER, Paul
1/28/60C

DELTA Airlines
3/14/61H

DELVALLE, Max
3/24/68D, 3/25/68D,
3/26/68D

DE MIRANDA, Bonifacio
11/10/67A, 11/14/67A

DEMIREL, Suleyman
2/4/66B

DEMOCRACY and the Student Left (book)
9/25/68J

DEMOCRATIC Institutions, Center for the Study of
5/21/62I

DEMOCRATIC Party—See also PRESIDENTIAL Campaign headings
5/22/60G
Advisory Council
1/18/60F
Campaign Funds
6/8/62F
Congress, U.S.
1/6/60F, 1/7/65F
Elections
11/6/62F
Factions
10/28/66F
Finances
1/17/63F
Issues & Policies
5/19/62F, 6/7/62F, 5/5/67G
Kennedy Assassination
11/26/63F
National Committee
7/16/60F
Negroes
1/29/67F
New York State
1/8/67F
Presidential Campaign of 1968
10/8/68F
Realignment
11/14/64F, 11/16/64F
South, U.S.
9/16/64F
Southern Wing
2/19/63F
Vietnam War
8/27/67G, 12/9/67G,
1/13/68G, 1/14/68G

DEMOGRAPHIC Yearbook
9/1/62A

DEMONSTRATIONS & Riots
6/11/68F, 11/19/68F
Law & Legislation
6/19/67F

DEMPSEY, Jack
8/7/60J

DEMPSEY, John
2/18/61H, 7/9/63F

DENGLER, Dieter
9/13/66E

DENHAM Springs, La.
8/18/67F

DENMARK
Atomic Energy & Weapons
7/28/63A
Cyprus
7/17/64B
Deaths
2/19/60B
Elections
9/22/64B
European Economic Community (EEC) (Common Market)
5/10/62B
Foreign Trade
1/4/60B
Germany, West
3/11/60B
Government & Politics
2/21/60B, 11/15/60B,
8/31/62B, 9/3/62B
Greece
5/5/67B, 2/29/68B
North Atlantic Treaty Organization (NATO)
9/3/60B
United Nations (U.N.)
12/15/61A
Vietnam War
8/21/64E

DENNIS, K.D.
5/26/66F

DENNISON, Robert L.
2/29/60G, 4/29/63G

DENTISTRY & Dental Goods
Education
2/24/61F
Tooth Decay
5/13/61I
Tooth Transplants
2/10/69I

DENVER, University of
3/25/63J, 3/7/64J

DEPARTMENTS & Agencies, U.S.
6/16/65F, 8/31/65F,
1/16/67H

Defense Contracts
4/17/62F

Proposed
1/24/62F

DE PORRES, Martin
5/6/62J

DE PRIETO, Ines Cuervo
9/7/63J

DE Profundis (manuscript)
1/2/60J

DEPUTY, The (play)
2/26/64J, 5/30/64J

DE QUAY, Jan Eduard
1/2/62E, 1/20/62E,
7/24/63B

DE RUDDER, Marcel
4/21/66I, 4/26/66I

Petroleum
1/19/61D
Police
1/18/65D
Press
6/14/61D
Protests & Rallies
10/18/61D, 10/29/65D
Rebellions & Revolutions
12/30/62D, 4/24/65D,
4/25/65D, 4/26/65D,
4/27/65D, 4/28/65D,
4/28/65G, 4/30/65D,
5/1/65D, 5/2/65D, 5/3/65D,
5/6/65D, 5/7/65D, 5/8/65D,
5/11/65D, 5/13/65D,
5/14/65D, 5/15/65D,
5/16/65D, 5/20/65G,
5/31/65D, 6/15/65D,
6/16/65D, 6/17/65D,
6/21/65D, 6/25/65D,
7/2/65D, 7/4/65D,
7/10/65D, 7/22/65D,
9/12/65D, 9/26/65D,
9/28/65D, 10/19/65D,
10/20/65D, 10/23/65D,
12/19/65D, 12/20/65D,
12/21/65D, 12/29/65D
Strikes & Settlements
11/28/61D, 11/30/61D,
5/8/64D, 12/17/65D
Sugar
8/23/60G, 9/1/60G,
9/28/60D, 2/17/61G,
3/21/61G, 4/1/61D,
12/17/65D
Terrorism
12/4/61D, 6/11/64D
Truce
5/19/65D, 5/20/65D,
5/22/65A, 5/22/65D,
5/23/65D
Union of Soviet Socialist Republics (USSR)
5/21/65A
United Nations (U.N.)
9/9/60D, 11/21/61D,
11/24/61D, 5/18/65A,
5/21/65A, 5/22/65A,
5/27/65A, 6/9/65A
United States
2/26/60D, 8/26/60D,
9/1/60G, 9/2/60G,
9/28/60D, 1/19/61D,
11/18/61D, 11/19/61D,
11/20/61D, 11/21/61D,
11/24/61D, 12/3/61D,
1/6/62D, 1/17/62D,
1/22/62D, 3/8/62D,
1/10/63D, 9/25/63D,
10/4/63D, 10/31/63D,
12/14/63D, 4/26/65D,
5/11/65G, 5/14/65A,
5/14/65B, 5/18/65G,
5/19/65D, 5/20/65G,
5/21/65A, 5/26/65B,
5/29/65D, 5/31/65G,
6/2/65G, 6/17/65G,
9/4/65G, 9/15/65G,
12/1/65D, 1/13/66A,
6/2/66G, 7/1/66D,
9/19/66D, 7/3/69D
Uruguay
5/4/65A
U.S. Troops
4/28/65G, 4/29/65G,
4/30/65D, 5/1/65D,
5/1/65G, 5/2/65G, 5/3/65D,
5/4/65A, 5/4/65D, 5/6/65C,
5/6/65D, 5/7/65G,
5/21/65G, 9/24/65D
Venezuela
2/15/60D, 3/18/60D,
8/20/60D, 10/23/60D,
11/30/60D

DON, Tran Van
11/1/63E
DONALD, David
5/1/61J
DONG, Pham Van
9/1/67E
DONLON, Roger
12/5/64G
DONOVAN, Bernard
9/6/66F
DONOVAN, James
2/10/62A, 4/22/63D
DON Rodrigo (opera)
2/22/66J
DOOLEY, 3d, Thomas A.
1/18/61I
DORJI, Jigme
4/5/64E
DORNIER, Claude
12/5/69J
DORSCHEL, Peter
6/23/67B
DORTICOS Torrado, Osvaldo
11/2/60D, 1/13/61D,
2/5/61D, 4/27/61D,
4/28/61D, 10/4/61D,
11/29/61D, 1/30/62D,
10/8/62D, 1/1/63D
DOSSIN, Francois
9/3/63I
DOUBLEDAY & Co.
6/9/67J, 8/18/67J, 10/6/67J,
11/17/67J, 11/24/67J,
3/22/68J, 5/18/68J, 7/5/68J,
9/27/68J
DOUBLE Helix, The (book)
2/26/68J
DOUGLAS, Paul
12/4/60H
DOUGLAS, William O.
11/13/60G, 3/30/61G
DOUGLAS-HOME, Alec
7/27/60B, 7/28/60B,
1/2/61E, 8/5/63A,
10/19/63B, 10/22/63B,
10/23/63B, 11/12/63B,
11/29/63B, 12/12/63B,
2/8/64B, 4/9/64B, 5/7/64C,
9/25/64B
Elections
11/7/63B
Government & Politics
10/15/64B
Rhodesia
7/15/64C
United States
2/13/64B
DOW Chemical Co.
5/28/66G, 2/22/67G,
10/18/67F, 11/11/68F,
2/13/69F
DOW Jones & Co.
2/4/62J
DOWNES, Terry
7/11/61J, 4/7/62J,
11/30/64J
DOYLE, James
6/23/60F
DOYLE, Joseph
10/20/61I
DRAFT
4/18/60G, 4/18/64G,
2/27/67H, 3/16/67G

Call
7/26/61G, 1/5/62G,
7/11/65G, 7/23/65G,
7/28/65G, 8/3/65G,
8/18/65G, 8/26/65G,
10/14/65G, 10/26/65G,
8/4/66G, 11/2/67G,
11/9/67G, 12/3/67G,
12/7/67G, 12/9/67G
Card Burning
10/18/65G, 7/1/66F,
7/29/66F, 2/13/67F
Conscientious Objectors
1/20/64G, 4/5/67G,
4/30/67G
Cuts
9/19/69G
Deferments
3/6/61G, 5/14/66G,
2/27/67H, 2/16/68F,
1/13/69F, 3/10/69F
Demonstrations & Riots
10/19/67F, 12/5/67G,
12/7/67G, 12/8/67G,
2/23/69D
Doctors & Dentists
11/14/60G
Evasion
10/17/65G, 1/5/67G,
2/6/67F, 6/20/67F,
12/12/67F, 1/12/68F,
3/2/68F, 4/16/68F,
6/14/68F, 7/10/68F,
12/18/68F, 4/28/69F
Extension
3/11/63G, 3/29/63G,
5/11/67G
Inequities
6/22/66G
Lottery
11/19/69G, 11/26/69G,
12/1/69G
Lottery (Proposed)
5/17/67G
Marriages
9/10/63G
Negroes
1/13/68F
Opponents
9/3/64G, 10/17/65F,
1/6/66F, 1/8/66F, 1/10/66F,
3/30/66F, 12/5/66F,
1/30/67F, 12/7/67G,
12/9/67G
Protests & Rallies
3/22/66G, 5/18/66F,
10/16/67F, 10/27/67F,
11/2/67G, 11/9/67G
Reform
11/11/66G
Rejects
1/4/64G, 8/23/66G,
10/1/66F
Resisters
12/3/67G, 1/5/68F
DRAPER, Henry, Medal
3/25/61I
DRAPER, Jr., William
5/7/63G
DREADNOUGHT (ship)
10/21/60B
DROUGHTS
5/15/62D, 8/20/65H
DR. Strangelove (film)
1/29/64J

DRUGS, Addictive—See NAR-
COTICS
DRUGS & Drug Industry—See
also CANCER—Drug Therapy;
NARCOTICS
Amphetamines
8/26/60J
Antibiotics
3/11/61I, 5/16/61I, 7/15/61I
Cancer
1/5/60I
False Advertising
3/19/61H
Fertility
7/30/65I
Frauds
3/11/64H
Generic
9/5/63H
IUD
2/5/62I
New
4/29/62I
Pain-Killing Drugs
4/16/63I
Prices
6/27/61H, 7/6/61H
Reform
10/25/62H
Research & Development
3/5/64I
Safety
10/6/60H, 4/16/62I,
8/1/62H, 8/17/62H,
8/23/62H, 9/18/62F,
12/28/62H, 1/4/63H,
1/18/63I, 12/20/63H,
2/28/64H, 11/17/64I,
9/30/69I
DRUMMOND, Nelson
7/19/63G
DRURY, Allen
5/2/60J
DRYDEN, Hugh L.
6/1/60G
DRYSDALE, Don
11/15/62J
DR. Zhivago (book)
5/30/60J, 11/1/64B
DUBAI—See TRUCIAL States
DUBCEK, Alexander
6/25/63B, 1/5/68B,
3/16/68B, 3/23/68B,
3/26/68B, 5/5/68B,
7/18/68B, 4/8/68B,
8/27/68B, 9/14/68B,
9/20/68B, 9/23/68B,
9/24/68B, 10/25/68B,
11/17/68B, 11/18/68B,
1/24/69B, 4/3/69B,
4/17/69B, 5/18/69B,
8/23/69B, 10/15/69B
DUBLIN University
6/10/61I
DUBOIS, W.E.B.
12/22/61F, 8/27/63F
DUCHAMP, Marcel
10/1/68J
DUELS
4/20/67B
DUFFY, Martin
7/4/67F
DUHAMEL, Georges
4/13/66J
DUKE, Angier Biddle
9/12/61G
DUKE, Matthew
5/12/60D

DUKE, Patty
4/8/63J
DUKE of Palermo And Other
Plays, The (book)
2/21/69J
DUKE University
4/8/68F, 4/11/68F
DUKLA
8/6/61J
DULLES, Allen
1/26/60A, 11/10/60G,
5/2/61G, 9/27/61G,
1/29/69J
DULLES International Airport
11/17/62H
DU MAURIER, Daphne
8/18/67J
DUMONT, Donald
1/10/66C
DUNCAN, Elizabeth
8/8/62F
DUPAS, Ralph
7/13/62J
DUPLANTIER, Adrian
3/3/62F
DU Pont, E.I. de Nemours &
Co.
3/11/60H, 5/9/61I,
5/22/61H, 3/1/62H
DU PONT, Mrs. Richard
3/23/63J
DU PONT William
12/31/65J
DURFEE, James
4/21/60H
DURHAM, N.C.
5/20/63F
DURRELL, Lawrence
3/30/60J, 4/8/68J
DUSING, Erich
6/9/67B
DUTCHMAN (film)
2/27/67J
DUTSCHKE, Rudi
4/11/68B, 3/14/69B
DUVALIER, Francois
7/15/60D, 8/17/60D,
4/7/61D, 9/15/62D,
4/16/63D, 5/14/63D,
5/15/63D, 5/17/63G,
5/22/63D, 6/4/63D,
8/2/63D, 8/5/63D,
8/22/63D, 4/1/64D
DWIGHT Jr., Edward J.
3/30/63I
DYHRENFURTH, Norman
5/1/63J
DYKES, Jimmy
8/5/60J
DYMSHITS, Veniamin
7/18/62B
DYNAMITE
8/13/66F, 8/14/66F,
8/15/66F, 8/19/66F
DZU, Truong Dinh
5/1/68E

E

EARHART, Amelia
7/1/60J
EARLY Jazz (book)
4/11/68J

FRY, Franklin Clark
6/27/61J

FRY, Varian
9/13/67J

FUENTES, Carlos
2/22/69G

FUENTES, Miguel
1/10/61D

FUGITIVE Felon Act
10/4/61F

FULBRIGHT, James William
1/10/60H, 4/25/60G,
4/28/60G, 5/25/66G

Arts & Culture
12/3/63J

Atomic Energy & Weapons
8/26/63G

Berlin
9/30/61G

Books by
1/24/67J

Central Intelligence Agency
(CIA)
8/14/66G

China (Communist), People's
Republic of
10/10/60G

Cold War
4/5/64F, 9/8/64G

Congress, U.S.
5/4/67G

Congressional-Presidential
Relations
7/31/67G

Cuba
2/16/63G

Dominican Republic
9/15/65G

Espionage & Treason
6/28/60G

European Economic Com-
munity (EEC) (Common Mar-
ket)
1/24/63G

Foreign Aid
2/6/60G

Foreign Relations
10/20/60F, 1/6/61G,
6/29/61G, 8/2/63G,
3/25/64G, 3/26/64G,
3/27/64G, 3/28/64G,
3/31/64G, 5/17/66G,
5/19/69G

Government & Politics
11/29/60G

Laos
4/30/61G, 10/28/69G

Missiles & Rockets
9/16/67G

North Atlantic Treaty Organization (NATO)
10/29/63B

Presidential Campaign of
1964
9/8/64G

Thailand
8/8/69G

Vietnam, South
5/4/61G

Vietnam War
6/15/65G, 10/24/65G,
1/28/66G, 4/28/66G,
5/5/66G, 7/22/66G,
1/22/67G, 1/23/67G,
7/8/67G, 12/8/67G,
1/23/68G, 2/8/68G,
3/5/69G, 10/20/69G

FULBRIGHT Scholarships
11/9/64G

FULLER, Buckminster
11/15/69J

FULLMER, Gene
4/20/60J, 6/29/60J, 3/4/61J,
8/5/61J, 10/23/62J,
2/23/63J, 8/10/63J

**FUND-RAISING, American As-
sociation of**
12/7/60H, 5/8/61H,
6/4/63H, 7/26/64H

FUNGUS
7/15/61I

FUNK, Casimir
11/19/67J

FUNK, Walther
5/31/60B

FUNNY Girl (play)
3/26/64J

G

GABLE, Clark
11/16/60J

GABON

Canada
3/4/68D, 4/25/68D

Coups & Attempted Coups
2/17/64C

Deaths
11/28/67C

Demonstrations & Riots
3/3/64C

France
3/3/64C

Government & Politics
2/20/64C

Rebellions & Revolutions
3/16/64C

United States
3/16/64C

GAGARIN, Yuri
4/12/61I, 4/14/61I, 4/15/61I,
4/16/61I, 4/21/61I, 4/22/61I,
7/15/61B, 7/22/61I, 8/5/61I,
10/15/63I, 3/27/68B,
3/30/68B

GAINESVILLE, Fla.
6/4/63F

GAISSEAU, Pierre Dominique
1/4/68C, 1/8/68C

GAITSKELL, Hugh
2/13/60B, 3/16/61B,
11/2/61B, 6/16/62B,
1/18/63B

Atomic Energy & Weapons
3/27/60B, 5/23/60B,
10/5/60B

Government & Politics
11/3/60B

GALAHAD (book)
6/21/67J

GALAXIES
12/11/60I

GALBRAITH, John Kenneth
3/15/61G, 4/6/63G,
4/25/66G, 4/2/67G,
5/7/67G, 6/26/67J,
8/26/67G, 11/11/67G

India
10/29/62E

GALBRAITH, Thomas
11/8/62G

GALBREATH, John
5/4/63J, 6/8/63J

GALILEE, Sea of
1/26/60C, 8/20/63C,
9/3/63C, 11/14/64C,
11/23/64C, 12/21/64C,

5/4/66C, 6/15/66C,
8/7/66C, 8/20/66C,
2/13/67C, 4/12/67C,
2/14/69C

GALLAGHER, Gordon
4/22/69F

GALLIMARD, Michel
1/9/60J

GALLION, MacDonald
12/1/60F

GAMA e Silva, Luis
5/12/68D

GAMBIA

Government & Politics
6/12/62C, 10/3/63C

Independence
2/18/65C

GANDHI (book)
5/27/68J

GANDHI, Indira
1/14/60E, 1/22/67E,
2/21/67E, 3/14/68E,
4/21/68E, 7/16/69E,
7/22/69E

Atomic Energy & Weapons
6/18/67E

Demonstrations & Riots
4/11/66E

Government & Politics
1/19/66E, 2/18/66E,
11/17/69E

Pakistan
1/26/66E

Travel
4/3/66E

Union of Soviet Socialist Republics (USSR)
7/12/66B

United States
3/28/66G

**GANDHI, (Mahatma) Mohandas
Karamchand**
5/27/68J, 4/14/69J

GANDHI, Ramdas
4/14/69J

GANEY, J. Cullen
2/6/61H

GANGS
8/7/66F

GANTT, Harvey B.
1/28/63F

GARBER, LeRoy
10/23/67F

GARCIA, Carlos
2/20/60E, 3/16/60E,
4/4/60E, 11/14/61E

GARCIA-GODOY, Hector
9/3/65D, 1/6/66D, 1/7/66D,
2/12/66D, 2/26/66D,
3/3/66D, 3/10/66D,
4/7/66D, 6/1/66D, 6/2/66G

GARCIA Villasmil, Martin
4/29/69D

**GARDEN and Other Poems,
The** (poem)
1/7/62J

GARDNER, Bertram
6/24/66F

GARDNER, John
7/3/66F, 8/18/66F,
7/12/67H, 1/3/68H,
1/25/68F, 3/22/68F

GARIN, Vasco Viera
2/4/62B

GARMENT Industry—See
Clothing Industry

GARRETT, Henry F.
8/7/61I

GARRISON, James
2/18/67F, 2/22/67F,
2/24/67F, 2/26/67F,
3/1/67F, 3/17/67F,
4/15/67F, 4/24/67F,
5/8/67F, 5/22/67F,
6/11/67F, 6/19/67F,
6/26/67F, 6/27/67F,
9/21/67F, 12/9/67F,
12/29/67F

GARRISON, Jim
2/6/63F

GARY, Ind.
5/4/64F, 11/7/67F,
4/24/68F

Ethics
2/24/62F

Government & Politics
12/12/62F, 5/2/67F

Racial Unrest
7/27/68F, 7/28/68F,
7/29/68F, 7/30/68F

Strikes & Settlements
5/29/63H

GAS, Natural
2/4/69I

Depletion Allowance
12/1/69H

Deregulation
3/21/60H

Exploration & Discovery
5/12/60E

North Sea
9/21/65B

Output
12/31/61H

Prices
8/5/65H

GASS, William
3/27/68J

GATES, Jr., Thomas S.
1/6/60G, 1/11/60G,
1/19/60G, 1/20/60G,
3/16/60G, 4/27/60G,
6/2/60G, 8/17/60G,
10/7/60G, 12/1/60G,
1/7/61G

GAVILAN, Kid
6/23/64D

GAVIN, James
2/13/61G, 8/11/62G,
1/16/66G, 11/12/67G

GAZA Strip
11/28/65C, 12/19/65C,
8/27/66C, 9/4/66C,
6/12/67C

GBENYE, Christophe
10/29/64C, 11/5/64C

GDANSK, Poland
9/10/67B

GEISART, Harold L.
1/10/60D

GENDEBIEN, Oliver
6/26/60J, 6/11/61J,
6/24/62J

GENERAL Accounting Office
5/20/60G

GENERAL Dynamics Corp.
3/15/60G, 6/6/60H,
3/6/63G, 3/21/63G,
6/28/63G, 7/23/63G,
11/18/63G, 5/10/67G

GENERAL Electric Co.
1/12/60I, 10/2/60H,
10/22/60H, 12/8/60I,
3/14/61H, 3/29/61H,
7/28/62H, 4/26/64H,
10/14/66H, 10/17/66H,
12/31/66G, 7/1/68D,
10/26/69H, 10/27/69H

**GENERAL (Geneva) Agree-
ment on Tariffs & Trade**
11/19/60A, 11/22/67A,
7/1/68A, 7/19/68A,
2/25/69A, 12/3/69A

Great Britain
12/18/64A

Iceland
3/25/68A

Kennedy Round
11/16/64A

Rumania
11/11/68A

Tariff Cuts
1/1/69A

Unaligned Nations
12/1/64A, 11/24/67A

GENERAL Motors Corp.
3/11/60H,
4/12/61H, 5/22/61H,
9/11/61H, 9/20/61H,
3/1/62H, 1/27/64H,
9/25/64H, 10/5/64H,
10/25/64H, 7/7/65H,
7/27/65H, 10/26/65H,
3/9/66H, 11/18/66H,
2/15/67H, 3/10/67H,
12/15/67H, 6/20/69D

Finances
1/28/63H

Prices
9/11/69H

GENET, Jean
2/1/67J

GENETICS
5/21/60I, 10/18/60I,
12/19/61I, 9/9/62I, 3/3/63I,
9/10/63I, 5/3/64I, 11/19/64I,
11/24/64B, 3/16/67I,
10/14/68J, 11/19/68I,
11/22/69I

**GENEVA, International Com-
mission of Jurists**
10/13/61C

**GENEVA Agreement on Indo-
china (1954)**
1/16/61E

GENTILE, Robert
1/14/61D

GEOLOGICAL Society, U.S.
7/22/63H

GEOLOGICAL Survey, U.S.
8/13/60I

GEOPHYSICS
7/31/60I

GEORGETOWN Hospital
11/25/60F

GEORGETOWN University
7/30/60F

**GEORGE Washington, U.S.S.
(ship)**
4/29/60G, 11/15/60G

GEORGE Washington Award
2/22/63F

1/22/63B, 10/18/63B,
11/22/63B, 12/3/63B,
2/11/64B, 2/15/64B,
7/4/64B, 11/11/64B,
12/7/64B, 1/20/65B,
6/3/65B, 6/11/65B, 2/7/66B,
2/8/66B, 4/14/66B,
5/25/66B, 6/27/66G,
7/21/66B, 12/13/66B,
12/18/66B, 12/24/66B,
1/13/67B, 1/14/67B,
1/15/67B, 4/28/67B,
7/12/67B, 1/8/68B,
2/15/68B, 5/19/68B,
5/29/68B, 9/28/68B,
3/13/69B, 3/14/69B

Germany, East
4/11/60B, 8/16/60B,
9/30/60B, 12/6/60B,
12/29/60B, 1/4/63B,
12/2/64B, 1/7/65B,
6/14/65B, 1/31/66B,
6/29/66B, 10/7/66B,
4/12/67B, 5/23/67B,
5/17/68B, 6/14/68B,
12/6/68B, 2/15/69B,
2/17/69B, 4/18/69B,
7/25/69B, 10/6/69B,
10/28/69B, 12/21/69B

Germany, West
10/8/68A

Government & Politics
5/3/60B, 6/13/60B,
8/24/60B, 11/14/61B,
7/11/62B, 10/31/62B,
11/5/62B, 11/19/62B,
11/28/62B, 12/11/62B,
1/22/63B, 2/4/63B,
3/11/63B, 4/23/63B,
10/15/63B, 10/16/63B,
1/30/64B, 7/9/64B,
11/28/64B, 2/14/65B,
4/2/65B, 9/25/65B,
10/26/65B, 11/2/66B,
11/8/66B, 11/9/66B,
11/11/66B, 11/20/66B,
12/1/66B, 3/14/67B,
4/3/67B, 2/1/68B, 3/21/68B,
10/1/68B, 10/2/68B,
12/18/68B, 8/31/69B,
9/30/69B, 10/1/69B,
10/3/69B, 10/21/69B

Grain
10/20/64B, 12/1/64B

Great Britain
8/28/62B, 5/24/65B,
5/27/65B, 7/25/66B,
5/2/67B, 4/1/68B, 2/13/69B,
11/20/69B

Hungary
2/22/67B, 2/23/67B,
4/25/67B, 2/27/69B

Internal Security
5/10/68B, 5/11/68B,
5/12/68B

Iraq
3/16/65C, 5/12/65C

Israel
3/14/60A, 1/9/62C,
3/20/63C, 3/22/63C,
4/7/63C, 5/27/63C,
6/12/63C, 6/15/63B,
5/4/64C, 1/12/65C,
1/20/65C, 2/7/65C,
2/10/65B, 3/7/65B, 3/9/65C,
3/10/65C, 3/11/65C,
3/14/65C, 3/24/65B,
4/15/65B, 5/13/65C,
8/19/65C, 12/29/65B,
5/2/66A, 5/2/66C, 5/3/66C,
5/5/66C, 5/6/66C, 5/8/66C,
5/11/66B, 5/13/66B,
2/28/67C, 12/19/67B

Jews
1/4/60B, 1/5/60B, 1/6/60B,
1/7/60B, 1/11/60B,
1/14/60B, 1/16/60B,
1/17/60B, 1/27/60B,
1/30/60B, 2/6/60B,
2/17/60B, 3/14/60A,
3/19/61B, 11/24/64B

Jordan, Hashemite Kingdom of
2/28/67C

Korea, South
7/4/67B

Lebanon
3/16/65C

Libya
5/29/65C

Medicine & Health
2/13/69I, 2/14/69I

Middle East
3/9/65C, 3/16/65C,
8/15/65B

Missiles & Rockets
9/5/60B, 12/5/63C

Monetary Policy
3/4/61B, 5/9/69B, 9/24/69B,
9/29/69A, 9/29/69B

Monetary System
3/6/61B

Nazis & Neo-Nazi Parties
8/8/63B, 7/20/67B,
9/18/68B, 11/7/68B

Netherlands
4/8/60B

North Atlantic Treaty Organization (NATO)
4/1/60B, 8/19/60B, 9/5/60B,
3/31/61B, 4/17/61B,
5/14/61B, 5/20/61B,
11/26/61B, 1/9/62B,
1/15/63B, 2/4/63B,
2/28/63B, 8/30/63B,
11/11/64B, 11/14/64B,
12/21/65G, 2/27/67B,
3/3/67B, 3/5/67G,
3/20/67G, 4/28/67B,
8/18/68D

Nuclear Power
12/1/68B, 2/22/69B

Pakistan
1/23/61E

Poland
1/24/61B, 2/5/61B, 3/7/63B,
1/15/65B, 1/16/66B,
3/29/66B, 3/27/68B,
11/25/69B, 12/22/69B

Press
10/27/62B, 10/31/62B,
11/5/62B, 11/7/62B,
11/19/62B, 12/11/62B,
2/4/63B, 2/5/69B

Protests & Rallies
11/18/66B

Rumania
1/31/67B, 2/3/67B, 8/3/67B,
8/8/67B, 12/14/69B

Satellites
2/5/61H, 4/28/67B

Science & Technology
7/1/60I, 7/18/60I

Somalia, Republic of
11/10/63C

Spain
2/24/60B, 3/4/60B

Steel
12/19/67B

Sudan
5/16/65C

Union of Soviet Socialist Republics (USSR)
1/11/60B, 1/28/60B,
3/13/60B, 4/6/60B, 6/3/60B,
6/5/60B, 7/29/60B, 9/5/60B,

12/12/60B, 12/31/60B,
6/8/61B, 7/12/61B,
11/13/61B, 11/20/61B,
1/9/62B, 1/21/62B, 3/7/64B,
7/2/64A, 12/23/64B,
5/17/66B, 12/2/66B,
1/28/67B, 2/9/67B,
4/20/67B, 6/15/68B,
9/18/68B, 1/10/69B,
7/25/69B, 10/27/69B,
12/7/69B

United Arab Republic (UAR)
4/7/63C, 6/12/63C

United Nations (U.N.)
5/2/66A

United States
3/15/60B, 2/2/61B, 2/9/61B,
2/13/61B, 2/17/61B,
4/12/61B, 8/19/61B,
9/23/61B, 10/5/61B,
10/14/62B, 1/15/63B,
3/13/63G, 6/22/63B,
6/23/63B, 6/25/63B,
10/25/63B, 12/3/63B,
12/13/63B, 12/27/63B,
6/12/64B, 6/19/64B,
6/27/64B, 11/14/64B,
8/23/65G, 6/27/66G,
9/26/66G, 11/30/66G,
12/18/66B, 2/8/67A,
8/15/67G, 1/30/69B,
2/26/69G, 12/4/69G

United States Bases & Troops
11/26/60G, 10/1/63G,
1/2/64A, 4/20/66B,
5/12/66B, 5/13/66G,
9/27/66G, 5/2/67B,
5/9/67B, 6/20/67B,
3/11/68B, 3/12/68B,
3/19/68B, 5/9/68G,
5/10/68G, 6/10/68B,
9/16/68G, 1/6/69B,
3/30/69B

Vietnam War
6/4/65B, 1/30/68B

Yugoslavia
4/18/60B, 9/3/60B,
6/14/65B, 2/24/67B,
1/31/68B, 2/10/69B

GERM Warfare
8/18/61E, 11/25/69G

GEROW, Richard
8/9/64F

GERTRUDE (book)
3/7/69J

GESELL, Arnold
5/29/61I

GESSNER, George
6/9/64G

GESTIDO, Oscar Daniel
12/6/67D

GHANA—See also African
States, Union of
6/11/65C

African Federation (Proposed)
7/19/64C, 7/20/64C

Amnesties
5/5/62C

Angola
5/12/61C, 5/24/61C

Armed Forces & Defense
9/22/61C, 10/10/61C

Assassinations & Assassination Attempts
8/1/62C, 1/2/64C

Atomic Energy & Weapons
3/19/63C

Budget
7/29/62C

**China (Communist), People's
Republic of**
4/5/66C, 2/22/67C

Communists & Communism
2/22/67C

**Communists & Communism
(International)**
3/1/66C

**Congo, Republic of the (Leopoldville) (formerly Belgian
Congo)**
9/12/60C, 9/23/60C,
11/27/60C, 2/15/61C,
2/18/61C, 10/5/61C

Coups & Attempted Coups
2/24/66C, 4/17/67C,
5/5/67C

Courts
9/12/66C

Cuba
2/22/67C

Deaths
8/27/63F, 2/4/65J

Defectors & Political Exiles
12/28/66C, 1/25/67C

Demonstrations & Riots
2/5/64C

Energy & Power
6/8/66C

Espionage & Treason
6/9/66C

Executions
5/9/67C

Fish & Fishing
3/21/69C

Foreign Aid
12/16/61G, 1/13/62G,
4/13/65C

Foreign Relations
1/10/60C, 8/4/65A

France
2/13/60C, 3/15/60C

Germany, East
6/9/66C

Government & Politics
9/30/61C, 9/7/62C,
1/5/64C, 1/28/64C,
12/1/64C, 3/4/66C,
2/22/67C, 4/2/69C, 5/1/69C

Great Britain
2/15/60C, 1/25/67C

Guinea
3/2/66C, 3/10/66C,
3/14/66C, 10/29/66C,
11/5/66C

Independence
7/1/60C

Internal Security
4/8/61C, 10/3/61C,
12/24/63C, 5/1/64C,
2/8/65C

Ivory Coast
3/16/66C

Nationalization of Industry
10/9/60C

Nigeria
6/9/62C

Organization of African Unity (OAU)
2/28/66C

Peace Corps
8/28/61G

Political Prisoners
2/24/68C, 4/24/68C

Terrorism
9/9/62C, 9/10/62C,
9/22/62C, 10/16/62C

Togoland
2/4/60C, 3/15/60C

Union of Soviet Socialist Republics (USSR)
10/10/61C, 3/11/66C,
3/16/66C, 6/8/66C,

6/9/66C, 2/22/67C,
6/27/68C, 3/21/69C

United Nations (U.N.)
10/30/61A, 12/22/63C,
8/4/65A

United States
12/16/61G, 2/5/64C

GHANDI Society
6/21/63F

GHANIAN Times (newspaper)
9/10/62C

GHEORGHIU-DEJ, Gheorghe
6/25/60B, 4/26/68B

GHOST in the Machine, The
(book)
1/25/68J

GIACOMETTI, Alberto
1/11/66J

GIACOMO Joyce (book)
1/1/68J

GIANNATTASIO, Luis
2/7/65J

GIAP, Vo Nguyen
2/28/64E, 10/21/67E

GIARDELLO, Joey
4/20/60J

GIBRALTAR
3/31/65B, 2/28/66B,
5/18/66B, 5/26/66B,
10/24/66B, 1/5/67B,
4/12/67B, 4/13/67B,
4/25/67B, 6/9/67B,
3/18/68B, 10/9/68C

Foreign Labor
4/18/67B

Great Britain
1/5/67B, 4/12/67B,
4/13/67B

Referendum
6/14/67B, 6/15/67B,
9/1/67A, 9/10/67A,
9/10/67B

United Nations (U.N.)
9/1/67A, 9/10/67A

United States
1/24/68B

GIBSON, Althea
2/23/62J, 2/22/63J

GIBSON, Richard
5/16/61G

GIDE, Andre
5/20/68J

GIDEON, Clarence
3/18/63F

GIEDION, Sigfried
4/10/68J

GIELGUD, John
1/18/68J

GIFFORD, Frank
2/9/61J

GILBERT, Alfred
1/24/61J

GILBERT, Jean-Paul
1/6/69D

GILBERT, Stuart
11/14/60J

GILDERSLEEVE, Virginia
7/8/65J

GILLETTE Razor Co.
1/8/60J

GILLILAND, Whitney
4/21/60H

GILLMAN, Sid
1/7/60J

GILMORE, Voit
12/30/62H

10/7/67C, 4/20/68C,
8/12/69C
Government Employees
7/6/68C
Great Britain
7/3/67B
Guerrilla Warfare
4/25/68C, 4/26/68C,
11/3/68C, 11/21/68C,
2/16/69C, 4/10/69C
Immigration & Refugees
6/23/67C, 7/29/68C
Internal Security
4/29/63C
Iraq
4/27/63C, 12/2/68C,
12/3/68C
Israel
7/4/62C, 7/17/62C,
9/30/62C, 8/25/63C,
5/27/65C, 5/31/65C,
7/14/65C, 9/4/65C,
9/5/65C, 10/31/65C,
11/5/65C, 11/6/65C,
11/17/65C, 12/17/65C,
4/30/66C, 5/11/66C,
5/30/66C, 9/25/66C,
11/12/66C, 11/13/66C,
11/16/66A, 11/21/66A,
11/23/66C, 11/24/66C,
11/25/66A, 11/25/66C,
1/18/67C, 2/19/67C,
6/12/67G, 6/26/67A,
8/1/67C, 8/2/67C, 8/6/67C,
8/15/67A, 9/7/67C,
10/4/67C, 10/14/67C,
10/15/67C, 11/20/67C,
11/21/67C, 12/8/67C,
12/9/67C, 1/2/68C,
1/6/68C, 1/7/68C, 1/8/68C,
1/10/68C, 1/11/68C,
1/13/68C, 1/25/68C,
2/8/68C, 2/11/68C,
2/12/68C, 2/13/68C,
2/14/68C, 2/15/68C,
2/16/68C, 2/18/68C,
2/19/68C, 3/19/68A,
3/21/68C, 3/22/68C,
3/23/68C, 3/24/68A,
3/24/68C, 3/25/68C,
3/28/68C, 3/29/68C,
4/8/68C, 4/14/68C,
4/26/68C, 4/30/68C,
6/4/68C, 6/17/68C,
6/23/68C, 7/25/68A,
8/4/68C, 8/6/68C, 8/16/68A,
8/25/68C, 9/23/68C,
10/16/68C, 11/5/68C,
12/1/68C, 12/2/68C,
12/3/68C, 12/4/68C,
12/15/68C, 12/16/68C,
12/17/68G, 12/20/68C,
1/6/69C, 1/9/69C,
1/11/69C, 1/16/69C,
2/14/69C, 3/14/69C,
3/16/69C, 3/17/69C,
3/21/69C, 3/24/69C,
3/26/69C, 3/27/69A,
3/30/69C, 4/1/69A, 4/9/69C,
5/4/69C, 5/7/69C, 5/9/69C,
5/21/69C, 6/18/69C,
6/22/69C, 6/23/69C,
8/10/69C, 9/22/69C,
10/10/69A, 10/28/69A,
11/13/69C, 11/17/69C,
11/26/69C, 12/28/69C
Palestine Issue
2/29/60C
Palestinian Arab Refugees
2/20/68A
Saudi Arabia
8/29/62C, 11/4/62C,
2/3/63C, 5/24/67C, 6/9/68C

Syria
10/1/61C, 12/1/66C,
12/7/66C, 12/19/66C,
12/29/66C
Union of Soviet Socialist Republics (USSR)
10/3/67B, 10/4/67B,
10/5/67B
United Arab Republic (UAR)
3/12/60C, 10/3/60C,
10/1/61C
United Nations (U.N.)
3/21/68A
United States
2/2/66G, 4/2/66G,
11/21/66G, 1/18/67C,
6/28/67G, 11/8/67G,
2/14/68G, 3/28/68C,
5/30/68C, 4/8/69G
Vatican
7/6/67B
Water Supply
9/4/65C, 6/23/69C,
8/10/69C, 9/22/69C
Yemen
11/25/62C, 1/4/63C
JORDAN, Winthrop
4/24/69J
JORDAN River
2/11/60C, 3/18/60C,
12/8/63C, 5/5/64C,
9/11/64C, 9/13/64C,
1/24/65C, 5/15/66C,
9/5/66C, 6/20/67A, 7/2/67C,
8/6/67C, 8/7/67C,
8/24/67G, 9/23/67C,
9/24/67C, 9/27/67C,
9/27/67G, 1/6/68C,
1/13/68C, 2/8/68C,
2/11/68C, 2/15/68C,
2/16/68C, 3/3/68C,
3/22/68C, 3/24/68C,
3/29/68C, 4/4/68A,
4/14/68C, 4/28/68C,
4/30/68C, 6/8/68C,
6/16/68C, 6/17/68C,
6/18/68C, 6/22/68C,
6/23/68C, 6/28/68C,
7/9/68C, 7/17/68C,
8/25/68C, 11/5/68C,
11/26/68C, 1/6/69C,
4/9/69C, 5/17/69C,
6/11/69C, 8/20/69C
JORDEN, William
10/16/68B
JORNAL do Brazil (newspaper)
12/23/68D
JOSEPH, Raymond
5/22/68D
JOUHAUD, Edmond
4/13/62C, 6/5/62C,
12/22/67B
JOURNAL of the American Medical Association (magazine)
1/26/62I, 3/15/62I, 9/15/62I
JOURNAL of the Canadian Medical Association
5/12/62I
JOURNAL of the National Education Association (magazine)
1/2/64F
JOURNEY to the East (book)
4/29/68J
JOXE, Louis
5/26/61C
JOYCE, James
1/1/68J

JUAN Carlos de Borbon, Prince (Spain)
7/17/69B, 7/23/69B
JUAN of Bourbon, Don (Spanish pretender)
3/29/60B
JUDD, Walter
6/9/60F, 7/25/60F
JUDGMENT at Nuremburg (film)
4/9/62J
JUIN, Alphonse-Pierre
12/28/60B, 1/27/67J
JUMA, Saad
7/5/67C
JUNDI, Abdel Kerim al-
3/2/69C
JUNDI, Khalid al-
9/9/66C
JUPITER (Planet)
12/29/63I, 5/16/64I
JURGENS Byrne, Most Rev. Carlos Maria
3/26/69D
JURIES
4/6/64F, 4/21/64F
Negroes
7/7/64F, 1/19/66F,
1/24/66F, 3/24/66F,
4/10/67F, 10/16/67F
Women
11/20/61F, 10/11/63F
JURISTS, International Commission of
8/7/60E, 6/20/62C
JUSTICE, Department of
6/6/60F, 9/13/60F,
10/24/60G, 1/2/61H,
7/2/61H, 5/24/63F, 1/7/66F,
4/10/66F, 6/27/66F,
2/7/69H
Acquisitions & Mergers
10/1/63H
Antitrust & Monopolies
1/22/62H
Appointments
12/16/60F, 12/28/60F,
2/16/61F, 4/2/62F,
1/28/65F, 2/28/67F
Civil Rights
12/12/64F
Ethics
10/16/62F
Federal Marshals
4/24/63F
Protests & Rallies
6/3/68F
Racial Unrest
11/1/67F
Racketeering
1/3/64H
School Desegregation
4/26/61F, 8/26/69F
Suits
7/26/61F, 8/3/61F,
6/15/62F, 8/28/62F,
12/22/62F, 1/18/63F,
1/22/63F, 3/30/63F,
7/19/63F, 9/2/64F, 1/6/67F,
1/9/67F, 1/11/67F,
2/27/67F, 3/1/67F,
3/20/67F, 4/7/67F,
4/13/67F, 4/14/67F,
4/25/67F, 4/26/67F,
5/19/67F, 6/2/67F, 6/7/67F,
6/23/67F, 7/5/67F,
7/24/67F, 9/11/67F,
9/21/67F, 12/7/67F,
2/7/68F, 2/12/68F,
2/13/68F, 2/14/68F,
2/15/68F, 4/25/68F,

6/12/68F, 1/10/69F,
1/10/69H, 1/15/69F,
1/17/69F, 1/20/69F,
7/10/69F, 10/14/69F
Travel Restrictions
3/31/63D
Wiretapping
11/30/66F
JUVENILE Delinquency
5/11/61F, 5/23/63F
Federal & State Aid
1/26/60F

K

KABUL River
2/14/60E
KABYLIA Mountains
4/6/60C
KACHINGWE, Joe
2/5/68C
KADAR, Janos
3/21/63B, 10/27/64B,
11/28/66B, 2/22/67B,
4/25/67B, 5/20/68B
KAEL, Pauline
4/30/68J
KAGAWA, Toyohiko
4/23/60E
KAHN, Louis
4/11/60J
KAISER, Henry
8/24/67J
KAISER, Roger
3/1/61J
KALONJI, Albert
2/23/61C, 3/8/61C,
4/9/61C, 12/30/61C,
9/8/62C
KAMMAIR, Mikhail
9/24/65J
KAMPMANN, Viggo
2/21/60B, 11/15/60E,
8/31/62B, 9/3/62B
KANE, Maurice
11/28/65J
KANELLOPOULOS, Panayotis
1/1/67B, 4/14/67B,
4/21/67B
KANGAS, John
1/2/69F
KANSAS
7/26/62F,
KANSAS, University of
6/18/60J
KANSAS City, Mo.
4/9/68F
KANSAS City Athletics
12/20/60J
KANSAS City Star
1/20/60J
KAPEK, Antonin
10/12/68B
KAPLAN, Rabbi Jacob
11/29/67B, 1/1/68B
1/6/68B
KAPWEPWE, Simon
1/27/67C
KARAME, Rashid
10/25/61C
KARAMI, Rashid
5/14/60C, 4/24/69C,
10/22/69C, 11/25/69C

KARIBA Dam
12/1/65B, 12/3/65C,
12/4/65C
KARJALAINEN, Ahti
10/7/68B
KARLOFF, Boris
2/2/69J
KARP, Haskell
4/4/69I
KARRAS, Alex
4/17/63J, 3/16/64J
KARUME, Abeid
1/16/64C, 3/8/64C,
4/22/64C
KASAVUBU, Joseph
6/21/60C, 6/30/60C,
7/10/60C, 7/12/60C,
8/7/60C, 9/6/60C, 9/7/60C,
9/9/60C, 9/12/60C,
9/13/60C, 9/14/60C,
9/20/60C, 9/29/60C,
10/29/60A, 11/3/60A,
11/7/60A, 11/16/60A,
11/22/60C, 11/24/60C,
11/27/60C, 12/1/60C,
1/1/61C, 1/24/61C,
1/28/61C, 1/29/61C,
1/30/61C, 2/22/61C,
2/24/61C, 2/27/61C,
3/1/61C, 3/4/61C, 3/8/61C,
3/12/61C, 3/16/61C,
3/18/61C, 3/20/61C,
4/17/61C, 4/24/61C,
4/25/61C, 4/30/61C,
5/6/61C, 5/13/61C,
7/5/61C, 7/31/61C,
8/2/61C, 1/21/64C,
6/30/64C, 7/9/64C,
10/13/65C, 11/24/65C,
3/24/69J
KASHMIR
9/23/60E, 1/4/62E, 2/1/62E,
5/3/62E, 5/31/62E,
6/19/62E, 6/22/62E,
11/27/62E, 11/29/62E,
12/26/62E, 12/27/62E,
2/10/63E, 3/2/63E,
3/16/63E, 4/16/63E,
5/16/63E, 8/13/63E,
2/21/64E, 2/23/64E,
4/8/64E, 4/18/64E,
5/26/64E, 6/16/65E,
8/10/65E, 8/25/65E,
8/30/65E, 8/31/65E,
9/2/65E, 9/4/65E, 9/5/65E,
9/6/65E, 9/10/65E,
9/11/65E, 9/13/65E,
9/14/65E, 9/15/65A,
9/24/65E, 9/28/65E,
10/2/65E, 1/4/66E, 1/5/66E,
2/10/66E, 3/27/66E,
7/2/66E
Accidents & Disasters
9/2/63I
Cease-fire
9/21/65E, 9/22/65A,
9/22/65E, 9/23/65E,
9/25/65E, 9/27/65E,
9/27/65A, 9/29/65E,
9/30/65A, 10/2/65A,
10/14/65A, 11/4/65E,
12/20/65A
Disputed Territory
1/4/60E
Middle East
9/7/65C
Plebiscite
10/24/65E

Deaths
11/6/68J
Elections
3/24/68C
France
1/14/69B
Germany, West
3/16/65C
Government & Politics
5/14/60C, 7/3/60C,
7/20/60C, 10/25/61C,
9/23/64C, 4/9/66C,
4/24/69C, 10/22/69C,
11/25/69C
Guerrilla Warfare
4/24/69C, 4/25/69C,
5/5/69C, 5/6/69C, 5/8/69C,
5/12/69C, 7/30/69C,
8/11/69C, 10/22/69C,
10/27/69C, 10/28/69C,
10/29/69C, 10/30/69C,
10/31/69C, 11/1/69C,
11/2/69C, 11/3/69C,
11/7/69C, 11/20/69C,
12/3/69C
Iran
4/2/69C
Israel
1/24/65C, 6/3/65C,
10/28/65C, 10/29/65C,
1/14/67C, 5/5/67C,
5/5/68C, 5/12/68C,
6/15/68C, 1/1/69C,
1/2/69C, 1/6/69C,
7/30/69C, 8/11/69C,
8/18/69A, 8/18/69G,
8/26/69A, 9/5/69C, 9/6/69A,
10/28/69C, 12/3/69C
Narcotics
2/5/67A
Palestinian Arab Refugees
11/12/69C
Peace-Keeping
1/21/65C
Protests & Rallies
1/4/69C
Rebellions & Revolutions
9/18/62C
Syria
10/19/63C, 10/23/69C,
10/24/69C, 10/25/69B,
10/25/69C, 10/26/69C,
10/27/69C
Union of Soviet Socialist Republics (USSR)
10/18/66C
United States
10/18/66C
LE CARRE, John
10/21/68J
LECHIN Oquendo, Juan
4/27/64D
LE CORBUSIER
8/27/65J
LEE, Harper
7/11/60J, 5/1/61J
LEE, Robert E.
4/19/62J
LEE Ki Poong
4/28/60E
LEFEVRE, Theo
4/25/61B, 4/21/64B
LEGAL Profession
Civil Rights
1/14/63F, 7/6/63F
Deaths
10/6/60G, 1/1/65J, 1/8/65J,
5/4/65J, 12/24/65J,
10/12/68J
Indigent
3/3/63F

Negroes
1/3/66F
Public Defenders
3/8/63F, 3/18/63F,
10/14/63F, 8/20/64F,
11/13/67F
LEGER St. Leger, Alexis
10/26/60J
LEI Chen
10/8/60E
LEIGH, Vivian
7/8/67J
LEIPZIG Fair
2/17/69B
LEMA, Tony
7/10/64J, 9/13/64J
LEMASS, Sean
10/11/61B, 6/27/63B,
10/16/63B
LEMAY, Curtis
5/22/61G, 2/27/62G,
5/6/63G
LEMNITZER, Lyman
8/15/60G, 1/16/62G,
7/20/62G, 7/21/62B,
1/2/63G, 11/12/68B
LE Monde (newspaper)
11/11/60C, 3/22/63D,
3/8/66B, 4/16/66B,
12/24/66B
LEMUS, José
10/26/60D, 1/25/61D
LENART, Jozef
4/6/68D
LEND-LEASE
1/11/60A, 1/27/60A,
2/4/60A
LENIN, Nikolai
10/30/61B, 2/3/64A,
4/21/68B
LENIN Peace Prize
5/3/60A, 4/21/61J,
4/30/62J, 4/21/63I, 5/1/63C
LENSHINA, Alice
8/12/64C
LEONARDO da Vinci
11/23/65J
LEONE, Giovanni
6/19/63B, 6/20/63B,
7/11/63B, 11/5/63B,
6/25/68B
LEONEV, Aleksei
3/18/65I
LEONI, Raul
12/1/63D, 3/11/64D
LEON Valencia, Guillermo
8/7/62D
LE ROY, Marcel
2/10/66B
LESOTHO
Energy & Power
2/23/68C
Independence
10/4/66C
South Africa, Republic of (formerly Union of)
2/23/68C
LESSING, Doris
5/16/69J
LEUKEMIA
9/29/60I, 6/1/62H, 2/3/64I,
4/10/64I
Drug Therapy
12/4/67I
LEVIN, Ira
4/13/67J

LEVIN, Nora
1/5/68J
LEVIN, Rabbi Yehuda
6/17/68J, 6/19/68J
LEVITT, Arthur
9/7/61F
LEVY, Joseph
4/19/65J
LEWIS, Cecil Day
1/1/68J
LEWIS, Clarence Irving
2/3/64J
LEWIS, Rev. Cotesworth
11/12/67G
LEWIS, Henry
2/9/61J
LEWIS, John
1/6/66F
LEWIS, John L.
1/14/60H, 6/11/69J
LEWIS, Oren
8/24/61F
LEWIS, William
2/1/60H
LEXINGTON, N.C.
6/5/63F
LEZHNEV, Vsevolod
3/24/69J
LIAO Cheng-chin
12/19/62A
LIAQUAT Ali Khan, Begum (Pakistan)
1/4/62J
LIBBY, Willard F.
11/3/60I
LIBEL
4/19/60F, 5/27/60F,
5/30/60F, 7/15/60J,
9/6/60F, 10/23/61H,
3/19/62F, 6/28/62F,
8/30/62F, 8/20/63J,
3/9/64F, 9/24/64F,
11/23/64F
LIBERIA
Congo, Republic of the (Leopoldville) (formerly Belgian Congo)
3/3/61C
Elections
5/2/67C
Foreign Aid
1/13/62G
Government & Politics
1/4/60C, 2/9/66C
LIBERTY (ship)
6/8/67C, 6/8/67G, 5/28/68C
LIBRARIES
2/23/66F
LIBYA
Accidents & Disasters
2/22/63I
Arab Meetings
12/27/69C
Common Market
11/28/64C
Coups & Attempted Coups
9/1/69C, 9/1/69G, 9/4/69C,
9/15/69C
Egypt
5/29/65C
English Language
10/1/69C
Germany, West
5/29/65C

Great Britain
2/23/64C, 1/12/65B,
1/19/66C, 11/13/69B,
12/13/69B
United States
9/1/69G, 9/6/69G, 10/2/69C
United States Bases & Troops
2/23/64C, 8/22/64C,
9/25/69C, 9/28/69C
LICENSED Beverage Industries, Inc.
1/21/62H, 8/20/63H
LI Chi
5/25/66E
LICHTENBERGER, Arthur
11/15/61J
LIE, Trygve
12/30/68J
LIEB, Joseph
7/13/61H
LIFE (magazine)
11/30/60A, 12/9/62G,
4/13/64G, 11/23/64G,
10/30/67G, 5/4/69F
LIFE Span
8/9/62H
LIGHT Amplification
7/24/60I
LILIES of the Field (film)
4/13/64J
LIMA, University of
4/11/65D, 8/15/65D,
10/7/65D
LIMITS of Power, The (book)
10/9/67J
LINCOLN, Abraham
7/28/60F, 4/15/66D
LINCOLN, Murray
1/24/61G
LINCOLN Center for the Performing Arts (N.Y.C.)
9/23/62J, 10/12/65J,
9/16/66J, 7/1/69J
LINCOLN Memorial
8/28/63F, 12/22/63F
LINCOLN School (New Rochelle, N.Y.)
1/24/61F
LINDSAY, John V.
2/21/62G, 5/13/65F,
11/2/65F, 12/4/66H,
4/16/68F, 11/4/69F
Arab-Israeli Conflict
6/23/66G
Presidential Campaign of 1964
8/3/64F
Press
4/22/66H
Racial Unrest
7/23/66F
Strikes & Settlements
1/1/66H, 1/10/66H,
1/11/66H
Welfare
8/9/69F
LINDSTROM, Peter
5/10/63I
LINK, Fred
6/5/63F
LINK, Karl
10/22/60I
LINNER, Sture
1/10/62C, 1/26/62C

LIN Piao
6/19/66E, 8/18/66E,
8/31/66E, 11/13/67E,
1/20/67E, 3/19/67E
LION In the Garden (book)
5/28/68J
LIPCHITZ, Jacques
2/15/66J, 9/13/67J
LIPPINCOTT, J.B., Co.
1/30/67J
LIPPMANN, Walter
4/19/61B
LIPSCOMB, Gene
5/10/63J
LIQUOR—See Alcoholic Beverage Industry; Alcoholism
LISSER, Stanley
9/19/66F, 9/20/66F,
9/21/66F, 9/23/66F
LISTON, Charles (Sonny)
9/25/62J, 7/22/63J,
2/25/64J
LITERACY
1/25/62F, 5/24/62A,
6/29/65A, 12/25/65D,
2/10/67A
LITERARNI Listy (magazine)
7/26/68B
LITERATURE—See also Poetry
2/4/60J, 7/15/60J,
12/10/66J, 12/13/66J,
12/16/66J, 12/19/66J,
12/25/66J, 12/27/66J,
1/16/67J, 3/21/67J
Atomic Energy & Weapons
10/20/62G
Awards & Honors
5/2/60J, 10/26/60J,
12/1/60J, 3/14/61J,
4/11/61J, 4/19/61J, 5/1/61J,
5/10/61J, 10/26/61J,
11/20/61J, 3/20/62J,
5/7/62J, 10/25/62J,
11/19/62J, 3/12/63J,
5/6/63J, 11/19/63J,
3/10/64J, 3/26/64J,
10/22/64J, 10/15/65J,
3/15/66J, 4/21/66J,
10/20/66J, 3/8/67J, 5/1/67J,
5/2/67J, 5/24/67J,
10/19/67J, 3/6/68J,
12/31/68B, 4/24/69J,
10/23/69J
Bestsellers
1/20/64J, 1/30/67J
Censorship
1/12/60J, 3/25/60J,
11/2/60J, 1/10/61J, 2/8/66J,
4/23/68F
Deaths
1/4/60J, 1/12/60J, 1/24/60J,
5/30/60J, 7/16/60J,
11/28/60J, 1/10/61J,
7/2/61J, 7/6/62J, 8/9/62J,
5/2/63J, 10/11/63J,
11/22/63J, 2/25/64J,
4/14/64H, 8/3/64J,
8/12/64J, 1/12/65J,
6/30/65J, 7/20/65J,
10/8/65J, 11/21/65J,
12/15/65J, 4/10/66J,
4/13/66J, 3/7/67J, 5/22/67J,
6/7/67J, 9/1/67J, 9/29/67J,
10/9/67J, 10/14/67J,
6/1/68J, 11/25/68J,
12/20/68J, 12/21/68J,
10/21/69J
Fellowships
2/13/69J
Pornography & Obscenity
2/27/64J

8/10/66F, 8/23/66F,
8/31/66F, 9/12/66F,
9/13/66F, 9/14/66F,
9/16/66F, 12/29/66F,
1/9/67F, 4/10/67F,
8/10/67F, 8/13/67F,
8/15/67F, 8/17/67F,
8/18/67F, 1/16/69F
School Desegregation
8/17/64F, 1/11/67F,
8/26/67F, 1/15/68F
Voting Issues
1/13/64F
LOUISIANA State University
6/8/64F
LOUISIANA State University Press
10/30/67J
LOUISVILLE, Ky.
2/24/67F, 5/29/68F
Civil Rights
4/25/67F
Demonstrations & Riots
4/12/67F, 4/13/67F,
4/17/67F, 4/18/67F,
4/19/67F, 4/20/67F,
4/21/67F, 5/3/67F, 5/5/67F,
5/8/67F, 5/11/67F
Housing
12/16/67F
Negroes
4/14/67F
LOUISVILLE & Nashville R.R. Co.
10/16/61F
LOUISVILLE Symphony
9/21/66J
LOURIA, Donald
3/5/67I
LOUW, Eric
10/11/61A
LOVE, John
4/25/67F
LOVELL, Bernard
3/22/64I
LOVELL, Jr., James
9/17/62I, 11/15/66I
LOW, David
9/19/63J
LOWELL, Robert
1/30/67J, 5/19/69J
LOYALTY Oaths
8/11/64H
LOYOLA University
3/23/63J
LSD (Lysergic Acid Diethylamide)—See also Narcotics-Psychedelic Drugs
2/13/67D, 3/5/67I, 3/16/67I,
4/18/67I, 1/24/68A
LUCAS, Jerry
3/4/60J, 3/1/61J, 3/13/62J
LU Cheng-tsao
1/26/67E
LUCIANO, Charles (Lucky)
1/26/62F
LUDWIG, Horst
1/25/60B, 1/30/60B
LUEBKE, Heinrich
8/29/61B
LUISI, Hector
9/26/67A, 4/26/68D
LUMUMBA, Patrice
1/25/60C, 5/17/60C,
5/22/60C, 6/1/60C,
6/13/60C, 6/21/60C,

6/30/60C, 7/10/60C,
7/11/60C, 7/12/60C,
7/15/60A, 7/15/60C,
7/17/60C, 7/18/60C,
7/24/60C, 7/31/60A,
8/1/60C, 8/7/60C, 8/9/60C,
8/10/60C, 8/15/60C,
8/16/60C, 8/20/60C,
8/22/60A, 8/22/60C,
8/24/60C, 8/25/60C,
8/27/60C, 8/28/60C,
8/31/60C, 9/2/60C,
9/6/60C, 9/7/60A, 9/7/60C,
9/9/60C, 9/12/60C,
9/13/60C, 9/14/60A,
9/14/60C, 9/20/60C,
10/11/60C, 10/29/60A,
11/3/60A, 11/7/60A,
11/12/60C, 11/22/60C,
11/28/60C, 12/1/60C,
12/4/60C, 12/5/60C,
12/6/60C, 12/7/60C,
12/8/60C, 12/9/60C,
12/13/60C, 12/14/60A,
12/15/60C, 1/4/61C,
1/9/61C, 1/11/61C,
1/12/61C, 1/18/61C,
1/19/61C, 1/20/61C,
1/22/61C, 1/24/61C,
1/28/61C, 1/29/61C,
1/30/61C, 2/1/61A,
2/10/61C, 2/11/61C,
2/12/61C, 2/24/61C,
2/25/61C, 2/28/61C,
3/1/61C, 3/22/61C,
8/18/61C, 9/28/62C,
4/17/63C
Deaths
2/13/61C, 2/14/61A,
2/15/61A, 2/21/61A,
2/25/61C, 11/14/61C,
11/16/61C
LUNCH Counters—See Restaurants
LUNGS
3/28/60I, 3/7/62I, 3/12/62I
Black Lung Disease
1/26/69H, 2/18/69F,
3/8/69F, 3/11/69F
Cancer
10/24/66I
Smoking
1/11/64I, 1/16/64I, 6/10/64I
Transplants
4/13/69I
LUNS, Joseph
9/26/61E, 9/30/66A,
10/3/67A
LUOW, Eric H.
2/8/60C
LUTHERAN Church
4/10/60J, 4/22/60J,
10/14/60J, 8/13/63J,
7/6/65J
LUTHERAN World Federation
6/27/61J
LUTHULI, Albert John
10/23/61A, 7/21/67J
LU Ting-yi
7/10/66E
LUV (play)
11/11/64J
LUXEMBOURG
4/29/69B,
LUYT, Sir Richard
6/13/64D
LUYTEN, William
5/1/62I
LYNCHING
1/14/60F, 1/17/61F

LYND, Staughton
1/9/66G, 4/24/68J
LYNEN, Feodor
10/15/64I
LYNG, John
9/21/63B
LYSENKO, Trofim
8/8/61I, 4/5/62B, 11/19/64I,
11/24/64B

M

MAARIV (newspaper)
12/22/67C
MABACH, Karl
2/7/60I
MACALESTER College (Minn.)
12/15/68F
MACAO
12/5/66E, 1/3/67E, 6/1/67E
MACAPAGAL, Diosdado
12/30/61E, 5/14/62E,
6/26/62E, 10/6/64E
MACARTHUR, Douglas
7/2/61E, 7/5/61G,
12/24/62J, 1/19/63J,
4/5/64G
Korean War
4/8/64G, 4/9/64G
MACDONALD, Dave
5/30/64J
MACDOWELL, Edward
10/28/60J
MACDOWELL, Edward, Medal
8/19/61J
MACHINISTS, International Association of
6/6/60H, 6/7/60H, 7/21/62H
MACIAS Nguemo, Francisco
3/9/69C
MACK, Richard A.
10/13/60J
MACK, Russell V.
3/28/60F
MACKAWEE, Abdul Quawaee
3/11/67E
MACLEOD, Iain
2/1/60C, 5/5/60C, 5/19/60C
MACMILLAN, (Maurice) Harold
1/10/60C, 11/13/62B,
1/10/68J
Africa
2/3/60C, 2/8/60C, 2/15/60C
Armed Forces & Defense
9/9/61A
Arms Control & Disarmament
3/24/60A, 6/29/60B,
6/30/63B
Atomic Energy & Weapons
3/26/60A, 3/27/60B,
3/29/60A, 11/8/60B,
12/13/60B, 9/3/61A,
1/24/62A, 2/8/62B,
4/10/62A, 4/13/62A,
12/23/62B
Berlin
8/26/61B, 12/22/61B
Commonwealth of Nations
3/8/61A
Economy
2/23/61B
Espionage & Treason
7/12/60B, 6/17/63B,
6/21/63B, 6/22/63B,
9/26/63B

Europe, West
12/18/62B, 12/21/62B
European Economic Community (EEC) (Common Market)
6/13/61B, 7/31/61B,
1/21/63B, 1/30/63B,
2/3/63B, 2/11/63B,
2/12/63B
France
3/13/60B, 1/29/61B,
6/2/62B, 12/16/62B,
1/21/63B
Government & Politics
7/27/60B, 7/28/60B,
7/27/61B, 7/13/62B,
5/10/63B, 10/9/63B,
10/19/63B, 2/10/64B
Health
10/9/63B
Internal Security
5/15/61B
Israel
3/18/60C
Laos
3/26/61E
Nassau Accord
2/5/63B
Nigeria
1/16/60C
North Atlantic Treaty Organization (NATO)
8/11/60B, 4/7/61B
Pakistan
10/30/62E
Press
2/28/61B
Rhodesia
1/18/60C, 1/19/60C,
1/21/60C, 2/21/61C
South Africa, Republic of (formerly Union of)
3/14/61A, 3/19/61C
Summit Conferences & Proposals
5/15/60A, 5/17/60A,
5/20/60B, 8/5/60A,
10/7/60A, 10/15/60B,
12/20/60B, 1/24/61A
Travel
1/5/60C
Union of Soviet Socialist Republics (USSR)
6/2/60B, 6/29/60B,
10/4/60A, 4/26/62B,
4/29/62A
United Nations (U.N.)
9/29/60A, 2/5/62A
United States
10/25/60B, 11/1/60B,
4/4/61B, 4/8/61B, 6/5/61B,
12/23/62B
Vietnam, South
4/6/61E
MACMILLAN Co.
1/25/68J, 3/29/68J,
5/31/68J
MADAGASCAR
3/26/60C
MADDOX, Lester
9/22/61F, 7/3/64F,
7/22/64F, 8/10/64F,
8/13/64F, 12/14/64F,
9/28/66F, 1/11/67F,
4/16/67F
MADDOX (ship)
8/4/64E, 2/23/68G
MADRID, University of
2/25/65B, 3/9/65B,
3/28/65B, 6/26/65B,
8/14/65B, 11/3/65B,
12/11/65B, 4/4/66B,
4/29/66B, 5/2/66B, 5/5/66B,

5/6/66B, 12/19/66B,
1/28/67B, 1/30/67B,
1/31/67B, 2/1/67B, 5/3/67B,
11/30/67B, 12/1/67B,
12/2/67B, 12/4/67B,
12/5/67B, 1/10/68B,
1/11/68B, 1/22/69B,
2/21/69B
MAFIA—See Organized Crime
MAGAZINES—See Press;
names of publications
MAGNETS
1/22/69I
MAGNIN, Cyril
9/29/66F
MAGNUSON, Warren
4/29/68I
MAGRITTE, Rene
8/15/67J
MAHANDI River
8/25/60E
MAHDI, Saadik el
7/27/66C, 5/15/67C
MAHENDRA Bir Bikram Shah Deva, King (Nepal)
12/15/60E, 1/5/61E,
12/10/61E, 1/7/62E,
4/13/63E
MAHER Pasha, Aly
8/23/60C
MAHGOUB, Mohamed Ahmed
5/18/67C, 5/26/68C
MAHMOUD, Hamid
9/19/68C
MAHONEY, William
2/5/64C
MAILER, Norman
11/20/60J, 2/2/61J,
11/13/61J, 9/15/67J,
5/6/68J, 10/24/68J
MAIMONIDES Hospital (N.Y.C.)
12/6/67I
MAISONS a l'Estaque (art object)
10/14/65J
MAI Van Bo
2/22/67E
MAJALI, Abdel Wahab
8/7/67C
MAJALI, Hazza
8/29/60C, 9/6/60C,
12/29/60C
MAKARIOS, Archbishop
1/18/60B, 8/16/60B,
1/1/63B, 12/21/63B,
1/1/64B, 1/31/64B, 2/2/64B,
2/6/64B, 2/13/64B, 4/4/64B,
4/11/64B, 4/15/64B,
4/22/64B, 7/3/64B,
7/27/64B, 8/8/64B,
8/25/64B, 8/29/64B,
8/31/64B, 5/3/65B,
11/23/65B, 2/2/66B,
6/23/66B, 12/29/67B,
2/25/68B
MAKHOUS, Ibrahim
5/5/66C
MAKING of the President, 1960, The (program)
5/25/64J
MAKING of the President 1960, The (book)
5/7/62J
MALAGASY Republic
3/8/61C, 3/9/61C

9/3/65I, 2/24/69I, 2/27/69I,
7/30/69I, 7/31/69I, 8/5/69I,
9/11/69I, 9/15/69I

MARTELLI, Giuseppe
4/26/63B, 7/15/63B

MARTIN, Billy
8/4/60J, 8/22/60J

MARTIN, David
5/14/64F

MARTIN, Graham
1/18/67E

MARTIN, J. Robert
7/10/63F

MARTIN, Paul
9/5/64E, 6/16/67B

MARTIN, Ralph
1/23/69J

MARTIN, William H.
8/5/60G, 9/6/60A

MARTIN, William McChesney
7/17/62H, 2/1/63H,
2/7/63H, 5/4/66H,
9/14/67H, 12/4/67H,
4/19/68H, 10/17/69H

MARTINEZ, Rodolfo
11/19/62D

MARTINEZ Barrio, Diego
1/1/62B

MARTINIQUE
10/22/65D,

MARTI, Jose
1/28/60D

MARX, Chico (Leonard)
10/11/61J

MARX, Harpo (Arthur)
9/28/64J

MARX, Robert
9/5/60G

MARYLAND
Abortion
3/25/68F
Apportionment
7/26/62F, 2/3/64F
Church-State Relations
6/19/61F
Government Employees
11/6/67F
Negroes
2/16/60F, 7/11/61F,
9/13/61F, 9/25/61F,
11/3/61F, 11/8/61F,
11/11/61F, 2/17/63F,
3/1/63F, 6/14/63F, 7/7/63F,
2/26/64F, 5/12/66F,
5/22/66F, 5/23/66F,
1/9/67F, 3/3/67F, 7/24/67F,
7/25/67F, 7/26/67F,
8/14/67F, 3/27/68F,
3/28/68F, 3/29/68F,
3/30/68F, 5/18/68F,
5/19/68F
Prisons & Prisoners
7/8/66F

MARYLAND, University of
11/24/62J, 1/8/64I

MASAPAGAL, Diosdado
11/14/61E

MASARYK, Jan
4/2/68B, 4/3/68B, 4/16/68B,
4/19/68B, 5/7/68B

MASARYK, Thomas
5/14/68B

MASEFIELD, John
5/10/61J

MASFERRER Rojas, Rolando
1/4/67F

MASPES, Antonio
8/28/62J

MASSACHUSETTS
8/12/61F
Accidents & Disasters
4/11/66I
Birth Control & Family Planning
5/10/66I, 4/6/67F
Elections
11/6/62F
Government & Politics
3/14/62F, 6/9/62F,
6/16/62F, 9/18/62F
Negroes
6/18/63F, 9/7/63F,
12/25/68F

**MASSACHUSETTS, University
of**
2/13/69F

**MASSACHUSETTS Institute of
Technology**
4/24/62I, 5/10/62I, 5/12/63I,
9/15/63I, 12/14/69J

MASSAMBA-DEBAT, Alphonse
8/15/63C, 8/15/64C,
8/1/68C, 8/2/68C, 8/3/68C,
8/4/68C

MASSE, Marcel
6/22/67D

MASS Transit—See Transit Sys-
tems

MASSU, Jacques
1/19/60C, 1/22/60C,
1/24/60C

MASTERS, William
4/18/66J

MASURIUM (Element)
12/7/60I

MA Szu-tsung
4/12/67J

**MATHEMATICAL Association
of America**
1/25/62I

**MATHEMATICAL Sciences,
Conference Board of the**
1/23/61I

MATHEMATICS
1/23/61I, 2/26/62J
Awards & Honors
1/25/62I
Deaths
8/10/60I
Study & Teaching
3/6/67A

MATHEWS, Herbert
5/5/69J

MATOS, Huber
1/3/68D

MATSU—See Quemoy & Matsu

MATTERHORN
2/4/62J

MATTHEWS, Thomas
3/29/64I

MAUDLING, Reginald
4/3/63B

MAUGHAM, W. Somerset
5/10/61J, 12/15/65J

MAULDING, Reginald
4/14/64B

MAURER, Ion
6/23/67A

MAURITANIA
3/25/68C
Independence
10/19/60C, 11/28/60C

Morocco
11/28/60C
United Nations (U.N.)
12/4/60A, 4/19/61A,
10/27/61A
Water Supply
1/22/69C

MAURITIUS
1/20/68C, 1/21/68C,
1/22/68C, 1/23/68C,
3/17/68C, 3/18/68C
Independence
8/22/67C, 3/12/68C
Rebellions & Revolutions
5/13/65B
United Nations (U.N.)
4/24/68A

MAUROIS, Andre
5/23/66J, 10/9/67J

**MAX Planck Society for the
Promotion of Sciences**
5/19/60I

MAXWELL, Jr., Allison
5/24/62H

MAYER, Jacquelyn
9/8/62J

MAYER, Maria
11/5/63I

MAYORS, U.S.
12/4/66F, 11/7/67F

MAYORS, U.S. Conference of
6/15/66F, 6/19/67F,
6/21/67F

MAYS, Willie
1/28/60J, 2/20/63J,
1/15/64J

MAZEROSKI, Bill
10/13/60J

MAZZILLI, Paschoal
4/2/64D, 4/11/64D

MBA, Leon
9/11/62C, 2/17/64C,
2/20/64C, 3/3/64C,
3/16/64C, 11/28/67C

MCCARRAN Act (1950)
6/5/61F

**MCCARRAN-WALTER Immi-
gration Act of 1952**
5/23/62G

MCCARTHY, Eugene
10/9/67J, 10/26/67G
Armed Forces & Defense
4/22/68G, 8/9/68G
China (Communist), People's
Republic of
10/16/67G
Cuba
7/17/68G
Espionage & Treason
5/9/60G
Foreign Relations
1/24/66G
Government & Politics
4/21/68G
Labor
3/30/60H
Missiles & Rockets
7/10/68G
North Atlantic Treaty Organization (NATO)
4/19/68G
Presidential Campaign of
1964
7/30/64F
Presidential Campaign of
1968
11/30/67F, 12/2/67F,
1/3/68F, 1/5/68F, 1/6/68F,
1/8/68F, 3/12/68F,
3/19/68F, 3/25/68F,

3/27/68F, 4/2/68F,
4/23/68F, 5/7/68F,
5/14/68F, 5/19/68F,
5/28/68F, 6/1/68F, 6/4/68F,
6/11/68F, 6/12/68F,
6/18/68F, 6/22/68F,
6/28/68F, 6/29/68F,
6/30/68F, 7/20/68F,
8/21/68F, 8/30/68F,
10/8/68F, 10/9/68F,
10/29/68F
Vietnam War
5/9/66G, 12/10/67G,
1/1/68G, 1/12/68G,
1/14/68G, 4/1/68G,
4/2/68F, 5/22/68F,
6/13/68F, 6/23/68F,
7/7/68F, 7/23/68F

MCCARTHY, Joseph R.
10/6/60G, 1/17/69F

MCCARTHY, Mary
1/20/64J, 9/6/67J

MCCARTNEY, James
11/30/69J

MCCLELLAN, John
1/25/61H, 6/27/62F

MCCLELLAN, John L.
2/21/60F

MCCLOSKEY, Matthew
9/10/64F

MCCLOY, John J.
1/2/61G, 7/30/61A

MCCLURE, Wilbert
9/4/60J

MCCOMB, Miss.
9/23/64F, 10/11/64F,
10/23/64F

MCCONAUGHY, Walter P.
4/19/60G

MCCONE, John
10/3/60G, 12/18/60G,
1/3/61H, 9/27/61G,
1/19/62G, 1/31/62G,
2/6/63G, 2/19/63D,
8/16/63G, 2/13/64F

MCCONNAUGHY, Walter
2/8/61E

MCCORMACK, John W.
1/3/61F, 8/31/61F, 1/9/62F,
1/10/62F, 12/6/63F,
10/11/67G

MCCORMICK, Austin
2/15/68F

MCCRACKEN, Paul
12/4/68H

MCCULLERS, Carson
9/29/67J, 7/31/68J

MCDERMOTT, Terry
2/4/64J

MCDIVITT, James
9/17/62I

MCDONALD, David J.
9/19/60H, 9/23/60H,
5/6/63G

MCDONALD, Irving
11/21/60A

MCDONALD, Levi S.
5/10/60H

MCDOWELL, Cleve
9/24/63F

MCDOWELL, Harris
10/21/64G

MCGALTHERY, Dave
6/13/63F

MCGANNON, Donald H.
1/25/60J

MCGEE, Gale
6/1/66G

MCGILL, Ralph
2/4/69J

MCGILL University (Canada)
11/25/68D, 3/29/69D

MCGINLEY, Phyllis
5/1/61J

MCGOVERN, George
12/15/60G, 2/9/61G,
4/18/62F, 8/10/68F,
8/14/68G, 8/19/68G,
3/17/69G
Foreign Aid
5/6/61G
Vietnam War
5/29/66G

MCGRAW-HILL Book Co.
3/31/67J, 8/7/67J, 11/1/67J,
2/1/68J

MCGUIRE Air Force Base
6/7/60G

MCILVAINE, Robinson
10/30/66C

MCINTIRE, Carl
2/24/60F, 5/13/64F

MCKAY, John
12/8/62J, 1/9/63J

MCKECHNIE, Bill
1/28/62J

MCKEITHEN, John
8/17/67F

MCKELDIN, Theodore
5/23/66F

MCKEOWN, Sean
12/21/60A, 12/10/61C

MCKINLEY, Charles
2/11/62J

MCKINLEY, Chuck
7/7/61J, 7/6/63J, 12/28/63J

MCKISSICK, Floyd
6/20/63F, 6/2/66F, 6/7/66F,
7/2/66F, 3/30/67F

MCKNEALLY, Martin
8/26/60G

McKONE, John R.
1/27/61A

MCKOY, Roy
4/28/67F

MCLAREN, Bruce
6/3/62J, 11/18/62J

MCLUHAN, Marshall
3/1/67J

MCMILLAN, Edwin
7/30/63I

MCNAIR, Robert
2/9/68F

MCNAMARA, Robert
1/23/67G
Aircraft, Military
12/22/64G
Armed Forces & Defense
12/13/60G, 7/10/61G,
10/27/61G, 1/8/62G,
2/17/62G, 7/7/62H,
11/25/62G, 12/4/62G,
1/31/63G, 12/7/63G,
12/12/63G, 1/27/64G,
4/24/64G, 11/18/64G,
12/5/64G, 12/12/64G,
1/21/65G, 7/14/65G,
12/6/65G, 3/2/66G,

4/24/66G, 6/22/67F,
9/7/67F
Arms Control & Disarmament
1/23/67G, 5/18/67G,
11/11/68B
Astronautics
3/8/61G, 12/10/63I
Atomic Energy & Weapons
9/23/61G, 8/13/63G,
11/18/63G, 8/17/64G,
3/7/66G
Awards & Honors
6/3/66F, 6/8/66F
Berlin
8/25/61G
Books by
8/28/68J
China (Communist), People's Republic of
12/15/65G, 2/23/66G
Civil Defense
7/26/61G, 2/9/62G
Civil Rights
7/26/63F, 12/26/67F
Cuba
10/23/62A, 10/23/62G,
2/28/63D, 3/29/63G
Defense Contracts
3/12/63G
Draft
8/23/66G
Elections
11/6/66G
Espionage & Treason
7/19/63G
Ford Motor Co.
11/9/60H
Foreign Relations
5/18/66G
Germany, West
9/28/62B
Government & Politics
2/27/67G
Greece
5/11/67G
Korea, North
2/4/68G
Labor
1/19/61H
Laos
11/18/64E
Missiles & Rockets
9/18/67G, 11/3/67G
North Atlantic Treaty Organization (NATO)
7/24/61B, 12/17/63B,
4/30/66G, 9/23/66G
Presidential Campaign of 1964
8/17/64G
Ships, U.S. Navy
10/14/63G
Union of Soviet Socialist Republics (USSR)
11/10/66G, 11/3/67G,
2/1/68G
United States Bases & Troops
5/13/66G
Vietnam, North
3/5/64E
Vietnam, South
1/16/62G, 3/15/62E,
4/9/62G, 5/9/62E,
7/23/62G, 9/21/63G,
9/29/63G, 10/2/63G,
11/20/63G, 12/19/63E,
12/21/63E, 12/21/63G,
1/27/64E, 2/18/64G,
3/8/64E, 3/17/64E,
3/17/64G, 3/26/64E,
3/26/64G, 3/29/64E,
4/24/64G, 5/12/64G,

5/13/64E, 5/14/64E,
5/15/64G
Vietnam War
8/6/64G, 9/19/64E,
4/26/65G, 7/20/65G,
11/27/65E, 11/29/65G,
1/24/66G, 3/30/66G,
6/11/66G, 10/10/66E,
11/5/66G, 1/23/67G,
2/1/67G, 2/15/67G,
2/24/67G, 3/1/67G,
4/27/67G, 7/7/67E,
7/8/67E, 7/9/67E, 7/10/67E,
7/11/67E, 7/12/67G,
8/25/67G, 9/7/67G
World Bank
11/29/67G, 9/30/68A
MCNEELEY, Tom
12/4/61J
MCSHANE, Terence
9/26/60H, 10/28/60H
MCSORLEY, Edward
4/19/61J
MEADVILLE, Miss.
11/6/64F
MEANY, George
1/11/60H, 2/15/60H,
10/7/60G, 1/19/61H,
4/24/61H, 10/10/61H,
5/25/62H, 11/9/62F,
11/12/62H, 11/14/63H,
11/18/63H, 2/20/64H,
5/5/65H, 2/3/67H,
2/24/67H, 5/8/67H,
12/4/67H, 12/11/67H,
12/12/67G, 2/19/68H,
2/21/68H, 8/30/69H
Civil Rights
11/11/61F
Collective Bargaining
2/26/62H
Ethics
10/23/61H
Government & Politics
2/21/67H, 2/23/67H
Negroes
2/22/66H
Strikes & Settlements
1/11/66H
Taxes
6/29/62H, 8/23/67H
Vietnam War
12/30/65G
Wages & Hours
8/31/63H
MEASLES
3/24/67D
Vaccine
3/15/62I, 3/21/63I
MEAT
11/3/65H
MEAT Industry
5/10/60I
Income
8/1/60H
Inspection
12/6/67H, 12/15/67H
Strikes & Settlements
1/2/60H, 1/7/60H,
2/19/60H, 3/10/60H
MEDAWAR, Peter B.
10/20/60I
MEDICAID
3/22/60F, 12/9/69F
MEDICAL Quackery, National Conference on
10/7/61I
MEDICARE
3/30/60F, 5/4/60F, 5/5/60F,
6/3/60F, 6/29/60F,
8/13/60F, 8/17/60F,

8/23/60F, 8/29/60F,
1/11/61F, 2/13/61F,
2/21/61F, 1/6/62F,
1/11/62F, 2/27/62F,
3/28/62F, 5/20/62F,
5/21/62F, 5/23/62F,
6/29/62F, 7/5/62F,
7/17/62F, 1/4/63F,
2/21/63F, 5/17/63F,
2/10/64F, 5/6/64F,
10/3/64F, 10/24/64F,
2/7/65I, 2/16/65H, 4/6/65F,
4/8/65F, 7/9/65F, 7/21/65F,
7/30/65F
Social Security
12/2/64F
MEDICINE & Health—See also Atomic Energy—Health Hazards; Drug & Drug Trade; Osteopathy; Viruses; disease names
3/29/68F
Astronautics
3/17/62I
Awards & Honors
10/20/60I, 10/22/60I,
9/16/64I, 10/14/65I,
10/13/66J, 10/18/67I,
11/19/68I, 10/16/69I
Communicable Diseases
4/8/64I
Costs
8/23/66H
Deaths
1/13/60I, 5/7/60I, 5/24/60E,
7/15/60I, 7/17/60I, 8/31/60I,
9/4/60I, 9/20/60I, 11/2/60I,
11/9/60I, 12/29/60I,
1/18/61I, 2/1/61I, 3/4/63J,
9/15/64I, 3/28/65I, 9/5/65J,
11/19/67J, 12/22/67J,
2/21/68J, 6/24/68J
Discrimination
6/19/62F, 3/7/66F, 9/1/66F,
2/13/68F
Doctors
11/14/60G, 5/1/61I
Education
2/24/61F, 4/24/63H,
9/12/63H
Expenditures
2/1/62H
Federal Aid
1/12/61F, 1/30/61F,
2/21/61F, 10/5/61F,
1/18/62F, 9/19/64I, 3/1/66F,
3/7/66F
Finances
12/6/62H
Government Controls
6/20/67I
Health Insurance
5/7/60F, 5/5/64H, 4/30/66F,
7/17/69F
Health Workers
3/4/68F
Hospital Ship
9/22/60G
Lobbying
8/5/66F
Personnel
4/26/68F
Research & Development
10/2/60F, 8/24/66F,
1/13/67I, 12/14/67I,
4/13/69I, 9/10/69I,
10/30/69I
Smoking
6/27/62I
State of
5/21/62I
Women
6/8/61I

MEDICO Inc.
1/18/61I
MEDINA, Capt. Ernest
12/4/69F
MEDITERRANEAN Sea
5/30/67B, 1/24/68B,
1/27/68B, 6/25/68B,
2/16/69B, 4/10/69B
MEDIUM is the Message: An Inventory of Effects, The (book)
3/1/67J
MEES, Charles Edward Kennet
8/15/60I
MEET the Press (program)
12/18/60G, 11/19/61F,
11/19/67G
MEIN, John
8/28/68D
MEINSCHEIN, Warren
3/16/61I
MEIR, Golda
3/20/63C, 4/12/69C,
6/30/69C, 9/25/69G
Arab-Israeli Conflict
10/9/61C, 4/30/69C
Economy
12/29/69C
Government & Politics
1/10/66C, 3/3/69C,
3/17/69C
United Nations (U.N.)
10/10/60C
United States
11/16/69C
Vietnam War
11/16/69C
War Crimes
6/14/60A
MEITNER, Lise
10/27/68J
MELBOURNE University
10/20/60I
MELEKH, Igor
10/27/60A, 11/4/60A,
11/28/60A, 3/24/61A
MELLAH, Amar
5/7/68C
MELLON, Paul
6/6/64J, 3/3/67J
MELNICK, Joseph
2/3/64I
MEMOIRS (book)
6/23/67J, 3/6/68J
MEMOIRS: 1925-1950 (book)
11/6/67J
MEMPHIS, Tenn.
2/6/62F, 2/12/68F
Civil Rights
2/25/68F
Demonstrations & Riots
4/4/69F
Racial Unrest
3/25/68F, 11/10/69F
Strikes & Settlements
2/23/68F, 3/5/68F,
3/13/68F, 3/14/68F,
3/29/68F, 4/16/68F

MENADIONE
3/29/63I
MENDERES, Adnan
4/30/60B, 5/5/60B,
5/15/60B, 5/21/60B,
5/22/60B, 5/27/60B,
6/1/60B, 6/3/60B, 9/29/60B,
10/6/60B, 10/14/60B,
4/20/61B, 9/15/61B,
9/17/61B, 5/31/62B
MENDES-FRANCE, Pierre
9/25/61B, 11/27/67J
MENDEZ Montenegro, Julio Cesar
3/6/66D, 4/10/66D,
7/1/66D, 8/29/68D
MENINGITIS
4/28/62I, 10/30/69I
MEN in Prison (book)
11/6/69J
MENNINGER, William Claire
9/6/66J
MENNINGER Foundation
9/6/66J
MENON, V. K. Krishna
4/6/60E, 4/9/60E,
12/18/61E, 10/31/62E,
2/21/67E, 4/23/67E
MENSHIKOV, Mikhail
3/30/62B
MENTAL Health
5/31/60I, 1/5/61I, 2/5/63F,
10/9/68J, 10/14/68J,
12/7/69I
Civil Rights
1/12/67F
Deaths
7/25/63I, 9/6/66J, 3/17/68J,
11/30/69J
Desegregation
4/26/66F
Drug Therapy
1/8/64I, 3/5/64I
Psychoanalysis
9/28/65J
Research & Development
5/10/63I
MENTAL Retardation
12/9/61H, 10/15/62F,
2/5/63F, 9/10/63H,
9/13/63F, 10/24/63F,
2/24/69F
MENZEL, Jiri
10/15/67J
MENZIES, Robert
1/20/66E
MERCHANT, Livingston
11/7/61E
MERCHANT Marine—See Shipping & Shipbuilding Industry
MERCK, Sharp & Dohme
1/4/68I
MERCOURI, Melina
10/18/60J
MERCURY (Planet)
4/20/65I
MERCY Killings
3/7/69B
MEREDITH, James
6/25/62F, 9/10/62F,
9/20/62F, 9/27/62F,
9/28/62F, 9/30/62F,
10/1/62F, 10/3/62F,
10/17/62F, 11/1/62F,

Indonesia
6/27/65C
Jordan, Hashemite Kingdom of
6/15/67C
Libya
2/23/64C
Personal
7/24/68C, 7/26/68C
Saudi Arabia
12/18/69C
Summit Conferences & Proposals
9/30/60A
Unaligned Nations
11/19/61A
Union of Soviet Socialist Republics (USSR)
5/24/64C, 12/23/68C, 12/24/68C, 6/13/69C
United Nations (U.N.)
9/27/60C
United States
5/7/60C, 12/28/64G, 4/18/65C, 7/23/69C
Yemen
5/1/66C
Yugoslavia
7/12/68B

NASSER, Mohammed
7/4/65C, 7/12/65C

NASUTON, Abdul
2/21/66E

NATCHEZ, Miss.
12/3/65F
Bombings & Bomb Plots
2/27/67F
Racial Unrest
10/5/65F

NATCHEZ, Tenn.
3/2/67F, 3/4/67F

NATIONAL—For those organizaitons not found here, see key word

NATIONAL Academy of Engineering (Proposed)
4/23/63I

NATIONAL Academy of Foreign Affairs (Proposed)
2/11/63G

NATIONAL Academy of Sciences
1/9/63H, 4/17/63G, 4/23/63I, 4/19/64I, 4/29/64I

NATIONAL Academy of Television Arts & Sciences
5/25/64J

NATIONAL Aeronautics & Space Administration (NASA)
3/9/60I, 6/11/60H, 7/1/60I, 7/28/60I, 8/4/60I
Appropriations
2/4/64I, 7/13/64I

NATIONAL Airlines
1/4/60H, 1/14/60H, 1/20/60H, 10/13/60J, 3/14/61H

NATIONAL Archives
11/1/66F, 1/5/68I

NATIONAL Association for the Advancement of Colored People (NAACP)
1/4/60F, 1/10/60C, 2/23/60F, 6/25/60F, 7/10/60F, 4/7/61F, 5/22/61F, 9/23/61F, 4/5/62F, 1/14/63F, 3/4/63F, 7/4/63F, 1/8/66F, 3/8/66F,

4/27/66F, 3/5/67F, 10/13/67F, 2/7/69F
Alabama
12/29/61F
Black Power
3/23/63F, 7/4/66F, 7/5/66F, 7/6/66F, 1/17/68F
Boycotts
3/3/66F
Colleges & Universities
5/12/69F
Conventions
7/12/61F, 7/13/61F, 7/16/61F, 7/1/63F, 7/5/63F, 6/24/64F, 6/27/64F, 7/10/67F, 7/11/67F, 7/14/67F
Courts
6/26/61F
Deaths
8/27/63F
Demonstrations & Riots
7/16/67F
Draft
5/17/67G
Equal Opportunity
6/18/63F
Government & Politics
1/2/62F, 1/3/67F,
Housing
8/10/66F
Labor
10/16/62F, 11/9/62F
Law & Legislation
5/10/61F
Marches
3/4/67F
Police Brutality
11/19/67F
Presidential Campaign of 1964
9/6/64F
Racial Unrest
4/20/67F
School Desegregation
8/24/61F, 2/11/62F, 4/20/62F, 5/18/63F, 5/16/66F
Suits
10/10/61F, 5/31/66F, 1/19/67F, 7/12/67F, 9/3/69F
Vietnam War
4/10/67F, 7/15/67F
Voting Issues
7/9/61F, 5/28/63F
Zoning Laws
12/6/69F

NATIONAL Association for the Prevention of Addiction to Narcotics
9/11/63F

NATIONAL Association of British Manufacturers
9/16/62B

NATIONAL Association of Broadcasters
4/3/62J

NATIONAL Association of Manufacturers (NAM)
12/6/61H, 12/5/62H, 12/4/63H, 7/13/67H, 8/21/67H

NATIONAL Association of Real Estate Boards
7/26/66F

NATIONAL Basketball Association (NBA)
3/25/60J, 4/9/60J, 5/17/60J, 3/10/62J, 5/1/63J

NATIONAL Board of Review
12/21/62J

NATIONAL Book Awards
3/14/61J, 3/12/63J, 3/10/64J, 3/15/66J, 3/8/67J, 3/6/68J, 3/10/69J

NATIONAL Boxing Association
3/5/60J, 10/25/60J

NATIONAL Broadcasting Co. (NBC)
1/8/60J, 2/11/60J, 2/16/60J, 4/25/60F, 9/17/60G, 12/18/60G, 2/12/63B, 10/5/63E, 1/5/64G, 6/19/67F, 11/19/67G

NATIONAL Cancer Institute
1/5/60I, 9/15/61I, 7/17/63I, 10/15/63I, 9/19/64I

NATIONAL Catholic Welfare Conference
3/1/62F

NATIONAL Center of Atmospheric Research
6/26/60I

NATIONAL Civic Union
9/30/61D

NATIONAL Collegiate Athletic Association
1/6/60J, 4/26/60J, 1/13/62J, 12/24/62J, 1/19/63J, 12/18/63J, 3/21/64J

NATIONAL Conference of Catholic Bishops
4/11/67J

NATIONAL Council of Churches
1/4/60G, 6/1/60J, 9/13/62J

NATIONAL Council on the Arts
9/3/64J

NATIONAL Defense Education Act of 1958
6/15/60F, 7/30/60F, 9/12/61F, 10/3/61F, 10/2/62F

NATIONAL Education Association (NEA)
7/1/60F, 4/25/61F, 6/30/61F, 7/6/62H, 9/21/62F, 1/30/63H, 5/11/64H, 5/19/64H

NATIONAL Farmers Organization
8/31/62H

NATIONAL Farmers Union
3/19/63H, 3/15/67F

NATIONAL Farm Workers Association
4/6/66H, 6/21/66H

NATIONAL Fire Protection Association
5/11/60H, 1/2/63H

NATIONAL Football Foundation
12/5/61J

NATIONAL Football League
1/26/60J, 2/8/60J, 3/9/60J, 6/17/60J, 12/26/60J, 1/8/62J, 5/21/62J

NATIONAL Foreign Trade Convention
10/31/62H

NATIONAL Gallery (London)
8/23/61J

NATIONAL Gallery of Art (Washington, D.C.)
1/8/63J, 2/20/67J

NATIONAL Board of Review
12/21/62J

NATIONAL Geographic Society
7/22/61I

NATIONAL Goals, President's Commission on
2/3/60F, 11/27/60G, 11/27/60H, 11/27/60I

NATIONAL Guard
1/7/60H, 7/11/61G, 8/1/61G, 9/19/61G, 12/4/61G, 4/4/62G, 5/28/64H, 7/26/64F, 12/12/64G, 3/18/65F, 3/19/65F, 3/20/65F, 9/2/65F, 7/15/66F, 7/19/66F, 7/20/66F, 8/24/66F, 8/31/66F, 9/2/66F, 9/28/66F, 5/2/67F, 6/12/67F, 7/19/67F, 7/26/67F, 7/30/67F, 8/10/67F, 8/17/67F, 11/5/67F, 2/9/68F, 2/11/68F, 5/20/68F, 5/26/68F, 7/25/68F, 12/18/68F, 4/3/69F, 5/25/69F
Civil Rights
6/14/63F
Negroes
6/27/63F, 1/7/69F
Reorganization
12/4/62G

NATIONAL Highway Safety Agency
2/16/67H

NATIONAL Hockey League
12/1/60J

NATIONAL Industrial Conference Board
2/13/61H, 6/12/66F

NATIONAL Industrial Recovery Act
11/27/60F

NATIONAL Institute of Arts & Letters
3/20/62F, 4/17/62J

NATIONAL Institute of Dental Research
5/13/61I

NATIONAL Institute of Neurological Diseases & Blindness
7/26/62I

NATIONAL Institutes of Health
6/1/61J, 12/19/61I, 12/28/62F

NATIONAL Invitational Tournament
3/21/64J

NATIONAL Labor Relations Board (NLRB)
4/4/60H, 8/26/60H, 9/2/60H, 9/14/60H, 9/15/60H, 12/29/60H, 4/17/61H, 7/20/61H, 7/2/64H

NATIONAL League (Baseball)
7/13/60J, 7/18/60J, 8/2/60J, 10/17/60J, 10/18/60J, 11/17/60J, 11/23/60J, 4/22/61J, 5/8/61J, 10/10/61J, 7/20/62J, 6/21/64J

NATIONAL Museum (Jerusalem)
1/6/60J

NATIONAL Observer, The (newspaper)
2/4/62J

NATIONAL Research Council
1/13/69I

NATIONAL Safety Council
1/29/60H, 12/27/60H, 7/6/61H, 2/19/62H

NATIONAL Science Foundation
6/26/60I, 6/21/61F, 1/14/62G, 12/20/62I, 9/3/63I

NATIONAL Security Agency
8/5/60G, 9/6/60A, 9/6/60G, 9/16/60G, 11/21/61G

NATIONAL Security Council
6/29/61B, 1/21/64G

NATIONAL Service Corps
8/14/63F

NATIONAL Student Association
3/31/61G, 9/2/65G, 2/13/67F

NATIONAL Traffic Safety Agency
3/21/67H, 3/30/67H

NATIONAL Urban League
1/8/60F, 9/8/60F, 1/8/67F

NATIONAL Wilderness Preservation System
9/6/61H

NATIONAL Wilderness System Act of 1964
10/3/64F

NATURAL Gas—See Gas, Natural

NATURAL Resources
1/9/63H, 3/31/63H

NATURE (magazine)
5/21/60I

NAVAL Academy, U.S. (Annapolis, Md.)
3/29/60G

NAVAL Medical Research Institute
6/22/62I

NAVIGATION
4/13/60I

NAVY, Department of the
Appointments
12/27/60G
Appointments & Resignations
10/14/63G
Resignations
12/20/61F

NAVY, U.S.
2/11/60G, 2/16/60D, 2/19/60G, 5/4/61I
Astronautics
3/8/61G
Deaths
3/30/64G
Peace Movement
12/10/67G
Personnel
8/16/61G
Reserves
8/25/61G

NAVY Band, U.S.
2/25/60D

NAZI & Neo-Nazi Parties
3/10/60B, 3/26/60F, 5/3/60B, 6/22/60F, 8/30/60F, 9/29/60C, 10/17/60J, 10/26/60F, 11/30/60A, 11/13/61F, 7/11/62B, 5/12/64D, 11/18/64B, 11/19/64B, 8/25/67F, 9/18/68B, 11/7/68B

NUCLEAR Disarmament, Campaign for
1/6/60B

NUCLEAR Power—See under Atomic Energy & Weapons

NUCLEAR Research, European Organization for (CERN)
2/5/60I, 9/21/67B

NUDITY
12/11/69B

NUGENT, Frank
12/30/65J

NUGENT, Luci Johnson
6/21/67J

NUGENT, Patrick John
8/6/66J

NUREYEV, Rudolf
6/16/61J

NUSUNTARA (newspaper)
9/27/60E

NUTTER, Donald
1/25/62F

NWAKO, M.P.K.
10/4/67A

NYASALAND—See also Malawi
Demonstrations & Riots
4/1/60C
Government & Politics
8/4/60C, 12/19/62C, 2/1/63C
Great Britain
12/19/62C
Independence
11/23/62C, 9/26/63C
Internal Security
6/16/60C
United Nations (U.N.)
12/18/61A

NYERERE, Julius
2/10/60C, 9/1/60C, 11/8/62C, 4/22/64C, 7/20/64C, 9/15/66C, 2/6/67C, 2/11/67C, 5/3/68C, 7/7/68C, 2/21/69C, 10/9/69C

O

OAKLAND, Calif.
10/19/66F, 12/18/67G

OAS—See Organization of American States (OAS)

OBANDO Candia, Alfredo
11/4/64D

OBERDORFER, Don
6/1/60F

OBERLAENDER, Theodor
5/3/60B

OBOTE, Milton
4/30/62C, 2/22/66C, 5/20/66C, 5/23/66C, 6/10/66C, 12/20/69C

O'BRIEN, David
7/1/66F

O'BRIEN, Parry
1/22/61J

OBSCENITY—See Pornography

OBSERVER, The (newspaper)
5/26/68B, 7/24/68B

OBSOLETE Communism (book)
1/20/69J

O'CASEY, Sean
9/18/64J

OCCULT
3/3/67J

OCEAN Drive Beach, S.C.
3/25/67F

OCEAN Hill-Brownsville (N.Y.C.)
12/2/68F, 12/5/68F

OCEANOGRAPHY
1/7/60I, 7/29/63I, 4/25/64I, 4/16/65I, 10/1/66H, 3/9/67H, 9/23/68I, 8/7/69I
Records & Achievements
1/23/60I, 11/6/62I

OCEANS—See also Sea, Law of the
6/9/67A

OCEAN Voyages
7/21/60J, 7/4/62J, 4/22/69J

O'CONNOR, Flannery (Mary)
8/3/64J, 5/12/69J

O'CONNOR, Timothy
1/24/60F

ODAKA, Sam
5/25/68C

ODETS, Clifford
8/15/63J

ODINGA, Oginga
3/13/66C, 4/14/66C, 4/19/66C, 4/22/66C, 6/26/66C, 11/9/67J, 1/24/69C

ODRIA, Manuel
5/13/61D

OERTER, Al
9/7/60J, 7/1/62J, 4/27/63J, 4/25/64J

OFFICE Buildings
3/7/63H

OFFICE of Economic Opportunity (OEO)
1/14/67F, 1/23/67F, 1/27/67F, 2/2/67F, 2/8/67F, 2/23/67F, 2/24/67F, 2/27/67F, 3/1/67F, 3/8/67F, 3/10/67F, 5/3/67F, 1/29/68F

OGANIA, Juan Carlos
6/27/68D

O'HARA, John
3/26/64J, 11/23/67J, 11/28/68J

O'HARA, Thomas
1/16/60H, 2/3/64J, 3/6/64J

OHIO
7/23/68F
Accidents & Disasters
7/4/69I, 7/7/69I
Elections
1/17/64F
Negroes
10/27/63F, 3/14/64F, 4/20/64F, 2/26/66F, 6/23/66F, 6/24/66F, 7/18/66F, 7/19/66F, 7/20/66F, 7/24/66F, 8/17/66F, 8/18/66F, 9/1/66F, 9/2/66F, 4/16/67F, 5/2/67F, 6/14/67F, 9/19/67F, 10/13/67F, 11/7/67F, 11/28/67F, 4/8/68F, 7/24/68F, 7/25/68F, 7/26/68F, 7/27/68F, 9/30/69F

OHIO River
3/13/64I

OHIO State University
3/19/60J, 3/25/61J, 3/26/61J, 3/12/62J, 3/24/62J, 4/26/68F

OIL, Chemical & Atomic Workers International Union
5/11/67F

OIL and Gas Journal (newspaper)
12/27/60H

OJUKWU, Chukwuemaka Odumegwu
3/13/67C, 4/20/67C, 9/2/67C, 4/23/68C, 7/18/68C

O'KEEFE Center for the Performing Arts
3/29/60J

O'KELLY, Sean
11/23/66J

OKINAWA
6/19/60E, 8/17/63I, 7/31/65E, 4/28/69E, 6/2/69G, 6/3/69E, 7/18/69E, 10/29/69G, 11/20/69G, 11/21/69G
Government & Politics
11/13/60E
United States
2/10/63A

OKLAHOMA
Accidents & Disasters
5/6/60I, 4/22/66I
Apportionment
6/19/62F, 7/26/62F
Education
11/9/64H
Negroes
6/16/66F, 7/10/67F

OKLAHOMA, University of
1/6/60J, 3/25/63J, 1/11/64J

OKLAHOMA (play)
8/23/60J

OKLAHOMA State University
3/27/64J

OKSANEN, Enio
4/19/62J

OLD Northeast: Pioneer Period, 1815-1840, The (book)
4/25/68J

OLENGA, Nicholas
8/5/64C

O'HARA, John

OLIVA, Tony
11/28/64J

OLIVERO, Magda
10/19/69J

OLIVIER, George Berg
2/19/62B, 3/3/62B

OLIVIER, Sir Laurence
10/5/60J

OLMSTEAD, Freeman
1/27/61A

OLYMPIC Committee, International
8/23/60J

OLYMPIC Games
Accidents & Disasters
8/26/60J
Amateurs
9/27/62J
Civil Rights
5/4/64J
Demonstrations & Riots
9/1/68D
Indonesia
6/26/64J
Korea
1/25/63J

Participants
2/7/63J
Records & Achievements
2/2/64J
Rifle Competition
10/16/64J
Summer
8/25/60J, 8/26/60J, 9/1/60J, 9/3/60J, 9/4/60J, 9/7/60J, 9/11/60J, 10/18/63J, 10/10/64J, 10/24/64J
Swimming
10/18/64J
Track & Field
10/15/64J, 10/17/64J
Tryouts
9/13/64J
Winter
2/9/64J
Winter (1960)
2/18/60J, 2/28/60J
Winter (1964)
1/28/64J, 1/29/64J, 2/4/64J

OLYMPIO, Sylvanus E.
2/4/60C, 1/13/63C

OMAHA, Neb.
7/3/66F, 7/4/66F, 7/6/66F, 7/30/66F

OMAN
11/30/67A
South Yemen, People's Republic of
12/1/67C, 12/3/67C
United Nations (U.N.)
12/11/63C, 12/18/68A

ONASSIS, Aristotle
10/13/63J, 10/20/68J

ONASSIS, Jacqueline Bouvier Kennedy (Mrs. Aristotle Onassis)
Family
11/25/60F, 4/15/63F, 8/7/63F, 8/9/63F, 1/16/67J
Kennedy Assassination
12/10/66J, 12/13/66J, 12/16/66J
Personal
10/20/68J
Travel
12/16/61D, 10/13/63J, 11/21/63F
White House
2/14/62J, 9/23/62J

ONE Day in the Life of Ivan Denisovich (book)
1/22/63J, 9/11/68J

O'NEIL, John (Buck)
5/29/62J

O'NEILL, Eugene
2/5/65J

O'NEILL, Terence
12/11/68B

ONE Man's Destiny (book)
6/12/67J

ONENKO, Ramogi Achieng
4/25/66C

ONE Very Hot Day (book)
1/15/68J

ONGANIA, Juan Carlos
6/28/66D, 6/29/66D, 7/12/66D, 7/23/66D, 8/25/67D, 8/28/67D, 8/20/68D, 3/31/69D

ON TARGET (magazine)
11/12/64F

OPERA
10/27/64J, 5/31/66J, 5/19/68F
Conductors
3/14/66J

Deaths
3/4/60J, 7/15/60J, 9/9/60J, 7/29/66J
Debuts & Premiers
1/29/65J, 2/22/66J, 2/7/68J, 10/19/69J
Houses
4/16/66J, 6/24/66J, 9/16/66J, 1/17/67J
Performers
5/15/65J, 3/18/66J
Productions
9/18/67J, 9/16/68J, 6/25/69J
Strikes & Settlements
8/28/61H, 12/13/69J

OPHUL, Max
4/20/69J

OPIUM
2/5/67A

OPPEN, George
5/5/69J

OPPENHEIMER, J. Robert
4/5/63G, 2/18/67J

ORAL Contraceptives—See under Birth Control

ORANGE, N.J.
5/16/63F

ORANGEBURG, S.C.
2/5/68F, 2/6/68F, 2/7/68F, 2/8/68F, 2/9/68F, 2/10/68F, 2/11/68F, 2/13/68F, 2/15/68F, 2/26/68F

ORBS (ballet)
12/26/66J

OREGON
10/8/62F

OREGON State University
11/27/61J

ORFEO ed Euridice (opera)
2/7/68J

ORGANIZATION of African Unity (OAU)
2/28/66C, 7/1/66C

ORGANIZATION of American States (OAS)
Cuba
6/27/60D, 7/18/60D, 7/19/60A, 8/2/60D, 8/7/60D, 8/22/60D, 8/23/60D, 8/25/60D, 8/28/60D, 8/30/60D, 10/28/60D, 12/21/60D
Dominican Republic
3/18/60D, 6/8/60D, 6/9/60D, 8/18/60D, 8/20/60D, 8/23/60G, 8/26/60D, 9/9/60D, 9/28/60D
Foreign Ministers' Conference (1960)
8/8/60D, 8/16/60D, 8/18/60D, 8/22/60D, 8/23/60D, 8/25/60D, 8/26/60D, 8/28/60D, 8/30/60D
ORGANIZED Crime
6/28/67F, 7/4/67F
Appalachin Conspiracy Trial
11/28/60F
Convictions
4/7/60F
Deaths
1/26/62F
Federal Crackdown & Investigations
9/27/63F, 10/10/63F

POOR People's Campaign—See under Poverty, U.S.

POOR People's Conferences
4/14/66F

POPE, Allen L.
4/29/60E

POPE, Jr., George
5/5/62J

POPES—See names

POPOVIC, Koca
7/13/61B, 4/21/62B

POPOVICH, Pavel
8/12/62I, 8/21/62I

POPULAR Front for the Liberation of Palestine
4/11/68C

POPULATION & Census Reports
6/27/62H, 8/1/68I
Birth Rate
5/12/60F
Farm
2/20/60H
Foreign Trade
2/1/62H
Jews
7/26/62A
Labor
12/19/62H
Negroes
3/14/61F, 12/27/61F, 1/5/62F, 11/2/67F
Population Explosion
8/13/61A, 4/17/63G, 4/24/63G, 5/7/63G, 8/30/64A, 10/5/64A, 3/23/65A, 5/2/67D
Population Growth
3/17/69J
Poverty, U.S.
8/14/67F
Rural Areas
3/10/63F
Shifts in
11/15/60F
United Nations (U.N.)
5/24/69A
Vital Statistics
1/5/60H, 6/16/60F, 11/15/60F, 8/12/61F, 4/21/62F, 5/8/62F, 12/4/62F, 12/31/62F, 9/27/63H, 1/1/64F, 8/31/64F, 7/27/66F, 8/11/66F, 11/21/67F
World Population
9/1/62A, 10/6/63A

POPULATION Reference Bureau
10/6/63A

PORNOGRAPHY & Obscenity
3/25/60J, 11/2/60J, 2/18/63F, 7/10/63J, 3/21/66F

PORTER, Cole
10/15/64J

PORTER, H.K. Co.,
6/23/67F

PORT Gibson, Miss.
1/27/67F

PORTMAN, Eric
12/7/69J

PORTNOY'S Complaint (book)
2/21/69J

PORT of N.Y. Authority
1/18/64H

PORTS
Contracts
12/16/64H
Labor
8/2/64H, 1/20/69F
Strikes & Settlements
12/21/62H, 12/31/62H, 1/16/63H, 1/26/63H, 3/14/64H, 10/1/64H, 4/1/66H, 2/14/69H

PORTUGAL—See also names of colonies, territories & former
1/3/62B
Accidents & Disasters
11/26/67B
African Unity, Organization of
7/18/64C, 7/21/64C
Angola
3/8/60C, 6/30/61A, 6/30/61B, 7/25/61C, 11/28/61C, 1/30/62C
Arms Sales
7/31/63C
Biafra, Republic of
10/20/67C
Birth Control & Family Planning
11/22/68J
Brazil
2/3/61B, 7/13/69D
Church-State Relations
1/18/68B
Cold War
3/24/66B
Colonies & Territories
8/28/61C, 12/7/61E, 12/18/61E, 12/19/61A, 12/19/61E, 12/21/61E, 12/30/61E, 1/3/62B, 3/14/62E, 12/15/62C, 7/31/63C, 8/12/63C, 12/11/63C, 12/7/64C, 3/15/65B, 5/13/65A, 6/10/65B, 9/26/65C, 12/12/65B, 11/17/67A, 1/9/68B, 11/29/68A, 4/14/69B, 4/21/69B
Communists & Communism
1/28/65B
Congo, Republic of the (Leopoldville) (formerly Belgian Congo)
7/7/67A, 11/10/67A, 11/12/67B, 11/14/67A, 11/15/67A
Damao
1/3/62B
Deaths
10/31/68B
Defectors & Political Exiles
1/22/61B, 1/23/61B, 1/27/61B, 2/7/61C, 1/9/63B, 3/21/68B, 11/10/68B
Demonstrations & Riots
2/3/61B, 3/27/61B, 1/31/62B, 5/1/62B, 10/5/68B, 10/31/68B, 11/20/68B
Elections
11/11/61B
Foreign Trade
1/4/60B, 7/13/69D
Government & Politics
5/3/61B, 8/14/68B, 9/16/68B, 9/27/68B, 11/24/69B, 12/9/69B
Great Britain
2/3/61B
Guerrilla Warfare
1/6/67C
Human Rights
2/6/61B, 2/8/61B

India
10/15/60E, 8/17/61E, 12/7/61E, 12/30/61E
Internal Security
5/12/61B, 1/13/68B
Pan-African Freedom Movement
2/9/62C
Political Prisoners
8/25/65B, 1/19/68B, 3/1/68B, 3/20/68B, 5/11/68B, 5/16/68B, 5/20/68B, 10/26/68B
Press
2/8/61B, 1/19/68B, 5/11/68B, 5/20/68B
Protests & Rallies
10/4/69B, 10/5/69B
Rebellions & Revolutions
1/1/62B
Rhodesia
4/6/66C, 4/13/66B
Senegal
4/24/63C
South Africa, Republic of (formerly Union of)
4/13/61A
Sweden
10/14/69B
Union of Soviet Socialist Republics (USSR)
1/30/62C
United Arab Republic (UAR)
6/29/63C
United Nations (U.N.)
1/3/62B, 8/10/62C, 12/15/62C, 7/31/63C, 12/11/63C, 12/7/64C, 5/13/65A, 11/17/67A, 11/29/68A
United States
3/17/60G, 1/23/61B, 2/3/61B, 3/27/61B, 6/30/61B, 6/28/62B
United States Bases & Troops
2/4/62B
Zambia
4/6/68C, 8/7/69C

PORTUGAL Grand Prix
8/14/60J

PORTUGUESE Guinea
8/28/61C, 8/12/63C
Casualties
1/9/68B
Government & Politics
12/15/62C
Rebellions & Revolutions
7/17/63C

PORUMBEANU, Andre
4/6/60J

POSION Gas—See Chemical Warfare

POST, Emily
9/25/60J

POSTAL Service
Appointments
12/17/60F, 9/9/63H
Appropriations
8/22/61H, 7/28/64H
Commemorative
11/13/62H
Communists & Communism
5/24/65F
Construction
3/2/61H
Discrimination
11/10/62F
Firearms
6/12/68F, 7/9/68F, 7/24/68F, 9/18/68F, 10/10/68F

Fraud
12/7/60H, 7/13/61H, 4/15/63F
Rates
3/11/60H, 4/14/61H, 1/24/62H, 10/11/62H, 1/7/63H
Thefts
8/14/62F

POST-PRISON Writings and Speeches (book)
2/27/69J

POSUN Yun
8/12/60E

POTSDAM Conference (1945)
6/12/64B

POTTERY
9/28/68I

POULTRY
8/2/68F, 8/18/68H

POUND, Ezra
9/4/63J

POVERTY, U.S.—See also Appalachia
12/13/63H, 1/8/64F, 1/17/64F, 1/20/64H, 6/21/65F
Anti-Measures
1/21/64H, 2/22/64H, 3/15/64F, 3/16/64H, 5/6/64F, 5/9/64F, 5/14/64F, 7/23/64H, 8/8/64H, 9/22/64H, 10/3/64F, 11/24/64H, 1/17/65F, 7/22/65F, 8/12/65F, 12/25/66F, 12/30/66F, 3/1/67F, 3/14/67F, 3/15/67F, 6/21/67F, 11/2/67F, 6/2/69F
Education
7/2/65F, 10/20/65F
Federal Aid
5/23/68F, 12/18/69F
Food Aid
6/12/68F
Food Food
6/16/68F
Law & Legislation
12/18/63F, 8/11/64H, 8/20/64H, 10/3/64F
Poor People's March
3/4/68F, 3/13/68F, 3/26/68F, 4/26/68F, 4/29/68F, 5/2/68F, 5/3/68F, 5/6/68F, 5/8/68F, 5/9/68F, 5/10/68F, 5/11/68F, 5/24/68F, 5/25/68F, 5/28/68F, 5/30/68F, 5/31/68F, 6/3/68F, 6/4/68F, 6/6/68F, 6/7/68F, 6/20/68F, 6/21/68F, 6/23/68F, 6/24/68F, 6/26/68F
Protests & Rallies
10/16/67F
Rural Areas
12/9/67F
State Programs
12/12/69F
Vital Statistics
8/14/67F

Poverty Programs
2/22/64H

POWELL, Adam Clayton
1/22/60F, 4/22/60F, 4/13/61F, 2/5/63F, 2/20/63F, 3/23/63F, 4/27/63F, 12/24/66F, 1/2/67F, 1/3/67F, 1/7/67F, 1/8/67F, 1/10/67F, 1/19/67F, 1/22/67F, 2/13/67F, 2/23/67F, 3/1/67F, 3/2/67F, 3/6/67F,

3/7/67F, 3/8/67F, 3/13/67F, 3/17/67F, 4/11/67F, 3/22/68F, 6/16/69F

POWELL, Anthony
3/5/69J

POWELL, Enoch
6/10/66B, 4/20/68B, 4/21/68B, 4/23/68B, 4/24/68B, 4/26/68B, 4/28/68B, 10/12/68B, 11/16/68B, 11/21/68B, 11/22/68B

POWELL, Wesley
3/7/60F

POWER, Thomas S.
2/2/60G

POWERS, Francis Gary
5/7/60A, 8/17/60A, 8/22/60B, 8/26/60G, 2/10/62A, 2/13/62G, 3/6/62G

PRACTITIONER, The (magazine)
10/2/61I

PRADO y Ugarteche, Manuel
6/7/60D, 4/25/61D, 7/16/62D, 7/29/62D

PRAGUE Film Festival
7/10/61J

PRASAD, Rajendra
8/17/61E

PRATHER, Victor
5/4/61I

PRATT, Edwin
1/26/69F

PRAVDA (newspaper)
2/17/60B, 8/13/60A, 11/5/60C, 4/16/61B, 7/30/61B, 2/23/62B, 1/7/63A, 2/10/63A, 3/15/63D, 4/15/63C, 4/24/63I, 6/23/63I, 3/3/64J, 9/2/64A, 9/15/64B, 10/17/64A, 10/17/64B, 12/6/64B, 1/14/66B, 9/16/66B, 7/16/67B, 7/19/67B, 3/28/68B, 7/11/68B, 6/2/69B

PRAXIS (magazine)
7/23/68B

PRCHLIK, Vaclav
7/15/68B, 7/25/68B

PRECOCIOUS Autobiography, A (book)
3/27/63B, 8/7/63B

PREGNANCY—See Birth and Pregnancy

PRELUDE, A (book)
6/21/67J

PREMINGER, Otto
12/15/60J

PRENSA, La (newspaper)
1/24/67D, 1/26/67D, 2/2/67D

PRENSA Confidencial (magazine)
2/28/68D

PRESBYTERIAN Church
5/3/60F, 12/4/60J, 9/29/61J, 3/8/62F, 5/22/62J, 5/22/63J, 4/25/64F, 5/21/64J

PRESBYTERIAN-St. Luke's Hospital (Chicago)
9/4/61I

RICKOVER, Hyman
5/1/67G

RIDGEWAY, Matthew
10/6/67J

RIESSEN, Martin
6/22/63J

RIFAI, Abdel Moneim
4/21/68C, 8/12/69C

RIFAI, Samir el-
4/20/63C

RIFKIND, Simon
5/8/60H

RIGHT to Know—See Information, Freedom of

RIGOLETTO (opera)
6/25/69J

RIGORES, José
6/3/61J

RINALDI, Giulio
6/10/61J

RING Magazine (magazine)
4/6/63J

RINZLER, Seymour
10/7/64I

RIO Defense Treaty
3/1/60D

RIO de Janeiro, University of
10/11/65D, 12/22/65D,
4/9/66D, 8/10/66D,
6/20/68D, 6/23/68D

RIO de la Plata
5/19/68D, 5/20/68D,
1/28/69D, 4/23/69D

RIOT Control Command
4/26/68F

RIPPON Society
4/6/66G

*RISE and Fall of the Third
Reich, The* (book)
10/17/60J, 3/14/61J

RIVAS, Victor Manuel
7/20/65J

RIVERA Caminero, Francisco
1/7/66D

RIVERO, Felipe
7/11/67F

RIVERS, Larry
1/4/68C, 1/8/68C

RIVERS, L. Mendel
3/22/61F, 1/5/68G

RIZOR, Joseph
5/2/68I, 5/5/68I

RIZZO, Frank
11/19/67F, 11/22/67F

ROA, Raul
1/2/60A, 7/11/60A,
8/25/60D, 10/25/60A,
11/18/60D, 12/31/60A,
4/5/61D, 4/15/61D,
11/23/61D, 3/5/63D

ROADS—See Highways

ROBARTS, John
8/24/67D

ROBB, Charles
9/10/67J, 12/9/67J

ROBBERIES
8/14/62F
Great Britain
8/8/63J, 8/15/63B,
12/10/63J, 3/26/64B

ROBERT Collier Trophy
10/10/63I

ROBERTO, Holden
7/1/61C, 7/18/63C, 1/3/64C

ROBERTS, Arch
4/19/62G, 4/27/62G

ROBERTS, Sir Frank
1/21/61E, 3/23/61A

ROBERTS, Glenn
7/2/64J

ROBERTSON, Floyd
5/9/64J

ROBERTSON, Oscar
3/4/60J, 3/10/62J

ROBERTSON, Stokes
11/17/64F

ROBESON, Paul
12/22/63J

ROBINSON, Brooks
11/24/64J

ROBINSON, Ermer
10/4/62J

ROBINSON, Frank
11/22/61J

ROBINSON, G. Canby
8/31/60I

ROBINSON, Jackie
1/22/62J, 2/23/62J

ROBINSON, M. K.
4/4/67I

ROBINSON, Sugar Ray
1/22/60J, 4/2/60J, 6/10/60J,
3/4/61J

ROBINSON, Willie
3/21/64J

ROBINSON-PATMAN Act
2/18/63H

ROBLAIN, Clovis
4/28/68I, 4/30/68I

ROBLES, Marco Aurelio
5/13/64D, 11/24/64D,
1/8/65D, 6/26/67D,
2/28/68D, 3/4/68D,
3/6/68D, 3/7/68D,
3/14/68D, 3/15/68D,
3/24/68D, 3/25/68D,
4/1/68D

ROBSON, Edwin
3/24/61A

ROC, Eduardo
2/23/68D

ROCHESTER, N.Y.
7/26/64F, 6/23/67F,
11/17/67F

ROCKEFELLER, Jr., John D.
5/11/60H

ROCKEFELLER, Mary Todhunter
11/17/61F

ROCKEFELLER, Michael
11/19/61J

ROCKEFELLER, Nelson A.
7/14/63F
Arab-Israeli Conflict
6/23/66G
Arms Control & Disarmament
8/8/62G
Atomic Energy & Weapons
4/25/63G
Cities
4/18/68F
Civil Defense
1/25/60G, 2/21/60G
Civil Rights
9/8/60F, 2/12/63F, 3/4/63F,
10/20/63F
Cold War
11/16/63G
Courts & Legal System
3/3/64F

Economy
12/5/62H, 4/6/63H
Education
1/25/60F
Family
5/11/60H
Foreign Relations
7/25/68G
Government & Politics
8/6/63F, 11/16/64F,
3/6/67F
Governor
3/11/61H, 4/22/61J
Johnson, Lyndon B.
1/10/64F
Latin America
5/11/69D, 5/14/69D,
5/16/69D, 5/19/69D,
5/23/69D, 5/24/69G,
5/27/69D, 5/30/69D,
5/31/69D, 6/1/69D,
6/3/69D, 6/16/69D,
6/17/69D, 6/18/69D,
6/19/69D, 6/22/69D,
6/29/69D, 7/1/69D, 7/3/69D
Law & Legislation
4/27/66F, 4/30/66F,
6/24/66J, 6/28/66H,
7/1/66H
Narcotics
11/5/66F
North Atlantic Treaty Organization (NATO)
2/9/63G
Personal
11/17/61F, 11/19/61J,
3/16/62F, 5/4/63F
Presidential Campaign of 1960
3/4/60F, 6/26/60F,
7/23/60F, 7/26/60F,
1/5/61F
Presidential Campaign of 1964
11/4/61F, 3/29/63F,
4/16/63F, 10/22/63F,
11/7/63F, 12/14/63F,
3/10/64F, 4/28/64F,
5/15/64F, 6/2/64F,
6/15/64F, 7/17/64F,
8/6/64F
Presidential Campaign of 1968
7/25/65G, 11/14/65G,
11/19/66F, 2/24/68F,
3/21/68F, 4/30/68F,
6/30/68F
Racial Unrest
7/26/64F
Railroads
9/11/61H
Republican Party
11/29/60F, 10/12/63F
Vietnam War
7/13/68G
Welfare
7/18/61F, 1/17/64F

ROCKEFELLER, Winthrop
2/3/67F, 2/5/68F

ROCKEFELLER Foundation
12/12/60G, 12/9/68F

ROCKEFELLER Institute
9/16/64I

ROCKETS—See Missiles & Rockets; Aircraft, Military; Cape Canaveral; Cape Kennedy

ROCKWELL, George Lincoln
8/30/60F, 2/14/61F,
11/13/61F, 8/25/67F

RODGERS, Richard
8/23/60J

RODRIGUES, Urbano Tavares
1/19/68B

RODRIGUEZ, Carlos Rafael
2/14/62D, 4/27/69D,
5/17/69D

RODRIGUEZ, Luis
3/21/63J, 6/8/63J

RODRIGUEZ Alfonso, Marcos
4/2/64D

RODRIGUEZ Echavarria, Rafael
1/16/62D

RODRIQUEZ Astiarzarain, Nicolas
4/3/67A

ROETHKE Memorial Poetry Award, Theodore
5/11/68J

ROGER, Muriel
5/3/64I

ROGERS, Edith Nourse
9/10/60F

ROGERS, William
8/6/63G, 12/11/68G,
4/7/69G
Arab-Israeli Conflict
12/10/69C, 12/22/69G
Arms Control & Disarmament
6/6/69G
Vietnam War
3/27/69G, 6/5/69G,
7/2/69G, 9/16/69A,
10/12/69G, 11/18/69G,
12/23/69G

ROGERS, William P.
1/12/60F, 1/26/60F,
12/1/60F

ROHAN, Michael
10/6/69C

ROKOSSOVSKY, Marshal Konstantine
8/3/68J

ROLLS-ROYCE, Ltd.
7/31/66G

ROMAN Catholic Church—See Catholics, Roman

ROMAN Catholic University (Argentina)
8/5/66D

ROME, University of
9/6/65B, 11/21/65B,
12/5/65B, 12/23/65B,
4/5/66B, 5/30/66B,
2/23/68B, 3/12/68B,
3/16/68B, 3/18/68B,
6/3/68B, 2/21/69B,
6/21/69B

ROMEO & Juliet (film)
10/8/68J

ROMNEY, George
1/5/60H, 2/10/62F,
11/6/62F, 3/4/63F,
5/28/64H, 8/31/66F,
8/16/67G, 5/12/69H
Government & Politics
11/4/64F
Presidential Campaign of 1964
1/7/64F, 6/7/64F
Presidential Campaign of 1968
7/2/67F, 9/17/67F,
1/12/68F, 2/28/68F
Vietnam War
9/4/67G, 9/17/67F

ROOSA, Robert
9/13/67H

ROOSEVELT, Eleanor (Mrs. Franklin D. Roosevelt)
Awards & Honors
12/24/60J, 12/26/61J,
4/18/63J
Cuba
5/20/61D, 5/22/61D
Deaths
11/7/62F
Peace Corps
3/30/61G
Wiretapping
10/31/65F
Women's Rights
3/13/61F, 12/14/61F

ROOSEVELT, Franklin D.
9/28/60J, 11/9/60A,
11/23/63F, 1/8/64F,
4/18/69J

ROPER Associates
11/7/60F

ROQUE, Jacqueline
3/2/61J

ROSE, Billy
1/6/60J

ROSELLE, Pete
2/8/60J

ROSEMARY'S Baby (book)
4/13/67J, 6/12/68J

ROSENBERG, Julius
10/24/60G

ROSENCRANTZ and Guildenstern Are Dead (play)
10/16/67J, 4/21/68J,
4/25/68J

ROSENTHAL, Benjamin
1/16/67H

ROSHCHIN, Aleksei
10/10/67A

ROSS, Donald
5/19/62J

ROSSELLINI, Roberto
6/13/60J

ROSSIDES, Zenon
2/10/68A

ROSTOW, Walt
1/19/61G, 2/4/67G

ROSWELL Park Memorial Institute
4/7/61I

ROTH, Philip
2/21/69J

ROTHSCHILD de Koenisgswarter, Kathleen
4/21/60F

ROTZ, John
5/19/62J

ROUND Table (horse)
7/4/63J

ROUS, Francis
10/13/66J

ROUSE, Milford
6/20/67I

ROUSH, EDD
1/28/62J

ROUSSELOT, John
3/31/61F, 1/6/63G

ROUTE 40 (Maryland)
11/3/61F, 11/8/61F

ROVENSTINE, Emery
11/9/60I

ROWAN, Carl
1/10/62F, 12/10/62F,
1/21/64G

ROWING
3/23/63J

SIBERIA
10/14/69I

SIDERATOS, Michael
4/8/68B

SIDEY, Hugh
7/8/68J

SIDNEY, Ann
11/12/64J

SIERRA Leone
1/25/69C
Coups & Attempted Coups
3/24/67C, 4/18/68C,
5/7/68C
Deaths
4/27/64C
Elections
3/17/67C
Government & Politics
3/26/67C, 4/3/67C
Independence
5/3/60C, 4/27/61C
Internal Security
11/20/68C
Press
4/2/67C
United Nations (U.N.)
9/27/61A

SIERRA Maestra Mountains
4/15/60D

SIFFORD, Charles
3/3/63J

SIGNALS
11/8/63I

SIHANOUK, Prince (Cambodia)
9/29/60E, 12/26/60E,
9/22/61A, 11/19/63E,
11/21/63E, 2/11/64E,
3/11/64E, 3/21/64E,
3/22/64E, 3/27/64E,
6/26/64E, 10/6/64E,
10/27/64E, 4/30/69E

SIKKIM
11/25/65E, 12/14/65E,
9/11/67E

SILBER, Bernard
4/14/60F

SILENT Spring (book)
4/14/64H

SILES Salinas, Louis Adolfo
9/26/69D

SILVER
2/20/62H, 6/4/63H,
10/6/63H, 6/8/65H

SILVESTER, Jay
8/20/61J

SIMON & Schuster, Inc.
1/12/68J, 6/5/68J, 8/5/68J

SIMON Foundation, Norton
3/19/65J

SIMON Fraser College (Canada)
11/20/68D

SIMONS, Elwyn
7/2/68I

SIMPSON, Floyd
4/29/63F, 9/13/63F

SIMPSON, Richard M.
1/7/60F, 6/19/60F

SIMPSON, Varnado
11/26/69F

SINAI Peninsula
2/25/60C, 6/27/67A,
12/13/67C, 5/17/68C,
12/10/68C, 8/3/69C

SINATRA, Frank
12/11/63J

SINATRA Jr., Frank
12/11/63J, 12/14/63J

SINCLAIR, Upton
11/25/68J

SINCLAIR Oil Co.
10/9/62H

SINGAPORE—See also Malaysia, Federation of
7/31/62E, 8/11/65E
Communists & Communism
8/9/65E
Demonstrations & Riots
10/31/65E, 2/1/66E
Executions
10/17/68D
Great Britain
7/18/67B, 1/16/68G
Indonesia
4/17/66E
Internal Security
3/2/63E
International Monetary Fund (IMF)
8/3/66E
Malaya
9/20/61E
Malaysia, Federation of
7/9/65E, 8/8/65E, 9/15/65E
Racial Unrest
9/12/64E
Union of Soviet Socialist Republics (USSR)
9/15/65E
United States
4/4/66E
Vietnam War
12/13/69E

SINGAPORE, University of
10/31/65E

SINGER, Isaac Bashevis
5/2/66J, 10/30/67J,
10/14/68J

SINGER Manufacturing Co.
6/17/63H

SINGH, Dinesh
4/8/69E

SINGH, Swaren
5/10/66E

SINGH, Tara
8/15/61E, 10/1/61E

SINISTER Twilight A. The Fall of Singapore (book)
8/23/68J

SINYAVSKY, Andrei
1/12/66B, 2/14/66B

SIOPRAES, Sergio
1/27/63J

SIQUEIROS, David Alfaro
8/9/60D

SIRHAN, Sirhan
6/6/68F, 6/7/68F, 6/19/68F,
1/7/69F, 4/17/69F,
4/23/69F, 5/21/69F

SIROKY, Viliam
9/21/63B

SISCO, Joseph
1/30/69G

SITWELL, Sir Osbert
5/4/69J

SIX Crises (book)
3/29/62F

SKATING, Ice
3/3/63J, 1/17/64J
Accidents & Disasters
2/15/61J
Championships
1/30/60J, 1/28/61J, 2/9/64J

Figure Skating
1/11/64J
Speed-skating
2/19/61J, 2/2/64J, 2/4/64J,
2/16/64J
Titles
3/3/60J

SKIING
3/25/63J, 3/7/64J
Awards & Honors
3/2/63J
Deaths
4/12/64J
Titles
2/25/62J

SKIN
12/14/66I

SKOBLIKOVA, Lidiya
2/2/64J, 2/16/64J,
12/28/64J

SKYSCRAPERS
3/1/60J, 8/26/69J

SLANSKY, Rudolf
8/22/63B

SLAUGHTERHOUSE Five (book)
3/31/69J

SLAVERY
3/21/67A

SLAYTON, Donald
3/15/62I

SLEDDING
1/27/63J

SLIM, Sir William
2/2/60E

SLIPHER, Vesto
11/9/69J

SLOAN, Boyd
1/6/60F

SLOAN-KETTERING Institute for Cancer Research (N.Y.)
1/5/60I, 4/9/60I, 4/18/60I,
9/23/60I, 9/29/60I, 4/9/61I,
3/13/62I, 12/4/67I

SMALL Business Administration (SBA)
4/5/61H, 9/5/61H

SMALL Businesses—See under Business & Industry

SMALLPOX
9/16/62I, 2/10/63I,
4/19/67E, 11/29/69A

SMALL Town in Germany, A (book)
10/21/68J

SMIRNOV, Andrei A.
3/13/60B

SMITH, Alfred E.
1/2/60F

SMITH, Eugene G.
3/18/60F

SMITH, Howard K.
5/15/61F, 11/11/62F,
12/5/63F

SMITH, Ian
4/13/64C, 10/24/64C,
10/25/64C, 5/7/65A,
5/7/65C, 9/19/65C,
10/1/65C, 10/7/65B,
10/9/65B, 10/18/65C,
11/20/65C, 1/1/66C,
1/2/66C, 1/17/66C,
7/7/66C, 8/25/66C,

9/24/66C, 11/30/66B,
12/3/66C, 12/6/66C,
11/3/67A, 11/8/67C,
11/9/67C, 11/10/67C,
3/19/68C, 4/6/68C,
7/15/68C, 7/26/68C,
7/27/68C, 9/13/68C,
10/9/68C, 10/13/68C

SMITH, Margaret Chase
2/1/60J, 9/21/61G,
9/23/61G, 7/8/63J,
1/27/64F, 4/14/64F,
5/11/64J

SMITH, Norman
4/6/63J

SMITH, Perry E.
1/3/60F, 3/29/60F

SMITH, Ralph
4/25/60F

SMITH Act (1940)
6/5/61F

SMITHERMAN, Joseph
3/17/65F

SMITHSONIAN Astrophysical Observatory
1/3/67I

SMOKING—See Cancer—Smoking; Heart—Smoking; Tobacco

SMOLEN, Michael
10/12/64D

SMRKOVSKY, Josef
8/29/68B, 3/31/69B

SNAKES
6/17/66F

SNEAD, Sam
5/7/61J, 11/11/62J

SNELL, Peter
1/27/62J, 2/3/62J, 2/10/62J,
6/2/62J

SNODGRASS, William D.
5/2/60J

SNOW
1/10/65I, 12/25/66I,
1/17/67I, 2/8/67I, 3/17/67I

SNOW, Sir Charles P.
12/26/60A

SNYDER, M.G.
5/14/64F

SOARES, Mario
1/13/68B, 3/1/68B,
3/20/68B, 3/21/68B,
5/16/68B, 11/10/68B

SOBELL, Morton
1/14/69F

SOBLE, Jack
11/29/60G

SOBLEN, Robert
11/29/60G, 8/7/61G,
6/28/62G, 7/1/62G,
9/11/62G

SOBOLEV, Arkady
7/19/60A

SOBUKWE, R. M.
5/4/60C

SOCCER
8/6/61J, 4/28/62J, 6/17/62J,
8/5/62J, 11/24/62J, 4/6/63J,
8/4/63J, 8/7/63J, 9/11/63J,
5/27/64J, 8/2/64J
American Challenge Cup
8/6/60J
Demonstrations & Riots
5/24/64J

SOCIALISM
12/19/68J

SOCIALIST International
9/2/64B

SOCIAL Security
5/5/60F, 5/7/60F, 6/3/60F,
6/29/60F, 8/17/60F,
8/23/60F, 1/11/61F,
2/2/61H, 2/13/61F,
2/21/61F, 4/20/61F,
1/11/62F, 2/27/62F,
3/28/62F, 10/24/64F,
10/14/66F
Cost-of-Living Link
9/25/69F
Deaths
5/20/60H
Increased Benefits
1/23/67F, 12/3/69H,
12/5/69H, 12/8/69H
Law & Legislation
6/26/61F, 6/29/61F

SOCIAL Services
1/17/63F

SOCIOLOGY
1/29/60J

SOGLO, Christophe
12/17/67C, 12/19/67C

SOIL Bank Program
1/6/60H, 2/3/60H

SOKOLOV, Aleksandr
10/2/64G

SOLAR Flares & Rays
9/3/63I, 1/22/69I

SOLH, Sami es-
11/6/68J

SOLIDARITY (newspaper)
4/15/61H

SOLOMON Islands
10/5/64E

SOLTI, Georg
12/17/68J

SOLZHENITSYN, Aleksandr
1/22/63J, 6/5/67B,
6/21/67B, 2/6/68B,
9/11/68J, 10/15/68J,
11/4/69B, 11/22/69B

SOMALIA, Republic of
7/1/60C, 9/20/68C
Armed Forces & Defense
11/10/63C
Assassinations & Assassination Attempts
10/15/69C
Ethiopia
2/8/64C, 2/15/64C,
3/26/64C, 3/30/64C
Germany, West
11/10/63C
Independence
5/5/60C
Kenya
4/30/67C, 5/2/67C,
8/18/67C, 10/28/67C,
1/31/68C
Union of Soviet Socialist Republics (USSR)
11/10/63C
United States
11/10/63C
Uranium
3/15/68C

SOMOZA de Bayle, Jr., Anastasio
2/5/67D, 4/13/67J, 5/1/67C

SONATRACH
5/9/68C

SONG Yo Chan
5/20/60E, 7/10/62E,
9/4/63E, 9/6/63E

YOULOU, Fulbert
6/9/61G, 8/15/63C,

YOUNG, A.Z.
9/13/66F

YOUNG, Cy
11/3/60J, 11/8/61J,
11/15/62J, 11/9/64J

YOUNG, James
7/27/65J

YOUNG, John
9/17/62I

YOUNG, Milton
3/8/61F

YOUNG, Whitney
6/9/63F, 7/2/63F, 7/27/63F,
7/29/64F, 5/21/69J

YOUNG Americans for Freedom
3/7/62F

YOUNG Democratic Clubs of America
11/18/67G

YOUSSOUPOFF, Prince Felix
9/27/67J

YOUSUF, Mohammed
3/19/63E

YOUTH—See Children; Labor—Youth; specific programs

YPSILANTI, Mich.
8/13/66F

YUGOSLAVIA
Accidents & Disasters
7/26/63I, 8/5/63I, 8/11/63I,
5/20/65B
Agriculture
7/1/61B
Albania
11/30/67B, 9/29/68B,
12/23/68B, 12/25/68B
Amnesties
3/13/62B
Armed Forces & Defense
10/13/61G, 9/24/68B,
11/18/68B, 2/11/69B
Arts & Culture
7/23/62B
Atomic Energy & Weapons
4/1/60I
Austria
11/26/60B, 9/30/68B
Bombings & Bomb Plots
1/29/67D
Bulgaria
9/29/68B
China (Communist), People's Republic of
1/23/63A, 12/13/64B,
4/10/67E, 10/15/68E
Church-State Relations
1/10/60B, 2/8/60B,
2/17/60B, 10/17/60B
Colleges & Universities
6/9/68B

Communists & Communism
1/27/63A, 2/10/63A,
12/13/64B, 1/20/67B,
3/21/67B, 4/11/67B,
4/24/67B, 4/27/67B,
6/26/68B, 7/23/68B,
10/20/68B
Congo, Republic of the (Leopoldville) (formerly Belgian Congo)
1/22/61C, 1/26/61A,
2/15/61C
Constitution
11/28/60B, 4/7/63B
Croats
2/8/60B
Cuba
12/13/62B
Czechoslovakia
8/9/68B, 8/11/68B,
8/12/68B, 10/14/68A
Deaths
2/10/60B
Demonstrations & Riots
6/2/68B, 11/27/68B
Economy
11/28/60B
Egypt
8/11/67C, 7/12/68B
Espionage & Treason
12/7/62B
European Economic Community (EEC) (Common Market)
10/27/65B
Finances
12/27/60B
Food
12/31/66B
Foreign Aid
8/11/63I, 2/18/64D
Foreign Population
11/27/68B, 12/23/68B
Foreign Trade
12/27/60B, 5/4/63B,
3/26/64B, 2/10/69B
France
10/15/68B
Germany
10/3/62B
Germany, West
4/18/60B, 9/3/60B,
6/14/65B, 2/24/67B,
1/31/68B, 2/10/69B
Government & Politics
4/19/67B, 5/17/67B
Greece
5/15/67B, 9/11/68B
Internal Security
5/14/62B
Israel
6/13/67B
Italy
9/11/68B
Language & Linguistics
3/17/67B, 3/19/67B
North Atlantic Treaty Organization (NATO)
11/15/68G

Pakistan
1/23/61E
Political Prisoners
1/20/61B, 4/19/67B
Purges
1/12/68B, 4/15/69B
Rumania
2/6/69B
Serbo-Croatian Nationalism
3/26/67B, 3/27/67B,
4/11/67B
Union of Soviet Socialist Republics (USSR)
12/26/60B, 7/13/61B,
4/21/62B, 9/21/62B,
10/3/62B, 12/4/62B,
2/10/63A, 8/20/63B,
8/27/63A, 1/28/67B,
11/30/68B, 3/11/69B
United Nations (U.N.)
9/22/60A, 1/22/61C
United States
4/1/60I, 2/8/61G, 7/1/61B,
10/13/61G, 5/4/63B,
7/28/63G, 10/17/63B,
3/26/64B, 11/9/64G,
12/31/66B, 10/16/68G

YUGOV, Anton
11/5/62B, 11/19/62B

YUN, Posun
10/15/63E

Z

ZADKINE, Ossip
11/25/67J

ZAGLEBIE
8/2/64J

ZAHIR, Mahammad
10/6/61E

ZAIRE
3/22/66C, 4/13/66C,
7/30/66C

ZAJIC, Jan
2/25/69B

ZAKHAROV, Matvei
3/28/63B

ZAMBIA
10/24/64C, 5/20/68C
Angola
8/7/69C
Armed Forces & Defense
2/19/69C
China (Communist), People's Republic of
4/15/65C, 5/26/65A
Commonwealth of Nations
8/30/66C
Congo, Republic of the (Leopoldville) (formerly Belgian Congo)
9/17/67C
Copper
11/26/65C, 7/22/66C
Deportations
1/12/68C

Foreign Aid
1/26/68C
Foreign Trade
1/2/66C
Government & Politics
2/12/68C, 8/14/68C
Great Britain
7/23/66C, 12/9/66A,
2/1/67B, 1/26/68C,
2/19/69C
Independence
5/19/64C
Nationalization of Industry
4/19/68C, 4/24/68C
Portugal
4/6/68C, 8/7/69C
Railroads
7/31/66C, 4/8/68C
Rhodesia
10/29/65G, 11/13/65C,
11/26/65C, 12/4/65C,
12/8/65C, 12/18/65C,
1/1/66C, 1/2/66C,
7/22/66C, 11/16/66C,
1/27/67C, 2/1/67B,
8/19/67C, 8/23/67C,
8/25/67C, 8/27/67C,
4/27/68C, 7/22/68C,
3/26/69C
South Africa, Republic of (formerly Union of)
5/18/67C, 1/12/68C
United Nations (U.N.)
12/9/66A
United States
10/29/65G, 12/3/65C

ZANZIBAR
Agriculture
3/8/64C
China (Communist), People's Republic of
1/19/64C, 3/31/64C,
6/8/64C
Cuba
1/19/64C
Demonstrations & Riots
6/11/61C
Foreign Aid
6/8/64C
Government & Politics
6/24/63C, 7/2/63C
Great Britain
6/1/61C, 2/23/64C
Independence
11/7/60C, 12/10/63C
Nationalization of Industry
3/8/64C
Political Prisoners
2/21/69C
Rebellions & Revolutions
1/12/64C, 1/18/64C,
1/19/64C
Union of Soviet Socialist Republics (USSR)
3/31/64C
United Nations (U.N.)
12/16/63A,
United States
1/16/64C, 2/23/64C

U.S. Bases & Troops
6/24/63C

ZARO, Nadim
10/30/68C

ZARUBA, Jan
9/10/68B

ZAVATT, Joseph
1/24/64F

ZAYAS, Jorge
1/7/60D

ZAYEN, Yussef
2/25/66C

ZAYYAT, Mohammed el-
7/6/68C, 7/7/68C

ZEFFIRELLI, Franco
3/8/67J, 10/8/68J

ZELLER, Andre
5/31/61B

Z (film)
5/23/69J, 12/29/69J

ZHIVKOV, Todor
11/19/62B, 11/14/66B

ZIEGLER, Ronald
11/15/68G, 12/11/68G,
12/16/68G

ZINN, Walter
4/5/60I

ZIONISM
12/27/60C, 1/15/61J,
4/15/64C, 8/14/67F,
8/15/67F

ZIONIST Organizations of America
8/27/60F

ZOG I (Ahmed Bey Zogu) (Ex-King of Albania)
4/9/61B

ZOLI, Adone
2/20/60B

ZOLLINGER, Louis
1/20/66B

ZONING
12/6/69F

ZORACH, William
1/14/61J

ZORIN, Valerian
11/19/60A, 12/8/60C,
1/12/61A, 4/5/61A,
10/13/61A, 12/22/61A,
4/20/62A, 12/23/62B,
6/25/64A, 7/2/64A,
1/12/66B

ZPRAVY (book)
11/28/68B

ZUCERT, Eugene
5/13/64G

ZURLINI, Valerio
9/8/62J